# STATISTICAL METHODS IN EDUCATION AND PSYCHOLOGY

## second edition

**GENE V GLASS**

**KENNETH D. HOPKINS**

*Laboratory of Educational Research*
*University of Colorado*



PRENTICE-HALL, INC., *Englewood Cliffs, New Jersey 07632*

*Library of Congress Cataloging in Publication Data*

Glass, Gene V
Statistical methods in education and psychology.

Bibliography: p.
Includes index.
1. Education statistics. 2. Psychometrics.
I. Hopkins, Kenneth D. II. Title.
LB2846. G55 1984 519 84-1954
ISBN 0-13-844944-9

Editorial/production supervision and
interior design: Marion Osterberg and Fred Bernardi
Cover design: Wanda Lubelska Design
Manufacturing buyer: Ron Chapman

*To the graduates of the Laboratory of Educational Research, University of Colorado-Boulder, who teach and apply statistics all over the world, for their contributions to our thinking about statistical methods.*



Printed in the United States of America

10 9 8 7 6 5 4 3 2

ISBN 0-13-844944-9 01

Prentice-Hall International, Inc., *London*
Prentice-Hall of Australia Pty. Limited, *Sydney*
Editora Prentice-Hall do Brasil, Ltda., *Rio de Janeiro*
Prentice-Hall Canada Inc., *Toronto*
Prentice-Hall of India Private Limited, *New Delhi*
Prentice-Hall of Japan, Inc., *Tokyo*
Prentice-Hall of Southeast Asia Pte. Ltd., *Singapore*
Whitehall Books Limited, *Wellington, New Zealand*

# CONTENTS

## 10 STATISTICAL INFERENCE: SAMPLING AND INTERVAL ESTIMATION 173



## 11 INTRODUCTION TO HYPOTHESIS TESTING 202



## 12 INFERENCES ABOUT THE DIFFERENCE BETWEEN MEANS 229

## 13 INFERENCE REGARDING VARIANCES 255



## 14 INFERENCES REGARDING PROPORTIONS 275



## 15 INFERENCES AMONG CORRELATION COEFFICIENTS 300

## APPENDIX 512



## TABLES 521



## BIBLIOGRAPHY 557

## AUTHOR INDEX 567

## SUBJECT INDEX 570

# PREFACE

This textbook is designed for a one- or two-semester course in applied statistics. The methods are applicable to empirical research in many disciplines. We have drawn applications from several disciplines, although most come from education and psychology. In most instances, the data are not hypothetical but are from actual studies.

Our selection of topics has been guided by three considerations: (1) What are the most useful statistical methods? (2) Which statistical techniques are the most widely used in scholarly journals in the behavioral and social sciences? (3) Which statistical concepts and methods are fundamental to further study?

This text attempts to produce a more thorough coverage of analysis of variance techniques than usually appears in basic statistics texts for social scientists. Edgington (1974) found that more than 70 percent of all articles published in journals of the American Psychological Association employed this extremely versatile and powerful technique. According to the survey of Wick and Dirkes (1973), more than 95 percent of the doctoral dissertations in education use the statistical techniques that are treated in this text.

This edition of *Statistical Methods in Education and Psychology* (*SMEP*) differs from the first edition in both substance and style. The substantive changes include (1) an expanded and integrated treatment of multiple comparisons, including trend analysis, (2) a new chapter on multiple regression, (3) a new chapter on inferential methods with proportions, and (4) expanded treatment of more complex applications of the analysis of variance and covariance.

The pedagogical improvements include (1) diagnostic mastery tests following each chapter, (2) reorganization of content involving separate chapters on inferences regarding means, variances, proportions, and correlation coefficients, and (3) an attempt to provide more options in course content and emphasis. *SMEP* has endeavored to continue to be "extraordinary in its collection of examples, exercises, and statistical tables" (Schmidt, 1972, p. 169).

The approach of this text is conceptual, not mathematical or "cookbookish." Deriving a formula is no proof of real understanding, nor is the ability to plug numbers into formulas and "turn the crank." Indeed, the number of formulas used is kept small; the verbal-to-mathematical ratio of text material would rank high among statistics texts. We have stressed concepts rather than derivation and proof.

We have pruned away much deadwood present in some other statistics texts. Although every text claims to reflect the latest influences of electronic computers and hand calculators, obsolete techniques of calculating the mean, variance, and correlation coefficient from "grouped" data continue to be taught. These "shortcut" methods lead to roundabout formulas that, in addition to being less accurate, impede conceptualizing the meaning of the statistic being calculated.

We have tried to be sensitive to changes in statistical pedagogy occasioned by the rapid spread of hand calculators. We strongly advise students to purchase a hand calculator having at least one memory and the square root ($\sqrt{x}$) and reciprocal ($1/X$) features; better yet would be one with preprogrammed functions for mean, standard deviation, and correlation.

In this edition, we have tried to maintain the high professional standards of the first edition of *SMEP*. Michael (1970, pp. 1015 and 1018) found that the first edition of *SMEP* "probably affords the most nearly current and best balanced treatment of statistical methodology to be found in any well-known introductory text. . . . This volume should set the standard for many years to come."

In *Twenty-Five Years of Recommended Readings in Psychology*, Solso (1979) found that *SMEP* was among the 25 most recommended books by graduate departments of psychology, a distinction recorded by only one other statistics book (and it was less popular than *SMEP*). In their survey of statistics professors in graduate departments of education, Gay, Campbell, and Gallagher (1978) found that *SMEP*, in comparison to the other common statistics texts studied, had the highest ratings of (1) technical accuracy, (2) breadth of coverage, and (3) depth of topic coverage. *SMEP* was judged (1) to have no statistics prerequisites for comprehension, (2) to have a good sequence of topics, and (3) to be appropriate for undergraduate and graduate work, and (4) to have an orientation that is appropriate for both research consumers and producers. Stein and Kuenne (1979) found *SMEP* to have the lowest (easiest) readability of the seven statistics and research textbooks they studied. In a recent survey of the 100 top research-producing universities in education, *SMEP* was the most-used text (Brinzer & Sinatra, 1982). During the two years this text was being revised, our colleagues and students contributed in innumerable ways to our efforts. We cannot name them all here, but the following colleagues deserve special thanks for contributing recently to our education in statistical methods: Julian Stanley deserves credit for his influence as mentor and his contributions to the first edition. His modesty and heavy research commitments led to his decision not to remain a co-author for the second edition. Roberta Flexer, Stuart Kahl, Jason Millman, and Lorrie Shepard made several suggestions based on extensive classroom experience with *SMEP* that improved it as a text. Others made technical or pedagogical contributions: Maurice Tatsuoka, Edward Cureton, William Michael, Lorrie Shepard, James Collins,

Roberta Flexer, Stuart Kahl, Victor Willson, Todd Rogers, Arlen Gullickson, Percy Peckham, Bob Hopkins, Mary Lee Smith, James Sanders, Stephen Jurs, Gregory Camilli, George Kretke, James Morrow, Frank B. Baker, and Carol Vojir.

We are indebted to Bob Hopkins, Mark Chisholm, James Rosenthal, Rick Kroc, Thomas Hughes, Lynn Sherretz, Alan Davis, Paul Kelter, and Carol Vojir for critically reading various chapters and providing answers to problems and exercises.

The tedious tasks of deciphering, typing, and correcting various drafts of the manuscript were shared by Sue Reissig, Karen O'Grady, Mary Ann Gardner, and Sheryl Vriesman.

*Gene V Glass*
*Kenneth D. Hopkins*

# 1

# INTRODUCTION

## 1.1 THE "IMAGE" OF STATISTICS

Popular attitudes toward statistics contain a mixture of awe, cynicism, suspicion, and contempt. Freudian slips have transformed statistics into "sadistics," and "Don't become a statistic" is taken to mean "Don't let something evil befall you."

Statisticians have been scornfully placed in the company of liars and accused of "statisticulation"–the art of lying with statistics while maintaining an appearance of objectivity and rationality. Someone once remarked: "If all the statisticians in the world were laid end to end–it would be a good thing." A statistician has been depicted as a person who drowns while wading in a river having an average depth of 3 ft., or who sits with his head in a refrigerator and his feet in an oven and reports, "On the average, I feel fine."

W. H. Auden wrote, "Thou shalt not sit among statisticians, nor commit a social science." But nonsense can be expressed as readily verbally as it can be quantitatively. Knowledge of logic is a good safeguard against uncritical acceptance of verbal nonsense, and knowledge of statistics is the best defense against quantitative nonsense. The study of statistical concepts and methods will certainly reduce numerical credulity and help one be a wise consumer of quantitative information. The first step toward replacing popular images of statistics with more realistic ones is to study the structure of the discipline of "statistical methods" and its historical antecedents.

Some persons avoid statistics because of philosophical bias, apprehension about its rigors, or misconceptions about the discipline. Some prefer to operate on the basis of tradition, intuition, authoritative judgment, or "common sense." But it is increasingly recognized that there is a place for systematic, objective, and empirical research for which statistics is a tool.

Knowledge of statistical methods is becoming necessary for scholarship in most empirical disciplines. In the past twenty years, most graduate schools have acknowledged its importance as a research tool by accepting course work in statistics as a substitute for one of the two foreign languages traditionally required for a Ph.D. degree. The substitution is apt: statistics is an increasingly important means of communicating knowledge.

There were two widely divergent influences on the early development of statistical methods. Statistics had a mother who was dedicated to keeping orderly records of governmental units (*state* and *statistics* come from the same Latin root, *status*) and a gambling father who relied on mathematics to increase his skill at playing the odds in games of chance. From the mother sprang counting, measuring, describing, tabulating, ordering, and the taking of censuses—all of which led to modern *descriptive statistics.* From the father eventually came modern *inferential statistics*, which is based squarely on theories of probability. This text offers an introduction to the descriptive and inferential statistics that are most widely used in educational and behavioral research (Edgington, 1974; Wick and Dirkes, 1973; Willson, 1980). Descriptive statistics are emphasized in Chapters 2 through 8. Beginning with "Probability" in Chapter 9 and extending through Chapter 15, topics from inferential statistics are covered. Chapters 16 through 20 present the considerations and inferential techniques especially important in the design and analysis of experiments.

## 1.2 DESCRIPTIVE STATISTICS

Descriptive statistics involves tabulating, depicting, and describing collections of data. These data may be either *quantitative*, such as measures of height or intelligence—variables that are characterized by an underlying continuum—or the data may represent *qualitative* variables, such as sex, college major, or personality type. Large masses of data generally must undergo a process of summarization or reduction before they are comprehensible.

The human mind cannot extract the full import of a mass of data (How do they vary? About how large are they? Is one set useless in reducing uncertainty about the other?) without the aid of special techniques. Thus descriptive statistics serves as a tool to describe or summarize or reduce to manageable form the properties of an otherwise unwieldy mass of data.

## 1.3 INFERENTIAL STATISTICS

Inferential statistics is a formalized body of methods for solving another class of problems. This general class of problems involves attempts to infer the properties of a large collection of data from inspection of a sample of observations. For example, a school superintendent wishes to determine the proportion of children in a large school system who come in without breakfast (have used drugs, have been vaccinated for Asian flu, or whatever). Having a little knowledge of statistics, the superintendent would know that it is unnecessary and inefficient to question each child; the proportion for the entire district could be estimated fairly accurately from a sample of as few as 100 children.

Thus the purpose of inferential statistics is to predict or estimate characteristics of a population from a knowledge of the characteristics of only a sample of the population. The descriptive characteristics of a sample can be generalized to the entire population, with a known margin of error, using the techniques of inferential statistics.

The design and analysis of experiments is an important branch of inferential statistical methods. These methods were developed for testing causal relationships among variables. Experimental design is so important for the study of causal relationships that in some philosophical systems an experiment constitutes an operational definition of a causal relationship. Adults make causal inferences during all their waking moments. The frequent use of the word "because" reveals this: "The school bond failed to pass because it was not well publicized" or "He scored poorly on the intelligence test because he was overly anxious about the consequences of the score." Statistical methods assist researchers in describing data, in drawing inferences to larger bodies of data, and in studying causal relationships.

## 1.4 STATISTICS AND MATHEMATICS

The discipline of statistics is a branch of applied mathematics. Mastering statistical methods requires some mathematical proficiency, but less than commonly assumed. Do not think statistics is accessible only to the specially trained. In this book, much use is made of intuition, logical reasoning, and simple arithmetic. Much of the rationale of applied statistics and many of its techniques can be learned without advanced mathematical skills.

If you have not studied mathematics, logic, or any other rigorous and deductive discipline recently, you may find studying statistics uncomfortable for a while. In many disciplines characterized by vague verbal discourse and personalistic use of language, a student can sustain sloppy and erroneous thinking for long periods without being aware of it. A speaker might receive an enthusiastic audience reaction to the statement, "Viable individualized, democratic, and creative alternatives are necessary to meet the needs of the whole child." If the statement is scrutinized, however, its meaning is so ambiguous and imprecise that it is essentially meaningless. The student of statistics is likely to be confronted abruptly and uncomfortably with the results of careless thinking. If you are inclined toward critical and precise thought, this restrictive and confining mantle will soon begin to feel comfortable. The satisfying reassurance of knowing that you are mastering a logical and unambiguous language will outweigh the work involved in learning it. Being wrong on occasion is the price we must pay for knowing when we are correct. Not knowing if we are speaking nonsense is too expensive a luxury to entertain in an age in which sense is scarce.

*A word to the wise:* "Be ye doers of the word, and not hearers only, deceiving your own selves" (James 1:22). By far the greatest demand that the study of statistics exacts from the student is thorough, detailed, and careful attention to the subject. A quick reading of this book will not produce a mastery of statistics. A statistics text is not a novel. The material simply cannot be acquired through casual reading. It is recommended that each chapter be read at least twice, once before and once after the concepts are presented in class. Reading the material before hearing a lecture will pay dividends. Most chapters should be studied carefully and thoughtfully, because the related topics and concepts are prerequisites for subsequent chapters. The Mastery Tests that follow each chapter are a novel feature. These items have been carefully designed to assess all fundamental ideas introduced in the chapter. The Mastery Tests will help you diagnose deficiencies in skills and understanding. Skip the Mastery Test, and you may never know what you do not know about statistics. Problems and Exercises are also provided for each chapter to enhance your knowledge of the subject.

## Our Targets

The student who applies attention consistently to the task can expect to gain the following fruits from this labor: a general functional literacy for information expressed quantitatively; a "consumer's knowledge" of statistics that will help gain access to more than half of the published empirical research in the field; a command of skills in statistical methods that can contribute significantly to many research efforts under the supervision of an experienced researcher; and a knowledge of statistical methods sufficient to support more advanced study, which will contribute to being a relatively independent empirical researcher.

The study of statistics not only will improve your ability to read and evaluate research literature but should help you become a more informed citizen and consumer by being better equipped to evaluate data and other quantitative evidence used to support claims, conclusions, and points of view. You may find your excursion into statistics rewarding and even enjoyable.

# 2

# VARIABLES, MEASUREMENT, AND SCALES

## 2.1 VARIABLES AND THEIR MEASUREMENT

Descriptive and inferential statistics are concerned almost entirely with the study of variables. Variables are nonuniform characteristics of observational units. Units are the "entities" on which *observations* are obtained. The most common units used in behavioral sciences and education are persons. But other units are also frequently encountered, such as families, cities, census tracts, and classrooms of students. Examples of variables on persons (*personological* variables) are height, age, reading speed, socioeconomic status, sex, grade-point average, ethnicity, IQ, occupation, auditory discrimination, marital status, and the like. Examples of variables defined on a classroom unit might include class size (number of students), ability (average IQ), ethnicity ratio (proportion of nonwhite pupils), and attendance (average daily attendance).

Statistics describe characteristics of observational units. In this book many examples will be drawn from education and the behavioral and social sciences and will pertain to personological variables. Hence persons will be the most common observational unit. Of course the concepts and methods will apply equally to other units.

## 2.2 MEASUREMENT: THE OBSERVATION OF VARIABLES

Before a variable can be treated statistically, it must be observed—that is, classified, measured, or quantified. As you come to know a person, you naturally make observations (assessments) on many variables: attractiveness, speech style, vocabulary, self-confidence, ethnicity, likeability, eye color, and even political or religious persuasion. When observations are quantified or categorized, they can be treated statistically. A measurement is a quantified or categorized observation. If these measurements differ among the units, the observations represent a variable.

*Measurement* involves assigning numbers to things according to rules. To measure a person's height is to assign a number to the distance between the top of a person's head and the bottom of his feet with the use of a ruler. Measurement of a child's IQ is the assignment of a number to the sum of the correct responses that she makes to a group of standard problems. Measurement transforms attributes into more familiar and tractable things, numbers. Is it not adequate for a physicist to know that iron melts at a high temperature or for a traveler that Chicago is "down the road a piece"? Measurements should be as precise and as valid as possible.*

## 2.3 MEASUREMENT SCALES: NOMINAL MEASUREMENT

The ideas of "scales of measurement" are deeply embedded in the pedagogy of research methods.† Four different scales and their implications for statistics will be discussed briefly.

Nominal measurement (giving a *name* or *names*) scarcely deserves to be called "measurement." It is the process of grouping objects into classes so that all those in a single class are equivalent (or nearly so) with respect to some attribute or property. The classes are then names or numerals given for identification, which may account for the title "nominal measurement." Classificatory schemes in biology are examples of nominal measurement. Researchers often code "sex" by assigning "0" to female and "1" to male—an example of nominal measurement.

When measurement is merely nominal, one uses only the property of numbers that 1 is distinct from 2 or 4 and that if object $A$ has a 1 and object $B$ a 4, then $A$ and $B$ are different with respect to the attribute measured. It does not necessarily follow that $B$ has any more of the attribute than $A$. Common examples of nominal scales include college major, ethnicity, and geographic region.

*The principles and theory of measurement are found in many sources such as Hopkins and Stanley (1981) or Nunnally (1978).

†The names of the scales of measurement used here and many of the concepts are from Stevens (1951).

The remaining scales of measurement which follow make use of three additional properties of numbers: numbers can be ordered by size, they can be added, and they can be divided.

## 2.4 ORDINAL MEASUREMENT

Ordinal measurement is possible when differing degrees or amounts of an attribute or property can be detected. Ordinal measurement is achieved when a group of things can be ranked from low to high. The numeric values of the measurements reflect differing amounts of the characteristic. Athletic awards are usually made on the basis of an ordering of performance: first place, second place, and so on. Some tests measuring interests require people to order certain activities according to their preferences. A list of priorities represents an *ordinal scale.*

An ordinal scale commonly used in college admission is "percentile rank in high school class." Indeed, percentile rank on any characteristic represents a kind of ordinal scale. States are frequently rank ordered on certain variables, since the rank order may be more easily understood than a raw measurement.

## 2.5 INTERVAL MEASUREMENT

Interval scales represent a more highly refined measurement than ordinal scales. With interval scales, the numbers describe the magnitude of the differences among the things. The difference between 50 and 60°F is the same as the difference between 90 and 100°F. But 100°F is *not* twice 50°F in terms of heat or molecular motion. With interval measurement, the zero point on the scale is arbitrary and does not correspond to the absence of the characteristic measured. For example, an object at 0°C or 0°F is *not* the total absence of heat or temperature. Any interval scale can be converted easily to an ordinal scale, but ordinal scales cannot usually be transformed into interval scales. If the daily "highs" are known, the days of July can be placed in rank order from the hottest to the least hot. But if the rank order is known, one cannot transform ranks into degrees Fahrenheit. The numbering of calendar years is an interval scale. The year 1 was set originally as the year of the birth of Christ.* The unit of measurement is a span of $365\frac{1}{4}$ days.

Interval measurement involves assigning numbers to objects in such a way that equal differences in the numbers correspond to equal differences in the amounts of the attribute measured. The zero point of the interval scale can be placed arbitrarily and does not indicate absence of the property measured.

Occasionally ordinal measurement is more useful than interval or ratio measurement. For example, to know that a ten-year-old boy is 50 in. tall and weighs 80 lb. is less

*Actually the chronologer Dionysius Exiguus (AD 500–560) made an error: Christ was born 6–3 BC. The incorrect zero point, however, does not affect the interval scale properties of the BC–AD scale.

informative than to know that his percentile ranks are 5 and 95 in height and weight, respectively.

## 2.6 RATIO MEASUREMENT

Ratio measurement differs from interval measurement only in that the zero point indicates the absence of the property measured instead of being arbitrarily assigned. The measurer can perceive the absence of the property and has a unit of measurement with which to record differing amounts of the property. As with interval scales, equal differences between the numbers assigned in measurement reflect equal differences in the amount of the property possessed by the things measured. Furthermore, since the zero point is not arbitrary but absolute, it is meaningful to say that $A$ has two, three, or four times as much of the property as $B$. Age, height, and weight are examples of ratio measurement scales. Zero height is no height at all, and a man six feet tall is twice as tall as a three-foot-tall boy. This scale is so named because the ratios of numbers on a ratio scale are meaningful. These ratios can be interpreted as ratios of amounts of the objects measured. A ratio statement about a strictly interval scale has no meaning in terms of the amounts of the attribute. For example, if June 3 had a high temperature of 90°F and March 17 had a high of 45°F, it is *not* correct to say that June 3 had twice as much heat or temperature as March 17. One cannot make ratio-type comparisions on measures of attitude, achievement, personality, intelligence or sociometric status. An IQ of 140 does not represent twice as much intelligence as an IQ of 70!

Much measurement in the behavioral and social sciences occurs below the ratio level. Fig. 2.1 is a summary of definitions and examples of scales of measurement.

**FIGURE 2.1. Summary of characteristics of scales of measurement.**

| *Scale* | *Characteristic of Scale* | *Examples* |
|---|---|---|
| RATIO | Numbers represent equal units from absolute zero. Observations can be compared as ratios or percentages. | Distance, age, time, weight |
| INTERVAL | Equal differences between numbers represent equal differences in the amounts of the attribute measured. | Year (A.D.), °F |
| ORDINAL | Numbers indicate rank order of observations. | Percentile norms, social class |
| NOMINAL | Numbers represent categories. Numbers do not reflect differences in magnitude. Numbers serve to distinguish groups. | Sex, nationality, clinical diagnosis, college major |

## 2.7 INTERRELATIONSHIPS AMONG MEASUREMENT SCALES

Identifying the level of measurement is really not as simple as it first appears. Measurement of some variables does not fall neatly into one of the four levels of measurement. What about IQ scores from Stanford-Binet or Wechsler intelligence tests? One cannot say that an IQ of 130 represents 30% more intelligence than a score of 100 (a ratio interpretation). But is the difference between IQ scores of 70 and 100 the same as the difference between scores of 100 and 130 (an interval interpretation)? Probably not, but neither do IQ scores represent only an ordinal scale. Indeed, if only ordinal-level measurement were achieved, only ranks (percentile ranks) should be reported. Certainly the difference in intellectual ability between the 99th percentile rank (IQ = 137) and the 94th percentile rank (IQ = 125) is much larger than the difference between the 55th (IQ = 102) and 50th (IQ = 100) percentile ranks. The IQ scale defies categorization as strictly ordinal or interval.

In the past, some textbooks have exaggerated the importance of the level of measurement, claiming that the mean, variance, and many other statistical measures and methods require an interval scale. Since many educational and psychological variables do not achieve this level of measurement, considerable emphasis was devoted to *nonparametric* statistics—methods which make fewer assumptions but are also less efficient. It has now been shown that the disenchantment with the classical methods was premature. Heermann and Braskamp (1970, pp. 30–110) give the principal papers and studies on this issue.

## 2.8 CONTINUOUS AND DISCRETE VARIABLES

Intuition and experience show that some variables are *continuous* (i.e., measurements of them could theoretically take on any value within a certain range), such as weight, age, or reaction time. But some variables are *discrete* (i.e., measurements of them can take on only separated values), such as number of children. The most familiar discrete variables are those that are measured by counting. "Number of children" can give rise to the numbers 0, 1, 2, 3, . . . . It is not possible for this variable to take on intermediate values such as 1.75.

The *actual* or *exact* measurement of a continuous variable is something that can never be attained, because measurement must always stop short of the *exact value*. The *reported value* is the value that the measuring process produced.

The reported and actual values of a variable do not coincide, but the reported values are approximations that yield bounds for the actual values. For example, if a person's height is 62 in. measured to the nearest inch, the actual height at that time and under those conditions is considered to be between $61\frac{1}{2}$ in. and $62\frac{1}{2}$ in.

One sometimes wishes to establish limits around a reported value within which the exact value lies. For example, what are the lowest and highest actual heights that will result in a reported height of 58 in. if height is measured to the nearest inch? The limits for the exact value around any reported value are found by adding and subtracting one-half the unit of measurement from the reported value. Thus a person with a reported height of 58 in. has an actual height between

$$58 \text{ in.} - \frac{1 \text{ in.}}{2} = 57\frac{1}{2} \text{ in.} \quad \text{and} \quad 58 \text{ in.} + \frac{1 \text{ in.}}{2} = 58.5 \text{ in.}$$

The following examples should clarify this procedure.

| *Variable* | *Unit of Measurement* | *Reported Value* | *Limits of Exact Value* |
|---|---|---|---|
| Weight | lb. | 130 lb. | 129.5–130.5 lb. |
| Height | in. | 66 in. | 65.5–66.5 in. |
| Reaction time | 1/100 sec. | .53 sec. | .525–.535 sec. |
| Running speed | .1 sec. | 49.5 sec. | 49.45–49.55 sec. |

## CHAPTER SUMMARY

A *variable* is a characteristic on which observational units differ. *Measurement* is the process of assigning numbers to observations of a variable. These numbers have characteristics and can be roughly classified into one of four measurement scales. *Nominal scales* represent a nonordered classification. *Ordinal scales* represent a sequential ordering of the things measured in relation to amount or degree of the variable. An *interval scale* has equal units of measurement but an arbitrary zero point. A *ratio scale* is an interval scale that has an absolute zero. The scale of measurement depends not only on the measurement procedure, but on the interpretation to be given the numbers.

## *MASTERY TEST*

The mastery tests that follow each chapter are designed for self-evaluation and diagnosis. Answers are given following the exercises.

1. Which one of the following is least likely to be *variable* among persons in a statistics class?
   a. socioeconomic status
   b. typing speed
   c. nationality
   d. assertiveness
   e. religious affiliation
   f. speaking ability
   g. favorite food
   h. muscial ability
   i. year of birth
   j. age
2. Which three variables in Question 1 would most likely be measured on nominal scales?
3. Which option in Question 1 best illustrates an interval but not a ratio scale?
4. Which two variables in Question 1 are most likely to be measured by ratio scales?
5. As typically measured, which four variables in Question 1 represent at least ordinal scales but probably not true interval scales?
6. Can observations on an interval or ratio scale be converted to an ordinal scale (ranks)?
7. To say, "$X_1$ is 25% greater than $X_2$" illustrates what level of measurement?

8. Order the four levels of measurement from the least to the most refined: ratio, nominal, ordinal, and interval.
9. When persons are measured on an interval scale (e.g., date of birth), are differences between persons measured on a ratio scale?
10. Is the measure "number of books listed in a library's card catalog" continuous or discrete?
11. Does the measure qualify as a ratio scale?
12. If A, B, C, D, and F grades were used for statistical purposes, the letters would be converted to 4, 3, 2, 1, and 0. a. Does this represent a ratio scale? b. Is it at least an ordinal scale?

Questions 13 to 15 involve a study conducted to see how well reading success in first grade could be predicted from various kinds of information obtained in kindergarten: reading readiness, age, sex, and socioeconomic status (SES).

13. Which of the variables represents a nominal scale?
14. Which variable could be measured on a ratio scale?
15. Would you recommend measuring age in months or in years as the unit of measurement? Why?

## *MASTERY TEST ANSWERS*

1. Probably c
2. c, e, g
3. i
4. b, j
5. a, d, f, h
6. Yes
7. Ratio
8. Nominal, ordinal, interval, ratio
9. Yes
10. Discrete
11. Yes
12. a. no, not a ratio scale. b. yes, at least an ordinal scale
13. Sex
14. Age
15. Months is a more precise unit than years.

# 3
# FREQUENCY DISTRIBUTIONS

## 3.1 TABULATION OF DATA

Data can be interpreted more easily if they are organized and summarized. Table 3.1 shows a class record for a test. The scores are listed in alphabetical order as they appear in the teacher's record book. However, the scores mean little in this form. One can tell only with some difficulty whether, for example, the first-listed pupil (David A.), with a score of 90 points out of a possible 128, is superior or just average.

## 3.2 RANK-ORDER DISTRIBUTIONS

A possible first step in organizing data for interpretation is to arrange the scores by size, usually from highest to lowest. This is called a rank-order distribution. If the number of observations is small, nothing more than a rank-order distribution may be needed to comprehend their important properties. Table 3.2A shows the same thirty-eight scores as Table 3.1, arranged in order from 112 to 44. This table also shows the rank order of the

**TABLE 3.1 A Class Record of Test Scores ($n$ = 38)**

| *Student* | *Score* | *Student* | *Score* | *Student* | *Score* | *Student* | *Score* |
|---|---|---|---|---|---|---|---|
| David A. | 90 | Robert D. | 59 | Jerome L. | 75 | Paul S. | 81 |
| Barbara B. | 66 | Dan F. | 95 | Rosa M. | 75 | Richard S. | 71 |
| Charles B. | 106 | Larry F. | 78 | Billy N. | 51 | Robert S. | 68 |
| Robert B. | 84 | Richard G. | 70 | Nancy O. | 109 | William S. | 112 |
| Mildred C. | 105 | Grover H. | 47 | Carrie P. | 89 | Jean T. | 62 |
| Robin C. | 83 | Robert H. | 95 | Ralph R. | 58 | Adolfo W. | 91 |
| Robert C. | 104 | Sylvia H. | 100 | George S. | 59 | Dolores W. | 93 |
| Diney D. | 82 | Warren H. | 69 | Gretta S. | 72 | Richard W. | 84 |
| Jim D. | 97 | Clarence K. | 44 | Jack S. | 74 | | |
| John D. | 97 | David K. | 80 | Mary S. | 75 | | |

pupils (1st, 2nd, . . . , 38th) and the scores tabulated without further grouping. It is now easy to see that David A.'s score of 90 gives him a rank of thirteen in a class of thirty-eight or about one-third of the way from the top. Similarly, it is easy to interpret each of the other scores in terms of rank. But ties are likely to occur, especially in classes of twenty or more pupils. Notice, for example, that two pupils made a score of 97. Since it is not correct to say that one ranks higher than the other, they must be assigned the same rank. Since there are six students who rank higher (1, 2, 3, 4, 5, 6), the next two ranks, 7 and 8, are averaged, giving 7.5. There are three students with scores of 75, and there are twenty-one students who rank above this score; the average of the next three ranks (22, 23, and 24) is 23, which is the rank assigned to each of the scores of 75. In addition to the time and trouble required to determine these ranks, the list is long, unwieldy, and inadequate for making comparisons with other classes that are much larger or much smaller; ranking 19th in a group of thirty-eight students is not nearly as good as 19th in a group of seventy students.

## 3.3 THE UNGROUPED FREQUENCY DISTRIBUTION

The list of scores can be made shorter by arranging the scores in a frequency distribution, sometimes simply called a *distribution.* The third and fourth columns of Table 3.2B show this ungrouped frequency distribution. The scores are arranged in order of size, here from 112 to 44, and to the right of each score is recorded the number of times it occurs. Each entry to the right of a score is its frequency. The total of the frequencies is represented by $n$.

For data representing interval and ratio scales, a rank-order distribution does not adequately depict the nature and characteristics of the distribution. The properties of a distribution become evident if the observations are grouped into classes. The number of classes or groups is arbitrary—usually between five and fifteen classes are used, depending on the purpose. The complete grouping arrangement is usually referred to as a *grouped frequency distribution.*

**TABLE 3.2 Scores from Table 3.1 Arranged in a Rank-Order Distribution and in an Ungrouped Frequency Distribution**

*A. Rank-Order Distribution*

| Score | Rank |
|---|---|
| 112 | 1 |
| 109 | 2 |
| 106 | 3 |
| 105 | 4 |
| 104 | 5 |
| 100 | 6 |
| 97 | 7.5 |
| 97 | 7.5 |
| 95 | 9.5 |
| 95 | 9.5 |
| 93 | 11 |
| 91 | 12 |
| 90 | 13 |
| 89 | 14 |
| 84 | 15.5 |
| 84 | 15.5 |
| 83 | 17 |
| 82 | 18 |
| 81 | 19 |
| 80 | 20 |
| 78 | 21 |
| 75 | 23 |
| 75 | 23 |
| 75 | 23 |
| 74 | 25 |
| 72 | 26 |
| 71 | 27 |
| 70 | 28 |
| 69 | 29 |
| 68 | 30 |
| 66 | 31 |
| 62 | 32 |
| 59 | 33.5 |
| 59 | 33.5 |
| 58 | 35 |
| 51 | 36 |
| 47 | 37 |
| 44 | 38 |

*B. Ungrouped Frequency Distribution*

| Score | Frequency | |
|---|---|---|
| 112 | 1 | |
| 109 | 1 | |
| 106 | 1 | |
| 105 | 1 | |
| 104 | 1 | |
| 100 | 1 | |
| 97 | 2 | |
| 95 | 2 | Sum = 19 = $n/2$ |
| 93 | 1 | |
| 91 | 1 | |
| 90 | 1 | |
| 89 | 1 | |
| 84 | 2 | |
| 83 | 1 | |
| 82 | 1 | |
| 81 | 1 | |
| - - - - - | - - - - - | Midpoint of Frequencies |
| 80 | 1 | |
| 78 | 1 | |
| 75 | 3 | |
| 74 | 1 | |
| 72 | 1 | |
| 71 | 1 | |
| 70 | 1 | |
| 69 | 1 | Sum = 19 = $n/2$ |
| 68 | 1 | |
| 66 | 1 | |
| 62 | 1 | |
| 59 | 2 | |
| 58 | 1 | |
| 51 | 1 | |
| 47 | 1 | |
| 44 | 1 | |
| | $n$ = 38 | = 19 + 19 |

## 3.4 GROUPED FREQUENCY DISTRIBUTIONS

To organize data into a grouped frequency distribution, (1) *determine the range*, (2) *select the classes (invervals) into which the data are to be grouped*, and (3) *tally the observations in the classes.*

### (1) Determine the Range:

*The range* is the difference between the largest observation,* $X_{max}$, *and the smallest observation,* $X_{min}$. That is,

$$\text{Range} = X_{max} - X_{min} \tag{3.1}$$

From Table 3.2,

$$X_{max} = 112, \text{ and } X_{min} = 44$$

Hence,

$$\text{Range} = 112 - 44 = 68$$

### (2) Select the Classes Into Which the Data Are to be Grouped

As a preliminary indication of the class width needed, divide the range by the *number* of classes (intervals) to be used, usually around ten. That is,

$$\text{Approximate class width } w = \frac{\text{Range}}{10} \tag{3.2}$$

The approximate class width $w$, is $\frac{68}{10} = 6.8$; this value should be "rounded" up or down to arrive at a convenient whole number.

For computational purposes, odd interval widths are preferred to even-numbered class sizes, because the latter have midpoints that are not whole numbers. The midpoint of the 7-point wide class 42–48 is 45 [(42 + 48)/2 = 45]; the midpoint of 49–55 is 52. Each class should begin with a multiple of the class width.

In the example, $X_{min}$ is 44 and the class width is 7. From Table 3.3 note that the first class begins with 42, the second begins with 49, the third with 56, and so on—each interval begins with a multiple of the class width. Note also that the classes are defined so that every observation falls into one and only one of the mutually exclusive classes. Thus the first class is 42–48 and the second 49–55 (not 42–49 and 49–56).

*Some statisticians define the range as $X_{max} - X_{min} + 1$ so that it extends from the upper real limit of $X_{max}$ (i.e., $X_{max} + .5$) to the lower real limit of $X_{min}$ (i.e., $X_{min} - .5$). The value yielded by Equation 3.1 is more common and is termed the exclusive range, which is 1 less than the inclusive range, $X_{max} - X_{min} + 1$.

**TABLE 3.3 An Illustration of the Process of Constructing a Grouped Frequency Distribution**

*Original Scores (from Table 3.1)*

90
66
106
84
105
83
104
82
97
97
59
95
78
70
47
95
100
69
44
80
75
75
51
109
89
58
59
72
74
75
81
71
68
112
62
91
93
84

*Steps in Constructing the Distribution*

*Step 1.* Determine the range.

| | |
|---|---|
| Largest score ($X_{max}$): | 112 |
| Smallest score ($X_{min}$): | 44 |
| Range = $X_{max}$-$X_{min}$ | = 68 |

*Step 2.* Determine class width $w$ and classes.*

$$w \doteq \frac{\text{Range}}{10} = \frac{68}{10} = 6.8, \text{ round to } 7 = w$$

*Step 3.* Tally the data.

A. Grouped Frequency Distribution

| *Class* | *Tally* | *Frequency* |
|---|---|---|
| 112–118 | 1 | 1 |
| 105–111 | 111 | 3 |
| 98–104 | 11 | 2 |
| 91–97 | ~~1111~~ 1 | 6 |
| 84–90 | 1111 | 4 |
| 77–83 | ~~1111~~ | 5 |
| 70–76 | ~~1111~~ 11 | 7 |
| 63–69 | 111 | 3 |
| 56–62 | 1111 | 4 |
| 49–55 | 1 | 1 |
| 42–48 | 11 | 2 |
| | | $n = 38$ |

B. Stem-and-Leaf Display

| | |
|---|---|
| 11 | 2 |
| 10 | 04569 |
| 9 | 0135577 |
| 8 | 0123449 |
| 7 | 0124558 |
| 6 | 2689 |
| 5 | 1899 |
| 4 | 47 |

*The symbol "≐" means "is approximately equal to."

### (3) Tally the Observations Into the Classes

A tally is made for each observation that falls within a class, as illustrated in Table 3.3. These tallies are counted and expressed as a numeral in the "Frequency" column. If all observations have been tallied correctly, the sum of the frequencies should equal the total number of observations $n$.

When the number of observations in the distribution is large, the tally scheme suggested by Tukey (1977) is convenient. Instead of "picket-fence" tallies (like those in Table 3.3), the first four scores are denoted by dots, the next four enclose the "square," followed by two crossed lines—to provide a convenient counting unit of ten. For example, 1 = ., 2 = :, 3 = :., 4 = ::, 5 = |:, 6 = L:, 7 = ⊔, 8 = □, 9 = ⧄, 10 = ⊠, 11 = ⊠ ., etc. This tallying technique is illustrated in Figure 4.1 (sec. 4.2)*.

## 3.5 GROUPING AND LOSS OF INFORMATION

Note that some information is lost when the observations are grouped. In general, the fewer the classes, the greater the loss. Any summary fails to tell the entire story. Statistics often involve a tradeoff between more usable, comprehensible data and less precise information. The question of how many classes to employ is answered by some arbitrary weighting of accuracy versus the ease of communication, the intended audience, and the use to be made of the information.

In the era before electronic computers, applied statistics books contained many procedures for classifying observations into grouped frequency distributions to facilitate the computation of means, standard deviations, and other statistics. For such purposes, at least ten to twenty intervals were commonly recommended. Even though grouping speeds up computations, it complicates the formulas and obscures their conceptual meaning. Fortunately, electronic computers and hand calculators have eliminated these computational considerations from the grouping decision. The grouping that best reveals or portrays the important features of a collection of scores is now the sole consideration. In the chapters that follow, calculations will be made directly from the raw observations. Thus simpler formulas can be used and more accurate results obtained; no information is lost by grouping.

## 3.6 GRAPHING A FREQUENCY DISTRIBUTION: THE HISTOGRAM

An ordinary frequency distribution does not always give a very clear picture of the important properties of a group of scores. There are three common methods of graphing a distribution: the histogram or bar graph, the frequency polygon, and the ogive curve.

The histogram is a series of columns, each having as its base one class interval and as its height the number of cases, or frequency, in that class. Figure 3.1 is a histo-

*There are numerous instances in which you will be referred to figures, tables, and equations in other chapters in the book; the associated section number will usually be given to expedite its location.

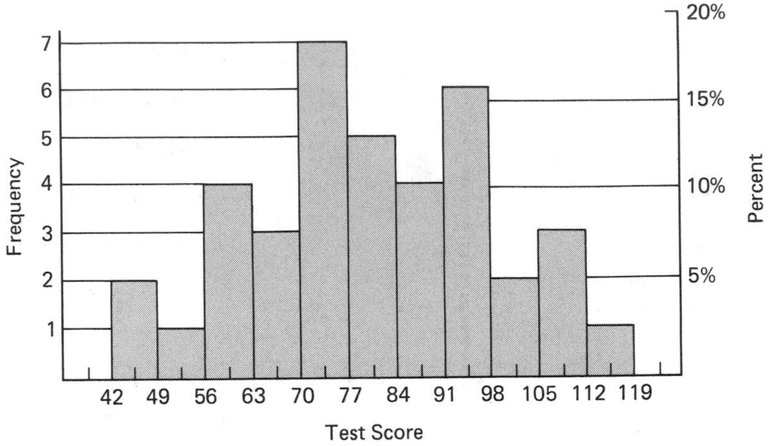


**FIGURE 3.1. Histogram of the test scores (n = 38) (from Table 3.1).**

gram showing the distribution of the thirty-eight test scores given in Tables 3.1 to 3.3. Since the greatest frequency is 7 in the 70-76 class, it is not necessary to extend the vertical frequency scale at the left above 7 (see Table 3.3). Since the scores range from the 42-48 class to the 112-118 class, one needs to draw the horizontal scale only through that distance. For clarity, however, it is customary to extend the scale one class interval above that range. To avoid having the figure appear too flat or too steep, it is usually well to arrange the scales so that the width of the histogram itself is one to two times its height—that is, the ratio of height to width should ordinarily be approximately between 1:1 and 1:2. A column is centered around the midpoint of the score-class interval when the class size is an odd number. Software is now available for virtually all microcomputers that will construct histograms (and other forms of graphic displays) from numerical data.

Histograms are often used to represent percentage instead of (or in addition to) frequency. Percentages sometimes mean more than simple frequencies. Note in Figure 3.1 that a second vertical axis is given on the right which is expressed in percentage units. Thus the reader has the choice of interpreting in frequencies or percentages. Percentage histograms are especially useful when more than one frequency distribution is represented in the figure.

Figure 3.2 gives the percentages for eight countries of the male and female populations ages 15 to 18 that are enrolled in education (Golladay, 1976). The percentage histogram allows the relevant information to be grasped more easily. A frequency histogram would be less illuminating due to the large differences in population sizes of the eight countries.

## 3.7 FREQUENCY AND PERCENTAGE POLYGONS

Constructing a frequency polygon (a figure having many angles) is much like constructing a histogram. In the histogram the top of each column is indicated by a horizontal line

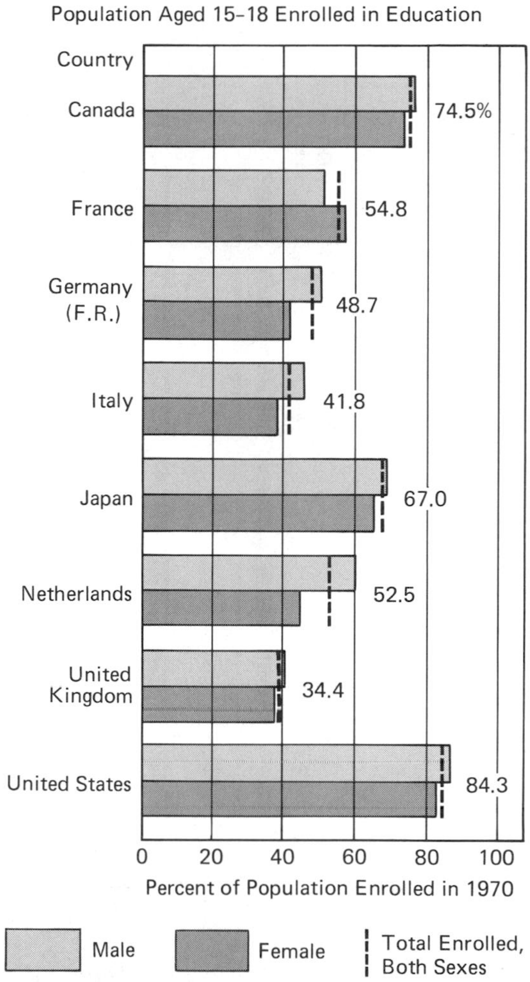


**FIGURE 3.2**
**A histogram showing United States teenage enrollment in education is higher than elsewhere for both sexes (from Golladay, 1976).**

placed at the height equal to the frequency in that class. But in the polygon a point is located above the *midpoint* of each class interval to represent the frequency in that class. These points are then joined by straight lines. The values on the baseline variable are always recorded with low values to the left and high values to the right. Figure 3.3 illustrates a frequency polygon superimposed on a histogram. The data are IQ scores on the Wechsler Intelligence Scale for Children (WISC) from a nationally representative sample of 2,200 children ages 6 to 16. Notice that the *Y*-axis (vertical axis or *ordinate*) is labeled in units of both frequency (on the left) and percent (on the right); hence Figure 3.3 illustrates both a frequency polygon and a percentage polygon. As noted earlier, percents are more useful than frequencies when the number of observations is arbitrary, as in the number of persons in a sample. But it is a simple matter to give both frequency and percent in the same figure by labeling the vertical axis on both the right and left like Figure 3.3 or Figure 3.1. When one is comparing two distributions that are based on unequal numbers of observations, percents are preferable.

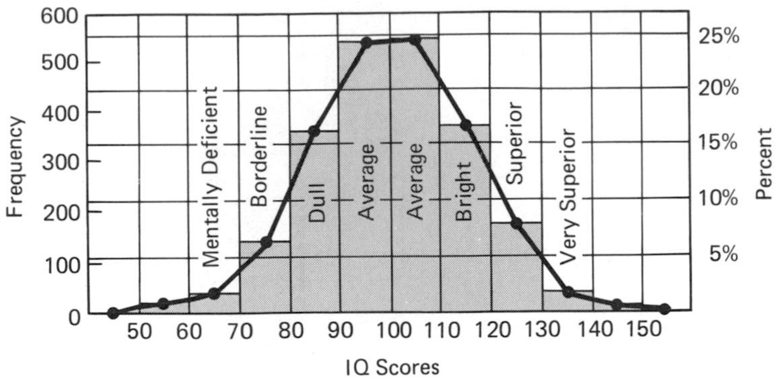


**FIGURE 3.3. Frequency and percentage polygon and histogram of 2,200 IQ scores on the Wechsler Intelligence Scale for Children–Revised (Wechsler, 1974).**

## 3.8 DESCRIBING DISTRIBUTIONS

Statisticians have a special vocabulary for describing various types of distributions. Notice in Figure 3.3 how the observations are approximately *symmetrical* and "bell-shaped". Such distributions approximate the *normal distribution.* Figure 3.4A depicts a normal curve. Many human characteristics are approximately normally distributed, for example, height, weight, and IQ scores. Much will be said about normal distributions in Chapter 6 and thereafter. Curve $B$ in Figure 3.4 is symmetrical but not normal. Distributions that have two modes (that is, two distinctly different points around which scores cluster) are called *bimodal.* For example, if the heights of adults were plotted, a bimodal distribution would result. The heights of females would cluster around their mode of approximately 64 in., and the male heights would cluster around a mode of about 69 in.

A *rectangular distribution* is shown as curve $C$ in Figure 3.4. The frequency is constant for all values of $X$. If a single die were tossed 10,000 times, a rectangular distribution of frequencies would result.

*Skewed distributions* are represented in curves $D$ and $E$. These curves are not symmetrical; they are *asymmetrical.* The degree to which a frequency distribution is asymmetrical is its *skewness.* Distribution $D$ is *positively skewed*, that is, the scores "bunch up" at the low end and "tail off" at the high or positive end. *Negative skewness* is depicted in curve $E$; the high scores are clustered together and "tail off" toward the left (the low or negative values). The terms *positive* and *negative* result from the statistical formulas that describe numerically the degree of skewness in a distribution.

If a distribution were drawn for days absent from work during a year for a group of persons, it would be positively skewed–most persons miss only a few days each year, but a few individuals miss several days because of illness. Annual family income in the United States is also skewed positively, as is number of traffic citations received by motorists.

Skewness can vary from mild to extreme. The statistical formulas for quantifying the degree of skewness in a distribution are given in Chapter 6 (Sec. 6.8).

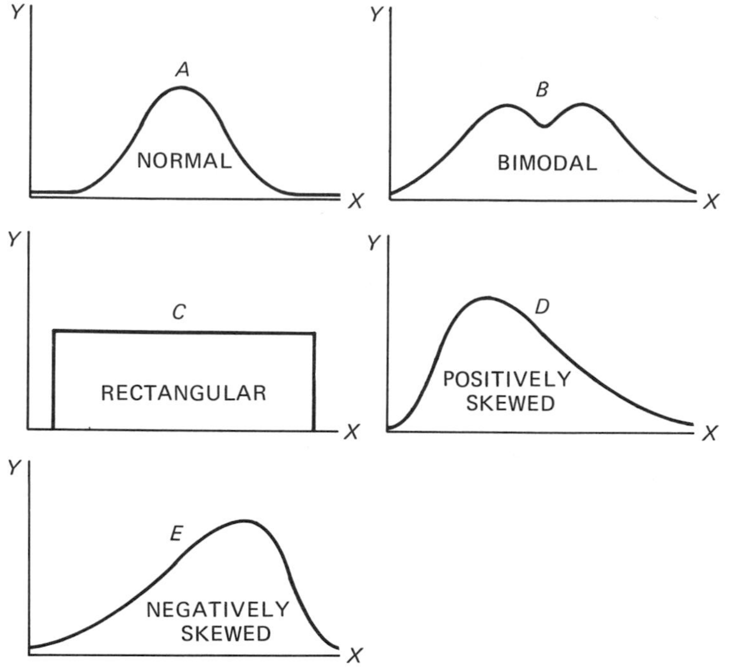


**FIGURE 3.4. Common types of frequency distributions. (The *Y*-axis represents frequency, and the *X*-axis represents the numerical value of the observations.)**

## 3.9 CUMULATIVE DISTRIBUTIONS

Frequency and percentage polygons can be readily converted into cumulative distributions. The *cumulative percentage* or *ogive curve* is the most common type of cumulative distribution. Figure 3.5A gives the same information as Figure 3.3 but displays the distribution using an ogive curve. With cumulative percentage distributions, the *Y*-axis represents cumulative percentages, those within a class plus the percentages falling below that class. The computation procedures are evident from Table 3.4. They convert the class frequencies to cumulative percentages:

Step 1. Divide the class frequency by $n$, the total number of observations, to obtain the *proportion* of cases falling within that class.

Step 2. Multiply this proportion by 100 (move the decimal point two places to the right) to obtain the *percent* of cases falling within that interval (see the "Percent" column of Table 3.4).

Step 3. Add the percent within the class to the cumulative percent falling *below* that class to obtain the cumulative percent for that class.

Step 4. Plot the cumulative percent values against the *upper limits* of the class as illustrated in Figure 3.5A.

Step 5. Label the *X*-axis.

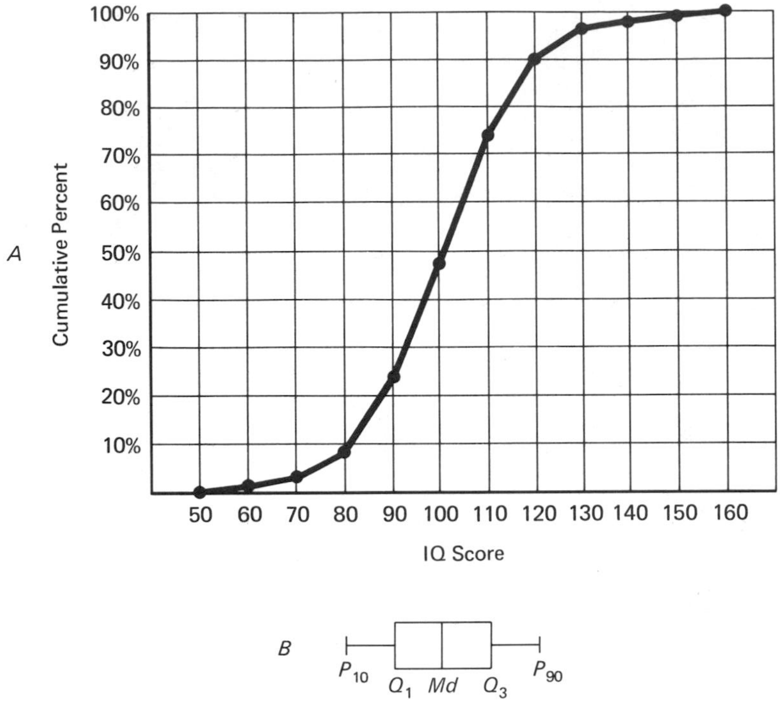


FIGURE 3.5. Ogive curve (*A*) and box-and-whisker plot (*B*) of IQ scores from a nationally representative sample of 2,200 persons (see Figure 3.3).

**TABLE 3.4 Computation of Cumulative Percentage Data Required for the Ogive Curve (IQ Scores from Figure 3.3)**

| *Class* | *Frequency* | *Percent* | *Cumulative Percent* |
|---|---|---|---|
| 150–159 | 1 | .05 | 100.00 |
| 140–149 | 6 | .27 | 99.95 |
| 130–139 | 44 | 2.0 | 99.7 |
| 120–129 | 163 | 7.4 | 97.7 |
| 110–119 | 363 | 16.5 | 90.3 |
| 100–109 | 548 | 24.9 | 73.8 |
| 90–99 | 539 | 24.5 | 48.9 |
| 80–89 | 356 | 16.2 | 24.4 |
| 70–79 | 132 | 6.0 | 8.2 |
| 60–69 | 41 | 1.9 | 2.2 |
| 50–59 | 6 | .27 | .32 |
| 40–49 | 1 | .05 | .05 |
| | $n$ = 2,200 | 100.00% | |

## 3.10 PERCENTILES

An ogive curve provides a useful and efficient method for determining *percentiles*. Percentiles are points in a distribution below which a given percent $P$ of the cases lie. From Figure 3.5, it can be seen that $P_{90}$ corresponds to an IQ score of approximately 120; hence, only 10% of the IQ scores exceeded 120. (Follow an imaginary line horizontally from the cumulative percent of 90 on the $Y$-axis until it intersects to ogive curve; then read vertically until reaching the $X$-axis to find the IQ score, 120, that corresponds to $P_{90}$.)

Similarly, an IQ score 110 can be converted to a percentile rank by proceeding upward from an IQ of 110 on the $X$-axis until the ogive curve is intersected. The height of the curve at that point indicates the cumulative percent, that is, the percentile rank (75) of the IQ score of 110. Percentile norms are employed for many purposes. Percentile scores also allow relative performance on two different variables to be compared.

In the next chapter attention is given to the most widely used percentile, the *median*, which is the 50th percentile. Other commonly reported percentiles are $P_{25}$ (which is also the *first quartile* $Q_1$ which defines the point below which the bottom quarter of observations falls), and $P_{75}$ (the *third quartile* $Q_3$). We saw earlier from Figure 3.5 that for the distribution of IQ scores $P_{75} = 110 = Q_3$. It is also evident that $P_{25} = 90 = Q_1$. Hence the middle 50% of the IQ scores falls between 90 and 110. Also notice from Figure 3.9 that the median IQ ($P_{50}$ or $Q_2$) $\doteq$ 100. (The symbol $\doteq$ means "is approximately equal to.")

### Computing Percentiles

The percentile or percentile rank of an observation is the percent of a distribution that falls below its midpoint; one-half of the observation is said to fall below its midpoint. Thus, if there are 40 scores in a distribution, and Tom's score exceeds those of 37 students, the percentile rank of his score is 37.5/40 × 100. Expressed mathematically, the percentile rank, $PR$, of the score having rank $R_i$ in the rank-order distribution (Sec. 3.2) is

$$PR_i = 100\left(1 - \frac{R_i - .5}{n}\right) \tag{3.3}$$

where $R_i$ is the rank of the score $X_i$ (ranked from highest to lowest) and $n$ is the number of observations in the distribution. Using Equation 3.3, the percentile rank of Tom's score is $PR = 100(1 - (3 - .5)/40) = 93.75$ or 94.

## 3.11 BOX-AND-WHISKER PLOTS

The box-and-whisker plot is a simple and very useful graph for exploring and summarizing an array of data. It takes little time or space to construct. A box-and-whisker plot of Wechsler IQ scores is given in Figure 3.5B. The "box" extends from $Q_1$ to $Q_3$ (termed "hinges" by Tukey), thus describing the middle 50% of the distribution, in this case IQs

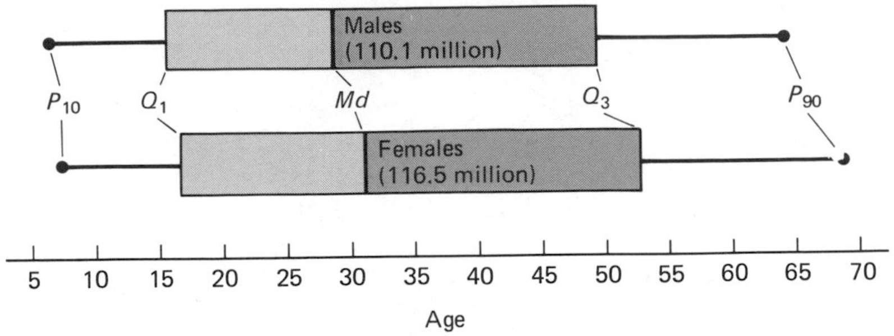


**FIGURE 3.6. Box-and-whisker plots depicting the age distributions of the populations of males and females in the United States (1980 U.S. census).**

of 90–110. The median or midpoint in the distribution falls in the box, halfway between $Q_1$ and $Q_3$ when the distribution is symmetrical, as in Figure 3.4. The whiskers extend beyond $Q_1$ and $Q_3$, often to $P_{10}$ and $P_{90}$, the points beyond which the lowest and highest scoring 10% of the distribution fall. (When further detail is desired, one can extend "dots" from the whiskers to $P_5$ and $P_{95}$.*)

Figure 3.6 gives box-and-whisker plots showing the age distributions of United States males and females in 1974 (Golladay, 1976). Note the greater longevity of females. Notice that whereas the proportions do not differ markedly at the young age, the female distribution extends considerably farther to the right. Notice that both distributions are skewed positively. Skewness is indicated (1) when the whiskers differ in length, (2) when $(Md - Q_1) \neq (Q_3 - Md)$, or (3) when $(Md - P_{10}) \neq (P_{90} - Md)$.

## 3.12 STEM-AND-LEAF DISPLAYS

Another method of portraying a *batch* of data suggested by Tukey (1977) is the *stem-and-leaf display*, which is a refined grouped frequency distribution. Instead of tally marks, the last (or next) digit of the observation is used to indicate an observation. A stem-and-leaf display of the data in Table 3.3 is given in panel B. The line is the stem and each observation is a leaf. Notice that less information is lost in the stem-and-leaf displays in panel B than in the conventional grouped frequency in panel A of Table 3.3.

Figure 3.7 illustrates a more typical stem-and-leaf display and a box-and-whisker plot for the same data set. Each of the 560 observations is a leaf—a correlation coefficient between self-esteem and achievement from an exhaustive review and meta-analysis (Glass, McGaw, and Smith, 1981) of the literature. Notice that the negative skewing is evident in both the stem-and-leaf display and the box-and-whisker plot.

*The whiskers on some box-and-whisker plots extend to $P_{12.5}$ and $P_{87.5}$ to denote the mid-values in the lowest and highest quarters of the distribution (see Fig. 3.7B). This and several other of Tukey's exploratory data analysis (EDA) techniques are available in a set of computer programs described by Vellman and Hoaglin (1981).

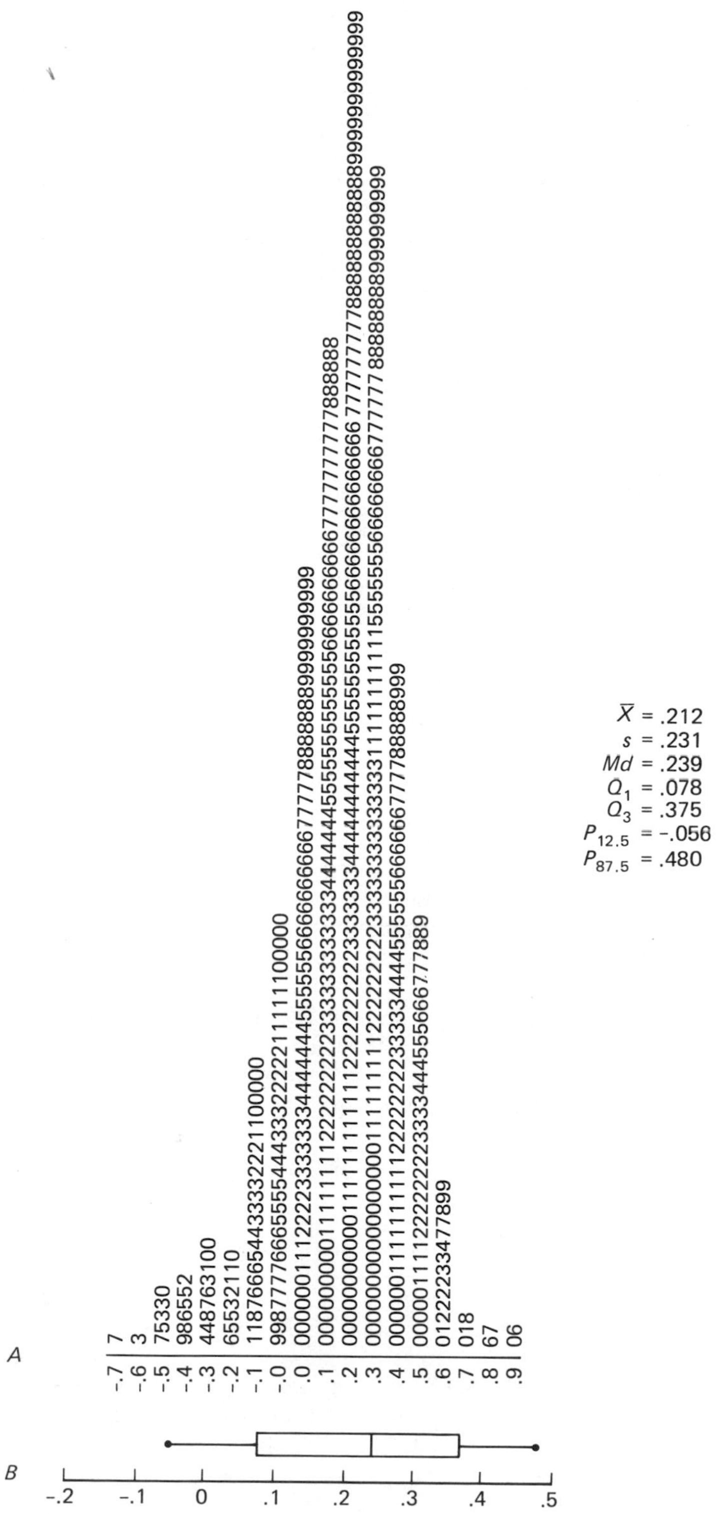


**FIGURE 3.7**
**Stem-and-leaf display (panel *A*) and box-and-whisker plot (panel *B*) of correlations between self measures and performance achievement (adapted from Hansford and Hattie, 1982).**

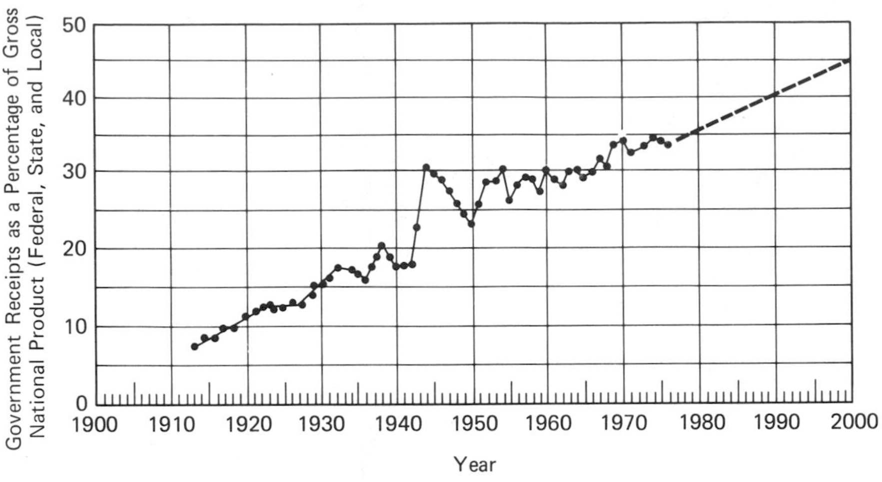


**FIGURE 3.8. An illustration of a time-series graph, "The Demise of Free Enterprise" (from Augustine, 1978).**

## 3.13 TIME-SERIES GRAPHS

The *time-series graph*, a standard statistical technique in business and economics, is becoming common in some areas of psychology (Glass, Willson, and Gottman, 1975). It can be very informative about trends in ways that no static representation of data can be. A time-series graph is a polygon in which the *X*-axis, or baseline, is time; the ordinate is a measure of the variable of interest. The time dimension can be measured in minutes, hours, days, weeks, months, years, and so on. The ordinate variable can be measured in many ways, depending on the variable of interest. Familiar examples of time-series graphs include the Dow-Jones stock price average plotted across days, the Consumer Price Index plotted across months, a patient's body temperature plotted across hours, and school enrollment plotted across years. Figure 3.8 is an illustrative time-series graph "The Demise of Free Enterprise," provided by Augustine (1978). The extrapolated projections into the future are shown by the dashed line. Obviously such projections into the distant future must be viewed with a large margin for error.

## CHAPTER SUMMARY

Statistical methods are tools for simplifying, summarizing, and systematizing a set of observations. Statistical tables, figures, graphs, and charts are means of organizing otherwise unwieldy quantities of data. The "Gestalt" or configuration of a distribution becomes evident if the observations are grouped into between five and fifteen classes. Much data in the behavioral and social sciences are normally distributed, but other types of curves are common. Skewed distributions result when observations pile up at the low or high end and drop off gradually toward the other end. The term *positive skewness* describes a distribution where the tail "points" to the high scores; the converse is true with negative skewness.

Frequency distributions can be expressed graphically using a number of different methods. Histograms (bar graphs) are especially useful with qualitative or nominal baseline ($X$-axis) variables. Frequency and percentage polygons are more useful with quantitative baseline variables. Ogive (cumulative percentage) curves are useful for determining percentiles (the percentage of a distribution that falls below a given point), such as $Q_1$ ($P_{25}$), the median ($P_{50}$), and $Q_3$($P_{75}$). Box-and-whisker plots are also useful graphs for conveying salient features of a distribution.

## MASTERY TEST

1. Which term least belongs with the others?
   a. ordinate b. $Y$-axis c. vertical axis d. $X$-axis
2. Which one of these types of distribution is best for conveying the shape of the frequency distribution of 150 test scores?
   a. rank-order distribution
   b. ungrouped frequency distribution
   c. a histogram
3. If the largest observation in a set of scores is 99 and the smallest is 71, what is the range?
4. For visually representing data in a grouped frequency distribution, how many classes are generally recommended?
   a. less then 5 b. approximately 10 c. more than 20
5. If the lowest score in a distribution is 51, with a class width of 5, what would the first interval be?
   a. 51–55 b. 47–51 c. 50–55 d. 50–54
6. If the baseline variable represents a nominal variable (such as ethnic groups), which method of graphic representation is preferred, histograms or frequency polygons?
7. Can a percentage polygon and a frequency polygon for one set of data be represented in the same figure?
8. Which term does not belong with the others?
   a. $X$-axis b. $Y$-axis c. horizontal axis d. abscissa
9. Which four of these are depicted in Figure 3.3?
   a. frequency histogram e. percentage polygon
   b. percentage histogram f. box-and-whisker plot
   c. ogive curve g. stem-and-leaf display
   d. frequency polygon h. time-series graph
10. Which of these graphs is best for determining percentiles?
    a. histogram b. percentage polygon c. ogive curve
11. If an IQ score of 90 is at $P_{25}$, what percent of scores *exceed* 90?
12. Which term does not belong?
    a. $Q_1$ b. median c. $P_{50}$ d. $Q_2$

In questions 13–17, match the verbal and graphic descriptions:

13. Rectangular distribution

14. Bimodal distribution

15. Positively skewed distribution

16. Negatively skewed distribution

a. b. c. d. e.

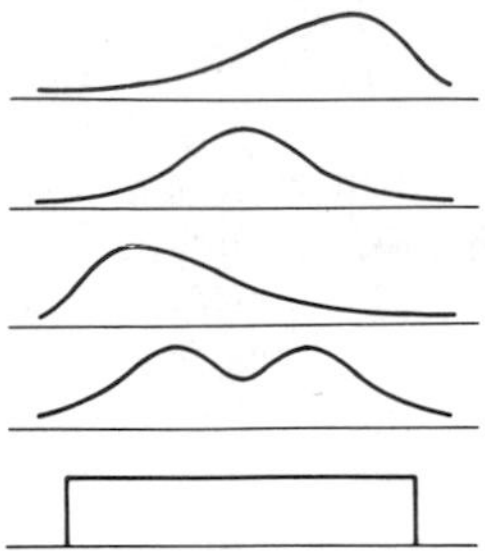

17. Which of the above curves (a–e) are symmetrical?

18. Indicate which of the following distributions is probably negatively skewed.
    a. family income in dollars per year
    b. age at graduation from college
    c. populations of cities in the United States
    d. scores on a very easy test

19. In a box-and-whisker plot, what percent of the observations fall in the box?

20. In a box-and-whisker plot, if the left-hand whisker is longer than the right-hand whisker, the distribution is probably
    a. normal
    b. bimodal
    c. postively skewed
    d. negatively skewed

## PROBLEMS AND EXERCISES

1. This problem is an exercise in constructing a grouped frequency distribution. The following data are Stanford-Binet IQ scores for 50 adults:

| | | | | |
|---|---|---|---|---|
| 141 | 87 | 115 | 91 | 96 |
| 92 | 118 | 98 | 101 | 107 |
| 97 | 124 | 118 | 146 | 108 |
| 106 | 135 | 97 | 108 | 129 |
| 107 | 110 | 101 | 129 | 109 |
| 83 | 127 | 116 | 113 | 105 |
| 127 | 114 | 112 | 114 | 139 |
| 109 | 102 | 113 | 106 | 89 |
| 108 | 92 | 102 | 102 | 134 |
| 104 | 101 | 131 | 86 | 123 |

   a. Determine the range ($X_{max}$-$X_{min}$).
   b. The class width recommended (range/10) is ___ .
   c. If a class width of 7 is used, the first (lowest) interval will begin with the score ___ .
   d. Using a class width of 5, construct a grouped frequency distribution of the fifty scores.

2. a. Construct a histogram from the fifty scores in Problem 1 using a class width of 7.
   b. Superimpose a frequency polygon in the same figure (as illustrated in Fig. 3.3).
   c. Label "Percent" on the right-hand vertical axis.

3. Add the "Percent" and "Cumulative Percent" columns to the frequency distribution in Problem 1c. Construct an ogive curve and estimate
   a. $Q_1$  b. *Md*  c. $Q_3$
   d. How do these values compare with the national parameters (see Fig. 3.5; Sec. 3.9)?
   e. Construct a box-and-whisker plot for the data in Problem 1.
   f. Construct a stem-and-leaf display for the scores in Problem 1.
4. Plot two percentage polygons on the same graph from the following grouped frequency distributions of the grade equivalent scores in reading and math on the Cooperative Test of Basic Skills for fourth-grade students in a moderate-sized school district.

| *Grade Equivalent Interval* | *Reading* | | *Math* | |
|---|---|---|---|---|
| | Frequency | Percent | Frequency | Percent |
| 11.0– | 48 | 2.9 | 9 | 0.6 |
| 10.0–10.9 | 71 | 4.3 | 13 | 0.8 |
| 9.0–9.9 | 114 | 7.0 | 35 | 2.2 |
| 8.0–8.9 | 188 | 11.5 | 58 | 3.6 |
| 7.0–7.9 | 252 | 15.4 | 160 | 9.9 |
| 6.0–6.9 | 357 | 21.8 | 453 | 27.9 |
| 5.0–5.9 | 295 | 18.0 | 442 | 27.2 |
| 4.0–4.9 | 166 | 10.1 | 267 | 16.4 |
| 3.0–3.9 | 120 | 7.3 | 142 | 8.7 |
| 2.0–2.9 | 26 | 1.6 | 39 | 2.4 |
| 1.0–1.9 | 3 | .2 | 6 | .4 |
| | $n$ = 1,640 | 100.1 | $n$ = 1,624 | 100.1 |

   a. Which distribution has more very low scores (below 4.0)?
   b. Which distribution has more very high scores (8.0 and above)?
   c. Which distribution has the higher median?
   d. Plot these distributions as ogives on the same graph. Which distribution shows the steeper slope (more nearly vertical) between 4.0 and 7.0?
   e. Construct box-and-whisker plots. Use percentile points from the ogive curve.
   f. What accounts for the fact that the percent columns did not add up to exactly 100.0%?

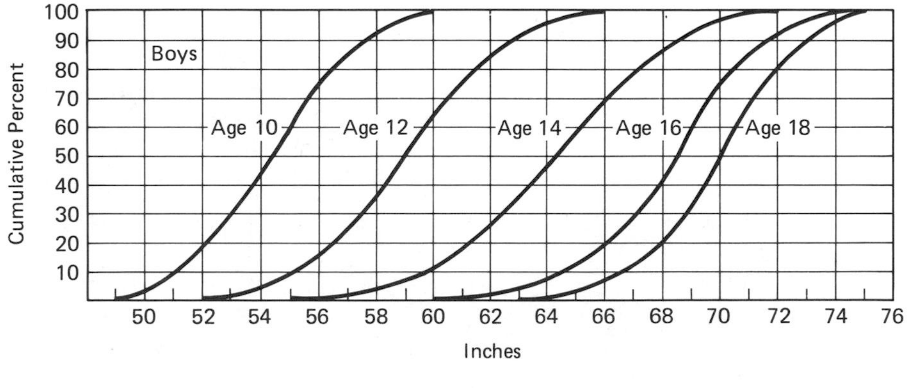

5. The preceding ogive curves for boy's heights were prepared from data compiled by National Center for Health Statistics (*NCHS Growth Charts*, 1976).
   a. What is the median height for boys at age 12?
   b. How much growth in height does the median boy make between age 12 and 14?
   c. At age 16 Kenny Dean was 64 in. tall; two years later he was 72 in. tall. His percentile rank increased from about the ____ at age 16 to about the ____ at age 18.
   d. The most growth occurs for the median boy during which two-year interval?
   e. The distance between $Q_3$ and $Q_1$ is termed the *interquartile range.* Which curve has the largest interquartile range? How much taller is the boy at $P_{75}$ than the boy at $P_{25}$ at that age?
   f. Construct box-and-whisker graphs for the five distributions using the same $X$-axis. Is skewness more apparent from these figures than from the ogive curves?
6. Women who called for help at a suicide prevention center were classified in relation to their menstrual cycles (Mandell and Mandell, 1967). The menstrual cycle for each woman was grouped into seven periods of days beginning with the onset of the menstrual period. The incidence of the eighty-seven suicide calls for each of the seven periods was 27, 7, 5, 15, 6, 9, 18. Construct a frequency and percentage polygon to portray graphically these data.

## *ANSWERS TO MASTERY TEST*

1. d
2. c
3. Range = $X_{max} - X_{min} = 99 - 71 = 28$
4. b
5. d. 50–54, since 50 is the largest multiple of the class width (5) that is below the lowest score of 51
6. Histograms
7. Yes
8. b
9. a, b, d, and e
10. c
11. 75%
12. a
13. e
14. d
15. c
16. a
17. b, d, and e
18. d
19. 50%
20. d

## *ANSWERS TO PROBLEMS AND EXERCISES*

1. a. Range = 146 − 83 = 63
   b. 63/10 = 6.3, hence $w$ = 6 or 7
   c. 77
3. a. $Q_1 \doteq 97.5$ (the symbol $\doteq$ is read, "is approximately equal to");
   b. $Md \doteq 106$
   c. $Q_3 \doteq 125.5$
   d. The national values are lower.
4. a. math
   b. reading
   c. reading
   d. math
   f. rounding error
5. a. 59 in.
   b. $5\frac{1}{2}$ in.
   c. 8th, 80th
   d. 12–14
   e. age 14; $Q_3 - Q_1 = 66.5 - 61.5$ in. = 5 in.
   f. yes

# 4 MEASURES OF CENTRAL TENDENCY

## 4.1 INTRODUCTION

Measures of *central tendency* are statistics that describe typical, average, or representative scores. They indicate the location of the bulk of scores in a distribution, but they tell little else about the shape of the distribution. Many different measures of central tendency exist—perhaps a dozen or more; in this chapter only a half-dozen will be mentioned and of these, only three will be studied in detail. The most common measures of central tendency (mean, median, and mode) are quite different in conception and calculation. They reflect different notions of the "center" of a distribution, and at times one of them may be more useful than another. Measures of central tendency are the most widely used statistical descriptions of data, not only in research but also for quantitative information reported to the public.

## 4.2 THE MODE

The *mode* is the score that *occurs most frequently*. In the set of scores (2,6,6,8,9,9,9,10) the mode is 9 because it occurs more often than any other score. The mode is the most

| *Height* | *Tally* | *f* | *Cumulative f* | |
|---|---|---|---|---|
| 75 | | 1 | 192 | Mode = 68 in. |
| 74 | | 2 | 191 | Median = 68.38 in. |
| 73 | | 5 | 189 | Mean = 68.44 in. |
| 72 | | 10 | 184 | Midrange = 69 in. |
| 71 | | 19 | 174 | Midhinge = 68.48 in. |
| 70 | | 25 | 155 | Trimean = 68.43 in. |
| 69 | | 30 | 130 | |
| 68 | | 34 | 100 | |
| 67 | | 30 | 66 | |
| 66 | | 14 | 36 | |
| 65 | | 12 | 22 | |
| 64 | | 8 | 10 | |
| 63 | | 2 | 2 | |

$n = 192$

**FIGURE 4.1**
**Frequency distribution of the height of 192 adult males.**

frequent *score* (9 in this example) and not the frequency of that score (3 in this example). The modal letter grade given in a history course may be "B." "Smith" is the modal name in the United States. The mode can be employed even with qualitative, categorical variables—data that represent only a nominal scale of measurement. For example, there are 100 females to every ninety-five males in the United States; hence, the modal sex is female.

When observations have been grouped into classes, the midpoint of the class with the largest frequency is used as an estimate of the mode. Notice that the mode of the heights of the adult males in Figure 4.1 is 68 in.,—the midpoint of the most "popular" interval. Table 3.3 and Figure 3.1 show that the mode of the grouped frequency distribution is estimated to be 73, the midpoint of the 70-76 class. This value (73) differs little from the precise value of the mode (75) found from the ungrouped frequency distribution given in Table 3.2 (Sec. 3.3).

In the group of scores (10,11,11,11,11,12,12,13,14,14,14,17) both 11 and 14 are modes; the distribution is said to be *bimodal.* Large sets of scores are often referred to as bimodal when they present a frequency polygon that looks like a two-humped camel's back, even if the frequencies at the two peaks are not strictly equal. This slight twisting of the definition is allowed because the term *bimodal* is convenient and descriptive. A distinction can be made between *major* and *minor modes* in these instances.

## 4.3 THE MEDIAN

*The median is the 50th percentile of a distribution*—the point below which half of the observations fall. In any distribution there will always be an equal number of cases above and below the median. For an odd number of untied scores (such as 11,13,18,19,20) the median is the middle score when they are arranged in rank order ($Md = 18$). For an even number of untied scores, (such as 4,9,13,14) the median is the point halfway between the two central values when the scores are arranged in rank order: $Md = (9 + 13)/2 = 11$.

If tied scores occur in the data, particularly at or near the median, a frequency tabulation of the scores will probably be necessary. Interpolation within a score class will often be necessary in such instances. For example, in Figure 4.1 there will be $n/2$ (or $192/2 = 96$) scores below (and above) the median. In the cumulative frequency column of Figure 4.1 it can be seen that sixty-six of the observations fall below the interval within which the median falls, 68 in. One needs $96 - 66 = 30$ more scores to reach the median. Because there are thirty-four observations in this interval, the median is located 30/34 of the distance into the interval. Because $30/34 = .88$ and the interval has a width ($w$) of 1 in., the median ($Md$) is .88 in. above the lower limit ($L$) of the interval, that is, $Md = 67.50$ in. + .88 in. = 68.38 in.

The procedure for calculating the median from a grouped frequency distribution is described in Equation 4.1.

$$Md = L_M + w\left(\frac{n/2 - {}_{cum}f}{f_M}\right) \tag{4.1}$$

where, *for the interval that contains the median*, $L_M$ is its lower limit, $w$ is its width, $f_M$ is its frequency, ${}_{cum}f$ is number of observations falling below it, and $n$ is number of scores in the entire distribution.

For example, in Table 3.3 $n = 38$ and the median falls within the 77–83 interval; thus $L_M = 76.5$, $f_M = 5$, and $w = 7$. There are seventeen scores below this interval; hence ${}_{cum}f = 17$ and, from Equation 4.1,

$$Md = 76.5 + 7\left(\frac{38/2 - 17}{5}\right) = 76.5 + 2.8 = 79.3$$

The median can be found for any distribution that can be ordered, that is, it requires only an ordinal scale of measurement. If members of Congress are ranked on a liberal-conservative scale, the middlemost Congressperson represents the median of the group even though only a rank order is involved. The median can be estimated graphically, as illustrated in the ogive curve in Chapter 3. Although the median determined from a grouped frequency distribution is less precise than if the ungrouped observations were employed, occasionally one does not have the raw observations available, as in Figure 4.1.

## 4.4 SUMMATION NOTATION, Σ

Before learning about the mean, one must become familiar with the summation operator, $\Sigma$. $X_1, X_2, \ldots, X_n$ stands for a group of $n$ numbers, any one of which can be referred to as $X_i$, the $i$th number. $X_1 + X_2$ stands for the *sum* of the first and second numbers. The ordering of the subscripts is usually completely arbitrary: $X_2 + X_1$ could be used to designate the sum of the first and second numbers instead.

If there are five numbers in the group, $n = 5$ and the sum of all the numbers is $X_1 + X_2 + \ldots X_5$. Using $\Sigma$ notation, one can denote this sum by $\Sigma_{i=1}^{n=5} X_i$ or $\Sigma_{i=1}^{5} X_i$.

The sum of all $n$ numbers in a group when $n$ is not specified is $X_1 + X_2 + \ldots + X_n$, which is abbreviated as $\Sigma_{i=1}^{n} X_i$. Thus*

$$\sum_{i=1}^{n} X_i = X_1 + X_2 + \ldots + X_n \tag{4.2}$$

$\Sigma$ is the capital Greek letter sigma. $\Sigma_{i=1}^{5} X_i$ is read "the sum of $X_i$ as $i$ runs from 1 to 5." $\Sigma_{i=1}^{n} X_i$ is read "the sum of $X_i$ as $i$ runs from 1 to $n$." In most applications in this book the summation is for all $n$-values. Hence the lower and upper limits will be eliminated from the summation sign unless they are needed to avoid ambiguity, that is, $\Sigma_{i=1}^{n} X_i = \Sigma X_i$. Occasionally $\Sigma_i$ will be used to denote $\Sigma_{i=1}^{n}$, the $i$ being a concise way of $i$ indicating that the summation begins at $i = 1$ and continues through $i = n$, that is $\Sigma_{i=1}^{n} X_i = \Sigma_i X_i = \sum\limits_{i} X_i = \Sigma X_i$, or even $\Sigma X$ if there is no ambiguity.

## 4.5 THE MEAN

The mean, or arithmetic mean,† of a set of observations is simply their sum, $\Sigma_i X_i$, divided by the number of observations $n$.

$$\overline{X} = \frac{\Sigma X_i}{n} \quad \text{or more explicitly} \quad \overline{X} = \frac{\sum_{i=1}^{n} X_i}{n} \tag{4.3}$$

The mean is the familiar "average." People often use the word "average" for any one of the three aforementioned measures of central tendency. The name "mean," being less ambiguous, is preferred. The common symbol for the mean is $\overline{X}$. The bar above $X$ indicates that an average has been taken. If $X_1 = 40$, $X_2 = 45$, and $X_3 = 65$, the sum of the $n = 3$ scores, $\Sigma X_i$, is $40 + 45 + 65 = 150$. The mean is $\overline{X} = \Sigma X_i/n$ $150/3 = 50$. The sum of the $n = 192$ $X_i$'s in Figure 4.1 is 13,141, thus $\overline{X} = 13{,}141/192 = 68.44$.

It should be apparent that the concepts of mean and median are virtually meaningless with categorical variables such as college major or nationality. (What is the mean or median occupation in the United States?) But the mode has meaning even with nominal scales (categorical variables, see Sec. 2.3).

*It is conventional to locate the lower and upper limits for the summation just below and above the summation sign respectively, as in Equation 4.2. However when the limits occur in the text, they will be positioned to the immediate right of the $\Sigma$ to improve legibility.

†Since the term *mean*, without a modifier, always denotes the arithmetic mean, hereafter we will use *mean* without the modifier. However, there are other kinds of means, e.g., the harmonic mean $(= n/\Sigma_i 1/X_i)$ and the geometric mean $(= n/\sqrt{(X_1)(X_2)\cdots(X_n)})$ that have occasional uses in applied statistics. These are not of sufficient importance to be a part of a basic course in statistics.

## 4.6
## MORE SUMMATION NOTATION

Before certain properties of the mean are discussed, more needs to be said about the summation operator $\Sigma$.

Adding numbers after something has been done to them, such as multiplying each number by 6, or squaring each number is as common as simply adding the numbers as they are. Suppose one wants to multiply each of $n$ numbers by 2 and add together the resulting $n$ products. The desired sum will be $2X_1 + 2X_2 + \ldots + 2X_n$. This sum is the same as $2(X_1 + X_2 + \ldots + X_n)$. Using $\Sigma$ notation, $X_1 + X_2 \ldots + X_n$ can be replaced by $\Sigma_{i=1}^{n} X_i$ (see Equation 4.2). The result can be summarized as follows.

$$2X_1 + 2X_2 + \ldots + 2X_n = \sum_{i=1}^{n} 2X_i = 2 \sum_{i=1}^{n} X_i$$

This result did not come about because of any magic in the number 2; if $c$ stands for any constant number (i.e., a number that does not change regardless of what $i$ is), then

$$cX_1 + cX_2 + \ldots + cX_n = \sum_{i=1}^{n} cX_i = c \sum_{i=1}^{n} X_i \qquad \text{(Rule 1)} \qquad \textbf{(4.4)}$$

If a constant number $c$ is to be added to each of $n$ numbers, one writes $X_1 + c, X_2 + c, \ldots, X_n + c$. The sum of these $n$ new numbers is

$$(X_1 + c) + (X_2 + c) + \ldots + (X_n + c) = \sum_{i=1}^{n} (X_i + c)$$

With addition, numbers can always be regrouped in any order.

$$\sum_{i=1}^{n} (X_i + c) = (X_1 + X_2 + \ldots + X_n) + (c + c + \ldots + c)$$

The first sum in parentheses on the right-hand side above is $\Sigma_{i=1}^{n} X_i$. The second sum equals $nc$. Consequently,

$$\sum_{i=1}^{n} (X_i + c) = \sum_{i=1}^{n} X_i + \sum_{i=1}^{n} c = \sum_{i=1}^{n} X_i + nc \qquad \text{(Rule 2)} \qquad \textbf{(4.5)}$$

Recall from Equation 4.3 that

$$\overline{X} = \frac{1}{n}(X_1 + X_2 + \ldots + X_n) = \frac{1}{n}\sum_{i} X_i$$

## 4.7 ADDING OR SUBTRACTING A CONSTANT

What would happen to the value of the mean if a constant were added to every score? Suppose 3 is added to each of the five scores in Section 4.9. The scores 3,4,4,6,8 are obtained; their mean is $(3 + 4 + 4 + 6 + 8)/5 = 25/5 = 5$. It is no coincidence that the mean is 3 points greater than the original mean.

If a constant $c$ is added to each score in a group whose mean is $\overline{X}$, the resulting scores will have a mean equal to $\overline{X} + c$. Proof:

$$\frac{1}{n} \sum_i (X_i + c) = \frac{1}{n} \sum X_i + \frac{1}{n} \sum c = \overline{X} + \left(\frac{1}{n}\right) nc = \overline{X} + c \tag{4.6}$$

Obviously the proof holds when $c$ is a negative number, that is, when a constant is subtracted from every observation in a distribution, the mean of the augmented distribution is $\overline{X} - c$.

## 4.8 MULTIPLYING OR DIVIDING BY A CONSTANT

If each score in a set whose mean is $\overline{X}$ is multiplied by a constant $c$, the mean of the resulting scores is $c\overline{X}$, because

$$\frac{\sum_{i=1}^{n} cX_i}{n} = \frac{c\sum_i X_i}{n} = c\overline{X}. \tag{4.7}$$

Recall that dividing by $c$ is equivalent to multiplying by $1/c$. Thus if every observation in a distribution is divided by $c$, the mean of the augmented distribution is $(1/c)(\overline{X}) = \overline{X}/c$.

## 4.9 SUM OF DEVIATIONS

What if $\overline{X}$ were subtracted from the score $X_1$? The resulting difference is a *deviation score*, which can be either negative or positive. If one were to find the deviation score for each of the $n$ scores in the set, *the sum of all* n *deviation scores would be exactly zero*.*

*The proof follows that the sum of the deviation scores $\Sigma\, x_i$ is zero:

$$\sum_{i=1}^{n} x_i = \sum_{i=1}^{n} (X_i - \overline{X}) = \sum_i X_i - \sum_i \overline{X} = \sum_i X_i - n\overline{X}$$

$$= \sum_i X_i - n \frac{\sum_i X_i}{n} = \sum_i X_i - \sum_i X_i = 0$$

| *Data* | *Score* ($X_i$) | − | *Mean* ($\overline{X}$) | = | *Deviation* ($x_i$) |
|---|---|---|---|---|---|
| 0,1,1,3,5 | 0 | − | 2 | = | −2 |
| $n = 5$ | 1 | − | 2 | = | −1 |
| $\overline{X} = 2$ | 1 | − | 2 | = | −1 |
| | 3 | − | 2 | = | 1 |
| | 5 | − | 2 | = | 3 |
| | | | | | $\Sigma_i x_i = 0$ |

## 4.10
## SUM OF SQUARED DEVIATIONS

A fourth property of the mean concerns the $n$ deviation scores. *The sum of the squared deviations of scores from their mean is less than the sum of the squared deviations around any point other than* $\overline{X}$.

That is, $(X_1 - \overline{X})^2 + (X_2 - \overline{X})^2 + \ldots + (X_n - \overline{X})^2$ is smaller in value than $(X_1 - b)^2 + (X_2 - b)^2 + \ldots + (X_n - b)^2$, where $b \neq \overline{X}$. (For proof, see Glass and Stanley, 1970, p. 65.)

For example, the sum of the squared deviations of 0,1,1,3,5 around 2, their mean, is $(0 - 2)^2 + (1 - 2)^2 + (1 - 2)^2 + (3 - 2)^2 + (5 - 2)^2 = (-2)^2 + (-1)^2 + (-1)^2 + (1)^2 + (3)^2 = 16$. The sum of the squared deviations of 0,1,1,3,5 around 1 is equal to 21, which is greater than 16.

## 4.11
## THE MEAN OF THE SUM OF TWO OR MORE SCORES

Later chapters use a composite variable created by adding two or more scores for each of the $n$ subjects. Suppose $K$ scores are obtained for each subject and their sum forms a composite. The mean of a sum is simply the sum of the $K$ means, as defined in Equation 4.8.

$$\overline{X}_{1+2\ldots+K} = \overline{X}_1 + \overline{X}_2 + \ldots + \overline{X}_K = \sum_{K=1}^{K} \overline{X}_K \tag{4.8}$$

If the mean of two midterm examinations are $\overline{X}_1 = 40$ and $\overline{X}_2 = 45$, and the mean of the final examination is $\overline{X}_3 = 65$, what is the mean of the total scores $\overline{X}_{1+2+3}$? From Equation 4.8:

$$\overline{X}_{1+2+3} = \overline{X}_1 + \overline{X}_2 + \overline{X}_3$$

$$= 40 + 45 + 65 = 150$$

## 4.12 THE MEAN OF A DIFFERENCE

Suppose a difference or gain score is formed for each person by subtracting one score from another. For example, if $X_1$ is a pretest and $X_2$ is a posttest, what is the mean gain $\overline{X}_{2-1}$? The pretest score could be subtracted from the posttest score for each of the $n$ subjects, and the mean of these differences could be found using Equation 4.3. This mean difference is equivalent to the difference in the means:

$$\overline{X}_{2-1} = \overline{X}_2 - \overline{X}_1 \tag{4.9}$$

The mean difference ($\overline{X}_{2-1}$) between test 1 ($\overline{X}_1 = 40$) and test 2 ($\overline{X}_2 = 45$) is $45 - 40 = 5$.

## 4.13 MEAN, MEDIAN, AND MODE OF TWO OR MORE GROUPS

Suppose the means, medians, and modes of scores from three separate groups are known and one wishes to find the same measures of central tendency for all three groups combined.* This will be a simple matter in the case of the mean, but for the median and mode it will be necessary to go back to the original data and make new calculations. The ease with which the mean of the combined groups is found reveals one of the advantages of summary statistics defined in terms of simple algebraic operations, such as adding and dividing, and having every score in a group exert an influence on the statistic. The median and mode are found by the operations of ranking and inspecting the data, respectively.

The means and $n$'s for three ethnic groups on a 100-item standard reading test for a representative sample of fifth-grade students in Colorado were:

| | | |
|---|---|---|
| Whites | $\overline{X}_1 = 64.70$ | $n_1 = 2{,}367$ |
| Blacks | $\overline{X}_2 = 49.80$ | $n_2 = 138$ |
| Hispanics | $\overline{X}_3 = 47.40$ | $n_3 = 534$ |

The total $n_{\bullet}$ of all three groups combined is equal to $n_{\bullet} = n_1 + n_2 + n_3 = \Sigma_{j=1}^{J=3} n_j$ 3,039. The mean of the combined groups is simply the sum of all 3,039 scores divided by 3,039. The combined group mean is *not* the average of the three group means. The sum of the scores in any group is simply $\Sigma X_i = n\overline{X}$. For example, the sum of the scores of group 3 is (534)(47.40) = 25,312. Similarly, for groups 1 and 2, the sums of the scores are 153,145, and 6,872, respectively. The sum of all scores for all three groups is then 185,329. Thus the mean score of all these schools combined is 185,329/3,039 = 60.98.

*Note that the mean of the aggregate of two *groups* of scores (Sec. 4.13) is different from the mean of the composite of two scores ($X = X_1 + X_2$ in Sec. 4.11). In Section 4.11 a composite score for each of the $n$ subjects is formed. In Section 4.13, $n_2$ additional subjects are added to the $n_1$ subjects in the distribution to form a distribution of $n_{\bullet} = n_1 + n_2$ subjects.

Symbolically, the grand mean of the combined groups $\overline{X}_{\bullet}$ is

$$\overline{X}_{\bullet} = \frac{n_1\overline{X}_1 + n_2\overline{X}_2 + n_3\overline{X}_3}{n_1 + n_2 + n_3} = \frac{n_1\overline{X}_1 + n_2\overline{X}_2 + n_3\overline{X}_3}{n_{\bullet}}$$

The general equation for the grand mean $\overline{X}_{\bullet}$ of the $n_{\bullet}$ scores in the $J$ groups is given in Equation 4.10:

$$\overline{X}_{\bullet} = \frac{n_1\overline{X}_1 + n_2\overline{X}_2 + \ldots + n_J\overline{X}_J}{n_{\bullet}} = \frac{\sum_{j=1}^{J} n_j\overline{X}_j}{n_{\bullet}} \tag{4.10}$$

Hence, if there are four groups ($J = 4$) to be combined, Equation 4.10 becomes the following:

$$\overline{X}_{\bullet} = \frac{n_1\overline{X}_1 + n_2\overline{X}_2 + n_3\overline{X}_3 + n_4\overline{X}_4}{n_{\bullet}}$$

Notice that if each group is based on the same number of frequencies, $n_1 = n_2 = n_3 = n$, then Equation 4.10 becomes for $J = 3$

$$\overline{X}_{\bullet} = \frac{n(\overline{X}_1 + \overline{X}_2 + \overline{X}_3)}{3n} = \frac{\overline{X}_1 + \overline{X}_2 + \overline{X}_3}{3}$$

This shows that if the three groups are the same size, the mean of the combined group is the same as the unweighted average of the three means. Of course, this is true for combining any number of means of equal-size groups. A common statistical error is committed when one assumes that the mean of combined groups is the average of the constituent group means when the individual groups are of different sizes. A recent study (see Hopkins and Stanley, 1981, p. 70) reported that the mean scores of approximately 4,000 anthropology majors, 37,000 psychology majors, and 5,000 sociology majors on the verbal test of the Graduate Record Examination were 571, 533, and 494, respectively. The mean score for these 46,000 behavioral science majors, from Equation 4.10, is then

$$\overline{X}_{\bullet} = \frac{(4{,}000)(571) + (37{,}000)(533) + (5{,}000)(494)}{46{,}000} = 532.1^*$$

Attempting to find the median or the mode of combined groups is a different matter, however. For both the mode and median, the original data must be in hand before these measures of central tendency on combined groups can be found.

*Do not be concerned if the answers to your computations differ slightly from those in the book. Very small discrepancies will result from intermediate points at which rounding is done. If you are using a hand calculator, rounding intermediate values is unnecessary. At least three figures (other than preceding zeros) should be retained in the final answer.

## 4.14
## INTERPRETATION OF MODE, MEDIAN, AND MEAN

Each measure of central tendency can be thought of as resulting in a different set of errors if it were used to represent the entire distribution of scores. The sense in which the mode is the most representative score or the score which best "takes the place of all of the scores" is fairly obvious. If one score were selected to stand for every score in a group, the mode would most often correspond to a score in the distribution.

The interpretation of the median is less obvious. Suppose that the scores 1,3,6, 7, and 8 are placed along a number line:

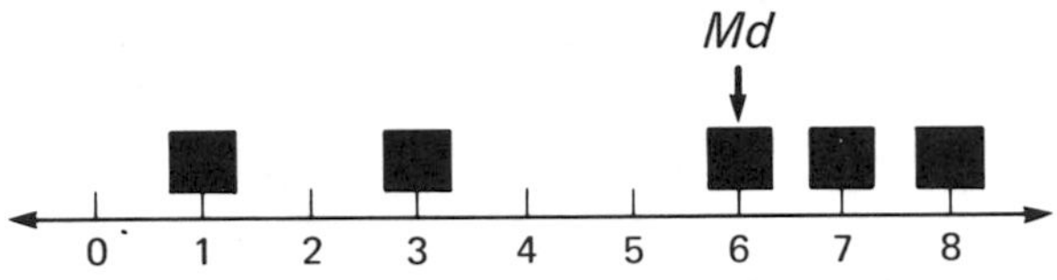


*Md* indicates the median of the group, $Md = 6$. The distance between 6 and 1 is 5 units; between 6 and 3, 3 units; between 6 and 6, 0 units; between 6 and 7, 1 unit; between 6 and 8, 2 units. The sum of these distances, $5 + 1 + 0 + 1 + 2 = 11$, is smaller than would be the sum of the distances of the five points from any other point on the line. *The median of a group of scores is that point on the number line such that the sum of the distances of all scores in the group to that point is smaller than the sum of distances to any other point.* If the median is substituted for every score in the group, less error results than if the mean, mode, or any other value is used as the reference point, where "error" is defined as the sum of the absolute distances of all scores from the reference point (Horst, 1931).

*The mean of a group of scores is that point on the number line such that the sum of the squared distances of all scores to that point is smaller than the sum of the squared distances to any other point.* If the mean is taken in place of every score in the group, the sum of the squared errors that result is at a minimum. This is termed the *least-squares criterion* in statistics: the sum of squared deviations of scores from a point is *least* about the mean than about any other point (see Sec. 4.10).

## 4.15
## OTHER MEASURES OF CENTRAL TENDENCY

Several other "midsummary" measures of central tendency are occasionally used, especially for exploratory data analyses (Tukey, 1977): *the Midrange* $= (X_{max}-X_{min})/2$, *the Midhinge* $= (Q_1 + Q_3)/2$, and *the Trimean* $= (Q_1 + 2Md + Q_3)/4$. The midhinge is the middle of the box in box-and-whisker plots. For the data in Figure 4.1, Midrange $= (75 + 63)/2 = 69$, Midhinge $= (66.90 + 70.06)/2 = 68.48$, and Trimean $= [66.90 + 2(68.38) + 70.06]/4 = 68.43$. The trimean is halfway between the median and the midhinge; ordinarily it will fall between the median and the mean. In distributions that are approximately symmetric, the values of the various measures of central tendency will differ little, as illustrated in Figure 4.1.

## 4.16 CENTRAL TENDENCY AND SKEWNESS

In *unimodal, symmetric distributions*, such as the normal curve in Figure 4.2A, *the mean* ($\overline{X}$), *median* (*Md*), *and mode* (*Mo*) (and the other measures of central tendency mentioned in this chapter) *will be the same.* For example, the mean, median, and mode IQ scores are all 100. In symmetric distributions, such as in Figure 4.2B and C, *the mean and median will be the same.* Note that a true rectangular distribution, such as Figure 4.2C, has no mode, but Figure 4.2B has two modes. Hence it is *bimodal.*

In skewed distributions like Figure 4.2D and E, the mean is "pulled" toward the "tail"; that is, the mean has the largest value of the three measures of central tendency in a positively skewed distribution, but the smallest value in a distribution that is negatively skewed. The median falls between the mean and mode in skewed distributions—usually closer to the mean than to the mode. With unimodal curves of moderate asymmetry, the distance from the median to the mode is approximately twice that of the distance between the median and the mean. The following equation can be used to obtain an estimate of the mode when the mean and median are provided:

$$\text{Mode} \doteq 3Md - 2\overline{X} \tag{4.11}$$

Using Equation 4.11, if $Md = 102$ and $\overline{X} = 103$, confirm that Mode $\doteq 100$.

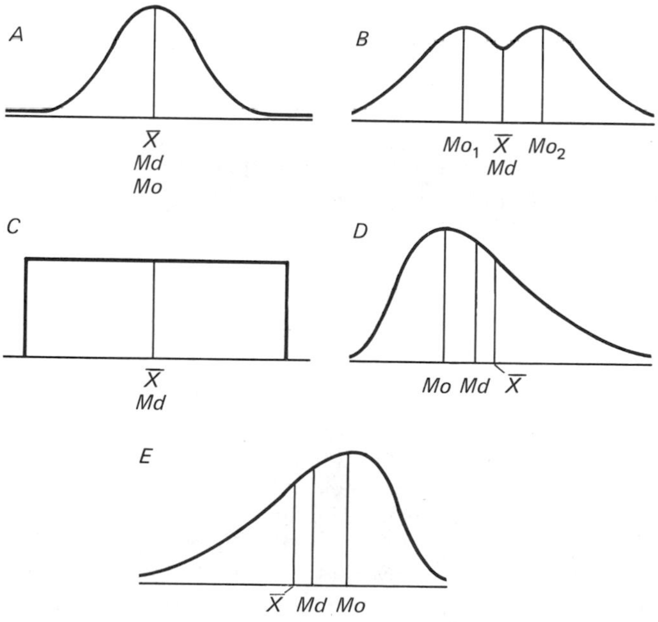


**FIGURE 4.2**
**The relationships between measures of central tendency and shape of distribution.**

## 4.17 MEASURES OF CENTRAL TENDENCY AS INFERENTIAL STATISTICS

When used inferentially, measures from a sample are viewed as estimates of the corresponding values in the population called parameters. If 100 ten-year-old girls were randomly sampled from the entire population of ten-year-old girls and weighed, would the mean, median, and mode of the 100 weights be precisely the same as the mean, median, and mode of the population? Intuitively one realizes that the values for the sample and those for the population would differ to some degree. This difference is termed *sampling error:*

$$\text{Sampling error} = \text{Parameter} - \text{estimate of parameter (an inferential statistic)} \quad \textbf{(4.12)}$$

For example, the difference between a sample mean, $\overline{X}$, and the population mean or parameter, $\mu$, is sampling error. Lowercase Greek letters are used to denote parameters. Thus the parameter $\mu$ is said to be estimated by the inferential statistic $\overline{X}$.

Inferential statistics and sampling error are discussed in subsequent chapters. The mean will be used much more frequently than the median or mode, even though the median is usually a better *descriptive* measure of central tendency. One reason for the dominance of the mean is that, on the average, there is less sampling error associated with the mean than with the median, and the mode tends to have more sampling error than the median. In other words, the difference between the statistic $\overline{X}$ and the parameter $\mu$ tends to be less than for the corresponding values for the sample, median ($Md$) and population median ($Md_{pop}$).

As inferential measures, the mean has greater precision than the median, which is more precise than the mode. To achieve the same degree of precision that $\overline{X}$ possesses for estimating $\mu$ with $n$ scores, more than half again the number of scores ($1.57n$ when the distribution is normal and $n$ is large) is needed for estimating the population median from the sample median (Dixon and Massey, 1969, p. 488).

In one sense the issue of precision has carried undue weight in the choice of statistical measures. Which measure is the most useful for the intended purposes should be the principal criterion. Relative precision should often be a secondary consideration. A less precise estimate of a more meaningful parameter is preferred to a more precise estimate of a less meaningful parameter.

## 4.18 WHICH MEASURE IS BEST?

There is no single answer to the question of which measure is best. If the variable under consideration represents only a nominal scale (such as political affiliation, college major, or occupation), there is no choice—only the mode is meaningful.

The mean lends itself more readily to further statistical treatment than the other two measures of central tendency. But the mean lies far from the bulk of scores in extremely skewed distributions. Perhaps two-thirds of American families have an annual income less than the nationwide average when the average is defined as the mean. Hence the median is often the preferred descriptive measure with skewed distributions. For estimating $\mu$, the mean of the sample $\overline{X}$ is more precise (has less sampling error) than is the sample median for estimating the median of the population.

## CHAPTER SUMMARY

There are three common measures of central tendency. The mean is the most widely used and the most precise for inferential purposes and is the foundation for statistical concepts that will be introduced in subsequent chapters. The mean is the ratio of the sum of the observations to the number of observations. The value of the mean is influenced by the value of every score in a distribution. Consequently, in skewed distributions it is "drawn" toward the elongated tail more than is the median or mode.

The median is the 50th percentile of a distribution. It is the point in a distribution from which the sum of the absolute differences of all scores are at a minimum. If these differences were squared, however, the minimum total would be about the mean, not the median. Hence the mean is the least-squares measure of central tendency. In perfectly symmetrical distributions the median and mean have the same value. When the mean and median differ greatly, the median is usually the most meaningful measure of central tendency for descriptive purposes.

The mode, unlike the mean and median, has descriptive meaning even with nominal scales. The mode is the most frequently occurring observation. When the median or mean is applicable, the mode is the least useful measure of central tendency. In symmetric unimodal distributions the mode, median, and mean have the same value.

## *MASTERY TEST*

Questions 1 to 4 refer to the following distribution of observations:

1,3,6,8,9,9,10,10,10

1. What is the mode?
2. What is the value of $n$? What is the median?
3. What is the value of $\Sigma_{i=1}^{n} X_i$? What is the mean?
4. Describe the shape of the distribution.

Questions 5 to 18 pertain to the three common measures of central tendency.

5. Which requires only nominal scale?
6. Which requires only ranked observations?
7. Which is the point below and above which half the observations fall?
8. Which is influenced by the specific value of every observation?
9. Which will be equal in a symmetrical distribution?
10. Will all three be equal in a normal distribution?
11. Which will have the largest value in a positively skewed distribution?
12. Which will have the largest value in a negatively skewed distribution?

13. Which of the three is neither the largest nor the smallest in skewed distributions?
14. Which lends itself (best) to other arithmetic operations?
15. Which is used most widely in more advanced statistical methods?
16. Which can be estimated accurately from ogive curves?
17. Which is easily estimated from histograms or frequency polygons?
18. Which is equal to $P_{50}$ and $Q_2$?
19. In a distribution of scores for which $\overline{X} = 65.5$, $Md = 64$, and Mode = 60, it was found that a mistake had been made on one score. Instead of 70, the score should have been 90. Consequently, which measure of central tendency would certainly be incorrect?
20. If there were forty observations in the distribution in Question 19, what would be the correct value for the mean?
21. If the mean salary for the ten female faculty members in a department is $28,000 and for the forty male faculty members is $30,000, what is the mean salary for all fifty faculty members?
22. If most students in your statistics class had read this chapter so carefully that they knew the answers to almost all questions on this Mastery Test, the scores would be expected to be
    a. normally distributed
    b. skewed negatively
    c. skewed positively
    d. bimodal
    e. rectangular

For Questions 23 and 24, assume the mean of Test 1 is 40 and the mean of Test 2 is 50.

23. What is the mean of the sum of the two tests, $\overline{X}_{1+2}$?
24. What is the mean difference between the two tests, $\overline{X}_{2-1}$?

## *PROBLEMS AND EXERCISES*

1. Find the mean, median, and mode of the following set of scores:

   1.2, 1.5, 1.7, 2.1, 2.4, 2.4, 2.7, 2.8, 3.0, 3.0, 3.0, 3.0, 3.1, 3.1, 3.4

2. Suppose the number 0.5 is added to each of the fifteen scores in the preceding problem. What will be the value of the mean and median of these 15 augmented scores?
3. Suppose that each of the fifteen scores in the distribution in Problem 1 is multiplied by 3. What would be the values of the mean and median of the resulting scores?
4. Find the median and estimate the mode of the 100 scores in the following grouped frequency distribution:

| *Score Interval* | *Frequency* |
|---|---|
| 45–49 | 8 |
| 40–44 | 12 |
| 35–39 | 40 |
| 30–34 | 26 |
| 25–29 | 10 |
| 20–24 | 4 |
| | $n = 100$ |

5. If the midpoint of each of the score intervals in Problem 4 is multiplied by its frequency, and these products are summed and divided by 100, a value of 35.50 results. Name this statistic.
6. Group $A$ contains ten scores, the mean and median of which are 14.5 and 13, respectively. Group $B$ contains twenty scores, the mean and median of which are 12.7 and 10, respectively. What are the mean and median of the thirty scores obtained from combining Groups $A$ and $B$?
7. During a recent decade, the mean income in the South increased 74% for whites and 113% for nonwhites. What was the mean increase for both groups combined? Among every 100 workers, eighty-two were white.
8. The seven members of the Sunday Afternoon Picnic Society (SAPS) live along a straight stretch of Highway 101. They are also members of the Determined Oppressors of the Polluters of Ecology Society (DOPES). Their homes are positioned along the highway as follows:

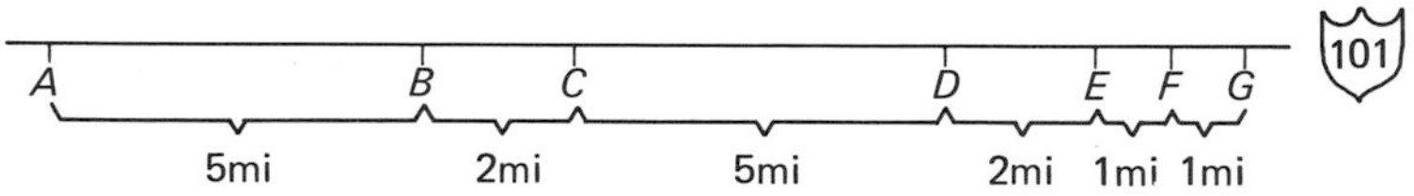


Since any point along Highway 101 is a fine place for a picnic, at which point along the road should the members hold their picnic so as to require the minimum amount of gasoline for travel? (Their conservation commitment stops short of doing without their automobiles.) The point represents which measure of central tendency?

## *ANSWERS TO MASTERY TEST*

1. 10
2. $n = 9$, $Md = 9$
3. $\Sigma X = 66$, $\overline{X} = 7.33$
4. Skewed negatively
5. Mode
6. Median
7. Median
8. Mean
9. Mean and median
10. Yes
11. Mean
12. Mode
13. Median
14. Mean
15. Mean
16. Median
17. Mode
18. Median
19. Mean
20. 66.0
21. $\overline{X}_{\bullet} = \$29,600$
22. b
23. 90
24. 10

## *ANSWERS TO PROBLEMS AND EXERCISES*

1. $\overline{X} = 2.56$; $Md = 2.8$; Mode = 3.0
2. $\overline{X} = 3.06$; $Md = 3.3$
3. $\overline{X} = 7.68$; $Md = 8.4$
4. $Md = 35.75$; Mode $\doteq 37$
5. The mean
6. Mean = 13.3; combined median cannot be determined from a knowledge of individual medians and $n$'s only.
7. $\overline{X}_{\bullet} = 81.02$ or 81%
8. Point $D$, the median

# 5 MEASURES OF VARIABILITY

## 5.1 INTRODUCTION

The two most important statistical characteristics of any distribution of observations are its central tendency and its variability. Most empirical research studies in education and in the social sciences give the reader at least one measure of central tendency and at least one measure of variability. Measures of central tendency do not indicate the differences that exist among the scores; other statistical measures are required to describe the variation in the distribution of scores. This chapter discusses common measures of variability. Important distinctions between populations and samples and between parameters and statistics are also considered.

## 5.2 THE RANGE

The range is the difference between the largest ($X_{max}$) and the smallest ($X_{min}$) scores in a distribution. For example, the range of the scores 10, 12, 13, 13, 15, and 18 is 18 - 10 = 8. The scores -0.2, 0.4, 0.8, and 1.6 have a range of 1.6 - (-0.2) = 1.8. Although the meaning of the range as a measure of variability is quite clear, it has certain drawbacks. Because the range is determined by just two scores in the group, it ignores the spread of all scores except the largest and smallest. One aberrant score or "outlier" can greatly increase the range. The five distributions in Figure 3.4 have approximately the same range, even though they differ considerably in the degree of dispersion within the groups.

## 5.3 H-SPREAD AND THE RANGE INTERQUARTILE

In Section 3.11 the quartiles of a distribution of scores were defined: the first quartile $Q_1$, the point on the scale below which 25% of the scores lie, $Q_2$ (the median), and the point above which 25% of the scores lie, $Q_3$. The distance between the first and third quartiles of a group of scores, that is, $Q_3 - Q_1$, is called the *interquartile range.* A synonyn for $Q_3 - Q_1$ is *H-spread* (Tukey, 1977), the distance between the lower hinge $Q_1$ and the upper hinge $Q_3$. The *semi-interquartile range* $Q$ is half the distance between the third and first quartiles, that is,

$$Q = \frac{Q_3 - Q_1}{2} . \tag{5.1}$$

$Q$ is an easily obtained and a useful measure of variability. For most descriptive purposes it is superior to the range. If two groups of scores have the same value of $Q$, they are much more likely to possess similar patterns of heterogeneity than are two groups with the same range. In distributions that are nearly symmetrical around the median, $Q$ can be used to reconstruct the score limits between which approximately 50% of the scores are contained.

On most intelligence tests, $Md$ is approximately 100 and $Q$ is about 10 (see Figure 3.5). Therefore, approximately 50% of persons have IQ scores that lie between $Md - Q = 100 - 10 = 90$ and $Md + Q = 100 + 10 = 110$. Obviously, if instead of the median, the *midhinge* $(Q_1 + Q_3)/2$ (Sec. 4.15) is used as the point of reference, then midhinge $\pm\, Q$ will reproduce the H-spread and always contain the middle 50% of the scores.

## 5.4 DEVIATION SCORES

Note that the range, the H-spread and the semi-interquartile range do not involve every individual score in a group of scores. Other measures are influenced by the value of every score. Deviation scores, $x_i = X_i - \overline{X}$, reflect something about the variation in a set of scores. A set of scores with great heterogeneity will have some large deviation scores. Conversely, what would the deviation scores be if all the scores in the set were identical, for example, 9? The mean would be 9; hence every deviation score would be $9 - 9 = 0$.

## 5.5 SUM OF SQUARES

The sum of the deviation scores is always exactly zero: $\Sigma_{i=1}^{n} x_i = \Sigma_i (X_i - \overline{X}) = 0$ (see Sec. 4.9). Thus it is useless as a measure of variability. But each deviation could be regarded as positive (that is, their absolute values taken) and the mean deviation found. The mean deviation is rarely used as a measure of variability because the process of taking absolute values often leads to intractable mathematics for inferential purposes. Instead of working with the absolute values of deviation scores, it is preferable to square each deviation score and then sum them to obtain a quantity known as the *sum of squares;* $\Sigma_i x_i^2$. For a set of $n$ scores, the sum of squares is the following:

$$\sum_{i=1}^{n} x_i^2 = \sum_i (X_i - \overline{X})^2 = (X_1 - \overline{X})^2 + \ldots + (X_n - \overline{X})^2 = x_1^2 + \ldots + x_n^2 \qquad (5.2)$$

## 5.6 MORE ABOUT THE SUMMATION OPERATOR Σ

If the summation operation ($\Sigma$) is applied to a term that is raised to a power (for example, $\Sigma_{i=1}^{n} x_i^2$), the multiplication indicated by the exponent must be carried out before the summation. If $x_1 = 3$, $x_2 = -1$, and $x_3 = -2$, then $\Sigma_{i=1}^{n} x_i^2 = (3)^2 + (-1)^2 + (-2)^2 = 14$. Note that $\Sigma_{i=1}^{n} x_i^2 \neq (\Sigma_{i=1}^{n} x_i)^2$. In the example, $\Sigma_{i=1}^{n} x_i^2 = 14$, the quantity $(\Sigma_{i=1}^{n} x_i)^2 = [3 + (-1) + (-2)]^2 = (0)^2 = 0$.

A common expression in statistical analysis is

$$\sum_{i=1}^{n} (X_i + c)^2 = (X_1 + c)^2 + (X_2 + c)^2 + \ldots + (X_n + c)^2$$

Now $(X_i + c)^2 = (X_i + c)(X_i + c)$, which equals $(X_i^2 + 2cX_i + c^2)$. The expression within the parentheses may be written $n$ times as follows:

$$\begin{array}{l} X_1^2 + 2cX_1 + c^2 \\ X_2^2 + 2cX_2 + c^2 \\ \vdots \qquad \vdots \\ X_n^2 + 2cX_n + c^2. \end{array}$$

What is the sum of the first column? It is $X_1^2 + X_2^2 + \ldots + X_n^2 = \Sigma_{i=1}^{n} X_i^2$. And the second column sums to $2cX_1 + 2cX_2 + \ldots + 2cX_n = 2c(X_1 + X_2 + \ldots + X_n)$, which may be written concisely as $2c\, \Sigma_i X_i$. The sum of the third column is $c^2 + c^2 + \ldots + c^2 = nc^2$. Putting together these three column sums gives

$$\sum_{i=1}^{n} (X_i + c)^2 = \sum_i X_i^2 + 2c \sum_i X_i + nc^2. \qquad (5.3)$$

Though it is correct to proceed in this way (by writing each individual expression and summing colums) it is not necessary. Instead, one can "distribute the summation sign" before each term, as follows, and secure the same result more directly:

$$\begin{aligned}\sum_{i=1}^{n}(X_i + c)^2 &= \sum_i (X_i^2 + 2cX_i + c^2)\\ &= \sum_i X_i^2 + \sum_i 2cX_i + \sum_i c^2\\ &= \sum_i X_i^2 + 2c\sum_i X_i + nc^2.\end{aligned}$$

Note carefully how the summation sign was placed in front of *each* of the three terms *after* squaring.

## 5.7 THE VARIANCE OF A POPULATION

When all $N$ observations in the population are represented in a distribution, the variance $\sigma^2$ (lowercase Greek sigma) of that set of observations is the mean of the squared deviation scores (called "mean square" for short) as defined by Equation 5.4. Indeed, *mean square* is a synonym for variance.

$$\sigma^2 = \frac{\sum_i x_i^2}{N} = \frac{\sum_i (X_i - \mu)^2}{N} \tag{5.4}$$

In other words, Equation 5.4 shows that the variance in a population of observations is equal to the sum of the squared deviations from the population mean, divided by the total number of observations in the population.

## 5.8 THE VARIANCE ESTIMATED FROM A SAMPLE

An observed set of scores rarely contains all the $N$ observations in the population. Equation 5.4 should not be used when one is working with a sample of $n$ observations from the entire population of $N$ observations. If one has IQ scores from a random sample of 100 persons, the mean of the 100 observations is symbolized by $\overline{X}$, not $\mu$. Obviously there is going to be some sampling error in the selection of the 100 persons that would cause the sample mean $\overline{X}$ to differ to some degree from the mean of all observations in the population. One would not be surprised if $\overline{X}$ were 98 or 101 even though in this example it is known that $\mu$ is 100.

Obviously, the value of the sum of squares would differ somewhat, depending on whether $\overline{X}$ or $\mu$ is used as the point of reference for deviation scores. In Chapter 4 you learned that the value of the squared deviations is less from $\overline{X}$ than from any other point.

Hence, in a sample, the value of $\Sigma_i (X_i - \overline{X})^2$ would be less than $\Sigma_i (X_i - \mu)^2$ (unless, of course, $\overline{X} = \mu$).

Ideally, a sample variance would be based on $\Sigma_i (X_i - \mu)^2$; except this is impossible since $\mu$ is not known if one has only a sample of $n$ cases. The result of substituting $\overline{X}$ for the unknown $\mu$ results in a quantity slightly smaller than the ideal value of $\Sigma_i (X_i - \mu)^2$. One could correct for this bias by dividing by a factor somewhat less than $n$; but precisely how much less? The bias in estimating the variance in the population that accrues from deviating the $X$'s from the statistic, $\overline{X}$ (rather than from the parameter, $\mu$) is exactly compensated for by dividing the sum of squares by $n - 1$ rather than by $n$ (compare Eqs. 5.4 with 5.5). The expression, $n - 1$, is said to be the *degrees of freedom* for the variance estimate; throughout this book degrees of freedom will be denoted by the lowercase Greek letter "nu," $\nu$. The variance $s^2$ yielded by Equation 5.5 is an unbiased estimate of the parameter $\sigma^2$.

$$s^2 = \frac{\sum_i x_i^2}{n - 1} = \frac{\sum_i x_i^2}{\nu} = \frac{\text{Sum of squares}}{\text{Degrees of freedom}} \tag{5.5}$$

## Calculating $s^2$.

The following data will be used to illustrate the calculation of the variance $s^2$ of a set of six scores.

| $X_i$ | $x_i = X_i - \overline{X}$ | $x_i^2$ |
|---|---|---|
| 1 | $1 - 2 = -1$ | 1 |
| 3 | $3 - 2 = 1$ | 1 |
| 3 | $3 - 2 = 1$ | 1 |
| 0 | $0 - 2 = -2$ | 4 |
| 4 | $4 - 2 = 2$ | 4 |
| 1 | $1 - 2 = -1$ | 1 |
| $\Sigma_i X_i = 12$ | | $\Sigma_i x_i^2 = 12$ |

$$\overline{X} = \frac{\sum_i X_i}{n} = \frac{12}{6} = 2.00$$

$$s^2 = \frac{\sum_i x_i^2}{n - 1} = \frac{12}{6 - 1} = \frac{12}{5} = 2.40$$

In the preceding example $s^2$ was easily calculated because the mean was a whole number. Without a hand calculator, computation of $s^2$ by Equation 5.5 is tedious when the mean is not a whole number, for example, 2.173. For this reason a formula for $s^2$ that uses raw scores rather than deviation scores is desirable. It can be arrived at by the following derivation:

$$\sum_{i=1}^{n} x_i^2 = \sum_{i=1}^{n} (X_i - \overline{X})^2 = \sum_i (X_i^2 - 2\overline{X}X_i + \overline{X}^2) = \sum_i X_i^2 - 2\overline{X} \sum_i X_i + \sum_i \overline{X}^2$$

Noting that $\Sigma_i X_i = n\overline{X}$, one can write the preceding expression as follows:

$$\sum_i x_i^2 = \sum_i X_i^2 - 2n\overline{X}^2 + n\overline{X}^2 = \sum_i X_i^2 - n\overline{X}^2 \tag{5.6}$$

Equivalently, the sum of squares is

$$\sum_i x_i^2 = \sum_i X_i^2 - \left(\sum_i X_i\right)^2 \Big/ n \tag{5.6A*}$$

Thus, the variance is

$$s^2 = \frac{\sum_i X_i^2 - n\overline{X}^2}{n - 1} \tag{5.7}$$

The calculation of $s^2$ by means of Equation 5.7 will be illustrated on the six scores used in the previous example: 1, 3, 3, 0, 4, 1.

| $X$ | $X^2$ |
|---|---|
| 1 | 1 |
| 3 | 9 |
| 3 | 9 |
| 0 | 0 |
| 4 | 16 |
| 1 | 1 |
| $\Sigma X_i = 12$ | $\Sigma X_i^2 = 36$ |

$$\overline{X} = \frac{\Sigma X_i}{n} = \frac{12}{6} = 2.00$$

*Final calculations*

$$\sum_i x_i^2 = \sum_i X^2 - n\overline{X}^2 = 36 - 6(2.0)^2$$

$$= 36 - 24 = 12$$

$$s^2 = \frac{\Sigma x_i^2}{\nu} = \frac{12}{6 - 1} = \frac{12}{5} = 2.40$$

## 5.9 THE STANDARD DEVIATION

A measure of variability closely related to the variance is the standard deviation. The *standard deviation*, denoted by $\sigma$ (or $s$) is defined as the positive square root of the variance $\sigma^2$ (or $s^2$). If the variance $s^2$ is 16, then

$$s = \sqrt{s^2} = \sqrt{16} = 4.0$$

*Equation 5.6A was preferred to Equation 5.6 before the wide availability of hand calculators, because it resulted in less rounding error. Since hand calculators retain eight or more figures, the two formulas now are equally satisfactory.

In Chapter 6 the standard deviation is used extensively. Its meaning and value are more fully developed there.*

## 5.10 ADDING OR SUBTRACTING† A CONSTANT

Recall from Equation 4.6 that if a constant $c$ is added to each score in a distribution, then the mean of the augmented distribution is the mean of the original distribution $\overline{X}$ plus the constant $c$.

The deviation score of the $i$th observation in the augmented distribution then is $(X_i + c) - (\overline{X} + c) = X_i + c - \overline{X} - c = X_i - \overline{X}$. Thus adding (or subtracting) a constant has no effect on the value of any deviation score and hence does not change the value of the sum of squares, $\Sigma_{i=1}^{n} x_i^2$, the variance, the standard deviation, or any other common measure of variability. Thus the variance of the distribution 5, 8, 9 has the same value as the variance of the distribution 15,18,19. Obviously the standard deviations and ranges of the two distributions are also equal.

## 5.11 MULTIPLYING OR DIVIDING‡ BY A CONSTANT

If each score in a distribution is multiplied by a constant $c$, the mean of the transformed distribution is $c\overline{X}$ (see Sec. 4.8). The sum of squares of the new distribution $cX_1, cX_2, \ldots, cX_n$ is $\Sigma_{i=1}^{n} (cX_i - c\overline{X})^2$. The constant $c$ can be factored out of the expression within the parentheses as follows: $\Sigma_i (cX_i - c\overline{X})^2 = \Sigma_i [c(X_i - \overline{X})]^2 = \Sigma_i c^2(X_i - \overline{X})^2 = c^2 \Sigma_i (X_i - \overline{X})^2 = c^2 \Sigma_i x_i^2$. Thus the variance of the transformed distribution is $s^2c^2$:

$$\text{Variance of } cX_i = \frac{\text{Sum of squares}}{\nu} = \frac{c^2 \sum_i x_i^2}{n - 1} = c^2 s^2 \tag{5.8}$$

For example, if $s = 4$ for a given distribution and if each score in that distribution is multiplied by 3, the variance of the augmented distribution is $(3)^2(4)^2 = 144$.

Since the standard deviation is the square root of the variance, the standard deviation of the transformed distribution in which each score has been multiplied by a

*The coefficient of variation ($CV$) is another measure of variability that can be useful if the measure represents a ratio scale (see Sec. 2.6). It is the ratio of the standard deviation to the mean, expressed as a percent: $CV = 100\ s/\overline{X}$. Suppose one wishes to estimate the relative variability in wages of teachers in 1970 and 1980. If in 1970 $s_1$ = \$3,000 and $\overline{X}_1$ = \$10,000 and in 1980 $s_2$ = \$6,000 and $\overline{X}_2$ = \$20,000, the $CV$ is 3 in each instance even though $s_2$ is twice as large as $s_1$. (For an additional description, see Snedecor and Cochran, 1980, p 37.)

†Subtracting a constant $c$ is equivalent to adding $c$ when $c$ carries a negative value (see Sec. 4.7).

‡Recall that dividing by a constant $c$ is equivalent to multiplying by the reciprocal of the constant $1/c$ (see Sec. 4.8).

constant is $\sqrt{c^2 s^2} = |c|s$.* If $X_1, X_2, \cdots, X_n$ has a standard deviation $s$, what is the standard deviation of the transformed distribution, $X_1/s, X_2/s, \ldots, X_n/s$? Since $c = 1/s$, then $\sqrt{c^2 s^2} = \sqrt{(1/s)^2 s^2} = 1$. This transformation will be used in Sec. 6.3.

## 5.12 VARIANCE OF A COMPOSITE DISTRIBUTION†

In Chapter 4 the mean of a set of scores formed by pooling scores from two separate samples was found to be a simple weighted average of the means of the two groups (see Eq. 4.11). The comparable situation for variances is more complicated. It will be seen that the variance of the entire set of scores formed by pooling scores from groups 1 and 2 depends on both the variances and means of the two groups. Notice that group 1 comprises the scores 3, 3, and 3, and group 2 is 5, 5, and 5, then the variance of the composite distribution (3, 3, 3, 5, 5, 5) is not zero even though $s_1^2 = s_2^2 = 0$.

Suppose that 1 and 2 denote two separate sets of scores:

| | *Group 1* | *Group 2* |
|---|---|---|
| Group size | $n_1 = 10$ | $n_2 = 20$ |
| Mean | $\overline{X}_1 = 50$ | $\overline{X}_2 = 41$ |
| Variance | $s_1^2 = 36$ | $s_2^2 = 30$ |

The variance $s_\bullet^2$ of the set of $n_1 + n_2 = n_\bullet$ scores formed by combining groups 1 and 2 is

$$s_\bullet^2 = \frac{[(n_1 - 1)s_1^2 + (n_2 - 1)s_2^2 + n_1(\overline{X}_1 - \overline{X}_\bullet)^2 + n_2(\overline{X}_2 - \overline{X}_\bullet)^2]}{n_1 + n_2 - 1}$$

Or more generally

$$s_\bullet^2 = \frac{\sum_{j=1}^{J} (n_j - 1)s_j^2 + \sum_{j=1}^{J} n_j(\overline{X}_j - \overline{X}_\bullet)^2}{n_\bullet - 1} \tag{5.9}$$

where $n_\bullet = \Sigma_{j=1}^{J} n_j$ and the grand mean $\overline{X}_\bullet$ (Sec. 4.13) equals $\Sigma_{j=1}^{J} \Sigma_{i=1}^{n_j} X_{ij}/n_\bullet$.

Using Equation 5.9, the variance $s_\bullet^2$ for the $n_1 = n_2 = n_\bullet = 30$ scores in the two groups combined into a single composite distribution in which $\overline{X}_\bullet = 44$ is

$$s_\bullet^2 = \frac{(10 - 1)(36) + (20 - 1)(30) + 10(50 - 44)^2 + 20(41 - 44)^2}{30 - 1} = 49.45$$

*The vertical lines around $c$ indicate that the absolute value of $c$ should be taken. The absolute value of a number is its magnitude without sign. Thus $|3| = 3$ and $|-3| = 3$. Consequently, a variable cannot be given a negative standard deviation by multiplying it by a negative constant.

†See Section 7.13 for the variance of a sum; for the variance of a difference, see Section 7.14.

## 5.13 INFERENTIAL PROPERTIES OF THE RANGE, $s^2$, AND $s$

For each measure of variability (and other statistical measures), sampling error (Eq. 4.12) tends to decrease as sample size ($n$) increases. This property is known as *consistency.*

### Expected Values and Unbiasedness

The variance $s^2$ as a measure of variability has a very desirable statistical property. Its value on any random sample of observations from the population is an unbiased estimate of the variance of all observations in the population. That is, the statistic $s^2$ in Equation 5.5 is an unbiased estimator of the parameter $\sigma^2$. An unbiased estimator is one for which the sample overestimates and underestimates tend to balance out in the long run. In other words, an unbiased statistic tends to be neither larger nor smaller, on the average, than the parameter it estimates.

Statisticians say that if a statistic is unbiased, the "expected value" of the statistic is equal to the parameter it estimates. The *expected value* of a sample statistic is its long-run mean value across all possible samples from the population. For example, as shown by the following expression, since the expected value of the variance $E(s^2)$ is equal to the variance in the population $\sigma^2$, then $s^2$ is said to be an unbiased estimator of $\sigma^2$:

$$E(s^2) = \sigma^2 \tag{5.10}$$

Thus the average of the sample variance over all possible samples of size $n$ from the population is exactly equal to the population variance $\sigma^2$. This would not have been true if the sample variance had been defined in Equation 5.5 with $n$ instead of $n - 1$ in the denominator. It is also true that $E(\overline{X}) = \mu$; that is, the sample mean $\overline{X}$ is an unbiased estimator of the population mean $\mu$. Other things being equal, unbiased statistics are preferred.

It appears that if $E(s^2) = \sigma^2$, then $s$ should also be an unbiased estimate of $\sigma$. Strangely, however, square roots of unbiased statistics are not unbiased estimates of the square root of the related parameters; that is $E(s) \neq \sigma$. Fortunately, the bias in using $s$ as an estimator of $\sigma$ is negligible unless $n$ is very small. $s$ tends to underestimate $\sigma$, but the bias is very small—only 5% [i.e., $E(s) = .95\sigma$] when $n = 6$, and only 1% [i.e., $E(s) = .99\sigma$] when $n = 20$.* Since published research usually involves $n$'s larger than 20, the degree to which $s$ underestimates $\sigma$ is inconsequential, and the amount of bias is disregarded.

A related and additional shortcoming of the range as a measure of variability is that its value is greatly affect by sample size. Since the range is determined by only the largest and smallest observations, other things being equal, the larger the sample, the larger the range. This is not the case with $s^2$. The expression $E(s^2) = \sigma^2$ does not depend on $n$; the statement is true regardless of $n$, the size of the sample.

*The degree of bias for other values of $n$ can be found using the formula: the expected value of $\{1 + 1/[4(n - 1)]\}s = \sigma$ if $X$ is normally distributed. The formula can be used to convert any $s$ to an unbiased estimate of $\sigma$. A graphic representation of the degree of bias with respect to $n$ is given by Hopkins and Glass (1978, p. 82).

**TABLE 5.1 The Expected Values of the Range, Variance, and Standard Deviation as a Function of Sample Size ($n$) in a Representative Sample from a Normal Distribution in which $\sigma = 10$**

| | *When* $\sigma = 10$ | | |
|---|---|---|---|
| $n$ | Expected Value of the Range | Expected Value of $s^2$ | Expected Value of $s$ |
| 2 | 11 | 100 | 8.0 |
| 5 | 23 | 100 | 9.4 |
| 10 | 31 | 100 | 9.73 |
| 20 | 37 | 100 | 9.87 |
| 50 | 45 | 100 | 9.95 |
| 100 | 50 | 100 | 9.97 |
| 200 | 55 | 100 | 9.987 |
| 500 | 61 | 100 | 9.993 |
| 1,000 | 65 | 100 | 9.997 |

Table 5.1 shows the influence of sample size on the range. The comparison of the range with the variance $s^2$ and the standard deviation $s$, are given using $\sigma = 10$ as an example. Table 5.1 gives the range, $s^2$, and $s$ in scores that would be expected in a random sample from the population where $\sigma = 10$ for example sizes ranging from 2 to 1,000.

Table 5.1 shows that the expected size of the range varies markedly with the sample size, while the expected variance and standard deviation do not. As a consequence, the range has very limited value as an inferential statistic. It is, however, frequently useful to describe a sample, and helps identify obvious errors in scoring or recording. The range also has value as a check on the accuracy of the calculation of $s$. For example, if the range is reported to be less than $2s$ or more than $8s$, one can be nearly certain that a computational error was made. The range should be considered a complement to, and not a substitute for, $s^2$ or $s$.

## CHAPTER SUMMARY

If a distribution contains all of the observations in the population, the measures of central tendency and variability are parameters. The variance and standard deviation in the population are symbolized by $\sigma^2$ and $\sigma$, respectively.

If the distribution contains only a sample of $n$ observations from the population, the measures of central tendency and variability are called sample statistics (or inferential statistics). Estimates of the population variance and standard deviation are symbolized by $s^2$ and $s$, respectively.

The variance ($s^2$), standard deviation ($s$), and range are common measures of variability. Each has the statistical property of consistency. But only $s^2$ is an unbiased estimate of the corresponding parameter $\sigma^2$. The sample standard deviation $s$ underestimates the related parameter $\sigma$, although the degree of bias is negligible unless $n$ is very small. The range is an unstable measure and is greatly influenced by $n$.

If a constant is added to each score in a distribution, the values of variance and other measures of variability are unchanged. If each score in a distribution is multiplied by a constant $c$, the standard deviation of the transformed distribution is $|c|s$, where $s$ is the original standard deviation.

## *MASTERY TEST*

Given the sample of three scores 40, 45, 50:

1. What is the value of the range?
2. $\overline{X}$ =?
3. The sum of squares $\Sigma_{i=1}^{n} x_i^2$?
4. For computing $s^2$, how many degrees of freedom $\nu$, are there?
5. What is the value of $s^2$?
6. What is the value of $s$?
7. If each score is increased by ten points, will the values of $s^2$ and $s$ be affected?
8. If each score is multiplied by 10, what are the new values of $s^2$ and $s$?
9. What is the value of $\Sigma_i X_i^2$? Is $\Sigma_i X_i^2 = (\Sigma_i X_i)^2$?
10. Complete the analogy: ____ is to a *sample* as *parameter* is to ____.

Answer Questions 11–17 regarding these three measures of variability for data obtained from a random sample of $n$ observations: range, standard deviation ($s$), and variance ($s^2$).

11. Which is unbiased even for small $n$?
12. Which has a value that, on the average, is much greater when $n = 100$ than when $n = 20$?
13. Which is technically biased but for practical purposes is essentially unbiased if $n$ is 20 or more?
14. Which is simplest to calculate?
15. Which has the same expected value regardless of sample size?
16. Do all have the property of consistency?
17. Which is *not* expressed in the same units as the original observations?
18. If all scores are not equal; will the range always be larger than the standard deviations?
19. To compute $s$ or $s^2$, is the sum of squares divided by the sample size $n$ or by $n - 1$?
20. What symbol represents the population standard deviation?
21. What symbol represents the size of a sample?
22. What symbol represents the mean of a population?
23. If the variance of IQ scores is found to be 225, what is the value of the standard deviation?
24. Using Table 5.1, and assuming that a sample of 100 IQ scores is randomly drawn from a population with standard deviation 15, estimate the range.
25. The heights of American women are approximately normally distributed with $\mu \doteq 54.5$ in. and $Q \doteq 1.5$ in. The middle 50% of heights fall between ____ and ____.
26. Which one of these is one-half the other two: $Q$, H-spread, or interquartile range?

27. When does $Md \pm Q$ precisely define $Q_1$ and $Q_3$?
28. Group 1: 7, 8, 12
Group 2: 15, 16, 20
The variance in group 1, $s_1^2$, is equal to 7.0; by inspection, what is $s_2^2$?
29. The variance of the composite distribution, $s_{\bullet}^2$, formed by combining groups 1 and 2 in Question 28 will be
    a. less than 7
    b. 7
    c. greater than 7.

## *PROBLEMS AND EXERCISES*

1. Calculate the a. range, b. interquartile range, c. $Q$, d. $s^2$, and e. $s$ of the following set of scores. (*Hint*: to simplify calculations, first subtract 100 from all scores; this will not change the value of any of the measures of variability):

| | | | |
|---|---|---|---|
| 125 | 116 | 114 | 111 |
| 122 | 115 | 113 | 106 |
| 118 | 114 | 112 | 102 |

f. Are the relative sizes of the range and $s$ reasonable (see Table 5.1)?

2. Calculate the standard deviation of the composite distribution in Mastery Test Question 28.
3. In a perfectly normal distribution $Q = .674\sigma$, using data from Mastery Test Question 25, a. rearrange the equation such that $\sigma$ = ____ $Q$ = ____. How much difference in inches between the tallest and shortest women in a random sample would you expect if b. $n = 5$, c. $n = 10$, d. $n = 50$, e. $n = 100$, and f. $n = 1{,}000$? g. Does this phenomenon explain why basketball teams from large high schools tend to be taller than teams from small high schools? (See Table 5.1.)

## *ANSWERS TO MASTERY TEST*

1. 10
2. 45
3. 50
4. 2
5. 25
6. 5
7. No
8. $s^2 = (10)^2(25) = 2{,}500$; $s = 10(5) = 50$
9. $\Sigma_i X_i^2 = 6{,}125$; no, $(\Sigma_i X_i^2 = (135)^2 = 18{,}225$
10. Statistic or inferential statistic/population (or $s$, $\sigma$; $\overline{X}$, $\mu$)
11. Variance
12. Range (see Table 5.1)
13. Standard deviation
14. Range
15. Variance
16. Yes
17. Variance
18. Yes
19. $n - 1$
20. $\sigma$
21. $n$
22. $\mu$
23. 15
24. $5(15) = 75$
25. 53 in. and 56 in.
26. $Q$
27. When the distribution is perfectly symmetrical
28. 7.0
29. c

## *ANSWERS TO PROBLEMS AND EXERCISES*

1. a. 23
   b. $Q_3 - Q_1 = 117 - 111.5 = 5.5$
   c. 2.75
   d. 38.91
   e. 6.24
   f. yes
2. $s_{\bullet} = 4.98$
3. a. $\sigma = 1.48\ Q = 2.23$ in.
   b. 5.1 in.
   c. 6.9 in.
   d. 16 in.
   e. 11.1 in.
   f. 14.5 in.
   g. yes

# 6

# THE NORMAL DISTRIBUTION AND STANDARD SCORES

## 6.1 THE IMPORTANCE OF THE NORMAL DISTRIBUTION

The normal distribution (Gaussian curve, normal probability curve) is the most fundamentally important distribution in statistics. The normal curve is used extensively in all subsequent chapters. Its use in this chapter will be illustrated by describing and evaluating the performance of an individual or group via standard scores. Other more important applications of the normal distribution will be evident in the following chapters. Measures of *skewness* and *kurtosis*, which describe and quantify the extent to which a distribution deviates from a true normal distribution, will also be considered.

### Historical Background

The study of the normal distribution dates from at least the seventeenth century. It was noticed, for example, that if an object were weighed repeatedly, the observed weights were not identical; there was some variation among the measurements. If enough measurements were taken, the distribution of the observations displayed a regular pattern, a pattern now recognized to be the normal distribution. Errors of observation of many kinds were found to follow this same pattern. In fact, the distribution was initially referred to as the "normal curve of errors."

It was soon discovered that observations other than measurement error resulted in normal or approximately normal curves. If a fair coin were flipped ten times, the number of heads recorded, and the procedure repeated many times (actually an infinite number), the distribution in Figure 6.1 would result. Note that the expected value for the number of heads is 5, which is the mean ($\mu$) of the theoretical distribution shown in Figure 6.1. In normal distributions the mean is also the mode—$\mu$ occurs more frequently than any other number. Figure 6.1 shows that almost 25% of the set of ten tosses results in five heads but, for 75% of the sets of ten flips, the number of heads is not five, but varies systematically about five; four and six heads were each observed in more than 20% of the sets. The distribution is approximately normal, but note that it does not result from errors of measurement but from the laws of chance. No collection of empirical observations would look *exactly* like the normal distribution since the latter is a mathematical abstraction. For example, the distribution of number of heads in Figure 6.1 has gaps; there are no points between 4 and 5 or between 5 and 6, for instance. The true normal distribution is continuous—that is, without gaps; and if the number of coin flips were increased—for example, if the number of heads in 1,000 flips were recorded—the distribution of heads would approach the mathematical normal distribution much more closely.

Late in the nineteenth century Francis Galton, an Englishman, took systematic measurements of a number of physical, psychological, and psychomotor variables on large numbers of persons and found that the distributions of many of the measurements were very close approximations to the normal distribution. Figure 6.2 illustrates his findings using the heights of 8,585 adult men born in Great Britain during the nineteenth century.

Refined measures of most cognitive, psychomotor, and many affective and other human characteristics have empirical distributions that are approximately normal, as illustrated by the distribution of heights in Figure 6.2 and IQ in Figure 3.3 (Sec. 3.7). Stated differently, "God loves the normal curve."

No set of data is ever perfectly described by the normal distribution, but the shape is often extremely close to the theoretical normal curve. Even if a variable were perfectly normally distributed, the observed distribution would never be perfectly normal because of measurement imperfections and sampling error. The error is frequently so small, however, that it can be disregarded for practical purposes. For example, the shaded "background" in Figure 6.2 represents a true normal distribution. Its shape is almost indistinguishable from that of the distribution of the empirical data.

**FIGURE 6.1. The distribution of the expected number of heads in 10 flips of a fair coin.**

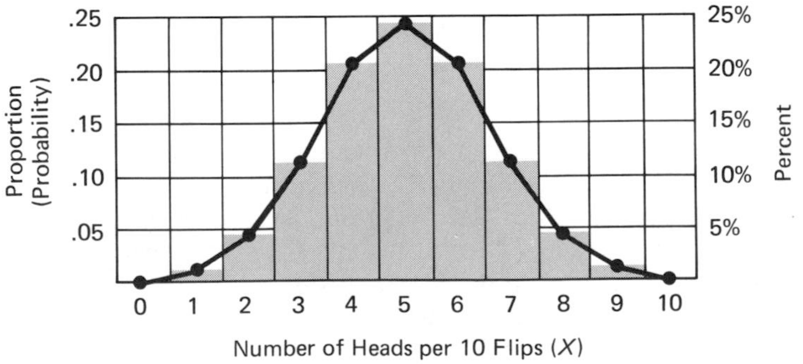

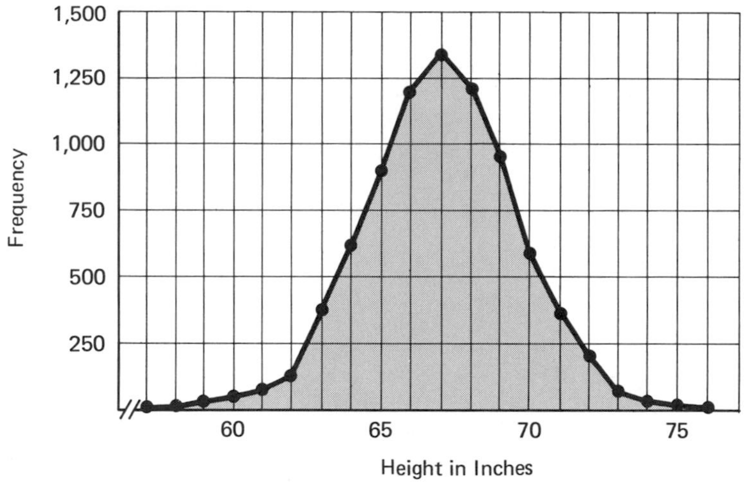


**FIGURE 6.2. Frequency polygon for heights of 8,585 adult men born in Great Britain during the nineteenth century ($\mu$ = 67.02, $\sigma$ = 2.56 in.). Shaded background depicts a true normal distribution.**

Building on the work of Pascal (1623-1662), de Fermat (1601-1665), and Bernoulli (1654-1705), Abraham DeMoivre (1667-1754) was able to show that the mathematical curve that approximates the curve that connects the tops of the lines in Figure 6.1 (and the curve for almost any other such problem) has the following formula:

$$u = \frac{1}{\sigma\sqrt{2\pi}}\, e^{-1/2\,(X-\mu/\sigma)^2} \qquad \textbf{(6.1)}$$

where $u$ is the height of the curve directly above any given value of $X$ in the plotted frequency distribution,

$\pi$ is the ratio of the circumference of any circle to its diameter,

$$\pi = 3.14159\ldots$$

$e$ is the base of the system of natural logarithms, $e = 2.71828\ldots$ and

$\mu$ and $\sigma$ are the mean and the standard deviation of the distribution.

Equation 6.1 is the formula for the *normal distribution*. We shall have little to do with the formula as such.

Recall from Figure 3.3 that the distribution of IQ scores is almost perfectly normal between 70 and 130. Although the commonly observed empirical bell-shaped curves of errors, height, IQ, and other variables have piqued the curiosity of scientists of many different stripes, *the prominence of the normal distribution in statistics is primarily due to its mathematical properties.* No other distribution has such desirable properties with which the mathematical statistician can do magic. Very many technical problems in statistics have been solved only by assuming the observations in the population are normally distributed. Specific instances will appear in later chapters.

The ubiquity of the normal curve sometimes leads to the mistaken notion that there is a necessary link between it and virtually any good set of data. But many variables are definitely *not* normally distributed. For example, many sociological variables, such as social class, socioeconomic status, income, level of education, and family size, are skewed. Certain social and political attitudes, such as attitude toward abortion, have bimodal distributions. Such variables as age, ethnicity, religion, and college major obviously are not normally distributed.

## 6.2 THE NORMAL CURVE

The graph of Equation 6.1 yields the familiar, symmetric, bell-shaped curve known as the *normal curve.* One speaks of a normal curve, because Equation 6.1 imparts a characteristic shape to the graph. All normal curves have the following properties: one mode, symmetric, points of inflection* at $\mu \pm \sigma$, tails that approach (but never quite touch) the horizontal axis† as they deviate from $\mu$. The normal curve has a smooth, altogether handsome countenance. (But not all curves with these characteristics are normal, see Sec. 6.9).

## 6.3 THE UNIT-NORMAL DISTRIBUTION AS A STANDARD: *z*-Scores

A raw score of 42 on a test means little; but a score that is $1\frac{1}{2}$ standard deviations ($1.5\sigma$) above the mean is quite large relative to the others in the distribution. If the mean and standard deviation are known the observation can be visualized in relation to that of others in the distribution. Observations expressed in standard deviation units from the mean are termed *z-scores*. For example, in Figure 3.3, where $\mu$ is 100 and $\sigma$ is 15, an IQ score of 130 can be transformed to a *z-score* of 2–it is two standard deviations above the mean. A *z-score* of $-2$ is two standard deviations *below* the mean, or equivalent to an IQ score of 70. Equation 6.2 is the definition of a *z-score*:

$$z_i = \frac{X_i - \mu}{\sigma} \quad \text{or} \quad \frac{x_i}{\sigma} \quad \text{or,} \quad z_i = \frac{\text{Deviation of } X_i \text{ from the mean}}{\text{Standard deviation}} \tag{6.2}$$

It will be most useful in the future if all references to scores in normal distributions are in terms of deviations from the mean $\mu$, in standard deviation $\sigma$ units, that is, *z-scores*. For almost any application of the normal curve, one wants to know how many standard deviations a score lies above or below the mean. Knowing this, questions about the area between points or scores, $X_1$ and $X_2$, (or heights of the curve above any point)

*A point of inflection is the precise point at which a curve changes from convex (down-sloping) to concave (up-sloping). It is, via calculus, the point at which the second derivative equals zero.

†The mathematician would say that "the curve approaches the $X$-axis *asymptotically*" or "the $X$-axis is the asymptote of the curve."

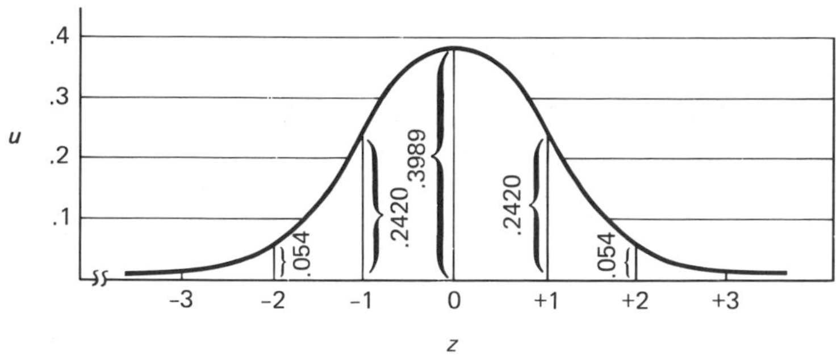


**FIGURE 6.3. The unit normal distribution, $\mu = 0$ and $\sigma = 1$.**

can be answered by reference to the unit normal curve (see Table A in the Appendix). The *shape* of a curve does not change when a *constant* is added or subtracted from each score or when each score is multiplied or divided by a *constant.* Thus when $\mu$ is subtracted from each score and these differences are divided by $\sigma$ (see Eq. 6.2), the shape of the distribution is not affected.

Any set of scores with mean $\mu$ and standard deviation $\sigma$ can be transformed into a different set of scores with mean 0 and standard deviation 1 so that the transformed score immediately tells one the distance in standard deviation units of the original score from the mean. These points are summarized in the following statement:

If $X$ has a normal distribution with mean $\mu$ and standard deviation $\sigma$, then $z_i = (X_i - \mu)/\sigma$ has a normal distribution with mean 0 and standard deviation 1, i.e., $z_i = (X_i - \mu)/\sigma$ has normal distribution.

By making use of this definition of a $z$-score in Equation 6.2, Equation 6.1 can be simplified:

$$u = \frac{1}{\sqrt{2\pi}} e^{-(z^2/2)} \tag{6.3}$$

The normal curve in Equation 6.3 and Figure 6.3 is a special one because it has been chosen as a standard. It is called the *unit normal curve* or *z-distribution*.

## 6.4 ORDINATES OF THE UNIT-NORMAL DISTRIBUTION

It is occasionally necessary to find the ordinate $u$ (the height of the curve) at a given value of $z$. Solving Equation 6.3 for $u$ when $z$ is given is far too inconvenient (unless one is proficient with a hand calculator which has a variable exponent function). Table A in the Appendix gives the ordinate $u$ of the unit normal curve. The highest point on the curve is above $z = 0$ (see Fig. 6.3 and Table A); when $z = 0$ is inserted in Equation 6.3, the height (ordinate) $u$ is .3989. Notice in Figure 6.3 that the ordinate $u$ equals .2420 at $z \pm 1.0$, and that $u = .0540$ at $z \pm 2.0$. For practice, locate these values in Table A.

## 6.5 AREAS UNDER THE NORMAL CURVE

In many applications of statistics it is necessary to know the area of the normal curve (that is, the proportion of the distribution) that falls below a particular value of $z$. To find the proportion of scores that fall below any particular score in a normal distribution, the score is converted to a $z$-score. The proportion is then read from the normal curve table (Table A). For example, in Figure 6.2, what proportion of the men are shorter than 70 in.?* Stated differently, what is the percentile rank of 70 in.? Assuming a normal distribution with a mean of 67.02 in. and a standard deviation of 2.56 in., $X_1 = 70$ in. expressed as a $z$-score, using Equation 6.2, is

$$z_1 = \frac{70 - 67.02}{2.56} = \frac{2.98}{2.56} = 1.16$$

One then finds $z = 1.16$ in Table A and in the adjacent column reads $p$, the proportion of the curve that falls below $z_1 = 1.16$. For $z_1 = 1.16$, $p_1 = .8770$; thus 87.7% of the area in a normal distribution falls below a $z$-score of 1.16 (see Figure 6.4). Or, stated differently, only $1 - .8770 = .1230$ (12.3%) of the men were taller than 70 in.

What proportion of the heights in Figure 6.2 fall *between* 66 and 70 in.? If the proportion of heights below $X_2 = 66$ in. is subtracted from the proportion below 70 in., the difference is the proportion between 66 and 70 in.. A height of 66 in. corresponds to a $z$-score of $-.40$ ($z_2 = (66 - 67.02)/2.56 = -.398$, which rounds to $-.40$). From Table A the area below $z_2 = -.40$ is found to be .3446 (see Figure 6.4). Of the .8770 of the heights below 70 in., .3446 are below 66 in.; therefore, $.8770 - .3446 = .5324$ (or 53.24%) of the cases fall between 66 and 70 in.†

The steps just illustrated can be summarized as follows: The area between $X_1$ and $X_2$ in the normal distribution with mean $\mu$ and standard deviation $\sigma$ is the same as the area between $z_1 = (X_1 - \mu)/\sigma$ and $z_2 = (X_2 - \mu)/\sigma$ in the unit normal distribution.

## 6.6 OTHER STANDARD SCORES

It is more convenient to work with standard scores than with raw scores. *With standard scores the mean and standard deviation are fixed and known to the user.* To learn that an IQ score on the Stanford-Binet Intelligence Scale is 120 means little unless it is also known that $\mu = 100$; to know that $\sigma = 16$ makes the score of 120 mean much more.

The $z$-scale ($\mu = 0$, $\sigma = 1$) is the most widely used standard score scale in statistics, but *any observation expressed in standard deviation units from the mean is a standard*

*The heights in Figure 6.2 are not representative of the United States distribution which in 1976 was $\mu \doteq 69.7$ in. and $\sigma \doteq 2.6$ in.

†*Chebyshev's inequality* proves that the proportion of the area *in any distribution* that is beyond the points $\pm z$ is less than $1/z^2$. Thus there is never more than $1/2^2 = .25$ of the distribution that is more than two standard deviations ($z = 2$) from the mean. For symmetric unimodal distributions, the maximum area beyond $\pm z$ is $4/(9z^2)$ (Dixon and Massey, 1969). Thus there can be no more than $4/[(9(2)^2] = \frac{1}{9}$ or 11.1% of the area falling in the tails beyond the points $z = -2$ and $z = +2$ in symmetric unimodal distributions.

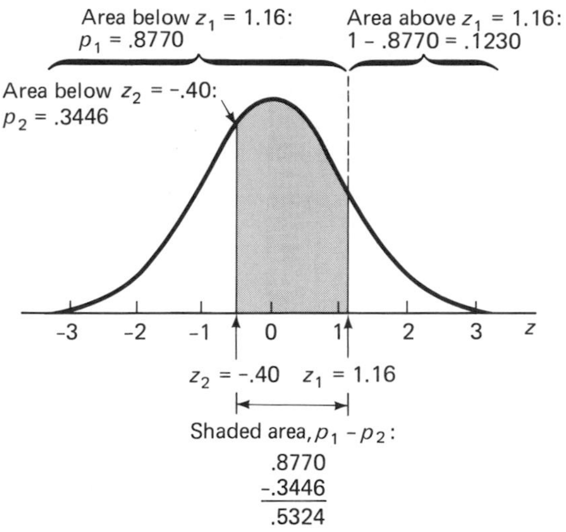


**FIGURE 6.4**
**The area under the normal curve between two values of *z*.**

*score*. Most standardized tests of intelligence, achievement, interest, and personality report performance in standard scores. Such measures rarely use *z*-scores, however, because other standard-score scales that do not involve negative numbers or decimals are easier to use.

A *z*-score can be converted to any other standard score ($S$) using the general formula in Equation 6.4.

$$S = \mu_S + (\sigma_S)(z) \tag{6.4}$$

where $S$ is the new standard score equivalent to $z$
$\mu_S$ is the mean for the new standard-score scale ($z$)
$\sigma_S$ is the standard deviation for the new standard-score scale
$z$ is the $z$-score for any observation as defined in equation 6

## T-Scale

A very commonly used standard-score scale is the *T*-scale* where $\mu_T = 50$ and $\sigma_T = 10$. To convert *z*-scores to *T*-scores, Equation 6.4 becomes

$$T = 50 + 10z \tag{6.5}$$

An example will illuminate certain advantages of standard scores. Suppose a 10-year-old boy is 46 in. tall and weighs 76 lb. Are his height and weight commensurate? Who knows without norm tables? But expressed as *T*-scores, 30 and 70, respectively, his weight problem becomes readily apparent—he is at the 2nd percentile in height but the 98th percentile in weight.

*The *T*-scale was originally proposed as a "normalized" standard score (Sec. 6.11); in most applications, however, *T*-scores are not normalized but are simply a linear transformation (Sec. 7.9) of raw scores.

If a student in grade 5.1 (first month of grade 5) received an IQ score of 130 and grade-equivalent scores of 6.4 and 6.1 on the standardized reading and arithmetic tests, respectively, how does his achievement compare with his measured scholastic aptitude (IQ)? The corresponding $T$-scores of 70, 60, and 60 show that the student's superiority on the intelligence test was twice as great as his superiority on the reading and arithmetic tests.*

Figure 6.5 shows the relation of $z$-scale, $T$-scale, and several other standard score scales. Observe that converting raw scores to standard scores does not alter the shape of the distribution or affect the percentile ranks of any observation. But standard scores have the advantage of having a known and constant mean and standard deviation, with which performance on all variables can be expressed.

Notice that the frequently-mentioned Wechsler IQ scale is a standard-score scale with $\mu = 100$ and $\sigma = 15$. The scale employed by the historic Stanford-Binet Intelligence Scale differs little ($\mu = 100$, $\sigma = 16$).† An IQ score of 145 on the Wechsler Intelligence Scale for children then has the same percentile ranks as a Stanford-Binet score of 148.

One may wonder why statisticians bothered to invent standard scores since they appear to provide only percentile information which is readily obtained from the simple calculation of percentiles. For all the clarity and simplicity of percentile scores, they do not lend themselves to many statistical operations such as averaging and correlating scores. The difference in actual measured heights between two men at the 50th and 52nd percentiles is very much smaller than the height difference between two men at the 97th and 99th percentiles. Compare the $z$-scores in the normal distribution at the 50th and 52nd versus the 97th and 99th percentiles: $P_{50} = 0.00$ and $P_{52} = .05$, but $P_{97} = 1.88$ and $P_{99} = 2.33$, a difference of $.05\sigma$ versus $.45\sigma$—the latter being nine times larger! In terms of the heights in Figure 6.2 the difference between $P_{50}$ and $P_{52}$ is only .128 in., whereas the difference between $P_{97}$ and $P_{99}$ is 1.152 in. Or, in IQ units $P_{50}$ and $P_{52}$ differ by less than one IQ point, whereas $P_{97}$ differs from $P_{99}$ by almost seven points. Standard scores avoid this problem and lend themselves readily to meaningful summary statistical calculations.

## 6.7 AREAS UNDER NORMAL CURVE IN SAMPLES

This chapter has assumed that the population mean ($\mu$) and standard deviation ($\sigma$) of a normal distribution are known. If the mean and standard deviation are estimated from a sample (i.e., $\bar{X}$ and $s$ are used since $\mu$ and $\sigma$ are not known) and inferences are made to the population, the proportion found in Table A is an approximation; the accuracy of the approximation is determined by how accurately $\bar{X}$ and $s$ estimate $\mu$ and $\sigma$.

*If more explanation and practice with the standard deviation, the normal distribution, or standard scores are desired, you may find the programmed instruction in Chapter 2 and 3 of Hopkins and Stanley (1981) helpful.

†Prior to the 1960 revision of the Stanford-Binet, IQ equaled the ratio of mental age to chronological age multiplied by 100. With this method the same IQ score had different interpretations at different ages since $\sigma$ varied considerably from age to age. The $\sigma = 16$ was selected because the average standard deviation across the various ages was found to be about 16.

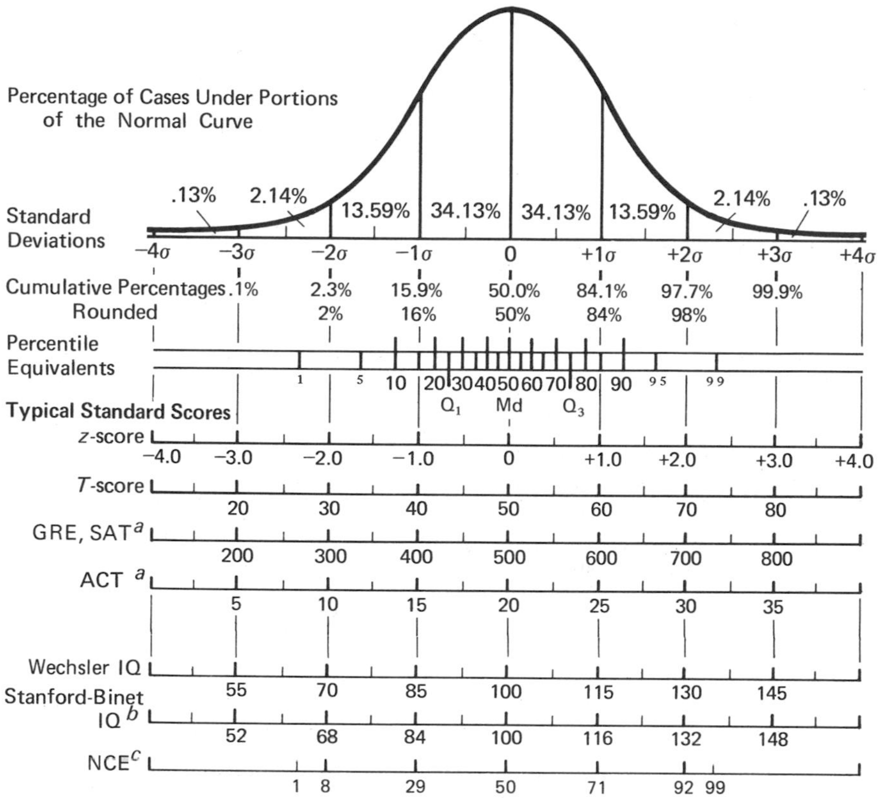


THE NORMAL CURVE, PERCENTILES, AND STANDARD SCORES

Distribution of scores of many standardized educational and psychological tests approximate the form of the normal curve shown at the top of this chart. Below it are shown some of the systems that have been developed to facilitate the interpretation of scores by converting them into numbers which indicate the examinee's relative status in a group.

The zero (0) at the center of the baseline shows the location of the mean (average) raw score on a test, and the symbol σ (*sigma*) marks off the scale of raw scores in standard deviation units.

Cumulative percentages are the basis of the percentile-equivalent scale.

Several systems are based on the standard deviation unit. Among these standard score scales, the *z*-score and the *T*-score, are general systems which have been applied to a variety of tests. The others are special variants used in connection with tests of the College Entrance Examination Board, the Graduate Records Examination, and other intelligence and ability scales.

Tables of norms, whether in percentile or standard score form, have meaning only with reference to a specified test applied to a specified population. The chart does not permit one to conclude, for instance, that a percentile rank of 84 on one test necessarily is equivalent to a *z*-score of +1.0 on another; this is true only when each test yields essentially a normal distribution of scores and when both scales are based on identical or very similar groups of people.

[a] Score points (norms) on the scales refer to university students and not to general populations. (GRE = Graduate Records Examination, SAT = Scholastic Aptitude Test of the College Entrance Examination Board, ACT = American College Testing Assessment.) These norms are not rescaled to better allow comparisons over time. Consequently current means are lower than means given above.

[b] Standard-score IQs with $\sigma = 16$ are also used on several other current intelligence tests.

[c] The NCE ("normal curve equivalent") scale is an ill-conceived normalized scale used in the evaluations of certain federally funded educational programs. The NCE scale has $\mu = 50$ and $\sigma = 21$; the NCE unit is 1/98 of the distance between the 1st and 99th percentiles, expressed in z-score units.

**FIGURE 6.5. Types of standard score scales. (Adapted from Test Service Bulletin No. 48. The Psychological Corporation, New York, by permission of The Psychological Corporation.)**

When the random sample contains 100 or more scores, the $z$-value for an observation ($X$) using $\overline{X}$ and $s$ will differ from the true $z$-value (i.e., the $z$-value using $\mu$ and $\sigma$) by .1 or less in most situations.* This degree of precision is adequate for most purposes. One should be wary of using Table A for inferential purposes if $\overline{X}$ and $s$ are based on very small samples and when the frequency distribution is not normal.

## 6.8 SKEWNESS

The degree of asymmetry, or skewness, of a distribution is an important characteristic. The nature and extent of asymmetry is apparent from well-constructed frequency polygons and histograms, but these are rarely available in published research. Moreover, mere observation of a curve is imprecise and cannot be communicated accurately in words or numbers. There are two widely used measures of skewness.

Recall (Sec. 4.16) that skewness affects the mean, median, and mode predictably. Figure 6.6 was constructed to illustrate various degrees of skewness. All the curves have the same mean and standard deviation but differ in skewness. Of course, the differences among the mean, median, and mode increase as the magnitude of the skewness increases. Indeed, Karl Pearson suggested Formula 6.6 as a useful and an easily interpreted measure of skewness in the population:

$$\varsigma\kappa = \frac{\mu - \text{Mode}}{\sigma} \tag{6.6}$$

Notice that $\varsigma\kappa$ describes the distance from the mean to the mode parameters in sigma units.

Because the sample median has much less sampling error than the mode, and the distance between the mean and mode is approximately three times the distance between the mean and the median for unimodal distributions (see Eq. 4.11, Sec. 4.16) Equation 6.7 provides a useful alternative expression for estimating $\varsigma\kappa$ from the sample mean and median.

$$sk = \frac{3(\overline{X} - Md)}{s} \tag{6.7}$$

Pearson proposed another measure of skewness, $\gamma_1$. If each of the $N$ scores in a frequency distribution is transformed to a $z$-score and then cubed, the mean of the $z^3$-scores is $\gamma_1$.

$$\gamma_1 = \frac{\sum_{i=1}^{N} z_i^3}{N} \tag{6.8}$$

*Technically only $(X - \mu)/\sigma$ is a $z$-ratio; $(X - \overline{X})/s$ is termed a $t$-ratio. If $n$ is large, there will be little difference between the $z$ and the $t$ associated with an observation. The $t$-distribution is widely used in statistics and will be used extensively beginning in Chapter 11.

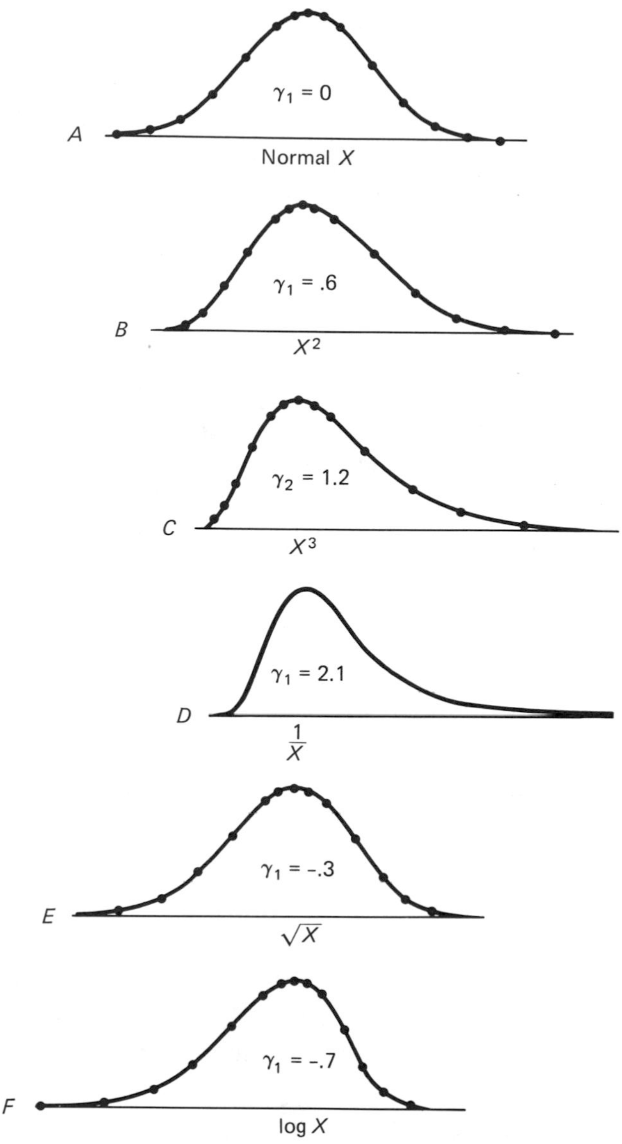


**FIGURE 6.6**
**Distributions illustrating various degrees of positive and negative skewness. (The authors are indebted to Carol Vojir for providing these transformations.)**

In actual practice $\varsigma\kappa$ and $\gamma_1$ do not differ greatly in value.* $\varsigma\kappa$ is more informative for visualizing the degree of skewness and reconstructing the frequency distribution; $\gamma_1$ is superior for certain inferential purposes (Snedecor and Cochran, 1980, pp. 78-79).

*$\varsigma\kappa$ can be perfectly determined from $\gamma_1$ when the kurtosis $\gamma_2$ (see Sec. 6.9) of the distribution is known (Kendall and Stuart, 1961, p. 85):

$$\varsigma\kappa = \frac{\gamma_1(\gamma_2 + 6)}{2(5\gamma_2 - 6\gamma_1^2 + 6)}$$

Although it is not yet common practice, researchers should routinely report the degree of skewness in distributions of interest to help the reader visualize the shape of the distribution and better interpret the associated statistical information such as correlation coefficients that can be substantially affected by skewness.

Figure 6.6 illustrates several degrees of positive and negative skewness. Curves $B$ through $F$ were obtained by performing mathematical transformations on the normally distributed values in curve $A$.

## 6.9 KURTOSIS

Up to this point three properties or features of groups of scores have been described: central tendency, variability, and symmetry. A fourth property, kurtosis, completes the set of features of distributions of scores that are generally of interest in analyzing data. One may wish to know something about how peaked or flat a distribution is. The customary measure of kurtosis, $\gamma_2$, is the mean of the frequency distribution of $z^4$-scores (i.e., $z$'s raised to the fourth power) minus the constant 3 (which is the mean $z^4$-value for the normal curve).*

$$\gamma_2 = \frac{\sum_{i=1}^{N} z_i^4}{N} - 3 \tag{6.9}$$

Figure 6.7 gives distributions differing in kurtosis but having the same means and standard deviations. The top four curves have fewer extremely high or low scores than does the normal distribution. They have negative $\gamma_2$- values and are termed *platykurtic* distributions. (The prefix "platy" means flat or broad.) The normal distribution has a $\gamma_2$-value of 0 and is said to be *mesokurtic* ("meso" means intermediate). The bottom curve has more extreme scores than the normal distribution (and hence fewer scores near the mean), which gives it a positive value. Such curves are described as *leptokurtic*. (The prefix "lepto" means slender or narrow.) Highly skewed distributions tend to be leptokurtic because they have more scores that are far from the mean than does the normal distribution.

Ordinarily there is far less interest in the kurtosis of a distribution than in its central tendency, variability, and skewness.

## 6.10 TRANSFORMATIONS†

Many statistical methods assume that population distributions follow normal curves. Although many of these methods work quite well even when the assumption is not satisfied, it is sometimes desirable to convert the original scores to another metric in which the dis-

*In some sources −3 is absent from the formula for kurtosis; thus the normal distribution would have kurtosis of 3.

†More explicitly, this should read *nonlinear transformations* (i.e., transformations that alter the shape of a distribution). The $z$-scale and $T$-scale (Eq. 6.2 and 6.5) are linear transformations of $X$ (Sec. 7.9).

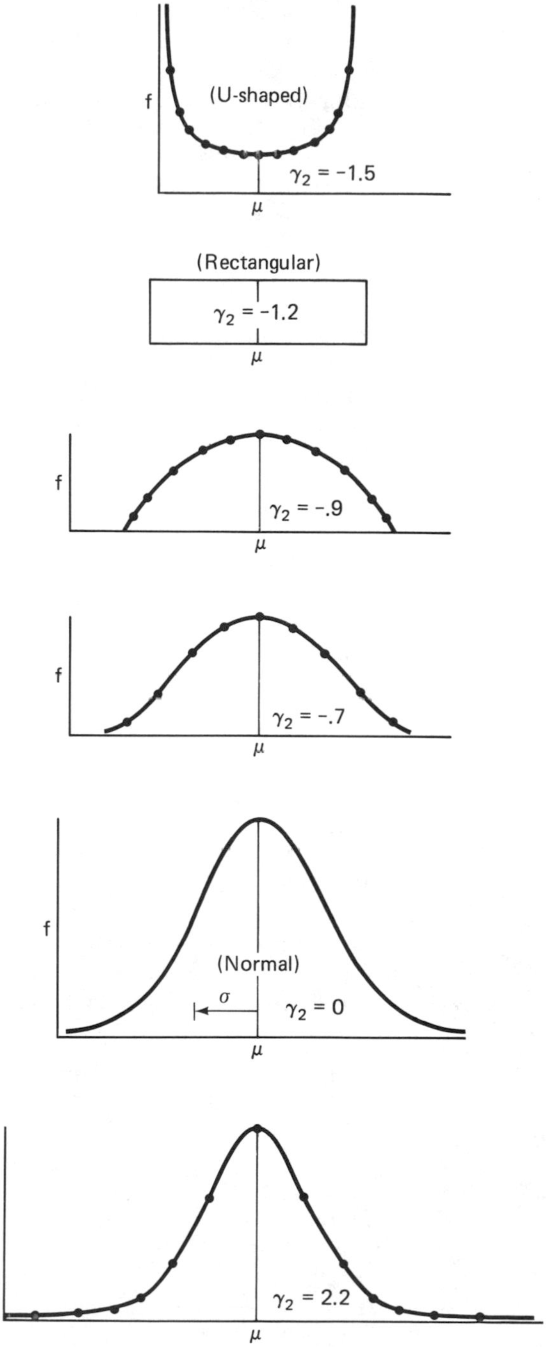


**FIGURE 6.7**
**Symmetric curves differing in kurtosis.**

tribution is more nearly normal. It often happens that an appropriate change of scale, such as using the square root, reciprocal, or logarithm of the observations, will result is less skewness.

Figure 6.6 illustrates how the shape of a normal distribution is altered by five common transformations. Notice that if the mathematical process is reversed, the normal distribution would be reproduced. For example, distributions $E$ and $F$ show that positive skewness can be reduced when the square root and log transformations are applied. If the square root transformation is applied to distribution $B$, a normal distribution ($A$) would result. Thus root and log transformations reduce positive skewness and power transformations reduce negative skewness.

The best transformation is often difficult to determine, and success in finding a good transformation is frequently a matter of trial and error. Additional guidelines can be found in Kirk (1982, pp. 81-84), Winer (1971, pp. 397-402), Lee (1975, pp. 288-291), Dixon and Massey (1969, Chapter 16), Snedecor and Cochran (1980, Chapter 15), and Tukey (1977, Chapter 3).

## 6.11 NORMALIZED SCORES

When it can be assumed that the variable underlying the observed distribution is normally distributed, the observed distribution is sometimes normalized, i.e., transformed to "force" the curve to approximate the normal distribution as closely as possible. This transformation is monotonic (the rank order of $X$'s is maintained) but is nonlinear (the relative distances between scores is not maintained, see Sec. 7.9).

Usually normalized scores are expressed using the $T$-score scale ($\mu = 50$, $\sigma = 10$). Normalized $T$-scores are obtained by first converting the original scores to percentiles and then converting each percentile to the score corresponding to that percentile in a normal distribution. In other words, this sequence is followed: $X_i \to P_i \to z_i \to T_i$. If a score is at the 10th percentile in its original distribution, from Table A in the Appendix one sees that a $z$-score of $-1.282$ corresponds to $P_{10}$ in the normal distribution. Using Equation 6.5, the $T$-score corresponding to $z = -1.282$ is $50 + 10(-1.282) = 37.18$ or 37. Unless the observed distribution deviates substantially from the normal distribution, normalized $T$-scores will differ little from nonnormalized $T$-scores.*

*On rare occasions one may need to know the mean and standard deviation within a *segment* of the normal distribution. The mean $z$-score of a section of the normal distribution between the points $z_a$ and $z_b$ (where $z_b > z_a$) is the difference in the corresponding ordinates $u_a$ and $u_b$ at $z_a$ and $z_b$ divided by the proportion of cases in the section $p$. Thus, $\mu_z = (u_a - u_b)/p$. To find the mean of scores falling between the median and $Q_3$ expressed as a $z$-score, do the following. From Table A, read that the ordinates corresponding to $z_a$ and $z_b$ are $u_a = .3989$ and $u_b = .3178$. Hence $\mu_z = (.3989 - .3178/.25 = .3244$. The same procedure can be used to find the mean of the scores in the tail of the normal distribution (Kelley, 1939). The mean $z$-score in the top quarter of normally distributed scores is $\mu_z = (.3178 - 0)/.25 = 1.27$; conversely, the mean of scores below $Q_1$ is $\mu_z = (0 - .3178)/.25 = -1.27$.

The variance of $z$-scores within a section of the normal distribution is $\sigma_z^2 = [p(z_a u_a - z_b u_b) - (u_a - u_b)^2]/p^2$. The variance of $z$-scores between the median and $Q_3$ is $\sigma_z^2 = \{.25[(0)(.3989) - (.674)(.3178)] - (.3989 - .3178)^2\}/(.25)^2 = .0380$, and $\sigma_z = .195$. For the top (or bottom) quarter of the normal distribution, $\sigma_z = .490$.

## CHAPTER SUMMARY

The measurement of many variables in the social and behavioral sciences have distributions that are closely approximated by the normal distribution.

The normal distribution is symmetrical, unimodal, and "bell-shaped." There is a known proportion of the curve below any $z$-score in a normal distribution. These proportions can be found from Table A after the observation is expressed as a $z$-score—the number of standard deviations that the observation falls from the mean [i.e., $z_i = (X_i - \mu)/\sigma$].

In addition to $z$-scores there are other widely used standard-score scales; the most popular is the $T$-scale that sets $\mu = 50$ and $\sigma = 10$.

Skewness and kurtosis indices describe some of the ways in which a distribution differs from the normal distribution. Nonnormal distributions can often be made to be more nearly normal by using certain mathematical transformations on the scores.

## *MASTERY TEST*

Information on certain standardized intelligence and achievement tests is given. Answer Questions 1 to 10 assuming the scores are normally distributed.

| | | *Iowa Test of Basic Skills Grade-Equivalent Scores* | | | |
|---|---|---|---|---|---|
| | | Reading | | | Arithmetic |
| | *Wechsler IQ* | Grade 3 | Grade 5 | Grade 8 | Grade 5 |
| $\mu$ | 100 | 3.0 | 5.0 | 8.0 | 5.0 |
| $\sigma$ | 15 | 1.0 | 1.4 | 1.9 | 1.1 |

1. An IQ score above 115 is obtained by what percent of the population?
2. If a fifth-grade pupil obtains a percentile rank of 84 in reading, what is her grade-equivalent score?
3. What is the grade-equivalent score for the same relative performance as in Question 2 ($P_{84}$) in arithmetic at grade 5?
4. Jack was reading at 6.1 when he entered grade 8. If his Wechsler IQ is equivalent to the same percentile rank, what is it?
5. If Jack's score in Question 4 is valid, he reads better than about what percentage of children in his grade?
6. Upon entering grade 3, approximately one out of how many third-grade children
   a. obtains a reading grade-equivalent score of 4.0 or better?
   b. obtains a score of 5.0 or better?
7. On the reading test, what percent of beginning third-grade students (3.0) score at least as high as the *average* beginning fourth-grade students (4.0)?
8. At grade 5, is a grade-equivalent score of 6.0 relatively better (i.e., does it have a higher percentile equivalent) in arithmetic than in reading?
9. In reading, what percentages of third-grade students score below grade-equivalent scores of 2.0, 3.0, 4.0, and 5.0, respectively?

10. How much reading "growth" in grade-equivalent units is required during the five years between grades 3.0 and 8.0 to
   a. maintain a percentile equivalent of 50?
   b. maintain a percentile rank of 84?

11. If $X = 176$ with $\mu = 163$ and $\sigma = 26$, express $X$ as
   a. a $z$-score b. a $T$-score c. a percentile equivalent

12. If IQ's were perfectly normally distributed, how many persons in the United States would have IQ's exceeding 175? (Assume $\mu = 100$, $\sigma = 15$, and $N = 200{,}000{,}000$.)

13. What percentage of IQ scores would fall between
   a. 90 and 110? b. 80 and 120? c. 75 and 125?

14. If men's heights are distributed normally, how many men in 10,000 will be 6ft. 6in. or taller? (Use $\mu = 68.5$ in., $\sigma = 2.6$ in.)

15. Which of these is *not* characteristic of a normal distribution?
   a. symmetrical b. unimodal c. skewed d. mesokurtic

16. Which of these reflects the poorest performance on a test?
   a. $P_{10}$ b. $z = -1.5$ c. $T = 30$

17. With a sample of 1,000 representative observations, which of these is probably least accurately characterized by the normal distribution?
   a. scores on a musical aptitude test
   b. number of baby teeth lost by age eight
   c. size of reading vocabulary of twelve-year-old children
   d. number of times attended church in past year
   e. scores on an inventory measuring interest in politics

18. If raw scores are changed to $z$-scores, would the shape of the distribution be changed?

19. If $z$-scores are multiplied by 10, the standard devation increases from ____ to ____.

20. What is the variance in a distribution expressed as
   a. $z$-scores? b. $T$-score?

21. Small changes in $z$-scores near the mean (e.g., from 0 to .5) correspond to (a. large or small) changes in percentile equivalents? But large $z$-score changes near the extremes (e.g., 2.0 to 2.5) correspond to (b. large or small) changes in percentile equivalents?

22. If for a class of gifted children $\mu = 140$, $\sigma = 10$, and $_S\kappa = .6$, estimate the mode and median of the distribution of scores.

23. What is the $_S\kappa$ skewness index for the distribution in Figure 3.7? (Use Eq. 6.7.)

24. The square root and log transformations will reduce ____ (positive or negative) skewness in a distribution. (See Fig. 6.6.)

## PROBLEMS AND EXERCISES

1. Let $z$ stand for the unit normal variable, i.e., the normally distributed variable with mean 0 and standard deviation 1. Find the area under the unit normal curve which lies:
   a. above $z = 1.00$
   b. below $z = 2.00$
   c. above $z = 1.64$
   d. below $z = -1.96$
   e. between $z = 0$ and $z = 3.00$
   f. above $z = -.50$
   g. between $z = -1.50$ and $z = 1.50$

2. Find the ordinates of the unit normal distribution above each of the following $z$ scores:
   a. $z = 2.25$  b. $z = -.15$

3. Find the $z$-scores which are exceeded by the following proportions of the area under the unit normal distribution:

| | *Proportion of Area Above z-score* | *z-score* |
|---|---|---|
| a. | .50 | 0 |
| b. | .16 | +1.00 |
| c. | .84 | |
| d. | .05 | |
| e. | .005 | |
| f. | .995 | |
| g. | .10 | |

4. If in the general population of children, Stanford-Binet IQ's have a nearly normal distribution with mean 100 and standard deviation 16 (see Fig. 6.5), find the percentile equivalent of each of the following IQ's:

| | *IQ* | *Percentile equivalent* |
|---|---|---|
| a. | 100 | 50 |
| b. | 120 | |
| c. | 75 | |
| d. | 95 | |
| e. | 140 | |

5. Suppose Mary obtained the following percentiles on five subtests on the McCarthy Scales of Children's Abilities:

| *Subtest* | *Percentile* |
|---|---|
| Verbal | 98 |
| Perceptual | 99.9 |
| Quantitative | 50 |
| Memory | 84 |
| Motor | 16 |

Use Figure 6.5 to answer Exercises a to d.

a. If Mary's Motor performance improved by $1\sigma$, the percentile equivalent would increase from 16 to ____, or ____ percentile units.
b. If the Verbal score improved by $1\sigma$, the percentile equivalent on the Verbal tests would increase from 98 to ____, or ____ percentile units.
c. In standard deviation units, is the size of the *difference* between Mary's performance on the Verbal and Perceptual tests the same as the difference between her Motor and Quantitative scores?
d. If expressed in $T$-scores, would the change from $P_{16}$ to $P_{50}$ in Exercise a. be equal to the change from $P_{98}$ to $P_{99.9}$ in Exercise b?

6. The manual for the *Metropolitan Achievement Tests* (MAT, 1978) contains no report of standard deviations for the grade equivalent (GE) scales but does give percentile ranks as indicated:

| *Percentile for Fall of Grade 5* | *GE* Reading | Math |
|---|---|---|
| 84 | 9.0 | 6.8 |
| 50 | 5.0 | 5.0 |
| 16 | 3.0 | 3.4 |

a. Estimate the GE standard deviation for the reading and math tests. $[\sigma \doteq (P_{84} - P_{16})/2]$
b. Which distribution is more severely skewed?
c. Would the mean GE be greater on the reading or the math test? Explain.
d. Using the estimated standard deviation on the math test, approximately what percent of beginning fifth-grade students obtain GE scores above 6.0 on the MAT? Assuming normal distributions, compare this figure with the corresponding figure for the ITBS Arithmetic Test (see data preceding Question 1 on the Mastery Test).

7. "Grading on the normal curve" was popular in some circles a few decades ago. The most common method used the following conversion:

| *Grade* | *z-score* |
|---|---|
| A | above 1.5 |
| B | .5 to 1.5 |
| C | −.5 to .5 |
| D | −1.5 to −.5 |
| F | below −1.5 |

Using this system, what percent of A's, B's, C's, D's, and F's are expected with a normal distribution of scores?

8. If a large number of naive examinees guess randomly to each of the 100 items on a true-false test, the mean would be expected to be $50 = \mu$, with $\sigma = 5$. What percent of the examinees would be expected to earn scores of 65 or more?

9. Each of eleven students in a club were asked to respond to a sociometric measure in which they identified the three persons who had showed the most leadership ability. The scores (number of nominations) for each student are given:

| $X_i$ | $x_i$ | $z_i$ | $z_i^2$ | $z_i^3$ | $z_i^4$ |
|---|---|---|---|---|---|
| 9 | 6 | 2.4 | 5.76 | 13.824 | 33.1776 |
| 5 | 2 | .8 | .64 | .512 | .4096 |
| 5 | 2 | ___ | ___ | ___ | ___ |
| 4 | 1 | .4 | ___ | ___ | ___ |
| 3 | 0 | .0 | .00 | .000 | .0000 |
| 2 | −1 | −.4 | .16 | ___ | ___ |
| 2 | −1 | −.4 | .16 | −.064 | .0256 |
| 1 | −2 | −.8 | .64 | −.512 | .4096 |
| 1 | −2 | −.8 | .64 | −.512 | .4096 |
| 1 | −2 | −.8 | .64 | −.512 | .4096 |
| 0 | −3 | ___ | 1.44 | −1.728 | 2.0736 |
| $\Sigma X_i =$ ___ | $\Sigma x_i =$ ___ | $\Sigma z_i =$ ___ | $\Sigma z_i^2 =$ ___ | $\Sigma z_i^3 =$ ___ | $\Sigma z_i^4 =$ ___ |

a. What are the mean, median, and mode of the distribution?
b. Supply the missing $z$-score ($\sigma = 2.5$).
c. Supply the missing values in the $z_i^2$, $z_i^3$, and $z_i^4$ columns, and determine the sums of each column.
d. Determine the skewness and kurtosis indices of the distribution.

10. Suppose a student can qualify for $100 in additional state aid designated for special remedial reading by scoring 2.0 or more grade equivalents below his current grade level status. For a typical, representative school district with approximately 4,000 students per grade level, how much more state aid would the district receive for its fifth graders if if used the Metropolitan (MAT) rather than the Iowa (ITBS)? The standard deviations are 3.0 and 1.4 for the MAT and ITBS, respectively; use 5.0 for both means. Assume normality and round $z$-scores to the second decimal place.
11. Knowing $\sigma = 15$ on the Wechsler IQ scale, estimate $Q$.
12. The Miller Analogies Test is used by some psychology departments in selecting graduate students. Although only raw scores are reported, it is known that for students applying for graduate study the mean and standard deviation are approximately 48 and 17, respectively. If applicants at a certain prestigious university are expected to be in the upper 10%, what is the minimum raw score expected on the Miller?
13. Prove that $\Sigma_{i=1}^{N} z_i^2 = N$

## *ANSWERS TO MASTERY TEST*

1. 16%
2. 6.4
3. 6.1
4. 85
5. 16%
6. a. 6, i.e. 1 of 6
   b. 50, i.e. 1 of 50
7. 16%
8. Yes
9. 16%, 50%, 84%, and 98%
10. a. 5.0
    b. 5.9
11. a. .5
    b. 55
    c. $P_{69}$
12. $z = \dfrac{175 - 100}{15} = 5.0;$
    (.0000003)(200,000,000) = 60
13. a. .7486 - .2514 = .4972 or about 50%
    b. .9082 - .0918 = .8164 or 82%
    c. .9525 - .0475 = .9050 or 91%
14. 1 or 2; $z = \dfrac{78 - 68.5}{2.6} = 3.65$
15. c
16. c
17. d
18. no
19. 1.0 to 10
20. a. $(1)^2 = 1$
    b. $(10)^2 = 100$
21. a. large b. small
22. Mode $\doteq$ 134, $Md \doteq$ 138 (See Eq. 4.11)
23. -.35
24. Positive

## *ANSWERS TO PROBLEMS AND EXERCISES*

1. a. 1587
   b. .9772
   c. .0505
   d. .0250
   e. .4987
   f. .6915
   g. .8664
2. a. .0317 b. .3945

3. a. 0.00
   b. +1.00
   c. −1.00
   d. +1.645
   e. +2.58
   f. −2.58
   g. +1.28
4. b. 89
   c. 6
   d. 38
   e. 99
5. a. 50; 34
   b. 99.9, 1.9
   c. Yes, $1\sigma$ in each instance
   d. Yes, *T*-score increase of 10 in each instance
6. a. $\sigma_R \doteq 3.0$, $\sigma_M \doteq 1.7$
   b. reading
   c. reading; greater positive skewness
   d. MAT: $z = .58$, 28% above 6.0
      ITBS: $z = .91$, 18% above 6.0
7. A: 7%
   B: 24%
   C: 38%
   D: 24%
   E: 7%
8. .0013 or .13% or roughly one student in 1,000
9. a. Mean = 3.0, median = 2, mode = 1
   b. .8 and −1.2
   c. $\Sigma X = 33$, $\Sigma x = 0$, $\Sigma z = 0$, $\Sigma z^2 = 10.88$, $\Sigma z^3 = 11.52$, $\Sigma z^4 = 37.3760$
   d. $\gamma_2 = 11.52/11 = 1.05; = 37.3760/11 - 3 = .40$
10. MAT: $z = -.67$, $.2514 \times 4{,}000 \times 100 = \$100{,}560$.
    ITBS: $z = -1.43$, $.0764 \times 4000 \times 100 = \$30{,}560$ or \$70,000 more using MAT
11. From Table A, $Q = .6740$, $Q = 10$
12. 70
13. $$\sum_1^N z_i^2 = \sum_1^N \frac{(X_i - \mu)^2}{\sigma^2} = \frac{1}{\sigma^2}\sum_1^N (X_i - \mu)^2 = \frac{1}{\sigma^2}(N\sigma^2) = N$$

# 7 CORRELATION: THE MEASUREMENT OF RELATIONSHIP

## 7.1 INTRODUCTION

Measures of correlation are used to describe the degree of relationship between two variables. Moreover, correlation is an integral part of many other statistical techniques. In this chapter the meaning, use, and computation of measures of relationship are studied.

Researchers are often concerned with the association between two variables for a group of persons, schools, cities, or the like. For example: Is absenteeism related to socioeconomic status? Is class size related to gains in achievement during the course of a school year? Do less competitive cultures have a smaller incidence of peptic ulcers? To answer questions such as these, measures of relationship or correlation are needed.

Most people have a general understanding of *correlation.* Two variables are correlated if they tend to "go together." If high scores on variable $X$ tend to be accompanied by high scores on variable $Y$, then the variables $X$ and $Y$ are correlated. The degree of correlation between variables can be described by such terms as "strong," "low," "positive," or "moderate," but these terms are not very precise. If a coefficient of correlation is computed between the sets of scores, the relationship is described more accurately. A coefficient of correlation is a statistical summary of the degree and direction of relationship or association between two variables.

## 7.2
## THE CONCEPT OF CORRELATION

There is a substantial, but by no means perfect, positive correlation between persons' income and the taxes they pay. Husbands and wives *tend* to be alike in age, amount of education, and many other ways. The sons of tall fathers tend to be taller than average, and the sons of short fathers tend to be shorter than average. Children resemble their parents in intelligence more closely than they resemble their cousins. Some degree of positive correlation between members of families is usually found for almost any characteristic, such as personality, attitude, interest, or ability.

Statistical measures have been devised to quantify the relationships among variables. Karl Pearson (1857-1936) derived a measure of relationship called the *product-moment coefficient of correlation* (signified by $r$ in a sample and by $\rho$, the Greek letter *rho*, for the population parameter). Since about 1900, this correlation coefficient has been employed in almost all social sciences.

## 7.3
## THE MEASUREMENT OF CORRELATION

Pearson's correlation coefficient summarizes the magnitude and direction of the relationship between two variables (such as height and weight of individuals) or between the same variable on *pairs* of observations (like the height of fathers and sons). It makes no difference whether the variables being correlated are history grades ($X$) and geography grades ($Y$), speed of running the 100-yard dash ($X$) and skill in playing the violin ($Y$), or political conservatism ($X$) and age ($Y$). In all situations the correlation coefficient can have values that range from $-1.0$ for a perfect inverse (negative) relationship, through 0 for no correlation, and up to $+1.0$ for perfect direct (positive) relationship.

The sign (+ or −) of the correlation coefficient indicates the *direction* of the relationship. When low scores on $X$ are accompanied by low scores on $Y$ and high scores on $X$ by high scores on $Y$, the correlation between $X$ and $Y$ is positive; if high scores on $X$ are associated with low scores on $Y$ and vice versa, the correlation is negative.

Correlation coefficients allow us to compare the strength and direction of association between different pairs of variables. For example, by comparing the respective correlation coefficients, one can say that siblings are more similar in scholastic achievement ($\rho \doteq .8$) than they are in intelligence ($\rho \doteq .5$). Or the correlation coefficient can be used to establish that the relationship between musical and psychomotor abilities ($\rho \doteq .2$) is less than the relationship between verbal and mathematical abilities ($\rho \doteq .6$). The IQ scores of adopted children are more highly related to the IQ scores of their biological parents ($\rho \doteq .4$) than to the IQ scores of their adopting parents ($\rho \doteq .25$) (see Munsinger, 1975).

### The Use of Correlation Coefficients

A classic example of the use of correlation coefficients is illustrated in the nature-nurture studies of intelligence. Table 7.1 gives correlation coefficients between measured intelligence (IQ) and varying degrees of genetic and environmental similarity. Data on

**TABLE 7.1 Correlation Coefficients of Intelligence, Academic Achievement, Height, and Weight for Persons of Varying Genetic and Environmental Similarity**

| | *Identical Twins Reared* | | *Fraternal Twins Reared* | *Siblings Reared* | | *Unrelated Children Reared* | |
|---|---|---|---|---|---|---|---|
| | Together | Apart | Together | Together | Apart | Together | Apart |
| Intelligence (IQ) | .91 | .67 | .64 | .50 | .40 | .23 | .00 |
| Achievement | .96 | .51 | .88 | .81 | .53 | .52 | .00 |
| Height | .96 | .94 | .47 | .50 | .54 | .00 | .00 |
| Weight | .93 | .88 | .59 | .57 | .43 | .24 | .00 |

Source: Data from Newman, Freeman, and Holzinger (1937) and Erlenmeyer-Kimling and Jarvik (1963).

academic achievement, height, and weight are also given in Table 7.1. Notice that environment has a much greater influence on scholastic achievement than it does on IQ. For example, in Table 7.1 the correlation between the scholastic achievement of pairs of unrelated children reared together is .52; but the correlation between their IQ scores is only .23. Notice also that although height is less influenced by environment than weight, a strong hereditary factor is evident in weight (e.g., $r$ = .88 for identical twins reared apart).

## 7.4 SCATTERPLOTS

An intuitive understanding of the meaning of correlation coefficients (such as those given in Table 7.1) is enhanced by studying some illustrative *scatterplots* (also called *scatter diagrams*). In a scatterplot of "dots" or tallies, each mark represents the intersection of two scores (one pair of observations) such as heights of father and son or, for persons: age paired with racial prejudice rating or, in a sample of cities: crimes per 10,000 residents versus number of police officers. *The chief purpose of the scatter diagram is for the study of the nature of the relationship between two variables.* The scatterplot also enables one to surmise whether or not a computed $r$ will accurately summarize the relationship between the two variables. For *linear* correlation, it will. The relationship between two variables is linear if a straight line called a *regression line*, more closely fits the dots of the scatterplot than does a curved line or, equivalently, if the means of vertical "slices" (class intervals) would not deviate substantially from a straight line. A perfect positive linear relationship ($r$ = 1.00) is shown in Figure 7.1—the dots fall in a straight line from low-low to high-high. For example, centigrade and Fahrenheit temperatures would correlate +1.0.

A perfect *negative* relationship ($r$ = −1) is illustrated in Figure 7.2. The time required to travel 1 mile correlates − 1 with velocity. Or, if everyone attempted all items on an objective test, the number of right answers would correlate −1.0 with the number of wrong answers. Actually obtained relationships rarely yield $r$'s of exactly −1, or 1, but values of .5, .7, .3, and so on are common.

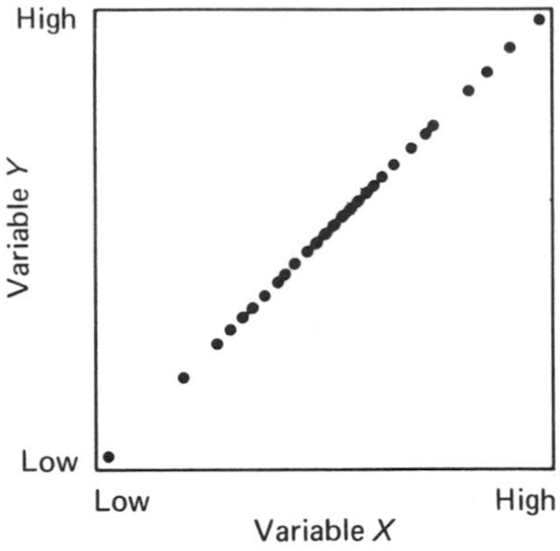


FIGURE 7.1
**An illustration of a perfect positive correlation, $r = 1$.**

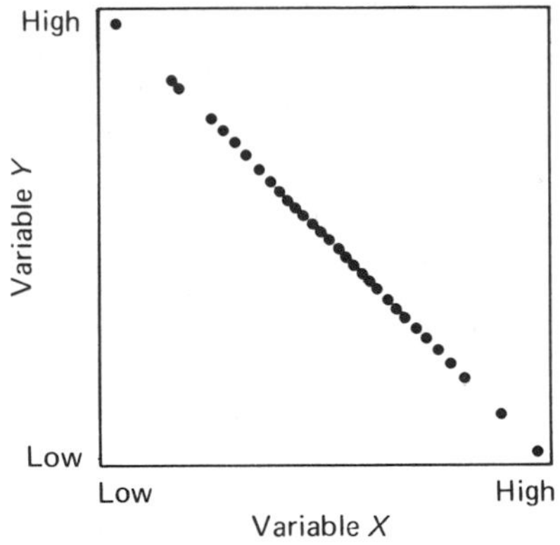


FIGURE 7.2
**An illustration of a perfect negative relationship, $r = -1$.**

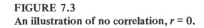

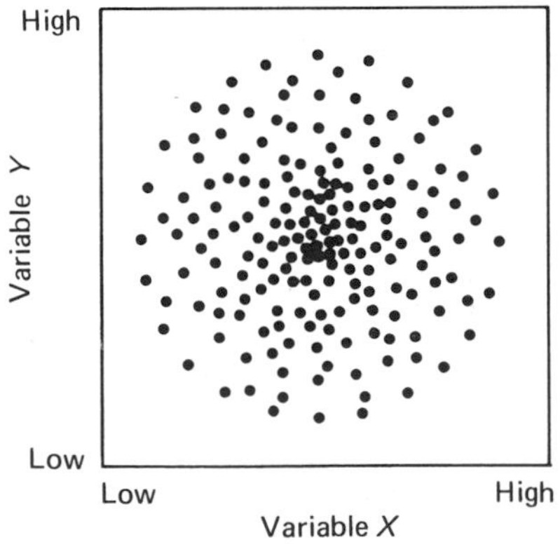


FIGURE 7.3
**An illustration of no correlation, $r = 0$.**

In Figure 7.3 the scatterplot depicts no relationship between variables $X$ and $Y$ ($r = 0.0$). An individual with a high score on $X$ could have either a high, middle, or a low score on $Y$.

## 7.5 LINEAR AND CURVILINEAR RELATIONSHIPS

Of all the possible ways in which measurements on two variables can be related, $r$ (or $\rho$) measures only one type; the value of $r$ is a measure of the degree of linear relationship between $X$ and $Y$. If $X$ and $Y$ are perfectly linearly related (i.e., $r = 1.0$ or $r = -1.0$), the points in the scatter diagram will fall on a straight line, as illustrated in Figures 7.1 and 7.2. If the points in a scatterplot "swarm" around a straight line that could be drawn through the points, a linear relationship exists between $X$ and $Y$ of some degree. If the points in a scatter diagram appear to be about a curved line rather than a straight line, the relationship between $X$ and $Y$ is *curvilinear*. Since $r$ measures *only* the linear relationship between $X$ and $Y$, if the actual relationship is curvilinear, the value of $r$ may be close to 0. This illustrates the importance of examining scatterplots in studying the relationship between variables. A substantial but *curvilinear* relationship can exist, and yet the computed value of $r$ can be zero. If $X$ and $Y$ are generally linearly related, the meaning of $r$ is unequivocal. However, if $X$ and $Y$ have some sort of curvilinear relationship, the value of $r$ will underestimate the true degree of relationship.

Figures 7.3 and 7.4 show two different scatter diagrams, each of which has a correlation coefficient of approximately zero. However, there is obviously a considerable relationship between $X$ and $Y$ in Figure 7.4, but no systematic relationship in Figure 7.3. The single illustration of Figure 7.4 should be sufficient warning never to draw a rash conclusion that two variables are unrelated merely because $r$ is zero. The relationship between age ($X$) and distance run in 12 min ($Y$) for boys between twelve and seventeen is similar to that illustrated in the scatterplot given in Figure 7.4 (Morrow, Jackson, and Bell, 1978).

A major purpose of scatterplots is to insure that the relationship is roughly linear before assuming that $r$ is an accurate indication of the degree of relationship between $X$

**FIGURE 7.4**
**An illustration of a substantial curvilinear relationship, but yields $r \doteq 0$.**

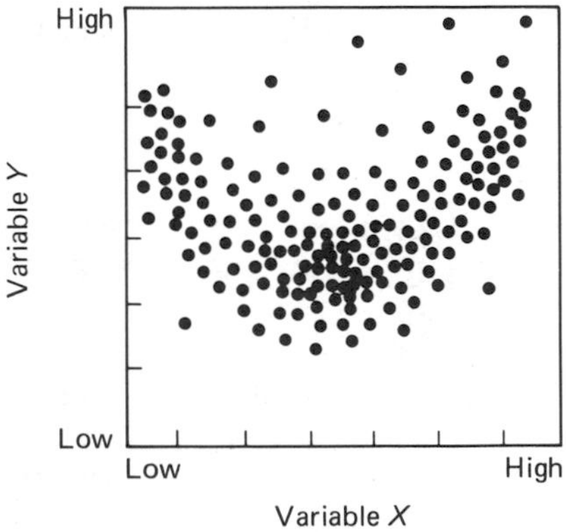

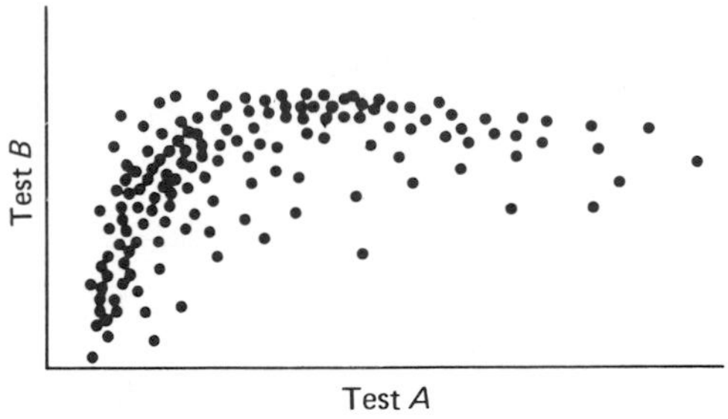


FIGURE 7.5
The scatterplot of scores for test $A$ (which is skewed positively) and test $B$ (which is skewed negatively).

and $Y$. The "eyeball" check is sufficient to detect any substantial degree of nonlinearity unless $n$ is small.

Fortunately, many variables in the behavioral sciences and education are linearly related. Well over 90% of all correlation coefficients reported in research literature in the behavioral sciences are Pearson $r$'s. There is a curvilinear relationship in adults between age and many psychomotor skills that involve coordination. Curvilinear relationships are rare, however, between cognitive and psychomotor skills, although spurious curvilinearity can result from poorly developed measures. For example, educational and psychological test scores frequently show "ceiling" or "cellar" effects with atypical groups of persons; that is, the test may be too easy or too difficult, with the result that many persons obtain very high or very low scores. In Figure 7.5 scores for Test $A$ are skewed positively because it is too difficult for these examinees; scores on Test $B$ are negatively skewed because of inadequate test "ceiling."

The value of $r$ for the data in Figure 7.5 is not large; it is probably only about .30. It appears, however, that if test $B$ were made more difficult and test $A$ easier without radically altering the content of either test, the value of $r_{AB}$ for these persons would increase substantially. The scatter diagram of the test scores for such altered tests would probably show substantial linear relationship. Note, however, that $r$ gives a conservative, minimum estimate of the relationship between two variables—a curvilinear correlation coefficient will never be less than $r$ for any set of data. The value of $r$ would be expected to increase if the scores in the two distributions were transformed to distributions which were more nearly normal (see Secs. 6.10 to 6.11). But these correlations would remain considerably less than if the measures were more adequate. (In the next chapter (Sec. 8.27) the correlation coefficient $\eta$ (eta) is introduced which does not require the relationship between $X$ and $Y$ to be linear.)

## 7.6 CALCULATING THE PEARSON PRODUCT-MOMENT CORRELATION COEFFICIENT $r$

The Pearson correlation coefficient is formed from the standard deviations of two variables, $X$ and $Y$, and their *covariance*. The covariance is a perfectly good measure of association in many problems in the physical sciences and engineering. The covariance is an adequate measure as long as the scales (means and variances) of the variables are not arbitrary. But most variables in the social and behavioral sciences are measured on an arbitrary scale; hence correlation coefficients are preferred to covariances as measures of relationship. Recall that variance $s_X^2$ was defined in Equation 5.3 as

$$s_X^2 = \frac{\sum_{i=1}^{n} x_i^2}{n-1} = \frac{\sum_i (X_i - \bar{X})^2}{n-1} \quad \text{or} \quad \frac{\sum_i (X_i - \bar{X})(X_i - \bar{X})}{n-1}$$

The *covariance of variables X and Y*, denoted by $s_{XY}$ is defined similarly, as shown in Equation 7.1:

$$s_{XY} = \frac{\sum_{i=1}^{n} x_i y_i}{n-1} = \frac{\sum_i (X_i - \bar{X})(Y_i - \bar{Y})}{n-1} \tag{7.1}$$

where $X$ and $Y$ are raw scores and $\bar{X}$ and $\bar{Y}$ are the means for variables $X$ and $Y$. If there is no association between $X$ and $Y$, the covariance will be zero; but unlike the correlation coefficient, it has no numerical upper or lower limits. The Pearson product-moment* correlation is obtained when the covariance $s_{XY}$ is divided by each standard deviation, $s_X$ and $s_Y$, as shown in Equation 7.2.

$$r = \frac{s_{XY}}{s_X s_Y} \tag{7.2}$$

## 7.7 A COMPUTATIONAL ILLUSTRATION OF *r*

Unless $n$ is very small, procedures for calculating $r$ are very time consuming unless a calculator is available. Fortunately, most calculations where $n$ is large are now performed using electronic computers or hand calculators preprogrammed to compute $r$ automatically. However, working a few problems by hand removes some of the mystery about correlation coefficients. Since one almost always wants to know $\bar{X}$, $\bar{Y}$, $s_X$, and $s_Y$ as well as $r$, Equation 7.2 is particularly useful.

The standard deviations of $X$ and $Y$ in Formula 7.2 can be obtained conveniently using Equation 5.7. A related simple computational formula for the covariance of $X$ and $Y$ is as follows:

$$s_{XY} = \frac{\sum_i X_i Y_i - n\bar{X}\bar{Y}}{n-1} \tag{7.3}$$

*The term *product-moment* results from the fact that the *products* of the first *moments* are used in defining $r$. The term *moment* in physics refers to a function of the distance of an object from the center of gravity, which is the mean of a frequency distribution. Hence, $x_i = X_i - \bar{X}$ and $y_i = Y_i - \bar{Y}$ are *moments* and $xy$ is a *product of the moments*. Unless otherwise indicated, the terms *correlation* and *correlation coefficient* are short for "Pearson product-moment correlation coefficient."

**TABLE 7.2 The Computation of Pearson *r* Between Scores on the Graduate Record Examination Verbal and Final Examination Scores for Twenty Students in Introductory Statistics**

| Student | GRE Verbal $X$ | Final Examination $Y$ |
|---|---|---|
| 1 | 280 | 64 |
| 2 | 350 | 43 |
| 3 | 380 | 55 |
| 4 | 470 | 73 |
| 5 | 480 | 45 |
| 6 | 490 | 64 |
| 7 | 500 | 69 |
| 8 | 510 | 69 |
| 9 | 510 | 77 |
| 10 | 550 | 65 |
| 11 | 570 | 84 |
| 12 | 580 | 76 |
| 13 | 590 | 79 |
| 14 | 590 | 80 |
| 15 | 600 | 58 |
| 16 | 620 | 68 |
| 17 | 630 | 69 |
| 18 | 630 | 75 |
| 19 | 710 | 69 |
| 20 | 760 | 78 |
| $n = 20$ | $\Sigma X_i = 10{,}800$ | $\Sigma Y_i = 1{,}360$ |
| | $\overline{X} = 540.00$ | $\overline{Y} = 68.00$ |

*Step 1.* **Compute** $s_X = \sqrt{\dfrac{\Sigma x_i^2}{n-1}}$

$$\Sigma x_i^2 = \Sigma X_i^2 - n\overline{X}^2$$

$$\Sigma X_i^2 = 280^2 + 350^2 + \cdots + 760^2 = 6{,}086{,}800$$

$$\Sigma x_i^2 = 6{,}086{,}800 - (20)(540)^2 = 254{,}800$$

$$s_X = \sqrt{\frac{\Sigma x_i^2}{n-1}} = \sqrt{\frac{254{,}800}{20-1}}$$

$$\mathbf{s_X = \sqrt{13{,}410.5} = 115.80}$$

*Step 2.* **Compute** $s_Y = \sqrt{\dfrac{\Sigma y_i^2}{n-1}}$

$$\Sigma y_i^2 = \Sigma Y_i^2 - n\overline{Y}^2$$

$$\Sigma Y_i^2 = 64^2 + 43^2 + \cdots + 78^2 = 94{,}788$$

$$= 94{,}788$$

$$\Sigma y_i^2 = 94{,}788 - (20)(68.00)^2 = 2{,}308$$

$$s_Y = \sqrt{\frac{\Sigma y_i^2}{n-1}} = \sqrt{\frac{2{,}308}{20-1}}$$

$$\mathbf{s_Y = \sqrt{121.47} = 11.02}$$

**TABLE 7.2 (Continued)**

*Step 3.* **Compute** $s_{XY} = \dfrac{\Sigma x_i y_i}{n-1}$

$$\Sigma x_i y_i = \Sigma X_i Y_i - n\overline{X}\overline{Y}$$

$$\Sigma X_i Y_i = (280)(64) + (350)(43) + \cdots + (760)(78) = 747{,}570$$

$$\Sigma x_i y_i = 747{,}570 - (20)(540)(68)$$

$$\Sigma x_i y_i = 13{,}170$$

$$s_{XY} = \frac{\Sigma x_i y_i}{n-1} = \frac{13{,}170}{20-1}$$

$$s_{XY} = \mathbf{693.16}$$

*Step 4.* **Obtain** $r$

$$r = \frac{s_{XY}}{s_X s_Y} = \frac{693.16}{(115.8)(11.02)}$$

$$r = \mathbf{.543}$$

Some actual data will be used to illustrate the computation of $r$. GRE verbal and final examination scores of twenty students in an introductory statistics course are given in Table 7.2. The steps for computing $r$ (compute $s_X$, $s_Y$, and $s_{XY}$, and insert the results into Equation 7.2) are also illustrated in Table 7.2.

## Scatterplots

The $X$ and $Y$ values in Table 7.2 are represented in the scatterplot in Figure 7.6. The figure allows a visual check if a computation error has been made as well as if the relationship appears to be linear. From Figure 7.6, it is apparent that the correlation is moderate, linear, and positive; hence, the computed value of .543 for $r$ appears reasonable. The $X$-variable is always plotted on the horizonal axis with values from left to right; the $Y$-variable is plotted in the vertical axis with smaller values toward the bottom.

It is good practice to study the scatterplot for any important relationship to insure that *outliers* (extremely deviant, and often aberrant scores) are not present. The value of $r$ can be distorted by even one or two outliers, as they are such deviant cases (either $x$ or $y$ is very large, or both). Consequently, outliers can have a large effect on $\Sigma xy$, and hence $r$. Frequently outliers are not from the same population as remaining observations.*

*For additional reading on outliers see Tukey (1977), Snedecor and Cochran (1980), and Winer (1971).

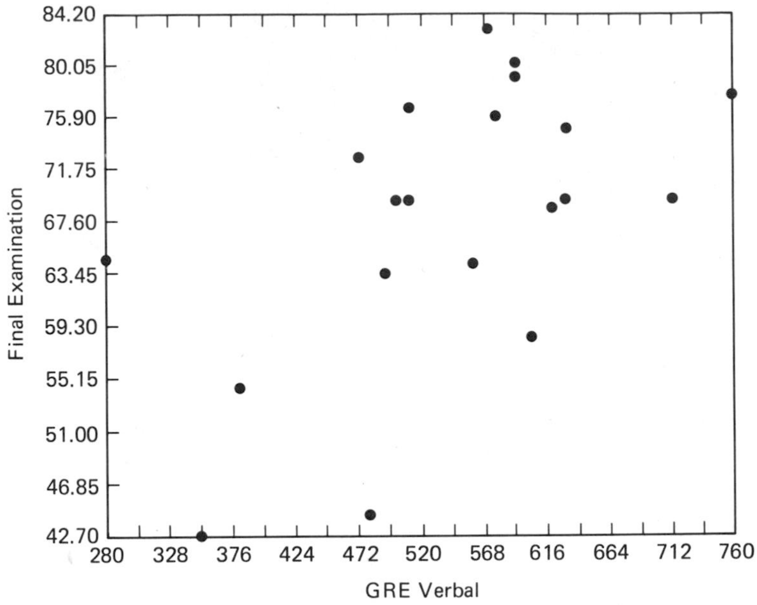


**FIGURE 7.6. Scatterplot of GRE verbal scores and final examination scores for 20 students in introductory statistics.**

## 7.8 ALTERNATIVE COMPUTATIONAL FORMULAS FOR *r*

Equation 7.2 is definitional and not always convenient for computing $r$. A formula more convenient for calculating $r$ shall now be derived, given the raw scores $X$ and $Y$. Note that Equation 7.2 can be rewritten

$$r = \frac{s_{XY}}{s_X s_Y} = \frac{\dfrac{\Sigma x_i y_i}{n-1}}{\sqrt{\dfrac{\Sigma x_i^2}{n-1}}\sqrt{\dfrac{\Sigma y_i^2}{n-1}}} = \frac{\dfrac{\Sigma x_i y_i}{n-1}}{\dfrac{\sqrt{\Sigma x_i^2}}{\sqrt{n-1}}\ \dfrac{\sqrt{\Sigma y_i^2}}{\sqrt{n-1}}}$$

And since the square of a square root is the quantity itself, $(\sqrt{n-1})(\sqrt{n-1}) = n - 1$; and since $\sqrt{\Sigma x_i^2}\sqrt{\Sigma y_i^2} = \sqrt{\Sigma x_i^2\ \Sigma y_i^2}$,

$$r = \frac{\dfrac{\Sigma x_i y_i}{n-1}}{\dfrac{\sqrt{(\Sigma x_i^2)(\Sigma y_i^2)}}{n-1}} = \frac{\Sigma x_i y_i}{n-1} \div \frac{\sqrt{(\Sigma x_i^2)(\Sigma y_i^2)}}{n-1} = \left(\frac{\Sigma x_i y_i}{\cancel{n-1}}\right)\left(\frac{\cancel{n-1}}{\sqrt{(\Sigma x_i^2)(\Sigma y_i^2)}}\right)$$

$$r = \frac{\Sigma x_i y_i}{\sqrt{(\Sigma x_i^2)(\Sigma y_i^2)}}$$

For hand computation, an equivalent expression, Equation 7.4, is less vulnerable to computational errors and takes less time (especially if a calculator is available). Recall from Equation 5.6 (Sec. 5.8) that the sum of squares is equal to $\Sigma x_i^2 = \Sigma X_i^2 - n\overline{X}^2$; a similar formula for obtaining $\Sigma x_i y_i$ is given in the numerator of Equation 7.4. Hence,

$$r = \frac{\Sigma x_i y_i}{\sqrt{(\Sigma x_i^2)(\Sigma y_i^2)}} = \frac{\Sigma X_i Y_i - n\overline{X}\overline{Y}}{\sqrt{(\Sigma X_i^2 - n\overline{X}^2)(\Sigma Y_i^2 - n\overline{Y}^2)}} \tag{7.4}$$

## Expressing $r$ in Terms of $z$-scores

For conceptual purposes it is useful to derive the formula for $r$ when both variables are expressed using $z$-scores. Since by definition the standard deviation of any distribution expressed in $z$-scores is exactly 1, when $X$ and $Y$ are expressed on the $z$-scale

$$r = \frac{s_{XY}}{s_X s_Y} = s_{XY} \tag{7.5}$$

Equation 7.5 shows that when both $X$ and $Y$ are expressed as $z$-scores that the values of $r$ and covariance are one and the same. Since the mean of any $z$-score distribution is zero, each $z$-score is also a deviation score. Thus

$$r = s_{XY} = \frac{\sum_{i=1}^{n} z_{X_i} z_{Y_i}}{n - 1} \tag{7.6}$$

Note that when $r = 1$, $\Sigma_{i=1}^{n} z_{X_i} z_{Y_i} = n - 1$; $r$ will equal 1 only when the two $z$-scores are identical for all $n$ persons.

# 7.9 LINEAR TRANSFORMATIONS AND CORRELATION

Any transformation of $X_i$'s (or $Y_i$'s) that does not change the corresponding $z$-scores does not affect the correlation coefficient. A special class of transformations called *linear* (namely, $X' = aX + b$) results in identical *z-scores* for the original, and the transformed

**TABLE 7.3 Illustrations of the Fact that Linear Transformations of Variables Affect Means and Standard Deviations, But Not the Correlation Between the Variables**

| | *Variable X* | | | *Variable Y* | | |
|---|---|---|---|---|---|---|
| Scores | Mean | Standard Deviation | Scores | Mean | Standard Deviation | r |
| a. $X_i$ | $\overline{X}$ | $s_X$ | $Y_i$ | $\overline{Y}$ | $s_Y$ | .50 |
| b. $(X_i + 50)$ | $(\overline{X} + 50)$ | $s_X$ | $Y_i$ | $\overline{Y}$ | $s_Y$ | .50 |
| c. $(X_i - 100)$ | $(\overline{X} - 100)$ | $s_X$ | $10Y_i$ | $10\overline{Y}$ | $10s_Y$ | .50 |
| d. $\frac{(X_i - \overline{X})}{s_X}$ | 0 | 1 | $\frac{10(Y_i - \overline{Y})}{s_Y} + 50$ | 50 | 10 | .50 |

scores, hence $r_{XX'} = 1.0$, and $r_{YX} = r_{YX'}$. Thus the correlation between $X$ and $Y$ will be identical if computed between raw scores, $z$-scores, $T$-scores, or other linear transformations of $X$ or $Y$. This fact is illustrated in Table 7.3. Notice that the addition of a constant to all $X$-values (or $Y$-values) does not affect $r$. This is also true for subtracting, multiplying, or dividing by non-zero constants—these are all linear transformations.

Height in inches correlates approximately .5 with weight in pounds. What is $r$ if height is expressed in centimeters and weight in kilograms? These transformations are linear; thus the correlation will be unaffected by the unit used for variable $X$ or $Y$.

## 7.10 THE BIVARIATE NORMAL DISTRIBUTION

The theory of correlation has close historical ties with the normal distribution and the *bivariate normal distribution.* Correlation describes the way in which scores on a variable $X$ are paired with scores on a second variable $Y$ for the same persons. Thus these questions concern bivariate relationships, that is, relationships between two variables.

If a large group of persons is measured in two ways—for example, each person's IQ ($X$) and school attitude ($Y$)—the data can be represented in a bivariate frequency distribution. For each person there is a pair of scores, a score on $X$ and a score on $Y$. A bivariate frequency distribution is a picture of the frequency with which different pairs of $X$ and $Y$ scores occur in a group of persons. Figure 7.7 is a bivariate frequency distribution for a group of persons measured on IQ ($X$) and school attitude ($Y$).

From Figure 7.7 approximately twenty persons had IQ scores of 110 (variable $X$) and thirty on the attitude variable $Y$. The height of the line at the intersection of 125 and 60 must be measured against the vertical scale of frequencies.

A large number of bivariate frequency distributions built from data gathered in educational and psychological settings show a characteristic shape. A surface drawn through the endpoints of the columns which represent the frequencies in a bivariate frequency distribution often looks like a bell—in three dimensions—that has been stretched in the $X$ and $Y$ directions and rotated around its center in the $XY$-plane. This smooth,

**FIGURE 7.7. Bivariate frequency distribution for a large group of persons measured on IQ ($X$) and attitude ($Y$).**

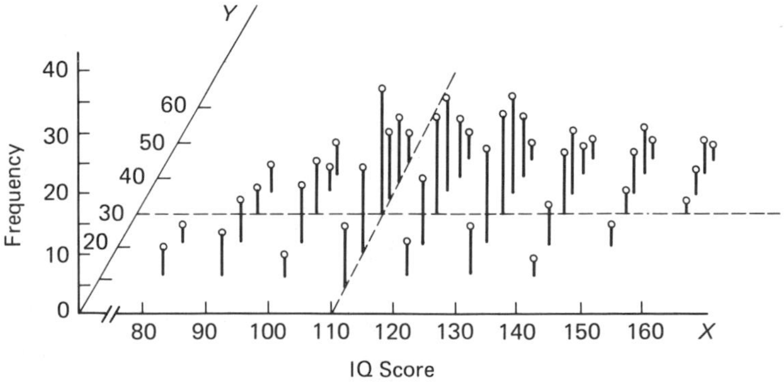

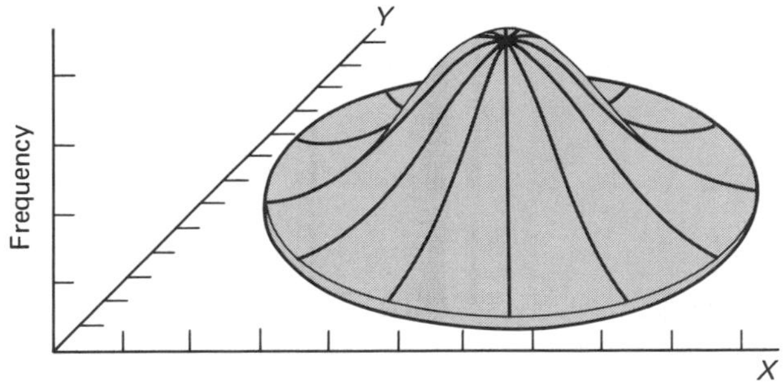


**FIGURE 7.8**
**One of the family of bivariate normal distributions.**

continuous, bell-shaped surface provides a mathematically convenient and satisfactory representation of numerous bivariate frequency distributions.

As was true of the normal distribution, the bivariate normal distribution is a family of three-dimensional surfaces. One member of this family appears in Figure 7.8.

All bivariate normal distributions have the following characteristics:

1. For each value of $X$, the distribution of the associated $Y$-values is a normal distribution, and vice versa.
2. The $Y$-means for each value of $X$ fall on a straight line—the relationship is linear. The same is true for $X$-means for each value of $Y$.
3. The scatterplots possess *homoscedasticity*—the variance in the $Y$-values is uniform across all values of $X$. Conversely, the variance in $X$-values is constant for all values of $Y$.

## 7.11 THE PEARSON *r* AND MARGINAL DISTRIBUTIONS

The maximum value of $r$ is 1.0.* However, $r$ can equal 1.0 only when the marginal distributions of $X$ and $Y$ have precisely the same shape. (The "marginal distribution" of $X$ is simply the frequency distribution of the $X$'s; the marginal distribution of $Y$ is the frequency distribution of the $Y$'s.) If $X$ is normally distributed and $Y$ is skewed negatively, the maximum value of $r$ is less than 1. How much less? The less similar the shapes, the lower the maximum value for $r$ (Carroll, 1961). With a little practice one can visualize the shape of the marginal frequency distributions from data in the scatterplot. Is it apparent that both $X$ and $Y$ appear to be normally distributed in Figures 7.1, 7.2, and 7.3? Is it evident that $X$ is skewed positively in Figures 7.4 and 7.5? There are too few cases in Figure 7.6 to give a good representation of the shapes of the marginal distributions,

*To prove that the value of $r$ cannot exceed +1, expand $\Sigma_1^n(z_X - z_Y)^2$, which is always greater than or equal to zero, and use the fact that

$$\sum z_X^2 = \sum z_Y^2 = n - 1 \qquad \text{and} \qquad r_{XY} = \frac{\Sigma z_X z_Y}{(n-1)}$$

To show that $r_{XY}$ cannot be less than −1, work with $\Sigma(z_X + z_Y)^2$.

unless there were extreme departures from normality. When scores on one or both variables are subjected to nonlinear transformation to make the two distributions more similar in shape, small increases in the value of $r$ would be anticipated.

## 7.12 EFFECTS OF VARIABILITY ON CORRELATION

A major, and often ignored, influence on $r$ is the variance in the sample. Other things being equal, *the greater the variability among the observations, the greater the value of r*. For example, in a school having students with relatively homogeneous socioeconomic status (SES) backgrounds, the correlation between SES and achievement (or between SES and any other variable) will be much less than in a school that is more heterogeneous in SES.

Figure 7.9 illustrates the common phenomenon of range restriction and its consequences on correlation coefficients. There is only a moderate correlation remaining between the two variables within the selected group (shaded area), yet a substantial correlation exists for the entire group (the ellipse). Much misinterpretation of correlation has resulted from the lack of understanding of this concept. The correlation between achievement and IQ will be far less for gifted students than for a representative group of students. A correlation between test performance and job performance of .64 for a total group ($n$ = 1,031) of aspiring pilots dropped to a correlation of only .18 for those ($n$ = 136) who eventually qualified (Thorndike, 1949)—that is, $r_I$ was .64, whereas $r_1$ was only .18.

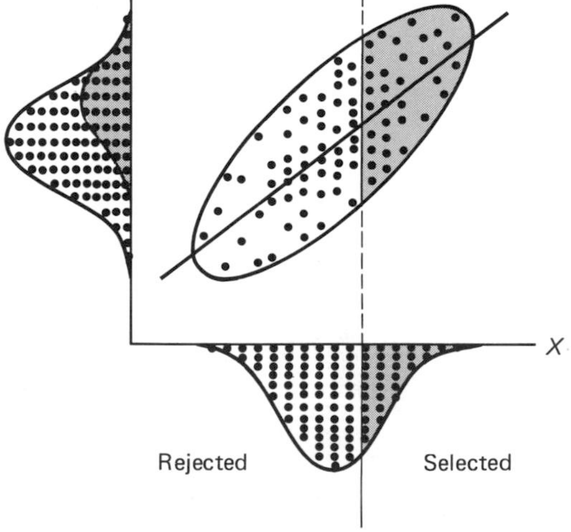


**FIGURE 7.9**
**An illustration of the effect of restricted variability on the correlation between $X$ and $Y$. The correlation coefficient *within* the selected and more homogeneous group ($\rho_1$) underestimates the magnitude of the relationship for the unrestricted range ($\rho_I$).**

## Correcting for Restricted Variability

If one knows the correlation for the restricted group ($\rho_1$) and the standard deviation of $X$ for the restricted($\sigma_1$) and unrestricted group ($\sigma_I$), the correlation for the unrestricted group ($\rho_I$) can be obtained from Equation 7.7. The principal importance of Equation 7.7 is *not* for the apparent purpose of estimating $\rho_I$—its value is basically in illuminating the substantial consequence of restricted (or exaggerated) variability on the value of the observed correlation coefficient.

$$\rho_I^2 = \frac{\rho_1^2(\sigma_I/\sigma_1)^2}{1 + \rho_1^2(\sigma_I/\sigma_1)^2 - \rho_1^2} \tag{7.7}$$

Suppose all applicants for college $A$ with a College Board SAT Verbal Score of below 600 were rejected, and all those with scores of 600 or higher were accepted. For the selected applicants, the correlation between SAT and GPA was .5. Estimate the correlation $\hat{\rho}_I$ if all applicants were admitted.* The standard deviation in the selected group is 50, half the value of 100 for the unrestricted group. Therefore,

$$\hat{\rho}_I^2 = \frac{(.5)^2(100/50)^2}{1 + (.5)^2(2)^2 - (.5)^2} = \frac{(.25)(2)^2}{1 + (.25)(4) - .25} = \frac{1.00}{1.75} = .5714$$

$$\hat{\rho}_I = \sqrt{.5714} = .7559 \quad \text{or} \quad .76$$

The validity of Equation 7.7 rests on the assumptions of bivariate normality (Sec. 7.10). The assumptions appear to be met in Figure 7.9. In many instances, however, these assumptions are suspect. For example, in the illustration with SAT scores, the linearity assumption is probably untenable as many professors are reluctant to give low marks. In other instances where linearity is known from previous research Equation 7.7 has been shown to be quite accurate.

Equation 7.7 should be used only for large samples where the $s$ and $r$ are very accurate estimates of $\sigma$ and $\rho$, respectively, and where the conditions of linearity and homoscedasticity are met. [See Gullickson and Hopkins (1976) for more detailed information on the accuracy of Eq. 7.7.]

## 7.13 THE VARIANCE OF A SUM†

The variance of a sum of two or more scores is needed frequently in statistics. The standard deviation on each of the Verbal ($X$) and Quantitative ($Y$) sections of the Graduate Record Examination (GRE) is approximately 100. If a combined $X + Y$ score is obtained

*When a "hat" appears above a symbol for a parameter, the "^" denotes that the value is not the parameter but an *estimate* of the parameter; thus $r = \hat{\rho}$, $s = \hat{\sigma}$, $\bar{X} = \hat{\mu}$, etc.

†Sections 7.13 and 7.14 are a belated completion of Chapter 5; since the concept of correlation is used, the delay was necessary. Note that in Section 7.13 two observations are summed for each of the $n$ subjects, whereas in Section 5.12 additional subjects are being added to a distribution.

for each examinee, what is its variance (or standard deviation)? The variance of a sum of two scores is the following (see Glass and Stanley, 1970, pp. 127-129, for proof):

$$s_{X+Y}^2 = s_X^2 + s_Y^2 + 2r_{XY}s_Xs_Y \tag{7.8}$$

where $s_X^2$ is the variance of variable $X$, $s_Y^2$ is the variance of variable $Y$, and $r_{XY}$ is the correlation between variables $X$ and $Y$. From Equation 7.2 it can be seen that the expression $r_{XY}s_Xs_Y$ equals the covariance between variables $X$ and $Y$. Notice that if the two variables are independent (i.e., $r_{XY} = 0$), the variance of the sum equals the sum of the variances:

$$s_{X+Y}^2 = s_X^2 + s_Y^2 \tag{7.9}$$

The variance of the composite variable, $X + Y$, given that $r = .543$ is as follows:

$$\begin{aligned} s_{X+Y}^2 &= (100)^2 + (100)^2 + 2(.543)(100)(100) \\ &= 30{,}860 \\ s_{X+Y} &= 175.67 \text{ or } 176. \end{aligned}$$

Suppose that both of Lola's GRE scores are 600. She is one standard deviation above each mean ($P_{84}$) of each test. But is her composite score, $X + Y$, also precisely one standard deviation above the mean? Because the mean of the composite scores, $X + Y$, is 1,000 (Sec. 4.11), and the standard deviation is 176, Lola's composite score of 1,200 is $\frac{200}{176} = 1.14$ standard deviations above the mean composite score. Although she is at the 84th percentile on each of the two tests, Table A shows she is at the 87th percentile for the composite.

If a variable is formed from the sum of three scores, its variance can be found from Equation 7.10; the logic underlying Equation 7.8 is extended to three addends in Equation 7.10.

$$s_{W+X+Y}^2 = s_W^2 + s_X^2 + s_Y^2 + 2r_{WX}s_Ws_X + 2r_{WY}s_Ws_Y + 2r_{XY}s_Xs_Y \tag{7.10}$$

Notice that if the variables are uncorrelated, the variance of the sum is the sum of the variances, just as in Equation 7.9. The logic on which Equation 7.10 is based is easily extended to any number of variables.

Equations 7.8 to 7.10 yield the parameter for the variance of the composite if $s$ and $r$ are replaced by the corresponding parameters $\sigma$ and $\rho$.

## 7.14 THE VARIANCE OF DIFFERENCE SCORES

In later chapters use is made of the difference between two scores $X$ and $Y$ (i.e., $X - Y$) and the variance of the distribution of difference scores, $s_{X-Y}^2$, which can be determined from Equation 7.11:

$$s_{X-Y}^2 = s_X^2 + s_Y^2 - 2r_{XY}s_Xs_Y \tag{7.11}$$

As expected, the equation shows that the larger the value of $r_{XY}$, the smaller the variance of the difference scores.

The variance of the difference between GRE $V$ and $Q$ scores, given that, $s_V = s_Q = 100$, and $r_{VQ} = .543$ is

$$s_{V-Q}^2 = (100)^2 + (100)^2 - 2(.543)(100)(100)$$
$$= 9{,}140$$

and the standard deviation of the difference, $s_{V-Q}$, is 95.6.

Is it rare for one's $V$ and $Q$ scores to differ by as much as 100 points? Since $z = (100 - 0)/95.6 = 1.05$, from Table A we find that almost 30% of the examinees have a difference of 100 points or more; half with $V$ being the higher score, and half with $Q$ being higher.

# 7.15
# ADDITIONAL MEASURES OF RELATIONSHIP:
## The Spearman Rank Correlation

In the sections to follow, situations will be considered in which one or both of the variables are in the form of ranks or dichotomies.

### Spearman Rank Correlation, $r_{ranks}$.

Raw data may be converted to ranks, or ranks may be gathered as the original data. "Rank in graduating class" is an example of the conversion of scores to ranks: grade-point averages are computed for each of 500 students; a rank of 1 is assigned the highest GPA, 2 to the next highest, . . . , 500 to the lowest. "Judges' rankings of excellence of a recitation" is an example of gathering ranks as original data: ten students recite a passage, and a judge assigns the rank 1 to the best recitation, 2 to the second best recitation, . . . , and 10 to the worst. Data are often gathered in this form when more refined measurements are not convenient, needed, or possible. Regardless of how the ranks $1, 2, \ldots, n-1, n$ are generated, two sets of ranks for the same $n$ persons can be correlated in the same way.

The Spearman rank correlation* $r_{ranks}$ is only a shortcut version of product-moment formulas 7.2, 7.4, or 7.6, that is, tailor-made to fit situations in which both variables are expressed as ranks.†

The Spearman rank correlation between highway speed limits and traffic fatalities is computed in Table 7.4. Note that $r$ could not be computed unless West Germany was excluded or a numerical value such as 90 or 100 mph was supplied as the speed limit—both options are undesirable. These difficulties can be avoided by using rank correlation. In addition, the outlier (namely, the extremely high fatality figure for Turkey) will have much less influence on $r_{ranks}$ than on $r$ (it is 4.2 standard deviations above the mean).

*Attributed to the British psychologist Charles Spearman (1863–1945).

†Another measure of relationship between two sets of ranks is Kendall's tau (see Glass and Stanley, 1970, pp. 176–179). Due to its infrequent use, it is not discussed here.

**TABLE 7.4 Computation of the Spearman Rank Correlation Between Highway Speed Limits and Traffic Fatalities (per 100,000,000 mi Driven) in 1977**

| | | | *Ranks* | | *Difference in Ranks* | |
|---|---|---|---|---|---|---|
| *Country* | *Speed Limit* | *Fatalities* | *X* | *Y* | *D* | $D^2$ |
| West Germany | none | 7.9 | 1 | 8 | 7 | 49 |
| Italy | 87 mph | 6.4 | 2 | 9 | 7 | 49 |
| France | 81 | 8.0 | 3 | 7 | 4 | 16 |
| Hungary | 75[a] | 14.5 | 5[a] | 3 | 2 | 4 |
| Belgium | 75 | 10.5 | 5 | 6 | 1 | 1 |
| Portugal | 75 | 22.5 | 5 | 2 | 3 | 9 |
| Britain | 70 | 4.0 | 7 | 14 | 7 | 49 |
| Spain | 62 | 12.4 | 10 | 5 | 5 | 25 |
| Denmark | 62 | 4.8 | 10 | 11 | 1 | 1 |
| Netherlands | 62 | 6.0 | 10 | 10 | 0 | 0 |
| Greece | 62 | 12.9 | 10 | 4 | 6 | 36 |
| Japan | 62 | 4.7 | 10 | 12 | 2 | 4 |
| Norway | 56 | 4.2 | 13.5 | 13 | .5 | .25 |
| Turkey | 56 | 32.2 | 13.5 | 1 | 12.5 | 156.25 |
| United States | 55 | 3.3 | 15 | 15 | 0 | 0 |

$\Sigma D^2 = 399.5$

$$r_{ranks} = 1 - \frac{6 \Sigma D^2}{n(n^2 - 1)}$$

$$= 1 - \frac{6(399.5)}{15(225 - 1)}$$

$$= 1 - \frac{2{,}397}{3{,}360}$$

$$= 1 - .7134$$

$$= .2866 \text{ or } .29$$

[a]When ties occur on $X$ or $Y$, assign the average of the ranks involved to each score, e.g., $(4 + 5 + 6)/3 = 5$ for $X = 75$.

When $X$ and $Y$ are ranks and there are no ties, both distributions have the same mean and the same variance, the values of which are governed solely by $n$, the number of pairs. The formula for $r$ thus can be simplified to Equation 7.12,*

$$r_{\text{ranks}} = 1 - \frac{6 \sum_{i=1}^{n} D_i^2}{n(n^2 - 1)} \tag{7.12}$$

*See Glass and Stanley (1970, pp. 173–175) for derivation.

where $n$ is the number of pairs and $D_i$ is the difference between the two ranks for the $i$th case. Thus $r_{\text{ranks}}$ is a special case of $r$ (Eqs. 7.2 and 7.4); $r$ will yield identical values of $r_{\text{ranks}}$ when $X$ and $Y$ are ranks (when there are no tied ranks).* When tied ranks occur, Equation 7.12 is not equivalent to the $r$ between the ranks. Even though the mean of the numbers 1, 2, . . . , $n$ does not change when ties in the ranks occur [it is still $(n + 1)/2$], the variance of the ranks is less than for the rectangular distribution assumed in Equation 7.12. Consequently, the variance simplifications in the formula for $r$ that led to Equation 7.12 are not exact. Fortunately, even when there are ties, $r$ and $r_{\text{ranks}}$ will differ trivially. For example, although there are many ties on $X$ in Table 7.4, the value of $r$ between the two sets of ranks is .27, whereas $r_{\text{ranks}}$ is .29.†

## 7.16 THE PHI COEFFICIENT: BOTH *X* AND *Y* ARE DICHOTOMIES

When both $X$ and $Y$ are dichotomous variables, the data can be thought of as arranged in two columns of 0's and 1's where each row corresponds to one person's two "scores." For example, ten students in academic trouble in their sophomore year of college might be observed on the variables "marital status" and "dropped out of college" (see Table 7.5). Arbitrarily, 1 means married and 0 means not married on variable $X$, and 1 denoted "dropped out" and 0 remaining in school on variable $Y$. One measure of the relationship between $X$ and $Y$ is simply $r$, the Pearson product-moment coefficient. The Pearson product-moment coefficient calculated on dichotomous data is called the *phi coefficient* and is denoted by $r_\phi$ (or $\phi$)‡. The value of $r_\phi$ for the data in Table 7.5 is .408, but this was not found with the usual computation formula for $r$. That formula can be replaced with a still simpler but algebraically identical formula when the data on $X$ and $Y$ are dichotomous.

Let $p_x$ be the proportion of people scoring 1 on $X$; $q_x$, the proportion scoring 0 on $X$, will be equal to $1 - p_x$. The proportion scoring 1 on $Y$ is denoted by $p_y$, and $q_y = 1 - p_y$. One more definition is necessary: $p_{xy}$ is the proportion of people scoring 1 on *both* $X$ and $Y$. If one were to operate on the formula for $r$ with these new definitions,

*There are three possible ways to proceed in the calculation of $r_{\text{ranks}}$ when tied ranks occur: (1) use the computational formula for $r$ (Eq. 7.2) on the data—this will always give $r_{\text{ranks}}$ whether any ranks are tied or not; (2) compute an approximation via Equation 7.12; (3) use a formula (see Kendall, 1955) that incorporates corrections of $s_X^2$ and $s_Y^2$ for the ties in the ranks. With the current availability of calculators and computers, when extreme precision is needed we suggest method (1)—that you compute the $r$ between the ranks using Equation 7.2 or 7.4, assigning ranks to tied measurements by the averaging method described.

†When it can be assumed that the underlying variable expressed in ranks is normally distributed, ranks are sometimes transformed to normalized $T$-scores. If both $X$ and $Y$ are ranks and both have underlying normal distributions, the $r$ between their normalized scores will tend to be slightly greater than $r_{\text{ranks}}$. On the other hand, if both underlying variables were distributed rectangularly, $r$ would be slightly less than $r_{\text{ranks}}$. To normalize ranks (or scores), the percentile ($p_i$) associated with each of the $n$ ranks ($R_i$) is determined using the equation: $p_i = 1 - (R_i - .5)/n$. Using Table A, each percentile, ($p_i$) is transformed to a $z$-score, which is converted to a $T$-score using Equation 6.5 (see Sec. 6.6).

‡Although $\phi$ is frequently used to denote the correlation coefficient, we will use $r_\phi$ to be consistent with the use of Greek letters to represent parameters.

**TABLE 7.5 Illustration of the Calculation of the Phi Coefficient $r_\phi$**

| *Student No.* | *X* *Marital Status* *(Married = 1; Not Married = 0)* | *Y* *Attrition* *(Dropped Out = 1; Remained = 0)* | *Calculations* |
|---|---|---|---|
| 1 | 0 | 0 | $p_x = \frac{4}{10} = .4 \quad q_x = \frac{6}{10} = .6$ |
| 2 | 1 | 1 | |
| 3 | 0 | 1 | |
| 4 | 0 | 0 | $p_y = \frac{5}{10} = .5 \quad q_y = .5$ |
| 5 | 1 | 1 | |
| 6 | 1 | 0 | |
| 7 | 0 | 0 | $p_{xy} = \frac{3}{10} = .3$ |
| 8 | 1 | 1 | |
| 9 | 0 | 0 | |
| 10 | 0 | 1 | $r_\phi = \frac{p_{xy} - p_x p_y}{\sqrt{p_x q_x p_y q_y}}$ |
| | $\Sigma X = 4$ | $\Sigma Y = 5$ | |
| | | | $r_\phi = \frac{.3 - (.4)(.5)}{\sqrt{(.4)(.6)(.5)(.5)}} = .408$ |

it would simplify algebraically to the following convenient form:

$$r_\phi = \frac{p_{xy} - p_x p_y}{\sqrt{p_x q_x p_y q_y}} \tag{7.13}$$

Equation 7.13 is a convenient way to compute the phi coefficient. The following derivation shows that $r_\phi$ is the Pearson product-moment correlation between two variables, each of which is scored 0, 1.

If both the numerator and the denominator of Equation 7.4 are divided by $n$, the expression for $r$ becomes

$$r = \frac{(1/n)\,\Sigma X_i Y_i - \overline{X}\,\overline{Y}}{\sqrt{[(1/n)\,\Sigma X^2 - \overline{X}^2]\;[(1/n)\,\Sigma Y^2 - \overline{Y}^2]}} \tag{7.14}$$

If $X$ and $Y$ are measured dichotomously, $\overline{X}$ and $\overline{Y}$ are simply the proportions of 1's on each variable. Thus $\overline{X}$ and $\overline{Y}$ can be replaced with $p_x$ and $p_y$, respectively. Now $X_i Y_i$ will be different from zero only when the $i$th person "scores" 1 on both variables, in which case $X_i Y_i = 1 \cdot 1 = 1$. Surely, then, $\Sigma X_i Y_i$ is simply a count of the number of persons scoring 1 on both $X$ and $Y$; hence $(1/n)\,\Sigma XY = p_{xy}$. Since $X$ is 0 or 1 and because $0^2 = 0$ and $1^2 = 1$.

$$\frac{\Sigma X^2}{n} = \frac{(0^2 + 1^2 + \ldots + 0^2 + 0^2)}{n} = p_x$$

Therefore, substituting such expressions into Equation 7.14 produces

$$r = r_\phi = \frac{p_{xy} - p_x p_y}{\sqrt{(p_x - p_x^2)(p_y - p_y^2)}} = \frac{p_{xy} - p_x p_y}{\sqrt{p_x(1 - p_x)p_y(1 - p_y)}} = \frac{p_{xy} - p_x p_y}{\sqrt{p_x q_x p_y q_y}} \quad \textbf{(7.15)}$$

When one has no particular interest in the proportions $p_x$ and $p_y$ and finds it more convenient to tabulate dichotomous bivariate data in a *contingency table* (a table showing the joint occurrences of pairs of scores on two variables in a group), $r_\phi$ can be calculated with a convenient raw score formula.

Students in an introductory statistics class were asked whether they regularly ate breakfast. The results, broken down separately for males and females, are given in Table 7.6. Is there a relationship between gender and breakfast eating?

Suppose that in each cell of a contingency table like Table 7.6 a letter is substituted for the actual frequencies so that we can deal with the computation of $r_\phi$ more generally. The number of persons scoring 0 on $X$ and 1 on $Y$ is denoted by $a$. The total number of persons scoring 0 on $X$ is $a + c$. The total number of persons represented in the table is $n$.

It can be shown by substituting such equivalences as $p_x = (b + d)/n$, $p_y = (a + b)/n$, and $p_{xy} = b/n$ into Equation 7.15 that the phi coefficient for the data arranged in a contingency table like Table 7.6 is

$$r_\phi = \frac{bc - ad}{\sqrt{(a + c)(b + d)(a + b)(c + d)}} \quad \textbf{(7.16)}$$

To illustrate the calculation of $r_\phi$ by Equation 7.16, the data in Table 7.6 will be used.

$$r_\phi = \frac{(6)(9) - (8)(4)}{\sqrt{(17)(10)(14)(13)}} = \frac{22}{\sqrt{30{,}940}} = \frac{22}{175.9} = .125$$

The positive value of $r_\phi$ indicates that persons with 1's on $X$ are more likely to have 1's on $Y$; thus males had a slightly greater tendency to eat breakfast regularly.

**TABLE 7.6 Contingency Table Depicting the Relationship Between Sex and Breakfast for Twenty-seven Students in Introductory Statistics**

| | | $X$: Sex | | |
|---|---|---|---|---|
| | | Female (0) | Male (1) | Totals |
| $Y$: Breakfast? | Yes (1) | 8 = $a$ | 6 = $b$ | 14 = $a + b$ |
| | No (0) | 9 = $c$ | 4 = $d$ | 13 = $c + d$ |
| | Totals | 17 = $a + c$ | 10 = $b + d$ | 27 = $n$ |

Recall that $r$ can never attain the value of +1 or −1 unless the marginal distributions of $X$ and $Y$ are identical in shape (Sec. 7.11). Likewise $r_\phi$ can have a theoretical maximum absolute value of 1 only if $p_X = p_Y$.

## 7.17
## THE POINT-BISERIAL COEFFICIENT

When one dichotomous variable (e.g., sex, pass-or-fail) is correlated with a continuous measure, the formula for the product-moment correlation coefficient can be simplified. Pearson (1901) derived the formula and called it the *point-biseral correlation coefficient*—denoted by $r_{pb}$. (The term *biserial* refers to the fact that there are *two series* of persons being observed on $Y$: those who "scored" 0 and those who "scored" 1 on the dichotomous measure, $X$.) A simplified formula for $r_{pb}$ follows:

$$r_{pb} = \frac{\overline{Y}_1 - \overline{Y}_0}{s_Y} \sqrt{\frac{n_1 n_0}{n_\bullet(n_\bullet - 1)}} \tag{7.17}$$

where $\overline{Y}_1$ is the mean on $Y$ of those who scored 1 on $X$; $\overline{Y}_0$ is the mean on $Y$ of those who scored 0 on $X$; $s_Y$ is the standard deviation of all $n$ scores on $Y$; $n_1$ is the number of persons scoring 1 on $X$; $n_0$ is the number of persons scoring 0 on $X$; and $n_\bullet = n_1 + n_0$.

Equation 7.17 represents an algebraic simplification of the Pearson product-moment correlation coefficient formula when $X$ is a dichotomous variable. Notice that the initial portion of Equation 7.17 is simply the difference in means of the two groups, expressed in standard deviation units. The calculation of $r_{pb}$, describing the degree of relationship between sex and height for twenty-seven adults, is illustrated in Table 7.7.

Notice that the two means differ by 1.48 standard deviations, which is approximately twice the value of $r_{pb}$. Except when $n_0$ and $n_1$ are grossly unequal, $\overline{Y}_1$ and $\overline{Y}_0$ will differ by approximately $2r_{pb}$ standard deviations.

Of course $r_{pb}$ can never attain a value of 1 because the two marginal distributions can never be the same shape (unless $Y$ is also a dichotomy, in which case $r_\phi$ is the proper coefficient, not $r_{pb}$).

## 7.18
## THE BISERIAL CORRELATION

Suppose that a variable is measured dichotomously even though one might think that more extensive or refined techniques could produce a nearly normal distribution of scores.

**TABLE 7.7 Illustration of the Calculation of the Point-Biserial Correlation Coefficient**

Females: $n_0 = 17$, $\overline{Y}_0 = 64.35$ in.
Males: $n_1 = 10$, $\overline{Y}_1 = 69.90$ in.
$s_Y = 3.75$ in. $n_\bullet = 17 + 10 = 27$

$$r_{pb} = \frac{\overline{Y}_1 - \overline{Y}_0}{s_y}\sqrt{\frac{n_1 n_0}{n_\bullet(n_\bullet - 1)}} = \frac{69.90 - 64.35}{3.75}\sqrt{\frac{(10)(17)}{(27)(27-1)}} = (1.48)\sqrt{.2422} = .728$$

Such measurement is dichotomous with an underlying normal distribution. The dichotomy is not a true dichotomy, such as sex, but is an artifact of crude measurement. The next two coefficients to be studied are estimates of what the Pearson product-moment coefficients would be *if* the two crude categories were replaced by a refined measure that yields scores that are normally distributed.

The biserial correlation coefficient is an estimate of the product-moment correlation between $Y$ and the normally distributed scores on $X$ that are assumed to underlie the dichotomous (0 or 1) scores. For example, the $Y$ scores might be scores on the Scholastic Aptitude Test, and the $X$ scores might be 0's and 1's on a test item measuring cognitive flexibility. With more elaborate tests of cognitive flexibility, it might be possible to produce a wide range of cognitive flexibility scores ($X$ scores) that are nearly normally distributed. These two arrays of normally distributed scores on $X$ and $Y$ could be correlated and $r$ found. What do the $Y$ scores and the dichotomous scores on $X$ tell about the value of $r$? The answer to this question lies in the biserial correlation coefficient $r_{bis}$.

It is important to emphasize that $r_{bis}$ is a projected estimate of $r$; it does not describe the relationship between the *observed* $X$ and $Y$ values; that is the function of $r_{pb}$. Suppose one wishes to study the relationship between IQ scores and the amount of time students need to complete a test. But what if the allotted testing time has expired and twelve of the forty students have not finished? If one uses the data on the twenty-eight students who finished the test, the range of testing time (variable $X$) will be restricted and the resulting $r$ will underestimate the true relationship (see Sec. 7.12). Variable $X$ could be reduced to two categories, "completed" and "did not complete" the test, and $r_{pb}$ could be computed but $r_{pb}$ would underestimate the degree of relationship since the individual differences among persons within the two categories are ignored. The best alternative is to obtain an "extrapolated" estimate of $r$–to compute $r_{bis}$. The computation of $r_{bis}$ using Equation 7.18 is illustrated in Table 7.8,

$$r_{bis} = \frac{\overline{Y}_1 - \overline{Y}_0}{s_Y}\left(\frac{n_1 n_0}{u n_{\bullet}^2}\right) \tag{7.18}$$

where $u$ is the ordinate of the unit normal distribution at $p$, (found using Table A), and $p$ is the proportion of cases in group 1 (i.e., $p = n_1/n_{\bullet}$); other symbols were defined previously in Equation 7.17.

A word or two about the range of possible values for $r_{bis}$ is in order. Unlike almost any other commonly used correlation coefficient, $r_{bis}$ can sometimes take on values below $-1$ and above $+1$. The only significance of these extreme values of $r_{bis}$ is that they reflect either (1) incorrectness of the assumption that the $Y$-scores are normally dis-

**TABLE 7.8 Illustration of the Calculation of the Biserial Correlation Coefficient**

Did not finish: $n_0 = 12$, $\overline{Y}_0 = 105.1$
Finished: $n_1 = 28$, $\overline{Y}_1 = 113.3$
$s_Y = 16.0$, $n_{\bullet} = 40$

$u = .3477$ (To find $u$ from Table A, enter $p = n_0/n_{\bullet}$ in the column "Proportion of Area Below $z$," and read $u$ in the adjacent column.)

$$r_{bis} = \frac{\overline{Y}_1 - \overline{Y}_0}{s_Y}\left(\frac{n_1 n_0}{u n_{\bullet}^2}\right) = \frac{113.3 - 105.1}{16.0}\left(\frac{(28)(12)}{(.3477)(40)^2}\right) = (.5125)(.6040) = .310$$

tributed, or (2) sampling error (when $n$ is small) that produces a markedly platykurtic distribution of $Y$'s in the sample. The unpleasant fact remains that for $n$'s of 15 and smaller, values of $r_{bis}$ exceeding 1.00 are occasionally obtained. When $n$ is small, $r_{bis}$ is a very crude estimate of $r$; indeed it is probably best not to use $r_{bis}$ when $n$ is small, especially when $p$ differs considerably from .5.

Another caution pertaining to $r_{bis}$ results from the fact that if the variable underlying $X$ is not normally distributed, or the relationship is not linear, $r_{bis}$ and $r$ can differ by as much as .2 (Nunnally, 1978, p. 137). For these reasons $r_{bis}$ should not be viewed as an adequate substitute for $r$ but only as a crude approximation, unless (1) the underlying assumptions are known to be met and (2) $n$ is large (at least 100).

## 7.19 BISERIAL VERSUS POINT-BISERIAL CORRELATION COEFFICIENTS

For any set of data, $r_{pb}$ can be transformed to $r_{bis}$ by Equation 7.19:

$$r_{bis} = r_{pb} \sqrt{\frac{n_1 n_0 (n_{\bullet} - 1)}{u^2 n_{\bullet}^3}} \qquad \textbf{(7.19)}$$

In comparing the values of $r_{bis}$ with $r_{pb}$, it is useful to know that the minimum value of the factor under the radical in Equation 7.19 is approximately 1.25 (i.e., when $n_1 = n_0$ and $n_{\bullet}$ is large). Consequently, $r_{bis} > 1.25 r_{pb}$. As the proportion ($p$) of the observations in the larger (or smaller) group deviates from .5, $r_{bis}$ will be more than 25% larger than $r_{pb}$; for $p = .6$, .7, .8, .9, and .95, then $r_{bis}/r_{pb}$ increases to 1.27, 1.32, 1.43, 1.71, and 2.11, respectively.

## 7.20 THE TETRACHORIC COEFFICIENT

When *both* $X$ and $Y$ are artificial dichotomies with underlying normal distributions, the tetrachoric correlation coefficient $r_{tet}$ provides a projected estimate of $r$. Before computers, the computation of $r_{tet}$ was commonly used to circumvent the huge computational burden required when many $r$'s were needed. If twenty-five variables are being studied and the $r$ between each pair is desired, 300 $r$'s would have to be correlated! Its use declined dramatically as computers became accessible. Nevertheless, situations arise in which $r$ cannot be computed directly, but an estimate is desired of what $r$ would be if variables $X$ and $Y$ are characterized by bivariate normality. For example, suppose two yes-no questions on an attitude survey were

$X$: Do you favor the legalization of marijuana?

$Y$: Do you approve of the legalization of abortion?

It is reasonable to assume there are gradations in attitudes on both $X$ and $Y$. If more refined scales were developed for detecting the shades of gray in both attitudes, what would

**TABLE 7.9 Illustration of the Calculation of the Tetrachoric Correlation Coefficient**

| | | Question $X$ No | Question $X$ Yes | Totals | Proportions |
|---|---|---|---|---|---|
| Question $Y$ | Yes | 90 ($a$) | 110 ($b$) | 200 | .50 ($p_y$) |
| | No | 190 ($c$) | 10 ($d$) | 200 | .50 ($q_y$) |
| | Totals | 280 | 120 | 400 ($n_\bullet$) | |
| | Proportions | .70 ($q_x$) | .30 ($p_x$) | | |

$u_x = .3477$
$u_y = .3989$
[To find $u_x$ (and $u_y$) from Table A, enter $p_x$ (and $p_y$) in the "Proportion . . . " column and read $u_x$ (and $u_y$) in the adjacent column.]

$$r_{tet} = \frac{bc - ad}{u_x u_y n_\bullet^2} = \frac{(110)(190) - (90)(10)}{(.3477)(.3989)(400)^2}$$

$$r_{tet} = .901$$

be the value of $r$? Using the data from the fourfold $2 \times 2$ table, Equation 7.20 for $r_{tet}$ can be used to estimate $r$.

$$r_{tet} = \frac{bc - ad}{u_x u_y n_\bullet^2} \tag{7.20}$$

where $a$, $b$, $c$, and $d$ are cell frequencies as defined in Table 7.6 and $u_x$ and $u_y$ are ordinates of the unit normal distribution at $p_x$ and $p_y$, where $p_x$ and $p_y$ are the proportions responding "1" (e.g., Yes = 1) on measures $X$ and $Y$, respectively, and $n_\bullet$ is the total number of cases. The computation of $r_{tet}$ is illustrated in Table 7.9.

The interpretation of $r_{tet}$ is similar to $r_{bis}$ in that it is an estimate of what the observed $r$ would be if both variables would yield normal distributions that would be linearly related if measured more accurately. Even when these conditions are met, $n$ must be quite large (200 or more) before $r_{tet}$ estimates of $r$ are reasonably accurate.

How do $r_{tet}$ and $r_\phi$ compare for the data in Table 7.9? From Equation 7.16, $r_\phi$ is found to be .546–much less than the $r_{tet}$ of .901. The observed relationship between the two dichotomies is described by $r_\phi$, whereas $r_{tet}$ gives an estimate of the relationship when the measures of $X$ and $Y$ are characterized by bivariate normality.

## 7.21 THE RANK-BISERIAL CORRELATION COEFFICIENT

One coefficient for correlating a dichotomous variable $X$ and an ordinal variable $Y$ has been studied by Cureton (1956) and Glass (1966b). This coefficient will be denoted by $r_{rb}$, the rank-biserial $r$.

**TABLE 7.10 Illustration of the Calculation of the Rank-Biserial Coefficient**

| *Ranks on Y for* | | |
|---|---|---|
| $X = 1$ | $X = 0$ | *Calculations* |
| 10 | 8 | $r_{rb} = \frac{2}{n_\bullet}(\overline{Y}_1 - \overline{Y}_0)$ |
| 9 | 6 | |
| 7 | 5 | |
| 2 | 4 | $r_{rb} = \frac{2}{10}(7.00 - 4.50) = \frac{2.50}{5} = .50$ |
| $\Sigma Y_1 = 28$ | 3 | |
| $(n_1 = 4)$ | 1 | |
| $\overline{Y}_1 = \frac{28}{4} = 7.00$ | $\Sigma Y_0 = 27$ | |
| | $(n_0 = 6)$ | |
| | $\overline{Y}_0 = \frac{27}{6} = 4.50$ | |

Let $X$ be a dichotomous variable and $Y$ a variable comprising the $n$ untied ranks $1, 2, \ldots, n_\bullet$. The $r_{rb}$ coefficient is descriptive of the relationship between $X$ and $Y$. Glass (1966b) derived the simplest formula for $r_{rb}$:

$$r_{rb} = \frac{2}{n_\bullet}(\overline{Y}_1 - \overline{Y}_0) \quad \textbf{(7.21)}$$

where $\overline{Y}_1$ is the average rank of those scoring 1 on $X$ and $\overline{Y}_0$ is the average rank of those scoring 0 on $X$. The calculation of $r_{rb}$ by Equation 7.21 is illustrated in Table 7.10.

## 7.22 CAUSATION AND CORRELATION

Figure 7.10 shows the extremely high relationship ($r = .95$) between the number of storks observed and the population of Oldenburg, Germany, for each of seven years.* Have we been misled all these years?

The presence of a correlation between two variables does not necessarily mean there exists a causal link between them.† Even though concomitance (correlation) between events can be useful in identifying causal relationships when coupled with other methodological approaches, it is a dangerous and potentially misleading test for causation when used alone. First, even when one can presume that a causal relationship does exist between the two variables being correlated, $r_{XY}$ can tell nothing by itself about whether $X$ causes $Y$ or $Y$ causes $X$. Second, often variables other than the two under consideration could be responsible for the observed association. Third, the relationships that exist among variables in behavioral and social sciences are almost always too complex to be explained in terms of a single cause. Juvenile delinquency, to take one of many possible

*These data, along with the primary sources, can be found in Box, Hunter, and Hunter (1978).

†For an excellent modern treatment of the concept of causation in the social sciences, see Cook and Campbell (1979).

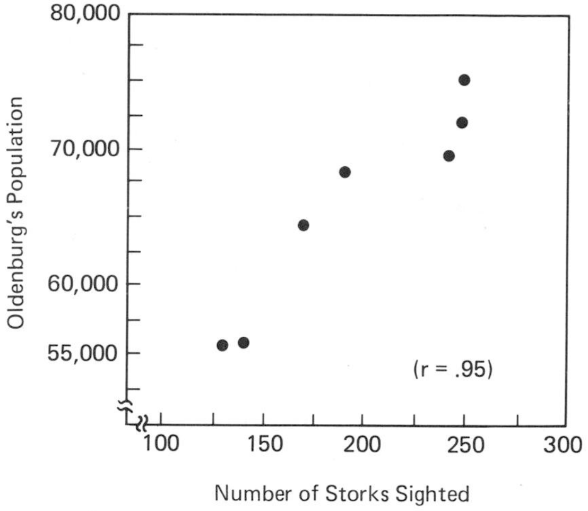


**FIGURE 7.10**
**Scatterplot of the population of Oldenburg, Germany, at the end of each year with the number of storks observed in that year (1930-1936).**

examples, is the result of numerous influences, in addition to being a complex concept itself that cannot be described adequately by any single measurement.

Some examples of the problems that arise in attempts to unearth causal relationships with correlational techniques will help illustrate these points. For example, it is probably true that in the United States there is a positive correlation between the average salary of teachers in high schools and the percentage of the schools' graduates who enter college. Does this imply that well-paid teaching staffs *cause* better trained high school graduates? Would the percentage of high-school graduates entering college rise if the pay of teachers were increased? Certainly affirmative answers to these questions are not justified by the association alone. The relationship between the two factors is not simple, but one prominent variable not yet mentioned is the financial and economic condition of the community that largely determines its ability to pay *both* teachers' salaries and college tuitions. Moreover, the economic and financial condition of the community is in part dependent upon the intellectual powers of its citizens, another variable that contributes to both higher teachers' salaries and greater college attendance among the young people.

It has been found that the percentage of dropouts in each of a number of high schools is negatively correlated with the number of books per pupil in the libraries of those schools. But common sense tells us that piling more books into the library will no more affect the dropout rate than hiring a better truant officer will bring about a magical increase in the holdings of the school library. If only common sense always served us so well!

Some researchers do not stop with one fallacious conclusion—that is, that correlation is prima facie evidence for causation—but draw a second one as well. They assume a certain direction for the causal relationship. This is only natural, since our minds are often made up as to the nature of a causal relationship between two phenomena before they gather data and compute $r_{XY}$. Let's investigate a plausible example more closely. Numerous studies have reported correlation coefficients of -.2 or so between test anxiety ($X$) and performance on intelligence tests ($Y$). Does this imply that high anxiety has caused the pupils to perform poorly on the test and that low-anxiety pupils, not being handicapped by fear, were able to perform up to a fuller measure of their ability? This conclusion has successfully tempted some researchers. Why is it not equally plausible that intelligence differences cause anxiety? Might not dull pupils become anxious when their intelligence is tested, while bright students find the experience pleasant and not anxiety producing? What is involved here is the question of whether $X$ can be said to cause $Y$ or $Y$ to cause $X$. A simple correlation coefficient between $X$ and $Y$ cannot lend evidence in support of either claim. Suffice to say here that studies of association alone, without experimental substantiation, are often difficult to interpret causatively. Experimental approaches to this same problem that involve making one group of pupils anxious and comparing their scores on the intelligence test with those of a control group have not found a cause-and-effect relationship (Allison, 1970; French, 1962; Chambers, Hopkins, and Hopkins, 1972).

Failure to recognize that correlation may not mean causation is a widespread logical error. Going to Sunday school is generally believed to be valuable in many ways, but a positive relationship between the rate of Sunday school attendance and honesty, for example, does not *necessarily* imply that children are honest *because* they attend Sunday school. Underlying and causing both attendance and honesty may be, for example, training in the home. A crucial but ethically unacceptable test of the hypothesis that Sunday school makes children more honest would involve prohibiting a comparable group of children from attending Sunday school to see if an increase in dishonesty resulted.

## Zero Correlation and Causation

Just as a positive correlation cannot be said to represent causation, so *a zero correlation does not necessarily demonstrate the absence of a causal relationship*. For example, some studies with college students have found no correlation between hours of study for an examination and test performance. Does this mean that the amount of study by a student had no effect on his test score? Of course not. Some bright students study little and still achieve average scores, whereas some of their less gifted classmates study diligently but still achieve an average performance. A controlled experimental study would almost certainly show some causal relationship.

## Negative Correlation and Causation

*Even a negative correlation does not rule out the possibility of a positive, direct causative relationship*. For example, suppose 1,000 high-school seniors were rated on two proficiencies: ability to play the piano and ability to play basketball. It is possible that, in general, those who excel at the piano have little time to practice basketball and vice versa. A negative correlation might be observed between the two proficiencies even though the refined finger coordination developed by playing the piano might improve basketball proficiency. In other words, an experimental study might find that piano playing improves basketball proficiency even though a correlational study might reveal a negative relationship.

From the preceding discussion it should be clear that one must be very careful not to infer causation from correlation coefficients. Likewise, one cannot conclude that there is no causative relationship between $X$ and $Y$ on the basis of zero or negative correlation coefficients. Nonzero correlation coefficients *do* indicate that $Y$ can be *predicted* better if $X$ is known than if unknown. (Or, equivalently, knowlege of $Y$ improves the predictability of $X$). Prediction does not necessarily require any information or assumptions about causation.

## CHAPTER SUMMARY

The need for an objective and precise measure to describe the degree of relationship between two variables is obvious. The Pearson product-moment correlation $r$ (or $\rho$ for parameter) is the most common measure of the degree of relationship between two variables. The degree of relationship can vary from −1.0, through 0, to +1.0. The magnitude of the relationship is indicated by the absolute value of the correlation coefficient. The sign (+ or −) of a coefficient only indicates the *direction* of the relationship. A coefficient of 0.0 indicates no *correlation* between two variables.

A positive correlation indicates that "high numbers on $X$ are associated with high numbers on $Y$" and that "low numbers on $Y$ are associated with low numbers on $X$."

The correlation coefficients, $r$ and $r_{\text{ranks}}$, accurately describe the degree of association between $X$ and $Y$ when $X$ and $Y$ are linearly related; the true association is underestimated if a curvilinear relationship exists between $X$ and $Y$. Scatterplots allow visual checks of linearity.

The correlation between two variables is unaffected by linear transformations of one or both variables. A linear transformation does not alter the shape of a distribution, the percentile rank of any observation, the number of standard deviations any observation deviates from the mean ($z$-score), or the correlation coefficients with any other variable.

The value of the correlation coefficient is greatly influenced by the heterogeneity of the sample—the less the variability, the lower the value of $r$ and vice versa.

The general formula for the Pearson product-moment $r$ is applicable when either or both $X$ and $Y$ are ranks or dichotomous, but the resulting coefficients are denoted by special names. The product-moment formula can also be simplified for hand computation purposes. When both $X$ and $Y$ are expressed as ranks, the Spearman rank correlation is obtained. When one variable is a dichotomy, the correlation is termed a point-biserial coefficient; if both variables are dichotomies, the correlation is a phi coefficient. When a dichotomous variable is not a true dichotomy, but can be assumed to have an underlying normal distribution and a linear relationship with the other variable, extrapolated estimates of $r$ are provided by the biserial coefficient. If both variables are viewed as artificial dichotomies, the tetrachoric coefficient estimates the $r$ that would be obtained if both variables were measured precisely.

The rank biserial coefficient describes the correlation between a dichotomous variable and a variable expressed in ranks. Correlation must be carefully distinguished from causation. There can be correlation without causation and vice versa.

## *MASTERY TEST*

1. Which of these correlation coefficients indicates the strongest relationship?
   a. .55 b. .09 c. −.77 d. .1

2. With which of the coefficients given as options to Question 1 do the $X$-observations below $\overline{X}$ tend to be associated with $Y$-observations above $\overline{Y}$?
3. Suppose a measure of political conservatism is administered to representative samples of persons of ages 15, 20, 30, 45, and 60 and that the respective means were 60, 85, 80, 70, and 65. The correlation between age and political conservation is
   a. 1.0 c. linear
   b. -1.0 d. curvilinear.

In Questions 4 to 8 select the scatter diagram that best matches the relationships described.

| *Value of r* | *Description of linear relationship* | *Scatter diagram* |
|---|---|---|
| 4. +1.00 | Perfect direct relationship | a. 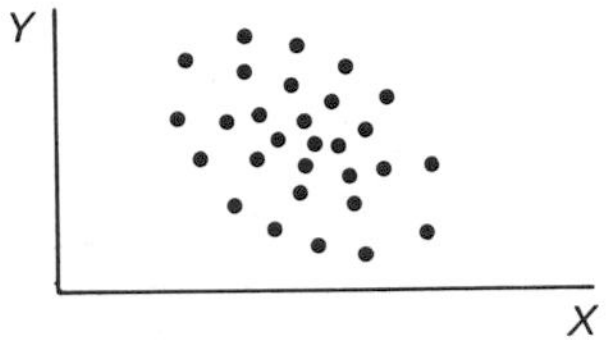 |
| 5. About +.50 | Moderate direct relationship | b.  |
| 6. .00 | No relationship (i.e., 0 covariation of $X$ with $Y$) | c.  |
| 7. About -.50 | Moderate inverse relationship | d. 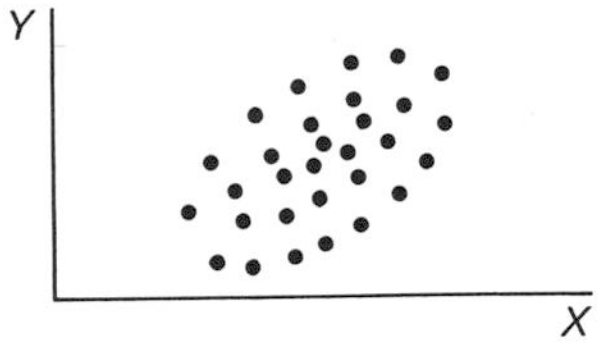 |
| 8. -1.00 | Perfect inverse relationship | e. 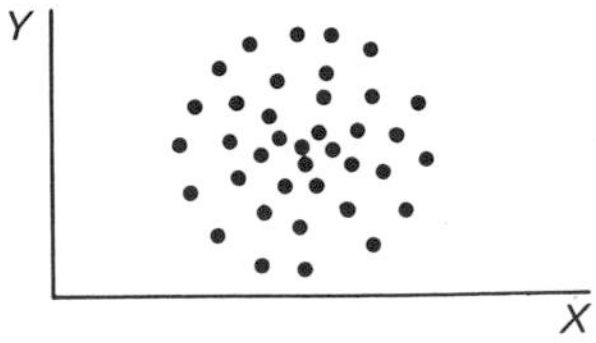 |

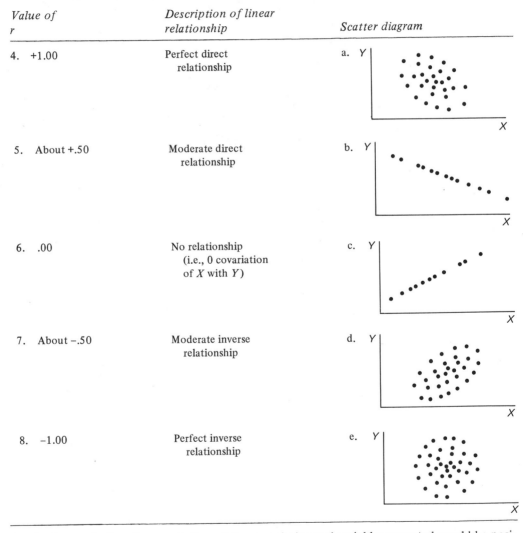

9. Indicate whether the correlation of the two designated variables expected would be positive, negative, or zero. (Assume the population for the following items a to g is all persons in grade 10 in the United States.)
   a. $X$, height in inches; $Y$, weight in pounds

b. $X$, age in months; $Y$, time in seconds required to run fifty yards
c. $X$, reading achievement in grade-placement units; $Y$, arithmetic achievement in grade-placement units.
d. $X$, shoe size; $Y$, "citizenship" rating of student on a 10-point scale by his teacher
e. $X$, arithmetic achievement in $T$-score units; $Y$, number of days absent from school during the year
f. $X$, Social Security numbers; $Y$, IQ's (ignore persons without Social Security numbers)
g. $X$, interest in sports; $Y$, interest in politics
h. $X$, total miles traveled by a car; $Y$, year in which the car was manufactured
i. $X$, maximum daily temperature; $Y$, amount of water used by residents

10. If $r_{XY} = -.8$ in part h of Question 9, what would the value of $r_{XY}$ be if $Y$ were changed from "year in which the car was manufactured" to "age of vehicle?"
11. The correlation of $X$ with $Y$ is .60; the correlation of $X$ with $W$ is $-.80$. Is $X$ more closely linearly related to $Y$ or to $W$?
12. If the correlation between $X$ and $Y$ is .5, what will the value of $r$ be if the $X$-values are linearly transformed to $T$-scores and then correlated with $Y$?
13. If $r = 1$ and $z_X = -.5$, what is $z_Y$?
14. If $r = -1$ and $z_Y = .8$, what is $z_X$?
15. The IQ's using Test $A$ are consistently 10 points higher than the IQ's using Test $B$. What is the largest possible value for $r$?
16. Brown calculated the covariance of height in ($X$) in feet (e.g., 67in. becomes 5.58 ft) and running speed in seconds ($Y$). He obtained a covariance of 2.30 on a sample of fifty students. From the same original data that Brown collected, Smith calculated the covariance of height in inches ($X$) and running speed in minutes ($Y$) (e.g., 60 sec becomes 1.15 min). Smith obtained a value of .46. Compare the correlations between $X$ and $Y$ obtained by Brown and Smith.
17. For a particular set of data, $s_X = 15$ and $s_Y = 3$. What is the largest that $s_{XY}$ could possibly be? (*Hint:* $r$ cannot be larger than +1; $r = s_{XY}/s_X s_Y$.)
18. Suppose by observation alone you estimated the heights ($X$) and weights ($Y$) of each of your classmates and that you calculated the correlation coefficient ($r_1$) between these observations. How would this coefficient $r_1$ compare with the coefficient $r_2$ using data from a scale and tape measure to determine $X$ and $Y$? Why?
19. One study on heart attacks reported that persons who attend church regularly had a lower risk of heart attacks than nonchurchgoers. Assuming the information is valid, which one of the following statements is correct?
    a. If you start attending church more regularly, your chances of a heart attack are certain to be reduced.
    b. There is definitely no causal relationship between the two variables.
    c. If you are a regular churchgoer, you are less likely to have a heart attack than if you are a nonchurchgoer.
    d. The correlation provides definitive information pertaining to causation.
20. In which college would you expect the correlation between IQ and grade-point average to be greatest?

| | *College* | | |
|---|---|---|---|
| | *A* | *B* | *C* |
| Mean IQ | 108 | 112 | 120 |
| s | 10 | 12 | 8 |

21. Which college in Question 20 would you expect to have the lowest value for $r$?
22. One study reported the correlation between IQ and creativity as being quite low ($r = .2$). The standard deviation of the IQ scores of the sample was approximately 5. What would be the effect on $r$ if the sample did not have restricted variability in IQ?

Identify the type of correlation coefficient appropriate for measuring the relationship between $X$ and $Y$.

| | |
|---|---|
| 23. $X$: handedness (R or L); $Y$: IQ | a. $r$ |
| 24. $X$: sex; $Y$: pass (1) or fail (0) | b. $r_{pb}$ |
| 25. $X$: height (in inches); $Y$: weight (in pounds). | c. $r_{bis}$ |
| 26. $X$: height (ranks); $Y$: weight (ranks) | d. $r_{\phi}$ |
| 27. $X$: sex; $Y$: rank in class (1 to $n$) | e. $r_{rb}$ |
| 28. $X$: IQ; $Y$: GPA (above or below 2.5) | f. $r_{tet}$ |
| 29. $X$: IQ (above or below 100); $Y$: GPA (above or below 2.5) | g. $r_{ranks}$ |

## *PROBLEMS AND EXERCISES*

1. a. Compute the Pearson correlation coefficient $r$ between the following ten pairs of arithmetic and IQ scores:

| *Pupil* | *IQ* | *Arithmetic* | *Pupil* | *IQ* | *Arithmetic* |
|---|---|---|---|---|---|
| A | 105 | 15 | F | 96 | 10 |
| B | 120 | 23 | G | 107 | 4 |
| C | 83 | 11 | H | 117 | 30 |
| D | 137 | 22 | I | 108 | 18 |
| E | 114 | 17 | J | 130 | 14 |

   b. Plot a scatter diagram for the ranks in Problem 1. (Scale the plot so that the horizontal and vertical spans for $X$ and $Y$ are approximately equal.) Does the relationship appear to be curvilinear? Does the value of $r$ seem reasonable?

   c. On the IQ variable, how do the mean and standard deviation of the sample in Problem 1 compare with corresponding national parameters ($\mu = 100, \sigma = 15$)?

2. One study reported the importance of eight morale factors for employees and employers as indicated:

| | *Rank* | |
|---|---|---|
| *Factor* | Employers | Employees |
| A. Credit for work done | 1 | 7 |
| B. Interesting work | 2 | 3 |
| C. Fair pay | 3 | 1 |
| D. Understanding and appreciation | 4 | 5 |
| E. Counseling on personal problems | 5 | 8 |
| F. Promotion based on merit | 6 | 4 |
| G. Good working conditions | 7 | 6 |
| H. Job security | 8 | 2 |

a. Compute $r_{\text{ranks}}$.
b. Compute Pearson $r$ using the ranks for the $X$- and $Y$-values.
c. Which two factors contributed most to the negative correlation?

3. The data given in the table below show the relationship between verbal and nonverbal IQ's from the Lorge-Thorndike Intelligence Test (LT) and reading and arithmetic achievement as measured by the Iowa Test of Basic Skills (ITBS). At each grade level, each correlation is based on approximately 2,500 nationally representative pupils.

| | *Verbal IQ* | | | *Nonverbal IQ* | | |
|---|---|---|---|---|---|---|
| | Grade | | | Grade | | |
| | 3 | 5 | 7 | 3 | 5 | 7 |
| Reading | .68 | .76 | .81 | .53 | .65 | .67 |
| Arithmetic | .66 | .72 | .74 | .61 | .68 | .71 |

On the basis of this information, are the following statements true or false?

a. The correlation between the intelligence and achievement measures appears to increase with grade level.
b. The nonverbal IQ's correlate as highly with achievement as verbal IQ's.
c. Verbal and nonverbal IQ's tend to correlate slightly higher with reading than with arithmetic.
d. The correlation between both measures of achievement and both measures of intelligence is substantial at each of the three grade levels.

4. A researcher demonstrated a correlation of $-.52$ between average teacher's salary ($X$) and the proportion of students who drop out of school before graduating ($Y$) across 120 high schools in her state. She concluded that increasing teacher's salaries would reduce the dropout rate. Comment on her conclusion.

5. A researcher correlated the MTAI scores of a group of 100 experienced secondary school teachers with the number of students each teacher failed in a year. He obtained an $r$ of $-.39$. He concluded that teachers tend to fail students because they do not have "accepting" attitudes toward students. Comment on the researcher's methods and conclusions.

6. a. When heights of girls (or boys) at ages three and twenty are expressed as $T$-scores, the covariance is approximately 70. What is the correlation coefficient between height at the two ages?
b. What is the covariance if the two variables are expressed as $z$-scores?
c. If it were learned that at age three height was expressed in inches, but at age eighteen it was expressed in centimeters, would the value of $r$ be affected?
d. If it were learned that shoes were removed before taking measurement at age three but not at age twenty, would the inconsistency have a consequential effect on $r$?
e. If the subjects were measured with and without shoes on both occasions, which correlation would be slightly larger?

7. In Question 22 of the Mastery Test, assume the statistics are parameters, assume a linear and homoscedastic relationship between IQ and creativity, and estimate the correlation in the population ($\rho_I$) using $\sigma_I = 15$ and Equation 7.7.

8. A correlation ($\rho_I$) is .8 in the unrestricted population in which the standard deviation equals 10. Use Equation 7.7 to estimate the correlation ($\rho_1$) in a group in which the standard deviation is 5.

9. Examine the scatterplot at the beginning of the Problems and Exercises section in Chapter 8. The scatterplot shows the relationship between IQ scores at grades five and seven for 354 students on the California Test of Mental Maturity.
   a. Does the relationship appear to be linear?
   b. Does the scatterplot appear to have the property of homoscedasticity?
   c. Does the reported $r$ of .83 appear to be reasonable in view of the degree of "scatter" in the scatterplot?

10. Measures of spelling ability and spatial ability were given to 10,000 representative high-school seniors, half of which were girls (Bennett, Seashore, and Wesman, 1974). The means and standard deviations for each sex were

| | *Spelling* | | *Spatial* | |
|---|---|---|---|---|
| | Mean | $s$ | Mean | $s$ |
| Boys (1) | 71.8 | 17.3 | 34.3 | 13.0 |
| Girls (0) | 80.2 | 14.5 | 30.9 | 11.9 |

The standard deviation for the distribution combining boys and girls into one distribution was found to be 16.5 and 12.6 for spelling ability and spatial ability, respectively. Compare the two point-biserial correlation coefficients (Eq. 7.17) to determine which ability is more highly related to sex.

11. One study found that of the twenty-seven beginning first-grade children scoring below 40 on the Metropolitan Readiness Test, only one received a letter grade of B or better in reading at the end of first grade (Hopkins and Stanley, 1981, p. 100). For the 125 pupils scoring 40 or better, sixty-eight received a grade of B or better. Assuming there is a normal distribution underlying each of these variables and that they are linearly related (Sec. 7.20), estimate the value of $r$ had refined, continuous measures been obtained for both variables.

12. Themes written by ten pupils were judged to be either "creative" ($X = 1$) or "not creative" ($X = 0$). A ranking of the same students on intelligence $Y$ was available (10 = highest, 1 = lowest). Calculate the rank-biserial correlation coefficient from these data:

| *Student* | $X$ | $Y$ |
|---|---|---|
| A | 1 | 9 |
| B | 1 | 5 |
| C | 1 | 10 |
| D | 0 | 4 |
| E | 0 | 8 |
| F | 0 | 1 |
| G | 1 | 2 |
| H | 1 | 6 |
| I | 0 | 7 |
| J | 0 | 3 |

## *ANSWERS TO MASTERY TEST*

1. c
2. c
3. d
4. c

5. d
6. e
7. a
8. b
9. a. positive
   b. zero
   c. positive
   d. zero
   e. negative
   f. zero
   g. zero
   h. negative
   i. positive
10. .8
11. *W*
12. .5
13. $z_Y = -.5$
14. $z_X = -.8$
15. 1.0
16. Since the relative standings (ranks and corresponding standard scores) of the *X*'s and *Y*'s are unaffected, *r* is unaffected by the metric employed. In other words, "feet" to "inches" and "seconds" to "minutes" are both examples of linear transformations which do not affect the correlation between the two variables.
17. Maximum covariance is $s_X s_Y = (3)(15) = 45$.
18. $r_2$ would be higher since it would contain less measurement error.
19. c
20. College *B*, because *s* is greatest
21. College *C*
22. The *r* would increase considerably.
23. b
24. d
25. a
26. g
27. e
28. c
29. f

## *ANSWERS TO PROBLEMS AND EXERCISES*

1. a. $r = .517$
   b. No; yes
   c. $\overline{X} = 111.7$ (considerably above $\mu = 100$); $s = 15.7$ (very similar to $\sigma = 15$)
2. a. $r_{\text{ranks}} = -.095$
   b. $r = -.095$
   c. *A* and *H*
3. a. true
   b. false
   c. false (with verbal IQ, true; with nonverbal IQ, false)
   d. true
4. The researcher is inferring a causal relationship solely from correlational evidence. She has no justification for doing so. If may well be the case—and probably is—that teachers' salaries and the dropout rate are *both* functions of the social and economic status of the community and that increasing teachers' salaries in a given school would not bring about a decrease in the dropout rate.
5. The researcher mistakenly assumed correlation equals causation.
6. a. $.7 = [70/(10 \times 10)]$
   b. .7
   c. no
   d. no, since roughly a constant was added to height at age 20.
   e. without shoes, because heel thickness would introduce a small amount of uncontrolled and irrelevant variation (measurement error)
7. $\hat{\rho}_I^2 = .273$, $\hat{\rho}_I = .52$
8. $\hat{\rho}_1 = .55$
9. a. yes
   b. yes
   c. yes
10. Spelling: $r_{pb} = -.25$; Spatial: $r_{pb} = .13$
11. $r_{tet} = .71$
12. $r_{rb} = .36$

# 8

# LINEAR AND MULTIPLE REGRESSION

How are observations on one variable used to predict those on another variable? What is the margin of error in these predictions? Regression (prediction) and correlation are variations of the same theme.

## 8.1 PURPOSES OF REGRESSION ANALYSIS

One major use of statistical methods is to forecast or predict future events. Insurance companies sometimes set premiums on the basis of statistical predictions. The cost of automobile insurance for minors is greater than that for adults because age often correlates with—that is, predicts—accident frequencies. Colleges usually admit and reject applicants primarily on the basis of predictions about their probable future scholastic performance made from scholastic aptitude tests and academic performance in high school. Delinquency and dropout prevention programs frequently use early indicators (predictors) in identifying persons who appear likely to become delinquents or dropouts. In vocational counseling and personnel selection, implicit or explicit predictions of various job-related criteria are made from variables such as age, interests, aptitudes, sex, and experience. These examples involve prediction. The degree of reliance on statistical considerations in making these predictions varies greatly from one application to another. Insurance companies rely heavily on statistical (actuarial) predictions, whereas the selection of employees is rarely made on purely statistical considerations.

By using statistical methods, the accuracy of predictions of a *dependent variable* (a criterion or outcome variable) from one or more *independent* (*predictor*) *variables* can be maximized. In statistical parlance, the dependent variable $Y$ is said to be a function of the independent variable $X$. No causal association is assumed. Indeed, causation is beside the point in forecasting. The higher the correlation, the better the prediction; the lower the correlation, the greater the margin of error in the predictions. Initially the simplest type of prediction—predicting the dependent variable $Y$ from one independent variable $X$ when both $X$ and $Y$ represent variables that are normally distributed and linearly related—will be treated.

The underlying concepts and rationale of simple regression extend to more complex applications such as multiple regression in which there are two or more independent variables.

## 8.2 THE REGRESSION EFFECT

*Unless $r = 1.0$ or $-1.0$, all predictions of $Y$ from $X$ involve a regression toward the mean.* Francis Galton (1822-1911) first documented this *regression effect* in studying the relationship between the characteristics of parents and their children. The heights of 192 father-son combinations arc tallied in Figure 8.1. In addition to the *bivariate* distribution (i.e., the scatterplot), frequency distributions of $X$ (father's height) and $Y$ (son's height) are given in Figure 8.1 at the top and to the right, respectively. The tallying method used in these two marginal distributions is that of Tukey (1977) (Sec. 3.4). Notice that $\bar{X}$ and $s_X$ appear to be approximately equal to $\bar{Y}$ and $s_Y$, respectively, and that both variables appear to be normally distributed (when allowance is made for sampling error).

If all sons had exactly the same height as their fathers, all tallies in Figure 8.1 would fall in the shaded "boxes" and $r$ would be 1.0. Study Figure 8.1 and observe, as Galton did, that the sons of tall fathers tend to be taller than average, but not as tall as their fathers; that is, the sons *regressed* toward the mean. Similarly, there is a trend for the sons of short fathers to be taller than their fathers, but shorter than average—they also *regressed* toward the mean.*

The mean height of the sons of fathers of a given height are plotted within each column of Figure 8.1. The sons' (column) means have been connected by a broken line. For example, for fathers who were 63 in. tall, the mean height of the sons was 66.5 in.; fathers who were 73 in. tall had sons whose mean height was 72 in.

Notice that the more the fathers' height ($X$) deviates from its mean ($\bar{X}$), the greater the *difference* in the sons' mean height (i.e., the dashed line) and that of their fathers (the straight line drawn through the shaded area). This is always true whenever the absolute value of $r$ is less than 1.0; the more $X$ deviates from $\bar{X}$, the greater will be the amount of regression. Note that in Figure 8.1 the distributions of $X$ and $Y$ have means

*Apparently, Galton did not initially recognize the ubiquity of this phenomenon and termed it "the law of filial regression." Actually, there is a regression effect when any two variables are not perfectly correlated.

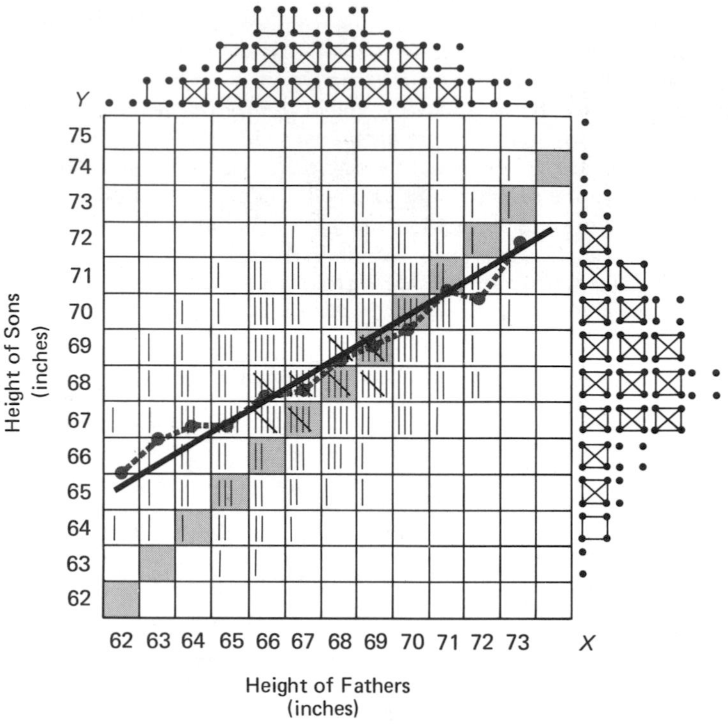


**FIGURE 8.1**
**An illustration of the regression effect. (Data from McNemar, 1962.) Univariate distributions of *X* and *Y* are given at the top and to the right.**

and standard deviations that are essentially equal; the distributions of $X$ and $Y$ are equally heterogeneous even with the regression effect. The sons were not more homogeneous in height than were their fathers, yet as a general rule the percentile ranks of sons, given a certain percentile rank for fathers, tend to be closer to 50 than that of the fathers.

## 8.3 THE REGRESSION EQUATION EXPRESSED IN STANDARD Z-SCORES

The most illuminating way of statistically expressing the regression phenomenon (or, equivalently, the prediction of $Y$ from $X$) occurs when $X$ and $Y$ are expressed as $z$-scores. Equation 8.1 is the simplest form of the regression equation—it shows that the predicted $z$-score of the dependent variable $\hat{z}_{Y_i}$ (the "hat" above $\hat{z}_{Y_i}$ denotes "predicted value of" $z_{Y_i}$), is the product of the $z$-score on $X$ and the correlation coefficient between $X$ and $Y$:

$$\hat{z}_{Y_i} = r z_{X_i} \tag{8.1}$$

In other words, if $r = .60$ and $z_{X_i} = 1.0$, then $\hat{z}_{Y_i} = .6$; or if $r = .60$ and $z_X = -2.0$, then $\hat{z}_Y = -1.2$. Notice, *except when the correlation is perfect, the absolute value of* $\hat{z}_Y$ *is always less than* $z_X$; that is, the $\hat{z}_Y$-value *regresses* toward the mean. But how much less is $\hat{z}_Y$ than $z_X$? If Equation 8.1 is rearranged, it is apparent that $r$ is the ratio of $\hat{z}_Y$ to $z_X$

(i.e., $r = \hat{z}_Y / z_X$) and $r$ can be seen as the "rate of change" in $\hat{z}_Y$ per unit of change in $z_X$. The correlation coefficient between $X$ and $Y$ in Figure 8.1 is approximately .5. Hence, from Equation 8.1, it is evident that, on the average, sons tend to be only half (.5) as many standard deviations from their mean as their fathers are from their mean. For example, for fathers who are two standard deviations below the mean ($z_X = -2.0$), the sons' average is only one standard deviation below the mean ($\hat{z}_Y = -1.0$); thus fathers who were at the 98th percentile had sons who were at the 84th percentile, on the average (see Fig. 8.1).

Since $r = \hat{z}_Y / z_X$, one can see the sense in which the correlation coefficient can be directly interpreted as a proportion or a percentage. If $r = .8$ and if $X$ and $Y$ are expressed as standard $z$-scores, for any given score on the independent variable the expected $z$-score on the dependent variable ($\hat{z}_Y$) is only .8 (or 80%) as far from its mean as $z_X$ is from its mean. For example, if $r = .8$ and $z_X = 1.0$, then $\hat{z}_Y = .8$, which is 80% as far from the mean of the dependent variable as $z_X$ is from the mean of the independent variable. In other words, $(1 - r) \times 100\%$ gives the percentage of regression involved in the predictions.

## 8.4 USE OF REGRESSION EQUATIONS

It may seem peculiar to talk about predicting $Y$ from $X$, because, as in the example, one must have both $X$ and $Y$ to compute the $r$ which is required in (the regression) Equation 8.1. Obviously, if one has the examination scores (the $Y$'s, as in Table 8.1), Equation 8.1 would not be used to predict them. These particular scores are known, and it would make no sense to predict them. However, not only does the correlation coefficient between $X$ and $Y$ describe the degree of association between $X$ and $Y$, but this correlation will also facilitate the prediction of examination scores ($Y$'s) for other GRE-*Q* scores ($X$'s) that were not represented in the data in Table 8.1. The purpose of a regression equation is to make predictions on a new sample of observations from the findings on a previous sample of observations.

For intuitive and conceptual purposes, regression and prediction have been discussed in terms of $z$-scores. The underlying concepts are best understood without the distractions resulting from unequal means and unequal variances of $X$ and $Y$. In actual practical application, however, it is more convenient to use regression equations that predict raw scores, $\hat{Y}$'s (not $\hat{z}_Y$'s), from observations on $X$ (not $z_X$). But before proceeding further with the discussion of this topic, some geometry should be reviewed.

## 8.5 CARTESIAN* COORDINATES

A *Cartesian* coordinate system is depicted in Figure 8.2. The axes of the coordinate system—the perpendicular $X$ and $Y$ lines—divide the plane. This coordinate system is a means of marking off the plane so that every point can be identified by a pair of numbers, $(X, Y)$. The point (0, 0) is called the *origin* of the system and lies at the point

*Named after the French philosopher-mathematician René Descartes.

**TABLE 8.1 Determination of the Regression Equation for Predicting Final Examination Scores in Statistics from GRE-*Q* Scores ($n = 20$)**

| *GRE-Q* $X$ | *Examination* $Y$ | *Computation* |
|---|---|---|
| 620 | 65 | $\hat{Y}_i = bX_i + c$ |
| 600 | 73 | |
| 590 | 85 | $b = r\,\frac{s_Y}{s_X} = \frac{(.6076)(11.245)}{(91.39)} = .0748$ |
| 590 | 80 | |
| 580 | 64 | |
| 560 | 69 | $c = \overline{Y} - b\overline{X} = 68.15 - (.0748)(495)$ |
| 550 | 78 | |
| 540 | 70 | Hence, $\hat{Y}_i = .0748X_i + 31.12$ |
| 530 | 79 | |
| 530 | 70 | |
| 500 | 77 | |
| 480 | 69 | |
| 480 | 64 | |
| 460 | 76 | |
| 440 | 59 | |
| 430 | 44 | |
| 390 | 75 | |
| 380 | 69 | |
| 370 | 54 | |
| 280 | 43 | |
| $\overline{X} = 495.00$ | $\overline{Y} = 68.15$ | |
| $s_X = 91.39$ | $s_Y = 11.245$ | |
| | $r = .6076 = .608$ | |

where the two axes intersect. The first number of any pair is the distance one must travel *horizontally* from the origin (the $X$ distance) to reach the point, and the second number is the distance the point lies *vertically* from the origin. The point $A$ in Figure 8.2 corresponds to the pair of numbers (0, 1). The first number is called the *X-coordinate;* the second number is called the *Y-coordinate.* The point $B$ corresponds to the pair of numbers (2, 2); it lies two units to the right of the origin along the $X$ axis and two units above the origin along the $Y$ axis.

Eventually, a method of predicting a set of scores will be detailed that uses a straight line in a plane to describe the set of predicted scores. It will be useful to know the manner in which any straight line in a plane can be completely described by a simple equation.

In Figure 8.2 the straight line $L$ crosses the $Y$ axis at point $A$ (0, 1). For each unit on the $X$ axis that the moving point which describes the line moves to the right, it rises one-half unit on the $Y$ axis. The following points lie on line $L$: (0, 1), (1, 1.5), (2, 2), (3, 2.5), (4, 3) etc. The value of $Y$ in the description of the point $(X, Y)$ is systematically related to the value of $X$. For the line $L$ in Figure 8.2, the $Y$ value of any point on the line equals one-half the $X$ value plus 1, i.e., $Y = .5X + 1$. The equation $Y = .5X + 1$ is the equation for the straight line in Figure 8.2. The *Y intercept* of line $L$ is 1 because it

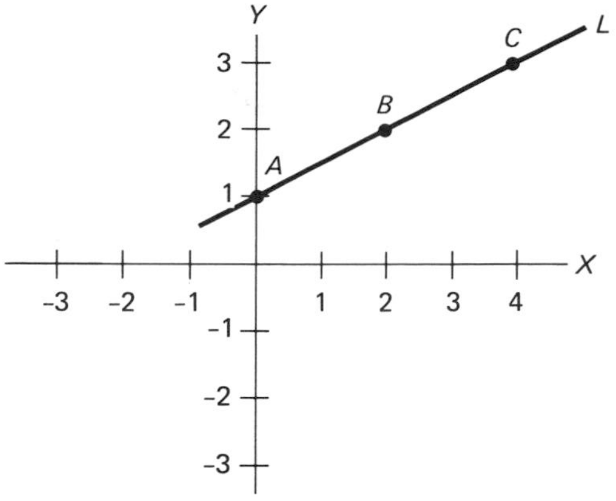


**FIGURE 8.2**
**Two-dimensional ($X$ and $Y$) Cartesian coordinate system.**

is the value of $Y$ where line $L$ intersects the $Y$ axis. The number .5 is the *slope* of the straight line $L$. The slope is the number of units the line rises for each unit of movement to the right on the $X$ axis, here 1 : 2.

The equation $Y = bX + c$ is called the *equation for a straight line.* It says simply that the pairs of points ($X$, $Y$) that lie on any straight line are related in such a way that for any $X$ value the $Y$ value paired with it can be found by multiplying $X$ by some number $b$, and adding a second number $c$ to this product. This is a linear transformation of $X$ to secure $Y$.

## 8.6 ESTIMATING $Y$ FROM $X$: THE RAW-SCORE REGRESSION EQUATION

Given an individual's score on variable $X$, what prediction can be made about his score on variable $Y$? For example, how accurately can test scores in statistics be predicted from the $Q$ (quantitative) portion of the GRE?

To derive the equation for predicting the score of a person on the dependent variable $Y$ from scores on the independent variable $X$, one must know the correlation between $X$ and $Y$. Data must be gathered on some number $n$ of students who have taken the GRE and who subsequently take the statistics course. Next an equation (called a *regression equation*) must be established that predicts the score on $Y$ for any $X$, using the least squares criterion (see Sec. 8.9). This equation then could be used with students whose scores on $X$ are known and whose scores on $Y$ one wants to estimate. Equation 8.2 is the regression equation in raw-score form. The predicted criterion score for individual $i$, $\hat{Y}_i$, is the product of the *regression coefficient* $b$,* and the raw score on $X_i$ plus a constant $c$, the *intercept.*

*We have consistently tried to use subscripts for variables only when ambiguity would otherwise result. Thus we use $s$ if only one variable is involved, but $s_X$ and $s_Y$ if we are dealing with two variables. Likewise, the "$XY$" subscript for $r_{YX}$ is unnecessary and $r$ suffices if only two variables are involved. Since we are predicting $Y$ (i.e., $\hat{Y}$) in Equation 8.2, it follows that the regression coefficient required is $b_{Y.X}$; hence the subscript "$Y.X$" is unnecessary.

$$\hat{Y}_i = bX_i + c \tag{8.2}$$

where

$$b_{Y.X} = b = r\left(\frac{s_Y}{s_X}\right) \tag{8.2A}$$

and

$$c = \overline{Y} - b\overline{X} \tag{8.2B}$$

Illustrative data for twenty students for whom GRE-$Q$ scores and subsequent scores on the comprehensive final examination in introductory statistics are given in Table 8.1 and graphed in Figure 8.3. Using Equation 8.2, the regression equation for the data in Table 8.1 is found to be, $\hat{Y}_i = .0748X_i + 31.12$. What examination score would be predicted for a student having a GRE-$Q$ score of 400? The predicted score on the examination, $\hat{Y}_i$, for student $i$ with $X_i = 400$ is

$$\hat{Y}_i = (.0748)(400) + 31.12 = 61.04$$

**FIGURE 8.3. Scatterplot and regression line for data in Table 8.1.**

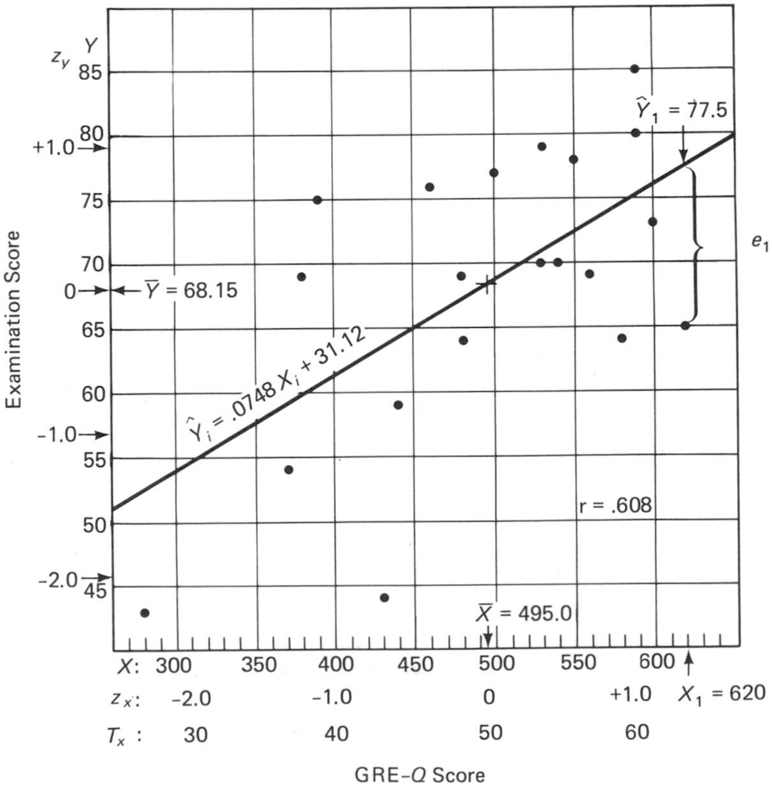

## 8.7
## ERROR OF ESTIMATE

Obviously $\hat{Y}_i$ will rarely equal $Y_i$ except when $r = 1.0$. Even with the "best" linear (straight regression line) prediction equation, the prediction is imperfect—there is some error in estimating $Y$ from $X$, that is, $\hat{Y}_i$ will rarely precisely equal $Y_i$. In other words, $\hat{Y}_i$ + residual$_i$ = $Y_i$ where residual$_i$ is the *error of estimate* for the $i$th person, or

$$\text{residual}_i = Y_i - \hat{Y}_i = Y_i - (bX_i + c) = e_i \tag{8.3}$$

The residual for the first student in the list in Table 8.1 is illustrated in Figure 8.3. The actual GRE-$Q$ score is $620 = X_1$, and the observed examination score is $65 = Y_1$. Using the regression equation, the predicted examination score is $\hat{Y}_1 = (.0748)(620) + 31.12 = 77.5$. Thus for the first student the residual or error of estimate is $e_1 = Y_1 - \hat{Y}_1 = 65 - 77.5 = -12.5$. The negative value for the residual indicates that the observed score was less than the predicted score—all scores below the regression line in Figure 8.3 will have negative residuals.

## 8.8
## PROPORTION OF PREDICTABLE VARIANCE, $r^2$

In Table 8.2 the observed scores ($Y_i$'s), the predicted scores ($\hat{Y}_i$'s), and residuals ($Y_i - \hat{Y}_i$'s) are given for the twenty students in Table 8.1 (and Figure 8.3). Table 8.2 is given only for the purpose of illustrating how $r^2$ can be interpreted as the proportion of variance in $Y$ that is predictable from $X$.

Notice that the means of the $Y$ and $\hat{Y}$ distributions are equal and that the mean of the residuals is 0.00; these are checks on our computational accuracy. Observe that the sum of squares in the $\hat{Y}$'s ($SS_{\hat{Y}}$) plus the sum of squares in the residuals ($SS$ residuals) equals the total sum of squares in the observed scores ($\Sigma y^2$ or $SS_Y$):

$$SS_Y = SS_{\hat{Y}} + SS_{\text{residuals}} \tag{8.4}$$

$SS_{\hat{Y}}$ is the sum of squares due to the regression, that is, in the predicted values of the dependent variable ($\hat{Y}_i$'s). $SS_{\text{residuals}} = SS_e$ is the sum of the squared residuals. The ratio of $SS_{\hat{Y}}$ to $SS_Y$ gives the proportion of the sum of squares that are predictable using the regression equation. This ratio is equal to $r^2$: $887/2403 = .369 = r^2$, or $r = .608$.

The pattern is the same for variances, that is,

$$s_Y^2 = s_{\hat{Y}}^2 + s_e^2 \tag{8.5}$$

or, in Table 8.2, $126.5 = 46.7 + 79.8$. The proportion of the total variance in $Y$ that is predictable from the regression equation is the ratio of $s_{\hat{Y}}^2$ to $s_Y^2$, which equals $r^2$:

$$r^2 = \frac{\text{Predictable variance}}{\text{Total variance}} = \frac{s_{\hat{Y}}^2}{s_Y^2} \tag{8.6}$$

Or, in our example, $r^2 = 46.7/126.5 = .369; r = .608$.

**TABLE 8.2 Observed Score ($Y_i$), Predicted Score ($\hat{Y}_i$), and Residual ($Y_i - \hat{Y}_i$) for the Twenty Students in Table 8.1**

| | $Y_i$ | | $\hat{Y}_i$ | | $e_i$ (*residual*) |
|---|---|---|---|---|---|
| | 65 | | 77.50 | | -12.50 |
| | 73 | | 76.00 | | -3.00 |
| | 85 | | 75.25 | | 9.75 |
| | 80 | | 75.25 | | 4.75 |
| | 64 | | 74.50 | | -10.50 |
| | 69 | | 73.01 | | -4.01 |
| | 78 | | 72.26 | | 5.74 |
| | 70 | | 71.51 | | -1.51 |
| | 79 | | 70.77 | | 8.23 |
| | 70 | | 70.77 | | -0.77 |
| | 77 | | 68.52 | | 8.48 |
| | 69 | | 67.03 | | 1.97 |
| | 64 | | 67.03 | | -3.03 |
| | 76 | | 65.53 | | 10.47 |
| | 59 | | 64.04 | | -5.04 |
| | 44 | | 63.29 | | -19.29 |
| | 75 | | 60.30 | | 14.70 |
| | 69 | | 59.55 | | 9.45 |
| | 54 | | 58.80 | | -4.80 |
| | 43 | | 52.08 | | -9.08 |
| Mean: | 68.15 | = | 68.15 | | 0.00 |
| Sum of Squares: | 2403 | = | 887 | + | 1516: $SS_Y = SS_{\hat{Y}} + SS_e$ |
| Variance: | 126.5 | = | 46.7 | + | 79.8: $s_Y^2 = s_{\hat{Y}}^2 + s_e^2$ |
| Standard Deviation: | 11.2 | | 6.83 | | 8.93 |

The proportion of variance in $Y$ that is unpredictable using the regression equation is $s_e^2/s_Y^2 = 79.8/126.5 = .631$. Obviously that proportion of the variance that is *not* unpredictable is predictable. Thus

$$r^2 = 1 - \frac{\text{Unpredictable variance}}{\text{Total variance}} = 1 - \frac{s_e^2}{s_Y^2} \tag{8.7}$$

## 8.9 LEAST-SQUARES CRITERION

What statistical criterion was used to arrive at the values for $b$ and $c$? The equations for $b$ and $c$ satisfy the *least-squares criterion.** The equations yield values such that the sum of the squared residuals is as small as possible—the sum of the *squared* residuals:

*See Glass and Stanley (1970, Appendix C) for mathematical proof.

$$\sum_{i=1}^{n} (Y_i - \hat{Y}_i)^2 = (Y_1 - \hat{Y}_1)^2 + (Y_2 - \hat{Y}_2)^2 + \cdots + (Y_n - \hat{Y}_n)^2 = e_1^2 + e_2^2 + \cdots + e_n^2$$

has the minimal value.

The use of the least-squares criterion is computationally convenient and is generally preferred on statistical inferential grounds. However, other criteria are possible (even though there has never been a serious contender for the criterion for fitting the regression line).

One criterion is that $b$ and $c$ could be chosen so that the sum of the *absolute* values of errors made in prediction is as small as possible, that is, so that $|e_1| + \cdots + |e_n|$ is minimized. This criterion leads to a "median regression line." (You will recall that the median of a group of scores is the point around which the sum of the absolute deviations of the scores from that point is minimal, whereas the mean is the "least-squares" measure of central tendency.) Although the median regression line is easily calculated, it does not have the inferential theoretical superstructure that the least-squares regression line has.*

No knowledge of the shapes of the frequency distributions of $X$ and $Y$ is needed to derive the least-squares regression coefficients $b$ and $c$. The values of $b$ and $c$ in Equation 8.2 produce the straight line that minimizes the sum of squared residuals, regardless of the nature of the scatter diagram of the $X$ and $Y$ scores.

Nothing has been said to this point about whether the dependent and independent variables are normally distributed or distributed in any other special way. But if some plausible assumptions are made about the distributions of large numbers of $X$ and $Y$ scores, one is likely to be rewarded by being able to perform a more penetrating prediction study. A study does gain much, in fact, if one assumes that $X$ and $Y$ have a *bivariate normal distribution.*

## 8.10 HOMOSCEDASTICITY AND THE STANDARD ERROR OF ESTIMATE

Property 3 of the bivariate normal distribution (Sec. 7.10) indicates that if there are nineteen persons with a score of 75 on $X$ and twenty-one persons with a score of 80 on $X$, the two variances of the two subsets of associated $Y$ scores should be about the same. This condition of equal variance of $Y$ scores for each value of $X$ is known as *homoscedasticity* (the roots of this word mean *equal spread*). The scatter diagram in Figure 8.4 should help in gaining an understanding of this condition.

It is important to note that *homoscedasticity* is a property of very large bodies of bivariate data. One should not expect equality of variances of $Y$ scores for any two values of $X$ when the $n$'s are small, say of the order of 100 or less. For $n$'s of 19 and 21 the variances of the $Y$ scores for $X_1 = 75$ and $X_2 = 80$ in Figure 8.4 are $s^2_{Y.X_1} = 5.54$ and $s^2_{Y.X_2} = 6.85$. These two variances are not equal, but they are reasonably close. With

*The use of the criterion of least squares for establishing a prediction line is over 150 years old. Karl Gauss (1777–1855), German mathematician, physicist, and astronomer, is generally credited with having developed the criterion of least squares. In one form or another it underlies a large portion of theoretical and applied statistical work.

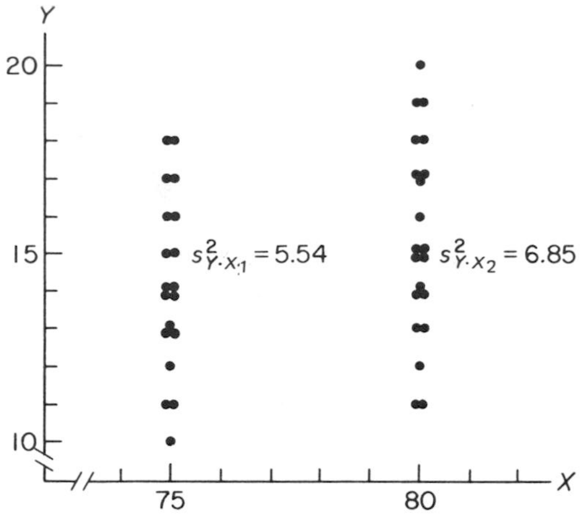


**FIGURE 8.4**
**Scatter diagram for 19 persons scoring 75 on *X* and 21 persons scoring 80 on *X* which exhibits nearly the same variance of *Y* scores for both values of *X*.**

such small numbers of persons one cannot ascertain very well whether the condition of homoscedasticity is satisfied, but at least it seems somewhat plausible for $X$ equals 75 and 80 after inspection of data of Figure 8.4.

Obviously the sizes of the errors made in estimating $Y$ from $X$ are an indication of the accuracy of estimation. For the data in hand, that is, the $n$ pairs of $X$ and $Y$ scores, the differences between the actual $Y$ scores and the predicted $Y$ scores are measures of the errors that would result if $X$ is used to estimate $Y$. These errors are called errors of estimate or residuals (see Eq. 8.3).

Would the mean of these $n$ errors of estimate, $\bar{e}$, be a suitable measure of how well $Y$ is predicted from $X$? No, because *the average error of estimate is always zero** when it is calculated on the same $n$ pairs of scores that produced $b$ and $c$. For this reason it is not a suitable measure of the accuracy of predicting $Y$ from $X$.

Remember that the sample mean had the property that $\Sigma\,(X_i - \overline{X}) = 0$. The principle of estimation that makes the least-squares regression line a minimum-variance estimator of $Y$ scores is the same principle that makes $\overline{X}$ a minimum-variance summary measure of central tendency. If a single score had to be used in place of, or to estimate, every score in a group, the sample mean $\overline{X}$ would do so with the smallest sum of squared errors of estimate.†

One of several possibilities for a measure of the accuracy of predicting $Y$ from $X$ is the variance of the $n$ errors of estimate, $e_i$. This quantity will be independent of the mean of the errors, which is always zero, and the number of such errors, because it in-

*Proof:

$$n\bar{e} = \sum_{i=1}^{n} e_i = \sum_i (Y_i - bX_i - c) = \sum_i Y_i - b\sum_i X_i - \sum_i c$$
$$= n\overline{Y} - nb\overline{X} - nc = n\overline{Y} - nb\overline{X} - n(\overline{Y} - b\overline{X}) = 0$$

(Recall from Eq. 8.2B that $c = \overline{Y} - b\overline{X}$.)

†Formally, $\Sigma_i\,[X_i - (\overline{X} + P)]^2 > \Sigma_i\,(X_i - \overline{X})^2$ when $P \neq 0$. Confirm this for yourself by squaring the left-hand member of the inequality, "distributing the summation sign," and simplifying algebraically. Hint: $X_i - (\overline{X} + P) = (X_i - \overline{X}) - P$.

volves division by $n - 1$. The variance of the $n$ scores $e_i = Y_i - \hat{Y}_i$ is called the *variance error of estimate* and is denoted by $s^2_{Y.X}$ (i.e., the variance in $Y$, holding $X$ constant).

$$s^2_{Y.X} = \frac{\sum_{i=1}^{n} (e_i - \bar{e})^2}{n - 1} = \frac{\sum_i e_i^2}{n - 1}. \tag{8.8}$$

There is a means of expressing $s^2_{Y.X}$ in terms of $s^2_Y$ and the correlation $r$ between $X$ and $Y$ that illuminates some of the relationships between correlation and prediction. One can write

$$s^2_{Y.X} = \frac{\sum_i e_i^2}{n - 1} = \frac{\sum_i (Y_i - bX_i - c)^2}{n - 1}\text{; and since } c = \bar{Y} - bX,$$

$$= \frac{\sum (Y_i - bX_i - \bar{Y} + b\bar{X})^2}{n - 1} = \frac{\sum [(Y_i - \bar{Y}) - b(X_i - \bar{X})]^2}{n - 1}$$

$$s^2_{Y.X} = \frac{\sum_i (Y_i - \bar{Y})^2}{n - 1} + \frac{b^2 \sum_i (X_i - \bar{X})^2}{n - 1} - 2\left[\frac{b \sum_i (X_i - \bar{X})(Y_i - \bar{Y})}{n - 1}\right]$$

$$= s^2_Y + b^2 s^2_X - 2bs_{XY}.$$

However,

$$b = rs_Y/s_X \text{ and } b^2 = r^2 s^2_Y/s^2_X \text{ (see Eq. 8.2A).}$$

Therefore,

$$s^2_{Y.X} = s^2_Y + r^2 s^2_Y - 2bs_{XY}$$

Now, note that

$$2bs_{XY} = \frac{2rs_Y s_{XY}}{s_X}$$

Since $r = s_{XY}/(s_X s_Y)$ (Eq. 7.2), the quantity $s_{xy}/s_x$ must equal $rs_y$. Therefore,

$$2bs_{XY} = 2r^2 s^2_Y$$

Finally,

$$s^2_{Y.X} = s^2_Y + r^2 s^2_Y - 2r^2 s^2_Y = s^2_Y(1 - r^2) \tag{8.9}$$

Equation 8.9 gives the variance error of estimate in terms of $r$ and the variance of $Y$.

The positive square root of the variance error of estimate is called the *standard error of estimate:*

$$s_{Y.X} = s_Y \sqrt{1 - r^2} \tag{8.10}$$

The standard error of estimate can be used to set limits around a predicted score $\hat{Y}_i$, within which a person's actual score is likely to fall. If it can be assumed that the persons whose scores determined the prediction line $\hat{Y}_i = bX_i + c$ came from what is roughly a bivariate normal distribution, then $\hat{Y}_i$ can be viewed as the mean of the $Y_i$'s for persons having $X$-scores of $X_i$. The $e_i$'s are normally distributed and have a standard deviation that is estimated by Equation 8.10. If the prediction equation is applied to a large group of persons, the procedures used to determine areas under the normal curve (Sec. 6.5) can be applied:

1. Approximately 68% will have actual scores that lie within one $s_{Y.X}$ of their predicted score $\hat{Y}_i$.
2. Approximately 95% will have actual scores that lie within two $s_{Y.X}$'s of their $\hat{Y}_i$.

These statements are valid because if the bivariate normality assumption is correct, the distribution of actual $Y$ scores is normal around a mean of $bX + c$ and with a standard deviation of $s_{Y.X}$ for any $X$.* (Notice that although the *mean* of the normal

**FIGURE 8.5. A scatterplot with broken lines marking off 1 and 2 standard errors of estimate above and below the regression line.**

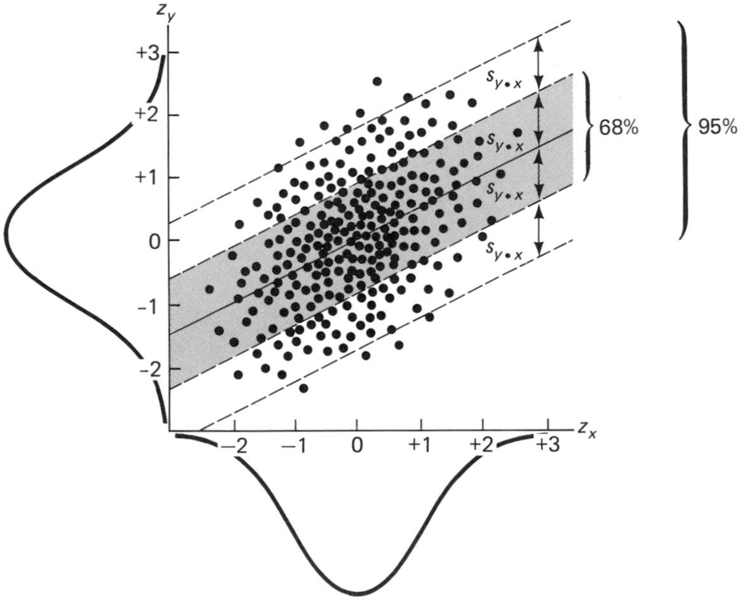


*For the *exact* estimation procedures that remove the "approximately" from statements 1 and 2 see Dixon and Massey (1969, pp. 199–200). The statements are precise only when $X_i = \bar{X}$. Actual percentages will be less than the figures given in Statements 1 and 2 as $X_i$ deviates from $\bar{X}$, especially if $n$ is small and $X_i$ deviates more than $2s_X$ from $\bar{X}$.

distribution of the $Y$ scores differs from one value of $X$ to the next, the standard deviation $s_{Y.X}$ does not depend on $X$.) These relationships are illustrated in Figure 8.5.

Note that the greater *range* in the residuals near the mean does not suggest a lack of homoscedasticity. Recall from Table 5.1 that $n$ greatly affects the range. Suppose $\sigma_1^2 = \sigma_2^2$ and $n_1 > n_2$; then $\text{range}_1 > \text{range}_2$. Since there are more observations near the mean of $X$, the range of the residuals is greater, even though about 68% of them are within one standard error of estimate of the predicted value.

## 8.11 REGRESSION AND PRETEST-POSTTEST GAINS

One of the most subtle sources of invalidity in behavioral research is the phenomenon of regression. Even seasoned researchers have frequently failed to detect its presence. Hence it has spoiled many otherwise good research efforts. Studies of atypical and special groups have probably been the victims of the regression phenomenon more often than those in any other single area of inquiry. A simple statistical truism is that when subjects are selected because they deviate from the mean on some variable, regression will occur.

Many studies on academic remediation and treatment of the handicapped and other deviant groups follow this pattern. Those in greatest "need" are selected on a "pretest," a treatment is administered, and a reassessment on a "posttest" then follows. For example, suppose all children having IQ scores below 80 were given some special (alleged cognitively beneficial) treatment (e.g., glutamic acid) over a period of a year and were then retested. Assume that the time interval between testings was such that there was absolutely no practice effect. If the treatment had absolutely no effect, how would the experimental group fare on the posttest? For purposes of illustration, assume a correlation of .6 between pretest and posttest IQ scores for young children. Figure 8.6 depicts the illustrative situation—that is, no treatment or practice effects are present. The means and variances are identical in both distributions (as they are in most tests where standard

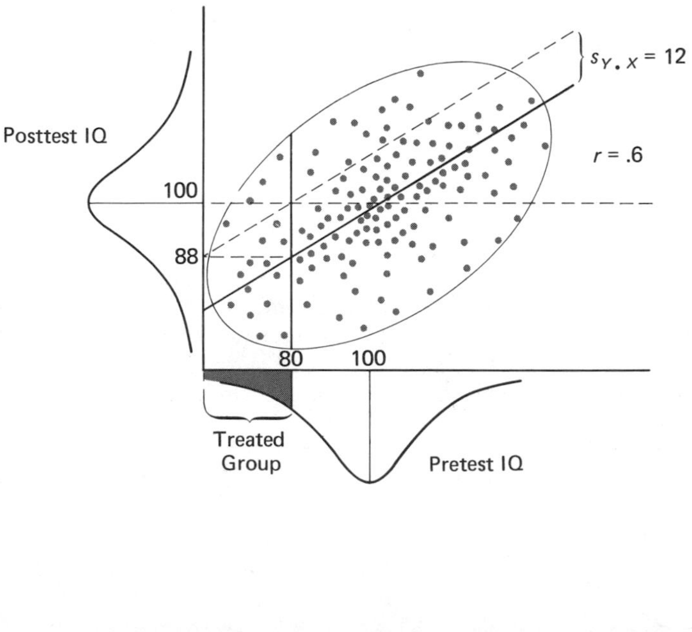


**FIGURE 8.6**
**Hypothetical situation in which a deviant group is selected and administered an inefficacious treatment.**

scores are employed). Figure 8.6 illustrates that there is a definite and pronounced tendency for subjects to regress toward the mean to the extent that subjects tend to be, on the average, only six-tenths as far from the posttest mean as they were on the pretest. That is, on the average, examinees tend to deviate only 60% as much from the posttest mean as they did from the pretest mean. Those examinees with pretest IQ scores of 80 would, on the average, be only 60% as far below the posttest mean—they would be expected to have an average posttest score of 88, a substantial "gain" of 8 points. Those initially having IQ scores of 70 would appear to have gained 12 points, with a posttest mean of about 82.

The standard error of estimate ($s_{Y.X} = s_Y \sqrt{1 - r^2} = 15 \sqrt{1 - (.6)^2}$) gives the standard deviation of posttest scores of persons having the same pretest scores. In this example, $s_{Y.X} = 12$ IQ points. Using the standard error of estimate ($s_{Y.X}$), one can accurately predict the proportion of those with a given pretest score who will fall above (or below) any other IQ score on the posttest (provided the common assumptions of linearity and homoscedasticity between the two variables are met). Those scoring 70 on the first test will have a mean of 82 on the second test, with a standard deviation of 12 IQ points. Using a normal curve table, it is readily apparent that about 84% will regress and hence receive higher IQ scores on the posttest even without any practice effect. One-half will "gain" 12 or more IQ points; one-sixth will have IQ's that "increased" by 24 or more points (i.e., obtain IQ scores of 94 or more). Further, about 7% of those with an initial IQ of 70 will obtain an IQ score of 100 or more on the second test, apart from any treatment or practice effect. Obviously, what may appear to a naive investigator to be striking improvements in a deviant population can result solely from the regression phenomenon. The following example will also serve to illustrate the problems.

One study treated infants born to mentally retarded mothers with an extensive regimen of sensory stimulation. The offspring were found to have much higher IQ scores than their mothers, and the authors uncritically attributed the increase to the sensory stimulation experiences. But from regression alone, what would the difference have been? Since the parent-child correlation of IQ's is known to be approximately .5, for mothers with an IQ score of 70, we would expect the children to have a mean of 85 even without the sensory stimulation.

There are numerous other examples in which ignorance of the regression effect has resulted in its being interpreted as a treatment effect. Studies using "matched pairs" usually also suffer from a lack of control over the regression effect (see Hopkins, 1969, and Shepard and Hopkins, 1977).

## 8.12 PART CORRELATION

Concepts from simple linear regression and correlation are combined in *part correlation* and *partial correlation.* These concepts are of interest in themselves. They are also useful for understanding the subsequent topics of multiple regression and multiple correlation. This section will begin with the development of part correlation, since partial correlation is a logical extension of part correlation.

A researcher wishes to determine the correlation between a measure of intelligence $X_1$ and achievement gains during an instructional unit. He chooses to define $X_1$ as

IQ scores on the Stanford-Binet Intelligence Test. But he faces some important decisions about how to measure achievement gains. Posttest scores $X_2$ on a valid achievement test are not what this researcher means by achievement gains. A large correlation of IQ with the achievement-test score $r_{12}$ would be expected even though no learning took place during instruction.

Administering a parallel form of the achievement test before ($X_3$) and after ($X_2$) instruction and subtracting each student's initial score from his postinstruction score produces a measure that is far closer to the researcher's notion of a measure of "achievement gain." One difficulty remains. Such a posttest-minus-pretest measure, $X_2 - X_3$, is contaminated by the regression effect (Sec. 8.2)—the gain scores, $X_2 - X_3$, would correlate negatively with pretest scores $X_3$.

It is certain that these "gain scores" will have a negative correlation with the pretest scores, that is, $r_{3,2-3} < 0$ unless $r_{32} = 1$. This is considered a defect of gain scores when there is reason to believe that amount of learning should not necessarily correlate negatively with pretest status.

A better method to measure gain or change is to predict posttest scores ($\hat{X}_2$) from pretest scores ($X_3$) and use the deviation $X_2 - \hat{X}_2$ as a measure of gain above and beyond what is predictable from the pretest. Note that this deviation is a residual from the regression line in which $X_2$ is predicted from $X_3$. This deviation, sometimes called a residual gain score, is illustrated in Figure 8.7 where $X_3$ and $X_2$ denote the pretest and posttest, respectively.

The residual gain score is denoted by $e_{2.3}$ because it is precisely the same as the error made in predicting $X_2$ from $X_3$ by the least-squares regression line. From previous experience with the regression model, the correlation of $e_{2.3}$ with $X_3$ is always zero. As a measure of learning, then, $e_{2.3}$ has the property that the measure of how much has been learned is unrelated ($r = 0$) with initial performance. The researcher would consider this property desirable.

The correlation of $X_1$ with $e_{2.3}$ is called a *part correlation* (also called *semipartial correlation*). It is the correlation of $X_1$ with $X_2$ after the portion of $X_2$ that can be

**FIGURE 8.7. Illustration of the definition of the residual gain score.**

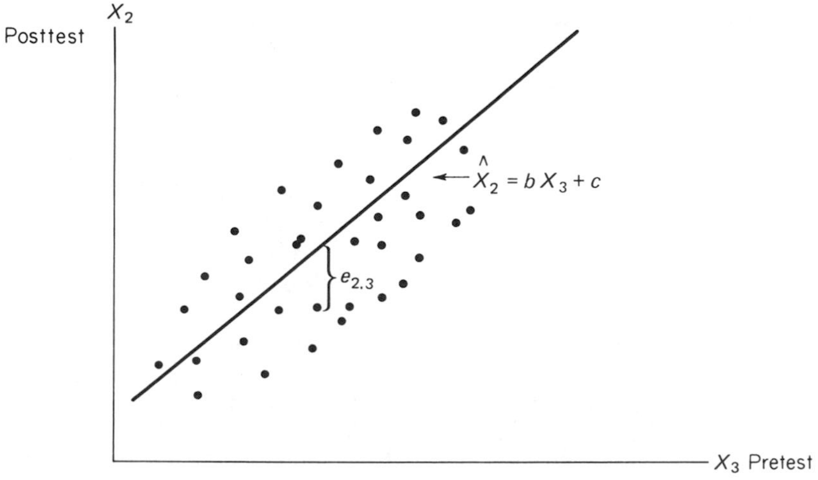

predicted from $X_3$ has been removed from $X_2$—it is the correlation of $X_1$ with the *residuals* from the prediction of $X_2$ from $X_3$. For example, in Table 8.2 the residuals are given on a statistics test that has been predicted from the GRE. If these residuals are correlated with age, the resulting correlation is a part correlation—the correlation of age with that part of the test scores that are not predictable from the GRE. The computational labor of computing this correlation is unnecessary when $r_{12}, r_{13}$, and $r_{23}$ are known. The part (or semipartial) correlation of variable 1 with the residuals on variable 2 having been predicted by variable 3 is

$$r_{1(2.3)} = \frac{r_{12} - r_{13}r_{23}}{\sqrt{1 - r_{23}^2}} \tag{8.11}$$

## 8.13 PARTIAL CORRELATION

*Partial correlation* is a simple extension of part correlation. The correlation of $X_1$ and $X_2$ with $X_3$ "held constant," "removed," or "partialed out" is a partial correlation—it is the correlation of the residuals $e_{1.3}$ and $e_{2.3}$, that is, $r_{e_{1.3}e_{2.3}}$. More simply, the partial correlation of $X_1$ and $X_2$ with $X_3$ partialed out is symbolized by $r_{12.3}$.

As in the case of part correlation, the actual calculation of the errors of estimate for all $n$ persons is unnecessary in the calculation of $r_{12.3}$. The partial correlation coefficient can be calculated directly from $r_{12}, r_{13}$, and $r_{23}$ by using the following formula:

$$r_{12.3} = \frac{r_{12} - r_{13}r_{23}}{\sqrt{(1 - r_{13}^2)(1 - r_{23}^2)}} \tag{8.12}$$

What interpretation can be given to $r_{12.3}$? One might hypothesize that there exists a positive correlation between reading performance $X_1$ and visual perceptual ability $X_2$ (as evidenced by eye coordination, scanning speed, etc.). Suppose a large sample of children, ranging in age ($X_3$) from six years to fifteen years, yields a correlation of $X_1$ with $X_2$ of .64. The conclusion that some children read better than others because of greater perceptual abilities is tempting, but the cautious researcher will avoid drawing it. It is obvious that as children grow older they develop greater eye coordination and other perceptual abilities as a part of natural maturation. Moreover, the same children receive instruction in school which helps make them better readers year after year, up to a point. Could it not be that measures of both $X_1$ and $X_2$ increase (improve) with age, in the one case as a consequence of physical maturation, and in the other of increased exposure to instruction? This certainly could be the case. If the correlation of $X_1$ and $X_2$ were zero at any one level of chronological age (instead of over the range from six years to fifteen years), the $r_{12}$ of .64 for the sample of children has far different implications. Indeed, the observed $r_{12}$ of .64 would not appear to be due to any direct or causal relationship between $X_1$ and $X_2$. How can one find what the value of $r_{12}$ would be for any single value of the chronological age variable $X_3$? Under suitable assumptions, this desired correlation equals the partial correlation of $X_1$ and $X_2$ with $X_3$ held constant: $r_{12.3}$.

Provided that $X_3$ has a linear relationship with both $X_1$ and $X_2$ and that the strength of the linear relationship between $X_1$ and $X_2$ is the same for persons at each level of $X_3$, then $r_{12.3}$ equals the value of $r_{12}$ obtained by correlating $X_1$ and $X_2$ for a group of persons having the same age. For example, in the preceding illustration suppose that $r_{12} = .64, r_{13} = .80$, and $r_{23} = .80$. The value of $r_{12.3}$ from Equation 8.8 is

$$r_{12.3} = \frac{.64 - (.80)(.80)}{\sqrt{1 - .80^2}\sqrt{1 - .80^2}} = \frac{.64 - .64}{(.60)(.60)} = .00$$

Thus one would estimate the value of $r_{12}$ for children of the *same chronological age* to be zero. If enough children of the same chronological age were available, $r$ could be calculated for them alone to check the previous result. The partial correlation coefficient serves the purpose of estimating $r_{12}$ for a single level of chronological age even when there is an insufficient number of persons at any single chronological age to do the estimating by direct calculation.

## 8.14 SECOND-ORDER PARTIAL CORRELATIONS

$r_{12.3}$ is called a *first-order* partial-correlation coefficient because the influence of *one* variable $X_3$ is partialed out. Partial correlation can be used to remove the influence of more than one variable. A *second-order* partial correlation coefficient extends the rationale for controlling the effects to two variables. The partial correlation between $X_1$ and $X_2$ with the influence of both $X_3$ and $X_4$ removed is

$$r_{12.34} = \frac{r_{12.3} - r_{14.3}r_{24.3}}{\sqrt{(1 - r_{14.3}^2)(1 - r_{24.3}^2)}} \tag{8.13}$$

The second-order partial correlation coefficient is the correlation between the residuals for $X_1$ with those for $X_2$ when each has been predicted from a multiple regression equation using the two variables $X_3$ and $X_4$ as predictors.

## 8.15 MULTIPLE REGRESSION AND MULTIPLE CORRELATION

The prediction of a dependent variable from one independent variable was considered in Section 8.6. In many applications, however, more than one predictor variable is involved. *Multiple regression* is the statistical term for predicting $Y$ from two or more *optimally* combined independent variables. For example, most colleges use two variables (high-school rank-in-class and SAT scores) to predict GPA in college. Stated broadly, the purpose of multiple prediction is the estimation of a variable $Y$, the dependent variable, from a linear combination of $m$ independent variables $X_1, X_2, \cdots, X_m$.

From Section 8.9, when one variable $X$ is used to estimate a second variable $Y$, the estimation criterion of "least squares" is equivalent to choosing values for $b$ and $c$ so that the sum of the squared residuals $\Sigma e_i^2$ is as small as possible. The equation $\hat{Y}_i =$

$bX_i + c$ provides the least-squares estimate $\hat{Y}_i$ of the $i$th person's score on the variable $Y$. This type of estimation is sometimes termed simple or *univariate* prediction because there is only one "predictor variable." A *multivariate* prediction of the $Y$ variable given scores on $m$ independent variables is

$$\hat{Y}_i = b_1 X_{1_i} + b_2 X_{2_i} + \cdots + b_m X_{m_i} + c \tag{8.14}$$

Equation 8.14 provides the raw-score multiple regression equation. It is a *linear* regression equation because the independent variables (the $X$'s) have exponents of 1. The least-squares criterion is employed in determining the values of the regression coefficients $(b_1, b_2, \cdots, b_m)$ and the intercept $c$—their values are such that the squared residuals,

$$\sum_{i=1}^{n} e_i^2 = \sum_i (Y_i - \hat{Y}_i)^2 = \sum_i [Y_i - (b_1 X_{1_i} + b_2 X_{2_i} + \cdots + b_m X_{m_i} + c)]^2, \tag{8.15}$$

are at a minimum for a given set of values of $Y$ and $X_1, X_2, \cdots, X_m$.

A second sense in which the $b$'s and $c$ are "best" is that they weight the $m$ predictors such that the correlation between $\hat{Y}$ and $Y$ is maximal.

The Pearson product-moment correlation between $Y$ and $\hat{Y}$, $r_{Y\hat{Y}}$, is a measure of how well the "best" linear weighting of the independent variables $X_1, \cdots, X_m$ predicts or correlates with the single dependent variable $Y$. This special case of Pearson's $r$ is called the multiple correlation coefficient and is denoted by $R_{Y.1,2,\cdots,m}$. Thus the regression coefficients and intercept in Equation 8.14 not only provide $\hat{Y}_i$'s, the least-squares estimates of $Y_i$'s (i.e., $\Sigma e_i^2$ is minimized), but also yield the highest possible correlation between the $\hat{Y}_i$'s and the $Y_i$'s—the $m$ independent variables are optimally weighted by the $b$'s.

## 8.16 THE STANDARDIZED REGRESSION EQUATION

The raw-score regression equation (Eq. 8.14) simplifies when all variables are expressed as standard $z$-scores—in the standardized regression equation all variables have a mean of 0 and a standard deviation of 1.

Equation 8.1, $\hat{z}_{Y_i} = r z_{X_i}$, is a standardized regression equation when there is a single independent variable. Similarly, with $m$ predictors, each expressed in standard $z$-score form, the standardized regression equation is

$$\hat{z}_{Y_i} = \hat{\beta}_1 z_{1_i} + \hat{\beta}_2 z_{2_i} + \cdots + \hat{\beta}_m z_{m_i} \tag{8.16}$$

The regression coefficients $\beta_1, \beta_2, \cdots, \beta_m$ are termed "beta weights,"* standardized regression coefficients, or, more explicitly, standard partial regression coefficients—standard to denote $z$-scale, and partial because the effects of the other variables are "held constant." In other words, $\beta_1$ is short for $\beta_{Y1.23\ldots m}$.

*The use of the Greek lowercase letter beta ($\beta$) is conventional, but it is not to be confused with the typical use of Greek letters to represent parameters.

## An Illustration with Two Independent Variables

How well can reading performance in grade one ($Y$) be predicted prior to grade one using reading readiness (RR) test scores ($X_1$) and IQ scores ($X_2$)? What is the optimal weighting of RR and IQ for predicting $Y$? End-of-year grades in reading given by pupils' first-grade teachers will serve as the criterion ($Y$). In this example with $m = 2$, Equation 8.16 becomes

$$\hat{z}_{Y_i} = \hat{\beta}_1 z_{1_i} + \hat{\beta}_2 z_{2_i} \tag{8.16A}$$

The least-squares estimates of the beta weights when $m = 2$ are given by

$$\hat{\beta}_1 = \frac{r_{Y1} - r_{Y2}r_{12}}{1 - r_{12}^2} \qquad \hat{\beta}_2 = \frac{r_{Y2} - r_{Y1}r_{12}}{1 - r_{12}^2} \tag{8.17}$$

The correlation between all pairs of variables is necessary in arriving at a regression equation. The matrix of intercorrelations for sample problems is given in Table 8.3.

Table 8.3 shows that both RR and IQ correlated substantially with the criterion (.612 and .541). How can the information on $X_1$ and $X_2$ be weighted optimally to maximize the accuracy in predicting $Y$? The beta weights are found from Equation 8.17, using the $r$'s in Table 8.3:

$$\hat{\beta}_1 = \frac{(.612) - (.541)(.466)}{1 - (.466)^2} = \frac{.3599}{.7828} = .460$$

and

$$\hat{\beta}_2 = \frac{(.541) - (.612)(.466)}{1 - (.466)^2} = .327$$

Thus the standardized regression equation is

$$\hat{z}_{Y_i} = .460 z_{1_i} + .327 z_{2_i}$$

To illustrate the use of this equation, predict $Y$ for students who are one standard deviation above the mean on both $X_1$ and $X_2$, that is, $z_1 = 1$ and $z_2 = 1$. When $z_1 =$

**TABLE 8.3 Intercorrelations Between Reading Performance ($Y$), IQ, and Reading Readiness (RR) Scores for 157 First-grade Pupils (Data from Hopkins and Sitkei, 1969)[a]**

| | $X_2$ | $Y$ | *Mean* | $s$ |
|---|---|---|---|---|
| RR Test Scores: $X_1$ | .466 | .612 | 49.0 | 10.3 |
| IQ Test Scores: $X_2$ | | .541 | 102.8 | 14.7 |
| Reading Score: $Y$ | | | 26.0 | 8.10 |

[a] $X_1$: Lee-Clark Reading Readiness Test raw scores
$X_2$: California Test of Mental Maturity, total IQ
$Y$: Lee-Clark Reading Test raw scores

1 and $z_2 = 1$ are substituted into the standardized regression equation, the predicted $z$-score on $Y$ is obtained: $\hat{z}_Y = .460(1) + .327(1) = .787$. The mean grade for such students is .787 standard deviations above $\overline{Y}$. From Table 8.3, $\overline{Y} = 26.0$ and $s_Y = 8.1$; thus $\hat{Y} = 26.0 + .787(8.1) = 32.4$. From the norm tables, a raw score of 32.4 is found to be equivalent to a grade-equivalent score of 2.6 (sixth month of grade two).

It is inconvenient to convert $X_1, X_2, \cdots, X_m$ to $z$-scores and to convert $\hat{z}_Y$ to $\hat{Y}$. The raw-score regression equation is more expedient for making predictions.

## 8.17 THE RAW-SCORE REGRESSION EQUATION

What is the predicted average reading grade for students having an RR score of 55 and an IQ score of 120? These scores could be converted to $z$-scores ($z_1 = .583$ and $z_2 = 1.17$), and $\hat{z}_Y$ could be obtained using the standardized regression equation ($\hat{z}_Y = .651$). $\hat{Y}$ could then be found ($\hat{Y} = 31.27$). But the raw-score regression equation makes the $z$-scale transformations unnecessary:

$$\hat{Y}_i = b_1 X_{1_i} + b_2 X_{2_i} + \cdots + b_m X_{m_i} + c \tag{8.18}$$

where

$$b_m = \hat{\beta}_m \frac{s_Y}{s_m}$$

$$c = \overline{Y} - b_1 \overline{X}_1 - b_2 \overline{X}_2 - \cdots - b_m \overline{X}_m$$

Notice that $b$'s and $\beta$'s will be equal when the standard deviations $s_Y$ and $s_m$ are equal. The raw-score regression coefficients can be obtained from the beta weights and the values for the standard deviations, found in Table 8.3:

$$b_1 = \frac{(.460)(8.10)}{10.3} = .362 \qquad \text{and} \qquad b_2 = \frac{(.327)(8.10)}{14.7} = .180$$

And, from Equation 8.18, the intercept $c$ is

$$c = 26.0 - (.362)(49.0) - (.180)(102.8) = -10.24$$

The raw-score form of the regression equation, therefore, is

$$\hat{Y}_i = .362 X_{1_i} + .180 X_{2_i} - 10.24$$

For students with $X_1 = 55$ and $X_2 = 120$, the predicted reading score is

$$\hat{Y} = .362(55) + .180(120) - 10.24 = 31.27$$

Notice how much more convenient the raw-score regression equation is to use, compared to the standardized regression equation. The latter equation, however, is more useful for evaluating the relative contributions of the independent variables. Notice that beta weights (Eq. 8.17) are close relatives of part and partial correlations (Eqs. 8.11 and 8.12).

## 8.18 MULTIPLE CORRELATION

The correlation between $Y$ and $\hat{Y}$ when the prediction is based on two or more independent variables is termed *multiple correlation.* When there are two predictors, as in the reading example, the multiple correlation coefficient, $R_{Y.12}$, can be obtained from Equation 8.19 using its square, $R^2_{Y.12}$, which describes the proportion of variance in $Y$ that is predicted by the regression equation

$$R^2_{Y.12} = \frac{r^2_{Y1} + r^2_{Y2} - 2r_{Y1}r_{Y2}r_{12}}{1 - r^2_{12}} \tag{8.19}$$

Supplying the $r$'s from Table 8.3 into Equation 8.19,

$$R^2_{Y.12} = \frac{(.612)^2 + (.541)^2 - 2(.612)(.541)(.466)}{1 - (.466)^2} = .458$$

and $R_{Y.12} = .677$. Notice that the correlation between $Y$ and $\hat{Y}$ increased to .677 when both IQ and RR scores were used to predict $Y$, whereas the correlation was .612 when the better of the two predictors was used singly. Stated differently, the proportion of the variance in $Y$ that was predictable increased from $(.612)^2 = .375$ to .458.

Notice that the multiple correlation would have been much higher if the two independent variables were not correlated—if $r_{12} = 0$, then $R^2_{Y.12} = r^2_{Y1} + r^2_{Y2}$. In a sense, $r_{12}$ is a measure of redundancy between the two independent variables; if $r_{12} = 1.0$, there is no unique information in the second variable, hence the ability to predict any criterion is not improved by using both $X_1$ and $X_2$. But to the extent that $r_{12}$ approaches 0, $X_1$ and $X_2$ do not contain common information.

The concepts of unique and redundant variance are illustrated in Figure 8.8, where the variance of each variable is depicted as a square.

**FIGURE 8.8**
**Redundant and unique variance among two independent variables and a dependent variable, based on data in Table 8.3.**

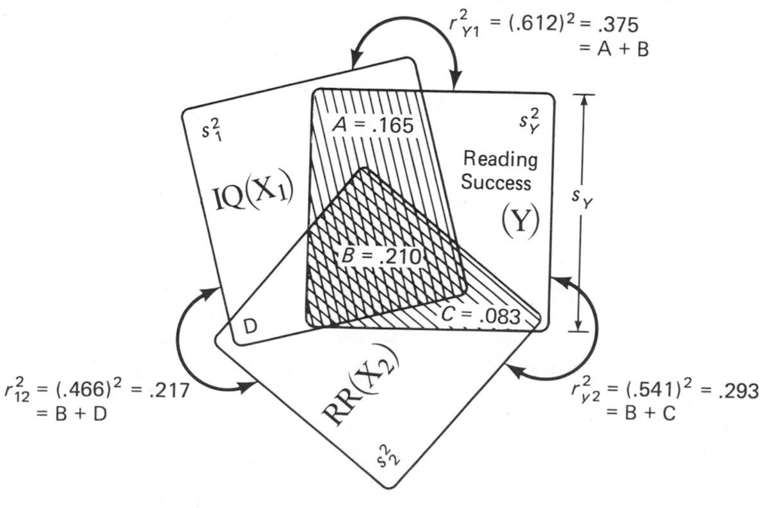

Areas $A$ and $B$ represent the variance in $Y$ that is predictable from $X_1$—$A + B = r_{Y1}^2 = (.612)^2 = .375$ or 37.5% of the $Y$ variance is predictable from $X_1$. The proportion of variance in $Y$ that is predictable from $X_2$, $r_{Y2}^2 = (.541)^2 = .293$, is depicted by areas $B$ and $C$. Likewise, areas $B + D$ represent the common variance between $X_1$ and $X_2$, $r_{12}^2 = (.466)^2 = .217$ or 21.7%. Thus the relevant and unique variance in $X_2$ for predicting $Y$ is shown as area $C$. Since $R_{Y.12}^2 = .458$, and area $A + B = .375$, area $C = .458 - .375 = .083$. Area $B$ represents relevant variance in $X_2$ for predicting $Y$, but variance already accounted for by $X_1$. Since $B + C = .293$, and $C = .083$, $B = .210$.

The total variance in $Y$ that is predictable from $X_1$ and $X_2$ is represented by areas $A + B + C = .458$. How does this figure compare to the figure that would result if $X_1$ and $X_2$ contained no redundant information—if $r_{12} = 0$? In this situation $R_{Y.12}^2 = r_{Y1}^2 + r_{Y2}^2 = .375 + .293 = .668$, hence $R_{Y.12} = .817$. It is apparent that in multiple regression it is desirable to have independent variables that correlate highly with the dependent variable, but have low intercorrelations with each other.

In rare instances, predictors that do not correlate with the criterion can increase the multiple correlation by "suppressing" irrelevant variance in other independent variables. For example, if $r_{Y1} = .5$, $r_{Y2} = 0$, and $r_{12} = .4$, then (from Eq. 8.19) $R_{Y.12} = .55$; thus variable 2 increased the predictable variance in $Y$ even though $r_{Y2} = 0$ by suppressing irrelevant variance in variable 1. Variables like variable 2 are termed *suppressor variables.*

## 8.19 MULTIPLE REGRESSION EQUATIONS WITH THREE OR MORE INDEPENDENT VARIABLES

The computations of regression coefficients ($\hat{\beta}$'s or $b$'s) for three or more independent variables, although not theoretically complex, are tedious and time-consuming when done by hand. Fortunately, the actual computations for three or more independent variables are almost always done using standard computer programs available at virtually all university computing facilities. Standardized and raw-score multiple regression equations were employed for the case in which two independent variables, $X_1$ and $X_2$, are used to predict $Y$. The underlying rationale and applications extend logically to situations in which there are three or more independent variables. The independent variables can include any combination of demographic, cognitive, psychomotor, affective, and variables such as age, IQ, GPA, height, sex, socioeconomic status, reaction time, interests, and ethnicity.

## 8.20 STEPWISE MULTIPLE REGRESSION

In Section 8.18 an additional predictor was demonstrated effective to the extent that it contributes relevant and unique variance to the set of predictor variables. If $r_{Y1} = .5$, $r_{Y2} = .5$, and $r_{Y3} = .4$, will $R_{Y.12}$ necessarily be larger than $R_{Y.13}$? Certainly not. If $r_{12} = 1$, then $X_2$ would be totally redundant and would not increase the ability to predict $Y$ over what could be done by $X_1$ alone, whereas if $r_{13} = 0$, $R_{Y.13} = .64$.

Much—if not most—behavioral research that employs multiple regression equations utilizes "stepwise" multiple regression computer programs to show the increment added by each predictor. In stepwise multiple regression the best predictor is selected in Step 1, and a one-predictor regression equation is provided along with the correlation $r_{Y\hat{Y}}$ and various other statistics such as the standard error of estimate. In Step 2 the variable that would contribute the most additional relevant variance is selected and a two-predictor regression equation is selected and $R_{Y.12}$ is determined. The variable selected in Step 2 is the variable that has the highest correlation with $Y$ when the previously entered independent variable is partialed out. Each successive step progresses in like manner—the next predictor variable entered into the regression equation will be the variable that has the largest correlation with the criterion when all variables already included in the previous regression equation have been partialed out.

## 8.21 AN ILLUSTRATION OF STEPWISE MULTIPLE REGRESSION

The independent variables in Table 8.3 are only two of five predictors that were studied for the purpose of forecasting reading success in grade one. The larger study asked the question, how accurately can end-of-year first-grade reading performance be predicted from a child's age (CA), sex, socioeconomic status (SES), reading readiness (RR), and IQ scores when a standardized reading test is used as a criterion? Table 8.4 gives the intercorrelations, means, and standard deviations for the variables of the study. Notice that all five independent variables correlated positively with the criterion, although the correlations for CA, SES, and sex are low: .050, .209, and .197, respectively.

The stepwise multiple regression is summarized in Table 8.5. The regression equation after Step 2 is the same equation that was worked out previously. Notice in Step 3 that the sex variable was selected because it complements $X_1$ and $X_2$ more than SES, even though SES has a slightly higher ("zero-order partial") correlation with the dependent variable. In other words, the second-order partial correlation $r_{Y5.12}$ (.201) was higher than either $r_{Y4.12}$ (.069) or $r_{Y3.12}$ (−.038); thus variable 5 was added in Step 3.

**TABLE 8.4 Intercorrelations of Variables Used in Predicting First-grade Reading Performance ($n$ = 157)**

| | (*IQ*) $X_2$ | (*CA*) $X_3$ | (*SES*) $X_4$ | (*Sex*) $X_5$ | $Y$ | *Mean* | *s* | *Measure* |
|---|---|---|---|---|---|---|---|---|
| RR: $X_1$ | .466 | .252 | .160 | .055 | .612 | 49.0 | 10.3 | Lee-Clark RR Test |
| IQ: $X_2$ | | −.119 | .265 | .072 | .541 | 102.8 | 14.7 | CTMM IQ Test |
| CA: $X_3$ | | | −.053 | −.081 | .050 | 76.8 | 4.11 | Age in Months |
| SES: $X_4$ | | | | −.040 | .209 | 32.3 | 21.6 | Duncan Scale |
| Sex: $X_5$ | | | | | .197 | 1.48 | .501 | (Male = 1, Female = 2) |
| $Y$ | | | | | | 26.0 | 8.10 | Lee-Clark Reading Test |

**TABLE 8.5 Stepwise Multiple Regression for Variables in Table 8.4**

| | | | | | *Partial r's* | | | | |
|---|---|---|---|---|---|---|---|---|---|
| *Step* | $R_{Y.1\ldots m}$ | $SS_{res}$ | $s_{Y.1\ldots m}$ | *Variable Entered* | RR $X_1$ | IQ $X_2$ | CA $X_3$ | SES $X_4$ | Sex (M = 1, F = 2) $X_5$ |
| 0 | . . . | 10237.0 | 8.1007 | . . . | .612 | .541 | .050 | .209 | .197 |
| 1 | .612 | 6405.4 | 6.428 | $X_1$(RR) | | .366 | −.135 | .142 | .206 |
| $(\hat{Y}_i = .481X_{1_i} + 2.41)$ | | | | | | | | | |
| 2 | .677 | 5549.6 | 6.003 | $X_2$(IQ) | | | −.038 | .069 | .201 |
| $(\hat{Y}_i = .362X_{1_i} + .180X_{2_i} - 10.24)$ | | | | | | | | | |
| 3 | .693 | 5325.3 | 5.900 | $X_5$(Sex) | | | −.021 | .083 | |
| $(\hat{Y}_i = .358X_{1_i} + .175X_{2_i} + 2.40X_{5_i} - 13.16)$ | | | | | | | | | |
| 4 | .69526 | 5288.5 | 5.899 | $X_4$(SES) | | | −.017 | | |
| $(\hat{Y}_i = .356X_{1_i} + .167X_{2_i} + 2.46X_{5_i} + .023X_{4_i} - 13.01)$ | | | | | | | | | |
| 5 | .69537 | 5286.95 | 5.917 | $X_3$(CA) | | | | | |
| $(\hat{Y}_i = .360X_{1_i} + .165X_{2_i} + 2.44X_{5_i} + .023X_{4_i} - .026X_{3_i} - 10.95)$ | | | | | | | | | |

## 8.22 DICHOTOMOUS AND CATEGORICAL VARIABLES AS PREDICTORS

Dichotomous variables such as sex can be used as independent variables if they are numerically coded, as in this example (M = 1, F = 2). The code must be known before the point-biserial *r*'s can be properly interpreted. Notice in Table 8.4 that sex correlated .197 with *Y* (reading test scores). The positive *r* indicates that the sex given the higher numerical code (females in this case) had higher test scores. If the code M = 2, F = 1 had been used, $r_{Y5}$ would have been −.197—the sign of *r* would have been reversed.

Categorical variables having $J = 3$ or more categories must be broken down into $J - 1$ dichotomies before they can be used for prediction purposes. For example, if there are three ethnic groups, two independent variables are required: $X_1$ is "Do you belong to ethnic group *A*?" with responses coded: No = 1, Yes = 2. The $X_2$ variable follows the identical pattern: "Do you belong to ethnic group *B*?" But what about the individuals in the third ethnic group? They are defined indirectly by having 1's (No's) for $X_1$ and $X_2$. These types of independent variables are often referred to as *dummy variables.**

*See Kerlinger and Pedhazur (1973, Part 2) for further details and illustrations of dummy coding.

## 8.23 THE STANDARD ERROR OF ESTIMATE IN MULTIPLE REGRESSION

Returning to the stepwise multiple regression equations in Table 8.5, is there any point to retaining CA as a predictor? Not really. The multiple correlation increment was only .0001! Moreover, the standard error of estimate $s_{Y.12345} = 5.917$ is actually larger than the value for the previous step, $s_{Y.1245} = 5.899$. How can this be in view of the fact that $R_{Y.12345} > R_{Y.1245}$? And, the sum of the squared residuals is less in Step 5 than in Step 4. Is not $s^2_{Y.12...m} = s^2_Y(1 - R^2_{Y.12...m})$ as one would expect, extrapolating from Equation 8.9? It is true that $s^2_{Y.12...m} \doteq s^2_Y(1 - R^2_{Y.12...m})$. But more precisely,

$$s^2_{Y.12...m} = \frac{SS_{\text{residuals}}}{n - m - 1} = \frac{SS_{\text{residuals}}}{\nu} \tag{8.20}$$

The denominator $n - m - 1$ defines the degrees of freedom ($\nu$). Recall from Section 5.8 that the sum of squares divided by its degrees of freedom is a variance—in this case the variance of the residuals. From Step 4 to Step 5, the decrease in the numerator of Equation 8.20 was proportionately less than the decrease in the denominator. Thus the ratio (i.e., $s^2_{Y.12345}$) in Step 5 is greater than the ratio in Step 4 (i.e., $s^2_{Y.1245}$).

Notice in Table 8.5 that Steps 4 and 5 provided virtually no increase in the multiple correlation; this is not unusual. In most prediction studies in the behavioral sciences there is little increase in $R_{Y.12...m}$ after the best three or four predictors have been included in the multiple regression equation. In actual practice the regression equation with the three independent variables $X_1$, $X_2$, and $X_5$ would be employed; variables 3 and 4 added virtually no relevant *unique* information.

## 8.24 THE MULTIPLE CORRELATION AS AN INFERENTIAL STATISTIC: CORRECTION FOR BIAS

The regression coefficients are determined in such a way as to yield the highest possible correlation between $Y$ and $\hat{Y}$, $r_{Y\hat{Y}}$, which is the multiple correlation $R_{Y.12...m}$. But in the process of weighting the predictors there is a certain amount of capitalizing on chance. To the extent that there is sampling error (Eq. 4.12) in the $r$'s in the correlation matrix and in the standard deviations of the independent and dependent variables, the optimizing procedures involved in obtaining the multiple regression equation cause the correlation $r_{Y\hat{Y}}$ to tend to be systematically higher than the corresponding parameter $\rho_{Y\hat{Y}}$, where the $\hat{Y}$'s in $\rho_{Y\hat{Y}}$ are from a regression equation derived using $\rho$'s and $\sigma$'s (not $r$'s and $s$'s).

Several "shrinkage" formulas have been proposed to remove the "error fitting" from the multiple correlation $R_{Y.12...m}$. Olkin and Pratt (1958) derived a formula for the unbiased estimate of $\rho^2_{Y\hat{Y}}$, that is, $\hat{R}^2_{Y.12...m}$. But a much simpler formula (Eq.

8.21) by Wherry yields results that are only trivially different (Lord and Novick, 1968, p. 286; Carter, 1979):

$$\hat{R}^2_{Y.12\ldots m} = 1 - (1 - R^2_{Y.12\ldots m})\left(\frac{n-1}{n-m-1}\right) \tag{8.21}$$

where $\hat{R}^2_{Y.12\ldots m}$ is an estimate of $\rho^2_{Y\hat{Y}}$, and $R^2_{Y.12\ldots m}$ is the square of the multiple correlation from the regression equation based on $n$ cases and $m$ variables. In the sample problem with $n = 157$, $m = 5$, and $R^2_{Y.12345} = (.69537)^2 = .48354$, the corrected multiple correlation, estimated from Equation 8.21 is

$$\hat{R}^2_{Y.12345} = 1 - (1 - .48354)\left(\frac{157-1}{157-5-1}\right) = 1 - (.51646)(1.0331)$$

$$= .466445$$

$$\hat{R}_{Y.12345} = .6830$$

The multiple $R$ after the correction is slightly lower than the value reported in Table 8.5 of .69537.* The correction would have been much greater if $n$ had been much smaller and/or $m$ had been much larger. For example, if $n = 25$, other things remaining constant, the corrected $R$ would have been .59. Or if $m = 25$, other things remaining constant, the corrected $R$ would have become .62. As the ratio $m/n$ increases, the amount of error fitting (bias) increases. Apply Equation 8.21 to the situation in which $m = 25$, $n = 50$, and $R_{Y.12\ldots 25} = .5$, and find that the corrected multiple $R$ has shrunk to .24! In one study the authors obtained a multiple $R$ of .6 based on twenty-one variables on sixty persons. The corrected multiple $R$ of .08 illustrates that almost all the relationship was due to error fitting. The common terms in Equations 8.20 and 8.21 are no accident. Indeed the rationale underlying Equation 8.21 is to estimate the square of the multiple correlation, not on the proportion of sum of squares in the criterion that is predictable, but using unbiased estimators of unpredictable and total variance:

$$\hat{R}^2_{Y.12\ldots m} = 1 - \frac{s^2_{Y.12\ldots m}}{s^2_Y} \tag{8.22}$$

where $s^2_{Y.12\ldots m}$ is obtained from Equation 8.20. Thus, in the sample problem in Table 8.5,

$$\hat{R}^2_{Y.12345} = 1 - \frac{(5.917)^2}{(8.1007)^2} = .4665 \qquad \text{and} \qquad \hat{R}_{Y.12345} = .6830$$

the identical value found using Equation 8.21. In other words, Equation 8.22 estimates the parameter $\rho^2_{Y\hat{Y}}$ by entering the unbiased estimates of the parameters $\sigma^2_{Y.12\ldots m}$ and $\sigma^2_Y$. If Equation 8.20 is used to determine the value of the standard error of estimate, then the corrected multiple correlation can be estimated directly from Equation 8.22, and Equation 8.21 is unnecessary.

*Using the Olkin-Pratt procedure, the corrected multiple correlation was .6854. Equation 8.21 results in a very slight overcorrection (Carter, 1979), but is simpler to use than the Olkin-Pratt formula.

## 8.25 ASSUMPTIONS

The regression procedures that have been discussed and illustrated make three assumptions:

1. The $Y$ scores are *normally distributed* at all points along the regression line; that is, the residuals are normally distributed. (There is no assumption that the independent variables are normally distributed.)
2. There is a *linear relationship* between the $Y$'s and $\hat{Y}$'s—at all points along the straight regression line, the residuals have a mean of zero.
3. The variance of the residuals is homogeneous at all points along the regression line. This characteristic is known as *homoscedasticity.*

In most regression models an additional assumption is listed, namely, that the independent variables are fixed, not random. Fixed variables have values which are selected by the investigator and are not the result of random sampling. Sex and chronological age in the sample multiple regression problem (Sec. 8.21) are examples of fixed independent variables: both sexes in the population are represented and overaged and underaged pupils were excluded. The other three independent variables, IQ, RR, and SES, are random variables—not all the particular values within the population to which the regression equation might be applied are represented in the sample. Fortunately the regression methods that interest us yield identical results whether the independent variables are fixed or random (Snedecor, 1956, p. 133).

## 8.26 CURVILINEAR REGRESSION AND CORRELATION

Most cognitive and psychomotor variables that are measured on refined instruments have linear relationships. But if the relationships are nonlinear, one should try various transformations (Sec. 8.28) to see if the relationship can be accurately described by a straight line. If these procedures are unsuccessful, more complex regression equations can be used—equations that allow the independent variables to be raised to powers other than one, polynomial regression equations. Fortunately most computer program packages have programs for determining polynomial regression equations as well as multiple regression equations.

## 8.27 MEASURING NONLINEAR RELATIONSHIPS BETWEEN TWO VARIABLES; THE CORRELATION RATIO $\eta^2$

This section appears here for the sake of completeness and logical continuity. You may find it more meaningful after you are familiar with one-factor analysis of variance (Chapter 16).

Although we have repeatedly pointed out that the Pearson product-moment $r$ measures only the degree of *linear* relationship between $X$ and $Y$, we have yet to indicate a descriptive measure to use when the relationship between $X$ and $Y$ is predominantly nonlinear. As an example of a nonlinear relationship, consider the hypothetical data in Figure 8.9 relating age $X$ to psychomotor performance $Y$.

Although the Pearson $r_{XY} = -.077$, a visual inspection of the scatterplot indicates that the relationship is nonlinear; hence $r$ is an inappropriate measure of the degree of relationship between $X$ and $Y$. Although in the example there are an equal number of persons in each of the $J = 7$ age groups, the procedures are identical when the numbers per group are not equal.

It is obvious from Figure 8.9 that the scores on this subtest rise in straight-line fashion from age ten to a peak at age twenty-five and then decline rather rapidly.

The data depicted in Figure 8.9 are tabulated in Table 8.6.

A measure of the linear *or* nonlinear relationship between $X$ and $Y$ is denoted by the parameter $\eta^2$ and $\hat{\eta}^2$ in a sample (read "eta squared"), also called the *correlation ratio*. The correlation ratio has the following definitional form:

$$\hat{\eta}^2_{Y.X} = 1 - \frac{SS_{within}}{SS_{total}} \tag{8.23}$$

where $SS_{total} = \Sigma_j \Sigma_i (Y_{ij} - \overline{Y}_{\bullet})^2$, that is, the sum of the squared deviations of each $Y$ score for the mean of all $n_{\bullet}$ scores, $\overline{Y}_{\bullet}$.

$SS_{within}$ is obtained in the following manner: for each of the $J = 7$ different $X_j$'s, the corresponding $Y_{ij}$-scores are deviated from their own mean, $\overline{Y}_j$, and the sum of squares for each of the $J$ groups is calculated. For example, in Table 8.6 the sum of squares for group $j = 1$ (age ten) is $(7 - 8.5)^2 + (8 - 8.5)^2 + (9 - 8.5)^2 + (10 - 8.5)^2 = 5.0$. This process is repeated for each of the $J$ groups. In group 2 (age fifteen), the sum of the squared deviations of the $Y_{i2}$'s about their mean is also 5.0. Finally, the $J = 7$ sums of squared deviations are combined; the result is $SS_{within}$.

For the data in Table 8.6, the value of $SS_{total}$ is 54.43 and the value of $SS_{within}$

**FIGURE 8.9**
**Relationship between age and psychomotor performance.**

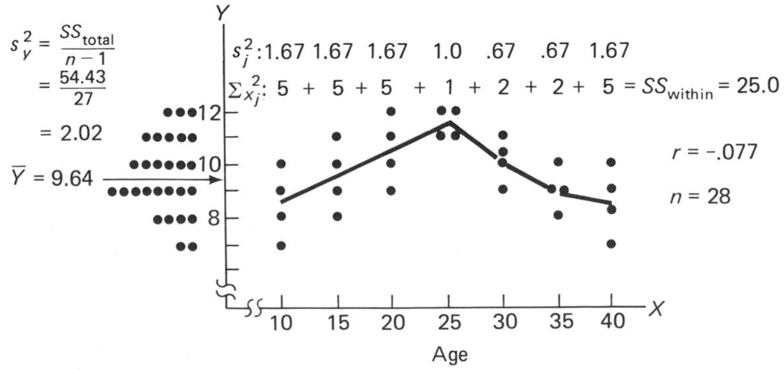

**TABLE 8.6 Psychomotor Test Scores of 28 Persons in Eight Equally Spaced Age Groups**

| | *Age* | | | | | | | |
|---|---|---|---|---|---|---|---|---|
| | *10* | *15* | *20* | *25* | *30* | *35* | *40* | |
| *j*: | *1* | *2* | *3* | *4* | *5* | *6* | *7 = J* | |
| | 7 | 8 | 9 | 11 | 9 | 8 | 7 | |
| | 8 | 9 | 10 | 11 | 10 | 9 | 8 | |
| | 9 | 10 | 11 | 12 | 10 | 9 | 9 | |
| | 10 | 11 | 12 | 12 | 11 | 10 | 10 | |
| Means: | 8.5 | 9.5 | 10.5 | 11.5 | 10.0 | 9.0 | 8.5 | $\overline{Y}_{\bullet} = 9.64$ |
| $SS_j$: | 5.0 | 5.0 | 5.0 | 1.0 | 2.0 | 2.0 | 5.0 | |

$$\sum_j SS_j = SS_{within} = 25.00$$

is 25.00; hence, the value of $\hat{\eta}^2_{Y.X}$ is

$$\hat{\eta}^2_{Y.X} = 1 - \frac{25.00}{54.43} = 1 - .459 = .541$$

The following considerations bear on the interpretation of $\hat{\eta}^2_{Y.X}$. The coefficient $\hat{\eta}^2_{Y.X}$—notice that $Y$ precedes the dot and $X$ follows it—is a measure of the extent to which $Y$ is predictable from $X$ by a "best-fitting" line that may be either straight or curved.

It is important to note that $\hat{\eta}^2_{Y.X}$ and $\hat{\eta}^2_{X.Y}$ will generally have different values. This is contrary to our experience with $r$, for which $r_{XY} = r_{YX}$. We can give the fact that $\hat{\eta}^2_{Y.X}$ may not equal $\hat{\eta}^2_{X.Y}$ some intuitive appeal with the data in Table 8.6. If a person's age is ten, his score can be fairly confidently predicted to be near 8.6. However, if a person's $Y$ score is 8, his age $X$ may either be low, around ten, or high, around thirty-eight. Hence, $Y$ can be predicted from $X$ reasonably well; but $X$ cannot be predicted well from $Y$. These facts are reflected in the values of $\hat{\eta}^2_{Y.X} = .545$ and $\hat{\eta}^2_{X.Y}$ which was not calculated but which is close to zero, $\hat{\eta}^2_{X.Y} = .016$.

The value of $\hat{\eta}^2_{Y.X}$ should be compared with the value $r^2_{XY}$ instead of $r_{XY}$. We saw that $r^2_{XY} = 1 - (s^2_e/s^2_Y)$, which is equal to

$$r^2_{XY} = 1 - \frac{SS_e}{SS_{total}} \tag{8.24}$$

Equation 8.24 shows $r^2_{XY}$ to be 1 minus the proportion of the sum of squares of $Y$ that remain after prediction by the least-squares regression line. Equation 8.24 shows $\hat{\eta}^2_{Y.X}$ to be 1 minus the proportion of the sum of squares of the $Y$-scores that are around a prediction line that passes through the mean $\overline{Y}_j$, for each $\overline{X}_j$. The curvilinear prediction line for predicting $Y$ from $X$ appears in Figure 8.9.

As with $r_{XY}^2$, $\hat{\eta}_{Y.X}^2$ must always be less than or equal to 1 and greater than or equal to 0. Furthermore, $\hat{\eta}_{Y.X}^2 \geqslant r_{XY}^2$. The difference, $\hat{\eta}_{Y.X}^2 - r_{XY}^2$, is a measure of the degree of nonlinearity of a best-fitting line for predicting $Y$ from $X$ (see Glass and Hakstian, 1969). Use of this fact is made to test for nonlinearity (Chap. 16).

## 8.28 TRANSFORMING NONLINEAR RELATIONSHIPS INTO LINEAR RELATIONSHIPS

A nonlinear relationship can often be converted to a linear relationship by a mathematical transformation of $X$ or $Y$ (or both). For example, the strong nonlinear relationship in Figure 8.10 becomes more nearly linear if the abscissa is log $X$ rather than $X$.

Another important fact is illustrated in Figure 8.10: even though correlation coefficients are useful indices to describe relationships between variables, scatterplots often illuminate aspects of the relationship that are not revealed in $r$ or $\hat{\eta}$. For example, notice in Figure 8.10 that life expectancy reaches a plateau at "four score and ten" when the annual income is about $2,000 per person.

## CHAPTER SUMMARY

Correlation and regression are opposite sides of the same coin. If $r = 1.0$, there is no regression toward the mean; if $r = .5$, scores tend to regress half the distance to the mean in standard-score units.

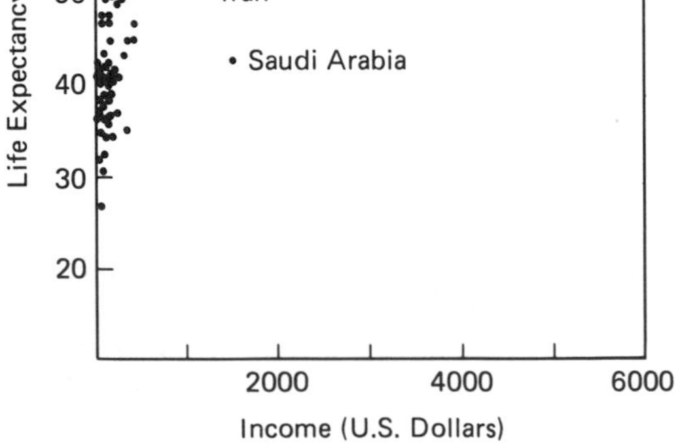

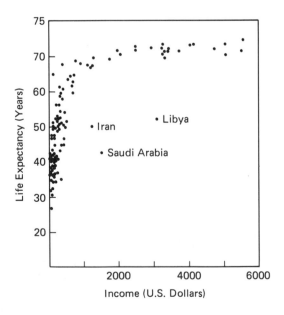

**FIGURE 8.10**
**Scatterplot of life expectancy versus income for nations (from Leinhardt and Wasserman, 1979).**

The expression $\hat{z}_Y = rz_X$ is the simplest form of the regression equation; equivalently, $r = \hat{z}_Y/z_X$ shows $r$ as an expected rate of change in $z_Y$ per unit $z_X$. The correlation between $\hat{z}_Y$-values and actual $z_Y$-values is the same as $z_Y$ with $z_X$-values since $\hat{z}_Y$ is simply a linear transformation of $z_X$. The variance in $\hat{z}_Y$-values is $r^2$ and is the proportion of variance in the criterion that is predictable from the independent variable.

The difference in observed $Y$'s from predicted $\hat{Y}$'s are residuals. The standard deviation of residuals is the standard error of estimate; $s_{Y.X}$ can be used with $\hat{Y}$ to determine the proportion of $Y$-values that are expected to fall above or below any point, assuming bivariate normality. Bivariate normal distributions are three-dimensional bell-shaped "hats," with varying degrees of elongation. Linearity and homoscedasticity are characteristics of all bivariate normal distributions.

The regression line is defined by the least-squares criterion. No other straight line can be drawn that will have so small a sum of the squared residuals. In multiple regression, two or more predictors are used to predict a dependent variable. The resulting correlation between the predictors, optimally weighted, yields the highest correlation with $Y$; this is termed multiple correlation. Multiple $R$'s overestimate the values of the corresponding parameters because they capitalize on sampling error. The degree of bias increases as the number of predictors increases and the sample size decreases.

Partial correlation can be useful to estimate the correlation between two variables with the effects of one or more other variables statistically removed. Partial correlations are correlations between residuals.

Standardized regression equations express all variables as $z$-scores. Their regression coefficients are called beta weights; they more directly reflect the influence of each predictor variable than do the raw-score regression coefficients.

In stepwise multiple regression the variable that correlates most highly with the criterion is selected first. The second variable entered into the regression equation is that variable which adds the most relevant, unique variance, that is, has the highest partial correlation with the dependent variable.

Although the degree of variability greatly influences the correlation coefficient, it does not affect the predicted values on the dependent variable or the standard error of estimate. When regression is nonlinear and cannot be made linear by transformations, the relationship can be described by the correlation ratio $\hat{\eta}^2_{Y.X}$; it describes the proportion of variance in the criterion that is predictable allowing curvature in the regression line.

## *MASTERY TEST*

1. Which term least belongs with the other three?
   a. independent variable
   b. predictor variable
   c. $X$-variable
   d. criterion variable
2. Which term least belongs with the other three?
   a. dependent variable
   b. independent variable
   c. predicted variable
   d. criterion variable

3. Which term least belongs with the other three?
   a. percentile
   b. correlation
   c. regression
   d. prediction
4. If $r = .5$ and $z_X = 2.0$, what is $\hat{z}_Y$?
5. The $\hat{z}_Y$ from Question 4 would be expected to correspond to what percentile in the entire distribution of $Y$?
   a. $P_{50}$
   b. $P_{75}$
   c. $P_{84}$
   d. $P_{98}$
6. If $r = .5$, for persons at $P_2$ on $X$, what is their average percentile on $Y$?
   a. $P_{50}$
   b. $P_{75}$
   c. $P_{16}$
   d. $P_2$
7. If $r = -.6$ and $z_X = -1.5$, what is $\hat{z}_Y$?
8. If $r = 1.0$, are scores on $X$ and $Y$ *identical* for all pairs of observations?
9. If $r$ is greater than .0, is the variance in predicted $z$-scores on $Y(\hat{z}_Y$'s) less than 1.0?
10. If $r = .8$, do persons below the mean on $X$ tend to have higher $z$-scores on $Y$ than on $X$?
11. If for $z_X = 1.0$, $\hat{z}_Y = .75$, is $r = .75$?
12. Other things being equal, as $r$ increases, does the standard error of estimate increase?
13. If $s_Y = s_X = 15$, does $r = b$?
14. In a bivariate normal distribution, is the regression of $Y$ on $X$ always linear?
15. In $z$-score units, will $s_{Y.X}$ always equal $s_{X.Y}$?
16. If $s_Y = 10$ and $r = .6$, what is the value of $s_{Y.X}$? Use Equation 8.10.
17. a. If $s_{Y.X} = 8$, what percentage of the actual $Y$-scores will be within 8 points of the predicted values?
    b. What percentage of the observations on $Y$ will be more than 8 points higher than predicted?
    c. Will the percentage underpredicted by more than 8 points be expected to be the same as in part b?
18. Assume that the correlation between a parent's IQ score and the IQ score of an offspring is about .5; moreover, we know that $\mu_X = \mu_Y = 100$ and that $\sigma_X = \sigma_Y = 15$.
    a. Estimate the average IQ of children of mothers with IQ = 130.
    b. Estimate the average IQ of children of fathers with IQ = 90.
    c. Estimate the average IQ of children of mothers with IQ = 100.
19. The average IQ of both parents correlates approximately .6 with their offspring's IQ ($Y$). What is the value of the standard error of estimate for predicting $Y$?
20. If $s_{Y.X} = 12$, the observed IQ scores will be within 12 points of the predicted IQ's for what percentage of the children?
21. For high multiple correlations, one wants independent variables that correlate (high or low?) with the dependent variable and correlate (high or low?) with each other.
22. To estimate the correlation between variables $Y$ and $X$ with the effects of variable $Z$ removed, one would use
    a. partial correlation
    b. multiple regression
    c. simple correlation

23. Match the term in the left-hand column with its definition in the right-hand column.

| | | | |
|---|---|---|---|
| A. | $r_{XY.Z}$ | a. | regression coefficient |
| B. | $b_{Y.X}$ | b. | simple correlation |
| C. | $r$ | c. | standard error of estimate |
| D. | $s_{Y.X}$ | d. | multiple correlation |
| E. | $R_{Y.XZ}$ | e. | second-order partial correlation |
| F. | $\hat{Y}$ | f. | predicted $z$-score on $Y$ |
| G. | $\hat{z}_Y$ | g. | predicted score on $Y$ |
| H. | $r_{X(Y.Z)}$ | h. | beta weight |
| I. | $\beta_1$ | i. | correlation ratio (eta squared) |
| J. | $\hat{Y}_i - Y_i$ | j. | residual |
| K. | $r_{12.34}$ | k. | part correlation |
| L. | $\eta^2_{Y.X}$ | l. | first-order partial correlation |

24. If variable $Y$ is predicted from variable $X$ and the resulting residuals are correlated with variable $Z$, this correlation is a
    a. part correlation
    b. partial correlation
    c. multiple correlation
    d. stepwise multiple correlation
    e. beta weight

25. The correlation in the previous questions would be denoted as
    a. $r_{ZY.X}$
    b. $r_{Z(Y.X)}$
    c. $R_{Z.YX}$
    d. $\beta_{Z.YX}$

26. When all variables are standardized using the $z$-scale, the regression coefficients for the $m$ predictor variables are
    a. equal
    b. beta weights
    c. equal to raw-score regression coefficients
    d. parameters

27. If $r_{Y1} = 0$, $\hat{\beta}_1$
    a. may be positive
    b. may be negative
    c. may be zero
    d. two of the above
    e. all of the above

28. If $r_{Y1} = r_{Y2} = r_{12} = .5$, what is the value of the multiple correlation, $R_{Y.12}$? (See Eq. 8.19).

29. If $r_{YA} = .4$, $r_{YB} = .5$, $r_{YC} = .4$, $r_{AB} = .5$, $r_{AC} = 0$, and $r_{BC} = 0$, which of the predictor variables, $A$, $B$, or $C$, will be selected in Step 1, a stepwise multiple regression?

30. Which independent variable will be entered in Step 2?

31. Using the related multiple regression equation in Table 8.5 (Step 3), predict the reading test score for a girl having an IQ score of 130 and a RR score of 60. What is the predicted score for a boy with the same scores?

32. In a multiple regression involving five predictors and 206 persons, the sum of the squared residuals is 800. What is the value of the standard error of estimate $s_{Y.12345}$? (Use Eq. 8.20.)

33. In the previous question, estimate $\hat{R}_{Y.12345}$ if $s_Y^2 = 8$ (see Eq. 8.22).

34. When viewed as an inferential statistic, the observed multiple correlation $R_{Y.12\ldots m}$
   a. is unbiased
   b. tends to overestimate the value of the parameter
   c. tends to underestimate the value of the parameter

35. The degree of bias in $R_{Y.12\ldots m}$ will be least in which of these situations?
   a. $n$ is large and $m$ is large
   b. $n$ is small and $m$ is large
   c. $n$ is large and $m$ is small
   d. $n$ is small and $m$ is small

36. Which one of these is not assumed in multiple regression?
   a. Variable $Y$, the dependent variable, is normally distributed
   b. All independent variables are normally distributed
   c. The scatterplot possesses homoscedasticity
   d. The relationship between the $Y$'s and $\hat{Y}$'s is linear

37. Eta, $\hat{\eta}$, will exceed $r$ except when
   a. $SS_{within} = SS_{residuals}$
   b. $SS_{within} < SS_{total}$
   c. $SS_{total} = SS_{residuals}$
   d. $r = 0$.

38. Does $r_{YX} = r_{XY}$? Does $\hat{\eta}_{Y.X}$ usually have exactly the same value as $\hat{\eta}_{X.Y}$?

## *PROBLEMS AND EXERCISES*

1. The figure on page 149 is a computer-produced scatterplot of IQ scores from the California Test of Mental Maturity obtained by 354 children tested at grade five ($X$) and two years later in grade seven ($Y$). We will determine the regression equation $Y_i = bX_i + c$ for predicting $Y_i$ from $X_i$. The essential information is given in the figure.
   a. What were the lowest and highest IQ scores obtained at grade five?
   b. What were the lowest and highest IQ scores obtained at grade seven?
   c. Does the regression appear linear?
   d. Does the scatterplot appear to possess homoscedasticity?
   e. Does the scatterplot appear to be approximately bivariately normal?
   f. Compute $b_{Y.X} = r\left(\frac{s_Y}{s_X}\right) = b$.
   g. Compare $c = \overline{Y} - b\overline{X}$.
   h. Express the regression equation using $b$ and $c$ previously determined.
   i. Bob obtained a CTMM IQ score of 140 at grade five. Predict his IQ score on the same test at grade seven.
   j. Sam's IQ score at grade five was 70. Predict his grade seven IQ score.
   k. Draw in the regression line in the figure (use $X$'s and $\hat{Y}$'s from Exercises 1i and 1j).
   l. Compute the standard error of estimate ($s_{Y.X}$).
   m. What percentage of the grade seven predictions will be within seven points of the observed values?
   n. Draw in dotted lines one $s_{Y.X}$ above and one $s_{Y.X}$ below the regression line.
   o. Chances are about 2 in 3 that Bob's IQ score at grade seven will be between ___ and ___ and than Sam's IQ score will be between ___ and ___.
   p. Assuming bivariate normality, what percentage of those who score 140 at grade five will score as high or higher at grade seven?

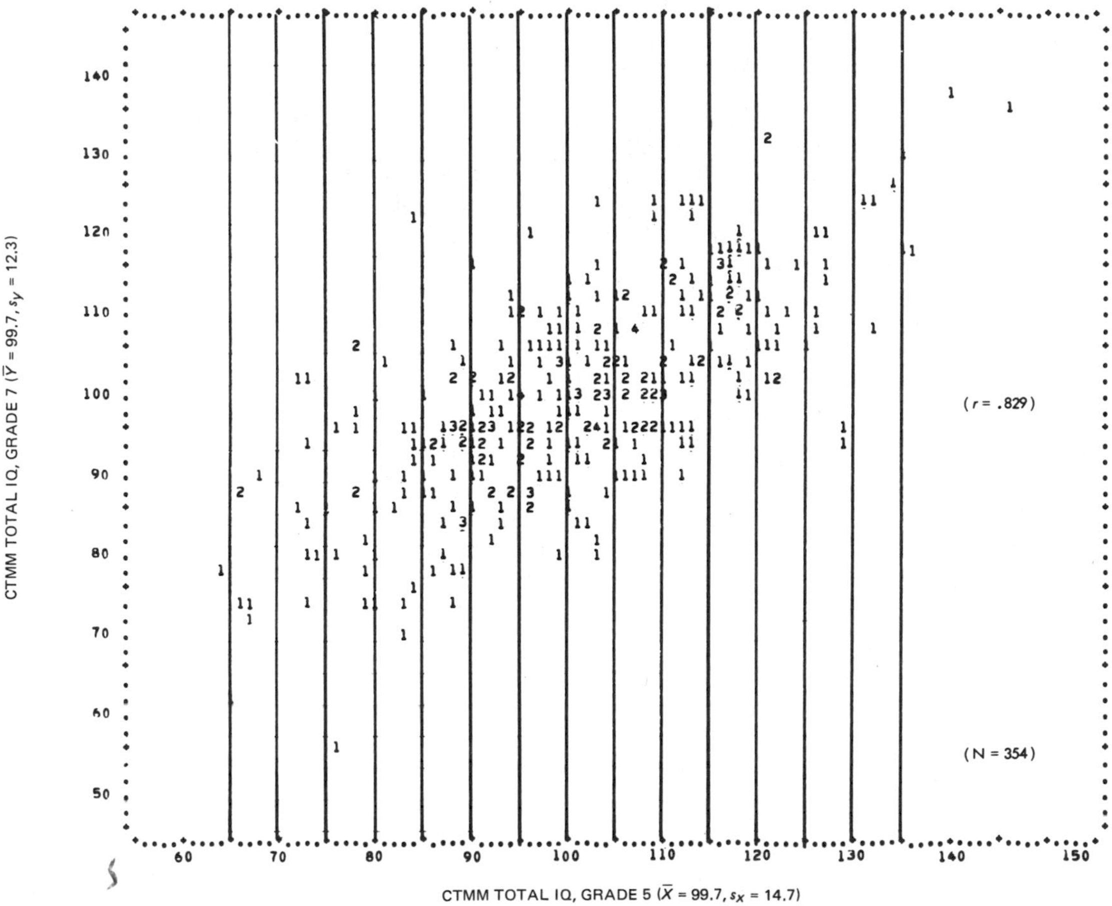


q. Assuming bivariate normality, for every 1,000 persons scoring 70 at grade five, how many would be expected to receive "average" scores of 100 or better at grade seven?

In the same study (Hopkins and Bibelheimer, 1971), grade-three IQ scores ($\bar{W}$ = 104.4, $s_W$ = 15.6) correlated .755 and .651 with IQ scores at grades five (X) and seven (Y), respectively.

r. What is $R_{Y.XW}$?

s. How much of the grade-seven IQ variance is predictable using both $X$ and $W$ as predictors? Compare with $r^2_{YX}$. Does variable $W$ add substantial relevant variance to that found in variable $X$? Determine the standardized multiple regression equation:

$$\hat{z}_{Y_i} = \hat{\beta}_X X_i + \hat{\beta}_W W_i$$

u. Persons who exceeded $\bar{X}$ and $\bar{W}$ each by one standard deviation, tended to exceed $\bar{Y}$ by ___ standard deviation.

v. Determine the raw-score multiple regression equation:

$$\hat{Y}_i = b_X X_i + b_W W_i$$

w. Predict the grade seven IQ score for a pupil having an IQ score of 140 at grades three and five. Compare with part i.
x. Correct $R_{Y.XW}$ to estimate the corresponding parameter. Why does $\hat{R}_{Y.XW}$ differ so little from $R_{Y.XW}$?
y. What is the correlation between IQ scores as grades five and seven for persons who had the same IQ score at grade three (i.e., hold grade three IQ scores constant).
z. By inspecting the scatterplot, how would the value of $\hat{\eta}_{Y.X}$ compare with $r_{YX}$?

2. In the national standardization of the Lorge-Thorndike Intelligence Test and the Iowa Test of Basic Skills, nonverbal IQ scores correlated .82 with reading grade-equivalent scores at grade eight:

| | *IQ* | *Reading* |
|---|---|---|
| $\mu$ | 100 | 8.0 |
| $\sigma$ | 15 | 2.0 |

$\rho = .82$

a. Determine the regression equation to predict grade-equivalent scores in reading from the nonverbal IQ scores. Assume bivariate normality.
b. What is the average reading score for persons with IQ scores of 100 at grade 8.0?
c. Persons with IQ scores of 90 have what average reading score at grade 8.0?
d. Compare the percentile equivalents in exercise 2c for $X$ and $\hat{Y}$.
e. What percentage of the entering eighth-grade pupils with IQ = 90 read above grade level (8.0)? What is the value of $s_{Y.X}$?
f. What percentage of students at grade 8.0 with IQ = 90, score 9.1 or higher on the reading test?
g. What is the average reading score for beginning eighth graders at $P_{98}$ on the intelligence test?
h. What is the reading score in percentile units? (See 2g above.)
i. What percentage of students at grade 8.0 with IQ scores of 130, obtain reading scores below grade level (8.0)?

3. One large remedial reading study selected seventh-grade students who were reading 2.0 grades or more below grade level (7.0) on a standardized reading test. These students were given special reading treatment and tested one year later with the standardized reading test. The mean scores of the treated groups increased 1.4 grade equivalents from 4.5 to 5.9 during the year interval between the pretest and posttest. Answer the remaining exercises using the following information given from the test manual; assume these "norms" were based on a large representative sample that was tested at the beginning of grade seven (7.0), and again one year later (8.0).

| *Grade 7* | *Grade 8* |
|---|---|
| $\bar{X} = 7.0$ | $\bar{Y} = 8.0$ |
| $s_X = 1.8$ | $s_Y = 1.9$ |

$r = .8$

a. What is the regression coefficient $b$?
b. What is the intercept $c$?
c. What is the predicted score on the posttest, corresponding to the mean pretest score for the treated group?
d. How does the actual gain compare with the predicted gain?

4. The correlation of the mother's height is about .5 with the height of her sons or daughters. The correlation of the father's height with his offspring is the same. The correlation of heights of husbands and wives has been found to be approximately .3.
   a. How accurately can children's height be predicted—that is, what is the multiple correlation—using the height of both parents as predictors?
   b. Other things being equal, what would be the multiple correlation if, instead of .3, the husband-wife correlation were 0.0?
   c. Other things being equal, what would be the effect on $R$ if the husband-wife correlation were greater than .3?
   d. Estimate the correlation between height of mother ($M$) and of daughter ($D$) with no variation in father's height ($F$). For example, for 1,000 daughters whose fathers are 5 ft 8 in., what is the correlation between the daughters' height with their mothers' heights?
   e. Why is $r_{DM.F}$ less than $r_{DM}$ in Exercise 4d?
   f. Commercial speed-reading clinics often quote research showing the correlation of reading speed ($S$) with reading comprehension ($C$), suggesting that if speed is improved, comprehension will also be enhanced. The partial correlation between speed and comprehension drops to nearly zero when intelligence is partialed out. Explain.
5. If teaching success could be predicted in advance, the information could be used for selection purposes. The predictability of teaching ability of graduate teaching assistants was studied using various predictors including Graduate Record Examination verbal ($V$) and quantitative ($Q$) scores and undergraduate GPA($G$) (Vecchio and Costin, 1977). Student satisfaction ratings on a five-point scale were used as the criterion ($Y$). The results are given:

| | *Q* | *G* | *Y* | *s* | *Mean* |
|---|---|---|---|---|---|
| *V* | .53 | .32 | .34 | 75 | 623 |
| *Q* | | .16 | .17 | 87 | 637 |
| *G* | | | .00 | .30 | 4.56 |
| *Y* | | | | .41 | 3.67 |

   a. Determine Step 1 of the stepwise multiple regression equation $\hat{Y}_i = bX_i + c$.
   b. From the partial correlations $r_{YQ.V}$ and $r_{YG.V}$ determine which predictor variable will be added in Step 2.
   c. Determine the standardized multiple regression equation at Step 2.
   d. What is the $\hat{z}_Y$ for a person who is $+1s$ above the mean of both predictor variables?
   e. Determine the multiple regression equation at Step 2 in raw-score form.
   f. What is the predicted criterion score for a person with $V = 700$ and $G = 3.2$?
   g. What is the multiple correlation $R_{Y.VG}$ associated with Step 2?
   h. How much of the variance in the criterion is predictable using $V$ and $G$?
   i. If Step 3 were carried out, would $R_{Y.VGQ}$ be negligibly increased over $R_{Y.VG}$? If the proportion of variance in $Y$ that is predictable from $V$, $G$, and $Q$ is .1225, what is $R_{Y.VGQ}$?

## *ANSWERS TO MASTERY TEST*

1. d
2. b
3. a
4. $\hat{z}_Y = 1.00$
5. c
6. c

7. +.9
8. Not necessarily, but each pair would have identical $z_X$ and $z_Y$ scores.
9. Yes
10. Yes, $\hat{z}_Y = .8z_X$
11. Yes
12. No, it decreases.
13. Yes, $b_{Y.X} = r\left(\frac{s_Y}{s_X}\right) = r\left(\frac{15}{15}\right) = r$
14. Yes
15. Yes (but not in raw-score units)
16. $s_{Y.X} = 10\sqrt{1 - .36} = 8$
17. a. 68%
    b. 16%
    c. yes
18. a. 115
    b. 95
    c. 100
19. 15(.8) = 12
20. 68%
21. High; low
22. a
23. A–l
    B–a
    C–b
    D–c
    E–d
    F–g
    G–f
    H–k
    I–h
    J–j
    K–e
    L–i
24. a
25. b
26. b
27. e
28. .577
29. B
30. C
31. 35.9, 33.5
32. 2.0
33. $\sqrt{.5} = .707$
34. b
35. c
36. b
37. a
38. Yes, no

## *ANSWERS TO PROBLEMS AND EXERCISES*

1. a. 64 and 146
   b. 55 and 138
   c. Yes
   d. Yes
   e. Yes
   f. $b_{Y.X} = \dfrac{.829(12.3)}{14.7} = .694$
   g. $c = 99.7 - (.694)(99.7) = 30.5$
   h. $\hat{Y} = .694X + 30.5$
   i. $\hat{Y} = .694(140) + 30.5 = 128$
   j. $\hat{Y} = .694(70) + 30.5 = 79$
   l. $s_{Y.X} = 12.3\sqrt{1 - (.829)^2} = 12.3(.559) = 6.88$ or approximately seven points
   m. approximately 68%
   o. 121, 135(128 ± 7); 72, 86(79 ± 7)
   p. $\dfrac{Y - \hat{Y}}{s_{Y.X}} = \dfrac{140 - 128}{6.88} = 1.74$; from Appendix Table A; only 4%
   q. $\dfrac{Y - \hat{Y}}{s_{Y.X}} = \dfrac{100 - 79}{6.88} = 3.05$; from Appendix Table A; only about one person per 1,000.
   r. .830
   s. .6887 is negligibly greater than .6872
   t. $\hat{z}_{Y_i} = .785z_{X_i} + .058z_{W_i}$
   u. .84
   v. $\hat{Y}_i = .657X_i + .046W_i + 29.4$
   w. $\hat{Y} = 127.8$ or 128
   x. $\hat{R}_{Y.XW} = .829$ because $n$ is large and $m$ is only 2.
   y. $R_{YX.W} = .678$
   z. Eta would be negligibly larger than $r$ because the relationship is linear.

2. a. $b = \frac{(.82)(2.0)}{15} = .11;$
$c = 8.0 - (.11)(100)$
$= -2.93; \hat{Y} = bX + c$
$= .11X - 2.93$

b. 8.0

c. $\hat{Y} = .11(90) - 3 = 9.9 - 3 = 6.9$

d. An IQ of 90 is equivalent to $z = \frac{90 - 100}{15} = -.67$, and from Appendix Table B, $P_{25}$; a reading score of 6.9 is equivalent to $\frac{6.9 - 8.0}{2.0} = -.55$, and from Table B; $P_{29}$.

e. $\hat{Y} = 6.9;$
$s_{Y.X} = 2.0\sqrt{1 - (.82)^2}$
$= 2.0(.572) = 1.1$; hence,
$z = \frac{8.0 - 6.9}{1.1} = 1.0;$
hence, only 16%

f. $z = \frac{9.1 - 6.9}{1.1} = 2.0;$
hence, about 2%

g. $P_{98}$ = IQ of 130, $\hat{Y} = .11(130) - 3 = 11.3$

h. $z = \frac{11.3 - 8.0}{2.0} = \frac{3.3}{2.0}$
$= 1.65$ or $P_{95}$

i. $z = \frac{8.0 - 11.3}{1.1} = -3$ or .13%

3. a. $b = r\left(\frac{s_Y}{s_X}\right) = .8\left(\frac{1.9}{1.8}\right) = .84$

b. $c = \overline{Y} - b\overline{X} = 8.0 - (.84)(7.0)$
$= 2.1$

c. $\hat{Y} = (.84)(4.5) + 2.1 = 5.9$

d. They are equal: 1.4 grade equivalents.

4. a. $R^2 = .385; R = .62$

b. $R^2 = .5; R = .71$

c. $R$ would decrease.

d. $r_{DM.F} = .42$

e. Since $R_{MF}$ is greater than zero, if we hold the father's height constant, we restrict the variance in the mother's height, and, other things being equal, the less the variance in $X$, the lower the correlation $r_{YX}$. (See Fig. 8.4.)

f. The correlation between speed and comprehension appears to result from the correlation of each with IQ. For persons of the same IQ, there is little correlation between speed and comprehension. Hence, since an increase in reading speed will not increase IQ, it would be expected to have little effect on comprehension.

5. a. $\hat{Y}_i = .00186V_i + 2.51$

b. $r_{YQ.V} = -.013, r_{YG.V}$
$= -.122$; $G$ will be selected since its absolute value is greatest.

c. $\hat{z}_{Y_i} = .379z_{V_i} - .121z_{G_i}$

d. .258

e. $\hat{Y}_i = .00207V_i - .165G_i + 3.133$

f. 4.06

g. .349

h. .122 or 12.2%

i. Yes, .35

# 9
# PROBABILITY

## 9.1 INTRODUCTION

Researchers often attempt to generalize from their observations. Even when they are most cautious and least want to make inferences, they sometimes make a tacit assumption that the set of data has some generalizibility—if they gathered more data tomorrow, it would reflect approximately, though not exactly, the same trend. Inferences differ in their likelihood of being correct all the way from "extremely unlikely" to "almost certain." From the standpoint of logic, all inferences contain uncertainty.

Much of the work of the statistician is the development of methods that assign probabilities to inferences. This is indeed a useful endeavor. Inferential reasoning is a principal method of science. The imprecise language of everyday life—"extremely unlikely" or "almost certain"—does not serve research purposes very well. It is far better when researchers can independently arrive at a statement regarding the probability that an inference is correct—that the statement can be made in unambiguous terms that convey the same meaning for all.

Statisticians are not unanimous on deciding how to assign probabilities to statements or choosing to which statements to assign probabilities. Nonetheless, their preference for objectivity and quantification springs from values regarding the nature and methods of science. Their systems are open for all to see, and to understand. Although statisticians do not always agree on the proper method, their methods of assigning probabilities to inferences are far better than the use of everyday language and unquantified subjective estimates.

Many of the remaining chapters deal with assigning a probability value to an inference. The methods that statisticians have developed that allow one to state, for example, "There is a positive relationship between IQ and grade-point average, and the probability is only .01 that the statement is not true," will be examined. One can expect to learn only certain basics of probability in a single chapter: probability is a large and complex body of knowledge. One can learn enough, however, to make the probability statements associated with inferential statistics meaningful.

## 9.2 PROBABILITY AS A MATHEMATICAL SYSTEM

Probability can be viewed as a system of definitions and operations pertaining to a *sample space*. The idea of a sample space is basic. Every probability statement is related to a sample space of some sort. Indeed, statements of probability are simple statements about sample spaces and their characteristics.

The notion of a sample space is actually a relatively recent development in probability theory, dating back only to the 1920s and the work of von Mises (1931). A *sample space* is a set of points. These points can represent anything: persons, numbers, balls, and so on. An *event* is an observable happening like the appearance of "heads" when a coin is flipped, or the observation that a person about to be selected at random from a telephone book is watching television. There may be several points in the sample space, each of which is an example of an event. For instance, the sample space may be a set of six white and three black balls in an urn. This sample space has nine points. An event might be "A ball is white." This event has six sample-space points. How many points in the sample space does the event "A ball is black" have? The event "A ball in this urn is red" has no sample points. "A ball in this urn is either white or black" is also an example of an event. Notice that many different events can be defined on the same sample space.

A statement of probability is made about the relative frequency of an event that is associated with a sample space. A capital letter, $A$, $B$, $C$, . . . , will stand for an event; the "probability of the event $A$" will be denoted by $P(A)$.

Definition: The probability of the event $A$, $P(A)$, is the ratio of the number of sample points that are examples of $A$ to the total (finite) number of sample points in the sample space, assuming all sample points are equally likely.

Let $A$ be the event "a '3' when a die is cast," where the sample space is the set of the six faces of a die. How many sample points are examples of the event $A$? Obviously, the answer is 1. What is the total number of sample points? The answer is 6. Hence, the probability of the event $A$ ("3") is

$$P(A) = \frac{\text{Number of examples of A}}{\text{Total number of sample points}} = \frac{1}{6} \tag{9.1}$$

If $B$ is the "an even numeral" in this die-tossing example, find $P(B)$. $B$ can be restated as "a 2 or 4 or 6". Since $B$ consists of three points in the sample space of six points, $p(B) = \frac{3}{6} = \frac{1}{2}$. What is $P(C)$ if $C$ is the event "7?" $P(C)$ is $\frac{0}{7} = 0$, since "7" is not in the sample space of this problem. If $D$ is the event "an even or odd numeral," what is $P(D)$? The answer is $\frac{6}{6} = 1$.

Suppose there is an urn which has four white balls in it and a finite but unspecified number of black balls. The probability of an event cannot be determined. A probability statement can be made only when the sample space is defined completely.

There exists an alternative route by which the definition of the probability of an event can be expressed. Consider a sample space composed of a specified number of sample points. Denote each of the sample points by "$a_i$": $a_1, a_2, \ldots, a_n$. Every event that is defined within the sample space is composed of a related set of sample points.

Definition: A probability function is a rule of correspondence that associates with each event $A$ in the sample space a number $P(A)$ such that

1. $P(A) \neq 0$, for any event $A$
2. The sum of the probabilities for all distinct events is 1
3. If $A$ and $B$ are mutually exclusive events, that is, have no sample points in common, the $P(A \text{ or } B) = P(A) + P(B)$.

If it is assumed that the probability of every elementary event $a_i$ is $1/N$, where $N$ is the total number of sample points, then the probability of the event $A$ that is composed of $n$ sample points is

$$P(A) = \frac{1}{N} + \frac{1}{N} + \cdots + \frac{1}{N} = \frac{n}{N} \tag{9.2}$$

The probability of event $A$, $P(A)$, is the ratio of the number of sample points that are examples of $A$ to the total number of sample points, $N$, that is, $n/N$.

Both routes bring us to the same definition for $P(A)$. While the second definition might have the preference of the mathematician, the first definition of $P(A)$ is easier to comprehend.

## Combining Probabilities

Suppose an urn contains five red, three white, and two black balls. Three events might be of interest: (1) $A$, a ball is red, (2) $B$, a ball is white, or (3) $C$, a ball is black. These three events are *mutually exclusive*: each sample point is an example of one and only one event.

The question arises, "What is the probability that a ball is red *or* white?" This event, the "union" of $A$ and $B$, shall be denoted by the symbol $A \cup B$ and its probability by $P(A \cup B)$.

# 9.3 FIRST ADDITION RULE OF PROBABILITIES

*When the events $A$ and $B$ are mutually exclusive, $P(A \cup B)$, the probability of either $A$ or $B$ is*

$$P(A \cup B) = P(A) + P(B) \tag{9.3}$$

In the example,

$$P(A \cup B) = P(A) + P(B) = \frac{5}{10} + \frac{3}{10} = \frac{8}{10} \quad \text{or} \quad .8$$

Find $P(A \cup C) = P(A) + P(C)$; [.5 + .2 = .7]. What is the value of $P(B \cup C)$? [.3 + .2 = .5].

## Nonindependent Events

In some sample spaces two events may not be mutually exclusive; a single sample point may be an example of both events $A$ and $B$. A playing card can be both an ace and a diamond. Consider the possible outcomes ("heads" or "tails") of flipping a fair coin three times in a row. The eight possible outcomes make up the sample space:

1. H H H
2. H H T
3. H T H
4. H T T
5. T H H
6. T H T
7. T T H
8. T T T

Assume that each of the eight outcomes is equally likely, that is, each has probability $\frac{1}{8}$. What is the probability of "heads" on the first "flip?" The answer is $\frac{4}{8}$ or $\frac{1}{2}$. What is the probability of "heads" on flips 1 *and* 2? The answer is $\frac{2}{8}$ or $\frac{1}{4}$.

Now define two events, $A$ and $B$, using the sample space just defined:

$A$: "'heads' on flips 1 and 2"
$B$: "'heads' on flips 2 and 3"

The sample points that are examples of event $A$ are the first two events (*HHH* and *HHT*) in the sample space. The first and fifth outcomes (*HHH* and *THH*) are the sample points corresponding to event $B$. The symbol $A \cap B$ shall denote the new event, the "intersection" of $A$ and $B$. (Note the symbols "$\cup$" and "$\cap$" are analogous to the words "or" and "and.") In the example, $A \cap B$ is the event "heads" on flips 1 and 2 *and* "heads" on flips 2 and 3. *Assuming that all the sample points are equally likely, the probability of the event $A \cap B$ is*

$$P(A \cap B) = \frac{\text{Number of sample points that are examples of } A \cap B}{\text{Total number of sample points}} \tag{9.4}$$

The total number of sample points is 8. Only one sample point, *HHH*, is an example of the event $A$ ("'heads' on flips 1 and 2") *and* $B$ ("'heads' on flips 2 and 3"). So the probability of the event $A \cap B$ is $\frac{1}{8}$.

Look back at the first addition rule of probabilities (Sec. 9.3) and notice the condition that the two events $A$ and $B$ are mutually exclusive. In the example just discussed $A$ and $B$ were not mutually exclusive. The outcome *HHH* was an example of both events $A$ and $B$. But what is the probability of $A$ or $B$, $P(A \cup B)$, when $A$ and $B$ are *not* mutually exclusive?

## 9.4 SECOND ADDITION RULE OF PROBABILITIES

*The probability of either event A or event B or both,* $P(A \cup B)$, *is* $P(A) + P(B) - P(A \cap B)$.

This expression might look strange; a Venn diagram (Fig. 9.1) illustrating the relationship between the events defined within sample spaces should help clear up the mystery of the term "$-P(A \cap B)$." The events $A$ and $B$ are not mutually exclusive, that is, they have sample points in common in the sample space $S$. It is assumed that the probability of event $A$ is represented by the area of circle $A$ and that the probability of event $B$ is represented by the area of circle $B$.

The probability of $A$ or $B$, or both, is that area covered by the intersecting circles, $A$ and $B$. The shaded portion in Figure 9.1 is that set of sample points in both events $A$ and $B$, that is, those points in the intersection $A \cap B$.

How does one find the entire area covered by $A$ and $B$? First, find the area of $A$ that is not shared by $B$. Add to it the area of $B$ not shared by $A$, and then add the area of *A and B*:

$$P(A \cup B) = [P(A) - P(A \cap B)] + [P(B) - P(A \cap B)] + P(A \cap B)$$

The first two terms following the equal sign, $P(A) - P(A \cap B)$, give the area of $A$ minus the area in common with $B$. $P(B) - P(A \cap B)$ gives the area of $B$ minus its area in common with $A$. The desired area is found by adding in the area common to $A$ and $B$, $P(A \cap B)$. The previous equation simplifies to

$$P(A \cup B) = P(A) + P(B) - P(A \cap B) \qquad \textbf{(9.5)}$$

Hence the second addition rule of probabilities has been established. Notice that if one had simply added $P(A)$ and $P(B)$ to find $P(A \cup B)$, the portion in common to $A$ and $B$, $P(A \cap B)$, would contribute twice to the sum, since $A$ and $B$ are not mutually exclusive areas. The intersection must be restored only once, so consequently it must be subtracted as shown in Equation 9.5.

Notice the first addition rule of probabilities (Eq. 9.3) is just a special case of the second rule (Eq. 9.5), that is, the case when $P(A \cap B) = 0$.

If $A$ and $B$ are mutually exclusive events in $S$, then they do not overlap. See

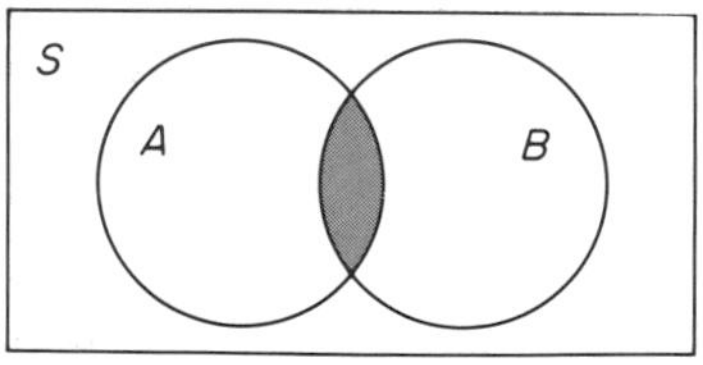


**FIGURE 9.1**
**Venn diagram of the intersecting events $A$ and $B$ in the sample space $S$.**

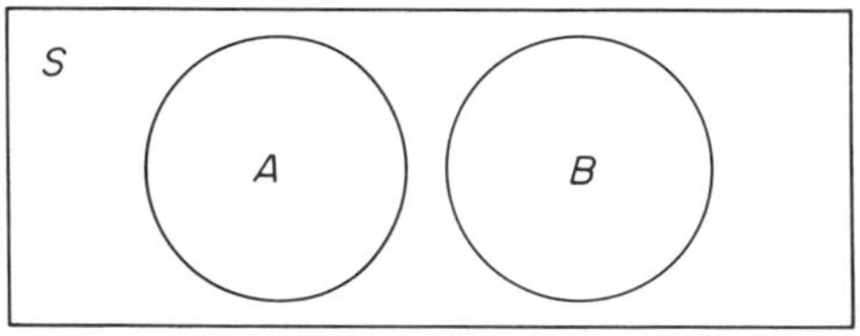


**FIGURE 9.2**
**Venn diagram of the mutually exclusive events $A$ and $B$ in the sample space $S$.**

Figure 9.2, where there is no area in common to $A$ and $B$; hence $P(A \cap B) = 0$. More generally, $P(A \cup B) = P(A) + P(B) - P(A \cap B)$. But if $A$ and $B$ are mutually exclusive, then $P(A \cap B) = 0$. Therefore, if $A$ and $B$ are mutually exclusive then

$$P(A \cup B) = P(A) + P(B) - 0 = P(A) + P(B)$$

So far probability has been treated rather abstractly. In much the same manner as the mathematical systems of geometry and algebra, probability theory can be developed from a small set of axioms and definitions. But also in the same manner as geometry and algebra, probability theory can serve as a model for what is going on in a certain class of events in the world around us.

James Bernoulli (1654–1705) was the first to relate probability statements to physical events. An example of the application of a formal probability statement to an actual set of actions will illustrate the relationship between theory and application.

Suppose an urn contains four white and six black balls. The balls are identical in size, shape, and weight and thoroughly mixed so that if one were to reach in and pull one out, it is equally likely that any one of the ten balls would be selected; each ball has one chance in ten of being chosen. A ball is taken out and its color is recorded. The ball is returned to the urn, the balls in the urn are stirred thoroughly, and the act is repeated under the same conditions. This act is performed a very large number of times, say, 10,000. After the ten-thousandth drawing of a ball, suppose a count is taken of the number of times a white ball was drawn. Intuition says that the ratio of the number of times a white ball is drawn to 10,000 will be very close to $\frac{4}{10}$. It is unlikely the ratio is exactly $\frac{4}{10}$, but it will be very close.

If the ten balls are regarded as a sample space, and if $A$ is the event "a ball is white," then $P(A)$ is exactly $\frac{4}{10}$. The question arises, "Will the formal probability of an event as calculated from theory correspond closely to the relative frequency of the occurrence of the event?" The answer to this question is the key to the relationship of probability theory and its application. The answer is "yes" when the underlying assumptions are closely approximated. Suppose an event $A$ either does or does not occur on every trial of an act. The probability that $A$ will occur, $P(A)$, is the same for all trials of the act. For example, the act may be flipping a fair coin, $A$ may be the event "heads," and it is assumed that the probability of heads ($\frac{1}{2}$) is the same from one flip to the next. It is also assumed that every trial is *independent* of (in no way affected by) every other trial. Now after $n$ trials of the act, the proportion of times $A$ has occurred is $p$. It can be proved that $p$ gets closer and closer to $P(A)$ as $n$ becomes larger and larger. The proportion of times $A$ occurs can be made closer and closer to $P(A)$ (the probability calculated from the sample space) by performing the act an increasing number of times. So $P(A)$ tells what will happen *in the long run* if the actions under the conditions laid down previously are actually performed.

The preceding paragraph is a statement of the *law of large numbers*. The law of large numbers is important for the application of probability, of which statistical inference is one such application. The law of large numbers is closely related to the statistical property of consistency, encountered previously in Chapter 5.

## 9.5 MULTIPLICATIVE RULE OF PROBABILITIES

There exists a multiplicative rule for probabilities that will be of considerable importance in later work. Suppose a coin is flipped five times in a row. Assume that the probability of "heads" is $\frac{1}{2}$ on each flip and that the flips are independent (the outcomes are uncorrelated and have no influence on one another). The *multiplicative rule for probabilities* states that the probability of getting five straight "heads" is $\frac{1}{2} \cdot \frac{1}{2} \cdot \frac{1}{2} \cdot \frac{1}{2} \cdot \frac{1}{2} = \frac{1}{32}$. A general statement of the rule follows:

Multiplicative Rule of Probabilities: The probability that $A$, which has probability $P(A)$ of occurring on any one trial, will occur $n$ times in $n$ independent trials is

$$P(A) \cdot P(A) \cdot \ldots \cdot P(A) = P(A)^n \tag{9.6}$$

### An Illustration

The following examples illustrate the probability rules developed so far. Consider a roll of a pair of dice; one die is red and the other is green. The sample space of possible outcomes has 36 points, as shown in Table 9.1. Let event $A$ be "a 1 on the red die" and event $B$ "a 1 on the green die." $P(A \cap B)$ is found by dividing the number of sample points that are examples of $A \cap B$ (both $A$ and $B$) by the total number of sample points (36). Verify that the probability that both $A$ and $B$ occur: $P(A \cap B)$ is equal to $P(A) \cdot P(B)$, or $\frac{1}{6} \cdot \frac{1}{6} = \frac{1}{36}$.

Find $P(A \cup B)$, the probability of event $A$ or event $B$, remembering that $P(A \cup B) = P(A) + P(B) - P(A \cap B)$. $P(A \cap B)$ is $\frac{1}{36}$ since only the point "1, 1" is common to $A$ and $B$; thus, $P(A \cup B) = \frac{6}{36} + \frac{6}{36} - \frac{1}{36} = \frac{11}{36}$.

Two events are independent if and only if $P(A \cap B) = P(A) \cdot P(B)$. Independence is an important concept in statistics and probability, and more will be said about it later.

**TABLE 9.1 Sample Space of Outcomes of Tossing a Pair of Dice**

| | | | | | |
|---|---|---|---|---|---|
| 1, 1 | 2, 1 | 3, 1 | 4, 1 | 5, 1 | 6, 1 |
| 1, 2 | 2, 2 | 3, 2 | 4, 2 | 5, 2 | 6, 2 |
| 1, 3 | 2, 3 | 3, 3 | 4, 3 | 5, 3 | 6, 3 |
| 1, 4 | 2, 4 | 3, 4 | 4, 4 | 5, 4 | 6, 4 |
| 1, 5 | 2, 5 | 3, 5 | 4, 5 | 5, 5 | 6, 5 |
| 1, 6 | 2, 6 | 3, 6 | 4, 6 | 5, 6 | 6, 6 |

## 9.6 CONDITIONAL PROBABILITY

*If $P(A)$ and $P(B)$ are known, the "conditional" probability of B given A, that is, $P(B|A)$, is*

$$P(B|A) = \frac{P(A \cap B)}{P(A)} \tag{9.7}$$

In Figure 9.1 note that the conditional probability $P(B|A)$ (read "the probability of $B$ given $A$") is represented by the ratio of the area $A \cap B$ to the area $A$. In the example in Section 9.5, $P(A) = \frac{1}{6}$ and $P(A \cap B) = \frac{1}{36}$; thus using Equation 9.7, the probability of $B$ given $A$ is $\frac{1}{36} \div \frac{1}{6} = \frac{1}{6}$. Given $A$ (a "1 on die 1"), the probability of $B$ (a "1 on die 2") is $\frac{1}{6}$.

Suppose that the sample space is American adults and $B$ is "a woman" and $A$ is "a college graduate." Given that a college graduate is selected, what is the probability that it is a woman, that is, what is $P(B|A)$? Currently, the probability of selecting a college graduate is $.26 = P(A)$, and the probability of selecting a woman college graduate is $.115 = P(A \cap B)$. Given $A$, that a college graduate is selected, the probability of $B$, a woman, is

$$P(B|A) = \frac{.115}{.26} = .44$$

Notice that $P(B|A)$ is not equal to $P(A|B)$. In this example given $B$ (a woman), $P(B) = .5$, the probability of $A$ (a college graduate) is:

$$P(A|B) = \frac{P(A \cap B)}{P(B)} = \frac{.115}{.5} = .23$$

## 9.7 BAYES' THEOREM

Equation 9.7 is the simplest version of Bayes' theorem,* a theorem that describes the relationship among various conditional probabilities. Equation 9.7 may be expressed alternatively as

$$P(B|A) = \frac{P(A|B)\,P(B)}{P(A|B)\,P(B) + P(A|\overline{B})\,P(\overline{B})} \tag{9.8}$$

where $\overline{B}$ is read "not $B$."

*The theorem is named for its originator, the English clergyman and mathematician Thomas Bayes (1702–1761), who first used probability inductively and established a mathematical basis for probabilistic inference.

Let event $B$ be "an automobile accident during the next year" and event $A$ be "a course in driver education." What is the probability of event $B$ (an accident in the next year), given $A$ (driver education), that is, what is $P(B|A)$? Assume that $P(B) = .1$; thus $P(\bar{B}) = 1 - P(B) = .9$. Also assume that $P(A|B)$, the probability of having driver education given that a person has had an accident, is .50, and that $P(A|\bar{B})$, the probability of having driver education given that a person has not had an accident, is .7. From Equation 9.8, the probability of an accident ($B$) given driver education ($A$) is

$$P(B|A) = \frac{(.5)(.1)}{(.5)(.1) + (.7)(.9)} = \frac{.05}{.68} = .0735$$

Thus the probability of an accident has been reduced by 26.5%, from .10 to .0735, given the person had driver education.

Bayes' theorem provides exact results, providing the "prior" probabilities (the probabilities entered into Eq. 9.8) are accurate. Obviously the practical difficulty in the application of the theorem lies in knowing the prior probabilities. These probabilities have often been viewed as degrees of belief ("personal probabilities"). The topic has occasioned much controversy among statisticians who favor a strict relative-frequency interpretation of probability and those who would allow for a more subjective interpretation.

## 9.8 PERMUTATIONS

Two additional concepts that crop up repeatedly in probability illustrations are *permutations* and *combinations* (Sec. 9.9).

*A permutation of a set of objects* (the letters A, B, and C, for example) *is an arrangement of them in which order is considered.* A different ordering of the objects is a different permutation. How many different permutations (orderings) are there of the letters A, B, and C? To find out, one can set about the task of writing them down and counting them, as shown in Table 9.2.

The first letter can be either A, B, or C. Suppose it is A (this is the top third of Table 9.2). If the first letter is A, the second letter can be either B or C. If the second letter is B, then the third letter must be C. So ABC is one possible permutation. There are three possible letters for the first position. After one letter is assigned to the first

**TABLE 9.2 Permutations of Three Letters: A, B, and C.**

| *1st letter* | *2nd letter* | *3rd letter* | *Permutation* |
|---|---|---|---|
| A | B | C | 1. A B C |
| | C | B | 2. A C B |
| B | A | C | 3. B A C |
| | C | A | 4. B C A |
| C | A | B | 5. C A B |
| | B | A | 6. C B A |

position, there are two possible letters for the second position. Hence the number of possible permutations of the three letters A, B, and C is (3)(2)(1) = 6.

*If there are n distinct objects, one can make* $n(n-1)(n-2)\cdots(2)(1)$ *different permutations of them.* Instead of writing $n(n-1)(n-2)\cdots(2)(1)$, one can denote this product simply by $n!$ (read "$n$ factorial"). $n!$ is the product of the numbers from 1 through $n$ and equals the number of permutations of $n$ distinct objects. (0! is defined to equal 1.)

The value of $n!$ increases dramatically as $n$ increases. Would you work for 10! pennies a year? Most people would, since 10! = 3,628,800 or $36,288! To give an idea of the size of 12!, imagine that you have one dozen eggs in a carton and that you want to form every possible permutation (arrangement) of them in an egg carton. Assume you can make a new arrangement every minute of your eight-hour working day. If you keep at this job five days a week fifty-two weeks a year, you would require longer than 3,500 years to make every possible arrangement! Descendants of a family who began at the start of the Roman Empire would not yet be finished.

## 9.9 COMBINATIONS

The concept of combinations arises when one is selecting some number $r$ of objects from a set of $n$ objects, where $r \neq n$. *A combination of objects is a distinct set of objects in which order is not considered.* When $r = n$, that is, $n$ objects are selected from $n$ objects, all the objects are selected and there is only one combination. If $r = 1$, one object is selected from $n$ objects, and there are $n$ combinations. The problem is to find a general expression for the number of combinations that exist when $r$ things are selected from $n$.

Consider four objects, A, B, C, and D. How many different combinations can be made by selecting two letters at a time from these four? The answer is six: AB, AC, AD, BC, BD, CD. Notice that for combinations, order is not considered; AB is one combination, and BA is the same combination. (See the first two columns of Table 9.2, where the six permutations form three combinations.)

Suppose $r$ objects are being selected from $n$ objects. How many different combinations are there? For the time being, regard order as important, and then later combine all the sets that are different only because of order. If $r$ objects are being selected from $n$, then there are $n$ choices for the first object, $(n-1)$ choices for the second, $(n-2)$ for third, $(n-3)$ for the fourth, and so on until there are $(n-r+1)$ choices for the $r$th object. So *the total of different permutations of r objects from n objects, where order is considered, is equal to*

$$n(n-1)(n-2)\ldots(n-r+1) \qquad \textbf{(9.9)}$$

How many permutations are there for $n = 4$ objects, taking $r = 3$ at a time? The answer is 4(3)(2) = 24 permutations (see Eq. 9.9). There are $r$ terms in this product corresponding to the $r$ objects selected. However, for each unique combination of $r$ objects, there are $r!$ permutations; in the example, $r = 3$ and $r! = 3! = 6$. Hence *the number of combinations of r objects selected from n objects such that the order among the r objects is not considered, is the number of permutations of the n objects* (Eq. 9.9) *divided by the number of permutations within a combination.*

$$\binom{n}{r} = \frac{n(n-1)(n-2)\ldots(n-r+1)}{r!} \tag{9.10}$$

The symbol $\binom{n}{r}$ denotes "the number of combinations of $r$ things taken from $n$ things."

It can be shown* that the number of permutations of $r$ objects taken from $n$ objects is

$$n(n-1)(n-2)\ldots(n-r+1) = \frac{n!}{(n-r)!} \tag{9.11}$$

When this substitution is made in Equation 9.10, the number of combinations of $n$ things taken $r$ at a time is given by

$$\binom{n}{r} = \frac{n!}{r!\,(n-r)} \tag{9.12}$$

## Examples

How many different combinations are there of $r = 3$ things taken from $n = 5$ things?

$$\binom{5}{3} = \frac{5!}{3!(5-3)!} = \frac{5!}{3!2!} = \frac{5\cdot 4\cdot \not{3}\cdot \not{2}\cdot \not{1}}{(\not{3}\cdot \not{2}\cdot \not{1})(2\cdot 1)} = \frac{5\cdot 4}{2\cdot 1} = \frac{20}{2} = 10$$

Note from Equation 9.9 that there are $(5)(4)(3) = 60$ permutations of five things taken three at a time. Each combination has $r! = 3! = 6$ permutations; thus the sixty permutations represent $60/6 = 10$ combinations. Each of the ten combinations of five things taken three at a time has $(3)(2)(1) = 6$ permutations.

Ten persons are eligible to serve on a committee. The committee must be composed of only five persons. How many different five-member ($r = 5$) committees could be formed from the ten available persons ($n = 10$)? From Equation 9.12

$$\binom{10}{5} = \frac{10!}{5!(10-5)!} = \frac{10\cdot 9\cdot 8\cdot 7\cdot 6\cdot 5\cdot 4\cdot 3\cdot 2\cdot 1}{(5\cdot 4\cdot 3\cdot 2\cdot 1)(5\cdot 4\cdot 3\cdot 2\cdot 1)} \quad \frac{30{,}240}{120} = 252$$

## 9.10 INTUITION AND PROBABILITY

The study of probability can be interesting and entertaining. Historically, probability concepts arose in connection with games of chance. Those who make use of probability

*Note that $n! = n(n-1)(n-2)\ldots[(n-r)+1](n-r)[(n-r)-1]\ldots(1)$. Write out $n!$ in the numerator and $(n-r)!$ in the denominator and cancel the terms common to both numerator and denominator and express $(n-r)[(n-r)-1]\ldots(1)$ as $(n-r)!$ to obtain Equation 9.11.

theory are generally awed by the intricacy and excitement of the system and the way in which it produces results which are often quite in disagreement with intuition, unless one's intuition has been developed by experience with calculated probabilities. A few examples of surprising results will illustrate the untrustworthiness of intuition.

What is the probability that at least two people in a group of twenty-three have the same birthday? Assume that the people are drawn randomly from a population of persons in which all 365 birthdates (not counting 29 February) are equally likely. Is the probability .10 or .0001 or even smaller? Actually, the probability that at least two people out of twenty-three have the same birthdate is .507! One should expect more than "coincidence" to occur in slightly more than half the groups of size twenty-three. It is practically certain that in a group of 150 persons at least two people will have the same birthdate. (See Feller, 1957, pp. 31-32.)

What is the probability that a student will obtain a score of 75 on a 100-item true false test solely from guessing randomly on each question, given that $\mu = 50\%$ and $\sigma = 5\%$?* The score of 75 is $z = 5$ standard deviations above the chance mean. From Table A in the Appendix, the probability can be read as less than one chance in 1,000,000!

The "gambler's fallacy" represents another example in which intuitive notions of probability often lead to erroneous conclusions. If the football captain has won the coin flip by calling "heads" for the first three games, should he change to "tails" on the next flip? If a craps shooter failed to throw a "7" on ten straight throws of a pair of dice, is he more likely to throw a "7" on the next throw than if he has thrown three "7's" in a row? If the first four children in a family are boys, are the chances that the next child will be a girl different from what they would be if the four previous children had been two boys and two girls or all girls? If you think so, your thinking represents the "gambler's fallacy." If the probabilities of the event in question are independent, as they appear to be in the examples above, the probability of a future event is unaffected by any pattern of past results. Regardless of the number of "heads," prior to a given toss, the probability of "heads" on the next toss of a fair coin is .5. This is confirmed by the conditional probability equation (Eq. 9.7). In the sample space of four tosses of a coin there are sixteen events (permutations): *HHHH, HHHT, HHTH, HHTT, . . . TTTH, TTTT*. If $A$ is *HHH* for the first three tosses, then $P(A) = \frac{2}{16} = \frac{1}{8}$; and if $B$ is $H$ for the fourth toss, then $P(A \cap B) = \frac{1}{16}$, the probability of head ($B$) given three previous heads ($A$), that is

$$P(B|A) = \frac{P(A \cap B)}{P(A)} = \frac{1/16}{1/8} = .5$$

## 9.11 PROBABILITY AS AN AREA

The probabilities of observing values of continuous variables, for example, height, are conveniently represented by mathematical curves known as probability distributions. Suppose a continuous random variable $X$ takes on values from 0 to 10. For example, $X$ could be the time required for students to solve a certain puzzle. A student may solve it

*$\mu = k/a$, where $k$ is the number of items on the test and $a$ is the number of response options per item. The standard deviation of the chance score is $\sigma = \sqrt{k\pi(1 - \pi)}$, where $\pi = 1/a$ (see Hopkins and Stanley, 1981).

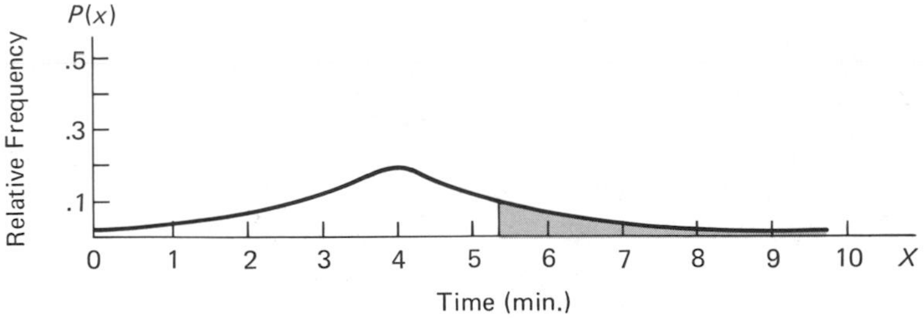


**FIGURE 9.3. The probability density function of the variable $X$, time required to solve a puzzle.**

almost immediately, or he may take as long as ten minutes. Presumably the length of time required to solve the problem is known for a huge number of different subjects. A graph is drawn in which the "time to solution" is graphed against "proportion of subjects requiring that time" (see Fig. 9.3).

The proportion of subjects requiring between two and four min. to solve the puzzle can be regarded as *the probability that a subject selected at random from the population will require between two and four min. to solve the puzzle.* The area under the curve in Figure 9.3 is 1, so the area under the curve between any two points $X_1$ and $X_2$ is the probability that a randomly selected subject will require between $X_1$ and $X_2$ minutes to solve the puzzle. The probability that a randomly selected subject will take more than 5.3 minutes is equal to the shaded area in Figure 9.3. What area corresponds to the probability that a randomly selected subject will take less than 0.5 minutes? (Theoretically, the probability of a subject's taking *exactly* four minutes, i.e., 4.000 . . . minutes is zero.) If the area under the curve in Figure 9.3 between 6 and 10 were .17, then in a group of 100 randomly chosen subjects we would expect about seventeen of them to take between six and ten minutes to solve the puzzle.

The statistician frequently plots the values a continuous random variable can assume in such a way that the area between any two values of the variable equals the probability that the variable will assume a value between those two values. The resulting graph is called a *probability density function.* The graph can often be expressed as a mathematical function in such a way that the ordinate $P(X)$ can be found by substituting any value of the random variable $X$. For example, assume $X$ is a random variable that can take on any value between 0 and 2 *with equal probability*. If $P(X) = \frac{1}{2}$ for all $X$, then the resulting graph (Fig. 9.4) will be the probability density function of $X$.

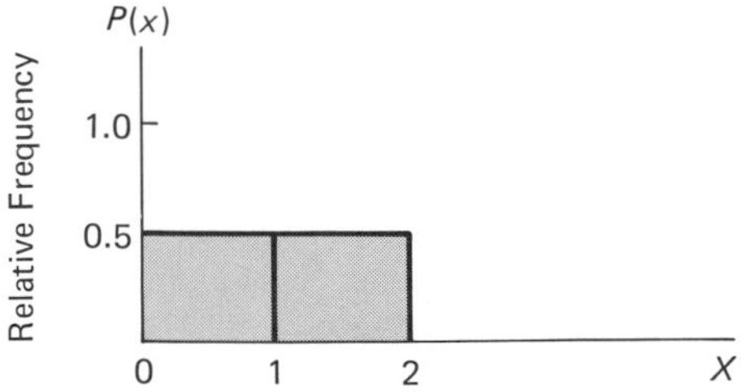


**FIGURE 9.4**
**Probability density function of the variable $X$ that assumes all possible values between 0 and 2 with equal probability.**

The area under the curve, for example, of the rectangle in Figure 9.4, is exactly 1 $(0.5 \cdot 2.0)$. The shaded area is the probability that $X$ takes on a value between 0 and 1. This probability equals .5.

## 9.12 EXPECTATIONS AND MOMENTS

Moments are characteristics of distributions defined in terms of expectations. The definition of the expectation of a random variable will be considered first.

Definition: If $X$ is a discrete random variable that takes on the values $X_1, X_2, \ldots, X_n$ with probabilities $p_1, p_2, \ldots, p_n$, then the expectation of $X$ denoted by $E(X)$ is defined as

$$E(X) = p_1 X_1 + p_2 X_2 + \ldots + p_n X_n = \sum_{j=1}^{n} p_j X_j \quad \textbf{(9.13)}$$

where $p_1 + p_2 + \ldots + p_n = 1 = \Sigma p_j$.

Another symbol denoting the expectation of $X$ is $\mu$, the Greek lowercase letter mu. $E(X) = \mu$, the mean of the population of $X$'s.

The names "expectation" and "expected value" are synonymous. Some examples of expectations are as follows:

1. Suppose $X$ is the random variable that has six possible values, $1, 2, \ldots, 6$. The events of the sample space could be the six sides of a die. *Assume* that a probability of $\frac{1}{6}$ is associated with each value of $X$. What is the value of $E(X)$? From Equation 9.13,

$$E(X) = \sum_{j=1}^{6} p_j X_j = \frac{1}{6}1 + \frac{1}{6}2 + \frac{1}{6}3 + \frac{1}{6}4 + \frac{1}{6}5 + \frac{1}{6}6 = \frac{1}{6}(1 + 2 + \ldots + 6)$$
$$= \frac{21}{6} = 3.5.$$

In this example, $E(X) = \mu = \frac{21}{6} = 3.5$. In repeatedly rolling the die one can "expect" to average 3.5 points.

2. A particular slot-machine has payoffs of \$0.00, \$0.50, \$1, \$2, and \$25. The probabilities associated with each of these occurrences are .80, .15, .04, .01, and .001, respectively. Define a random variable $X$ that takes on the four values 0, 50, 100, 200, and 2500 cents with probabilities .80, .15, .04, .01, and .001. What is the value of $E(X)$?

$$\mu = E(X) = .80(0) + .15(50) + .04(100) + .01(200) + .001(2500)$$
$$= 0 + 7.5 + 4.0 + 2.0 + 2.5 = 16$$

If it costs 25 cents for each trial on this slot-machine, would you like to play? If you feed \$25 into the machine, how much can you expect to lose? (\$9)

3. Let $X$ be the four random variables that corresponds to the number of "heads" in four flips of a fair coin. $X$ can take on the values 0, 1, 2, 3, and 4. Find $E(X)$. If you write out the sixteen equally probable events in the sample space, that is, *HHHH*, *HHHT*, . . . , *TTTT*, you will find the probabilities associated with 0, 1, 2, 3, 4 are $\frac{1}{16}$, $\frac{1}{4}$, $\frac{3}{8}$, $\frac{1}{4}$, and $\frac{1}{16}$, respectively. Thus,

$$E(X) = \sum_{j=1}^{4} p_j X_j = \frac{1}{16}(0) + \frac{1}{4}(1) + \frac{3}{8}(2) + \frac{1}{4}(3) + \frac{1}{16}(4) = 2$$

"In the long run" one can "expect" to average two heads in four random tosses of a fair coin.

If $X$ is a continuous variable instead of a discrete one, then an algebraic function describes the form of its probability distribution. If $X$ is continuous one cannot assign a probability to a single value of $X$. Instead, statements about the probability that $X$ lies in an interval are made. For these reasons the definition given for $E(X)$ in Equation 9.13 cannot be applied to a continuous random variable. Unfortunately for those without recourse to knowledge of integral calculus, it is difficult to define the expectation of a continuous variable.

Suppose $X$ is a continuous random variable and the probability distribution of $X$ looks like the one in Figure 9.5. There is an algebraic rule that gives the height of the curve in Figure 9.5 for every value of $X$. The area under the curve is 1 unit. The probability that $X$ will assume a value between, for example, 2 and 3 is equal to the area under the curve between those two points.

Definition: The *expectation* of the continuous random variable $X$ is the sum of the products formed by multiplying each value that $X$ can assume by the height of the probability function curve above that value of $X$.

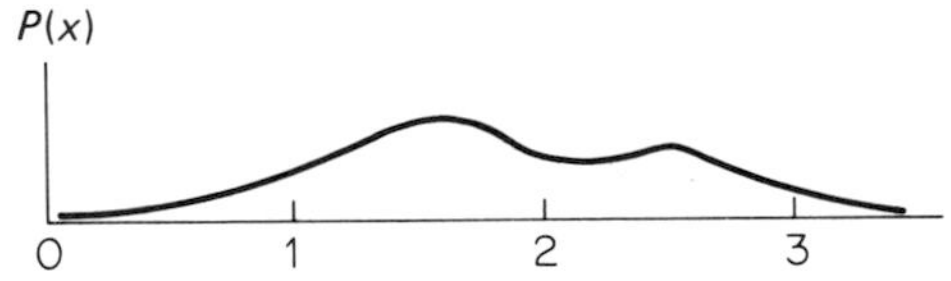


**FIGURE 9.5**
**Probability distribution of $X$.**

Since $X$ can take on infinitely many values, you might wonder how you could multiply each of the separate values of $X$ by the height of the curve at $X$ to find its expectation. This is the problem that recourse to the integral calculus solves. If you are not familiar with calculus, take it on faith that it can be done, in a precise but somewhat indirect way, by "integration."

The expectation of a continuous random variable $X$ is denoted by $E(X)$ or $\mu$, as is the expectation of a discrete variable.

## CHAPTER SUMMARY

The probability of event $A$ can be viewed as the ratio of the number of points of $A$ to the total number in the sample space. Often intuitive notions regarding probability are quite inaccurate.

If events $A$ and $B$ are mutually exclusive, the probability of either $A$ or $B$, $P(A \cup B)$, is $P(A) + P(B)$. If events $A$ and $B$ are not mutually exclusive, $P(A \cup B) = P(A) + P(B) - P(A \cap B)$, where the last term is the probability of both $A$ and $B$.

If event $A$ has probability $P(A)$, the probability that $A$ will occur $n$ times in $n$ independent trials is $P(A)^n$.

The probability of event $B$, given event $A$, is conditional probability, $P(B|A)$, and equals $P(A \cap B)/P(A)$. It is the simplest illustration of Bayes' theorem.

Each unique ordering or arrangement of $n$ objects is a permutation. There are $n!$ permutations of $n$ objects. The set of objects irrespective of order is a combination. The number of combinations of $n$ things taken $r$ at a time is $n!/[r!(n - r)!]$.

A function is any set of ordered pairs of elements, no two of which have the same first element. A random variable is a function in which all the first elements are points in sample space. Random variable may be discrete (take only certain fixed values) or continuous (assume any numerical value) on the number line.

The expected value $E(X)$ of a discrete random variable is the sum of the product of the $X$-values and their associated probabilities, $\Sigma_j p_j X_j$.

## *MASTERY TEST*

1. What is the probability of tossing a "6," $P(6)$, with one toss of a die?
2. How many sample points are there in the sample space in Question 1?
3. Are the sample points mutually exclusive?
4. What is the probability of not tossing "6," $P(\overline{6})$?
5. What is the probability of tossing "6's" in two tosses of a die?
6. Given that one "6" has been tossed, what is the conditional probability that the second toss will also be a "6"?
7. On a five-option multiple-choice test, what is the probability of selecting the correct answer from a random guess?
8. What is the probability of correctly guessing the right answer on all ten items of a five-option multiple-choice test?
9. Although 651412 and 214165 are different permutations, they represent a single ______ ______.
10. What is the probability of correctly guessing ten of ten true-false questions?
11. How many permutations are there in the previous question? (For example, T, T, F, T, T, F, F, F, T, T, is one permutation.)
12. How many different "doubles" teams in tennis are possible with a class of twenty members?
13. The probability of throwing two consecutive "snake eyes" with the toss of a pair of dice is $(\frac{1}{36})^2 = \frac{1}{1,296}$. If you have just tossed "snake eyes," what is the probability the next toss will be "snake eyes"?
14. Which of these random variables are discrete and which are continuous:
    a. number of students enrolled in a statistics class
    b. running speed of ten-year-olds
    c. result from the toss of a pair of dice
    d. height of adult males
15. What is the "expected" number of girls in two-child families if the probabilities associated with 0, 1, and 2 girls are $\frac{1}{4}$, $\frac{1}{2}$, and $\frac{1}{4}$, respectively?

16. Probability density pertains to
    a. continuous random variable
    b. discrete random variable
17. If 25% of the area in a probability distribution falls between 90 and 100, what is the probability that a case selected at random will fall between 90 and 100?
18. If event $A$ influences the probability of event $B$, events $A$ and $B$ are not ________.
19. What is the probability of drawing four aces without replacement from a deck of fifty-two cards? (*Hint:* probability of ace on first card is $\frac{4}{52}$; on second, $\frac{3}{51}$; etc.)

## *PROBLEMS AND EXERCISES*

1. Let a pack of fifty-two playing cards be the sample space $S$ of interest. Determine the probabilities of each of the following events:
    a. $A$ is "a card is the ace of spades." Find $P(A)$.
    b. $B$ is "a card is an ace." Find $P(B)$.
    c. $C$ is the event that "a card is a spade." Find $P(C)$.
    d. $D$ is "a card is a diamond," and $C$ is "a card is a spade." Find $P(D \cap C)$.
    e. $C$ is "a card is a spade" and $B$ is "a card is an ace." Find $P(C \cup B)$.
2. Suppose that in a certain locale 3% of the children of kindergarten age have severe perceptual problems and 6% of the children of the same age have emotional problems. Also, 1.5% of the same group of children have *both* perceptual and emotional problems. Children suffering from either problem or both must receive teaching apart from normal pupils. What is the probability that a child entering kindergarten will require special teaching, that is, will have either perceptual or emotional problems or both?
3. a. Find $15!/13!$
    b. Find $6!/[3!(6-3)!]$.
    c. What is the value of $n$ if $(n + 1)!$ is exactly ten times larger than $n!$?
4. An experimenter wishes to have subjects learn a list of paired associations in all possible orders of the six pairs. Each subject can learn the list only once. How many subjects would be required if a different subject is required for every possible ordering of the six pairs?
5. a. How many combinations are there of six things taken four at a time—find $\binom{6}{4}$.
    b. Find $\binom{5}{1}$, $\binom{5}{2}$, $\binom{5}{3}$, $\binom{5}{4}$, and $\binom{5}{5}$.
6. The varsity basketball team has twelve members. How many possible "starting fives"—the five players who start the game—could the coach form from his team of twelve players?
7. a. Verify that $\binom{4}{0} + \binom{4}{1} + \binom{4}{2} + \binom{4}{3} + \binom{4}{4}$ is equal to $2^4$. (In general, $\sum_{i=0}^{n} \binom{n}{i} = 2^n$.)
    b. How many different combinations are there of six things, in groups of size 0 to 6 inclusively, that is, what is $\sum_{i=0}^{6} \binom{6}{i}$?
8. How many five-item tests can be formed by ten items split into two tests of five items each?
9. A student takes a ten-item true-false test but does not know the answers to five of the items. If he guesses randomly between "true" and "false" on each of the five items
    a. what is the probability that he will earn a perfect score of 10?
    b. what is the probability that he will guess incorrectly on all five questions?
    c. what is the probability that his score will be 6, 7, 8, or 9?
    (*Hint:* subtract probabilities for scores of 5 and 10 from 1.00.)

10. In a fictitious experiment convicts volunteered for study of the causal relationship between smoking and lung cancer. The convicts were matched into five matched pairs so that both pair mates are of the same age. Within each pair of convicts a coin was flipped to determine which convict would continue smoking two packs of cigarettes a day and which one would not be allowed cigarettes for the duration of the experiment. At the end of the ten-year experimental period, the five smokers in each pair had lung cancer; none of the nonsmokers had lung cancer. Suppose that at the outset of the experiment, a convict in each pair had undiagnosed lung cancer.
    a. What is the probability that the five initially cancerous convicts would be randomly assigned to be the five experimental smokers?
    b. If there had been ten pairs, rather than five, what is the probability that the cancerous convict in each of the ten pairs would have been assigned to the smoking group?

11. In the general population, Stanford-Binet IQ's are nearly normally distributed with a mean of 100 and a standard deviation of 16. By referring to Table A in the Appendix, determine the following probabilities:
    a. that a randomly sampled person will have an IQ between 80 and 120.
    b. that a randomly sampled person will have an IQ above 140.
    c. that three independently randomly sampled persons will all have IQ's above 92.

12. The variable $X$ takes on the values 0, 1, 2, 3, and 4 with probabilities 0, $\frac{2}{5}$, $\frac{1}{5}$, $\frac{1}{5}$, and $\frac{1}{5}$, respectively. What is the value of $E(X)$, the expected value of $X$?

13. The sample space for tossing a pair of dice is given in Table 9.1.
    a. Determine the probability for each value of $X$, for 2, 3, 4, . . . , 12.
    b. What is the expected value of $X$, $E(X)$?
    c. What is probability that $X \neq 7$?
    d. What is the probability of "7" on three consecutive throws?
    e. Given the consecutive "7's," what is the probability of "7" on the next toss?

## ANSWERS TO MASTERY TEST

1. $\frac{1}{6}$
2. 6
3. Yes
4. $\frac{5}{6}$
5. $(\frac{1}{6})^2 = \frac{1}{36}$
6. $P(B|A) = (\frac{1}{36})/(\frac{1}{6}) = \frac{1}{6}$
7. $\frac{1}{5}$
8. $(\frac{1}{5})^{10} \doteq .0000001$
9. Combination
10. $(\frac{1}{2})^{10} = 1/1{,}024$
11. 1,024
12. $\binom{20}{2} = \dfrac{20!}{2!(20-2)!} = 190$
13. $\frac{1}{36}$
14. $a$ and $c$ are discrete, $b$ and $d$ are continuous.
15. $E(X) = \frac{1}{4}(0) + \frac{1}{2}(1) + \frac{1}{4}(2) = 1$
16. a
17. .25
18. Independent
19. $(\frac{4}{52})(\frac{3}{51})(\frac{2}{50})(\frac{1}{49}) = 24/(6{,}497{,}400)$ $\doteq .0000037$

## ANSWERS TO PROBLEMS AND EXERCISES

1. a. $P(A) = \frac{1}{52}$
   b. $P(B) = \frac{4}{52} = \frac{1}{13}$
   c. $P(C) = \frac{13}{52} = \frac{1}{4}$
   d. $P(D \cap C) = \frac{0}{52} = 0$
   e. $P(C \cup B) = \frac{13}{52} + \frac{4}{52} - \frac{1}{52} = \frac{16}{52} = \frac{4}{13}$

2. $A$: a child has perceptual problems.
   $B$: a child has emotional problems.
   $A \cap B$: a child has both perceptual and emotional problems.
   $P(A) = .03$, $P(B) = .06$, $P(A \cap B) = .015$.
   $P(A \cup B) = .03 + .06 - .015 = .075$
3. a. 210
   b. 20
   c. If $n = 9$, then $(n + 1)! = 10! = 10(9!)$.
4. $6! = 720$
5. a. 15
   b. 5, 10, 10, 5, and 1
6. $\binom{12}{5} = 792$
7. a. $1 + 4 + 6 + 4 + 1 = 16; 2^4 = 16$
   b. $2^6 = 64$
8. $\binom{10}{5} = 252$
9. a $P(A)^n = (\frac{1}{2})^5 = \frac{1}{32}$ or .03125
   b. $\frac{1}{32}$ or .03125
   c. $1 - \frac{1}{32} - \frac{1}{32} = \frac{30}{32} = \frac{15}{16}$ or .9375.
10. a. $(\frac{1}{2})^5 = \frac{1}{32}$;
    b. $(\frac{1}{2})^{10} = 1/1{,}024$
11. a. .7888
    b. .0062
    c. $(.6915)^3 = .3307$
12. $E(X) = 2\frac{1}{5}$
13. a. $\frac{1}{36}, \frac{1}{18}, \frac{1}{12}, \frac{1}{9}, \frac{5}{36}, \frac{1}{6}, \frac{5}{36}, \frac{1}{9}, \frac{1}{12}, \frac{1}{18}, \frac{1}{36}$
    b. $E(X) = \Sigma_j p_j X_j = 7$
    c. $\frac{5}{6}$
    d. $(\frac{1}{6})^3 = \frac{1}{216}$
    e. $\frac{1}{6}$

# 10

# STATISTICAL INFERENCE: SAMPLING AND INTERVAL ESTIMATION

## 10.1 THE PURPOSE OF STATISTICAL INFERENCE

In the preceding chapters statistical inference has been only a minor theme. Beginning with this chapter, we will be occupied with estimating and making statements about parameters using inferential statistical methods. One of the primary purposes of statistical methods is to allow generalizations about populations using data from samples. This chapter introduces concepts that are of fundamental importance in all succeeding chapters.

Virtually all public opinion polls and surveys, such as the Gallup and Harris polls, involve selecting a sample, obtaining data on that sample, and then making inferences about the entire population. Rarely are all members of the population observed—usually only a small fraction of the elements in the population is sampled. The Nielsen ratings of the popularity of television programs are based on the viewing habits of a sample of less than one home in 10,000 (.01%) in the population. The computerized projections of winners in political elections are nothing more than sophisticated applications of the concepts of this chapter. But before considering the theory underlying statistical inference, some fundamental definitions and concepts must be reviewed.

## 10.2 POPULATIONS AND SAMPLES: PARAMETERS AND STATISTICS

The principal use of statistical inference in empirical research is to obtain knowledge about a large class of persons or other statistical units from a relatively small number of the same elements. Inferential statistical methods employ inductive reasoning—reasoning from the particular to the general and from the observed to the unobserved. Inferential statistical reasoning addresses such questions as "What do I know about the age at which the average child in the United States (the population) utters his or her first sentence, knowing that for twenty-five children (the sample) the average was 202 weeks?" Any large (finite or infinite) collection or aggregation of things that we wish to study or about which we wish to make inferences is called a *population*. The term *population* takes on more meaning when coupled with the definition of a sample from a population: a *sample* is a part, or subset, of a population. A sample of $n$ elements should be selected in a deliberate fashion from the population of $N$ elements so that the characteristics of the population can be estimated with a known margin for error.

Measurements taken on members of a population can be described in the ways that have been discussed in the preceding chapters. Means, medians, variances, and percentiles can be computed on the data sampled from a population. The correlation between height and weight for sixteen-year-old females in the United States could be of interest. The values of various descriptive measures computed for *populations* are called *parameters*. For samples, these same descriptive measures are called *statistics.* As we have seen in previous chapters, the *parameter* describes a *population* in the way a *statistic* describes a *sample.* It is customary to denote statistics by Roman letters and parameters by Greek letters. The symbol $\overline{X}$ stands for the sample mean, and the Greek letter $\mu$ stands for the population mean. The sample variance is denoted by $s^2$ and the population variance by $\sigma^2$. The statistic $r$ is an estimate of the parameter $\rho$.

A statistic computed on a sample can be regarded as an estimate of the parameter in the population. An estimator is some function of the scores in a sample that produces a value, called the *estimate*. The estimate gives some information about a parameter. For example, the sample mean $\overline{X}$ is an estimate of the mean or average score in the population. A random sample of 100 eight-year-olds might yield 104.65 for a sample mean on the Stanford-Binet Intelligence Scale. This value, 104.65, would be an estimate of the mean test score in that population.

## 10.3 INFINITE VERSUS FINITE POPULATIONS

For most research purposes, populations are assumed to be *infinite*, *not finite*, in size. However, the truly infinite populations that come easily to mind are somewhat artificial or imaginary—for example, the collection of all positive numbers, the collection of all possible measurements of a person's weight, the collection of tosses of two dice which could be made throughout eternity, or all six-year-olds who will ever exist. Almost any interesting population of physical items (as opposed to conceptual possibilities) is finite in size—for example, all living persons in the Western Hemisphere, all possible orderings of twenty stimuli (20!), all public schools in the United States, or all social workers in New

York City. A finite population may be extremely large—the proverbial "grains of sand on earth," the number of census tracts in the United States, or all first-grade children in California. If it is conceivable that the process of counting the elements of the population could be completed, then the population is technically *finite*. Fortunately, it is generally not necessary to worry about the distinction between finite and infinite populations. As discussed later, unless the fraction of the elements sampled (i.e., the sampling fraction, $n/N$) is .05 (i.e., 5%) or greater, the techniques for making inferences to finite populations and those for infinite populations give essentially the same results. Even if the sampling fraction is as much as 10%, the results from using the simpler methods (which assume that $N$ is infinitely large) are only slightly less precise and efficient than the results from using procedures that take the sampling fraction into account.

In short, most applied statistical techniques are based on the assumption that an infinite population is being sampled. If the population is quite large and the sample from the population constitutes only a small proportion of the population (i.e., $n/N \leqslant .05$), the fact that the population is not actually infinite is of little concern. It is common to speak of a population as being "virtually infinite," that is, the population although finite, is very large, and statistical techniques that assume an infinite population will be used. In most illustrations and procedures of this chapter, the populations are virtually infinite in size.

## 10.4 RANDOMNESS AND RANDOM SAMPLING

The concept of random sampling is closely tied to probability (Chapter 9). The validity of a statistical inference depends on how representative the sample is of the population. To evaluate the preferences of all voters in the United States, common sense tells us not to interview people on a street corner.

*The method used to select the sample is of utmost importance in judging the validity of the inferences made from the sample to the population.* The novice is often more concerned with the size of a sample than with its *representativeness*. A representative sample of 100 may be preferable to an unrepresentative sample of 1,000,000.

A classic illustration of how not to sample occurred in 1936 in the presidential preference poll conducted by the now-defunct periodical *Literary Digest*. Postcards were sent to an unrepresentative sample of 12,000,000! The sample was selected from automobile owners and telephone directories. Even though the response rate was poor (21%), the 2,500,000 who returned the postcards constitute one of the largest samples on record. Although 57% of the respondents indicated a preference for the Republican candidate Alf Landon, Franklin Roosevelt was elected by the greatest majority in history up to that time, carrying all states except Maine and Vermont.

What went wrong? How can George Gallup's projections be presumed to be accurate with his sample of less the 2,000 persons when the *Literary Digest* was misled by a sample that was more than 1,000 times larger? *The size of a sample can never compensate for a lack of representativeness (bias).* Automobile owners and families with telephones were not a representative sample of voters in 1936. In addition the 21% who returned the questionnaire probably were not a representative sample even of the 12,000,000 who received the postcards. (The possible self-selection bias among those who return questionnaires continues to this day to be the greatest threat to the validity of mail surveys.)

The *Literary Digest* survey, apart from the biased sampling plan, utilized an extremely inefficient strategy. To anyone with a modicum of statistical understanding, it would have been evident that a sample only one-thousandth (.1%) as large as that used by the *Literary Digest*, if representative, would be *exceedingly* precise. Even in the era of the penny postcard, the postage for 12 million postcards would have been $120,000! Any statistician would have known that $120 ($n$ = 12,000) would have served as well.*

### Types of Samples

Samples, and the estimates calculated from them (statistics), serve to give information about the characteristics of the population sampled. There are several legitimate and illegitimate ways in which samples can be selected from a population. Simple random sampling is the most widely used and acceptable way to sample, though there are other appropriate methods.

## 10.5 ACCIDENTAL OR CONVENIENCE SAMPLES

Accidental or convenience sampling is the most common inappropriate method of obtaining a sample. Convenient but haphazard collections of observations are usually of little value in estimating parameters. Results from street-corner polls, polls of the audience of a particular television or radio program, or readers of a particular magazine cannot be generalized beyond such groups without great risks. Commercial advertisements often report data on their products obtained on samples of unknown representativeness. One should be wary of conclusions based on accidental samples.

## 10.6 RANDOM SAMPLES

As in all texts on statistical methods, the greatest emphasis in this and subsequent chapters is given to simple random sampling.† *Before a sample will adequately serve as a basis for making estimates of population parameters, it must be representative of the population.*

*Another common misinterpretation of surveys, especially political polls, is evidenced when the findings are generalized over a period of time—that is, to predict results of future elections. During the course of a campaign, voter preferences usually vacillate considerably as issues and positions are clarified or changed. In forecasting an election it is the population of *actual voters*—those who will in fact vote (not the registered voters or other adults) that is the relevant population. The population of actual voters is never a truly representative sample of the population of registered voters, which in turn is never a representative sample of those eligible to be registered voters. In interpreting any poll one must bear in mind the pollsters' definition of the population as well as the fact that the generalizability (or lack of it) of the results over time is not addressed by the statistics per se.

†More sophisticated sampling plans, such as stratified sampling, cluster sampling, and two-stage sampling, are dealt with in textbooks devoted exclusively to sampling, such as William Cochran's *Sampling Techniques* (1973) and Leslie Kish's *Survey Sampling* (1965).

However, this criterion of representativeness presents a problem. How would one know for certain whether a sample is representative of a population unless the characteristics of the entire population are known? And if the characteristics of the entire population are known, why does one need a sample with which to estimate them? This quandary is resolved when one realizes that *random sampling of a population will produce samples which in the long run are representative of the population.*

*If a sample is randomly drawn, it is representative of the population in all respects*—that is, the statistic differs from the parameter only by chance on any variable, real or illusory, measured or not measured. Through the "magic" of statistical theory, the degree of this difference can be estimated. The method of random selection of samples will ensure, within a certain known margin of error, representativeness of the samples and hence will permit establishing limits within which the parameters are expected to lie with a particular probability.

*The ability to estimate the degree of error due to chance (sampling error) is an important feature of a random sample*—the ability to determine the accuracy of the statistical inferences. It is not possible to estimate the error with accidental sampling and many other sampling strategies since they contain unknown types and degrees of bias in addition to sampling error. For example, if one were to choose the first fifty households in the telephone directory one would not have a random sample of the population of households in a city. This sample of fifty is not representative of the population, and it is nonrepresentative in unknown ways and to an unknown extent. However, if fifty households were randomly sampled from the population, it would be possible to answer such questions as "How likely is it that a randomly drawn sample of fifty households will have a mean income that differs by less than $500 from the mean income of all households in the directory?"*

The process of inferential statistical reasoning involves finding an estimate of a parameter from a sample and then determining how representative such a sample can be expected to be for the purpose of estimating the parameter. It is not surprising, then, that inferential statistics is based on the assumption of random sampling from populations.

The following is an example of random sampling using a table of random digits. From the 3,000 students at Fairview High School, Principal Howe wishes to estimate the percent of students currently using drugs. It is impractical to try to have all students respond to an anonymous questionnaire. By methods that will be introduced later, Howe determines that the percent using drugs in the random sample of 100 probably will not differ by more than 5% from the corresponding percent in the population of 3,000. It can be said that the sampling error will almost certainly be less than 10%. Howe instructs her secretary to assign a four-digit number from 0001 to 3000, starting at the beginning of the alphabetical file of the student roster. She then goes to her table of random numbers (such as Table B in the Appendix) to make the selection.† The first task is to determine a point of entry into the table. With the book open to the first page, she lays the point of her pencil on the page of random digits with her eyes closed. Suppose the two digits closest to her pencil point are 6 and 5. She then moves to the intersection of row 6 and column 5 of the table to begin making selections. Moving along row 6 and starting with column 5, Howe sees the digits 2861. By grouping digits into groups of four and reading down, the numbers 1572, 2993, 4477, 8488, 2169 . . . are obtained. Her

*Of course the households in the city and the households listed in the telephone directory are not always the same. A few households have no telephone; others have unlisted numbers.

†Most microcomputers have a built-in function for generating random numbers.

secretary will now compile the names of those persons who have identification numbers 1572, 2993, 2169, and so on. But what about 4477 and 8488? There are only 3,000 persons, so no one has these identification numbers. These numbers are simply disregarded. What happens if the same number comes up a second time? If it does, it is disregarded the second time it comes up. The sampling continues as though nothing had happened. In this manner Principal Howe can be assured of the randomness of her sample. Each member of the population has an equal and independent chance of being chosen in the sample.

Why should Howe have gone to this trouble to obtain a random sample? Why did she not just go through the files and choose 100 persons she thought would be representative of all 3,000? Would this judgment not give a more representative sample than leaving the process to mindless chance? No, the random sample will probably be better than a judgmental sample. Numerous factors can operate on the principal's judgment to make her judgmental sample unrepresentative. If the principal were more likely to select those she knew by name, her judgmental sample would be biased in several possible ways. It might have a greater proportion of student leaders, scholars, or troublemakers than in the population. If she selects her sample via the random number table, these biases cannot affect the selection. Randomized selection prevents any systematic biases.

## 10.7 INDEPENDENCE

An example of sampling in which the observations are not independent will illustrate what will be avoided when random sampling is used. Suppose a researcher wants to estimate the average IQ of childern who have a twin brother or sister. Assume that 1,000 children (500 pairs of twins) constitute the available population, and the researcher can administer intelligence tests to thirty children. He decides that his work will be simplified if each time he chooses one child at random, he also tests the child's twin; hence fifteen pairs of twins are tested. Does he then have a random sample of thirty children? Of course not. The thirty observations have not been selected *independently*. If they were, the selection of one child would not have made the selection of his twin any more likely than the selection of any other child. As it was, the selection of a child made the probability of the selection of his twin equal to 1, a certainty. The researcher does not have a simple random sample of thirty children from the population of 1,000. He is justified in saying, however, that he has obtained a simple random sample of fifteen twin pairs from a population of 500 pairs. He could average the two IQ's in the twin set to obtain an observation appropriate to his sampling technique. (Drawing twin pairs is an example of cluster sampling.)

Nonindependence of the observations in a sample that is presumed to be a random sample is a prevalent fault in experimental studies. A surprising number of experiments are analyzed incorrectly because the experimenter was not aware of what is and what is not a random sample. Countless theses and many other published studies stumble on this basic problem.

A common fault of researchers in education is to choose "classrooms" randomly to participate in an experiment and then to analyze the data as if "students" had been chosen randomly. If the twenty-five students in classroom $A$ are chosen for method $E$

and the twenty-five students in classroom $B$ are chosen for method $C$, then although the condition of equiprobability obtains, surely the selection of "students" has not been an independent one. If Sue and George are both in classroom $A$, then Sue and George must both receive method $E$. There is no chance for Sue to receive $E$ and George to receive $C$. Any simple analysis that treats the twenty-five students in each $E$ and $C$ as though they constituted a random sample of fifty separate observations is likely to be inaccurate because the two classrooms are just two "cluster samples" of students. The proper method of sampling and the associated statistical analysis sometimes manages to elude even sophisticated researchers (Sec. 19.22).

This section on random sampling is concluded with an alternative statement of the definition of simple random sampling. This statement on simple random sampling is equivalent to the one given earlier in this section:

> If the sampling of $n$ observation from a population of $N$ observations is random, then regardless of what the first $n$ choices were, the probability of any particular observation $X_i$ being chosen on the $(n + 1)st$ selection is $1/(N - n)$.

## 10.8 SYSTEMATIC SAMPLING

To draw a sample of the 100 students from the 3,000 students at Fairview High School (a sampling fraction of $n/N = 1/30$), Principal Howe could select a random number between one and thirty from the table of random numbers and then pick the student corresponding to that number and every thirtieth student thereafter from the student roster. For example, if the random number selected were thirteen, the 13th, 43rd, 73rd, 103rd, . . . , 2,983rd students from the list would comprise the sample. A sample of this kind is known as a *systematic sample*. Likewise, selecting every hundredth word in a dictionary would yield a 1% systematic sample of words.

A practical advantage of systematic samples is that they are easier to obtain than random samples. Systematic samples of persons are usually representative samples. Indeed, the results from systematic samples tend to be slightly more accurate than results from simple random samples, but inconsequentially so. The orderly sampling process allows less opportunity for sampling error to occur. The chief disadvantage of systematic sampling is that there is no satisfactory way to determine precisely how accurate the estimates are in the long run. What is usually done is to behave as if the sample were drawn randomly. In most instances samples of persons utilizing systematic sampling will differ little from simple random samples. Unlike accidental sampling, systematic sampling is an acceptable sampling technique (the differences between a systematic and a random sample of persons are almost always inconsequential). Properly employed, findings on random and systematic samplings are said to be generalizable; that is, one can be confident that the findings on the sample are not biased and that they are generalizable (within a given margin of sampling error) to the parent population.*

*Systematic sampling is hazardous only if the data are cyclic (as they often are in time sampling) and the sampling fractions happen to coincide with the cycle. For example, if boys and girls were required to sit in alternate seats and a systematic sample of every second desk (e.g., desks 2, 4, 6, etc.) was selected, the sample would result in a disproportionate number of one sex.

## 10.9 POINT AND INTERVAL ESTIMATES

In previous chapters all inferential statements involved *point estimates*; that is, a single point or value was considered to be the estimate of a parameter. The expression $E(\overline{X}) = \mu$ suggests that the single value of $\overline{X}$ is an unbiased point estimate of $\mu$. An *interval estimate* builds on the concept of the point estimate but in addition conveys the degree of accuracy of the estimate. Interval estimation is a valuable, but much underused, inferential statistical method in behavioral research.

As the term suggests, an interval estimate is a range or band within which the parameter is presumed to fall. For example, the mean recognition vocabulary size of university students has been estimated at 156,000 words. The point estimate of the parameter is 156,000, but if the sample of students on which this statistic was obtained is small, the interval estimate could extend for example, from 112,000 to 200,000. Hence, we would know the point estimate (156,000) is not a very precise estimate of the parameter and that the true average vocabulary size is probably somewhere in the interval indicated. On the other hand, if the interval estimate were 152,000-160,000, it would be evident that $\mu$, the parameter, was estimated rather precisely.

The understanding of the underlying rationale for interval estimates demands a grasp of *the most fundamentally important concept of inferential statistics, the concept of the sampling distribution*. Subsequent chapters cannot be fully comprehended without understanding the concept of a sampling distribution. Mastering the concept presents a challenge, but the fruit is well worth the effort.

## 10.10 SAMPLING DISTRIBUTIONS

The concept of a sampling distribution is critical in inferential statistics. In this chapter the concept of the sampling distribution of the mean is illustrated. Once the concept of a sampling distribution is mastered, it is easily extended to other statistical measures such as variances or correlation coefficients.

The statistician assesses the degree of precision to be expected from random samples by studying *sampling distributions*. A statistic or estimator calculated on a sample is said to possess a certain sampling distribution. You can imagine the process of choosing sample after sample of size $n$ from a certain population and recording for each sample the value of some estimator, for example, the sample mean, $\overline{X}$. If this process of drawing a sample from the population were repeated thousands of times, it would be possible to construct a frequency distribution of the thousands of sample statistics (means) that were obtained. The frequency distribution of the statistics (means) so constructed would be a sampling distribution (of the mean) based on $n$ observations.

## 10.11 THE STANDARD ERROR OF THE MEAN WHEN $X$ IS NORMALLY DISTRIBUTED

An illustration will first be presented in which the variable $X$ in the parent population is normally distributed, and in which $\mu$ and $\sigma$ are known. Bear in mind that the purpose at this point is conceptual. By specifying these conditions, some important concepts about sampling distributions can be illustrated without distracting qualifying statements. In Chapter 11 the more typical situation in which $\mu$ and $\sigma$ are not known will be considered.

On many intelligence scales the IQ parameters $\mu$ and $\sigma$ are 100 and 15, respectively. If twenty-five observations are randomly drawn from the normal distribution, how close will the mean of our twenty-five observations ($\overline{X}$) be to the parameter ($\mu$), that is, how great is the sampling error ($\overline{X} - \mu$)?

Equation 10.1 gives the standard deviation of the sampling distribution of the sample means ($\overline{X}$'s), called the *standard error of the mean* and denoted by $\sigma_{\overline{X}}$. The standard error of the mean is the standard deviation of the sampling error in $\overline{X}$'s when a random sample of size $n$ is employed.*

$$\sigma_{\overline{X}} = \frac{\sigma}{\sqrt{n}} \tag{10.1}$$

In the example with $\sigma = 15$ and $n = 25$, the parameter $\sigma_{\overline{X}}$ is found to have a value of 3.0 by using Equation 10.1:

$$\sigma_{\overline{X}} = \frac{15}{\sqrt{25}} = \frac{15}{5} = 3.0$$

The $\sigma_{\overline{X}}$ value of 3 indicates the following: if a random sample of twenty-five observations were drawn from the parent population, the mean ($\overline{X}$) of these twenty-five $X$'s was computed, and this process was repeated, again determining the mean ($\overline{X}$) of the second set of twenty-five random observations, and this process was repeated an infinite number of times, the standard deviation of this sampling distribution, $\sigma_{\overline{X}}$, would be 3. In other words, the standard deviation of the normal distribution of sampling error in the $\overline{X}$'s, ($\overline{X} - \mu$), is 3. Sampling error is the difference in the statistic (in this case $\overline{X}$) and the corresponding parameter (in this case $\mu$).

## 10.12 RELATIONSHIP OF $\sigma_{\overline{X}}$ TO $n$

As the sample size $n$ increases, the magnitude of sampling error decreases, as shown in Equation 10.1. For example, with $\sigma = 15$ and $n = 25$, $\sigma_{\overline{X}} = 3$. But if $n = 100$, $\sigma_{\overline{X}} = 1.5$; and if $n = 225$, $\sigma_{\overline{X}} = 1$. This is illustrated in Figure 10.1. Note that the value of $\sigma_{\overline{X}}$ is halved when $n$ is quadrupled.

Regardless of $n$, the $\overline{X}$-values are normally distributed and have a mean of $\mu$. The expression $E(\overline{X}) = \mu$ is just another way of saying that the mean of the sampling distribution of $\overline{X}$'s is $\mu$. To say that the expected value of a sample mean is equal to the parameter—or, in our IQ illustration, to say that $E(\overline{X}) = \mu = 100$—simply indicates that 100 is the mean of the sampling distribution of means. The expected value of any statistic is the mean of its sampling distribution.

*Equation 10.1 assumes that the $N$ observations in the population is infinitely large. Occasionally in surveys the sample of $n$ observations represents a nonnegligible proportion of $N$. In this case the variance in the sampling distribution is precisely described by the equation $\sigma^2_{\overline{X}} = (1 - n/N)\sigma^2/n$. But unless the sampling fraction $n/N$ is .10 or more, the precise value for $\sigma_{\overline{X}}$ is *at most* 5% smaller than the value yielded by Equation 10.1 (see Sec. 10.3).

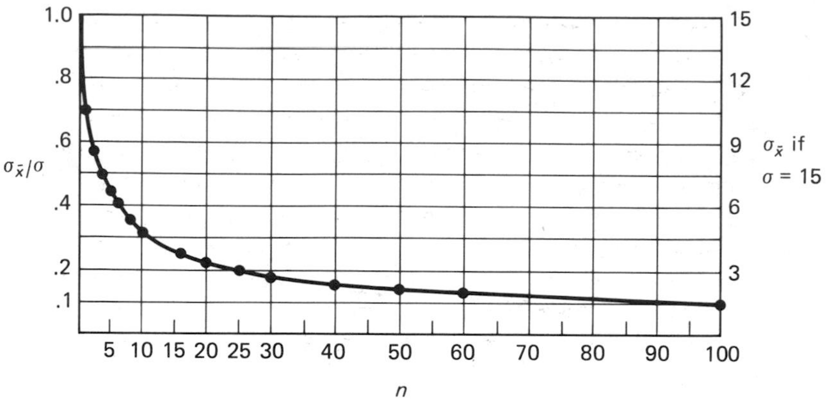


**FIGURE 10.1. The relationship of $n$ and $\sigma_{\bar{X}}$.**

## 10.13 CONFIDENCE INTERVALS

In the hypothetical illustration of IQ scores, the mean of the parent population ($\mu$) is known. Consequently there is no need to use $\bar{X}$ to estimate $\mu$. But imagine for the moment the unlikely situation in which $\sigma$ was known, but $\mu$ was not known. How could $\bar{X}$ be used to estimate $\mu$? For any value of $n$, $E(\bar{X}) = \mu$, but this does not tell how much sampling error is to be expected in the $\bar{X}$-value. If $n = 225$, then $\sigma_{\bar{X}} = \sigma/\sqrt{n} = 1.0$; hence, 68% of the means in the sampling distribution would differ 1.0 point or less from $\mu$. For example, many different random samples with $n = 225$ were selected; if we placed a band of $\sigma_{\bar{X}} = 1.0$ points above and below ($\pm$) each of the many $\bar{X}$-values, the value of $\mu$ would fall within that interval for 68% of the sample means. In other words, the .68 *confidence interval* is $\bar{X} \pm \sigma_{\bar{X}}$, as shown in Equation 10.2. The lower limit of the .68 confidence interval (CI) is $\bar{X} - \sigma_{\bar{X}}$; the upper limit of the interval is $\bar{X} + \sigma_{\bar{X}}$. The ".68" refers to the confidence coefficient of the confidence interval:

$$.68\text{CI} = \bar{X} \pm \sigma_{\bar{X}} \qquad \textbf{(10.2)}$$

Equation 10.2 indicates that if $\sigma_{\bar{X}}$ is added to, and subtracted from, each $\bar{X}$-value in the sampling distribution, of the intervals formed (in the example from one point below each $\bar{X}$ to one point above each $\bar{X}$), the parameter $\mu$ would lie within 68% of such intervals.

In practice one has just the one mean, $\bar{X}$, which is based upon a sample of $n$ observations. One has no way of knowing whether or not the particular mean ($\bar{X}$) is one of the 68% that falls within one standard error ($\sigma_{\bar{X}}$) of $\mu$. Consequently, one usually wants to have more than ".68 confidence" that the interval estimate contains $\mu$. Hence a wider confidence interval, the .90 or .95 CI is more commonly used. The .90 CI is defined as

$$.90\text{CI} = \bar{X} \pm 1.645\,\sigma_{\bar{X}} \qquad \textbf{(10.3)}$$

The parameter $\mu$ will be contained within 95% (nineteen out of twenty) of .95 confidence intervals in the long run.

$$.95\text{CI} = \bar{X} \pm 1.96\sigma_{\bar{X}} \tag{10.4}$$

Or, equivalently, probability $(\bar{X} - 1.96\sigma_{\bar{X}} < \mu < \bar{X} + 1.96\sigma_{\bar{X}}) = .95$. More generally,

$$(1 - \alpha)\text{CI} = \bar{X} \pm {}_{1-\alpha/2}z\,\sigma_{\bar{X}} \tag{10.5}$$

Recall from the normal curve table (Table A) that a $z$-score of $-1.96$ corresponds to $P_{2.5}$, the 2.5th percentile, and that $z = 1.96$ corresponds to $P_{97.5}$. Equation 10.4 shows that if $1.960\ \sigma_{\bar{X}}$ is added to and subtracted from the sample mean ($\bar{X}$), one can be "95% confident" that the parameter $\mu$ lies somewhere within the $\bar{X} \pm 1.96\sigma_{\bar{X}}$ interval. To be even more confident, one can find the .99 confidence interval in Table A by using $\bar{X} \pm 2.576\sigma_{\bar{X}}$, since ${}_{.995}z = 2.576$.

## 10.14 CONFIDENCE INTERVALS WHEN $\sigma$ IS KNOWN: AN EXAMPLE

An example will now be presented of how an interval estimate is used. The example will be developed in considerable detail so that the rationale of the underlying theory can be illustrated.

Consider a researcher who has set out to determine the average IQ of the approximately 500,000 adopted children in the United States as measured by the Wechsler Intelligence Scale for Children (WISC). The WISC is an individual verbal and performance intelligence test that must be administered by trained examiners and therefore is quite expensive compared to group intelligence tests. The available funds for this study will cover 100 test administrations, but no more. The researcher has good reason to believe that the adopted children are no more heterogeneous than the population of children used in the norming of the WISC, but there is reason to believe that their average score might differ from the norm (100). Hence, the standard deviation of WISC total IQ's is 15—the same as in the norm group.*

A random sample of 100 WISC IQ scores will be taken from the parent population of 500,000 in which $\sigma = 15$. The researcher will calculate $\bar{X}$ as a point estimate of the unknown $\mu$, but he also should establish a confidence interval around $\bar{X}$. He would like the confidence coefficient for this interval to be .95. With samples as large as 100,

*The argument that $\sigma$ is known and $\mu$ is not known is somewhat artificial. In almost all instances $\mu$ and $\sigma$ are either both known or both unknown. We assumed here that $\sigma$ is known and $\mu$ is unknown in order to keep the problem of interval estimation simpler than it would be if both $\sigma$ and $\mu$ had to be estimated from the same sample. This latter case, in which both $\sigma$ and $\mu$ are unknown, is by far the more realistic situation. The solution to the problem of interval estimation of $\mu$ when $\sigma$ is unknown was the first step in the development of modern inferential statistical methods; this solution was not presented until early in this century. It is due to W. S. Gossett, who wrote under the pseudonym of "Student" (1908).

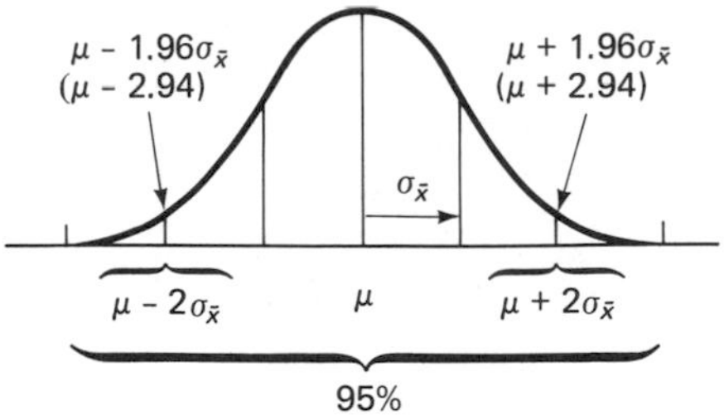


**FIGURE 10.2**
**Sampling distribution of $\overline{X}$ for random samples of size 100 from a parent population with $\sigma = 15$, hence $\sigma_{\overline{X}} = 1.5$ and an unknown mean $\mu$.**

one can be confident in this situation that in repeated random samples, the distribution of $\overline{X}$-values is very nearly normal with a mean, $\mu$, and with a standard deviation, $\sigma_{\overline{X}}$, or $\sigma/\sqrt{n} = 15/\sqrt{100} = 1.5$. We have already seen from Equation 10.4 (or Table A) that 95% of the area under the unit normal curve lies within 1.96 standard deviations of the mean ($\pm 1.96\sigma$). The sampling distribution of $\overline{X}$ for samples of 100 from a normal population with $\sigma = 15$ appears in Figure 10.2, $\sigma_{\overline{X}} = 1.5$. Thus 95% of the area under this curve lies within $\mu \pm 2.94$ because $1.96(1.5) = 2.94$.

Suppose the researcher found the mean of the 100 IQ scores was 105.0. The .95 confidence interval for $\mu$ then is $105.0 \pm 2.94$, or 102.06 to 107.94. In other words, the value of $\mu$ for the population of adopted children is probably at least 102 and perhaps as high as 108. If more precision is desired—that is, a narrower confidence interval—the sample size must be increased. From Equation 10.1, one sees that if $n = 225$, then $\sigma_{\overline{X}} = 1.0$; if $n = 400$, then $\sigma_{\overline{X}} = .75$; if $n = 900$, then $\sigma_{\overline{X}} = .5$.

Confusion will result unless the distinction between $\mu \pm 1.96\sigma_{\overline{X}}$ and $\overline{X} \pm 1.96\sigma_{\overline{X}}$ is clear. It is true that samples of $n = 25$ or more can be relied upon to yield a very nearly normal sampling distribution of means, even when the frequency distribution in the parent population is not normal, as will be demonstrated in Figure 10.3. Although 95% of $\overline{X}$'s fall within $\mu \pm 1.96\sigma_{\overline{X}}$, $\mu$ does not vary; it either is, or is not, within $\overline{X} \pm 1.96\sigma_{\overline{X}}$.

## 10.15 CENTRAL LIMIT THEOREM

*A Demonstration of the Central Limit Theorem.* Since the central limit theorem is vital for a proper understanding and application of statistical methods, it will be illustrated extensively with empirical sampling distributions in which sample size ($n$) and the shape of the parent population have been varied. A primary purpose of all the figures to follow (Fig. 10.3) is to demonstrate the central limit theorem. Many (actually 10,000) random samples of $n$ observations were drawn from three different types of parent populations—normal, rectangular, and skewed. The effect of sample size $n$ and nonnormality in the parent population on the sampling distribution is illustrated by using sample sizes ($n$'s) of 1, 2, 5, 10 and 25. As Figure 10.3 is perused, the basis for the following two generalizations should become apparent:

1. Even for nonnormal parent populations, the shape of the sampling distributions rapidly approaches normality as $n$ increases.

2. As $n$ increases, the variability of the sampling distribution of $\overline{X}$ decreases; the decrease is accurately described by Equation 10.1 ($\sigma_{\overline{X}} = \sigma/\sqrt{n}$) even if the parent population is nonnormal.

Three parent populations are defined such that all have equal means ($\mu_1 = \mu_2 = \mu_3 = 100$) and equal standard deviations ($\sigma_1 = \sigma_2 = \sigma_3 = 15$). But the populations differ in shape—one is normal, another rectangular (kurtosis, $\gamma_2 = -1.2$), and the third is highly skewed ($\varsigma\kappa = .7$). These three parent populations are shown in Panel A of Figure 10.3. Each bar in the percentage histograms gives the percentage of observations for each IQ score. For example, in the parent populations the percentage of IQ scores of 100 (where $\mu = 100$ and $\sigma = 15$) is 2.66% for the normal distribution (see Panel A-I), 1.89% for the rectangular distribution (see Panel A-II), and 2.58% for the skewed distribution (see Panel A-III) shown in Figure 10.3.

Note that *Panels B, C, and D of Figure 10.3 are empirical sampling distributions in which $n$ = 1, 2, and 5, respectively.* For example, for Panel D-I, a sample of five observations was selected randomly from the *normal* parent population, the mean of these five observations was computed, and this process was repeated 10,000 times. The figure in Panel D-I is the frequency distribution of these 10,000 means*—that is, the figure in Panel D-I is an empirical sampling distribution of the mean when $\mu = 100$, $\sigma = 15$, and $n = 5$. If the process had been repeated, not 10,000 but 1,000,000 times, the empirical sampling distribution would have become almost perfectly symmetrical and normal—the small amount of irregularity evident in column I of Figure 10.3 would virtually disappear and the empirical sampling distribution would coincide with the theoretical sampling distribution.

Observe that the mean of the sampling distributions (the mean of the $\overline{X}$'s) is approximately $100 = \mu$ in each figure. Indeed, the expression $E(\overline{X}) = \mu$ is another way of saying that the mean of the sampling distribution of an infinite number of samples (not just 10,000 as in Fig. 10.3) is the parameter $\mu$. In Panels B to E of Figure 10.3, the sample sizes are small; hence, some degree of nonnormality in the parent population continues to be evident in the sampling distribution, but progressively less so as $n$ increases. Panel F gives the three corresponding empirical sampling distributions when $n$ was increased to 25. Notice that these sampling distributions are very similar yet $n$ is only 25. To the untrained eye the distributions in Panel D may not appear to be normal, but this is only because the vertical ("Percent") axis has been scaled uniformly in Panels A to F so that the decrease in the variability of the sampling distribution would be evident.

The sampling distributions in Figure 10.3 demonstrate that even in nonnormal distributions the standard deviation of the $\overline{X}$'s—that is, the standard error of the mean—equals the standard deviation of the parent population divided by the square root of the sample size: $\sigma_{\overline{X}} = \sigma/\sqrt{n}$. In Table 10.1 the standard errors, $s_{\overline{X}}$ (each based on 10,000 means for the various sampling distributions) are reported along with the theoretical value, $\sigma_{\overline{X}} = \sigma/\sqrt{n}$. For example, when samples of $n = 25$ were drawn from a skewed parent population, the resulting 10,000 sample means had a standard deviation of 2.98, which agrees almost perfectly with the theoretical standard error of the mean,

*The authors are indebted to George Kretke for the data for this demonstration, obtained via computer simulation. It is estimated that this project done by hand with only the aid of a table of random numbers and a hand calculator would have required approximately 2,500 hours—approximately a full working year!

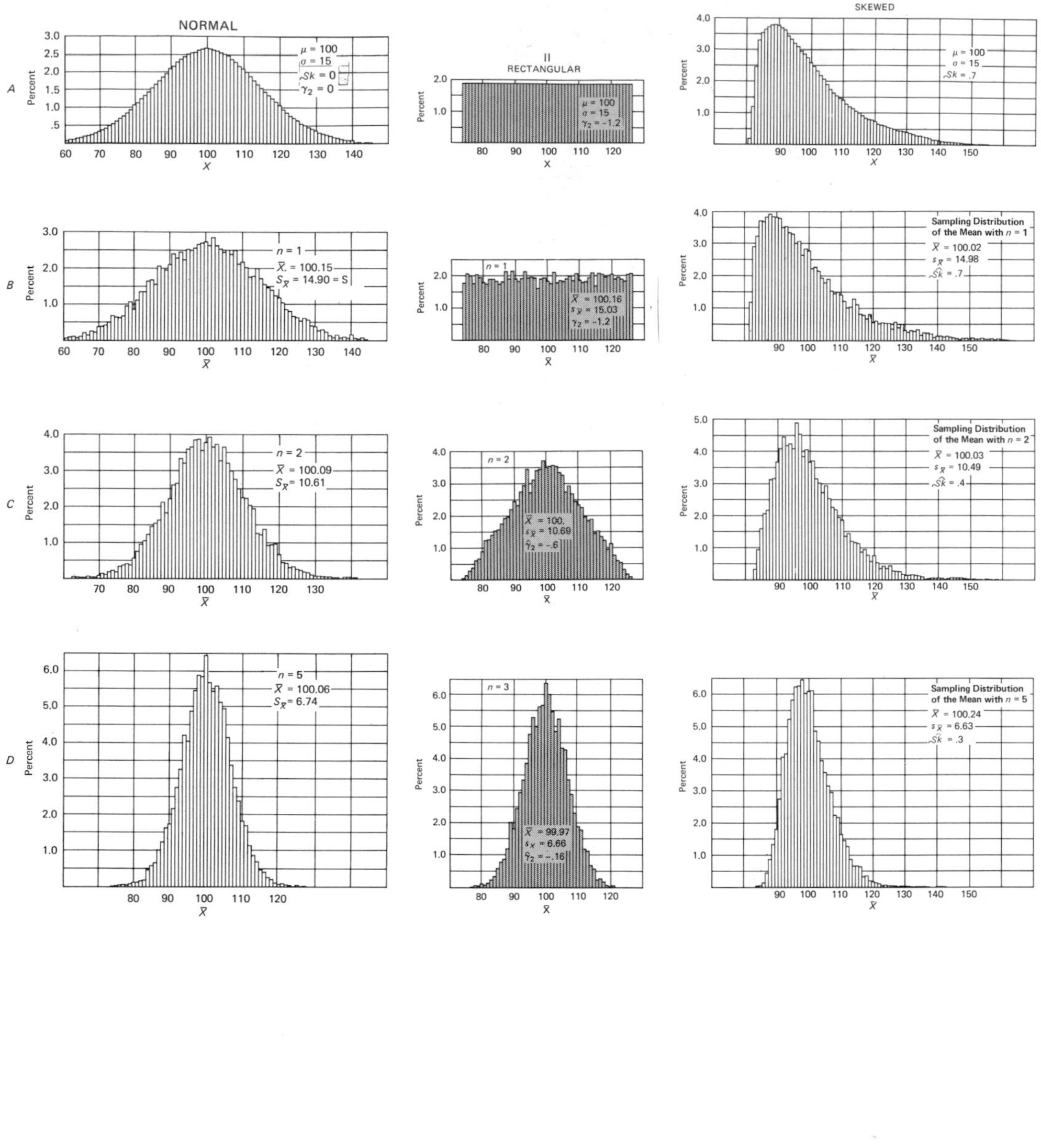

FIGURE 10.3. Empirical sampling distributions of 10,000 means of $n$ observations drawn randomly from normal (col. I), rectangular (col. II), and skewed (col. III) parent distributions in which $\mu = 100$ and $\sigma = 15$. Sample size ($n$) is 1, 2, and 5 in Panels B, C, and D, respectively. Panels E and F give sampling distributions for $n = 10$ and $n = 25$ (p. 187).

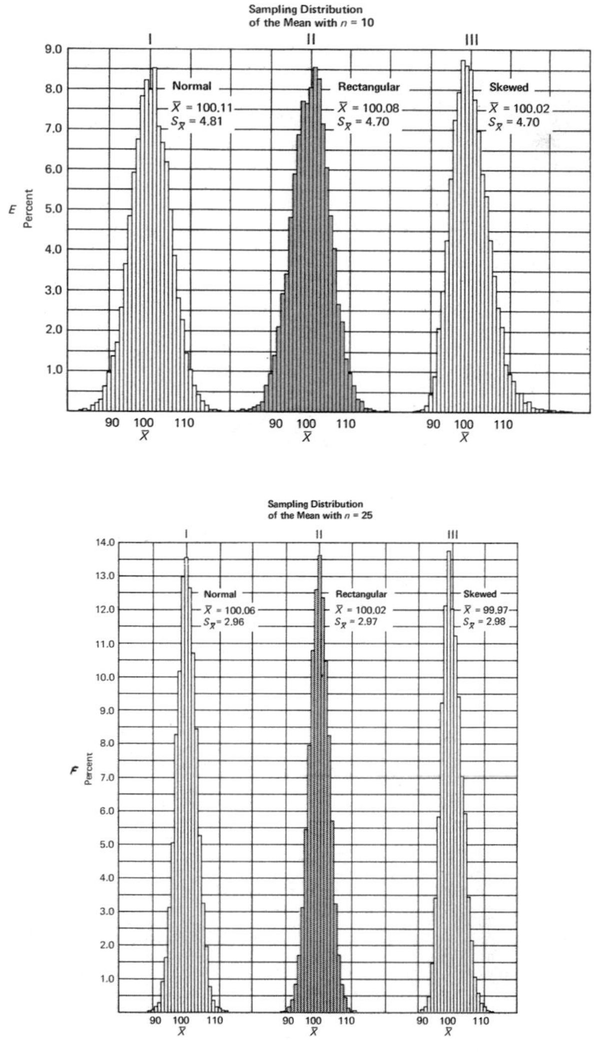


FIGURE 10.3. (cont.)

**TABLE 10.1 A Comparison of Observed Values of $s_{\bar{X}}$ (Based on 10,000 $\bar{X}$'s) and Theoretical Values of $\sigma_{\bar{X}}$ for Various Sample Sizes When the Three Parent Populations (Normal, Rectangular, and Skewed) Sampled Have Equal Means and Standard Deviations ($\mu$ = 100 and $\sigma$ = 15)**

| *Parent Population* | $s_{\bar{X}}$ | | | | | |
|---|---|---|---|---|---|---|
| | $n = 1$ | $n = 2$ | $n = 5$ | $n = 10$ | $n = 25$ | $n = 100$ |
| Normal | 14.90 | 10.61 | 6.74 | 4.81 | 2.96 | 1.498 |
| Rectangular | 15.03 | 10.69 | 6.66 | 4.70 | 2.97 | 1.487 |
| Skewed | 14.98 | 10.49 | 6.63 | 4.70 | 2.98 | 1.479 |
| $\sigma_{\bar{X}} = \sigma/\sqrt{n}$ | 15 | 10.61 | 6.71 | 4.74 | 3.00 | 1.500 |

$\sigma/\sqrt{n} = 15/\sqrt{25} = 3$. In other words, *even when the parent population is not normal, the formula $\sigma_{\bar{X}} = \sigma/\sqrt{n}$ accurately depicts the degree of variability in the sampling distribution.*

## 10.16 THE USE OF SAMPLING DISTRIBUTIONS

The notion of a sampling distribution is used by the theoretical statistician to derive the techniques of inferential statistics. *The researcher does not seek to create his own sampling distribution by repeatedly drawing samples from a population.* That would be costly and unnecessary. In practice only one sample of $n$ cases is drawn; then the theory underlying the sampling distribution is used to establish a confidence interval. For example, an investigator might draw a sample of $n$ = 200 cases and establish a single confidence interval—say, the .95 confidence interval—around $\bar{X}$. He does *not* draw many samples or attempt to construct an actual sampling distribution of $\bar{X}$. Instead, he has a single interval, extending perhaps from 46.5 to 51.5. Is $\mu$ in this interval? It's impossible to know *for certain.* Is it rational to act as though $\mu$ is in this interval? Indeed it is, since in the long run $\mu$ would be missing from only 5% of the intervals constructed in like manner. The technique of interval estimation is based on the theoretical concept of the sampling distribution with its notion of infinitely many samples drawn and their means distributed in some known fashion.

## 10.17 PROOF THAT $\sigma^2_{\bar{X}} = \sigma^2/n$

The proof that regardless of the shape of the parent population, the sampling distribution of $\bar{X}$ has a mean of $\mu$ and variance of $\sigma^2/n$, where $\mu$ and $\sigma^2$ are the mean and variance of the population sampled and $n$ is the sample size, is straightforward: $X$ is the variable being measured on the population; its mean is $\mu$ and its variance is $\sigma^2$. A random sample of size $n$ has a first element $X_1$, a second element $X_2, \cdots$, and an $n$th element $X_n$; $X_1$ is merely the *first* score chosen in each sample, not the smallest score. Therefore, the collection of all possible $X_1$'s, that is, all first scores chosen in all possible random samples from the population, forms a population with mean $\mu$ and variance $\sigma^2$. Thus, $X_1, X_2, \cdots, X_n$ are each random variables from a population with a mean of $\mu$ and a variance of $\sigma^2$.

The sample mean equals $(X_1 + X_2 + \cdots + X_n)/n$. The mean of the sampling distribution of means equals the *expected value of* $\bar{X}$

$$E(\bar{X}) = E[(X_1 + X_2 + \cdots + X_n)/n]$$

$$= \frac{1}{n} E(X_1 + X_2 + \cdots + X_n)$$

$$= \frac{1}{n} [E(X_1) + E(X_2) + \cdots + E(X_n)] \quad \textbf{(10.6)}$$

Now $X_1$ has the same distribution over samples as does $X_2$ or any other $X_i$. Its population mean and variance are $\mu$ and $\sigma$, hence the last term in Equation 10.6 equals

$$E(\bar{X}) = \frac{1}{n} (\mu + \mu + \cdots + \mu) = \frac{1}{n} (n\mu) = \mu$$

Stated in words, regardless of the shape of the parent population, the expected value of $\bar{X}$ is the mean $\mu$ of the sampling distribution of the sample means, which is also the mean of the population being sampled.

How much will $\bar{X}$ vary from sample to sample? If each sample contains more than one observation, the variance of the sample means will be smaller than the variance of the parent population. Notice that if $n = 1$, the sampling distribution of the mean would be the same as the frequency distribution of the parent population, as shown in Panel B of Figure 10.3. If samples with $n = 1$ were repeatedly drawn and a sampling distribution of these "sample means" were constructed, the variance of the original population, $\sigma^2$, and the variance of the sampling distribution of the "means" of samples of size 1 would be the same; $\sigma^2/n = \sigma^2/1 = \sigma^2$.

$$E(s_{\bar{X}}^2) = \sigma_{\bar{X}}^2$$

What is the variance of the means of samples of size $n = 2$ from a population? Let the population variance be $\sigma^2$. For each sample, $\bar{X} = (X_1 + X_2)/2$ is calculated. $X_1$ and $X_2$ are arbitrary designations for the first and second observations randomly drawn and are not related to the size of the scores. Consequently, over all random samples, $X_1$ has variance $\sigma^2$ and so does $X_2$. Because the samples are randomly drawn, there is no relationship ($\rho = 0$) between the values of the first and second observations in any sample. Since $X_1$ and $X_2$ are uncorrelated, the correlation and covariance between the first and second observations in a sample over infinitely many random samples from a population is zero.

Now the variance over random samples of $\bar{X} = (X_1 + X_2)/2$ is denoted as follows:

$$\sigma_{\bar{X}}^2 = \sigma_{(X_1 + X_2)/2}^2$$

When a variable is multiplied by a constant (in this instance, $\frac{1}{2}$), the variance of the resulting variable is the original variance multiplied by the square of the constant (Sec. 5.11). Therefore,

$$\sigma^2_{(X_1+X_2)(1/2)} = \left(\frac{1}{2}\right)^2 \sigma^2_{(X_1+X_2)}$$

If two variables are uncorrelated, then the variance of the sum of the two variables is the sum of their variances (Eq. 7.8). We argued that $X_1$ and $X_2$ are uncorrelated.

$$\left(\frac{1}{2}\right)^2 \sigma^2_{X_1+X_2} = \frac{1}{4}(\sigma^2_{X_1} + \sigma^2_{X_2} + 2\rho_{X_1X_2}\sigma_{X_1}\sigma_{X_2}) = \frac{1}{4}(\sigma^2_{X_1} + \sigma^2_{X_2})$$

The variance of $X_1$ over repeated random samples is $\sigma^2$, and so is the variance of $X_2$: $\sigma^2_{X_1} = \sigma^2_{X_2} = \sigma^2$. Therefore, the equation can be written as follows:

$$\left(\frac{1}{4}\right)(\sigma^2_{X_1} + \sigma^2_{X_2}) = \left(\frac{1}{4}\right)(2\sigma^2) = \sigma^2/2$$

The equation expresses the conclusion of the argument: the variance of the mean of samples of size 2 from a population with variance $\sigma^2$ is equal to $\sigma^2/2$. In this instance $n = 2$ and $\sigma^2_{\bar{X}} = \sigma^2/2$. This is no coincidence. It is true in general that for random samples of size $n$, $\sigma^2_{\bar{X}} = \sigma^2/n$.

If random samples of size $n$ are taken from a population with variance $\sigma^2$, then the variance of the mean, $\bar{X} = (X_1 + X_2 + \cdots + X_n)/n$, over samples is given by

$$\sigma^2_{\bar{X}} = \sigma^2_{(X_1+X_2+\cdots+X_n)/n}$$

The right-hand side of the previous equation shows $\sigma^2_{\bar{X}}$ to be the variance of $(1/n)$ times the sum of the variance of the $n$ *uncorrelated* variables $X_1, X_2, \ldots X_n$. Therefore,

$$\sigma^2_{\bar{X}} = \left(\frac{1}{n}\right)^2 \sigma^2_{(X_1+X_2+\cdots+X_n)}$$

Each variable $X_i (i = 1, 2, \ldots, n)$ has a variance of $\sigma^2$ and is uncorrelated with the other $n - 1$ variables. Therefore, the variance of the sum of the $n$ uncorrelated variables is the sum of the variances of the variables, because each of the $n(n - 1)/2$ covariance is 0. Thus

$$\left(\frac{1}{n}\right)^2 \sigma^2_{(X_1+X_2+\cdots+X_n)} = \left(\frac{1}{n}\right)^2 (\sigma^2_{X_1} + \sigma^2_{X_2} + \cdots + \sigma^2_{X_n})$$

Because each variable has the same variance $\sigma^2$, the previous equation can be written as

$$\left(\frac{1}{n}\right)^2 (\sigma^2 + \sigma^2 + \cdots + \sigma^2) = \left(\frac{1}{n}\right)^2 (n\sigma^2) = \frac{\sigma^2}{n} \qquad \textbf{(10.7)}$$

A fundamental relationship is expressed in Equation 10.7. *The variance of the means of random samples of size n from a population with variance* $\sigma^2$ *is equal to* $\sigma^2/n$.

The expression $\sigma^2/n$ has traditionally been called the *variance error of the mean.* Its positive square root, Equation 10.1, is another important expression known as the *standard error of the mean*:

$$\sigma_{\overline{X}} = \sigma/\sqrt{n} \tag{10.1}$$

The standard error of the mean, Equation 10.1, is the standard deviation of the sampling distribution of the means of an infinite number of samples, each of size $n$, from a population with variance $\sigma^2$. Notice that in Table 10.1 and Figure 10.3 that the population from which samples were drawn had a standard deviation of 15, and the standard deviation of the sampling distribution of means of random samples of various sizes is consistent with Equation 10.1. For example, when $n = 10$: $\sigma_{\overline{X}} = \sigma/\sqrt{n} = 15/\sqrt{10} = 4.74$, whereas in Table 10.1 the values of $s_{\overline{X}}$ were 4.81, 4.70, and 4.70 for the normal, rectangular, and skewed distributions, respectively.

## 10.18 PROPERTIES OF ESTIMATORS

An estimate is a value of a sample statistic that gives information about a population parameter. For example the sample mean $\overline{X}$ is an estimator of the population mean $\mu$. There is a close analogy between the way in which a sample mean is calculated and the way in which one might calculate a population mean. It is logical to think of $\overline{X}$ as estimating $\mu$. However, there are other ways of treating sample data to arrive at a value that estimates $\mu$. Why not use the sample median or the sample mode as an estimate of $\mu$? It is certainly possible to do this; however, by the criteria used in assessing the properties of an estimator, $\overline{X}$ turns out to be a better estimator of $\mu$ than either the sample median or the sample mode (Sec. 4.17).

In this section the properties of estimators of parameters will be examined. What are the different ways in which parameters can be estimated? Is one estimator to be preferred over all others for estimating a certain parameter, and why? The properties of unbiasedness, consistency, and efficiency will be considered.

## 10.19 UNBIASEDNESS

As discussed in Section 5.13, an estimator $\hat{\theta}$, is said to be *unbiased* for estimating a parameter, $\theta$, if the mean of the sampling distribution of the estimator equals the value of the parameter being estimated. Equivalently, an estimator $\hat{\theta}$ is unbiased if its expected value $E(\hat{\theta})$ is equal to the parameter being estimated, $\theta$.

Regardless of the nature of the population being sampled, the sample mean $\overline{X}$ is an unbiased estimator of the population mean $\mu$. Notice in Figure 10.3 that the value of the population mean $\mu$ is 100 and that the mean of any of the sampling distributions of $\overline{X}$ also approaches 100. This example illustrates the unbiasedness of $\overline{X}$ as an estimator of

$\mu$. If samples are drawn randomly from a normal distribution or some other symmetric distribution, then the sample median is also an unbiased estimator of the population mean $\mu$. In other words, the average of the medians on an infinite number of random samples from a normal distribution equals $\mu$, the mean of the normal distribution (which is, of course, also its median and its mode).

There are many examples of *biased* estimators. Suppose one wishes to estimate $\rho$, the correlation between two variables that have a bivariate normal distribution in the population. Imagine that for a particular population $\rho = .75$. The mean of the sampling distribution of the sample correlation coefficient $r$ will be slightly *less than* .75 for any finite sample size. Thus, $r$ is in general a negatively *biased* estimator of $\rho$*. When the expected value of a statistic is less than the parameter being estimated, it is said to be negatively biased. Conversely, if $E(\hat{\theta}) > \theta$, $\hat{\theta}$ is said to be positively biased.

In Equation 5.5 the variance in a sample is defined as $s^2 = \Sigma(X_i - \overline{X})^2/(n - 1)$. It might have been more natural to measure variability by simply taking the *average* of the $n$ squared deviations around the sample mean, but instead it was decided to place $(n - 1)$ and not $n$ in the denominator of $s^2$ *because the quantity* $s^2$ *is an unbiased estimator of the population variance* $\sigma^2$, *whereas* $\Sigma(X_i - \overline{X})^2/n$ *is negatively biased as an estimator of* $\sigma^2$. That is,

$$E\left[\frac{(X_i - \overline{X})^2}{n}\right] \leqslant \sigma^2$$

Suppose that we took many random samples from any population with variance $\sigma^2$ and calculated $s^2$ each time. The average of a huge number of these sample variances would be exactly equal to $\sigma^2$. Hence, $s^2$ is an unbiased estimator of $\sigma^2$. If $\Sigma(X_i - \overline{X})^2/n$ had been calculated on each sample instead, the average of these quantities would have been smaller than $\sigma^2$, namely $[(n - 1)/n]\,\sigma^2$. Of course, if $n$ were quite large—100 or more for example—the difference between $s^2$ and $\Sigma(X_i - \overline{X})^2/n$ would be very small, because the value of $(n - 1)/n$, the ratio of the degrees of freedom to sample size would approach 1, and the estimator would contain only a small bias as an estimator of $\sigma^2$.

Suppose that one has a normal distribution with mean $\mu = 0$ and variance $\sigma^2 = 100$. If an infinite number of random samples of size $n = 6$ were drawn from the population and both $s^2$ and $\Sigma(X_i - \overline{X})^2/6$ were calculated for each sample, the two sampling distributions in Figure 10.4 would be obtained.

Notice that the mean of the sampling distribution of $s^2$ is 100 the value of $\sigma^2$. This illustrates the unbiasedness of $s^2$ in this instance, that is, $E(s^2) = \sigma^2$. The mean of the sampling distribution of $\Sigma(X_i - \overline{X})^2/6$ is equal to 83.33. In this instance the bias

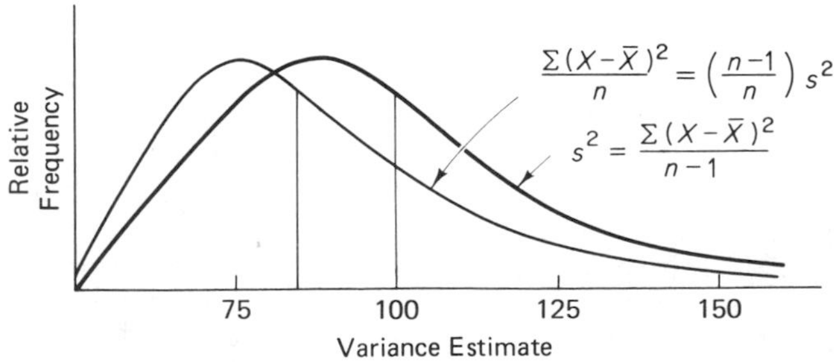


**FIGURE 10.4**
**Sampling distributions of $s^2$ and $\Sigma(X_i - \overline{X})^2/6$ for random samples of size 6 from a normal distribution with variance $\sigma^2 = 100$.**

*The extent of the bias is exceedingly small—less than .01 if $n > 25$ (Olkin, 1967, p. 111).

introduced into the estimation of $\sigma^2$ by using $n$ in place of $(n - 1)$ in the denominator of the sample variance is sizable—that is, $(n - 1)/n = \frac{5}{6}$ here.

How was it determined that the denominator (i.e., the degrees of freedom $\nu$) of the sample variance should be $n - 1$ in order for $E(s^2) = \sigma^2$? It was *not* determined empirically that $n - 1$ gives the unbiased estimator. There are several ways of proving mathematically that $s^2$ is an unbaised estimator of $\sigma^2$. The algebraic proof is cumbersome and will not be presented here.*

The quantity $s^2$ is an unbiased estimator of $\sigma^2$. Does this imply that $s$, the sample standard deviation, is an unbiased estimator of $\sigma$, the population standard deviation? It does not (Sec. 5.13). A nonlinear transformation (Sec. 7.9, e.g., $\sqrt{X}$) of an unbiased estimator ($X$) does not produce an unbiased estimator.

The sample standard deviation is a *biased* estimator of the population standard deviation. The amount of bias depends on the shape of the population being sampled. *If the population is normal*, the mean of the sampling distribution of $s$, $\mu_s$, is slightly less than $\sigma$. Specifically,

$$E(s) = \mu_s = \left(\frac{4n - 4}{4n - 3}\right) \sigma \tag{10.9}$$

Equation 10.9 can be rearranged to provide an unbiased estimate of $\sigma$.

$$E\left\{\left[1 + \frac{1}{4(n - 1)}\right] s\right\} = \sigma \tag{10.10}$$

It is obvious from Equation 10.10 that the amount of bias—the difference between $\mu_s$ and $\sigma$—is $s/[4(n - 1)]$.† The bias in $s$ is quite small unless $n$ is very small. For example, even if $n$ is 26, the average $s$ will underestimate $\sigma$ by only 1%.

Table 10.2 presents some parameters, their estimators, and statements that the

**TABLE 10.2 Biasedness or Unbiasedness of Various Estimators of Parameters of Various Populations**

| *Parameter* | *Nature of population* | *Estimator (statistic)* | *Status of the bias in the estimator* |
|---|---|---|---|
| Range | Any population | Range | Negatively biased |
| $\mu$ | Any population | $\bar{X}$ | Unbiased |
| $\mu$ | Symmetric | *Md* | Unbiased |
| $\mu$ | Symmetric and unimodal | *Mo* | Unbiased |
| $\mu$ | Skewed | *Md* | Biased |
| $\mu$ | Skewed | *Mo* | Biased |
| $\sigma^2$ | Any population | $s^2$ | Unbiased |
| $\sigma$ | Normal | $s$ | Negatively biased |
| $\rho$ | Bivariate-normal | $r$ | Negatively biased |

*It can be found in Edwards (1964, pp. 29-36).

†If $n$ is very small, a negligible degree of bias remains in Equation 10.10. For example, if $n = 2$, 3, and 4, Equation 10.10 yields 1.25$s$, 1.125$s$, and 1.083$s$, respectively, whereas the precise values for perfectly unbiased estimates are trivially larger: 1.253$s$, 1.128, and 1.085, respectively (Dixon and Massey, 1969). For interesting discussions of unbiased estimation of the standard deviation, see Cureton (1968*b*), Jarrett (1968), Cureton (1968*c*), and Bolch (1968) in that order.

estimator is biased or unbiased. As you study Table 10.2, notice that the sample median and sample mode can be used to estimate the parameter $\mu$. Note that for certain statistics, whether the estimator is biased or unbiased depends upon the shape of the distribution of the population from which samples are drawn.

## 10.20 CONSISTENCY

A second property of estimators is their *consistency*. A consistent estimator, even though it may be biased, tends to get closer and closer to the value of the parameter it estimates as the sample size becomes larger. All commonly used estimators, such as those in Table 10.2, whether biased or unbiased, are consistent. For example, the sample standard deviation is a biased but consistent estimator of $\sigma$. By taking a large sample, the mean $s$ will be close to $\sigma$ in value. The larger the sample becomes, the closer the mean $s$ gets to $\sigma$. This can be seen algebraically when $n$ approaches infinity in Equation 10.9.

## 10.21 RELATIVE EFFICIENCY

The third property of estimators is their *efficiency*. Efficiency refers to the precision with which an estimator estimates a parameter. It refers to the variability of the estimates from sample to sample–the degree of sampling error associated with the estimator. Efficiency is more important in the application of statistics than either unbiasedness or consistency. The variance error of the sample mean $\sigma_{\overline{X}}^2$ is a measure of efficiency of $\overline{X}$, as an estimator of $\mu$. The variance (or standard) error of an estimator is one of its most important properties. The *variance error* of any statistic is the variance of the sampling distribution of the statistic.

Suppose the value of the population mean of a particular normal distribution is to be estimated. One way of estimating $\mu$ is to find the mean $\overline{X}$ of a sample of size $n$. However, the sample median *Md* is also an unbiased estimator of $\mu$ (See Table 10.2). Both are consistent estimators of $\mu$. Which is to be preferred? This question could be answered by considering the *relative efficiencies* of the two estimators. Which estimator of $\mu$, the sample mean or the sample median, varies less from sample to sample? Which has a smaller variance error?

If the variance $\sigma^2$ of the normal population sampled is 225 and sample size $n$ is 9, then the variance of the sampling distribution of $\overline{X}$'s is (Eq. 10.7) $\sigma^2/n = 225/9$ or $\sigma_{\overline{X}} = 5$.

What about the variance error of the sample median $\sigma_{Md}^2$? If thousands and thousands of random samples, each of size $n$, are drawn from a normal population with mean $\mu$ and variance $\sigma^2$, and the median *Md* is calculated for each sample, the frequency distribution of these sample medians, that is the sampling distribution, will be normal with mean $\mu$ and, if $n$ is large, its variance is given in Equation 10.11.

$$\sigma_{Md}^2 = 1.57\sigma^2/n = 1.57\sigma_{\overline{X}}^2 \qquad \textbf{(10.11)}$$

**FIGURE 10.5**
**Sampling distributions of the sample mean $\overline{X}$ and the sample median $Md$ for random samples of size 9 from a normal population with mean $\mu = 100$ and variance $\sigma^2 = 225$.**

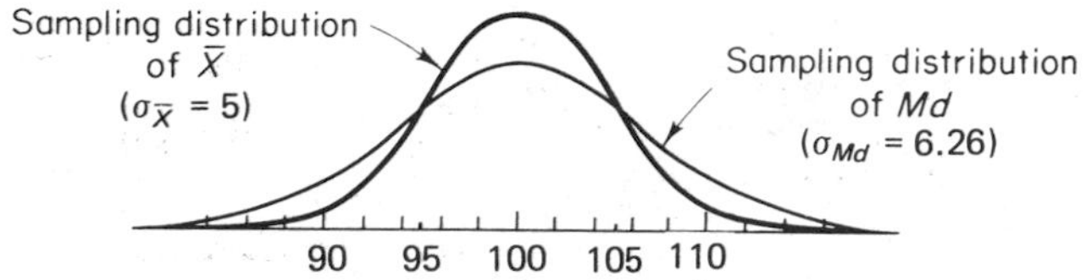


Note the variance error of the sample median is $(1.57)\sigma_{\overline{X}}^2$. Figure 10.5 depicts the sampling distributions of $\overline{X}$, and $Md$ for samples of size 9 from a normal distribution with $\sigma = 15$.

The variance error of the sample median in Figure 10.5 is equal to $(1.57)\sigma^2/n = (1.57)(25) = 39.25$ or $\sigma_{Md} = 6.26$. The figure reveals that the sample median will vary more than the sample mean over repeated samples. Note that only 16% of the sample means will be larger than 105 while about 21% of the sample medians will be larger than 105. $\overline{X}$ is a more efficient estimator of $\mu$ than $Md$; relative efficiency is the ratio of the variance of the more efficient estimator to the variance of the less efficient estimator.

The *efficiency* of $Md$ *relative to* $\overline{X}$ *is* the ratio of their variance errors. In this instance when $n$ is large,

$$\textit{Relative efficiency of Md} = \frac{\sigma_{\overline{X}}^2}{\sigma_{Md}^2} = \frac{\sigma^2/n}{(1.57)\sigma^2/n} = \frac{1}{1.57} = .637 = 63.7\%$$

meaning that for normally distributed measures the median is less than two-thirds as efficient as the arithmetic mean, regardless of the magnitude of $n$.

One interpretation of relative efficiency is that if the median of a sample of 100 observations is used to estimate $\mu$, the same degree of precision of estimation could be attained by drawing a sample of sixty-four observations and computing $\overline{X}$. More precisely, the relative efficiency of $\overline{X}$ versus $Md$ is influenced by $n$. Figure 10.6 shows that the

**FIGURE 10.6. The efficiency of the median and the midrange relative to $\overline{X}$ for estimating the parameter $\mu$. Relative efficiency = $\sigma_{\overline{X}}^2/\sigma_{Md}^2$ or $\sigma_{\overline{X}}^2/\sigma_{\text{Midrange}}^2$.**

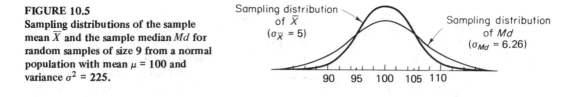

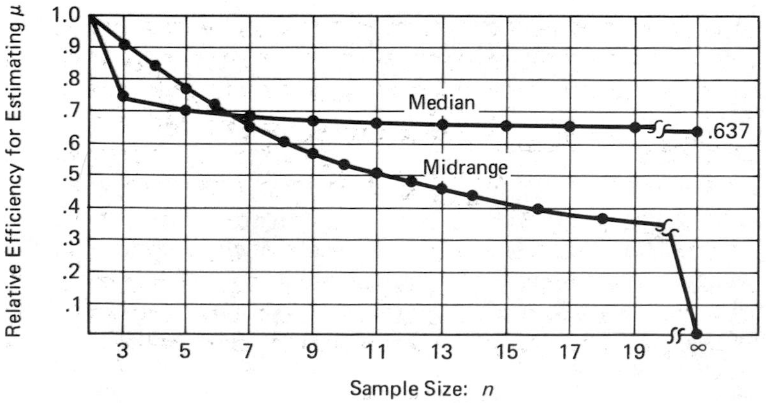

relative efficiency of $\overline{X}$ and $Md$ in normal populations are equal when $n = 2$, but that $Md$ rapidly approaches its asymptote of .637 as $n$ increases. Figure 10.6 also shows that the efficiency of the midrange, $(X_L - X_S)/2$ (Sec. 4.15), is greater than that of the $Md$ for $n \leqslant 6$, but continues to decline progressively as $n$ increases. Statisticians have generally combined the criteria of unbiasedness and efficiency when making their choice of a "best" estimator of a parameter. Because all commonly used estimators have the property of consistency, and all have little or no bias when $n$ is large, the criterion of efficiency becomes the major criterion for applied use of inferential statistics. The greater efficiency of the mean is the principal reason it is used more than the median in statistical inference, in spite of the fact that the median often has superior descriptive and interpretive properties (Sec. 4.17).

## CHAPTER SUMMARY

Most applications of inferential statistics actually involve parent populations of finite size, not infinite populations. The ratio of the sample size $n$ to the size of the population is known as the sampling fraction ($n/N$). Unless the sampling fraction is at least .05, there are negligible differences in using the simpler inferential techniques which assume $N$ is infinite.

The most important characteristic of a sample is representativeness. Representativeness is characteristic of random samples. In random sampling each unit (person, school, city, etc.) has an equal and independent chance of being selected for the sample. Random samples are often obtained using a list of random numbers. Most well-designed systematic samples and random samples differ inconsequentially. Accidental samples should not be used for inferential purposes.

Point and interval estimation are both useful. If $\overline{X} = 56.0$, 56.0 is a point estimate of $\mu$. If the .95 confidence interval is 54–58, 54–58 is an interval estimate for the value of $\mu$. Properly employed, 95% of the .95 confidence intervals around any statistic will include the corresponding parameter being estimated.

A sampling distribution is a frequency distribution of statistics, such as $\overline{X}$, $Md$, $s^2$, $r$, and so on. In this chapter the sampling distribution of the mean was examined extensively.

The central limit theorem states that even if the parent population is not normal, the sampling distribution will be approximately normal as $n$ increases. If $n \geqslant 25$, the sampling distribution of $\overline{X}$ is essentially normal and confidence intervals for $\mu$ can be assumed to be accurate even for nonnormal populations.

A major purpose of this chapter has been to present the theory and a portion of the practice of interval estimation. This has been done in considerable detail because the comprehension of the rationale of this highly useful inferential statistical technique is critical. In subsequent chapters numerous examples of the construction of confidence intervals will be met. In each instance some of the particulars of the calculation of the confidence interval will be different from those presented in this chapter.

In this chapter $\sigma$ was assumed to be known even though in practice this is rarely the case. This allowed us to avoid many distracting qualifying statements. In Chapter 11 we will face the more typical situation in which $\sigma$ is not known. The second major branch of inferential statistics, hypothesis testing, will also be introduced.

## *MASTERY TEST*

The selection of a random sample requires which of the following? (Answer T or F.)

1. The observations must be normally distributed.
2. Each observation must have an equal chance of being chosen for the sample.
3. The selection of any one observation must be independent of that for all other observations.

In a mail survey, of the randomly sampled 400 social workers who were sent questionnaires, 240 returned them.

4. Can the 240 be considered a random sample of the population of social workers?
5. Can the 240 be considered a representative sample of the 400?
6. Can the 60% of the sample who responded be considered to represent approximately 60% of the population—the 60% who would have responded had they been sent questionnaires?
7. A sample of 100 families was randomly selected for a structured interview survey. Interviews with eighteen of the families were not conducted because of the unwillingness to cooperate, incorrect addresses, "vicious dogs," or "nobody home." Can the eighty-two be viewed as a random sample of the original population sampled?
8. A psychologist followed up a group of chronic alcoholics who had undergone two weeks of intensive therapy at a state hospital by a treatment team composed of psychiatrists, clinical psychologists, social workers, and vocational counselors. Only about thirty-six of 108 could be located eight weeks after treatment. Twenty-five of the thirty-six were coping satisfactorily. Can it be concluded that about two-thirds (i.e., $\frac{25}{36} = .69$) of those treated appear to be getting along adequately? Why?

A sample of twelfth-grade students at Lincoln High School is to be tested. Which of the following procedures will result in a random sample of 100 students from the population of seniors at the school?

9. Test twenty twelfth-grade students in each of five randomly selected classes.
10. Select the first 100 seniors who arrive at school on a given day.
11. Use a table of random numbers and select 100 seniors from those who volunteered to participate.
12. Randomly select 100 seniors from those present on a given day.
13. Randomly draw 100 seniors from an alphabetical listing of all students.
14. If every tenth name on the roster were selected after randomly selecting the initial name, what kind of a sample would result? Would this be a representative sample?

On the Wechsler Intelligence Scales, IQ's are normally distributed with $\mu = 100$, $\sigma = 15$. Suppose a random sample of nine persons was tested, the mean computed, and this process repeated 1,000 times.

15. Estimate the value of the standard deviation of the 1,000 means.
16. About what percentage of the sample means with $n = 9$ would exceed 105? 110?
17. About what percentage of the means would fall between 95 and 105? Between 90 and 110?
18. Would the $\overline{X}$'s be normally distributed?
19. What is the variance of this distribution of $\overline{X}$'s?
20. If $n = 225$ (not 9), what would be the value of $\sigma_{\overline{X}}$?
21. If $n = 225$, what percentage of $\overline{X}$'s would deviate *by less than* 1 point from 100—that is, would be expected to fall within the interval 99.0–101.0?

22. If the observations in a frequency distribution are not normally distributed and $n$ is small, will the sampling distribution of sample means be *precisely* normally distributed?
23. Will the sampling distribution of means be approximately normal if $n$ is 25 or so, even if the frequency distribution of $X$-values is not normal?
24. What is the mathematical theorem that indicates that the sampling distribution of $\overline{X}$ approaches normality as $n$ increases, regardless of the shape of the distribution in the parent population?
25. Suppose that instead of selecting a truly random sample, for convenience the last name on each page of a telephone directory was selected. Would this sample probably be quite representative of the population of listings in the telephone directory?
26. Assuming that $\sigma$ is known for a normal distribution of observations, is it true that $\overline{X} \pm 1.96\sigma_{\overline{X}}$ yields a .95 confidence interval for any value of $n$?
27. When the distribution is normal and $\sigma$ is known, if two samples of 100 observations are drawn randomly from the same parent populations, will the two resulting .68 confidence intervals be identical?

Are the following pairs of terms synonymous and equivalent?

28. (1) The standard error of $\overline{X}$ and (2) the standard deviation of the sampling distribution of $\overline{X}$.
29. (1) $\sigma^2/n$ and (2) the standard error of $\overline{X}$.
30. (1) $\sigma^2_{\overline{X}}$ and (2) the variance of the sampling distribution of $\overline{X}$.
31. (1) The population variance $\sigma^2$ and (2) $n$ times the $\sigma^2_{\overline{X}}$.
32. (1) The mean of the sampling distribution of $\overline{X}$ and (2) $\sigma^2_{\overline{X}}$.
33. (1) $E(\overline{X})$ and (2) $\mu$.
34. (1) $\mu$ and (2) $(\Sigma X)/n$.
35. (1) $\overline{X}$ and (2) $(\Sigma x)/n$.
36. (1) $s^2$ and (2) $\Sigma x^2/(n - 1)$.
37. If you conducted many studies on many different topics, in the long run, what percentage of your .95 confidence intervals would be expected to contain the parameter you were estimating?
38. Where would an increase in $n$ of 20 have the greatest effect on reducing the size of the confident intervals?
    a. increasing $n$ from 5 to 25
    b. increasing $n$ from 10 to 30
    c. increasing $n$ from 40 to 60
39. Which type of estimate, point or interval, more properly conveys the degree of accuracy in the estimate?
40. In a normal distribution is $E(Md) = E(\overline{X}) = \mu$?
41. The statistical property denoted in the previous question is
    a. consistency b. efficiency c. unbiasedness
42. Using the options in the previous question, which property is primarily responsible for the greater use of the mean instead of the median or mode in inferential statistics?
43. Using Figure 10.6, the same degree of precision using $Md$ to estimate $\mu$ with $n = 100$ can be obtained using $\overline{X}$ with a sample size of_____.

## *PROBLEMS AND EXERCISES*

1. By using the table of random digits (Table B in the Appendix), draw a random sample of five students from the following set of sixteen:

| | | | |
|---|---|---|---|
| John | Al | Joan | Phil |
| Mary | Tom | Susan | Paul |
| Alice | Maurice | Martha | Edith |
| Bob | Barbara | Jack | Warren |

2. Enter the table of random numbers (Table B) and select two random digits. Determine the mean of these two numbers and repeat the process until you have twenty-five means. Tally the twenty-five means into a sampling distribution.
   a. What is the shape of the frequency distribution of the individual random digits (not means)?
   b. Does the distribution of the twenty-five $\overline{X}$'s appear to be bell-shaped?
   c. Compute the mean of these twenty-five means. What parameter is being estimated? What is the numerical value of $\mu$?
   d. Compare the mean of your means (part c) with $\mu$.
   e. If you continued finding means for pairs of random numbers until you had 100 means, would the sampling distribution be expected to appear more symmetrical? Would the sampling distribution be expected to appear more nearly normal? Would the range of the distribution of $\overline{X}$'s be expected to increase?
   f. If, instead of finding the mean for two numbers, you determined the mean of eight random numbers, and repeated the process twenty-five times, would the value of $\mu$ be altered?
   g. In part f would the value of $\sigma_{\overline{X}}$ decrease?
   h. In part f would the sampling distribution be more nearly normal?
   i. What mathematical principle accounts for the approximate normality of the sampling distribution as $n$ becomes larger?
   j. If you computed the standard deviation of the set of twenty-five means, what is the appropriate symbol?
   k. What is the parameter being estimated in part j?
3. A sample of size $n$ is to be drawn randomly from a population with mean $\mu$ and variance $\sigma^2$. The sample size is sufficiently large that the sampling distribution of $\overline{X}$ can be assumed to be normal. Determine the probabilities with which $\overline{X}$ will be between the following pairs of points:
   a. $\mu + \sigma_{\overline{X}}$ and $\mu - \sigma_{\overline{X}}$
   b. $\mu + 1.96\sigma_{\overline{X}}$ and $\mu - 1.96\sigma_{\overline{X}}$
   c. $\mu + 2.58\sigma/\sqrt{n}$ and $\mu - 2.58\sigma/\sqrt{n}$
   d. $\mu + .675\sigma_{\overline{X}}$ and $\mu - .675\sigma_{\overline{X}}$
4. A sample of size $n$ is to be drawn from a population of normally distributed $T$-scores with mean 50 and variance 100. Complete the following table by calculating the variance error and standard error of $\overline{X}$ for various sample sizes.

| | $n$ | $\sigma^2_{\overline{X}}$ | $\sigma_{\overline{X}}$ |
|---|---|---|---|
| a. | 1 | ___ | ___ |
| b. | 2 | ___ | ___ |
| c. | 4 | ___ | ___ |
| d. | 8 | ___ | ___ |
| e. | 16 | ___ | ___ |
| f. | 100 | ___ | ___ |
| g. | 200 | ___ | ___ |
| h. | 400 | ___ | ___ |
| i. | 1,000 | ___ | ___ |

   j. As $n$ is doubled, how was $\sigma^2_{\overline{X}}$ affected?
   k. As $n$ is quadrupled, how was $\sigma_{\overline{X}}$ affected?
   l. If $n = 1$, is the sampling distribution of $\overline{X}$ identical to the frequency distribution, and does $\sigma = \sigma_{\overline{X}}$ when $n = 1$?

5. In 1976 the mean height of women in the United States was found to be $\mu \doteq 64.5$ in. with a standard deviation of $\sigma \doteq 2.3$ in.
   a. Estimate the standard deviation of the sampling distribution if $n = 100$.
   b. If $n = 100$, find the width of the .95 confidence arrival for $\sigma = 2.3$ in. (assume that $\mu$ was unknown).
   c. How large a sample is required in order for $\sigma_{\overline{X}}$ to equal .10?
6. When $n$ is small, the sampling distribution of $s^2$ is positively skewed with a mean of $\sigma^2$ (see Fig. 10.4). Recall the relationship between the mean and median in a positively skewed distribution. Is the probability of obtaining a value of $s^2$ that exceeds $\sigma^2$ greater than, equal to, or less than .50?

## *MASTERY TEST ANSWERS*

1. F
2. T
3. T
4. No
5. No
6. Yes
7. No
8. No–the thirty-six are probably not a representative sample of the 108.
9. No
10. No
11. No
12. No
13. Yes
14. A systematic sample; yes
15. $\sigma_{\overline{X}} = 15/\sqrt{9} = 5$
16. $z = \dfrac{105 - 100}{5} = 1.0$, 16%; $z = 2.0$, 2.3%
17. 68%; 95%
18. Yes
19. $\sigma^2_{\overline{X}} = (5)^2 = 25$
20. $\sigma_{\overline{X}} = 15/\sqrt{225} = 1.0$
21. 68%
22. No, but the difference will be negligible unless $n$ is very small.
23. Yes
24. The central limit theorem
25. Yes (but probably not the population of homes with telephones because of unlisted numbers)
26. Yes (but the value of $\sigma_{\overline{X}}$ will differ for each value of $n$)
27. No, .68 CI = $\overline{X} \pm \sigma_{\overline{X}}$, but the value of $\overline{X}$ will vary from sample to sample
28. Yes
29. No, $\sigma^2/n$ equals $\sigma^2_{\overline{X}}$, not $\sigma_{\overline{X}}$
30. Yes
31. Yes–square both sides of the equation $\sigma_{\overline{X}} = \sigma/\sqrt{n}$; $\sigma^2_{\overline{X}} = \sigma^2/n$, and rearrange to obtain $\sigma^2 = n\sigma^2_{\overline{X}}$
32. No: $\mu \neq \sigma^2_{\overline{X}}$
33. Yes
34. No: rarely is $\overline{X}$ precisely equal to $\mu$
35. No: $\overline{X} = (\Sigma X)/n$, not $(\Sigma x)/n$; $\Sigma x = 0$.
36. Yes
37. 95%
38. a
39. Interval estimates
40. Yes
41. c
42. b
43. 64

## *ANSWERS TO PROBLEMS AND EXERCISES*

2. a. rectangular
   b. It should.
   c. $\mu$, the mean of the population of single random digits: $\mu = (0 + 1 + \cdots + 9)/10 = 4.5$
   d. Yes (except for about 1% of students)
   e. Yes, yes, yes (see Table 5.1)
   f. No
   g. Yes: $\sigma_{\overline{X}} = \sigma/\sqrt{n}$ ; if $n = 8$, $\sigma_{\overline{X}}$

is only one-half the value of $\sigma_{\overline{X}}$ for $n = 2$

h. Yes

i. The central limit theorem

j. $s_{\overline{X}}$

k. $\sigma_{\overline{X}}$

3. a. .68

b. .95

c. .99

d. .50

4.

| | $\sigma^2_{\overline{X}}$ | $\sigma_{\overline{X}}$ |
|---|---|---|
| a. | 100 | 10 |
| b. | 50 | 7.07 |
| c. | 25 | 5 |
| d. | 12.5 | 3.54 |
| e. | 6.25 | 2.5 |
| f. | 1 | 1 |
| g. | .5 | .707 |
| h. | .25 | .5 |
| i. | .1 | .316 |

j. $\sigma^2_{\overline{X}}$ for $2n$ is one-half $\sigma^2_{\overline{X}}$ for $n$.

k. $\sigma^2_{\overline{X}}$ for $4n$ is one-fourth $\sigma^2_{\overline{X}}$ for $n$ hence, $\sigma_{\overline{X}}$ for $4n$ is one-half $\sigma_{\overline{X}}$ for $n$

l. yes

5. a. $\sigma_{\overline{X}} = 2.3/\sqrt{100} = .23$ in.

b. $\pm 1.96\sigma_{\overline{X}} = \pm 1.96(.23 \text{ in.}) = \pm .45$ in.; width = .90 in.

c. $n = 529$

6. Less than .50

# 11

# INTRODUCTION TO HYPOTHESIS TESTING

## 11.1 INTRODUCTION

In Chapter 10 the inferential technique known as interval estimation, one of the most useful techniques of statistical inference, was developed. In this chapter another important inferential technique, hypothesis testing, is introduced.

Hypothesis testing has become an ubiquitous feature of research in education and the behavioral sciences. Many professional journals can be only partially comprehended if the reader is not aware of the theory and some of the techniques of hypothesis testing. Most empirical research in the behavioral sciences uses interval estimation or hypothesis testing.

The concepts of hypothesis testing to be introduced and comprehended will make the discussion to follow a challenge, and mastery of these concepts for most students will require several careful readings. Fortunately, most concepts utilized in interval estimation also play central roles in hypothesis testing. The concepts of random samples, sampling distributions, and probability values associated with confidence intervals are also building blocks for hypothesis testing. Hypothesis testing and interval estimation are carried out with different languages, but we shall see that they usually produce equivalent results, or results that are easily converted from one to the other. The basic question addressed by both procedures is: "How does one make inferences regarding the population from a sample of observations?"

## 11.2 STATISTICAL HYPOTHESES AND EXPLANATIONS

Statistical hypothesis testing began in the early eighteenth century. Perhaps the earliest example of a formal statistical hypothesis test appears in a publication dated 1710 and written by John Arbuthnot (1667-1735), titled "An Argument for Divine Providence, Taken from the Constant Regularity Observed in the Births of Both Sexes." Noting that for eighty-two consecutive years the records showed a greater number of males born than females, Arbuthnot argued that the hypothesis that male and female births are equally likely (each with a probability of $\frac{1}{2}$) was refuted by these data, for if the probability of a male birth were precisely $\frac{1}{2}$, then the probability of eighty-two consecutive years in which more males than females were born would be infinitesimally small: $(\frac{1}{2})^{82}$ to be exact. Arbuthnot concluded that the greater portion of male births to female births was an act of Divine Providence; the sacred institution of monogamy was being maintained since males were more likely to be killed in war or work before reaching adulthood.

Arbuthnot's study illustrates a critically important point in empirical research that employs statistics. Statistics allow one to determine the probability of some event, given certain conditions and assumptions. But *statistics* per se *never supply the explanation or interpretation*. If you toss a coin ten times and get ten heads, the probability of this result given a fair coin is $(\frac{1}{2})^{10} = 1/1{,}024 \doteq .001$. You will conclude that there is an explanation other than "chance," but statistics do not tell you whether the coin was biased, the tossing was unfair, whether psychokinesis was operating, whether you are a "winner," or whether God ordained it.

Arbuthnot's statistics were unimpeachable, but you may or may not find his explanation cogent. You may have another theory to explain the phenomenon such as the sperm carrying the Y-chromosome has slightly less mass to propel, hence wins the race to the ovum more than 50% of the time. Like Arbuthnot, the modern researcher is much concerned with the probabilistic consideration of various hypotheses.

## 11.3 STATISTICAL VERSUS SCIENTIFIC HYPOTHESES

The decision that the researcher will supposedly make is a decision about the truth or falsity of a statistical hypothesis. There are at least two types of hypotheses it would be well to identify and distinguish: scientfic hypotheses and statistical hypotheses. A scientific hypothesis is a suggested solution to a problem. It is an intelligent, informed, and educated guess, and is generally stated as a proposition. The formulation of a good scientific hypothesis is truly a creative act.

The strategy of hypothesis testing involves a decision regarding a statistical hypothesis, $H_0$—a decision about whether or not $H_0$ is false. A statistical hypothesis is simply a numerical statement about an unknown parameter. In Table 11.1 illustrative

**TABLE 11.1** Illustrative Statistical Hypotheses

| | |
|---|---|
| $A.\ H_0: \mu = 100$ | The population mean is 100. |
| $B.\ H_0: \mu = 0$ | The population mean is 0 |
| $C.\ H_0: \sigma = 15$ | The standard deviation in the population is 15. |
| $D.\ H_0: \mu_1 - \mu_2 = 0$ (or $\mu_1 = \mu_2$) | The means of populations 1 and 2 are equal—there is no difference in the parameters $\mu_1$ and $\mu_2$. |
| $E.\ H_0: \sigma_1^2 - \sigma_2^2 = 0$ (or $\sigma_1^2 = \sigma_2^2$) | The variance in population 1 is equal to the variance in population 2; that is, $\sigma_1^2 = \sigma_2^2$. |
| $F.\ H_0: \rho_{XY} = 0$ | The correlation coefficient between $X$ and $Y$ in the population is 0. |
| $G.\ H_0: \rho_1 - \rho_2 = 0$ (or $\rho_1 = \rho_2$) | The difference between $\rho_{XY}$ in population 1 and $\rho_{XY}$ in population 2 is 0; that is, $\rho_1 = \rho_2$. |
| $H.\ H_0: \mu_1 = \mu_2 = \mu_3$ | The means in populations 1, 2, and 3 are equal. |
| $I.\ H_0: \pi = .5$ | The proportion in the population ($\pi$) is .5. |

statistical hypotheses are given. Note that the nine hypotheses in Table 11.1 are statements about *parameters*. Each $H_0$ specifies a numerical value for some parameter or difference between parameters (which is itself a parameter). For example, hypothesis $A(H_0: \mu = 100)$ is a statistical hypothesis; it is a statement that the numerical value of the mean of a population is 100.

Hypothesis $B$ indicates that if all observations in the population were included—that is, if $n = N$—the value of the mean would be 0. In this chapter we will be particularly concerned with testing statistical hypotheses like $A$ and $B$.

Hypothesis $C$ in Table 11.1 states that a particular population has a standard deviation of 15. $H_0: \sigma^2 = 225$ is, of course, equivalent to hypothesis $C$. Hypothesis $D$ states that there is no difference in the means of two populations. Hypothesis $D$ is an example of a two-sample test of means in contradistinction to hypotheses $A$ and $B$ which are one-sample tests of means. Procedures for testing hypotheses like $D$ through $I$ are treated in subsequent chapters.

Fortunately, once the procedures and concepts are understood for testing hypotheses regarding the mean, it is a relatively straightforward matter to apply the concepts to the testing of other statistical hypotheses (like $C$ through $I$ in Table 11.1).

It is important to distinguish scientific and statistical hypotheses. It is quite possible to test statistical hypotheses about very mundane matters that possess limited generality and not a whit of scientific importance. Not all scientific hypotheses need to be tested statistically; and by no means are all statistical hypotheses of scientific interest.

## 11.4 TESTING STATISTICAL HYPOTHESES ABOUT $\mu$

A statistical hypothesis is presumed to be either true or false; by using inferential statistical methods the researcher makes a decision (within a certain margin of error) as to whether the statistical hypothesis—for example, $H_0: \mu = 100$ is tenable or whether it must be rejected as false. To reject $H_0$ is to reject the statement that $\mu = 100$; to reject $H_0: \mu = 100$ is to conclude that $\mu \neq 100$. The four steps required for the testing of any statistical hypothesis are given in Table 11.2.

**TABLE 11.2** The Four Steps in Testing Hypotheses About $\mu$

Step 1. *State the statistical hypothesis $H_0$ to be tested* (e.g., $H_0 : \mu = 100$).

Step 2. *Specify the degree of risk of a type-I error*, that is, the risk of *incorrectly* concluding that $H_0$ is false (i.e., if it is true). This risk, stated as a probability, is denoted by $\alpha$ (alpha) and is the probability of a type-I error (e.g., $\alpha = .05$).

Step 3. *Assuming $H_0$ to be correct, determine the probability ($p$) of obtaining a sample mean ($\overline{X}$) that differs from $\mu$ by an amount as large or larger than that which was observed* (e.g., if $\mu = 100$, and $\overline{X} = 108$, calculate the probability of observing a difference between $\overline{X}$ and $\mu$ of 8 or more points).

Step 4. *Make a decision regarding $H_0$—whether or not to reject it* [e.g., if the probability ($p$) from Step 3 is less than $\alpha$ (Step 2), $H_0$ is rejected and we conclude that $\mu \neq 100$].

The purpose of hypothesis testing is to make a decision about whether or not a statistical hypothesis is tenable. If the probability ($p$) of what was observed in the sample is small if $H_0$ were indeed true (i.e., smaller than the maximum acceptable risk, $\alpha$), the researcher will conclude that the statistical hypothesis $H_0$ is false. The statistical hypothesis will be rejected at the $\alpha$-level of significance.

Suppose you are observing a game of craps in which a stranger wins consistently. The thought crosses your mind that the dice may be loaded toward 7's. The statistical hypothesis that you entertain is that the dice are fair, not wanting to accuse someone falsely. You observe the stranger roll the dice and note that "7" appeared in eight of the ten tosses (i.e., data are gathered). The probability of this happening *if* the dice are true is very small. Intuition tells you that something is operating in the system other than chance, even though you may not be able to determine the probability mathematically. You make a mental note to avoid the stranger (i.e., you reject the statistical hypothesis). You are a wise and an unprejudiced soul, and a hypothesis tester of sorts.

## 11.5 TESTING $H_0$: $\mu = K$, A ONE-SAMPLE $z$-TEST

To illustrate the four steps in testing hypotheses about $\mu$ (Table 11.2), suppose one wants to determine whether the mean IQ of adopted children differs from the mean for the general population of children (known to be 100).

1. The statistical hypothesis is $H_0 : \mu = 100$.
2. Set $\alpha = .05$ (.05 is the most commonly chosen value for $\alpha$).
3. On a random sample of $n = 25$ adopted children, a mean, $\overline{X}$, of 96.0 is obtained. The probability, $p$, is determined that one would obtain a sample mean, $\overline{X}$, for twenty-five observations that differs from 100 by 4 or more points, if indeed the population mean, $\mu$, is 100.
4. If the probability ($p$) is smaller than .05 ($\alpha$), the statistical hypothesis ($H_0 : \mu = 100$) will be rejected at the .05 level of significance. If $p > \alpha$, $H_0$ is not rejected; hence, it continues to be tenable.

The decision, then, regarding $H_0$ is either to "reject" $H_0$ (hence conclude $\mu \neq 100$) or "accept" $H_0$ (that is, conclude that $\mu = 100$ is tenable). The decision is based on the probability that one would observe a difference between $\overline{X}$ (96.0) and $\mu$ (100.0) (i.e., sampling error) as large as the four-point difference observed if, indeed, $H_0$ were true. With a sample mean of 96.0 for a sample of twenty-five adopted children, is $H_0$ tenable, or must it be rejected at the $\alpha$-level of significance?

If $\mu = 100$ and $n = 25$, how frequently would a sample mean, $\overline{X}$, of 96 or less be observed? How frequently would sample means be expected to differ by four or more points from the population mean? From the test norms, it is known that $\sigma = 15$. Hence, the standard deviation of the sampling distribution of means (i.e., standard error of the mean, $\sigma_{\overline{X}}$) of twenty-five random observations is shown by Eq. 10.1 to be $15/\sqrt{25} = 3.0$.

Recall from Equation 6.2 that to find the area beyond any point in a normal distribution, the deviation of an observation in a distribution from the mean of the distribution—that is, $x = X - \mu$—is divided by the standard deviation of the distribution, $\sigma$, to obtain the $z$-ratio as shown:

$$z = \frac{X - \mu}{\sigma} = \frac{x}{\sigma}$$

But since we are dealing with a sampling distribution, the "observations" in the normal distribution are means ($\overline{X}$'s) and the standard deviation is the standard error of the mean ($\sigma_{\overline{X}}$); hence, the $z$-ratio or $z$-test becomes

$$z = \frac{\overline{X} - \mu}{\sigma_{\overline{X}}} \qquad \textbf{(11.1)}$$

By entering the $z$-value in the normal-curve table (Appendix Table A), the probability of obtaining a sample mean of 96.0 or less, if indeed $H_0$ is true, can be determined. In the example with $\overline{X} = 96.0$,

$$z = \frac{\overline{X} - \mu}{\sigma_{\overline{X}}} = \frac{96 - 100}{3.0} = \frac{-4.0}{3.0} = -1.33$$

From Table A, the proportion of the normal curve falling below the point $z = -1.33$ is found to be .0918. Hence, when $\mu = 100$, we would observe $\overline{X}$'s that are below 96 in .0918 (9.18%) of samples of twenty-five observations. Similarly, we would expect $\overline{X}$'s to be 104 or greater in 9.18% of the samples of twenty-five cases. Thus $p = 2(.0918) = .1836 > \alpha = .05$, hence $H_0$ is not rejected.

## 11.6 TYPES OF ERRORS IN HYPOTHESIS TESTING

If $\mu = 100$ and $n = 25$, the probability of the mean of a sample, $\overline{X}$, differing from 100 by four or more points is $2(.0918) = .1836$. If $H_0: \mu = 100$ is consistently rejected when the sample mean is below 96 or above 104, the risk of error is approximately 18% ($\alpha = .18$) if $H_0$ is true. If $H_0$ is true, yet it is rejected, a type-I error has been made. $H_0$ is rejected when the probability, $p$, that the sample mean deviates from the hypothesized $\mu$ by the amount of the observed difference is less than the prespecified $\alpha$. $H_0$ continues to be tenable if $p$ is greater than $\alpha$.* That is, $H_0$ is not rejected if $p > \alpha$. In our example we would not reject $H_0$, since $p = .18 > \alpha = .05$. Notice, however, that we have not proven $H_0$ to be true; we have only decided that it is tenable. The probability is only .18 that we would observe a value of $\overline{X}$ that differs by four or more points from 100 if $H_0$ is true. But the probability does exceed the maximum risk of a type-I error that we decided to take, that is, $p > \alpha = .05$. To "accept" $H_0$ simply indicates that we will continue to entertain the possibility that $H_0$ is true, that is, the truth of $H_0$ is not unreasonable. But notice that $H_0$ has not been proven to be correct. Likewise, the rejection of $H_0$ would be a statistical decision attended by a risk of error; it would not be "proof" of the falsity of $H_0$. The failure to make such distinctions as the difference in meaning between "not rejecting $H_0$" and "proving $H_0$ to be correct" has led to the misinterpretation of much research.

Statistical inferential techniques can never establish the truth of a hypothesis with certainty—no statistical hypothesis can be accepted or rejected with 100% confidence. Rejecting $H_0$ when it is true is termed a *type-I error.* Conversely, when $H_0$ is "accepted," $H_0$ is not proven to be true—just that the evidence against the proposition is not sufficiently strong to reject it. Failure to reject $H_0$ when it is false is termed a *type-II error.* The probability of a type-I error is symbolized by $\alpha$, the probability of a type-II error is denoted by $\beta$. Of course, no errors are involved when a true $H_0$ is accepted and a false $H_0$ is rejected.

## An Example in Which $H_0$ is Rejected

Suppose that, instead of 96, the random sample of twenty-five adopted children had a mean IQ score of 108. The $z$-ratio would then be $z = (\overline{X} - \mu)/\sigma_{\overline{X}} = (108 - 100)/3 = 2.67$. From the normal curve in Appendix Table A, it is found that only .0038 of the area in a normal curve falls above a point 2.67 standard deviations above the mean. Note the black portion of the curve in Figure 11.1. The black portion of each "tail" represents .0038 of the area under the curve. Hence, when $\mu = 100$, the probability of observing a

**FIGURE 11.1**
**The sampling distribution for $\overline{X}$'s when $\mu = 100$, $\sigma = 15$, and $n = 25$. The probability of obtaining a sample mean that deviates by 4 or more points from $\mu$ is shown by areas $A$ and $B$. (The black "tails" of areas $A$ and $B$ reflect the probability of obtaining a sample mean that deviates by 8 or more points from $\mu = 100$.)**

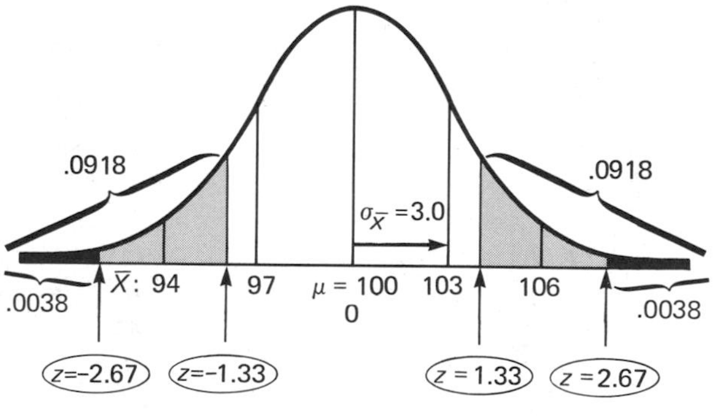


*For no good reason other than convenience and simplicity, a 5% risk of a type-I error ($\alpha = .05$) has become conventional. As you progress in your understanding of statistical inference, you will be able to make intelligent decisions regarding the type-I error risk that is appropriate in a given situation, rather than adhering slavishly to $\alpha = .05$. In certain situations it is appropriate to set $\alpha = .1$ or even higher; in other instances, $\alpha$ should be set at .01 or even .001.

value for $\overline{X}$ that differs from $\mu = 100$ by eight or more points is $p = 2(.0038) = .0076$, that is, 76 chances in 10,000.* In other words, there is less than one chance in 100 that sampling error $(\overline{X} - \mu)$ would be as large as eight points when $H_0: \mu = 100$ is true. What then is the decision regarding the truth of $H_0: \mu = 100$ when $\overline{X} = 108$ is observed? $H_0$ would be rejected at the .05 level (indeed, even at the .01 level) of statistical significance—there is a statistically significant difference between $\overline{X} = 108$ and $\mu = 100$. The probability of making a type-I error in such situations, when the absolute value of $z$ is 2.67, is less than .01. Although we were willing to take a 5% risk of a type-I error, the risk is less than 1%. It is evident that the .01 level gives us greater assurance than the .05 level that indeed $H_0$ is false.

In summary the steps in testing hypotheses of the type, $H_0: \mu = K$ are the following: (1) explicate the statistical hypothesis; (2) specify $\alpha$; (3) estimate the probability $p$ of observing an event as deviant or more deviant than that which was observed, entertaining for the moment that $H_0$ is true; (4) if $p$ is less than $\alpha$, reject $H_0$ and conclude that the parameter being estimated has a value different from that stated by $H_0$. If $p > \alpha$, $H_0$ is not rejected, and $H_0$ continues to be tenable.

Notice that when $H_0$ is not rejected, we did not say that it is probably true. We might say that the evidence against the truthfulness of the defendant ($H_0$) is not sufficient to convict him—a reasonable doubt remains.

## 11.7 HYPOTHESIS TESTING AND CONFIDENCE INTERVALS†

> Probably the *greatest ultimate importance* among all types of statistical procedures we now know, belongs to *confidence procedures* which, by making interval estimates, attempt to reach as strong conclusions as are reasonable by pointing out, not single likely values, but rather whole classes (intervals, regions, etc.) of *possible* values, so chosen that there can be high confidence that the "true" value is *somewhere among them.* Such procedures are clearly quantitative conclusion procedures. They make clear the essential "smudginess" of experimental knowledge. (Tukey, 1960, p. 429.)

If a confidence interval is set about $\overline{X}$, one can see the high degree of correspondence between hypothesis testing and interval estimation. If $\overline{X} = 108$, $\sigma = 15$, and $n = 25$, the .99 confidence interval on $\mu$ is $\overline{X} \pm 2.576\,\sigma_{\overline{X}} = 108 \pm 2.576(3)$ or $108 \pm 7.73$, which extends from 100.27 to 115.73. *Notice that the .99 confidence interval does not contain the hypothesized value of 100 for $\mu$. When the .99 confidence interval is symmetrical around $\overline{X}$ and does not include the value of the parameter specified by the statistical hypothesis, this is tantamount to stating that the statistical hypothesis is rejected at the*

*The probability of a type-I error is generally not reported as .0076 as it might appear from Figure 11.1. The high degree of precision implicit in the .0076 value is accurate only if all statistical assumptions are perfectly achieved. Hence, researchers usually report statistical significance at the .05, .02, .01, or .001 level, rather than a value that appears to be extremely precise, such as .0064 or .0122.

†The procedures we employ are eclectic, being drawn from both Neyman-Pearson and Fisher, and are not an orthodox example of either.

*.01 level of significance.* Likewise, if one rejects $H_0 : \mu = K$ at the .05 level, the .95 confidence interval will *not* include the hypothesized value $K$ for the parameter.

On the other hand, as in the initial example with $\bar{X} = 96$ in which $H_0$ is not rejected at the .05 level, one then knows that the value for the parameter specified by $H_0$ falls within the .95 confidence interval. With $\bar{X} = 96$, the .95 confidence interval is $\bar{X} \pm 1.96\sigma_{\bar{X}} = 96 \pm 1.96(3.0) = 96 \pm 5.88$ (i.e., 90.12 - 101.88). Note that the value of 100 specified in the statistical hypothesis for $\mu$ lies with the .95 confidence interval; hence, $H_0$ was *not* rejected at the .05 level.

These examples serve to illustrate how the inferential techniques of interval estimation and hypothesis testing are closely related. *From a confidence interval, one can easily determine the outcome of testing a hypothesis about* $\mu$. Conversely, however, from the knowledge that $H_0 : \mu = 100$ was rejected at the $\alpha = .05$ level, one does *not* know the .95 confidence interval for $\mu$ without a little extra computation.

It might be instructive to see the preceding argument in its mathematical form. From Eq. 11.1,

$$z = \frac{\bar{X} - \mu}{\sigma_{\bar{X}}} \qquad \sim N(0, 1)$$

where "$\sim N(0, 1)$" means "is distributed normally, with population mean 0 and population variance 1." Therefore, the probability ($p$) that the observed $z$ will be less than $|1.96|$ is .95:

$$p\left(-1.96 < \frac{\bar{X} - \mu}{\sigma_{\bar{X}}} < 1.96\right) = .95 \qquad \textbf{(11.2)}$$

Multiplying the inequality in parentheses by $\sigma_{\bar{X}}$ gives the following expression:

$$p\,(-1.96\sigma_{\bar{X}} < \bar{X} - \mu < 1.96\sigma_{\bar{X}}) = .95$$

Thus in the example in which $n = 25$ and $\sigma = 15$, $\sigma_{\bar{X}} = 3$; the probability, $p$, that $(-5.88 < \bar{X} - \mu < 5.88) = .95$. Or equivalently, if $\bar{X}$ differs by 5.88 from the hypothesized value of $\mu$, $H_0$, can be rejected at the .05 level of significance.

## 11.8 TYPE-II ERROR, $\beta$, AND POWER

Quite literally, so far in this chapter only half the story of statistical hypothesis testing has been told. In this section the other side of the story will be presented.

The standard technique for testing an hypothesis, such as $H_0 : \mu = 100$ using the $z$-test, is to select a level of significance $\alpha$, determine the critical values of $z$ (Table A), draw a sample and compute $\bar{X}$ and then, depending on the value of $z$, accept or reject $H_0$. In the previous section we showed how to determine the probability of a given value for $\bar{X}$ when $H_0$ was in fact true.

It was acknowledged that the decision "$H_0$ is false" could be incorrect and that, in the long run, this probability is $\alpha$. Now we acknowledge that the decision to "accept"

$H_0$, that is, to conclude that "$H_0$ is true" could also be incorrect. In other words, we could accept $H_0$ when it is false, for example, conclude that $\mu = 100$ when in fact $\mu \neq 100$. The error of accepting a false $H_0$ is termed an error of the second kind or a type-II error, and its probability will be calculated.

To test $H_0$ the investigator would establish critical regions of $\overline{X}$ that lead to the rejection of $H_0$, as was done in Figure 11.1. Since $\alpha = .05$ a $z$-ratio of 1.96 or larger or $-1.96$ or smaller would be required to reject $H_0$. Note from Table A that .025 of the area falls below $z = -1.96$ in a normal distribution.

If $\mu$ is actually 100, there is one chance in twenty ($\alpha = .05$) that the investigator will reject $H_0: \mu = 100$, even though it is true, i.e., that the investigator will make a type-I error.

## 11.9 POWER

However, what if $\mu$ is really 110? In this case $H_0: \mu = 100$ should be rejected in favor of the conclusion that $\mu$ is different from 100. But what is the probability that $H_0$ will be rejected? This probability of rejecting a false $H_0$ is the *power* of a statistical test. If $\mu =$ 110, the power is depicted by the unshaded area in the right-hand curve in Figure 11.2.

The upper critical region for $\overline{X}$ is at a $z$-value of 1.96, or $\overline{X}$ values above 105.88: $100 + (1.96)(3) = 105.88$. Hence, the power of the hypothesis test to reject $H_0$ when $\mu = 110$ is the area above $\overline{X} = 105.88$ under the right-hand curve that represents the sampling distribution of $\overline{X}$ for samples of size twenty-five when $\mu = 110$. This area is approximately 91% of the total area under the curve on the right in Figure 11.2. Thus the power is approximately .91.

How was the figure of .91 obtained? The standard error, $\sigma_{\overline{X}}$, is not affected by the value of $\mu$, thus $\sigma_{\overline{X}} = 3$ for both curves in Figure 11.2. The value of 105.88 corresponds to a $z$-score of $(105.88 - 110)/3 = -1.37$ in the right-hand distribution. In Table A we find that $.0853 \doteq .09$ (i.e., $\beta = .09$) of the area falls below the critical value needed to reject $H_0$.*

**FIGURE 11.2. Illustration of the power of the test of $H_0$: $\mu = 100$ against $H_1$: $\mu \neq 100$ for the case in which $\mu = 110$, $\sigma_{\overline{X}} = 3$, and $\alpha = .05$.**

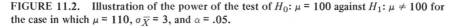

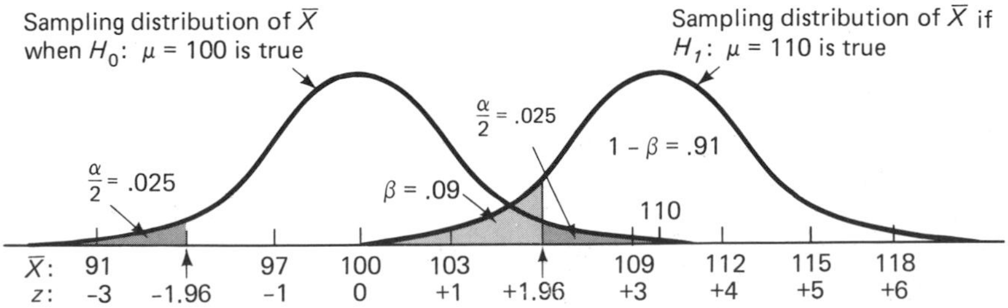


*Actually there also exists an infinitesimal chance ($p = .0000003$) that $H_0$ will be rejected in favor of the alternative hypothesis $H_1$ when $\mu = 110$ and $\overline{X}$ is below 94.12. This bit of esoterica is sometimes termed a type-III error, that is, when $H_0$ is rejected but the direction of the difference is incorrect.

The area under the curve on the right in Figure 11.2 (the sampling distribution of $\overline{X}$ when $\mu = 110$) *below* 105.88 is a measure of the probability that $\overline{X}$ will fail to exceed the critical value even though $H_0$ is false; this area measures $\beta$, the probability of a type-II error. The area in question is about 9% of the total area under the curve. Hence, $\beta$ is approximately .09. Since $\mu$ is actually 110, the probability of not committing a type-II error, that is, the power of the test, is given by $1 - \beta = .91$. Now try to convince yourself that if $\mu$ were equal to 90, the same hypothesis-testing procedure would run the same risk of a type-II error and have the same power, .91, as when $\mu = 110$.

## 11.10 EFFECT OF $\alpha$ ON POWER

Suppose one had chosen to test $H_0 : \mu = 100$ against $H_1 : \mu = 110$, but with $\alpha = .10$. If $\mu = 110$, refer to Figure 11.2 to confirm that the power of this test is greater than with $\alpha = .05$. From Table A, the critical $z$-values for $\alpha = .10$ are found to be $-1.645$ and $+1.645$—$\alpha/2 = .05$ of the critical area is found in each tail. The minimum value of $\overline{X}$ for which $H_0$ will be rejected is $1.645\ \sigma_{\overline{X}}$ or $1.645(3) = 4.94$ points from the value of 100 that is stated in the statistical hypothesis. Power at $\alpha = .10$ is then the proportion of the right-hand curve in Figure 11.2 that falls above 104.94. The value of 104.94 corresponds to a $z$-score of $-1.687 = (104.94 - 110)/3$ in the *right-hand* distribution, thus $\beta = .046$ and power $(1 - \beta)$ for $\mu = 110$ and $\alpha = .10$ is .954.

It will further extend the concepts being developed if the power of the test of $H_0 : \mu = 100$ (with $\alpha = .05$ and $\sigma_{\overline{X}} = 3$) is determined when $\mu = 105$ instead of 110. The critical regions of the test remain the same as in Figure 11.2—94.12 and below and 105.88 and above. The sampling distribution of $\overline{X}$ for samples of size twenty-five is unchanged from Figure 11.2 when $H_0$: $\mu = 100$ is true. It appears in Figure 11.3 along with the sampling distribution of $\overline{X}$ for $n = 25$ and $\sigma = 15$ when $\mu = 105$.

From an exact measure of the area under the curve on the right (with $\mu = 105$) that falls above the critical value of 105.88 in Figure 11.3, it can be shown that $z = (105.88 - 105)/3 = .27$ and the power of the test of $H_0 : \mu = 100$ is only .39. Of course it follows that $\beta = .61$.

It is almost never the case in behavioral research that the power of a hypothesis test for just one alternative value of the parameter is sufficient for designing research.

**FIGURE 11.3. Illustration of the power of the test of $H_0 : \mu = 100$ against $H_1 : \mu \neq 100$ for the case in which $\mu = 105$, $\sigma_{\overline{X}} = 3$ and $\alpha = .05$.**

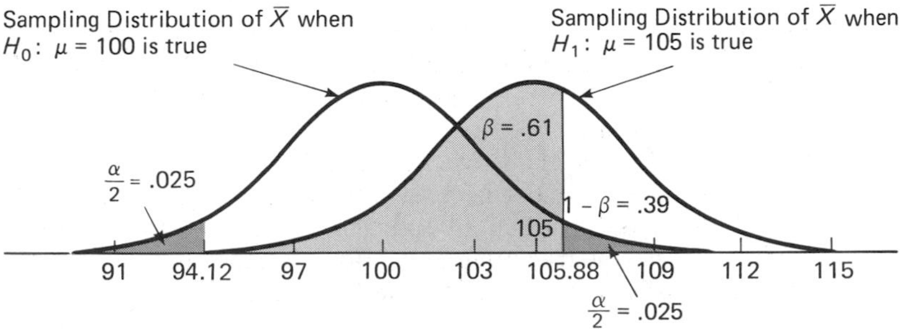

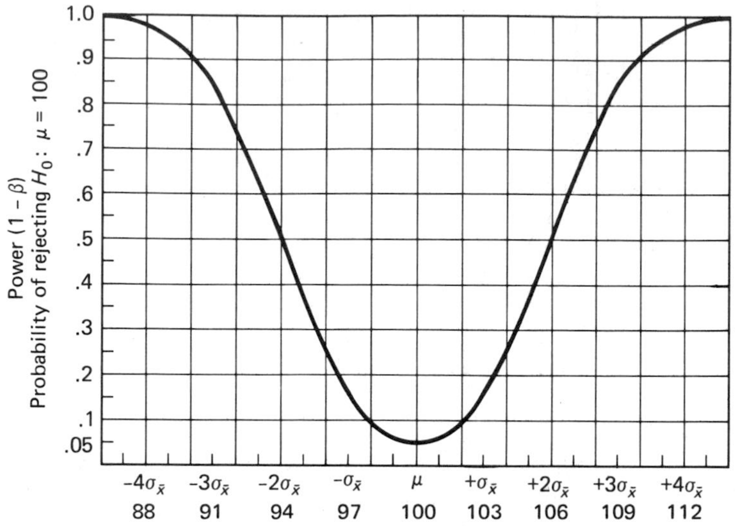


**FIGURE 11.4. Power curve for the test of $H_0 : \mu = 100$ against $H_1 : \mu \neq 100$ for $\sigma_{\overline{X}} = 3$ and $\alpha_2 = .05$.**

Generally one wants to determine the power of the test for several values of the parameter. Often the power is determined for (1) the largest value of the parameter that is reasonable, (2) the smallest value of the parameter that would be of practical interest, and (3) an intermediate value that represents the most reasonable expectation or "best guess." If additional values for the parameter are taken, a power curve like Figure 11.4 can be constructed.

## 11.11 POWER AND THE VALUE HYPOTHESIZED IN THE ALTERNATIVE HYPOTHESIS

The values of the power are plotted against the various values of the parameter ($\mu$ in this case) and then the points are connected by a smooth line. The resulting *power curve*, the power of the test against all alternative values of the parameter, is determined. The power curve for the test of $H_0 : \mu = 100$ against $H_1 : \mu \neq 100$ for $\sigma_{\overline{X}} = 3$ and $\alpha = .05$ appears as Figure 11.4.

Note in Figure 11.4 that the values of the power for $\mu = 110$ and $\mu = 105$ are .91 and .39, respectively, as they were calculated to be in Figures 11.2 and 11.3. Notice also that when $\mu = 100$ (that is, if $H_0$ is true) there is a probability equal to $\alpha = .05$ of making a type-I error—of rejecting $H_0$ when it is true.

It is apparent in Figure 11.4 that the power of the test increases and approaches 1 as the true value of $\mu$ differs more and more from the hypothesized value of $\mu$ (100 in this case). This is comforting to know, but it is a contingency not under the control of the investigator as he does not "set" the true value of $\mu$. However, the sample size $n$ and the level of significance $\alpha$ are usually under the researcher's control. For any value of $\mu$

(other than the hypothesized value of 100) the power of the test of $H_1 : \mu \neq 100$ increases as $n$ is increased.

Observe that if $n$ is increased from 25 to 100 and $\sigma_{\bar{X}}$ is reduced from 3 to $15/\sqrt{100} = 1.50$ (Eq. 10.1), $H_0 = 100$ will be rejected if $\bar{X} \geqslant (1.96)(1.50) + 100 = 102.94$. When $\mu = 105$, 91% of the right-hand sampling distribution falls above 102.94 (i.e., $z = (102.94 - 105)/1.5 = -1.37$), hence power is .91. The correspondence of this result with that from $\mu = 110$ and $n = 25$ is not accidental: when $n$ is quadrupled, the power remains constant for a difference, $(\mu_1 - \mu_2)$, this is half that which was associated with $n$.

Ordinarily one is well advised to take the largest sample that is practical and then determine if this sample size has good power for detecting a difference large enough to be of interest. If a sample is so large that the power of the test of $H_0$ is .99, for example, even when the true value of the parameter is only slightly different from the value specified in $H_0$, then it is unnecessary to use such a large sample. It may well be true that the power would drop to only .97 if a sample only half as large is taken. If so, the size of the sample can be reduced with trivial loss. Sometimes a person settles for equality of type-I and II error probabilities. More often, however, one finds that power is low even for detecting differences of a magnitude such that they are practically important. For example, using a "two-tailed" (Sec. 11.13) test, the power for detecting a five-point difference in the mean IQ in Figure 11.3 was only .39 with $n = 25$ and $\alpha = .05$. The power increases to .91 if $n = 100$.

## 11.12 METHODS OF INCREASING POWER

The following can be said about hypothesis-testing procedures in general:

1. For a given value of the parameter being tested, the power of the test of $H_0$ increases as the sample size, $n$, increases.
2. For a given value of the parameter being tested, the power of the test of $H_0$ increases as $\alpha$ (the probability of rejecting a true null hypothesis) is increased, for example, from .05 to .10.
3. Other things being equal, the power of the test of $H_0$ increases as the true value of the parameter being tested deviates further from the value hypothesized for it in $H_0$. For example, in the situation depicted in Figure 11.4, the power when testing $H_0 : \mu = 100$ is much greater when $\mu$ equals 110 (or 90) than when $\mu$ equals 105 (or 95).

The first two relationships are quite important since, to some extent, $\alpha$ and $n$ can be controlled by the investigator. It might be advisable in some circumstances to run a risk of a type-I error as large as .10, that is, $\alpha = .10$, to insure a reasonable power for a test. The third relationship is often not under the control of the investigator.

The popular notion among practicing researchers is that the statistician is the person who tells them "how large a sample to take." Presumably the statistician derives this decision about sample size from studying cost per observation, costs of committing type-I and type-II errors, and the power of the test for different sample sizes and particular alternative values of the parameter about which a hypothesis is to be tested. The theory is very accommodating when these costs and specific alternative values of the parameter can be specified. However, in research in education and the social sciences it is rare that they can be specified with any confidence.

## 11.13 NONDIRECTIONAL AND DIRECTIONAL ALTERNATIVES: TWO-TAILED VERSUS ONE-TAILED TESTS

An alternative hypothesis, $H_1$, can be designated as either nondirectional ("two-tailed") or directional ("one-tailed"). The alternative $H_1 : \mu \neq 0$ is nondirectional in that it states only that $\mu$ is not equal to 100 and not in which direction (above or below) it deviates from zero. Consider the pair of hypotheses $H_0 : \mu = 100$ and $H_1 : \mu > 100$. In this instance the alternative hypothesis is directional: it is presumed that either $\mu$ equals 100 or it is greater than 100. The investigator believes that $\mu$ could not possibly be less than 100. Evidence will be gathered that will either support the hypothesis that $\mu$ is above 100 or that will allow $H_0 : \mu = 100$ to remain tenable.

One consequence of stating the directional alternative $H_1 : \mu > 100$ is that now all the critical region for rejection of $H_0$ in favor of $H_1$ is in one tail of the sampling distribution of $\overline{X}$ when $\mu = 100$. In other words, only $\overline{X}$-values above 100 will lead one to decide in favor of $H_1$ over $H_0$; hence, all of the critical region for rejection of $H_0$ is in the *right-hand* tail of the sampling distribution of $\overline{X}$ when $\mu = 100$, as indicated in Figure 11.5. A value of $\overline{X}$ below 100 certainly does not favor the hypothesis that $\mu > 100$ over the hypothesis that $\mu = 100$. Since only the two conditions $\mu = 100$ or $\mu > 100$ are covered by the hypotheses, a $\overline{X}$ of less than 100 would imply the tenability of $H_0$.

If $\alpha_1 = .05$, from Table A it is found that 5% of the area in a normal distribution exceed the $z$-ratio of 1.645. One-tailed tests shall be distinguished from two-tailed by the subscripts $\alpha_1$ and $\alpha_2$; if no subscript is given, a nondirectional hypothesis is implicit. If $\alpha_1 = .05$, the critical region, as shown in Figure 11.5, includes all points above $\mu$ +

**FIGURE 11.5. Illustration of critical region for testing $H_0 : \mu = 100$ against $H_1 : \mu > 100$ for $\sigma_{\overline{X}} = 3$ and $\alpha_1 = .05$.**

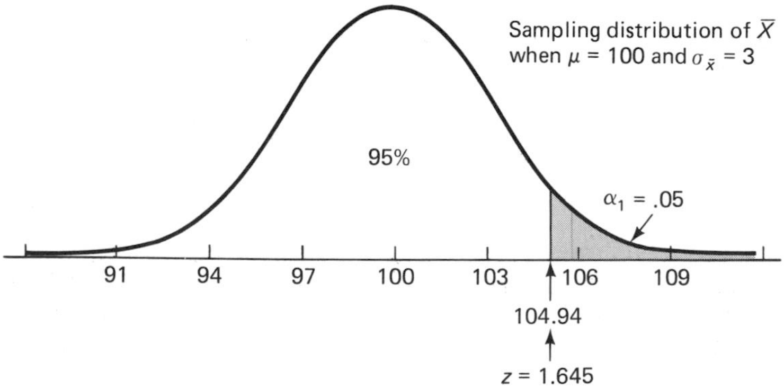

$1.645\,\sigma_{\overline{X}}$; if $\sigma_{\overline{X}} = 3$, all values of $\overline{X}$ above $100 + (1.645)(3) = 104.94$ will allow $H_0$ to be rejected with $\alpha_1 = .05$.

It should be apparent from comparing Figures 11.5 and 11.3 that the directional hypothesis will have greater power for rejecting $H_0$ when $\mu > 100$. Note in Figure 11.3 that power with $\alpha_2 = .05$ was approximately .39, whereas the power at $H_1 : \mu > 100$ and $\alpha_1 = .05$ is approximately .50.

The fact that the critical region lies in one tail of the sampling distribution of the statistic under the null hypothesis as illustrated in Figure 11.5, has made popular the phrase *one-tailed test* for a significance test of a directional hypothesis. This usage is sometimes ambiguous, however. The important distinction is between nondirectional and directional alternative hypotheses. If a test statistic has grown out of the history of statistics in such a manner that one or two tails of a sampling distribution lie above the critical values of a statistic is quite arbitrary. (We shall see in Chapter 16, for example, that a nondirectional hypothesis about a set of population means is tested by referring a test statistic to one tail of the $F$-distribution.)

The potential for misusing directional hypothesis tests is great. For example, one who hypothesizes that $\mu = 100$ against $\mu > 100$ must look the other way and conclude that $H_0$ is tenable even if a sample of 1000 yields a $\overline{X}$ of 80.

It is imperative that the researcher specify the directional alternative hypothesis *before* conducting the study. One must commit oneself to a directional test prior to collecting any data or obtaining any empirical "clue" as to how the results are turning out. If a researcher claims to have made a directional test with $\alpha_1 = .05$ after seeing the data—that is, if he hypothesizes $\mu > 100$ because he sees that $\overline{X}$ is larger than 100—he is deluding himself; the actual probability of a type-I error in this instance is $\alpha_2 = .10$, not $\alpha_1 = .05$. If the researcher has not definitely committed himself to a directional hypothesis before inspecting the data, he must resist the temptation to make a one-tailed test later on. Otherwise, the probability of a type-I error is spurious. The following are some illustrations in which a directional hypothesis might be justified:

1. Does early cognitive enrichment increase IQ scores?
2. Do ten-year-olds make greater progress in learning to play the piano than eight-year-olds?
3. Does stature increase between ages eighteen and twenty?
4. Are students who have not had a statistics course able to obtain scores higher than a chance score on a statistics examination?
5. Is life expectancy less for smokers than for nonsmokers?
6. Do children receiving balanced diets have better school attendance than children whose diet is nutritionally inadequate?

## 11.14 STATISTICAL SIGNIFICANCE VERSUS PRACTICAL SIGNIFICANCE

When $n$ is very large, even a trivial difference may be large enough to be highly statistically significant. For example, if $n = 2{,}000$ and $\overline{X} = 101$, one would reject $H_0 : \mu = 100$ at the .01 level of statistical significance. Obviously a one-point IQ difference has little or no practical significance even though it may be highly significant in a statistical sense. It is unfortunate that the term "significant" was ever chosen to denote the untenability of $H_0$.* Perhaps the term "reliable" would have been a better term for describing sample results and would less often be confused with practical significance or importance.

> Significance testing in general has been a greatly overworked procedure, and in many cases where significance statements have been made it would have been better to provide an interval within which the value of the parameter would be expected to lie. (Box, 1978, p. 109.)

The use of confidence intervals can reduce the likelihood of this misinterpretation since confidence intervals force one to look at the boundaries within which the parameter can be expected to fall. As previously stated, rejecting $H_0$ at $\alpha$ only indicates that the symmetrical $1\text{-}\alpha$ confidence interval does not include the value for the parameter that was specified by $H_0$. For example, in the illustration in which $\overline{X} = 101$, $\sigma = 15$, and $n = 2{,}000$, the .99 confidence interval for $\mu$ extends from 100.13 to 101.87. Thus the CI reduces the opportunity of confusing a highly statistically significant IQ difference with a practically significant IQ difference.

## 11.15 CONFIDENCE LIMITS FOR THE POPULATION MEDIAN

If $n$ is small, a confidence interval for the population median can be determined from a random sample of $n$ observations of a continuous (i.e., ordinal, interval, or ratio) variable from any normal or nonnormal population. If in a rank-order distribution of $n$ observations, the subscripts denote the low-to-high ordinal rank (thus $X_1$ and $X_n$ represent the lowest and highest scores, respectively), the $(1 - \alpha)$ CI for the population median falls between $X_L$ and $X_U$, where $U$ is determined from Equation 11.3 (Snedecor and Cochran, 1980).

$$U \geqslant \frac{(n+1)}{2} + \frac{{}_{1-\alpha/2}z\sqrt{n}}{2} \tag{11.3}$$

and

$$L = n - U + 1 \tag{11.4}$$

Thus for .95 CI, ${}_{.975}z = 1.96$, hence

$$U \geqslant (n+1)/2 + (1.96\sqrt{n})/2$$

$$U \geqslant (n+1)/2 + .98\sqrt{n} \tag{11.3A}$$

*Among attempts to clear away confusion about statistical hypothesis testing, the most successful in our opinion is William Kruskal's contribution to the *International Encyclopedia of the Social Sciences* (1968) entitled "Tests of Significance."

For example, if $n = 25$, $U \geqslant (25 + 1)/2 + .98\sqrt{25} = 13 + 4.9$, hence, $U = 13 + 5 = 18$ (fractional values must be rounded upward), and $L = 25 - 18 = 8$. Therefore, the lower limit for the .95 CI about the population median is $X_8$ and the upper limit is $X_{18}$. Confirm in Table 8.1 that the .95 CI for the population median extends from 440 ($X_6$) to 560 ($X_{15}$).

## 11.16 INFERENCES REGARDING $\mu$ WHEN $\sigma$ IS NOT KNOWN: $t$ VERSUS $z$

For pedagogical purposes,* the concepts and procedures of hypothesis testing have been illustrated with the $z$-test—the ratio of an observed difference to the parameter for its standard error, or in this instance

$$z = \frac{\overline{X} - \mu}{\sigma_{\overline{X}}}, \qquad \text{where} \qquad \sigma_{\overline{X}} = \frac{\sigma}{\sqrt{n}}$$

But the examples used are not typical of actual research; rarely is the value of the parameter $\sigma$ known. If the parameter $\sigma$ is unknown, the value of $\sigma_{\overline{X}}$ cannot be determined and must be estimated. Can the statistic $s$ be used to estimate $\sigma$? Yes, but not without introducing some sampling error (i.e., $e = s - \sigma$) into the system. When $\sigma$ is not known, the standard error of the mean is estimated by Equation 11.5:

$$s_{\overline{X}} = \frac{s}{\sqrt{n}} \tag{11.5}$$

When the parameter $\sigma_{\overline{X}}$ is not known and an estimate, $s_{\overline{X}}$, must be used, the ratio in Equation 11.6 is termed a $t$-ratio rather than a $z$-ratio:

$$t = \frac{\overline{X} - \mu}{s_{\overline{X}}} \tag{11.6}$$

When $n$ is large, $s$ and $s_{\overline{X}}$ become very accurate approximations of $\sigma$ and $\sigma_{\overline{X}}$, respectively. Hence, $t$ and $z$ differ negligibly for large $n$. But when $n$ is small, $t$ and $z$ may differ considerably. The use of $s_{\overline{X}}$ rather than $\sigma_{\overline{X}}$ results in sampling distributions that, although symmetrical, are not perfectly normal. These distributions are known as *student's† t-distributions.*

There is not just one $t$-distribution (as there is for the $z$ or unit-normal distribution), there exists a family of $t$-distributions. There is a different $t$-distribution for every

*Otherwise we would have to face the distracting complexity of nonnormal sampling distributions before the concept of sampling distributions was understood.

†The solution to the problem of hypothesis testing when $\sigma$ is unknown might well be taken as the dawn of modern inferential statistical methods. It was found in 1908 by William S. Gosset who published it under the pseudonym "Student," hence the term "Student's" $t$-distribution.

distinct number of degrees of freedom, where $\nu$ is the degrees of freedom* of the estimate of the parameter in the denominator of the $t$-test—in this case $\nu = n - 1$ (see Eq. 5.5). When $H_0$ is true, the $t$-distribution is denoted as the *central* $t$-distribution.

## 11.17 THE $t$-DISTRIBUTION

All the central $t$-distributions are described by symmetric, unimodal curves with a mean of 0. Whereas the variance of the $z$-distribution is 1, the variance of the $t$-distribution with $\nu$ degrees of freedom is greater than 1, that is, the variance of the $t$-distribution is $\nu/(\nu - 2)$. When $\nu$ is small, $t$-distributions are leptokurtic (see Sec. 6.9). Leptokurtic distributions have "thicker" tails than the normal distribution, thus for $\alpha_2 = .05$ the corresponding critical $t$-value is larger than 1.96 because the area of the $t$-distribution exceeding $|t| = 1.96$ is greater than .05. As the degrees of freedom become larger and larger, the $t$-distribution begins to look more and more like a normal distribution (see Fig. 11.6). For example, when $\nu = 5$, the kurtosis,† $\gamma_2 = 6$, but when $\nu = 25$, $\gamma_2 = .3$.

When $\nu$ is infinitely large—a theoretical possibility that is empirically impossible—the $t$-distribution is the same as the $z$-distribution. The $t$-distributions with degrees of freedom 1, 5, and 25 appear along with the normal distribution in Figure 11.6. Figure 11.7 graphically depicts the relationship between the critical $t$-ratios and degrees of freedom for common values of $\alpha$. Notice that the critical $t$-values rather quickly approach the corresponding critical values for $z$ as $\nu$ increases. Figures 11.6 and 11.7 illustrate that as $\nu$ increases, ${}_pt$ approach ${}_pz$.‡

**FIGURE 11.6. The $t$-distributions with 1, 5, and 25 degrees of freedom and the unit-normal distribution.**

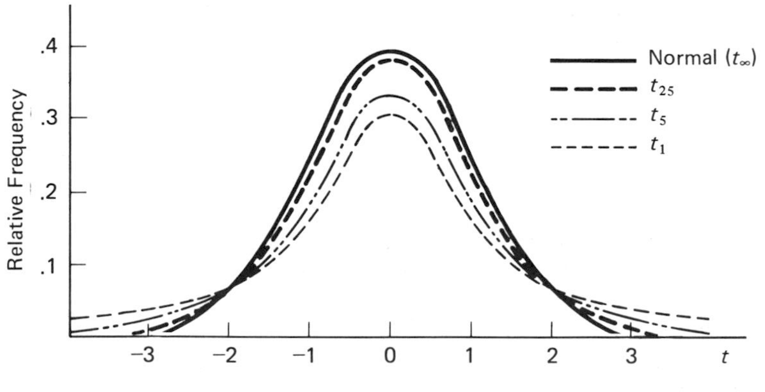


*The expression *degrees of freedom* ($\nu$) will be encountered many times in subsequent chapters. It is a statistical concept that has to do with "what is left over" after allowance is made for the number of mathematical restrictions imposed on a set of data. Do not expect a "flash of insight" that will give this complex statistical concept rich intuitive meaning.

†The kurtosis of a $t$-distribution is $\gamma_2 = 6/(\nu - 4)$.

‡This is expressed mathematically as $\lim_{\nu \to \infty} {}_pt_\nu = {}_pz$.

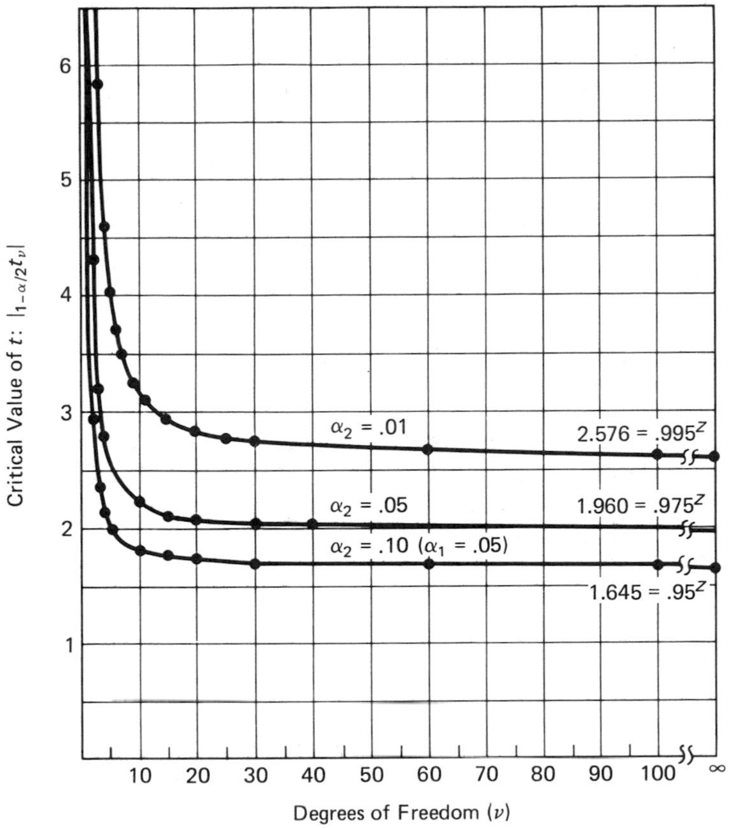


**FIGURE 11.7. Critical value of $t$ as related to degrees of freedom for $\alpha_2$ = .10, .05, and .01.**

In subsequent discussions of statistical inference, selected percentile points in a $t$-distribution (e.g., critical values of $t$) will have to be found. The $p$th percentile in the $t$-distribution with $\nu$ degrees of freedom will be denoted by ${}_pt_\nu$. The most often used percentiles in the $t$-distributions appear in Table C in the Appendix. There one reads, for example, that the 95th percentile in the $t$-distribution with ten degrees of freedom, that is, ${}_{.95}t_{10}$, is equal to $1.812 \doteq 1.81$.

Only the upper-percentile points in the $t$-distributions appear in Table C. Because of a simple relationship, it is unnecessary to tabulate both upper- and lower-percentile points. The symmetry of all $t$-distributions implies that

$$ {}_{1-p}t_\nu = -{}_pt_\nu, \quad \text{or} \quad |{}_{1-p}t_\nu| = |{}_pt_\nu| \tag{11.7} $$

that is, the negative of the $p$th percentile in the $t$-distribution with $\nu$ degrees of freedom equals the $(1-p)$th percentile in the same distribution. For example, ${}_{.95}t_{10} = 1.81$, therefore ${}_{.05}t_{10} = -1.81$. The critical $t$-values with $\alpha_2 = .10$ and $\nu = 10$ are $\pm 1.81$ or $|1.81|$.

## An Illustration

Suppose ten overweight persons went on a particular diet for one month and lost an average of 3.11 lb, ($\overline{X} = 3.11$, $s = 5.62$). Can $H_0: \mu = 0$ be rejected with $\alpha_2 = .10$? Using Equation 11.5, the standard error of the mean is found.

$$s_{\overline{X}} = \frac{s}{\sqrt{n}} = \frac{5.62}{\sqrt{10}} = 1.78$$

The null hypothesis can be tested using the $t$-test given in Equation 11.6.

$$t = \frac{\overline{X} - \mu}{s_{\overline{X}}} = \frac{3.11 - 0}{1.78} = 1.75$$

To find the critical $t$-value, ${}_{.95}t_9$, enter Table C at $\nu = n - 1 = 9$, and $\alpha_2 = .10$ and find the critical value of $t$ to be 1.83. Thus, an observed $t$-value greater than $|1.83|$ is required to reject $H_0$ with $\alpha_2 = .10$. Consequently, we cannot reject the hypothesis that the mean weight change in the population ($\mu$) is 0 because to do so would be taking a risk greater than .10. By studying Table C, we can see that $.20 > p > .10$; that is, the absolute value of the observed $t$-ratio (1.75) is greater than the critical $t$-value at $\alpha_2 = .20$ (${}_{.90}t_9 = 1.38$). Hence, $.20 > p > .10$.

But what if Lady Luck has played a trick on us: what if $\mu \neq 0$? Suppose that the entire population of overweight persons like those in the illustration were treated and measured and $\mu$ was $> 0$. If this is the case, we have made a type-II error—we failed to reject $H_0$ even though it was incorrect. Indeed, with such a small $n$ (10), type-II errors are common (see Hopkins, 1973).

## 11.18 CONFIDENCE INTERVALS USING THE $t$-DISTRIBUTION

Somewhat wider confidence intervals result when $s_{\overline{X}}$ is used than when $\sigma_{\overline{X}}$ is known. For example, regardless of $n$ the .95 confidence interval is $\overline{X} \pm 1.96\,\sigma_{\overline{X}}$ when $\sigma$ (and hence, $\sigma_{\overline{X}}$) is known. But when $\sigma$ is unknown and must be estimated from the sample, the .95 confidence interval for $\mu$ is

$$.95 \text{ CI} = \overline{X} \pm {}_{.975}t_\nu s_{\overline{X}}, \quad \text{where} \quad \nu = n - 1 \tag{11.8}$$

More generally,

$$(1 - \alpha)\text{CI} = \overline{X} \pm {}_{1-\alpha/2}t_\nu s_{\overline{X}} \tag{11.9}$$

Table C gives the critical value of $t$—the number of standard errors of the mean ($s_{\overline{X}}$) which must be added to and subtracted from $\overline{X}$ for the .90, .95, and .99 and other $1 - \alpha$ confidence intervals for various values of $\nu$. For example, when $\nu = n - 1 = 9$, the .90 CI is $\overline{X} \pm 1.83\,s_{\overline{X}}$. Or, as in this example, .90 CI = 3.11 ± 1.83 (1.78) = 3.11 ± 3.26 or −.15 to 6.37. The true weight change in the population may be anywhere from a loss of 6.37 lb to a gain of .15 lb, that is, 3.11 ± 3.26 lb. We make this statement with .90 confidence;

this means that if we replicated the study many times, only 10% of the .90 CI's will fail to encompass the parameter.

Would a "one-tailed" test be appropriate in this example? Hardly, since it is not unthinkable that the postweights will be greater than the preweights.

In summary to determine a confidence interval when $\sigma$ is unknown:

1. Compute $\overline{X}$ and $s_{\overline{X}}$ ($s_{\overline{X}} = s/\sqrt{n}$) on the random sample of $n$ observations from the parent population.
2. Find the critical value of $t$ required using $\nu = n - 1$ using the desired confidence coefficient ${}_{1-\alpha/2}t_\nu$ in Appendix Table C.
3. Use these values in Equation 11.9: $\overline{X} \pm {}_{1-\alpha/2}t_\nu s_{\overline{X}}$.

## 11.19 ACCURACY OF CONFIDENCE INTERVALS WHEN SAMPLING NONNORMAL DISTRIBUTIONS

The data in Figure 10.3 (Sec. 10.14) allow the validity of confidence intervals to be demonstrated empirically. Table 11.3 gives the observed percentage of 10,000 sample

**TABLE 11.3 Proportion of .68 Confidence Intervals That Included the Value of $\mu$ in 10,000 Samples from Normal, Rectangular, and Skewed Parent Populations**

| *Sample Size* | *Parent Population* | *Proportion of .68 Confidence Intervals Capturing $\mu$* |
|---|---|---|
| $n = 1$ | Normal | .682 |
| | Rectangular | .574 |
| | Skewed | .752 |
| $n = 2$ | Normal | .682 |
| | Rectangular | .667 |
| | Skewed | .714 |
| $n = 5$ | Normal | .686 |
| | Rectangular | .679 |
| | Skewed | .695 |
| $n = 10$ | Normal | .674 |
| | Rectangular | .681 |
| | Skewed | .689 |
| $n = 25$ | Normal | .682 |
| | Rectangular | .678 |
| | Skewed | .704 |
| $n = 100$ | Normal | .679 |
| | Rectangular | .687 |
| | Skewed | .690 |

means that actually included $\mu$ in their .68 confidence intervals when drawn from normal, rectangular, and skewed populations when Equation 11.9 is employed. It is evident from Table 11.3 that the confidence intervals are quite accurate even for nonnormal distributions with samples as small as $n = 5$.

## CHAPTER SUMMARY

Hypothesis testing is the most widely employed technique of statistical inference in educational and behavioral research. This chapter illustrated the hypothesis-testing procedure using statistical hypotheses of the type $H_0 : \mu = K$—that is, testing whether $\mu$ is equal to some specified number. In hypothesis testing one determines the probability ($p$) of observing a difference as large or larger than $(\overline{X} - \mu)$ if $H_0$ is true. If $p$ is smaller than the prespecified risk of a type-I error, $\alpha$ (usually .05), we reject $H_0$ (and accept $H_1 : \mu \neq K$) at the $\alpha$-level of statistical significance. If one rejects $H_0$ at $\alpha = .05$, in the long run type-I errors (rejecting $H_0$ when it is true) will be made in about one such decision in twenty (5%) in which $H_0$ is true. If $H_0$ is rejected at the .01 level, a type-I error will be made in less than one such decision in 100. If $H_0$ is not rejected, a type-I error cannot be made but a type-II error is a possibility. A type-II error is the failure to reject $H_0$ when it is incorrect.

The smaller the risk of a type-I error (rejecting a true $H_0$), $\alpha$, the greater the risk of a type-II error (failing to reject a false $H_0$), $\beta$. Conversely, one has greater power (i.e., less likelihood of making a type-II error) when $\alpha = .10$ than when $\alpha = .05$ or $\alpha = .01$. The probability of not making a type-II error is termed power, that is, $1 - \beta$. Power is increased by increasing $n$, "relaxing" $\alpha$ (e.g., from .05 to .10), or making a directional hypothesis when it is appropriate.

When $\sigma$ is known (and hence $\sigma_{\overline{X}}$ can be determined), the $z$-ratio, $z = (\overline{X} - \mu)/\sigma_{\overline{X}}$, is the proper test statistic. The critical values of $z$ are fixed and do not vary with $n$. If $\sigma$ is unknown, the $t$-ratio $t = (\overline{X} - \mu)/s_{\overline{X}}$, is employed. Sampling error appears in both the numerator and denominator of the $t$-test.

Whereas there is one normal distribution, there are an infinite number of central $t$-distributions, one for each "degree of freedom" associated with the $s_{\overline{X}}$ estimate. With few degrees of freedom, the $t$-distribution is highly leptokurtic (large tail area and very peaked near the center), but quickly approaches a normal distribution as the number of degrees of freedom increase. In the limit ($\nu = \infty$), the $t$-distribution is a normal distribution. The critical values of $t$ depend on the number of degrees of freedom ($\nu$) associated with the denominator of the ratio ($\nu = n - 1$ in this instance). The critical values of $t$ approach the critical values for $z$ as $n$ increases.

Hypothesis testing and interval estimation convey essentially the same information. To say that $H_0$ is rejected at $\alpha_2 = .05$ is equivalent to saying that the .95 confidence interval around $\overline{X}$ does not contain the hypothesized value of $\mu$. If a .99 confidence interval ranges from 60 to 66, any statistical hypothesis for $\mu$ having a value less than 60 or greater than 66 would be rejected at the .01 level of significance. Statistical significance (even at the .001 level) does not necessarily imply practical significance. Conversely, without establishing statistical significance one has not established significance of any type.

## *MASTERY TEST*

1. $z$ is to $\sigma_{\bar{X}}$ as $t$ is to ___.
   a. $\sigma$ b. $\sigma^2$ c. $s$ d. $s_{\bar{X}}$
2. Which of these can be properly regarded as statistical hypotheses?
   a. $\bar{X} = 63.0$ c. $\sigma = 10$ e. $s = 10.0$
   b. $\mu = 1.2$ d. $\rho = .50$ f. $r = 0$
3. Do statistical hypotheses pertain to parameters or statistics?
4. When are $\sigma_{\bar{X}}$ and $\sigma$ equal?
5. How large must $n$ be for the standard deviation of the sampling distribution of the mean $\sigma_{\bar{X}}$ to be only 10% as large as the standard deviation of the frequency distribution $\sigma$?
6. If $z = 2.0$, we can reject $H_0$
   a. at the .01 level of significance
   b. at the .05 level of significance, but not at the .01 level
   c. at neither the .01 nor the .05 levels
7. Which one of the following is least likely to have occurred by chance, that is, the result of sampling error?
   a. $z = -3.1$ b. $z = .00$ c. $z = 2.0$ d. $z = 2.58$
8. When $H_0$ is true, is the probability of observing a $z$-value greater than 1.31 the same as the probability of observing a $z$-value less than $-1.31$?
9. What is the symbol that denotes the risk of a type-I error that one is willing to tolerate?
10. Assuming $H_0$ is true, the probability of observing a sample mean which deviates as far from $\mu$ as the $\bar{X}$ obtained is denoted by the letter ___.
11. If $p < \alpha$, would $H_0$ be rejected?
12. If $p > \alpha$, does $H_0$ continue to be tenable?
13. If a particular .95 confidence interval for $\mu$ extends from 47.2 to 63.4, which two of the following statistical hypotheses would be rejected at the .05 level of significance?
    a. $\mu = 45$ b. $\mu = 50$ c. $\mu = 55$ d. $\mu = 60$ e. $\mu = 65$
14. Assume $H_0 : \mu = 100$ was rejected with $\alpha = .01$.
    a. Would the value of 100 fall within the .99 confidence interval?
    b. Would the value of 100 fall within the .95 confidence interval?
15. To reject $H_0$, which one of the following significance levels requires the largest difference between $\bar{X}$ and the hypothesized value of $\mu$?
    a. the .01 level b. the .05 level c. the .10 level
16. The $t$-statistic is used to test $H_0 : \mu = K$ when ___ is not known.
    a. $n$ b. $\bar{X}$ c. $\sigma$ d. $\alpha$
17. When $n = 20$, are the critical values slightly larger for $t$ than for $z$?
18. In which one of the following cases do the critical values of $z$ and $t$ differ most?
    a. $n = 5$ b. $n = 10$ c. $n = 100$ d. $n = \infty$
19. In testing $H_0 : \mu = K$, where $K$ is some numerical constant, which is more commonly employed as a test statistic, $z$ or $t$? Why?
20. Is the $t$-distribution a true, normal distribution?
21. For the following values of $n$, what are the associated degrees of freedom in testing $H_0 : \mu = K$?
    a. 11 b. 60 c. 101
22. If $H_0$ is true but has been rejected, what type of error has been made?
    a. type-I error b. type-II error c. no error

23. If $H_0$ is true and has not been rejected, has a type-II error been made?
24. When $H_0$ is true, what is the probability $H_0$ will be rejected at the .05 level, that is, the probability of a type-I error?
25. If $\alpha = .05$ and $H_0$ is not rejected, do we know the probability of a type-II error?
26. If $\alpha = .05$, yet $p < .01$, can $H_0$ be rejected at the .01 level of significance?
27. At the same $\alpha$-level, the absolute value of the critical $t$-ratio is greater for tests of
    a. nondirectional hypotheses b. directional hypotheses
28. If the critical $t$-values are 2.1 and $-2.1$, and the .05 level is selected,
    a. a one-tailed test is being employed b. a two-tailed test is being employed
29. If $\alpha = .05$ and $\nu = 20$, what are the critical $t$-values for making the following?
    a. a two-tailed $t$-test b. a one-tailed $t$-test
30. In Question 29, what is the probability of a type-I error for the following?
    a. a nondirectional hypothesis b. a directional hypothesis
31. If a directional hypothesis is appropriate and $\alpha = .05$, which will have greater power?
    a. a one-tailed test b. a two-tailed test
32. If $H_0$ is false and we fail to reject it, we have made
    a. a type-I error
    b. a type-II error
    c. a type-I error and a type-II error
    d. no error
33. ___ is to $\alpha$ as type-II error is to ___.

Use the following information to answer Questions 34 through 37: if $H_0 : \mu = 100$, $\alpha_2 = .05$, $\sigma = 15$, and $n = 25$, but $\mu$ is actually 105.

34. What is $\beta$? (Use Fig. 11.3.)
35. What is the probability of rejecting $H_0$?
36. Are the answers to Questions 34 and 35 consistent with those obtained using Figure 11.4?
37. If $n$ is increased from 25 to 100, the value of the standard error of the mean, $\sigma_{\overline{X}}$, will be reduced from 3 to ___.
38. Using Table A, determine the critical value for $z$ for $\alpha_2 = .10$. Is it identical with that for $\alpha_1 = .05$?
39. If $H_0$ is false and $\alpha$ is increased (relaxed) from .01 to .05, other things remaining constant, power will
    a. decrease b. remain constant c. increase
40. If the parent population is skewed, the proportion of .68 CI's that captured $\mu$ in Table 11.3 was $\geqslant .68$
    a. only when $n$ was large
    b. only when $n$ was $\geqslant 25$
    c. only when $n \leqslant 25$
    d. when $n \geqslant 1$.

## PROBLEMS AND EXERCISES

1. Give definitions of each of the following:
    a. null hypothesis, $H_0$
    b. alternative hypothesis, $H_1$
    c. type-I error
    d. type-II error
    e. level of significance, $\alpha$
    f. power of a test, $1 - \beta$
    g. critical region

2. The mean height $\mu$ of the population of adult males in the United States is 69.5 in. and the standard deviation $\sigma$ is 3 in. Suppose the mean height $\overline{X}$ of a sample of twenty-five mentally retarded males was found to be 67.5 in. Does $\overline{X}$ differ significantly from the $\mu$ of 69.5 in.? Using this information answer the following questions:
   a. State $H_0$ numerically.
   b. From the information provided, would you employ $z$ or $t$ as the test statistic?
   c. Is it appropriate to specify $H_1 : \mu < 69.5$ *after* finding that $\overline{X} = 67.5$?
   d. What is the value of $\sigma_{\overline{X}}$?
   e. What is the value of $z$?
   f. Will $H_0$ be rejected with $\alpha_2 = .01$?
   g. Would the critical values for $z$ remain the same if $n$ were increased to 100?
   h. Would $\sigma_{\overline{X}}$ remain the same if $n$ were increased to 100?
3. In each of the following instances indicate whether a type-I error, type-II error, or no error was committed by the researcher:

| | $H_0$ | $H_1$ | *True value of* $\mu$ | *Reseacher's decision based on* $\overline{X}$ |
|---|---|---|---|---|
| a. | $\mu = 0$ | $\mu \neq 0$ | 0 | Reject $H_0$ |
| b. | $\mu = 0$ | $\mu \neq 0$ | 5 | Reject $H_0$ |
| c. | $\mu = 0$ | $\mu \neq 0$ | 0 | Do not reject $H_0$ |
| d. | $\mu = 0$ | $\mu \neq 0$ | −3 | Do not reject $H_0$ |

4. The hypotheses $H_0 : \mu = 0$ and $H_1 : \mu \neq 0$ were tested with a sample of $n = 50$ $\alpha_1 = .05$. The sample $\overline{X}$ was sufficiently large that $H_0$ was rejected. What is the probability that a type-II error was committed? (*Hint*: can one commit a type-II error when one rejects $H_0$?)
5. A researcher draws a sample of $n = 100$ observations from a normal distribution for which $\sigma = 10$. He reasons correctly that if $\mu = 50$, the sampling distribution of $\overline{X}$ will be normally distributed with a mean of 50 and a standard deviation of 1. Further, he decides to reject $H_0 : \mu = 50$ if $\overline{X}$ is above 52 or below 48. What is the probability that he will commit a type-I error? (*Hint*: approximately what proportion of the sampling distribution falls below 48 or above 52? What is the approximate value of $\alpha$? Which symbol is appropriate, $\alpha_1$ or $\alpha_2$?)
6. In each of the following instances, indicate whether the critical region for rejection of $H_0$ lies in the upper (right) tail, lower (left) tail, or is divided between both tails of the sampling distribution of $\overline{X}$. If $\alpha = .05$ and, $\mu = 0$, in each instance give the proportion of the critical area that will fall in the upper tail.
   a. $H_0 : \mu = 0, H_1 : \mu \neq 0$
   b. $H_0 : \mu = 0, H_1 : \mu > 0$
   c. $H_0 : \mu = 0, H_1 : \mu < 0$
7. Jack is testing $H_0 : \mu = 10$ at the $\alpha_2 = .05$ level with a sample size of $n = 25$. Jill is testing $H_0 : \mu = 10$ at the $\alpha_2 = .05$ level with a sample of $n = 100$,
   a. Does Jack or Jill have the larger probability of committing a type-I error, or is this probability the same for both?
   b. If $\mu$ is actually 12, does Jack or Jill have the larger probability, $\beta$, of committing a type-II error? Who will have greater power?
   c. If $\sigma = 10$ and $\mu = 12$, approximately how much power will Jack have? How much power will Jill have? (Try to answer without using Figure 11.4.)
8. From Figure 11.4, estimate the power of the test of $H_0 : \mu = 100$ against $H_1 : \mu \neq 100$, for $n = 25$, $\sigma_{\overline{X}} = 3$, and $\alpha_2 = .05$ when:

| | | | |
|---|---|---|---|
| a. $\mu = 96$ | c. $\mu = 106$ | e. $\mu = 110$ | g. $\mu = 114$ |
| b. $\mu = 104$ | d. $\mu = 108$ | f. $\mu = 112$ | h. $\mu = 100$ |

9. If $\mu = 0$ and $\sigma_{\overline{X}} = 2$, how large ($\pm$) must $\overline{X}$ be to allow $H_0$ to be rejected? (If $H_1$ is directional, assume $H_1 : \mu > 0$.)
   a. $\alpha_1 = .10$
   b. $\alpha_2 = .10$
   c. $\alpha_1 = .05$
   d. $\alpha_2 = .05$
   e. $\alpha_1 = .01$
   f. $\alpha_2 = .01$
   g. What is $\alpha_2$ if the critical $z$-value is 3.29?
   h. In order to reduce the values in $\sigma_{\overline{X}}$ by one-half, the sample size $n$ would need to be increased to ___.
   i. If the sample size were increased to $16n$, the value of $\sigma_{\overline{X}}$ would equal ___.
10. Suppose a standardized reading test was given to a *sample* of sixteen sixth-grade students enrolled in a special reading enrichment program. In the eighth month of the school year their mean grade-equivalent score was 8.00. Suppose that the value of $\sigma$ is unknown, but $s$ for the sixteen pupils was 1.80. The investigator is curious about whether he can conclude that the *population* of pupils in the enrichment program have a mean which differs from 6.8, which represents the mean of all pupils in the nation in the eighth month of the sixth grade.
    a. What is $H_0$?
    b. Should $z$ or $t$ be used?
    c. What is the value for the denominator of the $t$-ratio?
    d. Calculate $t$.
    e. What are the critical values for $t$ at $\alpha_2 = .05$ and $\alpha_2 = .01$?
    f. Can $H_0$ be rejected at .05? at .01?
    g. Construct the .95 and .99 CI for $\mu$; are the results consistent with those in part f?
    h. Can we be certain that the significantly higher mean is the result of the special enrichment program?
11. The sixteen GE scores in Question 10 are given: 4.6, 5.2, 5.5, 6.4, 7.2, 8.1, 8.4, 8.5, 8.7, 8.9, 9.2, 9.6, 9.8, 9.9, 10.0, 10.0
    a. Construct the .95 CI for the population using median Equations 11.3A and 11.4.
    b. Is $H_0$ : population median = 6.8 tenable with $\alpha_2 = .05$?
    c. Construct the .68 CI using Equations 11.3 and 11.4.

## *MASTERY TEST ANSWERS*

1. d
2. b, c, and d
3. Parameters
4. When $n = 1$, ($\sigma_{\overline{X}} = \sigma/\sqrt{n}$)
5. $n = 100$; hence, $\sigma_{\overline{X}} = \sigma/\sqrt{100} = .1\sigma$.
6. b
7. a
8. Yes
9. $\alpha$
10. $p$
11. Yes
12. Yes
13. a and e
14. a. no b. no
15. a
16. c
17. Yes, with $\alpha_2 = .05$, critical value of 1.96 is required for $z$ ($_{.975}z = 1.96$), but 2.093 for $t$ ($_{.975}t_{19} = 2.093$)
18. a
19. $t$, because $\sigma$ is usually not known
20. No, although the $t$-distribution rapidly approximates a normal distribution as $n$ increases
21. a. $\nu = 10$
    b. $\nu = 59$
    c. $\nu = 100$
22. a

23. No: a type-II error results when $H_0$ is false and yet has not been rejected.
24. .05
25. No
26. Yes: $\alpha$ represents the maximum risk that we are willing to take.
27. a
28. b
29. a. ${}_{.975}t_{20} = \pm 2.09$
    b. ${}_{.95}t_{20} = 1.72$
30. .05 in both ($\alpha_1 = .05, \alpha_2 = .05$)
31. a
32. b
33. type-I error, $\beta$
34. .61
35. .39
36. Yes
37. 1.5
38. Yes
39. c
40. d

## *ANSWERS TO PROBLEMS AND EXERCISES*

1. a. The null hypothesis $H_0$ is a hypothesis about a parameter or parameters of a distribution that may or may not be "nullified" (rejected) on the basis of evidence provided by a sample from the distribution.
   b. The alternative hypothesis $H_1$ is a hypothesis about a parameter of a distribution that specifies values of the parameter other than that specified in $H_0$. If $H_0$ is rejected $H_1$ is accepted, and *vice versa.*
   c. A type-I error is the rejection of $H_0$ when it is true.
   d. A type-II error is the acceptance of $H_0$ when it is false.
   e. The level of significance $\alpha$ is the probability of committing a type-I error.
   f. The power of a test $1 - \beta$ is the probability of rejecting $H_0$ when it is false.
   g. The critical region is all those values of a sample statistic for which the investigator will reject $H_0$ if his sample yields one such value.
2. a. $H_0 : \mu = 69.5$
   b. $z$ (since $\sigma$ is known)
   c. no
   d. $\sigma_{\overline{X}} = \sigma/\sqrt{n} = 3/\sqrt{25} = .6$
   e. $z = (\overline{X} - \mu)/\sigma_{\overline{X}} = 67.5 - 69.5/.6 = -3.33$
   f. yes: $|z| = 3.33 > 2.576$
   g. yes
   h. no; $\sigma_{\overline{X}}$ would be equal to $\sigma/\sqrt{n} = 3/\sqrt{100} = .3$
3. a. type-I error
   b. no error
   c. no error
   d. type-II error
4. A type-II error cannot be committed if $H_0$ were rejected since the definition of a type-II error is that it is the failure to reject a false $H_0$.
5. $1 = \sigma_{\overline{X}}; 2(.0228) = .0456 \doteq .05 = \alpha_2$
6. a. Critical region is split between both tails, .025.
   b. upper tail, .05
   c. lower tail, 0
7. a. The probability of a type-I error is the same for both researchers; $\alpha = .05$.
   b. Jack has a larger probability of committing a type-II error when $\mu = 12$; Jill has more power.
   c. Jack: power $\doteq .16$;
      Jill: power $\doteq .50$
8. a. $\doteq .27$
   b. $\doteq .27$
   c. $\doteq .52$
   d. $\doteq .76$
   e. $\doteq .91$
   f. $\doteq .98$
   g. $\doteq .99$
   h. 0. One cannot fail to reject a false $H_0$ (and commit a type-II error) when indeed $H_0$ is true. The probability of rejecting $H_0$

is .05, but since $\mu = 100$, $.05 = \alpha$, which is the probability of making a type-I error.

9. a. $2(1.282) = 2.564$
   b. $2(1.645) = 3.290$
   c. $2(1.645) = 3.290$
   d. $2(1.96) = 3.92$
   e. $2(2.326) = 4.652$
   f. $2(2.576) = 5.152$
   g. $\alpha_2 = .001$
   h. $4n$
   i. .5

10. a. $H_0: \mu = 6.8$
   b. $t$
   c. $s_{\overline{X}} = s/\sqrt{n} = 1.8/\sqrt{16} = .45$
   d. $t = (\overline{X} - \mu)/s_{\overline{X}} = 8.0 - 6.8/.45 = 2.67$
   e. Since $\nu = n - 1 = 15$, critical $t$-values are 2.13 and 2.95 for $\alpha_2 = .05$ and $\alpha_2 = .01$, respectively.
   f. yes at .05, no at .01
   g. Yes: .95 CI $= \overline{X} \pm 2.13\ s_{\overline{X}} = 8.0 \pm 2.13(.45) = 8.0 \pm .96$, or (7.04, 8.96); 99 CI $= 8.0 \pm 2.95(.45) = 8.0 \pm 1.33$, or (6.67, 9.33). The value of 6.8 falls within .95 CI.
   h. No, perhaps they were bright students who performed excellently in spite of a poor enrichment program. Causal statements like this require the use of control groups.

11. a. $U = (16 + 1)/2 + .93\sqrt{16} = 8.5 + 3.72 = 12$, 22 or 13 (fractional values are rounded *upwards*). $X_{13} = 9.8$; $L = 16 - 13 + 1 = 4$, .95 CI $= (X_4, X_{13}) = 6.4$ to 9.8.
   b. yes, since .95 CI "captures" 6.8.
   c. $U = 8.5 + 1.00\sqrt{16}/2 = 10.5$ or 11; $L = 16 - 11 + 1 = 6$, .95 CI $= (X_6, X_{11})$ or (8.1, 9.2).

# 12

# INFERENCES ABOUT THE DIFFERENCE BETWEEN MEANS

## 12.1 INTRODUCTION

In this chapter the inferential techniques used in examining the difference between two means will be explained and illustrated. In most cases the techniques of both testing the significance of a statistic and constructing a confidence interval around it will be given.

The discussion of the inferential techniques will take the following form: (1) statement of the null **hypothesis** $H_0$ and the alternative hypothesis $H_1$—the alternative hypothesis will always be "nondirectional" unless stated otherwise; (2) statement of the **assumptions** made in making the test; (3) identification of the **test statistic** employed in testing $H_0$; (4) statement of the **sampling distribution** of the test statistic under both $H_0$ and $H_1$; (5) determination of **critical values** of the test; (6) construction of a **confidence interval** around the sample statistic; (7) an **illustration**; and (8) **special considerations**, if any.

## 12.2 TESTING STATISTICAL HYPOTHESES INVOLVING TWO MEANS

In Chapter 11 hypotheses of the type $H_0$: $\mu = K$ were tested. Methods for determining whether $\overline{X}$ differed significantly from the numerical value ($K$) that was hypothesized for the parameter $\mu$ were developed. Far more frequently, however, the interest is in *differences* in means–is there a difference in the means of populations 1 and 2? For example, for each of the following questions, the statistical hypothesis is $H_0$: $\mu_1 = \mu_2$. Is the treatment effective? Do girls read better than boys? Does drug $X$ reduce hyperactivity more than a placebo? Does anxiety level influence test performance? Is there a difference between the number of dollars per student spent for children of middle versus lower socioeconomic status?

## 12.3 THE NULL HYPOTHESIS, $H_0 : \mu_1 - \mu_2 = 0$

In each of the preceding questions the statistical hypothesis is $H_0$: $\mu_1 = \mu_2$, or equivalently, $H_0$: $\mu_1 - \mu_2 = 0$; that is, the means in populations 1 and 2 are equal–there is no difference in the parameters. The "no-difference" statistical hypothesis is widely known as the *null hypothesis.* The null hypothesis is a statistical hypothesis in which the parameter in question is hypothesized to be zero. Thus, the hypotheses $\mu = 0$, $\rho = 0$, and $\mu_1 - \mu_2 = 0$ are all examples of null hypotheses.

When two sample means are compared–for example, the mean of a treatment group, $\overline{X}_E$, versus the mean of a control group, $\overline{X}_C$–one is interested in whether the treatment had *any* effect, that is, whether $\mu_E = \mu_C$ is implausible. If the treatment were without effect, the difference in sample means $\overline{X}_E - \overline{X}_C$ results only from chance (sampling error) and $\mu_E$ equals $\mu_C$, and $\mu_E - \mu_C = 0$, as stated in the null hypothesis.

When comparing two means, the value hypothesized for the difference between $\mu_1$ and $\mu_2$ is almost always zero; that is, $H_0$: $\mu_1 - \mu_2 = 0$, although any value for the $\mu_1 - \mu_2$ difference (e.g., 10) can be specified by the statistical hypothesis. It is rare, however, that any value other than zero is hypothesized. In other words, *in behavioral research, the statistical hypothesis is almost always a null hypothesis.*

## 12.4 THE *t*-TEST COMPARING TWO INDEPENDENT MEANS*

If a random sample of persons receives a special treatment and a separate random sample does not, the two resulting means, $\overline{X}_1$ and $\overline{X}_2$, are said to be *independent*. But if a sample is pretested, then receives the treatment, and then posttested, pretest scores $X_1$'s and

*The *t*-test for means is mathematically equivalent to the analysis of variance (Chapter 16) when the number of groups equals 2. The *t*-test is widely used to test many hypotheses, not just those involving means. It is frequently encountered in published research in many disciplines.

posttest scores $X_2$'s will be correlated, that is, not independent. The case of dependent samples is treated in Section 12.12.

*Statistical Hypothesis.* The **hypothesis** tested is that the difference between the means of two populations, $\mu_1 - \mu_2$, is equal to zero against the alternative hypothesis that it is different from zero:

$$H_0: \mu_1 - \mu_2 = 0$$

$$H_1: \mu_1 - \mu_2 \neq 0$$

*Assumptions.* It is **assumed** that $X_1$ is *normally* distributed with mean $\mu_1$ and variance $\sigma^2$ and that $X_2$ is *normally* distributed with mean $\mu_2$ and *the same variance* $\sigma^2$. The assumption of equal variances in the two populations is referred to as the assumption of *homogeneous variances* or *homoscedasticity* (literally, "same spread"). Furthermore, it is assumed that a sample of size $n_1$ is randomly drawn from population 1 and that an *independent* sample of size $n_2$ is randomly drawn from population 2.

The major consequence of this assumption of independent samples is that the two sample means $\overline{X}_1$ and $\overline{X}_2$ will be perfectly uncorrelated $\rho_{\overline{X}_1\overline{X}_2} = 0$ across infinitely many pairs of samples. The independence assumption would be violated if, for example, sample 1 were a random sample of ten-year-old boys and sample 2 were composed of their sisters. The two means of brother-sister paired samples would correlate on most variables one might observe.

*Test Statistic.* $H_0: \mu_1 - \mu_2 = 0$ is tested by means of the **test statistic**, $t$. A general statement of the $t$-statistic (or $t$-test) is:

$$t = \frac{\textit{Difference} \text{ between the observed statistic and the hypothesized parameter}}{\textit{Estimate} \text{ of the standard deviation of this } \textit{difference}}$$

$$= \frac{\text{Sampling error if } H_0 \text{ is true}}{\text{Estimate of standard error}}$$

For testing the difference between two means, the $t$-test becomes

$$t = \frac{(\overline{X}_1 - \overline{X}_2) - (\mu_1 - \mu_2)}{s_{\overline{X}_1 - \overline{X}_2}} \tag{12.1}$$

or, simply, in the typical situation in which $H_0: \mu_1 - \mu_2 = 0$, Equation 12.1 simplifies to

$$t = \frac{\overline{X}_1 - \overline{X}_2}{s_{\overline{X}_1 - \overline{X}_2}} \tag{12.2}$$

Note that, unlike in the $z$-test, the denominator of the $t$-test is not a parameter; it is subject to sampling error.* The sampling error (the difference between $s_{\overline{X}_1 - \overline{X}_2}$ and $\sigma_{\overline{X}_1 - \overline{X}_2}$)

*If $\sigma_1^2$ and $\sigma_2^2$ are known, the $z$-test is used to test $H_0$: $\mu_1 - \mu_2 = 0$, and the assumption, $\sigma_1^2 = \sigma_2^2$, would be unnecessary: $\sigma^2_{\overline{X}_1 - \overline{X}_2} = \sigma^2_{\overline{X}_1} + \sigma^2_{\overline{X}_2}$ when means are independent; or when observations are paired (Sec. 12.12), $\sigma^2_{\overline{X}_1 - \overline{X}_2} = \sigma^2_{\overline{X}_1} + \sigma^2_{\overline{X}_2} - 2\rho\sigma_{\overline{X}_1}\sigma_{\overline{X}_2}$. The critical value for $|z|$ with $\alpha_2 = .05$ is 1.96 regardless of $n$. But $\sigma_1^2$ and $\sigma_2^2$ are rarely known, thus the $z$-test is the asymptote which is approached by the $t$-test as $\nu$ increases, that is, as $s_{\overline{X}_1 - \overline{X}_2}$ approaches $\sigma_{\overline{X}_1 - \overline{X}_2}$.

in the denominator causes the distribution of $t$-ratios to deviate from perfect normality, even if the original observations (the $X$'s) are normally distributed as assumed in the mathematical derivation.

## 12.5 COMPUTING $s_{\bar{X}_1-\bar{X}_2}$

Recall from Equation 5.5 (Sec. 5.8) that a variance estimate, $s^2$, is the ratio of the sum of squares ($\Sigma x^2$) to degrees of freedom ($\nu$):

$$s^2 = \frac{\text{Sum of squares}}{\text{Degrees of freedom}} = \frac{\Sigma x^2}{\nu}$$

But notice that when there are two samples, there are two separate estimates of $\sigma^2$, that is, $s_1^2$ and $s_2^2$:

$$s_1^2 = \frac{\Sigma x_1^2}{n_1 - 1}, \qquad s_2^2 = \frac{\Sigma x_2^2}{n_2 - 1}$$

Regardless of $n$, both $s_1^2$ and $s_2^2$ are unbiased estimates of $\sigma_1^2$ and $\sigma_2^2$, respectively. But if $\sigma_1^2 = \sigma_2^2$, as indicated in the assumptions in Section 12.4, then both $s_1^2$ and $s_2^2$ are independent estimates of the same parameter; that is, $\sigma_1^2 = \sigma_2^2 = \sigma^2$. It would be inefficient to use either $s_1^2$ or $s_2^2$ to estimate $\sigma^2$. Hence, the data from both samples are "pooled" to obtain the best, most efficient estimate of $\sigma^2$—that is, divide the pooled sums of squares from within groups by the pooled degrees of freedom to obtain the estimate of variance from within groups, $s_w^2$.

$$s_w^2 = \frac{\Sigma x_1^2 + \Sigma x_2^2}{(n_1 - 1) + (n_2 - 1)} = \frac{\text{Sum of squares within groups}}{\nu_1 + \nu_2} = \frac{SS_w}{\nu_w} \qquad \textbf{(12.3)}$$

The pooled within-groups variance estimate $s_w^2$ is based on the pooled degrees of freedom $(n_1 - 1) + (n_2 - 1)$ (i.e., $\nu_w = n_1 + n_2 - 2$). The pooled estimate is more precise than a variance estimate based on only $n_1 - 1$ or $n_2 - 1$ degrees of freedom—it can be expected to have less sampling error than either $s_1^2$ or $s_2^2$.

Once $s_w^2$, the unbiased estimate of the population variance, is obtained from the distribution of individual observations, it is a simple matter to estimate the variance in the sampling distribution of differences in sample means, $s_{\bar{X}_1-\bar{X}_2}^2$, and its square root, the standard error of the differences in means, $s_{\bar{X}_1-\bar{X}_2}$, by using Equation 12.4:

$$s_{\bar{X}_1-\bar{X}_2}^2 = s_w^2\left(\frac{1}{n_1} + \frac{1}{n_2}\right) \quad \text{or} \quad s_{\bar{X}_1-\bar{X}_2} = s_w\sqrt{\frac{1}{n_1} + \frac{1}{n_2}} \qquad \textbf{(12.4)}$$

*Sampling Distribution.* When $H_0$ is true, the sampling distribution of $t$ (Eq. 12.1) over pairs of samples is that of Student's $t$ with $\nu_w = n_1 + n_2 - 2$ degrees of freedom. When $H_1$ is true and hence $\mu_1 - \mu_2$ is different from zero, the distribution of $t$ in Equation 12.1 has a shape that is a function of the $t$-distribution; its mean is not 0 (the mean of a *noncentral* $t$-distribution is a function of $\mu_1 - \mu_2$).

*Critical Value.* For testing $H_0$ against $H_1$ at the $\alpha_2$-level of significance, the following critical values in the central $t$-distribution are determined and compared against the obtained value of $t$ from Equation 12.1:

$$_{\alpha/2}t_\nu = -({}_{1-\alpha/2}t_\nu) \quad \text{and} \quad {}_{1-\alpha/2}t_\nu, \qquad \text{or simply} \qquad |{}_{1-\alpha/2}t_\nu|^*$$

where $\nu = n_1 + n_2 - 2$. (Or, for a one-tailed $t$-test, the critical value is $_{1-\alpha}t_\nu$.)

*Confidence Interval.* The $1 - \alpha$ confidence interval on $\mu_1 - \mu_2$ around $\overline{X}_1 - \overline{X}_2$ is constructed as follows:

$$(1 - \alpha)CI = (\overline{X}_1 - \overline{X}_2) \pm {}_{1-(\alpha/2)}t_\nu s_{\overline{X}_1 - \overline{X}_2} \tag{12.5}$$

## 12.6 AN ILLUSTRATION

Suppose one wished to ascertain whether an intensive treatment of environmental stimulation will increase the intelligence of infants. The eighteen infants in the experimental group were randomly assigned from the thirty-six available, the remaining eighteen infants serving as the control group. After two years of the treatment, an intelligence test was administered to all thirty-six children. Hypothetical results for each group are given in Table 12.1. The $t$-test procedures outlined in Sections 12.4 and 12.5 are illustrated in Table 12.1, with $\alpha_2 = .05$.

Note in the example that $H_0$ cannot be rejected. The critical value of $t$ with 30 degrees of freedom for $\alpha_2 = .05$, that is $_{.975}t_{30} = 2.04$.† Since the obtained $t$-ratio of 1.87 is less than the critical $t$ of 2.04, $H_0$ cannot be rejected. The evidence is not strong enough to reject chance (sampling error) as the explanation for the difference between $\overline{X}_1$ and $\overline{X}_2$—at least it is not strong enough if one must maintain $\alpha_2 = .05$ protection against a type-I error. It is worth noting, however, that with $\alpha_2 = .10$, the difference is significant.

Note that the value of the pooled variance estimates $s_w^2$ (242.5) is the mean of the two sample values $s_1^2$ and $s_2^2$. This will be true when $n$'s are equal, that is, $s_w^2 = (s_1^2 + s_2^2)/2$ when $n_1 = n_2$.

Note also that the value of the denominator of the $t$-test is heavily influenced by sample size. Other things being equal, the larger the value of $n$, the smaller the value of $s_{\overline{X}_1 - \overline{X}_2}$. The smaller denominator results in a larger $t$-ratio for a fixed mean difference. This illustrates why one is less likely to make type-II errors with large $n$'s: even small mean differences can result in large $t$-ratios if $n$'s are large.

*For the $t$-ratio using a one-tailed test, the mean of the group predicted to have the smaller mean must be subtracted from the mean of the group predicted to have the larger mean. For a two-tailed test, it is inconsequential whether the numerator is $\overline{X}_A - \overline{X}_B$ or $\overline{X}_B - \overline{X}_A$, since the absolute value of $t$ will not be affected.

†Since $\nu = 34$ is not recorded in Table C, the closest smaller value for $\nu$ is used. The difference in $_{.975}t_{30}$ and $_{.975}t_{35}$ is negligible: $2.042 = {}_{.975}t_{30} > {}_{.975}t_{34} > {}_{.975}t_{35} = 2.030$. If more precision is desired, one can interpolate and estimate $_{.975}t_{34} = 2.032$. Many computer programs yield $p$'s along with significance tests.

**TABLE 12.1 A Computational Illustration of the *t*-Test Comparing Means for Independent Groups**

| *Experimental Group* | *Control Group* |
|---|---|
| $\overline{X}_1 = 108.10$ | $\overline{X}_2 = 98.40$ |
| $n_1 = 18$ | $n_2 = 18$ |
| $s_1^2 = 289.00$ | $s_2^2 = 196.00$ |
| $\Sigma x_1^2 = 4{,}913$[a] | $\Sigma x_2^2 = 3{,}332.$ |

$$t = \frac{\overline{X}_1 - \overline{X}_2}{s_{\overline{X}_1 - \overline{X}_2}} \quad \text{where} \quad s^2_{\overline{X}_1 - \overline{X}_2} = s^2_w\left(\frac{1}{n_1} + \frac{1}{n_2}\right);$$

and

$$s_w^2 = \frac{\Sigma x_1^2 + \Sigma x_2^2}{\nu_1 + \nu_2} = \frac{4{,}913 + 3{,}332}{17 + 17} = \frac{8{,}245}{34} = 242.50$$

Hence

$$s^2_{\overline{X}_1 - \overline{X}_2} = 242.50\left(\frac{1}{18} + \frac{1}{18}\right) = 26.944, \text{ thus } s_{\overline{X}_1 - \overline{X}_2} = 5.19$$

Therefore,

$$t = \frac{108.10 - 98.40}{5.19} = \frac{9.70}{5.19} = 1.87; \quad {}_{.975}t_{34} \doteq 2.04$$

$|t| < 2.04$, that is, $p > .05$, hence $H_0$ is tenable with $\alpha = .05$

[a]If necessary, the sum of squares $\Sigma x^2$ can easily be determined from $n$ and $s^2$: since $s^2 = \Sigma x^2/(n-1)$, then $\Sigma x^2 = s^2(n-1)$. $\Sigma x^2$ can also be determined from Equation 5.6: $\Sigma x^2 = \Sigma X^2 - n\overline{X}^2$.

The central *t*-distribution with 30 degrees of freedom is graphed in Figure 12.1. The associated *t*-values at percentiles .5, 2.5, 5, 95, 97.5, and 99.5 are indicated. For example, when $H_0$ is true and $\nu = 30$, a *t*-ratio of $-1.70$ or less would be observed in 5% of the *t*-tests. One would observe *t*-values of +1.70 or higher 5% of the time. In other words, when $\alpha_2 = .10$, the critical value for $t$ is $\pm 1.70$—if $|t| \geqslant 1.70$, $H_0$ is rejected at $\alpha = .10$. Five percent of the area under the curve in Figure 12.1 falls to the left of the point $t = -1.70$, another 5% to the right of $t = 1.70$. In the example $\alpha_2$ was set at .05; hence, $H_0$ would be rejected only if the observed $t$ is below $-2.04$ or greater than 2.04. When $H_0$ is true, 95% of the obtained $t$'s would fall in the range $\pm 2.04$.

If $\mu_1 \neq \mu_2$, the observed *t*-values will tend to be larger since the expected value of $\overline{X}_1 - \overline{X}_2$ is $\mu_1 - \mu_2$, not 0. $E(\overline{X}_1 - \overline{X}_2) = 0$ only when $\mu_1 = \mu_2$. Hence, a false $H_0$ will be rejected in more than 5% of the *t*-tests when $\alpha = .05$. If the observed *t*-ratio exceeds, in absolute value, the critical *t*-value, one will reject $H_0$ and be correct in the decision

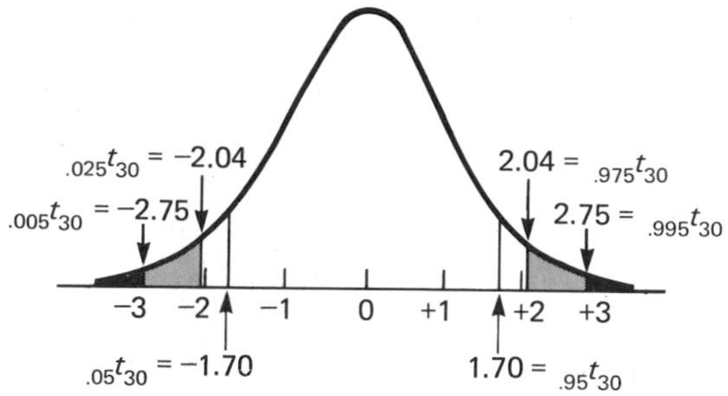


**FIGURE 12.1**
**A central $t$-distribution with 30 degrees of freedom. Critical areas are shown for $\alpha_2 = .10$, $\alpha_2 = .05$, and $\alpha_2 = .01$.**

when $\mu_1 \neq \mu_2$. But if $|t| <$ critical $t$, a type-II error will be made if $\mu_1 \neq \mu_2$. Observe in Figure 12.1 that the smaller the probability of a type-I error ($\alpha$), the larger the associated critical $t$-values. Recall (Chapter 11) that there is a greater risk of a type-II error ($\beta$) at $\alpha = .01$ than at $\alpha = .05$. If $\alpha$ had been set equal to .10 in Table 12.1, $H_0$ would have been rejected at the .10 level of statistical significance, since $1.87 > 1.70$.

Notice again the tradeoff: the greater the risk of making a type-I error ($\alpha$), the less the risk of making a type-II error ($\beta$). Accordingly, power is decreased as $\alpha$ is changed from .05 to .01, or from .10 to .05.

It is good practice to report probability values ($p$) as precisely as possible; $p$ is the observed level of significance—the proportion of the central $t$-distribution beyond the absolute value of the observed $t$. Rather than report $p > .05$, it is more informative to report $.10 > p > .05$. Always give the minimum level at which $H_0$ can be rejected. Even if one sets $\alpha = .05$, $H_0$ can be rejected at the .01 level if the obtained $t$-ratio exceeds the critical $t$ for $\alpha = .01$. As a reader of research reports, one is not obligated to operate at the same value for $\alpha$ used by the researcher. One may decide the 10% risk of a type-I error is more than offset by increased power—the decreased chance of a type-II error.

## 12.7 CONFIDENCE INTERVALS ABOUT MEAN DIFFERENCES

Recall from Chapter 11 that the .95 confidence interval for $\mu$ is

$$.95\,\text{CI} = \overline{X} \pm ({}_{.975}t_\nu)s_{\overline{X}}$$

Similarly, using Equation 12.6, one can set a CI for a difference in means irrespective of whether $H_0$: $\mu_1 = \mu_2$ is rejected. Equation 12.6 gives the expression for the .95 confidence interval around mean differences:

$$.95\text{CI} = \overline{X}_1 - \overline{X}_2 \pm ({}_{.975}t_\nu)s_{\overline{X}_1-\overline{X}_2} \qquad \textbf{(12.6)}$$

For the data given in Table 12.1, the observed mean difference ($\overline{X}_1 - \overline{X}_2$) was 9.70, with $s_{\overline{X}_1-\overline{X}_2} = 5.19$ and $\nu = 34$. Thus, by substituting into Equation 12.6, we can be 95%

confident that the true value of $\mu_1 - \mu_2$ is contained within the .95 confidence interval:

$$.95\text{CI} = 9.70 \pm (2.04)5.19$$
$$= 9.70 \pm 10.59 \quad \text{or between} \quad -.89 \quad \text{and} \quad 20.29$$

In other words, the true treatment effect $(\mu_1 - \mu_2)$ probably lies between $-.9$ and 20.3. Since the .95 confidence interval includes the value of 0, $H_0$ is not rejected at $\alpha_2 = .05$.

## 12.8 EFFECT SIZE

When the dependent variable is expressed in a metric that is well understood (e.g., inches, pounds, dollars, and minutes) a confidence interval is expressed in numbers that need no further explanation. Measures of IQ, GPA, and grade equivalents also allow the reader to attach some nonarbitrary meaning to the magnitude of differences.

But differences in means expressed in raw-score units on tests of arbitrary length are often difficult to interpret. A difference in means of five points on a twenty-five-item test would be expected to become a difference of twenty points if a 100-item test had been used. Using percentage scores rather than raw scores on cognitive and psychomotor measures is a step in the right direction. But scores are not very useful on attitude and many other kinds of scales where right-wrong scoring usually makes no sense.

In situations in which the metric of dependent variable is arbitrary the use of *effect size* to convey the magnitude of a difference can be helpful (Glass, McGaw, and Smith, 1981). Most often the effect size is used to describe the difference between the mean of experimental $(\overline{X}_E)$ and control $(\overline{X}_c)$ groups.

The effect size is simply the $z$-score of the mean of the experimental group $(\overline{X}_E)$ referenced in the frequency distribution of the control group, that is, $\overline{X}_E - \overline{X}_C$ expressed in standard deviation units. In terms of parameters

$$\Delta = \frac{\mu_E - \mu_C}{\sigma}; \qquad \text{in terms of estimators,} \qquad \hat{\Delta} = \frac{\overline{X}_E - \overline{X}_C}{\hat{\sigma}} \tag{12.7}$$

where $\hat{\sigma} = s_w$.

Thus, for the data in Table 12.1, where $\hat{\Delta} = (108.10 - 98.40)/15.6 = .62$—the difference in the two means is estimated to be .62 standard deviations.

When $\sigma$ is not known, it can be estimated by $s_w^*$.

### $t$-Test Assumptions and Robustness

The three assumptions (Sec. 12.4) made in the mathematical derivation of the central $t$-distribution (i.e., the sampling distribution of $t$-ratios when $H_0$ is true) are as follows: (1) the $X$'s within each of the two populations are normally distributed; (2) the two population variances ($\sigma_1^2$ and $\sigma_2^2$) are equal; and (3) the individual observations ($X$'s) are independent.

*In certain instances in which the treatment can affect the heterogeneity as well as the mean of the treatment group, $s_{control}$ should be used in the denominator of Equation 12.7. The statistical properties of $\hat{\Delta}$ have been examined by Hedges (1981).

## 12.9 NORMALITY

The statistician makes the assumption of normality not only because the normal curve is approximated by the distributions of many variables, but because of an important mathematical property of normal distributions. The mean and variance of samples from a normal distribution are statistically independent (the values of $\bar{X}$'s and $s^2$'s over repeated samples from the same *normal* population would correlate zero). In the past researchers have gone to great lengths to insure that the observations are normally distributed (Sec. 6.10). For example, if the dependent variable were positively skewed, instead of analyzing the actual scores, their square roots might be analyzed (if $X$'s are positively skewed, the distribution of $\sqrt{X}$'s will be less skewed).

Fortunately, much research has revealed (see Glass, Peckham, and Sanders, 1972) that violation of the assumption of normality has almost no practical consequences in using the $t$-test. Figure 12.2 is based on research by Boneau (1960) and Hsu and Feldt (1969); it illustrates the proportion of $t$-tests in which the null hypothesis was rejected when it was true (i.e., the proportion of type-I errors) when the nominal $\alpha_2$ was set at .05—that is, when the critical $t$-values from Appendix Table C were used. For example, the third row of Figure 12.2 shows that when $n_1 = 5$ and $n_2 = 5$ and both population distributions are skewed, $H_0$ will be rejected in approximately 3% of the tests with the nominal $\alpha$-value "$\alpha_2$" = .05; the fourth row reveals that $H_0$ will be rejected at "$\alpha_2$" = .05 in about 4% of the tests when $n_1 = n_2 = 15$. The bars extending out from .01 depict the proportion of $H_0$'s rejected when the nominal value for *alpha* ("$\alpha_2$") is set at .01. Note that when the $n$'s were 15 or more, the actual proportion of type-1 errors was within 1% of the nominal value for alpha for both the .05 and .01 levels, a negligible discrepancy for

**FIGURE 12.2**
**Actual proportion of type-I errors in 1.00 $t$-tests when nominal $\alpha_2$ was set at .01 and .05. Data from Boneau (1960) and Hsu and Feldt (1969).**

| Population I | $n_1$ | Population II | $n_2$ | Actual Proportion of Type-I Errors at Nominal $\alpha$-values of .01 and .05 (.01 .02 .03 .04 .05 .06) |
|---|---|---|---|---|
| Rectangular | 5 | Rectangular | 5 | |
| " | 15 | " | 15 | |
| Skewed | 5 | Skewed | 5 | |
| " | 15 | " | 15 | |
| Normal | 5 | " | 5 | |
| " | 15 | " | 15 | |
| " | 25 | " | 25 | |
| Rectangular | 5 | " | 5 | |
| " | 15 | " | 15 | |
| Dichotomous* | 11 | Dichotomous | 11 | |
| " ($\pi$ = .5) | 51 | " ($\pi$ = .5) | 51 | |
| " ($\pi$ = .6 | 11 | " ($\pi$ = .6) | 11 | |
| " " | 51 | " " | 51 | |
| " ($\pi$ = .75) | 11 | " ($\pi$ = .75) | 11 | |
| " " | 51 | " " | 51 | |

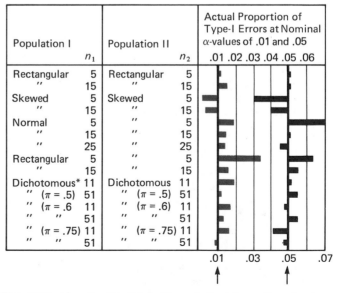

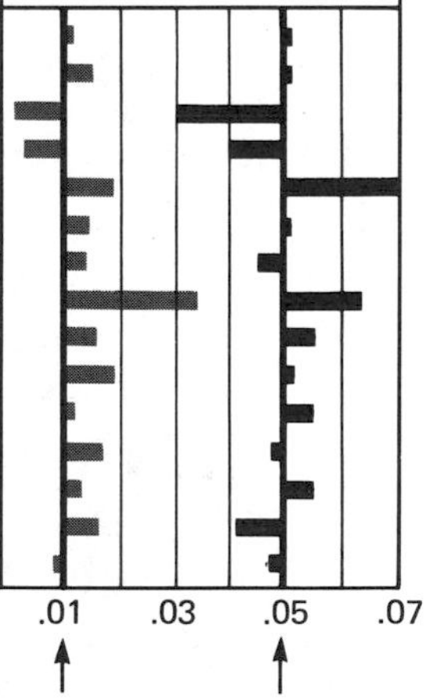


*The value of $\pi$ is the proportion of the observations in the population in one category of the dichotomy. The proportion in the other category is 1-$\pi$.

practical purposes. Observe that even when the dependent variable was dichotomous (i.e., yes or no response), the nominal "$\alpha$" was negligibly in error from the actual $\alpha$ when $n_1 = n_2$.

Boneau (1960) also found that the probability of a type-II error (power) is virtually unaffected by marked nonnormality. Consequently, the condition of normality can be largely disregarded as a prerequisite for using the $t$-test. The $t$-test is "robust" with respect to failure to meet the normality assumption.

## 12.10 HOMOGENEITY OF VARIANCE

The homogeneity-of-variance assumption* legitimizes the use of a single variance estimate from the aggregate of the sum of squares from both groups ($ss_w$) and the associated pooled degrees of freedom ($\nu_w$). The precision of the resulting variance estimate is greatest when the assumption that $\sigma_1^2 = \sigma_2^2$ is valid. If $\sigma_1^2 = \sigma_2^2$, then the expected value of both $s_1^2$ and $s_2^2$ is the parameter $\sigma^2$; that is, $E(s_1^2) = E(s_2^2) = \sigma^2$. If both $s_1^2$ and $s_2^2$ are unbiased estimates of a common parameter ($\sigma^2$), it would be inefficient not to combine (pool) the information from both to achieve a better, more accurate estimate of the parameter $\sigma^2$.

### Consequences of Heterogeneous Variances

Several researchers have studied the empirical consequences of violating the assumption of homogeneity of variance. This research has been extensively reviewed by Glass, Peckham, and Sanders (1972). It has been shown that the $t$-test is robust with respect to violation of the homogeneity-of-variance assumption when $n_1 = n_2$. Indeed, for practical purposes one need not even test the assumption of homogeneity of variance *when n's are equal*. Figure 12.3 illustrates the effects of heterogeneous variance when $n$'s are equal and when they are not. The relative size of $\sigma_1^2$ and $\sigma_2^2$ is given along the baseline; for example, if $\sigma_1^2/\sigma_2^2 = 2$, $\sigma_2^2$ is one-half as large as $\sigma_1^2$. The *relative* size of the $n$'s is given to the right of the "curves."

Note that when the larger sample is associated with the population with the larger variance—that is, when $n_1/n_2 > 1$ and $\sigma_1^2/\sigma_2^2 > 1$—the $t$-test is conservative with respect to committing type-I errors. The three lower curves indicate that when the critical $t$-values from Table C are used and "$\alpha_2$" is set at .05, the probability of rejecting a true null hypothesis is less than .05. For example, if $n_1$ is twice as large as $n_2$ ($n_1/n_2 = 2$) and $\sigma_1^2$ is five times larger than $\sigma_2^2$ ($\sigma_1^2/\sigma_2^2 = 5$), then the null hypothesis will be rejected in less than 2% of such situations when it is true. Hence, when $n_1 > n_2$ and $\sigma_1^2 > \sigma_2^2$, an even smaller risk of a type-I error is taken than is claimed when $H_0$ is rejected.† If $H_0$ is rejected at the ".05" level when $\sigma_1^2 > \sigma_2^2$ and $n_1 > n_2$, one need have no concern about violating the homogeneity-of-variance assumption. In Figure 12.3 we can see that the true probability of a type-I error is always less than the nominal probability when the larger $n$ and larger variance are paired.

*The principal reason Gosset ("Student") assumed homogeneity of variance was, no doubt, to simplify the mathematics; otherwise he would have been faced with the "Behrens-Fisher" problem.

†This added protection would be comforting if it were not that it also represents less power for rejecting a false $H_0$.

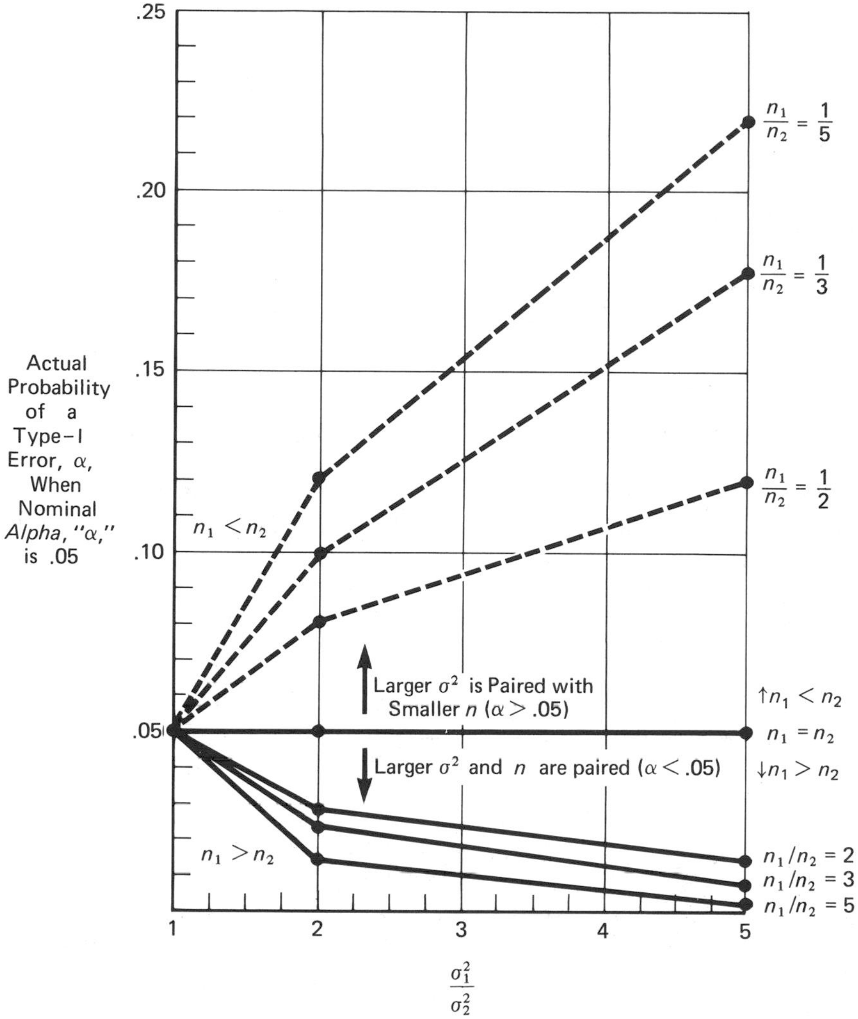


**FIGURE 12.3. The effect of heterogeneity of variance on *alpha* (α), the probability of a type-I error, for various ratios of $\sigma_1^2/\sigma_2^2$ and $n_1/n_2$, using the two-tailed $t$-test when the nominal significance, "α," is .05. (Data from Scheffé [1959] and Hsu [1938].)**

The three upper curves give the true $\alpha$ when $n_2 > n_1$ and $\sigma_1^2 > \sigma_2^2$. When the larger sample has the smaller variance, the true $\alpha$ is greater than the nominal (apparent) probability of a type-I error, "α." How much greater? In Figure 12.3 note that if $\sigma_1^2/\sigma_2^2 = 5$ and $n_1/n_2 = \frac{1}{5}$, and if the critical $t$-value for $\alpha_2 = .05$ from Table C is used, the probability of a type-I error is not .05 but .22! If $n_1/n_2 = \frac{1}{10}$ or less, the true $\alpha$ would be even higher. Of course, $\sigma_1^2/\sigma_2^2 = 5$ are extremely heterogeneous variances that would not often be encountered with actual data. But situations in which $n_1/n_2 = \frac{1}{10}$ or less are not rare. When a larger sample has the smaller variance, the true $\alpha$ will exceed "α," the apparent probability of a type-I error. If $\sigma_1^2 > \sigma_2^2$ and $n_2 > n_1$, and $H_0$ is not rejected, why does one need not be concerned about violating the homogeneity-of-variance assumption? If $H_0$ is rejected when the true $\alpha$ is greater than .05, $H_0$ would not be rejected if the true $\alpha$ is .05. For example, if $p > .06$ or $p > .10$, it is superfluous to inquire whether $p < .05$.*

## 12.11 INDEPENDENCE OF OBSERVATIONS

Independence simply means that the observations within or between the two groups are not paired, interdependent, or associated in any way. If the scores are paired, the *t*-test for paired observations should be used. If variable *A* is a pretest and variable *B* is a posttest, the observations would not be independent, but correlated. In certain situations it is difficult to ascertain whether the condition of independence is met (Sec. 19.22). If John copies some of his answers from Mary, $X_{\text{John}}$ and $X_{\text{Mary}}$ obviously would not be independent.

The condition of independence of observations is important. Without it, probability statements pertaining to type-I or type-II errors can be seriously affected. With proper experimental control, dependency among the observations can usually be prevented or taken into account in the analysis. More will be said regarding independence in subsequent chapters; the special case of nonindependence in which two sets of observations are paired will now be considered.

## 12.12 TESTING $H_0: \mu_1 = \mu_2$ WITH PAIRED OBSERVATIONS

When each observation in group 1 can be linked to or paired with an observation in group 2, the two sets of observations are dependent or correlated.† The procedures for testing paired observations differ in only two respects from those for independent observations: procedures for determining $s_{\overline{X}_1-\overline{X}_2}$ and degrees of freedom.

*Statistical Hypothesis.* Population 1 has mean $\mu_1$ and population 2 has mean $\mu_2$. The **null hypothesis** to be tested is the same as in Section 12.3.

$$H_0: \mu_1 - \mu_2 = 0$$

$$H_1: \mu_1 - \mu_2 \neq 0$$

*If $n_1 \neq n_2$ and $\sigma_1^2 \neq \sigma_2^2$ (Chapter 13 describes methods for testing $H_0$: $\sigma_1^2 = \sigma_2^2$), the hypothesis $H_0$: $\mu_1 = \mu_2$ can be evaluated using the quasi *t*-test:

$$t' = (\overline{X}_1 - \overline{X}_2)\Big/\sqrt{s_{\overline{X}_1}^2 + s_{\overline{X}_2}^2}$$

The $t'$-distribution closely approximates a *t*-distribution with $\nu$ degrees of freedom obtained from the Welch formula: $\nu = \nu_1\nu_2/\nu_2c^2 + \nu_1(1-c)^2$, where $c = s_{\overline{X}_1}^2/(s_{\overline{X}_1}^2 + s_{\overline{X}_2}^2)$. Thus, if $\nu_1 = n_1 - 1 = 10$, $\nu_2 = n_2 - 1 = 20$, $s_{\overline{X}_1}^2 = 7$, and $s_{\overline{X}_2}^2 = 3$: $c = .7$, and $\nu = (10)(20)/20(.7)^2 + 10(.3)^2 = 18.7$ or 19, the critical $t'$-value at $\alpha_2 = .05$ is ${}_{.975}t_{19} = 2.09$.

†The rare exception to this statement would occur if the variable on which the observations were paired did not correlate with the variable on which the two groups are to be compared. Obviously it would be pointless to pair observations in such situations.

*Assumptions.* It is assumed that samples 1 and 2 are randomly drawn from *normal* populations with the *same variance* $\sigma^2$. In this instance the samples need not be independent, that is, there may exist a correlation between $\overline{X}_1$ and $\overline{X}_2$ over repeated pairs of samples. The following are examples of dependent samples: sample 1 is a sample of one-year-old infants and sample 2 consists of the fraternal twin-mates of the children in sample 1; sample 1 is a group of boys and sample 2 is the group of their sisters; sample 1 is the collection of scores on a reaction-time test made by a group of persons before administration of a drug and sample 2 is the collection of scores made by the same persons after taking the drug.

*Test Statistic.* It will always be possible to "pair off" data from two dependent samples. The pairs may be defined by "brother-sister," "before-after," "twin 1, twin 2," "matched partner 1, matched partner 2," etc. Hence, data gathered from dependent samples will be in the form of $n$ pairs of observations $X_{1i}$ and $X_{2i}$ for $i = 1, \ldots, n$. This pairing of the data from dependent samples will be used to test the hypothesis that $\mu_1 - \mu_2 = 0$. The hypothesis that $X_1$ and $X_2$ have the same mean, that is, that $\mu_1 = \mu_2$, is equivalent to the hypothesis that $X_1 - X_2$ has a mean of 0 in the population. The $n$ differences, $X_{1i} - X_{2i}$, between the normally distributed variables $X_1$ and $X_2$ is itself assumed to be normally distributed.

When observations are paired, Equation 12.8 (and not Eq. 12.4) should be used to determine $s_{\overline{X}_1 - \overline{X}_2}$, the denominator of the $t$-test.* The degrees of freedom for the $t$-test for paired observations is $\nu = n - 1$, where $n$ is the number of pairs (not the number of scores).

$$s^2_{\overline{X}_1 - \overline{X}_2} = s^2_{\overline{X}_1} + s^2_{\overline{X}_2} - 2rs_{\overline{X}_1}s_{\overline{X}_2} \tag{12.8}$$

where $s^2_{\overline{X}_1} = \dfrac{s_1^2}{n}$ and $s^2_{\overline{X}_2} = \dfrac{s_2^2}{n}$,

with $\nu = n - 1$ degrees of freedom.

*Sampling Distribution.* If $H_0: \mu_1 - \mu_2 = 0$ is true, then $t$ in Equation 12.1 (and 12.2) will follow the central $t$-distribution with $\nu = n - 1$. If $H_1: \mu_1 - \mu_2 \neq 0$ is true, then $t$ in Equation 12.1 (and 12.2) will have a distribution identical in shape to the Student's $t$-distribution with $\nu = n - 1$, but the distribution will have a mean that is different from zero in a direction and by an amount depending on the size of $\mu_1 - \mu_2$.

*Critical Value.* The critical values for testing $H_0$ against $H_1$ at the $\alpha$-level of significance by means of the $t$-statistic in Equations 12.1 and 12.2 are as follows:

$$-({}_{1-(\alpha/2)}t_\nu) \quad \text{and} \quad {}_{1-(\alpha/2)}t_\nu$$

*CI.* The $1 - \alpha$ confidence interval on $\mu_1 - \mu_2$ around $\overline{X}_1 - \overline{X}_2$ is constructed as follows in Equation 12.5:

$$(1 - \alpha)\text{CI} = \overline{X}_1 - \overline{X}_2 \pm {}_{1-(\alpha/2)}t_\nu s_{\overline{X}_1 - \overline{X}_2}$$

where $\nu = n - 1$.

*Note that Equation 12.8 is an application of Equation 7.8. The $r$ in Equation 12.8 is the correlation between $\overline{X}_1$ and $\overline{X}_2$ over repeated samples, that is, $r_{\overline{X}_1\overline{X}_2}$. When observations are randomly selected, the correlation between the observations $r_{12}$ estimates the correlation between the means.

*Illustration.* A study was made (Wechsler, 1967) to estimate the "practice effect" on the Wechsler Preschool and Primary Scale of Intelligence (WPPSI). Fifty five-year-old children were tested, then retested two to four months later. Obviously there would be some correlation between the two sets of scores. Note that if there is no correlation between variables 1 and 2, since $n_1 = n_2$, Eq. 12.8 is mathematically equivalent to Eq. 12.4, which gives $s_{\overline{X}_1 - \overline{X}_2}$ for independent observations. Notice in Equation 12.8 that as $r$ increases, the value of $s_{\overline{X}_1 - \overline{X}_2}$ decreases. The $t$-test for dependent observations is illustrated in Table 12.2 using Wechsler's (1967) data.

Note that the mean practice effect was highly significant—$H_0$ is rejected at the .001 level.* But a highly satistically significant difference (e.g., $p < .001$) does not necessarily indicate a large difference in means. If $n$ is large or $r$ is high, even a small difference in means can result in a large $t$-ratio, and a highly significant difference. Level of statistical significance should never be used to convey the magnitude of a difference. Rather the effect size $\Delta$ (Sec. 12.8) and the CI for the difference in the population means should

**TABLE 12.2 An Illustration of the $t$-Test for Correlated Observations ($n$ = 50) Using Data from Wechsler (1967)**

| *Retest*[a] | *1st Test* | |
|---|---|---|
| $\overline{X}_1 = 109.2$ | $\overline{X}_2 = 105.6$ | $s_{\overline{X}_1} = \dfrac{s_1}{\sqrt{n_1}} = \dfrac{(13.3)}{\sqrt{50}} = 1.88$ |
| $s_1 = 13.3$ | $s_2 = 14.8$ | |
| $r = .91$ | | $s_{\overline{X}_2} = \dfrac{s_2}{\sqrt{n_2}} = \dfrac{(14.8)}{\sqrt{50}} = 2.09$ |

$$s^2_{\overline{X}_1 - \overline{X}_2} = s^2_{\overline{X}_1} + s^2_{\overline{X}_2} - 2rs_{\overline{X}_1}s_{\overline{X}_2}$$

$$= (1.88)^2 + (2.09)^2 - 2(.91)(1.88)(2.09)$$

$$s^2_{\overline{X}_1 - \overline{X}_2} = 7.90 - 7.15 = .75$$

$$s_{\overline{X}_1 - \overline{X}_2} = .866$$

$$t = \frac{\overline{X}_1 - \overline{X}_2}{s_{\overline{X}_1 - \overline{X}_2}} = \frac{109.2 - 105.6}{.866} = \frac{3.6}{.866} = 4.16; \quad {}_{.9995}t_{49} \doteq 3.50$$

Reject $H_0$ at .001 level ($p < .001$)

$$.95 \text{ CI} = \overline{X}_1 - \overline{X}_2 \pm {}_{.975}t_{49}s_{\overline{X}_1 - \overline{X}_2}$$

$$= 3.6 \pm (2.01)(.866) = 3.6 \pm 1.74 \text{ or } (1.86, 5.34)$$

Effect size[b], $\hat{\Delta}$, (Eq. 12.7): $(109.2 - 105.6)/15 = .24\sigma$

[a]We selected the group having the larger mean as group 1. This designation is arbitrary when testing non-direction hypotheses.
[b]Since from the test norms $\sigma = 15$, it can be used in Eq. 12.7. If one uses $\hat{\sigma} = s = \sqrt{(s_1^2 + s_2^2)/2} = 14.0$, $\hat{\Delta} = .26\hat{\sigma}$.

*Actually, a directional or one-tailed hypothesis could have been justified in this situation, since the possibility that the retest $\mu_2$ is less than $\mu_1$ is essentially nil.

be reported. As illustrated in Table 12.2, the effect size is shown to be $.24\sigma$, and the difference in population means ($\mu_2 - \mu_1$) is presumed to lie within the range of 1.86 to 5.34 IQ points. The CI limits can also be expressed in standard deviation units, that is, .95 CI for $\Delta$ extend from $1.86/15 = .12\sigma$, to $5.34/15 = .36\sigma$. If $H_0$ is true, there is less than one chance in 1,000 of obtaining a mean difference as large as that which was observed (3.6 points) for $n = 50$; that is, it is extremely improbable that the practice effect is zero.

## 12.13 DIRECT-DIFFERENCE METHOD FOR THE $t$-TEST WITH DEPENDENT OBSERVATIONS

Suppose the IQ scores were used to form pairs of students—the two members of each pair have the same IQ score. If we randomly assigned one member of each pair to the method-$A$ group and the other member to the method-$B$ group, the paired observations on the dependent variable would be correlated. Within group $A$, the students with higher IQ scores would probably tend to score higher on the posttreatment achievement test. The pattern would be expected to be the same in group $B$. The degree of correlation between the paired observations should be taken into account in the analysis. This type of research design is generally more powerful than a simple random assignment of persons to method without equating pairs of students ("stratifying") on IQ (see Sec. 12.14). This correlation $r$ could be computed, and Equation 12.8 could be used to obtain $s_{\bar{X}_1-\bar{X}_2}$. But there is a more direct computational procedure that avoids the necessity of computing $r$. A $t$-test formula for dependent samples that is mathematically equivalent to the procedure used in Panel A of Table 12.3 is as follows:

$$t = \frac{\bar{X}_1 - \bar{X}_2}{s_{\bar{X}_1-\bar{X}_2}} = \frac{\bar{X}_d}{s_{\bar{X}_d}} \qquad \textbf{(12.9)}$$

where $\bar{X}_d$ is the mean difference $(\bar{X}_1 - \bar{X}_2)$, $X_{di} = X_{1i} - X_{2i}$, and $s_{\bar{X}_d}$ is the standard error of the mean difference,

$$s_{\bar{X}_d} = \frac{s_{X_d}}{\sqrt{n}} = s_{\bar{X}_1-\bar{X}_2} \qquad \textbf{(12.10)}$$

(Notice that Equation 12.9 is simply an application of Equation 11.6 in which $\mu = 0$.)

### Computational Steps

The scores of ten brain-damaged children on two different Wechsler intelligence subtests (Verbal and Performance) are given in Table 12.3. Note the simple steps in computing $t$ for correlated samples using the direct-difference method.

1. Take the *difference* ($X_d$) between the paired observations for each of the $n$ pairs and determine the mean difference ($\bar{X}_d$).
2. Find the variance ($s^2_{X_d}$) of the difference scores (find the sum of squares $\Sigma x^2_d$ by using Eq. 5.6).

**TABLE 12.3 Using the Direct-Difference Method *t*-Test for Correlated Observations Comparing IQ Scores of Ten Brain-Damaged Students on Intelligence Tests**

| *Person* | *Verbal (1)* | *Performance (2)* | *Difference:* $X_{di} = X_{1i} - X_{2i}$ |
|---|---|---|---|
| 1 | 80 | 70 | +10 |
| 2 | 100 | 80 | +20 |
| 3 | 110 | 90 | +20 |
| 4 | 120 | 90 | +30 |
| 5 | 70 | 70 | 00 |
| 6 | 100 | 110 | −10 |
| 7 | 110 | 80 | +30 |
| 8 | 120 | 120 | 00 |
| 9 | 110 | 80 | +30 |
| 10 | 90 | 70 | +20 |
| | $\overline{X}_1 = 101.0$ | $\overline{X}_2 = 86.0$ | $\Sigma X_d = 150$ |
| | $(s_1 = 16.6)$ | $(s_2 = 17.1)$ | $\overline{X}_d = 15.0$ |

A. *Direct-Difference Method* (Eq. 12.10)

$$\overline{X}_d = \frac{\Sigma X_d}{n} = \frac{150}{10} = 15.0$$

$$s^2_{X_d} = \frac{\Sigma x_d^2}{n-1}$$

$$\Sigma x_d^2 = \Sigma X_d^2 - n\overline{X}_d^2 = (10)^2 + (20)^2 + \cdots + (20)^2 - 10(15.0)^2$$

$$\Sigma x_d^2 = 4100 - 2250 = 1850$$

$$s^2_{X_d} = \frac{\Sigma x_d^2}{n-1} = \frac{1850}{9} = 205.6$$

$$s^2_{\overline{X}_d} = \frac{s_d^2}{n} = \frac{205.6}{10} = 20.56, \quad s_{\overline{X}_d} = 4.53$$

$$t = \frac{\overline{X}_d}{s_{\overline{X}_d}} = \frac{15.0}{4.53} = 3.31, \quad {}_{.995}t_9 = 3.25$$

Reject $H_0$ at .01 level ($p < .01$)

$$.95 \text{ CI} = \overline{X}_d \pm {}_{1-\alpha/2}t_\nu s_{\overline{X}_d}$$

$$= 15.0 \pm (2.26)(4.53) = 15.0 \pm 10.2 \text{ or } (4.8, 25.2)$$

B. (Eq. 12.8) ($r_{12} = .64$)

$$s^2_{\overline{X}_1 - \overline{X}_2} = s^2_{\overline{X}_1} + s^2_{\overline{X}_2} - 2rs_{\overline{X}_1}s_{\overline{X}_2}; \quad s^2_{\overline{X}_1} = \frac{s_1^2}{n} = \frac{(16.6)^2}{10} = 27.7$$

$$s^2_{\overline{X}_2} = \frac{(17.1)^2}{10} = 29.2$$

$$= 27.7 + 29.2 - 2(.64)(\sqrt{27.6})(\sqrt{29.2})$$

$$= 20.5$$

$$s_{\overline{X}_1 - \overline{X}_2} = 4.53$$

$$t = \frac{\overline{X}_1 - \overline{X}_2}{s_{\overline{X}_1 - \overline{X}_2}} = \frac{101.0 - 86.0}{4.53} = 3.31$$

3. Find the standard error of the mean difference ($s_{\overline{X}_d} = s_{X_d}/\sqrt{n}$).
4. The ratio of $\overline{X}_d$ to $s_{\overline{X}_d}$ is $t$; compare $t$ with the critical $t$-value, that is, the appropriate percentile in the central $t$-distribution with $\nu = n - 1$ degrees of freedom ($n$ is the number of *pairs*, not the total number of observations).

In the example in Table 12.3, the obtained $t$ of 3.31 was greater than the critical $t$ of 3.25 for $\alpha_2 = .01$; hence, $H_0$ was rejected at the .01 level. Panel B shows that if the correlation between the Verbal and Performance tests had been computed ($r = .64$) and the standard error of the difference in means determined using Equation 12.8, the value of $s_{\overline{X}_1 - \overline{X}_2}$ would have been precisely .453—the two procedures are alternative routes to the same destination.

The effect size (Sec. 12.8) of the mean difference is $\hat{\Delta} = (101. - 86.)/15 = 1\sigma$.

## 12.14 CAUTIONS REGARDING THE MATCHED-PAIR DESIGNS IN RESEARCH

When properly used, a research design that results in correlated observations can be more powerful than a design in which the subjects are randomly assigned to two independent treatment groups. If subjects are grouped into homogeneous pairs on a variable (such as IQ) that correlates with the criterion (such as reading performance), and then one number of each pair is randomly assigned to each of the two treatment groups, the resulting $t$-test (for dependent groups) will have greater power than a design in which the same subjects are randomly assigned to treatment groups without pairing. This type of research design should not be confused with the conventional matched-pair design in which there is no random assignment following the pairing. Matched-pair designs have been widely used and misused in behavioral research. Their purpose is to match (pair) each person in group $A$ (e.g., delinquents) with a person in group $B$ (e.g., nondelinquents) on some variable (e.g., IQ), then compare the two groups on a dependent variable (e.g., reading ability). But the researcher is mistaken if he believes that he has fully equated the groups in intelligence. He may conclude erroneously that a significant difference on some dependent variable, such as reading proficiency, is due, not to intelligence differences, but to the delinquency factor. The fallacy of the matched-pair design is the assumption that matching equates the groups on the matching variable. If the groups have different means on that variable (and if not, why match?), the matching does not fully equate the groups on that variable. The pair members will each regress toward their respective means when they are retested. In other words, if we immediately retest our delinquents and nondelinquests on another intelligence test, the nondelinquents would regress toward their mean ($\doteq$100) and the delinquents would regress toward their mean ($\doteq$90). It is beyond the scope of this book to develop fully the underlying rationale for this subtlety;* the matching fallacy results primarily from measurement error and the regression effect (Sec. 8.11). But the practical consequences of the use of matched pair designs is that the groups are rarely truly equated on the variable on which they are matched.

*See Thorndike (1963), Hopkins (1969), and Shepard and Hopkins (1977) for a more complete treatment of the matched-groups fallacy.

## CHAPTER SUMMARY

When the hypothesized value for the parameter is 0, the statistical hypothesis is termed a null hypothesis. The null hypothesis states that any difference in the two means is attributable to chance (sampling error). If, assuming $H_0: \mu_1 - \mu_2 = 0$ is true, the probability of observing a difference in means as large as that which was observed is very small—that is, if $p < \alpha$—we reject $H_0$ and conclude either that $\mu_1 > \mu_2$ if $\overline{X}_1 > \overline{X}_2$ or that $\mu_2 > \mu_1$ if $\overline{X}_2 > \overline{X}_1$.

The $t$-test can be used to test the statistical hypothesis $H_0: \mu_1 - \mu_2 = 0$. The $t$-test allows one to determine the probability of observing a difference in means as large or larger than that which was observed when indeed the null hypothesis is true. There are three assumptions underlying the $t$-test: normality, homogeneity of variance, and independence.

The $t$-test is robust to violating the assumption of normality. It is also robust to violating the assumption of homogeneity of variance when $n$'s are equal. If $n_1 > n_2$ and $\sigma_1^2 > \sigma_2^2$, the true $\alpha$ is *less* than the nominal *alpha* ("$\alpha$"). But if $n_2 > n_1$ and $\sigma_1^2 > \sigma_2^2$, the true $\alpha$ is *greater* than "$\alpha$." The independence assumption is important; violating this assumption can result in serious errors in the estimations of probabilities of type-I and type-II errors. Unfortunately there is no simple way of evaluating whether the independence assumption is met. One type of nonindependence can be handled by the $t$-test for paired observations.

If the observations are matched or paired in some manner, the $t$-test for dependent observations should be used. Any positive correlation between the pairs of observations reduces the value of $s_{\overline{X}_1 - \overline{X}_2}$. The pairing reduces the degrees of freedom ($\nu$): when the means are independent, the $\nu = n_1 + n_2 - 2$, but when the observations are in the form of $n$ pairs, $\nu = n - 1$. Care must be exercised in the interpretation of matched-pair studies since rarely are the groups truly equated on the matching variable.

When the dependent variable is expressed in a metric that is arbitrary or lacks clear and precise meaning, the use of the *effect size* can be useful for conveying the magnitude of the difference in means. The effect size is the mean difference expressed in standard deviation units.

## *MASTERY TEST*

1. Which of the options are statistical hypotheses associated with testing for a *difference* in means?
   a. $H_0: \mu = 100$ b. $H_0: \mu_1 - \mu_2 = 0$ c. $H_0: \overline{X}_1 - \overline{X}_2 = 0$
2. Are the two expressions $\mu_1 - \mu_2 = 0$ and $\mu_1 = \mu_2$ identical in meaning?
3. Can hypothesis b in Question 1 be appropriately termed a null hypothesis?
4. If the "pretest" mean weight of 100 adults in a weight-loss program was compared to the posttest mean for the same 100 persons, would the two means be independent?
5. Which of these is *not* assumed for purposes of performing the $t$-test of differences between means of independent samples?
   a. $X$'s normally distributed within both populations
   b. $\sigma_1^2 = \sigma_2^2$
   c. $n$ very large

6. When testing $H_0: \mu_1 = \mu_2$ and $n_1$ and $n_2$ are very small, the shape of the $t$-distribution is
   a. normal  c. bimodal
   b. rectangular  d. leptokurtic
7. If all assumptions are met, in which of these situations will the central $t$-distribution differ least from a normal distribution?
   a. $n_1 = 10, n_2 = 10$
   b. $n_1 = 50, n_2 = 20$
   c. $n_1 = 20, n_2 = 20$
8. Is the central $t$-distribution for any value of degrees of freedom symmetric around 0?
9. Which of these denotes an *estimate* of the standard error of the difference between two means?
   a. $s_{\overline{X}_1 - \overline{X}_2}$  c. $\sigma_{\overline{X}_1 - \overline{X}_2}$
   b. $s_{\overline{X}}$  d. $s^2_{\overline{X}_1 - \overline{X}_2}$
10. Does ${}_{.10}t_{60} = -{}_{.90}t_{60}$?
11. If $\nu = 60$, what is the critical value for $t$, with $\alpha_2 = .10$, $\alpha_2 = .05$, and $\alpha_2 = .01$? (Use Table C.)
12. The probability of a type-I error is least for which one of the following?
   a. $\alpha_2 = .10$
   b. $\alpha_2 = .05$
   c. $\alpha_2 = .001$
   d. $\alpha_1 = .01$
13. Other things being equal, the probability of a type-II error is least for which one of the following?
   a. $\alpha_2 = .10$
   b. $\alpha_2 = .05$
   c. $\alpha_2 = .001$
14. With $\alpha = .05$, will the critical $t$-values decrease as $n$ increases?
15. With $\nu = 60$, $\alpha_2 = .05$, and $s_{\overline{X}_1 - \overline{X}_2} = 2.0$, how large must $\overline{X}_1 - \overline{X}_2$ be before $H_0$ would be rejected?
16. If $s_1^2 = 50$ and $s_2^2 = 100$, when will the pooled variance estimate $s^2$ equal 75.0?
17. If $s_1^2 = 60$ and $s_2^2 = 40$, will the within groups variance estimate, $s_w^2$, equal 50 if $n_1 = n_2$?
18. Square the expression:

$$s\sqrt{\frac{1}{n_1} + \frac{1}{n_2}}$$

19. If the observed $t$-ratio with $n_1 = 11$ and $n_2 = 11$ is 2.0, which of these are correct if $\alpha_2 = .05$?
   a. pooled $\nu = 20 = \nu_1 + \nu_2$
   b. critical $t$-value at $\alpha_2$ of $.05 = 2.09$
   c. $p > .05$
   d. $.10 > p > .05$
   e. $p < .05$
   f. $p < .10$
20. Does an increase in sample size decrease the probability of a type-I error?
21. For a fixed value of $\alpha$, does an increase in sample size decrease the probability of a type-II error?

22. Which of these are correct?
    a. $E(s) < \sigma$
    b. $E(s^2) = \sigma^2$
    c. $E(s^2_{\overline{X}_1 - \overline{X}_2}) = \sigma^2_{\overline{X}_1 - \overline{X}_2}$
23. If $s = 8$ and $n = 10$, what is $\Sigma x^2$?
24. If $s^2_{\overline{X}_1 - \overline{X}_2} = 1.0$ and $n_1 = n_2 = 10$, what is $s^2$?
25. If $n_1 = n_2 = n$, show that $s_{\overline{X}_1 - \overline{X}_2} = \sqrt{2}\, s_{\overline{X}}$.
26. In Question 25 how much more variable is the sampling distribution of mean *differences* $(\overline{X}_1 - \overline{X}_2)$ than the sampling distribution of means? (Compare $s_{\overline{X}_1 - \overline{X}_2}$ with $s_{\overline{X}}$.)
27. Which one of these is *not* a mathematical assumption underlying the $t$-test for independent means?
    a. The $X$'s are normally distributed within each group.
    b. $\sigma_1^2 = \sigma_2^2$
    c. Each observation is independent of the other observations.
    d. $n_1 = n_2$
28. If the null hypothesis is true, is it possible to make a type-II error?
29. If the null hypothesis is true, what is the most probable or expected value of $t$?
    a. $E(t) = 0$
    b. $E(t) = 1$
30. Suppose population variances are heterogeneous: $\sigma_1^2 = 300$, $\sigma_2^2 = 100$. In which of the following situations will the heterogeneous variance affect the researcher's conclusion regarding the null hypothesis? That is, in which situation must the investigator be concerned about the assumption that $\sigma_1^2 = \sigma_2^2$? ($H_0: \mu_1 = \mu_2$)
    a. $n_1 = n_2$ and $H_0$ is rejected
    b. $n_1 = n_2$ and $H_0$ is tenable
    c. $n_1 = 50$, $n_2 = 20$, and $H_0$ is rejected
    d. $n_1 = 50$, $n_2 = 20$, and $H_0$ is tenable
    e. $n_1 = 20$, $n_2 = 50$, and $H_0$ is rejected
    f. $n_1 = 20$, $n_2 = 50$, and $H_0$ is tenable
31. The assumption of normality must be tested before interpreting the $t$-test in which of the situations below?
    a. $n_1 = 5$, $n_2 = 5$
    b. $n_1 = 10$, $n_2 = 50$
32. For testing $H_0: \mu_1 = \mu_2$, in which of these situations can the assumption of homogeneity of variance be safely ignored?
    a. $n_1 = n_2 = 10$
    b. $n_1 = 100$, $n_2 = 200$
    c. $n_1 = 5$, $n_2 = 15$
    d. $n_1 = 50$, $n_2 = 50$
33. Which of these statements have been demonstrated empirically for the $t$-test?
    a. It is robust with respect to the normality assumption.
    b. It is robust with respect to the homogeneity-of-variance assumption when $n$'s are equal.
    c. It is robust with respect to the independence assumption.
34. In Figure 12.2 with $n_1 = n_2 = 15$ both populations I and II were skewed. What was the correct probability of a type-I error (i.e., what was the actual $\alpha$) when "$\alpha$" = .05?
35. Using Figure 12.3, if $\sigma_1^2 = 10$, $\sigma_2^2 = 5$, $n_1 = 10$, and $n_2 = 50$, estimate the correct probability of a type-I error if "$\alpha$" = .05.

36. In which of these situations are the observations correlated?
  a. Strength is measured at ages ten and twelve for the same twenty-one children.
  b. At age five, the reading scores of fifty boys and fifty girls are compared.
  c. Pretest and posttest IQ scores are compared for the treated group.
  d. Forty students taking general psychology are randomly assigned to either treatment $A$ or $B$ and $H_0 : \mu_A = \mu_B$ is tested.
  e. Delayed posttest achievement scores were compared with immediate posttest scores for all participants.
  f. Grade-equivalent scores in reading were compared with those in math for 100 bilingual students.

37. Suppose a researcher failed to recognize that the observations were positively correlated in Example a of item 36, and the $t$-test for independent observations was used. How would the results differ with the results from the appropriate $t$-test for correlated observations? Answer true or false for the following.
  a. The value of $\overline{X}_1 - \overline{X}_2$ would differ.
  b. The researcher's value for $s_{\overline{X}_1 - \overline{X}_2}$ would be too large.
  c. The researcher's value for the $t$-ratio would be too small.

38. For $\alpha_2 = .05$, the researcher in Question 37 probably uses a critical $t$-value of ___, whereas the appropriate critical $t$ value is ___.

39. Even though the correct analysis has a larger critical $t$-value, will the correct analysis have more power for rejecting $H_0 : \mu_{10} = \mu_{12}$?

40. To answer which of the following questions does a one-tailed test appear justified. (More than one answer may be correct.)
  a. Does going to college result in a change in measured intelligence (IQ)?
  b. Do bright college students (high scores on college board exams) study more or less than not-so-bright college students?
  c. Do math majors score higher than English majors on the Quantitative Aptitude Test of the Graduate Record Examination?
  d. Does the reaction time at age seventy differ from reaction time at age forty?

41. Table 12.3 illustrates the direct-difference method of testing for differences between correlated means; hence, $r$ was not computed. Suppose you wish to know the value of $r$. Rearrange Equation 12.8 below so that only $r$ is to the left of the equals sign.

$$s^2_{\overline{X}_1 - \overline{X}_2} = s^2_{\overline{X}_1} + s^2_{\overline{X}_2} - 2rs_{\overline{X}_1} s_{\overline{X}_2}$$

Hence, $r = ?$

42. If on the WAIS ($\sigma = 15$) $\overline{X}_E = 109$ and $\overline{X}_C = 100$, express the mean difference as an effect size.

## *PROBLEMS AND EXERCISES*

1. An experiment was conducted on the effects of "advance organizers" (introductory material that mentally organizes the material to be learned) on achievement in abstract mathematics. Fifty college students were randomly assigned to two groups: twenty-five subjects in group 1 studied a 1,000-word essay on topology after having been exposed to an advance organizer on the subject; twenty-five subjects in group 2 read the same essay on topology after having read a 1,000-word historical sketch of Euler and Riemann, two famous mathematicians. At the end of the experimental period, each group was

given an objective test on the topological concepts. The dependent variable $X$ was "number of correct answers." The following results were obtained:

| *Group 1* *(Advance Organizer)* | *Group 2* *(Historical Sketch)* |
|---|---|
| $n_1 = 25$ | $n_2 = 25$ |
| $\bar{X}_1 = 7.65$ | $\bar{X}_2 = 6.00$ |
| $s_1^2 = 6.50$ | $s_2^2 = 5.90$ |

a. State $H_0$.
b. What is the value of $s_w^2$, the pooled within groups variance estimate?
c. Compute $s_{\bar{X}_1 - \bar{X}_2}$.
d. Compute $t$.
e. What is the critical $t$-value if $\alpha_2 = .05$?
f. Is $H_0$ rejected?
g. Conclusion:
h. Give the .90 CI for $\mu_1 - \mu_2$.
i. Express the mean difference as an effect size (use $s_w$ from part b for the standard deviation).

2. In a test of reading achievement in a statewide assessment program fourteen reading items were included that had been previously administered to a national sample of students. The state and national percentages of students who correctly answered each of the fourteen items are given. Use the direct-difference $t$-test for correlated observations to determine whether $H_0$: $\mu_S = \mu_N$ is tenable with $\alpha_2 = .05$.

*Percentage Correct*

| Item | State $X_S$ | Nation $X_N$ | $X_S - X_N = X_d$ |
|---|---|---|---|
| 1 | 83% | 83% | 0 |
| 2 | 81 | 76 | 5 |
| 3 | 75 | 76 | −1 |
| 4 | 76 | 82 | −6 |
| 5 | 40 | 35 | 5 |
| 6 | 76 | 74 | 2 |
| 7 | 78 | 68 | 10 |
| 8 | 27 | 27 | 0 |
| 9 | 60 | 66 | −6 |
| 10 | 67 | 67 | 0 |
| 11 | 66 | 64 | 2 |
| 12 | 67 | 62 | 5 |
| 13 | 92 | 91 | 1 |
| 14 | 73 | 63 | 10 |
| | $\Sigma X_S = 961$ | $\Sigma X_N = 934$ | $\Sigma X_d = 27$ |
| | $\bar{X}_S = 68.64\%$ | $\bar{X}_N = 66.71\%$ | $\bar{X}_d = 1.93\%$ |

a. $s_{X_d}^2 = ?$
b. $s_{\bar{X}_d}^2 = ?$
c. $t = ?$
d. Is $H_0$ rejected?

e. .95 CI for $\mu_d$ = ?
f. Is the statistical unit persons or items?
g. Which of these interpretations of the .95 confidence interval is correct in this example?
   i. If these fourteen items had been administered to *all students* in both populations, we have .95 confidence that the value of $\mu_d$ falls between −.86% and +4.72%.
   ii. If a huge number of reading *items* like these fourteen were administered to these same samples, we have .95 confidence that the state average $\mu_S$ would be not less than −.86% below the national average $\mu_N$ nor more than 4.72% above $\mu_N$.

3. Suppose we wish to know whether a certain method of diet control has long-term efficacy for reducing weight. Ten adults were weighed ("pretested") prior to receiving a prescribed treatment and then were reweighed ("posttested") one year later.

   The pretest weight was subtracted from the posttest weight to obtain a "change" score ($X_i = X_{\text{Pre}_i} - X_{\text{Post}_i}$) for each person. The mean and standard deviation of this distribution of change scores were: $\overline{X}_d = 3.11$ and $s_{X_d} = 5.62$.
   a. Is $H_0: \mu = 0$ tenable at $\alpha_2 = .10$?
   b. Give the .90 CI for $\mu$.

4. In a remedial reading study the 125 students who scored more than 2.0 grade equivalents below their current grade level participated in a remedial reading program. The pupils were retested after eight months in the program. The results are given.

| *Pretest* | *Posttest* |
|---|---|
| $\overline{X}_{\text{Pre}} = 4.5$ | $\overline{X}_{\text{Post}} = 5.9$ |
| $s_{\text{Pre}} = 1.8$ | $s_{\text{Post}} = 1.9$ |
| $s_{\overline{X}_{\text{Pre}}} = .16$ | $s_{\overline{X}_{\text{Post}}} = .17$ |

$r = .8$

   a. Is a one-tailed test justified? What is the critical $t$ for $\alpha_1 = .01$?
   b. Did the mean increase significantly?
   c. Could $H_0: \mu_{\text{Pre}} = \mu_{\text{Post}}$ be rejected with $\alpha_1 = .001$?
   d. Was the gain in means greater than .8 grade equivalents—that is, can $H_0: \mu_{\text{Post}} - \mu_{\text{Pre}} = .8$ be rejected at $\alpha_1 = .0005$?
   e. Do these results prove the remedial reading program was very effective?

5. The effect of an all-day ($E$) versus the conventional ($C$) half-day kindergarten on subsequent reading performance was evaluated by comparing mean scores of the forty-one $E$ students and the thirty-five $C$ students on a standardized reading test administered at the end of grade two (De Rosia, 1980). The results are given:

| | *E* | *C* |
|---|---|---|
| $\overline{X}_j$ | 64.53 | 63.56 |
| $s_j$ | 11.1 | 10.4 |
| $n_j$ | 41 | 35 |

   a. Perform a $t$-test to evaluate $H_0: \mu_E = \mu_C$ at $\alpha_2 = .10$.
   b. Set .90 CI for $\mu_E = \mu_C$.
   c. Estimate the effect size $\hat{\Delta}$.
   d. Does the study prove there was absolutely no differential efficacy?

6. The authors surveyed an introductory statistics course and asked students to rate (anonymously) how well they liked statistics. The results for the twelve males were: $\overline{X}_M = 5.25$ and $s_M^2 = 6.57$; for the thirty-one females: $\overline{X}_F = 4.37$ and $s_F^2 = 7.55$.
   a. Is there a statistically significant ($\alpha_2 = .10$) difference in means?
   b. Set a .90 CI about *each mean* (not about the difference in means).
   c. Express the difference in means as an effect size $\hat{\Delta}$, (use $s_w$ for denominator).
   d. If $s_M^2$, $s_F^2$, $\overline{X}_M$, and $\overline{X}_F$ remained constant but the sample was quadrupled, would $H_0$ have remained tenable? Compare this $t$ with that in part a.

7. In a study of the effects of special curricular study of Mexican culture on students' stereotypes of Mexican-Americans, two-thirds of the students were randomly assigned to the experimental ($E$) and one-third to the control ($C$) group (Schon, Hopkins, and Vojir, 1982). All students responded anonymously to a posttest attitude inventory.
   a. For the following posttest scores, test $H_0: \mu_E = \mu_C$ at $\alpha_2 = .10$.

| | $E$ | $C$ |
|---|---|---|
| $\overline{X}_j$ | 53.25 | 54.42 |
| $s_i^2$ | 129.0 | 70.0 |
| $n_j$ | 59 | 31 |

   b. Contrast the posttest mean of the Mexican-American ($M$) students with that of the Anglo($A$) students. Using $\alpha_2 = .05$, and give the .95 CI for $\mu_M - \mu_A$.

| | $M$ | $A$ |
|---|---|---|
| $\overline{X}_j$ | 59.19 | 51.22 |
| $s_j^2$ | 53.2 | 112.4 |
| $n_j$ | 27 | 63 |

   c. A change score was obtained for each student by subtracting the posttest score from a pretest score. Statistics for these change scores are given. (1) Did the $E$ group change significantly? (2) With $\alpha_2 = .05$, did the $E$ group change significantly more (or less) than the $C$ group? (Note that the change scores are independent.)

| | *Change Scores* | |
|---|---|---|
| | $E$ | $C$ |
| $\overline{X}_j$ | 1.73 | 1.93 |
| $s_j$ | 8.10 | 5.44 |
| $n_j$ | 59 | 31 |

8. Show that when $n_1 = n_2$, the standard error of the difference between two means $s_{\overline{X}_1 - \overline{X}_2}$ (Eq. 12.4), is equivalent to $\sqrt{s_{\overline{X}_1}^2 + s_{\overline{X}_2}^2}$

## *ANSWERS TO MASTERY TEST*

1. b
2. Yes
3. Yes
4. No
5. c
6. d
7. b($\nu = 68$)
8. Yes
9. a
10. Yes
11. 1.67, 2.00, 2.66
12. c
13. a
14. Yes
15. If $|\bar{X}_1 - \bar{X}_2| \geqslant 4.0$, $|t| \geqslant 2.00$, and $H_0$ is rejected
16. When $n_1 = n_2$
17. Yes
18. $s^2\left(\frac{1}{n_1} + \frac{1}{n_2}\right)$
19. a, b, c, d, f
20. No
21. Yes
22. All are correct (see Sec. 5.13).
23. Since $s^2 = (8)^2 = 64$, $\Sigma x^2 = 9(64) = 576$.
24. $s^2_{\bar{X}_1-\bar{X}_2} = s^2\left(\frac{1}{n_1} + \frac{1}{n_2}\right)$;
$$s^2 = \frac{s^2_{\bar{X}_1-\bar{X}_2}}{\frac{1}{n_1} + \frac{1}{n_2}} = \frac{1.0}{\frac{1}{10} + \frac{1}{10}} = \frac{1.0}{.2}$$
$$= 5.0$$
25. $$s_{\bar{X}_1-\bar{X}_2} = s\sqrt{\frac{1}{n} + \frac{1}{n}} = s\sqrt{\frac{2}{n}} = s\frac{\sqrt{2}}{\sqrt{n}}$$
$$= \frac{\sqrt{2}\,s}{\sqrt{n}} = \sqrt{2}\,s_{\bar{X}}$$
26. Since $s_{\bar{X}_1-\bar{X}_2} = 1.414 s_{\bar{X}}$, $s_{\bar{X}_1-\bar{X}_1}$ is 41% larger than $s_{\bar{X}}$.
27. d
28. No
29. a
30. d and e
31. Neither a nor b
32. a and d
33. a and b
34. Actual $\alpha = .04$.
35. Actual $\alpha = .12$.
36. a, c, e, f
37. a. false
    b. true
    c. true
38. ${}_{.975}t_{40} = 2.02$, whereas ${}_{.975}t_{20} = 2.09$.
39. Yes, some positive correlation between the measurements at ages ten and twelve will reduce the value of $s_{\bar{X}_{10}-\bar{X}_{12}}$ and hence will yield a larger $t$-ratio for the same difference in means.
40. a, c, d
41. Add: $2rs_{\bar{X}_1}s_{\bar{X}_2}$ to both sides:
$s^2_{\bar{X}_1-\bar{X}_2} + 2rs_{\bar{X}_1}s_{\bar{X}_2} = s^2_{\bar{X}_1} + s^2_{\bar{X}_2}$.
Subtract $s^2_{\bar{X}_1-\bar{X}_2}$ from both sides:
$2rs_{\bar{X}_1}s_{\bar{X}_2} = s^2_{\bar{X}_1} + s^2_{\bar{X}_2} - s^2_{\bar{X}_1-\bar{X}_2}$.
Divide by $2s_{\bar{X}_1}s_{\bar{X}_2}$:
$$r = \frac{s^2_{\bar{X}_1} + s^2_{\bar{X}_2} - s^2_{\bar{X}_1-\bar{X}_2}}{2s_{\bar{X}_1}s_{\bar{X}_2}}.$$
42. $\hat{\Delta} = \frac{(\bar{X}_E - \bar{X}_C)}{\sigma} = \frac{9}{15} = .6$ or $.6\sigma$.

## *ANSWERS TO PROBLEMS AND EXERCISES*

1. a. $H_0: \mu_1 - \mu_2 = 0$
   b. $s^2_w = 6.20$;
   c. $s_{\bar{X}_1-\bar{X}_2} = 2.49\sqrt{\frac{1}{25} + \frac{1}{25}}$
   $= 2.49(.283)$
   $= .704$
   d. $t = \frac{7.65 - 6.00}{.704} = 2.34$
   e. $\nu = n_1 + n_2 - 2 = 48$: ${}_{.975}t_{40} = 2.02$. (The precise critical $t$-value would fall between ${}_{.975}t_{40} = 2.02$ and ${}_{.975}t_{50} = 2.01$: we use the closest, but smaller, $\nu$ value.
   f. yes
   g. $\mu_1 > \mu_2$; the advance organizer

appears to have facilitated achievement.

h. $.90 \text{ CI} = 1.65 \pm 1.68(.704)$
$= 1.65 \pm 1.18$
or $(.47, 2.83)$

i. $\hat{\Delta} = 1.65/2.49 = .66$

2\. a. $s^2_{X_d} = \dfrac{\Sigma x_d^2}{n-1}$;
$\Sigma x_d^2 = \Sigma X_d^2 - n\overline{X}_d^2$
$= 357 - 14(1.93)^2$
$= 304.9$
$s^2_{X_d} = \dfrac{\Sigma x_d^2}{n-1} = \dfrac{304.9}{13} = 23.5$

b. $s^2_{\overline{X}_d} = \dfrac{s^2_{X_d}}{n} = \dfrac{23.5}{14} = 1.68$,
$s_{\overline{X}_d} = 1.29$

c. $t = \dfrac{\overline{X}_d}{s_{\overline{X}_d}} = \dfrac{1.93}{1.29} = 1.50$

d. no: $t = 1.50 < 2.16 = {}_{.975}t_{13}$

e. $.95 \text{ CI} = \overline{X}_d \pm ({}_{.975}t_{13})(s_{\overline{X}_d}) =$
$1.93 \pm (2.16)(1.29) =$
$1.93 \pm 2.79$ or $-.86\%$ to $4.72\%$

f. items

g. ii

3\. a. $s_{\overline{X}} = 5.62/\sqrt{10} = 1.78$;
$t = 3.11/1.78 = 1.75$;
$H_0$ is tenable.

b. $3.11 \pm 1.83(1.78)$
$3.11 \pm 3.26$
$(-.15, 6.37)$

4\. a. yes: ${}_{.99}t_{124} \doteq 2.36$

b. yes,

$$t = \frac{5.9 - 4.5}{\sqrt{(.16)^2 + (.17)^2 - 2(.8)(.16)(.17)}}$$
$$= \frac{1.4}{.105} = 13.3, \quad p < .0005$$

c. yes

d. $$t = \frac{(\overline{X}_{\text{Post}} - \overline{X}_{\text{Pre}}) - (\mu_{\text{Post}} - \mu_{\text{Pre}})}{s_{\overline{X}_{\text{Post}} - \overline{X}_{\text{Pre}}}}$$
$$= \frac{(1.4) - (.8)}{.105} = \frac{.6}{.105} = 5.71$$

Yes: $H_0$ rejected at .0005 level; the increase in scores is significantly greater than .8 grade equivalent.

e. No, the posttest scores are influenced by the regression effect. The fact that $H_0$ can be confidently rejected only indicates that something more than *chance* is influencing the scores. In other words, a significance test never *explicates* the *cause* for the difference, but only indicates that the difference is greater than can be reasonably attributed to chance (sampling error). It is the design of the study that allows the researcher to specify causes. (This same example was used in Chapter 8's Problems and Exercise 3 in which the significant increase in posttest scores was attributable to regression.)

5\. a. $s_w^2 = 116.3, s_w = 10.78$
$s_{\overline{X}_E - \overline{X}_C} = 10.78\sqrt{(\frac{1}{41} + \frac{1}{35})}$
$= 2.48$
$t = .97/2.48 = .39$, $H_0$ is tenable.

b. $.90 \text{ CI} = .97 \pm (1.67)(2.48)$
$= (-3.17, 5.11)$

c. $\hat{\Delta} = .09$

d. no, failure to reject $H_0$ does not prove $H_0$ to be true.

6\. a. $t = .96$ (or $-.96$), $H_0$ is tenable.

b. .90 CI for $\mu_M$:
$5.25 \pm (1.80)(.740)$
$= (3.92, 6.58)$
.90 CI for $\mu_F$:
$4.37 \pm (1.70)(.494)$
$= (3.53, 5.21)$

c. $.88/2.70 = .33$

d. $t = 1.93$, ${}_{.90}t_{174} = 1.65$; reject $H_0$ at .10; $t$ is doubled

7\. a. $s_w = 10.44$, $s_{\overline{X}_E - \overline{X}_C} =$
$10.44\sqrt{\frac{1}{59} + \frac{1}{31}} = 2.31$; $t = -.51$,
$H_0$ is tenable.

b. $s_w = 9.74$, $s_{\overline{X}_M - \overline{X}_A} = 2.24$;
$t = 3.56$, reject $H_0$ at .001;
.95 CI: (3.52, 12.42)

c. No, $t = 1.73/1.05 = 1.64$,
$p > .05$; no, $t = -.12$

8\. When $n_1 = n_2 = n$,

$$s_{\overline{X}_1 - \overline{X}_2} = \sqrt{\frac{\Sigma x_1^2 + \Sigma x_2^2}{2(n-1)}\left(\frac{2}{n}\right)}$$
$$= \sqrt{\left(\frac{\Sigma x_1^2}{n-1} + \frac{\Sigma x_2^2}{n-1}\right)\left(\frac{1}{n}\right)}$$
$$= \sqrt{s_1^2/n + s_2^2/n}$$
$$= \sqrt{s^2_{\overline{X}_1} + s^2_{\overline{X}_2}}$$

# 13

# INFERENCE REGARDING VARIANCES

## 13.1 INTRODUCTION

In empirical research the hypotheses of greatest interest usually pertain to means, proportions, or correlation coefficients. At times, however, there is interest in questions of variance such as the following:

> Are the individual differences in achievement among boys greater than among girls?
>
> Does participation in discussion groups lead to group consensus or does it tend to polarize attitudes?

At other times tests of hypotheses pertaining to variances are performed to legitimize other analyses that rest on assumptions about variances. Recall in the independent groups *t*-test that $\sigma_1^2 = \sigma_2^2$ is assumed.

In testing statistical hypotheses of the type $H_0: \sigma^2 = K$, a family of sampling distributions that has not been used previously will be employed, namely the chi-square, $\chi^2$, distributions. We will digress from the immediate question of testing $H_0: \sigma^2 = K$ to give some introduction to, and rationale for, the chi-square distribution.

## 13.2 CHI-SQUARE DISTRIBUTIONS*

Imagine a population of scores that are normally distributed with mean 0 and standard deviation 1, that is, normally distributed $z$-scores. Denote the

$$\chi_1^2 = z^2 \tag{13.1}$$

that is, the square of a standardized score selected from a normal distribution is symbolized by $\chi_1^2$, where the exponent 2 indicates that squaring has taken place and the subscript 1 indicates that only one score has been used to produce $\chi^2$. Because of the squaring, $\chi^2$ can never be negative. We can conceive of repeating the process an unlimited number of times by which a value of $\chi_1^2$ was found. Each time a new $z$-score is randomly selected, it is squared and included in a frequency distribution of the values of $\chi_1^2$ so obtained. If this frequency distribution is based on many thousand $\chi_1^2$-values and if the scale of the ordinate is adjusted so that the area under the resulting curve is 1, the graph of the *chi-square distribution with one degree of freedom* would be obtained. A graph of this distribution appears in Figure 13.1.†

The area under the curve for $\chi^2$ is set equal to one unit so that $\chi^2$ is a probability distribution, for example the probability of obtaining a value of $\chi_1^2$ above 5 equals the area under the curve above 5. In Figure 13.1, .32 or 32% of the area under the curve lies to the right of $\chi^2 = 1$. Thus, the probability of obtaining a value of $z^2 = \chi_1^2$ that exceeds 1 is .32. In other words, 32% of the $z$ scores randomly selected from a normal distribution

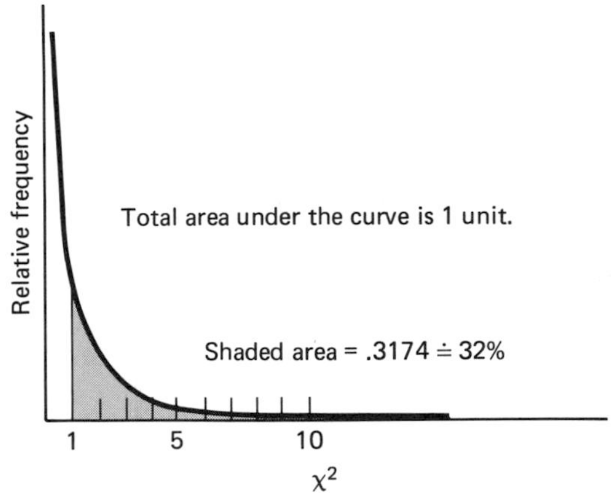


**FIGURE 13.1**
**Graph of the chi-square distribution with one degree of freedom. (The shaded area comprises 32% of the area under the curve.)**

*Section 13.2 provides the rationale for the chi-square distribution; understanding the theory of the $\chi^2$ distribution is not essential to applying the procedures for testing hypotheses pertaining to variances.

†The mathematical curve for the chi-square distribution was derived by Karl Pearson in 1900. The mathematical curve that is graphed in Figure 13.1 and that describes the distribution of $\chi_1^2$ has a complex formula given in Graybill (1961, p. 31).

will have squares that exceed 1. An equivalent statement of this fact is that the 68th percentile in the chi-square distribution with one degree of freedom equals 1.00, which can be written

$$_{.68}\chi_1^2 = 1.00$$

where $\chi_1^2$ denotes the chi-square distribution with one degree of freedom and .68 indicates the 68th percentile of that distribution. Notice that if $|z| < 1$, then $z^2 < 1$; thus in a unit-distribution 68% of the $z^2$-scores will be less than 1. Likewise 68% of the $\chi^2$ values will be less than 1. What is the value of $_{.95}\chi_1^2$? Since $\chi_1^2 = z^2$, if $|z| = 1.96$, $_{.95}\chi_1^2 = (1.96)^2 = 3.84$. Thus, the 95th percentile of $\chi_1^2$ is 3.84.

## $\chi_2^2$ AND $\chi_3^2$

Instead of drawing out just one $z$-score, draw two scores at random and independently from the original normal distribution of $z$-scores. Call the first score $z_1$ and the second $z_2$. Now square and sum the two $z$'s to form the quantity,

$$\chi_2^2 = z_1^2 + z_2^2 \tag{13.2}$$

This process of determining a $\chi_2^2$ could be repeated thousands of times with new pairs of $z$-scores. A frequency distribution of these $\chi_2^2$ scores could be constructed so that the area under the curve was one unit. The resulting curve would look like the graph of the mathematical curve $\chi_2^2$, the chi-square distribution with two degrees of freedom. Similarly $\chi_3^2 = z_1^2 + z_2^2 + z_3^2 = \Sigma_{i=1}^{\nu=3} z_i^2$. Figure 13.2 shows graphs of $\chi_2^2$ and $\chi_3^2$.

**FIGURE 13.2**
**Graphs of $\chi_2^2$ and $\chi_3^2$, the chi-square distributions, with two degrees and three degrees of freedom.**

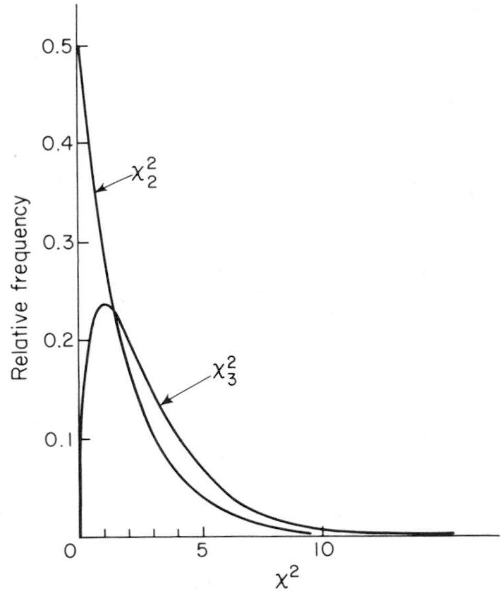

## 13.3 THE CHI-SQUARE DISTRIBUTION WITH $\nu$ DEGREES OF FREEDOM, $\chi^2_\nu$

A chi-square variable with $\nu$ degrees of freedom, $\chi^2_\nu$, is formed by adding together the squares of $\nu$ independent $z$-scores from a normal distribution:

$$\chi^2_\nu = z_1^2 + z_2^2 + \ldots + z_\nu^2 = \sum_{i=1}^{\nu} z_i^2 \tag{13.3}$$

If a large number of these $\chi^2$-values are generated from separate sets of $\nu$ $z$-scores, their frequency distribution will have the same shape as the mathematical curve $\chi^2_\nu$. Figure 13.3 illustrates the graphs of $\chi^2_\nu$ with $\nu = 1, 2, 4, 6,$ and $10$.

The area under each curve in Figure 13.3 is one unit. One-half the area under $\chi^2_{10}$ lies above the point 9.34, i.e., ${}_{.50}\chi^2_{10} = 9.34$. Hence, the probability is .50 that the sum of the squares of ten $z$-scores drawn at random from a normal distribution will exceed 9.34.

There is a different chi-square distribution for each integer value of $\nu$ (1, 2, 3, . . .).

**FIGURE 13.3. Distribution of chi-square for various degrees of freedom.**

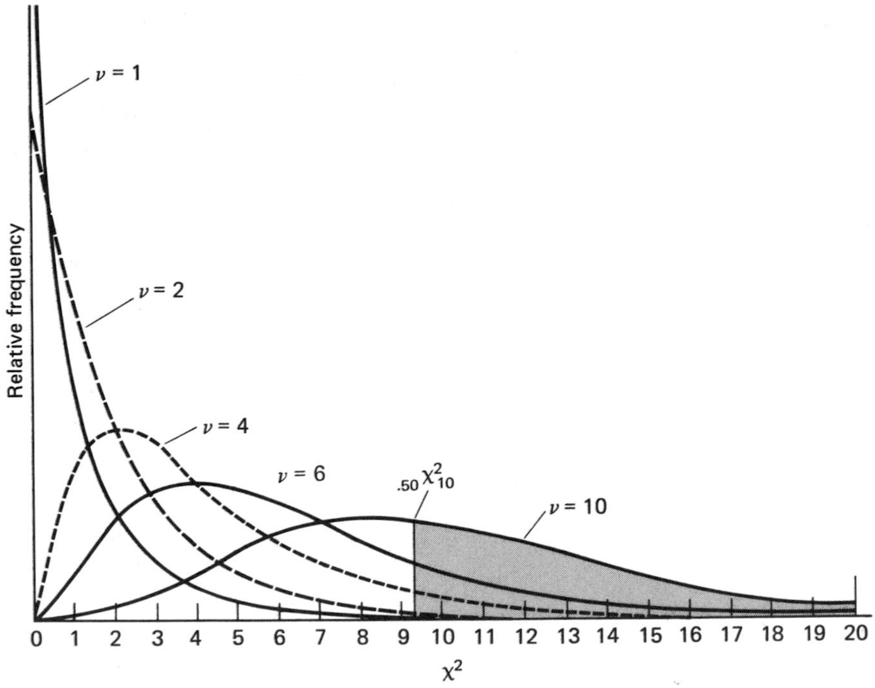


Distribution of chi-square for various degrees of freedom.

The properties of the curve $\chi^2_\nu$ depend upon the value of $\nu$. The following facts provide a partial description of the family of chi-square distributions:

1. The mean of a chi-square distribution with $\nu$ degrees of freedom is equal to $\nu$. For example, the average value of $\chi^2_{12}$ one would *expect* to obtain by squaring and summing twelve independent $z$-scores is 12.
2. The mode of $\chi^2_\nu$ is at the point $\nu - 2$ for $\nu \geqslant 2$.
3. The median is approximately $(3\nu - 2)/3$ (see Eq. 4.11) for $\nu \geqslant 2$.
4. The varance of $\chi^2_\nu$ is $2\nu$.
5. The skewness $\varsigma\kappa$ of $\chi^2_\nu$ is $\sqrt{2/\nu}$. Hence, every chi-square distribution is positively skewed, but the asymmetry decreases as $\nu$ increases. (But note in Table D that $\varsigma\kappa$ is still evident (.2) even with $\nu = 50$.
6. As $\nu$ becomes very large $\chi^2_\nu$ approaches more nearly a normal distribution with mean $\nu$ and standard deviation $\sqrt{2\nu}$.

The 100 $p$th percentile in the chi-square distribution with $\nu$ degrees of freedom is denoted by ${}_p\chi^2_\nu$. The percentiles of the chi-square distribution play a prominent role in inferential statistical techniques, particularly as applied to nominal data. Various percentiles in chi-square distributions for $\nu = 1$ up to $\nu = 100$ appear in Table D of the Appendix. The following is an example of how Table D is read: suppose one wishes to find the 95th percentile in the chi-square distribution with four degrees of freedom, that is ${}_{.95}\chi^2_4$. First, the *row* labeled 4 in Table D is located. Second, the *column* headed .95 is found. At the intersection of the appropriate row and column, the number 9.49 is read. This is the value of ${}_{.95}\chi^2_4$, the 95th percentile of the chi-square distribution with four degrees of freedom. Locate this point in the $\chi^2_4$ distribution in Figure 13.3; notice that only a small portion of the area of the curve exceeds 9.49.

## 13.4 INFERENCES ABOUT THE POPULATION VARIANCE: $H_0: \sigma^2 = K$

1. The **hypothesis** to be tested is that a population has a variance $\sigma^2$ equal to some number $K$ versus the hypothesis that $\sigma^2$ is different from $K$:

$$H_0:\ \sigma^2 = K$$

$$H_1:\ \sigma^2 \neq K$$

2. It must be **assumed** that the variable $X$ has a *normal* distribution in the population and that a *random* sample of $n$ observations has been selected from which $\sigma^2$ will be estimated by $s^2$ with $\nu = n - 1$ degrees of freedom.
3. The **test statistic** for testing $H_0$ against $H_1$ is the chi-square ($\chi^2_\nu$) statistic:

$$\chi^2 = \frac{\nu s^2}{\sigma^2}, \text{ where } \nu = n - 1 \qquad (13.4)$$

4. When $H_0$ is true, the **sampling distribution** of $\chi^2$ in Equation 13.4 is the chi-square distribution with $\nu = n - 1$, that is $\chi^2_\nu$; when $H_1$ is true and $\sigma^2$ is actually equal to some number $L$ (different from zero), the sampling distribution of $\nu s^2/\sigma^2$ will equal $L/\sigma^2$ times $\chi^2_\nu$. For example, the graphs of $\nu s^2/10$ are drawn in Figure 13.4 for the cases in which $\sigma^2 = 10$ and $n = 9$, that is, $H_0$ is true; and for $\sigma^2 = 20$.
   If, $\nu = 8$ and a $s^2$ of 21.40 was obtained, the value of the test statistic in Equation 13.4 would be:

$$\chi^2 = \frac{\nu s^2}{10} = \frac{8(21.40)}{10} = 17.12$$

   In Figure 13.4 a value of the test statistics as large as 17.12 or larger is relatively improbable when $\sigma^2 = 10$ but is quite reasonable when $H_1 : \sigma^2 = 20$ is true.
5. The **critical values** for testing $H_0$ against $H_1$ at the $\alpha$-level of significance are the $\alpha/2$ and $1 - (\alpha/2)$ percentile points in the chi-square distribution with $\nu = n - 1$, that is, ${}_{\alpha/2}\chi^2_\nu$ and ${}_{1-(\alpha/2)}\chi^2_\nu$.
6. The $1 - \alpha$ **confidence interval** on the unknown value of $\sigma^2$ is constructed as follows:

$$\frac{\nu s^2}{{}_{1-(\alpha/2)}\chi^2_\nu} < \sigma^2 < \frac{\nu s^2}{{}_{\alpha/2}\chi^2_\nu} \qquad \textbf{(13.5)}$$

7. *An example.* The standard deviation of the WISC Verbal IQ scores for a sample of thirty congenitally blind pupils ages nine to fifteen was found to be 16.0, whereas for the population, $\sigma = 15$ (Hopkins and McGuire, 1966). The data will be used to test the following hypotheses at the $\alpha_2 = .10$ level of significance:

$$H_0: \sigma^2 = (15)^2 = 225$$
$$H_1: \sigma^2 \neq 225$$

   For the sample of thirty IQ scores, $s^2 = 256$ and $\nu = 29$.
   From Equation 13.4.

$$\chi^2 = \frac{29(256)}{225} = 33.00$$

**FIGURE 13.4. Sampling distributions of $\nu s^2/\sigma^2$ when $H_0$: $\sigma^2 = 10$ is true and when $H_1$: $\sigma^2 = 20$ is true ($\nu = 8$).**

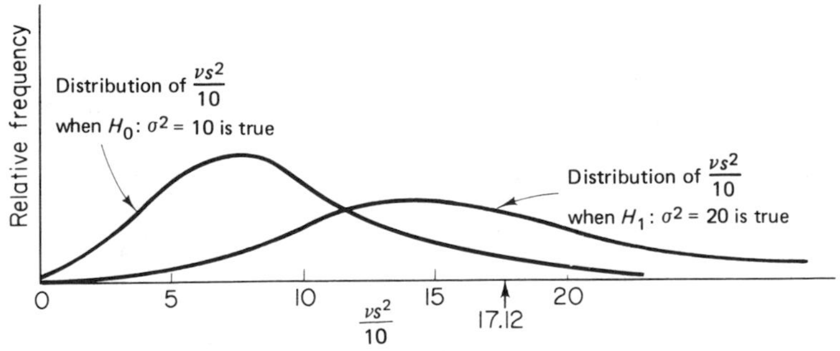

is compared with the critical values obtained from Table D,

$$_{.05}\chi^2_{29} = 17.71 \qquad _{.95}\chi^2_{29} = 42.56$$

and is seen not to be significant at the .10 level. (The probability $p$ of a value of $\chi^2$ equal to 42.56 or more given that $H_0$ is true is .05).

The .90 CI on $\sigma^2$ is found by substituting the sample data into Equation 13.5:

$$\frac{29(256)}{42.56} < \sigma^2 < \frac{29(256)}{17.71}, \text{ or } 174 < \sigma^2 < 419$$

The conclusion that the population which was sampled does not have a different variance from the general population continues to be tenable. The variance of the blind population is not very precisely estimated because of the small sample ($n = 30$); $\sigma$ is probably somewhere between $\sqrt{174} = 13.2$ and $\sqrt{419} = 20.5$.

8. Unlike hypothesis tests about means using Student's $t$-distribution, the assumption of sampling from a normal population cannot be taken lightly when testing hypotheses about population variances (see Scheffé, 1959, Chapter 10). If the population is nonnormal—particularly with respect to kurtosis—the hypothesis test previously outlined may be quite in error. Testing for normality is treated in Sec. 14.7.

Before going on to procedures for testing if two variance estimates differ significantly, a brief orientation to the $F$-distribution, which is used in testing $H_0: \sigma_1^2 = \sigma_2^2$, is necessary.

## 13.5 F-DISTRIBUTIONS*

Imagine that a chi-square value with ten degrees of freedom $\chi^2_{10}$ is formed from $z_1^2 + \ldots + z_{10}^2$. Now suppose a second, *independent* chi-square variable with five degrees of freedom $\chi^2_5$ is formed by sampling values from a unit-normal distribution, squaring, and summing the five squared terms. A ratio called an *F-ratio* with ten and five degrees of freedom is formed as follows:

$$F_{\nu_1, \nu_2} = \frac{\chi^2_{\nu_1}/\nu_1}{\chi^2_{\nu_2}/\nu_2} = F_{10,5} = \frac{\chi^2_{10}/10}{\chi^2_5/5} \qquad \textbf{(13.6)}$$

$F$-distributions with $\nu_1$ degrees of freedom for the numerator and $\nu_2$ degrees of freedom for the denominator have the following properties:

1. They are unimodal. Mode is $(\nu_2/\nu_1)(\nu_1 - 2)/(\nu_2 + 2)$ for $\nu_1 > 1$.

*An understanding of the theory in Section 13.5, like Section 13.2 is not essential to make tests of $H_0: \sigma_1^2 = \sigma_2^2$.

TABLE 13.1 **Descriptive Characteristics of Various $F$-distributions: $F_{\nu_1, \nu_2}$**

| | | $\nu_1 = 1$ | | | $\nu_1 = 3$ | | | | $\nu_1 = 10$ | | | |
|---|---|---|---|---|---|---|---|---|---|---|---|---|
| $\nu_2$ | $\mu$ | $_{.50}F$ | $\varsigma\kappa$ | $\sigma$ | Mode | $_{.50}F$ | $\varsigma\kappa$ | $\sigma$ | Mode | $_{.50}F$ | $\varsigma\kappa$ | $\sigma$ |
| 5 | 1.67 | .53 | .35 | 4.71 | .24 | .91 | .43 | 3.33 | .57 | 1.01 | .41 | 2.69 |
| 10 | 1.25 | .49 | .58 | 2.17 | .28 | .85 | .70 | 1.38 | .67 | 1.00 | .60 | .97 |
| 25 | 1.09 | .47 | .66 | 1.64 | .31 | .81 | .78 | .99 | .74 | .96 | .57 | .61 |
| 50 | 1.04 | .46 | .68 | 1.52 | .32 | .80 | .80 | .90 | .77 | .95 | .52 | .52 |
| 100 | 1.02 | .46 | .70 | 1.42 | .33 | .79 | .80 | .86 | .78 | .94 | .50 | .48 |
| $\infty$ | 1.00 | .46 | .71 | 1.41 | .33 | .79 | .80 | .82 | .80 | .93 | .44 | .45 |

2. They are positively skewed.
3. They have a median of 1 when $\nu_1 = \nu_2$. If $\nu_2 > \nu_1$, $_{.50}F_{\nu_1,\nu_2}$ is less than 1.
4. They have a mean equal to $\nu_2/(\nu_2 - 2)$ for $\nu_2 > 2$. Thus $\lim_{\nu_2 \to \infty} (\mu) = 1$.
5. They have variance equal to $[2\nu_2{}^2(\nu_1 + \nu_2 - 2)]/[\nu_1(\nu_2 - 4)(\nu_2 - 2)^2]$.

Descriptive data on selected $F$-distributions are given in Table 13.1. Observe the following:

1. As $\nu_2$ increases, $\mu$ approaches its limit of 1; $\mu$ is unaffected by $\nu_1$.
2. As $\nu_2$ increases the mode increases but the median decreases.
3. The variance decreases as $\nu_2$ increases.
4. The distribution remains substantially skewed unless both $\nu_1$ and $\nu_2$ are very large.

## 13.6 INFERENCES ABOUT TWO INDEPENDENT VARIANCES: $H_0: \sigma_1^2 = \sigma_2^2$

1. Testing if two variances are equal occurs more frequently than testing if a population has a variance equal to some hypothesized value. Suppose one wishes to test the **hypothesis** that the variance of populations 1 and 2, $\sigma_1^2$ and $\sigma_2^2$ are equal:

$$H_0: \sigma_1^2 = \sigma_2^2$$
$$H_1: \sigma_1^2 \neq \sigma_2^2$$

2. It is **assumed** that a sample size of $n_1$ is drawn at *random* from a *normal* population with mean $\mu_1$ and variance $\sigma_1^2$: an *independent random* sample size of $n_2$ is drawn from a second normal population with mean $\mu_2$ and variance $\sigma_2^2$. The values of $\mu_1$ and $\mu_2$ are irrelevant in testing $H_0$.

**TABLE 13.1** (con't.)

| $\nu_1 = 25$ | | | | $\nu_1 = 100$ | | | | $\nu_1 = 500$ | | | |
|---|---|---|---|---|---|---|---|---|---|---|---|
| Mode | $_{.50}F$ | $\varsigma\kappa$ | $\sigma$ | Mode | $_{.50}F$ | $\varsigma\kappa$ | $\sigma$ | Mode | $_{.50}F$ | $\varsigma\kappa$ | $\sigma$ |
| .66 | 1.12 | .41 | 2.49 | .70 | 1.14 | .41 | 2.39 | .71 | 1.15 | .41 | 2.36 |
| .76 | 1.04 | .59 | .83 | .82 | 1.06 | .58 | .75 | .83 | 1.07 | .57 | .73 |
| .85 | 1.00 | .52 | .46 | .91 | 1.02 | .49 | .37 | .92 | 1.03 | .49 | .34 |
| .88 | .99 | .53 | .37 | .94 | 1.01 | .39 | .26 | .96 | 1.02 | .36 | .23 |
| .90 | .98 | .36 | .33 | .96 | 1.00 | .29 | .21 | .98 | 1.01 | .25 | .16 |
| .92 | .97 | .29 | .28 | .98 | .99 | .14 | .14 | 1.00 | 1.00 | .07 | .06 |

3. The **test statistic** for testing $H_0$ against $H_1$ is the ratio of the two sample variances:

$$F = \frac{s_1^2}{s_2^2} \tag{13.7}$$

4. When $H_0$: $\sigma_1^2 = \sigma_2^2$ is true, the **sampling distribution** of $F = s_1^2/s_2^2$ is the $F$-distribution with $\nu_1 = n_1 - 1$ and $\nu_2 = n_2 - 1$. When $H_1$: $\sigma_1^2 \neq \sigma_2^2$ is true, the distribution of $s_1^2/s_2^2$ is equal to $\sigma_1^2/\sigma_2^2$ times the $F$-distribution with $\nu_1$ and $\nu_2$ degrees of freedom. Thus if in reality $\sigma_1^2/\sigma_2^2 = 2$, the distribution of $s_1^2/s_2^2$ will look like the $F$-distribution transformed by a multiplicative factor of 2; its mean and standard deviation would be doubled (Secs. 4.8 and 5.11).
5. The **critical values** against which $F$ in Equation 13.7 is compared in testing $H_0$ against $H_1$ at the $\alpha_2$-level of significance are

$$_{\alpha/2}F_{\nu_1,\nu_2} \qquad \text{and} \qquad _{1-(\alpha/2)}F_{\nu_1,\nu_2}$$

that is, the $100(\alpha/2)$ and $100[1 - (\alpha/2)]$ percentile points in the $F$-distribution with $\nu_1$ and $\nu_2$. The upper percentile points in the $F$-distributions can be read directly from Table F. The lower percentile points are related as follows to the upper percentiles.*

$$_{\alpha/2}F_{\nu_1,\nu_2} = \frac{1}{_{1-(\alpha/2)}F_{\nu_2,\nu_1}} \tag{13.8}$$

6. The $1 - \alpha$ **confidence interval** on the *ratio* of $\sigma_1^2$ to $\sigma_2^2$ is constructed as follows:

$$(1 - \alpha)\ \text{CI} = {}_{\alpha/2}F_{\nu_2,\nu_1}\frac{s_1^2}{s_2^2} < \frac{\sigma_1^2}{\sigma_2^2} < {}_{1-(\alpha/2)}F_{\nu_2,\nu_1}\frac{s_1^2}{s_2^2} \tag{13.9}$$

*Notice that $\nu_1$ and $\nu_2$ switch positions, for example,

$$_{.05}F_{10,5} = \frac{1}{_{.95}F_{5,10}} = \frac{1}{3.33} = 0.30$$

The critical $F$-ratios in Table F are correct as they stand for a directional test (Sec. 11.13) of $H_0$: $\sigma_1^2 = \sigma_2^2$, in which the designation of group 1 is made prior to data collection. Thus $s_1^2$ will be placed in the numerator of Equation 13.7 even when it is smaller in value than $s_2^2$. Note, for example, if $\alpha_1 = .05$, $\nu_1 = 20$ and $\nu_2 = 40$, the critical $F$-ratio is ${}_{.95}F_{20,40} = 1.84$. Thus if $s_1^2 = 200$ and $s_2^2 = 100$, then $F = 2.00$ and $H_0$: $\sigma_1^2 = \sigma_2^2$ would be rejected at $\alpha_1 = .05$. But what if $s_1^2 = 100$ and $s_2^2 = 200$? In that case $F = .50$ and $H_0$ would have been judged tenable.

For nondirectional tests (e.g., $H_0$: $\sigma_1^2 = \sigma_2^2$ against $H_1$: $\sigma_1^2 \neq \sigma_2^2$) the use of Equation 13.7 to obtain the lesser critical $F$-ratio can be circumvented by defining the larger *observed* $s^2$ as $s_1^2$, thus the observed $F$-ratio will never take a value less than 1. But the $\alpha$-value in Table F must then be halved when a directional test has not been employed. Thus if $\alpha_2 = .05$, the critical $F$-ratio is *not* ${}_{.95}F_{20,40} = 1.84$, but ${}_{.975}F_{20,40} = 2.07$.

7. **Example.** Are men more variable in height than women? One study of the standing heights of United States adult males and females found estimates of their standard deviations to be 6.69 cm and 5.47 cm, respectively. Suppose the larger $s^2$ is placed in the numerator of Equation 13.7, but a nondirectional test of $H_0$: $\sigma_M^2 = \sigma_F^2$ with $\alpha_2 = .05$ is made. Each variance estimate was based on a sample of 200 observations.

The value of the test statistic in Equation 13.7 is

$$F = \frac{(6.69)^2}{(5.47)^2} = 1.496 \text{ or } 1.50$$

The critical-$F$ is ${}_{.975}F_{199,199} \doteq {}_{.975}F_{200,200} = 1.32$; since the observed $F$-ratio (1.50) exceeds the critical $F$-ratio (1.32), the null hypothesis can be rejected at $\alpha_2 = .05$. (Indeed, $H_0$ can be rejected at $\alpha_2 = .02$ since $1.50 > 1.39 = {}_{.99}F_{200,200}$.) The .95 $CI$ on $\sigma_M^2/\sigma_F^2$ can be constructed using Equation 13.9. Equation 13.8 is used to determine ${}_{.025}F_{199,199}$.

Hence, ${}_{.025}F_{199,199} \doteq 1/{}_{.975}F_{200,200} = 1/1.32 = .76$.

$$.95CI\text{: } (.76)(1.50) < \frac{\sigma_M^2}{\sigma_F^2} < (1.32)(1.50)\text{, i.e., } 1.14 < \frac{\sigma_M^2}{\sigma_F^2} < 1.98 \text{ or } (1.14, 1.98)$$

Thus the population variance of males $\sigma_M^2$ is estimated to be at least 14%, and perhaps as much as 98% greater than the population variance of females $\sigma_F^2$.

8. In the past it was customary to test $H_0$: $\sigma_1^2 = \sigma_2^2$ prior to performing a $t$-test of the hypothesis $H_0$: $\mu_1 - \mu_2 = 0$. The initial hypothesis is a statement of the homogeneous variances assumption made in testing the latter hypothesis. One was advised in the textbooks of the time not to proceed with the simple $t$-test of Section 12.4 if $s_1^2/s_2^2$ led to rejection of $H_0$: $\sigma_1^2 = \sigma_2^2$. Although such advice stemmed from an admirable concern for meeting the assumptions of the tests employed, it proved to be generally poor advice if $n_1 = n_2$ (see Fig. 12.3).

The assumption that $s_1^2$ and $s_2^2$ are derived from *independent* samples from *normal* populations cannot be taken lightly—unlike the normality assumption underlying the $t$-tests of means (Box, 1953; Glass, Peckham, and Sanders, 1972). In particular the preliminary test of homogeneous variances can be largely invalidated by nonnormality of the populations; but this same nonnormality is of no consequence to the validity of the $t$-test of $\mu_1 - \mu_2 = 0$. In fact if $n_1 = n_2$ there is no reason to be concerned about violation of the assumption of homogeneous variances. The only circumstance in which one might advisedly test $H_0$: $\sigma_1^2 = \sigma_2^2$ prior to testing $H_0$: $\mu_1 - \mu_2 = 0$ is when there is good evidence that the populations are normally distributed *and* $n_1$ and $n_2$ are quite unequal. It may be possible to find a simple transformation of the observations that will give them a more nearly normal distribution (Sec. 6.10).

Since Table F is constructed for directional hypotheses concerning $\sigma_1^2$ and $\sigma_2^2$, where the numerator of the $F$-test is selected *a priori,* great care is required in obtaining the critical $F$-ratio for nondirectional hypotheses concerning $\sigma_1^2$ and $\sigma_2^2$. The Hartley and Bartlett tests are alternative methods for testing for homogeneity of variance which have the additional advantage of being able to test $J \geqslant 2$ variances.

## 13.7 TESTING HOMOGENEITY OF VARIANCE: HARTLEY'S $F_{max}$ TEST

1. Occasionally there is the need for a very simple and quick omnibus test of $H_0$: $\sigma_1^2 = \sigma_2^2 = \ldots = \sigma_J^2$, where each of the $J$ $s_j^2$'s is based on $n$ observations. The alternative hypothesis is that not all the $J$ $\sigma^2$'s are equal.
2. The sampling distribution of $F_{max}$ when $H_0$ is true **assumes** each of the $J$ variance estimates, $s_j^2$, is based on an independent random sample of $n$ observations from a normal population.
3. The **test statistic** $F_{max}$ is the ratio of the largest $s^2$ to the smallest $s^2$ in the set of $J$ $s^2$'s.

$$F_{max} = \frac{s^2_{\text{largest}}}{s^2_{\text{smallest}}} \tag{13.10}$$

4. The **sampling distribution** of $F_{max}$ was derived by Hartley (1950).
5. **Critical values** for the $F_{max}$ test, ${}_{1-\alpha}F_{max_{J,\nu_j}}$ (where $\nu_j = n - 1$) are given in Table H. Note that the table is entered using the degrees of freedom *per* variance estimate, $\nu_j = n - 1$. It is designed for situations where $n_1 = n_2 = \ldots = n_J$.
6. When $J \geqslant 3$ **confidence intervals** are not very meaningful. Equation 13.5 can be used to form CI's for each of the $J$ variances.
7. **Example.** In Table 12.1 each of the two $s_j^2$'s is based on $n = 18$ scores; the values of $s^2_{\text{largest}}$ and $s^2_{\text{smallest}}$ are 289 and 196, respectively. From Equation 13.10:

$$F_{max} = \frac{289}{196} = 1.47$$

The critical $F_{max}$-value at $\alpha = .05$ for $J = 2$ and $\nu_j = n - 1 = 17$ is ${}_{.95}F_{max_{2,17}} \doteq 2.86$, thus $H_0$ is tenable.

8. The $F_{max}$ is not robust when the normality assumption is violated. If distributions are leptokurtic, that is, have positive kurtosis (Sec. 6.9), the test is liberal (Durrand, 1969)—the true probability of rejecting a true null hypothesis is greater than the nominal value of $\alpha$. Recall that skewed distributions tend to be leptokurtic. The $F_{max}$ test is conservative for platykurtic (negative kurtosis) distributions—rectangular, bimodal, and dichotomous distributions have negative kurtosis (Sec. 6.9). The $F_{max}$ test is less powerful than the Bartlett test (Sec. 13.8); its chief virtues are its simplicity and ease of computation.

## 13.8 TESTING HOMOGENEITY OF VARIANCE FROM *J* INDEPENDENT SAMPLES: THE BARTLETT TEST

1. $H_0$: $\sigma_1^2 = \sigma_2^2 = \ldots = \sigma_J^2$; the alternative hypothesis is that at least one of the $J$ variances differs from the rest.
2. It is **assumed** that a sample of $n_j$ observations was randomly and independently drawn from each of the $J$ *normal* populations.
3. The **test statistic** for testing $H_0$ against $H_1$ is chi-square.

$$\chi^2 = \nu_w \ln s_w^2 - \Sigma\nu_j \ln s_j^2, \text{ where } \nu_j = n_j - 1, \text{ and } \nu_w = \Sigma\nu_j \qquad \textbf{(13.11)}$$

and $\ln s_w^2$ is the natural logarithm of the within-group variance (see Equation 12.3).

4. When $\sigma_1^2 = \sigma_2^2 = \cdots = \sigma_J^2$, the **sampling distribution** of the $\chi^2$ statistic obtained using Equation 13.11 is closely approximated by the chi-square distribution with $J - 1$ degrees of freedom. If $s_1^2 = s_2^2 = \cdots = s_J^2$, then $\Sigma\nu_j \ln s_j^2 = \nu_w \ln s_w^2$; otherwise the latter term is larger, that is, $\nu_w \ln s_w^2 \geqslant \Sigma\nu_j \ln s_j^2$.
5. The **critical value** against which $\chi^2$ in Equation 13.11 is compared for testing $H_0$ at the $\alpha$-level of significance is ${}_{1-\alpha}\chi_\nu^2$, where $\nu = J - 1$ degrees of freedom.*
6. **Confidence intervals** are not meaningful when $J > 2$ (see Eq. 13.9 for $J = 2$). Equation 13.5 can be used to form CI's for each of the $J$ $\sigma^2$'s.
7. In a statewide assessment of the reading ability of fifth-grade pupils, the variance estimates given in Table 13.2 were obtained for each of four ethnic groups. Are the individual differences significantly ($\alpha = .05$) greater within certain groups than others? The computation of Bartlett's test is illustrated in Table 13.2. The observed $\chi^2$-value of 8.935 is greater than the critical value of 7.82, thus the null hypothesis is rejected at the .05 level of significance. The significance appears to result from less heterogeneity within the White group. To pursue the issue fur-

*The $\chi^2$ value obtained from Equation 13.11 is slightly positively biased. If the computed $\chi^2$ exceeds the critical $\chi^2$-value very slightly, the $\chi^2$-value obtained from Equation 13.11 can be made more accurate if it is divided by $c$ (see footnote in Table 13.2). For most practical purposes the correction can be ignored.

**TABLE 13.2 Computation of Bartlett's Test of Homogeneity of Variance**

| *Group* | $n_j$ | $\nu_j$ | $s_j^2$ | $\nu_j s_j^2$ | $\ln s_j^2$* | $\nu_j \ln s_j^2$ |
|---|---|---|---|---|---|---|
| Blacks | 138 | 137 | 841 | 115,217 | 6.735 | 923 |
| Hispanics | 534 | 533 | 702 | 374,166 | 6.554 | 3,493 |
| Indians | 52 | 51 | 956 | 48,756 | 6.863 | 350 |
| Whites | 2,367 | 2,366 | 645 | 1,526,070 | 6.469 | 15,306 |
| | | $\nu_W = 3{,}087$ | | $\Sigma\nu_j s_j^2 = 2{,}064{,}209$ | | $20{,}072 = \Sigma\nu_j \ln s_j^2$ |

$$s_W^2 = \frac{\Sigma\nu_j s_j^2}{\nu_W} = \frac{2{,}064{,}209}{3{,}087} = 668.7;\ \ln s_W^2 = 6.505$$

$$\chi^2 = \nu_W \ln s_W^2 - \sum_j \nu_j \ln s_j^2$$

$$= (3{,}087)(6.505) - 20{,}072 = 8.935;\ {}_{.95}\chi_3^2 = 7.82,\ p < .05\dagger$$

*There are two widely used logarithms. *Common logarithms* use the base number of 10. The *log* (logarithm) of a number $N$ is the exponent or power of 10 that will equal that number. The log of 100 is 2 because $10^2 = 100$. The log of 1,000 is 3 because $10^3 = 1{,}000$. What is the log of 10? (*Answer:* 1, because $10 = 10^1$.) More generally, the log of a number $N$ is $p$ if $10^p = N$; that is, $\log N = p$. Common logs are designated by "log" or "$\log_{10}$", for example, $\log 100 = 2$.

*Natural logarithms* do not use 10 as base but a number, "$e$," ($e = 2.718\ldots$). Hence, the natural log ($\log_e$ or ln) of a number, $N$, is $x$ if $N = e^x$, that is $\ln N = x$. The natural log of 10 is 2.3026 because $10 = e^{2.3026}$ or $10 = 2.718^{2.3026}$. Most scientific hand calculators yield ln $N$ by entering $N$, then pressing the [ln] key. If the calculator has only the [log] function, it can be easily converted to the ln function by using $\ln N = 2.3026 \log N$; thus $\log 100 = 3$, hence $\ln 1000 = 2.3026(3) = 6.9078$.

†The $\chi^2$-value obtained from Equation 13.11 is slightly positively biased. If the computed $\chi^2$ exceeds the critical $\chi^2$-value very slightly, the $\chi^2$-value obtained from Equation 13.11 can be made more accurate if it is divided by $c$, where

$$c = \frac{1}{1 + 3(J-1)}\left(\sum_j \frac{1}{\nu_j} - \frac{1}{\nu_W}\right)\text{; if } n\text{'s are equal, } c = 1 + (J+1)/(3\nu_W).$$

For the problem in Table 13.2, $c = 1/3(3)\ (1/137 + 1/533 + 1/51 + 1/2{,}366 - 1/3{,}087) = .0032$.

The $F$-distribution can also be used for the Bartlett test. $F = \nu_2\chi^2/(\nu_1(b - \chi^2)$ is approximately distributed by the central $F$-distribution $F_{\nu_1,\nu_2}$ when $H_0$ is true; $\chi^2$ is from Equation 13.11, $\nu_1 = J - 1$, $\nu_2 = (J+1)/c^2$, and $b = \nu_2/(1 - c + 2/\nu_2)$. For the data in Table 13.2, $\chi^2 = 8.935$, $\nu_1 = 3$, $c = .0032$, $\nu_2 = 5/(.0032)^2 = 485{,}512$, and $b = 485{,}512/(1 - .0032 + 2/485{,}412) = 487{,}074$, thus $F = [(485{,}512)(8.935)]/[3(487{,}074 - 8.935)] = 2.97 > {}_{.95}F_{3,\infty} = 2.60$, $p < .05$. The $F$-procedure is termed the Bartlett-Box test of homogeneity of variance in the SPSS computer programs (Nie et al., 1975).

ther a CI for each group's $\sigma^2$ could be set using the procedures given in Section 13.3.

8. The Bartlett test yields accurate results if the parent populations are normally distributed as assumed.* If distributions have positive kurtosis (leptokurtosis), the Bartlett test is liberal, that is, the probability of a type-I error exceeds $\alpha$. If distributions have negative kurtosis (platykurtic curves, e.g., rectangular dis-

*Some sources (e.g., Snedecor and Cochran, 1980) suggest that $n_j$ should be greater than 5 before the Bartlett test is used, but Durrand (1969) found the test provided accurate results for $n_j \geqslant 3$.

tributions), the Bartlett test is conservative, that is, it will reject a true $H_0$ with probability less than $\alpha$ (Durrand, 1969). If the nonnormality is due to skewness, the Bartlett test is liberal, that is, it will reject a true $H_0$ with probability greater than $\alpha$ (because skewed distributions are also leptokurtic [Sec. 6.9]). Thus if $H_0$ is tenable and distributions have positive kurtosis, one can be confident that $H_0$: $\sigma_1^2 = \sigma_2^2 = \cdots = \sigma_J^2$ remains tenable. A test for homogeneity of variance which is relatively insensitive to departures from normality has been proposed by Scheffé (1959, pp. 83-87); this test is discussed and illustrated in Section 16.23.*

## 13.9 INFERENCES ABOUT $\sigma_1^2/\sigma_2^2$ WITH PAIRED OBSERVATIONS

1. As in Section 13.6, the null **hypothesis** being tested here is that two populations have the same variance:

$$H_0: \sigma_1^2 = \sigma_2^2$$

$$H_1: \sigma_1^2 \neq \sigma_2^2$$

2. It is **assumed** that two possibly *dependent* samples are drawn, one of size $n$ from a *normal* population with variance $\sigma_1^2$ and the other of the same size $n$ from a *normal* population with variance $\sigma_2^2$. The values of $\mu_1$ and $\mu_2$ are not of interest. The nature of dependent samples was discussed in Section 12.11.
3. The **test statistic** used in testing $H_0$ against $H_1$ is

$$t = \frac{s_1^2 - s_2^2}{\sqrt{\dfrac{4s_1^2 s_2^2}{n-2}(1 - r_{12}^2)}} = \frac{s_1^2 - s_2^2}{2s_1 s_2\sqrt{\dfrac{1 - r_{12}^2}{\nu}}} \qquad \textbf{(13.12)}$$

where $s_1^2$ and $s_2^2$ are the variances of samples 1 and 2, respectively, $n$ is the number of *pairs* of observations, pairing each observation of sample 1 with a single observation in sample 2, $r_{12}$ is the correlation coefficient calculated on the $n$ paired observations, and $\nu = n - 2$.
4. When $H_0$: $\sigma_1^2 = \sigma_2^2$ is true, the **sampling distribution** of $t$ in Equation 13.12 is Student's $t$-distribution with $\nu = n - 2$ degrees of freedom.
5. The critical values for testing $H_0$ against $H_1$ at the $\alpha$-level of significance are:

$${}_{\alpha/2}t_\nu \text{ and } {}_{1-\alpha/2}t_\nu, \text{ or } |t| \geqslant {}_{1-\alpha/2}t_\nu$$

*Other common tests for homogeneity of variance are the Cochran (Winer, 1971) and the Levene (Glass and Stanley, 1970) tests. The Cochran employs $C$ as a test statistic, $C = s_{\text{largest}}^2/\Sigma s_j^2$, which requires a special table and equal $n$'s for orthodox use. The Cochran test has no advantage over the Bartlett test, even when $n$'s are equal, except for computational ease which has largely disappeared with the availability of inexpensive calculators that yield logarithms with the touch of a key. The Levene test performs a one-factor analysis of variance (Chap. 16) on the absolute deviations for each of the $J$ groups. Contrary to some preliminary indications, it has also been found to be sensitive to nonnormality (Durrand, 1969).

6. Constructing a confidence interval on $\sigma_1^2 - \sigma_2^2$ or $\sigma_1^2/\sigma_2^2$ when estimates of the variances are obtained from dependent samples presents difficulties beyond the scope of this textbook.
7. Lord (1963b) reported data gathered by William E. Coffman on the performance of a sample of ninety-five students on the Stanford Achievement Test in the seventh and eighth grades. One might wonder whether, in the population of students sampled, performance is more uniform (less variable) in the seventh or the eighth grade.

   Sample 1 is the set of scores on the Stanford Achievement Test earned by the ninety-five students in grade seven, and sample 2 is the set of scores earned by the *same* ninety-five students in grade eight. Thus the two samples are not independent. The following data were obtained to test $H_0$: $\sigma_1^2 = \sigma_2^2$ at $\alpha_2 = .10$.

| *Sample 1 (grade 7)* | *Sample 2 (grade 8)* |
|---|---|
| $n = 95$ | $n = 95$ |
| $s_1^2 = 134.56$ | $s_2^2 = 201.64$ |

$r_{12} = .876$

The value of $r_{12} = .876$ is the product-moment correlation coefficient between the ninety-five students' performance in the seventh and eighth grades. Thus from Equation 13.12,

$$t = \frac{134.56 - 201.64}{\sqrt{\dfrac{4(134.56)(201.64)}{95-2}(1 - .876^2)}} = -4.07$$

The critical value for $|t|$ with which the obtained $|t|$ of 4.07 is compared is found in Table C: ${}_{.95}t_{93} \doteq 1.662$, ${}_{.9995}t_{93} \doteq 3.402$.

Thus we see that evidence exists to conclude that in the populations sampled—seventh-grade students and eighth-grade students—the variances $\sigma_1^2$ and $\sigma_2^2$ are different. The probability of obtaining a value of $t$ as discrepant from zero as that obtained is less than .001 if $\sigma_1^2$ is truly equal to $\sigma_2^2$. Performance on the Stanford Achievement Test is more variable among eighth-grade than among seventh-grade students.

## 13.10 RELATIONSHIPS AMONG THE NORMAL, *t*, CHI-SQUARE, AND *F*-DISTRIBUTIONS

The $t$, $\chi^2$, and $F$-distributions are all based on the normal distribution. In each instance sampling from a normal distribution underlies the new distribution. For example, a chi-square variable is formed by summing squared, unit-normal $z$-scores; in turn, chi-square variables are combined to form $F$-variables. In this section the relationships among the various families of distributions will be made explicit.

It was earlier pointed out that a $t$-distribution with infinite degrees of freedom is the same as the normal distribution. Consider, then, the *square* of the $t$-variable with $\nu$ degrees of freedom.

$$t_\nu^2 = \frac{z^2}{\chi_\nu^2/\nu} \tag{13.13}$$

In the numerator of Equation 13.13 the square of a unit normal variable is *divided by* 1; in the denominator is an independent chi-square variable divided by its degrees of freedom. Stated in slightly different form,

$$t_\nu^2 = \frac{\chi_1^2/1}{\chi_\nu^2/\nu} \tag{13.14}$$

Equation 13.14 is now recognized to be an $F$-variable with 1 and $\nu$ degrees of freedom. *Therefore, the square of a t-variable with $\nu$ degrees of freedom is an F-variable with* 1 *and $\nu$ degrees of freedom.*

It is somewhat more difficult to prove another interesting fact, which shall simply be stated: *any F-distribution with $\nu$ degrees of freedom for the numerator and infinite degrees of freedom for the denominator is the same as the $\chi_\nu^2$ distribution divided by the constant $\nu$*: that is

$$F_{\nu,\infty} = \frac{\chi_\nu^2}{\nu}^{*} \tag{13.15}$$

The $p$th percentile in the $\chi_\nu^2$ distribution is the same as the $p$th percentile in the $\nu(F_{\nu,\infty})$ distribution. However, if the $p$th percentile in the $t$-distribution with $\nu$ degrees of freedom is squared, the $|2p - 1|$ percentile in the distribution $F_{1,\nu}$ is obtained. For example, the 95th percentile of the $t_\nu$-distribution is the $2(.95) - 1 = .90 = 90$th percentile of the $t_\nu^2 = F_{1,\nu}$-distribution. (This is true because 5% of the cases exceed the 95th percentile in $t_\nu$ and 5% lie below the 5th percentile. When the $t$ values are squared both the top 5% and the bottom 5% take on a positive sign; hence, 10% of the values in $F_{1,\nu}$ exceed the square of ${}_{.95}t_\nu$.)

## CHAPTER SUMMARY

There are two purposes in testing for homogeneity of variance, $H_0: \sigma_1^2 = \sigma_2^2 = \ldots = \sigma_J^2$: (1) to determine whether one population is more variable than another population, and (2) to assess the statistical assumption of homoscedasticity, which is required for the $t$-test of means (and certain other statistical tests). For practical purposes, violation of the assumption of homogeneity of variance can be disregarded when testing mean differences when sample sizes for each group are equal, but not when $n$'s differ.

The chi-square distribution is employed for testing $H_0: \sigma^2 = K$, for setting a confidence interval for $\sigma^2$, and in testing $H_0: \sigma_1^2 = \sigma_2^2 = \cdots = \sigma_J^2$ when the Bartlett test is

*The proof depends on the fact that $\lim_{\nu_2 \to \infty} \chi_{\nu_2}^2/\nu_2 = 1$.

used. The mean of a $\chi^2$-distribution with $\nu$ degree of freedom is $\nu$, but the most probable (modal) $\chi^2$-value is $\nu - 2$ for $\nu > 1$. The $\chi^2$-distribution is positively skewed, but the skewness decreases as $\nu$ increases.

In testing $H_0: \sigma^2 = K$ the test statistic $\chi^2 = \nu s^2/\sigma^2$ has $\nu = n - 1$ degrees of freedom, and a critical value of ${}_{1-\alpha}\chi^2_\nu$.

The $F$-distribution is the ratio of two independent variance estimates, $s_1^2/s_2^2$; it is used to test $H_0: \sigma_1^2 = \sigma_2^2$. Table F gives critical $F$-ratios for directional ("one-tailed") hypotheses, for example, $H_1: \sigma_1^2 > \sigma_2^2$, in which sample 1 is predicted to have the larger variance. If nondirectional tests of the two independent variances are made, $\alpha$'s in Table F must be doubled.

The Bartlett test can test for homogeneity of variance for any number of independent groups, $J$, with equal or unequal $n$'s. The Hartley $F_{max}$ test requires equal $n$'s.

For paired observations, the $t$-test is used to test $H_0: \sigma_1^2 = \sigma_2^2$ between the two dependent (correlated) variance estimates.

All methods of testing for homogeneity of variance assume that the $N$ observations in the parent populations are normally distributed. Unfortunately, these tests are not robust when the normality condition (kurtosis, $\gamma_2 = 0$) is violated. Leptokurtosis increases the probability of a type-I error such that it exceeds $\alpha$. Consequently the Bartlett test and other related tests for homogeneity of variance are liberal (i.e., the true $\alpha$ is greater than the nominal $\alpha$) if there is positive kurtosis (i.e., with leptokurtic distributions), and conservative if there is negative kurtosis (i.e., with platykurtic distributions). Highly skewed distributions are also leptokurtic and result in liberal tests. If distributions are not approximately normal, the Scheffé test of homogeneity (Sec. 16.23) of variance should be employed.

## *MASTERY TEST*

1. When can the assumption $\sigma_1^2 = \sigma_2^2$ be disregarded in making a $t$-test for differences between independent means?
2. If $n_1 = n_2$, why might one be interested in testing $H_0: \sigma_1^2 = \sigma_2^2$?
3. What is the name of the distribution that is formed by the ratio of two independent estimates of $\sigma^2$, that is, $s_1^2/s_2^2$?

For Questions 4 to 7, which distribution is ordinarily used:

4. to test $H_0: \sigma^2 = 225$?
   a. $F$ b. $t$ c. $\chi^2$
5. to test $H_0: \sigma_1^2 = \sigma_2^2$, when the variance estimates are independent?
6. to test $H_0: \sigma_1^2 = \sigma_2^2$, when the variance estimates are paired?
7. to test $H_0: \sigma_1^2 = \sigma_2^2 = \ldots = \sigma_J^2$, using the Bartlett test?
8. Tests of homogeneity are generally robust with respect to the assumption of normality. (T or F)
9. If populations are leptokurtic (positive kurtosis) Bartlett's test tends to result in more type-I errors than $\alpha$ would indicate. (T or F)
10. If a parent population is rectangular, the Bartlett test will be
    a. conservative b. liberal

11. If parent populations are highly skewed they also tend to have positive kurtosis (leptokurtosis). (T or F)
12. For $H_1: \sigma_1^2 > \sigma_2^2$, the critical values in Table F are correct for testing $H_0: \sigma_1^2 = \sigma_2^2$.
13. If $\nu_1 < \nu_2$, the median value of the $F$-distribution $_{.50}F_{\nu_1, \nu_2}$ is (use Table 13.1)
    a. $> 1$
    b. 1
    c. $< 1$

Match the distribution with the characteristics indicated in Questions 14 to 21.

14. Skewed negatively
15. Skewed positively
16. Always symmetrical
17. Has an expected value of approximately 1
18. $E(?) = 0$
19. Has a median value of 1 when $\nu_1 = \nu_2$
20. $E(?) = \nu$
21. More nearly resembles a normal distribution as degrees of freedom ($\nu$ or $\nu_1$ and $\nu_2$) increase.

a. $F$
b. $t$
c. $\chi^2$
d. $F$ and $t$
e. $F$ and $\chi^2$
f. $t$ and $\chi^2$
g. $F$, $t$, and $\chi^2$
h. None of these

Find the values of the following:

22. $_{.95}t_5$, $_{.975}t_5$
23. $_{.90}F_{1,5}$, $_{.95}F_{1,5}$
24. Is $_{1-\alpha/2}t_\nu = \sqrt{_{1-\alpha}F_{1,\nu}}$
25. $_{.95}\chi_1^2$, $_{.95}\chi_5^2$, $_{.99}\chi_5^2$
26. Does $\sqrt{_{.95}\chi_1^2} = {}_{.975}z$

## *PROBLEMS AND EXERCISES*

1. In one study the authors found that the standard deviation of reading grade equivalent (GE) scores for the eighty-one students who completed an ungraded curriculum was $.93 = s_U$. The corresponding parameter given in the test manual was 1.00.
    a. Assuming the eighty-one students were a random sample, does the ungraded curriculum appear to reduce significantly ($\alpha_2 = .10$) individual differences?
    b. Treating the eighty-one students as a random sample, set .90 CI for $\sigma_U^2$.
    c. For 103 comparable students in a conventionally graded curriculum, the standard deviation was $1.08 = s_G$. Assuming that before the study, it had been predicted that $\sigma_G^2 > \sigma_U^2$, test $H_0$ with $\alpha_1 = .05$.
2. The mean and standard deviation of IQ scores for the 195 girls and the 209 boys in the fifth grade of a school district are given.

| | *Boys* | *Girls* |
|---|---|---|
| $\bar{X}_j$ | 99.7 | 99.2 |
| $s_j$ | 15.5 | 14.3 |

a. Test $H_0: \sigma_B^2 = \sigma_G^2$ using the $F$-test with $\alpha_2 = .10$.
b. Since $n_B \neq n_G$, would a $t$-test of independent means be seriously in error if the variances are not homogeneous?
c. Could the $H_0$ in part a. have been tested using the Bartlett test?

3. In one study 543 sixth-grade students were retested with a social studies test that they had taken one year earlier as fifth graders. The observed correlation between the two sets of scores was .79, with $s_5 = 7.60$ and $s_6 = 7.91$. Test $H_0: \sigma_6^2 = \sigma_5^2$, with $\alpha = .05$.
4. Suppose the variances in GPA for 101 students drawn randomly from grades ten, eleven, and twelve are .25, .20, and .16, respectively. Is $H_0: \sigma_{10}^2 = \sigma_{11}^2 = \sigma_{12}^2$ tenable at $\alpha = .10$, using the Bartlett test?
5. The stereotypes of Mexican-Americans by Anglo and Mexican-American students were compared in Problem 7b, following Chapter 12. Were the perceptions among the Mexican-American students more homogeneous? Use the $F$-test, with $\alpha_2 = .05$.
6. Test $H_0: \sigma_1^2 = \sigma_2^2 = \sigma_3^2$ in Question 5 in Problems and Exercises following Chapter 16 using a. the Bartlett test, b. the Hartley $F_{max}$ test. Let $\alpha = .10$.
7. If ${}_{.95}F_{2,10} = 4.10$, ${}_{.05}F_{10,2} = ?$
8. The mean of the chi-square distribution with $\nu$ degrees of freedom is $\nu$. The one and only mode is at $\nu - 2$ for $\nu > 2$. The chi-square distribution is positively skewed. Recall from Equation 4.11 that the mode is estimated by $3Md - 2\overline{X}$.
   a. If $\nu = 10$, estimate ${}_{.50}\chi_{10}^2$. Compare this value with the value in Table D.
   b. Is the median of the chi-square distribution with $\nu$ degrees of freedom *above, below,* or *equal to* $\nu$?
9. For very large $\nu$, the chi-square distribution with $\nu$ degrees of freedom approximates a normal distribution. The mean and standard deviation are $\nu$ and $\sqrt{2\nu}$, respectively, regardless of the size of $\nu$. For $\nu = 50$, find the 95th percentile in the chi-square distribution from Table D and compare it with the 97.5 percentile in a normal distribution with mean $\nu = 50$ and standard deviation $\sqrt{2\nu} = \sqrt{100}$. For large $\nu$, does ${}_{1-\alpha}\chi^2 \doteq {}_{1-\alpha/2}z^2$?
10. Prove that the variance of the $t$-distribution with $\nu$ degrees of freedom is $\nu/(\nu - 2)$. (Hint: $t_\nu^2$ is the same as the $F$-distribution with 1 and $\nu$ degrees of freedom. Since $E(t_\nu) = 0$, and $\sigma_t^2 = E[t - E(t)]^2$, the variance of $t_\nu$ is $E(t_\nu^2)$.)

## *ANSWERS TO MASTERY TEST*

1. When $n_1 = n_2$.
2. When one is interested in comparing variances as an inferential question in its own right.
3. F
4. c
5. a
6. b
7. c
8. F
9. T
10. a
11. T
12. Yes
13. c
14. h
15. e
16. b
17. a
18. b
19. a
20. c
21. g
22. 2.015, 2.571
23. 4.06, 6.61
24. Yes
25. 3.84, 11.07, 15.09
26. Yes, for example, $\sqrt{3.841} = 1.96$

## *ANSWERS TO PROBLEMS AND EXERCISES*

1. a. No, $\chi^2 = 69.19$; ${}_{.05}\chi^2_{80} = 60.39$, ${}_{.95}\chi^2_{80} = 101.9$
   b. $(69.19/{}_{.05}\chi^2_{80},\ 69.19/{}_{.95}\chi^2_{80}) = (69.19/60.39,\ 69.19/101.9) = (1.15, .68)$ or $1.15 > \sigma^2 > .68$
   c. $F = (1.08)^2/(.93)^2 = 1.349$; ${}_{.95}F_{102,80} \doteq {}_{.95}F_{100,60} = 1.48$, $H_0$ is tenable
2. a. $F = (15.5/14.3)^2 = 1.175$; ${}_{.95}F_{208,194} \doteq {}_{.95}F_{200,200} = 1.26$; $H_0$ is tenable, $p > .05$
   b. No, because $n_B/n_G \doteq 1$ see Fig. 12.3
   c. Yes
3. $t = [(7.91)^2 - (7.60)^2]/[2(7.91)(7.60)\sqrt{[1 - (.79)^2]/541}\,] = 4.81/3.17 = 1.52 < 1.96 = {}_{.95}t_{541}$
4. $\chi^2 = [300(-1.5929) - (-482.83)]/1.0044 = 4.94 > 4.605 = {}_{.90}\chi^2_2$; reject $H_0$ at .10 level.
5. $F = 112.4/53.2 = 2.11 > 208 \doteq {}_{.975}F_{62,26}$; reject $H_0$ at the .05 level
6. a. $\chi^2 = .34$; $1.39 = {}_{.50}\chi^2_2$; $p > .50$
   b. $F_{max} = 1.43 < 5.34 = {}_{.95}F_{max(3,9)}$; $p > .05$
7. $1/4.10 = .244$
8. a. $9.33 \doteq 9.34 = {}_{.50}\chi^2_{10}$
   b. below
9. ${}_{.95}\chi^2_{50} = 67.51$; $50 + 1.96(10) = 69.10$
10. $\sigma_t^2 = E(t_\nu^2) = E(F_{1,\nu}) = \nu/(\nu - 2)$

# 14

# INFERENCES REGARDING PROPORTIONS

## 14.1 STATISTICS FOR CATEGORICAL DEPENDENT VARIABLES

Many research questions in education and the social sciences deal with proportions or percentages. For example, do the proportions of psychotic disorders, suicides, peptic ulcers, illiterates, unemployed, and so on differ among cultures? Heretofore, hypotheses about means and variances have been considered. Now attention is focused on methods of inference for testing hypotheses involving proportions in various *categories*—measurement of the variable here is at the *nominal* level. Notice that each of the following questions implies a hypothesis regarding a *categorical* variable.

On true-false tests, is the proportion of correct answers that are keyed "true" equal to .5? Does the suicide rate differ among social classes? Does the school dropout rate differ among blacks, whites, hispanics, and American Indians?

## 14.2
## THE PROPORTION AS A MEAN

Within the sample of $n$ units, the number $f$ who possess the characteristic in question is observed. The sample proportion $p$ is the ratio of $f$ to $n$:

$$p = \frac{f}{n}$$

The statistic $p$ is an estimator of the parameter $\pi$*. In fact, if one thinks of a dichotomously measured variable $X$ that equals 1 when the unit observed possesses the characteristic in question and 0 when it does not, then $p$ is to $\pi$ as $\overline{X}$ is to $\mu$. For example, suppose that "male gender" is the characteristic being measured. A child's "score" is denoted by $X_i$, which equals 1 if the child is male and 0 if female. If in a sample of $n$ children there are $f$ males ("1's scorers"), then

$$\sum_{i=1}^{n} X_i = X_1 + \ldots + X_n = f$$

Hence,

$$\overline{X} = \frac{\Sigma X}{n} = \frac{f}{n} = p \qquad \textbf{(14.1)}$$

The population mean of $X$ will be $\pi$. Thus $p$ possesses all the properties as an estimator of $\pi$ which $\overline{X}$ possesses as an estimator of $\mu$.

## 14.3
## THE VARIANCE OF A PROPORTION

A *dichotomously* "scored" $X$ variable has a *variance* in the population that equals

$$\sigma^2 = E(X - \pi)^2 = \pi(1 - \pi) \qquad \textbf{(14.2)}$$

*We will use the symbol $\pi$ (the Greek lowercase letter *pi*) to denote the proportion in the population that falls in a given category. The parameter $\pi$ is estimated by the corresponding proportion $p$ in the random sample. The symbol "$\pi$" should not be confused with its use in geometry where it is the ratio of the circumference to the diameter of a circle and has the value of about 3.14. Use of the $\pi$ and $p$ symbols is consistent with the use of Greek letters for parameters and Roman letters for sample estimates.

where $\pi$ is the population proportion.* Thus, the standard deviation of a dichotomous variable is

$$\sigma = \sqrt{\pi(1 - \pi)} \tag{14.3}$$

## 14.4 THE STANDARD ERROR AND SAMPLING DISTRIBUTION OF A PROPORTION

The central limit theorem states that regardless of the shape of the frequency distribution—even if it is bimodal, dichotomous, or some other configuration—the sampling distribution of the mean (in this case, $p$) will be approximately normal if $n$ is large. In other words, if one randomly selected a sample of 200 persons, determined the proportion $p$ who were left-handed, and replicated the study many times, the distribution of $p$'s for the many random samples would be normally distributed and have a mean of $\pi$, the proportion in the population that falls in the category (e.g., left-handed) being studied.

Suppose one wished to know the proportion of persons over fifty years of age in the United States that are male. How much would the proportion $p$, in the random sample of $n$ persons differ from the parameter, $\pi$, the proportion in the entire population of $N$ persons? The variance error and standard error of a proportion are given in Equation 14.4† and 14.5 respectively.

$$\sigma_p^2 = \frac{\sigma^2}{n} = \frac{\pi(1 - \pi)}{n} \tag{14.4}$$

**Derivation:* If in the *population* of observations, $X_1, X_2, \ldots, X_N$, the proportion of 1's is $\pi$ and the proportion of 0's is $1 - \pi$, hence

$$\sigma^2 = \frac{1}{N}\sum_{i=1}^{N}(X_i - \pi)^2 = \frac{1}{N}\left[N\pi(1 - \pi)^2 + N(1 - \pi)(-\pi)^2\right]$$

$$= \pi(1 - \pi)^2 + (1 - \pi)(-\pi)^2 = \pi(1 - \pi).$$

In a random sample of $n$ observations, $X_1, X_2, \ldots, X_n$, in which there are $p$ 1's and $(1 - p)$ 0's, the variance is

$$s^2 = \frac{n\Sigma X_i^2 - (\Sigma X)^2}{n(n-1)} = \frac{n(1^2 + 1^2 + \ldots + 1^2 + 0^2 + 0^2 + \ldots + 0^2) - (np)^2}{n(n-1)}$$

$$= \frac{n^2p - n^2p^2}{n(n-1)} = \frac{n^2p(1-p)}{n(n-1)} = \frac{n^2p(1-p)}{n(n-1)} = \frac{np(1-p)}{n-1} = p(1-p)\left(\frac{n}{n-1}\right).$$

†Most precisely, $\sigma_p^2 = (1 - n/N)\ \pi(1 - \pi)/n$; but in most statistical applications $N$ is very large hence Equation 14.4 results. Occasionally in survey research $N$ is a known finite value and the sampling fraction can be taken into account. If $n/N$ is small (e.g., .05 or less), the inclusion of the sampling fraction factor in the formula has only a trivial effect on the standard error. See Section 10.3 for additional discussion of finite population models.

$$\sigma_p = \sqrt{\frac{\pi(1-\pi)}{n}} \tag{14.5}$$

Suppose a random sample of 100 persons from the population is drawn and the proportion $p$ that are males is determined, and the process is repeated many times. The standard deviation of the $p$'s (i.e., the standard error of the proportion) would be approximately .05, as given by Equation 14.5:

$$\sigma_p = \sqrt{\frac{\pi(1-\pi)}{n}} = \sqrt{\frac{(.5)(1-.5)}{100}} = \sqrt{\frac{(.5)(.5)}{100}} = .05$$

In other words, when $n = 100$, about two-thirds (68%) of the $p$'s differ from $\pi$ by .05 or less ($\pi \pm \sigma_p = .45$ to .55); about 95% of the $p$'s would fall between .40 and .60 ($\pi \pm 2\sigma_p$). The sampling distribution of $p$ when $\pi = .5$ and $n = 100$ appears in Figure 14.1. Of course, only a single $p$ will be observed, the value from the random sample of 100 persons; this $p$ is just one of the many observations in the sampling distribution in Figure 14.1. But what is the probability that the value $p$ will be in error by .10 or more? Less than 5% of $p$'s differ from $\pi$ by as much as .10. In other words, if a band of width $\pm 2\sigma_p$ were placed about each $p$ in the sampling distribution, approximately 95% of such intervals would include the parameter $\pi$ (which, in this example, is .5). Stated differently, 95% of the .95 confidence intervals will "capture" the parameter $\pi$.

What if a sample of 2,500 persons had been used instead of $n = 100$? The standard deviation of the sample proportions (i.e., the standard error of $p$) would then be $\sigma_p = \sqrt{(.5)(.5)/2{,}500} = .01$. In other words, 95% of the sample $p$'s would be within .02 ($\pm 2\sigma_p$) of the parameter $\pi$. That the sample proportion $p$ based on $n = 2{,}500$ is rarely in error by more than $\pm .02$ from the population proportion illustrates the precision of modern methods of opinion polling and survey research. Thus, television ratings and voting preferences can be estimated quite accurately for the nation from a relatively small sample of voters or viewers. It seems paradoxical, but it is true, that the accuracy of a sample estimate depends on the size of the sample and almost not at all on the proportion of the population that is sampled. One thousand cases, drawn randomly, give an estimate of 50 million voters' preferences that is almost as accurate as 1,000 cases drawn randomly from a city of 10,000 voters. Intuitively, it would appear that the larger the population,

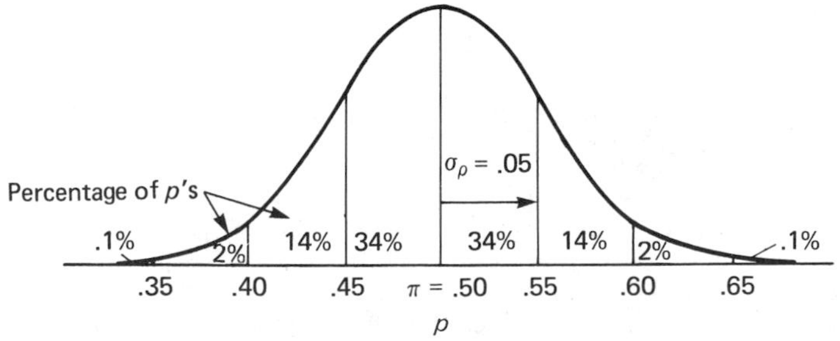


**FIGURE 14.1**
**The sampling distribution of $p$ when $\pi = .5$ and $n = 100$ ($\sigma_p = .05$).**

the larger the sample needed for a specified degree of accuracy. But this is not so (see Sec. 10.3).

The central limit theorem holds that the shape of the sampling distribution of $p$ will approach a normal distribution as $n$ increases. But how large does $n$ need to be before normality is a safe assumption? Research has shown that if $n\pi$ [or $n(1 - \pi)$, whichever is smaller] is 5 or greater, the error in treating the sampling distribution as if it were normal is negligible.

## 14.5 TESTING $H_0: \pi = K$

1. The **hypothesis** to be tested is that in the population, the proportion $\pi$ possessing a particular characteristic is equal to a value $K$ that lies between 0 and 1,

$$H_0: \pi = K$$
$$H_1: \pi \neq K$$

2. For purposes of testing $H_0$ against $H_1$ it need only be **assumed** that a *random* sample of size $n$ is drawn from the population.
3. $H_0$ is tested by means of the $z$-test. If $H_0$ is true (and if $n\pi$ and $n(1 - \pi)$ are each greater than 5) then the **sampling distribution** of

$$z = \frac{p - \pi}{\sigma_p} = \frac{p - \pi}{\sqrt{\pi(1 - \pi)/n}} \tag{14.6}$$

is approximately normally distributed over random samples of size $n$ with mean 0 and standard deviation 1.
4. To test $H_0$ against $H_1$ at the $\alpha_2$-level of significance, the value of $z$ in Equation 14.6 is compared with ${}_{\alpha/2}z$ and ${}_{1-(\alpha/2)}z$ in the unit-normal distribution. If $|z| \geqslant {}_{1-(\alpha/2)}z$, $H_0$ is rejected at the $\alpha_2$ level. (For directional hypotheses, $H_0$ is rejected at the $\alpha_1$ significance level and $H_1: \pi > K$ is accepted if $z \geqslant {}_{1-\alpha}z$).
5. The simplest method for determining the .95 and .99 **confidence interval** on $\pi$ for a proportion, $p$, is to use Figures 14.2 and 14.3. Suppose a random sample of $n = 100$ voters was surveyed for their preferred candidate and it was found that 20% ($p = .2$) favored candidate $A$. The .95 confidence interval for $\pi$ (the proportion in the entire population of voters who prefer candidate $A$) is found by locating $p$ (the sample proportion) on the baseline axis, then reading upward to find the two points where $p$ intersects with $n$, the curved lines that correspond to the sample size. From these two points, one reads across to the vertical axis to find the upper and lower limits of the confidence interval. Hence, for $p = .2$ and $n = 100$, the lower limit of the .95 confidence interval is .13, the upper limit is .30. In other words, one can be 95% confident that had the entire population been surveyed, between 13% and 30% would have stated a preference for

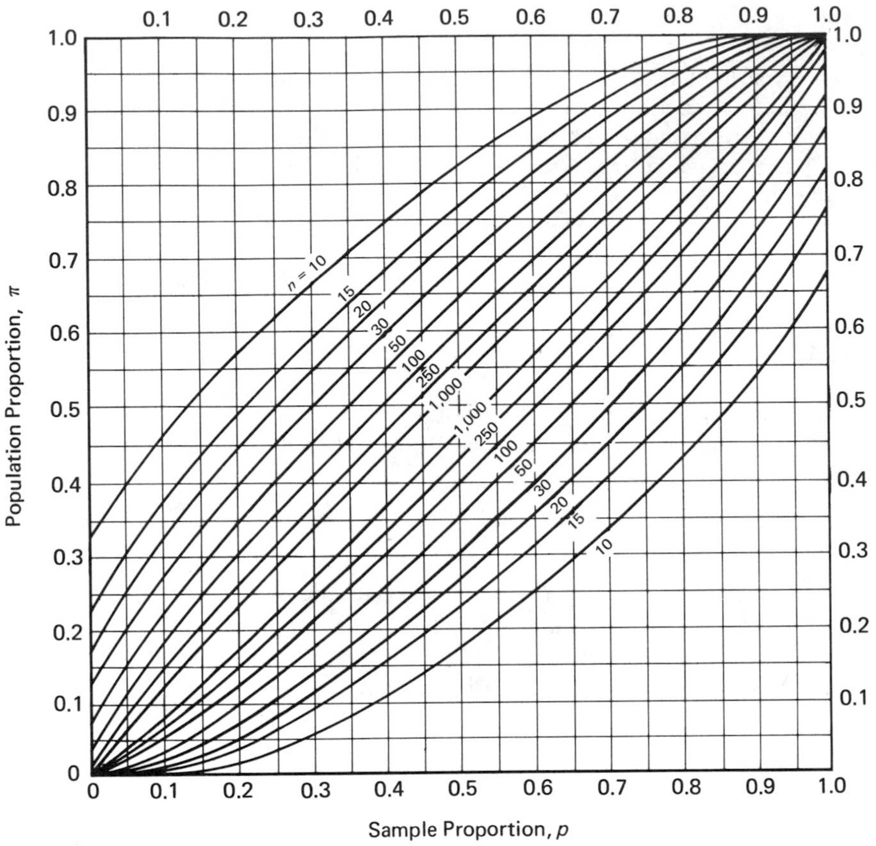


**FIGURE 14.2. Chart giving .95 confidence limits for the population proportion, $\pi$, given the sample proportion, $p$ and $n$. (The numbers on the curve indicate sample size, $n$.) (From E. S. Pearson and C. J. Clopper, "The Use of Confidence Intervals of Fiducial Limits Illustrated in the Case of the Binomial,"** ***Biometrika*****, 1934,** ***26*****, 404. Reproduced by permission of the** ***Biometrika*** **Trustees.)**

candidate *A*. The confidence intervals obtained from Figures 14.2 and 14.3 are slightly more accurate than those obtained by using procedures that assume $n$ is large enough to ensure that the sampling distribution is normal.*

6. **Example.** The superintendent of a school district wishes to take a poll one month before a city election to determine the chances of the proposed school

*For large $n$, .95 CI on $\pi \doteq p \pm 1.96 \sqrt{p(1-p)/n}$. More precisely, the lower and upper limits on $\pi$ for the $(1-\alpha)$CI are approximately $[n/(n + {}_{1-\alpha/2}z^2)][p + {}_{1-\alpha/2}z^2/2n \pm {}_{1-\alpha/2}z \sqrt{p(1-p)/n + {}_{1-\alpha/2}z^2/4n^2}]$. For example, if $p = .9$ and $n = 100$, the .95 CI is approximately $\{100/[100 + (1.96)^2]\}[.9 + (1.96)^2/200 \pm 1.96\sqrt{(.9)(.1)/100 + (1.96)^2/4(100)^2}] = .9630\,(.9192 \pm .06186) = (.826, .945)$. This procedure is quite accurate if $np$ [and $n(1-p)$] are greater than 5.

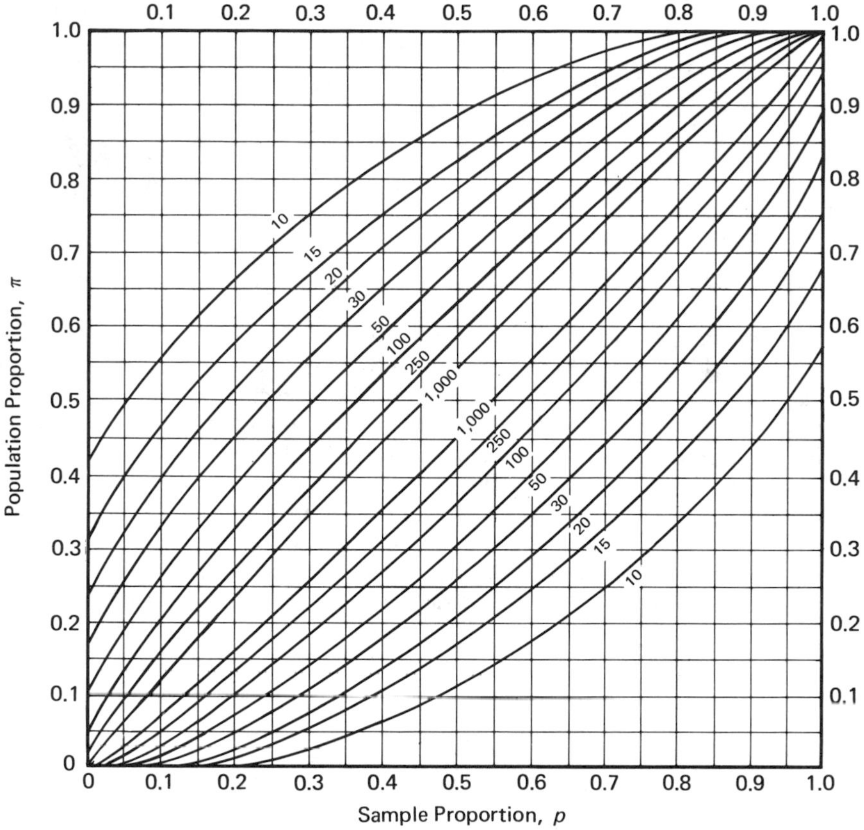


**FIGURE 14.3. Chart giving .99 confidence limits for the population proportion, $\pi$, given the sample proportion, $p$ and $n$. (The numbers on the curve indicate sample size.) (From E. S. Pearson and C. J. Clopper, "The Use of Confidence Intervals of Fiducial Limits Illustrated in the Case of the Binomial," *Biometrika*, 1934, *26*, 404. Reproduced by permission of the *Biometrika* Trustees.)**

bond receiving a majority of the votes that will be cast. The hypothesis to be tested at the $\alpha_2 = .01$ level of significance is that $\pi$, the proportion of the 25,000 registered voters favoring the school bond, is .50; the alternative hypothesis is that $\pi \neq .50$. A random sample of $n = 100$ registered voters is drawn; when questioned, $f$ = sixty-five voters indicated that they favored the school bond.

The value of $p$ is $f/n = .65$. The value of $z$ in Equation (14.6) is

$$z = \frac{p - \pi}{\sigma_p} = \frac{p - \pi}{\sqrt{\pi(1 - \pi)/n}} = \frac{.65 - .50}{\sqrt{.50(.50)/100}} = \frac{.15}{.05} = 3.00$$

The $z$ value of 3.00 is compared with the critical $|z|$-value of 2.576. It can be concluded that $p = .65$ is significantly greater than .50 at the .01 level.

The 95% confidence interval on $\pi$ is found from Figure 14.2 and extends from approximately .54 to .74. The .99 CI (Fig. 14.3) extends from approximately .52 to .78.

## 14.6 TESTING EMPIRICAL VERSUS THEORETICAL DISTRIBUTIONS: THE CHI-SQUARE GOODNESS-OF-FIT TEST

The chi-square ($\chi^2$) test statistic can be used to determine whether the observed proportions differ significantly from a priori or theoretically expected proportions. For example, on true-false exams when examinees do not know the correct answer, do they tend to guess "true" and "false" with equal frequency, or is there a response bias favoring one of the options? In one study of college students (Gustav, 1963) it was found that 62% of approximately 200 examinees guessed "true" when they did not know the correct answer. If $n = 200$, does the $p$-value of .62 differ significantly from chance, that is, differ significantly from $H_0$: $\pi = .50$? Recall that the $z$-test is the difference in a statistic and the corresponding parameter, measured in units of the standard error of the statistic. Hence, this hypothesis is tested using the $z$-test (Eq. 14.6):

$$z = \frac{p - \pi}{\sigma_p}$$

$$\sigma_p = \sqrt{\frac{\pi(1 - \pi)}{n}} = \sqrt{\frac{.5(1 - .5)}{200}} = .0354$$

$$z = \frac{.62 - .50}{.0354} = \frac{.12}{.0354} = 3.394$$

Recall that the null hypothesis is rejected at $\alpha_2 = .05$ if $|z| \geqslant 1.96$ and also rejected at $\alpha = .01$ if $|z| \geqslant 2.58$. Therefore, it is concluded that there is a significant ($p < .01$) response bias toward guessing "true" in the population sampled in the study.

This same null hypothesis—that the proportion of guesses for "true" ($\pi_1$) or for "false" ($\pi_2$) is .50 ($H_0$: $\pi_1 = \pi_2 = .50$)—can be tested using the chi-square statistic in the example.

| | *Category* | |
|---|---|---|
| | "True" | "False" |
| Observed | $p_1 = \frac{124}{200} = .62$ | $p_2 = \frac{76}{200} = .38$ |
| Hypothesized | $\pi_1 = .50$ | $\pi_2 = .50$ |

In other words, the proportion $p_1$ of "true" guesses was .62; the proportion $p_2$ of "false" guesses was .38 for the $n_\bullet = 200$ subjects ("$n_\bullet$" indicates the sum of all observations). Do .62 and .38 differ significantly from the hypothesized value for the parameters

$\pi_1 = .50$, $\pi_2 = .50$? The chi-square statistic $\chi^2$ represents the extent to which the *observed* proportions, $p_j$'s, differ from the hypothesized or *expected* proportions, $\pi$'s. The chi-square statistic is defined in Equation 14.7.*

$$\chi^2 = n_{\bullet} \sum_{j=1}^{J} \frac{(p_j - \pi_j)^2}{\pi_j} \tag{14.7}$$

In other words, in Equation 14.7 the *difference* in the observed and expected proportion for each of the $J$ categories is squared, then divided by the expected proportion for that category. The sum of these quotients for all $J$ categories multiplied by $n_{\bullet}$ is $\chi^2$. In the example there are two cells in which the two observed proportions were $p_1 = .62$ and $p_2 = .38$; the associated expected proportions $\pi_1$ and $\pi_2$ were both .50. Substituting these values into Equation 14.7, one finds

$$\chi^2 = n_{\bullet} \sum \frac{(p_j - \pi_j)^2}{\pi_j} = n_{\bullet} \left[\frac{(p_1 - \pi_1)^2}{\pi_1} + \frac{(p_2 - \pi_2)^2}{\pi_2}\right]$$

$$= 200 \left[\frac{(.62 - .5)^2}{.5} + \frac{(.38 - .5)^2}{.5}\right] = 200 \left[\frac{.0144}{.5} + \frac{.0144}{.5}\right]$$

$$= 200 \left(\frac{.0288}{5}\right) = 200(.0576) = 11.52$$

Is a chi-square of 11.52 significant at the .01 level? Table D in the Appendix gives the critical values for $\chi^2$ for various degrees of freedom. *In $\chi^2$ goodness-of-fit tests (like the one just illustrated) the number of degrees of freedom ($\nu$) is 1 less than the number of categories;* that is, $\nu = J - 1$, or, in our example, $2 - 1 = 1$. In Table D, the critical value of $\chi^2$ with $\alpha = .01$ and $\nu = 1$ is 6.64 (i.e., ${}_{.99}\chi_1^2 = 6.64$). Our $\chi^2$-value of 11.52 exceeds the critical $\chi^2$-value; hence, $p < .01$ and the null hypothesis ($H_0: \pi_1 = \pi_2 = .5$) is untenable. Indeed since $\chi^2 = 11.52 > {}_{.999}\chi_1^2 = 10.8$, the null hypothesis can be rejected at the .001 level.

Equation 14.7 expressed in percentages $P_j$ rather than proportions $p_j$ is

$$\chi^2 = \frac{n_{\bullet}}{100} \sum_{j=1}^{J} \frac{(P_j - 100\pi_j)^2}{100\pi_j} \tag{14.8}$$

*The formula for $\chi^2$ is given in most other textbooks as $\chi^2 = \Sigma[(f_O - f_e)^2/f_e]$, where $f_O$ and $f_e$, respectively, denote observed and expected *frequencies* in a category. This formula is mathematically equivalent to Equation 14.7, where its meaning is easier to grasp and it yields results that are directly interpretable. With the conventional formula, the values of observed and expected frequencies change as $n$ is increased or decreased, whereas the proportions $p$ and $\pi$ do not. Equation 14.7 was derived by substituting in the above formula $n_{\bullet}p$ for $f_O$ and $n_{\bullet}\pi$ for $f_e$ and factoring out $n_{\bullet}$. Notice that frequencies and proportions differ only by a constant factor of $n_{\bullet}$—testing the departure of observed from expected frequencies is equivalent to testing the departure of observed from expected proportions since $p = f/n_{\bullet}$, or $f = n_{\bullet}p$. Notice that $\pi_1 + \pi_2 + \ldots + \pi_J$ will always equal 1.

### $z$-Test versus $\chi^2$

Recall that when the $z$-test was used to test the hypothesis $H_0: \pi = .5$, the $z$-ratio of 3.394 was obtained. If this $z$ is squared, 11.52 is obtained—exactly the value observed for $\chi^2$. But $\chi^2$ is equivalent to the $z$-test *only* when there is 1 degree of freedom, that is, when there are only two categories ($J = 2$). The chi-square statistic has broader applications; it can accommodate three or more categories simultaneously whereas the $z$-test cannot. (See Sec. 13.2.)

*When the chi-square statistic is used to determine whether observed proportions are significantly different from theoretically expected proportions, it is usually termed the "$\chi^2$ goodness-of-fit test"*; $\chi^2$ reflects the degree to which the empirical observations "fit" the theoretical expectations. Note that in the true-false test example the expected proportion $\pi = .5$ was determined from "theory"—one-half of the choices should be "true" if the choices were made randomly. The $\chi^2$ goodness-of-fit test can assess whether any observed distribution differs from any theoretical distribution.

The chi-square goodness-of-fit test can be used to test whether a pair of dice is unbiased, whether a sample of questionnaires returned is geographically representative, whether the number of automobile fatalities differs by month or day of week, whether the percentage of extroverts varies by astrological sign, and so forth.

## 14.7
## TEST OF NORMALITY

The chi-square goodness-of-fit test can be employed to test if an empirical distribution departs significantly from the theoretical normal curve. In previous decades the test was used to legitimize the $t$-test and other tests based on the statistical assumption of normality. But since robustness studies have found that violations of this assumption have inconsequential effects on the accuracy of the probability statements about means, it is rarely used for that purpose today. Its principal use now is to address the inferential question of normality per se, not as a preliminary test for other analyses.

One of the largest representative samples of persons ever given an individual intelligence test occurred in the 1937 standardization of the Stanford-Binet Intelligence Scale. Table 14.1 gives the percentages ($P_j$) falling within ten-point intervals for the 3,184 persons. Based on the $\overline{X} = 101.8$ and $s = 16.4$ for the sample, the expected percentages ($100\pi_j$) are determined using Table A in the Appendix (see Sec. 6.5 and 6.6). The discrepancy ($P_j - 100\pi_j$) for each of the $J = 14$ categories is squared and divided by the expected percentage ($100\pi_j$), as implicit in Equation 14.8. The sum of these addends, multiplied by $n_{\bullet}/100$, determines the value of $\chi^2 = 27.39$. The critical $\chi^2$-value when $\chi^2$ is used as a test of normality has $J - 3$ degrees of freedom. In measuring the fit of any frequency distribution an additional degree of freedom is lost for each parameter that is estimated from the sample; here the mean and standard deviation had to be estimated and thus two additional degrees of freedom were lost. In Table 14.1 there are fourteen categories, thus $\nu = J - 3 = 11$; from Table D in the Appendix, ${}_{.95}\chi^2_{11} = 19.68$ and thus $H_0$ is not tenable ($p < .05$). (Indeed $H_0$ can be rejected at the .01 level since ${}_{.99}\chi^2_{11} = 24.72$.) The distribution is slightly leptokurtic; the index of kurtosis (see Sec. 6.9) is .5.* The

*That is, very similar to a $t$-distribution with $\nu = 16$ (see Table C in the Appendix).

**TABLE 14.1 The Chi-Square Goodness-of-Fit Test Employed as a Test for Normality Using Stanford-Binet IQ Scores (Data From Terman and Merrill, 1973, p. 18).**

| *IQ Category* | *Observed* $P_j$ | *Theoretically Expected* $100\pi_j$ | $P_j - 100\pi_j$ | $(P_j - 100\pi_j)^2$ | $\frac{(P_j - 100\pi_j)^2}{100\pi_j}$ |
|---|---|---|---|---|---|
| 160–169 | .03 | .027 | .003 | .000009 | .00033 |
| 150–159 | .2 | .15 | .05 | .0025 | .01667 |
| 140–149 | 1.1 | .89 | .21 | .0441 | .04955 |
| 130–139 | 3.1 | 3.5 | –.4 | .16 | .04571 |
| 120–129 | 8.2 | 9.5 | –1.3 | 1.69 | .17789 |
| 110–110 | 18.1 | 17.9 | .2 | .04 | .00223 |
| 100–109 | 23.5 | 23.7 | –.2 | .04 | .00169 |
| 90–99 | 23.0 | 21.8 | 1.2 | 1.44 | .06606 |
| 80–89 | 14.5 | 14.0 | .5 | .25 | .01786 |
| 70–79 | 5.6 | 6.3 | –.7 | .49 | .07778 |
| 60–69 | 2.0 | 1.95 | .05 | .0025 | .00128 |
| 50–59 | .4 | .42 | –.02 | .0004 | .00095 |
| 40–49 | .2 | .06 | .14 | .0196 | .32667 |
| 30–39 | .03 | .007 | .023 | .00053 | .07557 |
| | | | | | $.86024 = \sum \frac{(P_j - 100\pi_j)^2}{100\pi_j}$ |

$$\chi^2 = \frac{n_{\bullet}}{100} \sum \frac{(P_j - 100\pi_j)^2}{100\pi_j}$$

$$= \frac{3184}{100}(.86024) = 27.39.$$

$$_{.99}\chi^2_{11} = 24.72, \quad p < .01$$

empirical tails are larger than the tails of the true normal curve; there are more extreme scores than in a perfect normal distribution. Even though the discrepancies are small, they are great enough to allow the normality assumption to be rejected since the very large sample ensures high power even for relatively small departures from normality.*

## 14.8 TESTING DIFFERENCES IN PROPORTIONS: THE CHI-SQUARE TEST OF ASSOCIATION†

Suppose one wishes to determine whether school superintendents, principals, and teachers differ in attitude toward some question (e.g., collective bargaining) in a given state. A

*The Kolmogorov-Smirnoff (K-S) test of goodness-of-fit is more powerful than the chi-square goodness-of-fit test when the categories can be ordered along an underlying continuum and no parameters must be estimated from the data. It is described in Hollander and Wolfe (1971) and Ostle and Mensing (1975).

†A distinction is sometimes made between a chi-square test of independence and a chi-square test of homogeneity. The latter fixes the number of observations sampled within a category; the former classifies observations into categories after a sample has been drawn. The computation and practical interpretation of both procedures is identical. We use the "$\chi^2$ test of association" to subsume both types and will not distinguish between them.

random sample of forty superintendents, sixty principals, and 200 teachers is drawn. The results are given in the *contingency table* (Table 14.2); (the cross-tabulation of the frequencies for the combinations of categories of two variables is known as a contingency table). If a table has $R$ rows and $C$ columns, it is described as an $R$-by-$C$ contingency table. For example, Table 14.2 would be described as a "2-by-3" contingency table.

Do the attitudes toward collective bargaining differ among the three groups? The frequency in each cell in Table 14.2 can be divided by the number of observations in that column $n_{\bullet c}$ to find the proportion $p_{rc}$ of the observations in each column that fall into each row. For example, $n_{11}/n_{\bullet 1} = \frac{10}{40} = .25$ of the superintendents (column 1) favored collective bargaining—hence, the observed proportion $p_{11}$ for the cell is .25.

Likewise, the observed proportion of superintendents opposing the issue $p_{21}$ is $\frac{30}{40} = .75$. The observed proportions of the persons in each column (group) that fall into each cell is shown in parentheses in Table 14.2. Notice also that the row totals $n_{r\bullet}$ have been divided by $n_{\bullet\bullet}$ (the total number of all observations) to give the proportion of the observations that falls into each row: these bracketed proportions in Table 14.2 are *ex-*

**TABLE 14.2 Hypothetical Data for 300 Educators Classified by Group and Attitude Toward Collective Bargaining with Proportions by Column**[a]

| | | *Group* | | | | |
|---|---|---|---|---|---|---|
| | | Superintendents | Principals | Teachers | Row Totals | |
| *Attitude* | Favor | $n_{11} = 10$<br>$p_{11} = (.25)$ | $n_{12} = 12$<br>$p_{12} = (.20)$ | $n_{13} = 98$<br>$p_{13} = (.49)$ | $n_{r\bullet}$<br>120 | $\hat{\pi}_{r\bullet}$<br>[.40] |
| | Oppose | $n_{21} = 30$<br>$p_{21} = (.75)$ | $n_{22} = 48$<br>$p_{22} = (.80)$ | $n_{23} = 102$<br>$p_{23} = (.51)$ | 180 | [.60] |
| | | $n_{\bullet 1} = 40$ | $n_{\bullet 2} = 60$ | $n_{\bullet 3} = 200$ | $300 = n_{\bullet\bullet}$ | |

$$\chi^2 = \sum_{r=1}^{2}\sum_{c=1}^{3} n_{\bullet c}\frac{(p_{rc} - \hat{\pi}_{r\bullet})^2}{\hat{\pi}_{r\bullet}}$$

$$\chi^2 = 40\,\frac{(.25 - .40)^2}{.40} + 40\,\frac{(.75 - .60)^2}{.60} + 60\,\frac{(.20 - .40)^2}{.40} + 60\,\frac{(.80 - .60)^2}{.60}$$

$$+ 200\,\frac{(.49 - .40)^2}{.40} + 200\,\frac{(.51 - .60)^2}{.60}$$

$$= 40\left(\frac{.0225}{.40} + \frac{.0225}{.60}\right) + 60\left(\frac{.0400}{.40} + \frac{.0400}{.60}\right) + 200\left(\frac{.0081}{.40} + \frac{.0081}{.60}\right)$$

$$= 40(.09375) + 60(.16667) + 200(.03375)$$

$$\chi^2 = 20.50,\quad {}_{.999}\chi^2_2 = 13.82,\quad p < .001$$

[a]The value of $\chi^2$ will be the same regardless of which variable is designated as column or row variable. However, interpretation is facilitated if types of persons appear as columns; for example, it is usually more meaningful to ask, "What percentage of teachers favor collective bargaining," than "Of those favoring collective bargaining, what percentage are teachers?"

*pected proportions*, $\hat{\pi}_{r\bullet}$* for each cell in the respective rows. For example, if the null hypothesis is true, the proportions (.25, .20, and .49) in the first row differ only by chance from the expected proportion for the entire first row $\hat{\pi}_{1\bullet} = .4$. In other words, is the hypothesis tenable that the observed proportions in the first row (.25, .20, and .49) do not differ significantly from .4, and hence do not differ significantly from each other; that is, can all differences among the $p$'s within rows be attributable to sampling error? If the entire population of superintendents, principals, and teachers were queried, would the proportions who favor (or oppose) the issue be equal—is $H_0: \pi_{11} = \pi_{12} = \pi_{13}$ tenable?

In the chi-square test of association (unlike the chi-square goodness-of-fit test), the parameter of any expected proportion ($\pi$) is unknown. Hence, the parameter must be estimated. The best estimate of the parameter, $\pi_{1\bullet}$ (the proportion in the population who favor collective bargaining), is obtained by finding the proportion of the $n_{\bullet\bullet}$ observations that falls into the first row: $n_{1\bullet}/n_{\bullet\bullet} = .4$ in the example). With the $\chi^2$ test of association, the symbol $\hat{\pi}$ is used rather than $\pi$, since the parameter $\pi$ is unknown and must be estimated.

The formula for the $\chi^2$ test of association for an $R \times C$ contingency table may appear formidable, but it is not:

$$\chi^2 = \sum_{r=1}^{R} \sum_{c=1}^{C} n_{\bullet c} \frac{(p_{rc} - \hat{\pi}_{r\bullet})^2}{\hat{\pi}_{r\bullet}} \qquad \textbf{(14.9)}$$

In words, Equation 14.9 states that the contribution of each of the $R \times C$ cells to the value of the chi-square statistic is the square of the discrepancy between the observed and expected proportions, $(p_{rc} - \hat{\pi}_{r\bullet})^2$, which is divided by the expected proportion ($\hat{\pi}_{r\bullet}$) and multiplied by the number of observations in the column $n_{\bullet c}$ for that cell. The sum of this result for all cells is then the $\chi^2$ statistic for the contingency table.†

In the bottom portion of Table 14.2 the chi-square statistic is computed using Equation 14.9. In the chi-square test of association the chi-square statistic has degrees of freedom equal to $(R - 1)(C - 1)$, where $R$ is the number of rows and $C$ is the number of columns. In the example $R = 2$ and $C = 3$, hence $\nu = (2 - 1)(3 - 1) = 2$. In Table D the critical $\chi^2$-value at $\alpha = .001$ is found to be 13.8, that is, ${}_{.999}\chi^2_2 = 13.8$. Since the observed $\chi^2$ is larger than 13.8, $H_0$ is rejected at the .001 level.

If $H_0$ is true, discrepancies in $p$'s and associated $\hat{\pi}$'s as large as those that were observed would occur in less than one in every 1,000 replicated studies. Therefore, the null hypothesis is rejected at .001 level, and it is concluded that there is some association between the two variables—in the example whether one favors or opposes the question being posed is *associated* with the group to which one belongs. In other words, $\chi^2$ can be viewed as a test of association or relationship between the two factors in a contingency

*Recall that the caret ("hat") above a symbol for a parameter is a common way to denote an estimate for the parameter beneath. Thus $\hat{\mu}$ and $\hat{\sigma}$ are aliases for $\overline{X}$ and $s$. In the chi-square goodness-of-fit test the parameter $\pi$ is known; in the chi-square test of association an estimator of the parameter, $\hat{\pi}$, must be used.

†Equation 14.9, using percentages instead of proportions, becomes

$$\chi^2 = \sum_{r=1}^{R} \sum_{c=1}^{C} \frac{n_{\bullet c}}{100} \frac{(P_{rc} - 100\hat{\pi}_{r\bullet})^2}{100\hat{\pi}_{r\bullet}}$$

table. If the proportions of superintendents, principals, and teachers who favored the issue had been exactly the same, the value of $\chi^2$ would have been zero. The value of $\chi^2$ increases as the observed proportions differ among the groups being contrasted.

But does the significant chi-square indicate that each of the three groups differs significantly from the other two groups? Not at all. For example, teachers may differ significantly from principals and superintendents, but principals and superintendents may not differ. Procedures for making comparisons between two or more groups are called *multiple comparisons*. Procedures for making multiple comparisons among proportions are given in Section 17.23. In fact, the data in Table 14.2 are used in Section 17.23 to illustrate the technique. Teachers are found to differ significantly from both groups of administrators, but the principals do not differ significantly from the superintendents.*

When the data in a contingency table are given in frequencies and there is no need to convert these to proportions, the $\chi^2$-statistic can be computed directly and more expediently from $n$'s as defined in Equation 14.10.

$$\chi^2 = n_{\bullet\bullet} \left[ \sum_{r=1}^{R} \sum_{c=1}^{C} \frac{n_{rc}^2}{n_{r\bullet} n_{\bullet c}} - 1 \right] \tag{14.10}$$

where $n_{rc}$ is the number of observations in the ($rc$th cell of the contingency table; $n_{r\bullet}$ is the number of observations in the $r$th row of the table; $n_{\bullet c}$ is the number of observations in the $c$th column of the table; and $n_{\bullet\bullet}$ = the total number of observations. When $R = C = 2$, Equation 14.10 simplifies to

$$\chi^2 = \frac{n_{\bullet\bullet}(n_{11}n_{22} - n_{12}n_{21})^2}{n_{1\bullet}n_{2\bullet}n_{\bullet 1}n_{\bullet 2}} \tag{14.11}$$

Its use will be illustrated in Table 14.3.†

An alternative and mathematically equivalent test of equal proportions in two independent populations in 2 X 2 contingency tables is the $z$-test:

$$z \doteq \frac{p_{11} - p_{12}}{\sqrt{\hat{\pi}_{1\bullet}(1 - \hat{\pi}_{1\bullet})\left(\frac{1}{n_{\bullet 1}} + \frac{1}{n_{\bullet 2}}\right)}}$$

*It is not wise to pursue the topic of multiple comparisons among proportions until other basic concepts pertaining to them are developed. See also Goodman (1978) and Reynolds (1977).

†Until recently, it was thought that $\chi^2$ should not be used unless the *minimum* expected frequencies (i.e., $nP_e$) were five or more in each cell. Roscoe and Byars (1971, 1979), Conover (1974), and Camilli and Hopkins (1977, 1979) have shown that the $\chi^2$-statistic works well even when the *average* expected frequency is as low as 2. (Note that *average* expected frequency is less restrictive than *minimum* expected frequency.) In addition Camilli and Hopkins (1977) found that the Yates "correction for continuity" that is usually recommended for 2 X 2 $\chi^2$ tests of independence is not only unnecessary, but causes the already conservative values for $\alpha$ to be even more conservative. Fisher's exact probability test for 2 X 2 contingency tables with very small expected frequencies is often recommended, but is unnecessary since the $\chi^2$-test of association gives accurate probability statements even with very small $n$'s (Camilli and Hopkins, 1979).

**TABLE 14.3. Computational Illustration of the $\chi^2$ Median Test**

| | Males | Females | Row Totals |
|---|---|---|---|
| Above median | $n_{11} = 4$ | $n_{12} = 15$ | $n_{1\bullet} = 19$ |
| Below median | $n_{21} = 8$ | $n_{22} = 17$ | $n_{2\bullet} = 25$ |
| Column totals | $n_{\bullet 1} = 12$ | $n_{\bullet 2} = 32$ | $n_{\bullet\bullet} = 44$ |

Equation 14.10: $$\chi^2 = n_{\bullet\bullet}\left[\sum_{r=1}^{2}\sum_{c=1}^{2}\frac{n_{rc}^2}{n_{r\bullet}n_{\bullet c}} - 1\right]$$

$$\chi^2 = 44\left[\frac{4^2}{19(12)} + \frac{15^2}{19(32)} + \frac{8^2}{25(12)} + \frac{17^2}{25(32)} - 1\right]$$

$$= 44(.070175 + .370066 + .213333 + .361250 - 1)$$

$$= 44(1.014825 - 1)$$

$$\chi^2 = .652;\ {}_{.90}\chi^2 = 2.71,\ p > .10$$

Equation 14.11: $$\chi^2 = \frac{n_{\bullet\bullet}(n_{11}n_{22} - n_{12}n_{21})^2}{n_{1\bullet}n_{2\bullet}n_{\bullet 1}n_{\bullet 2}}$$

$$= \frac{44[4(17) - 15(8)]^2}{(19)(25)(12)(32)}$$

$$\chi^2 = .652$$

where $p_{11} = n_{11}/n_{\bullet 1}$, $p_{12} = n_{12}/n_{\bullet 2}$, and $\hat{\pi}_{1\bullet} = (n_{11} + n_{12})/n_{\bullet\bullet}$. When the $z$-test is used, $z^2 = \chi^2$ obtained from Equation 14.9 or 14.10. Notice the similarity of the $z$-test to the $t$-test for independent means (Eqs. 12.1 through 12.4). For an additional explanation see Glass and Stanley (1970, pp. 324-326).

## 14.9 THE $\chi^2$ MEDIAN TEST

The students in a beginning statistics course were asked to rate themselves (anonymously) on a 0 to 9 point scale to the degree that they considered themselves to be happy. The median for the forty-four students, that is, the grand median was 7.3. The number of males and females that rated themselves above or below the grand median is given in Table 14.3. The $\chi^2$ computation, viewing the males and females as random samples, is illustrated using Equations 14.10 and 14.11. (Since the ratings are in discrete units, there will not be precisely 50% above and below the median.)

Notice that each student appears only once; the student is either male or female and is either above or below the median. The observations are independent (see

Sec. 14.12) and the $\chi^2$ test is a valid test of whether males or females report higher or lower happiness ratings. This application of the $\chi^2$ test of association is known as the *median test* since it tests whether the medians of the groups are different. The obtained $\chi^2$ of .652 is less than the critical $\chi^2$-value with $(R-1)(C-1)=1$ degree of freedom ($_{.90}\chi_1^2 = 2.71$) hence, the null hypothesis that the two median parameters are equal cannot be rejected at the .10 level of significance. Although only 33% of the males were above the median compared to 47% of the females, the difference does not even approach significance because of the small sample size.

Of course, the *t*-test could have been used to compare attitude scale means; indeed, the *t*-test is considerably more powerful (i.e., more likely to detect differences in the parameters) than the $\chi^2$ median test. But the median test is much faster to compute and is often used as a quick preliminary check. In addition the median test is not limited to two groups as is the *t*-test. It is like the analysis of variance (Chap. 16) in that any number of groups can be compared simultaneously, that is, $H_0: \pi_1 = \pi_2 = \ldots = \pi_J$ can be evaluated with a single omnibus test.

## 14.10 CHI-SQUARE AND THE PHI COEFFICIENT

The value of $\chi^2$ is greatly influenced by $\nu$ and $n$, hence its numerical value is essentially useless as a measure of the degree of association between the two variables of a contingency table. But in a 2 X 2 contingency table, the chi-square test statistic for a test of association can be easily converted to its close relative, the phi coefficient, $r_\phi$ (see Sec. 7.16), as given in Equation 14.12:

$$r_\phi = \sqrt{\frac{\chi^2}{n}} \qquad \textbf{(14.12)}$$

where $n$ is the total number of observations in the contingency table. For example, if in the 2 X 2 contingency in Table 14.3 containing forty-four observations, $\chi^2 = .652$, then $r_\phi = \sqrt{.652/44} = \sqrt{.0148} = .12$.

Notice how easily Equation 14.10 is converted into a test of significance for $r_\phi$, $H_0: \rho_\phi = 0$.

$$\chi^2 = nr_\phi^2 \qquad \textbf{(14.13)}$$

Thus in Table 7.9, in which $r_\phi = .546$ and $n = 400$, from Equation 14.11, $\chi^2 = (400)(.546)^2 = 119.25$. The critical value at $\alpha = .001$ from Table D, $_{.999}\chi_1^2 = 10.83$; therefore $H_0: \rho_\phi = 0$ can be confidently rejected at the .001 level.*

*The degree of association between two measures, each with two or more levels, can be decribed by another close relative of the chi-square statistic, the *coefficient of contingency*, *C*:

$$C = \sqrt{\frac{\chi^2}{n + \chi^2}}$$

## 14.11 INDEPENDENCE OF OBSERVATIONS

The $\chi^2$-statistic can be used with any contingency table in which each observation is independent from the other observations. "Independence" in this context means that each observation qualifies for one and only one cell–that is, the categories are mutually exclusive, and there is only one entry per observation unit. The most common observational unit in educational and psychological research is a person. If some persons in Table 14.2 were both teachers and principals (as is the case in very small schools), the observations would not be completely independent. To be entirely independent, the 300 observations represented in Table 14.2 must be on 300 different persons.

Suppose a questionnaire of ten items on attitude toward school was administered to a sample of fifty elementary and fifty secondary school students. Each student responded with a positive or negative response to each of the ten questions. One could legitimately tally the responses separately for each question and apply the chi-square test of independence to see if there were a difference in the responses for elementary versus secondary school students. But the ten contingency tables could not be aggregated into a composite table of 1,000 "cases" since each person would be represented ten times–the observations would not be independent. The dependence would seriously affect the probability of a type-I error. One could, however, compare the two groups of students by obtaining each student's score on the set of ten questions, then employ the median test (Sec. 14.9), or the $t$-test (Sec. 12.2).

## 14.12 INFERENCES ABOUT $\pi_1 = \pi_2$ WHEN OBSERVATIONS ARE PAIRED*

Suppose a group of persons is asked a question to which each person answers "Yes" or "No." Some time later the same question is repeated to the same persons. In determining if the proportion responding "Yes" has changed, it is clear that the observations are correlated and that the chi-square test of association as described in Section 14.8 is inappropriate in this case.

The hypotheses to be tested are identical to those in Section 14.8, namely, $H_0$: $\pi_1 = \pi_2$ against $H_1$: $\pi_1 \neq \pi_2$. As with all techniques involving dependent samples, it is possible to establish "pairs" of observations, one member of each pair from sample 1 and the other member from sample 2. Thus samples 1 and 2 could comprise matched pairs, twin mates, "before" and "after" observations, and so on. The most frequent application of the procedures in this section is to problems in which samples 1 and 2 are the same group of persons observed at two different points in time. The number of persons "scoring" 1 on the dichotomous variable, that is, having the characteristic being observed, at time 1 is $n_{1\bullet}$ and $p_1 = n_{1\bullet}/n_{\bullet\bullet}$; at time 2, $n_{\bullet 2}$ persons have the characteristic, and $p_2 = n_{\bullet 2}/n_{\bullet\bullet}$.

Such data can be tabulated in a 2 X 2 contingency table, as shown in Figure 14.4.

*The techniques presented in this section are from McNemar (1947).

| | | Time 2: 0 | Time 2: 1 | |
|---|---|---|---|---|
| Time 1 | 1 | $a$ | $b$ | $n_{1\bullet}$ |
| | 0 | $c$ | $d$ | $n_{2\bullet}$ |
| | | $n_{\bullet 1}$ | $n_{\bullet 2}$ | $n_{\bullet\bullet}$ |

**FIGURE 14.4**
**2 × 2 contingency table for correlated proportions.**

For example, $b$ might be the number of persons who possess the characteristic being observed at both times 1 and 2.

The $\chi^2$ test statistic can be used to test $H_0$ against $H_1$:

$$\chi^2 = \frac{(d - a)^2}{d + a} \tag{14.14}$$

The critical values against which $\chi^2$ from Eq. 14.14 is compared in testing $H_0$ at the $\alpha$-level of significance is the chi-square distribution with $\nu = 1$ Suppose a sample of $n = 60$ persons is asked to indicate whether or not they approve of capital punishment both before and after being exposed to a film dealing with capital punishment. The data obtained are tabulated.

| | | *Before*: No | *Before*: Yes | Row Totals |
|---|---|---|---|---|
| *After* | Yes | $a = 13$ | $b = 20$ | $33 = n_{1\bullet}$ |
| | No | $c = 23$ | $d = 4$ | $27 = n_{2\bullet}$ |
| | | $n_{\bullet 1} = 36$ | $n_{\bullet 2} = 24$ | $60 = n_{\bullet\bullet}$ |

Notice that twenty-four of the sixty persons ($p_1 = \frac{24}{60} = .40$) approved of capital punishment prior to the film, whereas the proportion increased to $\frac{33}{60} = .55 = p_2$ after the film. Is the change statistically significant or does $H_0$: $\pi_1 = \pi_2$ remain tenable? From Equation 14.14.

$$\chi^2 = \frac{(d - a)^2}{d + a} = \frac{(4 - 13)^2}{4 + 13} = \frac{(-9)^2}{17} = 4.76$$

Since the observed chi-square value of 4.76 is larger than the associated critical value (Table D) of $3.84 = {}_{.95}\chi_1^2$, the null hypothesis is rejected at the .05 level.

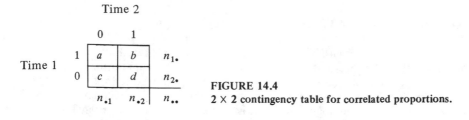

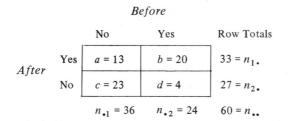

The significance test of this section is a test of the significance of the *difference* between $p_1 = n_{1\bullet}/n_{\bullet\bullet}$ and $p_2 = n_{\bullet 2}/n_{\bullet\bullet}$ and not of a hypothesis about "change." Change is evaluated by the significance test presented here only as it may be reflected in the difference between $\pi_1$ and $\pi_2$. Notice that if everyone who responded "Yes" before the film changed to "No" after the film, and if twenty-four of those responding "No" initially changed to "Yes" after the film, the chi-square statistic would have been 0 even though most persons changed between the pretest and the posttest.

## CHAPTER SUMMARY

For dichotomous variables, the sample proportion $p$ estimates the population proportion $\pi$. The sampling distribution of sample proportions, $p$, is approximated by the normal curve if the sample size $n$ is large. The standard error of $p$, $\sigma_p$, can be used to establish approximate confidence intervals for the parameter $\pi$. The $z$-test can be used to test whether a sample proportion differs significantly from the hypothesized value of the parameter $\pi$. Confidence intervals about a proportion can also be estimated easily using the charts in Figures 14.2 and 14.3.

The chi-square test is used to determine whether observed proportions (or percents) differ from expected proportions (or percents). When the expected proportions are determined a priori on the basis of theory, the $\chi^2$ test is referred to as a goodness-of-fit test. It determines how well the observed proportions fit the expected proportions. The chi-square goodness-of-fit test is commonly used as a test of normality.

When the expected frequencies (proportions) are estimated from the data to be analyzed, the $\chi^2$ test is termed a test of association. It answers the question, "Are the two factors independent, or is there some degree of association or correlation between them?" In such applications the degrees of freedom for the $\chi^2$ test are the product $(R - 1)$ $(C - 1)$, where $R$ and $C$ are the numbers of rows and columns, respectively. The median test is a special application of the $\chi^2$ test of association. The magnitude of the association in $2 \times 2$ tables can be described by the phi coefficient $r_\phi$. The statistical significance of this measure of association is evaluated by the chi-square test of association.

## *MASTERY TEST*

1. If $n$ is 100, the *largest* value for $\sigma_p$ will result when $\pi =$ ____. ($\sigma_p = \sqrt{\pi(1 - \pi)/n}$; find the answer by trial and error.)
2. If $n$ is 100 and $\pi = .5$, what is the value of $\sigma_p$?
3. If one repeatedly draws random samples with $n = 100$ from a population in which 50% ($\pi = .50$) favored candidate $A$, how often would a sample in which at least 60% ($p = .60$) favored candidate $A$ be obtained?
4. In Question 3 what percentage of repeated samples would show between .45 and .55 of the respondents favoring candidate $A$?
5. If 80% of the population of voters favor a bond issue, what is the value of $\sigma_p$ for the following value of $n$?
   a. $n_1 = 25$ b. $n_2 = 100$ c. $n_3 = 400$
6. What generalization regarding the precise relationship between $n$ and $\sigma_p$ is suggested in Question 5? (*Note*: $n_2 = 4n_1$, $n_3 = 4n_2 = 16n_1$.)
7. Suppose $\sigma_p = .05$ with $n = 100$. If $n$ is reduced to 25, what will be the value of $\sigma_p$?
8. In a sample of $n = 100$ teachers, fifty preferred merit pay. Set a .95 confidence interval around the sample proportion of .50. Use Equation 14.1 and $\pm 2\sigma_p$.

9. Use Figure 14.2 to determine the .95 confidence interval in Question 8. Compare the result with that for Question 8.

10. Use Figure 14.2 to establish the .95 CI for $\pi$ if:
    a. $p = .2, n = 50$ c. $p = .6, n = 50$
    b. $p = .4, n = 50$ d. $p = .6, n = 100$

11. Other things being equal, which of the confidence intervals will span the largest range of values?
    a. .90 CI b. .95 CI c. .99 CI

12. Which one of these symbols denotes the critical value for chi-square when $\alpha = .05$ with 2 degrees of freedom?
    a. ${}_{.90}\chi^2_2$ b. ${}_{.95}\chi^2_2$ c. ${}_{.95}\chi^2$

13. Which is largest?
    a. ${}_{.90}\chi^2_1$ b. ${}_{.95}\chi^2_1$ c. ${}_{.99}\chi^2_1$

14. Which is largest?
    a. ${}_{.95}\chi^2_1$ b. ${}_{.95}\chi^2_2$ c. ${}_{.95}\chi^2_3$

15. In the $\chi^2$ goodness-of-fit test are the expected proportions known prior to the collection of data?

16. In a $2 \times 5$ $\chi^2$ test of association, the critical value with $\alpha = .01$ is symbolized by which of the following?
    a. ${}_{.99}\chi^2_1$ b. ${}_{.99}\chi^2_4$ c. ${}_{.99}\chi^2_5$ d. ${}_{.01}\chi^2_4$

17. In Table D in the Appendix, study the pattern of ${}_{.50}\chi^2$-values for various degrees of freedom. What do you observe?

18. If the $\chi^2$ goodness-of-fit test is used to test for normality, and the data are grouped into ten classes, what is the critical value with $\alpha = .05$?

19. If the data from a $3 \times 3$ contingency table yield a chi-square value of 9, is the relationship between the two variables statistically significant with $\alpha = .05$?

20. Which $\chi^2$ test should be used to see if the proportion of left-handedness were significantly different for 116 boys from that for seventy-eight girls?
    a. goodness-of-fit test b. test of association.

21. In which of the following applications can the $\chi^2$-statistic be used?
    a. to compare proportions, $H_0$: $\pi_1 = \pi_2$
    b. to determine if two categorical variables are associated
    c. to compare medians in two groups
    d. to compare medians in three or more groups

22. In a $3 \times 4$ contingency table if $H_0$ were rejected using $\chi^2$, is it possible that $p = \hat{\pi}$ in some cells?

23. If the $\chi^2$computation involves only one variable or factor (i.e., does not involve a contingency table), we can be sure that it is which of the following?
    a. a goodness-of-fit $\chi^2$ test b. a $\chi^2$ test of association

24. If $r_\phi = .20$ and $n = 100$, a. can $H_0$: $\rho_\phi = 0$ be rejected at the .05 level? b. At the .01 level?

Suppose the 120 students who want to take Algebra I during period 3 have a choice of instructors. Four different instructors are available. Suppose a $\chi^2$ is used to determine if the proportion desiring (or avoiding) certain teachers differs significantly from chance.

25. What is the expected proportion ($\pi$) for each instructor?

26. What is the critical value for $\chi^2$ with $\alpha = .05$?

27. If the computed $\chi^2$ is 15.4, could $H_0$ be rejected at the .05 level? at the .01 level? at the .001 level?

## *PROBLEMS AND EXERCISES*

1. On true-false exams, is "true" as likely to be the correct answer as "false?" In one investigation (Metfessel and Sax, 1957) examinations developed by several different instructors were studied. The following result was typical:

*Ninety Items Classified by Correct Answer*

| "True" | "False" |
|---|---|
| 55 | 35 |

   a. What is the expected proportion for each of the two categories if the keying of the items is random?
   b. Is $H_0$: $\pi_1 = \pi_2 = .5$?
   c. What is the value of $\chi^2$?
   d. What is the critical value of $\chi^2$ at $\alpha = .05$?
   e. Is $H_0$ rejected at $\alpha = .05$?
   f. Is $H_0$ rejected at $\alpha = .01$?
   g. Set a .95 CI for $\pi_1$ (proportion "true").

2. Is the correct answer on a multiple-choice exam more likely to be in one response position than another? The following table gives the position for the correct answer for 100 items on the adult level of the Lorge-Thorndike Intelligence Test (Verbal):

*Item Classified by Position of Correct Option*

| Position | 1 | 2 | 3 | 4 | 5 | Total |
|---|---|---|---|---|---|---|
| Frequency | 16 | 24 | 25 | 21 | 14 | 100 |

   a. Convert the observed frequencies to observed percentages.
   b. What are the expected percentages ($100\pi_j$) for all five cells? (Or, $H_0$: $100\pi_j = ?$)
   c. Compute $\chi^2$ using percents.
   d. What are the degrees of freedom of this chi-square test?
   e. What is the critical value for $\chi^2$ at $\alpha = .05$?
   f. Is $H_0$ tenable?

3. A grouped frequency distribution of the scores of fifty-four introductory statistics students on a midterm examination ($\overline{X} = 70.49$, $s = 14.39$) is given. Viewing the scores as a sample representing a larger population, is the assumption of normality in the population of scores tenable at $\alpha = .10$?

| *Interval* | *Frequency* | *Observed Proportion p* | *Expected[a] Proportion π* |
|---|---|---|---|
| 90%– | 3 | .056 | ___ |
| 80%–89% | 14 | .259 | ___ |
| 70%–79% | 12 | .222 | ___ |
| 60%–69%' | 12 | .222 | .248 |
| 50%–59% | 9 | .167 | .152 |
| 40%–49% | 3 | .056 | .056 |
| 30%–39% | 0 | .000 | .014 |
| 20%–29% | 1 | .019 | .002 |

[a]Recall (Sec. 4.3) that the lower limit of the 90%-interval is 89.5%.

4. A classic study by Hartshorne and May (1928) investigated the relationship between pupil's socioeconomic status (SES) and cheating in school. The results are given for a sample of 400 children classified by SES and cheating.

| | | *SES* | | | |
|---|---|---|---|---|---|
| | | Lower | Middle | Higher | Row Totals |
| *Cheated* | Yes | 28 | 72 | 37 | $137 = n_{1\bullet}$ |
| | No | 16 | 71 | 176 | $263 = n_{2\bullet}$ |
| | Column Totals | $n_{\bullet 1} = 44$ | $n_{\bullet 2} = 143$ | $n_{\bullet 3} = 213$ | $400 = n_{\bullet\bullet}$ |

a. Can $H_0$ be stated as $H_0$: $\pi_1 = \pi_2 = \pi_3$?
b. Compute the "expected proportion" of cheating and not cheating.
c. Construct a table that gives the observed proportions ($p$'s) of each of the three SES groups who did and did not cheat.
d. What is the value of $\chi^2$?
e. Can $H_0$ be rejected at $\alpha = .001$?
f. Conclusion?
g. Determine the .95 confidence intervals for the proportion cheating in the lower and higher SES groups using Figure 14.2.

5. In a study of 1,405 high school and college students A study found the following relationships between religious participation and the question, "How happy has your home life been?" Observed percentages are given for each cell.

| | | *Participation in Religious Activities* | | | | |
|---|---|---|---|---|---|---|
| | | Not at all | Very little | Somewhat | Very much | Row Totals |
| *Answer to "How Happy has your Home Life Been"?* | Very happy | 105 (50%) | 257 (59%) | 368 (68%) | 151 (70%) | 881 [63%] |
| | Fairly happy | 78 (38%) | 149 (34%) | 153 (28%) | 52 (24%) | 432 [31%] |
| | Unhappy | 25 (12%) | 30 (7%) | 24 (4%) | 13 (6%) | 92 [7%] |
| | Column Totals | 208 | 436 | 545 | 216 | $1405 = n_{\bullet\bullet}$ |

a. What is the critical $\chi^2$-value at $\alpha = .001$?
b. Can $H_0$ be rejected with $\alpha = .001$?
c. Conclusion?

6. A large groups of men who smoked twenty or more cigarettes daily were compared with an equal number of similar men who had never smoked regularly (Hammond, 1964). The number of deaths during the following three-year period was more than twice as great among the smokers. Use Equation 14.11 and test the null hypothesis using the following data.

| | Smokers | Nonsmokers | Row Totals |
|---|---|---|---|
| Deaths | 1,385 | 662 | 2,047 |
| Living | 35,590 | 36,313 | 71,903 |
| Column Totals | 36,975 | 36,975 | 73,950 |

7. Based on 1,000 men within each group, the numbers of deaths within various age groups are given. Does the proportion of deaths differ among the four age groups? Use Equation 14.10

| | 40's | 50's | 60's | 70's | Row Totals |
|---|---|---|---|---|---|
| Smokers | 30 | 75 | 157 | 337 | 599 |
| Nonsmokers | 10 | 34 | 85 | 199 | 328 |
| Column Totals | 40 | 109 | 242 | 536 | 927 |

8. Using the data in Problem 6 following Chapter 3, determine whether the incidence of the eighty-seven suicide calls was significantly related to menstrual cycle. Use Eq. 14.8.

9. A sample of sixty-nine teachers (twenty-nine Caucasian and forty Black) were asked whether they perceived "poor children" to be generally responsible or irresponsible. A phi coefficient of correlation was calculated between the race of the teacher, $X$, and the teacher's perception of "poor children," $Y$. A value of $\phi = .24$ seemed to indicate a weak relationship between the variables. Caucasian teachers tended to perceive "poor children" as irresponsible more than did Black teachers. Using the techniques of Section 14.10, test the hypothesis at the .05 level of significance that in the population of teachers sampled "teacher's race" and "perception of 'poor children' as irresponsible" are uncorrelated.

10. In one study the relationship between student behavior and barometric pressure under conditions of high relative humidity was investigated. Four hundred thirteen classrooms were divided among three different *barometric pressures* (high, medium, low) and the teachers classified the *behavior of the class* as either normal, "squirmy," lethargic, or hyperactive.

| | | *Barometric Pressure* | | | |
|---|---|---|---|---|---|
| | | Low | Medium | High | Totals |
| *Class behavior* | Hyperproductive | 30 | 34 | 5 | 69 |
| | "Squirmy" | 79 | 39 | 16 | 134 |
| | Normal | 60 | 97 | 23 | 180 |
| | Lethargic | 13 | 15 | 2 | 30 |
| | Totals | 182 | 185 | 46 | 413 |

Using the chi-square test in Section 14.8, test the null hypothesis at the .05 level of significance that *barometric pressure* and class behavior are independent in the population of classrooms sampled.

11. Dyson (1967) studied the relationship between pupils' self-concepts (above average versus below average) and whether they were members of a homogeneous or hetrogeneous (with respect to classroom) group. The following data were obtained from a sample $n = 568$ seventh-grade pupils:

| | Homogeneous | Heterogeneous | Totals |
|---|---|---|---|
| Above | 137 | 159 | 296 |
| Below | 108 | 164 | 272 |
| Totals | 245 | 323 | 568 |

Use the $\chi^2$ median test to test the null hypothesis of independence of self-concept and classroom grouping in the population sampled at both the .10 and .05 levels of significance.

12. Use Equation 7.16 to determine the correlation $r_\phi$ between the attitudes, before and after the film, in the 2 X 2 contingency table in Section 14.12. Is $H_0: \rho_\phi = 0$ tenable at the .05 level?

## *ANSWERS TO MASTERY TEST*

1. For any value of $n$, the largest value of $\sigma_p$ occurs at $\pi = .5$.
2. $\sigma_p = \sqrt{\dfrac{(.5)(.5)}{100}} = .05$
3. $p = \pi + 2\sigma_p = .50 + 2(.05) = .60$ or $z = 2$, hence in approximately 2% of the samples, the observed $p$ would equal or exceed .60.
4. Approximately 68%, $(\pi \pm \sigma_p)$
5. $\sigma_p = \sqrt{\dfrac{(.8)(.2)}{n}} = \dfrac{.4}{\sqrt{n}}$
   a. $\sigma_p = \dfrac{.4}{5} = .08$
   b. $\sigma_p = \dfrac{.4}{10} = .04$
   c. $\sigma_p = \dfrac{.4}{20} = .02$
6. If $n$ is quadrupled, $\sigma_p$ is reduced by half.
7. $\sigma_p = .10$
8. .95 CI = .5 ± 2(.05) = .4 to .6
9. .95 CI = .4 to .6 (same result as in Question 8)
10. a. Approximately .10 to .35
    b. Approximately .27 to .55
    c. Approximately .45 to .73
    d. Approximately .50 to .70
11. c
12. b
13. c
14. c
15. Yes
16. b
17. The value of ${}_{.50}\chi^2$ (the median in the $\chi^2$-distribution) is approximately equal to the corresponding *df*-value, especially as *df* increases.
18. ${}_{.95}\chi^2_7 = 14.07$
19. No, $p > .05$; ${}_{.95}\chi^2_4 = 9.49$
20. b
21. In all four (a-d)
22. Yes
23. a
24. a. Yes, $\chi^2 = 100(.2)^2 = 4.0 > 3.84 = {}_{.95}\chi^2_1$
    b. No, ${}_{.99}\chi^2_1 = 6.64$
25. $\pi = \dfrac{30}{120} = .25$
26. ${}_{.95}\chi^2_3 = 7.82$
27. Yes, $15.4 > 7.82$; yes, $15.4 > 11.3$; no, $15.4 < 16.3 = {}_{.999}\chi^2_3$; $.01 > p > .001$

## *ANSWERS TO PROBLEMS AND EXERCISES*

1. a. $\pi_1 = \pi_2 = .5$
   b. yes
   c. $\chi^2 = n_\bullet \sum \dfrac{(p_j - \pi)^2}{\pi}$

$$= 90\left[\frac{(.611 - .50)^2}{.50} + \frac{(.389 - .50)^2}{.50}\right]$$

$$= 90\left[\frac{(.111)^2}{.50} + \frac{(.111)^2}{.50}\right]$$

$$= 90(.0493) = 4.44$$

   d. ${}_{.95}\chi^2_1 = 3.84$
   e. yes, since $4.44 > 3.84$, $p < .05$
   f. no: ${}_{.99}\chi^2_1 = 6.63$; $.05 > p > .01$;
   g. (.51, .71)

2. a. Since $n_\bullet = 100$, the observed frequencies are also the observed percentages.
   b. $H_0$: $100\pi = 20$
   c. $\chi^2 = \dfrac{n_\bullet}{100} \sum \dfrac{(P - 100\pi)^2}{100\pi}$

$$= \frac{\cancel{100}}{\cancel{100}} \times \left[\frac{(16-20)^2}{20} + \frac{(24-20)^2}{20} + \frac{(25-20)^2}{20} + \frac{(21-20)^2}{20} + \frac{(14-20)^2}{20}\right]$$

$$= \left[\frac{(4)^2 + (4)^2 + (5)^2 + (1)^2 + (6)^2}{20}\right]$$

$$= \frac{16 + 16 + 25 + 1 + 36}{20} = \frac{94}{20}$$

$= 4.70$

d. $\nu = J - 1 = 5 - 1 = 4$

e. ${}_{.95}\chi^2_4 = 9.49$

f. yes: $p > .05$

3. $$\chi^2 = 54\left[\frac{(.056 - .093)^2}{.093} + \frac{(.259 - .171)^2}{.171} + \ldots + \frac{(0 - .014)^2}{.014} + \frac{(.019 - .002)^2}{.002}\right]$$

$= 12.39 > 9.24 = {}_{.90}\chi^2_2$; Normality assumption is not tenable.

4. a. Yes, that is in the three populations, there is no difference in the proportions who would cheat—the differences among $p_1$, $p_2$, and $p_3$ are attributable to random sampling error.

b. cheating: $137/400 = .34$; not cheating: $263/400 = .66$

c.

| | SES | | | |
|---|---|---|---|---|
| Cheated? | L | M | H | Row Totals |
| | proportions | | | $\hat{\pi}$ |
| Yes | (.64) | (.50) | (.17) | [.34] |
| No | (.36) | (.50) | (.83) | [.66] |
| $n_{\bullet c}$ | 44 | 143 | 213 | 400 |

d. $$\chi^2 = \sum n_{\bullet c} \frac{(p - \hat{\pi}_e)^2}{\hat{\pi}}$$

$$= 44\frac{(.64 - .34)^2}{.34} + 44\frac{(.36 - .66)^2}{.66} + 143\frac{(.16)^2}{.34} + 143\frac{(-.16)^2}{.66} + 213\frac{(-.17)^2}{.34} + 213\frac{(.17)^2}{.66} = 44(.265 + .136)$$

$+ 143(.075 + .039) + 213(.085 + .044) = 17.644 + 16.302 + 27.477\ \chi^2 = 61.4$

e. yes: $\chi^2 = 61.4 > 13.8 = {}_{.999}\chi^2_2$, $p < .001$

f. There is a significant relationship between SES and cheating—the proportion of children who cheated was least for higher SES and greatest for lower SES.

g. lower: approximately .48 to .79; higher: .11 to .23

5. a. ${}_{.999}\chi^2_6 = 22.46$

b. $\chi^2 = 34.83 > 22.46$, $p < .001$

c. There was a positive relationship between amount of participation in religious activities and self-rated happiness of home life.

6. $\chi^2 = 262.6$, $p < .001$

7. No, $\chi^2 = 3.44$, $p > .10$, ${}_{.90}\chi^2_3 = 6.25$

8. $\chi^2 = 31.17$; $p > .001$, ${}_{.999}\chi^2_6 = 225$

9. $\chi^2 = 69(.24^2) = 3.97$, ${}_{.95}\chi^2_1 = 3.84$; reject $H_0$ at .05 level.

10. The obtained value of $\chi^2$ is 24.6. The 95th percentile in the $\chi^2$ distribution with six degrees of freedom is 12.59. Hence, reject the null hypothesis of "no association" between the two factors of classification at the .05 level. Indeed, reject $H_0$ at the .001 level since ${}_{.999}\chi^2_6 = 22.46$.

11. The obtained value of $\chi^2$ is approximately 2.50. The 90th and 95th percentiles in the $\chi^2$ distribution with one degree of freedom are 2.71 and 3.84, respectively; hence the obtained $\chi^2$ is nonsiginificant at the .10 ( and .05) level.

12. No, $r_\phi = .465$, $\chi^2 = 12.97$, $p < .001$.

# 15

# INFERENCES AMONG CORRELATION COEFFICIENTS

## 15.1 TESTING A STATISTICAL HYPOTHESIS REGARDING $\rho$

How does one decide whether a sample correlation coefficient, $r$, is significantly greater than zero—how is $H_0: \rho = 0$ tested? Suppose a sample of 200 persons was selected for the purpose of investigating the relationship between two variables, for example, anxiety and creativity. Measures are chosen for both variables; both measures are normally distributed. There is reason to believe that the sample is from a population in which the variables "anxiety" and "creativity" have a *bivariate normal distribution*.* This is an assumption that will not be tested explicitly even though it could be. Interest centers on $\rho$, the Pearson product-moment correlation between anxiety and creativity in the population.

Reasoning will proceed inductively from the sample ($r$) to the population ($\rho$)—a decision will be made about a hypothesis that asserts $\rho$ is a particular number. Partly out of habit, partly because of tradition, and partly because it is a sensible choice,† the hy-

*The bivariate normal distribution is described and illustrated in Section 7.10.

†The good sense in hypothesizing that $\rho = 0$ is at least twofold: (1) $\rho = 0$ is the midpoint between positive and negative correlations; (2) zero correlations between variables are particularly important—they indicate that the two variables are independent.

pothesis $H_0: \rho = 0$, will be tested, that is, the correlation between creativity and anxiety in the population is zero. *Our statistical hypothesis is a null hypothesis.* On the basis of the observed $r$ from the random sample of pupils, we will decide either to accept this hypothesis as tenable or to reject it as untenable.

What constitutes a sensible test of the hypothesis $H_0: \rho = 0$ in this situation? Should one compute $r$ for this sample and decide that $H_0$ is true if $r$ is zero or that $H_0$ is false if $r$ is not zero? Obviously not; too much is known about the erratic behavior of sample estimates (i.e., sampling error) to use such a plan. It is quite possible for $\rho$ to equal 0 in the population and for $r$ to be substantially different from 0 in a sample. In fact if $\rho = 0$, it is not even an impossibility that a sample will yield an $r$ of .5, .6, or even .9! Such $r$'s are extremely improbable when $\rho = 0$ unless $n$ is very small, but they are within the realm of possibility. This presents a perplexing problem. Even if $\rho = 0$ in the population, any value of $r$ from $-1$ to $+1$ is a "possibility" (i.e., has probability greater than zero) in a random sample of observations. Consequently, regardless of the value of $r$ for the sample, one cannot with absolute certainty conclude that $\rho$ is, or is not, zero. This important principle underlies all tests of statistical hypotheses: *In testing any statistical hypothesis, the researcher's decision that the hypothesis is true or that it is false is never made with certainty; a risk of making an incorrect decision is always present.* The purpose of statistical hypothesis testing is to enable one to control and assess that risk.

Suppose one measures the random sample of 200 pupils on both the anxiety and creativity tests. The correlation between the scores is computed and the value of $r$ for the sample is found to be +.09.

The uncertainty in the decision about whether $H_0: \rho = 0$ is due to *sampling error.* This is a familiar concept; the entire discussion of inferential statistics has been concerned with the problem of how to handle the estimation of a parameter from a statistic that is in error to some degree. As in previous chapters, the inferential problems of hypothesis testing are approached through the concept of a sampling distribution; the basic theory is the same as in Chapters 10 and 11, but it is applied to correlation coefficients instead of means.

## 15.2 TESTING $H_0: \rho = 0$* USING THE $t$-TEST†

When $\rho = 0$, the ratio defined in Equation 15.1 has a $t$-distribution with $\nu = n - 2$ degrees of freedom.

$$t = \frac{r}{\sqrt{\dfrac{1 - r^2}{n - 2}}} \qquad \textbf{(15.1)}$$

*For testing the hypothesis in which $\rho \neq 0$, the numerator in Equation 15.1 becomes $r - \rho$.

†The $t$-test for testing $H_0: \rho = 0$ is slightly more powerful than the $z$-test, where $z = r/\sigma_r$ and $\sigma_r = 1/\sqrt{n-1}$; or, the $z$-test using the Fisher $Z$-transformation of $r$ (Eqs. 15.3 and 15.4): $z = Z/(1/\sqrt{n-3})$. For practical purposes the difference between the $z$-test and the $t$-test is negligible; the decision regarding $H_0$ would almost always be the same for both.

For example, White and Hopkins (1975) found that for 511 elementary school pupils, socioeconomic status (SES) correlated .154 with scores on the Metropolitan Achievement Tests. Is this correlation significantly larger than zero; that is, is $H_0: \rho = 0$ tenable?

$$t = \frac{.154}{\sqrt{\dfrac{1 - (.154)^2}{511 - 2}}} = \frac{.154}{\sqrt{\dfrac{.9763}{509}}} = \frac{.154}{\sqrt{.001918}} = 3.52 > 3.32 = {}_{.9995}t_{509}$$

$$p < .001$$

The critical $t$-value is found from Table C in the Appendix. Although the correlation coefficient is very small, the $r$ is significantly greater than 0 at the .001 level, because $n$ is large.

Equation 15.1 can be rearranged to yield the minimum value for which $H_0: \rho = 0$ can be rejected (i.e., the critical value of $r$) by supplying the degrees of freedom ($\nu = n - 2$) and the critical value of $t$:

$$\text{Critical } r = \frac{t}{\sqrt{t^2 + \nu}} \qquad \textbf{(15.2)}$$

where $t$ is the critical $t$.* The critical $t$ for Equation 15.2 can be easily obtained from Table C. If the value of $\nu = n - 2$ and the associated critical $t$-value for $n - 2$ degrees of freedom are substituted into Equation 15.2 the minimum $r$ necessary to reject $H_0: \rho = 0$ can be found. For example, how large must $r$ be to reject the null hypothesis at $\alpha_2 = .05$, if $n = 25$? From Table C; ${}_{.975}t_{23} = 2.07$; hence:

$$\text{Critical } r = \frac{2.07}{\sqrt{(2.07)^2 + 25 - 2}} = \frac{2.07}{\sqrt{27.285}} = \frac{2.07}{5.22} = .396$$

Hence, if $n = 25$, one does not need to compute $t$ (Eq. 15.1) since the critical value for $r$ is .396; if $|r| < .396$, $H_0$ is tenable; if $|r| > .396$, $H_0$ is rejected at $\alpha_2 = .05$. The critical values of $r$ have been graphed in Figure 15.1 for various $n$'s and $\alpha$-values. For example, if $r = .3$ and $n = 50$, $H_0: \rho = 0$ would not be rejected at $\alpha_2 = .01$ because $r = .3$ is less than .37, the critical $r$ for $n = 40$.

Notice in Figure 15.1 how the critical value of $r$ decreases as $n$ increases. This relationship explains how the correlation of .154 between SES and academic achievement observed by White and Hopkins (1975), although very low, was significant at the .001 level—the sample size was large ($n = 511$). If $n$ is large, very small values of $r$ lead to rejection of $H_0: \rho = 0$. Figure 15.1 can also be used to determine the sample size $n$ associated with a particular critical value for $r$. For example, how large a sample is required to reject $H_0: \rho = 0$ if the observed value of $r$ is .4? The null hypothesis will be rejected at $\alpha_2 = .10$, $\alpha_2 = .05$, $\alpha_2 = .01$, and $\alpha_2 = .001$ if $n$'s are 18, 25, 40, and 65, respectively.

Table J in the Appendix gives the precise critical values of $r$ for one- and two-tailed tests at various values of $\alpha$ and $n$. For example, if $n = 1{,}000$ and $r \geqslant .104$, the null hypothesis ($\rho = 0$) would be rejected at $\alpha_2 = .001$.

*More explicitly, ${}_{1-\alpha/2}r_\nu = {}_{1-\alpha/2}t_\nu / \sqrt{{}_{1-\alpha/2}t_\nu^2 + n - 2}$.

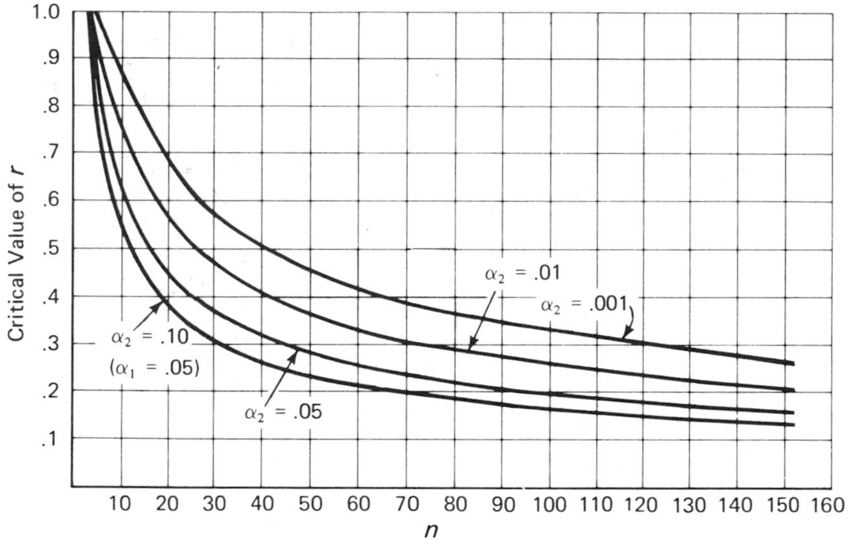


**FIGURE 15.1. Critical values of Pearson's $r$ for rejecting $H_0: p = 0$ with $\alpha_2 = .001$, $\alpha_2 = .01$, $\alpha_2 = .05$, and $\alpha_2 = .10$ ($\alpha_1 = .05$) for various sample sizes.**

## 15.3 DIRECTIONAL ALTERNATIVES: "TWO-TAILED" VERSUS "ONE-TAILED" TESTS

As with testing means, a statistical test for $H_0: \rho = 0$ can be designated as either *nondirectional* or *directional*. A nondirectional test leads to the conclusion either that $\rho > 0$ or that $\rho < 0$ when $H_0: \rho = 0$ is rejected. But if it is maintained by the investigator that if $\rho$ does not equal zero, it is greater than zero (i.e., that $\rho \geqslant 0$), a directional test is in order. The investigator believes that $\rho$ could not possibly be less than zero; the evidence will show that either $\rho$ is positive or that it is tenable to continue to hold that $\rho$ is zero.

One consequence of making a directional test is that the critical region for rejection of $H_0$ is in one tail of the sampling distribution of $r$ for $\rho = 0$. That the critical region "lies in *one* tail" of the sampling distribution of the statistic under the null hypothesis has made the term "*one-tailed test*" popular for a significance test of a directional hypothesis. This usage is somewhat ambiguous. The more precise usage is "nondirectional" versus "directional" alternative hypotheses. Notice in Figure 15.1 that if $n = 30$, $H_0: \rho = 0$ will be rejected with a nondirectional hypothesis only if $r$ is at least .36, whereas with a directional hypothesis $H_0$ can be rejected if $r \geqslant .31$ (with alpha = .05).

One should not employ directional tests thoughtlessly (Sec. 11.13). To be perfectly legitimate, for example, if $H_0$ is $\rho = 0$ and $H_1$ is $\rho > 0$, one must look the other way and refuse to budge from the conclusion that $\rho$ is zero even if a sample of 1,000 yields an $r$ of $-.9$! Once committed to testing a directional alternative, one cannot reverse position and perform a nondirectional test. However, when properly guided by sound theory or previous research, directional tests are appropriate and more powerful than nondirectional tests.

Directional tests might be justified in testing the correlations for the following pairs of variables, where expectations are strong that each pair of variables is positively correlated: reading vocabulary and speaking vocabulary; age and strength for pupils in grades one through twelve; spelling ability and IQ; musical aptitude and IQ; and socio-economic status and grade-point average.

A directional test for $H_1 : \rho > 0$ does not require knowledge that indeed $\rho > 0$; it only requires that negative values for $\rho$ can be safely regarded as unreasonable. Directional tests should not be employed when there is a reasonable possibility that the parameter $\rho$ could be either positive or negative. Unless otherwise specified, it is conventional to assume that statistical tests are nondirectional.

## 15.4
## SETTING CONFIDENCE INTERVALS ABOUT $r$: THE FISHER $Z$-TRANSFORMATION

The sampling distribution of $r$ for all values of $\rho$ other than 0 is not normal, but skewed to some degree. The correlation between verbal reasoning and numerical ability for the population of high-school students has been shown to be $\rho = .75$ (Bennett et al., 1974, p. 135).* But what if one had only a random sample of ten persons on which to estimate this parameter? If $n = 10$, the sampling distribution is neither normal nor symmetric.† Figure 15.2 illustrates the sampling distribution of $r$ with $n = 10$ from a population in which $\rho = .75$. Note from Figure 15.2 that with an $n$ of only 10 and $\rho = .75$, an $r$ of 0 or less will be observed occasionally and underestimate $\rho$ by .75 or more units! But can $r$ be overestimated by .75 unit? Since the maximum $r$ is 1.0, $r$ can exceed the parameter $\rho$ at most by .25 unit. Hence, the sampling distribution of $r$ is skewed. The more that $\rho$ differs from zero, the greater the skewness. When $\rho$ is greater than zero, the sampling distribution

FIGURE 15.2.   Sampling distribution of $r$ when $p = .75$ and $n = 10$.



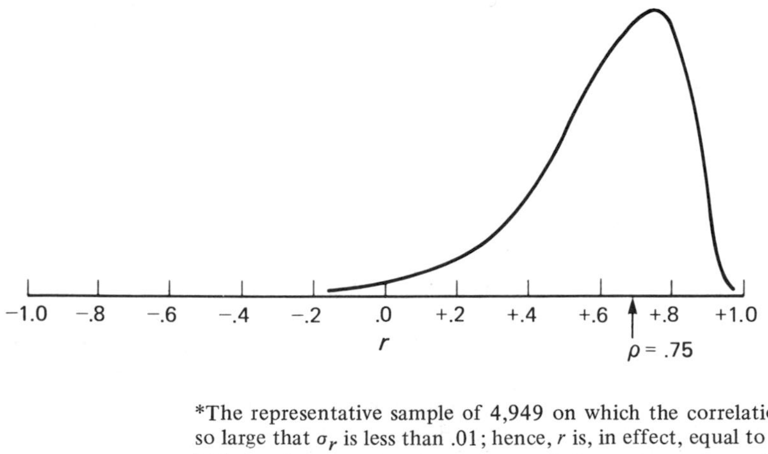

*The representative sample of 4,949 on which the correlation of about .75 was obtained is so large that $\sigma_r$ is less than .01; hence, $r$ is, in effect, equal to $\rho$ (i.e., $r = .75 \doteq \rho$).

†Obviously, this $n$ is ridiculously small for such a purpose, but the illustration was selected to illuminate the skewness in the sampling distribution.

is negatively skewed, as in Figure 15.2. When $\rho$ is negative, the situation is just the reverse, and the sampling distribution will be positively skewed. Obviously, if the sampling distribution is skewed, the common procedure for setting confidence intervals will not yield accurate limits. Fortunately, as $n$ increases the sampling distribution of $r$ rapidly become approximately normal.

R. A. Fisher devised a mathematical transformation, $Z$, of $r$ that has an approximately normal sampling distribution irrespective of $\rho$ or $n$. This transformation statistic, known as Fisher's $Z$,* is defined as one-half the natural logarithm† of the ratio given in Equation 15.3A.‡

$$|Z| = \frac{1}{2} \ln\left(\frac{1 + |r|}{1 - |r|}\right) \quad \textbf{(15.3A)}$$

Equivalently, but expressed in common logs:

$$|Z| = 1.1513 \log\left(\frac{1 + |r|}{1 - |r|}\right) \quad \textbf{(15.3B)}$$

If your calculator does not have the natural or common log function, Table E in the Appendix gives the value for $Z$ corresponding to values of $r$ from 0 to 1.00 in steps of .005. The sign of $Z$ is always the same as that of $r$. Verify from Table E that for $r$ = .395, $Z$ is .418 and that for $r$ = -.775, $Z$ is - 1.033.

Fisher showed that the sampling distribution of $Z$ for samples from a bivariate normal distribution approaches normality much more rapidly than does that of $r$. Its variance (unlike that of $r$) is essentially independent of the value of the parameter $\rho$ even if samples are not large.

Suppose a sampling distribution of $r$ were built by taking thousands of random samples each of 10 and computing $r$ for each sample. If the relationship between the two variables is bivariate normal (Sec. 7.10), the sampling distribution of the $r$'s would resemble that in Figure 15.2 if $\rho$ = .75. But if, instead of building a sampling distribution of the $r$'s, a sampling distribution of the corresponding $Z$'s were built, *the sampling distribution of the Z's would be nearly normal, with the mean equal to the parameter Z that corresponds to $\rho$—that is, $Z_\rho$.* The sampling distribution would look like the distribution in Figure 15.3. The standard error of Fisher $Z$'s is given in Equation 15.4. (Recall that standard deviations of sampling distributions are called standard errors.)

$$\sigma_Z = \frac{1}{\sqrt{n - 3}} \quad \textbf{(15.4)}$$

*Not to be confused with $z$ of the $z$-ratio or $z$-test. We will use the capital letter $Z$ when speaking of Fisher's $Z$; we will continue to use the lowercase $z$ for the $z$-test or $z$-score.

†A brief explanation of natural and common logarithms ("logs") is given in a footnote to Table 13.2.

‡Equivalently, $Z$ is the hyperbolic arctangent of $r$, that is, $Z = \tanh^{-1} r$. On most calculators with trigometric functions, $Z$ may be obtained by entering the value of $r$ (e.g., .4), pressing the "inverse" key, [INV], then pressing the [tanh] key. If for $r$ = .4, you get $Z$ = .42365, your procedures are correct. To convert $Z$ back to $r$, enter $Z$, then press the [tanh] key. On some calculators, one must use the [hyp] (for hyperbolic) and [tan⁻¹] keys to obtain $Z$ from $r$, and [hyp] [tan] to go from $Z$ to $r$.

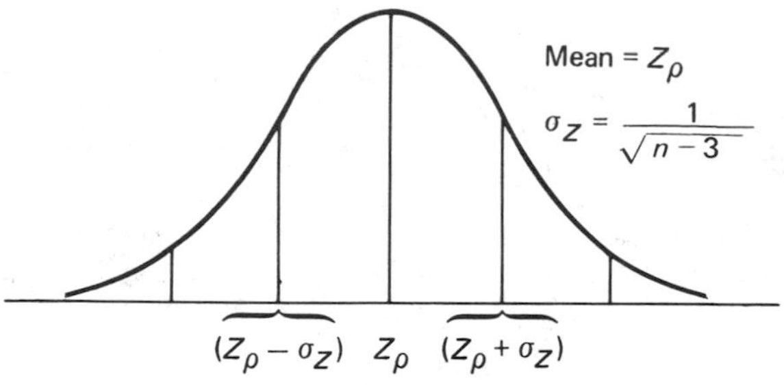


**FIGURE 15.3**
**Sampling distribution of Fisher's *Z*-transformation of *r* for random samples of size *n*.**

Fisher's $Z$-transformation provides what is needed for a solution to the problem of placing confidence intervals around $r$. The standard deviation of $Z$ over repeated random samples is $1/\sqrt{n-3}$, regardless of the value of $\rho$. Hence, 95% of the $Z$'s obtained in repeated random samples will lie within 1.96 standard deviations (a distance of $1.96\sigma_Z$) of $Z_\rho$; 99% of the $Z$'s will lie within a distance of 2.58 $\sigma_Z$ of $Z_\rho$; and so on. The distribution of $Z$ is approximately normal regardless of the size of $n$. Consequently, if $1.96\sigma_Z$ is added to $Z$ and subtracted from $Z$, the probability of capturing the parameter $Z_\rho$ within these intervals is .95. The procedure for forming .95 confidence intervals is illustrated in Figure 15.4.

To illustrate the steps outlined in Figure 15.4, one study reported an $r$ of .83 between the IQ's of thirty pairs of identical twins *reared apart*. Obviously, with $n = 30$, $r$ is not a precise estimate of $\rho$. Suppose a confidence interval with confidence coefficient .95 is desired. First, $r$ is transformed into $Z_r$ by reference to Table E (or directly using a calculator): for $r = .83$, $Z_r = 1.188$. Second, the standard error of $Z$ is found using Equation 15.4:

$$\sigma_Z = \frac{1}{\sqrt{n-3}} = \frac{1}{\sqrt{27}} = .1925$$

Third, the 95% confidence interval on $Z_\rho$ is found:

$$Z_r \pm 1.96\sigma_Z = 1.188 \pm (1.96)(.1925) = 1.188 \pm .377, \quad \text{or} \quad (.811, 1.565)$$

The interval .811 to 1.565 was generated by a process having a probability of .95 of producing an interval that captures the $Z$-transformation of $\rho$. The CI is more meaningful when expressed in units of $r$ than in Fisher $Z$-units. To accomplish this, the $Z$'s are transformed back into $r$'s.* What are the values of $r$ which correspond to $Z$'s of .811 and 1.565? A $Z$ of .811 corresponds to an $r$ of .670, and a $Z$ of 1.565 corresponds to an $r$ of .916. Therefore, the 95% confidence interval on $\rho$ extends from .670 to .916. One may feel quite confident that the value of $\rho$, the population correlation coefficient,

**FIGURE 15.4. Flowchart for setting .95 confidence intervals on *r*.**

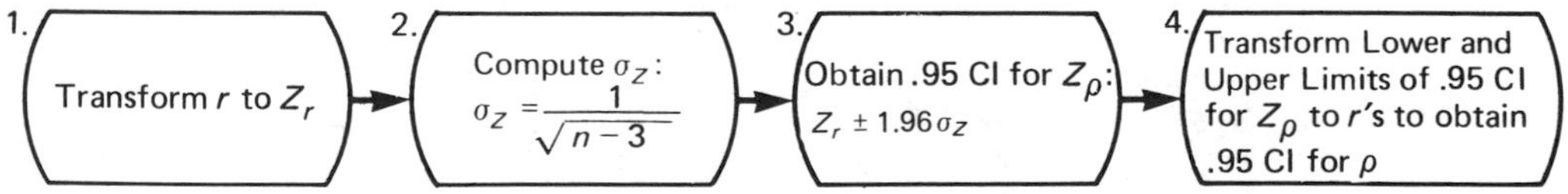


*See footnote on page 305.

is between .670 and .916. Notice that the limits of the .95 confidence interval, .670 and .916, are not equidistant from the observed $r$ of .83. This result is expected because this sampling distribution of $r$ is negatively skewed.

One study reported a correlation of .93 between IQ scores of eighty-three pairs of identical twins reared together. An $r$ of .93 corresponds to a $Z$ of 1.658. With $n = 83$, the standard error of $Z$, $\sigma_Z$, is .112; the .95 confidence interval therefore is

$$1.658 \pm 1.96\,(.112) = 1.658 \pm .220, \quad \text{or } (1.438, 1.878)$$

The transformation of the lower and upper $Z$-limits of the .95 confidence interval back to correlation coefficients yields limits on $\rho$ of .893 and .954.

## 15.5 DETERMINING CONFIDENCE INTERVALS GRAPHICALLY

If precision is not required, the limits of the .95 confidence interval for $\rho$ can be read directly from Figure 15.5. For example, if $r = .20$ with $n = 25$, enter the figure along the base axis at +.20 and read upward until the curved line for $n = 25$ is met; then read the value of that point on the vertical axis (−.21, for $r = .2$ and $n = 25$). The lower limit of the .95 confidence interval is then −.21. To find the upper limit, continue glancing upward until the other curved line for $n = 25$ is met; and again read the value on the vertical axis (+.55). The .95 confidence interval for $\rho$ with $r = .20$ and $n = 25$ extends, then, from approximately −.21 to +.55.

## 15.6 TESTING THE DIFFERENCE BETWEEN INDEPENDENT CORRELATION COEFFICIENTS: $H_0: \rho_1 = \rho_2$

Earlier, the .95 confidence intervals for $\rho$ both for identical twins reared apart and reared together were determined. But do the two $r$'s differ significantly, can the null hypothesis $H_0: \rho_1 = \rho_2$ be rejected? At such times, one is interested in hypotheses regarding *differences* in $\rho$'s. Are the IQ's of identical twins reared together correlated more highly than the IQ's of identical twins reared apart? If intellectual performance is determined solely by heredity, the $\rho$'s would be expected to be equal. To test the hypothesis, $H_0: \rho_1 = \rho_2$, the $z$-test will be employed. The $z$-test for testing the significance of the difference between independent $r$'s is given in Equation 15.5.

$$z = \frac{Z_1 - Z_2}{\sigma_{Z_1 - Z_2}} \tag{15.5}$$

where

$$\sigma_{Z_1 - Z_2} = \sqrt{\sigma^2_{Z_1} + \sigma^2_{Z_2}} = \sqrt{\frac{1}{n_1 - 3} + \frac{1}{n_2 - 3}}. \tag{15.5A}$$

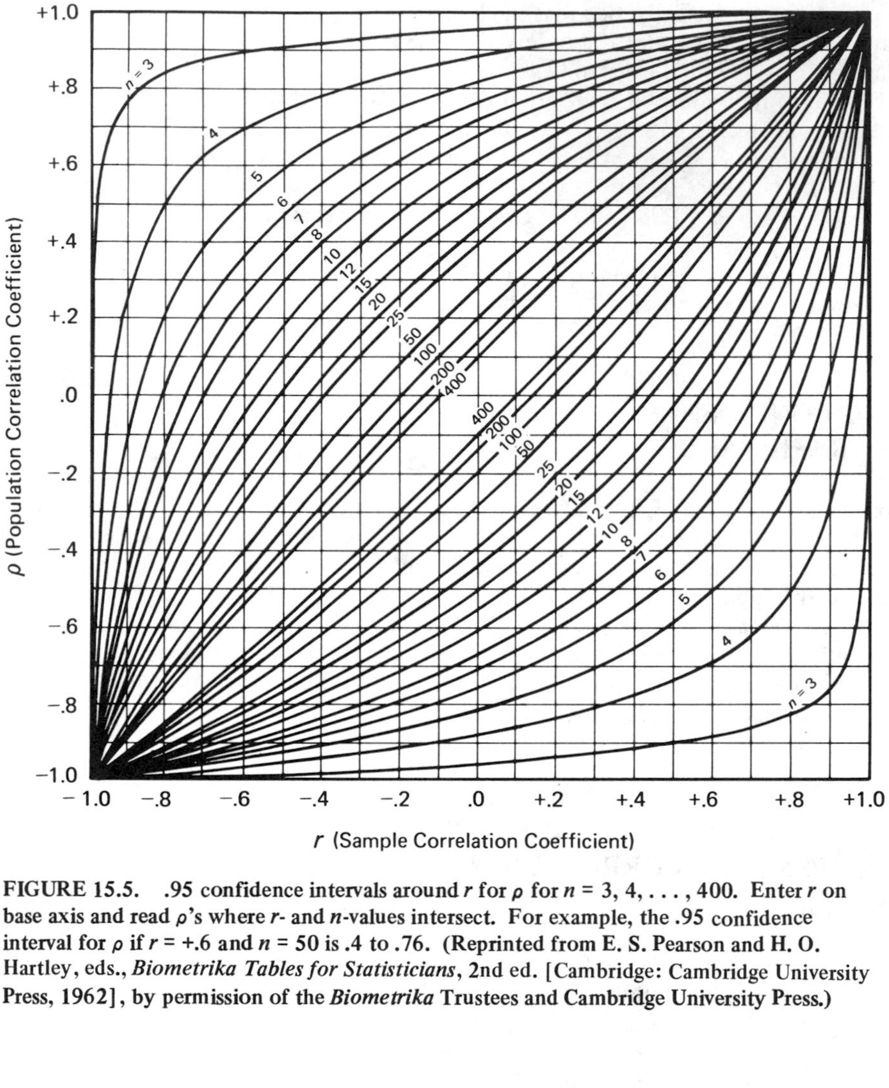


**FIGURE 15.5.** **.95 confidence intervals around $r$ for $\rho$ for $n = 3, 4, \ldots, 400$. Enter $r$ on base axis and read $\rho$'s where $r$- and $n$-values intersect. For example, the .95 confidence interval for $\rho$ if $r = +.6$ and $n = 50$ is .4 to .76. (Reprinted from E. S. Pearson and H. O. Hartley, eds., *Biometrika Tables for Statisticians*, 2nd ed. [Cambridge: Cambridge University Press, 1962], by permission of the *Biometrika* Trustees and Cambridge University Press.)**

The $r$'s for the IQ scores of identical twins reared apart and together were given in the preceding section:

| *Twins Reared Together* | *Twins Reared Apart* |
|---|---|
| $r_1 = .93$ | $r_2 = .83$ |
| $n_1 = 80$ | $n_2 = 30$ |
| $Z_1 = 1.658$ | $Z_2 = 1.188$ |
| $\sigma^2_{Z_1} = \dfrac{1}{n_1 - 3} = .0130$ | $\sigma^2_{Z_2} = \dfrac{1}{n_2 - 3} = .0370$ |

The $r$'s have been transformed to Fisher $Z$'s; the variances of the $Z$'s have been computed and the standard error of the difference in $Z$'s is determined from Equation 15.5A.

$$\sigma_{Z_1 - Z_2} = \sqrt{\sigma^2_{Z_1} + \sigma^2_{Z_2}}$$
$$= \sqrt{.0130 + .0370}$$
$$= \sqrt{.0500}$$
$$\sigma_{Z_1 - Z_2} = .2236$$

The $z$-ratio for testing $H_0: \rho_1 = \rho_2$ using Equation 15.5 is:

$$z = \frac{Z_1 - Z_2}{\sigma_{Z_1 - Z_2}} = \frac{1.658 - 1.188}{.2236} = \frac{.470}{.2236} = 2.10$$

The $z$-ratio 2.10 is compared with the critical $z$-value 1.96 with $\alpha_2 = .05$. Since $2.10 > 1.96$, $H_0: \rho_1 = \rho_2$ can be rejected at the .05 level. With these data the correlation of IQ's of identical twins reared together is significantly higher than the correlation of IQ's of identical twins reared apart.*

## 15.7 TESTING DIFFERENCES AMONG SEVERAL INDEPENDENT CORRELATION COEFFICIENTS: $H_0: \rho_1 = \rho_2 = \cdots = \rho_J$

The procedure in Section 15.6 works well when there are only two correlation coefficients to be compared. But what if there are three or more $r$'s? In one study it was found that the correlations of nonlanguage IQ's with reading appeared to increase with grade level, from .63 at grade four to .69 at grade eight. Are these differences large enough to allow $H_0: \rho_4 = \rho_5 = \cdots = \rho_8$ to be rejected? The hypothesis that all differences in the $r$'s are due to sampling error can be tested using Equation 15.6, where $w_j = n_j - 3$.

$$\chi^2 = \Sigma w_j Z_j^2 - w_{\bullet} \bar{Z}_w^2, \text{ where } \bar{Z}_w = \frac{\Sigma w_j Z_j}{w_{\bullet}}, \text{ and } w_{\bullet} = \Sigma w_j \qquad \textbf{(15.6)}$$

The procedure is illustrated in Table 15.1. Each of the $J = 5$ values of $r$ (column 4) is converted to the corresponding Fisher $Z$ (column 5); each $Z$ is then multiplied by its weight, $w_j = n_j - 3$ (column 3). The products (column 6) are summed and the sum is

*Could a directional hypothesis have been justified in this situation? Since it is not plausible that the IQ's of twins reared apart would correlate more highly than the IQ's of twins reared together, a directional hypothesis could have been justified *if it had been decided upon* before the data were inspected. Even if a "one-tailed" test had been used, the null hypothesis would not have been rejected at the .01 level; for $\alpha_1 = .01$, the critical value of $z$ is 2.326 (from Table A).

**TABLE 15.1 A Test of $H_0: \rho_1 = \rho_2 = \cdots = \rho_J$, where the $\rho$'s are Independent**

| (1) Grade | (2) $n_j$ | (3) $w_j = n_j - 3$ | (4) $r_j$[a] | (5) $Z_j$ | (6) $w_jZ_j$[b] | (7) $w_jZ_j^2$[b] |
|---|---|---|---|---|---|---|
| 4 | 2757 | 2754 | .63 | .741 | 2041.9 | 1513.9 |
| 5 | 2706 | 2703 | .65 | .775 | 2095.6 | 1624.7 |
| 6 | 2584 | 2581 | .65 | .775 | 2001.0 | 1551.4 |
| 7 | 2605 | 2602 | .67 | .811 | 2109.6 | 1710.3 |
| 8 | 2465 | 2462 | .69 | .848 | 2087.7 | 1770.2 |
| | | 13,102 ($w_\bullet$) | | | 10,335.8 ($\Sigma w_jZ_j$) | 8,170.6 ($\Sigma w_jZ_j^2$) |

$$\bar{Z}_w = \frac{\Sigma w_jZ_j}{w_\bullet} = \frac{10,335.8}{13,102} = .7889; (\bar{r} = .658)$$

$$\chi^2 = \Sigma w_jZ_j^2 - w_\bullet \bar{Z}_w^2$$
$$= 8,170.6 - 13,102\,(.7889)^2$$
$$= 8,170.6 - 8,154.2$$
$$\chi^2 = 16.37 > {}_{.99}\chi_4^2 = 13.3,\ p < .01$$

[a]Between Lorge-Thorndike nonlanguage IQ's and reading scores on the Iowa Test of Basic Skills.

[b]These figures result from transforming $r$ to $Z$ via a calculator. If you use Table E (or retain fewer decimal places in the $Z$'s), your results will differ slightly due to rounding error.

divided by the sum of the weights ($w_\bullet$) to obtain the weighted mean Fisher $Z, \bar{Z} = .7889$.* Column 7 ($w_jZ_j^2$) is the product of columns 5 ($Z_j$) and 6 ($w_jZ_j$); its sum ($\Sigma w_jZ_j^2$) is used in Eq. 15.6. If the $J$ values of $Z$ are all estimates of the same parameter, then the value yielded by Equation 15.6 will have a chi-square distribution with $\nu = J - 1$ degrees of freedom.

It is evident in Table 15.1 that the null hypothesis can be rejected at the .01 level. Although the differences in the $r$'s were not large, the large sample sizes result in very little sampling error in the correlation coefficients and, hence, in the null hypothesis being rejected with confidence.†

## 15.8 TESTING DIFFERENCES BETWEEN TWO DEPENDENT CORRELATION COEFFICIENTS: $H_0$: $\rho_{31} = \rho_{32}$

Two correlation coefficients cannot be assumed to be independent if they are based on the same sample. The situation would arise if one wished to compare the validity of

*The recommended procedure for averaging homogeneous $r$'s is to find $\bar{Z}_w$, then transform to the corresponding value of $r$; in this example $\bar{r} = .658$. Fisher noted that there is a slight bias in each $Z_j$-value, which accumulates to make $\bar{r}$ slightly too large. The correction is to reduce each $Z_j$ by $\bar{r}/(2(n_j - 1))$. But this correction can usually be ignored since its effects are trivial except when sample sizes are very small or $J$ is very large.

†Procedures for testing which of the $J$ values of $r$ differ significantly from which other of the $r$'s are in Section 17.23.

the College Board with the ACT for predicting GPA in college, and the two correlation coefficients were computed on the same students. For testing $H_0: \rho_{31} = \rho_{32}$, when $r_{31}$ and $r_{32}$ are based on the same sample, the *t*-test (Hotelling, 1940) in Equation 15.7 should be employed.

$$t = (r_{31} - r_{32}) \sqrt{\frac{(n-3)(1+r_{12})}{2(1 - r_{31}^2 - r_{32}^2 - r_{12}^2 + 2r_{31}r_{32}r_{12})}} \tag{15.7}$$

with $\nu = n - 3$ degrees of freedom.

In Table 8.4 the validities of pre-grade-one reading readiness (1) and IQ (2) scores for predicting subsequent reading success (3) were $r_{31} = .612$ and $r_{32} = .541$, respectively, with $r_{12} = .466$ and $n = 157$. Is $H_0: \rho_{31} = \rho_{32}$ tenable at $\alpha_2 = .10$? Using Equation 15.7:

$$t = (.612 - .541) \sqrt{\frac{(157-3)(1+.466)}{2[1 - (.612)^2 - (.541)^2 - (.466)^2 + 2(.612)(.541)(.466)]}}$$

$$= (.071)\sqrt{\frac{225.76}{.8484}} = 1.158$$

which is below the critical value of 1.66 (for $\alpha_2 = .10$ and $\nu = 154$), thus $H_0$ remains tenable, that is, one cannot conclude in this study that the IQ scores correlate less highly with later reading performance than do reading readiness scores.

In Equation 15.7 it is assumed that the sets of values associated with the predictor variables are fixed (Sec. 8.25); it is also assumed that the predicted variable, 3, has a normal distribution for each value of variable 1 and for each value of variable 2, with common variance (homoscedasticity).*

## 15.9 INFERENCES ABOUT OTHER CORRELATION COEFFICIENTS

In this section significance testing procedures for the correlation coefficients presented in Chapter 7 and 8 will be discussed. The presentation of inferential techniques will be greatly simplified since space does not permit detailed treatments such as those in the previous sections of this chapter. Procedures will be presented with which the null hypothesis of *no correlation* between variables $X$ and $Y$ can be tested against a nondirectional alternative hypothesis of most of the coefficients in Chapters 7 and 8.† Where

*There is an alternative large sample method proposed by Olkin (1967) which assumes all three variables are random variables and have a trivariate normal distribution (see Hendrickson and Collins, 1970). Olkin (1967) also describes procedures for testing $H_0: \rho_{12} = \rho_{34}$ when $r_{12}$ and $r_{34}$ are obtained on the same sample.

†Procedures for testing the significance of phi coefficients were treated in Section 14.10. For a discussion of significance tests for the rank-biserial correlation coefficient, $r_{rb}$, see Cureton (1956) and Glass (1966b).

possible, a test statistic will be defined that has a known or approximately known sampling distribution given that the two variables being correlated are unrelated—whether they are measured dichotomously, with ranks, or otherwise—that is, have a coefficient of zero in the population. In each instance the significance testing procedure will be illustrated.

## 15.10 THE POINT-BISERIAL CORRELATION COEFFICIENT $r_{pb}$

By inspection of the formula for $r_{pb}$ (Sec. 7.17), it can be seen that $r_{pb}$ is equal to zero if and only if $\overline{Y}_1 = \overline{Y}_0$:

$$r_{pb} = \frac{\overline{Y}_1 - \overline{Y}_0}{s_Y} \sqrt{\frac{n_1 n_0}{n_{\bullet}(n_{\bullet} - 1)}}$$

Equation 15.1 can be used to test $H_0: \rho_{pb} = 0$ by replacing $r$ with $r_{pb}$.

$$t = \frac{r_{pb}}{\sqrt{(1 - r_{pb}^2)/(n_{\bullet} - 2)}} \tag{15.8}$$

is approximately distributed as Student's $t$-distribution with $\nu = n_{\bullet} - 2$ when $\rho_{pb} = 0$. In a sample of size $n_{\bullet} = 27$ an $r_{pb}$ of .728 was found between sex and height (Table 7.7). The $t$-test (Eq. 15.8) of $H_0: \rho_{pb} = 0$ is

$$t = \frac{.728}{\sqrt{\dfrac{1 - (.728)^2}{27 - 2}}} = \frac{.728}{\sqrt{\dfrac{.4700}{25}}} = 5.31$$

The $t$-ratio of 5.31 exceeds the critical $t$ of 3.73 for $\alpha_2 = .001$ and $\nu = 25$ (Table C). Hence, it is extremely unlikely that $\rho_{pb}$ is zero for the population sampled, thus $H_0$ is rejected at the .001 level.

Table J in the Appendix can also be used to test $H_0: \rho_{pb} = 0$; note that the $r_{pb}$ of .728 exceeds the critical $r$ of .618 for $\alpha_2 = .001$, found in Table J for $\nu = 25$.

Testing the null hypothesis that a population value of the point-biserial correlation coefficient is zero is mathematically equivalent to testing the hypothesis that *in the population* those persons coded 1 on the dichotomous variable have a mean equal to the *population mean* of the persons coded 0 on the dichotomy, that is, $H_0: \mu_1 = \mu_0$. For example, the $r_{pb}$ of .728 was based on a sample of ten males whose mean height was 69.90 in. and seventeen females whose mean height was 64.35 in. If Equation 12.2 (Sec. 12.4) is used to test $H_0: \mu_1 = \mu_0$:

$$t = \frac{\overline{X}_1 - \overline{X}_0}{s_w\sqrt{\dfrac{1}{n_1} + \dfrac{1}{n_0}}} = \frac{69.90 - 64.35}{2.623\sqrt{\dfrac{1}{10} + \dfrac{1}{17}}} = 5.31$$

which is identical to the $t$ from Equation 15.8.

## 15.11 SPEARMAN'S RANK CORRELATION: $H_0: \rho_{ranks} = 0$

The sampling distribution of $r_{ranks}$, given zero correlation between two sets of ranks $X$ and $Y$ in the population, cannot be characterized in terms of any well-known statistical distribution for $n$ less than approximately 10. For $n > 10$, the sampling distribution when the population Spearman rank-correlation coefficient is zero is approximated by Student's $t$-distribution. In fact for $n > 30$, Equation 15.1 may be used, substituting $r_{ranks}$ for $r$.

$$t = \frac{r_{ranks}}{\sqrt{(1 - r_{ranks}^2)/(n - 2)}} \tag{15.9}$$

is approximately distributed as Student's $t$-distribution with $\nu = n - 2$ when the population value $\rho_{ranks}$ is zero.

The exact sampling distribution of $r_{ranks}$ when $n$ is less than 30 has been determined and is used in testing the null hypothesis of no relationship between the two ranked variables (see Kendall, 1962). Selected percentiles in the sampling distributions of $r_{ranks}$ for various values of $n$ have been determined and appear in Table K in the Appendix. As an example of how Table K is read, a value of $r_{ranks}$ greater than .794 or less than $-.794$ is required for significance at the $\alpha_2 = .01$ level when $n = 11$. By comparing Tables J and K it is evident that larger critical values are required for $r_{ranks}$ than for $r$, although the difference becomes negligible as $n$ increases.

## 15.12 PARTIAL CORRELATION, $H_0: \rho_{12.3} = 0$

Equation 15.10 can be used to test the null hypothesis that the first-order partial correlation (Sec. 8.13) in the population is 0 (Eq. 15.10 is identical to Eq. 15.1 for "zero-order" partial correlations, i.e., $r_{12}$).

$$t = \frac{r_{12.3}}{\sqrt{\dfrac{1 - r_{12.3}^2}{n - 3}}} \tag{15.10}$$

Expressed more generally for any partial correlation coefficient:

$$t = r_{12.3,\ldots,p}/\sqrt{(1 - r_{12.3,\ldots,p}^2)/\nu} \tag{15.11}$$

where $\nu = n - 2 - p$, and $p$ is the number of variables partialed out of $r_{12}$. For first-order partial correlations ($r_{12.3}$), $p = 1$; for second-order partial correlations ($r_{12.34}$), $p = 2$, and so on. Table J may also be used to test $H_0; \rho_{12.3,\ldots,p}$ by entering $\nu$ (not $n$). Thus if $n = 30$, $r_{12.34}$ must be at least .388 to allow rejection of $H_0$ at $\alpha_2 = .05$ ($\nu = 26$).

## 15.13 SIGNIFICANCE OF A MULTIPLE CORRELATION COEFFICIENT

The null hypothesis that the multiple correlation in the population is zero can be tested using the $F$-test in Equation 15.12.*

$$F = \frac{R^2_{Y.12\ldots m}}{(1 - R^2_{Y.12\ldots m})}\left(\frac{n - m - 1}{m}\right) \tag{15.12}$$

where $m$ is the number of predictor (independent) variables. When the null hypothesis is true, the distribution of the $F$-statistic is described by the central $F$-distribution with $\nu_1 = m$ degrees of freedom in the numerator and $\nu_2 = n - m - 1$ in the denominator. In Table 8.5 (Sec. 8.21) $R_{Y.12345} = .69537$ with $n = 157$. Is $H_0$ tenable? Using Equation 15.12:

$$F = \frac{(.69537)^2}{(1 - .48354)}\left(\frac{157 - 5 - 1}{5}\right) = (.9363)(30.2) = 28.27$$

which exceeds the critical value, ${}_{.999}F_{5,151} \doteq 4.42$, hence the multiple correlation coefficient is highly significant and the null hypothesis is untenable.

Equation 15.12 is equivalent to Equation 15.13, which is also widely used, where $\nu_1 = m$, and $\nu_2 = n - m - 1$.

$$F = \frac{\text{Sum of squares due to regression}/\nu_1}{\text{Residual sum of squares}/\nu_2} = \frac{SS_{\hat{Y}}/\nu_1}{SS_e/\nu_2} \tag{15.13}$$

From Equation 8.20, it can be seen that the denominator of Equation 15.13 is the variance error of estimate, $s^2_{Y.12\ldots m}$. Recall from Section 8.8 that $R^2$ gives the proportion of the total sum of squares (or variance) that is predictable from the $m$ predictors, hence $1 - R^2$ is the proportion of unpredictable (residual) variance. Thus if both the numerator and denominator of Equation 15.12 are multipled by $SS_{total}$, Equation 15.13 results. Most computer print-outs use Equation 15.13 to test the null hypothesis that the multiple correlation in the population is zero.

## 15.14 STATISTICAL SIGNIFICANCE IN STEPWISE MULTIPLE REGRESSION

As previously discussed in Section 8.20, the researcher often has access to many more predictor variables than are needed. Typically after the best three or four predictors are selected, the multiple correlation is essentially unaffected by the use of additional independent variables. Note in Table 8.5 (Sec. 8.21) that the multiple correlation coefficients

*Note that if $m = 1$, Equation 15.12 is the square of Equation 15.1; recall from Section 13.10 that when the numerator of the $F$-ratio has $\nu = 1$, that $F = t^2$.

were .612, .677, .693, .69526, .69537 when five independent variables were used in a stepwise multiple regression. Are all the increases statistically significant—does the addition of the "next best" predictor increase the multiple correlation enough so that the null hypotheses $H_{0_1}: \rho_{Y.1} = \rho_{Y.12}, H_{0_2}: \rho_{Y.12} = \rho_{Y.123}, H_{0_3}: \rho_{Y.123} = \rho_{Y.1234}$, and so on, can be rejected? Often the decision is made to use only the number of predictors that continue to increase significantly the multiple correlation. Equation 15.14 can be used to test $H_0: \rho_{Y.12...m_2} = \rho_{Y.12...m_1}$, where $m_2$ and $m_1$ are the number of predictors, and $m_2 > m_1$.

$$F = \frac{(R^2_{Y.12\ldots m_2} - R^2_{Y.12\ldots m_1})/(m_2 - m_1)}{(1 - R^2_{Y.12\ldots m_2})/(n - m_2 - 1)} \tag{15.14}$$

where $\nu_1 = m_2 - m_1$ and $\nu_2 = n - m_2 - 1$.

For example, to test whether the increase from $R_{Y.1} = .612$ to $R_{Y.12} = .677$ was statistically significant when $n = 157$, Equation 15.14 becomes

$$F = \frac{(R^2_{Y.12} - R^2_{Y.1})/(2 - 1)}{(1 - R^2_{Y.12})/(n - 2 - 1)} = \frac{(.677)^2 - (.612)^2}{(1 - .4583)/(157 - 3)} = 23.82$$

This is much larger than the critical value, ${}_{.999}F_{1,154} \doteq 11.4$, hence $H_{0_1}$ is rejected at the .001 level.*

Is the increase from $R_{Y.12} = .677$ to $R_{Y.123} = .693$ also significant? Using Equation 15.14

$$F = \frac{(.693)^2 - (.677)^2}{(1 - .4802)/153} = 6.45$$

which, from Table F in the Appendix, is found to be significant at the .025 level. Thus the use of the third independent variable significantly improved the accuracy of predictions.

But does step 4 increase the multiple correlation coefficient in the population—is $H_0: \rho_{Y.1234} = \rho_{Y.123}$ tenable? The use of Equation 15.14 yields $F = .92$, which does not approach significance. Thus for practical purposes, one can do as well with the three predictors in steps 1, 2, and 3 as with the addition of predictors 4 and 5. Predictors 4 and 5 add no significant relevant information.

## 15.15 SIGNIFICANCE OF THE BISERIAL CORRELATION COEFFICIENT $r_{bis}$

The exact sampling distribution of $r_{bis}$ (Sec. 7.18) is not known. McNamara and Dunlap (1934) argued that when the population biserial correlation coefficient is zero, then for

*This test is mathematically equivalent to testing $r_{Y2.1}$ for significance using Equation 15.11; for example, from Table 8.5, $r_{Y2.1} = .366$, which, using Equation 15.11 yields $t = 4.88$; hence $t^2 = 23.82 = F$ yielded by Equation 15.14. Other steps are similarly equivalent.

large samples $r_{bis}$ should be approximately normally distributed with mean 0 and standard deviation, i.e., $z = r_{bis}/\sigma_{r_{bis}}$, and

$$\sigma_{r_{bis}} \doteq \frac{\sqrt{n_0 n_1}}{u n_{\bullet} \sqrt{n_{\bullet}}} \tag{15.15}$$

where $n_{\bullet}$ is the sample size, $n_1$ and $n_0$ are the number of persons "scoring" 1 and 0, respectively, on the dichotomous variable ($n_{\bullet} = n_0 + n_1$), and $u$ is the ordinate on the unit normal curve at the point above which $n_1/n_{\bullet}$ proportion of the area under the curve lies.

When the population biserial correlation coefficient departs from zero, the value of $\sigma_{r_{bis}}$ is diminished by $1/\sqrt{n_{\bullet}}$ times the square of the population value of $r_{bis}$. When the population value, $\rho_{bis}$, is different from zero, the sampling distribution of $r_{bis}$ becomes nonnormal, being skewed toward zero.

Empirical sampling studies by Lord (1963a) and Baker (1965) have shown that the large-sample estimate of the standard error of $r_{bis}$ is quite nearly exact; in Baker's case this was true even for samples of size 15.

Suppose that for a sample of size 36 in which $n_1 = 16$ and $n_0 = 20$, the value of $r_{bis}$ is $-.145$. The value of $\sigma_{r_{bis}}$ when the population biserial coefficient is zero is

$$\sigma_{r_{bis}} = \frac{\sqrt{(16)(20)}}{(.3951)36\sqrt{36}} = .210$$

If the population value $\rho_{bis}$ is zero, $r_{bis}/\sigma_{r_{bis}}$ will be approximately normally distributed with mean 0 and standard deviation 1 over repeated random samples of size $n$.

$$z = \frac{r_{bis}}{\sigma_{r_{bis}}} = \frac{-.145}{.210} = -.69$$

A $z$-value of $-.69$ appears to be a not unusual observation to obtain in sampling from a unit normal distribution. Hence, evidence does not exist to allow rejection of the null hypothesis of a population biserial correlation coefficient of zero.

## 15.16 SIGNIFICANCE OF THE TETRACHORIC CORRELATION COEFFICIENT $r_{tet}$

When the null hypothesis of *no relationship* between $X$ and $Y$ (two normally distributed variables forced into dichotomies) is true, the sampling distribution of the sample tetrachoric correlation coefficient $r_{tet}$ is approximately normal for $n$ greater than about 20 with mean 0 and standard deviation, $\sigma_{r_{tet}}$:

$$\sigma_{r_{tet}} \doteq \frac{1}{u_x u_y} \sqrt{\frac{p_x p_y q_x q_y}{n_{\bullet}}}, \tag{15.16}$$

where $n_{\bullet}$ is the sample size, $u_x$ is the ordinate for the $z$-score in the unit-normal curve above which $p_x$ proportion of the area lies (Table A): ($p_x = n_x/n_{\bullet}$ = the proportion of persons "scoring" "1" on variable $X$), $u_y$ is the ordinate for the $z$-score in the unit-normal curve above which $p_y$ proportion of the area lies ($p_y = n_y/n_{\bullet}$ = the proportion of persons "scoring" "1" on the variable $Y$).

Thus, for moderately large and large $n$

$$z = \frac{r_{tet}}{\sigma_{r_{tet}}}$$

can be referred to the unit normal distribution to test the hypothesis that the population tetrachoric correlation coefficient is zero.

The data in Table 7.9 (Sec. 7.20) were gathered to study the relationship between two variables $X$ and $Y$ that are believed to be normally distributed but can only be measured dichotomously.

The value of $r_{tet}$ was found to be .90 and $n_{\bullet}$ was 400. Using Equation 15.16 and the data in Table 7.9, the standard error of $r_{tet}$ is estimated.

$$\sigma_{r_{tet}} = \frac{1}{(.3477)(.3989)} \sqrt{\frac{(.30)(.50)(.70)(.50)}{400}} = .0826$$

Thus the value of the $z$-ratio is $z = .90/.0826 = 10.90$, which far exceeds the critical value of $z$ of 3.29 with $\alpha_2 = .001$ (Table A in the Appendix). The hypothesis that the tetrachoric correlation in the population is zero is untenable.

## 15.17 SIGNIFICANCE OF THE CORRELATION RATIO

Recall that $\hat{\eta}$ is a measure of association that, unlike $r$, is not limited to describing the degree of linear correlation between two variables $X$ and $Y$ (Sec. 8.27). The $F$-statistic* (Eq. 15.17) can be used to test the null hypothesis that in the population, the correlation ratio (or coefficient eta) is zero, that is, $H_0 : \eta_{Y.X} = 0$.

$$F = \frac{\hat{\eta}^2_{Y.X}/(J - 1)}{(1 - \hat{\eta}^2_{Y.X})/(n - J)} \qquad (15.17)$$

where $J$ is the number of groups or categories of the $X$-variable into which the $n$ observations are grouped.

The value for the correlation ratio between age and scores on a test in Section 8.27 was found to be .541, based on $n = 28$ persons who were classified into $J = 7$ age groups.

*This may also be expressed in the terminology of analysis of variance (Chap. 16): $F = (SS_b/\nu_b)/(SS_w/\nu_w) = MS_b/MS_w$, where $SS$ = sum of squares, $MS$ = mean square, and the subscripts $_b$ and $_w$ denote "between" and "within," respectively.

Is this value significantly greater than 0? The $F$-ratio found using Equation 15.17 is

$$F = \frac{(.541)/(7 - 1)}{(1 - .541)/(28 - 7)} = 4.12$$

The critical $F$ is ${}_{1-\alpha}F_{(J-1),(n-J)}$, or in this case, ${}_{.99}F_{6,21} = 3.87$. Consequently the null hypothesis can be rejected at the .01 level.

## 15.18 TESTING FOR NONLINEARITY OF REGRESSION

The $F$-test in Equation 15.17 does not presume that there is a nonlinear relationship between $X$ and $Y$. Recall from Equations 8.23 and 8.24 (Sec. 8.27) that if the regression is perfectly linear, $\hat{\eta}^2$ and $r^2$ will be equal in value. But if the relationship is nonlinear, $\hat{\eta}^2$ will be larger than $r^2$; thus the difference in $\hat{\eta}^2$ and $r^2$ is a measure of nonlinearity. The $F$-test* for nonlinearity where the $n$ observations are grouped into $J$ groups is the following:

$$F = \frac{(\hat{\eta}^2_{Y.X} - r^2)/(J - 2)}{(1 - \hat{\eta}^2_{Y.X})/(n - J)} \tag{15.18}$$

(Note that the denominator is identical to that in Eq. 15.17.) For the illustration in Section 8.27 where $r = -.077$ and $r^2 = .0059$:

$$F = \frac{(.541 - .0059)/(7 - 2)}{(1 - .541)/(28 - 7)} = \frac{.1070}{.0219} = 4.89$$

which exceeds the critical ${}_{.99}F_{5,21} \doteq 4.10$, thus the statistical hypothesis that the relationship in the population is linear can be rejected at the .01 level.

## CHAPTER SUMMARY

The most direct method for testing the statistical hypothesis $H_0: \rho = 0$ is to enter Table J or Figure 15.1, which gives the critical value of $r$ needed to reject the null hypothesis. These critical values depend only on $n$ and $\alpha$. The critical values of $r$ decreases as $n$ increases and as $\alpha$ increases (e.g., from .01 to .05).

The sampling distribution of $r$ is normal when $\rho = 0$—it is skewed to the extent that $\rho$ deviates from 0. The skewness becomes progressively less and the sampling distribution becomes more nearly normal as $n$ increases.

*This may be expressed in analysis of variance terms (Sec. 17.21):

$$F = \frac{SS_{\text{nonlinear}}/(J - 2)}{SS_{within}/(n - J)}, \text{ whereas } SS_{\text{nonlinear}} = (1 - r^2)(SS_{total}) - SS_{within}$$

The Fisher $Z$-transformation has a distribution that is approximately normal irrespective of $n$ and $\rho$. It is used to set confidence intervals for $\rho$, although Figure 15.1 can be used for this purpose if high precision is not needed. Fisher $Z$-coefficients are also used in the $z$-test for independent $r$'s and in the $\chi^2$ test for $J$ independent $r$'s. If $r$'s are obtained on different subjects, they are independent; two $r$'s obtained on the same group of persons are not independent, and formulas that take the type and degree of dependency into account should be employed.

The $t$-tests for assessing the significance of point-biserial, Spearman rank, and partial correlation coefficients are very similar to testing $H_0: \rho = 0$. The critical values for $r_{ranks}$ are slightly larger than for $r$, but the differences become negligible as $n$ increases. The critical value for $r_{12.3\ldots p}$ is identical to that for $r$ except that it has $p$ fewer degrees of freedom for the same value of $n$.

The significance of (1) multiple correlation coefficients, (2) additional predictor variables in stepwise multiple correlation, (3) the correlation ratio, and (4) nonlinearity of regression are tested using the $F$-statistic. All procedures utilizing Pearson product-moment correlation coefficients assume that each relationship is characterized by bivariate normality.

The significance tests of biserial and tetrachoric correlations use the $z$-test and require large $n$'s to be precise.

## *MASTERY TEST*

1. Other things being equal, and $\rho \neq 0$, is the probability of a type-II error, $\beta$, greater with $\alpha_2 = .01$ or with $\alpha_2 = .05$?
2. Using Figure 15.1, determine how large a sample is needed to allow rejection of $H_0: \rho = 0$ with an $r$-value of .3 under the following circumstances.
   a. when $\alpha_2 = .001$
   b. when $\alpha_2 = .01$
   c. when $\alpha_2 = .05$
   d. when $\alpha_1 = .05$
   e. when $\alpha_2 = .10$
3. Assume $H_0: \rho = 0$ is true.
   a. Will the probability that it will be rejected increase as $n$ increases?
   b. Will the critical value of $r$ decrease as $n$ increases?
   c. Will the critical value of $r$ be larger at $\alpha = .05$ than at $\alpha = .01$?
4. Which one of these statements *best* describes the reason the Fisher $Z$-transformation is needed?
   a. The sampling distribution of $r$ is skewed when $\rho \neq 0$.
   b. The $t$-test and $z$-test for $H_0: \rho = 0$ are not powerful for small $n$'s.
   c. The sampling distribution of $r$ is not normal when $\rho = 0$.
5. If $r = .5$, which of the following .90 confidence intervals for $\rho$ are plausible?
   a. −.1 to .51
   b. −.2 to .84
   c. .42 to .57
   d. .48 to .55
6. Knowledge of which concepts were required in answering Question 5?
   a. The sampling distribution of $r$ is approximately normal with large $n$'s.
   b. The sampling distribution of $r$ is positively skewed when $\rho > 0$, unless $n$ is large.
   c. The sampling distribution of $r$ is negatively skewed when $\rho > 0$, unless $n$ is large.
7. Other things being equal, which of these will span the greatest distance (range of values)?
   a. the .67 CI b. the .95 CI c. the .99 CI

8. Which of these determine the value of $\sigma_Z$?
   a. $r$ b. $n$ c. $\rho$
9. Using Figure 15.5, determine the .95 confidence interval if $r = +.20$ and $n = 50$.
10. Given $n = 100$:
    a. Which one of the following $r$'s will have the confidence interval with the greatest numerical span? $r = -.5$, $r = .00$, $r = .5$, $r = .8$
    b. Which $r$ in part a will have the smallest range of values?
    c. Will the CI's for $r = -.5$ and $r = .5$ have the same width?
11. If $n = 30$, what is the critical value for each of the following to reject $H_0$ with $\alpha_2 = .01$?
    a. $r$ b. $r_{pb}$ c. $r_{ranks}$ d. $r_{12.345}$
12. In which of these situations would a directional alternative hypothesis about $\rho$ be reasonable?
    a. age and height among middle-school students
    b. male-female and popularity among high-school students
    c. neurotic traits and GPA in college
    d. SES and school achievement
    e. IQ and number of languages spoken
13. When used appropriately, directional tests of $H_0: \rho = 0$ are more powerful than nondirectional tests. (T or F)
14. In which of these situations are the correlation coefficients independent?
    a. $r_{\text{height, weight}}$ for boys compared to that for girls
    b. $r_{\text{IQ, achievement}}$ for this year's fourth graders with that for this year's fifth graders
    c. $r_{\text{IQ, achievement}}$ at grade four with that for the same students in grade five.
    d. $r_{\text{IQ, reading}}$ with $r_{\text{IQ, math}}$ for this year's fourth graders;
    e. $r_{\text{IQ, achievement}}$ for Anglos vs. Hispanics
    f. $r_{\text{GPA, IQ}}$ for this year's tenth graders, with those for this year's eleventh and twelfth graders
15. Which equation should be used in situations a, b, d, e, and f above?
16. The $t$-test for testing $H_0: \rho_{pb} = 0$ is identical to the $t$-test for testing $H_0$: _____.
17. If $R_{Y.123} = .30$ and $n = 104$, which equation should be used to determine if the null hypothesis is tenable at $\alpha_2 = .05$?
18. If, with the addition of a fourth independent variable in a multiple regression, the value of $R_{Y.1234}$ increased to .40, which equation would be used to see if the *increase* in the multiple correlation from .30 to .40 is statistically significant?
19. What is the central assumption underlying most of the inferential tests on correlation coefficients?
20. Which two of these equation are "large sample" methods? (Assume that $n$ is so large that there is virtually no sampling error in estimating the denominator of the test statistic.)
    15.1, 15.7, 15.11, 15.12, 15.14, 15.15, or 15.16?

## PROBLEMS AND EXERCISES

1. Using Table J, determine the minimum value of $r$ at which $H_0: \rho = 0$ will be rejected for $\alpha_1 = .05$, $\alpha_2 = .10$, $\alpha_2 = .05$, $\alpha_1 = .01$, and $\alpha_2 = .01$:
   a. with $n = 25$
   b. with $n = 100$
   c. If it is predicted that $\rho > 0$, with $n = 25$ and $r = .35$, would $H_0$ be rejected at the .05 level? At the .01 level?

2. a. Use Table J to determine the critical value for $r$ if $n = 1{,}000$ at $\alpha_2 = .01$
   b. If $r = .10$ and $n = 1{,}000$, would $H_0: \rho = 0$ be rejected at the .01 level?
   c. If $r = -.10$ and $n = 1{,}000$, would $H_0: \rho = 0$ be rejected at the .01 level?
3. If $r = .80$, compute the .68 confidence interval for $\rho$ (to two-decimal-place accuracy):
   a. if $n = 12$ c. if $n = 103$
   b. if $n = 28$ d. if $n = 403$
4. A correlation of .50 was observed on 236 students between verbal IQ's from group intelligence tests at grade one and IQ's ten years later (Hopkins and Bracht, 1975). The corresponding correlation for nonverbal IQ's was only .29.
   a. Can both null hypotheses ($H_0: \rho = 0$) be rejected at $\alpha_1 = .01$? (Use Table J)
   b. Use Figure 15.5 to establish .95 confidence intervals for the two corresponding parameters.
   c. Are these two correlations independent—could Equation 15.5 be used to test $H_0: \rho_1 = \rho_2$?
5. By studying the results from Problem 3, describe the effects of $n$ on the shape and variability of the sampling distribution of $r$.
6. On a group intelligence test, IQ scores of 150 girls at grade three correlated .75 with IQ scores four years later. The corresponding $r$ for 154 boys was .71 (Hopkins and Bibelheimer, 1971). Is $H_0: \rho_1 = \rho_2$ tenable at $\alpha_2 = .05$?
7. The correlation between numerical ability test scores and course grades in Spanish I was found to be .56 for a sample of 204 students. A correlation of .40 was reported between verbal reasoning test scores and grades in Spanish I for a different sample of 186 students (Bennett et al., 1974).
   a. Set .68 confidence intervals about each $r$ (to two-decimal-place accuracy) using Fisher's $Z$-transformation.
   b. In the population to which these two samples belong do grades in Spanish I correlate more highly with numerical than with verbal ability scores with $\alpha_2 = .05$?
8. Earlier in this chapter, it was found that the correlation of the IQ's of identical twins reared apart was significantly lower than the correlation for identical twins reared together. Compare the $r$'s (i.e., $H_0: \rho_1 = \rho_2$) for identical twins reared apart with those of fraternal twins reared together with $\alpha_2 = .01$.

| *Identical Twins Reared Apart* | *Fraternal Twins Reared Together* |
|---|---|
| $r_1 = .83$ | $r_2 = .54$ |
| $n_1 = 30$ | $n_2 = 172$ |

9. A correlation of .73 was observed between Instructor's Interest and Enthusiasm and the General Excellence of the Instructor with $n = 247$ (Houston, Crosswhite, and King, 1974). Establish the .95 confidence interval using Figure 15.1 and compare with the .95 confidence interval obtained using Fisher $Z$-coefficients. Is there a practical difference between the two .95 confidence intervals?
10. One study intercorrelated intelligence ($X$), reading rate ($Y$), and reading comprehension ($Z$) in a sample of $n = 80$ college students. The following correlation coefficients were obtained: $r_{xy} = -.034$, $r_{xz} = .422$, $r_{yz} = -.385$. Test the null hypothesis at the .10 level of significance that $\rho_{xy} = \rho_{xz}$, that is that intelligence is correlated with both reading rate and reading comprehension to the same degree. Can $H_0$ be rejected at the .01 level?
11. Estimate the partial correlation between reading rate and reading comprehension, holding IQ score constant (see Eq. 8.12). Use Table J to see if $H_0: \rho_{ZY.X} = 0$ can be rejected at the .001 level of significance. The number of degrees of freedom, $\nu = ?$ (See item 10.)

12. The correlation between high-school rank-in-class and college GPA was .50 for 200 students. When the college admissions test was used as a second predictor, the multiple correlation $R_{Y.12}$ became .55. Was the *increase* statistically significant? At what level?
13. The correlation of teachers' ratings and their students' reading ability was .80 for 103 primary students. On a separate group of 103 upper-elementary students the correlation was .70. On a group of 103 middle-school students the correlation was .60. Are these $r$'s significantly different at the .05 level? At the .01 level? What is the average correlation, $\bar{r}$?
14. Assume that the correlation ratio $\hat{\eta}^2_{Y.X}$ between age and height for 55 boys (five *at each age* 6, 7, · · · , and 16) was found to be .70
    a. Is the relationship statistically significant?
    b. If $r = .6$ is there a significant nonlinear relationship?

## *ANSWERS TO MASTERY TEST*

1. $\beta$ is greater with $\alpha_2 = .01$.
2. a. approximately 120
   b. approximately 72
   c. approximately 45
   d. approximately 31
   e. approximately 31
3. a. No; but if $\rho \neq 0$, the probability of rejecting $H_0$ will increase.
   b. Yes
   c. No; critical values of $r$ are greater at $\alpha = .01$ than $\alpha = .05$.
4. a.
5. a. no b. yes
   c. yes d. no
6. a and c
7. c
8. b; $\sigma_z = \dfrac{1}{\sqrt{n-3}}$
9. Approximately −.08 to +.46
10. a. .00 b. .8 c. yes
11. a. .463 c. .478
    b. .463 d. .487
12. a and d
13. T
14. a, b, e, f
15. a: 15.5, e: 15.5
    b: 15.5, f: 15.6
    d: 15.7
16. $H_0: \mu_1 = \mu_0$
17. 15.12
18. 15.14
19. Bivariate normality
20. 15.15, 15.16

## *ANSWERS TO PROBLEMS AND EXERCISES*

1. a. .337, .337, .396, .462, .505
   b. .165, .165, .196, .232, .256
   c. $H_0$ is rejected at the .05 level but not at the .01 level. With $n = 25$, critical $r$-values at $\alpha_1 = .05$ and $\alpha_1 = .01$ are .337 and .462, respectively.
2. a. .081
   b. Yes, $p < .001$.
   c. Yes; $\alpha_2 = .01$ indicates a nondirectional test; $|r| > .081$.
3. a. .64 to .89 (1.099 ± .333)
   b. .72 to .86 (1.099 ± .200)
   c. .76 to .83 (1.099 ± .100)
   d. .78 to .82 (1.099 ± .05)
4. a. Yes, both $r$'s (.50 and .29) exceed the critical value of $r$ (.164) for $n = 200$ and $\alpha_1 = .01$, indeed $p < .0005$.
   b. .95 CI with $r = 50$: .4 to .6; .95 CI with $r = .29$: .16 to .42.
   c. No, the $r$'s are not independent

since they were both obtained on the same 236 persons.

5. As $n$ increases, variance in sampling distribution decreases. As $n$ increases, sampling distribution becomes less skewed.

6. Yes, $z = \dfrac{.973 - .887}{.116} = .741 < 1.96$; therefore, $H_0$ is tenable.

7. a. for $r = .55$: .51 to .61 (.633 ± .071)
   for $r = .40$: .34 to .46 (.424 ± .074)

   b. Yes; $z = \dfrac{.633 - .424}{\sqrt{(.071)^2 + (.074)^2}} = \dfrac{.209}{\sqrt{.01052}} = 2.04, \quad p < .05$

8. $Z_1 = 1.188, Z_2 = .604, \sigma^2_{Z_1} = .0370, \sigma^2_{Z_2} = .0059$;

   $z = \dfrac{1.188 - .604}{\sqrt{.0370 + .0059}} = \dfrac{.584}{.207} = 2.82$; reject $H_0$ at $\alpha_2 = .01$.

9. .95 CI = .66 to .77; $\sigma_Z = .064$, $Z \pm 1.96\sigma_Z = .929 \pm .125 = .804$ to 1.054, or .67 to .78; no, the difference is inconsequential.

10. $t = 2.68$ (Eq. 15.7), $H_0$ rejected at the .05 and .01 levels.

11. $r_{YZ.X} = -.409$, yes, $\nu = 77$.

12. $F = 14.83$, ${}_{.999}F_{1,197} \doteq 11.2, p < .001$

13. $\chi^2 = 8.30$, yes, no $(.05 > p > .01)$; $\bar{r} = .71$.

14. a. Yes, $F = [(.70)/(11-1)]/[(1-.70)/(55-11)] = .070/.00682 = 10.27$ ${}_{.999}F_{10,44} \doteq 3.87, p < .001$

    b. Yes, $F = [(.70-.36)/(11-2)]/.00682 = 5.54$; ${}_{.99}F_{9,44} \doteq 4.02$, $p < .001$

# 16

# THE ONE-FACTOR ANALYSIS OF VARIANCE

## 16.1 INTRODUCTION

In Chapter 12 the means of two groups were compared. But what if there are three or more means? The statistical technique known as the *analysis of variance* (ANOVA)* is used to determine whether the differences among two or more means are greater than would be expected from sampling error alone. ANOVA is the most common of all inferential statistical techniques in education and the behavioral sciences (Edgington, 1974; Willson, 1980, Wick and Dirkes, 1973). In this chapter simple or one-factor ANOVA will be considered. Two-factor ANOVA, which allows the effects of two independent variables to be examined simultaneously, is treated in Chapter 18.

## 16.2 WHY NOT SEVERAL *t*-TESTS?

If the means of three groups are to be compared, why not make $t$-tests between each pair of means: that is, why not test the three null hypotheses separately: $\mu_1 = \mu_2$, $\mu_1 = \mu_3$,

*For an interesting historical account of the analysis of variance, see Kruskal (1980).

and $\mu_2 = \mu_3$? Or suppose that five groups (parents, students, teachers, principals, and superintendents) were to be compared on attitude toward school. How many different $t$-tests would be required to compare each group with every other group? If there are $J$ groups, the number of separate $t$-tests (i.e., pairwise comparisons) will be $J(J - 1)/2$. Since, in this example, $J$ is 5, the number of comparisons is 5(4)/2 or 10.

But if $J$ is 5, what is the probability of a type-I error, $\alpha$—what is the probability of rejecting a true null hypothesis? When one makes only one $t$-test with $\alpha = .05$, then $\alpha$ is indeed .05. *But whenever more than one t-test is made, the probability of one or more type-I errors is greater than* .05. Since ten $t$-tests would be required to make all possible pairwise comparisons when $J = 5$, and since in each of the ten there is a 5% chance of making a type-I error, the probability of incorrectly rejecting at least one null hypothesis is far greater than .05. Indeed, if all $t$-tests were independent, the probability of at least one type-I error would be .40!*

The dependency among the $t$-tests makes things even more complex—it is impossible to determine the actual value of $\alpha$ for several different, nonindependent $t$-tests.† Nevertheless it is evident that a major problem with multiple $t$-tests is that $\alpha$ becomes quite large as the number of groups increases.

The statistical technique known as the analysis of variance (ANOVA) was developed by the English statistician, Sir Ronald Fisher, in his classic, *Statistical Methods for Research Workers* (1925). ANOVA permits the control of $\alpha$ at a predetermined level when testing the simultaneous equality of any number of means. In ANOVA all differences for all pairs of $J$ means are examined simultaneously to see if one or more of the means deviate significantly from one or more of the other means. In other words, does at least one of the $J$ means differ from at least one of the other $J$ means by more than would be expected by sampling error? Or, is the variance among the $J$ means (an aggregated measure of all mean differences) greater than would be expected if the null hypothesis is true? Notice that in ANOVA the null hypothesis is an "omnibus" hypothesis:

$$H_0 : \mu_1 = \mu_2 = \mu_3 = \cdots = \mu_J$$

ANOVA is a powerful statistical technique; if the omnibus null hypothesis is tenable (i.e., if evidence is insufficient to reject it), one ordinarily does not proceed with further statistical comparisons of means.‡ The analysis of variance is a method of statistical inference that evaluates whether there is any *systematic* (i.e., nonrandom) difference among the set of $J$ means. Thus, ANOVA has three definite advantages over separate $t$-tests when $J > 2$: (1) It yields an accurate and known type-I error probability, whereas the actual $\alpha$ for the set of several separate $t$-tests is high yet undetermined; (2) It is more powerful (when $\alpha$ is held constant)—that is, if the null hypothesis is false, it is more likely to be rejected; (3) It can assess the effects of two or more independent variables simultaneously. For these reasons ANOVA has become the "workhorse" for comparative studies in education and the behavioral sciences (Edgington, 1974; Wick and Dirkes, 1973; Willson, 1980).

*$p = 1 - (1 - \alpha)^K$, if the $K$ comparisons are independent; or, for $\alpha = .05$: $p = 1 - (.95)^K$.

†It is known that the probability of a type-I error for the set of $K$ $t$-tests is never greater than $K\alpha$, where $\alpha$ is the value for each of the $K$-tests (see Eq. 17.13).

‡There are exceptions to this generalization, namely when certain select hypotheses are specified in advance, such as with planned orthogonal contrasts. These techniques are treated in Chapter 17.

Treatment (j)

| 1 | 2 | 3 |
|---|---|---|
| $X_{11}$ | $X_{12}$ | $X_{13}$ |
| $X_{21}$ | $X_{22}$ | $X_{23}$ |
| ⋮ | ⋮ | ⋮ |
| $X_{n1}$ | $X_{n2}$ | $X_{n3}$ |

**FIGURE 16.1**
**Layout of data from an experiment comparing three levels of the treatment factor ($j$ = 1, 2, 3 = $J$) and ($i$ = 1, 2, . . . , $n$ = 10) ten replicates.**

## 16.3 ANOVA NOMENCLATURE

As an example of a one-factor ANOVA, assume that one wants to know if anxiety affects test performance. Subjects will be randomly assigned to low, moderate, or high anxiety conditions. The *factor* in this study is anxiety condition or treatment, of which there are three; the three categories (subsets) of the treatment factor are termed *levels*. Suppose thirty students will be randomly assigned to one of the three levels; thus there will be ten students taking a test under high-anxiety conditions, ten different students will be taking the test under moderate (normal) anxiety conditions, and ten other students will take the test under low-anxiety conditions. Each student is said to be a *replicate*, thus there are ten replicates ($n$ = 10) for each of the three levels ($J$ = 3) of the treatment.

The purpose of the study is to see if test performance is influenced by the treatment (anxiety conditions), thus the treatment is said to be the *independent variable* (cause) and scores on the test would be the *dependent variable* (effect). The purpose of ANOVA is to evaluate if the differences in the $J$ means are larger than would be expected from sampling error ("chance").

In the present example the researcher wants to know if the different treatments (anxiety conditions) result in differences in test performance. The thirty test scores, the $X_{ij}$'s, can be tabulated as represented in Figure 16.1 (the actual scores are given later in Table 16.1). The "$j$" subscript defines the *level* of the treatment group (1, 2, or 3); the "$i$" subscript denotes the replicate (observation) (1, 2, . . . , 10 = $n$).

When there are the same number of replicates for every one of the $J$ levels of the factor, the design is said to be *balanced*, that is, $n_1 = n_2 = \ldots = n_J = n$ (subscripts for $n$ are superfluous in balanced designs, but are needed when all $n$'s are not equal).

## 16.4 ANOVA COMPUTATION

### *Sum of Squares*

In ANOVA extensive use is made of *sums of squares* ($SS$) in testing the null hypothesis. The total sum of squares ($SS_{\text{total}}$) in any set of data is a composite that reflects all treatment effects and sampling error. $SS_{\text{total}}$ is defined as the sum of the squared deviation of every score from the grand mean, $\bar{X}_{\bullet}$ (the mean of all the $n_{\bullet}$

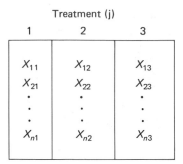

observations, $n_{\bullet} = n_1 + n_2 + \ldots + n_J$):

$$SS_{\text{total}} = \sum_{j=1}^{J} \sum_{i=1}^{n} x_{ij}^2 = \sum_j \sum_i (X_{ij} - \overline{X}_{\bullet})^2 = \sum_j \sum_i X_{ij}^2 - \left(\sum_j \sum_i X_{ij}\right)^2 \Big/ n_{\bullet} \quad \textbf{(16.1)}$$

In ANOVA the total sum of squares ($SS_{\text{total}}$) is decomposed into different effects or *sources of variation.* In one-factor ANOVA $SS_{\text{total}}$ is subdivided into two sources.* Part of the sum of squares is due to differences *between*† group means; a different part is the result of differences among the observations *within* the groups, that is,

$$SS_{\text{total}} = SS_{\text{between}} + SS_{\text{within}}$$

### $SS_b$: *Sum of Squares Between*

The between sum of squares results from the differences among group means, as defined in Equation 16.2. In other words, $\alpha_j$‡ is the difference between the mean of group $j$, $\mu_j$, and the grand mean, $\mu$, that is, $\alpha_j$ is said to be the *effect* of treatment $j$: $\alpha_j = \mu_j - \mu$; it is estimated by

$$\hat{\alpha}_j = \overline{X}_j - \overline{X}_{\bullet} \quad \textbf{(16.2)}$$

$SS_b$ is given by Equation 16.3 where $n_j$ is the number of observations in group $j$, and $\alpha_j$ is the effect of treatment $j$, that is,

$$SS_b = \sum_{j=1}^{J} n_j \hat{\alpha}_j^2 = \sum_j n_j (\overline{X}_j - \overline{X}_{\bullet})^2 \quad \textbf{(16.3)}$$

If the ANOVA design is balanced, Equation 16.3 simplifies to

$$SS_b = n \sum_j \hat{\alpha}_j^2 = n \sum_j (\overline{X}_j - \overline{X}_{\bullet})^2 \quad \textbf{(16.4)}$$

A common alternate formula for calculating $SS_b$ is given in Equation 16.5. Equations 16.3 and 16.4 are simplier and more directly related to the hypothesis being tested, but Equation 16.5 will result in less rounding error with hand computations. With the availability of hand calculators, rounding error no longer needs to be a consideration.

$$SS_b = \sum_{j=1}^{J} \frac{\left(\sum_{i=1}^{n_j} X_{ij}\right)^2}{n_j} - \frac{\left(\sum_j \sum_i X_{ij}\right)^2}{n_{\bullet}} \quad \textbf{(16.5)}$$

where $n_{\bullet} = \sum_j n_j$.

*In Chapter 18 two-factor and three-factor ANOVA are treated in which $SS_{\text{total}}$ is broken down into four and eight sources of variation, respectively.

† "Among" is proper grammatically, but "between" is standard terminology.

‡ This alpha is *not* related to the probability of a type-I error.

## $SS_w$: *Sum of Squares Within*

The sum of squares within groups, $SS_w = \Sigma_i x_{i1}^2 + \Sigma_i x_{i2}^2 + \cdots + \Sigma_i x_{iJ}^2$, can be computed directly using Equation 16.6.

$$SS_w = SS_1 + SS_2 + \ldots + SS_J \tag{16.6}$$

$$= \sum_{i=1}^{n_1} (X_{i1} - \bar{X}_1)^2 + \sum_{i=1}^{n_2} (X_{i2} - \bar{X}_2)^2 + \ldots + \sum_{i=1}^{n_J} (X_{iJ} - \bar{X}_J)^2$$

$$= \sum_{j=1}^{J} \sum_{i=1}^{n_j} (X_{ij} - \bar{X}_j)^2 = \sum_{j=1}^{J} SS_j$$

$SS_w$ can also be obtained indirectly*:

$$SS_w = SS_{\text{total}} - SS_b \tag{16.7}$$

In Chapter 5 it was seen that when a sum of squares is divided by its degrees of freedom, a variance estimate (Eq. 5.5) is obtained. ANOVA employs the $F$-test (Sec. 13.5), which is the ratio of two independent variance estimates. The computational procedures for a one-factor ANOVA are outlined in Figure 16.2.

When $SS_b$ and $SS_w$ are computed (steps 1 and 2) and are divided by their respective degrees of freedom (steps 3 and 4), two independent estimates of variance (called

**FIGURE 16.2. Computational procedures for one-factor ANOVA involving $J$ means and $n_{\cdot}$ total observations.**

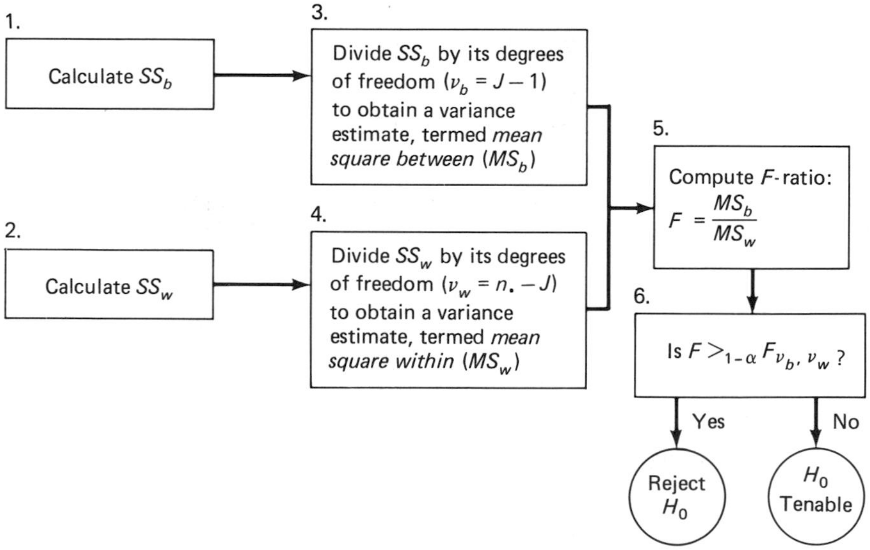


*Prior to the availability of hand calculators, Equation 16.7 was commonly used; now computing $SS_w$ directly using Equation 16.6 is equally convenient.

"mean squares") are obtained. The ratio $MS_b/MS_w$ is the $F$-ratio (step 5). When the null hypothesis is true, both variance estimates are estimating the same parameter, $\sigma^2$, the variance among the observations in the population, and the expected value of their ratio ($F$) is approximately 1.0.* But when $H_0$ is false—that is, when the population means are not equal—the numerator will tend to be larger than the denominator. Hence, when $H_0$ is false, the expected value of the $F$-ratio is greater than 1.0. When the observed $F$-ratio is greater than the critical $F$-ratio, $H_0$ is rejected (step 6).

Table F in the Appendix supplies the critical values for $F$ needed to reject $H_0$ for various combinations of degrees of freedom and $\alpha$-levels.

## 16.5 ANOVA COMPUTATIONAL ILLUSTRATION

To illustrate ANOVA calculations (Table 16.1), the example given in Section 16.3 will be used. An experimenter sought to determine the effect of three different treatments on test scores. Thirty subjects were randomly assigned to one of the three levels (ten to each level): (1) low-anxiety, (2) moderate-anxiety, and (3) high-anxiety conditions. A person's score was the number of items answered correctly on the test. These scores appear in Table 16.1.

The calculations for obtaining $SS_b$, $SS_w$, $MS_b$, and $MS_w$ are shown in Table 16.1. In panel B of Table 16.1 the data are summarized by the necessary quantities, $n$, $\Sigma X$, $\overline{X}$, and so on.

The null hypothesis $H_0: \mu_1 = \mu_2 = \mu_3$ is tested by comparing the obtained $F$-ratio ($F = MS_b/MS_w$) to the central $F$-distribution (i.e., the distributions of $F$ when $H_0$ is true) in Table F of the Appendix. The obtained value of $F$ is located relative to various percentile points of the $F$-distribution with 2 and 27 degrees of freedom to determine whether it could reasonably be regarded as an $F$-value randomly sampled from that distribution—which it must be if $H_0$ is true.

The value of the $F$-ratio for the data in Tables 16.1 is $F = 288.7/141.2 = 2.04$. In Table F we can find the following percentile points:

$$_{.99}F_{2,27} = 5.49$$

$$_{.95}F_{2,27} = 3.36$$

$$_{.90}F_{2,27} = 2.51$$

$$_{.75}F_{2,27} = 1.46$$

The obtained value of $F = 2.04$ from the data in Table 16.1 lies between the 75th and the 90th percentiles in the $F$-distribution with 2 and 27 degrees of freedom. Hence, if $H_0: \mu_1 = \mu_2 = \mu_3$ were true, an $F$-ratio as large or larger than 2.04 would occur with a probability $.25 > p > .10$. If $H_0$ were tested at the $\alpha = .05$ level, it would not be rejected. Even if $\alpha$ had been set at the .10 level of significance, $H_0$ would not have been rejected.

*More precisely, $E(F) = \nu_e/(\nu_e - 2)$; in the one-factor ANOVA $\nu_e = \nu_w$. A more thorough discussion of the theory related to the $F$-test appears later in this chapter.

**TABLE 16.1 Illustration of Calculations for a One-Factor ANOVA with Equal $n$'s ($n = 10$)**

| | Treatment | | | |
|---|---|---|---|---|
| | *1* *Low* | *2* *Moderate* | *3* *High* | |
| A. | 26 | 51 | 52 | |
| | 34 | 50 | 64 | |
| | 46 | 33 | 39 | |
| | 48 | 28 | 54 | |
| | 42 | 47 | 58 | |
| | 49 | 50 | 53 | |
| | 74 | 48 | 77 | |
| | 61 | 60 | 56 | |
| | 51 | 71 | 63 | |
| | 53 | 42 | 59 | |
| B. $\sum_{i=1}^{n=10} X_i$: | 484 | 480 | 575 | $1{,}539 = \sum_{j=1}^{J=3} \sum_{i=1}^{n=10} X_{ij}$ $\quad n_{\boldsymbol{\cdot}} = Jn = 30$ |
| $\overline{X}_j$: | 48.40 | 48.00 | 57.50 | $51.30 = \overline{X}_{\boldsymbol{\cdot}} = \sum_j \sum_i X_{ij}/n_{\boldsymbol{\cdot}} = 1{,}539/30$ |
| $\hat{\alpha}_j$: | −2.90 | −3.30 | 6.20 | (Eq. 16.2) |
| $SS_j$: | 1598.40 | 1352.00 | 862.50 | |
| $s_j^2$: | 177.60 | 150.22 | 95.83 | |

*Step*

C. 1.[a] $SS_b = \sum_j n_j \hat{\alpha}_j^2 = 10[(-2.9)^2 + (-3.3)^2 + (6.2)^2] = 577.4$ (Eq. 16.4)

## 16.6 ANOVA THEORY

In this section a theoretical explanation of ANOVA will be presented. Suppose that the null hypothesis $H_0 : \mu_1 = \ldots = \mu_J$ is true. That is, the $J$ population means about which one wishes to make an inference are all the same. This *hypothesis* when combined with the ANOVA *assumptions* (Sec. 16.7) implies that *there are J populations, all of which are normal in shape and which have identical means,* $\mu$, *and variances,* $\sigma^2$ (See Fig. 16.3, panels A and B). In effect, if the null hypothesis is true, there are not $J$ different populations, there is only one. Thus, when $J$ samples each of size $n$ are drawn, one is actually drawing $J$ independent samples from a single normal distribution.

**TABLE 16.1 (cont.)**

2.[b] $SS_w = \sum_j SS_j = 1598.4 + 1352.0 + 862.5 = 3812.9$ (Eq. 16.6)

3. $MS_b = \dfrac{SS_b}{\nu_b} = \dfrac{577.4}{2} = 288.7$

4. $MS_w = SS_w/\nu_w = 3812.9/27 = 141.2$

5. $F = MS_b/MS_w = 288.7/141.22 = 2.04$

6. $F = 2.04 < {}_{.95}F_{2,27} = 3.35$; $H_0$ is tenable

D. ANOVA Summary Table:

| *Source* | *SS* | $\nu$ | *MS* | *F* | *p* |
|---|---|---|---|---|---|
| Between | 577.4 | 2 | 288.7 | 2.04 | > .05 |
| Within | 3812.9 | 27 | 141.2 | | |

[a]If Equation 16.5 is used for $SS_b$:

$$SS_b = \sum_j \frac{\left(\sum_i X_{ij}\right)^2}{n} - \frac{\left(\sum_j \sum_i X_{ij}\right)^2}{n_{\bullet}} = \frac{(484)^2}{10} + \frac{(480)^2}{10} + \frac{(575)^2}{10} - \frac{(1{,}539)^2}{30} = 577.4$$

[b]If Equation 16.7 is used for $SS_w$:

$$SS_w = SS_{\text{total}} - SS_b$$

$$SS_{\text{total}} = \sum_j \sum_i X_{ij}^2 - \frac{\left(\sum_j \sum_i X_{ij}\right)^2}{n_{\bullet}} = (26)^2 + (34)^2 + \cdots + (59)^2 - (1539)^2/30 = 4{,}390.3$$

$$SS_w = 4{,}390.3 - 577.4 = 3812.9$$

## $MS_b$

In Chapter 11, it was demonstrated that when random samples of size $n$ are drawn from a distribution, the expected value of the mean of the sample means is $\mu$ and the expected value of their variance will be $\sigma^2/n$. The same is true here. If $J$ samples are drawn from a single population (i.e., $H_0$ is true), one expects the variance of those $J$ sample means to be $\doteq \sigma^2/n$. It follows then that $n$ times the variance of the $J$ sample means estimates $\sigma^2$ (See Fig. 16.3, panel C).

$$E(s_{\bar{X}}^2) = \frac{\sigma^2}{n}$$

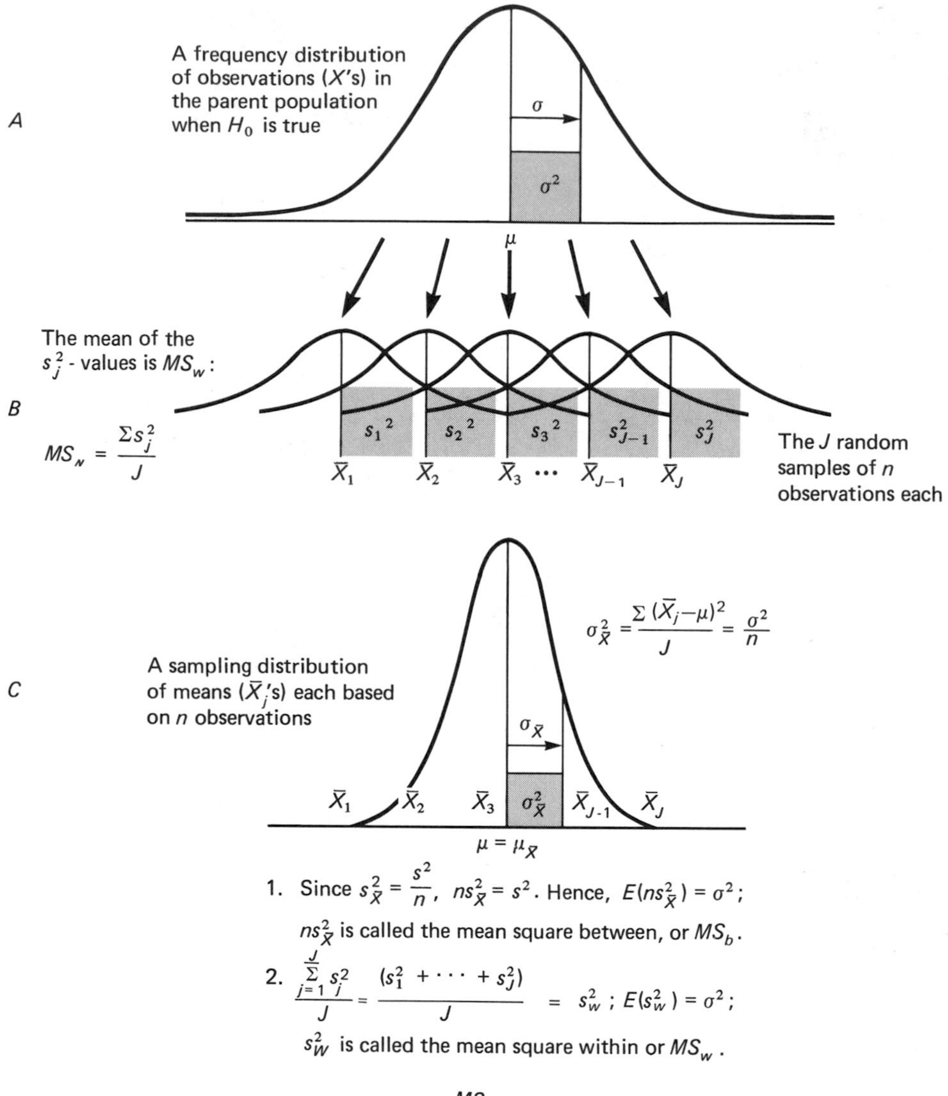


1. Since $s_{\bar{X}}^2 = \frac{s^2}{n}$, $ns_{\bar{X}}^2 = s^2$. Hence, $E(ns_{\bar{X}}^2) = \sigma^2$; $ns_{\bar{X}}^2$ is called the mean square between, or $MS_b$.
2. $\frac{\sum_{j=1}^{J} s_j^2}{J} = \frac{(s_1^2 + \cdots + s_J^2)}{J} = s_W^2$ ; $E(s_W^2) = \sigma^2$; $s_W^2$ is called the mean square within or $MS_w$.
3. Therefore, $F = \frac{MS_b}{MS_w}$ should be "about" 1 when the null hypothesis is true.

**FIGURE 16.3.** Theoretical basis of the ANOVA. The variance error of the mean, $s_{\bar{X}}^2$, when multiplied by $n$, gives an unbiased estimate of the variance among the observations in the frequency distribution of the parent population when the null hypothesis is true.

Hence,

$$E(ns_{\bar{X}}^2) = \sigma^2$$

Look more closely at $ns_{\bar{X}}^2$:

$$ns_{\bar{X}}^2 = n\sum_{j=1}^{J}\frac{(\bar{X}_j - \bar{X}_{\bullet})^2}{J-1} = \frac{n\Sigma\hat{\alpha}_j^2}{J-1} = MS_b \qquad \textbf{(16.8)}$$

Equation 16.8 gives the value of $MS_b$. Note that $MS_b$ is defined in just such a way that it estimates $\sigma^2$, the variance of the population sampled, when the null hypothesis regarding population means is true.

### $MS_w$

For the $J$ samples (Fig. 16.3, panel B), each gives an estimate $s_j^2$ of the population variance $\sigma^2$. If all these variance estimates were averaged an even better estimate of $\sigma^2$ would be obtained.

$$E\left(\frac{s_1^2 + \cdots + s_J^2}{J}\right) = \sigma^2$$

Recall that when $n$'s are equal, *mean square within*, $MS_w$, *is the average of the J sample variances.**

$$\sum_{j=1}^{J}\frac{s_j^2}{J} = \frac{s_1^2 + \cdots + s_J^2}{J} = MS_w \qquad \textbf{(16.9)}$$

Notice in Table 16.1 that $MS_w = \Sigma_j s_j^2/J = 423.65/3 = 141.2$. Therefore, $MS_w$ also estimates $\sigma^2$; and an important fact about $MS_w$ is that, unlike $MS_b$, *it estimates* $\sigma^2$ *whether or not the null hypothesis is true.*

## 16.7 THE *F*-TEST

If the null hypothesis ($H_0 : \mu_1 = \cdots = \mu_J$) is true, then $MS_b$ and $MS_w$ both estimate the same parameter—namely, $\sigma^2$. $MS_b$ and $MS_w$ will be *independent* estimates of $\sigma^2$ under these circumstances. If one compares $MS_b$ and $MS_w$—for example, by taking their ratio, $F = MS_b/MS_w$, one obtains evidence of whether they are estimating the same parameter $\sigma^2$. If the ratio of $MS_b$ to $MS_w$ is "about" 1, then it is reasonable to assume that they are both estimating $\sigma^2$, that is, that the null hypothesis is true. How much larger than 1 the ratio $MS_b/MS_w$ can be and still support the null hypothesis is best determined by referring the ratio to the central $F$-distribution (Table F), since this distribution describes the distribution of the ratio of two independent estimates of the same variance.

*If $n$'s are not equal, $MS_w = \sum_{j=1}^{J} \nu_j s_j^2/\nu_w$.

If the null hypothesis is false, then the variance estimate from the $J$ sample means will be larger than it is when $H_0$ is true. Thus, $MS_b$ estimates a number larger than $\sigma^2$ when $H_0$ is false. $MS_w$, however, is expected to estimate the same parameter $\sigma^2$ whether or not the null hypothesis about means is true, because it is based on variances *within* the $J$ samples and is insensitive to any difference among the means of the samples. Consequently, a false null hypothesis tends to yield a ratio of $MS_b$ to $MS_w$ greater than 1.

Such are the reasons for forming $F = MS_b/MS_w$, referring it to the $F$-distribution, regarding $H_0$ as tenable if the ratio $MS_b/MS_w$ is less than the critical-$F$: ${}_{1-\alpha}F_{J-1,n.-J}$, and rejecting it as false when $MS_b/MS_w$ is larger than the critical-$F$.

If $H_0 : \mu_1 = \mu_2 = \mu_3 = \cdots = \mu_J$ is rejected, does it necessarily follow that $\mu_1 \neq \mu_2 \neq \mu_3 \neq \cdots \neq \mu_J$? Certainly not; perhaps $\mu_1 > \mu_2 = \mu_3 \cdots = \mu_J$, or $\mu_1 = \mu_2 > \mu_3 = \cdots = \mu_J$, or any one of several patterns of results is possible. How, then, does one decide which means differ significantly from which other means? This is the topic addressed in Chapter 17.

## 16.8* A MODEL FOR THE DATA

The questions addressed in the one-factor ANOVA can be answered in more precise terms. Toward this end, it is assumed that any one of the thirty scores can be represented by a *linear model*. The term "linear" applies because the components are not squared, cubed, and so on.

Consider the following linear model for the $X_{ij}$'s:

$$X_{ij} = \mu + \alpha_j + \epsilon_{ij} \tag{16.10}$$

where $X_{ij}$ is the score for person $i$ in the $j$th group; $\mu$ is the grand mean (of all observations in the population); it is constant for all thirty scores—$\mu$ reflects the overall "elevation" of the scores; $\alpha_j$ is the effect of treatment $j$; it is a constant for all ten scores in group $j$. $\alpha_j$ reflects the elevation (or depression) in these scores that is associated with treatment $j$ (i.e., $\alpha_j = \mu_j - \mu$); $\epsilon_{ij}$ is the "error" in the linear model for the score, $X_{ij}$. It is the *residual* of the score, $X_{ij}$ when $\mu$ and $\alpha_j$ are used as predictors (i.e., $\epsilon_{ij} = X_{ij} - \mu - \alpha_j$).

Remember that $\mu$, $\alpha_j$, and $\epsilon_{ij}$ are numbers. If $\mu$ is 12, $\alpha_2$ is +2, and $X_{12}$ is 13, then $\epsilon_{12}$ is $13 - (12 + 2) = -1$. The main interest of the researcher concerns the $\alpha_j$'s: $\alpha_j$ reflects the effect treatment $j$ has on the scores. The grand mean $\mu$ is ordinarily of little interest (unless $X$ represents a gain score such as posttest - pretest). The original research question, "Do the effects of these three treatments differ?", can now be stated more precisely: "Is it true that $\alpha_1 = \alpha_2 = \alpha_3 = 0$, that is, $H_0 : \sigma_\alpha^2 = 0$?" Is the conclusion that the three treatments have the same effect tenable? This null hypothesis can be tested by the methods developed earlier in this chapter.

One needs a method of testing the hypothesis $H_0 : \alpha_1 = \alpha_2 = \alpha_3$ because each $\epsilon_{ij}$ does not equal 0. If there were no error in the linear model, the researcher could simply

*Sections 16.8 to 16.15 give a mathematical basis for ANOVA. Sections 16.1 to 16.7 should be thoroughly mastered before proceeding with Sections 16.8 to 16.15. A proper use of ANOVA does not require a mastery of Sections 16.8 to 16.15.

look at the means of the scores in the three groups to see if they were different and thus test the null hypothesis. But the $\epsilon_{ij}$'s are there and they must be dealt with. How do the $\epsilon_{ij}$'s arise? They come about in various ways. First, persons or whatever is measured are inherently different even when they are treated alike. Second, errors arise when an attempt is made to measure the students. These errors are due to unreliability (measurement error) of the measuring instrument, a test in this instance. Third, errors arise from all manner of uncontrolled happenings during the experiment. A student may break his pencil and have to obtain a new one; someone may not feel well; someone else may not like the researcher's looks and act uncooperatively. Additional error arises if the postulated linear model is not correct; it is possible that no linear model will give an exact description of the data. All these sources of error combine to make the results of the experiment today different from what would have been obtained yesterday or tomorrow on different groups of thirty students. The results of the experiment run at any one time will undoubtedly show differences between the three groups. It remains to be established, however, that the groups would be different if the experiment had been run on a different randomly chosen group of students under different conditions.

## 16.9 ESTIMATES OF THE TERMS IN THE MODEL

What one actually observes in an experiment are the 30 $X_{ij}$'s. The numbers $\mu$, $\alpha_j$, and $\epsilon_{ij}$ are unknown and unobservable; but certain estimates of them are possible. Statisticians have found a way to estimate the components of the linear model that has very useful and desirable properties. They obtain what are called *least-squares estimates* of $\mu$, $\alpha_j$, and $\epsilon_{ij}$. Denote these least-squares estimates by $\hat{\mu}$, $\hat{\alpha}_j$, and $\hat{\epsilon}_{ij}$. In the process of obtaining the least-squares estimates, the parameters of greatest interest, $\alpha_1, \ldots, \alpha_J$, are assumed to sum to zero, that is, $\alpha_1 + \cdots + \alpha_J = 0$. This is an entirely reasonable sort of restriction to adopt since the $\alpha_j$'s are thought of as "elevators" or "depressors" above or below a general level that is embodied in the parameter $\mu$. By placing this restriction on the $\alpha_j$'s, the statistician predetermines that the $\alpha_j$'s will have the properties of deviations from a mean $\mu$, since the sum of deviations around a mean is zero. The statistician has found that

$$\hat{\mu} = \overline{X}_{\bullet}$$

$$\hat{\alpha}_j = \overline{X}_j - \overline{X}_{\bullet}$$

$$\hat{\epsilon}_{ij} = X_{ij} - \overline{X}_j = e_{ij}$$

The estimates are made to fit the observed data in the sense that

$$X_{ij} = \hat{\mu} + \hat{\alpha}_j + e_{ij}$$

Notice that

$$X_{ij} = \overline{X}_{\bullet} + (\overline{X}_j - \overline{X}_{\bullet}) + (X_{ij} - \overline{X}_j) \qquad \textbf{(16.11)}$$

The first term on the right is $\hat{\mu}$, the second term is $\hat{\alpha}_j$ and the last term is $e_{ij}$.

## 16.10 SUMS OF SQUARES

To show that the total sum of squares is composed of two independent (orthogonal) components, $SS_b$ and $SS_w$, first, subtract the grand mean $\overline{X}_{\bullet}$ from each side of Equation 16.11:

$$X_{ij} - \overline{X}_{\bullet} = (\overline{X}_j - \overline{X}_{\bullet}) + (X_{ij} - \overline{X}_j) = \hat{\alpha}_j + e_{ij} \tag{16.12}$$

Second, square each side of the above equation and sum both sides over $j$ and $i$:

$$\sum_{j=1}^{J} \sum_{i=1}^{n} (X_{ij} - \overline{X}_{\bullet})^2 = \sum_j \sum_i (\hat{\alpha}_j + e_{ij})^2 \tag{16.13}$$

The quantity on the left in Equation 16.13 is the *total sum of squares*, $SS_{\text{total}}$. For the entire set of numbers obtained in a study the sum of the squared deviation of each number from the grand mean is the *total sum of squares*.

Now consider the right side of Equation 16.13. Notice that if we let $a$ stand for $\hat{\alpha}_j$ and $b$ stand for $e_{ij}$, then the right side involves the quantity $(a + b)^2 = a^2 + 2ab + b^2$. So it is easy to show that

$$SS_{\text{total}} = \sum_j \sum_i (\hat{\alpha}_j^2 + 2\,\hat{\alpha}_j e_{ij} + e_{ij}^2) \tag{16.14}$$

$$= \sum_j \sum_i \hat{\alpha}_j^2 + 2 \sum_j \sum_i \hat{\alpha}_j e_{ij} + \sum_j \sum_i e_{ij}^2$$

Within each of the $J$ groups, $\hat{\alpha}_j$ is a constant for all $n$ scores, hence

$$\sum_j \sum_i \hat{\alpha}_j^2 = \sum_j n\,\hat{\alpha}_j^2 = n \sum_j \hat{\alpha}_j^2$$

Because the sum of the deviations from the mean is zero (Sec. 4.9), and the $e_{ij}$'s within each group are these deviations (Eq. 16.12), the $e_{ij}$'s sum to zero. If each score in a distribution of scores that sum to zero is multiplied by a constant (in this case $\hat{\alpha}_j$), the sum of the products within each of the $J$ groups is also zero (Eq. 4.4):

$$\sum_{i=1}^{n} \hat{\alpha}_j e_{ij} = \hat{\alpha}_j \sum_i e_{ij} = 0$$

Thus the middle term in Equation 16.14 is equal to zero, and Equation 16.14 becomes

$$SS_{\text{total}} = \sum_{j=1}^{J} n\,\hat{\alpha}_j^2 + \sum_{j=1}^{J} \sum_{i=1}^{n} e_{ij}^2 = SS_b + SS_w \tag{16.15}$$

The total sum of squares ($SS_{\text{total}}$) has been partitioned (analyzed) into two additive components, the sum of squares between groups ($SS_b$) and the sum of squares within groups ($SS_w$). $SS_{\text{total}}$ reflects all the variation in the scores obtained. Thus the name "analysis of variance," or for short, ANOVA, has evolved. This analysis will be used to test the null hypothesis, $H_0 : \alpha_1 = \alpha_2 = \cdots = \alpha_J = 0$.

## 16.11 RESTATEMENT OF THE NULL HYPOTHESIS IN TERMS OF POPULATION MEANS

The null hypothesis $H_0 : \alpha_1 = \alpha_2 = \cdots = \alpha_J$ can be restated in an equivalent but slightly different form. The estimator of $\alpha_1$ was taken to be $\hat{\alpha}_1 = \overline{X}_1 - \overline{X}_{\bullet}$. Since $\hat{\alpha}_1$ is an unbiased estimator of $\alpha_1$, $E(\hat{\alpha}_1) = \alpha_1$ :

$$E(\hat{\alpha}_1) = E(\overline{X}_1 - \overline{X}_{\bullet}) = E(\overline{X}_1) - E(\overline{X}_{\bullet}) = \mu_1 - \mu = \alpha_1$$

Similarly, $\alpha_2 = \mu_2 - \mu$ and $\alpha_J = \mu_J - \mu$.

The null hypothesis can be written as

$$(\mu_1 - \mu) = (\mu_2 - \mu) = \cdots = (\mu_J - \mu)$$

Add $\mu$ to each of the three terms and it is the same as saying that $\mu_1 = \mu_2 = \cdots = \mu_J$. Hence the null hypothesis that $\alpha_1 = \alpha_2 = \cdots = \alpha_J = 0$ in the linear model, $X_{ij} = \mu + \alpha_j + \epsilon_{ij}$, is the same as the hypothesis that the means of the populations from which the samples are drawn are all equal, that is,

$$H_0 : \mu_1 = \mu_2 = \cdots = \mu_J$$

## 16.12 DEGREES OF FREEDOM

Associated with each sum of squares ($SS_{\text{total}}$, $SS_b$, and $SS_w$) is an integer, $\nu$, called the "degrees of freedom." Degrees of freedom is a name borrowed from the physical sciences where it denotes a characteristic of the movement of an object. If an object is free to move in a straight line only, it has one degree of freedom; an object that is free to move through any point in a plane, such as a bowling ball rolling down an alley, has two degrees of freedom; a ball in a handball court has three degrees of freedom: it can go from back to front, side to side, and floor to ceiling. Degrees of freedom enters into analysis of variance (ANOVA) by way of its geometric interpretation.*

*See the classic article by Helen Walker (1940) for an excellent explanation of the degrees of freedom concept.

### *Degrees of Freedom between Groups, $\nu_b$*

Consider first the degrees of freedom associated with $SS_b$; the definition of $SS_b$ (Eq. 16.3) is the following:

$$SS_b = \sum_{j=1}^{J} n_j(\overline{X}_j - \overline{X}_{\bullet})^2 = \sum_j n_j \hat{\alpha}_j^2$$

If the design is balanced, Equation 16.3 is simplified to

$$SS_b = n \sum_j \hat{\alpha}_j^2$$

and the group means (i.e., $\overline{X}_1, \overline{X}_2, \ldots, \overline{X}_J$) are related to $\overline{X}_{\bullet}$ by the equation:

$$\sum_{j=1}^{J} \overline{X}_j / J = (\overline{X}_1 + \overline{X}_2 + \cdots + \overline{X}_J)/J = \overline{X}_{\bullet}$$

If $J = 3$ and $\overline{X}_{\bullet} = 6$, $\overline{X}_1 = 3$, and $\overline{X}_2 = 7$, what must $\overline{X}_3$ be? $\overline{X}_3$ must be 8. If $\overline{X}_{\bullet} = 4$, $\overline{X}_2 = 3$, and $\overline{X}_3 = 4$, what must $\overline{X}_1$ be? $\overline{X}_1$ must be 5. If $\overline{X}_{\bullet}$ is a certain number, then when values are assigned to $J - 1$ means, the last mean is already determined—it must have a value that satisfies the equation. The degrees of freedom for $SS_b$ are one less than the number of groups, that is,

$$\nu_b = J - 1 \qquad \textbf{(16.16)}$$

### *Degrees of Freedom within Groups, $\nu_w$*

Consider the degrees of freedom associated with $SS_w$ (Eq. 16.6):

$$SS_w = \sum_{j=1}^{J} \sum_{i=1}^{n} (X_{ij} - \overline{X}_j)^2$$

For group 1, the computation of $SS_w$ involves

$$(X_{11} - \overline{X}_1)^2 + (X_{21} - \overline{X}_1)^2 + \cdots + (X_{n1} - \overline{X}_1)^2$$

How are $X_{11}, X_{21} \ldots X_{n1}$, and $\overline{X}_1$ related?

$$(X_{11} + X_{21} + \cdots + X_{n1})/n = \overline{X}_1$$

If $\overline{X}_1$ were a constant, say 12.40, to how many of the $n$ quantities $X_{11}$ through $X_{n1}$ could one assign any number and retain the value of 12.40 for $\overline{X}_1$? The answer is $n - 1$; thus the degrees of freedom for group, $\nu_1$, is $n_1 - 1$. Similarly, the degrees of freedom within group 2 is $\nu_2 = n_2 - 1$. Hence, the degrees of freedom within all $J$ groups, $\nu_w$, is

$$\nu_w = \sum_j \nu_j \tag{16.17}$$

Equation 16.17 can also be expressed as

$$\nu_w = n_\bullet - J \tag{16.17A}$$

For balanced designs, the following applies:

$$\nu_w = J\nu_j = J(n - 1) \tag{16.17B}$$

### *Total Degrees of Freedom*, $\nu_{\text{total}}$

$SS_{\text{total}}$ equals:

$$(X_{11} - \overline{X}_\bullet)^2 + (X_{21} - \overline{X}_\bullet)^2 + \cdots + (X_{nJ} - \overline{X}_\bullet)^2$$

The terms involved are related as follows:

$$(X_{11} + X_{21} + \cdots + X_{nJ})/n_\bullet = \overline{X}_\bullet$$

Of the $n_\bullet$ observations on the left of the equation, all but one ($n_\bullet - 1$) of them can be assigned numbers without restriction. The final ($n_\bullet$th) number is fixed, however, to satisfy the value of $\overline{X}_\bullet$. The degrees of freedom for $SS_{\text{total}}$ equals $n_\bullet - 1$, the total number of observations minus 1, that is,

$$\nu_{\text{total}} = n_\bullet - 1 \tag{16.18}$$

When $n$'s are equal (i.e., $n_1 = n_2 = \cdots = n_J$), then $\nu_{\text{total}} = Jn - 1$.

## 16.13 MEAN SQUARES: EXPECTATION OF $MS_b$ AND $MS_w$

A sum of squares ($SS$) divided by its degrees of freedom ($\nu$) is called a mean square ($MS$). In one-factor ANOVA only two mean squares will be of interest: the mean square between $MS_b$ which equals $SS_b/\nu_b$, and the mean square within $MS_w$ which equals $SS_w/\nu_w$.

*The expected value of a statistic is the mean of its sampling distribution.* The expected value of $MS_w$ is the long-term average of $MS_w$ from experiment to experiment. The expected value of $MS_w$ will be denoted by $E(MS_w)$. If an experiment were repeated an infinitely large number of times and each time $MS_w$ was computed, then the average of the population of $MS_w$ values would be $E(MS_w)$. $E(MS_w)$ can be written in terms of a characteristic of the normal populations from which the scores obtained in the experiment are a random sample.

First view $MS_w$ in a slightly different way. Here is a balanced ANOVA design:

$$MS_w = \frac{SS_w}{\nu_w} = \frac{\sum_{j=1}^{J} \sum_{i=1}^{n} (X_{ij} - \overline{X}_j)^2}{J(n-1)}$$

$$= \frac{1}{J}\left[\frac{\sum_i (X_{i1} - \overline{X}_1)^2}{n-1} + \frac{\sum_i (X_{i2} - \overline{X}_2)^2}{n-1} + \cdots + \frac{\sum_i (X_{iJ} - \overline{X}_J)^2}{n-1}\right]$$

Notice that $\Sigma_i (X_{i1} - \overline{X}_1)^2/(n-1)$ is the sample variance of group 1; it is denoted by $s_1^2$. The sample variance of group 2 is $s_2^2$, and so on. Therefore since the $n$'s are equal, $MS_w = (s_1^2 + s_2^2 + \cdots + s_J^2)/J$, that is, $MS_w$ is the mean of the sample variances of the $J$ groups. Earlier it was stated that $E(s_1^2)$ was $\sigma_1^2$, the variance of the population from which the scores in group 1 were sampled. If all the populations had the same variance, $\sigma^2$,

$$E(MS_w) = \frac{1}{J}\,E(s_1^2 + \cdots + s_J^2) = \frac{1}{J}\,[E(s_1^2) + \cdots + E(s_J^2)] \tag{16.19}$$

$$= \frac{1}{J}\,(\sigma^2 + \sigma^2 + \cdots + \sigma^2) = \frac{J\sigma^2}{J} = \sigma^2$$

*The expectation of $MS_w$ is $\sigma^2$.*

The size of $MS_w$ does *not* depend on the means of the populations underlying the groups in the experiment. $MS_w$ is "mean-free," reflecting only the variability among the measures *within* groups. Such variability is around *each* group mean, rather than around the grand mean of all the groups. Whether all of the groups are samples from the same normal population or all the normal populations have different means, $E(MS_w)$ will be the same, $\sigma^2$,* when the ANOVA assumptions are met.

The same cannot be said for $E(MS_b)$, however. If $H_0$ is true, that is, if all the populations underlying the samples in the experiment have the same mean (it was already assumed they have the same variance), then $E(MS_b)$ is $\sigma^2$. If, however, *any of the population means is different from any other*, then $E(MS_b)$ will be *larger than* $\sigma^2$. If all the population means are equal, then the null hypothesis, $H_0 : \mu_1 = \mu_2 = \cdots = \mu_J$ is *true.* If at least two population means are different, then the null hypothesis $H_0$ is false. Although no proof is given here, the exact value of the expectation of $MS_b$ is

$$E(MS_b) = \sigma^2 + \frac{n \sum_j \alpha_j^2}{J-1} \tag{16.20}$$

*To prove that this is indeed true, start with

$$E(MS_w) = E\,[(SS_{w_1} + SS_{w_2} + \cdots + SS_{w_J})/J(n-1)]$$

For each $SS_{w_j}$ substitute its equivalent, $(n-1)MS_{w_j}$. Then distribute the expectations and simplify. Further, note that the definition of $SS_{w_j}$ is $\Sigma_{i=1}^{n} (X_{ij} - \overline{X}_j)^2$, which does not involve the grand mean, $\overline{X}_{..}$

where $\sigma^2$ is the variance in each population, $n$ is the number of subjects in each group (10 in the example in Table 16.1), $J$ is the number of groups (3 in the example), $\alpha_j$ is the difference in the mean of the $j$th population and the grand mean (i.e., $\alpha_j = \mu_j - \mu$).

To summarize:

1. If $H_0$ is *true*, then

$$E(MS_w) = \sigma^2 \qquad \text{and} \qquad E(MS_b) = \sigma^2$$

2. If $H_0$ is *false*, then

$$E(MS_w) = \sigma^2 \qquad \text{and} \qquad E(MS_b) = \sigma^2 + \frac{n \sum \alpha_j^2}{J - 1}$$

which is greater than $\sigma^2$.

For simplicity, $\Sigma\alpha_j^2/(J - 1)$ is often denoted $\sigma_\alpha^2$, hence Equation 16.20 can be expressed more simply as

$$E(MS_b) = \sigma^2 + n\sigma_\alpha^2 \tag{16.21}$$

In any experiment $MS_b$ and $MS_w$ are calculated. By comparing $MS_b$ to $MS_w$, one can determine if $H_0$ is plausible. If $MS_b$ is very large relative to $MS_w$, then it is likely that $H_0$ is false. The $F$-test of the null hypothesis requires that the two variance estimates be independent; fortunately it can be proven mathematically that $MS_b$ and $MS_w$ are independent when the parent populations are normally distributed.

Suppose for the moment that three samples of ten scores are drawn at random from a normal population. This is exactly what would be done if, in the example experiment the three conditions were equal (in terms of their effects, if any, on the dependent measure). This is a case of $H_0$ being true. The thirty scores sampled could be placed in a table, such as Table 16.1, and the $MS_b$ and $MS_w$ could be computed. Would $MS_b$ and $MS_w$ be equal? No. Their expectations would be equal; but from one sampling to the next, $MS_w$ might be a little bigger than $MS_b$ this time, and maybe a lot smaller next time. The sample values of $MS_w$ and $MS_b$ will fluctuate independently from one sampling of thirty scores to the next (the experiment that was actually run is considered to be one case of sampling thirty scores). The cases that vex researchers are those in which $MS_b$ is large relative to $MS_w$. They would like to regard such an occurrence as evidence that $H_0$ is false. (If $H_0$ is false, they would expect $MS_b$ to be larger than $MS_w$.) But how can they be sure that a large value of $MS_b$ relative to $MS_w$ did not occur simply by random fluctuations in scores sampled from the same normal population? One can never be certain, but in the next section it will be seen how one can control the proportion of times that $H_0$ is said *incorrectly* to be false, that is, the probability of a type-I error.

## 16.14 SOME DISTRIBUTION THEORY

In Chapter 13 (Sec. 13.2) it was seen that a chi-square variable with one degree of freedom has the form

$$\frac{(X - \mu)^2}{\sigma^2} = z^2 \sim \chi_1^2$$

that is, the squared normal-deviate ($z^2$) is distributed as ($\sim$) chi square with 1 degree of freedom when $X$ is a normally distributed variable with population mean of $\mu$ and variance, $\sigma^2$. A concise notation for denoting this is $X \sim NID\,(\mu, \sigma^2)$ which specifies that the $X_{ij}$'s are independent, normally distributed, have a mean ($\mu$) of 0 and variance, $\sigma^2$.*

Suppose $n$ scores are randomly drawn from a normal distribution with mean and variance $\mu$ and $\sigma^2$. Since independent chi-square variables have the additive property (Sec. 13.2), the quantity

$$\frac{(X_1 - \mu)^2}{\sigma^2} + \frac{(X_2 - \mu)^2}{\sigma^2} + \cdots + \frac{(X_n - \mu)^2}{\sigma^2} \sim \chi_n^2$$

The sum of the squared $z$ scores has a chi-square distribution with $n$ degrees of freedom, that is, this sum computed on many repeated samples of $n$ scores has a known frequency distribution $\chi_n^2$, where $\nu = n$.

If $X_1, \ldots, X_n$ are $n$ independent observations from a normal population with variance $\sigma^2$, then (see Wilks, 1962)

$$\frac{(X_1 - \overline{X})^2}{\sigma^2} + \frac{(X_2 - \overline{X})^2}{\sigma^2} + \cdots + \frac{(X_n - \overline{X})^2}{\sigma^2} \sim \chi_{n-1}^2$$

Therefore,

$$\sum_{i=1}^{n} (X_i - \overline{X})^2/\sigma^2 \sim \chi_{n-1}^2$$

Also,

$$\sum_{i} (X_{ij} - \overline{X}_j)^2/\sigma^2 \sim \chi_{n-1}^2$$

Notice that $\overline{X}$, the sample mean of the $n$ observations, has replaced $\mu$, the mean of the population from which the observations were selected. Also, the chi-square variable has $n - 1$ instead of $n$ degrees of freedom.

For the experiment at the beginning of the chapter (see Table 16.1)

$$SS_w = \sum_{i=1}^{n} (X_{i1} - \overline{X}_1)^2 + \sum_{i} (X_{i2} - \overline{X}_2)^2 + \sum_{i} (X_{i3} - \overline{X}_3)^2$$

If the first quantity on the right of this equation is divided by $\sigma^2$, it would have the distribution $\chi_9^2$ (chi-square with 9 degrees of freedom). This is so because the scores in group 1 were *randomly* drawn from a *normal* population with *variance* $\sigma^2$. The same can be said for the other two quantities on the right of the equation. Since all three quantities are

*Some sources use $N(0, \sigma^2)$ rather than $NID(0, \sigma^2)$. The "$\sim$" symbol is short for "is distributed as."

distributed as $\chi^2_9$, then their sum divided by $\sigma^2$ is distributed as $\chi^2_{9+9+9}$ or $\chi^2_{27}$ (chi-square with 27 degrees of freedom). Hence, for the example

$$\frac{SS_w}{\sigma^2} \sim \chi^2_{27}$$

$SS_w$ divided by $\nu_w = 27$ is $MS_w$; then

$$\frac{SS_w/\nu_w}{\sigma^2} \sim \frac{\chi^2_{\nu_w}}{\nu_w} \quad \text{or} \quad \frac{MS_w}{\sigma^2} \sim \frac{\chi^2_{27}}{27}$$

This fact will be saved for future use.

In general how is the mean $\overline{X}$ of a group distributed? That is, what frequency distribution would result if $n$ scores were repeatedly sampled at random from a population and the mean computed for each sample? If the means, $\overline{X}$'s, are based on $n$ scores randomly drawn from a normal population, they will (1) be normally distributed themselves, (2) have mean $\mu$, and (3) have variance $\sigma^2/n$. In other words $\overline{X} \sim NID(\mu, \sigma^2/n)$.

Using these facts, one can see that $(\overline{X} - \mu)/\sqrt{\sigma^2/n}$ has a mean of zero and a variance of 1; hence, it is a $z$ score. Consequently,

$$\frac{(\overline{X} - \mu)^2}{\sigma^2/n} = \frac{n(\overline{X} - \mu)^2}{\sigma^2} \sim \chi^2_1$$

*If the null hypothesis is true*, then

$$\frac{\sum_{j=1}^{J} n(\overline{X}_j - \overline{X}_\bullet)^2}{\sigma^2} \sim \chi^2_{J-1}$$

because under that condition $E(\overline{X}_1) = E(\overline{X}_2) = E(\overline{X}_3) = E(\overline{X}_J) = E(\overline{X}_\bullet) = \mu$. That is, each of the three $\overline{X}_j$'s is an independent random sample from a normally distributed, infinite population of $\overline{X}_j$'s whose mean is $\mu$. The original assumption that the three populations sampled in the experiment had the same variance $\sigma^2$ permits this conclusion. In the example $J = 3$ and $n = 10$, hence if each side of the equation is divided by $J - 1 = 2$, then

$$\frac{\left[\sum_{j=1}^{3} 10(\overline{X}_j - \overline{X}_\bullet)^2\right]}{2\sigma^2} = \frac{MS_b}{\sigma^2} \sim \frac{\chi^2_2}{2}$$

provided $H_0$, the null hypothesis, is true.

From Eq. 13.6 (Sec. 13.5) the ratio of two independent chi-square variables each of which is divided by its degrees of freedom has an $F$-distribution.

$$\frac{\left[\sum_j 10(\bar{X}_j - \bar{X}_{\bullet})^2\right] \Big/ 2\,\sigma^2}{\left[\sum_j \sum_i (X_{ij} - \bar{X}_j)^2\right] \Big/ 27\,\sigma^2} = \frac{\left[\sum_j 10(\bar{X}_j - \bar{X}_{\bullet})^2\right] \Big/ 2}{\left[\sum_j \sum_i (X_{ij} - \bar{X}_j)^2\right] \Big/ 27} \sim F_{2,27} \qquad \textbf{(16.22)}$$

Notice that since $\sigma^2$ appears in both numerator and denominator it cancels itself.

The numerator of Equation 16.22 is $MS_b$ and the denominator is $MS_w$. To summarize then, *if the null hypothesis, $H_0 : \mu_1 = \mu_2 = \cdots = \mu_J$*, then

$$\frac{SS_b/\nu_b}{SS_w/\nu_w} \sim F\nu_b, \nu_w \qquad \text{or} \qquad \frac{MS_b}{MS_w} \sim F\nu_b, \nu_w \qquad \textbf{(16.23)}$$

In the example if $H_0$ is true, the ratio of the mean-square between, $MS_b$, to the mean-square within, $MS_w$, has an $F$-distribution with $\nu_b = 2$ and $\nu_w = 27$ degrees of freedom when $\mu_1 = \mu_2 = \mu_3$.

The ratio of the two independent variance estimates, $MS_b/MS_w$ is called the *F-ratio.* The $F$-ratio is the test statistic that will be used in the last steps of the test of $H_0$. When $H_0$ is true, the resulting $F$-distribution is described as the *central* $F$-distribution.

## 16.15
## THE *F*-TEST OF THE NULL HYPOTHESIS: RATIONALE AND PROCEDURE

To illustrate the distribution theory that has been developed, consider the act of repeatedly sampling at random three groups of ten scores each from the *same* normal distribution (note that under these conditions the null hypothesis is true). If each time this were done the $F$-ratio, $MS_b/MS_w$, were calculated and its value recorded, the frequency distribution of these $F$-ratios would look like the central $F$-distribution, $F_{2,27}$, in Figure 16.4. The $F$-ratios obtained by this procedure of repeatedly sampling, calculating, and recording would all be greater than zero and can be very large. With this knowledge, statisticians can calculate any percentile in the central $F$-distribution: for example, the $F$-ratio that will be exceeded by only 5% of the $F$-ratios ($_{.95}F_{2,27}$) can be determined. This is done assuming $H_0$ is true.

What if the sampling of the three groups of ten scores each was not done from the same normal population, that is, what if sampling is done under the condition in which the null hypothesis is false? Under these conditions one expects $MS_b$ to be larger than it would be if the null hypothesis were true. However, $MS_w$ would have the same expectation, $\sigma^2$. When the null hypothesis is false, $MS_b$ does *not* have a $\chi^2$ distribution and the ratios $MS_b/MS_w$ obtained from the sampling do *not* have a central $F$-distribution. However, the effect this sampling under conditions of a false null hypothesis has on the distribution of the $F$-ratios is known. They will be *on the average* larger than the $F$-ratios obtained by random sampling from a single normal population.

Suppose three groups of ten scores were randomly sampled repeatedly each from *one* normal population and the $F$-ratio calculated each time. The plot of the $F$-ratios

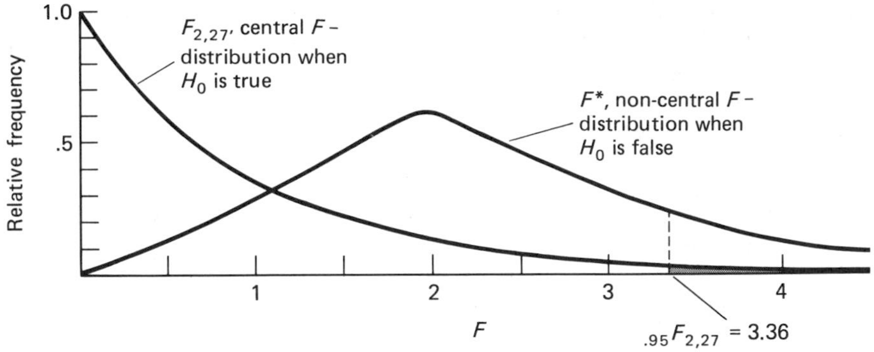


**FIGURE 16.4. Sampling distributions of $F = MS_b/MS_w$ when $H_0$ is true (curve $F_{2,27}$) and when $H_0$ is false (curve $F^*$).**

obtained looks like the central $F$-distribution in Figure 16.4. Now suppose two groups of ten scores each from a normal population with mean $\mu_1$, and one group of ten scores from a normal population with a different mean $\mu_2$ were repeatedly sampled. The null hypothesis is false, but in practice would not be known, because $\mu_1$ and $\mu_2$ are unknown characteristics of populations. The distribution of the $F$-ratios obtained would look something like the noncentral $F$-distribution, $F^*$ in Figure 16.4. Notice that the $F$-ratios in the noncentral distribution shift to the right (are larger) when sampling is done under conditions of a false null hypothesis instead of a true null hypothesis. Even so, some of the values in the central $F$-distribution, $F_{2,27}$, are larger than some of the values in non-central $F$-distribution, $F^*$. Is an $F$-ratio greater than 3.36 more likely to occur if one is sampling under conditions of a true or false null hypothesis? Compare the areas under the two curves to the right of the point 3.36 and see which area is larger (i.e., shows a greater probability of yielding a value of $F > 3.36$).

Statisticians can find the percentile points of the curve $F_{2,27}$; they can determine the value of $F$ such that only 5% or 1% of the values in the curve will exceed these points when $H_0$ is true. The 95th percentile in the curve $F_{2,27}$ is 3.36; the 99th percentile is 5.49. Table F in the Appendix reports the 75th, 90th, 95th, 97.5th, 99th, and 99.9th percentiles for various central $F$-distributions. As was seen in Chapter 13, the $F$-distribution depends on two values: the degrees of freedom for the numerator and the degrees of freedom for the denominator of the $F$-ratio. To find the $1 - \alpha$th percentile in the curve $F_{2,27}$, find the intersection of column 2 and row 26* and find the $F$-ratio associated with $\alpha$. For example, the value of $_{.95}F_{2,27} \doteq 3.36$.

What if the experiment were run and an $F$-ratio of 6.51 were obtained with 2 and 27 degrees of freedom? The 95th percentile of the curve, $_{.95}F_{2,27}$ is 3.36, and when the null hypothesis is true, the $F$-ratios form the curve $F_{2,27}$. If the null hypothesis were true, an $F$-ratio of 6.51 is a rare event indeed. Less than five times in 100 a value as large or larger than 3.36 would be obtained if the null hypothesis were true; an F-ratio of 5.49 or larger would occur only one time in 100, on the average. If the null hypothesis were false, then large values of $F$ are much more probable. The researcher reasons accordingly:

> If the value of the $F$-ratio obtained would occur less than five times in 100 (i.e., if it is greater than the 95th percentile of $F_{2,27}$) when the null hypothesis

*When the desired $\nu_e$ is not tabled, use the closest, lower value.

is true, then I shall conclude that the null hypothesis is false. It seems likely that such a value indicates a false null hypothesis since large values are more likely if the null hypothesis is false.

Choosing the 95th percentile of the curve $F_{2,27}$ as the point on which the decision about $H_0$ hinges is rather arbitrary. One could have chosen the 90th, 99th, or 99.9th percentile. What if the 50th percentile had been chosen? That is, what if one had agreed to reject the null hypothesis if the $F$-ratio were greater than the 50th percentile of $F_{2,27}$? If the null hypothesis were true, one would have a probability of $\frac{1}{2}$ of rejecting $H_0$ (calling it false). If researchers agreed on the 50th percentile point to make their decisions, half of them would be concluding that one method is better than another when the methods were actually no different. Researchers want to guard against these mistakes, type-I errors; so they agree to conclude that the null hypothesis is false when values equal to or greater than the value of $F$ obtained have a small probability of occurring when the null hypothesis is true. A "small probability" means .10, .05, or .01. These values correspond to using the 90th, 95th, and 99th percentiles, respectively.

## 16.16 TYPE-I VERSUS TYPE-II ERRORS: $\alpha$ AND $\beta$

It is *not* true that if the $F$-ratio from a study is large (e.g., 6.51), that the null hypothesis is *certainly* false. Such assertions are not possible in hypothesis testing. In making a conclusion such as "$H_0$ is rejected as a true statement about the means of the populations" or "$H_0$ is tenable" one is never absolutely certain of the truth of the conclusion. The conclusions will be correct a certain percent (90%, 95%, 99%, etc.) of the time they are made, given the truth or falsity of $H_0$.

Suppose the three anxiety conditions have absolutely no effect on tests scores. Suppose also that the experiment were repeated many times; each time an $F$-ratio is computed and the researcher draws a conclusion regarding $H_0$. Although unknown to the researcher, $H_0$ is true. The distribution $F_{2,27}$ that the obtained $F$-ratios will follow is the central $F$-distribution with 2 and 27 degrees of freedom. Five percent of the area under the $F_{2,27}$ curve lies to right of the point, $3.36 = {}_{.95}F_{2,27}$. Suppose the researcher has set $\alpha = .05$, hence $H_0$ will be rejected only when the obtained $F$-value exceeds 3.36. Since $H_0$ is true (in this illustration), the mistake of rejecting $H_0$ when it is true will be made 5% of the time, that is, $\alpha = .05$.

Notice the $\alpha$-value the researcher selects is arbitrary. If $\alpha = .01$ had been chosen, the critical $F$-ratio would be the 99th percentile point in the $F_{2,27}$ distribution; if $H_0$ is true, then on the average one time in 100 an $F$-ratio exceeding 5.49 would be obtained and the researcher would conclude (incorrectly) that $H_0$ is false. The size of $\alpha$ is under the researcher's control; it can be made as large or small as he wishes. There are two states that can exist as discussed in Sections 11.6 and 11.8: $H_0$ can be *true* or it can be *false*. A researcher agrees to make one of two conclusions after inspecting the data. Either $H_0$ will be *rejected* as the explanation, or $H_0$ will be *accepted* (i.e., viewed as a tenable explanation). The four possible outcomes of an experiment are shown in Figure 16.5.

If $H_0$ is true and is not rejected (lower left-hand cell), the decision is correct. If $H_0$ is false and is rejected (upper right-hand cell), the conclusion is also correct. How-

**FIGURE 16.5**
**Four possible outcomes of a test of a statistical hypothesis.**

| | $H_0$ is true | $H_0$ is false |
|---|---|---|
| Reject $H_0$ | Type I error ($\alpha$) | No error is made ($1-\beta$) |
| Do not reject $H_0$ | No error is made ($1-\alpha$) | Type II error ($\beta$) |

ever, if $H_0$ is rejected when it is true, a type-I error has been committed. If $H_0$ is false and is not rejected, a type-II error (Sec. 11.8) is the result.

The probability of committing a type-I error is denoted as $\alpha$. The size of $\alpha$ can be controlled, thus making the chances of incorrectly rejecting $H_0$ very large ($\alpha$ = .20 or .30) or very small ($\alpha$ = .01 or .001). It is customary to set $\alpha$ at .05 or .01, although the value should depend on the particular circumstances of a given analysis. If the number of subjects in a study is very small, $\alpha$ might be set at .10 or more.

The size of $\alpha$ is directly related to the probability of making a type-II error, $\beta$. The probability of failing to reject a false null hypothesis is under the control of the researcher to some extent. $\beta$ depends on the number of subjects in the experiment and the value of $\alpha$ chosen, among other things. The probability of correctly rejecting $H_0$ when it is false is denoted by $1 - \beta$; thus the probability of a type-II error is $\beta$. The power of a statistical test is the probability it will correctly reject $H_0$, which is $1 - \beta$. The larger the value of $\alpha$, the larger the value of $1 - \beta$. The value of $1 - \beta$ is of immense importance in planning research studies. All too often power considerations are neglected, even by otherwise competent researchers. All too frequently time and money are invested in an investigation in which the probability of discovering a true difference among treatments (i.e., power) is small, even if the treatment effects are as great as anticipated (Hopkins, 1973). That is, even if $H_0$ is false, the researcher has little chance of discovering it—there is a high probability that $H_0$ will not be rejected even though it is false.

It may happen if $\alpha$ is set at .05, the corresponding value of $1 - \beta$ might be .20; but if $\alpha$ were .10, $1 - \beta$ could be .50. Ordinarily it is prudent to take a slightly greater risk of a type-I error ($\alpha$) for a substantial increase in the probability, $1 - \beta$, of finding differences between the treatments. Just how large $\alpha$ and $\beta$ should be, or how $\alpha$ should be changed to compensate for a large $\beta$ are questions that go beyond the mathematics of

**FIGURE 16.6. Illustration of the probabilities of type-I and type-II errors for $J = 3$, $n = 10$, and a particular alternative hypothesis.**

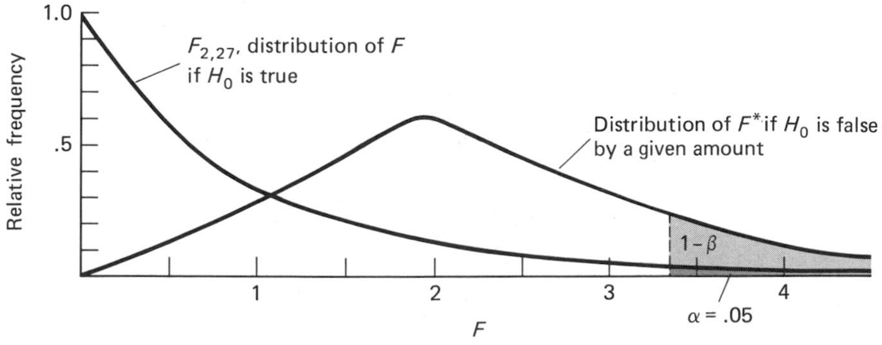

**TABLE 16.2 Illustration of Calculation of a One-Factor ANOVA with Unequal *n*'s Using Conformity Scores of Subjects Who Were Told That They Held Opinions of Low, Medium, or High Similarity to Students in General (see Fig. 16.2 for procedural steps)**

| | 1<br>*Low similarity* | 2<br>*Medium similarity* | 3<br>*High similarity* | |
|---|---|---|---|---|
| | 15 13 11 9<br>14 13 10 9<br>14 13 10 9<br>14 13 10 8<br>13 13 10 8<br>13 13 10 8 | 15 12<br>15 11<br>14 11<br>14 10<br>14 10<br>13 10 | 18 14 12 10<br>17 14 12 10<br>16 14 12 10<br>15 14 12 10<br>14 13 11 9<br>14 13 11 8 | |
| $n_j$: | 24 | 12 | 24 | $60 = n.$ |
| $\sum_{i=1}^{n_j} X_{ij}$: | 273 | 149 | 303 | $725 = \sum_{j=1}^{J=3} \sum_{i=1}^{n_j} X_{ij}$ |
| $\overline{X}_j$: | 11.375 | 12.417 | 12.625 | $12.083 = \overline{X}_{\bullet} = \frac{725}{60}$ |
| $\hat{\alpha}_j$: | −.708 | .333 | .542 | (Eq. 16.2) |
| $SS_j$: | 115.625 | 42.917 | 145.625 | |
| $s_j^2$: | 5.027 | 3.902 | 6.332 | |

$$SS_b = \sum_j n_j \hat{\alpha}_j^2 = 24(-.708)^2 + 12(.333)^2 + 24(.542)^2 = 20.411;^a$$

$$MS_b = \frac{SS_b}{\nu_b} = \frac{20.411}{2} = 10.205$$

$$SS_w = \sum_j SS_j = 115.62 + 42.917 + 145.625 = 304.162;^b$$

$$MS_w = \frac{SS_w}{\nu_w} = \frac{304.162}{57} = 5.356$$

ANOVA TABLE:

| *Source* | *SS* | $\nu$ | *MS* | *F* | | |
|---|---|---|---|---|---|---|
| Between Groups | 20.411 | 2 | 10.206 | 1.91 | $p > .10$ | $({}_{.90}F_{2,57} \doteq 3.15)$ |
| Within Groups | 304.162 | 57 | 5.336 | | | |

[a] Alternatively, if Equation 16.5 is used (values will differ trivially due to rounding error):

$$SS_b = \frac{(\Sigma_i X_{i1})^2}{n_1} + \frac{(\Sigma_i X_{i2})^2}{n_2} + \frac{(\Sigma_i X_{i3})^2}{n_3} - (\Sigma_j \Sigma_i X_{ij})^2/n.$$

$$= \frac{(273)^2}{24} + \frac{(149)^2}{12} + \frac{(303)^2}{24} - \frac{(725)^2}{60} = 20.417$$

[b] Alternatively, if Equation 16.7 is used:

$$SS_w = SS_{\text{total}} - SS_b$$

$$SS_{\text{total}} = \sum_{j=1}^{J} \sum_{i=1}^{n_j} X_{ij}^2 - \left(\sum_j \sum_i X_{ij}\right)^2 \Big/ n. = (15)^2 + (14)^2 + \cdots + (8)^2 - (725)^2/60$$

$$SS_w = 324.583 - 20{,}417 = 307.17$$

statistics. The questions are basically about the losses that ensue from errors and the benefits of being correct. These are not questions to which statisticians normally give more enlightened answers than other knowledgeable observers.

The definitions of $\alpha$ and $\beta$ and their relationship are depicted in Figure 16.6. The calculation of the power of the $F$-test of $H_0$ will be illustrated in Section 16.19 and Table 16.20.

## 16.17 COMPUTATIONAL PROCEDURES FOR THE ONE-FACTOR ANOVA

A study having $J$ levels of a treatment factor is run. Within each of the $J$ groups there are $n$ independent observations (replicates). The sequence for the ANOVA will be illustrated using the steps for testing a hypothesis employed in Chapter 13. A linear model is postulated to explain the data: $X_{ij} = \mu + \alpha_j + \epsilon_{ij}$, where $\alpha_j = \mu_j - \mu$, $\epsilon_{ij} = X_{ij} - \mu_j$, and $\Sigma_{j=1}^{J} n_j\alpha_j = 0$ (or when $n$'s are equal, $\Sigma_j \alpha_j = 0$).

1. *Hypotheses.*

$$H_0 : \mu_1 = \mu_2 = \cdots = \mu_J \text{ (or } H_0 : \alpha_1 = \alpha_2 = \cdots = \alpha_J = 0)$$

$$H_1 : \sum_j \alpha_j^2 \neq 0 \text{ (i.e., at least two } \mu_j\text{'s differ)}$$

2. *Assumptions.*

$$\epsilon_{ij} \sim NID(0, \sigma_\epsilon^2)$$

3. *Test Statistic,*

$$F = \frac{MS_b}{MS_w} = \frac{SS_b/\nu_b}{SS_w/\nu_w}$$

4. *Sampling Distribution*
If $H_0$ is true, the $F$-ratio has a central $F$-distribution with $\nu_b$ and $\nu_w$ degrees freedom, $F_{\nu_b, \nu_w}$.

5. *Critical Value.*
If $F > {}_{1-\alpha}F_{\nu_b, \nu_w}$, then $H_0$ is rejected at the $\alpha$ level of significance.

6. The $(1 - \alpha)$ CI for each of the $J$ means (see also Eq. 11.9) is

$$(1 - \alpha)\ \text{CI} = \overline{X}_j \pm \sqrt{_{1-\alpha}F_{1,\nu_w}(MS_w/n_j)} = \overline{X}_j \pm {}_{1-\alpha/2}t_{\nu_w}s_{\overline{X}_j}$$

7. In Table 16.2 data that represent the effects of perceived similarity to a social group on conformity were observed. A group of sixty experimental subjects was divided at random into three groups: low similarity—subjects ($n_1 = 24$) in this group were informed that their expressed opinions were generally at variance with those of college students in general: medium similarity—subjects ($n_2 = 12$) were told that their opinions agreed with those of college students in general only moderately often: high similarity—subjects ($n_3 = 24$) were told that their opinions were usually exactly like those of students in general. After subjects were thus informed, they were asked to express their opinions about eighteen questions (capital punishment, birth control, etc.). Before expressing their opinion, however, the subjects were told how students in general felt about each issue. The number of times out of eighteen questions that a subject's expressed opinion was the same as what was portrayed to be the opinion of students in general was taken to be the number of times the subject "conformed to majority opinion." The actual "conformity scores" for the $n_{\bullet} = 60$ subjects are presented in Table 16.2.

## 16.18 CONSEQUENCES OF FAILURE TO MEET THE ANOVA ASSUMPTIONS: THE "ROBUSTNESS" OF ANOVA

Recall that the following assumptions are made in a simple one-way fixed-effects model ANOVA:

$$X_{ij} = \mu + \alpha_j + \epsilon_{ij}, \qquad \text{where} \qquad \sum_j n_j \alpha_j = 0, \qquad \text{and}$$

$\epsilon_{ij} \sim NID\,(0, \sigma_\epsilon^2)$, that is, within each of the $J$ groups the observations are normally* and independently distributed about their mean $\mu_j$ with variance $\sigma_\epsilon^2$.†

The model implies that an observation can be thought of as the simple sum of three components: one reflecting the overall elevation of the measurements ($\mu$); a second reflecting the increment or decrement on the dependent variable resulting from all obser-

*Since for each level of the factor $\epsilon_{ij} = X_{ij} - \mu - \alpha_j$, and $\mu$ and $\alpha_j$ are constants, $\epsilon_{ij}$ is a linear transformation (Sec. 7.9) of $X_{ij}$; thus the ANOVA assumptions regarding the distributions of $\epsilon_{ij}$ and $X_{ij}$ are synonymous. Note that $\sigma_X^2 = \sigma_\epsilon^2 = \sigma_W^2$, which is often designated simply as $\sigma^2$.

†Normality can be tested via the $\chi^2$ goodness-of-fit test (Sec. 14.7); homogeneity of variance is treated in Sections 13.7, 13.8, and 16.23.

vations taken in group $j$ being exposed to treatment $j$; and a component $\epsilon_{ij}$ that comprises things usually referred to in the behavioral sciences as "individual differences" and "measurement error," among others. Various ways exist in which the linear model can fail to be correct. One is that the effect of treatment $j$ is not the same for all persons exposed to the treatment. For example, some students may benefit more from a particular treatment than others. Research suggests that the magnitude of the practice effect on mental ability tests is greater for brighter students than for duller ones. If this is expected, a two-factor ANOVA should be employed (see Chap. 18) so that possible differential effects by ability level can be examined statistically.

The assumptions, *NID* $(0, \sigma_\epsilon^2)$, state that the $\epsilon_{ij}$'s over repeated random samples have a normal distribution with a population mean (expectation) of 0 and variance of $\sigma_\epsilon^2$ and are independent. Three distinct violations of this assumption can be considered: (1) nonnormality, (2) heterogeneity of variance among groups, and (3) nonindependence. When these assumptions are met, the distribution of scores within each of the $J$ groups will differ from the normal distribution because of sampling error. Any difference in the $s_j^2$'s is also the result of sampling error. Furthermore, if repeated samples are drawn and a scatter diagram of the sample means for any one of the $[J(J - 1)/2]$ pairs of treatments is constructed, it will show zero correlation of the means because of the independence assumption. Failure to satisfy the independence assumption can be serious. The correlated or dependent groups $t$-test is an appropriate statistical technique (if only two treatments are being compared) when the nonindependence of the $\epsilon_{ij}$'s is due to pairing observations, such as when comparing pretest and posttest scores. (If $J > 2$ see Sec. 19.14.)

What follows is concerned with the effects of violations of the assumptions of normality, homogeneity of variance, and independence on the accuracy of the probability statements (i.e., $p$'s) and power. The paradigm for past research by mathematical statisticians has been somewhat like the following:

1. Given a true null hypothesis, find from the $F$-table the $1 - \alpha$ percentile in the $F$-distribution with $\nu_b = J - 1$ and $\nu_e = n_{\bullet} - J$: $({}_{1-\alpha}F_{\nu_b,\nu_e})$. (This percentile will be the value exceeded by $\alpha$ of the $F$-ratios obtained in an ANOVA when the null hypothesis is true *and the ANOVA assumptions are met.*)
2. By empirical or mathematical means, the *actual* percentage of $F$-ratios exceeding ${}_{1-\alpha}F_{\nu_b,\nu_e}$ is found when the null hypothesis is true and the variances are heterogeneous or the populations are nonnormal or both.
3. The *nominal* significance level $\alpha$, and the *actual* significance level (the percentage of $F$'s exceeding ${}_{1-\alpha}F_{\nu_b,\nu_e}$) are compared.

Fortunately, "robustness" studies have confirmed that the $t$-test findings associated with the normality and homogeneity of variance assumptions generalize to ANOVA (see Figs. 12.2 and 12.3; Secs. 12.9 and 12.10). The studies on the empirical consequences of failure to meet ANOVA assumptions have been reviewed by Glass, Peckham, and Sanders (1972) and are summarized in Table 16.3. Their principal conclusions were as follows:

1. Nonnormality has negligible consequences on type-I and type-II error probabilities unless populations are highly skewed, $n$'s are small, *and* directional ("one-tailed") tests are employed (see Fig. 12.2).

**TABLE 16.3 Summary of Consequences of Violation of Assumptions of the Fixed-Effects ANOVA[a]**

| | *Equal n's* | | *Unequal n's* | |
|---|---|---|---|---|
| *Type of Violation* | Effect on $\alpha$ | Effect on Power | Effect on $\alpha$ | Effect on Power |
| Nonindependence of errors | Nonindependence of errors seriously affects both the level of significance and power of the $F$-test whether or not $n$'s are equal. | | | |
| Nonnormality: Skewness | Skewed populations have very little effect on either the level of significance or the power of the fixed-effects model $F$-test; distortions of nominal significance levels of power values are rarely greater than a few hundredths. (However, skewed populations can seriously affect the level of significance and power of *directional*—or "one-tailed"—tests.) | | | |
| Kurtosis | Actual $\alpha$ is less than nominal $\alpha$ when populations are leptokurtic (i.e., $\gamma_2 > 0$). Actual $\alpha$ exceeds nominal $\alpha$ for platykurtic populations. (Effects are slight.) | Actual power is less than nominal power when populations are platykurtic. Actual power exceeds nominal power when populations are leptokurtic. Effects can be substantial for small $n$. | Actual $\alpha$ is less than nominal $\alpha$ when populations are leptokurtic (i.e., $\gamma_2 > 0$). Actual $\alpha$ exceeds nominal $\alpha$ for platykurtic populations. (Effects are slight.) | Actual power is less than nominal power when populations are platykurtic. Actual power exceeds nominal power when populations are leptokurtic. Effects can be substantial for small $n$'s. |
| Heterogeneous | Very slight effect on $\alpha$, which is seldom distorted by more than a few hundredths. Actual $\alpha$ seems always to be slightly increased over the nominal $\alpha$. | (No theoretical power value exists when variances are heterogeneous.) | $\alpha$ may be seriously affected. Actual $\alpha$ exceeds nominal $\alpha$ when smaller samples are drawn from more variable populations; actual $\alpha$ is less than nominal $\alpha$ when smaller samples are drawn from less variable populations. | (No theoretical power value exists when variances are heterogeneous.) |
| Combined nonnormality and heterogeneous variances | Nonnormality and heterogeneous variances appear to combine additively ("noninteractively") to affect either level of significance or power. (For example, the depressing effect on $\alpha$ of leptokurtosis could be expected to be counteracted by the elevating effect on $\alpha$ of having drawn smaller samples from the more variable, leptokurtic populations.) | | | |

[a] From Glass, Peckham, and Sanders (1972).

2. When $n$'s are equal, violation of the $\sigma_1^2 = \sigma_2^2 = \cdots = \sigma_J^2$ assumption has negligible consequences on probability statements (type-I error) (see Fig. 12.3) or power.* When the larger $\sigma_j^2$'s and $n_j$'s are associated, ANOVA is "conservative," that is, actual $\alpha <$ nominal $\alpha$. When the larger $n_j$'s are associated with the smaller $\sigma_j$'s, ANOVA yields "liberal" results (i.e., actual $\alpha >$ nominal $\alpha$).
3. The assumption of independence is necessary for accurate probability statements. The independence assumption is difficult to evaluate. Independence of observations requires that the observations within groups not be influenced by each other. Whenever the treatment is individually administered, observations are independent. But where treatments involve interaction among persons, such as "discussion" method and group counseling, the observations may influence each other. If the observations are analyzed as if the data were independent, the true probability of a type-I error is apt to be larger than the nominal $\alpha$. In other words, nonindependence of observations increases the probability that treatment effects will be claimed for ineffective treatments. (This concern is dealt with more fully in Sec. 19.22.)

## 16.19 THE POWER OF THE $F$-TEST

Recall from Section 16.8 that the linear model for a one-factor, fixed-effects ANOVA is $X_{ij} = \mu + \alpha_j + \epsilon_{ij}$. The power $(1 - \beta)$ of a particular $F$-test in a one-factor ANOVA (i.e., the probability that $H_0: \mu_1 = \mu_2 = \cdots = \mu_J$ will be rejected when it is false) is a function of the following (see Sec. 11.12):

1. The magnitude of the differences among the population means. This is measured by their weighted (i.e., $n_j$) effects, $n_j\alpha_j^2$, where $\alpha_j = \mu_j - \mu$, where $\mu$ is the grand mean of the variable $X$.
2. The error variance (residual variance in $X$ not predicted using the parameters, $\mu$, $\alpha_j$): $\sigma_\epsilon^2$. (In a one-factor ANOVA $\sigma_\epsilon^2 = \sigma_w^2$.)
3. The number of degrees of freedom associated with the numerator of the $F$-test $(MS_b)$: $\nu_b = J - 1$.
4. The number of degrees of freedom associated with the denominator of the ("error term") $F$-test ($MS_e$). In a one-factor ANOVA, $\nu_e = n_\bullet - J$.
5. The probability of a type-I error, $\alpha$. (Do not confuse $\alpha$ with $\alpha_j$, as defined in step 1.)

To determine the numerical value for power, one must first determine a *noncentrality* parameter, denoted by $\phi$ (not to be confused with the phi correlation coefficient).

$$\phi = \sqrt{\frac{\sum_j n_j\alpha_j^2}{J\sigma_\epsilon^2}} \tag{16.24}$$

*This conclusion is correct within the degree of variance heterogeneity one is apt to encounter in practice. If $\sigma^2$'s are inordinately heterogeneous (e.g., $\sigma^2_{\text{largest}} = 10\,\sigma^2_{\text{smallest}}$) $\alpha$ may be nonnegligibly distorted (Rogan and Keselman, 1977).

If the design is balanced ($n_1 = n_2 = \cdots = n_J = n$), Equation 16.24 simplifies* to

$$\phi = \sqrt{\frac{n \sum_j \alpha_j^2}{J\sigma_\epsilon^2}} \qquad \textbf{(16.25)}$$

## 16.20 AN ILLUSTRATION

Suppose an experiment is being designed to test a treatment to improve the cognitive functioning level of environmentally impoverished children, who otherwise have an average IQ of 90, that is, the control group's expected mean is 90. If the treatment increases Wechsler IQ scores by an average of ten points, what is the power, that is, how likely is it that the researcher will come to the correct conclusion regarding the null hypothesis and reject it? Thus, $\mu_1 = 100$, $\mu_2 = 90$, and from test norms it is seen that $\sigma = 15$. How large a sample is needed to have good power? Using Equation 16.25, and $\mu = (\mu_1 + \mu_2)/2 = 95$:

$$\phi = \sqrt{\frac{n[(100-95)^2 + (90-95)^2]}{2(15)^2}} = \sqrt{\frac{50n}{450}} = \sqrt{\frac{n}{9}} = \frac{\sqrt{n}}{3}$$

Suppose it is planned to have $n_1 = n_2 = 40$ and $\alpha = .01$. Thus,

$$\phi = \sqrt{40}/3 = 2.11$$

Once $\phi$ is known, the power of the $F$-test can be determined from Table G in the Appendix for $\alpha = .01$ (and $\alpha = .05$). The use of Table G requires some explanation.

1. Find the figure corresponding to $\nu_b$; $\nu_b$ is given in the upper left-hand corner of each figure. In the example $\nu_b = J - 1 = 1$.
2. Find the row of $X$-coordinates along the base-axis that corresponds to the particular $\alpha$-value being used (.05 or .01). (In our example $\alpha = .01$ corresponds to the numerical values immediately below the grid.)
3. Locate the noncentrality parameter $\phi$ that has been determined from Equation 16.24 or 16.25 on the base-axis ($\phi = 2.11$ in the example).
4. Read up from the $\phi$ value to the point where it intersects with the value of $\nu_e$ in the set of curves with the value for $\alpha$ being used. (In the example $\nu_e = n_{\bullet} - J = 78$ and $\alpha = .01$).
5. Read the value for power $(1 - \beta)$ on the vertical axis (in the example $\phi = 2.11$ and the curve for $\nu_e = 78$ would intersect at $1 - \beta \doteq .63$).

*Equation 16.25 can also be expressed as $\phi = \sqrt{n\sigma_\alpha^2/\sigma_e^2}$ since $\sum \alpha_j^2/J = \sigma_\alpha^2$.

Since the probability of making a type-II error is quite large ($\beta \doteq .37$), how can power be increased? If $\alpha$ is increased to .05, what is the power? Entering $\phi = 2.11$ on the $\alpha = .05$ base axis, one finds that power is much higher, $1 - \beta \doteq .84$. What is power if $n_1 = n_2 = n$ is increased to 60? Then, $\nu_e = 118$ and $\phi = \sqrt{60}/3 = 2.58$; at $\alpha = .01$, the power is approximately .85; and at $\alpha = .05$, the power is about .95.

## 16.21 POWER WHEN $\sigma$ IS UNKNOWN

Often one does not have a good estimate of $\sigma$ prior to the study. In such situations it is useful to consider mean differences in standard deviation units. For example in Section 16.20 the effect size $[\Delta = (\mu_1 - \mu_2)/\sigma = 10/15 = 2/3]$ is $2/3\sigma$, or $\Delta = .67$.

Suppose $\mu_1 - \mu_3 = \sigma$, and $\mu_2 - \mu_3 = .5\sigma$; or, expressed graphically:

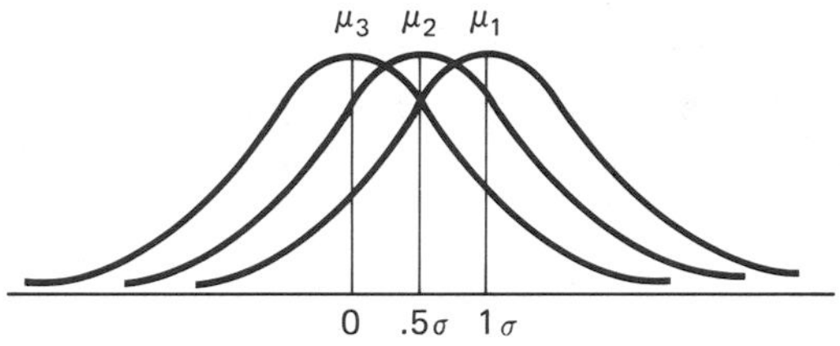


In other words $\mu_1$ exceeds $\mu_3$ by one standard deviation and exceeds $\mu_2$ by $.5\sigma$. If $n_1 = n_2 = n_3 = n = 20$, what is the power of the test at $\alpha = .05$? Since $\mu = .5$, then $\alpha_1 = .5$, $\alpha_2 = 0$, $\alpha_3 = -.5$, and $\Sigma\alpha^2 = .50$. Using Equation 16.25 with $J = 3$ and $\sigma_\epsilon = 1$,

$$\phi = \sqrt{n \sum_j \alpha_j^2 / J} = \sqrt{20(.50)/3} = 1.83$$

Reading the figure for $\nu_b = J - 1 = 2$ in Table G in the Appendix, one finds that $\alpha = .05$, and $\nu_e = 57$, the power of the test is approximately .80. But at $\alpha = .01$ the power drops to about .56.

## 16.22 $n$ REQUIRED FOR SPECIFIED POWER

For the situation described in the previous figure, what value of $n$ is required to achieve a power $(1 - \beta)$ of .90? Equation 16.25 can be rearranged as follows:

$$n = \frac{J\sigma_\epsilon^2 ({}_\alpha\phi_{1-\beta}^2)}{\Sigma\alpha_j^2} \qquad \textbf{(16.26)}$$

where ${}_\alpha\phi_{1-\beta}$ is the noncentrality parameter for power $= 1 - \beta$ at $\alpha(.01$ or $.05)$.

The noncentrality parameter associated with the power value $1 - \beta$ and $\alpha$ can be determined from Table G by reading ${}_{\alpha}\phi_{1-\beta}$ on the $X$-axis where $\nu_e$ and $1 - \beta$ intersect for the curves associated with $\alpha$. In the situation in Section 16.21 where $\Sigma\alpha_j^2 = .50$, $\sigma_\epsilon^2 = 1$, $\nu_b = 2$, and $\nu_e = 57$ one finds that ${}_{.05}\phi_{.90} \doteq 2.1$. When 2.1 is substituted into Equation 16.26, the number of persons per group is found:

$$n = \frac{(3)(1)(2.1)^2}{.5} = 26.5 \text{ or } 27$$

In other words if $n = 27$, the power is about .90 for rejecting $H_0: \mu_1 = \mu_2 = \mu_3$ at $\alpha = .05$ where $\mu_1 - \mu_3 = 1\sigma$ and $\mu_2 - \mu_3 = .5\sigma$. But for $\alpha = .01$, ${}_{.01}\phi_{.90}$ is equal to 3.5, hence the $n$ required is much greater:

$$n = \frac{3(3.5)^2}{.5} = 73.5 \text{ or } 74$$

Estimates of power $(1 - \beta)$ for very small $(.1\sigma)$ to very large $(1\sigma)$ effect sizes ($\Delta$, see Sec. 12.8) are given in Table 16.4 when $J = 2$ independent means are being compared via ANOVA (or the $t$-test). Power is given for various sample sizes ($n$/group) and the commonly used values of $\alpha$. For example, if the effect size $\Delta$ is .5 and $n = 50$, power is .46 at $\alpha = .01$ but .71 at $\alpha = .05$; if $n = 100$ and $\alpha = .05$, power increases to .94.

## 16.23 THE SCHEFFÉ TEST FOR HOMOGENEITY OF VARIANCE

Since the Scheffé test* (Scheffé, 1959, pp. 83–87) of $H_0: \sigma_1^2 = \sigma_2^2 = \cdots = \sigma_J^2$ requires a one-factor ANOVA, it was not illustrated in Chapter 13. Unlike the Bartlett, Hartley, and Cochran tests of homogeneity of variance, it is relatively insensitive to nonnormality. It has special applicability when (1) $n$'s are unequal, hence the homogeneity of variance assumption cannot be ignored in comparing means (Sec. 12.10); or (2) when parent populations are highly nonnormal, which confounds the interpretation of the Bartlett test (Sec. 13.8).

With the Scheffé test of homogeneity of variance, the scores within each of the $J$ groups are randomly subdivided into subgroups of approximately the same size. The data in Table 16.2 will be used to illustrate the test of $H_0: \sigma_1^2 = \sigma_1^2 = \sigma_3^2$, where $n_1 = 24$, $n_2 = 12$, and $n_3 = 24$. The scores within group $j$ are randomly subdivided into $k_j$ subgroups; the number per subgroup is arbitrary although there should be four or more subgroups

*Because several persons have made contributions to this test, it (or a slight variation) has been variously referred to as the Bartlett-Kendall test, the Box test, the Scheffé, and the Box-Scheffé test. In 1946 Bartlett and Kendall suggested performing an ANOVA on logarithmic transformations of the within-group variance estimates. In 1953, Box suggested dividing samples into subsamples and performing an ANOVA on logarithmic transformations of variance estimates computed on the subsamples. In 1959 this technique was generalized by Scheffé to accommodate unequal subsample sizes and sampling from nonnormal populations (see Martin and Games, 1977). Following Winer (1972), we designate the procedure as the Scheffé test.

**TABLE 16.4 Power for Various Effect Sizes for $J = 2$[a]**

| | | *Effect Size* $(\Delta)$[b] | | | |
|---|---|---|---|---|---|
| *n per group* | $\alpha_2$[c] | $\Delta = .1\sigma$ | $\Delta = .25\sigma$ | $\Delta = .5\sigma$ | $\Delta = \sigma$ |
| 5 | .01 | .01 | .01 | .03 | .10 |
| | .05 | .05 | .06 | .11 | .29 |
| | .10 | .10 | .12 | .19 | .43 |
| | .20 | .13 | .17 | .27 | .54 |
| 10 | .01 | .01 | .02 | .06 | .29 |
| | .05 | .05 | .08 | .18 | .57 |
| | .10 | .10 | .15 | .30 | .71 |
| | .20 | .14 | .23 | .42 | .81 |
| 15 | .01 | .01 | .02 | .09 | .50 |
| | .05 | .06 | .10 | .26 | .76 |
| | .10 | .11 | .19 | .39 | .86 |
| | .20 | .15 | .27 | .52 | .92 |
| 25 | .01 | .01 | .05 | .19 | .80 |
| | .05 | .06 | .14 | .42 | .94 |
| | .10 | .12 | .24 | .56 | .97 |
| | .20 | .17 | .35 | .68 | .99 |
| 50 | .01 | .02 | .09 | .46 | .99+ |
| | .05 | .07 | .24 | .71 | .99+ |
| | .10 | .14 | .36 | .81 | .99+ |
| | .20 | .22 | .49 | .89 | .99+ |
| 100 | .01 | .03 | .22 | .83 | .99+ |
| | .05 | .10 | .43 | .94 | .99+ |
| | .10 | .18 | .56 | .97 | .99+ |
| | .20 | .29 | .68 | .99 | .99+ |
| 200 | .01 | .05 | .48 | .99 | .99+ |
| | .05 | .16 | .69 | .99+ | .99+ |
| | .10 | .27 | .79 | .99+ | .99+ |
| | .20 | .39 | .86 | .99+ | .99+ |
| 400 | .01 | .11 | .78 | .99+ | .99+ |
| | .05 | .30 | .91 | .99+ | .99+ |
| | .10 | .42 | .95 | .99+ | .99+ |
| | .20 | .55 | .97 | .99+ | .99+ |

[a] For $J = 3$ and $J = 4$ or power if the analysis of covariance is used see Hopkins, Coulter, and Hopkins (1981).

[b] $\Delta = (\mu_1 - \mu_2)/\sigma$.

[c] To determine $\alpha_1$ for one-tailed test, divide $\alpha_2$ by 2. For example, for $\alpha_1 = .05$, power is same as for $\alpha_2 = .10$; for $\alpha_1 = .10$, use tabled values for $\alpha_2 = .20$.

**TABLE 16.5 An Illustration of the Scheffé Test of Homogeneity of Variance**

| *Group 1* | | | *Group 2* | | | *Group 3* | | |
|---|---|---|---|---|---|---|---|---|
| | $s_{1k}^2$ | $\ln s_{1k}^2$ | | $s_{2k}^2$ | $\ln s_{2k}^2$ | | $s_{3k}^2$ | $\ln s_{3k}^2$ |
| 15, 9, 14, 8 | 12.33 | 2.51 | 15, 14, 14, 10 | 4.92 | 1.59 | 18, 10, 15, 10 | 15.58 | 2.75 |
| 10, 13, 13, 9 | 4.25 | 1.45 | 10, 15, 10, 13 | 6.00 | 1.79 | 12, 14, 14, 10 | 3.67 | 1.30 |
| 11, 10, 14, 13 | 3.33 | 1.20 | 14, 11, 11, 12 | 2.00 | .69 | 12, 11, 16, 13 | 4.67 | 1.54 |
| 10, 9, 8, 10 | .92 | −.09 | | | | 12, 10, 8, 12 | 3.67 | 1.30 |
| 13, 13, 14, 13 | .25 | −1.39 | | | | 14, 14, 11, 14 | 2.25 | .81 |
| 13, 8, 10, 13 | 6.00 | 1.79 | | | | 17, 14, 9, 13 | 10.92 | 2.39 |

$\overline{X}_1{}^a = .91$ $\quad$ $\overline{X}_2 = 1.36$ $\quad$ $\overline{X}_3 = 1.68$

$SS_1 = 10.00$ $\quad$ $SS_2 = .69$ $\quad$ $SS_3 = 2.71$

$\hat{\alpha}_1 = \overline{X}_1 - \overline{X}_\bullet = .91 - 1.31 = -.40$ $\quad$ $\hat{\alpha}_2 = .05$ $\quad$ $\hat{\alpha}_3 = .37$

$\nu_1 = 5$ $\quad$ $\nu_2 = 2$ $\quad$ $\nu_3 = 5$

$$SS_b = \sum_j k_j \hat{\alpha}_j^2 = 6(-.40)^2 + 3(.05)^2 + 6(.37)^2 = 1.79$$

$$MS_b = SS_b/(J-1) = (1.79)/2 = .895$$

$$MS_w = \sum_j SS_j/\nu_w = (10.00 + .69 + 2.71)/12 = 1.117 \quad (\nu_w = \Sigma \nu_j = 12)$$

$$F = \frac{MS_b}{MS_w} = \frac{.895}{1.117} = .80; \quad {}_{.75}F_{2,12} = 1.56, p > .25$$

[a] To simplify notation, $\overline{X}_1 = \overline{X}_{\ln s_{1k}^2}$; the values of $\ln s_{1k}^2$ are treated as $X_{ij}$'s in the ANOVA.

per group (Winer, 1971). We shall use subgroups of size 4; a table of random numbers is used to form the $k_1 = 24/4 = 6$ subgroups of group 1, the $k_2 = 12/4 = 3$ subgroups of group 2, and the $k_3 = 6$ subgroups of group 3. These $k_{\bullet} = k_1 + k_2 + k_3 = 15$ subgroups and the computational procedures are given in Table 16.5.

Randomly assign each of the $n_j$ scores within each of the $J$ groups in $k_j$ subgroups.

1. Compute the variance ($s_{jk}^2$) of the set of scores in each of the $k_{\bullet}$ subgroups.
2. Find the natural logarithm ($\ln s_{jk}^2$) of each of the $k_{\bullet}$ variances.
3. Treat these $\ln s_{jk}^2$'s as observations in the $J$ groups and perform a one-factor ANOVA.
4. If $F = MS_b/MS_w \geqslant {}_{1-\alpha}F_{(J-1),(k_{\bullet}-J)}$, reject $H_0$.

In Table 16.5 $H_0: \sigma_1^2 = \sigma_2^2 = \sigma_3^2$ is tenable with $\alpha = .05, p > .25$.

## CHAPTER SUMMARY

If $J > 2$, performing several $t$-tests among the $J$ means is not recommended. When two or more means are to be compared, ANOVA should be used as an omnibus test of differences among the $J$ means: $H_0: \mu_1 = \mu_2 = \cdots = \mu_J$. When $J = 2$, ANOVA and the $t$-test are different paths to the same destination, that is, $F = t^2$.

ANOVA allocates the total sum of squares ($SS_{\text{total}}$) in a set of observations into two sources of variation: (1) that which is determined entirely from differences *between* the $J$ means ($SS_b$), and (2) that which results entirely from differences among the $n$ observations *within* the $J$ groups ($SS_w$). When $SS_b$ and $SS_w$ are divided by their degrees of freedom ($\nu_b$ and $\nu_w$, respectively), two independent estimates of variance, $MS_b$ and $MS_w$, are obtained. When $H_0$ is true, both $MS_b$ and $MS_w$ estimate the same parameter, $\sigma^2$, and the $F$-ratio, $MS_b/MS_w$, has an expected value of approximately 1. The distribution of $F$-ratios when $H_0$ is true is termed the *central F-distribution.* If $H_0$ is false, the expected value of $MS_b$ increases and consequently the expected value of $F$ increases.

The linear model for the common one-factor ANOVA is $X_{ij} = \mu + \alpha_j + \epsilon_{ij}$, where $\epsilon_{ij} \sim NID(0, \sigma_\epsilon^2)$. In ANOVA it is assumed that the $\epsilon$'s in the population (1) are normally distributed, (2) have equal variances, and (3) are independent. When $n$'s are equal, ANOVA is "robust" to violations of assumptions 1 and 2 (i.e., violations of statistical assumptions have negligible consequences on $\alpha$, the probability of a type-I error, or type-II error). When $n$'s are not equal, however, homogeneity of variance is necessary for accurate results. Homogeneity of variance can be tested using Scheffé's test which, unlike the tests treated in Chapter 13, is relatively accurate even with nonnormal populations.

The power of ANOVA is influenced by (1) the magnitude of the differences in the population means (i.e., $\Sigma\alpha_j^2$), (2) the number of groups, $J$, (3) the number of observations per group, $n$, and (4) the value of $\alpha$.

## MASTERY TEST

1. Suppose pupils in grades seven, eight, nine, ten, eleven, and twelve ($J = 6$) were compared with respect to absenteeism. If ANOVA were used rather than multiple $t$-tests, the probability of a type-I error would be less. (T or F)

2. How many different $t$-tests would be required to make all possible comparisons of pairs of means in Question 1? [$J(J - 1)/2$]
3. Write the null hypothesis for the omnibus $F$-test in Question 1. (Use grade levels for the subscripts for the respective means.)
4. If ANOVA were performed and the critical $F$-values associated with $\alpha = .05$ were used, is the probability of a type-I error equal to .05 if $H_0$ is true?
5. If $H_0$ is true, if multiple $t$-tests are used, and if the critical value for $t$ with $\alpha = .05$ is used, the probability of rejecting at least one of the 15 $H_0$'s is
   a. slightly less than .05
   b. .05
   c. slightly more than .05
   d. much greater than .05.
6. A "synonym" for sum of squares ($SS$) is
   a. $\overline{X}$ b. $\Sigma x_i^2$ c. $\Sigma X_i^2$ d. $(\Sigma X_i)^2$
7. The degrees of freedom for $SS_b$ are
   a. $J$ b. $J - 1$ c. 1 d. $n_{\bullet} - J$ e. $J(n - 1)$
8. The degrees of freedom for $SS_w$ are NOT
   a. $J - 1$ b. $n_{\bullet} - J$ c. $J(n - 1)$ d. $\Sigma_j \nu_j$
9. In ANOVA what is the numerator for the $F$-test?
   a. $MS_b$ b. $MS_w$
10. If $J = 3$ and $\overline{X}_1 = \overline{X}_2 = \overline{X}_3 = 11.0$, what will be the numerical value of the numerator of the $F$-test?
11. In Question 10, what is the value of the grand mean, $\overline{X}_{\bullet}$?
12. In Question 10, will $SS_{total} = SS_w$?
13. In ANOVA if $H_0: \mu_1 = \mu_2 = \cdots = \mu_J$ is true, are the expected values of $MS_b$ and $MS_w$ both equal to $\sigma^2$?
14. If the observed $F$-ratio is 1.00 or less, will the null hypothesis be rejected at an $\alpha = .25$?
15. The means of the thirty-one persons in the experimental group and the thirty-one persons in the control groups were compared using a $t$-test. The value of $t$ was 2.5. If ANOVA is performed on the same data, what will be the value of the $F$-ratio?
16. The critical value for $t$ in Question 15 with $\alpha = .05$ is 2.00; what is the critical $F$-value $({}_{.95}F_{1,60})$?

In Questions 17 to 19 indicate which $F$-value will be smallest. Study Appendix Table F for trends.

17. a. ${}_{.90}F_{2,30}$
    b. ${}_{.95}F_{2,30}$
    c. ${}_{.99}F_{2,30}$
18. a. ${}_{.95}F_{3,10}$
    b. ${}_{.95}F_{3,30}$
    c. ${}_{.95}F_{3,60}$
19. a. ${}_{.95}F_{1,60}$
    b. ${}_{.95}F_{2,60}$
    c. ${}_{.95}F_{3,60}$

Answer Questions 20 to 39 below assuming that $J$, the number of groups, is 4.

| *Source* | *SS* | $\nu$ | *MS* | *F* |
|---|---|---|---|---|
| Between | 30 | — | — | — |
| Within | — | 60 | 2.00 | — |

20. What is the value of $\nu_b$?
21. What is the value of $MS_b$?

22. What is the $F$-ratio?
23. If $\alpha = .05$, what is the critical value for $F$?
24. Will $H_0: \mu_1 = \mu_2 = \mu_3 = \mu_4$ be rejected at $\alpha = .05$?
25. Can $H_0$ be rejected at $\alpha = .01$?
26. Can $H_0$ be rejected at $\alpha = .001$?
27. What is the total number of observations, $n$, in this example?
28. What is the value of $SS_{\text{within}}$?
29. What is the value of $SS_{\text{total}}$?
30. Will nonnormality of $X$'s ordinarily lead to erroneous conclusions regarding the null hypothesis when ANOVA is used?
31. When using ANOVA with equal $n$'s does one need to be concerned about the homogeneity-of-variance assumption?
32. If $n_1 \neq n_2 \neq n_3 \neq n_4$, should one be concerned about the $\sigma_1^2 = \sigma_2^2 = \sigma_3^2 = \sigma_4^2$ assumption?
33. If $n_1 > n_2 > n_3 > n_4$ and $\sigma_1^2 > \sigma_2^2 > \sigma_3^2 > \sigma_4^2$ and $H_0$ is rejected, is the conclusion suspect?
34. If the larger $n$'s are paired with smaller variances and $H_0$ is not rejected, is the conclusion suspect?
35. In which of these situations is the independence-of-$X$'s assumption less apt to be satisfied?
    a. when the treatment is administered separately to each individual
    b. when the treatment is administered to a group of individuals simultaneously
36. If $n$'s are equal, is $\overline{X}_{\bullet} = \Sigma_{i=1}^{J} \overline{X}_j/J$?
37. Assuming $n_1 = n_2 = n_3 = n_4$, what is the average variance, $(s_1^2 + s_2^2 + s_3^2 + s_4^2)/4$, in the ANOVA table preceding Question 20?
38. The mean of the standard deviations within the four groups would be roughly
    a. 1 b. 1.5 c. 2.0 d. 2.5
39. If the ranges of scores within groups 1 through 4 are found to be 6, 5, 4, 5, is the value of $MS_w$ of 2.00 reasonable?

For items 40–46, using the linear model for ANOVA: $X_{ij} = \mu + \alpha_j + \epsilon_{ij}$

40. The treatment effects are represented by the symbol ___; the assumptions of normality, homogeneity of variance, and independence pertain to the ___ term.
41. The assumption of normality, independence, and homogeneity of variance can be denoted by ___.
42. If $\mu_1 = 23$, $\mu_2 = 19$, and $\mu_3 = 18$, and $n$'s are equal, $\mu =$ ___ and $\alpha_1 =$ ___.
43. If $X_{11} = 30$, $\epsilon_{11} =$ ___.
44. If $n = 10$ and $\sigma_\epsilon^2 = 7.5$, use Eqs. 16.19 and 16.20 to find $E(MS_w)$ and $E(MS_b)$.
45. If $s_1^2 = 6$, $s_2^2 = 5$, and $s_3^2 = 10$, $s_w^2 = MS_w =$ ____.
46. If $\alpha$ is changed from .05 to .01, power will be ____ (increased or decreased).

If $H_0: \mu_1 = \mu_2 = \cdots = \mu_J$ is true, then (items 47–48):

47. $\alpha_1 = \alpha_2 = \cdots = \alpha_J =$ ___; and $\sigma_\alpha^2 =$ ___.
48. $E(MS_b) = E(MS_w) =$ ___.

49. The noncentrality parameter $\phi$ used in determining power when $n$'s are equal is found from Equation 16.25:

$$\phi = \sqrt{\frac{n \sum \alpha_j^2}{J\sigma_\epsilon^2}}$$

Using Equation 16.25, supply the correct word (increases or decreases) in the following blanks. *Other things being equal*, power increases:

a. as $n$ _____,
b. as the variability among scores within the $J$ groups, $\sigma_\epsilon^2$, _____,
c. as the effect sizes for the $J$ groups, $\sum \alpha_j^2$, _____.

## *PROBLEMS AND EXERCISES*

1. Calculate the degrees of freedom for both $MS_b$ and $MS_w$ in each of the following instances:
   a. $J = 2, n = 4$  b. $J = 5, n = 2$
   c. $J = 3; n_1 = 3, n_2 = 6, n_3 = 4$  d. $J = 3; n_1 = 4, n_2 = 1, n_3 = 5$

2. Determine the critical value of $F = MS_b/MS_w$ for testing $H_0$ in each of the following instances:
   a. $J = 2; n = 6; \alpha = .01$  b. $J = 5; n = 7; \alpha = .10$
   c. $J = 3; n_1 = 4; n_2 = 6; n_3 = 8; \alpha = .05$

3. Which one or more of the following statements are equivalent to the alternative hypothesis $H_1$ in the one-factor ANOVA?
   a. $\mu_j \neq \mu_j'$ for some $j$ and $j'$  b. $\alpha_j \neq 0$ for some $j$'s
   c. $\sum_{j=1}^{J} (\mu_j - \mu)^2 \neq 0$  d. $\sum_j \alpha_j^2 \neq 0$
   e. $\sum_{j=1}^{J} \alpha_j = 0$

4. Given only the following data in an ANOVA table, determine $MS_B$, $MS_W$, and $F$. State $H_0$; is it tenable with $\alpha = .10$?

| *Source* | *SS* | *v* | *MS* | *F* |
|---|---|---|---|---|
| Between | 80 | 4 | — | — |
| Within | — | — | — | |
| Total | 480 | 44 | | |

5. One study experimented with the order of cognitive "organizers" that structure the material for the learner. A group of thirty persons were randomly split into three groups of ten each. Group I received organizing material before studying instructional materials on mathematics; group II received the "organizer" after studying the mathematics; group III received the math materials but no organizing material. On a ten-item test over the mathematics covered, the following scores were earned:

| *Group* I (*Postorganizer*) | *Group* II (*Preorganizer*) | *Group* III (*No-Organizer*) |
|---|---|---|
| 5 | 4 | 5 |
| 4 | 5 | 4 |
| 4 | 3 | 6 |
| 7 | 6 | 2 |
| 8 | 6 | 2 |
| 7 | 3 | 2 |
| 6 | 3 | 6 |
| 4 | 4 | 4 |
| 4 | 4 | 3 |
| 7 | 2 | 5 |
| $\overline{X}_j$: 5.60 | 4.00 | 3.90 |
| $s_j^2$: 2.49 | 1.78 | 2.54 |

Perform a one-factor ANOVA (see Fig. 16.1 and Table 16.1); test the null hypothesis $H_0: \mu_1 = \mu_2 = \mu_3$ at $\alpha = .05$ and at $\alpha = .01$.

6. Ten samples of twenty scores each are drawn at random from a single normal population with mean $\mu$ and variance $\sigma^2$. The sample *means* of the ten samples have a variance of 2.40 that is,

$$s_{\overline{X}}^2 = \frac{\sum_j (\overline{X}_j - \overline{X}_{\bullet})^2}{J - 1} = 2.40$$

Find an estimate of $\sigma^2$, the variance of the original normal population sampled.

7. A study (Hakstian, 1971) was designed to determine whether the type of examination anticipated (essay, objective, or a combination of both) had an effect on performance on objective or essay tests. On a common assignment, one-third of a class of thirty-three students expected an objective test, one-third expected an essay test, and one-third expected both types of items. The actual examination consisted of both an objective and essay test over the common material. The analysis of variance for the objective test is given. (The means for the three groups were $\overline{X}_E = 27.3$, $\overline{X}_O = 27.2$, and $\overline{X}_C = 29.1$ for the students expecting objective, essay and combination, respectively.)

| *Source* | $\nu$ | *MS* | *F* |
|---|---|---|---|
| Between | 2 | 12.57 | .54 |
| Within | 30 | 23.35 | |

a. What conclusion can be drawn from these results?
The ANOVA table for scores on the essay test is given:

| *Source* | $\nu$ | *MS* | *F* |
|---|---|---|---|
| Between | 2 | 259.49 | 1.44 |
| Within | 30 | 180.20 | |

b. If $H_0$ is true, using Table F, estimate the probability of obtaining an $F$-ratio as large as 1.44.

c. The three observed means on the essay test (graded anonymously) were as follows: $\overline{X}_O = 45.3$, $\overline{X}_E = 43.4$, and $\overline{X}_C = 52.6$. Recall that $s^2_{\overline{X}} = s^2/n$; hence, $ns^2_{\overline{X}} = s^2 = MS_B$. Thus, we can obtain an estimate of the population variance ($\sigma^2$) using only $n$ and $s^2_{\overline{X}}$. Compute $s^2_{\overline{X}}[s^2_{\overline{X}} = \Sigma\hat{\alpha}^2_j/(J - 1)]$, and estimate the population variance—that is, $ns^2_{\overline{X}}$. Compare the result with the mean square for between groups.

8. Calculators were randomly assigned to twenty students of the forty students in a statistics class. All students were instructed to work ten problems involving complex arithmetic operations. The mean of the calculator group was $\overline{X}_C = 6.40$; the mean of the hand-computation group was $\overline{X}_H = 5.90$; $\Sigma_j\Sigma_i X^2_{ij}$ was 1,662 and $\Sigma_j\Sigma_i X_{ij}$ was 246.
   a. Can $H_0$ be rejected at $\alpha = .10$? Perform an analysis of variance and present results in an ANOVA table.
   b. If instead of the one-factor ANOVA, a $t$-test had been employed to test $H_0: \mu_C = \mu_H$, the $t$-ratio would have been _____, and the critical $t$-value would have been ____.

9. (This problem is recommended only for students having access to a calculator because of the large amount of time that the arithmetic computation would require by hand. Use Equation 16.3 to obtain $SS_b$.) Fifth-grade students representing five ethnic groups from twenty-six school districts in Colorado were compared in school attitude (Hopkins, Kretke, Harms, Gabriel, Phillips, Rodriquez, and Averill, 1974). The means and $n$'s for each group were as follows:

| | *Blacks* | *Hispanics* | *American Indians* | *Orientals* | *White* | *Totals* |
|---|---|---|---|---|---|---|
| $\overline{X}_j$ | 54.9 | 55.8 | 54.5 | 55.1 | 55.6 | $\overline{X}_\bullet = 55.58$ |
| $n_j$ | 138 | 534 | 52 | 21 | 2,367 | $n_\bullet = 3,112$ |
| $\sum_i X_{ij}$ | 7,576 | 29,797 | 2,834 | 1,157 | 131,606 | |
| $s^2_j$ | 38.4 | 33.6 | 39.7 | 27.0 | 27.0 | |

   a. Is $H_0: \mu_B = \mu_H = \mu_I = \mu_O = \mu_W$ tenable at $\alpha = .05$?
   b. How could $H_0: \sigma^2_B = \sigma^2_H = \sigma^2_I = \sigma^2_O = \sigma^2_W$ be tested?

10. a. Use the Scheffé test of homogeneity of variance for the data in problem 5 with $\alpha = .05$. Use two subgroups per group and assume that the observations are randomly ordered and take the first five $X$'s for the first subgroup, and so on.
   b. Compare the results with those found using the Bartlett test and the Hartley $F_{max}$ test in Problem 6 following Chapter 13.

11. An investigator expects that the average math achievement in a school district on the annual criterion-referenced math tests can be increased 5% with a new instructional emphasis that monitors time-on-task. From previous years' results it is known that $\mu \doteq 80\%$ and $\sigma \doteq 10\%$. If the new program is going to be field tested in one school with 100 students (who will be randomly assigned to either the $E$ or $C$ group), and if the researcher's expectations are correct,
   a. Compute power for the $F$-test with $\alpha_2 = .05$.
   b. Compare your result with those read from Table 16.4.
   c. Using Table 16.4, what is the power if $\alpha_1 = .05$ and $\alpha_1 = .10$, respectively?
   d. If the effect size is only one-half that which is expected, how many pupils must be in each group in order to have power $\doteq .80$, even with a one-tailed test and taking a 5% chance of making a type-I error?

12. The null hypothesis, $H_0 : \mu_1 = \mu_2 = \mu_3$, is to be tested with $n = 21$ ($n_\bullet = 63$). Suppose that, unknown to the researcher, $\mu_1 = 70$, $\mu_2 = 72$, and $\mu_3 = 74$, and $\sigma^2 = 24$.
    a. What is the power of the $F$-test under these conditions at $\alpha = .05$ and $\alpha = .01$?
    b. How large must $n$ be to have power $(1 - \beta)$ equal to .90 with $\alpha = .05$?
13. Unknown to the experimenter, the value of $\sigma^2$ is 20, and $\mu_1 = 10$, $\mu_2 = 15$, and $\mu_3 = 20$ in the three populations from which he has samples of size $n = 10$. What is the expected value of $MS_b$ in this experiment, i.e., what would be the average value of $MS_b$ over an infinite number of replications of the same experiment?
14. Prove that $SS_w = \Sigma_{j=1}^{J}[\Sigma_{i=1}^{n}(X_{ij} - \overline{X}_j)^2]$ is equal to its computational formula $SS_w = \Sigma_{j=1}^{J}\Sigma_{i=1}^{n} X_{ij}^2 - \Sigma_{j=1}^{J}(\Sigma_{i=1}^{n} X_{ij})^2/n$. (*Hint*: First show that $\Sigma_{i=1}^{n}(X_{ij} - \overline{X}_j)^2$ equals $\Sigma_{i=1}^{n} X_{ij}^2 - (\Sigma_{i=1}^{n} X_{ij})^2/n$, as was done in Chapter 5. Then sum the $J$ sums of squares for each group across $j$.)
15. Prove that the value of $F = MS_b/MS_w$ is a one-way ANOVA with $J = 2$ equals the square of the value of $t$ for testing the significance of the difference between the two means, that is, prove that

$$t^2 = \frac{(\overline{X}_1 - \overline{X}_2)^2}{[(s_1^2 + s_2^2)/2](2/n)}$$

equals

$$F = \frac{n[(\overline{X}_1 - \overline{X}_\bullet)^2 + (\overline{X}_2 - \overline{X}_\bullet)^2]}{(s_1^2 + s_2^2)/2}$$

Start by noting that $\overline{X}_\bullet = (\overline{X}_1 + \overline{X}_2)/2$, and then manipulate the numerator of $F$ into the form $n(\overline{X}_1 - \overline{X}_2)^2/2$.

## *ANSWERS TO MASTERY TEST*

1. T
2. 15
3. $H_0 : \mu_7 = \mu_8 = \mu_9 = \mu_{10} = \mu_{11} = \mu_{12}$
4. Yes
5. d
6. b
7. b
8. a
9. a
10. 0; if $\overline{X}_1 = \overline{X}_2 = \cdots = \overline{X}_J$, $SS_b = 0$, and $MS_b = 0.0$
11. $\overline{X}_\bullet = 11.0$
12. Yes, since $SS_b = 0$
13. Yes
14. No; the expected value for $F$ when $H_0$ is true is approximately 1.
15. $(2.5)^2 = 6.25$ $(F = t^2)$
16. $_{.95}F_{1,60} = 4.00$ (when $J = 2$, $F = t^2$)
17. a
18. c
19. c
20. $\nu_b = J - 1 = 4 - 1 = 3$
21. $MS_b = SS_b/\nu_b = 30/3 = 10$
22. $F = MS_b/MS_w = 10/2 = 5.0$
23. $_{.95}F_{3,60} = 2.76$
24. Yes; $F = 5 > 2.76 = {}_{.95}F_{3,60}$
25. Yes; $F = 5 > 4.13 = {}_{.99}F_{3,60}$
26. No; $F = 5 < 6.17 = {}_{.999}F_{3,60}$
27. $n_\bullet = 64 = \nu_w + J$ (also, $n_\bullet = \nu_b + \nu_w + 1$)
28. 120 $[SS = (\nu)(MS)]$
29. 150 $[SS_{total} = SS_b + SS_w]$
30. No
31. No
32. Yes, ANOVA is robust to violating homogeneity of variance assumption only when $n$'s are equal.
33. No; when larger $n$'s and larger $\sigma^2$'s

are associated, the probability of type-I error is even less than the nominal $\alpha$.

34. No; when larger $n$'s are associated with smaller variances, the probability of a type-I error is greater then the nominal $\alpha$. Hence, if $H_0$ is not rejected at nominal $\alpha$, it certainly would not be rejected at true $\alpha$.
35. b
36. Yes
37. $MS_w = \Sigma s_j^2/J = 2.0$
38. b; since the average $s^2$ is 2.0, the average standard deviation within groups would be expected to be approximately 1.4–1.6.
39. Yes; with $n = 16$, the range is expected to span 3–4 standard deviations (see Table 5.1).
40. $\alpha_j$, $\epsilon_{ij}$
41. $NID \sim (0, \sigma_\epsilon^2)$
42. 20, 3
43. 7
44. $E(MS_w) = 7.5$, $E(MS_b) = 7.5 + 10(14)/2 = 77.5$
45. 7
46. Decreased
47. 0, 0
48. $\sigma^2$
49. a. increases
    b. decreases
    c. increases

## ANSWERS TO PROBLEMS AND EXERCISES

1. a. $\nu_b = 1, \nu_w = 6$
   b. $\nu_b = 4, \nu_w = 5$
   c. $\nu_b = 2, \nu_w = 10$
   d. $\nu_b = 2, \nu_w = 7$
2. a. $_{.99}F_{1,10} = 10.0$
   b. $_{.90}F_{4,30} = 2.14$
   c. $_{.95}F_{2,15} = 3.68$
3. a. Yes b. Yes c. Yes
   d. Yes e. No
4. $H_0: \mu_1 = \mu_2 = \mu_3 = \mu_4 = \mu_5$

| *Source* | *SS* | $\nu$ | *MS* | *F* |
|---|---|---|---|---|
| Between | 80 | 4 | (20) | (2.0) |
| Within | (400) | (40) | (10) | |
| | 480 | 44 | | |

$2.0 < 2.09 = {}_{.90}F_{4,40}$; $H_0$ is tenable.

5. $SS_b = 10([-.5)^2 + (1.1)^2 + (-.6)^2] = 18.2$
   $SS_w = 22.41 + 16.02 + 22.86 = 61.29$

| *SV* | *SS* | $\nu$ | *MS* | *F* |
|---|---|---|---|---|
| Between | 18.2 | 2 | 9.10 | 4.01 |
| Within | 61.29 | 27 | 2.27 | |

Can reject $H_0$ at $\alpha = .05$, $4.01 > 3.37 = {}_{.95}F_{2,26}$. Cannot reject $H_0$ at $\alpha = .01$, $4.01 < 5.53 = {}_{.99}F_{2,26}$.

6. Since $s_{\bar{X}}^2$ estimates $\sigma^2/n$, $ns_{\bar{X}}^2$ estimates $\sigma^2$. Hence, the estimate of $\sigma^2$ is $20(2.40) = 48.0$
7. a. The type of examination expected by the students had no discernible effect on performance on the objective test.
   b. $p \doteq .25$, $({}_{.75}F_{2,30} = 1.45)$
   c. $s_{\bar{X}}^2$

$$= \frac{(\bar{X}_O - \bar{X}_{\bullet})^2 + (\bar{X}_E - \bar{X}_{\bullet})^2 + (\bar{X}_C - \bar{X}_{\bullet})^2}{J - 1}$$

$$= \frac{(45.3 - 47.1)^2 + (-3.7)^2 + (5.5)^2}{3 - 1}$$

$$= \frac{3.24 + 13.69 + 30.25}{2} = \frac{47.18}{2}$$

$$= 23.59;\ 11(23.59) = 259.49 = MS_b$$

8. $SS_{total} = 1{,}662 - (246)^2/40 = 149.1$
   $SS_b = n\,\Sigma\hat{\alpha}_j^2$; $\hat{\alpha}_c = 6.40 - 6.15 = .25$;
   $\hat{\alpha}_H = 5.90 - 6.15 = -.25$
   $SS_b = 20[(.25)^2 + (-.25)^2] = 2.50$
   $SS_w = SS_{total} - SS_b = 149.1 - 2.50 = 146.6$

| *SV* | *SS* | $\nu$ | *MS* | *F* |
|---|---|---|---|---|
| Between | 2.50 | 1 | 2.50 | .65 |
| Within | 146.6 | 38 | 3.86 | |
| Total: | 149.1 | 39 | | |

$F < 1$; therefore, $H_0$ is tenable ($_{.90}F_{1,38} \doteq 2.85$).

b. $t = \sqrt{F} = \sqrt{.65} = .81$; $_{.95}t_{38} = \sqrt{_{.90}F_{1,38}} = 1.69$

9. $SS_b = \Sigma n_j \hat{\alpha}_j^2$; $\hat{\alpha}_B = 54.9 - 55.58$

$= -.68$ $\hat{\alpha}_C = .22$;

$\hat{\alpha}_I = -1.08$; $\hat{\alpha}_O = -.48$; $\hat{\alpha}_W = .02$

$$SS_b = 138(-.68)^2 + 534(.22)^2 + 52(-1.08)^2 + 21(-.48)^2 + 2{,}367(.02)^2$$

$$SS_b = 63.81 + 25.84 + 60.65 + 4.84 + 0.95 = 156.1$$

$$SS_w = \Sigma SS_j = \Sigma \nu_j s_j^2 = 137(38.4) + 533(33.6) + 51(39.7) + 20(27.0) + 2366(27.0) = 89{,}616.3$$

| *Source* | *SS* | $\nu$ | *MS* | *F* |
|---|---|---|---|---|
| Between | 156.1 | 4 | 39.03 | 1.353 |
| Within | 89,616.3 | 3,107 | 28.84 | |

a. $H_0$ is tenable—that is, differences in school attitude means are not statistically significant; indeed, $F = 1.353 > 1.35 = {_{.75}F_{4,\infty}}$, $p < .25$.

b. Bartlett's test (Sec. 13.8) or Scheffé's test (Sec. 16.23)

10. a. $MS_b = SS_b/\nu_b = 1.178/2 = .589$; $MS_w = SS_w/\nu_w = .489/3 = .163$; $F = 3.61 < {_{.90}F_{2,3}} = 5.46$, $p > 10$; $H_0: \sigma_1^2 = \sigma_2^2 = \sigma_3^2$ is tenable.

b. Results are comparable.

11. a. $= .71$ b. same

c. .81, .89 d. about 200

12. a. From Equation 16.24, the value of $\phi$ is $\sqrt{7/3} \doteq 1.53$, and $\nu_b = J - 1 = 2$; $\nu_w = n_\bullet - J = 60$. From Table G, the power of the $F$-test, $(1 - \beta)$, $= .60$ and .35 for $\alpha = .05$ and $\alpha = .01$, respectively.

b. From Table G, $_{.05}\phi_{.90} = 2.1$ for $\nu_b = 2$ and $\nu_e = \nu_w = 60$; from Equation 16.25:

$$n = 24(2)(2.1)^2/8 \doteq 40$$

13. (Eq. 16.21)

$$E(MS_b) = \sigma^2 + \frac{n \sum_j (\mu_j - \mu)^2}{(J - 1)}$$

$$= 20 + 250 = 270$$

# 17 MULTIPLE COMPARISONS

## 17.1 INTRODUCTION

The omnibus $F$-test in an analysis of variance (ANOVA) is a test of the hypothesis that the population means of all $J$ groups are equal, i.e., $H_0$: $\mu_1 = \mu_2 = \cdots = \mu_J$. There are two possible statistical conclusions following an ANOVA: either $H_0$ is tenable or it is rejected. If $H_0$ is rejected and if $J > 2$, the conclusion, "not all $J$ population means are equal," is not adequately explicit. The rejection of the null hypothesis tells nothing about which means differ significantly from which other means. In most studies, the omnibus $F$-test is a decision point: if the $F$-test is not statistically significant, $H_0$ is tenable and sampling error can be viewed as a reasonable explanation of the pattern of mean differences that was observed; but if $H_0$ is rejected, a search for which differences in means are significant is in order. These search procedures are termed *multiple comparison* (MC) techniques.

MC procedures are a relatively recent addition to the statistical arsenal; most MC techniques were developed during the 1950's, although their use in behavioral research was rare prior to the 1960's.*

*The most authoritative and comprehensive MC treatment to date is that of Miller (1966, 1977). See also O'Neill and Wetherill (1971) and Kirk (1982).

Historically, when $J > 2$ the $t$-test has been used following a rejection of $H_0$ in ANOVA. But a $t$-test applied to the largest and smallest of $J$ means cannot take into account how many groups (or means) are in the comparison set. Clearly if one draws $J = 10$ random samples from the same parent population and compares the extreme-most means, the observed $t$-ratio will exceed the critical $t$-ratio far more often than the probability denoted by the nominal value of alpha. When $J > 2$, the probability of a type-$I$ error will be larger than .05 when the nominal value of .05 is set for alpha (Sec. 16.2).*

There are several multiple comparison (MC) procedures available; the seven most useful will be developed in this chapter.

## An Example

One study examined the effects of "advance organizers" (interspersed test questions) on comprehension of an assigned reading task. There were $n = 20$ subjects randomly assigned to each of the $J = 7$ groups. Five groups received the advance organizer (AO) and two groups did not (See panel B of Table 17.1). One of the two no-AO groups was given special instructions to read carefully. Of the five groups receiving the AO, three

**TABLE 17.1 Sample Problem for Multiple Comparisons Illustrations: A One-Factor ANOVA with $J = 7$ Groups with $n = 20$ per Group**

| | *Source* | $\nu$ | *MS* | *F* |
|---|---|---|---|---|
| A. | Between (Treatments) | 6 | 467 | 2.25* |
| | Within (Error) | 133 | 207 | |

$^*p < .05$, ${}_{.95}F_{6,133} = 2.17$

B.

<table>
<tr><td colspan="5">Advanced Organizer (AO)</td><td colspan="2">No AO</td></tr>
<tr><td colspan="3">AO Before</td><td colspan="2">AO After</td><td rowspan="3">Control</td><td rowspan="3">"Read Carefully"</td></tr>
<tr><td colspan="5">Answers Provided for AO?</td></tr>
<tr><td>Yes</td><td>Yes</td><td>No</td><td>Yes</td><td>No</td></tr>
<tr><td>Blocked</td><td>Interspersed</td><td></td><td></td><td></td><td></td><td></td></tr>
<tr><td>36<br>$\bar{X}_4$</td><td>35<br>$\bar{X}_5$</td><td>30<br>$\bar{X}_7$</td><td>40<br>$\bar{X}_3$</td><td>43<br>$\bar{X}_1$</td><td>33<br>$\bar{X}_6$</td><td>42<br>$\bar{X}_2$</td></tr>
</table>

*Multiple $t$-tests following ANOVA is also commonly known as the "least-significant-difference" (LSD) method: LSD = (critical-$t$) $(s_{\bar{X}-\bar{X}}) = ({}_{1-\alpha/2}t_{\nu_e} s_{\bar{X}-\bar{X}})$, where $s_{\bar{X}-\bar{X}} = \sqrt{MS_w(2/n)}$ with a balanced design. In the example in Table 17.1 with alpha = .05, LSD = ${}_{.975}t_{133}(s_{\bar{X}-\bar{X}}) = 1.98\sqrt{(20.7)} = 9.01$. Any difference between a pair of means greater than 9.01 is judged to be statistically significant by the LSD method. For $C$ independent $t$-tests the probability of at least one type-I error is $\alpha_\Sigma = 1 - (1 - \alpha)^C$ (see Sec. 17.14). In Table 17.1 there are $C = 21$ possible pairwise comparisons. If they were independent and alpha is set at .05, the probability of at least one type-I error would be, $\alpha_\Sigma = 1 - (.95)^{21} = .66$. The dependency among multiple $t$-tests makes it impossible to determine the probability of a type-I error precisely.

received the AO before the reading, and two after. Within each of these two subsets of groups, one group did not receive answers to the test questions. The seven means are ordered by subscripts from the largest ($\overline{X}_1$) to the smallest ($\overline{X}_7$) in order to facilitate the MC computations. This recommended convention will be used throughout this chapter.

Panel A of Table 17.1 gives the ANOVA table: the $F$-ratio of 2.25 allowed the null hypothesis to be rejected at the .05 level. The next step is to select a MC procedure to evaluate which means differ significantly from which other means.

## 17.2 TESTING ALL PAIRS OF MEANS: The Studentized Range Statistic, $q$

The most typical situation in which MC methods are used is one in which the researcher wishes to compare each mean with each and every other mean. The maximum number of possible simple or pairwise contrasts among $J$ means is

$$C = J(J - 1)/2 \tag{17.1}$$

If school attendance rates are compared for all 12 grade levels of a school district, there would be $12(11)/2 = 66$ possible pairwise contrasts (hypotheses). Can you identify the $7(6)/2 = 21$ possible simple contrasts in the example in Table 17.1? To test the $C$ hypotheses or pairwise contrasts, the MC "method of choice" for this purpose makes use of the *studentized range statistic*, $q$.

Several MC procedures are based on the studentized *range* statistic, $q$. In a normal distribution, as the number in the sample ($n$) increases, the magnitude of the range also increases (Sec. 5.13). The same is true for sample means: in a set of $J$ means, the size of the difference between the largest mean, $\overline{X}_1$, and the smallest mean, $\overline{X}_J$ will increase as $J$ increases even when $H_0$ is true. Unlike multiple $t$-tests, the critical value of the studentized range statistic ($q$) is influenced by $J$.

The numerical value of $q$ is the difference between the larger and the smaller of two sample means, $\overline{X}_L - \overline{X}_S$, expressed in units of the standard error of the mean, $s_{\overline{X}}$:

$$q = \frac{\overline{X}_L - \overline{X}_S}{s_{\overline{X}}} \tag{17.2}$$

where $\overline{X}_L \geqslant \overline{X}_S$, and

$$s_{\overline{X}} = \sqrt{MS_{\text{error}}/n} \tag{17.3}$$

The value of $MS_{\text{error}}$ ($MS_e$) in Eq. 17.3 is the denominator of the $F$-test; in a one-factor ANOVA, or fixed-effects ANOVA (Chap. 18), $MS_e$ is always $MS_{\text{within}}$. In more complex ANOVA designs such as those considered in Chapter 19, $MS_{\text{error}}$, the denominator of the $F$-test, often is not $MS_w$.

If $n$'s are not equal*, the value of $s_{\overline{X}}$ for comparing pairs of means can be estimated from Eq. 17.4:

$$s_{\overline{X}} = \sqrt{\frac{MS_e}{2}\left(\frac{1}{n_L} + \frac{1}{n_S}\right)} \tag{17.4}$$

where $n_L$ and $n_S$ are the numbers of observations associated with the larger mean, $\overline{X}_L$, and the smaller mean, $\overline{X}_S$, respectively.

## 17.3 THE TUKEY METHOD OF MULTIPLE COMPARISONS

The Tukey method begins by testing the largest pairwise difference in the set of $J$ means, i.e., by testing $H_0: \mu_1 - \mu_J = 0$. Since the means are rank-ordered (denoted by subscripts, $_1$ to $_J$) in order of their size, $\overline{X}_1$ is the largest mean and $\overline{X}_J$ is the smallest mean. In the example in Table 17.1, the first hypothesis to be tested (Eq. 17.2) is $H_{0_1}: \mu_1 - \mu_7 = 0$. With alpha = .10, is $H_{0_1}$ tenable? Using Equation 17.2

$$q_1 = (\overline{X}_1 - \overline{X}_7)/s_{\overline{X}}$$

where from Equation 17.3,

$$s_{\overline{X}} = \sqrt{MS_e/n} = \sqrt{207/20} = 3.217$$

hence,

$$q_1 = (43 - 30)/3.217 = 4.04$$

The critical $q$-value is found from Table I in the Appendix, by locating the intersection of (1) $\nu_e$, the degrees of freedom for $MS_e$, (2) alpha, and (3) the number of means in the set, $r$ (no relation to the correlation coefficient); for the Tukey method, the value of $r$ is always $J$. Thus, the critical $q$-value for $J = 7$, $\nu_e = 133$ (use the closest, but smaller tabled value of $\nu_e$—in this instance, 120), and alpha = .10 is approximately 3.86 ($_{.90}q_{133,7} \doteq {}_{.90}q_{120,7} = 3.86$). The computation is shown in Panel C of Table 17.2. Since the observed value of $q_1$ of 4.04 exceeds the critical $q$-value of 3.86, the null hypothesis, $H_{0_1}: \mu_1 - \mu_7 = 0$ can be rejected at the .10 level, and it can be concluded that the mean of population 1 is greater than the mean of population 7.

*In the derivation of the studentized range statistic, all $J$ means are assumed to be based on the same number of observations so that $\sigma^2_{\overline{X}_1} = \sigma^2_{\overline{X}_2} = \cdots \sigma^2_{\overline{X}_J}$ would be true when $\sigma_1^2 = \sigma_2^2 = \sigma_J^2$. The logical modification proposed by Kramer (1956) given as Equation 17.4 has been shown to yield accurate results with unequal $n$'s (Smith, 1971; Myette & White, 1982). (The mathematical basis for the studentized range with unequal $n$'s is treated by Hochberg, 1975; and Spjotroll and Stoline, 1973).

**TABLE 17.2 Tukey Multiple Comparisons for the Sample Problem (Table 17.1)**

Ordered Means

| | | | | | | | |
|---|---|---|---|---|---|---|---|
| A. | $\overline{X}_1$ | $\overline{X}_2$ | $\overline{X}_3$ | $\overline{X}_4$ | $\overline{X}_5$ | $\overline{X}_6$ | $\overline{X}_7$ |
| | 43 | 42 | 40 | 36 | 35 | 33 | 30 |
| B. $\hat{\Delta}_j$: | (.90) | (.83) | (.70) | (.42) | (.35) | (.21) | . . . |

C. $q_1 = \dfrac{\overline{X}_1 - \overline{X}_7}{s_{\overline{X}}}$; $s_{\overline{X}} = \sqrt{\dfrac{MS_w}{n}} = \sqrt{\dfrac{207}{20}} = 3.217$

$$q_1 = \frac{43 - 30}{3.217} = 4.04; \quad p < .10, \quad {}_{.90}q_{133,7} = 3.86$$

$$q_2 = \frac{\overline{X}_1 - \overline{X}_6}{s_{\overline{X}}} = \frac{43 - 33}{3.217} = 3.11, \quad p > .10$$

$$q_3 = \frac{\overline{X}_2 - \overline{X}_7}{s_{\overline{X}}} = \frac{42 - 30}{3.217} = 3.73, \quad p > .10$$

If the difference between the extreme-most means had not been significant, the tests of differences between other pairs of means would have been superfluous. But since the largest difference in means was significant, one proceeds to test the second-largest difference involving group 1, $\overline{X}_1$ vs. $\overline{X}_{J-1}$, or $H_{0_2}$: $\mu_1 - \mu_6 = 0$. Panel C of Table 17.2 shows that $q_2 = 3.11$, which is less than the critical-$q$ of 3.86, hence there are no significant differences among set of means $\overline{X}_1$, $\overline{X}_2$, $\overline{X}_3$, $\overline{X}_4$, $\overline{X}_5$, and $\overline{X}_6$. The line in panel A of Table 17.2 which underscores this subset of means denotes that none of the pairwise differences among these six means is statistically significant.

After a nonsigificant range has been encountered with the largest mean, one proceeds to take the next-largest mean, $\overline{X}_2$, and test it against the smallest mean, $\overline{X}_J$; that is, $H_{0_3}$: $\mu_2 - \mu_7 = 0$. The computed value of the studentized range for this comparison, $q_3$, is shown in panel C to be: $q_3 = 3.73$, which is less than the critical $q$-value of 3.86, thus $H_{0_3}$: $\mu_2 = \mu_7$ is tenable. The lower line in panel A denotes that none of the six means underscored by this line (groups 2 through 7) differ significantly. Since there remain no two means that are *not* underscored by a common line, no further hypotheses need to be tested. The underscoring in panel A is a convention for summarizing the results of MC significance tests. It is particularly useful when $J > 3$. Since the only two means *not* underscored by a common line are those associated with groups 1 and 7, all other $H_0$'s are tenable except $H_{0_1}$: $\mu_1 - \mu_7 = 0$, when the Tukey method is used.*

*When $n$'s are equal, the entire Tukey method can be simplified for hand computation by finding the *minimum* difference between means necessary to reject the null hypothesis. This minimum difference is termed *honest significant difference* (HSD) or *wholly significant difference* (WSD). By inserting the critical $q$-value from Table I into Equation 17.2 and rearranging the equation, the value of HSD is obtained. For example, with alpha = .10, $J = 7$, with 133 degrees of freedom, from Table I the critical value of $q$ is found to be 3.86; thus HSD = $3.86 s_{\overline{X}}$ = (3.86) (3.217) = 12.43. Only one pair of means ($\overline{X}_1 - \overline{X}_7 = 13$) differed by more than 12.43, thus this is the only pair of means that differed significantly.

## 17.4 THE EFFECT SIZE OF MEAN DIFFERENCES

The *effect size* (Sec. 12.8) of a difference in means can be estimated by Equation 17.5:

$$\hat{\Delta}_j = (\overline{X}_j - \overline{X}_J)/s_w \tag{17.5}$$

where

$$s_w = \sqrt{MS_w} \tag{17.6}$$

In panel B of Table 17.2, the largest effect size, $\hat{\Delta}_1$, is shown to be .90: $\hat{\Delta}_1 = (\overline{X}_1 - \overline{X}_7)/\sqrt{MS_w} = (43 - 30)/\sqrt{207} = 13/14.4 = .90$ (or $.90\hat{\sigma}$). The effect-size metric is a useful descriptive estimate of the magnitude of the difference between means when the dependent variable has an arbitrary numerical scale (as with most measures in behavioral research, but unlike most measures in the physical and biological sciences). The effect size metric should not be limited to only those differences that are statistically reliable (Glass, McGaw & Smith, 1981). To express the magnitude of the mean differences, the effect size for each mean using the lowest mean, $\overline{X}_7$, as the point of reference is given in parenthesis in Panel B of Table 17.2. The effect size between any other pair of means is simply the difference between their respective $\hat{\Delta}_j$'s. For example, the estimated effect size between group 2 and 6 is $\overline{X}_2 - \overline{X}_6 = .83 - .21 = .62$.

## 17.5 THE BASIS FOR TYPE-I ERROR RATE: CONTRAST VERSUS FAMILY

In previous chapters, as in almost all other statistical applications, alpha pertains to the probability of a type-I error for a particular, explicit hypothesis (when $H_0$ is true). With MC methods, however, there is a choice between a type-I error rate per contrast (or specified hypothesis), $\alpha$, or a type-I error rate for a set or *family** of $C$ contrasts, $\alpha_\Sigma$.†

Two of the seven MC methods presented in this chapter use alpha per contrast; the other five MC techniques consider the set of $C$ contrasts as a family and base the type-I error rate on the entire set or family. The Tukey method (Sec. 17.3) uses a family-based type-I error rate, thus the probability of a type-I error in one or more of the $C = J(J - 1)/2 = 21$ (Equation 17.1) pairwise contrasts is alpha (in the example, .10). Other MC methods (like the Newman-Keuls, Sec. 17.6) risks a type-I error of $\alpha$ for each contrast tested.

*The term *experimentwise* error rate is commonly used synonymously with family error rate, but this terminology is confusing when there are two or more factors in the ANOVA (Chap. 18). Following Miller (1966, 1977), we will consistently use the expression *family* error rate, or error rate per family. The terms contrast and comparison are also synonymous (O'Neill & Wetherill, 1971).

†Multiple comparison hypotheses are rarely directional. A family-based type-I error rate for directional hypotheses is denoted by $\alpha_{\Sigma_1}$, otherwise $\alpha_\Sigma = \alpha_{\Sigma_2}$.

Which type of error rate is preferable is a matter of opinion and controversy. In the long run, the contrast-based error rate has greater power, but makes more type-I errors. Conversely, the family error rate results in fewer type-I errors, but more type-II errors. The rationale for a family error-rate is weakened by the arbitrariness of the decision as to what constitutes a family*, especially when there are two or more factors in the design (Chap. 18). The authors, like Miller (1966, 1977), feel that the contrast-based error rate is advantageous for most applications since it is consistent with almost all other alphas that researchers employ† and does not suffer from the overconservativeness of the family error rate, especially when $J$ is large.

## 17.6 THE NEWMAN-KEULS METHOD

The Newman-Keuls (NK) method of multiple comparisons is very similar to the Tukey method, except that it uses a per-contrast type-I error rate. Each pairwise hypothesis that is tested has a probability, $\alpha$, of a type-I error. The NK procedure is identical to that outlined in Table 17.2, except that the critical value of $q$ depends on the number of the means, $r$ (for range), in the set of means being considered in the particular comparison being made. For the initial hypothesis tested (that is, when the largest and smallest of the set of $J$ means are being compared, $H_0: \mu_1 - \mu_J$), the Tukey and NK procedures are identical. If this $H_0$ is not rejected, then all null hypotheses for every other pair of means are tenable. But if the initial $H_0$ is rejected (as it was in the example in Table 17.2), the two procedures differ with respect to the critical value of $q$ for all other contrasts. For the NK procedure, the critical $q$-value is not ${}_{1-\alpha}q_{\nu_e,J}$, but ${}_{1-\alpha}q_{\nu_e,r}$, where $r$ is the number of means in the set being compared in the particular hypothesis being tested. For $H_{0_2}$ and $H_{0_3}$ (Sec. 17.3), $r$ is 6. The range rationale is employed with both methods: whenever one finds a subset of means for which the difference between the largest and smallest means is not significant, no further comparisons are made within this subset of means.

The NK method is outlined below and is illustrated in Table 17.3.

1. The initial step is identical with the Tukey method (Eq. 17.2): in the set of $J$ means, the largest mean, $\bar{X}_L$, is compared with the smallest mean, $\bar{X}_S$. If this is not significant (at the specified alpha, .10 in the example), no further hypotheses are tested and all null hypotheses are tenable.

2. If the hypothesis for the extreme-most means is rejected (as it is in Table

*The term *experimentwise* error rate is commonly used synonymously with family error rate, but this terminology is confusing when there are two or more factors in the ANOVA (Chap. 18). Following Miller (1966, 1977), we will consistently use the expression *family* error rate, or error rate per family. The terms contrast and comparsion are also synonymous (O'Neill & Wetherill, 1971).

†For example, in factorial ANOVA (Chaps. 18–19), a per-contrast error rate is ordinarily used to test each effect, rather than a family-error rate for the entire "package" of main effects and interactions. Indeed, each $F$-test is a special case of planned orthogonal contrasts (Sec. 17.16). Miller (1966, p. 35) observed, "There are no hard-and-fast rules for where the family lines should be drawn, and the statistician must rely on his own judgment for the problem at hand. Large single experiments cannot be treated as a whole (family) without an unjustifiable loss in sensitivity."

**TABLE 17.3 Newman-Keuls Multiple Comparisons for the Sample Problem (Table 17.1)**

Ordered Means

| | | | | | | | |
|---|---|---|---|---|---|---|---|
| A. | $\overline{X}_1$ | $\overline{X}_2$ | $\overline{X}_3$ | $\overline{X}_4$ | $\overline{X}_5$ | $\overline{X}_6$ | $\overline{X}_7$ |
| | 43 | 42 | 40 | 36 | 35 | 33 | 30 |
| B. $\hat{\Delta}_j$: | (.90) | (.83) | (.70) | (.42) | (.35) | (.21) | . . . |

C. $q_1 = \dfrac{\overline{X}_1 - \overline{X}_7}{s_{\overline{X}}}$; $s_{\overline{X}} = \sqrt{\dfrac{MS_w}{n}} = \sqrt{\dfrac{207}{20}} = 3.217$

$q_1 = \dfrac{43 - 30}{3.217} = 4.04$; $p < .10$, ${}_{.90}q_{133,7} = 3.86$

$q_2 = \dfrac{\overline{X}_1 - \overline{X}_6}{s_{\overline{X}}} = \dfrac{43 - 33}{3.217} = 3.11$, $p > .10$; ${}_{.90}q_{133,6} = 3.71$

$q_3 = \dfrac{\overline{X}_2 - \overline{X}_7}{s_{\overline{X}}} = \dfrac{42 - 30}{3.217} = 3.73$, $p < .10$; ${}_{.90}q_{133,6} = 3.71$

$q_4 = \dfrac{\overline{X}_3 - \overline{X}_7}{s_{\overline{X}}} = \dfrac{40 - 30}{3.217} = 3.11$, $p > .10$, ${}_{.90}q_{133,5} = 3.52$

17.3), the mean of group 1 is contrasted with the mean of group $J - 1$ ($\overline{X}_6$ in the example). The critical $q$-value is based on $r = J - 1$. In panel C of Table 17.3, $H_{0_2}$: $\mu_1 - \mu_6 = 0$ cannot be rejected: $q = 3.11 < {}_{.90}q_{133,6} = 3.71$. If this $H_{0_2}$ is rejected, group 1 is tested against group $J - 2$, $J - 3$, etc., until a nonsignificant range is encountered. The subset of means, $\overline{X}_1$ through $\overline{X}_6$ is underscored to denote that there is no significant difference between any two means in this subset. Note that the only difference at step two between Tukey and the NK methods is that the NK has a smaller critical $q$-value.

3. If the means of groups 2 and $J$ are not underscored by a common line, one proceeds to test the second-largest mean, $\overline{X}_2$, against the mean of group $J$. In panel C of Table 17.3, $q_3$ is found to be 3.73 which is larger than the critical $q$-value of 3.71, thus $H_{0_3}$: $\mu_2 - \mu_7 = 0$ is rejected at the .10 level. Note, however, in step 2 that one does not proceed to test group 2 against group $J - 1 = 6$ because groups 2 and 6 were underscored by a common line in step 2 (denoting a nonsignificant subset); hence no further hypotheses are tested among means within this subset.

4. If the third-largest mean, $\overline{X}_3$, and the smallest mean, $\overline{X}_J$, are not underscored by a common line, one proceeds to test pairs of means within this subset until a nonsignificant range is found. In panel C of Table 17.3, for $H_{0_4}$: $\mu_3 - \mu_J = 0$, $q_4 = 3.11$, which is less than the critical $q$-value with $r = 5$ (3.52). Groups 3 through 7 are contained within a nonsignificant range, hence the subset is underscored as illustrated in panel A of Table 17.3. No further null hypotheses are tested because the remaining means are underscored by a common line.

Unlike the $t$-test, the Tukey and NK MC methods illustrate that the difference between means needed for statistical significance with MC techniques is influenced by the parameter, $J$.

## 17.7 THE TUKEY AND NEWMAN-KEULS METHODS COMPARED

Both the Tukey and the NK methods employ the studentized range statistic, $q$. The principal difference between them is that the Tukey procedure uses a family-based alpha, $\alpha_\Sigma$, whereas the NK method risks a type-I error with probability $\alpha$ for each null hypothesis that is tested. Consequently the NK method will have greater power than the Tukey method, except for the initial comparisons in which the two procedures are identical. If one can jump the initial hurdle, the NK method will tend to reject more $H_0$'s than the Tukey procedure, as illustrated in Tables 17.3 vs. 17.2. Notice that the critical value for $q$ with the Tukey method is 3.86 for all comparisons, whereas for the NK method, the critical $q$-values decrease progressively: 3.86, 3.71, 3.52, 3.28, 2.93, to 2.34, when there are $r = 7$, 6, 5, 4, 3, and 2 means, respectively, in the set of means being compared. The authors concur with Miller's (1966, p. 88) observation that:

> The Newman-Keuls [significance] levels provide a high degree of protection for the entire [omnibus] null hypothesis, and this is the multiple range test this author favors. Moreover, it does not suffer from the overconservatism of the Tukey test caused by utilizing just a single critical value.*

## 17.8 THE DEFINITION OF A CONTRAST

To describe, use, and properly evaluate other MC methods, it is necessary to understand (1) the formal definition of a *contrast*, (2) the distinction between simple and complex contrasts, and (3) the meaning of *planned* vs. *post-hoc* contrasts. These topics must be understood prior to dealing with other MC techniques.

Central to the use of MC methods is the notion of a contrast—*a contrast represents the mean difference between two subsets of means*. There may be only one mean in each subset, as in the pairwise contrast employed with the Tukey and NK methods, or there may be as many as $J - 1$ means in one of the subsets. Obviously there are many possible contrasts when there are four or more means.

*We have chosen not to include two multiple range MC methods that in our opinion are rarely, if ever, the MC method of choice. One, suggested by Tukey, uses a critical $q$-value which is the average of the critical $q$-values for the Tukey and NK methods (see O'Neill & Wetherill, 1971, p. 226). Another common method is that suggested by Duncan, and popularized by Edwards (1960), "Duncan's new multiple range test," in which the true value for alpha increases as $J$ increases. With the Duncan method the alpha for the largest observed pairwise difference in means is $1 - (1 - \alpha)^{J-1}$, or in our example with $J = 7$ and $\alpha = .10$, the probability of a type-I error when comparing the extreme-most means is $1 - (.90)^6 = .47$. The authors concur with Miller (1966, p. 87) that "... this violates the spirit of what simultaneous inference is all about, namely to protect a multiparameter null hypothesis from any false declaration [conclusion] due to the large number of declarations required."

*Definition:* A contrast, $\psi$, among the $J$ population means is a linear combination.

$$\psi = \sum_{j}^{J} c_j \mu_j = c_1\mu_1 + c_2\mu_2 + \cdots + c_J\mu_J \qquad (17.7)$$

such that, $\sum_{j}^{J} c_j = 0$

Or, in terms of unbiased estimators:

$$\hat{\psi} = c_1\bar{X}_1 + c_2\bar{X}_2 + \cdots + c_J\bar{X}_J = \sum_{j}^{J} c_j\bar{X}_j \qquad (17.7A)$$

The contrast coefficients,* $c_1, c_2, \cdots, c_J$, are simply positive and negative numbers that define the particular hypotheses to be tested. The meaning and interpretation of a contrast is enhanced if the positive $c_j$'s sum to +1, and the negative $c_j$'s sum to −1.†

## 17.9 SIMPLE VERSUS COMPLEX CONTRASTS

The difference between any two means is a contrast. For example, if $\psi = \mu_3 - \mu_6$, the coefficients for groups 3 and 6 are 1, and −1, respectively, with all other $c_j$'s being equal to 0. Contrasts which involve only two means, each mean having a contrast coefficient of either +1 or −1, are said to be *simple* or *pairwise* contrasts. If $J = 2$, there is only one possible contrast, $\mu_1 - \mu_2$ (or $\mu_2 - \mu_1$). If $J = 3$, there are three simple contrasts, $\mu_1 - \mu_2$, $\mu_1 - \mu_3$, and $\mu_2 - \mu_3$. Contrasts 1, 2, and 3 of panel C of Table 17.2 are simple contrasts. The null hypothesis states that the value of the parameter for every contrast is 0, that is, $H_0$: $\psi = 0$. The unbiased estimate of the contrast parameter is given in Equation 17.7A. The numerical value of each contrast for simple contrasts is the difference in the two sample means. The value of the contrast will be tested (by a *t*-test, or a near relative) to see if the observed value of the contrast differs significantly from the hypothesized value of 0.

Complex contrasts involve three or more means. The contrast, $\psi = \frac{1}{2}\mu_1 + \frac{1}{2}\mu_2 - \mu_3$, is a contrast involving three means; the significance test will respond to the question, "Is the average of means of groups 1 and 2 significantly different from the mean of group 3?"

Each contrast, $\psi$, is designed to answer a specific question in a research study. Six meaningful contrasts related to the example in Table 17.1 are listed below. These

*Not to be confused with $C$, the number of contrasts.

†This convention also allows the Tukey method to be used with complex contrasts (Geunther, 1964), although there are usually better MC alternatives for complex contrasts (Hopkins and Anderson, 1973).

contrasts are defined statistically in panels A and B of Table 17.4. Note that the corresponding null hypothesis is implicit from each contrast:

$\psi_1$: Is the effect of the AO when positioned *before* the reading selection different from the effect when positioned after the selection (when answers are not supplied)?

$\psi_2$: Is there a difference in the means of the two non-AO groups; that is, do the special directions to "read carefully" have an effect?

$\psi_3$: When the AO is positioned after the reading selection, does having answers to the questions have an effect on the mean?

**TABLE 17.4 Six Illustrative Contrasts from the Sample Experiment (from Table 17.1)**

| | Group Means | | | | | | |
|---|---|---|---|---|---|---|---|
| | $\overline{X}_1$ | $\overline{X}_2$ | $\overline{X}_3$ | $\overline{X}_4$ | $\overline{X}_5$ | $\overline{X}_6$ | $\overline{X}_7$ |
| | 43 | 42 | 40 | 36 | 35 | 33 | 30 |
| A. *Contrasts:* $\hat{\psi} = \sum_j c_j \overline{X}_j$, $H_0$: $\psi = 0$ | Contrast Coefficients | | | | | | |
| $\psi_1$: $\mu_1 - \mu_7$ | 1 | 0 | 0 | 0 | 0 | 0 | −1 |
| $\psi_2$: $\mu_2 - \mu_6$ | 0 | 1 | 0 | 0 | 0 | −1 | 0 |
| $\psi_3$: $\mu_1 - \mu_3$ | 1 | 0 | −1 | 0 | 0 | 0 | 0 |
| $\psi_4$: $\frac{1}{2}\mu_4 + \frac{1}{2}\mu_5 - \mu_7$ | 0 | 0 | 0 | $\frac{1}{2}$ | $\frac{1}{2}$ | 0 | −1 |
| $\psi_5$: $\frac{1}{2}\mu_1 + \frac{1}{2}\mu_3 - \frac{1}{3}\mu_4 - \frac{1}{3}\mu_5 - \frac{1}{3}\mu_7$ | $\frac{1}{2}$ | 0 | $\frac{1}{2}$ | $-\frac{1}{3}$ | $-\frac{1}{3}$ | 0 | $-\frac{1}{3}$ |
| $\psi_6$: $\frac{1}{5}\mu_1 + \frac{1}{5}\mu_3 + \frac{1}{5}\mu_4 + \frac{1}{5}\mu_5 + \frac{1}{5}\mu_7 - \frac{1}{2}\mu_2 - \frac{1}{2}\mu_6$ | $\frac{1}{5}$ | $-\frac{1}{2}$ | $\frac{1}{5}$ | $\frac{1}{5}$ | $\frac{1}{5}$ | $-\frac{1}{2}$ | $\frac{1}{5}$ |

B. $\hat{\psi}_1 = \overline{X}_1 - \overline{X}_7 = 43 - 30 = 13.0$

$\hat{\psi}_2 = 42 - 33 = 9.0$

$\hat{\psi}_3 = 43 - 40 = 3.0$

$\hat{\psi}_4 = (36 + 35)/2 - 30 = 5.5$

$\hat{\psi}_5 = (43 + 40)/2 - (36 + 35 + 30)/3 = 7.83$

$\hat{\psi}_6 = (43 + 40 + 36 + 35 + 30)/5 - (42 + 33)/2 = -.7$

C. $s_{\hat{\psi}_1} = \sqrt{MS_e\left(\sum_j c_j^2/n_j\right)} = \sqrt{207\left(\frac{2}{20}\right)} = 4.550$; $\quad s_{\hat{\psi}_1} = s_{\hat{\psi}_2} = s_{\hat{\psi}_3} = 4.550 = s_{\overline{X}-\overline{X}}$

$s_{\hat{\psi}_4} = \sqrt{207(1.5/20)} = 3.940$; $\quad s_{\hat{\psi}_5} = \sqrt{207(.833/20)} = 2.937$; $\quad s_{\hat{\psi}_6} = \sqrt{207(.7/20)} = 2.692$

D. $t_{\hat{\psi}} = \dfrac{\hat{\psi}}{s_{\hat{\psi}}}$; $\quad t_{\hat{\psi}_1} = \dfrac{13.0}{4.550} = 2.857$

$t_{\hat{\psi}_2} = 9.0/4.55 = 1.978$

$t_{\hat{\psi}_3} = .659$

$t_{\hat{\psi}_4} = 1.396$

$t_{\hat{\psi}_5} = 2.666$

$t_{\hat{\psi}_6} = -.260$

$\psi_4$: When the AO is positioned before the reading selection, does having answers to the questions have an effect on the mean?

$\psi_5$: Is the mean of the groups having the AO before the reading different from the mean of the groups having the AO after the reading?

$\psi_6$: Is the mean of the groups having the AO different from the mean of the groups that did not receive the AO?

The contrast coefficients for these six contrasts are given in panel A of Table 17.4; the observed difference in the two subsets of means for each of the six contrasts is given in panel B of Table 17.4*.

## 17.10 THE STANDARD ERROR OF A CONTRAST

The other MC methods of this chapter can use a modified $t$-ratio as the test statistic: the ratio of the estimate of the contrast, $\hat{\psi}$, to its estimated standard error, $s_{\hat{\psi}}$. The standard error of a contrast is given by Equation 17.8

$$s_{\hat{\psi}} = \sqrt{MS_e(c_1^2/n_1 + c_2^2/n_2 + \cdots + c_J^2/n_J)} \tag{17.8}$$

where $MS_e$ is the error mean square (the denominator of the $F$-test in the ANOVA).

In Equation 17.8, $c_j$ is the contrast coefficient for the mean, $\overline{X}_j$, and $n_j$ is the number of observations on which it is based, thus

$$s_{\hat{\psi}} = \sqrt{MS_e \sum_j c_j^2/n_j} \tag{17.8A}$$

Or if $n_1 = n_2 = \cdots = n_J$

$$s_{\hat{\psi}} = \sqrt{\frac{MS_e}{n}\left(\sum_j c_j^2\right)} \tag{17.8B}$$

For pairwise contrasts, with $n_1 = n_2 = n$:

$$s_{\hat{\psi}} = \sqrt{2MS_e/n} = \sqrt{2}s_{\overline{X}} \tag{17.8C}$$

In the example in Table 17.4, the standard error of contrast 1, $\hat{\psi}_1$, is (panel C):

$$s_{\hat{\psi}_1} = \sqrt{\frac{MS_e}{n}[(1)^2 + 0 + \cdots + (-1)^2]} = \sqrt{\frac{207(2)}{20}} = \sqrt{20.7} = 4.550$$

*The effect size of a contrast, $\psi$, is $\hat{\Delta} = \hat{\psi}/s_W$ (see Sec. 17.4).

All other pairwise contrasts (such as contrasts 2 and 3) would have the same value for their estimated standard error. Complex contrasts will have smaller standard errors. The more means that are involved in the contrast, the smaller will be the standard error of the contrast. For example, the standard error for contrast 6 found from Equation 17.8 is (see panel C of Table 17.4)

$$s_{\hat{\psi}_6} = \sqrt{207[(.2)^2 + (-.5)^2 + (.2)^2 + (.2)^2 + (.2)^2 + (-.5)^2 + (.2)^2]/20}.$$
$$= \sqrt{207(.7/20)} = 2.692$$

Standard errors for the other contrasts are given in panel C in Table 17.4.

## 17.11 THE $t$-RATIO FOR A CONTRAST

The $t$-ratio for a contrast is

$$t = \hat{\psi}/s_{\hat{\psi}} \tag{17.9}$$

The $t$-ratios for the six contrasts specified in panel A of Table 17.4 are given in panel D. Whether these $t$-ratios achieve statistical significance depends on which MC method is used—each will have different critical values for $t$ due to the different restrictions and conditions that are imposed. Before considering the remaining methods, a clarification of the distinction between planned and post hoc contrasts is needed.

## 17.12 PLANNED VERSUS POST HOC COMPARISONS

An important distinction must be made between the MC methods that are *planned* or use *a priori* contrasts versus those that allow *post hoc* or *a posteriori* contrasts. In planned contrasts, the hypotheses (contrasts) to be tested must be specified *prior* to data collection. MC methods which employ planned comparisons can be advantageous if the questions that the researcher is interested in are a relatively small subset of questions. The distribution theory and probability statements for these MC methods are valid only if there is no chance for the user to be influenced by the data in the choice of which hypotheses are to be tested. The rationale for planned contrasts is similar to that for "one-tailed" $t$-tests—to be valid, the decision must be made *a priori*. Post hoc MC techniques do not require advance specification of the hypotheses (contrasts) to be tested. The Tukey and NK MC methods are considered to be post hoc methods since there is no delimitation as to which pairs of means will be contrasted.

As in the case of one-tailed versus two-tailed tests, greater power ordinarily accrues to the use of planned MC methods.

Now with the meaning of a contrast, and the distinction between planned vs. post hoc contrasts in mind, other MC methods can be considered.

## 17.13 DUNN METHOD OF MULTIPLE COMPARISONS

The Dunn* (1961) MC method uses the *Bonferroni inequality* (Eq. 17.10, see Snedecor and Cochran, 1980, pp. 115-117) for determining the critical value of $t$. The probability of a type-I error in the family (Sec. 17.5) of $C$ independent or dependent contrasts is

$$\alpha_{\Sigma} \leqslant \alpha_1 + \alpha_2 + \cdots + \alpha_C \tag{17.10}$$

For example, it is evident from Equation 17.10 that if five significance tests are conducted, each with $\alpha = .01$, the probability of one or more type-I errors is not more than .05. The Dunn MC procedure requires that all $C$ contrasts be *planned* (Sec. 17.12), and defines the $C$ contrasts as a family which is the base for $\alpha_{\Sigma}$. The critical value of $t$, ${}_{1-\alpha/2}t_{\nu_e, C}$, for all $C$ contrasts is given in Table L in the Appendix. Note that the critical values of $t$ increase as $C$ increases. For example, with $\alpha_{\Sigma} = .10$, $\nu_e = 120$, and $C = 6$ as in Table 17.4), the critical $t$-value is 2.411, but if $C = 20$, the critical $t$-value is $2.843 = {}_{.90}t_{120, 20}$. When the absolute values of the $t$-ratios for each of the $C = 6$ contrasts in Table 17.4 are compared with the critical $t$-value of 2.411, two of the null hypotheses (for contrasts 1 and 5) can be rejected. For the other four contrasts (2, 3, 4, and 6), $H_0$ is tenable.

The Dunn MC method is very flexible; it allows any number of simple and/or complex contrasts, and uses a type-I error rate based on the family of $C$ contrasts. Its relative advantages and disadvantages in comparison to other MC procedures are reviewed after other methods are presented.

## 17.14 DUNNETT METHOD OF MULTIPLE COMPARISONS

The Dunnett MC method is tailor-made for the situation where the plan is to compare each of the $J - 1$ means with one (and only one) *predesignated* mean (usually the mean of the control group). Thus with the Dunnett method there are $C = J - 1$ planned pairwise contrasts—each contrast is against the mean of the predesignated "control" group, $\overline{X}_C$:

$$t_{\hat{\psi}_k} = \frac{\overline{X}_j - \overline{X}_C}{s_{\overline{X}-\overline{X}}} = \frac{\overline{X}_j - \overline{X}_C}{\sqrt{MS_e\left(\dfrac{1}{n_j} + \dfrac{1}{n_C}\right)}} \tag{17.11}$$

The critical $t$ values, ${}_{1-\alpha/2}t_{\nu_e, J-1}$, for the Dunnett method are given in Table M in the Appendix. If the Dunnett method is used to compare the mean of the control group ($\overline{X}_6$) with each of the other $C = J - 1 = 6$ group means, the critical value for $t$ for the six planned contrasts with $\alpha_{\Sigma} = .10$ is $2.32 = {}_{.90}t_{120,6}$.

*Also called the Bonferroni $t$ (Miller, 1966). The method can be used to estimate the maximum probability of a type-I error in any set of significance tests, not just those involving means.

Although the Dunn method could be used to test these same $C = J - 1 = 6$ planned contrasts, it is slightly less powerful than the Dunnett for this family of prespecified contrasts; the critical $t$-value for the sample problem with $\alpha_\Sigma = .10$, $C = 6$, and $\nu_e = 133$ are 2.32 and 2.41 for the Dunnett and Dunn MC methods, respectively.

In the example in Table 17.4, $s_{\overline{X}-\overline{X}} = 4.55$ (see panel C of Table 17.4); thus, if $\overline{X}_6$ (the control group) had been predesignated as $\overline{X}_C$, the $t$-ratio associated with the null hypothesis, $H_0: \mu_1 - \mu_6 = 0$ would be $t = (43 - 33)/4.55 = 2.20$ which is below the critical $t$-ratio of 2.32, thus, the null hypothesis cannot be rejected. The $t$-ratios for the other simple contrasts would be less than 2.20, thus, if the Dunnett (or Dunn) MC method were employed, none of the six null hypotheses ($H_0$: $\mu_j - \mu_6$) would be rejected.*

## 17.15 SCHEFFÉ METHOD OF MULTIPLE COMPARISONS

The Scheffé method† is the most widely presented MC method in textbooks of statistical methods (Hopkins and Anderson 1973); ironically it is rarely the MC method of choice for the questions of interest in terms of power efficiency. The Scheffé method is a very flexible post hoc MC method. It defines the family of contrasts as the family of *all possible* simple and complex contrasts, and employs a family-based type-I error rate $\alpha_\Sigma$. As a consequence of such latitude, the critical $t$-value for the Scheffé method is large relative to the other MC methods that have been presented, especially as the number of means, $J$, increases. One can be certain, however, that if the omnibus $F$-test is significant at a given alpha level, that at least one contrast will also be significant when the Scheffé MC method is used (Scheffé, 1959).

The critical $t$-ratio with the Scheffé method is

$$_{1-\alpha/2}t_{\nu_e, J} = \sqrt{(J-1)_{1-\alpha}F_{\nu_b, \nu_e}} \tag{17.12}$$

where $\nu_b = J - 1$, and $\nu_e$ is the degrees of freedom associated with $MS_e$.

In the example in Table 17.4, the critical value of $t$ for all contrasts for the Scheffé MC method with $\alpha_\Sigma = .10$ is found from Equation 17.12 to be

$$\sqrt{(7-1)_{.90}F_{6,120}} = \sqrt{6(1.82)} = 3.30$$

Notice that if the Scheffé method were employed in the sample problem, none of the contrasts specified in Table 17.4 would have approached statistical significance (see panel D).

The unique advantage of the Scheffé MC method is that it can be used for "data snooping"—for making any simple or complex contrasts even after inspecting

*In actual research applications, the optimal MC method for the questions of interest should be selected and used. In this chapter the various MC methods are all used with the sample problem so that the results can be compared.

†Also call $F$-projections (Miller, 1966), and the $S$-method (Scheffé, 1959).

the means. For example, is the mean of the three largest means in Table 17.4, significantly larger than the mean of the two groups having the lowest means:

$$H_0\colon \psi_7 = (\mu_1 + \mu_2 + \mu_3)/3 - (\mu_6 + \mu_7)/2 = 0$$

The value of this contrast ($\psi_7$) is estimated to be

$$\hat{\psi}_7 = (43 + 42 + 40)/3 - (33 + 30)/2 = 41.67 - 31.50 = 10.17$$

with

$$s_{\hat{\psi}_7} = s_{\hat{\psi}_5} = 2.94$$

(see panel C of Table 17.4):

$$t_{\hat{\psi}_7} = 10.17/2.94 = 3.46$$

which is greater than the critical $t$-value of 3.30, therefore, this null hypothesis can be rejected at $\alpha_\Sigma = .10$. Try your hand at interpreting this difference—the contrast has little apparent educational or psychological meaning.

The flexibility of the Scheffé method such that post hoc data snooping for any number of contrasts is allowed, causes it to be a very conservative and inefficient procedure in the usual research circumstance in which there is interest in only a limited subset of possible contrasts, such as all pairwise contrasts.

> The great versatility of the Scheffé technique is at the same time its major drawback . . . Although data-snooping with *F* projections [Scheffé] is an intellectually nice idea, it does not seem to be of too "great practical importance." For a prespecified subset of the possible contrasts the Dunn method will be usually more powerful than the Scheffé method.* (Miller 1966, p. 54)

For all possible pairwise contrasts the Tukey or Newman-Keuls methods are more sensitive.

## 17.16 PLANNED ORTHOGONAL CONTRASTS

When a researcher can accept the constraints imposed by *planned orthogonal contrasts* (POC), it is the most powerful test of mean differences. The POC method employs a contrast-based type-I error rate, $\alpha$. The notion of a planned contrast was treated in Section 17.12; the concept of *orthogonality* will now be considered.

*Contrary to popular opinion, both the Dunn and the Tukey (Guenther, 1963) methods are often more powerful than the Scheffé method for complex contrasts (Spjotvol and Stoline, 1973).

In the POC method all the sum of squares between groups, $SS_b$, is decomposed into $\nu_b = J - 1$ orthogonal (i.e., mathematically independent, mutually exclusive) parts. Each part is associated with a contrast. Thus, the $J - 1$ possible orthogonal contrasts contain unique, nonoverlapping information.

In balanced (i.e., equal $n$'s) designs the value of two contrasts, $\psi$ and $\psi'$ are orthogonal when the products of the corresponding contrast coefficients sum to zero:*

$$\sum_j c_j c_j' = c_1 c_1' + c_2 c_2' + \cdots + c_J c_J' = 0 \qquad (17.13)$$

when the two contrasts are orthogonal.

For example, for contrasts 1 and 2 in Table 17.4 $\Sigma_j c_j c_j' = (1)(0) + (0)(1) + (0)(0) + (0)(0) + (0)(0) + (0)(-1) + (-1)(0) = 0$, thus, $\psi_1$ and $\psi_2$ are orthogonal. But what about contrast 1 and 3? Since $\Sigma\, c_{j1} c_{j3} = (1)(1) + (0)(0) + (0)(-1) + (0)(0) + (0)(0) + (0)(0) + (-1)(0) = 1$, $\psi_1$ and $\psi_3$ are not orthogonal. Since $\psi_1$, $\psi_2$, and $\psi_3$ are not orthogonal, the POC method should not be used. Although contrasts 1 and 2, and contrasts 2 and 3 are orthogonal, each contrast must be orthogonal to every other contrast to achieve the condition of orthogonality.

POC is the MC method of choice only when (1) all research questions can be answered by $C = J - 1$ or fewer contrasts, and (2) all $C$ contrasts are orthogonal.

For POC the critical value is the central $t$-ratio found in Table C in the Appendix, where $\nu_e$ is the degrees of freedom for $MS_e$, that is, ${}_{1-\alpha/2}t_{\nu_e}$, where $\alpha$ is the probability of a type-I error for each contrast. With $\alpha = .10$, ${}_{.95}t_{133} = 1.66$.

Using the example in Table 17.4 five of the six contrasts (contrasts 2-6) are orthogonal. For purposes of illustration, assume that these contrasts were decided upon prior to the study. Two of the five orthogonal contrasts (contrasts 2 and 5) would achieve statistical significance when the POC method is used, whereas for the other three (contrasts 3, 4, and 6), the null hypothesis is tenable. Although contrast 1 would have been significant, it could not be included in the POC analysis since it is not orthogonal to the other contrasts.

The requirement that the contrasts be both planned and orthogonal makes the POC procedure very different from multiple $t$-tests, even though the critical $t$-ratio is ostensibly the same.

## 17.17 CONFIDENCE INTERVALS† FOR CONTRASTS

The 1-$\alpha$ confidence interval (CI) for the Tukey method is

$$(\bar{X}_j - \bar{X}_j') \pm {}_{1-\alpha}q_{\nu_e, J}\, s_{\bar{X}} \qquad (17.14)$$

*When $n$'s are not equal, orthogonality is maintained when $\Sigma_j\, c_j c_j'/n_j = 0$. Thus, with unbalanced designs orthogonality is achieved only at the expense of meaningfulness. In practice meaningfulness of the contrasts must be preserved even if some departure from ortogonality results.

†The Newman-Keuls and Duncan methods do not lend themselves to interval estimation.

Thus, in Table 17.2 the .90 CI for the *difference* in the mean of population 1 and the mean of population 7 (i.e., contrast 1 in Table 17.4), is (from Eq. 17.14)

$$13 \pm (3.86)(3.217) = 13 \pm 12.42 \quad \text{or} \quad (.58, 25.42)$$

For the MC methods for which the $t$-distribution was used, the .90 CI for a contrast $\psi$ is

$$\hat{\psi} \pm (\text{critical-}t)\, s_{\hat{\psi}} \tag{17.15}$$

where the critical $t$-ratios for the various MC methods* (using alpha = .10) for the sample problem were determined earlier when null hypotheses were being tested:

Dunn: ${}_{.95}t_{\nu_e, C}$

Dunnett: ${}_{.95}t_{\nu_e, C}$

Scheffé: $\sqrt{(J-1)\,{}_{.90}F_{J-1, \nu_e}}$

POC ${}_{.95}t_{\nu_e} = \sqrt{{}_{.90}F_{1, \nu_e}}$

The relative sizes of the CI for pairwise contrasts for the various MC methods are evident in Figure 17.1, which gives the minimum difference for a pairwise contrast required for statistical significance at the .10 level (i.e., one-half the width for the .90 CI) for the sample problem.

**FIGURE 17.1. Minimum difference between two means needed to reject $H_0$ (panel A) and estimated power for an effect size of $1\sigma$ (panel B) $H_0: \mu_j = \mu_{j'}$ at the .10 level for various multiple comparison methods using the data in Table 17.1 ($J = 7, MS_e = 207, \nu_e = 133, s_\psi = 4.55, s_{\bar{X}} = 3.217$).**

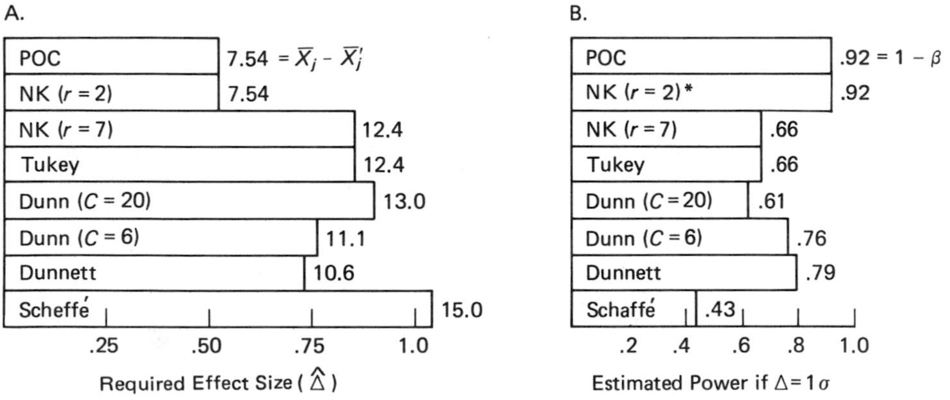


*Assuming the two means are *not* contained within a non-significant range.

## 17.18 RELATIVE POWER OF MULTIPLE COMPARISON TECHNIQUES

Notice that the mean difference required for significance for the various MC methods varies greatly. Observe in panel A of Fig. 17.1 that

1. POC requires the smallest mean difference for statistical significance.
2. The NK and the POC methods require the identical difference for signifcance between adjacently-ordered means. (Of course the NK method will never reach or allow this comparison if the two means fall within a nonsignificant range.)
3. The Tukey and NK methods require the identical difference for their initial comparison.
4. The Tukey is more powerful than the Dunn method if all pairwise contrasts are planned ($C = 21$).
5. The Dunn method requires a slightly larger mean difference for $J - 1 = 6$ planned contrasts than does the Dunnett.
6. The Scheffé technique requires a much larger difference than any of the other MC methods for simple contrasts.

To demonstrate further the relative power of the various MC techniques, assume for purposes of illustration that $\mu_j - \mu_{j'} = 10$. Using the design in Table 17.1, the estimated power for the various MC methods for correctly rejecting $H_0: \mu_j = \mu_{j'}$, is given in panel B of Figure 17.1. Notice that the Scheffé method is much less powerful than the other procedures. Although the POC method is much more powerful than the other techniques, the conditions of requiring contrasts to be planned and orthogonal greatly restricts its utility.

## 17.19 TREND ANALYSIS

Trend analysis is similar to planned orthogonal comparisons, but it is used in lieu of multiple comparisons when there is a continuum underlying the $J$ levels of the factor. When persons are grouped into levels of a factor such as age, grade, IQ, or SES, by using trend analysis, one can examine statistically the shape of the curve that results when the means of the dependent variable, $\overline{Y}_j$, are plotted for the $J$ levels of the factor (independent variable).* In such situations the use of trend analysis is usually more informative than multiple comparisons. Indeed, MC methods often fragment the whole configuration into seemingly contradictory parts when the $J$ levels of the factor represent a continuum. For example, suppose persons are classified into very low (1), low (2), medium (3), and high (4), and very high (5) levels of the factor "Anxiety," and the omnibus $F$-test for $H_0: \mu_1 = \mu_2 = \ldots = \mu_J$ is rejected and all pairwise comparisons are performed with the following

*In trend analysis, as in regression analysis and the analysis of covariance (Chapter 20), the dependent variable will be denoted by $Y$, and the independent variable by $X$.

result: $H_{0_1}: \mu_1 = \mu_5$ is rejected, but all the other $H_0$'s are tenable. It is implausible that the effects of anxiety are abrupt and operate only at levels 1 and 5.

Trend analysis will more explicitly illuminate the nature of the relationship between the $J$ levels of the independent variable, $X$, and the dependent variable, $Y$; that is, via trend analysis one is able to assess whether the relationship is linear or nonlinear. If nonlinear, what is the general shape of the best fitting regression (trend) line (of $Y$ on $X$)?

Trend analysis uses "orthogonal polynomials" to fit the trend line of the $J$ means. A polynomial is a mathematical equation that contains powers of the variable $X$ greater than one. For example,

$Y = a + bX$ is a linear or first-degree equation

$Y = a + bX + cX^2$ is a quadratic or second-degree equation

$Y = a + bX + cX^2 + dX^3$ is a cubic or third-degree equation

Examples of linear, quadratic, and cubic trends are illustrated in Figure 17.2

The general algebraic expression for an orthogonal polynomial in a trend analysis for a factor $X$ of $J$ levels is

$$Y = a + bX + cX^2 + dX^3 + \cdots + qX^{J-1} \tag{17.16}$$

As with POC, there are $C = J - 1$ *possible* orthogonal trend components. Trend analysis determines whether each term in Equation 17.16 contributes unique information. The correlation ratio (Sec. 8.28) describes the proportion of variance in $Y$ that is explicable or predictable from the orthogonal polynomial (curvilinear regression), whereas $r^2$ denotes the proportion of variance explicable from the first-degree (linear) equation ($a + bX$) alone. If there is no curvilinear relationship between the independent and dependent variables in the population, the second and higher degree equations will not improve significantly the prediction of $Y$, i.e., the degree of improvement will not be statistically significant and can be interpreted to be the result of sampling error (except when a type-I error is made).

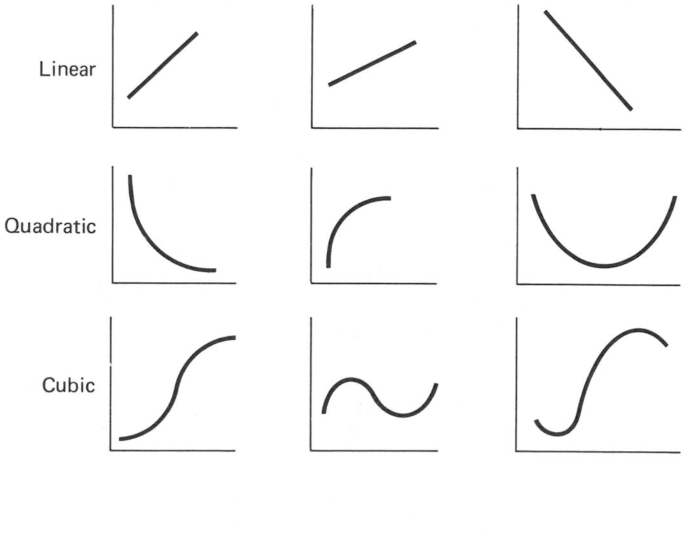


**FIGURE 17.2**
**Three examples of linear, quadratic, and cubic trends.**

The example in Table 17.5 illustrates that trend analysis is just a special application of planned orthogonal contrasts.* The example is from Table 8.6 (Sec. 8.27) in which $n = 4$ persons in each of $J = 7$ age groups are tested on psychomotor performance. The ANOVA table in panel A of Table 17.5 shows that the means of the seven age groups differ significantly. Is there a trend in the pattern of mean differences? Is there a linear trend among the seven means, that is, can a straight (linear) regression line predict $J$ means significantly better than the grand mean $\bar{X}_{\bullet} = 9.64$—is $H_0: \psi_{\text{linear}} = 0$ tenable?

A second and independent question is whether or not a quadratic component (a smooth curved line with a single bend—a parabola) would account for a significant amount of variance in the $\bar{Y}_j$'s over and above that provided by the grand mean and the linear contrast—is $H_0: \psi_{\text{quadratic}} = 0$ tenable? Notice that the orthogonality criterion defined in Equation 17.13 is met by the linear and quadratic contrasts given in panel B of Table 17.5: $\Sigma c_j c_j' = (-3)(5) + (-2)(0) + (-1)(-3) + (0)(-4) + (1)(-3) + (2)(0) + (3)(5) = 0$.

Similarly, a third and independent question asks if there is a significant cubic component—will a regression line allowing two "bends" better fit the data than a straight line and/or a curve with a single bend (quadratic)? Look at the scatterplot of the data in Figure 8.11 in Section 8.27. There does not appear to be a significant linear component (note that $r = -.077$). The means seem to increase up to a point, then decrease; this suggests that there is a quadratic component. There is not a second change of direction, which suggests that there is no cubic component in the relationship. These apparent trends should be evaluated for statistical significance to guard against overinterpretation. Notice that unlike POC's, the contrast coefficients do not have to be constructed; they are found in Table N in the Appendix. Panel B in Table 17.5 gives the $J = 7$ contrast coefficients for $\psi_{\text{linear}}$, $\psi_{\text{quadratic}}$, and $\psi_{\text{cubic}}$. Higher order trends could also be tested but such complex trends are rarely expected. The contrast coefficients are given for only the first five trends in Table N. Notice in panel D of Table 17.5 that the numerical values for $MS_{\hat{\psi}_{\text{linear}}}$ and $MS_{\hat{\psi}_{\text{cubic}}}$ are very small (only $-.32$ and $.67$), whereas $MS_{\hat{\psi}_{\text{quadratic}}}$ is much larger (24.11).

## 17.20 SIGNIFICANCE OF TREND COMPONENTS

Are the trend contrasts large enough to reject $H_0: \psi = 0$? Equation 17.9 can be used to provide a $t$-ratio for the trend contrast:

$$t_{\hat{\psi}} = \frac{\hat{\psi}}{s_{\hat{\psi}}} = \frac{\hat{\psi}}{\sqrt{MS_e \, \Sigma c_j^2 / n}}$$

The statistical significance of the contrast is ordinarily evaluated using the $F$-test, which is mathematically equivalent to $t^2$. A variance (mean square) is estimated from the value of

*Unlike POC's, the numerical values of these contrasts are not interpreted as a difference between the means of two subsets of means, consequently whole numbers are used for contrast coefficients to simplify the computations.

**TABLE 17.5 Means for Seven Age Levels on Psychomotor Test (Data from Table 8.6)**

A. ANOVA Table

| *Source* | *SS* | $\nu$ | *MS* | *F* | |
|---|---|---|---|---|---|
| Age (between) | 29.43 | 6 | 4.905 | 4.12 | $p < .10$ |
| Error (within) | 25.00 | 21 | 1.190 | | |
| Total | 54.43 | $27 = n_{.} - J$ | | | |

B.

| | $\bar{Y}_1$ | $\bar{Y}_2$ | $\bar{Y}_3$ | $\bar{Y}_4$ | $\bar{Y}_5$ | $\bar{Y}_6$ | $\bar{Y}_7$ | |
|---|---|---|---|---|---|---|---|---|
| Means: | (8.5) | (9.5) | (10.5) | (11.5) | (10.0) | (9.0) | (8.5) | |
| Contrast Coefficients: | $c_1$ | $c_2$ | $c_3$ | $c_4$ | $c_5$ | $c_6$ | $c_7$ | $\Sigma c_j^2$ |
| $\psi_{\text{linear}}$ | −3 | −2 | −1 | 0 | 1 | 2 | 3 | 28 |
| $\psi_{\text{quadratic}}$ | 5 | 0 | −3 | −4 | −3 | 0 | 5 | 84 |
| $\psi_{\text{cubic}}$ | −1 | 1 | 1 | 0 | −1 | −1 | 1 | 6 |

C. Estimated Contrasts

$$\hat{\psi}_{\text{linear}} = (-3)(8.5) + (-2)(9.5) + (-1)(10.5) + (0)(11.5) + (1)(10.0) + (2)(9.0) + (3)(8.5) = -1.5$$

$$\hat{\psi}_{\text{quadratic}} = (5)(8.5) + (-3)(10.5) + (-4)(11.5) + (-3)(10.0) + (5)(8.5) = -22.5$$

$$\hat{\psi}_{\text{cubic}} = -8.5 + 9.5 + 10.5 - 10.0 - 9.0 + 8.5 = 1.0$$

D. Significance Tests of Contrasts

$$MS_{\hat{\psi}} = \frac{\hat{\psi}_k}{\Sigma c_j^2/n}, \qquad MS_{\hat{\psi}_{\text{linear}}} = \frac{(-1.5)^2}{28/4} = \frac{2.25}{7} = .32$$

$$F_{\hat{\psi}_{\text{linear}}} = \frac{MS_{\hat{\psi}_{\text{linear}}}}{MS_e} = \frac{.32}{1.19} = .27, \qquad {}_{.75}F_{1,21} = 1.40, \; p > .25$$

$$MS_{\hat{\psi}_{\text{quadratic}}} = \frac{(-22.5)^2}{84/4} = 24.11, \qquad F_{\hat{\psi}_{\text{quadratic}}} = \frac{24.11}{1.19} = 20.26, \qquad {}_{.999}F_{1,21} = 14.8, \; p < .01,$$

$$MS_{\hat{\psi}_{\text{cubic}}} = \frac{(1.0)^2}{6/4} = .67, \qquad F_{\hat{\psi}_{\text{cubic}}} = \frac{.67}{1.19} = .56, \qquad p > .25$$

E. Trend Analysis Summary

| *Source* | *SS* | | *MS* | *F* |
|---|---|---|---|---|
| Age | 29.43 | 6 | 4.905 | 4.12[b] |
| Linear | .32 | 1 | .32 | .27 |
| Quadratic | 24.11 | 1 | 24.11 | 20.26[c] |
| Cubic | .67 | 1 | .67 | .56 |
| Remainder[a] | 4.33 | 3 | 1.44 | 1.21 |
| Error (within) | 25.00 | 21 | 1.190 | |

[a]This is an aggregate of quartic and other higher order curvilinear trends: $SS_{\text{remainder}} = SS_b - MS_{\text{linear}} - MS_{\text{quadratic}} - MS_{\text{cubic}} = 29.43 - .32 - 24.11 - .67 = 4.33$.

[b]$p < .01$.

[c]$p < .001$.

the contrast:

$$MS_{\hat{\psi}} = \frac{\hat{\psi}^2}{\Sigma c_j^2/n}$$

(Notice that the value of $\Sigma c_j^2$ is also given in Table N.) The $F = MS_{\hat{\psi}}/MS_e$; the critical $F$-ratio is the same as for POC's, ${}_{1-\alpha}F_{1,\nu_e}$.

The $F$-tests* for the linear, quadratic, and cubic trends are given in panel D of Table 17.5. Notice that only the quadratic component is significant.† The findings from the trend analysis are given in the ANOVA table in panel E of Table 17.5.

The sum of squares for the remaining components for the three higher order (quartic, etc.) trends can be aggregated, and tested as a composite, by subtracting the sum of squares accounted for by the three trends that have been evaluated (.32 + 24.11 + .67 = 25.10) from $SS_{\text{age}}$ = 29.43, to yield $SS_{\text{remainder}}$ (29.43 - 25.10 = 4.33). The remainder has $J - 1 - 3 = 3$ degrees of freedom. The mean square for the remainder is shown in panel E to be 1.44 (4.33/3).

The $F$-test for the composite of the remaining higher order trends is given in the fifth line of the ANOVA Table in panel E of Table 17.5. Since $F = 1.44/1.19 = 1.12$ and $p > .25$, it does not appear that there are higher order trends.‡

## 17.21 RELATION OF TRENDS TO CORRELATION COEFFICIENTS

There is a close parallel between the linear trend and the Pearson product-moment correlation coefficient $r$.

Indeed,

$$|r| = \sqrt{\frac{SS_{\text{linear}}}{SS_{\text{total}}}} \tag{17.20}$$

where $SS_{\text{linear}} = MS_{\text{linear}}$ since $\nu = 1$.
In the example using the results summarized in Table 17.5:

$$|r| = \sqrt{\frac{.32}{54.43}} = .077$$

which agrees with the $r$ of $-.077$ found in Section 8.28.

*Note that $F = \hat{\psi}^2/(MS_e \Sigma c_j/n) = t^2$.

†Ordinarily the curvilinear relationship is not expressed via a mathematical equation. But if this is desired, the particulars are given in Winer (1971, pp. 183–185), Kirk (1982, pp. 159–161), and Snedecor and Cochran (1980, pp. 404–407).

‡Some writers advocate a significant $F$-test of the remainder at each step before exploring further trends. We advocate this only after a priori contrasts have been examined individually. The logic is identical to that for POC's in relation to the omnibus $F$-test. The $SS_{\psi} = MS_{\psi}$ for the fourth-, fifth-, and sixth-order terms, if tested individually, are 3.14, .01, and 1.18, which sum to 4.33 = $SS_{\text{remainder}}$.

Likewise,

$$\hat{\eta}^2_{Y.X} = \frac{SS_{\text{between}}}{SS_{\text{total}}} = 29.43/54.43 = .541 \tag{17.21}$$

which agrees with the value for $\hat{\eta}^2_{Y.X}$ that was found in Section 8.28. $\hat{\eta}^2_{Y.X}$ defines the proportion of variance explained by the independent variable $X$.

Note in panel E of Table 17.5 that the $F$ of 4.12 for the Age ("between") effect is identical to the test for $H_0: \eta_{Y.X} = 0$ in Section 15.17. Similarly, the F-test for nonlinearity of regression in Section 15.18 yields $F = 4.89$ which is identical to testing the remaining $J - 2$ trend components after the linear component has been removed. That is, $SS_{\text{nonlinear}} = SS_{\text{between}} - SS_{\text{linear}} = 29.43 - .32 = 29.11$, and $MS_{\text{nonlinear}} = SS_{\text{nonlinear}}/(J - 2) = 29.11/5 = 5.82$. $F = MS_{\text{nonlinear}}/MS_e = 5.82/1.19 = 4.89$.

## 17.22 ASSUMPTIONS OF MC METHODS AND TREND ANALYSIS

In addition to the conditions that contrasts be planned and orthogonal assumed for valid use of certain MC methods, all methods discussed in this chapter have the same assumptions of normality, homogeneity of variance, and independence as the $t$-test and ANOVA.

The MC methods appear to be robust to departures from normality but cannot be presumed to be robust to large departures from homogeneity of variance (Petrinovich and Hardyck, 1969). For example, if $J = 4$, the nominal .05 $\alpha$-level is used, and $\sigma_1^2 > \sigma_2^2 > \sigma_3^2 > \sigma_4^2$, the MC tests of means from the more homogeneous populations (e.g., $H_0: \mu_3 = \mu_4$) will be liberal. Consequently, $H_0: \sigma_1^2 = \sigma_2^2 = \cdots = \sigma_J^2$ should be tested when using MC methods, especially for pariwise comparisons. If variances are very heterogeneous, a large sample MC test* can be used that does not assume homogeneity of variance (Marascuilo, 1966). However, the procedure (Sec. 17.23) is very conservative (Hopkins and Anderson, 1973)† for pairwise contrasts among means.

## 17.23 MULTIPLE COMPARISONS AMONG OTHER STATISTICS

The method described by Marascuilo (1966) defines a contrast similarly, but more generally, than Equation 17.7:

$$\hat{\psi} = \sum_{j=1}^{J} c_j \hat{\theta}_j \tag{17.22}$$

*A large sample statistical test is one in which the test requires knowledge of a parameter that is not known but, because $n$ is large, the sampling error in the estimate is viewed as negligible.

†See also Hochberg (1976).

**TABLE 17.6 Illustration of Multiple Comparison Among Proportion Using Data in Table 14.2**

| | Group 1 | Group 2 | Group 3 |
|---|---|---|---|
| $p_j$: | .25 | .20 | .49 |
| $n_j$: | 40 | 60 | 200 |
| $\hat{\sigma}^2_{p_j} = \dfrac{p_j(1-p_j)}{n_j}$ | .00469 | .00267 | .00125 |

$\psi_1$: $\pi_1 - \pi_3$; $\hat{\psi}_1 = .25 - .49 = -.24$; $\hat{\sigma}^2_{\hat{\psi}_1} = .00469 + .00125 = .00594$

$\psi_2$: $\pi_1 - \pi_2$; $\hat{\psi}_2 = .25 - .20 = .05$; $\hat{\sigma}^2_{\hat{\psi}_2} = .00736$

$\psi_3$: $\pi_2 - \pi_3$; $\hat{\psi}_3 = .20 - .49 = -.29$; $\hat{\sigma}^2_{\hat{\psi}_2} = .00392$

$$\chi^2_{\hat{\psi}_1} = \frac{\hat{\psi}_1^2}{\hat{\sigma}^2_{\hat{\psi}_1}} = \frac{(-.24)^2}{.00594} = 9.70 > 9.21 = {}_{.99}\chi^2_2,\ p < .01$$

$$\chi^2_{\hat{\psi}_2} = \frac{(.05)^2}{.00736} = .34,\ p > .80$$

$$\chi^2_{\hat{\psi}_3} = \frac{(-.29)^2}{.00392} = 21.45 > 13.82 = {}_{.999}\chi^2_2,\ p < .001$$

where $\hat{\theta}_j$ represents any of $J$ independent statistics ($p$, $r$, $\overline{X}$, $Md$, etc.) and $\Sigma\, c_j = 0$. The estimated variance of the contrast, $\hat{\sigma}^2_{\hat{\psi}}$, is the sum of the variance of the statistics involved in the contrast, weighted by the contrast coefficients.

$$\hat{\sigma}^2_{\hat{\psi}} = \sum_j^J c_j^2\, \hat{\sigma}^2_{\hat{\theta}_j} \tag{17.23}$$

for pairwise contrasts, $c_j^2 = 1$, hence $\hat{\sigma}^2_{\hat{\psi}} = \Sigma\hat{\sigma}^2_{\hat{\theta}_j}$.

If $n$ is large, the ratio $\hat{\psi}^2/\hat{\sigma}^2_{\hat{\psi}}$ has an approximate $\chi^2$-distribution with $\nu = J - 1$.

$$\chi^2 = \frac{\hat{\psi}^2}{\hat{\sigma}^2_{\hat{\psi}}} \tag{17.24}$$

The critical value ${}_{1-\alpha_\Sigma}\chi^2_\nu$ has a type-I error rate based on a family of any number of contrasts among the $J$ statistics.

The technique is illustrated in Table 17.6 using the proportions from Table 14.2 (Sec. 14.8). Note that $H_0$: $\pi_1 = \pi_2$ was tenable at $\alpha_\Sigma = .05$, whereas $H_0$: $\pi_1 = \pi_3$ and $H_0$: $\pi_2 = \pi_3$ were rejected.

## CHAPTER SUMMARY AND CRITERIA FOR SELECTING A MULTIPLE COMPARISON METHOD

There are several MC methods; the methods will often yield very different results. Some MC methods require planned (a priori) contrasts (Dunn, Dunnett, and planned orthogonal contrasts) while others are post hoc (Tukey, Newman-Keuls, Scheffé, and Marascuilo). The MC methods also differ with respect to the basis for $\alpha$; POC and NK use the contrast as the base; the others have a family-based significance level, $\alpha_\Sigma$. MC methods using contrast-based $\alpha$ will tend to have greater power, but have less protection against type-I errors. Other distinctions are reviewed in the decisions in the schema in Figure 17.3.

All methods except Marascuilo's assume homogeneity of variances; this assumption should be tested especially if $n$'s are not equal.

**FIGURE 17.3. Flow chart guide for the selection of multiple-comparison techniques.**

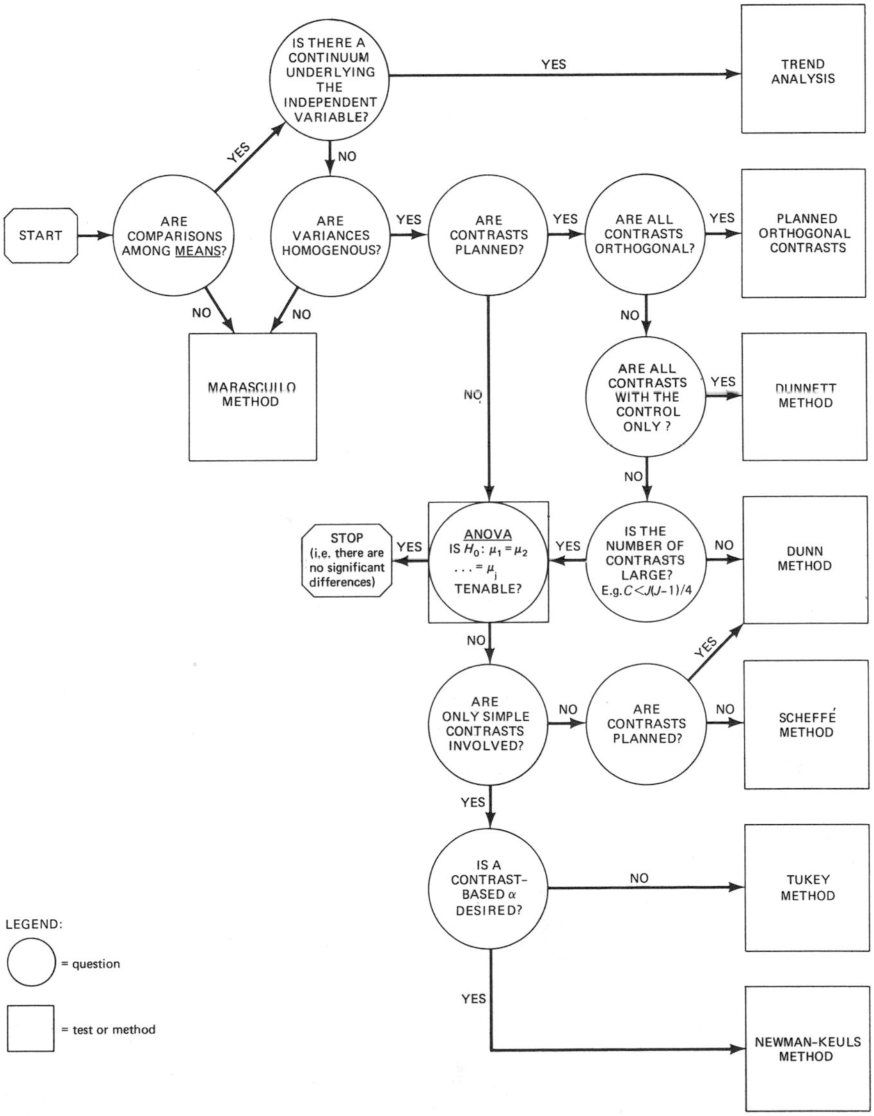

1. The large-sample method described by Marascuilo (1966) is needed when making MC's among correlation coefficients, proportions, and contingency tables and is recommended for contrasting means only when variances are not homogeneous.
2. If the $J$ levels are levels on an ordered continuum, such as age, grade, and trials, use trend analysis.
3. Make planned orthogonal contrasts if they will answer the relevant hypotheses (usually this will not be the case). Each comparison will have the contrast as the base for $\alpha$. If the contrasts are not planned, do an ANOVA (step 6).
4. If all comparisons of interest contrast the control group with each of the other $J - 1$ groups, use the Dunnett procedure. Using the Dunnett technique, the probability of a type-I error is $\alpha_\Sigma$ for the *set* of $J - 1$ tests.
5. If the number of comparisons $C$ is not large (e.g., $C < (J - 1)/4$), use the Dunn test.* The Dunn test is appropriate for simple contrasts (involving only two means, i.e., a pair of means) and complex contrasts (involving more than two means). If $C$ is large, do an ANOVA.
6. Compare $F$-ratio differences among the means obtained in the ANOVA with critical $F$-value required for significance. If $H_0$ cannot be rejected, one ordinarily should not look further for mean differences, although this is a logical rather than a purely statistical consideration. If the omnibus $F$ is not significant, it is tantamount to concluding that all differences among all means are attributable to random sampling error. Strictly speaking, none of the methods is contingent upon a significant omnibus $F$-test. Indeed, this recommendation makes the MC tests somewhat conservative (Myette and White, 1982). This sequence is logical, however, since the omnibus $F$-test is more powerful than the MC tests it precedes.
7. If only pairwise comparisons are to be made and a contrast-based $\alpha$ is desired, use NK.
8. If only $C = J(J - 1)/2$ pairwise comparisons are of interest and a family-based $\alpha$ is desired, the Tukey method should be used, since it is more powerful than the Dunn and Scheffé methods under such conditions (Scheffé, 1959, p. 76). If the number of hypotheses to be tested, $C$, is less than $J(J - 1)/2$ the Dunn (1961) method will usually be more powerful than either the Tukey or the Scheffé method.
9. If comparisons between complex combinations of means are desired, the Dunn method usually has more power than Scheffé unless $C$ is *very* large.
10. The Scheffé is rarely the MC method of choice except for "data snooping."

## *MASTERY TEST*

1. If a $t$-test is used to compare the largest mean with the smallest mean in a set of five means, which of the following is true? The probability of a type-I error is
   a. greater than
   b. equal to
   c. less than

   the $\alpha$ associated with the critical $t$-value.

*Tables 4 to 6 in Dunn (1961) provide precise figures for various $J$, $\alpha$, and $\nu_e$ combinations for which the Dunn method would be more powerful than the Scheffé method.

2. Are multiple $t$-tests recommended for locating significant differences when more than two means are involved?

3. If ten hypotheses are tested and the probability of a type-I error in any one (or more) of the $H_0$'s is $\leqslant .05$, the error rate is
   a. per comparison $\alpha$.
   b. per the family of ten contrasts, $\alpha_\Sigma$.

4. In making all pairwise comparisons among five means, MC methods that use a family type-I error rate, $\alpha_\Sigma$, will tend to make ____ (fewer or more) type-I errors and ____ (fewer or more) type-II errors than MC methods that employ a contrast-based type-I error rate, $\alpha$.

5. After inspecting the data, is it appropriate for a researcher to decide which "planned contrasts" she will make?

6. What is the distinction between $\psi$ and $\hat{\psi}$?

7. Which of these is not a valid contrast?
   a. $\hat{\psi}_1 = \overline{X}_2 - \overline{X}_3$
   b. $\hat{\psi}_2 = \overline{X}_1 + \overline{X}_2 + \overline{X}_3 = 0$
   c. $\hat{\psi}_3 = -\overline{X}_1/2 + \overline{X}_2 - \overline{X}_3/2$
   d. $\hat{\psi}_4 = \overline{X}_1 - \overline{X}_2 - \overline{X}_3 + \overline{X}_4$
   e. $\hat{\psi}_5 = \overline{X}_1 - (\overline{X}_2 + \overline{X}_3 + \overline{X}_4)/3$

8. Which of the valid contrasts above are "complex contrasts?"

9. What is the null hypothesis implicit in Question 7c?

10. Are these contrasts in Question 7 orthogonal?
    a. a and c
    b. a and d
    c. a and e
    d. c and e
    e. d and e

11. Which contrast in Question 7 could be used in comparing the freshmen mean with the average mean from the sophomores, juniors, and seniors?

Indicate which of the following methods is the proper MC method in the situations described in Question 12 to 17.

a. Dunnett method
b. Newman-Keuls method
c. planned orthogonal contrasts
d. Scheffé method
e. Tukey method
f. Dunn method
g. Marascuilo method

12. If a family error rate, $\alpha_\Sigma$, is desired and all hypotheses involved only pairs of means (not complex contrasts), which method should one select?

13. If $J = 6$ and hypotheses $H_{0_1}: \mu_1 = \mu_2$, $H_{0_2}: \mu_3 = \mu_4$, and $H_{0_3}: \mu_1 + \mu_2 = \mu_3 + \mu_4$ were to be tested, which would probably be employed?

14. Which methods use a type-I error rate per comparison (contrast)?

15. If one were only interested in comparing $\overline{X}_1$, $\overline{X}_3$, $\overline{X}_4$, and $\overline{X}_5$ with $\overline{X}_2$, which method would probably be selected?

16. To go "data snooping," which method is most general and makes fewest assumptions?

17. To make multiple comparisons among several independent proportions or correlation coefficients, which one would be chosen?

18. In which of these ways does the Scheffé method differ from POC, e.g., to test the $H_0$ in in Question 7c?
    a. in the coefficients employed for a given contrast
    b. in computing the value of $\hat{\psi}$
    c. in calculating $t$ (or $F$)
    d. in the critical value for the test statistic

19. Newman-Keuls and Tukey always give the identical result in testing a hypothesis for a contrast when:
    a. $J = 3$
    b. comparing the extreme-most means
    c. $r = 2$ (range of ordered mean $= r$)
    d. when $n$ is large
20. The assumption $\sigma_1^2 = \sigma_2^2 = \cdots = \sigma_J^2$ can be disregarded in making multiple comparisons if $n_1 = n_2 = \cdots = n_J$. (T or F)
21. Which method does not assume homogeneity of variance?
22. Which method is best for planned complex, nonorthogonal contrasts?

The figure below is from a recent review of the literature on the relationship between hours of television viewing (weekly) and school achievement for students in grades K through 12 (Williams et al. (1982). If a trend analysis were performed on these data, does it appear that there would be:

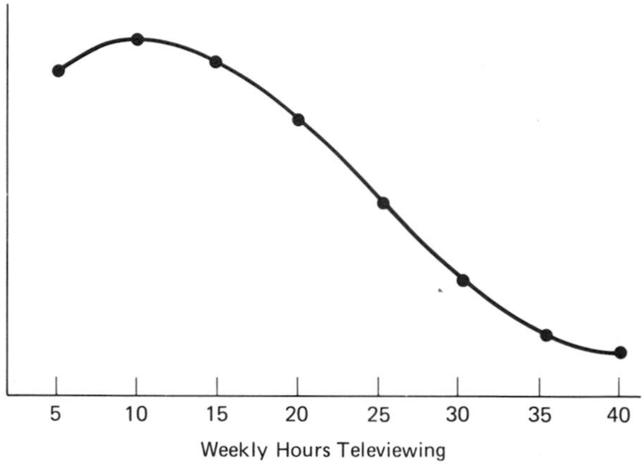


23. A linear trend?
24. A cubic trend?
25. A quartic (fourth-degree) trend?

The figures below depict the national trends in high school GPA and ACT scores for students taking the ACT test battery during 1969–1982. (From *The* American College Testing Program Newsletter, Feb., 1983, p. 2).

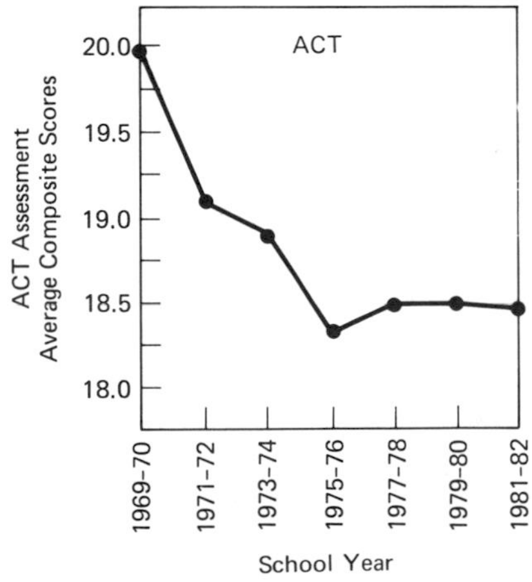


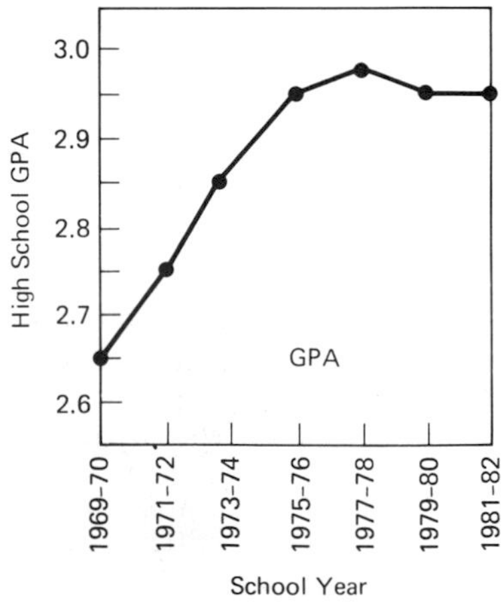

26. Which trend line(s) reflect a linear trend (linear component would be significant in a trend analysis)?
27. Is the nature of the linear trend in the two graphs logically congruent?
28. Which trend line(s) reflect a quadratic trend?
29. Which line(s) reflect a cubic trend?
30. How many orthogonal trends (including the linear, quadratic, and cubic trends), could be evaluated statistically in each figure?

## *PROBLEMS*

Use the following data from Problem 5 following Chapter 16:

| *Source* | $\nu$ | *MS* | *F* |
|---|---|---|---|
| Between | 2 | 9.10 | 4.01[a] |
| Within | 27 | 2.27 | |

[a] $p < .05$

| *Postorganizer Group* | *Preorganizer Group* | *Noorganizer Group* |
|---|---|---|
| $\bar{X}_1 = 5.6$ | $\bar{X}_2 = 4.0$ | $\bar{X}_3 = 3.9$ |

1. For the balanced design above ($n = 10$), use planned orthogonal contrasts with $\alpha = .05$, to test
   a. whether the means of the two "organizer" groups differ from the "no organizer" group, and
   b. the difference between the means of the two organizer groups.
2. If the two null hypotheses in the Problem 1 were tested using the Scheffé method, would both be tenable with $\alpha_\Sigma = .05$?
3. Use the Dunn method to test $H_0: \psi = 0$ for the two contrasts.
4. Use the Tukey-method to test all pairwise contrasts.
5. If the Newman-Keuls method were used, would the results agree with those of the Tukey-method?
6. Four methods of teaching percentage (case method, formula method, equation method, unitary analysis method) were compared (Sparks, 1963). Twenty-eight sixth-grade classes were randomly assigned to the four methods; seven classes studied under each method. The observational unit was the mean of each class, that is, $n_\bullet = 28$. At the conclusion of the teaching unit, a forty-five-item test on computing percentages were administered to each class. The following means were obtained, each based on seven observations:

Average test scores for each class

| *Case Method* | *Formula Method* | *Equation Method* | *Unitary Analysis Method* |
|---|---|---|---|
| $\bar{X}_4 = 41.5\%$ | $\bar{X}_3 = 47.2\%$ | $\bar{X}_2 = 61.9\%$ | $\bar{X}_1 = 72.3\%$ |

a. Fill in the blank in the ANOVA table:

| *Source* | $\nu$ | *MS* | *F* |
|---|---|---|---|
| Between (Treatments) | —— | 1366.6 | —— |
| Within (Error) | —— | 85.8 | |

b. Can $H_0: \mu_1 = \mu_2 = \mu_3 = \mu_4$ be rejected at $\alpha = .01$?
c. Use the NK method of multiple comparison at $\alpha = .01$ to find any untenable null hypotheses involving pairs of means.
d. Summarize the results using the underscoring procedure.

## *EXERCISES*

Given one ANOVA factor with five random-assigned treatment groups and $n_1 = n_2 = \cdots = n_5 = 9$.

The definitions of the five groups are given.

| | | |
|---|---|---|
| Group 1. | Frequently tested pupils with positive feedback | $(\overline{X}_1 = 65)$ |
| Group 2. | Infrequently tested pupils with positive feedback | $(\overline{X}_2 = 54)$ |
| Group 3. | Frequently tested pupils with negative feedback | $(\overline{X}_3 = 50)$ |
| Group 4. | Control | $(\overline{X}_4 = 47)$ |
| Group 5. | Infrequently tested pupils without feedback | $(\overline{X}_5 = 43)$ |

An ANOVA summary table is given.

| *Source* | *SS* | $\nu$ | *MS* | *F* |
|---|---|---|---|---|
| Treatments | 2545.2 | 4 | 636.3 | 6.3[a] |
| Error | 4000 | 40 | 100 | |

[a] $p < .01$; $_{.99}F_{4,40} = 3.83$

1. How many planned orthogonal contrasts are possible?
2. Could you have legitimately inspected the means prior to your selection of which $J - 1$ orthogonal contrasts should be tested?
3. Suppose you wished to test $H_0: \mu_1 - \mu_3 = 0$; what are the coefficients for this contrast $(\hat{\psi}_1 = \overline{X}_1 - \overline{X}_3)$?
4. Distinguish $\hat{\psi}$ from $\psi$.
5. Suppose you also had good reason to test $H_0: \mu_1 = \mu_5$. Would this be orthogonal with $\hat{\psi}_1$?
6. In addition to $\hat{\psi}_1$ give the coefficients to contrast the frequently versus the infrequently tested groups $(\hat{\psi}_2)$.
7. What is $H_0$ for $\hat{\psi}_3$ which has contrast coefficients of $\frac{1}{4}$, $\frac{1}{4}$, $\frac{1}{4}$, $-1$, and $\frac{1}{4}$?
8. Is $\hat{\psi}_2$ orthogonal with $\hat{\psi}_1$? with $\hat{\psi}_3$?

9. $\hat{\psi}_1 = ?$, $s_{\hat{\psi}_1} = ?$, $t_{\hat{\psi}_1} = ?$
10. For planned orthogonal contrasts, the critical $t$-value ($\alpha = .01$) in this problem is ——.
11. Is $H_0 \psi_1 = 0$ rejected with $\alpha = .01$?
12. Using the Scheffé method could the identical procedure be used to obtain $t_{\hat{\psi}_1}$?
13. For $H_0: \psi_1 = 0$, the Scheffé method would have a critical $t$-value of $\sqrt{(J-1)(_{.99}F_{J-1,\nu_e})} = ?$
14. How does the critical $t$-value for the Scheffé method compare with that for a planned orthogonal comparison? (See Exercises 10 and 13.)
15. Does the Scheffé approach require orthogonality among the $C$ contrasts?
16. Does the Scheffé method use a contrast-based or a family-based type-I error rate?
17. For the planned orthogonal contrasts would the critical $t$-value (2.70) be the same for each $(J - 1) = 4$ possible orthogonal contrasts?
18. Would the critical $t$-value for the S-method be constant for all the possible contrasts? In the sample problem can we be certain that at least one contrast somewhere in the set possible contrasts would reject $H_0: \psi = 0$ at $\alpha_\Sigma = .01$?
19. If the experimenter selected the Tukey method, the distribution theory involves the studentized range statistic, denoted by ___.
20. For the Tukey method, what is the critical value ($\alpha = .01$) for each comparison?
21. $s_{\overline{X}} = \sqrt{MS_e/n} = \sqrt{\quad} =$ ___.
22. Since the critical $q$-value is the same for all comparisons with the Tukey method, the minimum mean difference needed to reject $H_0$ (termed the honest significance difference, HSD) is HSD = $({}_{1-\alpha}q_{J,\nu_e})s_{\overline{X}}$ or HSD ( )( ) = ___, when $\alpha_\Sigma = .01$.
23. From the following matrix of pairwise differences between means, which $H_0$'s between pairs of means allow the associated $H_0$'s to be rejected at the .01 level, using HSD?

| | | *Smaller Mean,* $\overline{X}_s$ | | | |
|---|---|---|---|---|---|
| | | $\overline{X}_2$ | $\overline{X}_3$ | $\overline{X}_4$ | $\overline{X}_5 = 43$ |
| Larger Mean, $\overline{X}_L$ | $65 = \overline{X}_1$ | 11 | 15 | 18 | 22 |
| | $54 = \overline{X}_2$ | | 4 | 7 | 11 |
| | $50 = \overline{X}_3$ | | | 3 | 7 |
| | $47 = \overline{X}_4$ | | | | 4 |

24. The Newman-Keuls method, unlike the Tukey method (but like planned orthogonal contrasts), employs a type-I error rate, $\alpha$, per ___.
25. The NK method has ___ different critical values for $q$.
26. The minimum mean difference required to reject $H_0: \mu_L = \mu_S$ for the extreme-most means is identical for the ___ and ___ methods.
27. Is this always the case when $r = J$? $(r = L - S + 1)$
28. Therefore, for $\alpha_\Sigma = .01$ and $r = 5$, a difference between $\overline{X}_5$ and $\overline{X}_1$ of ___ is needed to reject $H_0$ (see Exercise 22).
29. Which $H_0$ was rejected for NK that was not with the Tukey method?
30. For the NK method, complete the summary figure using the underscoring procedure (any two means *not* underlined by the *same* line differ significantly at the .01 level).

$$\overline{X}_1 \quad \overline{X}_2 \quad \overline{X}_3 \quad \overline{X}_4 \quad \overline{X}_5$$

31. If the Dunnett method had been used to compare each of the $J - 1$ means with the control group ($\overline{X}_4$), $\psi: \mu_j - \mu_c$, the critical $t$-ratio (at $\alpha_\Sigma = .01$) would have been ___, and $s_\psi$ = ___ (see Exercise 9), hence for the Dunnett method, min $(\overline{X}_j - \overline{X}_c)$ = ___. Which of the four $H_0$'s could have been rejected with $\alpha_\Sigma = .01$?

32. If only ten of the possible comparisons were of interest, and some contrasts were complex, one would probably use the ___ method. The critical $t$-ratio ($\alpha_\Sigma = .01$) would be ___, and for the pairwise contrasts, min $(\overline{X}_L - \overline{X}_S)$ would be ___.

33. If the number of comparisons were limited to five, for the Dunn method, min $(\overline{X}_L - \overline{X}_S)$ = ___, ($\alpha_\Sigma = .01$).

34. The sensitivity of the various MC procedures can be seen from the relative values of min $(\overline{X}_L - \overline{X}_S)$ to reject $H_0: \mu_L = \mu_S$. At $\alpha = .01$,
    a. POC: $({}_{1-\alpha/2}t_{\nu_e})(s_{\hat{\psi}})$ = (___) (___) = ___ (see Exercise 9).
    b. Scheffé method: $\sqrt{(J-1)_{1-\alpha}F_{J-1,\nu_e}}\,(s_{\hat{\psi}})$ = (___) (___) = ___ (see Exercise 13).
    c. Tukey method: $({}_{1-\alpha}q_{J,\nu_e})(s_{\overline{X}})$ = ___ (see Exercise 22).
    d. NK ($r$ = J): $({}_{1-\alpha}q_{\nu_e,J})(s_{\overline{X}})$ = ___ (see Exercise 26).
    e. NK ($r$ = 2): $({}_{1-\alpha}q_{\nu_e,2})(s_{\overline{X}})$ = (___)(___) = ___ (see Exercise 28).
    f. Dunn ($K$ = 10): $({}_{1-\alpha/2}t_{\nu_e,C})(s_{\hat{\psi}})$ = ___ (see Exercise 31).
    g. Dunn ($K$ = 5): ___, (see Exercise 33).
    h. Dunnett: $({}_{1-\alpha/2}t_{\nu_e,J})(s_{\hat{\psi}})$ = (___)(___) = ___ (see Exercise 31).

## *ANSWERS TO MASTERY TEST*

1. a
2. No
3. b
4. Fewer, more
5. No, planned contrast must be a priori.
6. $\psi$ is a parameter, $\hat{\psi}$ is a statistic (estimate).
7. b
8. c, d, e
9. $H_0: \mu_2 - (\mu_1 + \mu_3)/2 = 0$ or $\mu_2 = (\mu_1 + \mu_3)/2$.
10. a. no
    b. yes
    c. yes
    d. no
    e. no
11. e
12. e
13. c
14. b, c
15. a
16. d
17. g
18. d
19. b
20. F
21. Marascuilo
22. Dunn
23. yes
24. yes
25. no
26. both
27. no; a downward trend (negative $r$ with year) for the ACT, but an upward trend with GPA
28. both
29. neither (when allowance is made for sampling error)
30. $J - 1 = 6$

## *ANSWERS TO PROBLEMS*

1. a. $\hat{\psi}_1 = \frac{1}{2}\overline{X}_1 + \frac{1}{2}\overline{X}_2 - \overline{X}_3 = .90$,
$s_{\hat{\psi}_1} = \sqrt{2.27(.5^2/10 + 5^2/10 + 1/10)}$
$= .584$
$t_{\hat{\psi}_1} = .90/.584 = 1.54$
${}_{.95}t_{27} = 2.05$, $\hat{\psi}_1$ not significant

b. $\hat{\psi}_2 = 5.6 - 4.0 = 1.6$,
$s_{\hat{\psi}_2} = \sqrt{2.27(.2)} = .674$
$t_{\hat{\psi}_2} = 1.6/.674 = 2.37, p < .02$

2. Yes, $\sqrt{(3-1)_{.95}F_{2,27}} \doteq \sqrt{2(3.37)} = 2.60$.
3. For Dunn, $_{.975}t_{27,2} \doteq 2.38$, both $H_0: \psi_1 = 0$ and $H_{0_2}: \psi_2 = 0$ are tenable.
4. $s_{\bar{X}} = \sqrt{2.27/10} = .476$,
$q_1 = (\bar{X}_1 - \bar{X}_3)/s_{\bar{X}} = 1.70/.476 = 3.55 > {}_{.95}q_{27,3} \doteq 3.53$
$q_2 = (\bar{X}_1 - \bar{X}_2)/s_{\bar{X}} = 1.6/4.76 = 3.36$, and $q_3 = (\bar{X}_2 - \bar{X}_3)/s_{\bar{X}} = .1/.476 = .21$; are not significant.
5. No, $q_2 = 3.36 > {}_{.95}q_{27,2} \doteq 2.92$, $p < .05$; $q_3$ is not significant
6. a.. $\nu_b = 3, \nu_e = 24, F = 15.93$
   b. yes; $15.93 > 7.55 = {}_{.999}F_{3,24}$
   c. $s_{\bar{X}} = \sqrt{85.8/7} = 3.50$
   $q_1 = (\bar{X}_1 - \bar{X}_4)/s_{\bar{X}} = 7.23 - 41.5/3.50 = 8.80, p < .01$
   $q_2 = (72.3 - 47.2)/3.50 = 7.17$, $p < .01$
   $q_3 = (72.3 - 61.9)/3.50 = 2.97 < 3.96 = {}_{.99}q_{24,2}, p > .01$
   $q_4 = (61.9 - 41.5)/3.50 = 5.83$
   $q_5 = (61.9 - 47.2)/3.50 = 4.20$
   $q_6 = (47.2 - 41.5)/3.50 = 1.63$
   d. $\underline{\bar{X}_1\bar{X}_2}\ \underline{\bar{X}_3\bar{X}_4}$, that is, all difference between means are significant except $X_1$ versus $X_2$ and $X_3$ versus $X_4$.

## *ANSWERS TO EXERCISES*

1. $J - 1 = 4$
2. No, a priori rationale would no longer apply.
3. 1, 0, −1, 0, 0; (or −1, 0, 1, 0, 0)
4. $\hat{\psi}$ is an *estimate* of the parameter, $\psi$.
5. No (see Eq. 17.12)
6. $\frac{1}{2}, -\frac{1}{2}, \frac{1}{2}, 0, -\frac{1}{2}$ better
7. $H_0: (\mu_1 + \mu_2 + \mu_3 + \mu_5)/4 - \mu_4 = 0$.
8. Yes, yes
9. $\hat{\psi}_1 = 65 - 50 = 15$;
$s_{\hat{\psi}} = \sqrt{100(1/9 + 1/9)} = 4.71$;
$t_{\hat{\psi}_1} = 3.18$
10. $_{.995}t_{40} = 2.70$
11. Yes, $p < .01$
12. Yes
13. $\sqrt{4({}_{.99}F_{4,40})} = \sqrt{4(3.83)} = 3.91$
14. It is much larger (3.91 versus 2.70).
15. No, any conceivable contrast is allowable.
16. Family-based $\alpha_\Sigma$
17. Yes
18. Yes; yes (since $p < .01$ for $F$-test)
19. $q$
20. 4.93
21. $\sqrt{100/9} = 10/3 = 3.33$
22. (4.93)(3.33) = 16.4. Therefore, in using the Tukey-method every $\hat{\psi}$ (usually a difference between a pair of means) greater than 16.4 would be judged significant, and $H_0: \psi = 0$ rejected at the .01 level.
23. $H_0: \mu_1 = \mu_5$, and $H_0: \mu_1 = \mu_4$
24. Contrast
25. $J - 1$
26. Tukey and Newman-Keuls
27. Yes
28. 16.4
29. $\underline{H_0: \mu_1 = \mu_3}$
30. $\underline{\bar{X}_1\bar{X}_2}\ \underline{\bar{X}_3\bar{X}_4\bar{X}_5}$
31. 3.19; 4.71; (3.19)(4.71) = 15.0, only $H_0: \mu_1 = \mu_4$ would be rejected.
32. Dunn, $_{.995}t_{40,10} = 3.549$
(3.549)(4.71) = 16.7
33. $_{.995}t_{40,5} = 3.305$
(3.305)(4.71) = 15.6
34. a. (2.70)(4.71) = 12.7
   b. (3.91)(4.71) = 18.4
   c. (4.93)(3.33) = 16.4
   d. same as T-method: 16.4
   e. 12.7
   f. 16.7
   g. 15.6
   h. 15.0

# 18

# TWO- AND THREE-FACTOR ANALYSIS OF VARIANCE An Introduction to Factorial Designs

## 18.1 INTRODUCTION

In Chapter 16 the rationale for one-factor analysis of variance (ANOVA) was considered along with procedures for testing whether or not the differences among two or more means were attributable to chance (sampling error). But ANOVA is not limited to a single independent variable: it can accommodate two or more factors simultaneously. If a two-factor ANOVA design is employed, three different hypotheses are testable. Two of these hypotheses are about *main effects*—each is essentially the same as the hypothesis of a one-factor design (Chap. 16): (1) whether the $J$ means of factor $A$ are equal in the population ($H_0: \mu_{1\bullet} = \mu_{2\bullet} = \cdots = \mu_{J\bullet}$); and (2) whether the $K$ means of factor $B$ are equal in the population ($H_{0_2}: \mu_{\bullet 1} = \mu_{\bullet 2} = \cdots = \mu_{\bullet K}$.* The third hypothesis is about a new concept, *interaction*—whether there is an interaction between factors $A$ and $B$; that is, are there certain combinations of the two factors that produce effects over and above those that would be expected from the two factors considered separately and independently? The concept of interaction is of central importance in this and subsequent chapters.

*Consistent with previous use, the "dot" subscripts denote aggregation; for example, $\mu_{2\bullet}$ is the mean of level 2 of factor $J$ with all levels of factor $K$ aggregated. If there are 3 levels of factor $J$ and 2 levels of factor $K$, and $\mu_{11} = 10$, $\mu_{12} = 20$, and $\mu_{13} = 9$, then $\mu_{1\bullet} = 13$; and if $\mu_{11} = 10$ and $\mu_{21} = 20$, then $\mu_{\bullet 1} = 15$.

The two-factor ANOVA design is the simplest design that encompasses the two essential notions of higher-order ANOVA designs: main effects and interaction.

## 18.2 THE MEANING OF INTERACTION*

In addition to interest in whether a treatment (independent variable) has an effect on the criterion (dependent variable) there is usually interest in whether the treatment is equally effective for certain types of individuals. Is the treatment effect greater at grade six than it is at grade three? Is the new method equally effective for high- and low-ability students? An interaction between two factors is said to exist if the mean differences among levels of factor $A$ are *not* constant across levels (categories) of factor $B$. For example, suppose two methods of teaching are being compared. If one teaching method is better for boys but the other method is better for girls, there is an interaction between the two factors, teaching method and sex.

### Interaction Examples

In recent years behavioral and educational research has become increasingly concerned with assessing interaction effects. Following are three examples of studies in which the interaction hypothesis was of particular interest. In a study of test-wiseness, two types of question (multiple-choice and free-response) were given to two ethnic groups (American and Indonesian students). The research question was not primarily concerned with either of the *two main effects*—whether the mean scores for the two nationalities differ, or whether mean scores differed on multiple-choice questions versus free-response items. The research focused on the possible *interaction* between nationality and type of item. Does one nationality perform *relatively* better than the other nationality on one type of item than they do on the other type of item—that is, is there an interaction between the two factors, nationality and type of item? If the degree of superiority of one nationality over the other is the same for both types of item, there is no interaction between the two factors. But, for example, if the mean difference between nationalities is significantly greater for multiple-choice items than for free-response items, a nationality-by-type-of-item interaction is said to exist.

In a learning experiment the effects of immediate versus delayed reinforcement on vocabulary acquisition were compared for pupils of low and middle socioeconomic status (SES). The researcher expected to find an interaction between the factors: treatment (timing of reinforcement) and SES. He hypothesized that delay of gratification is more characteristic of middle-SES families; hence, a substantial difference was expected between immediate and delayed reinforcement for low-SES students, but little difference was anticipated for middle-SES students. A graphic illustration of the researcher's hypothesis is given in Figure 18.1, with corresponding means on the dependent variable for each of the four combinations (cells) of the two factors, treatment and SES. A two-factor

*The concept of the interaction of two independent variables is due to the famed English statistician-geneticist, Ronald Fisher. It was Fisher's concepts of experimental control through randomization and the study of the effects of several factors and their interactions simultaneously that successfully overthrew the "one variable at a time" orthodoxy of experimental agriculture in the early 1900s. See Fisher (1925) and Stanley (1966).

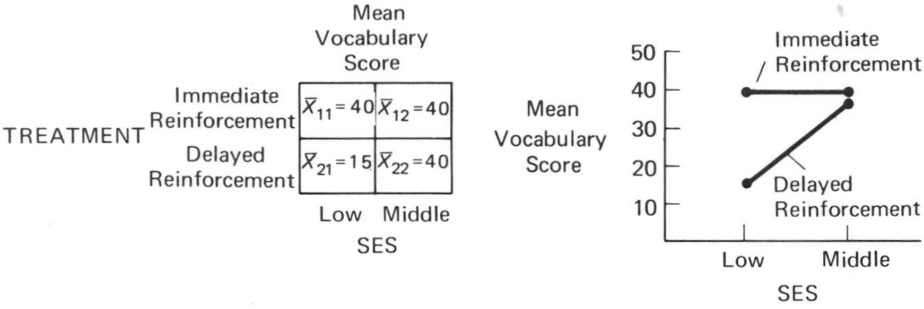


**FIGURE 18.1. An illustration of a two-factor (treatment-by-SES) interaction. Cell means are given on the left; the interaction graph is shown on the right.**

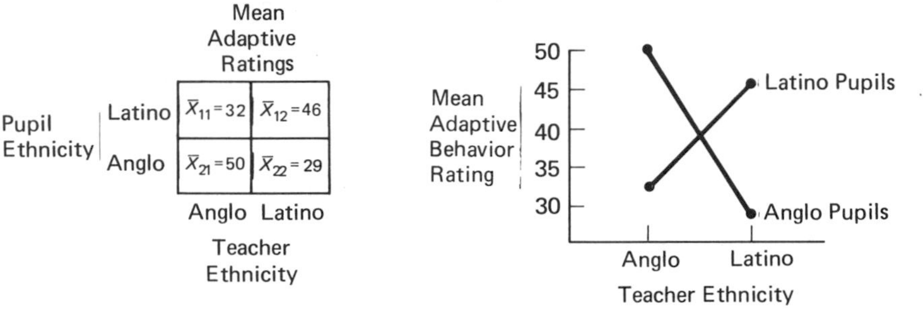


**FIGURE 18.2. An illustration of a significant interaction with neither main effect being significant.**

(treatment × SES—"treatment-by-SES") analysis of variance will reveal whether the hypothesized treatment-by-SES interaction is tenable.

A third interaction example is taken from a bilingualism-biculturalism study. The two factors are teacher ethnicity and pupil ethnicity. "Latino" and "Anglo" team teachers each independently rated the same Latino and Anglo students for "adaptive behavior" on a behavior rating scale. No significant difference was found between the means on the teacher ethnicity factor or between the means on the pupil ethnicity factor; that is, both null hypotheses for the two main effects were tenable. However, there was a significant interaction between the teacher ethnicity and pupil ethnicity factors, as shown in Fig. 18.2.

The interaction in Figure 18.2 shows that the two factors are interdependent. Latino teachers rated the behavior of Latino students as more adaptive than that of Anglo students, whereas the pattern was reversed for the Anglo teachers.

## 18.3 INTERACTION AND GENERALIZATION

Generalization involves making general inferences about the effect of some treatment. If there is no interaction between the treatment factor and characteristics of the subjects, the findings can be generalized with greater confidence. But if interaction is present, the generalization must be qualified. Perhaps bright students find the "new math" more interesting, while low-ability students find it less interesting than the "old math", and average students have equal interest in both. Notice that this question is not directly concerned with whether or not there are overall differences in average interest level, either between "old" versus "new" math, or between bright, average, and low-ability students. Questions about overall differences are questions about *main effects*. The interaction null hypothesis is that the effect (if any) of factor $A$ does not depend on factor $B$; that is, mean differences among the levels of factor $A$ are constant across all levels of factor $B$. If the $A \times B$ interaction is not significant, there is empirical support for generalizing the overall effect of factor $A$ to all levels of factor $B$ without qualification.

Often a second factor is included in a research design not because interaction is expected, but because the absence of interaction provides an empirical basis for generalizing the treatment effect to all levels of the second factor. For example, consider a hypothetical study in which two instructional methods ($E$ and $C$–experimental and control) are compared with students in an upper-middle-socioeconomic-status community. If the study contrasted only the means for the experimental and control groups (i.e., used a $t$-test or a one-factor ANOVA), the findings cannot be safely generalized to low-ability pupils since they were only a small proportion of the sample. But if a two-factor design was employed using, in addition to the treatment factor, several levels (categories) of a second factor, IQ, the treatment-by-IQ interaction would be statistically evaluated, as shown in Figure 18.3. That is, in addition to comparing the means of the $E$- and $C$-groups,

**FIGURE 18.3. Illustration of the absence of interaction between treatment and IQ factors, but with significant treatment and IQ effects.**

| TREATMENT | $B_1$ (80–90) | $B_2$ (90–100) | $B_3$ (100–110) | $B_4$ (110–120) | $B_5$ (120–130+) | $B_6$ (130+) |
|---|---|---|---|---|---|---|
| $E$: $A_1$ | 17 | 22 | 28 | 33 | 38 | 43 |
| $E$: $A_2$ | 6 | 10 | 16 | 21 | 27 | 32 |

Cell Means for a 2 X 6 Treatment-by-IQ Design

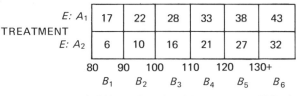

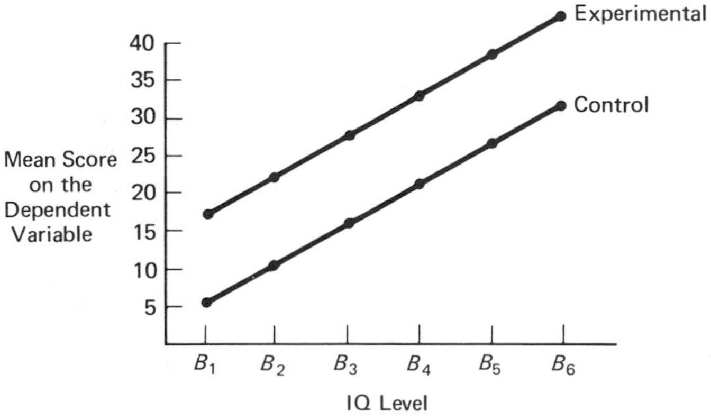

whether the treatment effect (if any) is constant at all IQ levels can be determined—whether or not there is a significant interaction between treatment and IQ level. Study Figure 18.3 to confirm that although there is no interaction, there are significant treatment and IQ effects.

Notice that the *difference* in *E*- and *C*-means is about the same for all IQ classifications; the treatment effect does *not* interact with IQ level. It is obvious that, even though the *E*- and *C*-groups may have had mean IQ's of 110 or so, the study is applicable to average or even below-average students, since the treatment effect was constant across the various IQ levels.

It should be clear that the examination of interaction between treatment and various subject characteristics (personological or organismic variables) contributes substantially to the generalizability of a study. If an interaction is not significant, one can generalize with greater confidence to various types of subjects than would otherwise be possible. If an interaction is significant, it should be graphed, as illustrated in Figures 18.1 to 18.3, and studied so that the proper interpretation can be made. In many research studies although an interaction is not expected, factors in addition to the treatment factor are often included so that the generalizability of the study can be empirically assessed.

Suppose the IQ factor in Figure 18.3 was replaced by a teacher factor—six teachers each tried the *E*-method with a random one-half of their students and the *C*-method with the other half. Whether the *E*-method (or *C*-method) is superior for all teachers, or whether the efficacy of the treatment depends on (i.e., interacts with) the particular teacher involved could be assessed. If there is no treatment-by-teacher interaction, one can be more confident that the *E*-method will result in superior performance with other teachers like those represented in the study. Indeed, a three-factor (treatment-by-teacher-by-IQ) ANOVA design could be employed (Sec. 18.20). Using the design, the treatment-by-IQ and treatment-by-teacher interactions would be tested in the same analysis, as well as the three-factor interaction (treatment-by-teacher-by-IQ). In the illustration the absence of a significant three-factor interaction would indicate that the pattern of results between treatment and IQ level was the same for all teachers. If the results shown in Figure 18.3 were obtained for all teachers, there would be no treatment-by-teacher-by IQ interaction.

## 18.4 INTERPRETING MAIN EFFECTS WHEN INTERACTION IS PRESENT

A two-factor interaction will be illustrated by using hypothetical data from an ESP experiment. There are two *levels* of the treatment factor: level 1 is the experimental group, which attempted to receive a mentally transmitted message, and level 2 is the control group. Suppose in this study that the null hypothesis, $H_0: \mu_1 = \mu_2$, was rejected. Does it necessarily follow that the "treatment" had an effect on all persons in the experimental group? Certainly not. It is possible that only certain persons in the *E*-group were "sensitive" to the treatment. Perhaps ESP is a sex-linked trait and appears only in females. Notice that if females were capable of ESP and males were not, the mean of the experimental group taken as a whole would exceed the control group mean as a consequence of the higher female scores. This fact is illustrated graphically in Figure 18.4—if the mean of

| | | SEX | | |
|---|---|---|---|---|
| | | Males | Females | Row Mean |
| TREATMENT | Experimental | $\bar{X}_{11} = 5.0$ | $\bar{X}_{12} = 15.0$ | $\bar{X}_{1\bullet} = 10.0$ |
| | Control | $\bar{X}_{21} = 5.0$ | $\bar{X}_{22} = 5.0$ | $\bar{X}_{2\bullet} = 5.0$ |
| | Column Mean | $\bar{X}_{\bullet 1} = 5.0$ | $\bar{X}_{\bullet 2} = 10.0$ | $\bar{X}_{\bullet\bullet} = 7.5$ |

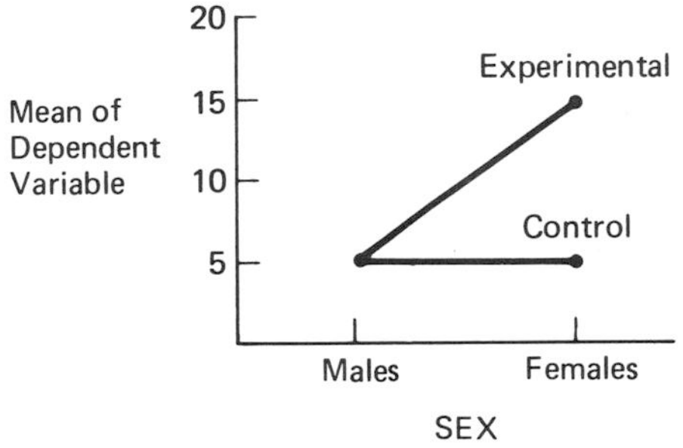


**FIGURE 18.4**
**Hypothetical data for two-factor ANOVA with a treatment-by-sex interaction. (Note: We will consistently denote the row ($j$) as the first subscript and the column factor ($k$) as the second subscript of a mean. For example, the mean of row 1, column 2, is $\bar{X}_{12}$. The symbol $\bar{X}_{1\bullet}$ is the mean of all observations in row (experimental group in the example). The grand mean, $\bar{X}_{\bullet\bullet}$, is based on all observations. Further explanation of notation appears later in Section 18.6.**

the females in the $E$-group ($\bar{X}_{12} = 15.0$) exceeds the mean of the females in the $C$-group ($\bar{X}_{22} = 5.0$), the mean of the experimental group ($\bar{X}_{1\bullet} = 10.0$) would exceed the control mean ($\bar{X}_{2\bullet} = 5.0$) even if the males in each of the $E$- and $C$-groups had equal means ($\bar{X}_{11} = 5.0$, $\bar{X}_{21} = 5.0$).

If only a one-factor ANOVA design had been employed for the data represented in Figure 18.4, the null hypothesis for the treatment effect, $H_0: \mu_E = \mu_C$, would have been rejected on the basis of $\bar{X}_E = 10.0$ and $\bar{X}_C = 5.0$. But using the treatment-by-sex design, it could be discovered that the ESP operated only with the females. If a two-factor design was employed, the pattern of results would be illuminated, as depicted in Figure 18.4. Since the treatment effect is not the same for both sexes, a "treatment-by-sex interaction" exists.

In many research studies interactions go unnoticed because of the failure to employ factorial designs, designs that examine the effects of two or more factors (independent variables) simultaneously. An interaction exists when the difference in row means is not the same across all levels of the column factor (or vice versa). In the ESP example there would be no interaction between the two factors, treatment and sex, if $\mu_{11} - \mu_{21} = \mu_{12} - \mu_{22}$; that is, the differences were equal. Notice in Figure 18.4 that the treatment factor interacts with the sex factor because the estimated treatment effect for males ($\bar{X}_{11} - \bar{X}_{21}$) is 0, but the estimated treatment effect for females ($\bar{X}_{12} - \bar{X}_{22}$) is 10.

The question of the statistical significance of this apparent interaction must be answered by means of an $F$-test. An ANOVA for the hypothetical data in Figure 18.4, assuming five observations per cell and an average within-cell variance ($MS_w$) of 10, is shown in Table 18.1, along with the corresponding three null hypotheses being tested.

**TABLE 18.1 Two-Factor ANOVA Table Corresponding to Hypothetical Data in Figure 18.4 with Corresponding Null Hypotheses Being Tested**

| *Source* | *SS* | $\nu$ | *MS* | *F* | $H_0$ |
|---|---|---|---|---|---|
| Treatment (*T*) | 125 | 1 | 125 | 12.5[a] | $H_{0_1}$: $\mu_{1\bullet} = \mu_{2\bullet}$ |
| Sex (*S*) | 125 | 1 | 125 | 12.5[a] | $H_{0_2}$: $\mu_{\bullet 1} = \mu_{\bullet 2}$ |
| $T \times S$ | 125 | 1 | 125 | 12.5[a] | $H_{0_3}$: $\mu_{11} - \mu_{12} = \mu_{21} - \mu_{22}$[b] |
| Error (within) | 160 | 16 | 10 | | |

[a] $p < .01$, ${}_{.99}F_{1,16} = 8.53$

[b] Or, equivalently, $\mu_{11} - \mu_{21} = \mu_{12} - \mu_{22}$, or $(\mu_{11} - \mu_{21}) - (\mu_{12} - \mu_{22}) = 0$

Null hypotheses $H_{0_1}$ and $H_{0_2}$ represent *main effects*, whereas $H_{0_3}$ represents an *interaction* hypothesis. The illustrative data represented in Figure 18.4, evaluated for statistical significance in the ANOVA table (Table 18.1), demonstrate that when a significant treatment-by-sex interaction exists, the interaction influences the interpretation of the main effects. It is certainly true that it can be concluded that $\mu_{1\bullet} > \mu_{2\bullet}$ and $\mu_{\bullet 2} > \mu_{\bullet 1}$, but a more precise and informative conclusion can be made if the treatment-by-sex interaction is considered.

The design that has been considered is described as a $2 \times 2$ *treatment-by-sex design*; there are two levels (*E* and *C*) of the treatment factor and two levels (*M* and *F*) of the sex factor.

## 18.5 TWO TYPES OF INTERACTION

In statistical literature a useful distinction is made (e.g., by Lubin, 1962) between two types of interaction: *ordinal* and *disordinal*. In the ordinal case the rank order of the categories of one factor on the basis of their dependent variable scores is the same within each level of the second independent variable. In Figure 18.5 an example of ordinal

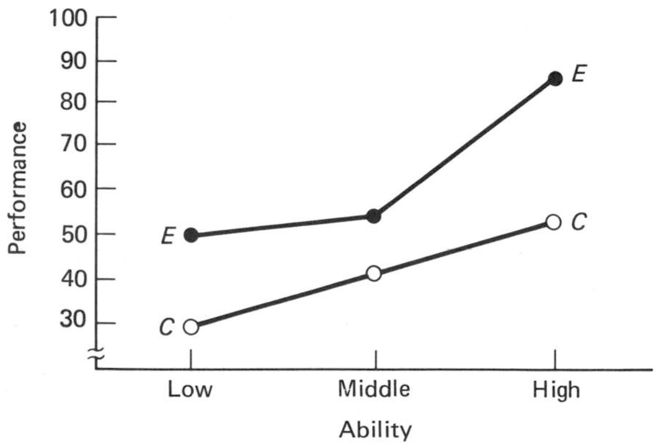


**FIGURE 18.5**
**Graphic representation of an ordinal interaction between treatment and ability.**

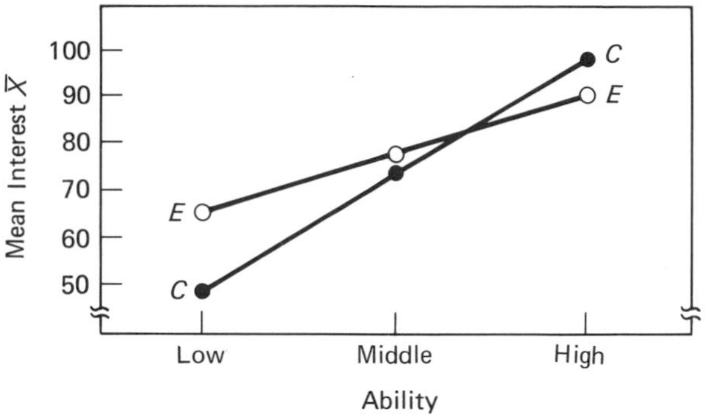


**FIGURE 18.6.**
**Graphic representation of a disordinal interaction.**

interaction is given. It is ordinal because the $E$ treatment is superior for all three ability levels.

Figure 18.6 presents an example of disordinal interaction. When the lines do not cross, interaction is said to be "ordinal"; when the lines cross, interaction is said to be "disordinal." The importance of this distinction for interpretation is that when interaction is ordinal–for example, when the $E$-group is higher than $C$ on the dependent variable–the superiority exists for all three ability levels. That is, even though an interaction exists, a single statement about the superior treatment can be made without qualification or reference to the second factor. However, when there is a disordinal interaction, the better treatment depends on the particular ability level in question. In Figure 18.6 the $E$-method works best with low-ability students, whereas the $C$-method is better for pupils of high ability. Whenever there is a significant interaction, one should plot the means for the various combinations.

It should be emphasized that whether or not the lines in the interaction graph cross sometimes depends on the choice between placing factor $A$ or factor $B$ on the abscissa when graphing an interaction. The same cell means can give an ordinal interaction when factor $A$ is on the abscissa and a disordinal interaction when factor $B$ is on the abscissa. If the "lines" in the graphs represent treatment, it is simpler to assess whether or not the relative treatment superiority needs to be qualified.

## 18.6 DATA LAYOUT AND NOTATION

Consider as an example of a two-factor design an experiment in which three methods of teaching beginning reading are compared. The pupils involved in this experiment can be classified in two ways: with respect to the teaching method under which they study (factor $A$) and by their sex (factor $B$). Factor $A$, teaching method, has three levels and factor $B$, sex, has two levels. Since both boys and girls study under each method in the experiment, six unique combinations of the levels of the two factors are possible. Suppose the variable that will be observed in the evaluation of the outcome of this experiment is reading comprehension, $X$. Observations on $X$ are taken by administering a standardized test of reading comprehension. If four boys and four girls were taught to read by method 1, four boys and four girls by method 2, and so on, the data could be tabulated as shown in Figure 18.7.

| | | | $B_1$ (boy) | | $B_2$ (girl) | |
|---|---|---|---|---|---|---|
| | $A_1$ | $\bar{X}_{11}$ | $X_{111}$ $X_{211}$ $X_{311}$ $X_{411}$ | $\bar{X}_{12}$ | $X_{112}$ $X_{212}$ $X_{312}$ $X_{412}$ | $\bar{X}_{1.}$ |
| Row Factor $A$ (Method) | $A_2$ | $\bar{X}_{12}$ | $X_{121}$ $X_{221}$ $X_{321}$ $X_{421}$ | $\bar{X}_{22}$ | $X_{122}$ $X_{222}$ $X_{322}$ $X_{422}$ | $\bar{X}_{2.}$ |
| | $A_3$ | $\bar{X}_{13}$ | $X_{131}$ $X_{231}$ $X_{331}$ $X_{431}$ | $\bar{X}_{32}$ | $X_{132}$ $X_{232}$ $X_{332}$ $X_{432}$ | $\bar{X}_{3.}$ |
| Column Means | | | $\bar{X}_{.1}$ | | $\bar{X}_{.2}$ | $\bar{X}_{..}$ |

Factor $B$ (Sex)

**FIGURE 18.7. Layout of data in a 3 × 2 two-factor ANOVA design with four observations per cell ($X_{ijk}$ notation, where $j$ = 1, 2, 3 for method, $k$ = 1, 2 for sex, and $i$ = 1, 2, 3, 4 for pupil within method-sex group.**

## Notation

Since there are two factors, two subscripts are necessary to identify cell means. Let $j$ in $\bar{X}_{jk}$ denote the row factor ($j$ = method) and $k$ define the column factor ($k$ = sex); the particular replicate, observation, person, or score in the $jk$ cell is denoted by $i$, that is, $X_{ijk}$.

In dot notation dots represent aggregation. For example, the mean of all observations in row 1 is $\bar{X}_{1\bullet}$. The dot subscript indicates that the row mean $\bar{X}_{1\bullet}$ is based on all the observations in row 1. The grand mean $\bar{X}_{\bullet\bullet}$ is based on all observations in all rows and columns, and hence has dots for both subscripts; $\bar{X}_{\bullet\bullet}$ is based on $n_{\bullet\bullet}$ observations. With a little practice, the notation can be used without ambiguity.

A total of twenty-four pupils participated in this experiment. $X_{111}$ represents the reading comprehension test score of the "first" (arbitrarily designated) boy ($k$ = 1) who studied under method 1 ($j$ = 1). $X_{132}$ stands for the first ($i$ = 1) pupil in method 3 ($j$ = 3) by a girl ($k$ = 2): the "3" stands for the method, "2" for the sex (male–1, female–2), and the "1" designates the arbitrary labeled first pupil in the group (of four) girls under method 3 (see Fig. 18.7).

In general an observation in a two-factor ANOVA design is denoted by $X_{ijk}$ where $j$ is a subscript for factor $A$ and takes on the values 1, 2, . . . , $J$; $k$ is the subscript for factor $B$ and takes on the values 1, 2, . . . , $K$; and $i$ is the subscript that identifies the replicate or observation within a *cell* (combination of levels of factors $A$ and $B$) of the design and takes on the values 1, 2, . . . , $n$.

The score of the third ($i = 3$) girl ($k = 2$) studying under the first method ($j = 1$) is denoted $X_{312}$. To summarize, in $X_{ijk}$:*

$i = 1, 2, \ldots, n$ for observations nested "within cells"

$j = 1, 2, \ldots, J$ for factor $A$

$k = 1, 2, \ldots, K$ for factor $B$

## 18.7 A MODEL FOR THE DATA

Our interest in gathering the data was to determine how the mean scores vary with the levels of the two factors, that is, whether or not boys score higher than girls, whether or not method 2 gives higher scores than method 1, and so on. Toward this end, we shall now devise a fairly abstract model—a generalization of that used with the one-factor ANOVA (Secs. 16.8 and 16.9)—to explain, in a general way, how the data are related to factors $A$ and $B$.

The fixed model for data in a two-factor ANOVA involves two terms for main effects: $\alpha_j$ which describes the effect of the $j$th level of factor $A$ ($\alpha_j = \mu_{j\bullet} - \mu$), and $\beta_k$ which describes the effect of the $k$th level of factor $B$ ($\beta_k = \mu_{\bullet k} - \mu$). As in Equation 16.10, $\mu$ is the grand mean—the mean of the $nJK$ observations; $\epsilon_{ijk}$ is the difference between the score, $X_{ijk}$, and $(\mu + \alpha_j + \beta_k)$. The discussion to follow assumes the design is balanced—there are $n$ observations in each of the $JK$ cells. Under this model, a score $X_{ijk}$ would be represented as follows.†

$$X_{ijk} = \mu + \alpha_j + \beta_k + \epsilon_{ijk} \tag{18.1}$$

For example, adult males in general tend to be 69 in. = $\mu$. Feeding them yoghurt tends to add 1 in. = $\alpha_1$ to their height and sleeping on a hard mattress tends to add $\frac{1}{2}$ in. = $\beta_1$ to their height. If one's unique individual history (environmental influence and heredity) explains the remainder ($\epsilon_{111} = X_{111} - (\mu + \alpha_1 + \beta_1)$), then if Joe is 66 in. tall, eats yoghurt, and sleeps on a hard mattress: $\epsilon_{111} = 66 - (69 + 1 + \frac{1}{2}) = -4\frac{1}{2}$, hence, $X_{111} = \mu + \alpha_1 + \beta_1 + \epsilon_{111} = 66 = 69 + 1 + \frac{1}{2} - 4\frac{1}{2}$.

A more useful and widely applicable model for the data in a two-factor ANOVA is slightly more complex than the model in Equation 18.1. It differs from Equation 18.1 by a term that denotes the effect of the *unique* result of combining level $j$ of factor $A$ with level $k$ of factor $B$. "Unique" in this context means that the outcome one would obtain from combining level $j$ of $A$ with level $k$ of $B$ may *not* be the simple sum of $\alpha_j$ and $\beta_k$. If not, a new term, $\alpha\beta_{jk}$, which is *not* the product of $\alpha_j$ and $\beta_k$, is needed to describe the scores in the $jk$th cell. Such a term is called an *interaction term.* If an interaction term is needed in the model to describe the scores, then knowing the general effect of level $j$ of $A$ and of level $k$ of $B$ is not enough to predict the mean of cell $jk$.

*The subscripts are arranged $ijk$ so that the left-most subscript can remain $i$ and always denote the observation number; the subscript $j$ is always associated with the first factor, $\alpha$, and $k$ is always associated with the second factor, $\beta$.

†A more explicit notation is unnecessary: $X_{ijk} = \mu_{\bullet\bullet} + \alpha_{j\bullet} + \beta_{\bullet k} + \epsilon_{ijk}$.

The expanded model, the model upon which the analyses in this chapter are based, is

$$X_{ijk} = \mu + \alpha_j + \beta_k + \alpha\beta_{jk} + \epsilon_{ijk} \tag{18.2}$$

Without any loss of generality the $\alpha$, $\beta$, and $\alpha\beta$ terms in the model are defined such that they sum to zero over both $j$ and $k$, that is, $\Sigma_j \alpha_j = \Sigma_k \beta_k = \Sigma_j \alpha\beta_{jk} = \Sigma_k \alpha\beta_{jk} = 0$. Please note that the $\alpha\beta_{jk}$ term is *not* the product of $\alpha_j$ and $\beta_k$; $\alpha\beta_{jk}$ represents the interaction effect of level $j$ of factor $A$ with level $k$ of factor $B$.

## 18.8 LEAST-SQUARES ESTIMATION OF THE MODEL

With data in hand and having adopted a particular model to explain them, the task of relating the data to the model remains. What features of the data influence the value of $\mu$ in Equation 18.2? How can the data be manipulated to disclose information about the values of the $\alpha_j$'s, the $\beta_k$'s, and the $\alpha\beta_{jk}$'s.

This is the same general problem when $Y$ is predicted from $X$ by means of a straight line (Chap. 8) or when there are differences between factor levels in a one-factor ANOVA (Secs. 16.8 and 16.9). The model in Equation 18.2 is fit to the data so that the least-squares criterion is satisfied. In this instance as in the others the criterion of least squares is as follows: (1) values are substituted into Equation 18.2 for $\mu, \alpha_1, \ldots, \alpha_J, \beta_1, \ldots, \beta_K, \alpha\beta_{11} \ldots, \alpha\beta_{JK}$; (2) these values along with the data $X_{ijk}$ determine, by subtraction, estimated values for the $nJK$, errors $\epsilon_{ijk}$; (3) when the sum of the squared errors so determined is as small as it is possible to make it, the least-squares estimates of $\mu$, the $\alpha_j$'s, the $\beta_k$'s, and the $\alpha\beta_{jk}$'s have been found.

For example, eight scores are gathered in a simple $2 \times 2$ design, with $n$ also 2, as shown in Figure 18.8. The following model is postulated for the data:

$$X_{ijk} = \mu + \alpha_j + \beta_k + \alpha\beta_{jk} + \epsilon_{ijk} \qquad \begin{aligned} j &= 1, 2 \\ k &= 1, 2 \\ i &= 1, 2 \end{aligned}$$

The hypothetical main and interaction effects underlie the data in Figure 18.8 in the model depicted in portion II of Figure 18.8. Hence it is assumed, for example that

$$X_{112} = \mu + \alpha_1 + \beta_2 + \alpha\beta_{12} + \epsilon_{112}$$

By subtraction of appropriate terms, it is seen that

$$\epsilon_{112} = X_{112} - (\mu + \alpha_1 + \beta_2 + \alpha\beta_{12}) \tag{18.3}$$

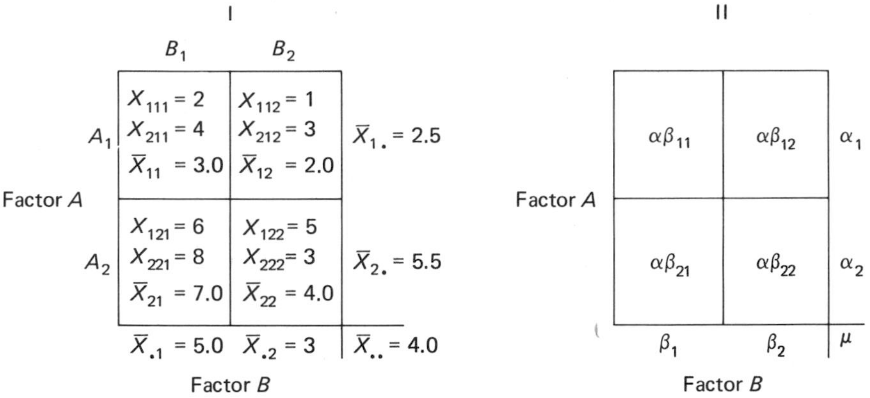


**FIGURE 18.8. Illustration of a 2 × 2 ANOVA design.**

The smallest sum of squared errors is produced by the following least-squares *estimates* of the parameters of the model:

$$\hat{\mu} = \bar{X}_{\bullet\bullet} = 4$$

$$\hat{\alpha}_1 = \bar{X}_{1\bullet} - \bar{X}_{\bullet\bullet} = -1.5 \qquad \widehat{\alpha\beta}_{11} = \bar{X}_{11} - (\bar{X}_{\bullet\bullet} + \hat{\alpha}_1 + \hat{\beta}_1) = 3.0 - (4 - 1.5 + 1) = -.5$$

$$\hat{\alpha}_2 = \bar{X}_{2\bullet} - \bar{X}_{\bullet\bullet} = 1.5 \qquad \widehat{\alpha\beta}_{12} = \bar{X}_{12} - (\bar{X}_{\bullet\bullet} + \hat{\alpha}_1 + \hat{\beta}_2) = .5$$

$$\hat{\beta}_1 = \bar{X}_{\bullet 1} - \bar{X}_{\bullet\bullet} = 1 \qquad \widehat{\alpha\beta}_{21} = \bar{X}_{21} - (\bar{X}_{\bullet\bullet} + \hat{\alpha}_2 + \hat{\beta}_1) = .5$$

$$\hat{\beta}_2 = \bar{X}_{\bullet 2} - \bar{X}_{\bullet\bullet} = -1 \qquad \widehat{\alpha\beta}_{22} = \bar{X}_{22} - (\bar{X}_{\bullet\bullet} + \hat{\alpha}_2 + \hat{\beta}_2) = -.5$$

The sum of the squared estimated errors, which were obtained by substituting the above least-squares estimates into Equation 18.2 along with the data $X_{ijk}$, is equal to 8.00, the smallest possible value for any choice of $\mu$, the $\alpha_j$, the $\beta_k$, and the $\alpha\beta_{jk}$. As was true in the one-factor ANOVA, the least-squares estimates of the terms in the model for the data are obtained by simple averaging of the data in various ways (see Table 18.2).

**TABLE 18.2 Least-Sqaures Estimation in the Two-Factor, Fixed Effects ANOVA**

| *Term in the model* | *Population value* | *Least-squares estimate* |
|---|---|---|
| $\mu$ | $\mu$ | $\hat{\mu} = \bar{X}_{\bullet\bullet}$ |
| $\alpha_1$ | $\mu_{1\bullet} - \mu$ | $\hat{\alpha}_1 = \bar{X}_{1\bullet} - \bar{X}_{\bullet\bullet}$ |
| $\alpha_2$ | $\mu_{2\bullet} - \mu$ | $\hat{\alpha}_2 = \bar{X}_{2\bullet} - \bar{X}_{\bullet\bullet}$ |
| $\beta_1$ | $\mu_{\bullet 1} - \mu$ | $\hat{\beta}_1 = \bar{X}_{\bullet 1} - \bar{X}_{\bullet\bullet}$ |
| $\beta_2$ | $\mu_{\bullet 2} - \mu$ | $\hat{\beta}_2 = \bar{X}_{\bullet 2} - \bar{X}_{\bullet\bullet}$ |
| $\alpha\beta_{11}$ | $\mu_{11} - (\mu + \alpha_1 + \beta_1)$ | $\widehat{\alpha\beta}_{11} = \bar{X}_{11} - (\bar{X}_{\bullet\bullet} + \hat{\alpha}_1 + \hat{\beta}_1)$ |
| $\alpha\beta_{12}$ | $\mu_{12} - (\mu + \alpha_1 + \beta_2)$ | $\widehat{\alpha\beta}_{12} = \bar{X}_{12} - (\bar{X}_{\bullet\bullet} + \hat{\alpha}_1 + \hat{\beta}_2)$ |
| $\alpha\beta_{21}$ | $\mu_{21} - (\mu + \alpha_2 + \beta_1)$ | $\widehat{\alpha\beta}_{21} = \bar{X}_{21} - (\bar{X}_{\bullet\bullet} + \hat{\alpha}_2 + \hat{\beta}_1)$ |
| $\alpha\beta_{22}$ | $\mu_{22} - (\mu + \alpha_2 + \beta_2)$ | $\widehat{\alpha\beta}_{22} = \bar{X}_{22} - (\bar{X}_{\bullet\bullet} + \hat{\alpha}_2 + \hat{\beta}_2)$ |

| | | Factor $B$ | | |
|---|---|---|---|---|
| | | $B_1$ | $B_2$ | Row means |
| Factor $A$ | $A_1$ | $\mu_{11}$ | $\mu_{12}$ | $\mu_{1.}$ |
| | $A_2$ | $\mu_{21}$ | $\mu_{22}$ | $\mu_{2.}$ |
| Column means | | $\mu_{.1}$ | $\mu_{.2}$ | $\mu_{..} = \mu$ |

**FIGURE 18.9**
**Expected values of cell and marginal means in a 2 × 2 ANOVA design.**

For example, the least-squares estimate of $\mu$ is just the mean of all eight scores in the 2 × 2 table. The least-squares estimate of $\alpha_1$ is just the mean of the four scores in row 1 of the table minus the mean of all eight scores. The least-squares estimate of $\beta_2$ is the mean of the four scores in column 2 minus the mean of all eight scores. The least-squares estimate of $\alpha\beta_{11}$ is the mean of the two scores in the cell at the intersection of row 1 and column 1 minus the mean of row 1 minus the mean of column 1 *plus* the mean of all eight scores.

Regarding notation, let $\mu_{jk}$ be the mean of the population of scores from which those scores in the $j$th row and the $k$th column of the data layout were sampled. Let $\mu_{j\bullet}$ be the average of the $K \mu_{jk}$'s in the $j$th row; let $\mu_{\bullet k}$ be the average of the $J \mu_{jk}$'s in the $k$th column; and let $\mu$ be the average of all the $\mu_{ij}$'s. For example, see Figure 18.9.

The least-squares estimates of the terms in the model for the 2 × 2 ANOVA design can be characterized in terms of their definition in the sample and their long-range average (or expected) value that they attain in the population. This has been done in Table 18.2.

## 18.9 STATEMENT OF NULL HYPOTHESES

If in Figure 18.7 factor $B$, "sex," was disregarded, the data would be identical to those gathered in a one-factor experiment comparing three teaching methods. Eight observations would have been gathered under each level of factor $A$, and the one-factor ANOVA model would be appropriate for a statistical inferential test of the hypothesis that the three population means underlying the teaching methods were equal. This null hypothesis, namely that the population means for the three teaching methods are equal, is identical to one null hypothesis of interest in the two-factor ANOVA. Specifically, we are interested in whether the data gathered in a two-factor ANOVA support or run counter to a decision to accept as tenable the statement $H_0: \mu_{1\bullet} = \mu_{2\bullet} = \mu_{3\bullet}$.

In any two-factor ANOVA the null hypothesis for factor $A$ can be stated as follows:

$$H_0: \mu_{1\bullet} = \mu_{2\bullet} = \ldots = \mu_{J\bullet}$$

Notice that the equality of the $J$ population means underlying the $J$ levels of factor $A$ has implications that can be used to state $H_0$ in several equivalent forms.

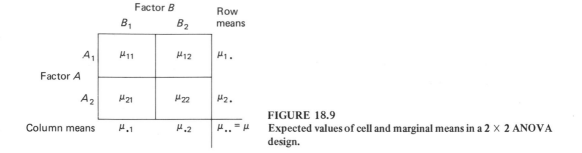

Because, when $i = 1, 2, \ldots, n$ for every $jk$th factor-level combination, $\mu$ is the average of the $JK$ population means (one for each cell), equality of the $\mu_{j\bullet}$'s implies that *each* $\mu_{j\bullet}$ equals $\mu$. If each $\mu_{j\bullet} = \mu$, then $\mu_{j\bullet} - \mu = 0$ for the $J$ levels of factor $A$. Since $\alpha_j$, the main effect for level $j$ of factor $A$, is equal to $\mu_{j\bullet} - \mu$, all $\alpha_j$'s equal zero if the null hypothesis is true. The following statements are equivalent ways of stating the null hypothesis for factor $A$:

1. $H_0: \mu_{1\bullet} = \ldots = \mu_{J\bullet}$
2. $H_0: \sum_{j=1}^{J} (\mu_{j\bullet} - \mu)^2 = 0$
3. $H_0: \alpha_1 = \alpha_2 = \ldots = \alpha_J = 0$
4. $H_0: \sum_{j=1}^{J} \alpha_j^2 = 0$

In the preceding discussion it was immaterial that attention was focused on factor $A$ instead of factor $B$. The development of the statement of the null hypothesis for factor $B$ is perfectly analogous to the development of $H_0$ for $A$. Specifically, as regards factor $B$, the interest is in rejecting or accepting the null hypothesis that the $K$ population means underlying the levels of factor $B$ are all equal. The following statements are equivalent ways of stating the null hypothesis for factor $B$:

1. $H_0: \mu_{\bullet 1} = \mu_{\bullet 2} = \ldots = \mu_{\bullet K}$
2. $H_0: \sum_{k=1}^{K} (\mu_{\bullet k} - \mu)^2 = 0$
3. $H_0: \beta_1 = \beta_2 = \ldots = \beta_k = 0$
4. $H_0: \sum_{k=1}^{K} \beta_k^2 = 0$

There are many ways in which the null hypothesis about a main effect, that is, about a single factor, can be false. For factor $A$, $\mu_{1\bullet}$ could equal 20.5 and the remaining $\mu_{j\bullet}$'s could equal 29.1, for example. Or $\mu_{1\bullet} = \mu_{2\bullet} = 16.65$ and $\mu_{3\bullet} = \mu_{4\bullet} = 17.80$. In both instances $H_0$ is false. All that it takes for $H_0$ to be false is for at least two population means to be unequal. The decision faced in an ANOVA is whether one should opt for the truth of $H_0$ or the truth of $H_1$, which is true when $H_0$ is false. $H_1$, the alternative hypothesis, can be stated in the following equivalent ways for factor $A$:

1. $H_1: \mu_{j\bullet} \neq \mu_{j'\bullet}$, where $j$ and $j'$ are distinct
2. $H_1: \sum_{j=1}^{J} (\mu_{j\bullet} - \mu)^2 \neq 0$
3. $H_1: \alpha_j \neq 0$ for *at least* one $j$
4. $H_1: \sum_{j=1}^{J} \alpha_j^2 \neq 0$

Each of the above equivalent statements will be true if and only if the null hypothesis for factor $A$ is false. Hence, if $H_0$ is rejected, $H_1$ is accepted automatically. The form of the alternative hypothesis for factor $B$ is perfectly analogous to the form of $H_1$ for factor $A$.

There remains one hypothesis of interest—the interaction term, $\alpha\beta_{jk}$. In Sections 18.2 to 18.4 attention was directed toward two sets of conditions: (1) the graph of the population means produced parallel lines; (2) the graph of the population means produced nonparallel lines.

In Section 18.3 it was seen that if no interaction exists between $A$ and $B$, that is, if the graph of the population means shows parallel lines, then as shown in Table 18.2, $\mu_{jk}$ will equal $\mu + (\mu_{j\bullet} - \mu) + (\mu_{\bullet k} - \mu) = \mu + \alpha_j + \beta_k$. An equivalent condition is that $\mu_{jk} = \mu_{j\bullet} + \mu_{k\bullet} - \mu$. Now if this condition is satisfied, then

$$\mu_{jk} - \mu_{j\bullet} - \mu_{\bullet k} + \mu = 0 \text{ for all the } \mu_{jk}\text{'s}$$

Or, in terms of the model in Equation 18.2

$$\alpha\beta_{jk} = 0 \text{ for all } j \text{ and } k$$

If the lines in the graph of the population cell means are *not* parallel at any single point on $A$, then at least one $\alpha\beta_{jk}$ is *not* equal to zero. Hence, parallel lines in the graph of the $JK$ population means correspond to all of the $\alpha\beta_{jk}$'s equaling zero; nonparallel lines correspond to *at least one* of the $\alpha\beta_{jk}$'s *not* equaling zero. These two conditions represent the null hypothesis and the alternative hypothesis, respectively, about the interaction of factors $A$ and $B$. There are several ways of stating the null hypothesis $H_0$ and the alternative hypothesis $H_1$ about the interaction effects. Some of these follow:

| *Equivalent statements of $H_0$ for the interaction of A and B* | *Equivalent statements of $H_1$ for the interaction of A and B* |
|---|---|
| 1. $H_0$: all $(\mu_{jk} - \mu_{j\bullet} - \mu_{\bullet k} + \mu) = 0$ | 1. $H_1$: $\mu_{jk} - \mu_{j\bullet} - \mu_{\bullet k} + \mu \neq 0$ for at least one $\mu_{jk}$ |
| 2. $H_0$: all $\alpha\beta_{jk} = 0$ | 2. $H_1$: $\alpha\beta_{jk} \neq 0$ for at least one $\alpha\beta_{jk}$ |
| 3. $H_0$: $\sum_{k=1}^{K}\sum_{j=1}^{J}(\mu_{jk} - \mu_{j\bullet} - \mu_{\bullet k} + \mu)^2 = 0$ | 3. $H_1$: $\sum_{k}\sum_{j}(\mu_{jk} - \mu_{j\bullet} - \mu_{\bullet k} + \mu)^2 \neq 0$ |
| 4. $H_0$: $\sum_{k=1}^{K}\sum_{j=1}^{J}\alpha\beta_{jk}^2 = 0$* | 4. $H_1$: $\sum_{k}\sum_{j}\alpha\beta_{jk}^2 \neq 0$ |

In summary there are three pairs of hypotheses that are typically of interest in the two-factor ANOVA: (1) $H_0$ and $H_1$ for factor $A$, (2) $H_0$ and $H_1$ for factor $B$, and (3) $H_0$ and $H_1$ for the interaction of $A$ and $B$. In the remaining sections of this chapter the data gathered in a two-factor experiment are brought to bear on the decision to reject $H_0$ for $A$, for $B$, and for the interaction of $A$ and $B$.

*Remember $\alpha\beta_{jk}$ is *not* a product of $\alpha_j$ and $\beta_k$; note $\alpha\beta_{jk}^2 = (\alpha\beta_{jk})^2$.

## 18.10 SUMS OF SQUARES IN THE TWO-FACTOR ANOVA

As in the one-factor ANOVA inferential tests of the three null hypotheses in the two-factor ANOVA employ sums of squares, degrees of freedom, mean squares, expected mean squares, and $F$-ratios.

There are four *sources of variation*, as they are called, in the two-factor ANOVA: (1) factor $A$, (2) factor $B$, (3) the interaction of $A$ and $B$, and (4) "within" cells or combinations of levels of $A$ and $B$. We shall define sum of squares for each source of variation in turn. It will be assumed throughout that the design is balanced, that is, $n_{11} = n_{21} = \ldots = n_{JK} = n$.

### Sum of Squares for Factor A

The sum of squares for factor $A$, denoted $SS_A$, is simply $nK = n_{j\bullet}$ times the sum of the squared least-squares estimates of the $\alpha_j$'s.

$$SS_A = nK \sum_{j=1}^{J} \hat{\alpha}_j^2 = nK \sum_j (\bar{X}_{j\bullet} - \bar{X}_{\bullet\bullet})^2 \tag{18.4}$$

Equivalently,*

$$SS_A = \sum_{j=1}^{J} \left( \sum_{k=1}^{K} \sum_{i=1}^{n} X_{ijk} \right)^2 \bigg/ n_{j\bullet} - \left( \sum_k \sum_j \sum_i X_{ijk} \right)^2 \bigg/ n_{\bullet\bullet}. \tag{18.4A}$$

Recall that $\alpha_j = \mu_{j\bullet} - \mu$ is estimated by the row mean minus the grand mean, that is, $\hat{\alpha}_j = \bar{X}_{j\bullet} - \bar{X}_{\bullet\bullet}$. The sum of squares for $\hat{\alpha}_j$ is $n_{j\bullet}\hat{\alpha}_j^2$. The sum over all $J$ levels of $A$ of these squared estimates, $n_{j\bullet}\hat{\alpha}_j^2$, (Equation 18.4) is called the *sum of squares for factor A*.

### Sum of Squares for Factor *B*

The sum of squares for factor $B$ is $nJ = n_{\bullet k}$ times the sum of the squared least-squares estimates of the $\beta_k$'s:

$$SS_B = nJ \sum_{k=1}^{K} \hat{\beta}_k^2 = nJ \sum_k (\bar{X}_{\bullet k} - \bar{X}_{\bullet\bullet})^2 = nJ \sum_k (\bar{X}_{\bullet k} - \bar{X}_{\bullet\bullet})^2 \tag{18.5}$$

*Traditionally Equation 18.4A has been more commonly used than Equation 18.4, (and Equation 18.5A than Equation 18.5), because less rounding error accrues. With hand calculators, however, rounding error is negligible. Equation 18.4 is much easier to understand and remember.

Notice that $n_{\bullet k}$ is the number of scores averaged to obtain $\overline{X}_{\bullet k}$ (just as $n_{j\bullet}$ was the number of scores averaged to obtain $\overline{X}_{j\bullet}$). Alternatively,

$$SS_B = \sum_{k=1}^{K} \left( \sum_{j=1}^{J} \sum_{i=1}^{n} X_{ijk} \right)^2 \Big/ n_{\bullet k} - \left( \sum_k \sum_j \sum_i X_{ijk} \right)^2 \Big/ n_{\bullet\bullet} \qquad \textbf{(18.5A)}$$

## Sum of Squares for the Interaction of $A$ and $B$

$$SS_{AB} = n \sum_{k=1}^{K} \sum_{j=1}^{J} \widehat{\alpha\beta}^2_{jk} = n \sum_k \sum_j [\overline{X}_{jk} - (\overline{X}_{\bullet\bullet} + \hat{\alpha}_j + \hat{\beta}_k)]^2$$

$$= n \sum_k \sum_j (\overline{X}_{jk} - \overline{X}_{j\bullet} - \overline{X}_{\bullet k} + \overline{X}_{\bullet\bullet})^2 \qquad \textbf{(18.6)}$$

Notice as before that $n_{jk} = n$, the factor multiplying the sum, is the number of scores averaged to obtain $\overline{X}_{jk}$. Alternatively, one may compute the composite of the sums of squares for $A$, $B$, and $AB$, that is, $SS_{A+B+AB}$, and subtract $SS_A$ and $SS_B$ to obtain $SS_{AB}$.

$$SS_{A+B+AB} = n \sum_k \sum_j (\overline{X}_{jk} - \overline{X}_{\bullet\bullet})^2 \qquad \textbf{(18.7)}$$

$$SS_{A+B+AB} = \sum_{k=1}^{K} \sum_{j=1}^{J} \left( \sum_{i=1}^{n} X_{ijk} \right)^2 \Big/ n - \left( \sum_k \sum_j \sum_i X_{ijk} \right)^2 \Big/ n_{\bullet\bullet} \qquad \textbf{(18.7A)}$$

$$SS_{AB} = SS_{A+B+AB} - SS_A - SS_B \qquad \textbf{(18.8)}$$

## Sum of Squares "Within" Cells

There remains one sum of squares, $SS_w$, the sum of squares within cells.

$$SS_w = \sum_k \sum_j \sum_i (X_{ijk} - \overline{X}_{jk})^2 = \sum_k \sum_j \sum_i x^2_{ijk} \qquad \textbf{(18.9)}$$

The meaning of these four sums of squares will begin to emerge when the corresponding mean squares and their expected values are considered in the following sections. The sum of the squared deviations of each of the $nJK = n_{\bullet\bullet}$ scores in a two-factor design around $\overline{X}_{\bullet\bullet}$ is exactly equal to $SS_A + SS_{AB} + SS_w$, that is

$$SS_{\text{total}} = \sum_k \sum_j \sum_i (X_{ijk} - \overline{X}_{\bullet\bullet})^2 = SS_A + SS_B + SS_{AB} + SS_w \qquad \textbf{(18.10)}$$

Or,

$$SS_{\text{total}} = \sum_k \sum_j \sum_i X_{ijk}^2 - \left(\sum_k \sum_j \sum_i X_{ijk}\right)^2 \Big/ n_{\bullet\bullet} \tag{18.10A}$$

The total sum of squares of $n_{\bullet\bullet}$ scores can be analyzed into four independent (orthogonal) components which, when divided by their respective degrees of freedom, yield four independent variance estimates, thus the expression *analysis of variance.* $SS_w$ is often obtained indirectly using Equation 18.11:

$$SS_w = SS_{\text{total}} - SS_A - SS_B - SS_{AB} \tag{18.11}$$

## 18.11 DEGREES OF FREEDOM

Each of the four sums of squares in the two-factor ANOVA is converted into a mean square (i.e., a variance estimate) by dividing it by its degrees of freedom. The degrees of freedom for a given sum of squares are the number of least-squares estimates of effects that comprise the sum of squares minus the number of independent linear restrictions placed on these estimates. This is a difficult and abstract notion, and it will be discussed in some detail.

$SS_A$ is calculated from the $J$ least-squares estimates $\hat{\alpha}_1, \ldots, \hat{\alpha}_J$. It was natural and unrestrictive to specify in the model in Equation 18.2 that $\alpha_1 + \ldots + \alpha_J = 0$. Furthermore, it was necessary to assume that $\hat{\alpha}_1 + \ldots + \hat{\alpha}_J = 0$ before the solution to the mathematical criterion of least-squares estimation could be found. Indeed, as they must, the least-squares estimates of the $\alpha_j$ satisfy this restriction, that is, $\hat{\alpha}_1 + \ldots + \hat{\alpha}_J = 0$. This is easy to demonstrate:

$$\sum_{j=1}^{J} \hat{\alpha}_j = \sum_j (\bar{X}_{j\bullet} - \bar{X}_{\bullet\bullet}) = 0$$

because $\bar{X}_{\bullet\bullet}$ is the mean of the $J$ means, $\bar{X}_{j\bullet}$.

There are $J$ least-squares estimates in the calculation of $SS_A$ and they must conform to the single linear restriction that their sum be zero. Hence, the degrees of freedom for $SS_A$ are $J - 1$. An exactly analogous line of reasoning would lead to the correct conclusion that $SS_B$ has degrees of freedom equal to $K - 1$.

The calculation of $SS_{AB}$ involves the $JK$ least-squares estimates of the $\alpha\beta_{jk}$ terms. The restrictions it was necessary to impose on these estimates to solve the least-squares problem were that summing the estimates across rows for any given column yields a sum of zero *and* summing the estimates across the columns for any given row yields a sum of zero, that is

$$\sum_{k=1}^{K} \widehat{\alpha\beta}_{jk} = 0 \text{ for each } j \tag{18.12}$$

$$\sum_{j=1}^{J} \widehat{\alpha\beta}_{jk} = 0 \text{ for each } k \tag{18.13}$$

The conditions in Equation 18.12 are $J$ in number; there are $K$ restrictions represented in Equation 18.13. Not all $J + K$ of these restrictions are independent, however. Namely, given the restrictions in Equation 18.12 and knowing that $\Sigma_{j=1}^{J} \widehat{\alpha\beta}_{jk}$ equals zero for $k = 1, \ldots, K - 1$, it must necessarily follow that $\Sigma_j \widehat{\alpha\beta}_{jK} = 0$. Hence, only $J + K - 1$ of the linear restrictions on the $JK$ values of $\widehat{\alpha\beta}_{jk}$ are independent. Therefore, the degrees of freedom for $SS_{AB}$ are

$$JK - (J + K - 1) = JK - J - K + 1$$

Notice that this expression can be factored into $(J - 1)(K - 1)$.

The sum of squares within cells, $SS_w$, is actually the sum of the squares of the $nJK$ least-squares estimates of the $\epsilon$-terms in the model in Equation 18.2. Any single $\epsilon_{ijk}$ is estimated by $e_{ijk} = X_{ijk} - \bar{X}_{jk}$.

Since $e_{ijk}$ is the deviation of a score from its cell mean, the sum of the $n$ $e_{ijk}$-values within each cell is zero. Thus, there are $JK$ independent linear restrictions on the $nJK$ values of $e_{ijk}$. Consequently, the degrees of freedom associated with $SS_w$ are $nJK - JK = JK(n - 1)$. The preceding results can be summarized as follows where there are $J$ levels of factor $A$, $K$ levels of factor $B$, and $n$ observations within each $JK$ combination.

| *Sum of squares* | *Degrees of freedom* |
|---|---|
| $SS_A$ | $J - 1$ |
| $SS_B$ | $K - 1$ |
| $SS_{AB}$ | $(J - 1)(K - 1)$ |
| $SS_w$ | $JK(n - 1)$ |

Now look at a very simple example of linear restrictions using the data in the $2 \times 3$ tables in Figure 18.10. (Try filling in the four missing cell entries and the missing row and column sum.)

If the number of degrees of freedom is the number of cells (here, $2 \times 3 = 6$) minus the number of independent linear restrictions on the data $[J + K - 1 = 4]$, how many degrees of freedom are there for a table of this type? Notice two cell entries are *free* to vary. This is analogous to the degrees of freedom for the interaction of factor $A$

| Row number | Column number 1 | 2 | 3 | Row sums |
|---|---|---|---|---|
| 1 | 1 | | | 7 |
| 2 | | 4 | | |
| Column sums | 4 | 6 | | **16** |

**FIGURE 18.10**
**An illustration of linear restriction.**

with factor $B$ in a $2 \times 3$ factorial design. For that ANOVA, the cell entries are interaction residuals, the six $(\overline{X}_{jk} - \overline{X}_{j\bullet} - \overline{X}_{\bullet k} + \overline{X}_{\bullet\bullet})$'s, and every row sum and column sum is zero.

## 18.12 MEAN SQUARES

For each sum of squares there is a mean square ($MS$), which is the sum of squares ($SS$) per degree of freedom ($\nu$): $MS = SS/\nu$.

$$MS_A = \frac{SS_A}{J - 1} \qquad MS_B = \frac{SS_B}{K - 1} \qquad MS_{AB} = \frac{SS_{AB}}{(J - 1)(K - 1)} \qquad MS_w = \frac{SS_w}{JK(n - 1)}$$

As in the one-factor ANOVA the mean squares are the final stage in calculations leading toward significance tests of the null hypotheses.

## 18.13 ILLUSTRATION OF COMPUTATION FOR THE TWO-FACTOR ANOVA

In this section the computational formulas are applied in finding the sums of squares and mean squares. For a two-factor ANOVA design in which factor $A$ has $J$ levels, factor $B$ has $K$ levels, and each of the $JK$ cells contain $n$ observations, the four sums of squares can be obtained most conveniently from the formulas used in Table 18.3.

A demonstration experiment was conducted in a statistics course on the effect of using electronic hand calculators on computational accuracy. Since the effect of the treatment (calculator) versus control (no calculator) might interact with the math background of the students, the students were categorized into two groups, those with college math and those with no college math. The result is two levels of both the treatment factor and the math-background factor. The forty students were classified into the math-background groups and then they were randomly assigned either the calculator or no-calculator group, resulting in ten students in each of the four cells.* All subjects were then given ten problems requiring complex arithmetic computations under speeded conditions. The raw scores and means appear in panel $A$ of Table 18.3.

### Sums of Squares

In steps 1 and 2, the sum of squares for factors $A$ and $B$, $SS_A$ and $SS_B$, are determined (panel $B$). In steps 3 and 4 the sum of squares for the interaction, $SS_{AB}$, is deter-

*Actually there were forty-three persons in the class; three students were randomly discarded so that there would be an equal number of students in the two levels of the math background. In two-factor ANOVA designs if $n$'s are equal, not only is the analysis simpler, the results are less ambiguous. In addition recall that the homogeneity-of-variance assumption can be disregarded only when $n$'s are equal (see Fig. 12.3).

**TABLE 18.3 Computational Illustration of a Two-Factor ANOVA with $n$ = 10 Observations Per Cell**

A.

| | | Factor B (Math Background): $B_1$ (College Math) | $B_2$ (No College Math) | A Main Effect |
|---|---|---|---|---|
| Factor A (Treatment) | $A_1$ (Calculator) | 4, 5, 6, 8, 10,<br>3, 5, 6, 8, 7<br>$\Sigma_i X_{i11} = 62$ $\quad \overline{X}_{11} = 6.20$<br>$\Sigma x_{11}^2 = 39.6$ $\widehat{\alpha\beta}_{11} = .35$<br>$s_{11}^2 = 4.40$ | 5, 5, 7, 8, 9,<br>4, 5, 6, 7, 8<br>$\Sigma_i X_{i12} = 64$ $\quad \overline{X}_{12} = 6.40$<br>$\Sigma x_{12}^2 = 24.4$ $\widehat{\alpha\beta}_{12} = .35$<br>$s_{12}^2 = 2.71$ | $\Sigma_k \Sigma_i X_{i1k} = 126$<br>$\overline{X}_{1\bullet} = 6.30$<br>$\hat{\alpha}_1 = .15$<br>$n_{1\bullet} = 20$ |
| | $A_2$ (Control) | 7, 5, 7, 8, 9<br>3, 4, 8, 6, 9<br>$\Sigma_i X_{i21} = 66$ $\quad \overline{X}_{21} = 6.60$<br>$\Sigma x_{21}^2 = 38.4$ $\widehat{\alpha\beta}_{21} = .35$<br>$s_{21}^2 = 4.27$ | 4, 5, 3, 4, 9,<br>3, 5, 6, 8, 7<br>$\Sigma_i X_{i22} = 54$ $\quad \overline{X}_{22} = 5.40$<br>$\Sigma x_{22}^2 = 38.4$ $\widehat{\alpha\beta}_{22} = -.35$<br>$s_{22}^2 = 4.27$ | $\Sigma_k \Sigma_i X_{i2k} = 120$<br>$\overline{X}_{2\bullet} = 6.00$<br>$\hat{\alpha}_2 = -.15$<br>$n_{2\bullet} = 20$ |
| | B Main Effect | $\Sigma_j \Sigma_i X_{ij1} = 128$ $\overline{X}_{\bullet 1} = 6.40$<br>$n_{\bullet 1} = 20$ $\quad \hat{\beta}_1 = .25$ | $\Sigma_j \Sigma_i X_{ij2} = 118$ $\overline{X}_{\bullet 2} = 5.90$<br>$n_{\bullet 2} = 20$ $\quad \hat{\beta}_2 = -.25$ | $\Sigma_k \Sigma_j \Sigma_i X_{ijk} = 246$<br>$\overline{X}_{\bullet\bullet} = 6.15$<br>$n_{\bullet\bullet} = 40$ |

B. 1. *Compute* $SS_A^a$: $SS_A = nK \sum_{j=1}^{J} \hat{\alpha}_j^2 = (10)(2)[(.15)^2 + (-.15)^2] = .90$ (Eq. 18.4)

2. *Compute* $SS_B^b$: $SS_B = nJ \sum_{k=1}^{K} \hat{\beta}_k^2 = (10)(2)[(.25)^2 + (-.25)^2] = 2.50$ (Eq. 18.5)

3. *Compute* $SS_{AB}$: $SS_{AB} = SS_{A+B+AB} - SS_A - SS_B$ (Eq. 18.8)

4. $SS_{A+B+AB}^c = n \sum_k \sum_j (\overline{X}_{jk} - \overline{X}_{\bullet\bullet})^2 = 10[(6.20 - 6.15)^2 + (6.60 - 6.15)^2 + (.25)^2 + (-.75)^2] = 8.30$ (Eq. 18.7)

$SS_{AB}^d = 8.30 - .90 - 2.50 = 4.90$

5. *Compute* $SS_w^e$: $SS_w = \sum_k \sum_j \sum_i x_{ijk}^2 = 38.4 + 38.4 + 39.6 + 24.4 = 140.8$ (Eq. 18.9)

C. 6. *Construct ANOVA table:*

| Source | $SS$ | $\nu$† | $MS$ | $F$* |
|---|---|---|---|---|
| Treatment ($A$) | .90 | 1 | .90 | .23 |
| College math ($B$) | 2.50 | 1 | 2.50 | .64 |
| $A \times B$ | 4.90 | 1 | 4.90 | 1.25 |
| Within (error) | 140.80 | 36 | 3.91 | |

* $_{.90}F_{1,36} = 2.86$, $p > .10$ for all three $H_0$'s.

† the degrees of freedom are $\nu_A = J - 1$, $\nu_B = K - 1$, $\nu_{AB} = (J-1)(K-1)$, and $\nu_w = JK(n-1)$.

---

[a]Or, using Equation 18.4A:

$$SS_A = \sum_j \left(\sum_k \sum_i X_{ijk}\right)^2 \Big/ n_{j\bullet} - \left(\sum_k \sum_j \sum_i X_{ijk}\right)^2 \Big/ n_{\bullet\bullet}$$

$$= [(126)^2 + (120)^2]/20 - (246)^2/40$$

$$SS_A = 1{,}513.80 - 1{,}512.90 = .90$$

[b]Or, using Equation 18.5A:

$$SS_B = \sum_k \left(\sum_j \sum_i X_{ijk}\right)^2 \Big/ n_{\bullet k} - \left(\sum_k \sum_j \sum_i X_{ijk}\right)^2 \Big/ n_{\bullet\bullet}$$

$$= [(128)^2 + (118)^2]/20 - 1{,}512.90 = 2.50$$

[c]Or, using Equation 18.7A:

$$SS_{A+B+AB} = \sum_k \sum_j \left(\sum_i X_{ijk}\right)^2 \Big/ n - \left(\sum_k \sum_j \sum_i X_{ijk}\right)^2 \Big/ n_{\bullet\bullet}$$

$$= [(62)^2 + (64)^2 + (66)^2 + (54)^2]/10 - 1{,}512.90$$

$$SS_{A+B+AB} = 1{,}521.20 - 1{,}512.90 = 8.30$$

[d]Or, computing $SS_{AB}$ directly, using Equation 18.6:

$$SS_{AB} = n \sum_k \sum_j \widehat{\alpha\beta}^2_{jk} = 10[(-.35)^2 + (.35)^2 + (-.35)^2 + (.35)^2] = 4.90$$

[e]Or, using Equations 18.10A and 18.11:

$$SS_w = SS_{total} - SS_A - SS_B - SS_{AB};\; SS_{total} = \sum_k \sum_j \sum_i X^2_{ijk} - \frac{\left(\sum_k \sum_j \sum_i X_{ijk}\right)^2}{n_{\bullet\bullet}}$$

$$= (4)^2 + (5)^2 + \ldots + (7)^2 - 1{,}512.90 = 1662 - 1{,}512.90 = 149.1$$

$$SS_w = 149.1 - .90 - 2.50 - 4.90 = 140.80$$

mined by finding the composite sum of squares for the $A$, $B$, and $AB$ effects ($SS_{A+B+AB}$) from which $SS_A$ and $SS_B$ are subtracted to obtain $SS_{AB}$.* In step 5 the sum of squares within cells is obtained by pooling the sum of squares for the $JK$ cells, that is, $SS_w = \Sigma_k \Sigma_j SS_{jk} = \Sigma_k \Sigma_j x_{jk}^2$. [In a balanced design the $SS_w$ step can be bypassed and $MS_w$ can be obtained directly from mean of the $JK$ cell variances, that is, $MS_w = \Sigma_k \Sigma_j s_{jk}^2/JK = (4.27 + 4.27 + 4.40 + 2.71)/4 = 3.91$.]

## Degrees of Freedom and Mean Squares

In step 6 (panel $C$) each of the four sums of squares is divided by its respective degrees of freedom; the four resulting mean squares given in the ANOVA table are obtained. The degrees of freedom for an interaction are simply the *product* of the $\nu$'s for all the factors involved. In the example the treatment factor has 1 degree of freedom, as does the math-background factor; hence, the $A \times B$ interaction has $1 \times 1 = 1$ degree of freedom.

## *F*-Tests

If all null hypotheses are true, the expected values of each of these four $MS$-values are equal to $\sigma^2$, the variance of observations in the parent population. Stated differently, if all null hypotheses are true, sampling error accounts for all the differences among the entries in the mean square column of the ANOVA table in panel $C$ of Table 18.3. But if the null hypothesis for a source of variation (e.g., treatment) is false, the expected $MS$-value for this source will increase, and hence the expected value for the $F$-ratio will increase. The bases for the $F$-test are treated more fully in Section 18.14.

In a one-factor ANOVA, $MS_A$ is divided by $MS_w$ to obtain the $F$-ratio to test $H_0: \mu_1 = \mu_2 = \ldots = \mu_J$. In a two-factor, fixed-effects ANOVA, the $MS$ for the two main effects ($A$ and $B$) and the $MS$ for the $AB$ interaction are each divided by $MS_w$ to obtain an $F$-ratio to determine whether or not the null hypothesis for that source is tenable.

The $F$-tests in the ANOVA table in panel $C$ of Table 18.3 indicate that none of the three null hypotheses ($H_{0_1}$: $\Sigma \alpha_j^2 = 0$, $H_{0_2}$: $\Sigma \beta_k^2 = 0$, $H_{0_3}$: $\Sigma_k \Sigma_j (\alpha\beta_{jk})^2 = 0$) can be rejected even with $\alpha = .10$ (i.e., all $F$'s are less than the critical $F$ of 2.86).

# 18.14 EXPECTED VALUES OF MEAN SQUARES

The computational aspects of the two-factor ANOVA are complete. Now it is time to turn attention once again to the purpose of the computations. A statistical inferential test is desired for deciding whether the data support the null hypothesis $H_0$ or the alter-

*This illustrates that a *balanced* factorial design is a special case of planned orthogonal contrasts (Sec. 17.16). If the four groups in Table 18.3 are viewed as a one-factor ANOVA, $\bar{X}_{11}$, $\bar{X}_{21}$, $\bar{X}_{12}$, $\bar{X}_{22}$, then the $A$ effect results from the contrast coefficients, $\frac{1}{2}, -\frac{1}{2}, \frac{1}{2}, -\frac{1}{2}$; similarly the coefficients for the $B$ effect are $\frac{1}{2}, \frac{1}{2}, -\frac{1}{2}$, and $-\frac{1}{2}$, and for the $AB$ interaction, $\frac{1}{2}, -\frac{1}{2}, -\frac{1}{2}$, and $\frac{1}{2}$.

native hypothesis $H_1$ for the main effects of factors $A$ and $B$ and their interaction effects. As was true in the one-factor ANOVA, expected values reveal how mean squares bear on the truth or falsity of the three null hypotheses.

### $E(MS_w)$

The expected value (or "long-run average value") of $MS_w$ is the mean of all the $MS_w$'s that *would* be obtained if the same two-factor ANOVA design were performed an infinite number of times with independent observations. Another way to look at $E(MS_w)$ is that it is the variance of the population from which the observations in any one cell of the two-factor ANOVA design have been sampled. Assume that the variance of the population from which the $n$ observations in any cell have been sampled is equal to $\sigma_\epsilon^2$. In other words, the variance of each of the populations underlying each of the $JK$ cells is equal to the same value, $\sigma_\epsilon^2$. This is an extension to the two-factor ANOVA of the assumption of homogeneous variances in the one-factor ANOVA.

If the $n$ observations in the $jk$th cell are assumed to have been drawn from a population with variance $\sigma_\epsilon^2$ then $E(s_{jk}^2) = \sigma_\epsilon^2$. $MS_w$ has the following form:

$$MS_w = \frac{SS_w}{\nu_w} = \frac{\sum_k \sum_j \sum_i (X_{ijk} - \bar{X}_{jk})^2}{JK(n-1)} = \frac{\sum_k \sum_j \sum_i x_{ijk}^2}{JK(n-1)} \tag{18.14}$$

In a balanced design $MS_w$ is the average of the $JK$ within cell sample variances:

$$MS_w = \frac{\sum_k \sum_j s_{jk}^2}{JK} \tag{18.14A}$$

For example, in Table 18.3 notice that

$$MS_w = \frac{(s_{11}^2 + s_{21}^2 + s_{12}^2 + s_{22}^2)}{JK} = \frac{(4.40 + 4.27 + 2.71 + 4.27)}{(2)(2)} = \frac{15.65}{4} = 3.91$$

And,

$$E(MS_w) = E\left[\frac{\sum_k \sum_j s_{jk}^2}{JK}\right] = \sum_k \sum_j \frac{E(s_{jk}^2)}{JK} = \sum_k \sum_j \frac{\sigma_\epsilon^2}{JK} = \frac{JK\sigma_\epsilon^2}{JK} = \sigma_\epsilon^2$$

The expected value of $MS_w$ is the average of an infinite number of $MS_w$'s, each one obtained from an independent replication of the same two-factor ANOVA design—$J$ levels of factor $A$, $K$ levels of factor $B$, and $n$ cases in each of the $JK$ cells. In the $2 \times 2$ experiment in the preceding section (Table 18.3) the value of $MS_w$ was 3.91. This is just one observation from a hypothetically infinite population of $MS_w$'s that could be generated by replicating the same treatment-by-math background experiment with a new set of forty, randomly drawn from the population. One does not know whether 3.91 is above or below the population average value of $MS_w$, that is,

$$E(MS_w) = \sigma_\epsilon^2$$

### $E(MS_A)$

From one replication of the experiment, only one value of $MS_A$ can be calculated. However, one cannot calculate the numerical value of the parameter, $E(MS_A)$; if one could, there would be no need for inferential statistics. The algebraic formula for $E(MS_A)$ in terms of the parameters of the model in Equation 18.2 can be found:

$$E(MS_A) = \sigma_\epsilon^2 + \frac{nK \sum_{j=1}^{J} \alpha_j^2}{J - 1} = \sigma_\epsilon^2 + nK\sigma_\alpha^{2}* \qquad \textbf{(18.15)}$$

where $nK = n_{j\bullet}$, $\sigma_\epsilon^2$ is the variance of the error term in Equation 18.2 and is estimated by $MS_w$, and $\alpha_j$ is the main effect of the $j$th level of factor $A$, that is, $\alpha_j = \mu_{j\bullet} - \mu$.

Suppose that, unknown to the researcher, the true value of $\sigma_\epsilon^2$ (the parameter for the "within cell" variance) is 15.0, and that $\mu_{1\bullet} = 12$ and $\mu_{2\bullet} = 22$. Since $\mu = \frac{1}{2}(12 + 22) = 17$, $\alpha_1 = 12 - 17 = -5$ and $\alpha_2$ is $22 - 17 = 5$. Substituting these values and $J = 2$ and $n = 12$ into Equation 18.15 yields

$$E(MS_A) = 15.0 + 10(2)\,\frac{[(-5)^2 + 5^2]}{2 - 1} = 1{,}015$$

The preceding calculations were performed to illustrate the nature of the terms in Equation 18.15. It must be emphasized that one never actually calculates a value for $E(MS_A)$. What *is* important is to note the relationship between the expression for $E(MS_A)$ and the truth or falsity of the null hypothesis about factor $A$. Notice that the fourth of several equivalent statements of $H_0$ for factor $A$ in Section 18.9 is $H_0\colon \Sigma_1^J\, \alpha_j^2 = 0$. The quantity hypothesized to be zero in $H_0$ for factor $A$ is the same quantity, $\Sigma\, \alpha_j^2$, that appears in the numerator of the second term for $E(MS_A)$. Thus, *if* $H_0$ is true—which means that $\Sigma\, \alpha_j^2 = 0$—then

$$E(MS_A) = \sigma_\epsilon^2 + \frac{nK(0)}{J - 1} = \sigma_\epsilon^2$$

On the other hand, *if* $H_0$ is false—which means that $\Sigma\, \alpha_j^2$ is positive—then

$$E(MS_A) = \sigma_\epsilon^2 + \frac{nK \sum_j \alpha_j^2}{J - 1} > \sigma_\epsilon^2$$

This is an important relationship to understand: *If $H_0$ is true, $MS_A$ is expected to be the same size as the true within-cell variance, $\sigma_\epsilon^2$; if $H_0$ is false, $MS_A$ is expected to be larger than $\sigma_\epsilon^2$.*

*For simplicity, $\Sigma_{j=1}^{J}\, \alpha_j^2/(J - 1)$ is often denoted $\sigma_\alpha^2$.

## $E(MS_B)$

The expected value of $MS_B$ has the form

$$E(MS_B) = \sigma_\epsilon^2 + \frac{nJ\sum_k \beta_k^2}{K-1} = \sigma_\epsilon^2 + nJ\sigma_\beta^2 \tag{18.16}$$

The null hypothesis for the main effect of factor $B$ is $H_0$: $\Sigma_k \beta_k^2 = 0$. *If $H_0$ for factor $B$ is true, then*

$$E(MS_B) = \sigma_\epsilon^2 + \frac{nJ(0)}{K-1} = \sigma_\epsilon^2$$

*If $H_0$ for factor $B$ is true, one expects $MS_B$ to be equal to $E(MS_w) = \sigma_\epsilon^2$; $MS_B$ can be expected to be larger than $\sigma_\epsilon^2$ when $H_0$ for factor $B$ is false.*

## $E(MS_{AB})$

The expected value of $MS_{AB}$ is

$$E(MS_{AB}) = \sigma_\epsilon^2 + \frac{n\sum_k \sum_j (\alpha\beta)_{jk}^2}{(J-1)(K-1)} = \sigma_\epsilon^2 + n\sigma_{\alpha\beta}^2 \tag{18.17}$$

The null hypothesis for the interaction of factors $A$ and $B$ can be stated as $H_0$: $\Sigma_j \Sigma_k (\alpha\beta)_{jk}^2 = 0$. Thus, *if $H_0$ for the interaction of $A$ and $B$ is true, then $E(MS_{AB})$ equals $\sigma_\epsilon^2$; if $H_0$ is false, then $E(MS_{AB}) > \sigma_\epsilon^2$.* These relationships are summarized in Table 18.4.

The comparison of $MS_A$ with $MS_w$ reflects on the truth of $H_0$: $\Sigma \alpha_j^2 = 0$. If $H_0$ is true, then $MS_A$ and $MS_w$ have the same expected value; if $H_0$ is false, then $MS_A$ has an expected value larger than $\sigma_\epsilon^2$ but the expected value of $MS_w$ is still $\sigma_\epsilon^2$. Naturally, if $MS_A$ proves to be much larger than $MS_w$ in a particular run of the experiment, one would be inclined to think that $H_0$ is false; if $MS_A$ and $MS_w$ are about the same size in a particular replication of the experiment, one would probably think that they are both estimating the same quantity, $\sigma_\epsilon^2$, which is the case when $H_0$ is true. Comparisons of either $MS_B$ or $MS_{AB}$ with $MS_w$ bear on the truth or falsity of the null hypotheses about the main effects of $B$ and the interaction effects of $A$ and $B$, respectively, in the same manner that comparing $MS_A$ with $MS_w$ tells us something about the plausibility of $\Sigma_j \alpha_j^2 = 0$ being true.

**TABLE 18.4 Relationships Between Null Hypothesis and Expected Values of Mean Squares**

| *Source of Variation* | *Mean square* | *Expected mean square when $H_0$ is true* | *Expected mean square when $H_0$ is false*[a] |
|---|---|---|---|
| Factor $A$ | $MS_A$ | $\sigma_\epsilon^2$ | $\sigma_\epsilon^2 + nK\sigma_\alpha^2$ |
| Factor $B$ | $MS_B$ | $\sigma_\epsilon^2$ | $\sigma_\epsilon^2 + nJ\sigma_\beta^2$ |
| Interaction of $A$ and $B$ | $MS_{AB}$ | $\sigma_\epsilon^2$ | $\sigma_\epsilon^2 + n\sigma_{\alpha\beta}^2$ |
| Within cells | $MS_w$ | $\sigma_\epsilon^2$ | $\sigma_\epsilon^2$ |

[a]More explicitly, $\sigma_\alpha^2 = \Sigma_j \alpha_j^2/(J-1)$; $\sigma_\beta^2 = \Sigma_k \beta_k^2/(K-1)$; $\sigma_{\alpha\beta}^2 = \Sigma_k \Sigma_j \alpha\beta_{jk}^2/[(J-1)(K-1)]$.

The problem of deciding when $MS_A$ ($MS_B$ or $MS_{AB}$) is sufficiently larger than $MS_w$ is a problem of the variability of the values of mean squares from one replication of the two-factor experiment to the next. This problem will be addressed in the next section.

## 18.15 THE DISTRIBUTION OF THE MEAN SQUARES

Before proceeding to the question of the statistical distributions of the four mean squares in a two-factor ANOVA design, it is advisable to clarify the nature of the statistical inference one makes in this situation. In the two-factor design in Section 18.3, ten observations were taken in each of the $2 \times 2 = 4$ cells of the design. These forty observations can be considered to be randomly drawn from four hypothetical populations (one for each cell) that contain the scores an infinite number of persons would obtain under the same experimental conditions. The forty observations in Table 18.3 will be called a *complete replication of the experiment.* This complete replication produced the following mean squares: $MS_A = .90$, $MS_B = 2.50$, $MS_{AB} = 4.90$, and $MS_w = 3.91$. A second complete replication of the experiment could be obtained by performing the same experiment with a different set of forty persons (ten in each cell); this second replication would yield different values for each of the four mean squares. Conceptually, third, fourth, fifth, and so on replications of the experiment could be run, and each replication would produce its own set of four mean squares. Now the question is, what will be the distribution of values of $MS_A$ obtained from an infinite number of replications of the experiment?

Before this question can be answered, it is necessary to add an assumption to our model in Equation 18.2. In Section 18.14 it was necessary to assume that the variances of the hypothetical populations underlying the *JK* cells of the experiment all have the same variance, $\sigma_\epsilon^2$. To these assumptions the assumption that these populations are normally distributed must be added.

### The Distribution of $MS_w$

With the addition of the normality assumption, the $n$ observations in any cell—the $jk$th cell—constitute a random sample from a normal distribution with mean $\mu_{jk}$ and variance $\sigma_\epsilon^2$. Each cell variance $s_{jk}^2$ is an unbiased estimator of $\sigma_\epsilon^2$. Furthermore,

$$\frac{s_{jk}^2}{\sigma_\epsilon^2} \sim \frac{\chi_{n-1}^2}{n-1} = \frac{\chi_\nu^2}{\nu}.$$

$s_{jk}^2/\sigma_\epsilon^2$ has a distribution equal to the chi-square distribution ($\nu = n - 1$) divided by $n - 1$. This statement is true for the *JK* independent cell variances $s_{jk}^2$. From the additive property of chi-square variables,

$$\sum_j \sum_k \frac{s_{jk}^2}{\sigma_\epsilon^2} \sim \frac{\chi_{n-1}^2}{n-1} + \cdots + \frac{\chi_{n-1}^2}{n-1} \sim \frac{\chi_{JK(n-1)}^2}{n-1}$$

Dividing the preceding quantities by $JK$ yields

$$\frac{\sum_j \sum_k \frac{s_{jk}^2}{\sigma_\epsilon^2}}{JK} = \frac{MS_w}{\sigma_\epsilon^2} \sim \frac{\chi^2_{JK(n-1)}}{JK(n-1)}$$

$MS_w/\sigma_\epsilon^2$ has a chi-square distribution, $\nu = JK(n-1)$, divided by $JK(n-1)$. For example, in the problem in Section 18.13, $J = K = 2$ and $n = 10$. Suppose the value of $\sigma_\epsilon^2$ is 5. Then

$$\frac{MS_w}{5} \sim \frac{\chi^2_{36}}{36}$$

and the single observed value of $MS_w = 3.91 \div 5$ is one observation from a chi-square distribution ($\nu = 36$) that has been rescaled by division by 36.

## The Distribution of $MS_A$

One must consider two cases in this instance: the distribution of $MS_A$ when $H_0\colon \Sigma \alpha_j^2 = 0$ is true and when $H_0$ is false. If $H_0$ is true, then

$$\frac{MS_A}{\sigma_\epsilon^2} \sim \frac{\chi^2_{J-1}}{J-1}$$

that is, $MS_A/\sigma_\epsilon^2$ has a distribution over complete replications of the two-factor design that is the chi-square distribution ($\nu = J - 1$) divided by $J - 1$.

If $H_0$ is false, then $MS_A/\sigma_\epsilon^2$ has what is called a *noncentral chi-square distribution* ($\nu = J - 1$) divided by $J - 1$. The noncentral chi-square distribution with $\nu = J - 1$ is a mathematical curve that has a higher mean and is generally to the right of the chi-square distribution ($\nu = J - 1$). The relationship of the chi-square distribution to the noncentral chi-square distribution is illustrated in Figure 18.11.

When $H_0$ is false, the values of $MS_A$ tend to be larger than those of $MS_A$ when

**FIGURE 18.11. Distributions of $MS_A/\sigma_\epsilon^2$ under "$H_0$ true" and "$H_0$ false."**

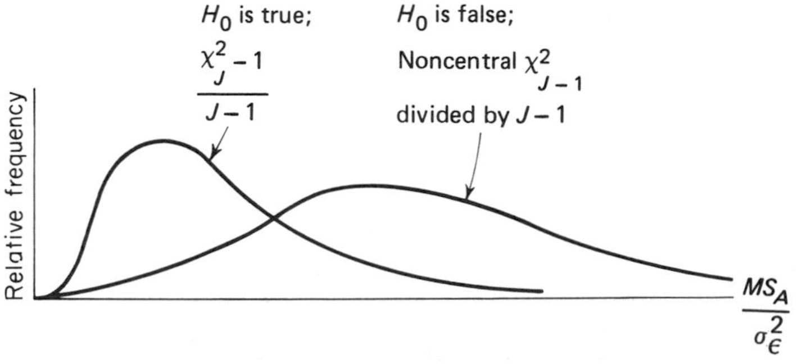

$H_0$ is true. This is reflected in the displacement to the right of the noncentral chi-square distribution. The larger the value of $\Sigma \alpha_j^2$, the further to the right of $\chi^2_{J-1}/(J-1)$ the values of $MS_A/\sigma_\epsilon^2$ will be displaced. Thus, the noncentral chi-square distribution in Figure 18.11 is for one particular value of $\Sigma \alpha_j^2$ only; there exists a separate noncentral $\chi^2$ distribution for each value of $\Sigma \alpha_j^2$.

## The Distribution of $MS_B$

The distributional statements that can be made about $MS_B$ are quite analogous to those for $MS_A$. If $H_0$: $\Sigma_k \beta_k^2 = 0$ is true, then

$$\frac{MS_B}{\sigma_\epsilon^2} \sim \frac{\chi^2_{K-1}}{K-1}$$

If $H_0$ is false, then $MS_B/\sigma_\epsilon^2$ has a noncentral chi-square distribution ($\nu = K - 1$) divided by $K - 1$.

## The Distribution of $MS_{AB}$

If $H_0$: $\Sigma_k \Sigma_j \alpha\beta_{jk}^2 = 0$, that is, if there is no interaction between factors $A$ and $B$, then

$$\frac{MS_{AB}}{\sigma_\epsilon^2} \sim \frac{\chi^2_{(J-1)(K-1)}}{(J-1)(K-1)}$$

$MS_{AB}/\sigma_\epsilon^2$ has a chi-square distribution, $\nu = (J-1)(K-1)$, divided by $(J-1)(K-1)$.

Again, if the null hypothesis about the interaction of $A$ and $B$ is false, $MS_{AB}/\sigma_\epsilon^2$ has a noncentral chi-square distribution, $\nu = (J-1)(K-1)$, divided by $(J-1)(K-1)$.

The facts can now be combined into the major results of this section. Recall that the ratio of two independent chi-square variables, each divided by its own degrees of freedom, has an $F$-distribution (see Sec. 13.5).

Suppose that $H_0$: $\Sigma \alpha_j^2 = 0$ is true; then $MS_A/\sigma_\epsilon^2 \sim \chi^2_{J-1}/(J-1)$. Regardless of whether $H_0$ is true or false, $MS_w/\sigma_\epsilon^2$ has a chi-square distribution divided by $JK(n-1)$. Now

$$\frac{MS_A/\sigma_\epsilon^2}{MS_w/\sigma_\epsilon^2} \sim F_{J-1, JK(n-1)}$$

But notice that

$$\frac{MS_A/\sigma_\epsilon^2}{MS_w/\sigma_\epsilon^2} = \frac{MS_A}{MS_w} \sim F_{J-1, JK(n-1)}$$

Fortunately, $\sigma_\epsilon^2$ can be eliminated without having to know its actual value.

The ratio of $MS_A$ to $MS_w$ has an $F$-distribution with $J - 1$ and $JK(n-1)$ degrees of freedom when $H_0$ is true. Thus if the value of $MS_A/MS_w$ for a replication of a two-factor experiment looks like a "typical" observation from the distribution $F_{J-1, JK(n-1)}$—by "typical" meaning that $MS_A/MS_w$ does not exceed the 90th, 95th, or 99th percentile

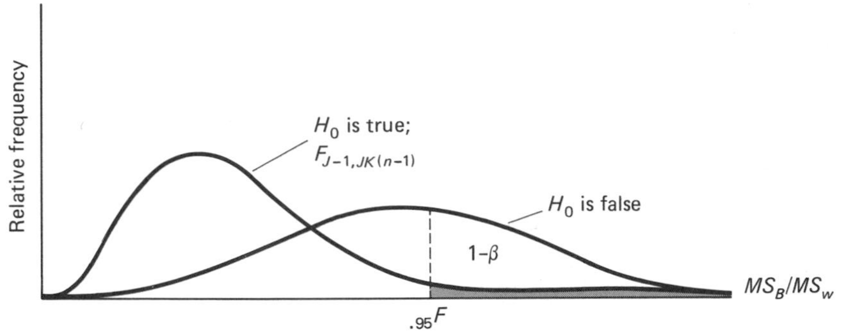


**FIGURE 18.12. Distribution of $MS_B/MS_w$ over complete replications of the two-factor design when $H_0$ is true and when it is false. (Shaded portion contains the 5% of the ratios that exceed the 95th percentile in the $F$-distribution.)**

of that distribution—one is inclined to think that $H_0$ is true. On the other hand, if $H_0$ is false, then the value of $MS_A$ is expected to be larger than the value of $MS_w$. Hence, if a very large value of $MS_A/MS_w$ is obtained—a value that *seems* not to have been drawn from $F_{J-1,JK(n-1)}$ since it exceeds the 99th percentile of that distribution—then $H_0$ is probably false.

When $H_0$: $\Sigma\, \beta_k^2 = 0$ is true,

$$\frac{MS_B/\sigma_\epsilon^2}{MS_w/\sigma_\epsilon^2} = \frac{MS_B}{MS_w} \sim F_{K-1,JK(n-1)}$$

When $H_0$: $\Sigma\Sigma\, \alpha\beta_{jk}^2 = 0$ is true, then

$$\frac{MS_{AB}/\sigma_\epsilon^2}{MS_w/\sigma_\epsilon^2} = \frac{MS_{AB}}{MS_w} \sim F_{(J-1)(K-1),JK(n-1)}$$

The effect of a false null hypothesis about either the main effects of factor $B$ or the interaction effects of $A$ and $B$ is to increase $MS_B$ or $MS_{AB}$ without systematically increasing $MS_w$, thus producing a distribution, over complete replications of the design, of mean squares that is displaced to the right of the $F$-distribution. These relationships are illustrated for factor $B$ in Figure 18.12. Note that the proportion of the noncentral $F$-distribution that exceeds the critical $F$-value (the vertical dashed line) is the power (the probability of not making a type-II error), $1 - \beta$.

## 18.16 HYPOTHESIS TESTS OF THE NULL HYPOTHESES

The discussion to this point has led to three ratios of mean squares that will be called $F$-ratios:

$$F_A = \frac{MS_A}{MS_w}, \qquad F_B = \frac{MS_B}{MS_w}, \qquad F_{AB} = \frac{MS_{AB}}{MS_w}$$

For the data in Table 18.3 these $F$-ratios have the following values:

$$F_A = \frac{.90}{3.91} = .23, \qquad F_B = \frac{2.50}{3.91} = .64 \qquad F_{AB} = \frac{4.90}{3.91} = 1.25$$

These *F-tests* are similar to the $F$-test in the one-factor fixed-effects ANOVA. The $F$-test will be illustrated with the main effects of factor $A$.

First, one adopts a level of significance $\alpha$, which is the probability of rejecting $H_0$: $\Sigma \alpha_j^2 = 0$ when it is in fact true. The $\alpha$ so chosen determines a critical region, that is, value of the ratio $MS_A/MS_w$ that will lead one to reject $H_0$: $\Sigma \alpha_j^2 = 0$. This critical region is all numbers greater than the $100(1 - \alpha)$ percentile in the distribution $F_{J-1, JK(n-1)}$, that is, all values larger than ${}_{1-\alpha}F_{J-1, JK(n-1)}$. If the calculated value of $F_A = MS_A/MS_w$ exceeds the critical value ${}_{1-\alpha}F_{J-1, JK(n-1)}$, then $H_0$ is rejected. If $F_A$ is less than the critical value, $H_0$ is not rejected.

The example in Table 18.3, can be used to illustrate the hypothesis tests. There it was found that $F_A = .23$. If $H_0$: $\Sigma \alpha_j^2 = 0$ were true, the distribution of $F_A$ over repeated complete replications of the $2 \times 2$ design would describe an $F$-distribution with $J - 1 = 1$ and $JK(n - 1) = 36$ degrees of freedom. One would not wish to conclude erroneously that $H_0$ is false when in fact it is true. Indeed, one wishes to adopt a decision rule for choosing between $H_0$ and $H_1$: $\Sigma \alpha_j^2 \neq 0$ that will lead to an erroneous decision to reject $H_0$ in favor of $H_1$ only one time in 10. Hence, one wants to adopt a risk of $\alpha = .10$ of committing a type-I error, rejecting $H_0$ when it is true. Since the only evidence in favor of $H_1$ is a large value of $F_A$, the entire critical region of the test should be placed in the upper tail of the distribution $F_{1,36}$; hence, the critical value for the test becomes ${}_{.90}F_{1,36}$. From Table $F$ in the Appendix, the 90th percentile in the $F$-distribution with 1 and 36 degrees of freedom is approximately 2.86.

Any $F$-ratio $F_A$ exceeding 2.86 will be taken to be evidence that the hypothesis $H_0$: $\Sigma \alpha_j^2 = 0$ is false. This statement constitutes the decision rule of the hypothesis test. If in reality $H_0$ is true, this decision rule will have a probability of $\alpha = .10$ of falsely rejecting $H_0$. Such is the magnitude of the risk one takes in agreeing to reject $H_0$ if $F_A$ is greater than 2.86. For the data in Table 18.3 the value of $F_A$ is .23. Since this $F$-ratio is less than the critical value of 2.86, the hypothesis that $\Sigma \alpha_j^2 = 0$ is tenable. One concludes that the two sample means $\bar{X}_{1\bullet}$ and $\bar{X}_{2\bullet}$ are not significantly different at the .10 level.

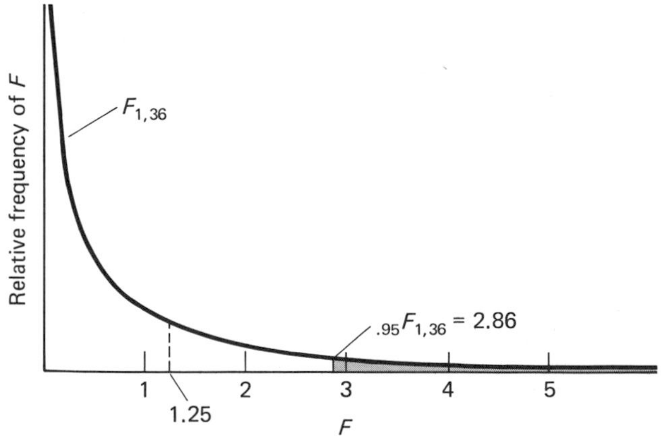


**FIGURE 18.13**
**Position of an $F$-ratio of 1.25 relative to the $F$-distribution with one and 36 degrees of freedom.**

The $F$-test of the hypothesis $H_0$: $\Sigma\,\beta_k^2 = 0$ proceeds along similar lines. Suppose it was decided to test $H_0$ with an $\alpha$ of .10. The $F$-ratio for factor $B$, .64, was well below the critical value of 2.86, hence $H_0$ remains tenable.

The $F$-test of the null hypothesis about the interaction of factors $A$ and $B$ is carried out in a similar manner. If $H_0$: $\Sigma\Sigma\,\alpha\beta_{jk}^2 = 0$ is true, then $F_{AB}$ has an $F$-distribution with $(J - 1)(K - 1) = 1$ and $JK(n - 1) = 36$ degrees of freedom. The value of $F_{AB}$ is $4.90/3.91 = 1.25$. The position of this obtained $F$-ratio relative to the central $F$-distribution—the distribution $F_{AB}$ would follow if $H_0$ were true—is illustrated in Figure 18.13.

By inspecting Figure 18.13, it would appear to be reasonable to regard 1.25 as having been drawn at random from the distribution $F_{1,36}$—to argue that the data support the null hypothesis that $\Sigma\Sigma\,\alpha\beta_{jk}^2 = 0$. Thus, the conlusion is to retain $H_0$.

## 18.17 DETERMINING POWER IN FACTORIAL DESIGNS

Procedures for determining power for a one-factor ANOVA were treated in Sections 16.19 to 16.22. The procedures for balanced designs having two or more factors are very similar: the $n$ in Equation 16.25 is the number of observations on which each of the $J$ means for the factor in question is based $n_{j\bullet}$. In Table 18.3 each row (and column) mean, $\bar{X}_{j\bullet}$ is based on twenty observations ($n_{j\bullet} = n_{1\bullet} = n_{2\bullet} = n_{\bullet 1} = n_{\bullet 2} = 20$), thus the value for $n$ in Equation 16.25 would be 20; $J$, $\alpha_j$, and $\sigma_\epsilon^2$ are virtually unchanged in definition. The variance in the error mean square $\sigma_\epsilon^2$, is the denominator of the $F$-test for testing the factor in question (the within-cell variance when all factors are fixed),* as they are in the examples in Table 18.3 (and Tables 18.5 and 18.6). Equation 16.25 extended to a two-factor ANOVA becomes:†

$$\phi_\alpha = \sqrt{\frac{nK \sum_j \alpha_j^2}{J\sigma_\epsilon^2}} \quad \text{and} \quad \phi_\beta = \sqrt{\frac{nJ \sum_k \beta_k^2}{K\sigma_\epsilon^2}} \tag{18.18}$$

for the $A$ and $B$ main effects, respectively.

Suppose in the study depicted in the 4 X 3 ANOVA design in Table 18.5 that factor $A$ is grade level and factor $B$ is treatment (anxiety conditions). If anxiety-reducing conditions ($B_1$) increase performance by $.25\sigma$ ($\beta_1 = \mu_{\bullet 1} - \mu = .25\sigma$), neutral conditions ($B_2$) have no effect on performance ($\beta_2 = 0$), and anxiety-producing conditions decrease performance by $.25\sigma$ ($\beta_3 = -.25\sigma$), estimate the power for detecting the $B$ main effect if there are $n = 12$ subjects per cell and $\alpha = .05$. Using the $z$-score metric (Section 16.21), $\sigma_\epsilon^2 = 1, \beta_1 = .25, \beta_2 = 0, \beta_3 = -.25, n_{\bullet k} = Jn = (4)(12) = 48$, and $K = 3$. Hence

$$\phi_\beta = \sqrt{\frac{nJ\,\Sigma\,\beta_k^2}{K\sigma_\epsilon^2}} = \sqrt{\frac{48[(-.25)^2 + (0) + (.25)^2]}{3(1)}} = \sqrt{2} = 1.414$$

*The distinction between fixed and random factors is treated in Section 19.2.

†The noncentrality parameters, $\phi$, in a three-factor ANOVA (Section 18.20) are

$$\phi_\alpha = \sqrt{\frac{nKL\,\Sigma\,\alpha_j^2}{J\sigma_\epsilon^2}}, \quad \phi_\beta = \sqrt{\frac{nJL\,\Sigma\,\beta_k^2}{K\sigma_\epsilon^2}}, \quad \phi_\gamma = \sqrt{\frac{nJK\,\Sigma\,\gamma_l^2}{L\sigma_\epsilon^2}}.$$

From Appendix Table G ($\nu_b = 2$), with $\alpha = .05$ and $\nu_e = 132$ (see panel *B* of Table 18.5), power would be estimated to be approximately .63.*

## 18.18 MULTIPLE COMPARISONS IN THE TWO-FACTOR ANOVA

As in the one-factor ANOVA, the rejection of a null hypothesis about a main effect implies only that the population means for the levels of that factor are not all equal. Obviously, if there are only two levels of a factor, multiple comparison procedures are not needed. But if there are three or more levels of a factor associated with a significant main effect, multiple comparison procedures are required to determine which of the pairs of sample means show differences large enough to permit the conclusion that the associated population means differ. Naturally, these remarks apply to both fixed factors in a two-factor design.

The MC procedures described in Chapter 17 extend logically to each fixed ANOVA factor, the only difference being that the $n$'s in the equations are the $n$'s for the marginal means for the factor being examined, that is, the number of observations on which the means being compared are based.

Panel *A* of Table 18.5 gives the set of means from a $J = 4$ by $K = 3$ two-factor ANOVA design; panel *B* gives the associated ANOVA table. The definition of a contrast (Eq. 17.7; Sec. 17.8) involving the means of factor *A* is

$$\hat{\psi} = \sum_{j=1}^{J} c_j \overline{X}_{j\bullet} = c_1 \overline{X}_{1\bullet} + c_2 \overline{X}_{2\bullet} + c_3 \overline{X}_{3\bullet} + c_4 \overline{X}_4$$

The standard error of contrasts (Eq. 17.4, Eq. 17.8A; Sec. 17.10) among means of factor *A* is

$$s_{\hat{\psi}} = \sqrt{MS_e \sum_j c_j^2 / n_{j\bullet}} \quad \text{and} \quad t = \frac{\hat{\psi}}{s_{\hat{\psi}}}$$

(Eq. 17.9; Sec. 17.11) where $MS_e = MS_w$, and $n_{j\bullet} = nK$. The degrees of freedom for the critical $t$-value for a contrast will be $\nu_e$; in Table 18.5, $\nu_e = 132$. If $H_{0_1}: \mu_1 - \mu_4 = 0$,

*Rarely is the power for detecting an interaction determined since the principal interest is usually in one or more of the main effects. The procedures are closely parallel: for example, in a two-factor ANOVA with $J = 4$ and $K = 3$:

$$\phi_{\alpha\beta} = \sqrt{\frac{n \sum_k \sum_j (\alpha\beta_{jk})^2}{JK\sigma_\epsilon^2}}$$

For a three-factor interaction:

$$\phi_{\alpha\beta\gamma} = \sqrt{\frac{n \sum_l \sum_k \sum_j (\alpha\beta\gamma_{jkl})^2}{JKL\sigma_\epsilon^2}}$$

See Cohen (1969) for computational examples.

**TABLE 18.5 Set of Means for a 4 × 3 Factorial Design in Which Each Cell Contains $n$ = 12 Observations (from Marascuilo and Levin, 1970)**

| | | $B_1$ | $B_2$ | $B_3$ | $\bar{X}_{j\bullet}$ |
|---|---|---|---|---|---|
| A. | $A_1$ | 15.67 | 13.83 | 12.08 | 13.86 |
| | $A_2$ | 14.67 | 13.67 | 10.50 | 12.95 |
| | $A_3$ | 17.17 | 8.42 | 12.00 | 12.53 |
| | $A_4$ | 14.83 | 9.00 | 10.17 | 11.33 |
| | $\bar{X}_{\bullet k}$ | 15.58 | 11.23 | 11.19 | $12.67 = \bar{X}_{\bullet\bullet}$ |

| | Source | Sum of Squares | $\nu$ | Mean Square | $F$ |
|---|---|---|---|---|---|
| B. | $A$ | 118.8 | 3 | 39.6 | 2.91[a] |
| | $B$ | 612.5 | 2 | 306.3 | 22.52[b] |
| | $A \times B$ | 271.1 | 6 | 45.2 | 3.32 |
| | Within (error) | 1789.5 | 132 | 13.6 | |

[a] $p < .05$
[b] $p < .001$

$c_1 = 1$ and $c_4 = -1$, then

$$\hat{\psi}_1 = \bar{X}_{1\bullet} - \bar{X}_{4\bullet} = 13.86 - 11.33 = 2.53$$

$$s_{\hat{\psi}_1} = \sqrt{13.6(\tfrac{1}{36} + \tfrac{1}{36})} = .869; \text{ and } t = 2.53/.869 = 2.91$$

If $\hat{\psi}_1$ were a planned orthogonal contrast (Sec. 17.16), the critical $t$-value at $\alpha = .01$ would be ${}_{.995}t_{132} \doteq 2.62$, therefore $H_{0_1}$ would be rejected at the .01 level. Similarly, if the studentized range statistic (Eq. 17.2) is used,

$$q = (\bar{X}_{1\bullet} - \bar{X}_{4\bullet})/s_{\bar{X}}, \text{ where } s_{\bar{X}} = \sqrt{\frac{MS_e}{n_{j\bullet}}} = \sqrt{\frac{13.6}{36}} = .615$$

thus $q_1 = 2.53/.615 = 4.12$, which is larger than the critical value at $\alpha = .05$; ${}_{.95}q_{132,4} \doteq 3.36$.

Multiple comparisons on factor $B$ differ only in that $n_{\bullet k} = nJ = 48$ (rather than $n_{j\bullet} = nK = 36$) is used in equations for $s_{\bar{X}}$ (or $s_{\hat{\psi}}$). Thus for the complex contrast, $H_{0_2}$: $\mu_{\bullet 1} - .5\mu_{\bullet 2} - .5\mu_{\bullet 3} = 0$, $\hat{\psi}_2 = 15.58 - (11.23 + 11.19)/2 \doteq 4.37$, and $s_{\hat{\psi}} = \sqrt{13.6(1/48 + (-.5)^2/48 + (-.5)^2/48)} = .652$, and $t = 4.37/.652 = 6.70$. If this were a post hoc hypothesis involving "data snooping" (i.e., the Scheffé test, Sec. 17.15) the critical $t$-value at $\alpha = .01$ would be

$$\sqrt{(K-1)_{.99}F_{(K-1),\nu_e}} = \sqrt{(2)_{.99}F_{2,132}} = \sqrt{2(6.85)} = 3.70$$

Thus $H_{0_2}$ is untenable.

If one wishes to make pairwise multiple comparisons among the twelve cell means, the procedure is identical to viewing the twelve means as twelve levels in a one-factor ANOVA. Hence Equation 17.8A becomes

$$s_{\hat{\psi}} = \sqrt{MS_e\left(\frac{1}{n} + \frac{1}{n}\right)} = \sqrt{13.6\left(\frac{1}{12} + \frac{1}{12}\right)} = 1.506$$

Critical values would continue to be based on the number of degrees of freedom associated with $MS_e$, in this case, $\nu_e = 132$.

## 18.19 CONFIDENCE INTERVALS FOR MEANS IN TWO-FACTOR ANOVA

Confidence intervals about all cell ($\bar{X}_{jk}$) or marginal ($\bar{X}_{j\bullet}$ or $\bar{X}_{\bullet k}$) means are constructed in the manner described in Section 11.18.

$$(1 - \alpha)\,\text{CI} = \bar{X}_{j\bullet} \pm {}_{1-\alpha/2}t_{\nu_e} s_{\bar{X}_{j\bullet}}$$

where $s_{\bar{X}_{j\bullet}} = \sqrt{MS_e/n_{j\bullet}}$, and for balanced two-factor designs, $n_{j\bullet} = nK$. In Table 18.5 for $\bar{X}_{1\bullet} = 13.86$ and $\alpha = .10$: $\nu_e = 132$, $n_{j\bullet} = nK = (12)(3) = 36$, and with ${}_{.95}t_{132} \doteq 1.66$.

$$.90\ \text{CI} = \bar{X}_{1\bullet} \pm {}_{.95}t_{132} s_{\bar{X}_{j\bullet}}, \quad \text{and} \quad s_{\bar{X}_{1\bullet}} = \sqrt{\frac{13.6}{36}} = .614$$

$$= 13.86 \pm 1.66(.614) = 13.86 \pm 1.02, \text{ or}$$

$$= (12.84, 14.88).$$

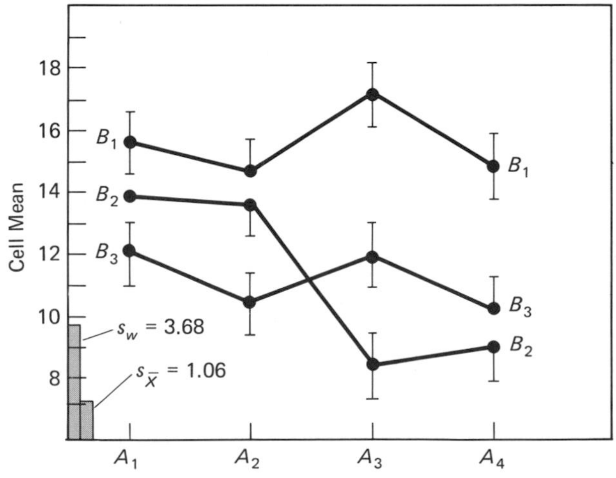


**FIGURE 18.14**
**Graphic representation of the interaction in Table 18.5.**

Similarly for cell means, for example, $\bar{X}_{11} = 15.67$ with $n = 12$:

$$s_{\bar{X}_{jk}} = \sqrt{\frac{MS_e}{n}} = \sqrt{\frac{13.6}{12}} = 1.06$$

hence .90 CI = 15.67 ± (1.66) 1.06 = 15.67 ± 1.76 or (13.91, 17.43)

Confidence intervals about cell means are helpful in interpreting interactions. For example, in Fig. 18.14 a band, $\pm s_{\bar{X}_{ij}}$, is set about each of the means in the interaction in Table 18.5 (except when the bands would overlap).

## 18.20 THREE-FACTOR ANOVA

Once the concepts of two-factor ANOVA are mastered, the building blocks are in place for ANOVA's with three and more factors. Indeed, the only new concept in the transition from a two-factor to a three-factor ANOVA is the three-factor interaction. The key to understanding a three-factor interaction is to view it as responding to the question, "Is the $A \times B$ interaction constant across all levels of factor $C$?" For example, if method $E$ is better for bright students but method $C$ is superior for not-so-bright students, there is a method-by-ability interaction. But do both boys and girls have the same pattern? This is the three-factor interaction question—is the two-factor interaction generalizable across both sexes?

In a balanced design all sources of variation are orthogonal. This indicates that the three-factor interaction is independent of the two-factor interactions. In other words, whether or not there is a three-factor interaction does not depend on the existence of any two-factor interaction. The three-factor interaction asks, "Is the $A \times B$ pattern, be the interaction zero or large, constant across all levels of factor $C$?" (Or, is the $A \times C$ pattern constant across all levels of $B$, and so on?) The example in Table 18.6 will be interpreted to illustrate the meaning of two- and three-factor interactions.

## 18.21 THREE-FACTOR ANOVA: AN ILLUSTRATION

To assess the effects of anxiety on test performance, three sets of instructions to examinees were used: (1) instructions designed to reduce anxiety, (2) neutral (standard) directions, or (3) directions designed to produce anxiety. Students were classified by sex, then randomly assigned to one of the three test conditions: $A_1$ (anxiety-reducing), $A_2$ (neutral), $A_3$ (anxiety-producing). Within each level of factor $A$, 5 boys and 5 girls took a standardized verbal ability test ($T_1$) and 5 other boys and 5 other girls took a standardized math ability test ($T_2$) previously calibrated to be of the same difficulty level as the verbal test.*

The basic statistical model for the analysis of the data is balanced $J = 3 \times K = 2 \times L = 2$ anxiety-condition ($A$) by test ($T$) by sex ($S$) design. For the three-factor

*The use of standard scores could have accomplished the same purpose.

**TABLE 18.6 Computational Illustration of a Three-Factor $A = 3 \times T = 2 \times S = 2$ Fixed-Effects ANOVA (cell variances given in parentheses, $n = 10$)**

*A.*

$A \times T \times S$

| | | $T_1$ (Verbal) $S_1(b)$ | $T_1$ (Verbal) $S_2(g)$ | $T_2$ (Math) $S_1(b)$ | $T_2$ (Math) $S_2(g)$ | $\bar{X}_{j..}$ | $\hat{\alpha}_j$ |
|---|---|---|---|---|---|---|---|
| Anxiety-reducing | $A_1$ | 12.7 (28.1) | 14.0 (25.0) | 16.0 (20.3) | 10.5 (18.5) | 13.30 | .30 |
| Neutral | $A_2$ | 13.0 (22.1) | 13.2 (26.0) | 12.6 (23.0) | 10.2 (25.0) | 12.25 | −.75 |
| Anxiety-producing | $A_3$ | 12.1 (27.0) | 16.3 (39.7) | 12.2 (43.6) | 13.2 (29.2) | 13.45 | .45 |
| | $\bar{X}_{.kl}$ | 12.60 | 14.50 | 13.60 | 11.30 | $13.00 = \bar{X}_{...}$ $n_{...} = 120$ | |

B.

$A \times T$

| | $T_1$ | $T_2$ | $\hat{\alpha}_j$ |
|---|---|---|---|
| $A_1$ | 13.35 | 13.25 | .30 |
| $A_2$ | 13.10 | 11.40 | −.75 |
| $A_3$ | 14.20 | 12.70 | .45 |
| $\bar{X}_{.k.}$ | 13.55 | 12.45 | |
| $\hat{\beta}_k$ | .55 | −.55 | |

$A \times S$

| | $S_1$ | $S_2$ |
|---|---|---|
| $A_1$ | 14.35 | 12.25 |
| $A_2$ | 12.80 | 11.70 |
| $A_3$ | 12.15 | 14.75 |
| $\bar{X}_{..l}$ | 13.10 | 12.90 |
| $\hat{\gamma}_l$ | .10 | −.10 |

$T \times S$

| | $S_1$ | $S_2$ |
|---|---|---|
| $T_1$ | 12.60 | 14.50 |
| $T_2$ | 13.60 | 11.30 |

C. *Step*

1. $SS_A = nKL\ \Sigma_j \hat{\alpha}_j^2 = 10(2)(2)[(.30)^2 + (-.75)^2 + (.45)^2] = 40(.855) = 34.20$
2. $SS_T = nJL\ \Sigma_k \hat{\beta}_k^2 = 10(3)(2)[(.55)^2 + (-.55)^2] = 60(.605) = 36.30$

ANOVA design the statistical model is: $X_{ijkl} = \mu + \alpha_j + \beta_k + \gamma_l + \alpha\beta_{jk} + \alpha\gamma_{jl} + \beta\gamma_{kl} + \alpha\beta\gamma_{jkl} + \epsilon_{ijkl}$, when $X_{ijkl}$ is the $i$th replicate (score) in cell $jkl$. The unbiased estimators of the parameters in the model are

$$\hat{\alpha}_j = \bar{X}_{j..} - \bar{X}_{...}$$
$$\hat{\beta}_k = \bar{X}_{.k.} - \bar{X}_{...}$$
$$\hat{\gamma}_l \equiv \bar{X}_{..l} - \bar{X}_{...}$$
$$\widehat{\alpha\beta}_{jk} = \bar{X}_{jk.} - (\bar{X}_{...} + \hat{\alpha}_j + \hat{\beta}_k)$$
$$\widehat{\alpha\gamma}_{jl} = \bar{X}_{j.l} - (\bar{X}_{...} + \hat{\alpha}_j + \hat{\gamma}_l)$$
$$\widehat{\beta\gamma}_{kl} = \bar{X}_{.kl} - (\bar{X}_{...} + \hat{\beta}_k + \hat{\gamma}_l)$$
$$\widehat{\alpha\beta\gamma}_{jkl} = \bar{X}_{jkl} - (\bar{X}_{...} + \hat{\alpha}_j + \hat{\beta}_k + \hat{\gamma}_l + \widehat{\alpha\beta}_{jk} + \widehat{\alpha\gamma}_{jl} + \widehat{\beta\gamma}_{kl})$$

The sum of each of the seven orthogonal effects is zero.

**TABLE 18.6 (cont.)**

3. $SS_{A+T+AT} = nL\ \Sigma_k \Sigma_j (\bar{X}_{jk.} - \bar{X}_{...})^2 = 10(2)[(.35)^2 + (.10)^2 + (1.20)^2 + (.25)^2 + (-1.60)^2 + (-.30)^2]$
$= 20(4.285) = 85.70$
$SS_{AT} = SS_{A+T+AT} - SS_A - SS_T = 85.70 - 34.20 - 36.30 = 15.2$
4. $SS_S = nJK\ \Sigma_l \hat{\gamma}_l^2 = 10(3)(2)[(.10)^2 + (-.10)^2 = 60(.02) = 1.20$
5. $SS_{A+S+AS} = nK\ \Sigma_l \Sigma_j (\bar{X}_{j.l} - \bar{X}_{...})^2 = (10(2)[(1.35)^2 + (-.20)^2 + (-.85)^2 + (-.75)^2 + (-1.30)^2 + (1.75)^2]$
$= 20(7.90) = 158.00$
$SS_{AS} = SS_{A+S+AS} - SS_A - SS_S = 158.00 - 34.20 - 1.20 = 122.60$
6. $SS_{T+S+TS} = nJ\ \Sigma_l \Sigma_k (\bar{X}_{.kl} - \bar{X}_{...})^2 = 10(3)[(-.40)^2 + (.60)^2 + (1.50)^2 + (-1.70)^2] = 30(5.66)$
$= 169.80$
$SS_{TS} = SS_{T+S+TS} - SS_T - SS_S = 169.80 - 36.30 - 1.20 = 132.30$
7. $SS_{A+T+S+AT+AS+TS+ATS} = n\ \Sigma_l \Sigma_k \Sigma_j (\bar{X}_{jkl} - \bar{X}_{...})^2 = 10[(-.3)^2 + (0)^2 + (-.9)^2 + (1.0)^2 + (.2)^2$
$+ (3.3)^2 + (3.0)^2 + (-.4)^2 + (-.8)^2 + (-2.5)^2 + (-2.8)^2 + (.2)^2]$
$= 10(36.76) = 367.60$
$SS_{ATS} = SS_{A+T+S+AT+AS+TS+ATS} - SS_A - SS_T - SS_{AT} - SS_{AT} - SS_{TS}$
$= 367.60 - 34.2 - 36.30 - 1.20 - 15.20 - 122.60 - 132.30 = 25.80$
8. $MS_w = \Sigma_l \Sigma_k \Sigma_j s_{jkl}^2 / JKL = (27.0 + 22.1 + \ldots + 18.5)^2/12 = 327.5/12 = 27.29$

**D.** *ANOVA Table*

| *Source* | *SS* | *ν* | *MS* | *F* |
|---|---|---|---|---|
| Anxiety Conditions (*A*) | 34.20 | 2 | 17.10 | .63 |
| Test (*T*) | 36.30 | 1 | 36.30 | 1.33 |
| Sex (*S*) | 1.20 | 1 | 1.20 | .04 |
| *AT* | 15.20 | 2 | 7.60 | .28 |
| *AS* | 122.60 | 2 | 61.30 | 2.25 |
| *TS* | 132.30 | 1 | 132.30 | 4.85[a] |
| *ATS* | 25.80 | 2 | 12.90 | .47 |
| Within (error) | 2,947.50 | 108 | 27.29 | |

[a] $p < .05$

The twelve cell means are given in panel *A* of Table 18.6. The three different combinations ($A \times T$, $A \times S$, and $T \times S$) of two-factor means are given in panel *B*, along with the estimates of the three main effects ($\hat{\alpha}_j$'s, $\hat{\beta}_k$'s, and $\hat{\gamma}_l$'s).

## 18.22 THREE-FACTOR ANOVA COMPUTATION

Using the data in panel *B*, the computation of a three-factor ANOVA proceeds as if three two-factor ANOVA's had been performed. The $A \times T$ summary table of means is used to obtain $SS_A$, $SS_T$, and $SS_{A \times T}$ applying the procedures outlined in steps 1 to 3 of Table 18.6.

Similarly in steps 4 and 5, the $A \times S$ summary table yields $SS_S$ and $SS_{AS}$. (Obviously, $SS_A$ does not need to be recomputed since its value was found previously from the $A \times T$ summary table.) Finally, $SS_{TS}$ is found in step 6 using the $T \times S$ summary table.

Only two remaining sources of variation are undetermined: (1) the three-factor ($A \times T \times S$) interaction, and (2) within cells. The rationale for the computation of the three-factor interaction is a logical extension of the procedures used in determining a two-factor interaction. Using the $A \times T \times S$ cell means in panel $A$, the source of variation for all aggregated effects is determined: $SS_{A+T+S+AT+AS+TS+ATS} = n\Sigma_l\Sigma_k\Sigma_j(\bar{X}_{jkl} - \bar{X}_{\bullet\bullet\bullet})^2$. The $SS$'s for all main effects and two-factor interactions are then subtracted; the residue then is $SS_{ATS}$. The computation of $SS_{ATS}$ illustrated in step 7 of Table 18.6, uses Eq. 18.19:

$$SS_{ABC} = SS_{A+B+C+AB+AC+BC+ABC} - SS_A - SS_B - SS_C - SS_{AB} - SS_{AC} - SS_{BC} \quad \textbf{(18.19)}$$

The procedure for finding $MS_w$ is parallel to that for a two-factor ANOVA: in a balanced design, $MS_w$ is the mean of the $JKL = (3)(2)(2) = 12$ cell variances.

$$MS_w = \sum_l \sum_k \sum_j s_{jkl}^2/JKL \quad \textbf{(18.20)}$$

Alternatively, $SS_w$ is $\Sigma_l\Sigma_k\Sigma_j SS_{jkl}$, which, divided by $\nu_w$ equals $MS_w$. $SS_w$ can also be calculated indirectly:

$$SS_w = SS_{\text{total}} - SS_{A+B+C+AB+AC+BC+ABC} \quad \textbf{(18.21)}$$

where

$$SS_{\text{total}} = \sum_l \sum_k \sum_j \sum_i X_{ijkl}^2 - \left(\sum_l \sum_k \sum_j \sum_i X_{ijkl}\right)^2 \bigg/ n_{\bullet\bullet\bullet}, \text{ and } n_{\bullet\bullet\bullet} = JKLn \quad \textbf{(18.22)}$$

The "within" degrees of freedom, $\nu_w$, are $JKL(n - 1)$, or in the example, (3)(2)(2) (10 − 1) = 108. In other words, $\nu_w$ equals the number of cells ($JKL$) times the degree of freedom per cell ($n - 1$).

## Results

The ANOVA table in panel $D$ of Table 18.5 summarizes the results. None of the three main effects is significant. The differences among the means of the three anxiety conditions ($\bar{X}_{1\bullet\bullet} = 13.30$, $\bar{X}_{2\bullet\bullet} = 12.25$, and $\bar{X}_{3\bullet\bullet} = 13.45$) do not approach statistical significance ($F = .63$, $p > .25$). Neither is the overall mean of the verbal test ($\bar{X}_{\bullet1\bullet} = 13.55$) reliably different from the overall mean of the math test ($\bar{X}_{\bullet2\bullet} = 12.45$). Thirdly, the difference in the means for the two sexes averaged across the two other factors is not significant ($\bar{X}_{\bullet\bullet1} = 13.10$ versus $\bar{X}_{\bullet\bullet2} = 12.90$). The only significant effect is the test-by-sex ($TS$) interaction; the other two two-factor interactions ($AT$ and $AS$) and the three-factor ($ATS$) interaction were not significant.

Recall that the absence of a two-factor interaction supports the generalizability of the pattern among the means of factor 1 across the levels of factor 2 (Sec. 18.3). Consequently, the absence of an $AT$ interaction indicates that the overall pattern among the means (in this case, small, nonsignificant differences) on factor $T$ (type-of-test) was

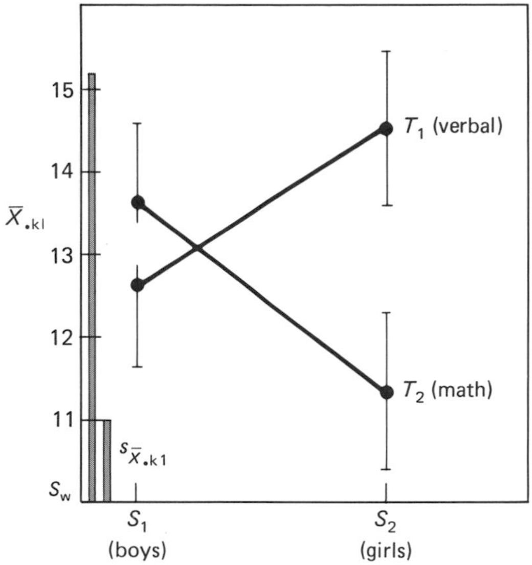


**FIGURE 18.15**
**A graph of the sex-by-test interaction.**

consistent across factor *A* (the three anxiety conditions). Likewise, the absence of a significant *AS* interaction shows that the overall pattern of means for the two sexes (factor *S*) generalized across the three levels of factor *A*.

The significant *TS* interaction indicates that the difference between the male and female means is *not* constant across factor *T* (type-of-test). The *TS* interaction is graphed in Figure 18.15 to clarify the nature of the interaction.

The disordinal interaction shown in Figure 18.15 reveals a familiar pattern: superior performance of females on verbal tests and better performance by males on math tests.

## 18.23 THE INTERPRETATION OF THREE-FACTOR INTERACTIONS

The null hypothesis of the three-factor interaction (*ATS*) is tenable. The most direct way to interpret a three-factor interaction is to view it as the generalizability of a two-factor configuration across the levels of the third factor, for example, is the *TS* interaction influenced by anxiety condition—does the pattern depicted in Fig. 18.15 vary depending on level of factor *A*? The absence of a significant *ATS* interaction indicates that the *TS* configuration in Figure 18.15 is not significantly affected by the anxiety treatment—the *TS* interaction does not have to be qualified regarding which level of factor *A* is involved.

## 18.24 CONFIDENCE INTERVALS IN THREE-FACTOR ANOVA

If we bear in mind that the *n* and degrees of freedom associated with the standard error of a mean, $s_{\bar{X}}$, and the critical *t*-value (Eqs. 11.8 to 11.9) pertain to the number of observations on which the particular mean in question is based, the extension of confidence intervals to cell means or other subgroup means is direct. For example, to determine the value of $s_{\bar{X}_{j..}}$ needed to set CI's about the level-means for factor $A$:

$$s_{\bar{X}_{j..}} = \sqrt{MS_e/n_{j\bullet\bullet}} \tag{18.23}$$

in the example in Table 18.5 $n_{j\bullet\bullet} = nKL = 40$, and

$$s_{\bar{X}_{j..}} = \sqrt{27.29/40} = .826$$

Likewise for factors $B$ and $C$:

$$s_{\bar{X}_{.k.}} = \sqrt{MS_e/n_{\bullet k\bullet}}, \text{ and } s_{\bar{X}_{..l}} = \sqrt{MS_e/n_{\bullet\bullet l}} \tag{18.23A}$$

To set confidence intervals about level means for factor $S$ (or factor $T$, since both factors have the same number of levels), $n_{\bullet k\bullet} = nJL = 60$, and

$$s_{\bar{X}_{.k.}} = \sqrt{MS_e/n_{\bullet k\bullet}} = \sqrt{27.29/60} = .674$$

Note that the CI's about the three means for factor $A$ will be $.826/.674 = 1.23$ times as wide as those for factors $S$ and $T$ because each $A$-mean is based on only forty scores, whereas each $S$-mean and each $T$-mean is based on sixty observations.

The CI's about cell means will be much larger than about level means because each cell mean is based on only $n = 10$ observations:

$$s_{\bar{X}_{jkl}} = \sqrt{MS_e/n} = \sqrt{27.29/10} = 1.652$$

Each of the four means in Figure 18.15 is based on $n_{\bullet kl} = nJ = 30$ scores, thus,

$$s_{\bar{X}_{.jk}} = \sqrt{MS_e/n} = \sqrt{27.29/30} = .977$$

This value is used to form the bands about the means in the interaction graph given in Figure 18.15. Notice that to set a confidence interval about any mean (marginal, cell, or other subgroup) the critical $t$-value is unchanged since its degrees of freedom is that associated with $MS_e$.*

## 18.25 MULTIPLE COMPARISONS WITH THREE-FACTOR ANOVA

For multiple comparisons, as with CI's the $n$ used in the equations for determining the standard error ($s_{\hat{\psi}}$ or $s_{\bar{X}}$) is the number of observations on which the means to be com-

*This will always be true when all factors are fixed because the error mean square is always the within-cell mean square. This is not the case in mixed model ANOVA (Chap. 19).

pared are based. The standard error of a pairwise contrast* (Eq. 17.8B) is

$$s_{\hat{\psi}} = \sqrt{\frac{2MS_e}{n}} \tag{18.24}$$

For factor $A$, where $n_{j\bullet\bullet} = nKL = 40$, the standard error of pairwise contrast, $s_{\hat{\psi}}$, among levels of factor $A$ is

$$s_{\hat{\psi}} = \sqrt{\frac{2(27.29)}{40}} = 1.168$$

For MC methods based on the studentized range statistic, $s_{\bar{X}}$ is determined as in Section 18.18. Factors $S$ and $T$ each have only two levels, hence multiple comparisons are redundant with the $F$-test.

## 18.26 FACTORIAL DESIGNS AND POWER

Even if one is not interested in a particular factor or its interaction with other factors, the inclusion of the factor in the design is often advisable because it can increase the power for identifying the other effects of principal interest. For example, if a one-factor ANOVA were performed on the factor $A$ for the data in Table 18.5 the ANOVA table in Table 18.7 would be the result.

Notice from Table 18.7 that the mean square for factor $A$ is not influenced by whether or not a second factor, $B$, was included in the design. This is always the case with balanced designs. In one-factor ANOVA all variance not associated with the main effect becomes within (error) variance (see Equation 16.10).

Notice the $F$-ratio for the $A$ effect in the one-factor ANOVA dropped from 2.91 (in Table 18.5) to 2.07 (in Table 18.7) because the error variance was 40% larger in the one-factor ANOVA; the $A$ effect is not significant in the one-factor ANOVA. Whenever a second factor is related to the dependent variable or interacts with first factor, the $MS_w$ for the two-factor ANOVA will be less than for a one-factor ANOVA, and the $F$-ratio for the first factor will be larger in the two-factor design than in a one-factor

**TABLE 18.7 ANOVA Table for the Data in Table 18.5 If Analyzed As a One-Factor ANOVA for Factor $A$.**

| *Source* | | *Sum of Squares* | | *ν* | *Mean Square* | *F* |
|---|---|---|---|---|---|---|
| $A$ | | 118.0 | | 3 | 39.6 | 2.07 |
| Within | ($B$: 612.5) | | ($B$: 2) | | | |
| | ($AB$: 271.1) | 2673.1 | ($AB$: 6) | 140 | 19.1 | |
| | (1789.5) | | (132) | | | |

*For complex contrast: $s_{\hat{\psi}} = \sqrt{(MS_e/n)\,\Sigma c^2}$.

ANOVA. But if the null hypotheses for the second factor and the interaction are true, the value of $MS_w$ will change little. For example, if a one-factor ANOVA is performed on the factor $A$ in Table 18.3, the value of $MS_w$ in the two-factor and one-factor ANOVA's differ little (3.91 versus 3.90) because neither one $B$ nor $AB$ effect is significant.

In general* the power for testing $H_0$: $\Sigma\alpha_j^2$ will be greater in a two-factor ANOVA than in a one-factor ANOVA if either $H_0$: $\Sigma\beta_k^2 = 0$ or $H_0$: $\Sigma\alpha\beta_{jk}^2 = 0$ is false.

## 18.27 FACTORIAL ANOVA WITH UNEQUAL *n*'s

When cell frequencies are unequal in factorial designs, complications arise in the analysis of such data. If the procedures in Table 18.3 were followed with unequal $n$'s, the sums of squares calculated directly (i.e., none of the $SS$'s was obtained by subtraction) would not add up to the $SS_{\text{total}}$; the $SS$'s associated with the various effects would not be orthogonal (Sec. 17.16). This nonorthogonality leads to $F$-tests for confounded effects unless certain adjustments are made.

What, then, is the analysis-of-choice in such situations? The most common alternative is to utilize multiple regression techniques with "dummy variables"† (Chap. 8). But there are several variations—different models relating to various orders for estimating the unknown parameters. In such siuations one should consult Snedecor and Cochran (1980, Chap. 20), Appelbaum and Cramer (1974), Carlson and Timm (1974), Herr and Gaebelein (1978), Bancroft (1968), Kerlinger and Pedhazur (1973), Marks (1974), Speed, Hocking, and Hackney (1978), and Spinner and Gabriel (1981),‡ or better, a statistician For most purposes, the authors favor the most conservative alternative in which the effect being tested is required to add unique information with respect to all other parameters in the model.§

## CHAPTER SUMMARY

ANOVA is a very useful statistical model; the effects of the two or more independent variables (factors) can be assessed separately and simultaneously. In this chapter, two-factor ANOVA has been considered—the simplest example of a factorial design. In addition to testing main effects, ANOVA can identify interactions between factors. If there are particular combinations of two factors that result in performance above or below what would be expected by considering the two factors separately, the factors are said to interact. The absence of interaction indicates that the pattern of results on factor $A$ is

*A rare exception could occur if the second factor greatly reduced the degrees of freedom for $MS_e$, $\nu_e$. For example, if $J = 2$ and $K = 5$, and $n_{\bullet\bullet} = 20$, the critical $F$ for a two-factor design with $\alpha = .05$ is ${}_{.95}F_{1,10} = 4.96$, and for a one-factor is ${}_{.95}F_{1,18} = 4.41$. This increase in critical value for $F$ might offset the larger observed $F$-ratio.

†See Kerlinger and Pedhazur (1973, part 2) for further details on the use of dummy coding in analyzing ANOVA with unequal $n$'s.

‡This is an excellent nonmathematical treatment of the issues and consequences of nonorthogonal designs.

§This is the "regression" option of the SPSS *analysis of variance and covariance* program (Nie et al., 1975, Chapter 22) and BMD 05V (Dixon, 1970).

constant across all levels of factor $B$; the results for factor $A$ are generalizable over all categories of factor $B$.

Significant interactions should be graphed to clarify the nature of the relationships. Three-factor interaction assesses the generalizability of two-factor configurations across the levels of the third factor.

In addition to detecting interaction and assessing generalizability, factorial designs usually are more powerful than one-factor ANOVA designs. The gain in power results when either (1) the second factor is related to the dependent variable or (2) there is an interaction between the factors.

In ANOVA with two or more factors it is assumed that the observations within each cell are independent and are a random sample from a population of observations that is normally distributed. It is further assumed that the cell variances in the population are equal. ANOVA is quite robust to nonnormality and, if the design is balanced, to violations of the homogeneity of variance assumption.

The procedures for two-factor ANOVA extend logically to ANOVA designs having three or more factors. In balanced ANOVA the mean squares for all main effects and interactions are orthogonal, hence each effect is assessing unique, nonredundant information. Any combination of significant effects is possible. In unbalanced ANOVA the effects are not orthogonal and the analyses and interpretations are much more complex.


## MASTERY TEST

For questions 1 to 10: suppose a study was made of attendance of elementary, junior high, and senior high school students for three ethnic groups (I, II, and III).

1. If a two-factor ANOVA were used, what are the two independent variables?

2. What is the dependent variable?

3. How many levels (categories) are there of each factor?

4. The design can be described as a ____ design.
   a.  2 × 2    d.  3 × 2
   b.  2 × 3    e.  3 × 4
   c.  3 × 3

5. Portions of the ANOVA table from the analysis are given. Complete the table.

| Source of Variation | SS | $\nu$ | MS | F |
|---|---|---|---|---|
| School level (S) | 900 | ☐ | ☐ | ☐ |
| Ethnicity (E) | ☐ | 2 | 250 | ☐ |
| $S \times E$ | 1,200 | ☐ | ☐ | ☐ |
| Within | 44,550 | 891 | ☐ | |

6. What are the critical $F$-values for the two main effects and for the interaction with $\alpha = .05$, $\alpha = .01$, and $\alpha = .001$?

7. Can the null hypotheses for the two main effects be rejected? At what level of significance?

8. Does the $F$-test for the $S \times E$ interaction indicate that the attendance trend did not follow the same pattern for the three ethnic groups; that is, is the $S \times E$ interaction statistically significant? Can the null hypothesis be rejected at $\alpha = .001$?

9. Which of the following figures (a), (b), or (c), is *consistent* with all the information in the ANOVA table in Question 5?

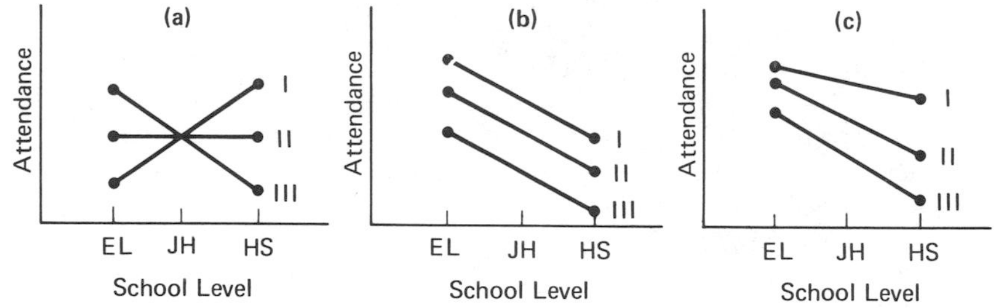


10. If a one-factor ANOVA had been performed comparing the three school levels, are the following true or false?
    a. The $F$-ratio for school level would have been less.
    b. The interaction of school level and ethnicity would not be tested.
11. Which of the following are advantages of two-factor ANOVA over a one-factor ANOVA?
    a. The denominator of the $F$-test is increased.
    b. The generalizability of the results is enhanced.
    c. Interaction between factors can be identified.
    d. Power is often increased.
12. Given a 2 X 4, $A \times B$ ANOVA: $SS_{total} = 100$
$$SS_{A+B+AB} = 50$$
$$SS_A = 25$$
$$SS_B = 10$$
    a. What is the value of $SS_{within}$?
    b. What is the value of $SS_{A \times B}$?
    c. What are the degrees of freedom for the $A \times B$ interaction?
    d. What is $MS$ for the $A \times B$ interaction?
13. Among $n_{\bullet 1}$, $n_{1 \bullet}$, and $n_{\bullet\bullet}$, which is the largest?
14. Graph the interaction of factor $B$, traditional orthography (TO) versus initial teaching alphabet (ITA), and factor $A$, sex, from the following cell means (expressed in grade-placement units) on a standardized reading test. Does the interaction appear to be significant?

| | | *Orthography* $B_1$ (TO) | $B_2$ (ITA) |
|---|---|---|---|
| *Sex* | Boys $A_1$ | $\bar{X}_{11} = 4.6$ | $\bar{X}_{12} = 4.5$ |
| | Girls $A_2$ | $\bar{X}_{21} = 4.9$ | $\bar{X}_{22} = 4.8$ |

15. The following figure represents cell, row, and column *population* means (parameters) in a two-factor ANOVA design.

| | | *Factor B* $B_1$ | $B_2$ | $B_3$ | |
|---|---|---|---|---|---|
| *Factor A* | $A_1$ | $\mu_{11} = 16$ | $\mu_{12} = 11$ | $\mu_{13} = 6$ | $\mu_{1\bullet} = 11$ |
| | $A_2$ | $\mu_{21} = 4$ | $\mu_{22} = 9$ | $\mu_{23} = 14$ | $\mu_{2\bullet} = 9$ |
| | | $\mu_{\bullet 1} = 10$ | $\mu_{\bullet 2} = 10$ | $\mu_{\bullet 3} = 10$ | $\mu_{\bullet\bullet} = \mu = 10$ |

a. Is $H_{0_1}$: $\Sigma \alpha_j^2 = 0$?
b. Is $H_{0_2}$: $\Sigma \beta_k^2 = 0$?
c. Is $H_{0_3}$: $\Sigma_k \Sigma_j (\alpha\beta_{jk})^2 = 0$?

16. Which hypotheses in Question 15 pertain to main effects and which to interaction?
17. In Question 9 do any of the interaction figures appear to be disordinal?
18. For the data in Question 14, assuming a balanced design,
Give the numerical values for
a. $\hat{\alpha}_1, \hat{\alpha}_2, \hat{\beta}_1, \hat{\beta}_2, \bar{X}_{\bullet\bullet}$
b. Estimate $\widehat{\alpha\beta}_{11}$; $\widehat{\alpha\beta}_{jk} = \bar{X}_{jk} - (\bar{X}_{\bullet\bullet} + \hat{\alpha}_j + \hat{\beta}_k)$
19. Assuming the ANOVA table in Question 5 is from a balanced ("equal $n$") design,
a. What is the value of $s_{\bar{X}_{j\bullet}} = \sqrt{MS_e/n_{j\bullet}}$?
b. If $\bar{X}_{2\bullet} = 10$, give the .95 CI for $\mu_{2\bullet}$.
20. How does the $F$-ratio for the school-level effect in Question 5 compare with what it would have been in a one-factor ANOVA?
21. In Question 5 $(s_{11}^2 + s_{12}^2 + \ldots + s_{33}^2)/9 = ?$
22. In a two-factor ANOVA the $JK$ within-cell variance estimates (the $s_{ij}^2$'s) are assumed to be from the same population, that is, $H_0$: $\sigma_{11}^2 = \sigma_{12}^2 = \ldots = \sigma_{JK}^2$. Generalizing from Chapter 16, when can this assumption be ignored? Which tests (presented in this text) could be used to test this assumption?
23. In Question 15, if $\sigma_\epsilon^2 = 60$ and $n = 10$,
a. what is the expected value of $MS_A$: $E(MS_A) = \sigma_\epsilon^2 + n_{j\bullet} \Sigma\alpha_j^2/(J-1)$?
b. what is the value of $E(MS_B)$?
c. what is the value of $E(MS_w)$?
24. In Question 14 if $n = 50$ and $MS_w = 2.0$, what is the .90 CI for $\mu_{22}$?

## *PROBLEMS AND EXERCISES*

1. Using a two-factor-ANOVA, analyze the following scores on a fifty-item vocabulary test administered to twenty-four students of high and average intelligence after one year of studying a foreign language under one of three methods with $\alpha = .10$ (see Table 18.3 for computational steps).

| | | *Method* | | |
|---|---|---|---|---|
| | | Aural-Oral Method (A) $B_1$ | Translation Method (T) $B_2$ | Combined Method (C) $B_3$ |
| High (IQ ≥ 115) | $A_1$ | 37<br>30<br>26<br>31 | 27<br>24<br>22<br>19 | 20<br>31<br>24<br>21 |
| Average (IQ ≤ 114) | $A_2$ | 32<br>19<br>37<br>28 | 20<br>23<br>14<br>15 | 17<br>18<br>23<br>18 |

2. Perform the Tukey HSD multiple comparisons for the method effect of Problem 1.
   a. $s_{\bar{X}_{\bullet k}} = \sqrt{MS_w / n_{\bullet k}} = ?$
   b. For $\alpha = .05$, what is $HSD_{.05} = {}_{1-\alpha}q_{\nu_e, J}(s_{\bar{X}})$?
   c. Which null hypotheses for difference in means can be rejected?
3. A researcher is studying the effects on learning of inserting questions into instructional materials. There is some doubt whether these questions would be more effective preceding or following the passage about which the question is posed. In addition the researcher wonders if the effect of the position of the questions is the same for factual questions and for questions that require the learner to compose a thoughtful and original response. A group of twenty-four students is split at random into four groups of six students each. One group is assigned to each of the four combinations of factor $B$, "position of question (before versus after the passage)" and factor $A$, "type of question (factual versus thought-provoking)." After ten hours of studying under these conditions, the twenty-four students are given a fifty-item test on the content of the instructional materials. The following test scores are obtained. (Round means to two decimal place.)

| | | | *Position of Question* | | | |
|---|---|---|---|---|---|---|
| | | | Before $B_1$ | | After $B_2$ | |
| *Nature of Question* | Fact | $A_1$ | 19 | 23 | 31 | 28 |
| | | | 29 | 26 | 26 | 27 |
| | | | 30 | 17 | 35 | 32 |
| | Thought | $A_2$ | 27 | 21 | 36 | 29 |
| | | | 20 | 26 | 39 | 31 |
| | | | 15 | 24 | 41 | 35 |

   a. Perform a two-factor ANOVA on the data. Test the null hypotheses for both main effects and the interaction effect with $\alpha = 10$.
   b. Graph the interaction using the procedure illustrated in Figure 18.14; place the nature-of-the-question factor on the abscissa.
4. A study by Carrier and Titus (1981) investigated the effects of pretraining in notetaking on learning from lectures. A second factor was the mode of test expected: one-third of the students were told they would be given a multiple-choice test, another third, an essay test; the final third were told only that they would be tested. A thirty-five-item objective test and an essay test were given following the lecture. Means and standard deviations for the 2 X 3 ANOVA design are given for the objective test.
   a. Perform the ANOVA assuming $n = 16$ students were randomly assigned to each cell, with $\alpha = .10$ for both main effects and the interaction.
   b. Graph the interaction to facilitate its interpretation.
   c. Use the Hartley $F_{max}$ test to test whether the heterogeneity of scores if affected by the treatment combinations ($\alpha = .05$).

| | | *Mode-of-test Expected* | | |
|---|---|---|---|---|
| | | MC | Essay | Unspecified |
| *Treatment* | Pretrained (*E*) | $\bar{X}_{11} = 28.1$<br>$s_{11} = 3.5$ | $\bar{X}_{12} = 23.6$<br>$s_{12} = 6.6$ | $\bar{X}_{13} = 25.3$<br>$s_{13} = 4.8$ |
| | Not Pretrained (*C*) | $\bar{X}_{21} = 25.1$<br>$s_{21} = 5.0$ | $\bar{X}_{22} = 26.6$<br>$s_{22} = 5.5$ | $\bar{X}_{23} = 26.7$<br>$s_{23} = 4.9$ |

5. For each of the following arrangements of data, graph the interaction of factor $B$, sex, with factor $A$, "treatments." Place factor $B$ on the abscissa so that each treatment level yields one line in the graph. Which cases show ordinal interaction (all questions of statistical significance aside)? Which show disordinal interaction?

(a)

| Treatments | Male | Female |
|---|---|---|
| 1 | $\bar{X}_{11} = 18.65$ | $\bar{X}_{12} = 21.68$ |
| 2 | $\bar{X}_{21} = 25.20$ | $\bar{X}_{22} = 14.17$ |
| 3 | $\bar{X}_{31} = 16.44$ | $\bar{X}_{32} = 17.89$ |

(b)

| Treatments | Male | Female |
|---|---|---|
| 1 | $\bar{X}_{11} = 19.63$ | $\bar{X}_{12} = 14.81$ |
| 2 | $\bar{X}_{21} = 10.21$ | $\bar{X}_{22} = 13.55$ |

(c)

| Treatments | Male | Female |
|---|---|---|
| 1 | $\bar{X}_{11} = 9.43$ | $\bar{X}_{12} = 13.95$ |
| 2 | $\bar{X}_{21} = 11.06$ | $\bar{X}_{22} = 15.58$ |

6. In one study a group of 240 sixth-grade pupils were randomly assigned to one of two levels of reading difficulty: "grade six reading difficulty" or "grade three reading difficulty." The pupils read a chapter in a science text, at either the third-grade or sixth-grade reading difficulty level. A 129-item multiple-choice test was administered at the end of the experiment to assess comprehension. Within both levels of reading difficulty, pupils were classified as either high, average, or low scorers on the reading section of the Stanford Achievement Test. The following data were obtained for the two levels of reading difficulty and three levels of reading achievement:

| Reading achievement | Reading difficulty: Grade 6 | Reading difficulty: Grade 3 |
|---|---|---|
| High | $n = 40$<br>$\bar{X}_{11} = 89.93$<br>$s_{11} = 12.02$ | $n = 40$<br>$\bar{X}_{12} = 93.89$<br>$s_{12} = 13.02$ |
| Average | $n = 40$<br>$\bar{X}_{21} = 70.79$<br>$s_{21} = 14.76$ | $n = 40$<br>$\bar{X}_{22} = 72.55$<br>$s_{22} = 15.90$ |
| Low | $n = 40$<br>$\bar{X}_{31} = 52.09$<br>$s_{31} = 11.30$ | $n = 40$<br>$\bar{X}_{32} = 56.84$<br>$s_{32} = 12.21$ |

a. Perform a two-factor ANOVA on these data. Test all three null hypotheses at the .05 level of significance (*Hint:* $MS_w$ is the average of the six within-cell *variances*.)

b. If the scores had been converted to percent-correct scores before the ANOVA, how would the ANOVA results have differed?

7. The following figure is based on the 1970, 1973, and 1977 National Assessments in Science. The results are given for three age levels (9, 13, and 17) and by content area (physical versus biological science). Each mean is based on a large, nationally representative sample. Assume a three-factor ANOVA was used to analyze these data.
   a. Identify the three factors.
   b. What is the dependent variable?
   c. Does the content-area ($C$) main effect appear to be significant?
   d. Does the year ($Y$) main effect appear to be significant (i.e., is an "achievement decline" evident in the data)?
   e. Aggregate the results to construct the year-by-content ($YC$) interaction graph. (Place "year" on the $x$-axis.)
   f. Does the $YC$ interaction appear to be significant? Explain. (Recall that the $n$'s are large.)
   g. Does the $YCA$ interaction appear to be significant? Explain.

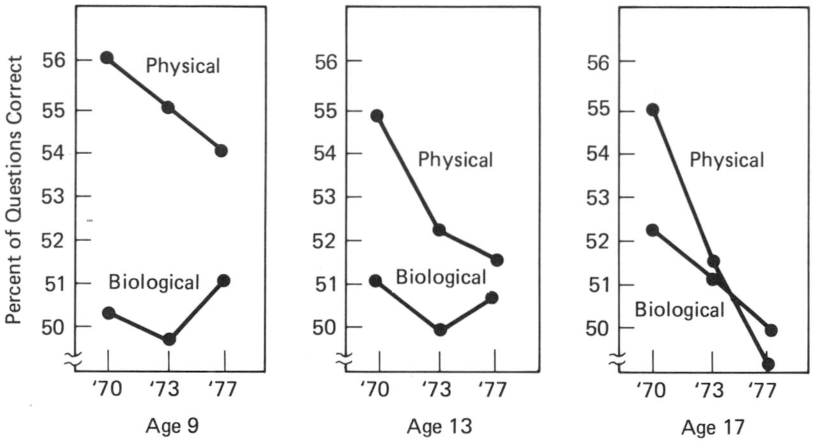


8. Given are the results of a three-factor ANOVA with five observations per cell ($n = 5$) (Hopkins and Kretke, 1976).
   a. Give the ANOVA table that would have resulted if the ethnicity factor had been ignored ($n = 10$).
   b. Give the ANOVA table if both ethnicity and sex had been ignored ($n = 20$).
   c. Was power lost as $n$/cell decreased?

**A Treatments-by-Sex-by-Ethnicity ANOVA of The Sixty Observations from Three Treatment Groups**

| *Source* | *SS* | $\nu$ | *MS* | *F* |
|---|---|---|---|---|
| Treatment ($T$) | 520.00 | 2 | 260.00 | 6.50 |
| Sex ($S$) | 60.00 | 1 | 60.00 | 1.50 |
| Ethnicity ($E$) | 240.00 | 1 | 240.00 | 6.00 |
| $T \times S$ | 120.00 | 2 | 60.00 | 1.50 |
| $T \times E$ | 280.00 | 2 | 140.00 | 3.50 |
| $S \times E$ | 93.75 | 1 | 93.75 | 2.34 |
| $T \times S \times E$ | 360.00 | 2 | 180.00 | 4.50 |
| Within | 1920.00 | 48 | 40.00 | |

9. Suppose prior to performing the study reported in the previous question that you were to estimate the power for detecting the treatment effect under conditions such that the treatment means, expressed as z-scores in the untreated population were $\mu_{1\bullet\bullet} = -.5$, $\mu_{2\bullet\bullet} = 0$, $\mu_{3\bullet\bullet} = .5$, and $\alpha = .05$.

## ANSWERS TO MASTERY TEST

1. School level and ethnicity
2. Attendance
3. Three levels of ethnicity and three of school type
4. c
5.

| *Source* | *SS* | $\nu$ | *MS* | *F* |
|---|---|---|---|---|
| School level (*S*) | 900 | 2 | 450 | 9.0 |
| Ethnicity (*E*) | 500 | 2 | 250 | 5.0 |
| $S \times E$ | 1,200 | 4 | 300 | 6.0 |
| Within | 44,550 | 891 | 50 | |

6. ${}_{.95}F_{2,891} \doteq 3.00$; ${}_{.95}F_{4,891} \doteq 2.38$
${}_{.99}F_{2,891} \doteq 4.62$; ${}_{.99}F_{4,891} \doteq 3.34$
${}_{.999}F_{2,891} \doteq 6.95$; ${}_{.999}F_{4,891} \doteq 4.65$
7. Yes. $H_{0_1}$: $\mu_E = \mu_J = \mu_S$ can be rejected at $\alpha = .001$; $9.0 > 6.95$; $p < .001$. $H_{0_1}$: $\mu_I = \mu_{II} = \mu_{III}$ can be rejected at $\alpha = .01$; $5.0 > 4.62$; $p < .01$.
8. Yes, $F = 6.0 > 4.65 \doteq {}_{.999}F_{4,891}$; $p < .001$. Yes, the null hypothesis can be rejected with $\alpha = .001$.
9. Only Figure C is consistent with the ANOVA table. (Figure A has no main effects for factors *A* and *B*; Figure B has no $A \times B$ interaction.)
10. a. True (the numerator of the *F*-ratio would remain unchanged, but the denominator of the *F*-ratio would have increased):

$$MS_w = \frac{500 + 1{,}200 + 45{,}000}{2 + 4 + 900} = 51.55$$

$$F = \frac{450}{51.55} = 8.73$$

b. true
11. b, c, and d
12. a. $SS_{\text{within}} = SS_{\text{total}} - SS_{A+B+AB} = 100 - 50 = 50$
b. $SS_{A \times B} = SS_{A+B+AB} - SS_A - SS_B = 50 - 25 - 10 = 15$
c. $(J - 1)(K - 1) = (2 - 1)(4 - 1) = 3$
d. $MS = SS/\nu = \frac{15}{3} = 5$
13. $n_{\bullet\bullet}$ is the largest; $n_{\bullet\bullet}$ is the total number of all observations, whereas $n_{\bullet 1}$ is the total from column 1 and $n_{1\bullet}$ is the total in row 1.
14. No

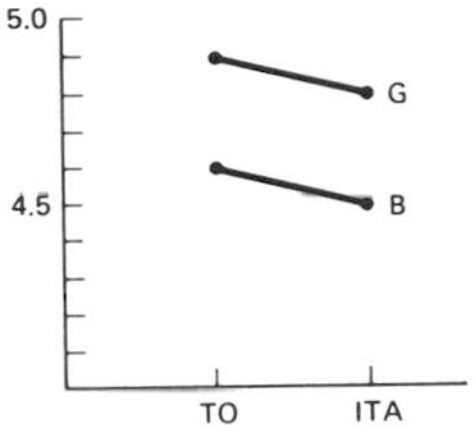


Or,

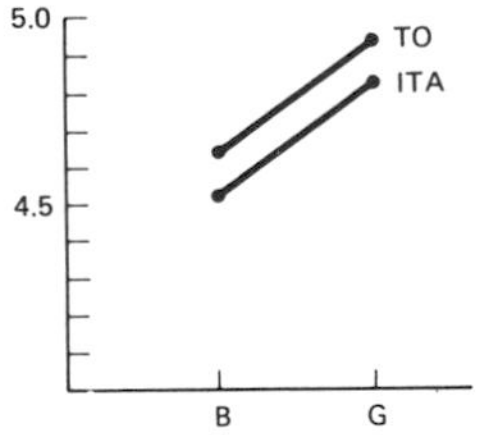


15. a. No
b. Yes
c. No
16. $H_{0_1}$ and $H_{0_2}$ pertain to main effects; the interaction null hypothesis is represented by $H_{0_3}$.
17. Yes, figure *a*
18. a. $\overline{X}_{1\bullet} = 4.55$, $\overline{X}_{2\bullet} = 4.85$, $\overline{X}_{\bullet\bullet} = 4.70$, $\overline{X}_{\bullet 1} = 4.75$, and $\overline{X}_{\bullet 2} = 4.65$, thus $\hat{\alpha}_1 = \overline{X}_{1\bullet} - \overline{X}_{\bullet\bullet} = -.15$, $\hat{\alpha}_2 = .15$, $\hat{\beta}_1 = .05$, $\hat{\beta}_2 = -.05$

b. $\widehat{\alpha\beta}_{11} = 4.60 - 4.70 - (-.15) - .05 = 0$

19. a. $s_{\bar{X}_{j.}} = \sqrt{50/300} = .41$
    b. $10 \pm (1.96)(.41) = 10 \pm .80$, or (9.20, 10.80)

20. It is larger.

21. $MS_w = 50$

22. When $n_{jk}$'s are equal; Bartlett, Hartley, or Scheffé tests

23. a. $E(MS_A) = 60 + 10(3)\,[(1)^2 + (-1)^2]/(2-1) = 120$
    b. 60
    c. 60

24. $s_{\bar{X}_{22}} = \sqrt{MS_w/n} = \sqrt{2.0/50} = .20$; .90 CI $= 4.80 \pm (2.01)(.20) = 4.80 \pm .40$, or (4.40, 5.20)

## *ANSWERS TO PROBLEMS*

1.

| | | Method | | | | |
|---|---|---|---|---|---|---|
| | | $B_1$ | $B_2$ | $B_3$ | $A$ Means | |
| IQ | $A_1$ | $\bar{X}_{11} = 31.0$<br>$s^2_{11} = 20.67$ | $\bar{X}_{12} = 23.0$<br>$s^2_{12} = 11.33$ | $\bar{X}_{13} = 24.0$<br>$s^2_{13} = 24.67$ | $\bar{X}_{1.} = 26.0$<br>$\hat{\alpha}_1 = 2$ | |
| | $A_2$ | $\bar{X}_{21} = 29.0$<br>$s^2_{21} = 58.00$ | $\bar{X}_{22} = 18.0$<br>$s^2_{22} = 18.00$ | $\bar{X}_{23} = 19.0$<br>$s^{23} = 7.33$ | $\bar{X}_{2.} = 22.0$<br>$\hat{\alpha}_2 = -2$ | $(n_{j.} = 12)$ |
| $B$ Means | | $\bar{X}_{.1} = 30.0$<br>$\hat{\beta}_1 = 6$ | $\bar{X}_{.2} = 20.5$<br>$\hat{\beta}_2 = -3.5$ | $\bar{X}_{.3} = 21.5$<br>$\hat{\beta}_3 = -2.5$ | $\bar{X}_{..} = 24.0$<br>$(n_{..} = 24)$ | |

$(n_{.k} = 8)$

$$SS_A = n_{k\bullet} \sum_j \hat{\alpha}_j^2 = 12[(2)^2 + (-2)^2] = 96; MS_A = 96$$

$$SS_B = nJ_k \sum_k \hat{\beta}_k^2 = 8[(6)^2 + (-3.5)2 + (-2.5)^2] = 436; MS_B = 218$$

$$SS_{A\text{-}B+AB} = n \sum_k \sum_j (\bar{X}_{jk} - \bar{X}_{\bullet\bullet})^2 = 4[(7)^2 + (5)^2 + \cdots + (-5)^2] = 544$$

$$SS_{AB} = 544 - 96 - 436 = 12; MS_{AB} = 12/2 = 6$$

$$MS_w = \sum_k \sum_j s_{jk}^2/(JK) = [20.67 + \cdots + 7.33)/6 = 23.3$$

| Source | $\nu$ | MS | F |
|---|---|---|---|
| $A$ | 1 | 96 | 4.12[a] |
| $B$ | 2 | 218 | 9.36[b] |
| $A \times B$ | 2 | 6 | .26 |
| Within | 18 | 23.3 | |

[a] $p < .10$; ${}_{.90}F_{1.18} = 3.01$, ${}_{.95}F_{1.18} = 4.41$, ${}_{.99}F_{2.18} = 6.01$, ${}_{.999}F_{2.18} = 10.4$

[b] $p < .01$

2. a. $s_{\bar{X}\cdot k} = \sqrt{23.3/8} = 1.71$
   b. ${}_{.95}q_{18,3} = 3.61$, $\text{HSD}_{.05} = (3.61)(1.71) = 6.17$
   c. $\bar{X}_A - \bar{X}_T = 30.0 - 20.5 = 9.5$; reject $H_0$
      $\bar{X}_A - \bar{X}_C = 30.0 - 21.5 = 8.5$; reject $H_0$
      $\bar{X}_C - \bar{X}_T = 21.5 - 20.5 = 1.0$; $H_0$ is tenable.

3. a.

| | $B_1$ | $B_2$ | $A$ Means | |
|---|---|---|---|---|
| $A_1$ | $\overline{X}_{11} = 24.00$ <br> $s_{11}^2 = 28.00$ | $\overline{X}_{12} = 29.83$ <br> $s_{12}^2 = 11.77$ | $\overline{X}_{1.} = 26.92$ <br> $\hat{\alpha}_1 = -.87$ | |
| $A_2$ | $\overline{X}_{21} = 22.17$ <br> $s_{21}^2 = 19.77$ | $\overline{X}_{22} = 35.17$ <br> $s_{22}^2 = 20.97$ | $\overline{X}_{2.} = 28.67$ <br> $\hat{\alpha}_2 = .87$ | $(n_{j.} = 12)$ |
| $B$ Means | $\overline{X}_{.1} = 23.08$ <br> $\hat{\beta}_1 = -4.71$ | $\overline{X}_{.2} = 32.50$ <br> $\hat{\beta}_2 = 4.71$ | $\overline{X}_{..} = 27.79$ <br> $(n_{..} = 24)$ | |

$(n_{.k} = 12)$

1. $SS_A = 12[(-.87)^2 + (.87)^2] = 18.17; MS_A = 18.17$
2. $SS_B = 12[(-4.71)^2 + (4.71)^2] = 532.42; MS_B = 532.42$
3. $SS_{A+B+AB} = 6[(22.27 - 27.79)^2 + (7.38)^2 + (-3.79)^2 + (2.04)^2]$
   $= 6(104.57) = 627.45$
4. $SS_{AB} = 627.45 - 18.17 - 532.42 = 76.86; MS_{AB} = 76.86$
5. $MS_w = (28.00 + 19.77 + 11.77 + 20.77)/4 = 20.13$

| *Source* | $\nu$ | *MS* | *F* |
|---|---|---|---|
| *A* (Question) | 1 | 18.17 | .90 |
| *B* (Position) | 1 | 532.42 | 26.45[a] |
| $A \times B$ | 1 | 76.86 | 3.82[b] |
| Within | 20 | 20.13 | |

[a] $p < .001$
[b] $p < .10$

b. $s_{\overline{X}} = \sqrt{20.13/6} = 1.83$
$s_w = \sqrt{20.13} = 4.49$

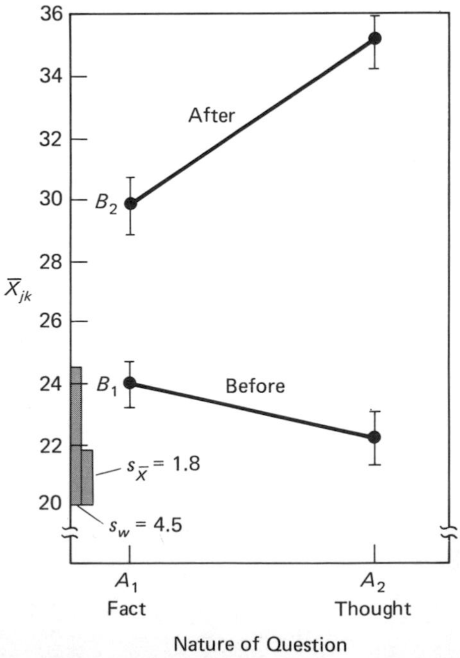

4. a.

| *Source* | $\nu$ | *MS* | *F* |
|---|---|---|---|
| Treatment (*T*) | 1 | 5.08 | .19 |
| Mode (*M*) | 2 | 18.24 | .69 |
| $T \times M$ | 2 | 77.08 | 2.93[a] |
| Within | 90 | 26.35 | |

[a] $p < .10$

c. $F_{max} = (6.6)^2/(3.5)^2 = 3.56$ not significant as the .05 level.

5. Case *a* shows a disordinal interaction. Case *b* shows an ordinal interaction. In case *c* there is no interaction since the two lines of the graph are parallel.
6. a. ANOVA table:

| *Source* | $\nu$ | *MS* | *F* |
|---|---|---|---|
| Reading achievement (*A*) | 2 | 28,103.97 | 158.86[a] |
| Reading difficulty (*D*) | 1 | 730.81 | 4.13[b] |
| $A \times D$ | 2 | 48.02 | 0.27 |
| Within | 234 | 176.91 | |

[a] $p < .001$

[b] $p < .05$

b. Since $X\% = (X/129) = .775X$, $s^2_{\%} = (.775)^2 s^2 = .60s^2$ (Sec. 5.11), hence all *MS*-values would be .60 of their value in the preceding ANOVA table. The *F*-ratios would be unchanged, as with any linear transformation of *X*.

7. a. Year (*Y*), age (*A*), and content-area (*C*)
b. percent-correct score on the science test
c. Yes, ($\bar{X}_{phys.} > \bar{X}_{biol.}$);
d. Yes, ($\bar{X}_{'70} > \bar{X}_{'73} > \bar{X}_{'77}$)
e.

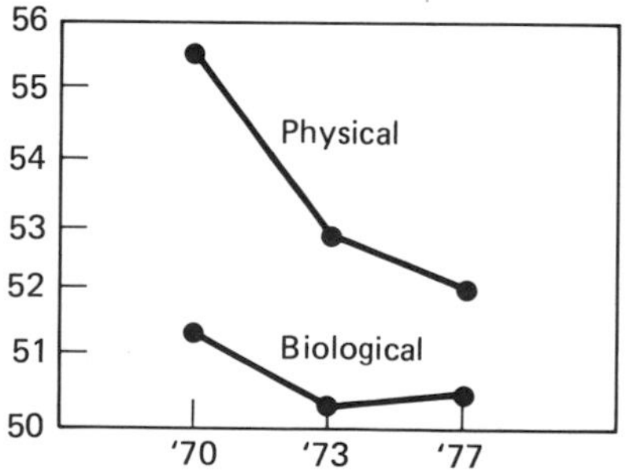

f. Yes; the *difference* between the content-area means decreased progressively between 1970 and 1977.

g. Yes; at age seventeen performance has steadily decreased in both physical and biological science, whereas at ages nine and thirteen the 1977 biological science scores "rebounded" to the 1970 levels. Thus an achievement decline in physical science is evidenced at all three age levels, in biological science only at age seventeen.

8. a.

| *Source* | *SS* | *v* | *MS* | *F* |
|---|---|---|---|---|
| Treatments (*T*) | 520.00 | 2 | 260.00 | 4.85 |
| Sex (*S*) | 60.00 | 1 | 60.00 | 1.12 |
| $T \times S$ | 120.00 | 2 | 60.00 | 1.12 |
| Within | 2893.75 | 54 | 53.59 | |

b.

| *Source* | *SS* | *v* | *MS* | *F* |
|---|---|---|---|---|
| Treatments (*T*) | 520.00 | 2 | 260.000 | 4.82 |
| Within | 3073.75 | 57 | 53.925 | |

c. No, on the contrary $MS_w$ is much less in three factor ANOVA where $n = 5$.

9. $$\phi = \sqrt{\frac{20[(-.5)^2 + 0 + (.5)^2]}{(3)1}} = 1.83,$$

and from Table G, power $\doteq .80$

# 19

# MULTI-FACTOR ANALYSIS OF VARIANCE: Random, Mixed, and Fixed Effects

## 19.1 INTRODUCTION

This chapter has three purposes: (1) to introduce the *random-effects* (or random) model (in contrast to the fixed-effects model presented in Chaps. 16 and 18); (2) to introduce the *mixed-effects* (or *mixed*) ANOVA model (a combination of the fixed and random ANOVA models); (3) to introduce the distinction between *nested* versus *crossed* factors.*

## 19.2 THE RANDOM-EFFECTS ANOVA MODEL

This section introduces an analysis of variance model and applications of the model that are fundamentally different from those of the fixed-effects ANOVA model of Chapters 16 and 18. Fortunately, many similarities between the techniques seen in Chapters 16 and 18 and those to be presented here should substantially facilitate learning the material

*The concepts of this chapter are complex. Careful reading and rereading will be required to assimilate its content and procedures.

in this chapter. The model that will now be developed is called the *random* or *random-effects* analysis of variance model, in contrast to the fixed-effects ANOVA model in Chapters 16 and 18. It is much simpler to comprehend the meaning of fixed effects when they can be contrasted with random effects. In the ANOVA model of Chapters 16 and 18 the primary interest was in making statistical inferences about the set of main effects $\alpha_1, \ldots, \alpha_J$. The inference to be made was from a set of sample data ($J$ groups of $n$ persons) to the $J$ groups in the population. In theory, in each of an infinite number of replications of the experiment there were $n$ persons within each of $J$ levels. The interest was in the $J$ means in the population—or equivalently, the $J$ main effects. Only replications of the experiment in which the *same* $J$ treatment levels appeared were considered. In a sense, then, the $J$ levels in the population were "fixed" (as opposed to varying, in the random model). With a random factor the *sample* of $J$ levels in each replication of the experiment is allowed to vary randomly across replications; levels $A$, $B$, and $C$ will be sampled this time and levels $D$, $E$, and $F$ next time.

This procedure would be adopted if one were interested in the amount of variance in the means of a large collection of levels, only a few of which could be observed in one experiment. For a given experiment a sample of $J$ levels could be randomly selected from a large collection of levels and then samples of size $n$ observations could be randomly selected from each level. If the experiment were run again, the levels would not be "fixed," so that the same $J$ levels would not be represented again; rather, a different random sample of $J$ levels would be drawn.

As there were "effects" of the form $\alpha_j = \mu_j - \mu$ in the fixed-effects model, so there are effects of the form $a_j = \mu_j - \mu$ for this new model.* However, whereas formerly the complete set of $J$ $\alpha_j$'s was present in every replication of the fixed-effects analysis, now the case of having only a *random* sample of the $a_j$ effects present in a replication of the experiment will be considered, hence the name *random* or *random-effects* ANOVA model. Figure 19.1 summarizes this distinction between the fixed-effects and random-effects models.

A study by Bennet (1972) illustrates a random-effects ANOVA model. He studied the magnitude of the teacher effect on first-grade pupils' reading performance and asked how much of the variance among pupils' end-of-year reading scores is attributable to differences among teachers? The random model answers how much the $\mu_j$'s

**FIGURE 19.1. Representation of fixed-effects and random-effects ANOVA models.**

| Fixed-effects model ($J = 3$) | | Random-effects model ($J = 3$) | |
|---|---|---|---|
| $X_{ij} = \mu + \alpha_j + \epsilon_{ij}$ | | $X_{ij} = \mu + a_j + \epsilon_{ij}$ | |
| Main effects: $\alpha_1, \alpha_2, \alpha_3$. | | Main effects: $a_1, a_2, \ldots, a_\infty$ | |
| Replication of experiment | Main effects present in replication | Replication of experiment | Main effects present in replication |
| 1 | $\alpha_1, \alpha_2, \alpha_3$ | 1 | $a_5, a_{31}, a_8$ |
| 2 | $\alpha_1, \alpha_2, \alpha_3$ | 2 | $a_{16}, a_3, a_9$ |
| 3 | $\alpha_1, \alpha_2, \alpha_3$ | 3 | $a_{21}, a_{11}, a_{50}$ |

*Lowercase Roman letters are commonly used to denote random effects, in contrast to the use of lowercase Greek letters for fixed effects.

differ and how variable are the $\mu_j$'s. The variance of the $\hat{\mu}_j$'s tells one what sort of differences to expect in the $\mu_j$'s.

To formalize the random-effects model, suppose there is a virtually infinite population of teachers, each one having a mean $\mu_j$. Denote the average of all these $\mu_j$'s by $\mu$. The $i$th student earns a score of $X_{ij}$ with the $j$th teacher. The difference between the $i$th student's score with teacher $j$ and the mean of all students' scores for that teacher is denoted by $\epsilon_{ij}$; hence,

$$X_{ij} = \mu_j + \epsilon_{ij} \tag{19.1}$$

where $X_{ij}$ is the score for student $i$ in level $j$ of the factor, that is, "teacher $j$," $\mu_j$ is the mean of all students' scores for the $j$th level of the random factor, and $\epsilon_{ij}$ is the deviation of the $i$th student's score from the mean of all students' scores at the $j$th level of the factor.

The model in Equation 19.1 will be altered in form slightly by deviating the $\mu_j$'s around $\mu$, the mean of all the $\mu_j$'s, as follows:

$$X_{ij} = \mu + (\mu_j - \mu) + \epsilon_{jj} \tag{19.2}$$

A notation simplification of Equation 19.2 will put the random-effects ANOVA model into its customary form:

$$X_{ij} = \mu + a_j + \epsilon_{ij} \tag{19.3}$$

where

$$a_j = \mu_j - \mu \quad \text{and} \quad \epsilon_{ij} = X_{ij} - \mu_j$$

Suppose that $\mu$, the mean test score of all students in the student population over all teachers in the population of teachers, is 30; and suppose that the population of students would average 4 points *above* 30 if they had teacher number 9, that is, $a_9 = 4$. Finally suppose that the fourth student scored 8 points *below* the average of all students having this teacher; that is, $\epsilon_{49} = -8$. If the model in Equation 19.3 holds, the test score of the fourth student will be

$$X_{ij} = \mu + a_j + \epsilon_{ij} = X_{49} = \mu + a_9 + \epsilon_{49} = 30 + 4 - 8 = 26$$

Initially, the interest was in the variance of the $\mu_j$'s. How has this concern changed now that the $\mu_j$'s have been "eliminated" from the model? Since $a_j$ is simply $\mu_j$ minus a constant, $\mu$, the variance of the $\mu_j$'s is the same as the variance of the $a_j$'s (Sec. 5.10). Thus, differences in test scores due to teacher differences will be reflected in the variance of the $a_j$'s, that is, in $\sigma_a^2$.

## 19.3 ASSUMPTIONS OF THE RANDOM ANOVA MODEL

Before proceeding to estimate $\sigma_a^2$ and making statistical inferential statements about it, it is necessary to make some assumptions about the model in Equation 19.3:

1. The random-effects, $a_j$, are independent and *normally* distributed with a mean of zero and a variance of $\sigma_a^2$, that is, $a \sim NID(0, \sigma_a^2)$.
2. The error components, $\epsilon_{ij}$'s, are independent and *normally* distributed with mean zero and variance $\sigma_\epsilon^2$, that is, $\epsilon \sim NID(0, \sigma_\epsilon^2)$.

These assumptions have several implications for the study of teacher effects. If the random-effects model is an adequate description of the data in the study of teacher effects, then:

1. The means ($\mu_j$'s) of populations of students' scores for all teachers in the population should appear to be normally distributed around $\mu$ and have a variance of $\sigma_a^2$. Since $a_j = \mu_j - \mu$, the $a_j$'s should have a normal distribution around zero with a variance of $\sigma_a^2$. $a_j$ is estimated by: $\hat{a}_j = \overline{X}_j - \overline{X}_\bullet$
2. The test scores $X_{ij}$ for all students for a given teacher (the $j$th teacher) should be normally distributed around a mean of $\mu_j$ with variance $\sigma_\epsilon^2$. Since $\epsilon_{ij} = X_{ij} - \mu_j$, $\epsilon_{ij}$ will be normally distributed around zero with variance $\sigma_\epsilon^2$. This is assumed to be true for all values of $j$. This is the homogeneous variances assumption.
3. If $e_{ij} = X_{ij} - \overline{X}_j$ and samples of $n$ test scores were taken from the populations of scores for a randomly selected $J$ teachers, the value of $a_j$ would give no information about whether the mean of the $e_{ij}$'s, $\overline{e}_j$, was above or below zero and similarly, the value of $\overline{e}_j$ would give no information about whether a different $\overline{e}_j'$ was above or below zero.

## 19.4 AN EXAMPLE

Techniques for actually estimating both $\sigma_a^2$ and $\sigma_\epsilon^2$ from data are needed. The problem to be solved is one of estimating the variability in test scores due to teachers, $\sigma_a^2$, and the variance among students having the same teacher, $\sigma_\epsilon^2$.

Theoretically, data are gathered in a two-phased sampling plan. First, $J$ levels of the random-effects factor are drawn at random. For example, $J = 5$ teachers from the population of teachers are *randomly* selected. Just as random sampling of persons from populations permits generalizations to the population of persons, randomly sampling levels of a factor allows generalization to a population of levels. Second, a random sample of $n$ observations is drawn from the populations in each of the $J$ levels. Theoretically, there is an infinite number of students for each teacher, even though perhaps only twenty or thirty are currently experimentally accessible. In the example $n = 7$ students are randomly drawn for each of the $J = 5$ teachers. Restricting the $n$'s to be equal is not a matter of convenience here; the methods of this section have never been fully developed for the unequal $n$'s case.

In the study suppose $J = 5$, hence $5a$'s and $Jn = 35\,\epsilon$'s have been sampled. The scores on a reading test are given in Table 19.1.

The computations for the one-factor random-effects ANOVA are identical to the one-factor fixed-effects ANOVA (Chap. 16). The variance of the $J$ sample means, $\overline{X}_1, \ldots, \overline{X}_J$, is used to estimate the variance of the $\mu_j$'s. Likewise, the variance of the $X$'s for each teacher yields an estimate of $\sigma_\epsilon^2$.

**TABLE 19.1 Hypothetical Data from a Study of Teacher Effects on Pupils' Reading Test Scores, $X_{ij}$**

| | | *Teacher (j)* | | |
|---|---|---|---|---|
| *1* | *2* | *3* | *4* | *5* |
| $X_{11} = 35$ | $X_{12} = 36$ | $X_{13} = 28$ | $X_{14} = 27$ | $X_{15} = 32$ |
| $X_{21} = 32$ | $X_{22} = 32$ | $X_{23} = 27$ | $X_{24} = 16$ | $X_{25} = 34$ |
| $X_{31} = 41$ | $X_{32} = 34$ | $X_{33} = 23$ | $X_{34} = 40$ | $X_{35} = 26$ |
| $X_{41} = 42$ | $X_{42} = 40$ | $X_{43} = 15$ | $X_{44} = 32$ | $X_{45} = 28$ |
| $X_{51} = 31$ | $X_{52} = 37$ | $X_{53} = 29$ | $X_{54} = 36$ | $X_{55} = 23$ |
| $X_{61} = 36$ | $X_{62} = 44$ | $X_{63} = 28$ | $X_{64} = 38$ | $X_{65} = 36$ |
| $X_{71} = 35$ | $X_{72} = 42$ | $X_{73} = 33$ | $X_{74} = 22$ | $X_{75} = 28$ |
| $\overline{X}_1 = 36.00$ | $\overline{X}_2 = 37.86$ | $\overline{X}_3 = 26.14$ | $\overline{X}_4 = 30.14$ | $\overline{X}_5 = 29.57$ |
| $s_1^2 = 17.33$ | $s_2^2 = 18.81$ | $s_3^2 = 32.81$ | $s_4^2 = 78.81$ | $s_5^2 = 21.29$ |

## 19.5 MEAN SQUARE WITHIN

As in the fixed-effects ANOVA model (Chaps. 16 and 18), each of the $J$ groups of scores produces a sample variance $s_j^2$ that is an unbiased estimator of $\sigma_\epsilon^2$, the variance of the population of scores for each teacher (level). Since $n$'s are equal, the average of these $J$ sample variances is the best estimator available for $\sigma_\epsilon^2$ (Sec. 16.6). The average within sample variance is called $MS_w$, the mean-square within:

$$MS_w = \frac{s_1^2 + \cdots + s_J^2}{J} = \frac{\sum_{j=1}^{J}\sum_{i=1}^{n}(X_{ij} - \overline{X}_j)^2}{J(n-1)} = \frac{\sum_{j=1}^{J}\sum_{i=1}^{n} x_{ij}^2}{J(n-1)} = \frac{SS_w}{\nu_w} \tag{19.4}$$

$MS_w$* is an estimator of $\sigma_\epsilon^2$ with the following properties:

1. The expected value of $MS_w$ is equal to $\sigma_\epsilon^2$, that is, $E(MS_w) = \sigma_\epsilon^2$. Thus, $MS_w$ is an unbiased estimator of $\sigma_\epsilon^2$, the variance of scores within each factor level.
2. Over replications of the study with $J$ factor levels and $n$ observations within each level, the sampling distribution of $MS_w$ is given by

$$MS_w \sim \sigma^2 \frac{\chi^2_{J(n-1)}}{J(n-1)} = \frac{\chi^2_{\nu_e}}{\nu_e}\sigma^2$$

*An alternate formula is preferred for computational purposes when a calculator is not available:

$$MS_w = \frac{SS_w}{\nu_w} = \frac{\sum_{j=1}^{J}\sum_{i=1}^{n} X_{ij}^2 - \frac{\left(\sum_{j=1}^{J}\sum_{i=1}^{n} X_{ij}\right)^2}{Jn}}{J(n-1)}$$

that is, the sampling distribution of $MS_w$ is $\sigma_\epsilon^2$ times a chi-square distribution with $J(n-1)$ degrees of freedom divided by $J(n-1)$.

It is simple to prove that the expected value of $MS_w$ is $\sigma_\epsilon^2$ if one remembers that the expected value of $\chi^2_{\nu_e}$ is simply $\nu_e$ (Sec. 13.3):

$$E(MS_w) = E\left[\frac{\sigma_\epsilon^2 \chi^2_{\nu_e}}{\nu_e}\right] = \frac{\sigma_\epsilon^2 \nu_e}{\nu_e} = \sigma_\epsilon^2 \qquad \textbf{(19.5)}$$

## 19.6 MEAN SQUARE BETWEEN

Recall from Chapters 16 and 18 that $MS_b$, the mean square between groups, is determined solely by differences among the means of the $J$ groups. Having defined $MS_b$ before, it can now be used in estimating $\sigma_a^2$, the variance of the population of $a_j$'s or, equivalently, the variance of the population of $\mu_j$'s. Since (see Equation 16.8)

$$MS_b = \frac{SS_b}{\nu_b} = \frac{n \sum_{j=1}^{J} (\overline{X}_j - \overline{X}_{\bullet})^2}{J-1} = \frac{n \sum_j \hat{a}_j^2}{J-1} \qquad \textbf{(19.6)}$$

that is, $MS_b$* is $n$ times the sample variance of the $J$ sample means, $\overline{X}_1, \ldots, \overline{X}_J$.

It can be shown that the expected value of $MS_b$ has the following form:

$$E(MS_b) = \sigma_\epsilon^2 + n\sigma_a^2 \qquad \textbf{(19.7)}$$

that is, on the average—the average $MS_b$ value across an infinite collection of independent replications of the same study with $J$ randomly chosen levels with $n$ randomly chosen observations at each level is $\sigma_\epsilon^2$, the same variance that is estimated by $MS_w$, plus $n$ times the variance of the population of $a_j$'s (which is the same as the variance of the population of $\mu_j$'s as shown in Equation 19.6).

Thus $MS_b$ estimates all that $MS_w$ estimates and more. The something "more" is $n$ times the quantity of interest, $\sigma_a^2$.

The sampling distribution of $MS_b$ is

$$MS_b \sim (\sigma_\epsilon^2 + n\sigma_a^2)\,\frac{\chi^2_{J-1}}{J-1} \qquad \textbf{(19.8)}$$

*A common formula for $MS_b$ that has less rounding error than Equation 19.6 when a calculator is not available is

$$MS_b = \frac{SS_b}{\nu_b} = \frac{\sum_{j=1}^{J} \frac{\left(\sum_{i=1}^{n} X_{ij}\right)^2}{n} - \frac{\left(\sum_{j=1}^{J}\sum_{i=1}^{n} X_{ij}\right)^2}{Jn}}{J-1}$$

**TABLE 19.2 Illustration of Calculation of $MS_b$ and $MS_w$ on the Data in Table 19.1, Where $J = 5$ and $n = 7$**

| | Teacher ($j$) 1 | 2 | 3 | 4 | 5 | |
|---|---|---|---|---|---|---|
| $\sum_{i=1}^{n} X_{ij}$: | 252 | 265 | 183 | 211 | 207 | |
| $\overline{X}_j$: | 36.00 | 37.86 | 26.14 | 30.14 | 29.57 | $\overline{X}_{\bullet} = 31.94$ |
| $\hat{a}_j = \overline{X}_j - \overline{X}$: | 4.06 | 5.92 | -5.80 | -1.80 | -2.37 | |
| $\sum_i x_{ij}^2$: | 104.00 | 112.86 | 196.86 | 472.86 | 127.74 | |
| $s_j^2$: | 17.33 | 18.81 | 32.81 | 78.81 | 21.29 | |

$$SS_b = n \sum_j \hat{a}_j^2 = 7[(4.06)^2 + (5.92)^2 + \cdots + (-2.37)^2] = 7(94.027) = 658.19$$

$$MS_b = \frac{SS_b}{J-1} = \frac{658.19}{4} = 164.55 \qquad \text{(Eq. 19.6)}$$

$$MS_w = \sum_j s_j^2/J = (17.33 + 18.81 + \cdots + 21.29)/5 = 169.05/5 = 33.81$$

ANOVA Table

| *Source* | $\nu$ | *MS* | *F* | $\hat{\sigma}_c^2$ |
|---|---|---|---|---|
| Between (Teachers) | 4 | 164.55 | 4.87* | 18.68 |
| Within | 30 | 33.81 | | 33.81 |

*$p < .01$

that is, over repeated random samplings of $J \times n$ data points (in which both factor levels and observations within levels are sampled), the sampling distribution of $MS_b$ is that of chi-square with $J - 1$ degrees of freedom multiplied by the constant $(\sigma_\epsilon^2 + n\sigma_a^2)/(J-1)$. Unlike the fixed-effects model, $MS_b$ has a sampling distribution that is a constant times the chi-square distribution even when there are differences among the $\mu_j$'s.

In Table 19.2 the calculations of $MS_b$ and $MS_w$ are illustrated using the data in Table 19.1. In Table 19.2 the best estimate of $\sigma^2$, the variance of the reading test scores in the population of students except for teacher effects is $MS_w$, which equals $33.81 = \hat{\sigma}_\epsilon^2$.

## 19.7 THE VARIANCE COMPONENT $\sigma_a^2$

The grand mean of all five groups $\overline{X}_{\bullet}$ is 31.94. It would be expected that scores on this reading test for the population of students being sampled is normally distributed around a mean of about 31.94, with a standard deviation of approximately $\sqrt{MS_w} = \sqrt{33.81} = 5.82$.

The value of $MS_b$ is an estimate of $\sigma_\epsilon^2 + n\sigma_a^2$ (Equation 19.7). An unbiased estimate of the variance in teachers' means, $\sigma_a^2$, can be obtained from $MS_b$ and $MS_w$ in the following manner:

$$E\left[\frac{MS_b - MS_w}{n}\right] = \frac{E(MS_b) - E(MS_w)}{n} = \frac{(\sigma_\epsilon^2 + n\sigma_a^2) - \sigma_\epsilon^2}{n} = \frac{n\sigma_a^2}{n} = \sigma_a^2 \quad \textbf{(19.9)}$$

An unbiased estimate of $\sigma_a^2$ is $\hat{\sigma}_a^2 = (MS_b - MS_w)/n$. The $F$-test in Table 19.2 shows that teacher differences were statistically significant. The variance component is needed to estimate the magnitude of the effect.

For the data in Table 19.1,

$$\hat{\sigma}_a^2 = \frac{MS_b - MS_w}{n} = \frac{164.55 - 33.81}{7} = 18.68$$

Thus the estimate $\hat{\sigma}_a^2$ of the variance of the means of population of teachers, that is, the *variance component*, $\hat{\sigma}_a^2$, is 18.68. The standard deviation of these population means is estimated to be $\sqrt{18.68} = 4.32$.

This estimate of $\sigma_a$ has some meaning in and of itself. For example, if the *metric* in the preceding example were converted to grade-equivalents in months by using a table of norms, and a $\hat{\sigma}_a$ of 4.32 was equivalent to 2.5 months, this would indicate that the magnitude of the teacher effect is substantial; students having a teacher whose $a_j$ is one $\sigma_a$ above the mean of the population of teachers will average about 2.5 months higher than the students having a teacher who is at the mean.* When the metric is arbitrary, such as raw scores on a test or inventory, $\sigma_a^2$ takes on meaning when compared with $\sigma_\epsilon^2$—the ratio of $\hat{\sigma}_a^2$ to $\hat{\sigma}_\epsilon^2$.

In our example $\hat{\sigma}_a^2/\hat{\sigma}_\epsilon^2$ is 18.68/33.81 = 0.55. In statistical parlance it is said that "the variance associated with 'teachers' is about half as great as the variance among students' test scores" (within teachers).

If $MS_w$ is larger than $MS_b$—which, because of sampling error, does happen occasionally—the estimate $\hat{\sigma}_a^2$ of $\sigma_a^2$ would be negative. But a variance can never be negative. Thus, if ever a negative estimate of $\sigma_a^2$ is obtained, it is said to be zero.

## 19.8 CONFIDENCE INTERVAL FOR $\sigma_a^2/\sigma_\epsilon^2$

Inferential questions of interest in the one-way random-effects model include (1) How can a confidence interval on $\sigma_a^2/\sigma_\epsilon^2$ be established around $\hat{\sigma}_a^2/\hat{\sigma}_\epsilon^2$? (2) How can the hypothesis that $\sigma_a^2 = 0$ be tested?†

*These data are hypothetical. Using fifty-one teachers, Bennet (1972) estimated the variance component for teachers at grade one to be .04 to .16 or $\hat{\sigma}_a$ = .2 to .4 grade equivalents.

†Unfortunately, the techniques for setting a confidence interval around $\hat{\sigma}_a^2$ on $\sigma_a^2$ cannot be derived in a straightforward manner from the original model. Approximate techniques are available; however, they are quite complex (see Scheffé, 1959, pp. 231–35; and Collins, 1970).

The $1 - \alpha$ confidence interval on $\sigma_a^2/\sigma_\epsilon^2$ is given in Equation 19.10:

$$\text{prob}\left\{\frac{1}{n}\left[\frac{MS_b}{MS_w}\left(\frac{1}{_{1-(\alpha/2)}F_{J-1,J(n-1)}}\right) - 1\right] \leqslant \frac{\sigma_a^2}{\sigma_\epsilon^2} \leqslant \frac{1}{n}\left[\frac{MS_b}{MS_w}\left(\frac{1}{_{\alpha/2}F_{J-1,J(n-1)}}\right) - 1\right]\right\} = 1 - \alpha \quad \textbf{(19.10)}$$

Both the $100[1 - (\alpha/2)]$ and the $100(\alpha/2)$ percentiles in $F_{J-1,J(n-1)}$ are required in Equation 19.10. Recall that

$$_{\alpha/2}F_{J-1,J(n-1)} = \frac{1}{_{1-(\alpha/2)}F_{J(n-1),J-1}} \quad \textbf{(19.11)}$$

To construct the 95% confidence interval on $\sigma_a^2/\sigma_\epsilon^2$ for the data in Table 19.1, find (from Table F in the Appendix) the value of $_{.975}F_{4,30} = 3.25$. Next, the value of $_{.025}F_{4,30}$, the other required percentile, is calculated using Equation 19.11.

$$_{.025}F_{4,30} = \frac{1}{_{.975}F_{30,4}} = \frac{1}{8.46} = 0.12$$

Substituting the two percentiles along with the values of $MS_b$, $MS_w$, and $n$ into Equation 19.10 yields the 95% confidence interval on $\sigma_a^2/\sigma_\epsilon^2$:

$$\frac{1}{7}\left[\frac{164.55}{33.81}\left(\frac{1}{3.25}\right) - 1\right] = .071, \quad \frac{1}{7}\left[\frac{164.55}{33.81}\left(\frac{1}{0.12}\right) - 1\right] = 5.65$$

The 95% confidence interval on $\sigma_a^2/\sigma_\epsilon^2$ extends from .071 to 5.65. The wide band shows that $\hat{\sigma}_a^2/\hat{\sigma}_\epsilon^2$ is a very crude estimate of $\sigma_a^2/\sigma_\epsilon^2$. The CI shows that $\sigma_a^2$ could be anywhere from less than one-tenth as large as, to over five times as large as $\sigma_\epsilon^2$. Both $J$ and $n$ must be fairly large to produce stable and accurate estimates of $\sigma_a^2$ and $\sigma_\epsilon^2$, or a narrow CI for $\sigma_a^2/\sigma_\epsilon^2$.* Testing the null hypothesis $H_0$: $\sigma_a^2 = 0$ is usually not of as much interest as was the corresponding test in the fixed model, $H_0$: $\Sigma\,\alpha_j^2 = 0$.

It is often implausible for all levels of a factor to have the same population mean, as must be true if $H_0$: $\sigma_a^2 = 0$ is true. Hence when the random ANOVA model is applied, in addition to testing whether $\sigma_a^2 = 0$ is tenable, interest will usually center on estimating the value of $\sigma_a^2$. The procedure for testing of $H_0$: $\sigma_a^2 = 0$ is similar to testing $H_0$: $\Sigma\,\alpha_j^2 = 0$. If $F = MS_b/MS_w$ exceeds $_{1-\alpha}F_{J-1,J(n-1)}$, $H_0$: $\sigma_a^2 = 0$ can be rejected at the $\alpha$-level of significance. For example, with the data in Table 19.2, $F = MS_b/MS_w = 164.55/33.81 = 4.87$, which exceeds 4.02, the 99th percentile in $F_{4,30}$. Thus, $H_0$: $\sigma_a^2 = 0$ can be rejected with $\alpha = .01$.

For all values of $\sigma_a^2$, the noncentral sampling distribution of $F = MS_b/MS_w$ is given by

$$F = \frac{MS_b}{MS_w} \sim \left(1 + \frac{n\sigma_a^2}{\sigma_\epsilon^2}\right)F_{J-1,J(n-1)} \quad \textbf{(19.12)}$$

*For approximate confidence limits with unequal $n$'s, see Snedecor and Cochran (1980, pp. 246–248).

**TABLE 19.3 Summary of the One-Factor Random-Effects ANOVA**

| *Source of Variation* | $\nu$ | *MS* | *E(MS)* | *Estimated Variance Component* ($\hat{\sigma}_c^2$) |
|---|---|---|---|---|
| Between levels | $J - 1$ | $n \sum_{j=1}^{J} \hat{a}_j^2/(J-1)$ | $\sigma_\epsilon^2 + n\sigma_a^2$ | $\hat{\sigma}_a^2 = \dfrac{MS_b - MS_w}{n}$ |
| Within levels | $J(n-1)$ | $\sum_{j=1}^{J} s_j^2/J$ | $\sigma_\epsilon^2$ | $\hat{\sigma}_\epsilon^2 = MS_w$ |

## 19.9 SUMMARY OF RANDOM ANOVA MODEL

Several major points developed in this section about the balanced one-factor random-effects ANOVA model are summarized in Table 19.3.

In the fixed-effects model, $X_{ij} = \mu + \alpha_j + \epsilon_{ij}$, the assumption, $\epsilon_{ij} \sim NID(0, \sigma_\epsilon^2)$, is made; in the random model, $X_{ij} = \mu + a_j + \epsilon_{ij}$, the *additional* assumption, $a_j \sim NID(0, \sigma_a^2)$, is made. Thus with the random-effects ANOVA model, one must deal with the assumptions of normality, homogeneity of variance, and independence for two components—both for the $a$'s and the $\epsilon$'s.

In Chapter 16 it was seen that the consequences on the validity of the fixed-effects ANOVA of violation of the normality assumption are negligible; in addition heterogeneous variances are immaterial in the fixed-effects model if all $n$'s are equal (see Glass, Peckham, and Sanders, 1972). Much less is known about the empirical consequences of violating the second set of assumptions in the random-effects ANOVA model (see Scheffé, 1959, pp. 334-337, and Box and Anderson, 1956). As with the $\epsilon$'s, it is likely that the consequences of meeting the assumptions regarding the $a$'s are less serious as the number of levels of the random factor, $J$, increases.

## 19.10 THE MIXED-EFFECTS ANOVA MODEL

The third and final analysis of variance model that will be dealt with is a combination of the fixed-effects and the random-effects models. This union of the two models into a *mixed* model is particularly useful in experimental research.

As the name "mixed-effects model" suggests, the mixed model involves at least one fixed and one random factor. The simplest form of the model describes data gathered in a two-factor design, similar in appearance to the two-factor fixed model of Chapter 18. One factor, for example, the row factor, comprises a set of $J$ fixed effects ($\alpha$'s); the column factor is a random sample of $K$ random effects ($b$'s) from a supposedly infinite population of normally distributed effects. Consider a hypothetical experiment in which three methods of counseling are compared. The experiment is designed as follows: ten counselors are chosen to participate, each having six clients, two of whom are randomly

**TABLE 19.4 Layout of Data from an Experiment Comparing Three Methods of Counseling**

| | | Counselor ($k$) 1 | 2 | 3 | 4 | 5 | 6 | 7 | 8 | 9 | 10 | Row means $\overline{X}_{j\cdot}$ | $\hat{\alpha}_j$ |
|---|---|---|---|---|---|---|---|---|---|---|---|---|---|
| Method ($j$) | 1 | 31, 27 | 21, 26 | 41, 40 | 24, 29 | 35, 28 | 36, 33 | 21, 21 | 31, 34 | 35, 40 | 24, 26 | 30.15 | −3.73 |
| | 2 | 39, 46 | 32, 30 | 46, 50 | 34, 32 | 42, 47 | 39, 43 | 26, 30 | 32, 35 | 44, 43 | 30, 27 | 37.35 | 3.47 |
| | 3 | 35, 28 | 31, 25 | 42, 39 | 36, 38 | 41, 37 | 38, 38 | 27, 25 | 29, 31 | 45, 41 | 31, 26 | 34.15 | .27 |
| Column means | $\overline{X}_{\cdot b}$ | 34.33 | 27.50 | 43.00 | 32.17 | 38.33 | 37.83 | 25.00 | 32.00 | 41.33 | 27.33 | $33.88 = \overline{X}_{\cdot\cdot}$ | |
| | $\hat{b}_k$ | .45 | −6.38 | 9.12 | −1.71 | 4.45 | 3.95 | −8.88 | −1.88 | 7.45 | −6.55 | | |

assigned to each of the three counseling methods. The dependent variable is an anonymous, self-report measure of neurotic symptoms. The data from the experiment may be laid out as in Table 19.4.

The general observation in Table 19.4 is denoted by $X_{ijk}$, where $j$ ranges over rows (methods) from 1 to 3, $k$ ranges over columns (counselors) from 1 to 10, and $i$ ranges over observations within cells (clients) from 1 to 2. In general $j = 1, \ldots, J$; $k = 1, \ldots, K$; and $i = 1, \ldots, n$. The notation is equivalent to that for the two-factor fixed-effects ANOVA of Chapter 18.

The two-factor design in Table 19.4 presents two sets of main effects, $\alpha$'s and $b$'s, plus an interaction effect, $\alpha b$. The two main effects are "method," which will be called factor $A$, and "counselor," factor $b$. Clearly it is not meaningful to consider the three methods as samples from a large population of methods; the researchers are not interested in generalizing to a hypothetical population of other methods from which these methods could have conceivably been sampled. Interest focuses on the question of which one of these methods is superior to the others.

Hence factor $A$ is considered "fixed." On the other hand, the ten counselors in the experiment can be considered to be a representative sample from a population of counselors; more important, the researchers do not want the results of their study to be generalizable only to the ten counselors of the experiment. One hopes that the conclusion about the relative superiority of the methods is generalizable beyond these ten counselors, that is, to other counselors "like these." Hence, the ten counselors are viewed as a random sample of levels of the random-effects factor $b$. One has, then, a fixed factor crossing a random factor in the same design. The structural model postulated for the observations in this design is aptly named the *mixed-effects model.*

$$X_{ijk} = \mu + \alpha_j + b_k + \alpha b_{jk} + \epsilon_{ijk} \qquad \textbf{(19.13)}$$

where $X_{ijk}$ is the $i$th observation in the $jk$th cell, $\mu$ is the grand population mean of all observations, $\alpha_j$ is the effect $(\mu_j - \mu)$ of the $j$th level of the fixed factor, $b_k$ is the effect $(\mu_k - \mu)$ of the $k$th level of the random factor, $\alpha b_{jk}$ is the interaction effect $[\mu_{jk} - (\mu + \alpha_j + b_k)]$ of the $jk$th combination of the fixed and random factor, and $\epsilon_{ijk}$ is the error, or "residual," component that accounts for variation of observations within the $jk$th cell.

The following restrictions (not assumptions) are placed on the terms of the mixed-effects model in Equation 19.13:

1. $\Sigma_{j=1}^{J} \alpha_j = 0$.
2. The population mean of the infinite number of $b_j$'s—only 10 of which are present in the counseling methods experiment—is zero.
3. $\alpha b_{1k} + \alpha b_{2k} + \cdots + \alpha b_{JK} = 0$ for all $K$.
4. The population of the infinite set of $\alpha b_{jk}$'s for a single $j$ (row) has a mean of zero.

These restrictions imply that if the fixed-effects and interaction effects are summed across the three rows of the data in Table 19.4, they will "add out," that is, sum to zero. However, summing across the columns of the design to obtain a particular row mean, for example, will not cause the $K$ values of $b_K$ or the $K$ values of $\alpha b_{jk}$ to sum to zero.

Suppose the means of methods 1 and 2 are compared. These two means, $\overline{X}_{1\bullet}$ and $\overline{X}_{2\bullet}$, have the following structure in terms of the model in Equation 19.13:

$$\overline{X}_{1\bullet} = \frac{1}{Kn}\left[\sum_1^K \sum_1^n (\mu + \alpha_1 + b_k + \alpha b_{1k} + \epsilon_{i1k})\right]$$

$$= \mu + \alpha_1 + \overline{b}_\bullet + \overline{\alpha b}_{1\bullet} + \overline{\epsilon}_{1\bullet}$$

where

$$\overline{b}_\bullet = \frac{\sum_{k=1}^K b_k}{K}, \qquad \overline{\alpha b}_{1\bullet} = \frac{\sum_{k=1}^K \alpha b_{1k}}{K},$$

and

$$\overline{\epsilon}_{1\bullet} = \frac{\sum_{k=1}^K \sum_{i=1}^n \epsilon_{i1k}}{nK}$$

$$\overline{X}_{2\bullet} = \mu + \alpha_2 + \overline{b}_\bullet + \overline{\alpha b}_{2\bullet} + \overline{\epsilon}_{2\bullet}$$

The difference between $\overline{X}_{1\bullet}$ and $\overline{X}_{2\bullet}$ is

$$\overline{X}_{1\bullet} - \overline{X}_{2\bullet} = (\alpha_1 - \alpha_2) + (\overline{\alpha b}_{1\bullet} - \overline{\alpha b}_{2\bullet}) + (\overline{\epsilon}_{1\bullet} - \overline{\epsilon}_{2\bullet})$$

Because the $\alpha b$'s do not necessarily sum to zero across the $K$ columns and because a replication of the experiment with a different set of $K$ random effects would produce different values of $\overline{\alpha b}_{1\bullet}$ and $\overline{\alpha b}_{2\bullet}$, the sampling variance of the difference between $\overline{X}_{1\bullet} - \overline{X}_{2\bullet}$ will contain a component for the interaction effects, $\alpha b$. This fact will be fully appreciated when the expected values of mean squares for the mixed model are discussed. But before that subject, the assumptions which must be made about the mixed model of Equation 19.13 need to be stated.

## 19.11 MIXED-MODEL ANOVA ASSUMPTIONS

The following assumptions are made about the terms of the model in Equation 19.13:

$$X_{ijk} = \mu + \alpha_j + b_k + \alpha b_{jk} + \epsilon_{ijk}$$

1. The random effects, $b_k = \mu_k - \mu$, are normally distributed with a mean of zero and a variance of $\sigma_b^2$.
2. The interaction effects $\alpha b_{jk}$ are normally distributed over $k$ for each $j$ with a mean of zero and a variance of $\sigma_{\alpha b}^2$.
3. The error components $\epsilon_{ijk}$ are distributed normally and independently of the $b$'s and $\alpha b$'s with mean zero and variance of $\sigma_\epsilon^2$.

There is a fourth assumption, compound symmetry (i.e., homogeneous variances and homogeneous covariances), in the hypothesis test of the fixed main effects, that is, to test $H_0: \mu_1 = \cdots = \mu_J$.

4. For all pairs of levels of the fixed factor, the covariance (across the population of random effects) of the scores for one level with the scores for the other level of the pair must be the same to achieve compound symmetry. For example, assuming $\sigma_{1\bullet}^2 = \sigma_{2\bullet}^2 = \sigma_{3\bullet}^2$, if in the population of all counselors the correlation of scores on method 1 with method 2 is $.5 = \rho_{12}$, then $\rho_{13}$ and $\rho_{23}$ must be .5 as well.

When assumption 4, compound symmetry, is violated, the $F$-test for the fixed effect becomes somewhat liberal, that is, true $\alpha >$ nominal $\alpha$. The extent of the bias is rarely large, however (Collier, Baker, Manderville, and Hayes, 1967).

With the model and its assumptions stated, consideration can be given to the methods by which null hypotheses about the fixed and random main effects and the interaction effects may be tested. The immediate purpose is to test the following three null hypotheses:

1. $H_0$: $\Sigma_{j=1}^J \alpha_j^2 = 0$ (versus $H_1$: $\Sigma \alpha_j^2 \neq 0$.)
2. $H_0$: $\sigma_b^2 = 0$ (versus $H_1$: $\sigma_b^2 \neq 0$.)
3. $H_0$: $\sigma_{\alpha b}^2 = 0$ (versus $H_1$: $\sigma_{\alpha b}^2 \neq 0$.)

## 19.12 MIXED-MODEL ANOVA COMPUTATION

As with other ANOVA models, the road to the hypothesis tests leads through the familiar sums of squares, degrees of freedom, mean squares, and expected values of mean squares; the computations of $SS$, $\nu$, and $MS$ in the two-factor mixed model are identical to the calculations in the two-factor fixed model. The two models do not part company until the $F$-ratios are formed. The computations in the two-factor mixed model for $SS$, $\nu$, and $MS$ are presented in Table 19.5, using the data of Table 19.4.

Once again, it is by way of the expected values of mean squares that one can see how various ratios of mean squares bear on the question of whether or not a null hypothesis is true. The expected mean square—long-run average values over replications of the experiment in Table 19.4 with different counselors and clients each time—is given in panel C of Table 19.5. The expected mean square for the fixed factor differs from the $E(MS_A)$ for the two-factor fixed-effects model; it includes the interaction component, $n\sigma_{\alpha b}^2$.

Consider first the problem of testing the null hypothesis for the fixed factor—that all the $\alpha_j$'s are zero, that is,

$$H_0: \sum_{j=1}^{J} \alpha_j^2 = 0$$

Unlike in the fixed model, here one does not divide $MS_A$ by $MS_w$ and refer the ratio to the $F$-distribution. Notice that $MS_A/MS_w$ does not bear solely on the question whether

**TABLE 19.5 Illustration of ANOVA Computations for a Two-Factor Mixed Model, Using Data from Table 19.4 ($n = 2$)**

A.

| Method ($j$) | | Counselor ($k$): $B_1$ | $B_2$ | $B_3$ | $B_4$ | $B_5$ | $B_6$ | $B_7$ | $B_8$ | $B_9$ | $B_{10}$ | $\overline{X}_{j\bullet}$ | $\hat{\alpha}_j$ |
|---|---|---|---|---|---|---|---|---|---|---|---|---|---|
| $A_1$ | $\overline{X}_{1k}$ | 29.0 | 23.5 | 40.5 | 26.5 | 31.5 | 34.5 | 21.0 | 32.5 | 37.5 | 25.0 | 30.15 | −3.73 |
| | $s_{1k}^2$ | 8.0 | 12.5 | .5 | 12.5 | 24.5 | 4.5 | 0.0 | 4.5 | 12.5 | 2.0 | | |
| $A_2$ | $\overline{X}_{2k}$ | 42.5 | 31.0 | 48.0 | 33.0 | 44.5 | 41.0 | 28.0 | 33.5 | 43.5 | 28.5 | 37.35 | 3.47 |
| | $s_{2k}^2$ | 24.5 | 2.0 | 8.0 | 2.0 | 12.5 | 8.0 | 8.0 | 4.5 | .5 | 4.5 | | |
| $A_3$ | $\overline{X}_{3k}$ | 31.5 | 28.0 | 40.5 | 37.0 | 39.0 | 38.0 | 26.0 | 30.0 | 43.0 | 28.5 | 34.15 | .27 |
| | $s_{3k}^2$ | 24.5 | 18.0 | 4.5 | 2.0 | 8.0 | 0.0 | 2.0 | 2.0 | 8.0 | 12.5 | | |
| | $\overline{X}_{\bullet k}$ | 34.33 | 27.50 | 43.00 | 32.17 | 38.33 | 37.83 | 25.00 | 32.00 | 41.33 | 27.33 | $33.88 = \overline{X}_{\bullet\bullet}$ | |
| | $\hat{b}_k$ | .45 | −6.38 | 9.12 | −1.71 | 4.45 | 3.95 | −8.88 | −1.88 | 7.45 | −6.55 | $(n_{\bullet\bullet} = 60)$ | |

B.

$$SS_A^* = nK \sum_j \hat{\alpha}_j^2 = 20[(-3.73)^2 + (3.47)^2 + (.27)^2] = 520.53; \; MS_A = \frac{SS_A}{J-1} = \frac{520.53}{3-1} = 260.27$$

$$SS_B = nJ \sum_k \hat{b}_k^2 = 6[(.45)^2 + (-6.38)^2 + \cdots + (-6.55)^2] = 2{,}059.68: \; MS_B = \frac{SS_B}{K-1} = \frac{2{,}059.68}{10-1} = 228.86$$

$$SS_{A+B+AB} = n \sum_k \sum_j (\overline{X}_{jk} - \overline{X}_{\bullet\bullet})^2 = 2[(29.0 - 33.88)^2 + (42.5 - 33.88)^2 + \cdots + (28.5 - 33.88)^2] = 2{,}848.68$$

$$SS_{AB} = SS_{A+B+AB} - SS_A - SS_B = 2{,}848.68 - 520.53 - 2{,}059.68 = 268.47; \; MS_{AB} = \frac{SS_{AB}}{(J-1)(K-1)} = \frac{268.47}{18} = 14.92$$

$$MS_w = \frac{\sum_k \sum_j s_{jk}^2}{JK} = \frac{(8.0 + 24.5 + \cdots + 12.5 = 237.5)}{(3)(10)} = \frac{237.5}{30} = 7.92$$

C.

| Source | $E(MS)$ | $\nu$ | $MS$ | $F$ | $\hat{\sigma}^2$ |
|---|---|---|---|---|---|
| $A$ (Methods) | $\sigma_\epsilon^2 + n\sigma_{\alpha b}^2 + nK\sigma_\alpha^2$ | 2 | 260.27 | 17.44[a] | |
| $B$ (Counselors) | $\sigma_\epsilon^2 + nJ\sigma_b^2$ | 9 | 228.86 | 28.90[b] | 36.82 |
| $A \times B$ | $\sigma_\epsilon^2 + n\sigma_{\alpha b}^2$ | 18 | 14.92 | 1.88[c] | 3.50 |
| Within | $\sigma_\epsilon^2$ | 30 | 7.92 | | 7.92 |

[a] $p < .001$, ${}_{.999}F_{2,18} = 10.4$. [b] $p < .001$, ${}_{.999}F_{9,30} = 4.39$. [c] $p > .05$, ${}_{.95}F_{18,30} \doteq 2.0$.

or not $\Sigma \alpha_j^2$ is zero. The quantity $\Sigma \alpha_j^2$ could be zero and yet $MS_A/MS_w$ might be large because $\sigma_{\alpha b}^2$ is not zero. The difference between $MS_A$ and $MS_w$ estimates two effects, $n\sigma_{\alpha b}^2 + nK \Sigma \alpha_j^2/(J-1)$, instead of just $nK \Sigma \alpha_j^2/(J-1)$, as it did in the two-factor fixed model. It can be seen by inspecting the previous expected mean squares that $E(MS_A)$ differs from $E(MS_{AB})$ only in that term, $\Sigma \alpha_j^2$, which is being tested. Thus, the size of the discrepancy between $MS_A$ and $MS_{AB}$, or the ratio of $MS_A$ to $MS_{AB}$, bears on the size of $\Sigma \alpha_j^2$. More specifically, given the assumptions of the mixed-effects model, $F = MS_A/MS_{AB}$ will have the $F$-distribution with degrees of freedom $J-1$ and $(J-1)(K-1)$ if $H_0$: $\Sigma \alpha_j^2 = 0$ is true. A positive value of $\Sigma \alpha_j^2$ will tend to inflate $MS_A$ above $MS_{AB}$ and give values of $F = MS_A/MS_{AB}$ that are larger than the typical values in the $F_{J-1,(J-1)(K-1)}$ distribution.

Although the null hypothesis $H_0$: $\sigma_b^2 = 0$ is usually of less interest than the hypothesis about the fixed main effects, it can be tested by referring the ratio $F = MS_B/MS_w$ to the table of the $F$-distribution with $K-1$ and $JK(n-1)$ degrees of freedom. Moreover, an unbiased estimate of the variance component, $\sigma_b^2$, can be obtained by $(MS_B - MS_w)/(nJ)$.

The $1-\alpha$ confidence interval on $\sigma_b^2/\sigma_\epsilon^2$ can be constructed by using Equation 19.10 of Section 19.8; $F_{K-1,JK(n-1)}$ is substituted for $F_{J-1,J(n-1)}$ in that equation. The null hypothesis $H_0$: $\sigma_{\alpha b}^2 = 0$ may be tested by referring $F = MS_{AB}/MS_w$ to the $F$-distribution with $(J-1)(K-1)$ and $JK(n-1)$ degrees of freedom.

For the data in Table 19.4, the three null hypotheses mentioned have been tested at the .05 level of significance. The results appear in the ANOVA table in panel $C$ of Table 19.5. The main effects for both the fixed (method) and random (counselor) factors are statistically significant: (1) there are differences among these three counseling methods in the populations of counselors and students, and (2) the population means of all counselors are not equal. The method-by-counselor interaction was not significant—the pattern of method differences is generalizable to the population of counselors.

## 19.13 MULTIPLE COMPARISONS IN THE TWO-FACTOR MIXED MODEL

Multiple comparisons (and trend analysis) are applied only to fixed factors. The procedures are the same as those presented in Chapter 17 (and 18), with the qualification that the error mean square, $MS_e$, denotes the denominator of the $F$-test for the fixed factor—in this case $MS_e = MS_{AB}$; likewise, $\nu_e = \nu_{AB}$.

To determine which of the three means differ significantly from which others, a post hoc multiple comparison method, such as the Newman-Keuls or the Tukey, could be employed. Using the Tukey-method (HSD) with $\alpha_\Sigma = .05$:

$$\text{HSD}_{.05} = ({}_{.95}q_{\nu_e,J})s_{\overline{X}_{j\bullet}}$$

where

$$s_{\overline{X}_{j\bullet}} = \sqrt{\frac{MS_e}{n_{j\bullet}}} = \sqrt{\frac{14.92}{20}} = .864$$

and

$$_{.95}q_{18,3} = 3.61 \text{ (Table I)}$$

Hence $\text{HSD}_{.05} = (3.61)(.864) = 3.12$. Note that $n_{j\bullet} = nK = 20$, is the number of observations on which each mean is based.

Since all pairs of counseling methods means differ by more than 3.12 points, each difference in pairs of means is statistically significant at the .05 level. ($H_0$: $\mu_2 - \mu_1 = 0$ can be rejected at the .001 level.)

## 19.14 REPEATED-MEASURES DESIGNS

The two-factor mixed-effects ANOVA model with $n = 1$ (i.e., one observation per cell) is frequently encountered. For example, five persons (i.e., $P = 5$ levels of the random factor $P$) may each be observed under six treatment conditions (i.e., $T = 6$ levels of the fixed factor $T$), as shown in panel $A$ of Table 19.6.* This design is commonly referred to as a *repeated-measures* design, because observations of persons (or the levels of a random factor, such as teachers or schools) are made several times instead of once. An observation in the repeated measures design will be denoted by $X_{pt}$, indicating the $t$th treatment on the $p$th person. The mean squares between rows, between columns, and for the interaction of rows and columns can all be calculated by means of the computational formulas in Table 19.5 noting that $n = 1$. Since $n = 1$, there are $PT(n - 1) = 0$ degrees of freedom for variation within cells; thus, there is no variance around the mean of the cell.† The analysis of variance table for the three sources of variation appear in panel $C$ of Table 19.6.

If for the $T$ levels of the fixed factor, $\sigma_1^2 = \cdots = \sigma_T^2$ and $\rho_{12} = \rho_{13} = \cdots = \rho = \rho_{(T-1)T}$, then $F = MS_T/MS_{PT}$ will have an $F$-distribution with $T - 1$ and $(P - 1)(T - 1)$ degrees of freedom when $H_0$: $\Sigma\,\alpha_t^2 = 0$ is true. Hence, $F = MS_T/MS_{PT}$ can be compared with $_{1-\alpha}F_{(T-1),(T-1)(P-1)}$ to test $H_0$ at the $\alpha$-level of significance. No tests of the null hypothesis $H_0$: $\sigma_{\alpha b}^2 = 0$ are possible in the mixed-effects model when $n - 1 = 0$ since there is no estimate of $\sigma_\epsilon^2$ (see panel $C$ of Table 19.5 for $E(MS)$'s.).

The probability statement for the $F$-test of $H_0$: $\Sigma\,\alpha_t^2 = 0$ will be precise in mixed models only when the condition of compound symmetry is met (Sec. 19.11). Violations of this assumption increase the actual probability of a type-I error above the value believed to hold, that is, the "nominal" value. When heterogeneous correlations among the pairs of levels of the fixed factor are suspected, special measures can be taken to insure

*The first letter of a factor is often used for mnemonic benefit, rather than $A$ or $B$.

†In theory the observation within each cell is viewed as a random sample with $n = 1$ from a population of observations (as defined in Eq. 19.13). Since there is only one score per cell, the variance in the $\epsilon$'s cannot be estimated separately from the $\sigma_{\alpha b}^2$. In such situations it is possible to test $H_0$: $\sigma_{\alpha b}^2 = 0$, by using a procedure devised by Tukey (Kirk, 1982, p. 400). If this null hypothesis is tenable, the $MS_{AB}$ can be viewed as an estimate of the variance in the $\epsilon$'s. Since $E(MS_{AB}) \geqslant E(MS_w)$, the consequences of using the interaction mean square for the error term when the desired mean square is $MS_w$ are conservative. For example, the $F$-ratio ($F = 50.07/.51 = 98.2$) for factor $P$ in panel $C$ of Table 19.6 is a minimal estimate.

**TABLE 19.6 ANOVA for a Two-Factor Repeated-Measures Design***

A.

| | | Treatment ($T$) 1 | 2 | 3 | 4 | 5 | 6 | $\Sigma_t X_{pt}$ | Person Means $\bar{X}_{p\bullet}$ | Person Effects $\hat{\alpha}_p$ |
|---|---|---|---|---|---|---|---|---|---|---|
| Person ($P$) | 1 | 0 | 0 | 0 | 1 | 1 | 1 | 3 | .50 | −3.27 |
| | 2 | 0 | 1 | 2 | 1 | 2 | 3 | 9 | 1.50 | −2.27 |
| | 3 | 2 | 3 | 4 | 3 | 5 | 5 | 22 | 3.67 | −.10 |
| | 4 | 4 | 4 | 5 | 6 | 7 | 8 | 34 | 5.67 | 1.90 |
| | 5 | 5 | 6 | 7 | 9 | 9 | 9 | 45 | 7.50 | 3.73 |
| $\Sigma_p X_{pt}$ | | 11 | 14 | 18 | 20 | 24 | 26 | $\Sigma_t \Sigma_p X_{pt} = 113$ | $\bar{X}_{\bullet\bullet} = 3.77$ | |
| Treatment Means, $\bar{X}_{\bullet t}$ | | 2.2 | 2.8 | 3.6 | 4.0 | 4.8 | 5.2 | | | |
| Treatment Effects, $\hat{\beta}_t$ | | −1.57 | −.97 | −.17 | .23 | 1.03 | 1.43 | | | |

B.

$$SS_P = T \sum_p \hat{\alpha}_p^2 = 6[(-3.27)^2 + (-2.27)^2 + \cdots + (3.73)^2] = 200.37; \; MS_P = \frac{200.37}{4} = 50.07$$

$$SS_T = P \sum_t \hat{\beta}_t^2 = 5[(-1.57)^2 + (-.97)^2 + \cdots + (1.43)^2] = 32.97; \; MS_T = \frac{32.97}{5} = 6.59$$

$$SS_{P+T+PT} = \sum_p \sum_t (X_{pt} - \bar{X}_{\bullet\bullet})^2 = (0 - 3.77)^2 + \cdots + (9 - 3.77)^2 = 243.37$$

$$SS_{PT} = SS_{P+T+PT} - SS_P - SS_T = 243.37 - 200.37 - 32.97 = 10.13; \; MS_{PT} = \frac{10.13}{20} = .51$$

C.

| *Source* | $\nu$ | $E(MS)$ | $\nu$ | $MS$ | $F$ |
|---|---|---|---|---|---|
| Persons ($P$) | $P - 1$ | $\sigma_\epsilon^2 + T\sigma_p^2$ | 4 | 50.07 | |
| Treatment ($T$) | $T - 1$ | $\sigma_\epsilon^2 + \sigma_{pt}^2 + p\sigma_t^2$ | 5 | 6.59 | 12.92[a] |
| $P \times T$ | $(P - 1)(T - 1)$ | $\sigma_\epsilon^2 + \sigma_{pt}^2$ | 20 | .51 | |

[a] $p < .001$

*Although it is arbitrary which factor is the row factor, in repeated-measures designs there is usually a chronological order for the levels of the repeated-measures factor (e.g., trial, age, pretest-posttest, etc.). Consequently, the column factor is conventionally viewed as the (fixed) repeated-measures factor. Note, however, the fixed factor in Table 19.5 is the row factor, and appears in the first line of that ANOVA table.

the validity of the $F$-test of the null hypothesis about the fixed main effects. Box (1954) showed that the effect of heterogeneous correlations of the fixed-factor levels was to produce a sampling distribution of $F = MS_T/MS_{PT}$ that has degrees of freedom *less than* $T - 1$ and $(T - 1)(J - 1)$ when $H_0$ is true. Greenhouse and Geisser (1959) showed that, at worst, the degrees of freedom could only be reduced to 1 and $T - 1$ for the sampling distribution of $F = MS_T/MS_{PT}$ under a true null hypothesis. If the conservative Greenhouse-Geisser test were used in Table 19.7, the $A$ effect would remain significant ($_{.975}F_{1,4} =$ 12.2). Fortunately, the probability statements using the nominal degrees of freedom,

$(T - 1)$ and $(T - 1)(K - 1)$, are rarely seriously underestimated* (Collier, Baker, Mandeville, and Hayes, 1967).

## 19.15 CROSSED AND NESTED FACTORS

All factors that have been illustrated up to this point (except the "within" source of variation) have been *crossed* factors; two factors are *crossed* if every level of one of the factors appears with every level of the other factor. That is, there must be at least one observation for every possible combination of levels of factors that are completely crossed. The levels of one factor may be crossed with those of another, or the levels of one or more factors may be *nested* within the levels of another factor. For instance, when three male raters and three female raters rate each of ten ratees on each of seven traits, raters are nested within sex, because no male rater is also a female rater (i.e., the rater levels do not cross the sex levels, though they do cross the ratee and the trait levels).

Nesting and crossing occur when there are at least two factors. In a given study there may be no nesting, no crossing, all of one or the other, or a mixture of nesting and crossing.

The experiment depicted in Table 19.7 will be used to illustrate crossed and nested factors. The factors of school ($S$) and method ($M$) are crossed: each of the five methods appears with each of the two schools—$5 \times 2 = 10$ combinations of levels appear. The number of levels of each factor will be denoted by the capital letter that denotes that factor, for example, $M = 5$, $S = 2$, and $T = 3$.

Note that the dependent variable in Table 19.7 is dichotomous (1 or 0). Bal-

*If extremely heterogeneous correlations are expected among the various levels of the repeated-measures factor, one can either use multivariate analysis of variance (MANOVA) (see Poor, 1973, and Gabriel and Hopkins, 1974) or employ the analysis strategy depicted (Glass and Hopkins, 1972) (where $\theta$ is a measure of the degree of heterogeneity in the variance-covariance matrix, see Winer, 1971, pp. 282–30):

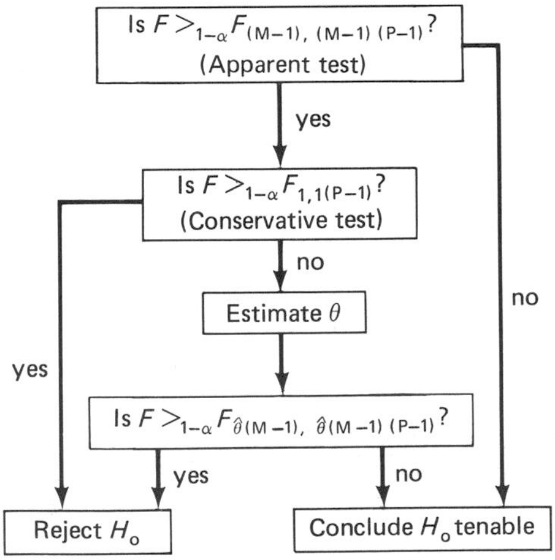

anced ANOVA designs have been shown to yield accurate results even with dichotomous dependent variables (Hsu and Feldt, 1969; Lunney, 1970; Glass, Peckham, and Sanders, 1972; also see Fig. 12.2, Sec. 12.9).

Factor $A$ is said to be *nested* within factor $B$ if each level of factor $A$ (the nested factor) appears in only one level of factor $B$. In the study represented in Table 19.7 teachers are nested within school. No teacher appears in more than one school, thus teachers ($T$) are said to be nested within school ($S$); this is denoted as, $T:S$, where ":" is read, "is nested within." If, however, in the unlikely event that the same teachers applied the methods in both schools (as, for example, would be the case if teachers were assigned to one school in the morning and to the other school in the afternoon), teachers would not be nested within schools, but would cross schools. Since teacher 1 ($T_1$) in Table 19.7 teaches only at school 1 ($S_1$), $T_1$ does not appear under school 2. The fact that the teacher subscripts, 1, 2, and 3, are not repeated at school 2 shows that three different teachers are involved at school 2.

The design in Table 19.7 is a three-factor design, but only two of the factors ($M$ and $S$) are completely crossed; the third factor ($T$) is nested within factor $S$, thus the three factors can be denoted as $M$, $S$, and $T:S$.

In practice nested factors are almost always random factors (like the teacher factor in this example). The converse is not true however—both fixed and random factors are frequently crossed. In the design in Table 19.7 it is desirable to view both teachers and schools as random effects so that the results can be generalized beyond these particular teachers and these two schools.*

Actually there has been a latent nested variable in the fixed ANOVA models, although it ordinarily is not described as such. In all examples given in Chapters 16 and 18 the replicate factor (usually persons) is nested within all other factors. Indeed, the "within" factor is a less explicit designation of the fact that persons are nested within all other factors. For example, "within" in Table 16.2 is "persons nested within treatments ($P:T$)"; in Table 18.3 "within" is "persons nested within factors $A$ and $B$ ($P:AB$)"; in Table 18.6 "within" is "persons nested within factors $A$, $S$, and $T$ ($P:ATS$)." Although the use of "within" as a source of variation is conventional, it is better practice to make this source of variation explicit.

## 19.16 COMPUTATION OF SUMS OF SQUARES FOR NESTED FACTORS†

The sum of squares for a nested effect, $T:S$, can be computed directly as with other effects, that is, $SS_\alpha = n\Sigma\hat{\alpha}^2$ where $n$ is the number of observations on which the means used to estimate the effect is based. To estimate the method effect in Table 19.7, each

*An unconventional practice that warrants more attention is the incremental inferential strategy proposed by Hopkins (1983) in which all factors (except the replicate factor) are viewed initially as fixed. If the effects are significant in this impoverished inferential context, the factors that ideally should be viewed as random are sequentially treated statistically as random.

†Computional procedures for a balanced design of any degree of complexity are given in the Appendix.

**TABLE 19.7 Illustration of a Design Having a Nested Factor. Three teachers are nested within each of two schools, and both teachers and schools cross methods.**

A.

| | $S_1$ | | | $S_2$ | | | Method Means $\bar{X}_{m\cdot\cdot}$ | Method Effects $\hat{\alpha}_m$ |
|---|---|---|---|---|---|---|---|---|
| | $T_1$ | $T_2$ | $T_3$ | $T_4$ | $T_5$ | $T_6$ | | |
| $M_1$ | 0, 1, 0<br>$\bar{X} = \frac{1}{3}$<br>$s^2 = \frac{1}{3}$ | 1, 1, 0<br>$\bar{X} = \frac{2}{3}$<br>$s^2 = \frac{1}{3}$ | 1, 0, 0<br>$\bar{X} = \frac{1}{3}$<br>$s^2 = \frac{1}{3}$ | 0, 0, 0<br>$\bar{X} = 0$<br>$s^2 = 0$ | 1, 0, 0<br>$\bar{X} = \frac{1}{3}$<br>$s^2 = \frac{1}{3}$ | 1, 0, 0<br>$\bar{X} = \frac{1}{3}$<br>$s^2 = \frac{1}{3}$ | .333 | −.100 |
| $M_2$ | 1, 1, 1<br>$\bar{X} = 1$<br>$s^2 = 0$ | 1, 1, 0<br>$\bar{X} = \frac{2}{3}$<br>$s^2 = \frac{1}{3}$ | 1, 1, 1<br>$\bar{X} = 1$<br>$s^2 = 0$ | 1, 1, 0<br>$\bar{X} = \frac{2}{3}$<br>$s^2 = \frac{1}{3}$ | 1, 0, 1<br>$\bar{X} = \frac{2}{3}$<br>$s^2 = \frac{1}{3}$ | 1, 0, 0<br>$\bar{X} = \frac{1}{3}$<br>$s^2 = \frac{1}{3}$ | .722 | .289 |
| $M_3$ | 1, 1, 0<br>$\bar{X} = \frac{2}{3}$<br>$s^2 = \frac{1}{3}$ | 0, 1, 0<br>$\bar{X} = \frac{1}{3}$<br>$s^2 = \frac{1}{3}$ | 0, 1, 1<br>$\bar{X} = \frac{2}{3}$<br>$s^2 = \frac{1}{3}$ | 0, 1, 0<br>$\bar{X} = \frac{1}{3}$<br>$s^2 = \frac{1}{3}$ | 1, 1, 0<br>$\bar{X} = \frac{2}{3}$<br>$s^2 = \frac{1}{3}$ | 1, 0, 0<br>$\bar{X} = \frac{1}{3}$<br>$s^2 = \frac{1}{3}$ | .500 | .067 |
| $M_4$ | 0, 1, 1<br>$\bar{X} = \frac{2}{3}$<br>$s^2 = \frac{1}{3}$ | 1, 0, 0<br>$\bar{X} = \frac{1}{3}$<br>$s^2 = \frac{1}{3}$ | 1, 1, 0<br>$\bar{X} = \frac{2}{3}$<br>$s^2 = \frac{1}{3}$ | 0, 1, 0<br>$\bar{X} = \frac{1}{3}$<br>$s^2 = \frac{1}{3}$ | 1, 1, 0<br>$\bar{X} = \frac{2}{3}$<br>$s^2 = \frac{1}{3}$ | 0, 0, 0<br>$\bar{X} = 0$<br>$s^2 = 0$ | .444 | .011 |
| $M_5$ | 0, 0, 0<br>$\bar{X} = 0$<br>$s^2 = 0$ | 0, 0, 1<br>$\bar{X} = \frac{1}{3}$<br>$s^2 = \frac{1}{3}$ | 1, 0, 0<br>$\bar{X} = \frac{1}{3}$<br>$s^2 = \frac{1}{3}$ | 0, 1, 0<br>$\bar{X} = \frac{1}{3}$<br>$s^2 = \frac{1}{3}$ | 0, 0, 0<br>$\bar{X} = 0$<br>$s^2 = 0$ | 0, 0, 0<br>$\bar{X} = 0$<br>$s^2 = 0$ | .167 | −.266 |
| School Means $\bar{X}_{\cdot\cdot s}$ | | .533 | | | .333 | | $\bar{X}_{\cdot\cdot\cdot} = .433$ | |
| School Effects $\hat{b}_s$ | | .100 | | | −.100 | | | |
| Teacher Means $\bar{X}_{\cdot ts}$ | .533 | .467 | .600 | .333 | .467 | .200 | | |
| Teacher (within school) effects $\hat{c}_{t:s}$ | .000 | −.066 | .067 | .000 | .134 | −.133 | | |

B. $X_{imst} = \mu + \alpha_m + b_s + c_{t:s} + \alpha b_{ms} + \alpha c_{mt:s} + \epsilon_{i:mst}$; where $\hat{\alpha}_m = \bar{X}_{m\cdot\cdot} - \bar{X}_{\cdot\cdot\cdot}$ $\hat{b}_s = \bar{X}_{\cdot\cdot s} - \bar{X}_{\cdot\cdot\cdot}$, $\hat{c}_{t:s} = \bar{X}_{\cdot t:s} - (\bar{X}_{\cdot\cdot\cdot} + \hat{b}_s)$, $\widehat{\alpha b}_{ms} = \bar{X}_{m\cdot s} - (\bar{X}_{\cdot\cdot\cdot} + \hat{\alpha}_m + \hat{b}_s)$, $\widehat{\alpha c}_{mt:s} = \bar{X}_{mt:s} - (\bar{X}_{\cdot\cdot\cdot} + \hat{\alpha}_m + \hat{c}_{t:s})$; where $i$ varies from 1 to $n$; $m$ varies from 1 to $M$; $s$ varies from 1 to $S$; and $t$ varies from 1 to $T$. In the preceding example $n = 3, M = 5, S = 2$, and $T = 3$.

**TABLE 19.7 (cont.)**

| C. *Source* | $\nu$ | $E(MS)$* | $\nu$ | $MS$ | $F$ |
|---|---|---|---|---|---|
| 1. Method ($M$) | $M-1$ | $\sigma^2_{p:tsm} + 3\sigma^2_{mt:s} + 9\sigma^2_{ms} + 18\sigma^2_m$ | 4 | .760 | 40.00[a] |
| 2. School ($S$) | $S-1$ | $\sigma^2_{p:tsm} + 15\sigma^2_{t:s} + 45\sigma^2_s$ | 1 | .900 | 5.17[b] |
| 3. Teacher *within* *School* ($T:S$) | $S(T-1)$ | $\sigma^2_{p:tsm} + 15\sigma^2_{t:s}$ | 4 | .167 | .65 |
| 4. $MS$ | $(M-1)(S-1)$ | $\sigma^2_{p:tsm} + 3\sigma^2_{mt:s} + 9\sigma^2_{ms}$ | 4 | .019 | .26 |
| 5. $MT:S$ | $(M-1)S(T-1)$ | $\sigma^2_{p:tsm} + 3\sigma^2_{mt:s}$ | 16 | .130 | .51 |
| 6. Pupils *within* *Teacher* ($P:TSM$) | $TSM(n-1)$ | $\sigma^2_{p:tsm}$ | 60 | .2556 | |

*The coefficient for a $E(MS)$ component is the product of $n, M, S, T$ that do *not* appear in the component's subscript as $p$, $m$, $s$, and $t$ respectively. Thus, the coefficient for $\sigma^2_m$ is $nST = (3)(2)(3) = 18$. See Sec. 19.19.

[a] $p < .01$, ${}_{.99}F_{4,4} = 16.0$

[b] $p < .10$, ${}_{.90}F_{1,4} = 4.54$

D.

$$SS_M = nST \sum \hat{\alpha}^2_m = 18[(-.100)^2 + (.289)^2 + \cdots + (-.266)^2] = 3.040;\ MS_M = 3.040/4 = .760$$

$$SS_S = nMT \sum \hat{b}^2_s = 45[(.100)^2 + (-.100)^2] = .900;\ MS_s = .900/1 = .900$$

$$SS_{T:S} = nM \sum_s \sum_t \hat{c}^2_{t:s} = 15[(.000)^2 + (-.066)^2 + \cdots + (-.133)^2] = .667;\ MS_{T:S} = .667/4 = .167$$

$$SS_{MS} = nT \sum_s \sum_m (\widehat{\alpha b}_{ms})^2 = SS_{M+S+MS} - SS_M - SS_S$$

$$SS_{M+S+MS} = nT \sum_s \sum_m (\overline{X}_{m\cdot s} - \overline{X}_{\cdots})^2 = 9[(\tfrac{4}{9} - .433)^2 + (\tfrac{8}{9} - .433)^2 + \cdots + (\tfrac{1}{9} - .433)^2] = 4.018$$

$$SS_{MS} = 4.018 - 3.040 - .900 = .078;\ MS_{MS} = .078/4 = .019$$

E.

$$SS_{MT:S} = n \sum_s \sum_t \sum_m (\widehat{\alpha c}_{mt:s})^2 = SS_{M+S+MS+T:S+MT:S} - SS_{M+S+MS} - SS_{T:S}$$

$$SS_{M+S+MS+T:S+MT:S} = n\left(\sum_s \sum_t \sum_m \overline{X}_{mt:s} - \overline{X}_{\cdots}\right)^2$$

$$= 3[(\tfrac{1}{3} - .433)^2 + (1 - .433)^2 + \cdots + (0 - .433)^2] = 6.767$$

$$SS_{MT:S} = 6.767 - 4.018 - .667 = 2.082;\ MS_{MT:S} = 2.082/16 = .130$$

$$MS_{P:TSM} = MS_w = \sum_t \sum_s \sum_m s^2_{mts}/MTS$$

$$= (\tfrac{1}{3} + 0 + \tfrac{1}{3} + \cdots + \tfrac{1}{3} + 0 + 0)/30 = 7.667/30 = .2556$$

method mean is based on eighteen observations, thus $SS_M = 18\ \Sigma_{m=1}^{M=5}\ \hat{\alpha}_m^2$. In estimating the school effect each school mean is based on $nTM = 45$ observations, hence $SS_s = 45\ \Sigma_{s=1}^{S=2}\ \hat{b}_s^2$. The procedure is similar with nested effects. For example, in the model in Table 19.7, the sum of squares for the $T{:}S$ effect (teacher-within-school, $\hat{c}_{t:s}$) is the number of observations per teacher ($nM = 15$) times the sum of the squared effects, where the estimated effect is $\hat{c}_{t:s} = \overline{X}_{\bullet t:s} - (\overline{X}_{\bullet\bullet\bullet} + \hat{b}_s)$, thus $SS_{T:S} = 15\ \Sigma_s\ \Sigma_t\ \hat{c}_{t:s}^2$. The estimated teacher-within-method effects, $\hat{c}_{t:s}$, are given in panel $C$ of Table 19.7.*

## 19.17 DETERMINING THE SOURCES OF VARIATION: THE ANOVA TABLE

Each line in an ANOVA table corresponds to an effect—a source of variation in the model. There is an effect for each factor (main effects), and each unique combination of factors (interactions). A nested factor interacts only with those factors that it crosses, that is, factors (or effects) that are *not* nested within it. For the design shown in panel $A$ of Table 19.7, the model is given in panel $B$. Note that there is no source of variation for a school-by-teacher interaction because teachers are nested within school. A source of variation for each component in the model (given in panel $B$) is shown in panel $C$.

## 19.18 DEGREES OF FREEDOM FOR NESTED FACTORS

If a factor is nested, its degrees of freedom are the number of nests, $U$, times the degrees of freedom per nest (one less than the number of observations per nest), that is, $U(n - 1)$. In Table 19.7 three teachers ($T = 3$) are nested within each of two schools ($S = 2$), hence the degrees of freedom for the $T{:}S$ source of variation are $S(T - 1) = 2(3 - 1) = 4$ (see panel $C$). For pupils, $P{:}TSM$, where there are 3, 2, and 5 levels, respectively, for factors $T$, $S$, and $M$, the number of nests is the product of the number of levels of factors $T$, $S$, and $M$, that is, $U = (3)(2)(5) = 30$. Thus, since there are three ($n = 3$) pupils per nest,

*Certain computer programs do not accommodate nested factors. But if the data are analyzed as if all factors were crossed, then various sums of squares can be combined to obtain the sum of squares for the nested effects. The rule for aggregation is: the sum of squares for any effect that is nested, includes itself plus all "interactions" of itself with the factor(s) under which it is nested. Thus,

$$SS_{A:B} = \text{``}SS_A\text{''} + \text{``}SS_{AB}\text{''}$$

$$SS_{AB:C} = \text{``}SS_{AB}\text{''} + \text{``}SS_{ABC}\text{''}$$

$$SS_{A:BC} = \text{``}SS_A\text{''} + \text{``}SS_{AB}\text{''} + \text{``}SS_{AC}\text{''} + \text{``}SS_{ABC}\text{''}$$

$$SS_{AB:CD} = \text{``}SS_{AB}\text{''} + \text{``}SS_{ABC}\text{''} + \text{``}SS_{ABD}\text{''} + \text{``}SS_{ABCD}\text{''}$$

(The associated degrees of freedom are carried along accordingly.)

The data in Table 19.7 could be analyzed as if it were a three-factor fully crossed ANOVA (as in Table 18.6, Sec. 18.22). Then "$SS_T$" and "$SS_{TS}$" would be aggregated to obtain $SS_{T:S}$, which divided by "$\nu_T$" + "$\nu_{TS}$" yields $MS_{T:S}$. Likewise, $SS_{MT:S}$ = "$SS_{MT}$" + "$SS_{MTS}$," and $\nu_{MT:S}$ = "$\nu_{TM}$" + "$\nu_{MTS}$".

the degrees of freedom for $P$: $TSM$ are $TSM(n - 1) = (30)(3 - 1) = 60$. Or, in Figure 19.4 there are two "levels" of the nested factor (pupils) nested within three levels of factor $M$ and ten levels of factor $C$; thus for $p$:$MC$, $\nu = MC(n - 1) = (3)(10)(2 - 1) = 30$.

As with crossed factors, $\nu$ for any interaction is the product of the $\nu$'s for the participating factors. For example in Table 19.7, for the method-teacher ($MT$:$S$) interaction, there are $(M - 1)S(T - 1) = 16$ degrees of freedom.

## 19.19 DETERMINING EXPECTED MEAN SQUARES

As designs become more complex, the $E(MS)$ for each source of variation is needed to determine the proper error term (denominator) for the $F$-test for a given source of variation. The expected mean square is also needed to determine variance components for random effects. Many sources exist that provide rules of thumb for finding some of the entries in an ANOVA table from some of the designs considered here (e.g., Glass and Stanley, 1970; Millman and Glass, 1967; and Cornfield and Tukey, 1956). The simplest method (Hopkins, 1976), requires only two complex rules, which must be practiced on several designs before they are mastered.

1. The *components* (addends) of expected mean square for any source of variation are the specified effect (a main effect or interaction, i.e., source of variation), plus (a) the interaction of the specified effect with any random effect (including combinations of random effects) and (b) any random effect nested within the specified effect.

In a one-factor ANOVA in which $n$ persons are nested within each of the $J$ methods the $E(MS)$ for the method effect includes, in addition to the method variance, $\sigma^2_M$, the variance from the random effect, persons, nested within method, $\sigma^2_{p:M}$ or $\sigma^2_{\text{within}} = \sigma^2_\epsilon$. In the two-factor fixed ANOVA design in Table 18.3 the effect nested within cells, persons, is a random effect; thus, the $E(MS)$ for factor $A$ is $\sigma^2_{p:ab} + nK\sigma^2_a$. The procedures for determining $E(MS)$'s are best learned inductively, using examples. Study the examples in Tables 19.6 and 19.7.

In a design in which the fixed effect, $A$, crosses random effects, $B$ and $C$, the $E(MS)$ for $A$ is $A + AB + AC + ABC$, that is, $\sigma^2_A + \sigma^2_{AB} + \sigma^2_{AC} + \sigma^2_{ABC}$. Note that each $E(MS)$ component in the mean square of $A$ included the specified effect, $A$, plus a term for each random factor, and combination of random factors that crossed the specified effect. Similarly, with the same design, the $E(MS)$ for the $AB$ interaction would be $AB + ABC$, that is, $\sigma^2_{AB} + \sigma^2_{ABC}$. If $B$ had been nested within $A$, the $E(MS)$ for $A$ would be $A + B{:}A + AC + CB{:}A$, that is, $\sigma^2_A + \sigma^2_{B:A} + \sigma^2_{AC} + \sigma^2_{CB:A}$. If $C$ had been nested within $B$, and $B$ nested within $A$, the $E(MS)$ for $A$ would become $A + B{:}A + C{:}BA$, that is, $\sigma^2_A + \sigma^2_{B:A} + \sigma^2_{C:BA}$. Note that in each instance each component included the specified effect, $A$, plus $A$ associated with a unique effect involving random factors.

2. The *coefficient** for any component is the product of the number of levels of all factors *not* denoted in the variance subscript for that component. Thus in

*The coefficients are needed only when variance components are to be determined (Sec. 19.7). The principal use of $E(MS)$'s is for selecting the correct error term for making $F$-tests for various effects.

panel $B$ of Table 19.7 the "within" component, that is, $\sigma^2_{P:TSM}$ has a coefficient of 1 because all factors (including pupils) appear in the subscript. Likewise, the coefficient for the method component has the coefficient of $nTS$ [or numerically, (3)(2)(3) = 18] since $p$, $T$, and $S$ do not appear in the subscript of the effect, $\sigma^2_M$. Equivalently, the coefficient for any component is the number of observations on which each of the means directly involved in the component is based. Thus for $\sigma^2_M$, each of the $M = 5$ means is based on eighteen observations, hence the coefficient of $\sigma^2_M$ is 18. Stated differently, the coefficient for any component is the total number of observations [in this case, $nTSM$ = (3)(3)(2)(5) = 90] divided by the product of the levels of the various factors represented in the subscripts.

Thus in Figure 19.7, for $\sigma^2_S$, where $S = 2$, the coefficient is 90/2 = 45. For $\sigma^2_{T:S}$, where $(T)(S) = (3)(2) = 6$, 90/6 = 15. And for $\sigma^2_{MT:S}$, $(M)(T)(S) = (5)(3)(2) = 15$, and 90/15 = 6. Panel $C$ of Table 19.7 gives the coefficients and components for each source of variation.

## 19.20 ERROR MEAN SQUARE IN COMPLEX ANOVA DESIGNS

The general form of an $F$-test is $F = (A + B)/B$, or, $F = (A + B + C)/(B + C)$, the denominator includes every component contained in the numerator *except* the effect to be tested. The null hypothesis states that the $A$ component is zero, hence when the null hypothesis is true, the numerator and denominator are independent estimates of the same parameter(s).

In panel $C$ of Table 19.7, the expected value for the $T$:$S$ mean square includes $\sigma^2_{p:tsm}$ in addition to $15\sigma^2_{t:s}$; thus the ratio of the $MS_{T:S}$ to $MS_{P:TSM}$ provides the $F$-ratio for testing the teacher differences with school. Note also, that $MS_{T:S}$ is the error term for testing the school effect since its $E(MS)$ includes all components in the numerator except the one to be tested, $\sigma^2_s$. Confirm from panel $C$ that the error terms for testing $M$, $S$, $T$:$S$, $MS$, and $MT$:$S$ effects are the mean squares associated with $MS$, $T$:$S$, $P$: $TSM$, $MT$:$S$, and $P$:$TSM$, respectively. If no appropriate $F$-ratio exists for testing an effect, approximate ("quasi-$F$") methods are sometimes applicable (see, e.g., Winer, 1971; Kirk, 1982; and Myers, 1979).*

*Notice in Table 19.7 that the $F$-test for the $M$ and $S$ effects have $\nu_e = 4$ and, hence, will have rather large critical $F$-values (e.g., ${}_{.95}F_{1,4} = 7.71$; ${}_{.95}F_{4,4} = 6.39$). A sequential analysis strategy often makes sense in such situations: analyze the data viewing all factors (except pupils) as fixed; then, if significance is obtained, treat the appropriate factors as random to see if the findings are generalizable to the appropriate population of levels. For example, in Table 19.7 one could initially treat schools and teachers as fixed factors, then treat teachers as random, and finally treat schools as a random factor as well. This strategy has the advantage of assessing the extent to which the results are generalizable, rather than settling for a single universe of inference (Hopkins, 1983). It also provides some insurance against type-I errors resulting from negatively biased $MS$-values–$MS$-values that have $F$-ratios below zero are suspect.

If in Table 19.7 school and teacher factors are fixed, hence one is assessing whether the findings are generalizable to the appropriate population of students for *these* schools and *these* teachers. In this case the error mean square for all effects is $\sigma^2_{p:tsm}$, and

## 19.21 MODEL SIMPLIFICATION AND POOLING

In certain situations, like that in Table 19.7, the error mean square for an $F$-test has very few degrees of freedom. In such situations some data analysts (Green and Tukey, 1960; Kirk, 1968; Winer, 1971; and Myers, 1979) recommend that the ANOVA model be evaluated to see if it can be simplified. If the model is simplified, any effect having an $F$-ratio below 1 (or below some other critical $F$-value, such as that for $\alpha = .25$) can be dropped from the model.

In Table 19.7 the $T{:}S$, $MS$, and $MT{:}S$ all have $F$-ratios below 1, thus it is tenable to view $\sigma^2_{t:s} = 0$, $\sigma^2_{ms} = 0$, and $\sigma^2_{mt:s} = 0$. Consequently, logic suggests that these components can be deleted from the model and from the $E(MS)$'s for the various effects. Thus, *sources* 3, 4, 5, and 6 could all be viewed as estimating a common parameter, $\sigma^2_{p:tsm}$. If the pooled $SS$ of 18.160 (i.e., the $SS$'s associated with $T{:}S$, $MS$, $MT{:}S$, and $P{:}TSM$) is divided by the pooled degrees of freedom (84), an error mean square $(18.160/84 = .216)$ with 84 rather than 4 degrees of freedom results. The $F$-ratios for the $M$ and $S$ effects are then $3.52(= .760/.216)$ and $4.16(= .900/.216)$, respectively, and both $H_0$'s can be rejected, $p < .05$.

In many instances, however, pooling is not an option because the observed $F$-ratios substantially exceed 1.0, and the model cannot be legitimately simplified. When pooling is employed, the results should be given before and after pooling so that readers can make their own evaluation of the conclusions.

## 19.22 THE EXPERIMENTAL UNIT AND THE OBSERVATIONAL UNIT

In the analysis of experiments a distinction must be made between the observational unit in the statistical analysis and the experimental unit. *Observational units* are the units on which the data (the actual numbers) that one considers to be outcomes of the study are obtained. The number of observational units in a statistical analysis is greater (by 1) than the total number of degrees of freedom from all the sources of variation in the ANOVA table. The *experimental* unit is that entity that is allocated to a treatment independently of the other entities. It may contain several observation units (Addelman, 1970) as, for example, in repeated-measures designs in which the experimental unit is usually persons and the observational unit is score on a trial or test or some other dependent measure.

There has been much confusion about the proper method of analysis in studies in which there are several observational units (e.g., students) per experimental unit (e.g.,

---

the $F$-ratios for $M$, $S$, $T{:}S$, $MS$, and $MT{:}S$ are 2.97, 3.52, .65, .07, and .51; the $M$ and $S$ effects are significant.

If in addition to pupils, teachers are also viewed as a random sample from a larger population of teachers to which one wishes to generalize, the $F$-ratio for the $M$, $S$, $T{:}S$, $MS$, and $MT{:}S$ are 5.85, 5.17, .65, .15, and .51, respectively. The $M$ effect continues to significant, strengthening the inference regarding method effects to the related population of teachers. If schools are also viewed as a random factor the analysis in panel $C$ of Table 19.7 results.

classes) (Peckham, Glass, and Hopkins, 1969; Hopkins, 1982). The most common recommendation in such situations has been to compute the class (or group) mean and make the observational unit identical with the experimental unit.

Three methods of analysis will be compared using data from a study (DeRosia, 1980) in which two methods of instruction are contrasted. Three teachers are nested within each method, twenty-five students are nested within each teacher. If the teacher factor is ignored in the analysis, the implicit model for the score for the $i$th student ($i = 1, \ldots, n$) in the $m$th ($m = 1, \ldots, M$) method is

$$X_{im} = \mu + \alpha_m + \epsilon_{i:m} \qquad \text{(Model } A\text{)}$$

The assumptions of normality, homogeneity of variance, and independence pertain to the $\epsilon$'s, that is, $\epsilon_{i:m} \sim NID(0, \sigma_\epsilon^2)$ [i.e., within each of the $M$ methods, the errors ($\epsilon$'s) are normally and independently distributed and have a mean of 0, and a common variance, $\sigma_\epsilon^2$]. The expected mean squares $E(MS)$ for model $A$ are given in panel $A$ of Table 19.8; the right-hand portion of panel $A$ gives the results of the analysis of the data using model $A$. Analyses such as this that use scores from individual students have been widely criticized since Lindquist (1940) because the method and teacher effects are confounded and cannot be sorted out; it is included for purposes of comparison. Any difference in "method" means may be due to teacher and/or method difference. The results using Model $A$ are shown in panel $A$ of Table 19.8.

**TABLE 19.8 Expected Mean Squares for a Balanced ANOVA Design (and Illustrative Analyses) in Which $n$ Students Are Nested Within $T$ Teachers, Which are Nested Within $M$ Methods, Using Three Models (from Hopkins, 1982)**

| | | | Example | | |
|---|---|---|---|---|---|
| *SV* | $\nu$ | $E(MS)$ | $\nu$ | *MS* | *F* |
| A. [Model $A$: $X_{im} = \mu + \alpha_m + \epsilon_{i:m}$] | | | | | |
| Methods ($M$) | $M - 1$ | $\sigma_{s:m}^2 + n\sigma_m^2$ | 1 | 2814.6 | $7.69^a$ |
| Students nested *within* method ($S:M$) | $M(n - 1)$ | $\sigma_{s:m}^2$ | 148 | 366.2 | |
| B. [Model $B$: $X_{tm} = \mu + \alpha_m + b_{t:m}$] | | | | | |
| Methods ($M$) | $M - 1$ | $\sigma_{t:m}^2 + T\sigma_m^2$ | 1 | 112.6 | 1.99 |
| Teachers nested *within* methods ($T:M$) | $M(T - 1)$ | $\sigma_{t:m}^2$ | 4 | 56.5 | |
| C. [Model $C$: $X_{itm} = \mu + \alpha_m + b_{t:m} + \epsilon_{i:tm}$] | | | | | |
| Methods ($M$) | $M - 1$ | $\sigma_{s:tm}^2 + n\sigma_{t:m}^2 + nT\sigma_m^2$ | 1 | 2814.5 | 1.99 |
| Teachers nested *within* methods ($T:M$) | $M(T - 1)$ | $\sigma_{s:tm}^2 + n\sigma_{t:m}^2$ | 4 | 1412.7 | $4.19^a$ |
| Students nested *within* teachers and methods ($S:TM$) | $MT(n - 1)$ | $\sigma_{s:tm}^2$ | 144 | 337.1 | |

$^a p < .01$.

If, instead of using student scores as the observational unit, class means for the $T$ teachers ($t = 1, \ldots, T$) were employed, the model becomes

$$X_{tm} = \mu + \alpha_m + b_{t:m} \qquad \text{(Model } B\text{)}$$

where $\beta_{t:m} \sim NID(0, \sigma_\beta^2)$. This is the model advocated by Lindquist (1940) and Campbell and Stanley (1966) for studies in which the treatment is group oriented and can result in nonindependence among the students' scores. The $E(MS)$'s for Model $B$ along with the analysis using Model $B$ is found in panel $B$ of Table 19.8. Notice that the "highly significant" ($p < .01$) methods effect that was found when Model $A$ (panel $A$) was used disappears ($p > .20$) when Model $B$ is employed.

When there are several observational units per experimental unit, both $[\beta_{t:m}]$ and $[\epsilon_{i:tm}]$ should be included in the model. Since both types of errors include variability due to factors unknown to or beyond the control of the experimenter, neither should be deleted from the model at the whim of the experimenter.

Model $C$ incorporates components both for teachers (or classes) and students; both are viewed as random effects because the desired inference is to a population of teachers "like these" as well as to a population of students "like these." The linear model for the design in which $n$ students are nested within $T$ teachers which, in turn, are nested within $M$ methods is

$$X_{itm} = \mu + \alpha_m + \beta_{t:m} + \epsilon_{i:tm} \qquad \text{(Model } C\text{)}$$

In Model $C$ there are two sets of assumptions, that is, $\epsilon_{i:tm} \sim NID(0, \sigma_\epsilon^2)$ and $\beta_{t:m} \sim NID(0, \sigma_\beta^2)$. In other words, since teachers are properly viewed as a random effect, a second "layer" of assumptions is required in the desired universe of inference.

If scores from individual students are used as observational units and the data are analyzed using Model $C$ (students are nested within teachers which are nested within methods), and if teachers are appropriately designated as a random factor, the expected mean squares for the effects are given in panel $C$ of Table 19.8. The analysis of the sample data using Model $C$ is given in the right-hand portion of panel $C$ in Table 19.8.

It is apparent from Table 19.8 that for balanced designs, the $F$-ratio for the *methods effect is the same whether class means or individual observations are used*, since the methods mean square would be divided by the teachers within-methods mean square ($T$:$M$) in both instances. Even though the mean squares for methods in Models $B$ and $C$ will differ (by a factor of $n$), the $F$-ratios for treatment will *be identical* in the two analyses and these $F$'s will have identical degrees of freedom and critical $F$'s.

Note that if the proper ANOVA model is employed, the question of the proper unit of analysis is taken care of implicitly. When the proper ANOVA model is used, although the analyses are identical as far as the method effect is concerned, the analyses using individual students in Model $C$ is preferred because the hypothesis concerning the teacher-within-method effect can be evaluated. In addition, by retaining individual scores in the analysis, the researcher can consider incorporating personological variables into the design so that interactions of these factors with treatment effects can be evaluated. These interactions speak directly to critical generalizability questions. An additional advantage of Model $C$ is that it allows the question of model simplification (pooling) to be considered.

## CHAPTER SUMMARY

When the levels of a factor represented in a study do not exhaust the levels in the population, but are viewed as a sample of the levels in the population, the factor is said to be random, not fixed. The levels of a random effect, $b$, are assumed to be distributed $NID(0, \sigma_b^2)$. In addition to $F$-tests for random effects, variance components are ordinarily calculated to estimate the variance among the means of the various levels in the population. Multiple comparisons and trend analysis (Chap. 17) are meaningful only for fixed factors.

When a random factor and a fixed factor cross, the resulting ANOVA model is said to be mixed. Although the procedures for determining mean squares for the various sources of variations are unaffected by whether factors are fixed or random, the associated $F$-ratios for fixed effects will change in the mixed model. The error mean square (error term) for any source of variation is defined by its expected mean square; the denominator of the $F$-test for that effect contains all the components of the numerator except for the effect to be tested.

In a repeated-measures design (mixed model) the covariances among the various levels of the fixed factor are assumed to be homogeneous (compound symmetry). Minor violations of the assumption do not appear to invalidate seriously the resulting probability statements.

Most ANOVA factors are crossed (i.e., each level of every factor appears in combination with each level of every other factor). When each level of a factor $b$ appears only within one level a second factor $A$, factor $b$ is said to be nested within $A$, that is, $b:A$. Interactions among nested factors cannot be assessed. Nested factors will ordinarily be viewed as random factors.

## *MASTERY TEST*

1. Which of the following factors would almost always be viewed as fixed?
   a. teachers b. raters c. treatments d. schools
2. In the random model $X_{ij} = \mu + a_j + \epsilon_{ij}$ which of the components are assumed to be normally distributed?
3. Does the random model in Question 2 assume $\sigma_a^2 = \sigma_\epsilon^2$?
4. If a factor is random, one ordinarily would
   a. determine the variance component for that factor.
   b. perform multiple comparisons on that factor if $H_0$ is rejected.
   c. perform a trend analysis on that factor if $H_0$ is rejected.
5. A repeated-measures ANOVA design is an example of a
   a. fixed model
   b. mixed model
   c. random model
6. If three teachers employ method $E$ and three other teachers employ method $C$,
   a. teachers are nested within method.
   b. teachers cross methods.
   c. methods are nested within teachers.

7. Which of the following denotes that teachers ($t$) are nested within method ($M$)?
   a. $M:t$  b. $t \times M$  c. $Mt$  d. $t:M$
8. Are $t:M$ and $M:t$ synonyms?
9. For crossed factors $A$ and $B$, is the $AB$ interaction synonymous with the $BA$ interaction?
10. Which of the following would rarely, if ever, be considered random factors?
    a. method  b. principal  c. test items  d. sex
    e. school  f. teacher  g. school district  h. type of school
    i. SES  j. ability level  k. rater (judge)  l. student (person)
11. If factor $A$ is a random factor and $a_j = \mu_j - \mu$, which of the following is *not* assumed?
    a. $\sigma_a^2 = 0$  b. the $a_j$'s are normally distributed  c. the $a_j$'s are independent
12. The interaction of factors $A$ and $B$ can be assessed only if
    a. both factors are fixed
    b. both factors are random
    c. factor $A$ is nested with factor $B$
    d. factor $B$ is nested within factor $A$
    e. factors $A$ and $B$ cross
13. In a balanced $2 \times 3$ ANOVA design with persons nested within both factors, $A$ and $B$, a *more explicit* notation of the "within" source of variation is
    a. $p:A$  b. $p:B$  c. $p:AB$  d. $AB:p$
14. Are all computations and $F$-tests in a *one-factor* random ANOVA model identical with those in a one-factor fixed model?
15. If the $H_0$ being tested is true, are the expected values of the numerator and the denominator of the proper $F$-test equal?
16. Is the expected value of $F$ equal to 0 when $H_0$ is true?
17. When will the condition of compound symmetry always be met in a repeated-measures design?

Factor $G$ (Grade Level)

| Factor $S$ School | | Person | $G_1$ | $G_2$ | $G_3$ |
|---|---|---|---|---|---|
| | $S_1$ | $P_1$ | | | |
| | | $P_2$ | | | |
| | | $P_3$ | | | |
| | | $P_4$ | | | |
| | | $P_5$ | | | |
| | | $P_6$ | | | |
| | $S_2$ | $P_7$ | | | |
| | | $P_8$ | | | |
| | | $P_9$ | | | |
| | | $P_{10}$ | | | |
| | | $P_{11}$ | | | |
| | | $P_{12}$ | | | |

18. In the preceding design which factor is fixed?

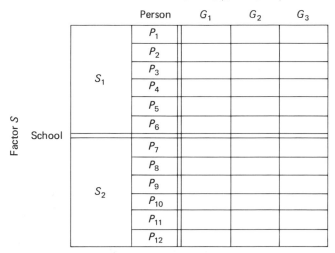

19. Which source of variation is nested?
20. Is the design a repeated-measures mixed ANOVA model?
21. Give the respective degrees of freedom for the sources of variation in the following ANOVA table.

| *Source* | $\nu$ | $E(MS)$ | $SS$ |
|---|---|---|---|
| $G$ | $(G-1) =$ ___ | $\sigma^2_{gp:s} + 6\sigma^2_{gs} + 12\sigma^2_g$ | 200 |
| $S$ | $(S-1) =$ ___ | $\sigma^2_{p:s} + 18\sigma^2_s$ | 50 |
| $GS$ | $(G-1)(S-1) =$ ___ | $\sigma^2_{gp:s} + 6\sigma^2_{gs}$ | 22 |
| $P{:}S$ | $S(P-1) =$ ___ | $\sigma^2_{p:s}$ | 200 |
| $GP{:}S$ | $(G-1)S(P-1) =$ ___ | $\sigma^2_{gp:s}$ | 200 |

22. The $E(MS)$ for each source of variation are given. Which source of variation is the error term for testing the $G$ effect? What will be the critical $F$-value if $\alpha = .10$? The $H_0$ for which effects are testable with this ANOVA model?
23. Using the $SS$-values in the preceding ANOVA table, compute the mean square for each effect; give the $F$-ratio for each testable effect.
24. Suppose the analysis is from a developmental study of attitude toward education. Were there significant differences ($\alpha = .10$) among the three grade levels? Were there significant differences between the two schools? Was the pattern of means across the grade levels very similar for both schools?
25. Estimate the variance component for schools, that is, $\hat{\sigma}^2_s = ?$
26. If in the population of persons, the variance in scores is the same at all three grade levels but the correlation between adjacent grade levels is higher than that between the first and third grade levels, the condition of ___ would not be met.
    a. normality  b. compound symmetry  c. $\sigma_1^2 = \sigma_2^2 = \sigma_3^2$
27. If multiple comparisons or a trend analysis were to be made among the three grade levels, the error mean square, $MS_e$, would have the value of ___.
28. In a balanced 2 X 3 ANOVA design with persons nested within factors $A$ and $B$, a *more explicit* denotation of $MS_{\text{within}}$ is
    a. $MS_{p:a}$  b. $MS_{p:b}$  c. $MS_{p:ab}$  d. $MS_{\text{error}}$
29. Is the computation of a *two*-factor ANOVA the same irrespective of whether the factors are fixed or random?
30. If a factor is random, $\mu_j - \mu$ is not denoted as $\alpha_j$ but ___.
31. The smallest unit which is independent assigned to treatment condition is the
    a. observational unit.
    b. experimental unit.
32. Must the observational unit be the same as the experimental unit in order for the statistical analysis to be valid?
33. If teachers are randomly assigned to experimental and control groups, but scores from each of the twenty students per class are used in the analysis, the observational unit is the ___, and the experimental unit is the ___.
34. Table 19.8 illustrates that if the ANOVA design is balanced, the statistical tests for the method main effect give identical results irrespective of whether the observational unit is the class (teacher), or student [if classes (teachers), and students are viewed as random effects]. (T or F)

## *PROBLEMS AND EXERCISES*

1. A random sample of ten raters was drawn from a population of raters. Each rater rated an independent and different random sample of $n = 20$ persons ($P$) on a 7-point scale of "emotional adjustment." The analysis of variance yielded the following results:

| *Source* | $\nu$ | *MS* | *E(MS)* |
|---|---|---|---|
| Rater ($R$) | 9 | 10.48 | $\sigma^2_{p:r} + 20\sigma^2_r$ |
| $P:R$ | 190 | 9.64 | $\sigma^2_{p:r}$ |

   a. Estimate the variance of raters, $\sigma^2_r$, from the data.
   b. Compare the sizes of $\hat{\sigma}^2_r$ and $\hat{\sigma}^2_{p:r}$.
   c. Establish the 95% confidence interval on $\sigma^2_r/\sigma^2_{p:r}$.

2. A population of 30,000 spelling words is identified. A test publisher is interested in how much variability is to be expected among 50-item spelling tests, $\sigma^2_t$, that could be formed from the pool of 30,000 words. (The total number of possible 50-item tests equal to the combinations of 30,000 items taken 50 at a time is incredibly large; see Eq. 9.10, Sec. 9.9.) A researcher constructs six 50-item spelling tests by randomly sampling items from the item pool. Thus, the $J = 6$ tests ($T$) can be considered to be randomly sampled from the population of all possible 50-item tests, and $t_j = \mu_j - \mu$. Each test is given to an independent random sample of $n = 12$ pupils. The following test scores (total number of correct spellings out of 50) are obtained:

| | *Test (J)* 1 | 2 | 3 | 4 | 5 | 6 | |
|---|---|---|---|---|---|---|---|
| | 21 | 34 | 44 | 12 | 30 | 27 | |
| | 14 | 19 | 31 | 26 | 18 | 32 | |
| | 11 | 26 | 36 | 22 | 14 | 26 | |
| | 27 | 31 | 24 | 30 | 29 | 29 | |
| | 19 | 39 | 40 | 35 | 36 | 34 | |
| | 32 | 42 | 38 | 14 | 27 | 20 | |
| | 21 | 27 | 42 | 19 | 30 | 15 | |
| | 23 | 14 | 35 | 24 | 25 | 25 | |
| | 18 | 25 | 27 | 23 | 25 | 31 | |
| | 25 | 29 | 29 | 31 | 20 | 39 | |
| | 24 | 33 | 30 | 27 | 32 | 23 | |
| | 23 | 36 | 33 | 25 | 19 | 29 | |
| $\overline{X}_j$: | 21.50 | 29.58 | 34.08 | 24.00 | 25.42 | 27.50 | $27.01 = \overline{X}_{\bullet}$ |
| $s^2_j$: | 31.73 | 64.81 | 38.27 | 44.91 | 42.63 | 41.18 | $\Sigma s^2_j/J = 43.9$ |
| $\hat{t}_j$: | -5.51 | 2.57 | 7.07 | -3.01 | -1.59 | .49 | |

   a. Using the one-factor random-effects ANOVA, give the two sources of variation, $T$ and $P:T$, the respective $\nu$'s, and their $E(MS)$'s (see Table 19.3).
   b. Estimate the variance among the population of spelling test means, $\hat{\sigma}^2_t$, and the estimate of the variance of pupils's scores within any spelling test, $\hat{\sigma}^2_{p:t}$. That is, calculate

$$\hat{\sigma}^2_t = \frac{MS_T - MS_{P:T}}{12} \quad \text{and} \quad \hat{\sigma}^2_{p:t} = MS_{P:T}$$

3. In a two-factor random-effects ANOVA with $J$ levels of factor $A$, $K$ levels of factor $B$, and $n$ observations per cell, the expected values of the mean squares are as follows:

$$E(MS_A) = \sigma^2 + n\sigma_{ab}^2 + nK\sigma_a^2$$
$$E(MS_B) = \sigma^2 + n\sigma_{ab}^2 + nJ\sigma_b^2$$
$$E(MS_{AB}) = \sigma^2 + n\sigma_{ab}^2$$
$$E(MS_w) = \sigma^2$$

Find a linear combination of the mean squares that provides an unbiased estimator of $\sigma_a^2$ and $\sigma_{ab}^2$. (*Hint:* Notice how $\sigma_b^2$ can be estimated.)

$$E\left[\frac{MS_B - MS_{AB}}{nJ}\right] = \frac{E(MS_B) - E(MS_{AB})}{nJ}$$
$$= \frac{\sigma^2 + n\sigma_{ab}^2 + nJ\sigma_b^2 - (\sigma^2 + n\sigma_{ab}^2)}{nJ} = \frac{nJ\sigma_b^2}{nJ} = \sigma_b^2$$

4. In Table 12.3, consider the "Persons" to be a random factor and the "Verbal IQ versus Performance IQ" to be a fixed factor. Using the repeated-measures ANOVA model, test the null hypothesis at the .05 level that populations of Verbal and Performance IQ's have the same mean for neurologically handicapped children. Does the $F$-test lead to the same decision that would be arrived at if a dependent-groups $t$-test of the hypothesis $\mu_1 = \mu_2$ were made? Compare $F$ with $t^2$, and ${}_{.99}F_{1,9}$ with ${}_{.995}t_9$. (Computation procedures are illustrated in Table 19.6.) Could the condition of compound symmetry be violated in this example?

5. Scores on the Information, Vocabulary, Digit Span, and Block Design subtests of the Wechsler Intelligence Scale for Children are tabulated for a group of twelve neurologically handicapped children.

| | | Test ($T$) | | | | Person Sum | Person Mean | Person Effect |
|---|---|---|---|---|---|---|---|---|
| | Person ($P$) | Information | Vocabulary | Digit Span | Block Design | $\Sigma_t X_{pt}$ | $\overline{X}_{p\bullet}$ | $\hat{\alpha}_p$ |
| | 1 | 7 | 8 | 7 | 7 | 29 | 7.25 | −2.50 |
| | 2 | 5 | 10 | 8 | 12 | 35 | 8.75 | −1.00 |
| | 3 | 9 | 11 | 9 | 11 | 40 | 10.00 | .25 |
| | 4 | 17 | 18 | 9 | 13 | 57 | 14.25 | 4.50 |
| | 5 | 4 | 7 | 7 | 9 | 27 | 6.75 | −3.00 |
| | 6 | 6 | 9 | 8 | 11 | 34 | 8.50 | −1.25 |
| | 7 | 11 | 11 | 7 | 7 | 36 | 9.00 | −.75 |
| | 8 | 10 | 14 | 12 | 7 | 43 | 10.75 | 1.00 |
| | 9 | 8 | 11 | 7 | 13 | 39 | 9.75 | .00 |
| | 10 | 12 | 11 | 5 | 9 | 37 | 9.25 | −.50 |
| | 11 | 13 | 16 | 6 | 18 | 53 | 13.25 | 3.50 |
| | 12 | 11 | 10 | 11 | 6 | 38 | 9.50 | −.25 |
| Test Sum: | $\Sigma_p X_{pt}$ | 113 | 136 | 96 | 123 | $468 = \Sigma_t \Sigma_p X_{pt}$ | | |
| Test Means: | $\overline{X}_{\bullet p}$ | 9.417 | 11.333 | 8.00 | 10.25 | $9.75 = \overline{X}_{\bullet\bullet}$ | | |
| Test Effect: | $\hat{\beta}_t$; | −.333 | 1.583 | −1.75 | .50 | $5{,}078 = \Sigma_t \Sigma_p X_{pt}^2$ | | |

WISC subtest scores are scaled to a mean of 10 and standard deviation of 3 for the general population. It has often been asserted that patterns of subtest scores on the WISC can be used to diagnose neurological handicaps.

a. Test the null hypothesis that the twelve test scores above were randomly sampled from four normal distributions with the same mean, with $\alpha = .05$. The design should be regarded as a repeated measures design.
b. If multiple comparisons were to be made among subtests, what is the numerical value of "$MS_e$?"

6. Twenty raters are drawn at random from a population of raters. Thirty-two ratees are drawn at random from a population of ratees. The eight traits of interest for this particular study are rated. Each of the twenty raters rated each of the thirty-two ratees once on each of the eight traits.
   a. How many ratings does this study yield?
   b. Which factors represent "random" effects and which "fixed?" Are any factors "nested" within any other factors? Which?
   c. How many sources of variation are there in these ratings? List them and the associated $\nu$'s.
   d. Work out all the expected mean squares for this design and indicate the appropriate error mean squares for each effect.
   e. Provide the formulas for estimating all estimable components of variance for random effects.

7. Two raters who were Democrats and two raters who were Republicans each rated three ratees who were prominent Democrats and three ratees who were prominent Republicans on each of four different traits. This yielded a total of $2 \times 2 \times 2 \times 3 \times 4 = 96$ ratings. The design is shown. There are five factors, two of which are "nested."

| Party of ratee | Ratee number | Trait rated | | | | | | | | | | | | | | | | |
|---|---|---|---|---|---|---|---|---|---|---|---|---|---|---|---|---|---|---|
| | | Intelligence | | | | Honesty | | | | Friendliness | | | | Generosity | | | | |
| | | *D* | | *R* | | *D* | | *R* | | *D* | | *R* | | *D* | | *R* | | Party of rater |
| | | 1 | 2 | 3 | 4 | 1 | 2 | 3 | 4 | 1 | 2 | 3 | 4 | 1 | 2 | 3 | 4 | Rater number |
| *R* | 1 | 7 | 6 | 8 | 7 | 8 | 2 | 8 | 7 | 5 | 1 | 8 | 2 | 5 | 0 | 10 | 5 | |
| | 2 | 7 | 7 | 6 | 7 | 7 | 6 | 6 | 6 | 6 | 6 | 9 | 1 | 5 | 6 | 8 | 2 | |
| | 3 | 6 | 6 | 4 | 5 | 8 | 9 | 8 | 6 | 10 | 5 | 9 | 8 | 9 | 5 | 10 | 6 | |
| *D* | 4 | 8 | 8 | 6 | 6 | 9 | 10 | 3 | 1 | 8 | 8 | 7 | 6 | 9 | 7 | 4 | 4 | |
| | 5 | 8 | 5 | 6 | 7 | 9 | 5 | 4 | 4 | 5 | 1 | 4 | 1 | 9 | 1 | 3 | 1 | |
| | 6 | 5 | 4 | 3 | 3 | 7 | 8 | 1 | 0 | 7 | 7 | 8 | 4 | 7 | 8 | 0 | 0 | |

a. Identify the two nested factors. Within what is each such factor nested?
b. Do the nested factors "cross" any other factors? Which ones?
c. Which factors does the "political party of rater" factor cross?
d. Which of the factors were probably considered as each having had its levels drawn randomly from an infinite (hypothetical) population of levels?
e. $\hat{\sigma}^2_{(\text{party of rater} \times \text{party of ratee})}$ contributed most to variation of the ratings. Would you have expected this result in advance of the rating procedure? What does this interaction probably mean?
f. The second largest estimated component of variance was that for party of rater $\times$ party of ratee $\times$ trait. What does this three-factor interaction mean? (One sometimes sees a three-factor interaction referred to as a "second-order" interaction, because a zero-order "interaction" would be a main effect, not interacting with anything. Thus

a two-factor interaction, such as that in part e, may be called a "first-order interaction.) For further results, see Stanley (1961).

## *ANSWERS TO MASTERY TEST*

1. c
2. $a_j$ and $\epsilon_{ij}$
3. No
4. a
5. b
6. a
7. d
8. No
9. Yes
10. a, d, h, i, j
11. a
12. e
13. c
14. Yes
15. Yes
16. No, $E(F) \doteq 1$ [more precisely, $E(F) = \nu_e/(\nu_e - 2)$]
17. When the number of levels of the repeated-measures factor is two (hence there is only one covariance term)
18. Grade level
19. Person, $P:S$
20. Yes
21. 2, 1, 2, 10, 20 for $G$, $S$, $GS$, $P:S$, and $GP:S$, respectively
22. $GS$; ${}_{.90}F_{2,2} = 9.00$; $G$, $S$, and $GS$
23. 

| *Source* | *MS* | *F* |
|---|---|---|
| $G$ | 100 | 9.09 |
| $S$ | 50 | 2.50 |
| $GS$ | 11 | 1.10 |
| $P:S$ | 20 | |
| $GP:S$ | 10 | |

24. Yes, no, yes
25. $\hat{\sigma}_s^2 = (MS_S - MS_{P:S})/18$
    $= (50 - 20)/18 = 1.67$
26. b
27. 11
28. c
29. No; although $MS$-values are not affected, $F$-ratios often are changed.
30. $a_j$
31. b
32. No
33. Student, teacher (or class)
34. T

## *ANSWERS TO PROBLEMS AND EXERCISES*

1. a. $\hat{\sigma}_r^2 = .042$.
   b. Based upon our estimates, the variance of ratings for persons being rated by the same rater is more than 200 times as large as the variance of raters, 9.64 versus .042.
   c. The 95% confidence interval on $\sigma_r^2/\sigma_{p:r}^2$ is (-.024, .131). Since it is impossible for $\sigma_r^2/\sigma_{p:r}^2$ to be negative, the interval could be set from 0 to .131.

2. a.

| *Source* | $\nu$ | $E(MS)$ |
|---|---|---|
| $T$ | 5 | $\sigma_{p:t}^2 + 12\sigma_t^2$ |
| $P:T$ | 66 | $\sigma_{p:t}$ |

   b. $MS_T = 237$; $MS_{P:T} = 43.9$
   $\hat{\sigma}_t^2 = (MS_T - MS_{P:T})/12 = 16.1$
   $\hat{\sigma}_{p:t}^2 = 43.9$

3. $\hat{\sigma}_a^2 = (MS_A - MS_{AB})/(nK)$
   $\hat{\sigma}_{ab}^2 = (MS_{AB} - MS_w)/n$

4. $F = 10.96 = (3.31)^2 = t^2$;
   ${}_{.99}F_{1,9} = 10.6 = (3.25)^2 = {}_{.995}t_9^2$.
   No, because there is only one covariance term.

5. a.

| *Source* | *SS* | $\nu$ | *MS* | *F* |
|---|---|---|---|---|
| $T$ | 71.15 | 3 | 23.72 | 3.39 |
| $P$ | 209.00 | 11 | 19.00 | |
| $TP$ | 230.82 | 33 | 6.99 | |

   b. 6.69

6. a. $20 \times 32 \times 8 = 5{,}120$.
   b. "Raters" and "ratees" are random factors; "traits" is a fixed factor. This is a fully crossed design; there is no nested factor.
   c. There are seven sources of variation in these data: three main effects, three two-factor interactions, and one three-factor interaction (residual). The sources of variation are as follows: Raters ($R$), Ratees ($P$), traits ($T$), $RP$, $RT$, $PT$, and $RPT$.
   d. Let raters be factor 1, ratees factor 2, and traits factor 3. Then

| $E(MS)$ | $\nu$ | Error MS |
|---|---|---|
| $E(MS_R) = \sigma_\epsilon^2 + 8\sigma_{rp}^2 + 256\sigma_r^2$ | $R - 1 = 19$ | $MS_{RP}$ |
| $E(MS_P) = \sigma_\epsilon^2 + 8\sigma_{rp}^2 + 160\sigma_p^2$ | $P - 1 = 31$ | $MS_{RP}$ |
| $E(MS_T) = \sigma_\epsilon^2 + \sigma_{rpt}^2 + 32\sigma_{rt}^2 + 20\sigma_{pt}^2 + 640\sigma_t^2$ | $T - 1 = 7$ | None[a] |
| $E(MS_{RP}) = \sigma_\epsilon^2 + 8\sigma_{rp}^2$ | $(19)(31) = 589$ | None |
| $E(MS_{RT}) = \sigma_\epsilon^2 + \sigma_{rpt}^2 + 32\sigma_{rt}^2$ | $(19)(7) = 133$ | $MS_{RPT}$ |
| $E(MS_{PT}) = \sigma_\epsilon^2 + \sigma_{rpt}^2 + 20\sigma_{pt}^2$ | $(31)(7) = 217$ | $MS_{RPT}$ |
| $E(MS_{RPT}) = \sigma_\epsilon^2 + \sigma_{rpt}^2$ | $(19)(31)(7) = 4{,}123$ | None |

[a]Although no source has the proper $E(MS)$ for testing the $T$ main effect, an error term can be "assembled" using variance components; for example, $MS_{PT} - MS_{RPT}$ estimates $20\sigma_{pt}^2$, which when added to $MS_{RT}$ produces a mean square with the desired ingredients. The resulting ratio is termed a "quasi-$F$." Special formulas are needed to estimate the degrees of freedom for "assembled" mean squares (see Winer, 1971, p. 375). Or, if $F = MS_{PT}/MS_{RPT} \doteq 1$ or $F = MS_{RT}/MS_{RPT} \doteq 1$, the model could be simplified by dropping out this component. Hence no mean square would need to be constructed.

   e.
$$\hat{\sigma}_r^2 = (MS_R - MS_{RP})/256$$
$$\hat{\sigma}_p^2 = (MS_P - MS_{RP})/160$$
$$\hat{\sigma}_{rp}^2 = MS_{RP}/8^*$$
$$\hat{\sigma}_{rt}^2 = (MS_{RT} - MS_{RPT})/32$$
$$\hat{\sigma}_{pt}^2 = (MS_{PT} - MS_{RPT})/20$$
$$\hat{\sigma}_{rpt}^2 = MS_{RPT}^*$$

7. a. The two nested factors are raters (nested within political party of rater) and ratees (nested within political party of ratee). It happens here that the political parties are the same for raters and ratees. This is a doubly nested design.

$^*\sigma_\epsilon^2$ is assumed to equal 0.

   b. Yes. Raters cannot cross political party of rater, and ratees cannot cross political party of ratee, but they can cross everything else. See Stanley (1961) for further details.
   c. "Political party of rater" crosses "trait," "party of ratee," and "ratee," that is, everything except "rater."
   d. Rater and ratee are likely to be considered random-effects factors.
   e. Democrat raters tended to rate Democrat ratees much higher than they rated Republican ratees, and Republican raters tended to rate Republican ratees much higher than they rated Democrat ratees. Thus raters tended to prefer the ratees who were prominent in their own party.
   f. The interaction of party of rater with party of ratee with trait rated suggests that raters' bias in favor of their own party was not uniform across traits. Raters tended to rate ratees of their own party relatively higher on some traits than on others, and similarly for ratees of the other party.

# 20

# AN INTRODUCTION TO THE ANALYSIS OF COVARIANCE

## 20.1 THE FUNCTIONS OF ANCOVA

The analysis of covariance (ANCOVA) is a method of statistical analysis devised by R. A. Fisher in 1932 that combines the analysis of variance with regression analysis (Chap. 8). It is used to (1) increase statistical power, and/or (2) reduce bias, that is, to equate (statistically) groups on one or more variables. ANCOVA can often accomplish the purpose of increasing power, but its ability to remove bias is fraught with technical difficulties that have been frequently ignored. Many novices have viewed ANCOVA as the Messiah of statistical methods; it has been asked to give signs and perform wonders—to reveal the truth amidst a bewildering array of uncontrolled and poorly measured confounding variables.

Some have mistakenly assumed that ANCOVA, in effect, transforms quasi experiments into randomized experiments. In reality ANCOVA is unable to give the results of a quasi-experiment* the same degree of credibility that is provided by randomized experiments.

*That is, studies in which the experimental units are not randomly assigned to treatments, but are taken as they occurred "naturally."

## An Illustration

An experiment is performed in the twenty elementary schools of a large school district. Ten of the schools are randomly designated to be the sites for adoption of an innovative science curriculum, "Science: A Process Approach" (SAPA). The SAPA materials are bought and placed in the ten schools; teachers will be trained to use them. The other ten elementary schools continue to use the district's traditional textbook-based science curriculum. After two years of study in the respective programs, sixth-grade pupils in all twenty schools are given the Science test (a 45-item measure of scientific methods, reasoning, and knowledge) of the *Sequential Tests of Educational Progress* (STEP). Each student's score is expressed as a percentage. There are fifty to 120 sixth-grade pupils in each school; but since the school itself (along with its teachers, administrators, surrounding neighborhoods, and the like) was randomly designated as either SAPA or Traditional (the two experimental conditions $E$ versus $C$), the school is the experimental unit.* The twenty schools' means of sixth-grade pupils' STEP-Science scores will be used as the observational unit in the statistical analysis. The data collected in the experiment are reproduced in Table 20.1.

# 20.2 ANOVA RESULTS

An analysis of variance will be performed on the dependent variable $Y$ so that the ANOVA results can be compared with those that will be obtained from the ANCOVA. In ANCOVA (as in multiple regression (Chap. 8) and trend analysis (Sec. 17.19) the dependent variable is usually designated by $Y$ (and the covariate by $X$); to avoid confusion when comparing results, $Y$ will be used to denote the dependent variable in both the ANOVA and ANCOVA. The model for this experiment is the usual fixed-effects ANOVA (Eq. 16.10; Sec. 16.8):

$$Y_{ij} = \mu + \alpha_j + \epsilon_{ij} \qquad \textbf{(20.1)}$$

where

$$\alpha_1 = \mu_1 - \mu$$

$$\alpha_2 = \mu_2 - \mu$$

*In practice the teacher factor should be included in the design, and the scores of individual students would ordinarily serve as the observational unit (Sec. 19.22), but this would complicate the illustration. Students would be nested within both teachers and schools, and schools would be designated as a random effect. When the design is balanced, the results for the treatment effect in both analyses would be identical when school is properly designated as a random factor (Hopkins, 1982). The use of students' scores as the observational units allows the examination of possible interactions of the treatment with learner characteristics such as ability level and sex. To avoid unnecessary complexity in notation, since the school means are the observational unit in the example, they will be denoted by $Y_{ij}$, not $\overline{Y}_{ij}$.

**TABLE 20.1 School Means from a Hypothetical Experiment Comparing Ten Experimental ($E$) Schools with Ten Control ($C$) Schools on the STEP Science Test**

*A.*

| *E Schools* ($n = 10$) | *C Schools* ($n = 10$) |
|---|---|
| 77.63% | 64.10% |
| 74.13 | 43.67 |
| 67.20 | 50.40 |
| 78.23 | 84.33 |
| 57.93 | 44.93 |
| 57.65 | 71.43 |
| 83.30 | 71.10 |
| 73.90 | 44.57 |
| 45.90 | 68.23 |
| 64.83 | 68.47 |
| $\bar{Y}_1 = 68.070\%$ | $\bar{Y}_2 = 61.123\%$ |
| $s_1^2 = 134.60$ | $s_2^2 = 201.50$ |

*B.* ANOVA Table

| *Source* | *SS* | $\nu$ | *MS* | *F* |
|---|---|---|---|---|
| Between Groups (Treatments) | 241.30 | 1 | 241.30 | 1.44 |
| Within Groups (Schools nested within Treatments) | 3,024.94 | 18 | 168.05 | |
| TOTAL | 3,266.24 | | | |

$_{.90}F_{1,18} = 3.01$, $p > .10$

and the customary assumptions (Sec. 16.18) of homogeneously, independently, and normally distributed errors, $\epsilon_{ij}$, are made, that is, $\epsilon \sim NID(0, \sigma_\epsilon^2)$. The ANOVA results are given in the ANOVA table in panel B of Table 20.1.

Since the critical value of $F$ at the 10% level of significance with 1 and 18 degrees of freedom is 3.01, the observed $F$-ratio of 1.44 is insufficient evidence on which to reject the null hypothesis of no difference between the means of populations of schools taught science with the SAPA ($E$) and with their traditional ($C$) curriculum.

## 20.3 ANCOVA MODEL

The analysis need not stop here. More attention to the unpredictable variance ("error") in the model could prove fruitful. The error $\epsilon_{ij}$ using the ANOVA model in Equation 20.1 represents the unpredictable deviation of any school from the mean of all schools in its same treatment group ($E$ or $C$); for example, each $E$ school (group 1) would have a predicted mean of $\mu_1 = \mu + \alpha_1$, and a given $E$ school $i$ would deviate from that expected value by an amount denoted by $\epsilon_{i1} = Y_{i1} - \mu_1$. For example, $Y_{i1} = \mu_1 + \epsilon_{i1}$. Note that the $\epsilon_{ij}$ is the residual or error of estimate (Sec. 8.7) when treatment group is the sole predictor.

If one knows absolutely nothing more about the twenty schools except which ten are in the $E$ group and which ten are in the $C$ group, then the errors, $\epsilon_{ij}$'s, are those in the ANOVA given in Table 20.1. It is often the case, however, that some characteristic, $X$, of the observational units (school IQ means in this illustration) correlates with the dependent variable $Y$ and hence can improve the accuracy in predicting $Y$ and decrease the residuals and, therefore, error variance. It is reasonable to expect, for example, that schools with high scholastic aptitude (IQ) will tend to have higher mean scores on the achievement test than schools of lower IQ means. Panel $A$ of Table 20.2 shows the groups of schools with achievement averages, $Y$, and IQ averages, $X$. (In this illustration $X$ is measured by a standardized scholastic aptitude test given prior to the treatment.) Thus, $X$ can be used to reduce the magnitude of the $\epsilon$'s. The variable $X$ is called the *covariate*.* Consequently, the error $\epsilon_{ij}$ in the ANOVA model can be separated into two independent, additive portions:

$$\epsilon_{ij} = \beta(X_{ij} - \mu_X) + \epsilon'_{ij} \tag{20.2}$$

where $X_{ij} - \mu_X$ is the deviation of the $i$th observation, $X_{ij}$, of the covariate in the $j$th treatment condition from the covariate mean, $\mu_X$, $\beta$ is a regression coefficient that describes the relationship of $X$ to $Y$, and $\epsilon'_{ij} \sim NID(0, \sigma^2_{\epsilon'})$.

The new error, $\epsilon'$, represents that portion of the old error, $\epsilon$, that remains when variance in $\epsilon$'s related to variance in $X$'s is excluded. In other words in ANCOVA the errors, $\epsilon'$'s, are residuals when treatment group ($E$ or $C$) and mean IQ are used as predictors, as in multiple regression (Chap. 8).

The fixed-effects ANOVA model now becomes the *fixed-effects analysis of covariance (ANCOVA)* model:

$$Y_{ij} = \mu + \alpha_j + \beta_w(X_{ij} - \mu_X) + \epsilon'_{ij} \tag{20.3}$$

or

$$Y_{ij} - \beta_w(X_{ij} - \mu_X) = \mu + \alpha_j + \epsilon'_{ij} \tag{20.3A}$$

Equation 20.3A shows that ANCOVA can be viewed as an ANOVA (Eq. 20.1) in which the dependent variable is not $Y$, but $Y - \beta(X_{ij} - \mu_X)$.

The term $\beta_w$ in the ANCOVA model represents the relationship between $X$ and $Y$ *within* the treatment groups. The assumption has been made that the regression of $Y$ onto $X$ is the same for each treatment condition, that is, $\beta_1 = \beta_2 \cdots = \beta_{\text{within}} = \beta_w$. This means that the slopes when $Y$ is regressed on $X$ within each of the $J$ groups differ only because of sampling error, that is, $E(b_1) = E(b_2) = \cdots = E(b_J) = \beta_w$. Peckham's (see Glass, Peckham, and Sanders, 1972) research suggests ANCOVA is relatively robust with respect to violations of this assumption.

The new errors, $\epsilon'$, will always sum to less than the old errors, $\epsilon$, except in the unlikely situation where $\beta$ is zero, hence ANCOVA usually will yield a more powerful test of the treatment effect than ANOVA. Notice in panel $C$ of Table 20.2 how the dependent variable $Y$ and the covariate $X$ are quite highly correlated within each of the two groups: $r_{XY}$ is +.931 for the $E$ group and +.805 for the $C$ group, that is, the average IQ of

*Also termed covariable and concomitant variable.

**TABLE 20.2 School Means on the Science Test ($Y$) and the IQ Test ($X$) for the Twenty Schools in the Hypothetical Curriculum Experiment[a]**

| | *E Schools* ($n = 10$) | | *C Schools* ($n = 10$) | | |
|---|---|---|---|---|---|
| *A.* | $X$ | $Y$ | $X$ | $Y$ | *Total* ($n_. = 20$) |
| | 105.7 | 77.63% | 101.2 | 64.10% | $\bar{X}_. = 100.63$ $\bar{Y}_. = 64.597$ |
| | 100.3 | 74.13 | 97.6 | 43.67 | $\Sigma x^2_{\text{total}} = 796.48$ |
| | 94.3 | 67.20 | 96.4 | 50.40 | $\Sigma y^2_{\text{total}} = 3{,}266.24$ |
| | 108.7 | 78.23 | 109.6 | 84.33 | $\Sigma xy_{\text{total}} = 1{,}145.97$ |
| | 93.1 | 57.93 | 94.0 | 44.93 | $r_{\text{total}} = .7105$ |
| | 96.7 | 57.65 | 105.4 | 71.43 | |
| | 106.9 | 83.30 | 102.4 | 71.10 | |
| | 100.3 | 73.90 | 100.6 | 44.57 | |
| | 86.5 | 45.90 | 104.2 | 68.23 | |
| | 96.1 | 64.83 | 112.6 | 68.47 | |
| *B.* | $\bar{X}_1 = 98.86$ | $\bar{Y}_1 = 68.070\%$ | $\bar{X}_2 = 102.40$ | $\bar{Y}_2 = 61.123\%$ | |
| | $s^2_X = 47.94$ | $s^2_Y = 134.60$ | $s^2_X = 33.60$ | $s^2_Y = 201.50$ | $\Sigma y^2_w = 3{,}024.94$ |
| | $\Sigma x^2_1 = 431.42$ | $\Sigma y^2_1 = 1{,}211.44$ | $\Sigma x^2_2 = 302.40$ | $\Sigma y^2_2 = 1{,}813.50$ | $\Sigma x^2_w = 733.82$ |
| *C.* | $\Sigma xy_1 = 672.78$ | | $\Sigma xy_2 = 596.10$ | | $\Sigma xy_w = 1{,}268.88$ |
| | $r_1 = .931$ | | $r_2 = .805$ | | $r_w = \dfrac{\Sigma xy_w}{\sqrt{(\Sigma x^2_w)(\Sigma y^2_w)}} = .8517$ |

*D.* $SS'_{\text{total}} = SS_{\text{total}}(1 - r^2_{\text{total}}) = 3{,}266.24\ [1 - (.7105)^2] = 1{,}617.58$

$SS'_w = SS_w(1 - r^2_w) = 3{,}024.94\ [1 - (.8517)^2] = 830.88$

$SS'_b = SS'_{\text{total}} - SS'_w = 1617.58 - 830.88 = 786.71$

the school is closely related to the average science achievement. Making use of this relationship will allow ANCOVA to result in a more powerful analysis than ANOVA.

Notice how the ANOVA of the data (in panel $B$ of Table 20.1) did not discover a significant treatment effect; the treatment effects $\hat{\alpha}_1$ and $\hat{\alpha}_2$ were not reliably different from 0, that is, $H_0\colon \mu_1 = \mu_2$ remained tenable. However, since the errors in the ANCOVA model will be smaller and have less variance than those in ANOVA, the main effects from the analysis of covariance may prove to be reliably greater than zero.

## 20.4 ANCOVA COMPUTATIONS: $SS_{\text{total}}$

To test the null hypothesis, $H_0\colon \mu_1 = \mu_2 = \cdots = \mu_J$, the various sums of squares must be *adjusted* for the effects of the covariate. Recall that the proportion of variance (or sum of squares) in variable $Y$ that is predictable from variable $X$ is described by $r^2_{XY}$. Thus, the adjusted total sum of squares ($SS'_{\text{total}}$) can be obtained using Equation 20.4

$$SS'_{\text{total}} = SS_{\text{total}}(1 - r^2_{\text{total}}) \tag{20.4}$$

**TABLE 20.2 (cont.)**

| E. Source | | $SS'$ | $\nu$ | $MS'$ | $F$ |
|---|---|---|---|---|---|
| Between | | 786.71 | 1 | 786.71 | $16.10^b$ |
| Within | | 830.88 | 17 | 48.88 | |
| | (TOTAL | 1,617.59 | 18) | | |

$^b\ {}_{.999}F_{1,17} = 15.7, p < .001$

F. $$b_w = \frac{\Sigma xy_w}{\Sigma x_w^2} = \frac{1{,}268.88}{733.82} = 1.73; \qquad \overline{Y}'_j = \overline{Y}_j - b_w(\overline{X}_j - \overline{X}_{\bullet})$$

$$\overline{Y}'_1 = 68.070 - 1.73(98.86 - 100.63) = 71.132$$

$$\overline{Y}'_2 = 61.123 - 1.73(102.40 - 100.63) = 58.061$$

G. $$s^2_{\overline{Y}'} = MS'_w\left[\frac{1}{n} + \frac{(\overline{X}_j - \overline{X}_{\bullet})^2}{\Sigma x_w^2}\right]$$

$$= 48.88\left[\frac{1}{10} + \frac{(98.86 - 100.63)^2}{733.82}\right] = 5.097$$

$s_{\overline{Y}'} = 2.258$

$$.90 \text{ CI for } \mu_1\!: \overline{Y}'_1 \pm {}_{.95}t_8 s_{\overline{Y}'} = 71.132 \pm (1.860)(2.258)$$

$$= 71.132 \pm 4.199$$

$$= (66.93, 75.33)$$

$$.90 \text{ CI for } \mu_2\!: \overline{Y}'_2 \pm 4.353 = (58.061 \pm 4.199)$$

$$= (53.86, 62.26)$$

[a]The authors wish to thank Alan Davis and Mark Chisholm for their assistance in these analyses.

where $SS_{\text{total}}$ is the total sum of squares obtained using ANOVA (i.e., the unadjusted, $\Sigma y^2$) and $r_{\text{total}}$ is the correlation between the covariate, $X$, and the dependent variable, $Y$, for all $nJ$ pairs of observations, viewed as a single group (i.e., treatment group membership is ignored).

If Equation 7.4 were employed with the twenty pairs of scores in Table 20.2, $r_{\text{total}}$ would result. In the right-hand portion of panel $A$ of Table 20.2, $r_{\text{total}}$ was found to be .7105 and the total sum of squares from the ANOVA of $Y$, $\Sigma y^2_{\text{total}}$, was found to be 3,266.24. In panel $D$ of Table 20.2, Equation 20.4 is used to find $SS'_{\text{total}} = (3{,}266.24)[1 - (.7105)^2] = 1{,}617.58$.

## 20.5 THE ADJUSTED WITHIN SUM OF SQUARES $SS'_w$

The adjusted within sum of squares, $SS'_w$ is given by Equation 20.5:

$$SS'_w = SS_w(1 - r_w^2) \qquad \textbf{(20.5)}$$

where $SS_w$ is the unadjusted sum of squares (from the ANOVA) and $r_w$ is the within groups (pooled) correlation coefficient between $X$ and $Y$.

Before the equation for determining $r_w$ is given, for simplicity in notation let*

$$\Sigma xy_w = \Sigma xy_1 + \Sigma xy_2 + \cdots + \Sigma xy_J$$
$$\Sigma x_w^2 = \Sigma x_1^2 + \Sigma x_2^2 + \cdots + \Sigma x_J^2$$
$$\Sigma y_w^2 = \Sigma y_1^2 + \Sigma y_2^2 + \cdots + \Sigma y_J^2$$

Then,

$$r_w = \frac{\Sigma xy_w}{\sqrt{(\Sigma x_w^2)(\Sigma y_w^2)}} \tag{20.6}$$

In the right-hand portion of panel $C$ in Table 20.2, $r_w$ was found to equal .8517, and in panel $D$, $SS'_w$ is shown to equal 830.88.

## 20.6 THE ADJUSTED SUM OF SQUARES BETWEEN GROUPS $SS'_b$

The adjusted sum of squares attributable to treatments, $SS'_b$, is the difference between $SS'_{total}$ and $SS'_w$; it must be computed indirectly using Equation 20.7.

$$SS'_b = SS'_{total} - SS'_w \tag{20.7}$$

In panel $D$ of Table 20.2, $SS'_b$ was found to be 786.71.

## 20.7 DEGREES OF FREEDOM IN ANCOVA AND THE ANCOVA TABLE

The degrees of freedom in ANCOVA are identical to those in ANOVA with one exception: one degree of freedom is lost from the "within" source of variation for the covariate. (If there is more than one covariate, one degree of freedom is lost for each covariate.)

*More explicitly.

$$\Sigma xy_w = \sum_{j=1}^{J} \sum_{i=1}^{n} x_{ij}y_{ij};$$

$$\Sigma x_w^2 = \sum_{j=1}^{J} \sum_{i=1}^{n} x_{ij}^2;$$

$$\Sigma y_w^2 = \sum_{j=1}^{J} \sum_{i=1}^{n} y_{ij}^2.$$

If the null hypothesis is true (hence $\mu_1 = \mu_2 = \cdots = \mu_J$ or $\alpha_1^2 = \cdots = \alpha_J^2 = 0$), then the ratio of the adjusted mean squares, $MS_b'/MS_w'$ will follow a central $F$-distribution with $J - 1$ and $n_{\bullet} - J - 1$ degrees of freedom.*

The ratio of $MS_A'$ to $MS_w'$ in panel $E$ of Table 20.2 is found to be 16.10, which exceeds the 99.9th percentile in the central $F_{1,17}$ distribution (15.7), thus leading to rejection of the null hypothesis ($H_0$: $\mu_1 = \mu_2$) or of zero treatment main effects. The results of the ANCOVA are summarized in a table like that used to report ANOVA results in panel $E$ of Table 20.2.

Recall that when the same data on $Y$, science achievement, were analyzed by an ANOVA (Table 20.1), taking no account of the correlation between $X$ (IQ means) and $Y$ (science means), the null hypothesis could not be rejected. By removing from $\epsilon$ in Equations 20.1 and 20.2 that portion which was predictable from $X$, a more powerful test of the difference between the means for the two treatment groups was obtained, and the null hypothesis was rejected at the .001 level of significance.†

## 20.8 ADJUSTED MEANS, $\overline{Y}_j'$

To interpret the ANCOVA results properly, one needs to know what the mean of each group would have been predicted to be if its covariate mean, $\overline{X}_j$, had been equal to the grand mean on the covariate, $\overline{X}_{\bullet}$. For this purpose, the adjusted mean of group $j$, $\overline{Y}_j'$, becomes

$$\overline{Y}_j' = \overline{Y}_j - b_w(\overline{X}_j - \overline{X}_{\bullet}) \tag{20.8}$$

where $\overline{Y}_j$ is the unadjusted mean of group $j$ on the dependent variable, $Y$, $\overline{X}_j$ is the mean of group $j$ on the covariate, $\overline{X}_{\bullet}$ is the grand mean on the covariate, and $b_w$ is the estimate of $\beta_w$, the slope (regression coefficient).

$$b_w = \frac{\Sigma\, xy_w}{\Sigma\, x_w^2} \tag{20.9}$$

The computation of $b_w$ and the adjusted means $\overline{Y}_1'$ and $\overline{Y}_2'$ are illustrated in panel $F$ of Table 20.2.‡ Notice that the difference between the adjusted means, $\overline{Y}_1' - \overline{Y}_2' = 71.13 - 58.06 = 13.07$, is much greater than the difference in unadjusted means, $\overline{Y}_1 - \overline{Y}_2 = 68.07 - 61.12 = 6.95$. Recall that $Y$ was the percent of the items answered correctly; hence, if both the $E$ and $C$ schools had the identical mean IQ of 100.63, the mean of the

*More generally, $\nu_e = n_{\bullet} - J - c$, where $c$ equals the number of covariates.

†Sometimes the covariate(s) is listed as a source of variation in the summary table. The sum of squares explained by the covariate(s) is the difference between $SS_{\text{total}}$ and $SS_{\text{total}}'$, that is, in the example $SS_{\text{covariate}} = 3266.24 - 1617.59 = 1{,}648.65$. $MS_{\text{covariates}} = SS_{\text{covariates}}/C$, where $C$ is the number of covariates. In the example in Table 20.2 $C = 1$, thus $MS_{\text{covariates}} = 1{,}648.65$. The test of the hypothesis, $H_0$: $\rho_{\text{total}} = 0$, is $F = MS_{\text{covariates}}/MS_w' = 1{,}648.65/48.88 = 33.73$, $p < .001$.

‡For a balanced design, an alternative formula is: $b_w = r_w\sqrt{MS_w/s_{wx}^2}$ where $MS_w$ and $s_{wx}^2$ are the average within-groups variance on $Y$ and $X$, respectively.

*E* schools would be expected to be 71.13% which is 13.07% higher than the predicted mean of the *C* schools (58.06%).*

In the example the main effects after being adjusted for the covariate are slightly larger than the unadjusted ANOVA main effects because, although the *E* schools scored higher on the achievement test than the *C* schools (presumably because of the superiority of the *E* curriculum), they had to overcome a very slight disadvantage in mean IQ. If there had been a large covariate (IQ) difference favoring the *E* group, the ANCOVA adjusted main effects would have been substantially smaller than the ANOVA unadjusted effects.†

If any event, for randomized experiments the adjustment of the means through covariance analysis will ordinarily be small when $n$ is large, since random assignment to treatment tends to make the groups only randomly different on the covariate. When $\overline{X}_j - \overline{X}_{\bullet}$ is quite small, the adjusted means will scarcely differ from the unadjusted means. When $n$ is small, the $\overline{Y}'$'s and $\overline{Y}$'s can differ considerably, even when units are randomly assigned to treatments (as in the curriculum experiment).‡

The more important consequence of employing the covariate, especially in experimental studies, is that its use reduces error variance and thus increases precision of estimates and the power of hypotheses tests. The relationship between the variance of $\epsilon'$ and $\epsilon$ is described in Equation 20.10

$$\sigma^2_{\epsilon'} = \sigma^2_{\epsilon}(1 - \rho^2_w)\left(1 + \frac{1}{\nu_e - 2}\right) \tag{20.10}$$

where $\nu_e$ is the degrees of freedom for the error mean square in an ANOVA. If $\nu_e$ is large

$$\sigma^2_{\epsilon'} \doteq \sigma^2_{\epsilon}(1 - \rho^2_w) \tag{20.10A}$$

or

$$MS'_w \doteq MS_w(1 - r^2_w) \tag{20.10B}$$

where $\sigma^2_{\epsilon'}$ (or $MS'_w$) is the error variance for ANCOVA, $\sigma^2_{\epsilon}$ (or $MS_w$) is the error variance for the corresponding ANOVA, and $\rho_w$ (or $r_w$) is the correlation of $X$ and $Y$ within treatment conditions.

*Expressing performance as percent-correct rather than raw scores can often be useful in conveying the magnitude of the treatment effect. To quantify effect size (Sec. 12.8), one should not use $MS'_w$, but continue to use the unadjusted $MS_w$, that is, $\hat{\Delta} = (\overline{Y}'_1 - \overline{Y}'_2)/\sqrt{MS_w}$.

†If the covariate $X$ were measured after the treatment was applied (e.g., suppose $X$ stood for IQ scores of sixth-graders and it was measured on the same day that the achievement test was given), then if $E$ also increased students IQ scores, the ANCOVA is likely to adjust out of the main effects on $Y$ some that are properly credited to the treatment. For this reason it is recommended that covariate $X$ be observed before treatments are applied, if it might be affected by the treatments.

‡The difference of 3.56 points in covariate means in Table 20.2 ($\overline{X}_1 = 98.86$ and $\overline{X}_2 = 102.40$) is well within the difference that would be expected from chance when $n = 10$. The difference would not be statistically significant ($F = 1.54, p > .20$).

Notice, for example, that if the covariate and the dependent variable are correlated, that $MS'_w$ is less than $MS_w$ (Eq. 20.10B).

## 20.9 CONFIDENCE INTERVALS AND MULTIPLE COMPARISONS FOR ADJUSTED MEANS

In setting confidence intervals one cannot use $MS'_w$ directly; the error variance must be increased by a factor which increases as a function of the degree of extrapolation employed:

$$s^2_{\overline{Y}'} = MS'_w \left[\frac{1}{n} + \frac{(\overline{X}_j - \overline{X}_\bullet)^2}{\Sigma x^2_w}\right] \tag{20.11}$$

where $\Sigma x^2_w = \Sigma_j \Sigma_i (X_{ij} - \overline{X}_j)^2$, and

$$.90\text{CI:} \quad \overline{Y}'_j \pm {}_{.95}t_{\nu_j} s_{\overline{Y}'} \tag{20.12}$$

where $\nu_j = n_j - 2$.

In panel $G$ of Table 20.2, the .90 confidence intervals for the population means of the $E$ and $C$ groups were found to be (66.93, 75.33) and (53.86, 62.26). Thus the true "percent-correct" means for the experimental could be as low as 66.93% or as high as 75.33%, in contrast to 53.86% to 62.26% for the control population.

For making multiple comparisons, the error mean square must be adjusted to reflect the magnitude of extrapolations among the $J$ means:

$$MS''_w = MS'_w \left[1 + \frac{\Sigma x^2_b}{(J-1)\,\Sigma x^2_w}\right] \tag{20.13}$$

where $\Sigma x^2_b$ and $\Sigma x^2_w$ are the "between" and "within" sums of squares on the covariate $X$, respectively.* Note in Equation 20.13 that $MS''_w$ will exceed $MS'_w$ to the extent that $J$ covariate means differ ($\Sigma x^2_b$).

## 20.10 ANCOVA ILLUSTRATED GRAPHICALLY

The sense in which covariance analysis adjusts $Y$ for concomitant variation in $X$ and thus hypothetically represents what might have been seen in $Y$ if all groups were equal in terms of $X$, is illuminated by Figure 20.1. The data from the elementary school science curriculum experiment are graphed and various features of the ANCOVA are depicted.

*Since there are only two means in the illustration, multiple comparisons are superfluous. Nevertheless, to illustrate the use of Equation 20.13, the error mean square for multiple comparisons, $MS''_w$, would be $MS''_w = 48.88\ \{1 + 62.66/[(2-1)733.82]\} = 53.05$, where $\Sigma x^2_b = \Sigma x^2_{\text{total}} - \Sigma x^2_w = 796.48 - 733.82 = 62.66$.

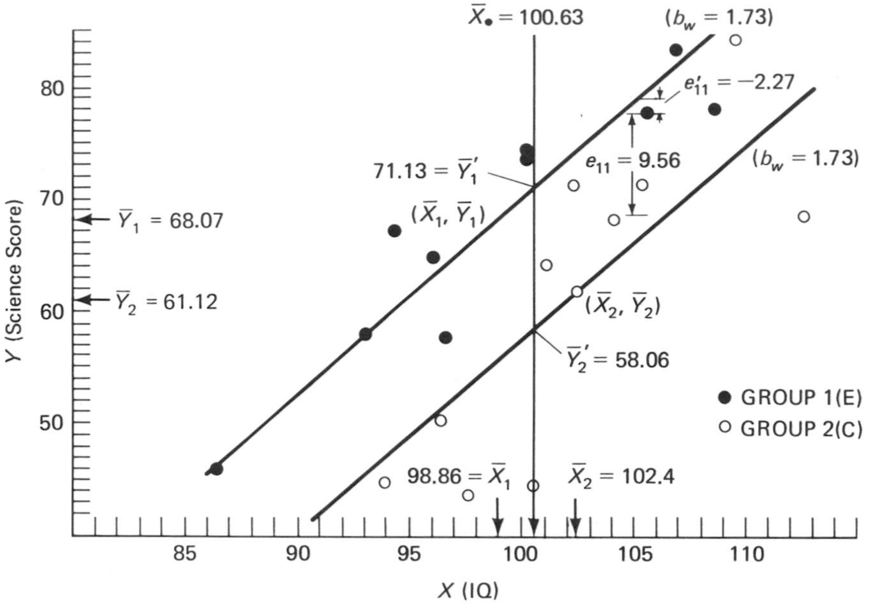


**FIGURE 20.1. ANCOVA illustrated graphically using data in Table 20.2.**

Figure 20.1 depicts the data in Table 20.2. The covariate $X$ is given along the $X$-axis and the dependent variable $Y$ is shown on the $Y$-axis. Notice that group $C$ has a slightly higher average on the covariate (IQ) than the $E$ group (102.4 versus 98.86), even though the difference is known to be due entirely to sampling error because schools were randomly assigned to $E$ or $C$ groups.

Each school is represented as a "dot" in the scatter plot. The $E$ and $C$ schools are denoted with "●" and "○," respectively, to help separate visually the data belonging to each group. The unadjusted means $\bar{Y}_1$ and $\bar{Y}_2$ are shown on the $Y$-axis. Recall from Table 20.1 that the difference in the unadjusted means was not statistically significant. The denominator in the ANOVA was the average within-group variance, $MS_w = s_w^2 = (s_1^2 + s_2^2)/2 = (134.60 + 201.50)/2 = 168.05$. $MS_w$ is approximately equal to the mean of the squared residuals ($x_{ij}^2 = (\bar{X}_{ij} - \bar{X}_j)^2$) within the two groups.

A visual examination of the "●'s" reveals a high correlation between $X$ and $Y$ within the $E$ group: $r_1 = .931$. The correlation is also high within the $C$ group: $r_2 = .805$. Pooling the information with each of the two groups, the within-group correlation, $r_w$, was found to be .852.

ANCOVA assumes $\beta_1 = \beta_2$, thus any difference between the regression slope in groups 1 and 2, that is, $b_1$ versus $b_2$, is viewed as sampling error. Pooling $\Sigma\, xy_1$ and $\Sigma\, xy_2$ to obtain $\Sigma\, xy_w$, and $\Sigma\, x_1^2$ and $\Sigma\, x_2^2$ to obtain $\Sigma\, x_w^2$ provides the data needed

*If $r_w$ is very low and $\nu_w$ is very small, for example, $r_w = .06$, it is possible for $MS'_w$ to be larger than $MS_w$, since the degrees of freedom are one less for $MS'$. This is rarely the case.

for the best estimate of the regression coefficient in the population, $b_w = \Sigma\, xy_w / \Sigma\, x_w^2 =$ 1.73.

Thus, for each unit that $\overline{X}_1$ is below $\overline{X}_{\bullet}$, $\overline{Y}_j$ is adjusted upward by 1.73 points. Conversely, since $\overline{X}_2 - \overline{X}_{\bullet} = 1.77$, $\overline{Y}_2'$ will be $(1.73)(1.77) = 3.06$ points less than $\overline{Y}_2$. $\overline{Y}_2' = 61.12 - 3.06 = 58.06$. In other words, $b_w$ is used to estimate what the $\overline{Y}_j$'s would have been if the mean of each group, the covariates, ($\overline{X}_1$ and $\overline{X}_2$) were precisely equal to the grand mean on the covariate ($\overline{X}_{\bullet}$).

In ANOVA error, $e_{11}$, for school 1 in group 1 is $e_{11} = Y_{11} - \overline{Y}_1 = 77.63 - 68.07 = 9.56$. The square of these residuals for all ten schools within each group summed for both groups is $SS_w$.

In ANCOVA, however, the error, $e_{11}'$, is the residual for school 1—the distance from $Y_{11}'$ to the regression line within group 1, that is, $e_{11}' = Y_{11} - Y_{11}'$; where $Y_{11}' = \overline{Y}_1 + b_w(X_{11} - \overline{X}_1) = 68.07 + 1.73(105.7 - 98.86) = 79.90$, thus, $e_{11}' = 77.63 - 79.90 = -2.27$, which is much less than the $e_{11}$ of 9.5. Find $e_{11}$ and $e_{11}'$ illustrated in Fig. 20.1.)

In other words $e_{11}'$ is the vertical distance from $Y_{11}$ to the regression line with slope, $b_w$, that passes through the centroid of its group ($\overline{X}_1$, $\overline{Y}_1$). The centroid for each group is marked "+" in Figure 20.1. When $X$ and $Y$ correlate, the residuals from ANCOVA will be smaller than from ANOVA, thus the sum of the squared residuals in ANCOVA ($SS_w'$) will be less than the sum of the squared residuals in ANOVA ($SS_w$); consequently, $MS_w'$ will be less than $MS_w^*$, and the ANCOVA will be more powerful than the ANOVA. $MS_w'$ is analogous to the square of the standard error of estimate (Sec. 8.10), that is, $MS_w' \doteq s_Y^2(1 - r_w^2)$.

The $F$-ratio of the adjusted treatment mean square $MS_b'$ to the adjusted within mean square $MS_w'$ provides a test of the hypothesis that treatment means on $Y$ would be equal if the groups were equal in their $X$ means.

## 20.11 ANCOVA ASSUMPTIONS

All the assumptions made regarding "errors," as defined in the ANOVA model, $\epsilon_{ij}$ in Equation 20.1 (Equation 16.10, see Secs. 16.8, 16.14, 16.18), are made for the adjusted errors, $\epsilon_{ij}'$ in the ANCOVA model in Equation 20.2; that is, $\epsilon_{ij}' \sim NID\ (0, \sigma_{\epsilon}^2)$. The general precautions that have been given regarding ANOVA (Sec. 16.18) would be observed in ANCOVA (Cochran, 1957; Glass, Peckham, and Sanders, 1972; Ragosa, 1980). Note that in testing for normality or heterogeneity of variance, the "observations" for each of the $J$ groups are the residuals ($\epsilon_{ij}' = Y_{ij}' - \overline{Y}_j$) about the regression line with slope $b_w$ that passes through the centroid ($\overline{X}_j$, $\overline{Y}_j$) of each group.

ANCOVA makes three additional assumptions that involve the regression of $Y$ on $X$.

1. *The regression lines for each group are assumed to be parallel*, that is, $\beta_1 = \beta_2 = \cdots = \beta_J = \beta_W$. If this is violated, the covariance adjustment may still improve the precision, but the meanings of the adjusted treatment means become cloudy, and the investigator may fail to discover the differential treatment effects—a point that might be

important for practical applications.* Violation of the parallel regression slopes appears to be inconsequential in a one-factor fixed-effects ANCOVA for a wide variety of conditions (Glass, Peckham, and Sanders, 1972). Heterogeneity of regression coefficients results when there is an interaction between treatment and covariate scores. For example, in Figure 18.6 view ability as a covariate and observe that the treatment-by-ability interaction would result in nonparallel regression lines.†

2. *The covariance procedure assumes that the correct form of regression equation has been fitted.* Virtually all ANCOVA applications assume a linear relationship between $X$ and $Y$. Nonlinearity will result in biased estimates of effects; the magnitude of the bias depends on the true form of the relationship between $X$ and $Y$. The bias will be least severe when subjects are randomly assigned to groups. The randomization ensures that the usual interpretations of standard errors and tests of significance are not seriously vitiated, although fitting the correct form of regression would presumably give a larger increase in precision. The danger of misleading results is much greater when there are real differences among treatment groups on the covariate. Fortunately, most cognitive and psychomotor variables are linearly related, and unless measurement procedures are faulty (e.g., the test that lacks ceiling), the linear regression model works well in most applications. Frequently, curvilinear relationships can often be made linear by mathematical transformations (Sec. 8.28) of either the dependent variable $Y$ or the covariate $X$ or both (see Li, 1964, for treatment of curvilinear ANCOVA).

*To test whether the slopes of the $J$ regression lines are from the same population, that is, $H_0$: $\beta_1 = \beta_2 = \cdots = \beta_J = \beta_w$, the sum of squares due to the variation among $b_1, b_2, \cdots, b_J$, is found by finding the squared residuals within each of the $J$ groups, allowing each group to determine its own least-squares regression line with slope $b_j$.

$$SS'_{w_j} = \sum_j \left[ \sum_i y_{ij}^2 (1 - r_j^2) \right]$$

In the curriculum experiment in Table 20.2.

$$\begin{aligned} SS'_{w_j} &= \Sigma y_1^2 (1 - r_1^2) + \Sigma y_2^2 (1 - r_2^2) \\ &= 1{,}211.44\ [1 - (.931)^2] + 1{,}813.50\ [1 - (.805)^2] \\ &= 161.41 + 638.31 = 799.72 \end{aligned}$$

Only when $b_1 = b_2$, does $SS'_{w_j}$ equal $SS'_w$; the difference between $SS'_w$ and $SS'_{w_j}$ is due to the difference in the $b_j$'s. The sum of squares accruing from variance in the $b_j$'s, $SS_{\sigma_b}$, is

$$SS_{\sigma_b} = SS'_w - SS'_{w_j} = 830.88 - 799.72 = 31.16$$

And,

$$F = \frac{SS_{\sigma_b}/(J - 1)}{SS'_{w_j}/[J(n - 2)]} = \frac{31.16/(2 - 1)}{799.72/[3(8)]^2} = \frac{31.16}{33.32} = .94$$

Therefore, $H_0$: $\beta_1 = \beta_2$ is tenable.

†There are ANCOVA models (Huitema, 1980, Chap. 13) which do not assume parallel regression lines and allow each of the $J$ groups to use its own regression coefficient, $b_j$, to adjust its mean. An undesirable complexity of these procedures is that the difference in the adjusted means depends on the point of reference on the covariate (see Ragosa, 1980).

3. An assumption in the usual ANCOVA model that is not widely recognized is that the covariate is fixed (Sec. 8.25) and contains no measurement error. Lord (1960) has shown how large errors in the covariate can produce misleading results. The effects of the less-than-perfectly reliable covariate are often predictable so the nature of the bias in the adjustment can be considered in any interpretation. It should be emphasized, however, that to the extent the covariate is unreliable, the groups will not be truly equated on the covariate. Measurement error will decrease the observed correlation between $X$ and $Y$, and hence the slope, $b_w$, and will affect the adjusted means.

## 20.12 ANCOVA PRECAUTIONS

Two or more groups differing on some characteristic (such as age, IQ, or pretest) can be studied to discover whether or not there is a significant difference among groups on the dependent variable when groups are "statistically equated" on the characteristic(s) on which they differ. Examples where randomized experiments are not practical or possible include studies contrasting cultures, social class comparisons, or public and private schools. In quasi-experimental studies it is widely realized that an observed association, even if statistically significant, may be due wholly or partly to other uncontrolled variables $X_1$, $X_2$ . . . in which the groups differ. A common device has been to match the groups for the disturbing variables thought to be most important. This matching often results in serious problems (Sec. 12.14; Hopkins, 1969). In the same way the $X$-variables can be treated as covariates and ANCOVA can be employed to remove (at least partly) the influence of $X$-variables.

Unfortunately, quasi-experimental studies are subject to difficulties of interpretation from which true experiments are free. Although ANCOVA has been skillfully applied, one can never be sure that bias may not be present from some confounding variable that was overlooked. Indeed, unless the covariate is perfectly reliable, ANCOVA does not remove all the bias due to $X$ itself. In true experiments the effects of all variables measured and unmeasured, real and illusory, are distributed among the groups by the randomization in a way that is taken into account in the standard tests of significance. There is no such safeguard in the absence of randomization.

Second, when the $X$-variables show real differences among groups—the case in which adjustment is needed most—covariance adjustments involve a degree of extrapolation. To illustrate by an extreme case, suppose that one were adjusting for differences in parents' income in a comparison of the achievement of private and public school children, and that the private school incomes ranged from \$20,000 to \$32,000 while the public school incomes ranged from \$8,000 to \$16,000. The covariance would adjust results so that they allegedly applied to a mean income of \$18,000 in each group, although neither group has any observations in which incomes are at or even near this figure.

Two consequences of this extrapolation should be noted. Unless the statistical assumption of linear and homogeneous regression holds in the region in which observations are lacking, covariance will not remove all the bias and in practice may remove only a small part of it. Second, even if the regression is valid in the "no man's land," the standard errors of the adjusted means become large (Eq. 20.11) because the standard error formula in a covariance analysis takes account of the degree extrapolation $(\overline{X}_j - \overline{X}_{\bullet})$

that is being employed. Consequently, the adjusted differences may become insignificant statistically merely because the adjusted comparisons are of low precision.

When groups differ widely on some confounding variable $X$, these difficulties imply that the interpretation of an adjusted analysis is speculative rather than definitive. While there is no sure way out of the difficulty, two precautions are worth observing. Consider what internal evidence exists to indicate whether or not the regression is valid in the region of extrapolation. Sometimes the fitting of a more complex regression formula serves as a partial check. Examine the confidence intervals for the adjusted group means (Sec. 20.9), particularly when differences are nonsignificant after adjustment. Confidence limits for the adjusted means will reveal the precision (or imprecision) of the adjusted comparison.

Researchers are frequently tempted to try to make ANCOVA compensate for the lack of randomization, that is, to equate groups on preexperimental characteristics. The tool is generally not up to the job it is asked to perform; what is worse, its defects may be hidden. For an even more cautious perspective on the use of ANCOVA in quasi experiments, see Reichardt (1979) and Cronbach et al. (1977).

## 20.13 COVARYING VERSUS STRATIFYING

If the covariate is obtained prior to the treatment, an alternative design and alternative analyses strategy should be considered by the experimenter. An ANOVA of simple gain scores (e.g., Posttest-Pretest) is a simple alternative, but will less powerful than ANCOVA.*

The measure to serve as the covariate, $X$, can also be used to form $n$ homogeneous "blocks" (groups) of $J$ subjects each, and then assign the $J$ subjects within each block randomly to the $J$ treatments. If this design is employed, the data are analyzed as a "randomized blocks design." This design can be preferable to ANCOVA if the experimenter's sole interest is to minimize the error mean square for purposes of increasing power (Eq. 20.1), although ANCOVA becomes more powerful when $\rho > .6$ (Feldt, 1958). Recall that the randomized blocks design is a single replicate design ($n = 1$ observation per cell), and hence has no within-cell variance estimate. The blocking variable $X$ is also assumed to be a random factor, otherwise no proper error term for testing the treatment main effect will result, unless the additional assumption is made that there is no interaction ($\alpha\beta = 0$) between the treatments and blocking variable. The assumption is the same assumption necessary for $\beta_1 = \beta_2 = \cdots = \beta_J = \beta_w$.

In behavior research a factorial design with $n = 2$ is usually preferred to a randomized blocks design because (1) the interaction between the treatment and stratifying factors can be tested; (2) the stratifying factor need not be a random factor, hence the $\alpha\beta = 0$ assumption is not required; and (3) the power of the factorial design is almost as great as that of the randomized blocks design, even when the latter is appropriate.†

In randomized experiments where the bias-reducing function of ANCOVA is not needed the two-factor ANOVA (stratifying on $X$) would often be preferred to ANCOVA,

*If the covariate and the dependent variate do not employ a common metric, both can be transformed to T-scores (Sec. 6.6) using the composite $X$ and composite $Y$ distributions.

†See Feldt (1958) to determine the optimal number of levels of $X$ and cell size, given $\rho_{XY}$ and the total number of subjects available.

primarily because it yields additional useful information regarding the generalizability of the treatment effects across the various levels of the second factor, $X$. In addition the factorial (and randomized blocks) design works well even when the relationship between $X$ and the dependent variable $Y$ is not linear. An additional disadvantage of ANCOVA is computational complexity. On the other hand, loss of experimental subjects creates even greater problems for randomized blocks and factorial designs than for ANCOVA, since nonorthogonal designs will result. Frequently ANCOVA and factorial designs are combined as in Problem 1 of *Problems and Exercises* following this chapter. More complex applications of ANCOVA, where there are two or more covariates in combination with factorial designs are found in Keppel (1982), Kirk (1982), Myers (1979), Winer (1971), and especially Huitema (1980).

## CHAPTER SUMMARY

ANCOVA has two principal functions: (1) to increase power and (2) to reduce bias. The within-groups mean square in ANOVA, $MS_w$, is reduced in ANCOVA to approximately $MS'_w \doteq MS_w(1 - r_w^2)$, where $r_w$ is the within-groups correlation between the covariate $X$ and the dependent variable $Y$. Although ANCOVA can reduce bias, it can never remove all possible sources of confounding. The ANCOVA model assumes that within each of the $J$ groups, the errors are independent, normally distributed, and have common variance. The covariate is assumed to be linearly related to the dependent variable and the slopes of regression lines within each of the $J$ groups differ randomly only from a common regression coefficient, $\beta$. The covariate is also assumed to be a fixed factor containing no measurement error. In randomized experiments it is usually preferrable to stratify on $X$, than to use $X$ as a covariate.

## *MASTERY TEST*

1. ANCOVA removes the need for random assignment of subjects to treatments, that is, ANCOVA makes a quasi-experiment as definitive as an experiment. (T or F)
2. When the covariate correlates +.5 with the dependent variable, the adjusted mean square within, $MS'_w$, will be less than the $MS_w$ from ANOVA. (T or F)
3. In Question 2, the ratio $MS'_w/MS_w \doteq$ ____ .
4. Can the $MS'_b$ from ANCOVA be less than the $MS_b$ from ANOVA?
5. Will the $F$-ratio for the treatment main effects always be larger when ANCOVA is used rather than ANOVA?

Which of these (Questions 6 to 9) are assumptions of ANCOVA? (T or F)

6. $\beta_1 = \beta_2 = \cdots = \beta_J$ (the within-groups regression slopes are equal).
7. $\epsilon'_{ij} \sim NID(0, \sigma_\epsilon^2)$; the errors are normally distributed, have common variance across groups, and are independent.
8. The covariate is a fixed variable without measurement error.
9. The dependent variable contains no measurement error.
10. ANCOVA results have greatest credibility when the groups being compared on $Y$ differ little on the covariate $X$. (T or F)

Use Figures $A$, $B$, and $C$ to answer Questions 11 to 20: • = $E$, ○ = $C$

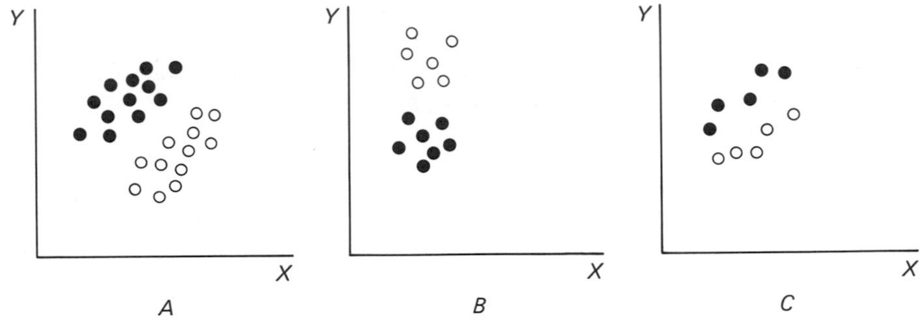


11. Which figure is least apt to be the result in a randomized experiment?
12. In which figure would the ANOVA and ANCOVA results be highly similar?
13. The within-groups correlation in Figure $B$ is approximately ____ .
14. In which figure would $MS'_w/MS_w$ be least?
15. In which figure would the adjusted means differ by more than the unadjusted means?
16. What is the value of $n$ in Figure $C$?
17. In which figure is $\overline{Y}'_C > \overline{Y}'_E$?
18. In which figure(s) does the relationship between $X$ and $Y$ (within groups) appear to be linear?
19. Making "visual" allowance for sampling error, does $\beta_E = \beta_C$ appear tenable in all figures?
20. Do the residuals $e'_{ij}$ appear to be heterogenous in any figure?

## *PROBLEMS AND EXERCISES*

The following gives the results of both an ANOVA and ANCOVA on the same data set. Subjects were classified by learning style (auditory, visual, and mixed) and sex, then randomly assigned to one of three treatments. Observations were randomly discarded from some cells to achieve a balanced design with $n = 5$ persons per cell. In the ANCOVA scores on a reading test served as the covariate.

| | *ANOVA* | | | *ANCOVA* | | |
|---|---|---|---|---|---|---|
| *Source* | $\nu$ | $MS$ | $F$ | $\nu$ | $MS'$ | $F$ |
| Treatment ($T$) | 2 | 661.11 | 21.34* | 2 | 713.87 | 26.13[a] |
| Learning Style ($L$) | 2 | 109.98 | 3.55 | 2 | 4.37 | .16 |
| Sex ($S$) | 1 | 48.02 | 1.55 | 1 | 62.84 | 2.30 |
| $TL$ | 4 | 4.33 | .14 | 4 | 10.38 | .38 |
| $TS$ | 2 | 5.58 | .18 | 2 | 5.46 | .20 |
| $LS$ | 2 | 23.54 | .76 | 2 | 32.51 | 1.19 |
| $TLS$ | 4 | 4.34 | .14 | 4 | 7.92 | .29 |
| Within ($p$: $SLT$) | 72 | 30.98 | | 71 | 27.32 | |

[a] $p < .001$

1. a. Do the adjusted means for the three treatment groups appear to differ greatly from the unadjusted means?
   b. Do the adjusted means for the three learning styles appear to differ less than the unadjusted means? What is the explanation?
   c. Did the ANCOVA result in a more powerful analysis than ANOVA?
   d. Estimate the "average" correlation between $X$ and $Y$ within the eighteen cells, that is, $r_w$.
   e. Estimate the standard error of estimate (Sec. 8.10) using the three predictors: learning style, sex, and covariate $X$ (reading test scores). (*Hint:* the standard error of estimate is the standard deviation of residuals within cells.)

2. Suppose there are three intact groups ($A$, $B$, $C$) and each was given a treatment. They were pretested ($X$) before the treatment and posttested following the treatment. Graph the data using $a$, $b$, and $c$ (not dots) to denote observations.

*Treatment*

| *A* | | *B* | | *C* | |
|---|---|---|---|---|---|
| $X$ | $Y$ | $X$ | $Y$ | $X$ | $Y$ |
| 2 | 5 | 14 | 7 | 20 | 20 |
| 4 | 8 | 16 | 8 | 18 | 22 |
| 5 | 7 | 15 | 10 | 23 | 26 |
| 8 | 9 | 19 | 13 | 25 | 28 |
| 6 | 11 | 11 | 12 | 24 | 24 |
| 5.0 | 8.0 | 15.0 | 10.0 | 22.0 | 24.0 |

$\bar{X}_{\bullet} = 14.0$ $\bar{Y}_{\bullet} = 14.0$
$\Sigma x^2_{total} = 818$
$\Sigma y^2_{total} = 846$
$r_{total} = .841$

$s^2_{X_1} = 5.0$ $s^2_{Y_1} = 5.0$ $s^2_{X_2} = 8.5$ $s^2_{Y_2} = 6.5$ $s^2_{X_3} = 8.5$ $s^2_{Y_3} = 10.0$

$\Sigma x_1^2 = 20$ $\Sigma y_1^2 = 20$ $\Sigma x_2^2 = 34$ $\Sigma y_2^2 = 26$ $\Sigma x_3^2 = 34$ $\Sigma y_3^2 = 40$

$\Sigma xy_1 = 15$ $\Sigma xy_2 = 5$ $\Sigma xy_3 = 30$

$r_1 = .75$ $r_2 = .168$ $r_3 = .813$

$\Sigma x^2_w = 88$
$\Sigma y^2_w = 86$
$\Sigma xy_w = 50$

   a. $r^2_w =$ ____.
   b. $SS_w =$ ____.
   c. $SS'_w =$ ____, $MS'_w =$ ____.
   d. $SS_{total} =$ ____, $SS'_{total} =$ ____.
   e. $SS'_b =$ ____, $MS'_b =$ ____.
   f. Construct an ANCOVA table. Is $H_0$ tenable using ANCOVA ($\alpha = .01$)?
   g. Using $b_w =$ ____, adjust the three means.
   h. Set a .90 CI around each mean. Why is the confidence interval for $\mu_B$ so much narrower than for $\mu_A$ and $\mu_C$?
   i. Show the adjusted means on a graph.
   j. Why might one lack confidence in the conclusions from this study?

3. One study (Gehler, 1979) compared a highly structured instructional approach ($E$) in kindergarten to the conventional method ($C$) on the end-of-year class performance on a composite measure $Y$, of cognitive perceptual and psychomotor kindergarten objectives. The experimental method emphasized behavioral objectives, diagnosis and prescription, and criterion-referenced assessment. Eight kindergarten teachers taught using the $E$ method, and eight others served as control teachers. To help control for differences in teacher quality, a confidential rating of teacher quality was obtained on each teacher (maximum

possible score of 100), which served as covariate $X$. Quality rating and the class means for each teacher are given.

| $E$ ($n = 8$) | | $C$ ($n = 8$) | |
|---|---|---|---|
| $X$ | $Y$ | $X$ | $Y$ |
| 65 | 105.8 | 96 | 129.1 |
| 52 | 111.0 | 61 | 113.1 |
| 76 | 95.3 | 77 | 90.8 |
| 81 | 109.6 | 68 | 114.1 |
| 99 | 111.3 | 76 | 121.6 |
| 82 | 118.4 | 84 | 120.7 |
| 95 | 122.8 | 65 | 118.1 |
| 79 | 119.7 | 94 | 115.4 |

a. Perform an ANOVA on the dependent variable $Y$.
b. Perform an ANCOVA on the dependent variable $Y$.
c. Contrast the ANOVA and ANCOVA results.
d. Were there significant differences between the two groups in teacher quality? ratings? What could account for such a small $F$-ratio?
e. Express $\overline{Y}'_E - \overline{Y}'_C$ as an effect size, $\hat{\Delta} = (\overline{Y}'_E - \overline{Y}'_C)/s_w$.

## ANSWERS TO MASTERY TEST

1. F  2. T  3. .75
4. Yes  5. No  6. T
7. T  8. T  9. F  10. T
11. A  12. B  13. 0
14. C  15. A  16. 5
17. B  18. A, B, and C
19. Yes  20. No

## ANSWERS TO PROBLEMS AND EXERCISES

1. a. No ($MS'_T$ and $MS_T$ do not differ greatly)
   b. Yes ($MS_L$ is much greater than $MS'_L$)
   c. Yes ($MS_w > MS'_w$)
   d. (a) $MS'_w = (MS_w)(1 - r^2_w)$; $r_w = .34$.
   e. (a) $s_{Y.X} = \sqrt{MS'_w} = \sqrt{27.32} = 5.23$

2. a. $r^2_w = \dfrac{(\Sigma xy_w)^2}{(\Sigma x^2_w)(\Sigma y^2_w)} = \dfrac{(50)^2}{(88)(86)} = .330$
   b. 86
   c. $SS'_w = SS_w(1 - r^2_w) = 86(1 - .330) = 57.62$; $MS'_w = 57.62/11 = 5.238$
   d. 846, 247.64
   e. $SS'_b = SS'_{\text{total}} - SS'_w = 190.02$; 95.01
   f.

| Source | $SS'$ | $\nu$ | $MS'$ | $F$ | |
|---|---|---|---|---|---|
| Between | 190.02 | 2 | 95.01 | 18.13 | $>9.65 = {}_{.99}F_{2,11}$; $H_0$ rejected |
| Within | 57.62 | 11 | 5.24 | | |

g. $b_w = \Sigma xy_w / \Sigma x_w^2 = 50/88$
$= 568;$
$\overline{Y}'_A = \overline{Y}_A - b_w(\overline{X}_A - \overline{X}_\bullet)$
$= 8.0 - (.568)(5 - 14)$
$= 13.112$, $\overline{Y}'_B = 9.432$, $\overline{Y}'_c$
$= 19.456$.

h. $s_{\overline{Y}'_A} = MS'_w\,[1/n + (\overline{X}_A - \overline{X}_\bullet)^2/$
$\Sigma x_w^2] = 5.238\,[1/5$
$+ (5 - 14)^2/88] = 5.869$,
$s_{\overline{Y}'_A} = 2.423$.
.90 CI for $\mu_A$: $\overline{Y}'_A \pm {}_{.95}t_3 s_{\overline{Y}'_A}$
$= 8.0 \pm (2.353)(2.423)$
$= 8.0 \pm 13.112$ or $(7.41, 18.81)$
$s^2_{\overline{Y}'_B} = 5.238\,[1/5 + 1/88]$
$= 1.107$, $s_{\overline{Y}'_B} = 1.052$;
.90 CI for $\mu_B = 10.0$
$\pm (2.353)(1.052)$
$= 10.0 \pm 9.432$ or $(6.95, 11.91)$
$s_{\overline{Y}'_c} = 2.204$; .90 CI for $\mu_c$
$= 24.0 \pm 19.456$ or $(14.27, 29.19)$
Because $\overline{X}_B$ differs little from $\overline{X}_1$, extrapolation error is minimal in group $B$ but large in groups $A$ and $C$.

j. Because of the large amount of extrapolation required in groups $A$ and $C$.

3. a.

| *Source* | *SS* | $\nu$ | *MS* | *F* |
|---|---|---|---|---|
| Between | 52.56 | 1 | 52.56 | .52 |
| Within | 1,414.56 | 14 | 101.04 | |

b.

| *Source* | *SS'* | $\nu$ | *MS'* | *F* |
|---|---|---|---|---|
| Between | 59.27 | 1 | 59.27 | .61 |
| Within | 1,265.46 | 13 | 97.34 | |

$\overline{Y}'_E = 111.62$, $\overline{Y}'_c = 115.48$

c. The ANOVA and ANCOVA results are very similar because (1) $\overline{X}_E$ and $\overline{X}_C$ are very similar, and (2) $r_w$ is very low. No.

d.

| *Source* | *SS* | $\nu$ | *MS* | *F* |
|---|---|---|---|---|
| Between | 4.00 | 1 | 4.00 | .02 |
| Within | 2,779.76 | 14 | 198.55 | |

No. Perhaps the experimenter did not randomly assign teachers to a group, but made the two groups more comparable than would have been expected from random assignment.

e. $\hat{\Delta} = \dfrac{(111.69 - 115.48)}{\sqrt{101.23}} = -.38$

# APPENDIX

## RULES OF THUMB FOR WRITING THE ANOVA TABLE

The following sections consist of "rules of thumb" for finding all entries in an analysis of variance (ANOVA) table for a large class of ANOVA models. For designs in which each pair of factors is completely crossed or nested, in which each factor is random or fixed, and in which the same number of replications (observations) are taken within the smallest subdivision of the design (cell), rules are provided that specify the possible sources of variation, the associated degrees of freedom, computational formulas for sums of squares, and expectations of mean squares.

Many sources exist that provide rules of thumb for finding some of the entries in an ANOVA table from some of the designs considered here (e.g., see Cornfield and Tukey, 1956; Henderson, 1959; Scheffé, 1959; Winer, 1971; Millman and Glass, 1967; and Hopkins, 1976). The presentation to follow is similar to that found in Henderson (1959) and Millman and Glass (1967).

The following experiment involving six classrooms will be used to illustrate the application of the rules presented. Three of six classrooms included in an experiment are from public schools ($P_1$) and three from private schools ($P_2$). Each classroom was administered five treatments. Suppose that within each class ten pupils were assigned randomly to treatment, and that two pupils responded independently under each of the

| Factor *P* Type of school | | Factor *C* Class | Factor *T* Treatments $T_1$ | $T_2$ | $T_3$ | $T_4$ | $T_5$ |
|---|---|---|---|---|---|---|---|
| | $P_1$ | $C_1$ | $X_1, X_2$ | . . . | | | |
| | | $C_2$ | ⋮ | | | | |
| | | $C_3$ | | | | | |
| | $P_2$ | $C_4$ | | | | | |
| | | $C_5$ | | | | | |
| | | $C_6$ | | | | | |

**FIGURE A.1. Data layout of the example used to illustrate the application of the ANOVA rules of thumb.**

five treatments. Thus, two observations, $X_1$ and $X_2$ on the single dependent variable $X$ exist for each classroom. This design is illustrated in Figure A.1.

# I. DEFINITIONS OF TERMS

## I-A. Crossed and Nested Factors

Two factors are *crossed* if every level (the different categories of a factor are called *levels*) of one of the factors appears with every level of the other factor. That is, there must be at least one observation for every possible combination of levels of factors that are completely crossed. Thus "type of school" and "treatments" (having two and five levels, respectively) are crossed since there are observations taken at each of the ten school-treatment combinations.

A factor is said to be *nested* in a second factor if each level of the first (the nested factor) appears in exactly one level of the second factor. In our experiment "classroom" is nested. No classroom appears in both a public ($P_1$) and a private ($P_2$) school. If, however, the same three classrooms were involved in both $P_1$ and $P_2$, then $C$ would not be nested in $P$. Nesting exists when one level of a variable does not appear with all levels of another variable. Since $C_1$ under $P_1$ is not the same class as $C_4$ under $P_2$, $C_1$ does not appear in both levels of $P$. Note that $C_1$ is combined with all levels of $T$ ("treatments"); the factor "classroom" is *not* nested in $T$. For the purposes of this discussion, *any nested factor must have the same number of levels in each level of the factor in which it is nested.* In our illustration there are three levels of "classroom" nested under both levels of "type of school."

## I-B. Random and Fixed Factors

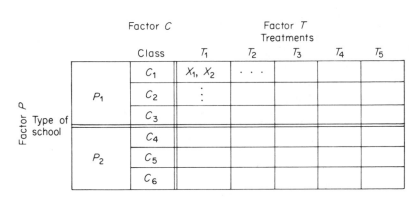

A factor may be considered *random* if the levels of that factor used in the study are a simple random sample from a population of levels with normally distributed effects. "Students" and "classrooms" are two factors frequently considered random. Results of an ANOVA may be generalized to the population of levels of a random factor. When all levels of a factor are in the study (e.g., male-female or high-average-low), when only the levels of interest to the investigator are in the study (e.g., method $A$ and method $B$ where the other methods are not of interest), or when a systematic selection of levels is used, the factor is considered *fixed.* Results of an ANOVA may be generalized only to the population of replications of the experiment in which the specific levels of the fixed factor included in the study are present. For example, a study that systematically selected grades three, six, nine, and twelve can generalize its results only to those four grades.

Actually, the status (fixed or random) of a factor depends as much upon the population of replications of a study to which one wishes to generalize as it does upon the way in which the levels were chosen. Five levels of a factor could be randomly sampled from a virtually infinite population of levels, but the factor would be "fixed" if one made inferences to replications of the study in which only those five levels chosen appear. This is an abstruse point about which we will have no more to say.

In our example "classrooms" is considered a random factor, and "type of school" and "treatments" are fixed. We shall also call "replication" within the smallest cell of a design a nested factor that is always random and is nested within *all* the other factors of the design. *This point is important and allows us to specify rules of thumb that are simpler than many others proposed.*

## II. DETERMINING THE POSSIBLE LINES (SOURCES OF VARIATION) OF THE ANOVA TABLE

### II-A. Notation

1. The source of variation for a factor that is not nested within any other factors is denoted by a capital letter, for example, $A, B, C, \ldots$.
2. The source of variation for a nested factor is denoted by a capital letter followed by a colon and then the letter or letters denoting the factors within which it is nested, for example, $A:B$ for factor $A$ nested within factor $B$.

### II-B. Rules

1. The ANOVA table has one line for each factor both crossed and nested (this includes the factor "replications").
2. The ANOVA table has one line for all possible (two-factor, three-factor, etc.) interactions among factors. To determine which interactions can exist, all possible pairs, trios, and so on of factors are formed by the following rules (if there is no nesting other than "replications," there will be $2^k - k - 1$ such interactions, where $k$ is the number of crossed factors):
    a. In the symbol denoting the interaction write to the left of the colon the letters to the left of the colons in the factors being combined. (If no colon appears in the notation for a factor, it is understood to be at the right of all letters.)
    b. Write following the colon, but with no repetition of a letter, those letters to the right of the colons in the factors being combined.
    c. Delete any combination having a letter to the left of the colon that is repeated to the right of the colon.

### II-C. Illustration of the Rules Under II-B (for the example)

1. $P$(types of school), $T$(treatments), $C:P$(classrooms nested within $P$), and $R:PCT$ (replications nested within $P, C, T$ combinations) represent the crossed and nested factors and are lines in the table by rule II-B.1.
2. The possible interactions among the factors above include
   $PT$ which is retained and may be written $TP$.
   $PC:P$ which is deleted because $P$ appears both before and after the colon (rule II-B.2c).
   $TC:P$ which is retained and may be written $CT:P$.
   $PTC:P$ which is also deleted because $P$ appears both before and after the colon.
   All the interactions involving $R:PCT$ are deleted because of rule II-B.2c.
3. Thus, the lines of the ANOVA table in our example consist of $P$, $C:P$, $T$, $PT$, $CT:P$, and $R:PCT$.

## III. DETERMINING THE DEGREES OF FREEDOM FOR SOURCES OF VARIATION

### III-A. Notation

1. The number of levels of a factor not nested within any other factor is denoted by the capital letter identifying the factor. In our example $P = 2$ and $T = 5$.
2. The number of levels of a nested factor within *each* level or combination of levels of the factors in which it is nested is denoted by the lowercase of the letter to the left of the colon identifying the nested factor. For example, in the nested classification $C:P$, the number of levels of $C$ in each level of $P$ is denoted by $c$, which is 3 in our example. In the nested classification $R:PCT$, $n$ denotes the number of replications within a cell, which equals 2 in our example.
3. The total number of observations $N$ equal the product of all the uppercase letters for the crossed and nested classifications. In our example this number is $P \times C \times T \times R = 2 \times 3 \times 5 \times 2 = 60$.

### III-B. Rules

1. The degrees of freedom for any line in the ANOVA table are found by subtracting one from each letter to the left of the colon and multiplying the grand product of these differences by the grand product of the letters to the right of the colon.
2. As a check, the computed degrees of freedom should add to $N - 1$.

### III-C. Illustration of the Rules Under III-B.2 (for the example)

1. The degrees of freedom for $P = P - 1 = (2 - 1) = 1$.
   The degrees of freedom for $C:P = (C - 1)P = (3 - 1)2 = 4$.
   The degrees of freedom for $T = (T - 1) = (5 - 1) = 4$.

The degrees of freedom for $PT = (P - 1)(T - 1) = (2 - 1)(5 - 1) = 4$.
The degrees of freedom for $CT{:}P = (C - 1)(T - 1)P = (3 - 1)(5 - 1)2 = 16$.
The degrees of freedom for $R{:}PCT = (n - 1)PCT = (2 - 1)(2)(3)(5) = 30$.

2. As a check, $1 + 4 + 4 + 4 + 16 + 30 = N - 1 = 59$.

# IV. COMPUTING SUMS OF SQUARES

## IV-A. Notation

1. Capital letter $X$ will be used to denote an observation on the dependent variable and will have as subscripts all the different lowercase letters used in expressing degrees of freedom. For example, $X_{pctr}$ is used to denote a general observation in our example.
2. Uppercase letters will also be used to denote the upper limits of subscripts. For example, $t = 1, 2, \ldots, T$, which means that the levels of variable $t$ are 1, 2, up to the *Tth* level, which is five in our example.

## IV-B. Rules

1. For each line in the ANOVA table write down the degrees of freedom ($\nu$) in their symbolic form and expand algebraically. For example, the line *PT* has degrees of freedom $(P - 1)(T - 1)$ which equals $+PT - P - T + 1$. The computational formula for the sum of squares of a source of variation will consist of as many terms as there are terms in the expanded symbolic expression for the degrees of freedom (four terms in the case of the *PT* interaction), and these terms will have the same algebraic signs as their corresponding terms in the symbolic expression for the $\nu$[+, −, −, and + in the case of the expansion of $(P - 1)$ $(T - 1)$ shown earlier].
2. For each term in the expanded algebraic representation for the $\nu$ write a multiple summation corresponding to each subscript of the general observation. Precede the summation with the algebraic sign of the term to which it corresponds. For example, for the term $+PT$ in the algebraic expansion of $(P - 1)(T - 1)$ one would write

$$+\sum_1^P \sum_1^T \sum_1^C \sum_1^n X_{ptcr}$$

3. For each multiple summation expression, place within parentheses $X$ and those summation signs whose upper limits do *not* appear in the corresponding term in the expanded expression for the $\nu$. For example, for the term $+PT$ one would place the parentheses as follows:

$$+\sum_1^P \sum_1^T \left(\sum_1^C \sum_1^n X_{ptcr}\right)$$

4. Square the expression inside the parentheses and divide by the total number of observations summed over to get the quantity inside the parentheses. This num-

ber will be the product of the upper limits of the summation signs inside the parentheses. If no summation sign appears inside the parentheses, one "sums" over 1 value, so the term is divided by 1. The part of the computational formula for the *PT* interaction that corresponds to the + term is then

$$\frac{+\sum_{1}^{P}\sum_{1}^{T}\left(\sum_{1}^{C}\sum_{1}^{n}X_{ptcr}\right)^2}{Cn}$$

## IV-C. Illustration of the Rules Under IV-B (for the example in Fig. A.1)

In Section II six sources of variation were identified for the example problem. Thus, six sums of squares must be calculated in the analysis of the design. Only the formulas for the sums of squares *PT* and *R*:*PCT* will be demonstrated. Attempt to write the remaining formulas by following rules IV-B.1 through IV-B.4. Four subscripts are needed to denote a general observation: $X_{pctr}$.

1. Sum of squares for *PT*.
   *Rule 1.* $(PT) = (P - 1)(T - 1) = PT - P - T + 1.$
   *Rule 2.* $PT - P - T + 1$:

$$\sum_{1}^{P}\sum_{1}^{C}\sum_{1}^{T}\sum_{1}^{n}X_{pctr} - \sum_{1}^{P}\sum_{1}^{C}\sum_{1}^{T}\sum_{1}^{n}X_{pctr} - \sum_{1}^{P}\sum_{1}^{C}\sum_{1}^{T}\sum_{1}^{n}X_{pctr} + \sum_{1}^{P}\sum_{1}^{C}\sum_{1}^{T}\sum_{1}^{n}X_{pctr}$$

*Rule 3:* $PT - P - T + 1$:

$$\sum_{1}^{P}\sum_{1}^{T}\left(\sum_{1}^{C}\sum_{1}^{n}X_{pctr}\right) - \sum_{1}^{P}\left(\sum_{1}^{C}\sum_{1}^{T}\sum_{1}^{n}X_{pctr}\right) - \sum_{1}^{T}\left(\sum_{1}^{P}\sum_{1}^{C}\sum_{1}^{n}X_{pctr}\right) + \left(\sum_{1}^{P}\sum_{1}^{T}\sum_{1}^{C}\sum_{1}^{n}X_{pctr}\right)$$

*Rule 4.* $PT - P - T + 1$:

$$\frac{\sum_{1}^{P}\sum_{1}^{T}\left(\sum_{1}^{C}\sum_{1}^{n}X_{pctr}\right)^2}{Cn} - \frac{\sum_{1}^{P}\left(\sum_{1}^{C}\sum_{1}^{T}\sum_{1}^{n}X_{pctr}\right)^2}{CTn} - \frac{\sum_{1}^{T}\left(\sum_{1}^{P}\sum_{1}^{C}\sum_{1}^{n}X_{pctr}\right)^2}{PCn} + \frac{\left(\sum_{1}^{P}\sum_{1}^{C}\sum_{1}^{T}\sum_{1}^{n}X_{pctr}\right)^2}{PCTn}$$

The result of the application of rule 4 is the computational formula for the sum of squares for the interaction of factors $P$ and $T$.

2. Sum of squares for $R:PCT$.
*Rule 1.* $\nu$ for $(R:PCT) = (n - 1)PCT = PCTn - PCT$.
*Rule 2.* $PCTn - PCT$.

$$\sum_1^P \sum_1^C \sum_1^T \sum_1^n X_{pctr} - \sum_1^P \sum_1^C \sum_1^T \sum_1^n X_{pctr}$$

*Rule 3.* $PCTn - PCT$:

$$\sum_1^P \sum_1^C \sum_1^T \sum_1^n (X_{pctr}) - \sum_1^P \sum_1^C \sum_1^T \left(\sum_1^n X_{pctr}\right)$$

*Rule 4.* $PCTn - PCT$:

$$\frac{\sum_1^P \sum_1^C \sum_1^T \sum_1^n (X_{pctr})^2}{1} - \frac{\sum_1^P \sum_1^C \sum_1^T \left(\sum_1^n X_{pctr}\right)^2}{n}$$

The preceding formula yields the sum of squares for replications (or "within").

# V. DETERMINING THE EXPECTATIONS OF MEAN SQUARES

## V-A. Notation

1. The symbol $\sigma^2$, having to the left of the colon in its subscript *only* letters corresponding to random or finite factors, denotes the variance of a random variable underlying those random and finite factors. For example, $\sigma^2_{c:p}$ denotes the variance of the effects associated with all the classrooms ($C$) included in the population of classrooms found in a particular type of school ($P$).
2. The symbol $\sigma^2$, having included to the left of the colon in its subscript lowercase letters corresponding to fixed factors, denotes a function of the sum of the squared effects of the variables represented to the left of the colon.* For example, $\sigma^2_t$ denotes a function of squared fixed effects associated with treatments, for example, $\sigma^2_t = \Sigma\alpha^2_t/(T - 1)$.

*Although it has become customary to adopt the $\sigma^2$ notation, the reader should keep in mind that for factors or combinations of factors involving fixed factors, the $\sigma^2$ is *not* a variance of a random variable; it is related to a sum of squared constants (the fixed effects).

## V-B. Rules

1. Unless deleted by rule V-B.2, the expectation of a mean square of any factor contains a $\sigma^2$ for each line in the ANOVA table that has in its denotation all the letters denoting the mean square under consideration.
2. Certain of the $\sigma^2$ components of an expectation for a mean square given in V-B.1 vanish according to the following rule: any $\sigma^2$ having to the left of the colon a letter denoting a fixed classification disappears except when the source of variation of the mean square includes this letter. Remember, if there is no colon in the subscript, the colon is by definition at the right of all letters.
3. The coefficient of a particular $\sigma^2$ in a particular mean square includes the product of all the uppercase letters not found in the subscript of $\sigma^2$.

## V-C. Illustrations of the Rules Under V-B (for the example in Sec. 18.3)

One way of determining the expected values of mean squares is first to list all possible $\sigma^2$, then to eliminate selected $\sigma^2$ by rule V-B.1, then eliminate more $\sigma^2$ by rule V-B.2, and finally to attach coefficients to the remaining components by rule V-B.3. This procedure will be followed here.

1. The expected mean square for any line *could* contain $\sigma_p^2$, $\sigma_t^2$, $\sigma_{c:p}^2$, $\sigma_{pt}^2$, and $\sigma_{ct:p}^2$ as well as $\sigma_{r:pct}^2$.* In the $E(MS)$ for $P$ delete $\sigma_t^2$ because $\sigma_t^2$ does not have a $p$ among its subscripts (rule V-B.1).

   In the $E(MS)$ for $C{:}P$ eliminate $\sigma_p^2$, $\sigma_t^2$, and $\sigma_{pt}^2$ because none of these has *both* a $c$ and a $p$ among its subscripts (rule V-B.1).

   In the $E(MS)$ for $T$ eliminate $\sigma_p^2$ and $\sigma_{c:p}^2$ (rule V-B.1).

   In the $E(MS)$ for $PT$ eliminate $\sigma_p^2$, $\sigma_{c:p}^2$, and $\sigma_t^2$ (rule V-B.1).

   In the $E(MS)$ for $CT{:}P$ eliminate all $\sigma^2$ except $\sigma_{ct:p}^2$ and $\sigma^2$ since none contains all the letters $c$, $t$, and $p$ in its subscripts (rule V-B.1).

   In the $E(MS)$ for $R{:}CTP$ eliminate all $\sigma^2$ except $\sigma^2$, since none contains all the letters $c, t, p$, and $r$ (rule V-B.1).
2. Recall that $C$ and $R$ are considered random, $P$ and $T$ fixed. In addition to $\sigma^2$, the $E(MS)$ for $P$ so far contains $\sigma_p^2$, $\sigma_{c:p}^2$, $\sigma_{pt}^2$, and $\sigma_{ct:p}^2$. Now $\sigma_p^2$ contains fixed factor $P$ to the left of the colon, but the mean square under consideration ($P$) contains (is) this letter, so $\sigma_p^2$ stays. $\sigma_{c:p}^2$ contains only random factor $C$ to the left of the colon, so $\sigma_{c:p}^2$ also stays. $\sigma_{pt}^2$ contains *fixed* factor $t$ to the left of the colon *and* $t$ is not part of the mean square under consideration ($P$), so $\sigma_{pt}^2$ is eliminated. For the same reason $\sigma_{ct:p}^2$ is eliminated. $\sigma^2$ (that is, $\sigma_{r:ptc}^2$) always remains since only the random factor $R$ is to the left of the colon.

   In addition to $\sigma^2$ the $E(MS)$ for $C{:}P$ contains so far only $\sigma_{c:p}^2$ and $\sigma_{ct:p}^2$. $\sigma_{c:p}^2$ is retained because $C$ is random, and it is also retained since $c$ is part of $C{:}P$.

*The expected mean square $E(MS)$ for the random factor replications within the smallest cell is usually denoted simply as $\sigma_{\text{residual}}^2$, or $\sigma_e^2$ ($e$ for "error"). This practice has been followed here. $\sigma^2$ always appears as a source of variation even if $n = 1$, in which case there are no degrees of freedom for this source.

**TABLE A.1 Summary ANOVA Table (for the example in Sec. 18.3)**

| *Source of Variation* | $\nu$ | *E(MS)* |
|---|---|---|
| $P$ | $(P-1) = 1$ | $\sigma^2 + 10\sigma^2_{c:p} + 30\sigma^2_p$ |
| $C:P$ | $P(C-1) = 4$ | $\sigma^2 + 10\sigma^2_{c:p}$ |
| $T$ | $(T-1) = 4$ | $\sigma^2 + 2\sigma^2_{ct:p} + 12\sigma^2_t$ |
| $PT$ | $(P-1)(T-1) = 4$ | $\sigma^2 + 2\sigma^2_{ct:p} + 6\sigma^2_{pt}$ |
| $CT:P$ | $P(C-1)(T-1) = 16$ | $\sigma^2 + 2\sigma^2_{ct:p}$ |
| $R:PCT$ | $PCT(n-1) = 30$ | $\sigma^2$ [a] |
| Total | $PCTn - 1 = N - 1 = 59$ | |

[a] More explicitly, $\sigma^2_{r:pct}$.

However, $\sigma^2_{ct:p}$ contains $t$ to the left of the colon and $T$ is *both fixed and* $t$ is not part of the mean square under consideration ($C:P$). Thus $\sigma^2_{ct:p}$ is eliminated.

In addition to $\sigma^2$ the *E(MS)* for $T$ contains so far $\sigma^2_t$, $\sigma^2_{pt}$, and $\sigma^2_{ct:p}$. $\sigma^2_t$ is retained because $t$ is part of $T$. $\sigma^2_{pt}$ is eliminated because $P$ is *fixed and* p is not part of $T$, the mean square under consideration. $\sigma^2_{ct:p}$ survives because $C$ is random. Note that $p$ is the the *right* of the colon, and thus not affected by rule V-B.2.

Similarly, it can be shown that the *E(MS)* for $PT$ is $\sigma^2$, $\sigma^2_{pt}$, and $\sigma^2_{ct:p}$; and the *E(MS)* for $CT:P$ is $\sigma^2$ and $\sigma^2_{ct:p}$.

3. The coefficients of the surviving components are found by a straightforward application of rule V-B.3. For example, the coefficient of $\sigma^2_{c:p}$ is $(T \times n) = (5)(2) = 10$. See Table A.1 for the final results.

# TABLES

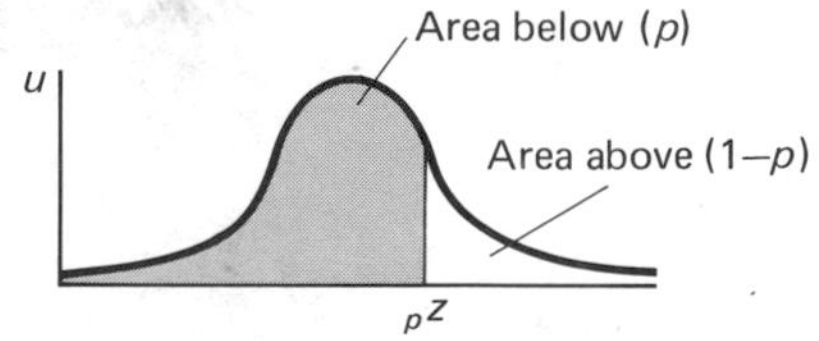


**TABLE A Areas of the Unit-Normal ($z$) Distribution**

| | *Proportion of Area* | | |
|---|---|---|---|
| $z^a$ | Below $z^b$ | Above $z$ | Ordinate $u$ |
| **0.000** | **.5000** | **.5000** | .3989 |
| 0.01 | .5040 | .4960 | .3989 |
| 0.02 | .5080 | .4920 | .3989 |
| 0.03 | .5120 | .4880 | .3988 |
| 0.04 | .5160 | .4840 | .3986 |
| 0.05 | .5199 | .4801 | .3984 |
| 0.06 | .5239 | .4761 | .3982 |
| 0.07 | .5279 | .4721 | .3980 |
| 0.08 | .5319 | .4631 | .3977 |
| 0.09 | .5359 | .4641 | .3973 |
| 0.10 | .5398 | .4602 | .3970 |
| 0.11 | .5438 | .4562 | .3965 |
| 0.12 | .5478 | .4522 | .3961 |
| **0.126** | **.5500** | **.4500** | **.3958** |
| 0.13 | .5517 | .4483 | .3956 |
| 0.14 | .5557 | .4443 | .3951 |
| 0.15 | .5596 | .4404 | .3945 |
| 0.16 | .5636 | .4364 | .3939 |
| 0.17 | .5675 | .4325 | .3932 |
| 0.18 | .5714 | .4286 | .3925 |
| 0.19 | .5753 | .4247 | .3918 |
| 0.20 | .5793 | .4207 | .3910 |
| 0.21 | .5832 | .4168 | .3902 |
| 0.22 | .5871 | .4129 | .3894 |
| 0.23 | .5910 | .4090 | .3885 |
| 0.24 | .5948 | .4052 | .3876 |
| 0.25 | .5987 | .4013 | .3867 |
| **0.253** | **.6000** | **.4000** | **.3863** |
| 0.26 | .6026 | .3974 | .3857 |
| 0.27 | .6064 | .3936 | .3847 |
| 0.28 | .6103 | .3897 | .3836 |
| 0.29 | .6141 | .3859 | .3825 |
| 0.30 | .6179 | .3821 | .3814 |
| 0.31 | .6217 | .3783 | .3802 |
| 0.32 | .6255 | .3745 | .3790 |
| 0.33 | .6293 | .3707 | .3778 |
| 0.34 | .6331 | .3669 | .3765 |
| 0.35 | .6368 | .3632 | .3752 |
| 0.36 | .6406 | .3594 | .3739 |
| 0.37 | .6443 | .3557 | .3725 |
| 0.38 | .6480 | .3520 | .3712 |
| **0.385** | **.6500** | **.3500** | **.3704** |
| 0.39 | .6517 | .3483 | .3697 |
| 0.40 | .6554 | .3446 | .3683 |
| 0.41 | .6591 | .3409 | .3668 |
| 0.42 | .6628 | .3372 | .3653 |
| 0.43 | .6664 | .3336 | .3637 |
| 0.44 | .6700 | .3300 | .3621 |
| 0.45 | .6736 | .3264 | .3605 |
| 0.46 | .6772 | .3228 | .3589 |
| 0.47 | .6808 | .3192 | .3572 |
| 0.48 | .6844 | .3156 | .3555 |
| 0.49 | .6879 | .3121 | .3538 |
| 0.50 | .6915 | .3085 | .3521 |
| 0.51 | .6950 | .3050 | .3503 |
| 0.52 | .6985 | .3015 | .3485 |
| **0.524** | **.7000** | **.3000** | **.3477** |
| 0.53 | .7019 | .2981 | .3467 |
| 0.54 | .7054 | .2946 | .3448 |
| 0.55 | .7088 | .2912 | .3429 |
| 0.56 | .7123 | .2877 | .3410 |
| 0.57 | .7157 | .2843 | .3391 |
| 0.58 | .7190 | .2810 | .3372 |
| 0.59 | .7224 | .2776 | .3352 |
| 0.60 | .7257 | .2743 | .3332 |

[a] If $z$ is negative, interchange the "area" columns, for example, if $z = -.10$, then .4602 of the area under the normal curve is below that point.

[b] Percentile points are commonly denoted as ${}_{p}z$, thus the 60th percentile is denoted ${}_{.60}z$ and equals .253. Commonly used percentile are given in boldface type.

**TABLE A (cont.)**

| | Proportion of Area | | | | | | |
|---|---|---|---|---|---|---|---|
| $z^a$ | Below $z^b$ | Above $z$ | Ordinate $u$ | $z^a$ | Below $z^b$ | Above $z$ | Ordinate $u$ |
| 0.61 | .7291 | .2709 | .3312 | 1.03 | .8485 | .1515 | .2347 |
| 0.62 | .7324 | .2676 | .3292 | **1.036** | **.8500** | **.1500** | **.2333** |
| 0.63 | .7357 | .2643 | .3271 | 1.04 | .8508 | .1492 | .2323 |
| 0.64 | .7389 | .2611 | .3251 | 1.05 | .8531 | .1469 | .2299 |
| 0.65 | .7422 | .2578 | .3230 | 1.06 | .8554 | .1446 | .2275 |
| 0.66 | .7454 | .2546 | .3209 | 1.07 | .8577 | .1423 | .2251 |
| 0.67 | .7486 | .2514 | .3187 | 1.08 | .8599 | .1401 | .2227 |
| **0.674** | **.7500** | **.2500** | **.3179** | 1.09 | .8621 | .1379 | .2203 |
| 0.68 | .7517 | .2433 | .3166 | 1.10 | .8643 | .1357 | .2179 |
| 0.69 | .7549 | .2451 | .3144 | 1.11 | .8665 | .1335 | .2155 |
| 0.70 | .7580 | .2420 | .3123 | 1.12 | .8686 | .1314 | .2131 |
| 0.71 | .7611 | .2389 | .3101 | 1.13 | .8708 | .1292 | .2107 |
| 0.72 | .7642 | .2358 | .3079 | 1.14 | .8729 | .1271 | .2083 |
| 0.73 | .7673 | .2327 | .3056 | 1.15 | .8749 | .1251 | .2059 |
| 0.74 | .7704 | .2296 | .3034 | 1.16 | .8770 | .1230 | .2036 |
| 0.75 | .7734 | .2266 | .3011 | 1.17 | .8790 | .1210 | .2012 |
| 0.76 | .7764 | .2236 | .2989 | 1.18 | .8810 | .1190 | .1989 |
| 0.77 | .7794 | .2206 | .2966 | 1.19 | .8830 | .1170 | .1965 |
| 0.78 | .7823 | .2177 | .2943 | 1.20 | .8849 | .1151 | .1942 |
| 0.79 | .7852 | .2148 | .2920 | 1.21 | .8869 | .1131 | .1919 |
| 0.80 | .7881 | .2119 | .2897 | 1.22 | .8888 | .1112 | .1895 |
| 0.81 | .7910 | .2090 | .2874 | 1.23 | .8907 | .1093 | .1872 |
| 0.82 | .7939 | .2061 | .2850 | 1.24 | .8925 | .1075 | .1849 |
| 0.83 | .7967 | .2033 | .2827 | 1.25 | .8944 | .1056 | .1826 |
| 0.84 | .7995 | .2005 | .2803 | 1.26 | .8962 | .1038 | .1804 |
| **0.842** | **.8000** | **.2000** | **.2799** | 1.27 | .8980 | .1020 | .1781 |
| 0.85 | .8023 | .1977 | .2780 | 1.28 | .8997 | .1003 | .1758 |
| 0.86 | .8051 | .1949 | .2756 | **1.282** | **.9000** | **.1000** | **.1754** |
| 0.87 | .8078 | .1922 | .2732 | 1.29 | .9015 | .0985 | .1736 |
| 0.88 | .8106 | .1894 | .2709 | 1.30 | .9032 | .0968 | .1714 |
| 0.89 | .8133 | .1867 | .2685 | 1.31 | .9049 | .0951 | .1691 |
| 0.90 | .8159 | .1841 | .2661 | 1.32 | .9066 | .0934 | .1669 |
| 0.91 | .8186 | .1814 | .2637 | 1.33 | .9082 | .0918 | .1647 |
| 0.92 | .8212 | .1788 | .2613 | 1.34 | .9099 | .0901 | .1626 |
| 0.93 | .8238 | .1762 | .2589 | **1.341** | **.9100** | **.0900** | **.1623** |
| 0.94 | .8264 | .1736 | .2565 | 1.35 | .9115 | .0885 | .1604 |
| 0.95 | .8289 | .1711 | .2541 | 1.36 | .9131 | .0869 | .1582 |
| 0.96 | .8315 | .1685 | .2516 | 1.37 | .9147 | .0853 | .1561 |
| 0.97 | .8340 | .1660 | .2492 | 1.38 | .9162 | .0838 | .1539 |
| 0.98 | .8365 | .1635 | .2468 | 1.39 | .9177 | .0823 | .1518 |
| 0.99 | .8389 | .1611 | .2444 | 1.40 | .9192 | .0808 | .1497 |
| 1.00 | .8413 | .1587 | .2420 | **1.405** | **.9200** | **.0800** | **.1487** |
| 1.01 | .8438 | .1562 | .2396 | 1.41 | .9207 | .0793 | .1476 |
| 1.02 | .8461 | .1539 | .2371 | 1.42 | .9222 | .0778 | .1456 |

**TABLE A (cont.)**

| | Proportion of Area | | |
|---|---|---|---|
| $z^a$ | Below $z^b$ | Above $z$ | Ordinate $u$ |
| 1.43 | .9236 | .0764 | .1435 |
| 1.44 | .9251 | .0749 | .1415 |
| 1.45 | .9265 | .0735 | .1394 |
| 1.46 | .9279 | .0721 | .1374 |
| 1.47 | .9292 | .0708 | .1354 |
| **1.476** | **.9300** | **.0700** | **.1342** |
| 1.48 | .9306 | .0694 | .1334 |
| 1.49 | .9319 | .0681 | .1315 |
| 1.50 | .9332 | .0668 | .1295 |
| 1.51 | .9345 | .0655 | .1276 |
| 1.52 | .9357 | .0643 | .1257 |
| 1.53 | .0370 | .0630 | .1238 |
| 1.54 | .9382 | .0618 | .1219 |
| 1.55 | .9394 | .0606 | .1200 |
| **1.555** | **.9400** | **.0600** | **.1191** |
| 1.56 | .9406 | .0594 | .1182 |
| 1.57 | .9418 | .0582 | .1163 |
| 1.58 | .9429 | .0571 | .1145 |
| 1.59 | .9441 | .0559 | .1127 |
| 1.60 | .9452 | .0548 | .1109 |
| 1.61 | .9463 | .0537 | .1092 |
| 1.62 | .9474 | .0526 | .1074 |
| 1.63 | .9484 | .0516 | .1057 |
| 1.64 | .9495 | .0505 | .1040 |
| **1.645** | **.9500** | **.0500** | **.1031** |
| 1.65 | .9505 | .0495 | .1023 |
| 1.66 | .9515 | .0485 | .1006 |
| 1.67 | .9525 | .0475 | .0989 |
| 1.68 | .9535 | .0465 | .0973 |
| 1.69 | .9545 | .0455 | .0957 |
| 1.70 | .9554 | .0446 | .0940 |
| 1.71 | .9564 | .0436 | .0925 |
| 1.72 | .9573 | .0427 | .0909 |
| 1.73 | .9582 | .0418 | .0893 |
| 1.74 | .9591 | .0409 | .0878 |
| 1.75 | .9599 | .0401 | .0863 |
| **1.751** | **.9600** | **0.400** | **.0861** |
| 1.76 | .9608 | .0392 | .0848 |
| 1.77 | .9616 | .0384 | .0833 |
| 1.78 | .9625 | .0375 | .0818 |
| 1.79 | .9633 | .0367 | .0804 |
| 1.80 | .9641 | .0359 | .0790 |
| 1.81 | .9649 | .0351 | .0775 |
| 1.82 | .9656 | .0344 | .0761 |
| 1.83 | .9664 | .0338 | .0748 |
| 1.84 | .9671 | .0329 | .0734 |
| 1.85 | .9678 | .0322 | .0721 |
| 1.86 | .9686 | .0314 | .0707 |
| 1.87 | .9693 | .0307 | .0694 |
| 1.88 | .9699 | .0301 | .0681 |
| **1.881** | **.9700** | **.0300** | **.0680** |
| 1.89 | .9706 | .0294 | .0669 |
| 1.90 | .9713 | .0287 | .0656 |
| 1.91 | .9719 | .0281 | .0644 |
| 1.92 | .9726 | .0274 | .0632 |
| 1.93 | .9732 | .0268 | .0620 |
| 1.94 | .9738 | .0262 | .0608 |
| 1.95 | .9744 | .0256 | .0596 |
| **1.960** | **.9750** | **.0250** | **.0584** |
| 1.97 | .9756 | .0244 | .0573 |
| 1.98 | .9761 | .0239 | .0562 |
| 1.99 | .9767 | .0233 | .0551 |
| 2.00 | .9772 | .0228 | .0540 |
| 2.01 | .9778 | .0222 | .0529 |
| 2.02 | .9783 | .0217 | .0519 |
| 2.03 | .9788 | .0212 | .0508 |
| 2.04 | .9793 | .0207 | .0498 |
| 2.05 | .9798 | .0202 | .0488 |
| **2.054** | **.9800** | **.0200** | **.0484** |
| 2.06 | .9803 | .0197 | .0478 |
| 2.07 | .9808 | .0192 | .0468 |
| 2.08 | .9812 | .0188 | .0459 |
| 2.09 | .9817 | .0183 | .0449 |
| 2.10 | .9821 | .0179 | .0440 |
| 2.11 | .9826 | .0174 | .0431 |
| 2.12 | .9830 | .0170 | .0422 |
| 2.13 | .9834 | .0166 | .0413 |
| 2.14 | .9838 | .0162 | .0404 |
| 2.15 | .9842 | .0158 | .0396 |
| 2.16 | .9846 | .0154 | .0387 |
| 2.17 | .9850 | .0150 | .0379 |
| 2.18 | .9854 | .0146 | .0371 |
| 2.19 | .9857 | .0143 | .0363 |
| 2.20 | .9861 | .0139 | .0355 |
| 2.21 | .9864 | .0136 | .0347 |
| 2.22 | .9868 | .0132 | .0339 |
| 2.23 | .9871 | .0129 | .0332 |

**TABLE A (cont.)**

| | *Proportion of Area* | | |
|---|---|---|---|
| $z^a$ | Below $z^b$ | Above $z$ | Ordinate $u$ |
| 2.24 | .9875 | .0125 | .0325 |
| 2.25 | .9878 | .0122 | .0317 |
| 2.26 | .9881 | .0119 | .0310 |
| 2.27 | .9884 | .0116 | .0303 |
| 2.28 | .9887 | .0113 | .0297 |
| 2.29 | .9890 | .0110 | .0290 |
| 2.30 | .9893 | .0107 | .0283 |
| 2.31 | .9896 | .0104 | .0277 |
| 2.32 | .9898 | .0102 | .0270 |
| **2.326** | **.9900** | **.0100** | **.0267** |
| 2.33 | .9901 | .0099 | .0264 |
| 2.34 | .9904 | .0096 | .0258 |
| 2.35 | .9906 | .0094 | .0252 |
| 2.36 | .9909 | .0091 | .0246 |
| 2.37 | .9911 | .0089 | .0241 |
| 2.38 | .9913 | .0087 | .0235 |
| 2.39 | .9916 | .0084 | .0229 |
| 2.40 | .9918 | .0082 | .0224 |
| 2.41 | .9920 | .0080 | .0219 |
| 2.42 | .9922 | .0078 | .0213 |
| 2.43 | .9925 | .0075 | .0208 |
| 2.44 | .9927 | .0073 | .0203 |
| 2.45 | .9929 | .0071 | .0198 |
| 2.46 | .9931 | .0069 | .0194 |
| 2.47 | .9932 | .0068 | .0189 |
| 2.48 | .9934 | .0066 | .0184 |
| 2.49 | .9936 | .0064 | .0180 |
| 2.50 | .9938 | .0062 | .0175 |
| 2.51 | .9940 | .0060 | .0171 |
| 2.52 | .9941 | .0059 | .0167 |
| 2.53 | .9943 | .0057 | .0163 |
| 2.54 | .9945 | .0055 | .0158 |
| 2.55 | .9946 | .0054 | .0154 |
| 2.56 | .9948 | .0052 | .0151 |
| 2.57 | .9949 | .0051 | .0147 |
| **2.576** | **.9950** | **.0050** | **.0145** |
| 2.58 | .9951 | .0049 | .0143 |
| 2.59 | .9952 | .0048 | .0139 |
| 2.60 | .9953 | .0047 | .0136 |
| 2.61 | .9955 | .0045 | .0132 |
| 2.62 | .9956 | .0044 | .0129 |
| 2.63 | .9957 | .0043 | .0126 |
| 2.64 | .9959 | .0041 | .0122 |
| 2.65 | .9960 | .0040 | .0119 |
| 2.66 | .9961 | .0039 | .0116 |
| 2.67 | .9962 | .0038 | .0113 |
| 2.68 | .9963 | .0037 | .0110 |
| 2.69 | .9964 | .0036 | .0107 |
| 2.70 | .9965 | .0035 | .0104 |
| 2.71 | .9966 | .0034 | .0101 |
| 2.72 | .9967 | .0033 | .0099 |
| 2.73 | .9968 | .0032 | .0096 |
| 2.74 | .9969 | .0031 | .0093 |
| 2.75 | .9970 | .0030 | .0091 |
| 2.76 | .9971 | .0029 | .0088 |
| 2.77 | .9972 | .0028 | .0086 |
| 2.78 | .9973 | .0027 | .0084 |
| 2.79 | .9974 | .0026 | .0081 |
| 2.80 | .9974 | .0026 | .0079 |
| 2.81 | .9975 | .0025 | .0077 |
| 2.82 | .9976 | .0024 | .0075 |
| 2.83 | .9977 | .0023 | .0073 |
| 2.84 | .9977 | .0023 | .0071 |
| 2.85 | .9978 | .0022 | .0069 |
| 2.86 | .9979 | .0021 | .0067 |
| 2.87 | .9979 | .0021 | .0065 |
| 2.88 | .9980 | .0020 | .0063 |
| 2.89 | .9981 | .0019 | .0061 |
| 2.90 | .9981 | .0019 | .0060 |
| 2.91 | .9982 | .0018 | .0058 |
| 2.92 | .9982 | .0018 | .0056 |
| 2.93 | .9983 | .0017 | .0055 |
| 2.94 | .9984 | .0016 | .0053 |
| 2.95 | .9984 | .0016 | .0051 |
| 2.96 | .9985 | .0015 | .0050 |
| 2.97 | .9985 | .0015 | .0048 |
| 2.98 | .9986 | .0014 | .0047 |
| 2.99 | .9986 | .0014 | .0046 |
| 3.00 | .99865 | .00135 | .0044 |
| 3.01 | .99869 | .00131 | .00430 |
| 3.02 | .99874 | .00126 | .00417 |
| 3.03 | .99878 | .00122 | .00405 |
| 3.04 | .99882 | .00118 | .00393 |
| 3.05 | .99886 | .00114 | .00381 |
| 3.06 | .99889 | .00111 | .00370 |
| 3.07 | .99893 | .00107 | .00358 |
| 3.08 | .99896 | .00104 | .00348 |
| 3.09 | .99900 | .00100 | .00337 |

**TABLE A (cont.)**

| | | *Proportion of Area* | | | | | |
|---|---|---|---|---|---|---|---|
| $z^a$ | Below $z^b$ | Above $z$ | Ordinate $u$ | $z^a$ | Below $z^b$ | Above $z$ | Ordinate $u$ |
| **3.0902** | **.999000** | **.001000** | **.00337** | 3.51 | .99978 | .00022 | .00084 |
| 3.10 | .99903 | .00097 | .00327 | 3.52 | .99978 | .00022 | .00081 |
| 3.11 | .99906 | .00094 | .00317 | 3.53 | .99979 | .00021 | .00079 |
| 3.12 | .99910 | .00090 | .00307 | 3.54 | .99980 | .00020 | .00076 |
| 3.13 | .99913 | .00087 | .00298 | 3.55 | .99981 | .00019 | .00073 |
| 3.14 | .99916 | .00084 | .00288 | 3.56 | .99981 | .00019 | .00071 |
| 3.15 | .99918 | .00082 | .00279 | 3.57 | .99982 | .00018 | .00068 |
| 3.16 | .99921 | .00079 | .00271 | 3.58 | .99983 | .00017 | .00066 |
| 3.17 | .99924 | .00076 | .00262 | 3.59 | .99983 | .00017 | .00063 |
| 3.18 | .99926 | .00074 | .00254 | 3.60 | .99984 | .00016 | .00061 |
| 3.19 | .99929 | .00071 | .00246 | 3.61 | .99985 | .00015 | .00059 |
| 3.20 | .99931 | .00069 | .00238 | 3.62 | .99985 | .00015 | .00057 |
| 3.21 | .99934 | .00066 | .00231 | 3.63 | .99986 | .00014 | .00055 |
| 3.22 | .99936 | .00064 | .00224 | 3.64 | .99986 | .00014 | .00053 |
| 3.23 | .99938 | .00062 | .00216 | 3.65 | .99987 | .00013 | .00051 |
| 3.24 | .99940 | .00060 | .00210 | 3.66 | .999873 | .000126 | .00049 |
| 3.25 | .99942 | .00058 | .00203 | 3.67 | .999879 | .000121 | .00047 |
| 3.26 | .99944 | .00056 | .00196 | 3.68 | .999883 | .000117 | .00046 |
| 3.27 | .99946 | .00054 | .00190 | 3.69 | .999888 | .000112 | .00044 |
| 3.28 | .99948 | .00050 | .00184 | 3.70 | .999892 | .000108 | .00042 |
| 3.29 | .99950 | .00050 | .00178 | 3.71 | .999896 | .000104 | .00041 |
| **3.2905** | **.999500** | **.000500** | **.00178** | **3.719** | **.9999000** | **.000100** | **.00040** |
| 3.30 | .99951 | .00048 | .00172 | 3.72 | .999900 | .000100 | .00039 |
| 3.31 | .99953 | .00047 | .00167 | 3.73 | .999904 | .000096 | .00038 |
| 3.32 | .99955 | .00045 | .00161 | 3.74 | .999908 | .000092 | .00037 |
| 3.33 | .99957 | .00043 | .00156 | 3.75 | .999912 | .000088 | .00036 |
| 3.34 | .99958 | .00042 | .00151 | 3.76 | .999915 | .000085 | .00034 |
| 3.35 | .99960 | .00040 | .00146 | 3.77 | .999918 | .000082 | .00033 |
| 3.36 | .99961 | .00039 | .00141 | 3.78 | .999922 | .000078 | .00031 |
| 3.37 | .99962 | .00038 | .00136 | 3.79 | .999925 | .000075 | .00030 |
| 3.38 | .99964 | .00036 | .00132 | 3.80 | .999928 | .000072 | .00029 |
| 3.39 | .99965 | .00035 | .00127 | 3.81 | .999931 | .000070 | .00028 |
| 3.40 | .99966 | .00034 | .00123 | 3.82 | .999933 | .000067 | .00027 |
| 3.41 | .99968 | .00032 | .00119 | 3.83 | .999936 | .000064 | .00026 |
| 3.42 | .99969 | .00031 | .00115 | 3.84 | .999939 | .000062 | .00025 |
| 3.43 | .99970 | .00030 | .00111 | 3.85 | .999941 | .000059 | .00024 |
| 3.44 | .99971 | .00029 | .00107 | 3.86 | .999943 | .000057 | .00023 |
| 3.45 | .99972 | .00028 | .00104 | 3.87 | .999946 | .000054 | .00022 |
| 3.46 | .99973 | .00027 | .00100 | 3.88 | .999948 | .000052 | .00021 |
| 3.47 | .99974 | .00026 | .00097 | 3.89 | .999950 | .000050 | .00021 |
| 3.48 | .99975 | .00025 | .00094 | **3.891** | **.9999500** | **.000050** | **.00021** |
| 3.49 | .99976 | .00024 | .00090 | 3.90 | .999952 | .000048 | .00020 |
| 3.50 | .99977 | .00023 | .00087 | 3.91 | .999954 | .000046 | .00019 |
| | | | | 3.92 | .999956 | .000044 | .00018 |

TABLE A (cont.)

| | Proportion of Area | | | | | | |
|---|---|---|---|---|---|---|---|
| $z^a$ | Below $z^b$ | Above $z$ | Ordinate $u$ | $z^a$ | Below $z^b$ | Above $z$ | Ordinate $u$ |
| 3.93 | .999958 | .000043 | .00018 | **4.265** | **.9999900** | **.0000100** | **.0000448** |
| 3.94 | .999959 | .000041 | .00017 | 4.417 | .9999950 | .0000050 | .0000231 |
| 3.95 | .999961 | .000039 | .00016 | 4.50 | .9999966023 | .0000033977 | .0000160 |
| 3.96 | .999963 | .000038 | .00016 | 5.00 | .9999997133 | .0000002867 | .00000149 |
| 3.97 | .999964 | .000036 | .00015 | 5.327 | .9999995000 | .0000005000 | .00000027 |
| 3.98 | .999966 | .000035 | .00014 | 5.50 | .9999999810 | .0000000190 | .00000011 |
| 3.99 | .999967 | .000033 | .00014 | 6.00 | .9999999990 | .0000000010 | .000000006 |
| 4.00 | .999968 | .000032 | .00013 | | | | |

**TABLE B Random Digits[a]**

| | | | | | | | | | | | | | | | | | | | |
|---|---|---|---|---|---|---|---|---|---|---|---|---|---|---|---|---|---|---|---|
| 60 | 36 | 59 | 46 | 53 | 35 | 07 | 53 | 39 | 49 | 42 | 61 | 42 | 92 | 97 | 01 | 91 | 82 | 83 | 16 |
| 83 | 79 | 94 | 24 | 02 | 56 | 62 | 33 | 44 | 42 | 34 | 99 | 44 | 13 | 74 | 70 | 07 | 11 | 47 | 36 |
| 32 | 96 | 00 | 74 | 05 | 36 | 40 | 98 | 32 | 32 | 99 | 38 | 54 | 16 | 00 | 11 | 13 | 30 | 75 | 86 |
| 19 | 32 | 25 | 38 | 45 | 57 | 62 | 05 | 26 | 06 | 66 | 49 | 76 | 86 | 46 | 78 | 13 | 86 | 65 | 59 |
| 11 | 22 | 09 | 47 | 47 | 07 | 39 | 93 | 74 | 08 | 48 | 50 | 92 | 39 | 29 | 27 | 48 | 24 | 54 | 76 |
| 31 | 75 | 15 | 72 | 60 | 68 | 98 | 00 | 53 | 39 | 15 | 47 | 04 | 83 | 55 | 88 | 65 | 12 | 25 | 96 |
| 88 | 49 | 29 | 93 | 82 | 14 | 45 | 40 | 45 | 04 | 20 | 09 | 49 | 89 | 77 | 74 | 84 | 39 | 34 | 13 |
| 30 | 93 | 44 | 77 | 44 | 07 | 48 | 18 | 38 | 28 | 73 | 78 | 80 | 65 | 33 | 28 | 59 | 72 | 04 | 05 |
| 22 | 88 | 84 | 88 | 93 | 27 | 49 | 99 | 87 | 48 | 60 | 53 | 04 | 51 | 28 | 74 | 02 | 28 | 46 | 17 |
| 78 | 21 | 21 | 69 | 93 | 35 | 90 | 29 | 13 | 86 | 44 | 37 | 21 | 54 | 86 | 65 | 74 | 11 | 40 | 14 |
| 41 | 84 | 98 | 45 | 47 | 46 | 85 | 05 | 23 | 26 | 34 | 67 | 75 | 83 | 00 | 74 | 91 | 06 | 43 | 45 |
| 46 | 35 | 23 | 30 | 49 | 69 | 24 | 89 | 34 | 60 | 45 | 30 | 50 | 75 | 21 | 61 | 31 | 83 | 18 | 55 |
| 11 | 08 | 79 | 62 | 94 | 14 | 01 | 33 | 17 | 92 | 59 | 74 | 76 | 72 | 77 | 76 | 50 | 33 | 45 | 13 |
| 52 | 70 | 10 | 83 | 37 | 56 | 30 | 38 | 73 | 15 | 16 | 52 | 06 | 96 | 76 | 11 | 65 | 49 | 98 | 93 |
| 57 | 27 | 53 | 68 | 98 | 81 | 30 | 44 | 85 | 85 | 68 | 65 | 22 | 73 | 76 | 92 | 85 | 25 | 58 | 66 |
| 20 | 85 | 77 | 31 | 56 | 70 | 28 | 42 | 43 | 26 | 79 | 37 | 59 | 52 | 20 | 01 | 15 | 96 | 32 | 67 |
| 15 | 63 | 38 | 49 | 24 | 90 | 41 | 59 | 36 | 14 | 33 | 52 | 12 | 66 | 65 | 55 | 82 | 34 | 76 | 41 |
| 92 | 69 | 44 | 82 | 97 | 39 | 90 | 40 | 21 | 15 | 59 | 58 | 94 | 90 | 67 | 66 | 82 | 14 | 15 | 75 |
| 77 | 61 | 31 | 90 | 19 | 88 | 15 | 20 | 00 | 80 | 20 | 55 | 49 | 14 | 09 | 96 | 27 | 74 | 82 | 57 |
| 38 | 68 | 83 | 24 | 86 | 45 | 13 | 46 | 35 | 45 | 59 | 40 | 47 | 20 | 59 | 43 | 94 | 75 | 16 | 80 |
| 25 | 16 | 30 | 18 | 89 | 70 | 01 | 41 | 50 | 21 | 41 | 29 | 06 | 73 | 12 | 71 | 85 | 71 | 59 | 57 |
| 65 | 25 | 10 | 76 | 29 | 37 | 23 | 93 | 32 | 95 | 05 | 87 | 00 | 11 | 19 | 92 | 78 | 42 | 63 | 40 |
| 36 | 81 | 54 | 36 | 25 | 18 | 63 | 73 | 75 | 09 | 82 | 44 | 49 | 90 | 05 | 04 | 92 | 17 | 37 | 01 |
| 64 | 39 | 71 | 16 | 92 | 05 | 32 | 78 | 21 | 62 | 20 | 24 | 78 | 17 | 59 | 45 | 19 | 72 | 53 | 32 |
| 04 | 51 | 52 | 56 | 24 | 95 | 09 | 66 | 79 | 46 | 48 | 46 | 08 | 55 | 58 | 15 | 19 | 11 | 87 | 82 |
| 83 | 76 | 16 | 08 | 73 | 43 | 25 | 38 | 41 | 45 | 60 | 83 | 32 | 59 | 83 | 01 | 29 | 14 | 13 | 49 |
| 14 | 38 | 70 | 63 | 45 | 80 | 85 | 40 | 92 | 79 | 43 | 52 | 90 | 63 | 18 | 38 | 38 | 47 | 47 | 61 |
| 51 | 32 | 19 | 22 | 46 | 80 | 08 | 87 | 70 | 74 | 88 | 72 | 25 | 67 | 36 | 66 | 16 | 44 | 94 | 31 |
| 72 | 47 | 20 | 00 | 08 | 80 | 89 | 01 | 80 | 02 | 94 | 81 | 33 | 19 | 00 | 54 | 15 | 58 | 34 | 36 |
| 05 | 46 | 65 | 53 | 06 | 93 | 12 | 81 | 84 | 64 | 74 | 45 | 79 | 05 | 61 | 72 | 84 | 81 | 18 | 34 |
| 39 | 52 | 87 | 24 | 84 | 82 | 47 | 42 | 55 | 93 | 48 | 54 | 53 | 52 | 47 | 18 | 61 | 91 | 36 | 74 |
| 81 | 61 | 61 | 87 | 11 | 53 | 34 | 24 | 42 | 76 | 75 | 12 | 21 | 17 | 24 | 74 | 62 | 77 | 37 | 07 |
| 07 | 58 | 61 | 61 | 20 | 82 | 64 | 12 | 28 | 20 | 92 | 90 | 41 | 31 | 41 | 32 | 39 | 21 | 97 | 63 |
| 90 | 76 | 70 | 42 | 35 | 13 | 57 | 41 | 72 | 00 | 69 | 90 | 26 | 37 | 42 | 78 | 46 | 42 | 25 | 01 |
| 40 | 18 | 82 | 81 | 93 | 29 | 59 | 38 | 86 | 27 | 94 | 97 | 21 | 15 | 98 | 62 | 09 | 53 | 67 | 87 |
| 34 | 41 | 48 | 21 | 57 | 86 | 88 | 75 | 50 | 87 | 19 | 15 | 20 | 00 | 23 | 12 | 30 | 28 | 07 | 83 |
| 63 | 43 | 97 | 53 | 63 | 44 | 98 | 91 | 68 | 22 | 36 | 02 | 40 | 08 | 67 | 76 | 37 | 84 | 16 | 05 |
| 67 | 04 | 90 | 90 | 70 | 93 | 39 | 94 | 55 | 47 | 94 | 45 | 87 | 42 | 84 | 05 | 04 | 14 | 98 | 07 |
| 79 | 49 | 50 | 41 | 46 | 52 | 16 | 29 | 02 | 86 | 54 | 15 | 83 | 42 | 43 | 46 | 97 | 83 | 54 | 82 |
| 91 | 70 | 43 | 05 | 52 | 04 | 73 | 72 | 10 | 31 | 75 | 05 | 19 | 30 | 29 | 47 | 66 | 56 | 43 | 82 |

[a]From *A Million Random Digits With 100,000 Normal Deviates* (New York: Free Press, 1955), by permission of the RAND Corporation.

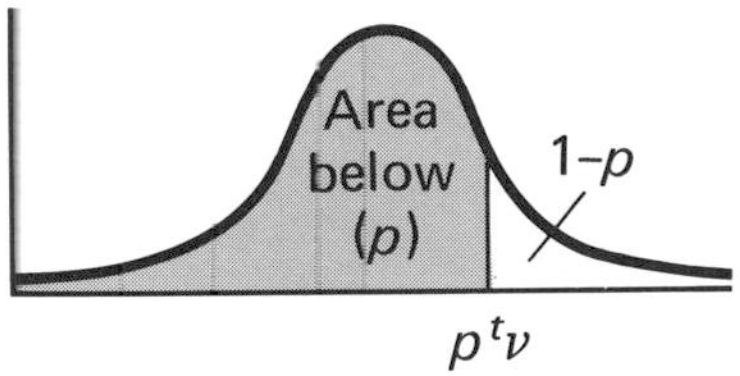


TABLE C Percentile Points of $t$-Distributions[a, b]

| | | | $\alpha_1 = .10$ | $\alpha_1 = .05$ | $\alpha_1 = .025$ | $\alpha_1 = .01$ | $\alpha_1 = .005$ | $\alpha_1 = .001$ | $\alpha_1 = .0005$ | | Kurtosis |
|---|---|---|---|---|---|---|---|---|---|---|---|
| | | | | $\alpha_2 = .10$ | $\alpha_2 = .05$ | $\alpha_2 = .02$ | $\alpha_2 = .01$ | $\alpha_2 = .002$ | $\alpha_2 = .001$ | | |
| $\nu$ | $_{.75}t$ | $_{.80}t$ | $_{.90}t$ | $_{.95}t$ | $_{.975}t$ | $_{.99}t$ | $_{.995}t$ | $_{.999}t$ | $_{.9995}t$ | $\nu$ | $\gamma_2$ |
| 1 | 1.000 | 1.376 | 3.078 | 6.314 | 12.706 | 31.821 | 63.657 | 318.309 | 636.619 | 1 | |
| 2 | .816 | 1.061 | 1.886 | 2.920 | 4.303 | 6.965 | 9.925 | 22.327 | 31.598 | 2 | |
| 3 | .765 | .978 | 1.638 | 2.353 | 3.182 | 4.541 | 5.841 | 10.214 | 12.924 | 3 | |
| 4 | .741 | .941 | 1.532 | 2.132 | 2.776 | 3.747 | 4.604 | 7.173 | 8.610 | 4 | |
| 5 | .727 | .920 | 1.476 | 2.015 | 2.571 | 3.365 | 4.032 | 5.893 | 6.869 | 5 | 6 |
| 6 | .718 | .906 | 1.440 | 1.943 | 2.447 | 3.143 | 3.707 | 5.208 | 5.959 | 6 | 3 |
| 7 | .711 | .896 | 1.415 | 1.895 | 2.365 | 2.998 | 3.499 | 4.785 | 5.408 | 7 | 2 |
| 8 | .706 | .889 | 1.397 | 1.860 | 2.306 | 2.896 | 3.355 | 4.501 | 5.041 | 8 | 1.5 |
| 9 | .703 | .883 | 1.383 | 1.833 | 2.262 | 2.821 | 3.250 | 4.297 | 4.781 | 9 | 1.2 |
| 10 | .700 | .879 | 1.372 | 1.812 | 2.228 | 2.764 | 3.169 | 4.144 | 4.587 | 10 | 1.0 |
| 11 | .697 | .876 | 1.363 | 1.796 | 2.201 | 2.718 | 3.106 | 4.025 | 4.437 | 11 | .86 |
| 12 | .695 | .873 | 1.356 | 1.782 | 2.179 | 2.681 | 3.055 | 3.930 | 4.318 | 12 | .75 |
| 13 | .694 | .870 | 1.350 | 1.771 | 2.160 | 2.650 | 3.012 | 3.852 | 4.221 | 13 | .67 |
| 14 | .692 | .868 | 1.345 | 1.761 | 2.145 | 2.624 | 2.977 | 3.787 | 4.140 | 14 | .60 |
| 15 | .691 | .866 | 1.341 | 1.753 | 2.131 | 2.602 | 2.947 | 3.733 | 4.073 | 15 | .55 |
| 16 | .690 | .865 | 1.337 | 1.746 | 2.120 | 2.583 | 2.921 | 3.686 | 4.015 | 16 | .50 |
| 17 | .689 | .863 | 1.333 | 1.740 | 2.110 | 2.567 | 2.898 | 3.646 | 3.965 | 17 | .46 |
| 18 | .688 | .862 | 1.330 | 1.734 | 2.101 | 2.552 | 2.878 | 3.610 | 3.922 | 18 | .42 |
| 19 | .688 | .861 | 1.328 | 1.729 | 2.093 | 2.539 | 2.861 | 3.579 | 3.883 | 19 | .40 |
| 20 | .687 | .860 | 1.325 | 1.725 | 2.086 | 2.528 | 2.845 | 3.552 | 3.850 | 20 | .38 |

**TABLE C (cont.)**

| | | | $\alpha_1 = .10$ | $\alpha_1 = .05$ | $\alpha_1 = .025$ | $\alpha_1 = .01$ | $\alpha_1 = .005$ | $\alpha_1 = .001$ | $\alpha_1 = .0005$ | | |
|---|---|---|---|---|---|---|---|---|---|---|---|
| | | | | $\alpha_2 = .10$ | $\alpha_2 = .05$ | $\alpha_2 = .02$ | $\alpha_2 = .01$ | $\alpha_2 = .002$ | $\alpha_2 = .001$ | | *Kurtosis* |
| $\nu$ | $_{.75}t$ | $_{.80}t$ | $_{.90}t$ | $_{.95}t$ | $_{.975}t$ | $_{.99}t$ | $_{.995}t$ | $_{.999}t$ | $_{.9995}t$ | $\nu$ | $\gamma_2$ |
| 21 | .686 | .859 | 1.323 | 1.721 | 2.080 | 2.518 | 2.831 | 3.527 | 3.819 | 21 | .35 |
| 22 | .686 | .858 | 1.321 | 1.717 | 2.074 | 2.508 | 2.819 | 3.505 | 3.792 | 22 | .33 |
| 23 | .685 | .858 | 1.319 | 1.714 | 2.069 | 2.500 | 2.807 | 3.485 | 3.767 | 23 | .32 |
| 24 | .685 | .857 | 1.318 | 1.711 | 2.064 | 2.492 | 2.797 | 3.467 | 3.745 | 24 | .30 |
| 25 | .684 | .856 | 1.316 | 1.708 | 2.060 | 2.485 | 2.787 | 3.450 | 3.725 | 25 | .29 |
| 26 | .684 | .856 | 1.315 | 1.706 | 2.056 | 2.479 | 2.779 | 3.435 | 3.707 | 26 | .27 |
| 27 | .684 | .855 | 1.314 | 1.703 | 2.052 | 2.473 | 2.771 | 3.421 | 3.690 | 27 | .26 |
| 28 | .683 | .855 | 1.313 | 1.701 | 2.048 | 2.467 | 2.763 | 3.408 | 3.674 | 28 | .25 |
| 29 | .683 | .854 | 1.311 | 1.699 | 2.045 | 2.462 | 2.756 | 3.396 | 3.659 | 29 | .24 |
| 30 | .683 | .854 | 1.310 | 1.697 | 2.042 | 2.457 | 2.750 | 3.385 | 3.646 | 30 | .23 |
| 35 | .682 | .852 | 1.306 | 1.690 | 2.030 | 2.438 | 2.724 | 3.340 | 3.591 | 35 | .19 |
| 40 | .681 | .851 | 1.303 | 1.684 | 2.021 | 2.423 | 2.704 | 3.307 | 3.551 | 40 | .17 |
| 50 | .680 | .849 | 1.299 | 1.676 | 2.008 | 2.403 | 2.678 | 3.261 | 3.496 | 50 | .13 |
| 60 | .679 | .848 | 1.296 | 1.671 | 2.000 | 2.390 | 2.660 | 3.232 | 3.460 | 60 | .11 |
| 70 | .678 | .847 | 1.294 | 1.667 | 1.994 | 2.381 | 2.648 | 3.211 | 3.435 | 70 | .09 |
| 80 | .678 | .847 | 1.293 | 1.665 | 1.990 | 2.374 | 2.638 | 3.195 | 3.416 | 80 | .08 |
| 90 | .678 | .846 | 1.291 | 1.662 | 1.987 | 2.368 | 2.632 | 3.183 | 3.402 | 90 | .07 |
| 100 | .677 | .846 | 1.290 | 1.661 | 1.984 | 2.364 | 2.626 | 3.174 | 3.380 | 100 | .06 |
| 120 | .677 | .845 | 1.289 | 1.658 | 1.980 | 2.358 | 2.617 | 3.160 | 3.373 | 120 | .05 |
| 200 | .676 | .844 | 1.286 | 1.653 | 1.972 | 2.345 | 2.601 | 3.131 | 3.340 | 200 | .03 |
| 300 | .676 | .843 | 1.285 | 1.650 | 1.968 | 2.339 | 2.592 | 3.118 | 3.323 | 300 | .02 |
| 400 | .676 | .843 | 1.284 | 1.649 | 1.966 | 2.336 | 2.588 | 3.111 | 3.315 | 400 | .015 |
| 500 | .676 | .843 | 1.284 | 1.648 | 1.965 | 2.334 | 2.586 | 3.107 | 3.310 | 500 | .012 |
| 1000 | .675 | .842 | 1.283 | 1.647 | 1.962 | 2.330 | 2.581 | 3.098 | 3.301 | 1000 | .006 |
| $\infty$ | .674 | .842 | 1.282 | 1.645 | 1.960 | 2.326 | 2.576 | 3.090 | 3.291 | $\infty$ | 0 |

[a]Table C is adapted from Table III of Fisher and Yates: *Statistical Tables for Biological, Agricultural and Medical Research*, published by Oliver & Boyd Ltd., Edinburgh, and by permission of the authors and publishers. (Certain corrections and additions from Federighi (1959); other values were calculated by George Kretke.

[b]The lower percentiles are related to the upper percentiles which are tabulated by the equation $_p t_\nu = -_{1-p} t_\nu$. Thus, the 10th percentile in the $t$-distribution with $\nu = 15$ equals the negative of the 90th percentile in the same distribution, that is, $_{.10}t_{15} = -1.341$. *Critical values* for nondirectional ($\alpha_2$) tests: $|_{1-\alpha/2}t|$; for directional ($\alpha_1$) tests: $_{1-\alpha}t$. Thus with $\alpha_2 = .05$ and $\nu = 20$: $|2.086|$; for $\alpha_1 = .05$ and $\nu = 20$, $|t| = 1.725$.

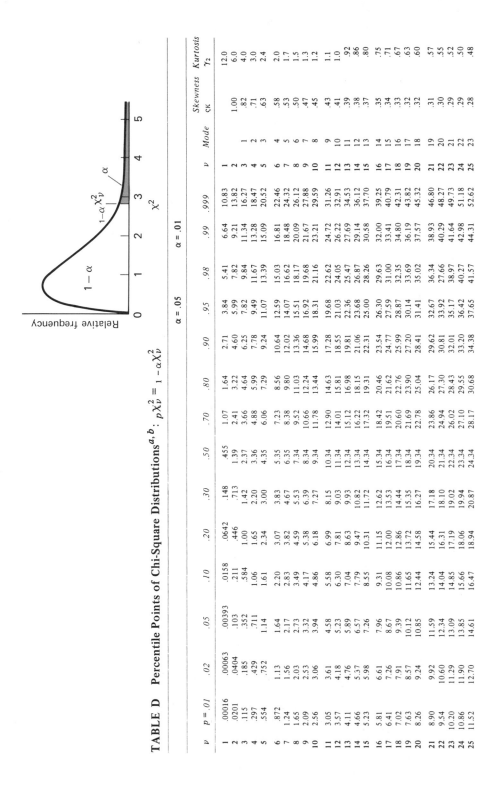

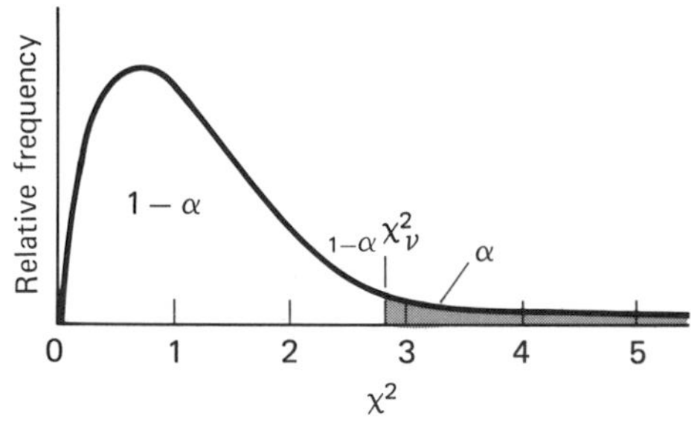


## TABLE D Percentile Points of Chi-Square Distributions[a, b]: $_p\chi^2_\nu = {}_{1-\alpha}\chi^2_\nu$

| | | | | | | | | | | | α = .05 | | α = .01 | | | | | |
|---|---|---|---|---|---|---|---|---|---|---|---|---|---|---|---|---|---|---|
| $\nu$ | *p* = .01 | .02 | .05 | .10 | .20 | .30 | .50 | .70 | .80 | .90 | .95 | .98 | .99 | .999 | $\nu$ | Mode | Skewness $\varsigma\kappa$ | Kurtosis $\gamma_2$ |
| 1 | .00016 | .00063 | .00393 | .0158 | .0642 | .148 | .455 | 1.07 | 1.64 | 2.71 | 3.84 | 5.41 | 6.64 | 10.83 | 1 | | | 12.0 |
| 2 | .0201 | .0404 | .103 | .211 | .446 | .713 | 1.39 | 2.41 | 3.22 | 4.60 | 5.99 | 7.82 | 9.21 | 13.82 | 2 | | 1.00 | 6.0 |
| 3 | .115 | .185 | .352 | .584 | 1.00 | 1.42 | 2.37 | 3.66 | 4.64 | 6.25 | 7.82 | 9.84 | 11.34 | 16.27 | 3 | 1 | .82 | 4.0 |
| 4 | .297 | .429 | .711 | 1.06 | 1.65 | 2.20 | 3.36 | 4.88 | 5.99 | 7.78 | 9.49 | 11.67 | 13.28 | 18.47 | 4 | 2 | .71 | 3.0 |
| 5 | .554 | .752 | 1.14 | 1.61 | 2.34 | 3.00 | 4.35 | 6.06 | 7.29 | 9.24 | 11.07 | 13.39 | 15.09 | 20.52 | 5 | 3 | .63 | 2.4 |
| 6 | .872 | 1.13 | 1.64 | 2.20 | 3.07 | 3.83 | 5.35 | 7.23 | 8.56 | 10.64 | 12.59 | 15.03 | 16.81 | 22.46 | 6 | 4 | .58 | 2.0 |
| 7 | 1.24 | 1.56 | 2.17 | 2.83 | 3.82 | 4.67 | 6.35 | 8.38 | 9.80 | 12.02 | 14.07 | 16.62 | 18.48 | 24.32 | 7 | 5 | .53 | 1.7 |
| 8 | 1.65 | 2.03 | 2.73 | 3.49 | 4.59 | 5.53 | 7.34 | 9.52 | 11.03 | 13.36 | 15.51 | 18.17 | 20.09 | 26.12 | 8 | 6 | .50 | 1.5 |
| 9 | 2.09 | 2.53 | 3.32 | 4.17 | 5.38 | 6.39 | 8.34 | 10.66 | 12.24 | 14.68 | 16.92 | 19.68 | 21.67 | 27.88 | 9 | 7 | .47 | 1.3 |
| 10 | 2.56 | 3.06 | 3.94 | 4.86 | 6.18 | 7.27 | 9.34 | 11.78 | 13.44 | 15.99 | 18.31 | 21.16 | 23.21 | 29.59 | 10 | 8 | .45 | 1.2 |
| 11 | 3.05 | 3.61 | 4.58 | 5.58 | 6.99 | 8.15 | 10.34 | 12.90 | 14.63 | 17.28 | 19.68 | 22.62 | 24.72 | 31.26 | 11 | 9 | .43 | 1.1 |
| 12 | 3.57 | 4.18 | 5.23 | 6.30 | 7.81 | 9.03 | 11.34 | 14.01 | 15.81 | 18.55 | 21.03 | 24.05 | 26.22 | 32.91 | 12 | 10 | .41 | 1.0 |
| 13 | 4.11 | 4.76 | 5.89 | 7.04 | 8.63 | 9.93 | 12.34 | 15.12 | 16.98 | 19.81 | 22.36 | 25.47 | 27.69 | 34.53 | 13 | 11 | .39 | .92 |
| 14 | 4.66 | 5.37 | 6.57 | 7.79 | 9.47 | 10.82 | 13.34 | 16.22 | 18.15 | 21.06 | 23.68 | 26.87 | 29.14 | 36.12 | 14 | 12 | .38 | .86 |
| 15 | 5.23 | 5.98 | 7.26 | 8.55 | 10.31 | 11.72 | 14.34 | 17.32 | 19.31 | 22.31 | 25.00 | 28.26 | 30.58 | 37.70 | 15 | 13 | .37 | .80 |
| 16 | 5.81 | 6.61 | 7.96 | 9.31 | 11.15 | 12.62 | 15.34 | 18.42 | 20.46 | 23.54 | 26.30 | 29.63 | 32.00 | 39.25 | 16 | 14 | .35 | .75 |
| 17 | 6.41 | 7.26 | 8.67 | 10.08 | 12.00 | 13.53 | 16.34 | 19.51 | 21.62 | 24.77 | 27.59 | 31.00 | 33.41 | 40.79 | 17 | 15 | .34 | .71 |
| 18 | 7.02 | 7.91 | 9.39 | 10.86 | 12.86 | 14.44 | 17.34 | 20.60 | 22.76 | 25.99 | 28.87 | 32.35 | 34.80 | 42.31 | 18 | 16 | .33 | .67 |
| 19 | 7.63 | 8.57 | 10.12 | 11.65 | 13.72 | 15.35 | 18.34 | 21.69 | 23.90 | 27.20 | 30.14 | 33.69 | 36.19 | 43.82 | 19 | 17 | .32 | .63 |
| 20 | 8.26 | 9.24 | 10.85 | 12.44 | 14.58 | 16.27 | 19.34 | 22.78 | 25.04 | 28.41 | 31.41 | 35.02 | 37.57 | 45.32 | 20 | 18 | .32 | .60 |
| 21 | 8.90 | 9.92 | 11.59 | 13.24 | 15.44 | 17.18 | 20.34 | 23.86 | 26.17 | 29.62 | 32.67 | 36.34 | 38.93 | 46.80 | 21 | 19 | .31 | .57 |
| 22 | 9.54 | 10.60 | 12.34 | 14.04 | 16.31 | 18.10 | 21.34 | 24.94 | 27.30 | 30.81 | 33.92 | 27.66 | 40.29 | 48.27 | 22 | 20 | .30 | .55 |
| 23 | 10.20 | 11.29 | 13.09 | 14.85 | 17.19 | 19.02 | 22.34 | 26.02 | 28.43 | 32.01 | 35.17 | 38.97 | 41.64 | 49.73 | 23 | 21 | .29 | .52 |
| 24 | 10.86 | 11.90 | 13.85 | 15.66 | 18.06 | 19.94 | 23.34 | 27.10 | 29.55 | 33.20 | 36.42 | 40.27 | 42.98 | 51.18 | 24 | 22 | .29 | .50 |
| 25 | 11.52 | 12.70 | 14.61 | 16.47 | 18.94 | 20.87 | 24.34 | 28.17 | 30.68 | 34.38 | 37.65 | 41.57 | 44.31 | 52.62 | 25 | 23 | .28 | .48 |

## TABLE D (cont.)

| | | | | | | | | | | | $\alpha = .05$ | | $\alpha = .01$ | | | | Skewness | Kurtosis |
|---|---|---|---|---|---|---|---|---|---|---|---|---|---|---|---|---|---|---|
| $\nu$ | $p = .01$ | .02 | .05 | .10 | .20 | .30 | .50 | .70 | .80 | .90 | .95 | .98 | .99 | .999 | $\nu$ | Mode | $\varsigma\kappa$ | $\gamma_2$ |
| **26** | 12.20 | 13.41 | 15.38 | 17.29 | 19.82 | 21.79 | 25.34 | 29.25 | 31.80 | 35.56 | 38.88 | 42.86 | 45.64 | 54.05 | **26** | 24 | .28 | .46 |
| **27** | 12.88 | 14.12 | 16.15 | 18.11 | 20.70 | 22.72 | 26.34 | 30.32 | 32.91 | 36.74 | 40.11 | 44.14 | 46.96 | 55.48 | **27** | 25 | .27 | .44 |
| **28** | 13.56 | 14.85 | 16.93 | 18.94 | 21.59 | 23.65 | 27.34 | 31.39 | 34.03 | 37.92 | 41.34 | 45.42 | 48.28 | 56.89 | **28** | 26 | .27 | .43 |
| **29** | 14.26 | 15.57 | 17.71 | 19.77 | 22.48 | 24.58 | 28.34 | 32.46 | 35.14 | 39.09 | 42.56 | 46.69 | 49.59 | 58.30 | **29** | 27 | .26 | .41 |
| **30** | 14.95 | 16.31 | 18.49 | 20.60 | 23.36 | 25.51 | 29.34 | 33.53 | 36.25 | 40.26 | 43.77 | 47.96 | 50.89 | 59.70 | **30** | 28 | .26 | .40 |
| **40** | 22.16 | 23.84 | 26.51 | 29.05 | 32.38 | 34.81 | 39.34 | 44.17 | 47.27 | 51.81 | 55.76 | 60.44 | 63.69 | 73.40 | **40** | 38 | .22 | .30 |
| **50** | 24.71 | 31.66 | 34.76 | 37.69 | 41.45 | 44.31 | 49.33 | 54.72 | 58.16 | 63.17 | 67.51 | 72.61 | 76.15 | 81.66 | **50** | 48 | .20 | .29 |
| **60** | 37.48 | 38.70 | 43.19 | 46.46 | 50.64 | 53.81 | 54.33 | 65.23 | 68.97 | 74.40 | 79.08 | 84.58 | 88.38 | 99.61 | **60** | 58 | .18 | .20 |
| **70** | 45.44 | 47.89 | 51.74 | 55.33 | 59.90 | 63.35 | 69.33 | 75.69 | 79.72 | 85.53 | 90.53 | 96.39 | 100.4 | 112.3 | **70** | 68 | .17 | .17 |
| **80** | 53.54 | 56.21 | 60.34 | 64.28 | 69.2 | 72.9 | 79.33 | 86.1 | 90.4 | 96.58 | 101.9 | 108.1 | 112.3 | 124.8 | **80** | 78 | .16 | .15 |
| **90** | 61.75 | 64.64 | 69.13 | 73.29 | 78.6 | 82.5 | 89.33 | 96.5 | 101.1 | 107.6 | 113.1 | 119.6 | 124.1 | 137.2 | **90** | 88 | .15 | .13 |
| **100** | 70.06 | 73.14 | 77.43 | 82.36 | 87.9 | 92.1 | 99.33 | 106.9 | 111.7 | 118.5 | 124.3 | 131.1 | 135.8 | 149.4 | **100** | 98 | .14 | .12 |

[a] Mode = $\nu - 2$, $\mu = \nu$, $\sigma_{\chi^2}^2 = 2\nu$, see Secs. 6.8 and 6.9 for definition of $\varsigma\kappa$ and $\gamma_2$. For large $\nu$:

$$_p\chi_\nu^2 = \nu\left(1 - \frac{2}{9\nu} + {}_pz\sqrt{\frac{2}{9\nu}}\right)^3$$

where $_pz$ is the normal deviate. For example $_{.95}\chi_{55}^2 = 55\,[1 - .00404 + (1.96)(.06356)]^3 = 55\ (1.1205)^3 = 77.38.$

[b] Values not found existing tables were calculated by George Kretke.

**TABLE E. Fisher's $Z$-transformation[a,b] of $r$: $|Z| = \frac{1}{2} \ln \left( \frac{1 + |r|}{1 - |r|} \right)$**

| $r$ | $Z$ | $r$ | $Z$ | $r$ | $Z$ | $r$ | $Z$ | $r$ | $Z$ |
|---|---|---|---|---|---|---|---|---|---|
| .000 | .000 | .200 | .203 | .400 | .424 | .600 | .693 | .800 | 1.099 |
| .005 | .005 | .205 | .208 | .405 | .430 | .605 | .701 | .805 | 1.113 |
| .010 | .010 | .210 | .213 | .410 | .436 | .610 | .709 | .810 | 1.127 |
| .015 | .015 | .215 | .218 | .415 | .442 | .615 | .717 | .815 | 1.142 |
| .020 | .020 | .220 | .224 | .420 | .448 | .620 | .725 | .820 | 1.157 |
| .025 | .025 | .225 | .229 | .425 | .454 | .625 | .733 | .825 | 1.172 |
| .030 | .030 | .230 | .234 | .430 | .460 | .630 | .741 | .830 | 1.188 |
| .035 | .035 | .235 | .239 | .435 | .466 | .635 | .750 | .835 | 1.204 |
| .040 | .040 | .240 | .245 | .440 | .472 | .640 | .758 | .840 | 1.221 |
| .045 | .045 | .245 | .250 | .445 | .478 | .645 | .767 | .845 | 1.238 |
| .050 | .050 | .250 | .255 | .450 | .485 | .650 | .775 | .850 | 1.256 |
| .055 | .055 | .255 | .261 | .455 | .491 | .655 | .784 | .855 | 1.274 |
| .060 | .060 | .260 | .266 | .460 | .497 | .660 | .793 | .860 | 1.293 |
| .065 | .065 | .265 | .271 | .465 | .504 | .665 | .802 | .865 | 1.313 |
| .070 | .070 | .270 | .277 | .470 | .510 | .670 | .811 | .870 | 1.333 |
| .075 | .075 | .275 | .282 | .475 | .517 | .675 | .820 | .875 | 1.354 |
| .080 | .080 | .280 | .288 | .480 | .523 | .680 | .829 | .880 | 1.376 |
| .085 | .085 | .285 | .293 | .485 | .530 | .685 | .838 | .885 | 1.398 |
| .090 | .090 | .290 | .299 | .490 | .536 | .690 | .848 | .890 | 1.422 |
| .095 | .095 | .295 | .304 | .495 | .543 | .695 | .858 | .895 | 1.447 |
| .100 | .100 | .300 | .310 | .500 | .549 | .700 | .867 | .900 | 1.472 |
| .105 | .105 | .305 | .315 | .505 | .556 | .705 | .877 | .905 | 1.499 |
| .110 | .110 | .310 | .321 | .510 | .563 | .710 | .887 | .910 | 1.528 |
| .115 | .116 | .315 | .326 | .515 | .570 | .715 | .897 | .915 | 1.557 |
| .120 | .121 | .320 | .332 | .520 | .576 | .720 | .908 | .920 | 1.589 |
| .125 | .126 | .325 | .337 | .525 | .583 | .725 | .918 | .925 | 1.623 |
| .130 | .131 | .330 | .343 | .530 | .590 | .730 | .929 | .930 | 1.658 |
| .135 | .136 | .335 | .348 | .535 | .597 | .735 | .940 | .935 | 1.697 |
| .140 | .141 | .340 | .354 | .540 | .604 | .740 | .950 | .940 | 1.738 |
| .145 | .146 | .345 | .360 | .545 | .611 | .745 | .962 | .945 | 1.783 |
| .150 | .151 | .350 | .365 | .550 | .618 | .750 | .973 | .950 | 1.832 |
| .155 | .156 | .355 | .371 | .555 | .626 | .755 | .984 | .955 | 1.886 |
| .160 | .161 | .360 | .377 | .560 | .633 | .760 | .996 | .960 | 1.946 |
| .165 | .167 | .365 | .383 | .565 | .640 | .765 | 1.008 | .965 | 2.014 |
| .170 | .172 | .370 | .388 | .570 | .648 | .770 | 1.020 | .970 | 2.092 |
| .175 | .177 | .375 | .394 | .575 | .655 | .775 | 1.033 | .975 | 2.185 |
| .180 | .182 | .380 | .400 | .580 | .662 | .780 | 1.045 | .980 | 2.298 |
| .185 | .187 | .385 | .406 | .585 | .670 | .785 | 1.058 | .985 | 2.443 |
| .190 | .192 | .390 | .412 | .590 | .678 | .790 | 1.071 | .990 | 2.647 |
| .195 | .198 | .395 | .418 | .595 | .685 | .795 | 1.085 | .995 | 2.994 |

[a]Values reported in this table were calculated by Thomas O. Maguire and are reproduced with his kind permission.

[b]Or $|Z| = 1.151 \log \left( \frac{1 + |r|}{1 - |r|} \right)$.

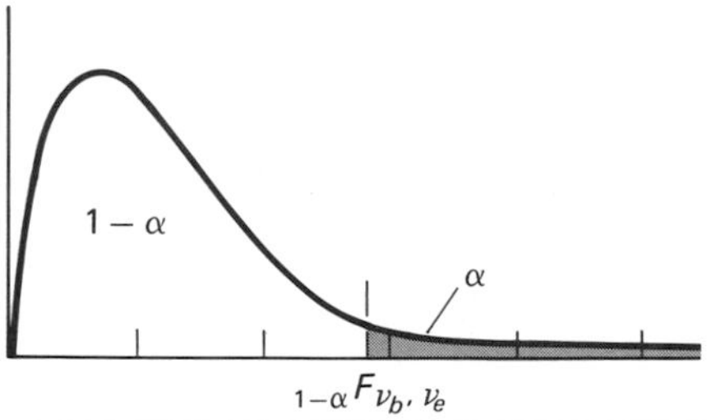


## TABLE F Critical Values of $F$[a]

| $\nu_e$ For Denominator | $\alpha$ | $\nu_b$ (Degrees of Freedom for Numerator) 1 | 2 | 3 | 4 | 5 | 6 | 7 | 8 | 9 | 10 | 12 | 15 |
|---|---|---|---|---|---|---|---|---|---|---|---|---|---|
| 1 | .25 | 5.83 | 7.50 | 8.20 | 8.58 | 8.82 | 8.98 | 9.10 | 9.19 | 9.26 | 9.32 | 9.41 | 9.49 |
| | .10 | 39.9 | 49.5 | 53.6 | 55.8 | 57.2 | 58.2 | 58.9 | 59.4 | 59.9 | 60.2 | 60.7 | 61.2 |
| | .05 | 161 | 200 | 216 | 225 | 230 | 234 | 237 | 239 | 241 | 242 | 244 | 246 |
| | .025 | 648 | 800 | 864 | 900 | 922 | 937 | 948 | 957 | 963 | 969 | 977 | 985 |
| | .01 | 4,052 | 5,000 | 5,403 | 5,625 | 5,764 | 5,859 | 5,928 | 5,982 | 6,022 | 6,056 | 6,106 | 6,157 |
| | .001 | [b] | [b] | [b] | [b] | [b] | [b] | [b] | [b] | [b] | [b] | [b] | [b] |
| 2 | .25 | 2.57 | 3.00 | 3.15 | 3.23 | 3.28 | 3.31 | 3.34 | 3.35 | 3.37 | 3.38 | 3.39 | 3.41 |
| | .10 | 8.53 | 9.00 | 9.16 | 9.24 | 9.29 | 9.33 | 9.35 | 9.37 | 9.38 | 9.39 | 9.41 | 9.42 |
| | .05 | 18.5 | 19.0 | 19.2 | 19.2 | 19.3 | 19.3 | 19.4 | 19.4 | 19.4 | 19.4 | 19.4 | 19.4 |
| | .025 | 38.5 | 39.0 | 39.2 | 39.3 | 39.3 | 39.3 | 39.4 | 39.4 | 39.4 | 39.4 | 39.4 | 39.4 |
| | .01 | 98.5 | 99.0 | 99.2 | 99.3 | 99.3 | 99.3 | 99.4 | 99.4 | 99.4 | 99.4 | 99.4 | 99.4 |
| | .001 | 998.5 | 999.0 | 999.2 | 999.2 | 999.3 | 999.3 | 999.4 | 999.4 | 999.4 | 999.4 | 999.4 | 999.4 |
| 3 | .25 | 2.02 | 2.28 | 2.36 | 2.39 | 2.41 | 2.42 | 2.43 | 2.44 | 2.44 | 2.44 | 2.45 | 2.46 |
| | .10 | 5.54 | 5.46 | 5.39 | 5.34 | 5.31 | 5.28 | 5.27 | 5.25 | 5.24 | 5.23 | 5.22 | 5.20 |
| | .05 | 10.1 | 9.55 | 9.28 | 9.12 | 9.01 | 8.94 | 8.89 | 8.85 | 8.81 | 8.79 | 8.74 | 8.70 |
| | .025 | 17.4 | 16.0 | 15.4 | 15.1 | 14.9 | 14.7 | 14.6 | 14.5 | 14.5 | 14.4 | 14.3 | 14.3 |
| | .01 | 34.1 | 30.8 | 29.5 | 28.7 | 28.2 | 27.9 | 27.7 | 27.5 | 27.4 | 27.2 | 27.1 | 26.9 |
| | .001 | 167 | 149 | 141 | 137 | 135 | 133 | 132 | 131 | 130 | 129 | 128 | 127 |
| 4 | .25 | 1.81 | 2.00 | 2.05 | 2.06 | 2.07 | 2.08 | 2.08 | 2.08 | 2.08 | 2.08 | 2.08 | 2.08 |
| | .10 | 4.54 | 4.32 | 4.19 | 4.11 | 4.05 | 4.01 | 3.98 | 3.95 | 3.94 | 3.92 | 3.90 | 3.87 |
| | .05 | 7.71 | 6.94 | 6.59 | 6.39 | 6.26 | 6.16 | 6.09 | 6.04 | 6.00 | 5.96 | 5.91 | 5.86 |
| | .025 | 12.2 | 10.7 | 9.98 | 9.60 | 9.36 | 9.20 | 9.07 | 8.98 | 8.90 | 8.84 | 8.75 | 8.66 |
| | .01 | 21.2 | 18.0 | 16.7 | 16.0 | 15.5 | 15.2 | 15.0 | 14.8 | 14.7 | 14.6 | 14.4 | 14.2 |
| | .001 | 74.1 | 61.3 | 56.2 | 53.4 | 51.7 | 50.5 | 49.7 | 49.0 | 48.5 | 48.1 | 47.4 | 46.8 |
| 5 | .25 | 1.69 | 1.85 | 1.88 | 1.89 | 1.89 | 1.89 | 1.89 | 1.89 | 1.89 | 1.89 | 1.89 | 1.89 |
| | .10 | 4.06 | 3.78 | 3.62 | 3.52 | 3.45 | 3.40 | 3.37 | 3.34 | 3.32 | 3.30 | 3.27 | 3.24 |
| | .05 | 6.61 | 5.79 | 5.41 | 5.19 | 5.05 | 4.95 | 4.88 | 4.82 | 4.77 | 4.74 | 4.68 | 4.62 |
| | .025 | 10.0 | 8.43 | 7.76 | 7.39 | 7.15 | 6.98 | 6.85 | 6.76 | 6.68 | 6.62 | 6.52 | 6.43 |
| | .01 | 16.3 | 13.3 | 12.1 | 11.4 | 11.0 | 10.7 | 10.5 | 10.3 | 10.2 | 10.1 | 9.89 | 9.72 |
| | .001 | 47.2 | 37.1 | 33.2 | 31.1 | 29.8 | 28.8 | 28.2 | 27.6 | 27.2 | 26.9 | 26.4 | 26.9 |
| 6 | .25 | 1.62 | 1.76 | 1.78 | 1.79 | 1.79 | 1.78 | 1.78 | 1.78 | 1.77 | 1.77 | 1.77 | 1.76 |
| | .10 | 3.78 | 3.46 | 3.29 | 3.18 | 3.11 | 3.05 | 3.01 | 2.98 | 2.96 | 2.94 | 2.90 | 2.87 |
| | .05 | 5.99 | 5.14 | 4.76 | 4.53 | 4.39 | 4.28 | 4.21 | 4.15 | 4.10 | 4.06 | 4.00 | 3.94 |
| | .025 | 8.81 | 7.26 | 6.60 | 6.23 | 5.99 | 5.82 | 5.70 | 5.60 | 5.52 | 5.46 | 5.37 | 5.27 |
| | .01 | 13.8 | 10.9 | 9.78 | 9.15 | 8.75 | 8.47 | 8.26 | 8.10 | 7.98 | 7.87 | 7.72 | 7.56 |
| | .001 | 35.5 | 27.0 | 23.7 | 21.9 | 20.8 | 20.0 | 19.5 | 19.0 | 18.7 | 18.4 | 18.0 | 17.6 |
| | $\alpha$ | 1 | 2 | 3 | 4 | 5 | 6 | 7 | 8 | 9 | 10 | 12 | 15 |

[a] Critical values with $\nu_b$ of 50, 100, 200, 500, and 1,000, or with $\nu_e$ for denominator of 200, 500, and 1,000 determined via computer thanks to Frank B. Baker, James R. Morrow, and Gregory Camilli. Other values are reprinted from table 18 in E. S. Pearson and H. O. Hartley (Eds.), *Biometrika Tables for Statisticians*, 3rd ed. (1966), by permission of the *Biometrika* Trustees.

[b] To obtain critical values for $\alpha = .001$ with 1 degree of freedom in the denominator, multiply critical values at $\alpha = .01$ by 100.

*Note*: As an example, the critical value of $F$ with $J = 3$ and $n = 2$ $(n_{\bullet} = 6)$ with $\alpha = .05$ is $_{1-\alpha}F_{\nu_b,\,\nu_e} = {}_{1-\alpha}F_{(J-1),\,(n_{\bullet}-J)} = {}_{.95}F_{2,3} = 9.55$.

| $\nu_b$ (Degrees of Freedom for Numerator) | | | | | | | | | | | | | |
|---|---|---|---|---|---|---|---|---|---|---|---|---|---|
| *20* | *24* | *30* | *40* | *50* | *60* | *100* | *120* | *200* | *500* | *1,000* | ∞ | α | $\nu_e$ |
| 9.58 | 9.63 | 9.67 | 9.71 | 9.74 | 9.76 | 9.78 | 9.80 | 9.82 | 9.84 | 9.85 | 9.85 | .25 | 1 |
| 61.7 | 62.0 | 62.3 | 62.5 | 62.7 | 62.8 | 63.0 | 63.1 | 63.2 | 63.3 | 63.3 | 63.3 | .10 | |
| 248 | 249 | 250 | 251 | 252 | 252 | 253 | 253 | 254 | 254 | 254 | 254 | .05 | |
| 993 | 997 | 1,001 | 1,006 | 1,010 | 1,010 | 1,010 | 1,014 | 1,020 | 1,020 | 1,019 | 1,018 | .025 | |
| 6,209 | 6,235 | 6,261 | 6,287 | 6,300 | 6,313 | 6,330 | 6,339 | 6,350 | 6,360 | 6,363 | 6,366 | .01 | |
| *b* | *b* | *b* | *b* | *b* | *b* | *b* | *b* | *b* | *b* | *b* | *b* | .001 | |
| 3.43 | 3.43 | 3.44 | 3.45 | 3.45 | 3.46 | 3.47 | 3.47 | 3.48 | 3.48 | 1.39 | 3.48 | .25 | 2 |
| 9.44 | 9.45 | 9.46 | 9.47 | 9.47 | 9.47 | 9.48 | 9.48 | 9.49 | 9.49 | 2.31 | 9.49 | .10 | |
| 19.4 | 19.5 | 19.5 | 19.5 | 19.5 | 19.5 | 19.5 | 19.5 | 19.5 | 19.5 | 3.00 | 19.5 | .05 | |
| 39.5 | 39.5 | 39.5 | 39.5 | 39.5 | 39.5 | 39.5 | 39.5 | 39.5 | 39.5 | 3.70 | 39.5 | .025 | |
| 99.5 | 99.5 | 99.5 | 99.5 | 99.5 | 99.5 | 99.5 | 99.5 | 99.5 | 99.5 | 4.63 | 99.5 | .01 | |
| 999 | 999 | 999 | 999 | 999 | 999 | 999 | 999 | 999 | 999 | 6.95 | 999 | .001 | |
| 2.46 | 2.46 | 2.47 | 2.47 | 2.47 | 2.47 | 2.47 | 2.47 | 2.47 | 2.47 | 1.37 | 2.47 | .25 | 3 |
| 5.18 | 5.18 | 5.17 | 5.16 | 5.15 | 5.15 | 5.14 | 5.14 | 5.14 | 5.14 | 2.09 | 5.13 | .10 | |
| 8.66 | 8.64 | 8.62 | 8.59 | 8.58 | 8.57 | 8.55 | 8.55 | 8.54 | 8.53 | 2.61 | 8.53 | .05 | |
| 14.2 | 14.1 | 14.1 | 14.0 | 14.0 | 14.0 | 14.0 | 14.0 | 13.9 | 13.9 | 3.13 | 13.9 | .025 | |
| 26.7 | 26.6 | 26.5 | 26.4 | 26.4 | 26.3 | 26.2 | 26.2 | 26.2 | 26.1 | 3.80 | 26.1 | .01 | |
| 126 | 126 | 125 | 125 | 125 | 125 | 124 | 124 | 124 | 124 | 5.46 | 123 | .001 | |
| 2.08 | 2.08 | 2.08 | 2.08 | 2.08 | 2.08 | 2.08 | 2.08 | 2.08 | 2.08 | 1.35 | 2.08 | .25 | 4 |
| 3.84 | 3.83 | 3.82 | 3.80 | 3.80 | 3.79 | 3.78 | 3.78 | 3.77 | 3.76 | 1.95 | 3.76 | .10 | |
| 5.80 | 5.77 | 5.75 | 5.72 | 5.70 | 5.69 | 5.66 | 5.66 | 5.65 | 5.64 | 2.38 | 5.63 | .05 | |
| 8.56 | 8.51 | 8.46 | 8.41 | 8.38 | 8.36 | 8.32 | 8.31 | 8.29 | 8.27 | 2.80 | 8.26 | .025 | |
| 14.0 | 13.9 | 13.8 | 13.8 | 13.7 | 13.7 | 13.6 | 13.6 | 13.5 | 13.5 | 3.34 | 13.5 | .01 | |
| 46.1 | 45.8 | 45.4 | 45.1 | 44.9 | 44.8 | 44.5 | 44.4 | 44.3 | 44.1 | 4.65 | 44.1 | .001 | |
| 1.88 | 1.88 | 1.88 | 1.88 | 1.88 | 1.87 | 1.87 | 1.87 | 1.87 | 1.87 | 1.33 | 1.87 | .25 | 5 |
| 3.21 | 3.19 | 3.17 | 3.16 | 3.15 | 3.14 | 3.13 | 3.12 | 3.12 | 3.11 | 1.85 | 3.10 | .10 | |
| 4.56 | 4.53 | 4.50 | 4.46 | 4.44 | 4.43 | 4.41 | 4.40 | 4.39 | 4.37 | 2.22 | 4.36 | .05 | |
| 6.33 | 6.28 | 6.23 | 6.18 | 6.14 | 6.12 | 6.08 | 6.07 | 6.05 | 6.03 | 2.58 | 6.02 | .025 | |
| 9.55 | 9.47 | 9.38 | 9.29 | 9.24 | 9.20 | 9.13 | 9.11 | 9.08 | 9.04 | 3.04 | 9.02 | .01 | |
| 25.4 | 25.1 | 24.9 | 24.6 | 24.4 | 24.3 | 24.1 | 24.1 | 23.9 | 23.8 | 4.14 | 23.8 | .001 | |
| 1.76 | 1.75 | 1.75 | 1.75 | 1.75 | 1.74 | 1.74 | 1.74 | 1.74 | 1.74 | 1.74 | 1.74 | .25 | 6 |
| 2.84 | 2.82 | 2.80 | 2.78 | 2.77 | 2.76 | 2.75 | 2.74 | 2.73 | 2.73 | 2.72 | 2.72 | .10 | |
| 3.87 | 3.84 | 3.81 | 3.77 | 3.75 | 3.74 | 3.71 | 3.70 | 3.69 | 3.68 | 3.67 | 3.67 | .05 | |
| 5.17 | 5.12 | 5.07 | 5.01 | 4.98 | 4.96 | 4.92 | 4.90 | 4.88 | 4.86 | 4.86 | 4.85 | .025 | |
| 7.40 | 7.31 | 7.23 | 7.14 | 7.09 | 7.06 | 6.99 | 6.97 | 6.93 | 6.90 | 6.89 | 6.88 | .01 | |
| 17.1 | 16.9 | 16.7 | 16.4 | 16.3 | 16.2 | 16.0 | 16.0 | 15.9 | 15.8 | 15.8 | 15.8 | .001 | |
| *20* | *24* | *30* | *40* | *50* | *60* | *100* | *120* | *200* | *500* | *1,000* | ∞ | α | $\nu_e$ |

**TABLE F** *(Continued)*

| $\nu_e$ For Denominator | $\alpha$ | $\nu_b$ (Degrees of Freedom for Numerator) 1 | 2 | 3 | 4 | 5 | 6 | 7 | 8 | 9 | 10 | 12 | 15 |
|---|---|---|---|---|---|---|---|---|---|---|---|---|---|
| 7 | .25 | 1.57 | 1.70 | 1.72 | 1.72 | 1.71 | 1.71 | 1.70 | 1.70 | 1.69 | 1.69 | 1.68 | 1.68 |
| | .10 | 3.59 | 3.26 | 3.07 | 2.96 | 2.88 | 2.83 | 2.78 | 2.75 | 2.72 | 2.70 | 2.67 | 2.63 |
| | .05 | 5.59 | 4.74 | 4.35 | 4.12 | 3.97 | 3.87 | 3.79 | 3.73 | 3.68 | 3.64 | 3.57 | 3.51 |
| | .025 | 8.07 | 6.54 | 5.89 | 5.52 | 5.29 | 5.12 | 4.99 | 4.90 | 4.82 | 4.76 | 4.67 | 4.57 |
| | .01 | 12.3 | 9.55 | 8.45 | 7.85 | 7.46 | 7.19 | 6.99 | 6.84 | 6.72 | 6.62 | 6.47 | 6.31 |
| | .001 | 29.3 | 21.7 | 18.8 | 17.2 | 16.2 | 15.5 | 15.0 | 14.6 | 14.3 | 14.1 | 13.7 | 13.3 |
| 8 | .25 | 1.54 | 1.66 | 1.67 | 1.66 | 1.66 | 1.65 | 1.64 | 1.64 | 1.63 | 1.63 | 1.62 | 1.62 |
| | .10 | 3.46 | 3.11 | 2.92 | 2.81 | 2.73 | 2.67 | 2.62 | 2.59 | 2.56 | 2.54 | 2.50 | 2.46 |
| | .05 | 5.32 | 4.46 | 4.07 | 3.84 | 3.69 | 3.58 | 3.50 | 3.44 | 3.39 | 3.35 | 3.28 | 3.22 |
| | .025 | 7.57 | 6.06 | 5.42 | 5.05 | 4.82 | 4.65 | 4.53 | 4.43 | 4.36 | 4.30 | 4.20 | 4.10 |
| | .01 | 11.3 | 8.65 | 7.59 | 7.01 | 6.63 | 6.37 | 6.18 | 6.03 | 5.91 | 5.81 | 5.67 | 5.52 |
| | .001 | 25.4 | 18.5 | 15.8 | 14.4 | 13.5 | 12.9 | 12.4 | 12.0 | 11.8 | 11.5 | 11.2 | 10.8 |
| 9 | .25 | 1.51 | 1.62 | 1.63 | 1.63 | 1.62 | 1.61 | 1.60 | 1.60 | 1.59 | 1.59 | 1.58 | 1.57 |
| | .10 | 3.36 | 3.01 | 2.81 | 2.69 | 2.61 | 2.55 | 2.51 | 2.47 | 2.44 | 2.42 | 2.38 | 2.34 |
| | .05 | 5.12 | 4.26 | 3.86 | 3.63 | 3.48 | 3.37 | 3.29 | 3.23 | 3.18 | 3.14 | 3.07 | 3.01 |
| | .025 | 7.21 | 5.71 | 5.08 | 4.72 | 4.48 | 4.32 | 4.20 | 4.10 | 4.03 | 3.96 | 3.87 | 3.77 |
| | .01 | 10.6 | 8.02 | 6.99 | 6.42 | 6.06 | 5.80 | 6.51 | 5.47 | 5.35 | 5.26 | 5.11 | 4.96 |
| | .001 | 22.9 | 16.4 | 13.9 | 12.6 | 11.7 | 11.1 | 10.7 | 10.4 | 10.1 | 9.89 | 9.57 | 9.24 |
| 10 | .25 | 1.49 | 1.60 | 1.60 | 1.59 | 1.59 | 1.58 | 1.57 | 1.56 | 1.56 | 1.55 | 1.54 | 1.53 |
| | .10 | 3.29 | 2.92 | 2.73 | 2.61 | 2.52 | 2.46 | 2.41 | 2.38 | 2.35 | 2.32 | 2.28 | 2.24 |
| | .05 | 4.96 | 4.10 | 3.71 | 3.48 | 3.33 | 3.22 | 3.14 | 3.07 | 3.02 | 2.98 | 2.91 | 2.85 |
| | .025 | 6.94 | 5.46 | 4.83 | 4.47 | 4.24 | 4.07 | 3.95 | 3.85 | 3.78 | 3.72 | 3.62 | 3.52 |
| | .01 | 10.0 | 7.56 | 6.55 | 5.99 | 5.64 | 5.39 | 5.20 | 5.06 | 4.94 | 4.85 | 4.71 | 4.56 |
| | .001 | 21.0 | 14.9 | 12.6 | 11.3 | 10.5 | 9.92 | 9.52 | 9.20 | 8.96 | 8.75 | 8.45 | 8.13 |
| 11 | .25 | 1.47 | 1.58 | 1.58 | 1.57 | 1.56 | 1.55 | 1.54 | 1.53 | 1.53 | 1.52 | 1.51 | 1.50 |
| | .10 | 3.23 | 2.86 | 2.66 | 2.54 | 2.45 | 2.39 | 2.34 | 2.30 | 2.27 | 2.25 | 2.21 | 2.17 |
| | .05 | 4.84 | 3.98 | 3.59 | 3.36 | 3.20 | 3.09 | 3.01 | 2.95 | 2.90 | 2.85 | 2.79 | 2.72 |
| | .025 | 6.72 | 5.26 | 4.63 | 4.28 | 4.04 | 3.88 | 3.76 | 3.66 | 3.59 | 3.53 | 3.53 | 3.33 |
| | .01 | 9.65 | 7.21 | 6.22 | 5.67 | 5.32 | 5.07 | 4.89 | 4.74 | 4.63 | 4.54 | 4.40 | 4.25 |
| | .001 | 19.7 | 13.8 | 11.6 | 10.4 | 9.58 | 9.05 | 8.66 | 8.35 | 8.12 | 7.92 | 7.63 | 7.32 |
| 12 | .25 | 1.46 | 1.56 | 1.56 | 1.55 | 1.54 | 1.53 | 1.52 | 1.51 | 1.51 | 1.50 | 1.49 | 1.48 |
| | .10 | 3.18 | 2.81 | 2.61 | 2.48 | 2.39 | 2.33 | 2.28 | 2.24 | 2.21 | 2.19 | 2.15 | 2.10 |
| | .05 | 4.75 | 3.89 | 3.49 | 3.26 | 3.11 | 3.00 | 2.91 | 2.85 | 2.80 | 2.75 | 2.69 | 2.62 |
| | .025 | 6.55 | 5.10 | 4.49 | 4.12 | 3.89 | 3.73 | 3.61 | 3.51 | 3.44 | 3.37 | 3.28 | 3.18 |
| | .01 | 9.33 | 6.93 | 5.95 | 5.41 | 5.06 | 4.82 | 4.64 | 4.50 | 4.39 | 4.30 | 4.16 | 4.01 |
| | .001 | 18.6 | 13.0 | 10.8 | 9.63 | 8.89 | 8.38 | 8.00 | 7.71 | 7.48 | 7.29 | 7.00 | 6.71 |
| 13 | .25 | 1.45 | 1.55 | 1.55 | 1.53 | 1.52 | 1.51 | 1.50 | 1.49 | 1.49 | 1.48 | 1.47 | 1.46 |
| | .10 | 3.14 | 2.76 | 2.56 | 2.43 | 2.35 | 2.28 | 2.23 | 2.20 | 2.16 | 2.14 | 2.10 | 2.05 |
| | .05 | 4.67 | 3.81 | 3.41 | 3.18 | 3.03 | 2.92 | 2.83 | 2.77 | 2.71 | 2.67 | 2.60 | 2.53 |
| | .025 | 6.41 | 4.97 | 4.35 | 4.00 | 3.77 | 3.60 | 3.48 | 3.39 | 3.31 | 3.25 | 3.15 | 3.05 |
| | .01 | 9.07 | 6.70 | 5.74 | 5.21 | 4.86 | 4.62 | 4.44 | 4.30 | 4.19 | 4.10 | 3.96 | 3.82 |
| | .001 | 17.8 | 12.3 | 10.2 | 9.07 | 8.35 | 7.86 | 7.49 | 7.21 | 6.98 | 6.80 | 6.52 | 6.23 |
| 14 | .25 | 1.44 | 1.53 | 1.53 | 1.52 | 1.51 | 1.50 | 1.49 | 1.48 | 1.47 | 1.46 | 1.45 | 1.44 |
| | .10 | 3.10 | 2.73 | 2.52 | 2.39 | 2.31 | 2.24 | 2.19 | 2.15 | 2.12 | 2.10 | 2.05 | 2.01 |
| | .05 | 4.60 | 3.74 | 3.34 | 3.11 | 2.96 | 2.85 | 2.76 | 2.70 | 2.65 | 2.60 | 2.53 | 2.46 |
| | .025 | 6.30 | 4.86 | 4.24 | 3.89 | 3.66 | 3.50 | 3.38 | 3.29 | 3.21 | 3.15 | 3.05 | 2.95 |
| | .01 | 8.86 | 6.51 | 5.56 | 5.04 | 4.69 | 4.46 | 4.28 | 4.14 | 4.03 | 3.94 | 3.80 | 3.66 |
| | .001 | 17.1 | 11.8 | 9.73 | 8.62 | 7.92 | 7.43 | 7.08 | 6.80 | 6.58 | 6.40 | 6.13 | 5.85 |
| 15 | .25 | 1.43 | 1.52 | 1.52 | 1.51 | 1.49 | 1.48 | 1.47 | 1.46 | 1.46 | 1.45 | 1.44 | 1.43 |
| | .10 | 3.07 | 2.70 | 2.49 | 2.36 | 2.27 | 2.21 | 2.16 | 2.12 | 2.09 | 2.06 | 2.02 | 1.97 |
| | .05 | 4.54 | 3.68 | 3.29 | 3.06 | 2.90 | 2.79 | 2.71 | 2.64 | 2.59 | 2.54 | 2.48 | 2.40 |
| | .025 | 6.20 | 4.77 | 4.15 | 3.80 | 3.58 | 3.41 | 3.29 | 3.20 | 3.12 | 3.06 | 2.96 | 2.86 |
| | .01 | 8.68 | 6.36 | 5.42 | 4.89 | 4.56 | 4.32 | 4.14 | 4.00 | 3.89 | 3.80 | 3.67 | 3.52 |
| | .001 | 16.6 | 11.3 | 9.34 | 8.25 | 7.57 | 7.09 | 6.74 | 6.47 | 6.26 | 6.08 | 5.81 | 5.54 |
| | $\alpha$ | 1 | 2 | 3 | 4 | 5 | 6 | 7 | 8 | 9 | 10 | 12 | 15 |

| $\nu_b$ (Degrees of Freedom for Numerator) | | | | | | | | | | | | | |
|---|---|---|---|---|---|---|---|---|---|---|---|---|---|
| 20 | 24 | 30 | 40 | 50 | 60 | 100 | 120 | 200 | 500 | 1,000 | ∞ | $\alpha$ | $\nu_e$ |
| 1.67 | 1.67 | 1.66 | 1.66 | 1.66 | 1.65 | 1.65 | 1.65 | 1.65 | 1.65 | 1.65 | 1.65 | .25 | 7 |
| 2.59 | 2.58 | 2.56 | 2.54 | 2.52 | 2.51 | 2.50 | 2.49 | 2.48 | 2.48 | 2.47 | 2.47 | .10 | |
| 3.44 | 3.41 | 3.38 | 3.34 | 3.32 | 3.30 | 3.27 | 3.27 | 3.25 | 3.24 | 3.23 | 3.23 | .05 | |
| 4.47 | 4.42 | 4.36 | 4.31 | 4.28 | 4.25 | 4.21 | 4.20 | 4.18 | 4.16 | 4.15 | 4.14 | .025 | |
| 6.16 | 6.07 | 5.99 | 5.91 | 5.86 | 5.82 | 5.75 | 5.74 | 5.70 | 5.67 | 5.66 | 5.65 | .01 | |
| 12.9 | 12.7 | 12.5 | 12.3 | 12.2 | 12.1 | 11.9 | 11.9 | 11.8 | 11.7 | 11.7 | 11.7 | .001 | |
| 1.61 | 1.60 | 1.60 | 1.59 | 1.59 | 1.59 | 1.58 | 1.58 | 1.58 | 1.58 | 1.58 | 1.58 | .25 | 8 |
| 2.42 | 2.40 | 2.38 | 2.36 | 2.35 | 2.34 | 2.32 | 2.32 | 2.31 | 2.30 | 2.29 | 2.29 | .10 | |
| 3.15 | 3.12 | 3.08 | 3.04 | 3.02 | 3.01 | 2.97 | 2.97 | 2.95 | 2.94 | 2.93 | 2.93 | .05 | |
| 4.00 | 3.95 | 3.89 | 3.84 | 3.81 | 3.78 | 3.74 | 3.73 | 3.70 | 3.68 | 3.68 | 3.67 | .025 | |
| 5.36 | 5.28 | 5.20 | 5.12 | 5.07 | 5.03 | 4.96 | 4.95 | 4.91 | 4.88 | 4.87 | 4.86 | .01 | |
| 10.5 | 10.3 | 10.1 | 9.92 | 9.80 | 9.73 | 9.57 | 9.53 | 9.46 | 9.39 | 9.35 | 9.33 | .001 | |
| 1.56 | 1.56 | 1.55 | 1.55 | 1.54 | 1.54 | 1.53 | 1.53 | 1.53 | 1.53 | 1.53 | 1.53 | .25 | 9 |
| 2.30 | 2.28 | 2.25 | 2.23 | 2.22 | 2.21 | 2.19 | 2.18 | 2.17 | 2.17 | 2.16 | 2.16 | .10 | |
| 2.94 | 2.90 | 2.86 | 2.83 | 2.80 | 2.79 | 2.76 | 2.75 | 2.73 | 2.72 | 2.71 | 2.71 | .05 | |
| 3.67 | 3.61 | 3.56 | 3.51 | 3.47 | 3.45 | 3.40 | 3.39 | 3.37 | 3.35 | 3.34 | 3.33 | .025 | |
| 4.81 | 4.73 | 4.65 | 4.57 | 4.52 | 4.48 | 4.42 | 4.40 | 4.36 | 4.33 | 4.32 | 4.31 | .01 | |
| 8.90 | 8.72 | 8.55 | 8.37 | 8.26 | 8.19 | 8.04 | 8.00 | 7.93 | 7.86 | 7.83 | 7.81 | .001 | |
| 1.52 | 1.52 | 1.51 | 1.51 | 1.50 | 1.50 | 1.49 | 1.49 | 1.49 | 1.48 | 1.48 | 1.48 | .25 | 10 |
| 2.20 | 2.18 | 2.16 | 2.13 | 2.12 | 2.11 | 2.09 | 2.08 | 2.07 | 2.06 | 2.06 | 2.06 | .10 | |
| 2.77 | 2.74 | 2.70 | 2.66 | 2.64 | 2.62 | 2.59 | 2.58 | 2.56 | 2.55 | 2.54 | 2.54 | .05 | |
| 3.42 | 3.37 | 3.31 | 3.26 | 3.22 | 3.20 | 3.15 | 3.14 | 3.12 | 3.09 | 3.09 | 3.08 | .025 | |
| 4.41 | 4.33 | 4.25 | 4.17 | 4.12 | 4.08 | 4.01 | 4.00 | 3.96 | 3.93 | 3.92 | 3.91 | .01 | |
| 7.80 | 7.64 | 7.47 | 7.30 | 7.19 | 7.12 | 6.98 | 6.94 | 6.87 | 6.81 | 6.78 | 6.76 | .001 | |
| 1.49 | 1.49 | 1.48 | 1.47 | 1.47 | 1.47 | 1.46 | 1.46 | 1.46 | 1.45 | 1.45 | 1.45 | .25 | 11 |
| 2.12 | 2.10 | 2.08 | 2.05 | 2.04 | 2.03 | 2.00 | 2.00 | 1.99 | 1.98 | 1.98 | 1.97 | .10 | |
| 2.65 | 2.61 | 2.57 | 2.53 | 2.51 | 2.49 | 2.46 | 2.45 | 2.43 | 2.42 | 2.41 | 2.40 | .05 | |
| 3.23 | 3.17 | 3.12 | 3.06 | 3.03 | 3.00 | 2.96 | 2.94 | 2.92 | 2.90 | 2.89 | 2.88 | .025 | |
| 4.10 | 4.02 | 3.94 | 3.86 | 3.81 | 3.78 | 3.71 | 3.69 | 3.66 | 3.62 | 3.61 | 3.60 | .01 | |
| 7.01 | 6.85 | 6.68 | 6.52 | 6.41 | 6.35 | 6.21 | 6.17 | 6.10 | 6.04 | 6.01 | 6.00 | .001 | |
| 1.47 | 1.46 | 1.45 | 1.45 | 1.44 | 1.44 | 1.43 | 1.43 | 1.43 | 1.42 | 1.42 | 1.42 | .25 | 12 |
| 2.06 | 2.04 | 2.01 | 1.99 | 1.97 | 1.96 | 1.94 | 1.93 | 1.92 | 1.91 | 1.91 | 1.90 | .10 | |
| 2.54 | 2.51 | 2.47 | 2.43 | 2.40 | 2.38 | 2.35 | 2.34 | 2.32 | 2.31 | 2.30 | 2.30 | .05 | |
| 3.07 | 3.02 | 2.96 | 2.91 | 2.87 | 2.85 | 2.80 | 2.79 | 2.76 | 2.74 | 2.73 | 2.72 | .025 | |
| 3.86 | 3.78 | 3.70 | 3.62 | 3.57 | 3.54 | 3.47 | 3.45 | 3.41 | 3.38 | 3.37 | 3.36 | .01 | |
| 6.40 | 6.25 | 6.09 | 5.93 | 5.83 | 5.76 | 5.63 | 5.59 | 5.52 | 5.46 | 5.44 | 5.42 | .001 | |
| 1.45 | 1.44 | 1.43 | 1.42 | 1.42 | 1.42 | 1.41 | 1.41 | 1.40 | 1.40 | 1.40 | 1.40 | .25 | 13 |
| 2.01 | 1.98 | 1.96 | 1.93 | 1.92 | 1.90 | 1.88 | 1.88 | 1.86 | 1.85 | 1.85 | 1.85 | .10 | |
| 2.46 | 2.42 | 2.38 | 2.34 | 2.31 | 2.30 | 2.26 | 2.25 | 2.23 | 2.22 | 2.21 | 2.21 | .01 | |
| 2.95 | 2.89 | 2.84 | 2.78 | 2.74 | 2.72 | 2.67 | 2.66 | 2.63 | 2.61 | 2.60 | 2.60 | .025 | |
| 3.66 | 3.59 | 3.51 | 3.43 | 3.38 | 3.34 | 3.27 | 3.25 | 3.22 | 3.19 | 3.18 | 3.17 | .01 | |
| 5.93 | 5.78 | 5.63 | 5.47 | 5.36 | 5.30 | 5.17 | 5.14 | 5.07 | 5.00 | 4.98 | 4.97 | .001 | |
| 1.43 | 1.42 | 1.41 | 1.41 | 1.40 | 1.40 | 1.39 | 1.39 | 1.39 | 1.38 | 1.38 | 1.38 | .25 | 14 |
| 1.96 | 1.94 | 1.91 | 1.89 | 1.87 | 1.86 | 1.83 | 1.83 | 1.82 | 1.80 | 1.80 | 1.80 | .10 | |
| 2.39 | 2.35 | 2.31 | 2.27 | 2.24 | 2.22 | 2.19 | 2.18 | 2.16 | 2.14 | 2.14 | 2.13 | .05 | |
| 2.84 | 2.79 | 2.73 | 2.67 | 2.64 | 2.61 | 2.56 | 2.55 | 2.53 | 2.51 | 2.49 | 2.49 | .025 | |
| 3.51 | 3.43 | 3.35 | 3.27 | 3.22 | 3.18 | 3.11 | 3.09 | 3.06 | 3.03 | 3.01 | 3.00 | .01 | |
| 5.56 | 5.41 | 5.25 | 5.10 | 5.00 | 4.94 | 4.80 | 4.77 | 4.70 | 4.69 | 4.62 | 4.60 | .001 | |
| 1.41 | 1.41 | 1.40 | 1.39 | 1.39 | 1.38 | 1.38 | 1.37 | 1.37 | 1.36 | 1.36 | 1.36 | .25 | 15 |
| 1.92 | 1.90 | 1.87 | 1.85 | 1.83 | 1.82 | 1.79 | 1.79 | 1.77 | 1.76 | 1.76 | 1.76 | .10 | |
| 2.33 | 2.29 | 2.25 | 2.20 | 2.18 | 2.16 | 2.12 | 2.11 | 2.10 | 2.08 | 2.07 | 2.07 | .05 | |
| 2.76 | 2.70 | 2.64 | 2.59 | 2.55 | 2.52 | 2.47 | 2.46 | 2.44 | 2.41 | 2.40 | 2.40 | .025 | |
| 3.37 | 3.29 | 3.21 | 3.13 | 3.08 | 3.05 | 2.98 | 2.96 | 2.92 | 2.89 | 2.88 | 2.87 | .01 | |
| 5.25 | 5.10 | 4.95 | 4.80 | 4.70 | 4.64 | 4.51 | 4.47 | 4.41 | 4.35 | 4.32 | 4.31 | .001 | |
| 20 | 24 | 30 | 40 | 50 | 60 | 100 | 120 | 200 | 500 | 1,000 | ∞ | $\alpha$ | $\nu_e$ |

**TABLE F (cont.)**

| $\nu_e$ For Denominator | α | $\nu_b$ (Degrees of Freedom for Numerator) 1 | 2 | 3 | 4 | 5 | 6 | 7 | 8 | 9 | 10 | 12 | 15 |
|---|---|---|---|---|---|---|---|---|---|---|---|---|---|
| 16 | .25 | 1.42 | 1.51 | 1.51 | 1.50 | 1.48 | 1.47 | 1.46 | 1.45 | 1.44 | 1.44 | 1.43 | 1.41 |
| | .01 | 3.05 | 2.67 | 2.46 | 2.33 | 2.24 | 2.18 | 2.13 | 2.09 | 2.06 | 2.03 | 1.99 | 1.94 |
| | .05 | 4.49 | 3.63 | 3.24 | 3.01 | 2.85 | 2.74 | 2.66 | 2.59 | 2.54 | 2.49 | 2.42 | 2.35 |
| | .025 | 6.12 | 4.69 | 4.08 | 3.73 | 3.50 | 3.34 | 3.22 | 3.12 | 3.05 | 2.99 | 2.89 | 2.79 |
| | .01 | 8.53 | 6.23 | 5.29 | 4.77 | 4.44 | 4.20 | 4.03 | 3.89 | 3.78 | 3.69 | 3.55 | 3.41 |
| | .001 | 16.1 | 11.0 | 9.00 | 7.94 | 7.27 | 6.81 | 6.46 | 6.19 | 5.98 | 5.81 | 5.55 | 5.27 |
| 17 | .25 | 1.42 | 1.51 | 1.50 | 1.49 | 1.47 | 1.46 | 1.45 | 1.44 | 1.43 | 1.43 | 1.41 | 1.40 |
| | .10 | 3.03 | 2.64 | 2.44 | 2.31 | 2.22 | 2.15 | 2.10 | 2.06 | 2.03 | 2.00 | 1.96 | 1.91 |
| | .05 | 4.45 | 3.59 | 3.20 | 2.96 | 2.81 | 2.70 | 2.61 | 2.55 | 2.49 | 2.45 | 2.38 | 2.31 |
| | .025 | 6.04 | 4.62 | 4.01 | 3.66 | 3.44 | 3.28 | 3.16 | 3.06 | 2.98 | 2.92 | 2.82 | 2.72 |
| | .01 | 8.40 | 6.11 | 5.18 | 4.67 | 4.34 | 4.10 | 3.93 | 3.79 | 3.68 | 3.59 | 3.46 | 3.31 |
| | .001 | 15.7 | 10.7 | 8.73 | 7.68 | 7.02 | 6.56 | 6.22 | 5.96 | 5.75 | 5.58 | 5.32 | 5.05 |
| 18 | .25 | 1.41 | 1.50 | 1.49 | 1.48 | 1.46 | 1.45 | 1.44 | 1.43 | 1.42 | 1.42 | 1.40 | 1.39 |
| | .10 | 3.01 | 2.62 | 2.42 | 2.29 | 2.20 | 2.13 | 2.08 | 2.04 | 2.00 | 1.98 | 1.93 | 1.89 |
| | .05 | 4.41 | 3.55 | 3.16 | 2.93 | 2.77 | 2.66 | 2.58 | 2.51 | 2.46 | 2.41 | 2.34 | 2.27 |
| | .025 | 5.98 | 4.56 | 3.95 | 3.61 | 3.38 | 3.22 | 3.10 | 3.01 | 2.93 | 2.87 | 2.77 | 2.67 |
| | .01 | 8.29 | 6.01 | 5.09 | 4.58 | 4.25 | 4.01 | 3.84 | 3.71 | 3.60 | 3.51 | 3.37 | 3.23 |
| | .001 | 15.4 | 10.4 | 8.49 | 7.46 | 6.81 | 6.35 | 6.02 | 5.76 | 5.56 | 5.39 | 5.13 | 4.87 |
| 19 | .25 | 1.41 | 1.49 | 1.49 | 1.47 | 1.46 | 1.44 | 1.43 | 1.42 | 1.41 | 1.41 | 1.40 | 1.38 |
| | .10 | 2.99 | 2.61 | 2.40 | 2.27 | 2.18 | 2.11 | 2.06 | 2.02 | 1.98 | 1.96 | 1.91 | 1.86 |
| | .05 | 4.38 | 3.52 | 3.13 | 2.90 | 2.74 | 2.63 | 2.54 | 2.48 | 2.42 | 2.38 | 2.31 | 2.23 |
| | .025 | 5.92 | 4.51 | 3.90 | 3.56 | 3.33 | 3.17 | 3.05 | 2.96 | 2.88 | 2.82 | 2.72 | 2.62 |
| | .01 | 8.18 | 5.93 | 5.01 | 4.50 | 4.17 | 3.94 | 3.77 | 3.63 | 3.52 | 3.43 | 3.30 | 3.15 |
| | .001 | 15.1 | 10.2 | 8.28 | 7.26 | 6.62 | 6.18 | 5.85 | 5.59 | 5.39 | 5.22 | 4.97 | 4.70 |
| 20 | .25 | 1.40 | 1.49 | 1.48 | 1.46 | 1.45 | 1.44 | 1.43 | 1.42 | 1.41 | 1.40 | 1.39 | 1.37 |
| | .10 | 2.97 | 2.59 | 2.38 | 2.25 | 2.16 | 2.09 | 2.04 | 2.00 | 1.96 | 1.94 | 1.89 | 1.84 |
| | .05 | 4.35 | 3.49 | 3.10 | 2.87 | 2.71 | 2.60 | 2.51 | 2.45 | 2.39 | 2.35 | 2.28 | 2.20 |
| | .025 | 5.87 | 4.46 | 3.86 | 3.51 | 3.29 | 3.13 | 3.01 | 2.91 | 2.84 | 2.77 | 2.68 | 2.57 |
| | .01 | 8.10 | 5.85 | 4.94 | 4.43 | 4.10 | 3.87 | 3.70 | 3.56 | 3.46 | 3.37 | 3.23 | 3.09 |
| | .001 | 14.8 | 9.95 | 8.10 | 7.10 | 6.46 | 6.02 | 5.69 | 5.44 | 5.24 | 5.08 | 4.82 | 4.56 |
| 22 | .25 | 1.40 | 1.48 | 1.47 | 1.45 | 1.44 | 1.42 | 1.41 | 1.40 | 1.39 | 1.39 | 1.37 | 1.36 |
| | .10 | 2.95 | 2.56 | 2.35 | 2.22 | 2.13 | 2.06 | 2.01 | 1.97 | 1.93 | 1.90 | 1.86 | 1.81 |
| | .05 | 4.30 | 3.44 | 3.05 | 2.82 | 2.66 | 2.55 | 2.46 | 2.40 | 2.34 | 2.30 | 2.23 | 2.15 |
| | .025 | 5.79 | 4.38 | 3.78 | 3.44 | 3.22 | 3.05 | 2.93 | 2.84 | 2.76 | 2.70 | 2.60 | 2.50 |
| | .01 | 7.95 | 5.72 | 4.82 | 4.31 | 3.99 | 3.76 | 3.59 | 3.45 | 3.35 | 3.26 | 3.12 | 2.98 |
| | .001 | 14.4 | 9.61 | 7.80 | 6.81 | 6.19 | 5.76 | 5.44 | 5.19 | 4.99 | 4.83 | 4.58 | 4.33 |
| 24 | .25 | 1.39 | 1.47 | 1.46 | 1.44 | 1.43 | 1.41 | 1.40 | 1.39 | 1.38 | 1.38 | 1.36 | 1.35 |
| | .10 | 2.93 | 2.54 | 2.33 | 2.19 | 2.10 | 2.04 | 1.98 | 1.94 | 1.91 | 1.88 | 1.83 | 1.78 |
| | .05 | 4.26 | 3.40 | 3.01 | 2.78 | 2.62 | 2.51 | 2.42 | 2.36 | 2.30 | 2.25 | 2.18 | 2.11 |
| | .025 | 5.72 | 4.32 | 3.72 | 3.38 | 3.15 | 2.99 | 2.87 | 2.78 | 2.70 | 2.64 | 2.54 | 2.44 |
| | .01 | 7.82 | 5.61 | 4.72 | 4.22 | 3.90 | 3.67 | 3.50 | 3.36 | 3.26 | 3.17 | 3.03 | 2.89 |
| | .001 | 14.0 | 9.34 | 7.55 | 6.59 | 5.98 | 5.55 | 5.23 | 4.99 | 4.80 | 4.64 | 4.39 | 4.14 |
| 26 | .25 | 1.38 | 1.46 | 1.45 | 1.44 | 1.42 | 1.41 | 1.39 | 1.38 | 1.37 | 1.37 | 1.35 | 1.34 |
| | .10 | 2.91 | 2.52 | 2.31 | 2.17 | 2.08 | 2.01 | 1.96 | 1.92 | 1.88 | 1.86 | 1.81 | 1.76 |
| | .05 | 4.23 | 3.37 | 2.98 | 2.74 | 2.59 | 2.47 | 2.39 | 2.32 | 2.27 | 2.22 | 2.15 | 2.07 |
| | .025 | 5.66 | 4.27 | 3.67 | 3.33 | 3.10 | 2.94 | 2.82 | 2.73 | 2.65 | 2.59 | 2.49 | 2.39 |
| | .01 | 7.72 | 5.53 | 4.64 | 4.14 | 3.82 | 3.59 | 3.42 | 3.29 | 3.18 | 3.09 | 2.96 | 2.81 |
| | .001 | 13.7 | 9.12 | 7.36 | 6.41 | 5.80 | 5.38 | 5.07 | 4.83 | 4.64 | 4.48 | 4.24 | 3.99 |
| 28 | .25 | 1.38 | 1.46 | 1.45 | 1.43 | 1.41 | 1.40 | 1.39 | 1.38 | 1.37 | 1.36 | 1.34 | 1.33 |
| | .10 | 2.89 | 2.50 | 2.29 | 2.16 | 2.06 | 2.00 | 1.94 | 1.90 | 1.87 | 1.84 | 1.79 | 1.74 |
| | .05 | 4.20 | 3.34 | 2.95 | 2.71 | 2.56 | 2.45 | 2.36 | 2.29 | 2.24 | 2.19 | 2.12 | 2.04 |
| | .025 | 5.61 | 4.22 | 3.63 | 3.29 | 3.06 | 2.90 | 2.78 | 2.69 | 2.61 | 2.55 | 2.45 | 2.34 |
| | .01 | 7.64 | 5.45 | 4.57 | 4.07 | 3.75 | 3.53 | 3.36 | 3.23 | 3.12 | 3.03 | 2.90 | 2.75 |
| | .001 | 13.5 | 8.93 | 7.19 | 6.25 | 5.66 | 5.24 | 4.93 | 4.69 | 4.50 | 4.35 | 4.11 | 3.86 |
| | α | 1 | 2 | 3 | 4 | 5 | 6 | 7 | 8 | 9 | 10 | 12 | 15 |

| $\nu_b$ (Degrees of Freedom for Numerator) | | | | | | | | | | | | | |
|---|---|---|---|---|---|---|---|---|---|---|---|---|---|
| 20 | 24 | 30 | 40 | 50 | 60 | 100 | 120 | 200 | 500 | 1,000 | ∞ | α | $\nu_e$ |
| 1.40 | 1.39 | 1.38 | 1.37 | 1.37 | 1.36 | 1.36 | 1.35 | 1.35 | 1.34 | 1.35 | 1.34 | .25 | 16 |
| 1.89 | 1.87 | 1.84 | 1.81 | 1.79 | 1.78 | 1.76 | 1.75 | 1.74 | 1.73 | 1.72 | 1.72 | .10 | |
| 2.28 | 2.24 | 2.19 | 2.15 | 2.12 | 2.11 | 2.07 | 2.06 | 2.04 | 2.02 | 2.02 | 2.01 | .05 | |
| 2.68 | 2.63 | 2.57 | 2.51 | 2.47 | 2.45 | 2.40 | 2.38 | 2.36 | 2.33 | 2.32 | 2.32 | .025 | |
| 3.26 | 3.18 | 3.10 | 3.02 | 2.97 | 2.93 | 2.86 | 2.84 | 2.81 | 2.78 | 2.76 | 2.75 | .01 | |
| 4.99 | 4.85 | 4.70 | 4.54 | 4.45 | 4.39 | 4.25 | 4.23 | 4.16 | 4.10 | 4.08 | 4.06 | .001 | |
| 1.39 | 1.38 | 1.37 | 1.36 | 1.35 | 1.35 | 1.34 | 1.34 | 1.34 | 1.33 | 1.33 | 1.33 | .25 | 17 |
| 1.86 | 1.84 | 1.81 | 1.78 | 1.76 | 1.75 | 1.73 | 1.72 | 1.71 | 1.69 | 1.69 | 1.69 | .10 | |
| 2.23 | 2.19 | 2.15 | 2.10 | 2.08 | 2.06 | 2.02 | 2.01 | 1.99 | 1.97 | 1.97 | 1.96 | .05 | |
| 2.62 | 2.56 | 2.50 | 2.44 | 2.40 | 2.38 | 2.33 | 2.32 | 2.29 | 2.26 | 2.26 | 2.25 | .025 | |
| 3.16 | 3.08 | 3.00 | 2.92 | 2.87 | 2.83 | 2.76 | 2.75 | 2.71 | 2.68 | 2.66 | 2.65 | .01 | |
| 4.78 | 4.63 | 4.48 | 4.33 | 4.24 | 4.18 | 4.04 | 4.02 | 3.95 | 3.89 | 3.87 | 3.85 | .001 | |
| 1.38 | 1.37 | 1.36 | 1.35 | 1.34 | 1.34 | 1.33 | 1.33 | 1.32 | 1.32 | 1.32 | 1.32 | .25 | 18 |
| 1.84 | 1.81 | 1.78 | 1.75 | 1.74 | 1.72 | 1.70 | 1.69 | 1.68 | 1.67 | 1.66 | 1.66 | .10 | |
| 2.19 | 2.15 | 2.11 | 2.06 | 2.04 | 2.02 | 1.98 | 1.97 | 1.95 | 1.93 | 1.92 | 1.92 | .05 | |
| 2.56 | 2.50 | 2.44 | 2.38 | 2.35 | 2.32 | 2.27 | 2.26 | 2.32 | 2.20 | 2.20 | 2.19 | .025 | |
| 3.08 | 3.00 | 2.92 | 2.84 | 2.78 | 2.75 | 2.68 | 2.66 | 2.62 | 2.59 | 2.58 | 2.57 | .01 | |
| 4.59 | 4.45 | 4.30 | 4.15 | 4.05 | 4.00 | 3.86 | 3.84 | 3.77 | 3.71 | 3.69 | 3.67 | .001 | |
| 1.37 | 1.36 | 1.35 | 1.34 | 1.33 | 1.33 | 1.32 | 1.32 | 1.31 | 1.31 | 1.31 | 1.30 | .25 | 19 |
| 1.81 | 1.79 | 1.76 | 1.73 | 1.71 | 1.70 | 1.67 | 1.67 | 1.65 | 1.64 | 1.63 | 1.63 | .10 | |
| 2.16 | 2.11 | 2.07 | 2.03 | 2.00 | 1.98 | 1.94 | 1.93 | 1.91 | 1.89 | 1.88 | 1.88 | .05 | |
| 2.51 | 2.45 | 2.39 | 2.33 | 2.30 | 2.27 | 2.22 | 2.20 | 2.18 | 2.15 | 2.14 | 2.13 | .025 | |
| 3.00 | 2.92 | 2.84 | 2.76 | 2.71 | 2.67 | 2.60 | 2.58 | 2.55 | 2.51 | 2.50 | 2.49 | .01 | |
| 4.43 | 4.29 | 4.14 | 3.99 | 3.90 | 3.84 | 3.71 | 3.68 | 3.61 | 3.55 | 3.53 | 3.51 | .001 | |
| 1.36 | 1.35 | 1.34 | 1.33 | 1.33 | 1.32 | 1.31 | 1.31 | 1.30 | 1.30 | 1.30 | 1.29 | .25 | 20 |
| 1.79 | 1.77 | 1.74 | 1.71 | 1.69 | 1.68 | 1.65 | 1.64 | 1.63 | 1.62 | 1.61 | 1.61 | .10 | |
| 2.12 | 2.08 | 2.04 | 1.99 | 1.97 | 1.95 | 1.91 | 1.90 | 1.88 | 1.86 | 1.85 | 1.84 | .05 | |
| 2.46 | 2.41 | 2.35 | 2.29 | 2.25 | 2.22 | 2.17 | 2.16 | 2.13 | 2.10 | 2.09 | 2.09 | .025 | |
| 2.94 | 2.86 | 2.78 | 2.69 | 2.64 | 2.61 | 2.54 | 2.52 | 2.48 | 2.44 | 2.43 | 2.42 | .01 | |
| 4.29 | 4.15 | 4.00 | 3.86 | 3.77 | 3.70 | 3.58 | 3.54 | 3.48 | 3.42 | 3.39 | 3.38 | .001 | |
| 1.34 | 1.33 | 1.32 | 1.31 | 1.31 | 1.30 | 1.30 | 1.30 | 1.29 | 1.29 | 1.28 | 1.28 | .25 | 22 |
| 1.76 | 1.73 | 1.70 | 1.67 | 1.65 | 1.64 | 1.61 | 1.60 | 1.59 | 1.58 | 1.57 | 1.57 | .10 | |
| 2.07 | 2.03 | 1.98 | 1.94 | 1.91 | 1.89 | 1.85 | 1.84 | 1.82 | 1.80 | 1.79 | 1.78 | .05 | |
| 2.39 | 2.33 | 2.27 | 2.21 | 2.17 | 2.14 | 2.09 | 2.08 | 2.05 | 2.02 | 2.01 | 2.00 | .025 | |
| 2.83 | 2.75 | 2.67 | 2.58 | 2.53 | 2.50 | 2.42 | 2.40 | 2.36 | 2.33 | 2.32 | 2.31 | .01 | |
| 4.06 | 3.92 | 3.78 | 3.63 | 3.53 | 3.48 | 3.35 | 3.32 | 3.25 | 3.19 | 3.17 | 3.15 | .001 | |
| 1.33 | 1.32 | 1.31 | 1.30 | 1.29 | 1.29 | 1.28 | 1.28 | 1.27 | 1.27 | 1.26 | 1.26 | .25 | 24 |
| 1.73 | 1.70 | 1.67 | 1.64 | 1.62 | 1.61 | 1.58 | 1.57 | 1.56 | 1.54 | 1.54 | 1.53 | .10 | |
| 2.03 | 1.98 | 1.94 | 1.89 | 1.86 | 1.84 | 1.80 | 1.79 | 1.77 | 1.75 | 1.74 | 1.73 | .05 | |
| 2.33 | 2.27 | 2.21 | 2.15 | 2.11 | 2.08 | 2.02 | 2.01 | 1.98 | 1.95 | 1.94 | 1.94 | .025 | |
| 2.74 | 2.66 | 2.58 | 2.49 | 2.44 | 2.40 | 2.33 | 2.31 | 2.27 | 2.24 | 2.22 | 2.21 | .01 | |
| 3.87 | 3.74 | 3.59 | 3.45 | 3.35 | 3.29 | 3.16 | 3.14 | 3.07 | 3.01 | 2.99 | 2.97 | .001 | |
| 1.32 | 1.31 | 1.30 | 1.29 | 1.28 | 1.28 | 1.26 | 1.26 | 1.26 | 1.25 | 1.25 | 1.25 | .25 | 26 |
| 1.71 | 1.68 | 1.65 | 1.61 | 1.59 | 1.58 | 1.55 | 1.54 | 1.53 | 1.51 | 1.51 | 1.50 | .10 | |
| 1.99 | 1.95 | 1.90 | 1.85 | 1.82 | 1.80 | 1.76 | 1.75 | 1.73 | 1.71 | 1.70 | 1.69 | .05 | |
| 2.28 | 2.22 | 2.16 | 2.09 | 2.05 | 2.03 | 1.97 | 1.95 | 1.92 | 1.90 | 1.89 | 1.88 | .025 | |
| 2.66 | 2.58 | 2.50 | 2.42 | 2.36 | 2.33 | 2.25 | 2.23 | 2.19 | 2.16 | 2.14 | 2.13 | .01 | |
| 3.72 | 3.59 | 3.44 | 3.30 | 3.21 | 3.15 | 3.02 | 2.99 | 2.92 | 2.86 | 2.84 | 2.82 | .001 | |
| 1.31 | 1.30 | 1.29 | 1.28 | 1.27 | 1.27 | 1.26 | 1.25 | 1.25 | 1.24 | 1.24 | 1.24 | .25 | 28 |
| 1.69 | 1.66 | 1.63 | 1.59 | 1.57 | 1.56 | 1.53 | 1.52 | 1.50 | 1.49 | 1.48 | 1.48 | .10 | |
| 1.96 | 1.91 | 1.87 | 1.82 | 1.79 | 1.77 | 1.73 | 1.71 | 1.69 | 1.67 | 1.66 | 1.65 | .05 | |
| 2.23 | 2.17 | 2.11 | 2.05 | 2.01 | 1.98 | 1.92 | 1.91 | 1.88 | 1.85 | 1.84 | 1.83 | .025 | |
| 2.60 | 2.52 | 2.44 | 2.35 | 2.30 | 2.26 | 2.19 | 2.17 | 2.13 | 2.09 | 2.08 | 2.06 | .01 | |
| 3.60 | 3.46 | 3.32 | 3.18 | 3.08 | 3.02 | 2.89 | 2.86 | 2.80 | 2.73 | 2.71 | 2.69 | .001 | |
| 20 | 24 | 30 | 40 | 50 | 60 | 100 | 120 | 200 | 500 | 1,000 | ∞ | α | $\nu_e$ |

## TABLE F (cont.)

| $\nu_e$ For Denominator | $\alpha$ | $\nu_b$ (Degrees of Freedom for Numerator) 1 | 2 | 3 | 4 | 5 | 6 | 7 | 8 | 9 | 10 | 12 | 15 |
|---|---|---|---|---|---|---|---|---|---|---|---|---|---|
| 30 | .25 | 1.38 | 1.45 | 1.44 | 1.42 | 1.41 | 1.39 | 1.38 | 1.37 | 1.36 | 1.35 | 1.34 | 1.32 |
| | .10 | 2.88 | 2.49 | 2.28 | 2.14 | 2.05 | 1.98 | 1.93 | 1.88 | 1.85 | 1.82 | 1.77 | 1.72 |
| | .05 | 4.17 | 3.32 | 2.92 | 2.69 | 2.53 | 2.42 | 2.33 | 2.27 | 2.21 | 2.16 | 2.09 | 2.01 |
| | .025 | 5.57 | 4.18 | 3.59 | 3.25 | 3.03 | 2.87 | 2.75 | 2.65 | 2.57 | 2.51 | 2.41 | 2.31 |
| | .01 | 7.56 | 5.39 | 4.51 | 4.02 | 3.70 | 3.47 | 3.30 | 3.17 | 3.07 | 2.98 | 2.84 | 2.70 |
| | .001 | 13.3 | 8.77 | 7.05 | 6.12 | 5.53 | 5.12 | 4.82 | 4.58 | 4.39 | 4.24 | 4.00 | 3.75 |
| 40 | .25 | 1.36 | 1.44 | 1.42 | 1.40 | 1.39 | 1.37 | 1.36 | 1.35 | 1.34 | 1.33 | 1.31 | 1.30 |
| | .10 | 2.84 | 2.44 | 2.23 | 2.09 | 2.00 | 1.93 | 1.87 | 1.83 | 1.79 | 1.76 | 1.71 | 1.66 |
| | .05 | 4.08 | 3.23 | 2.84 | 2.61 | 2.45 | 2.34 | 2.25 | 2.18 | 2.12 | 2.08 | 2.00 | 1.92 |
| | .025 | 5.42 | 4.05 | 3.46 | 3.13 | 2.90 | 2.74 | 2.62 | 2.53 | 2.45 | 2.39 | 2.29 | 2.18 |
| | .01 | 7.31 | 5.18 | 4.31 | 3.83 | 3.51 | 3.29 | 3.12 | 2.99 | 2.89 | 2.80 | 2.66 | 2.52 |
| | .001 | 12.6 | 8.25 | 6.60 | 5.70 | 5.13 | 4.73 | 4.44 | 4.21 | 4.02 | 3.87 | 3.64 | 3.40 |
| 60 | .25 | 1.35 | 1.42 | 1.41 | 1.38 | 1.37 | 1.35 | 1.33 | 1.32 | 1.31 | 1.30 | 1.29 | 1.27 |
| | .10 | 2.79 | 2.39 | 2.18 | 2.04 | 1.95 | 1.87 | 1.82 | 1.77 | 1.74 | 1.71 | 1.66 | 1.60 |
| | .05 | 4.00 | 3.15 | 2.76 | 2.53 | 2.37 | 2.25 | 2.17 | 2.10 | 2.04 | 1.99 | 1.92 | 1.84 |
| | .025 | 5.29 | 3.93 | 3.34 | 3.01 | 2.79 | 2.63 | 2.51 | 2.41 | 2.33 | 2.27 | 2.17 | 2.06 |
| | .01 | 7.08 | 4.98 | 4.13 | 3.65 | 3.34 | 3.12 | 2.95 | 2.82 | 2.72 | 2.63 | 2.50 | 2.35 |
| | .001 | 12.0 | 7.76 | 6.17 | 5.31 | 4.76 | 4.37 | 4.09 | 3.87 | 3.69 | 3.54 | 3.31 | 3.08 |
| 120 | .25 | 1.34 | 1.40 | 1.39 | 1.37 | 1.35 | 1.33 | 1.31 | 1.30 | 1.29 | 1.28 | 1.26 | 1.24 |
| | .10 | 2.75 | 2.35 | 2.13 | 1.99 | 1.90 | 1.82 | 1.77 | 1.72 | 1.68 | 1.65 | 1.60 | 1.55 |
| | .05 | 3.92 | 3.07 | 2.68 | 2.45 | 2.29 | 2.17 | 2.09 | 2.02 | 1.96 | 1.91 | 1.83 | 1.75 |
| | .025 | 5.15 | 3.80 | 3.23 | 2.89 | 2.67 | 2.52 | 2.39 | 2.30 | 2.22 | 2.16 | 2.05 | 1.94 |
| | .01 | 6.85 | 4.79 | 3.95 | 3.48 | 3.17 | 2.96 | 2.79 | 2.66 | 2.56 | 2.47 | 2.34 | 2.19 |
| | .001 | 11.4 | 7.32 | 5.79 | 4.95 | 4.42 | 4.04 | 3.77 | 3.55 | 3.38 | 3.24 | 3.02 | 2.78 |
| 200 | .25 | 1.33 | 1.39 | 1.38 | 1.36 | 1.34 | 1.32 | 1.31 | 1.29 | 1.28 | 1.27 | 1.25 | 1.23 |
| | .10 | 2.73 | 2.33 | 2.11 | 1.97 | 1.88 | 1.80 | 1.75 | 1.70 | 1.66 | 1.63 | 1.57 | 1.52 |
| | .05 | 3.89 | 3.04 | 2.65 | 2.42 | 2.26 | 2.14 | 2.06 | 1.98 | 1.93 | 1.88 | 1.80 | 1.72 |
| | .025 | 5.10 | 3.76 | 3.18 | 2.85 | 2.63 | 2.47 | 2.35 | 2.26 | 2.18 | 2.11 | 2.01 | 1.90 |
| | .01 | 6.76 | 4.71 | 3.88 | 3.41 | 3.11 | 2.89 | 2.73 | 2.60 | 2.50 | 2.41 | 2.27 | 2.13 |
| | .001 | 11.2 | 7.15 | 5.63 | 4.81 | 4.29 | 3.92 | 3.65 | 3.43 | 3.26 | 3.12 | 2.90 | 2.67 |
| 500 | .25 | 1.33 | 1.39 | 1.37 | 1.35 | 1.33 | 1.31 | 1.30 | 1.28 | 1.27 | 1.26 | 1.24 | 1.22 |
| | .10 | 2.72 | 2.31 | 2.10 | 1.96 | 1.86 | 1.79 | 1.73 | 1.68 | 1.64 | 1.61 | 1.56 | 1.50 |
| | .05 | 3.86 | 3.01 | 2.62 | 2.39 | 2.23 | 2.12 | 2.03 | 1.96 | 1.90 | 1.85 | 1.77 | 1.69 |
| | .025 | 5.06 | 3.72 | 3.14 | 2.81 | 2.59 | 2.43 | 2.31 | 2.22 | 2.14 | 2.07 | 1.97 | 1.86 |
| | .01 | 6.69 | 4.65 | 3.82 | 3.36 | 3.05 | 2.84 | 2.68 | 2.55 | 2.49 | 2.36 | 2.22 | 2.07 |
| | .001 | 11.0 | 7.00 | 5.50 | 4.69 | 4.17 | 3.81 | 3.54 | 3.33 | 3.16 | 3.02 | 2.80 | 2.57 |
| 1,000 | .25 | 1.33 | 1.39 | 1.37 | 1.35 | 1.33 | 1.31 | 1.29 | 1.28 | 1.27 | 1.26 | 1.24 | 1.22 |
| | .10 | 2.71 | 2.31 | 2.09 | 1.95 | 1.85 | 1.78 | 1.72 | 1.60 | 1.64 | 1.60 | 1.55 | 1.49 |
| | .05 | 3.85 | 3.00 | 2.61 | 2.38 | 2.22 | 2.10 | 2.02 | 1.95 | 1.89 | 1.84 | 1.76 | 1.68 |
| | .025 | 5.04 | 3.70 | 3.13 | 2.80 | 2.58 | 2.42 | 2.30 | 2.20 | 2.13 | 2.06 | 1.96 | 1.85 |
| | .01 | 6.66 | 4.62 | 3.80 | 3.34 | 3.04 | 2.82 | 2.66 | 2.53 | 2.43 | 2.34 | 2.20 | 2.06 |
| | .001 | 10.9 | 6.95 | 5.46 | 4.65 | 4.14 | 3.78 | 3.51 | 3.30 | 3.13 | 2.99 | 2.77 | 2.54 |
| $\infty$ | .25 | 1.32 | 1.39 | 1.37 | 1.35 | 1.33 | 1.31 | 1.29 | 1.28 | 1.27 | 1.25 | 1.24 | 1.22 |
| | .10 | 2.71 | 2.30 | 2.08 | 1.94 | 1.85 | 1.77 | 1.72 | 1.67 | 1.63 | 1.60 | 1.55 | 1.49 |
| | .05 | 3.84 | 3.00 | 2.60 | 2.37 | 2.21 | 2.10 | 2.01 | 1.94 | 1.88 | 1.83 | 1.75 | 1.67 |
| | .025 | 5.02 | 3.69 | 3.12 | 2.79 | 2.57 | 2.41 | 2.29 | 2.19 | 2.11 | 2.05 | 1.94 | 1.83 |
| | .01 | 6.63 | 4.61 | 3.78 | 3.32 | 3.02 | 2.80 | 2.64 | 2.51 | 2.41 | 2.32 | 2.18 | 2.04 |
| | .001 | 10.8 | 6.91 | 5.42 | 4.62 | 4.10 | 3.74 | 3.47 | 3.27 | 3.10 | 2.96 | 2.74 | 2.51 |
| | $\alpha$ | 1 | 2 | 3 | 4 | 5 | 6 | 7 | 8 | 9 | 10 | 12 | 15 |

| $\nu_b$ (Degrees of Freedom for Numerator) | | | | | | | | | | | | | |
|---|---|---|---|---|---|---|---|---|---|---|---|---|---|
| 20 | 24 | 30 | 40 | 50 | 60 | 100 | 120 | 200 | 500 | 1,000 | ∞ | α | $\nu_e$ |
| 1.30 | 1.29 | 1.28 | 1.27 | 1.26 | 1.26 | 1.25 | 1.24 | 1.24 | 1.23 | 1.23 | 1.23 | .25 | 30 |
| 1.67 | 1.64 | 1.61 | 1.57 | 1.55 | 1.54 | 1.51 | 1.50 | 1.48 | 1.47 | 1.46 | 1.46 | .10 | |
| 1.93 | 1.89 | 1.84 | 1.79 | 1.76 | 1.74 | 1.70 | 1.68 | 1.66 | 1.64 | 1.63 | 1.62 | .05 | |
| 2.20 | 2.14 | 2.07 | 2.01 | 1.97 | 1.94 | 1.88 | 1.87 | 1.84 | 1.81 | 1.80 | 1.79 | .025 | |
| 2.55 | 2.47 | 2.39 | 2.30 | 2.25 | 2.21 | 2.13 | 2.11 | 2.07 | 2.03 | 2.02 | 2.01 | .01 | |
| 3.49 | 3.36 | 3.22 | 3.07 | 2.98 | 2.92 | 2.79 | 2.76 | 2.69 | 2.63 | 2.61 | 2.59 | .001 | |
| 1.28 | 1.26 | 1.25 | 1.24 | 1.23 | 1.22 | 1.21 | 1.21 | 1.20 | 1.19 | 1.19 | 1.19 | .25 | 40 |
| 1.61 | 1.57 | 1.54 | 1.51 | 1.48 | 1.47 | 1.43 | 1.42 | 1.41 | 1.39 | 1.38 | 1.38 | .10 | |
| 1.84 | 1.79 | 1.74 | 1.69 | 1.66 | 1.64 | 1.59 | 1.58 | 1.55 | 1.53 | 1.52 | 1.51 | .05 | |
| 2.07 | 2.01 | 1.94 | 1.88 | 1.83 | 1.80 | 1.74 | 1.72 | 1.69 | 1.66 | 1.65 | 1.64 | .025 | |
| 2.37 | 2.29 | 2.20 | 2.11 | 2.06 | 2.02 | 1.94 | 1.92 | 1.87 | 1.83 | 1.82 | 1.80 | .01 | |
| 3.15 | 3.01 | 2.87 | 2.73 | 2.64 | 2.57 | 2.44 | 2.41 | 2.34 | 2.28 | 2.25 | 2.23 | .001 | |
| 1.25 | 1.24 | 1.22 | 1.21 | 1.20 | 1.19 | 1.17 | 1.17 | 1.16 | 1.15 | 1.15 | 1.15 | .25 | 60 |
| 1.54 | 1.51 | 1.48 | 1.44 | 1.41 | 1.40 | 1.36 | 1.35 | 1.33 | 1.31 | 1.30 | 1.29 | .10 | |
| 1.75 | 1.70 | 1.65 | 1.59 | 1.56 | 1.53 | 1.48 | 1.47 | 1.44 | 1.41 | 1.40 | 1.39 | .05 | |
| 1.94 | 1.88 | 1.82 | 1.74 | 1.70 | 1.67 | 1.60 | 1.58 | 1.54 | 1.51 | 1.49 | 1.48 | .025 | |
| 2.20 | 2.12 | 2.03 | 1.94 | 1.88 | 1.84 | 1.75 | 1.73 | 1.68 | 1.63 | 1.62 | 1.60 | .01 | |
| 2.83 | 2.69 | 2.55 | 2.41 | 2.31 | 2.25 | 2.12 | 2.08 | 2.01 | 1.94 | 1.91 | 1.89 | .001 | |
| 1.22 | 1.21 | 1.19 | 1.18 | 1.17 | 1.16 | 1.14 | 1.13 | 1.12 | 1.11 | 1.10 | 1.10 | .25 | 120 |
| 1.48 | 1.45 | 1.41 | 1.37 | 1.34 | 1.32 | 1.27 | 1.26 | 1.24 | 1.21 | 1.20 | 1.19 | .10 | |
| 1.66 | 1.61 | 1.55 | 1.50 | 1.46 | 1.43 | 1.37 | 1.35 | 1.32 | 1.28 | 1.27 | 1.25 | .05 | |
| 1.82 | 1.76 | 1.69 | 1.61 | 1.56 | 1.53 | 1.45 | 1.43 | 1.39 | 1.34 | 1.33 | 1.31 | .025 | |
| 2.03 | 1.95 | 1.86 | 1.76 | 1.70 | 1.66 | 1.56 | 1.53 | 1.48 | 1.42 | 1.40 | 1.38 | .01 | |
| 2.53 | 2.40 | 2.26 | 2.11 | 2.02 | 1.95 | 1.80 | 1.76 | 1.68 | 1.60 | 1.57 | 1.54 | .001 | |
| 1.21 | 1.20 | 1.18 | 1.16 | 1.14 | 1.12 | 1.11 | 1.10 | 1.09 | 1.08 | 1.08 | 1.06 | .25 | 200 |
| 1.46 | 1.42 | 1.38 | 1.34 | 1.31 | 1.28 | 1.24 | 1.22 | 1.20 | 1.17 | 1.16 | 1.14 | .10 | |
| 1.62 | 1.57 | 1.52 | 1.46 | 1.41 | 1.39 | 1.32 | 1.29 | 1.26 | 1.22 | 1.21 | 1.19 | .05 | |
| 1.78 | 1.71 | 1.64 | 1.56 | 1.51 | 1.47 | 1.39 | 1.37 | 1.32 | 1.27 | 1.25 | 1.23 | .025 | |
| 1.97 | 1.89 | 1.79 | 1.69 | 1.63 | 1.58 | 1.48 | 1.45 | 1.39 | 1.33 | 1.30 | 1.28 | .01 | |
| 2.42 | 2.29 | 2.15 | 2.00 | 1.90 | 1.83 | 1.68 | 1.64 | 1.55 | 1.46 | 1.43 | 1.39 | .001 | |
| 1.20 | 1.18 | 1.17 | 1.15 | 1.14 | 1.13 | 1.10 | 1.10 | 1.08 | 1.06 | 1.05 | 1.05 | .25 | 500 |
| 1.44 | 1.40 | 1.36 | 1.31 | 1.28 | 1.26 | 1.21 | 1.19 | 1.16 | 1.12 | 1.11 | 1.09 | .10 | |
| 1.59 | 1.54 | 1.48 | 1.42 | 1.38 | 1.35 | 1.28 | 1.26 | 1.21 | 1.16 | 1.14 | 1.11 | .05 | |
| 1.74 | 1.67 | 1.60 | 1.52 | 1.46 | 1.42 | 1.34 | 1.31 | 1.25 | 1.19 | 1.17 | 1.14 | .025 | |
| 1.92 | 1.83 | 1.74 | 1.63 | 1.57 | 1.52 | 1.41 | 1.38 | 1.31 | 1.23 | 1.20 | 1.17 | .01 | |
| 2.33 | 2.19 | 2.05 | 1.90 | 1.80 | 1.73 | 1.57 | 1.53 | 1.43 | 1.32 | 1.28 | 1.23 | .001 | |
| 1.19 | 1.18 | 1.16 | 1.15 | 1.13 | 1.25 | 1.10 | 1.09 | 1.07 | 1.05 | 1.04 | 1.03 | .25 | 1,000 |
| 1.43 | 1.39 | 1.35 | 1.30 | 1.27 | 1.33 | 1.20 | 1.18 | 1.15 | 1.10 | 1.06 | 1.06 | .10 | |
| 1.58 | 1.53 | 1.47 | 1.41 | 1.36 | 1.41 | 1.26 | 1.24 | 1.19 | 1.13 | 1.11 | 1.08 | .05 | |
| 1.72 | 1.65 | 1.58 | 1.50 | 1.44 | 1.50 | 1.32 | 1.29 | 1.23 | 1.16 | 1.13 | 1.10 | .025 | |
| 1.89 | 1.81 | 1.71 | 1.61 | 1.54 | 1.69 | 1.38 | 1.35 | 1.28 | 1.19 | 1.16 | 1.11 | .01 | |
| 2.30 | 2.16 | 2.02 | 1.87 | 1.77 | 1.72 | 1.53 | 1.49 | 1.38 | 1.27 | 1.22 | 1.15 | .001 | |
| 1.19 | 1.18 | 1.16 | 1.14 | 1.13 | 1.12 | 1.09 | 1.08 | 1.07 | 1.04 | 1.03 | 1.00 | .25 | ∞ |
| 1.42 | 1.38 | 1.34 | 1.30 | 1.26 | 1.24 | 1.18 | 1.17 | 1.13 | 1.08 | 1.06 | 1.00 | .10 | |
| 1.57 | 1.52 | 1.46 | 1.39 | 1.35 | 1.32 | 1.24 | 1.22 | 1.17 | 1.11 | 1.08 | 1.00 | .05 | |
| 1.71 | 1.64 | 1.57 | 1.48 | 1.43 | 1.39 | 1.30 | 1.27 | 1.21 | 1.13 | 1.09 | 1.00 | .025 | |
| 1.88 | 1.79 | 1.70 | 1.59 | 1.52 | 1.47 | 1.36 | 1.32 | 1.25 | 1.15 | 1.11 | 1.00 | .01 | |
| 2.27 | 2.13 | 1.99 | 1.84 | 1.73 | 1.66 | 1.50 | 1.45 | 1.34 | 1.21 | 1.15 | 1.00 | .001 | |
| 20 | 24 | 30 | 40 | 50 | 60 | 100 | 120 | 200 | 500 | 1,000 | ∞ | α | $\nu_e$ |

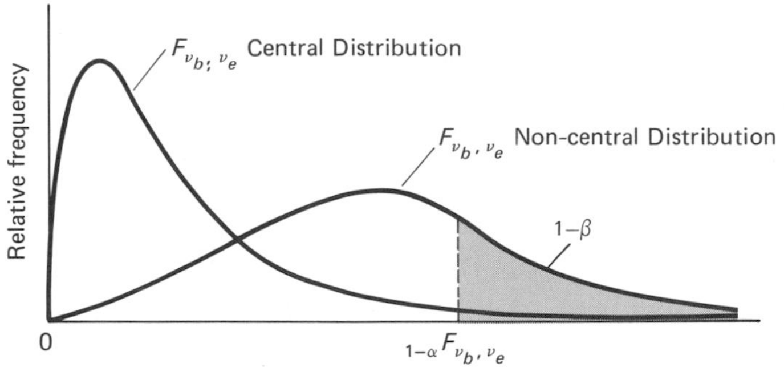


**TABLE G**[a] **Power $(1 - \beta)$ of the $F$-Test Associated with $\nu_b$ and $\nu_e$ for $\alpha = .05$ and $\alpha = .01$**[b]

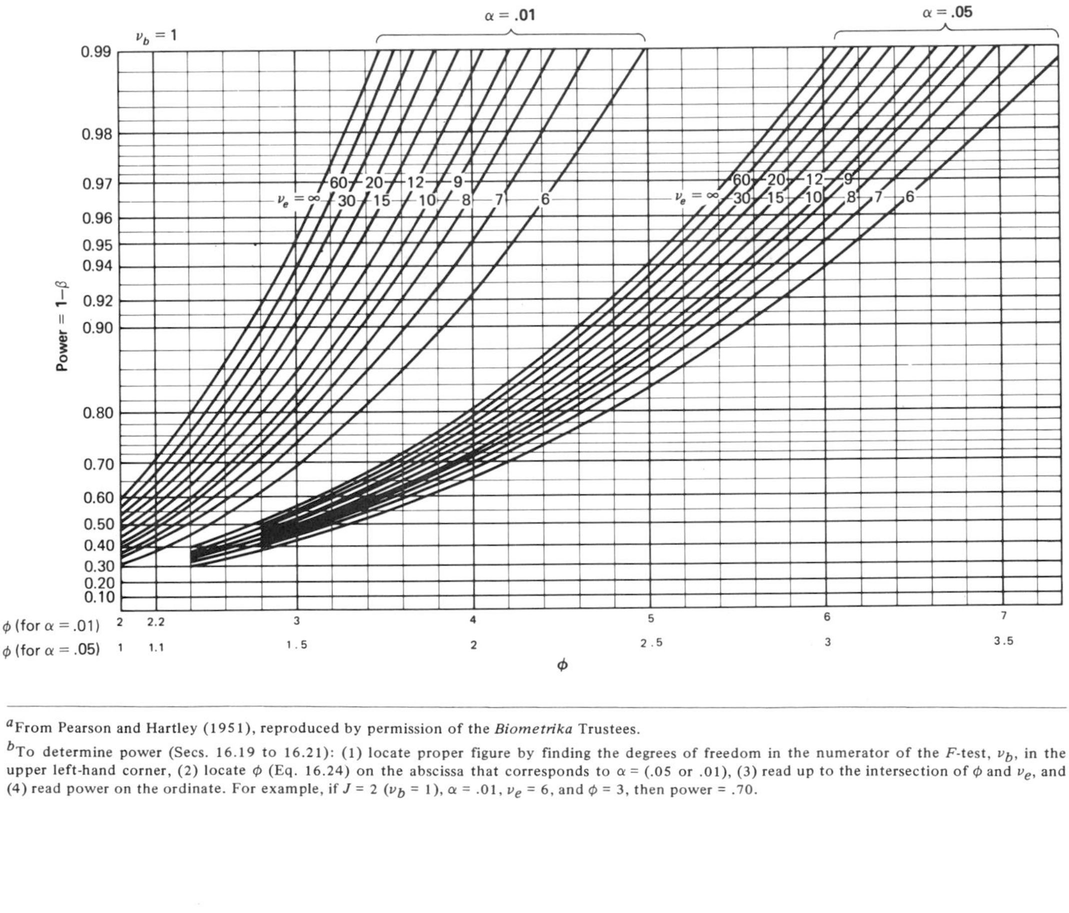


[a]From Pearson and Hartley (1951), reproduced by permission of the *Biometrika* Trustees.

[b]To determine power (Secs. 16.19 to 16.21): (1) locate proper figure by finding the degrees of freedom in the numerator of the $F$-test, $\nu_b$, in the upper left-hand corner, (2) locate $\phi$ (Eq. 16.24) on the abscissa that corresponds to $\alpha = (.05$ or $.01)$, (3) read up to the intersection of $\phi$ and $\nu_e$, and (4) read power on the ordinate. For example, if $J = 2$ $(\nu_b = 1)$, $\alpha = .01$, $\nu_e = 6$, and $\phi = 3$, then power = .70.

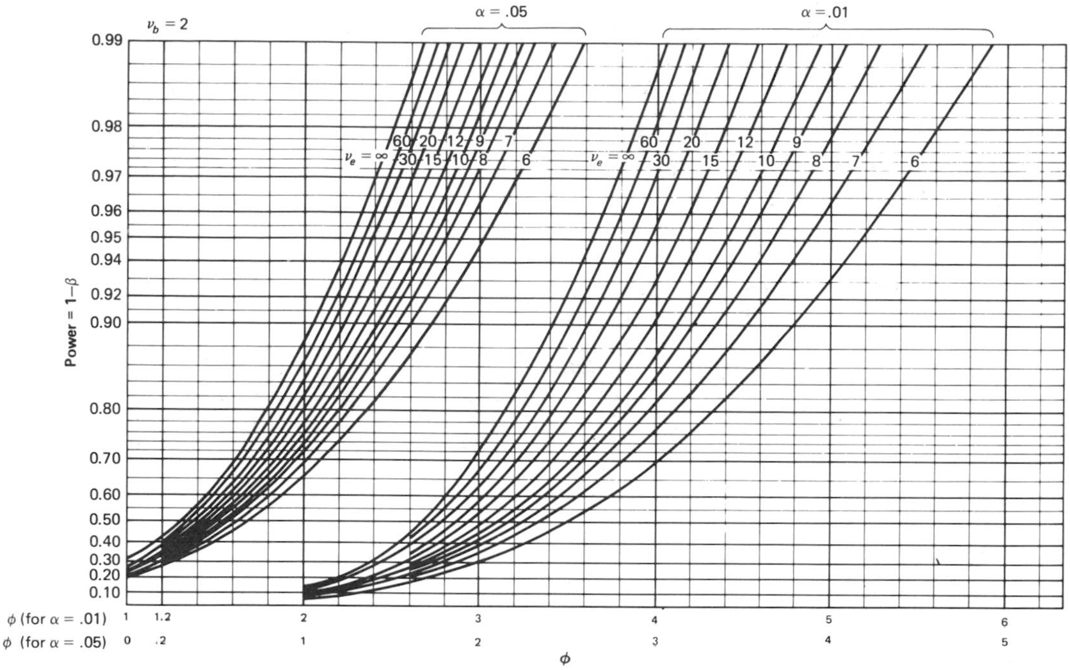
$\nu_b = 2$
$\alpha = .05$
$\alpha = .01$
$\nu_e = \infty$
60 20 12 9 7
30 15 10 8 6
60 20 12 9
30 15 10 8 7 6
Power = 1−β
0.99
0.98
0.97
0.96
0.95
0.94
0.92
0.90
0.80
0.70
0.60
0.50
0.40
0.30
0.20
0.10
$\phi$ (for $\alpha$ = .01) 1 1.2 2 3 4 5 6
$\phi$ (for $\alpha$ = .05) 0 .2 1 2 3 4 5
$\phi$

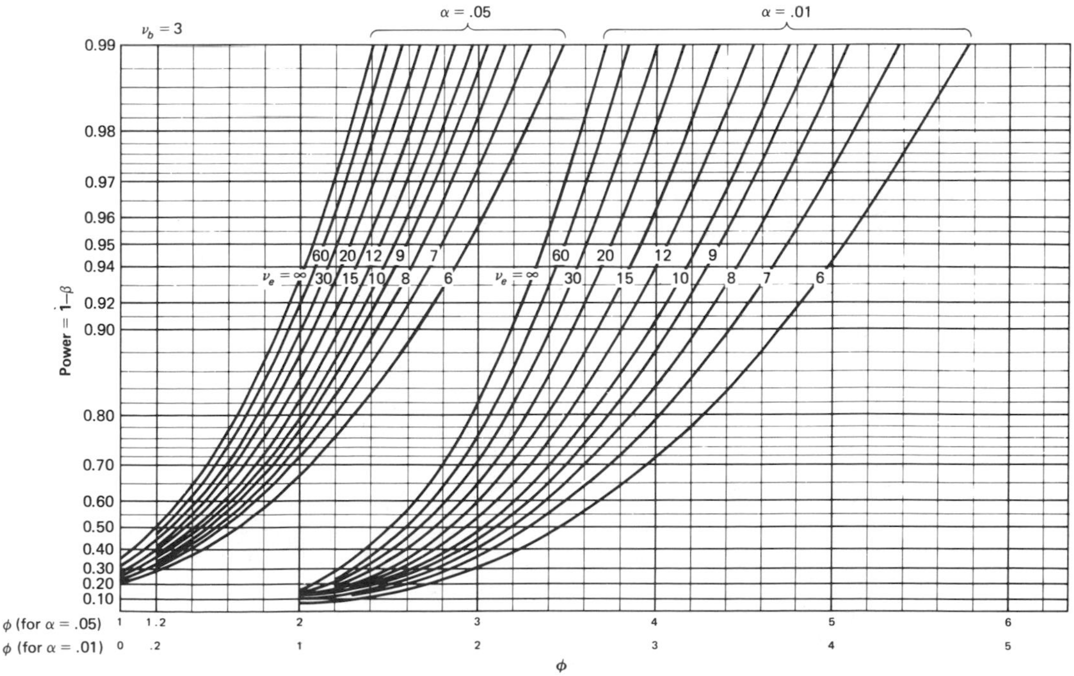
$\nu_b = 3$
$\alpha = .05$
$\alpha = .01$
$\nu_e = \infty$
60 20 12 9 7
30 15 10 8 6
60 20 12 9
30 15 10 8 7 6
Power = 1−β
0.99
0.98
0.97
0.96
0.95
0.94
0.92
0.90
0.80
0.70
0.60
0.50
0.40
0.30
0.20
0.10
$\phi$ (for $\alpha$ = .05) 1 1.2 2 3 4 5 6
$\phi$ (for $\alpha$ = .01) 0 .2 1 2 3 4 5
$\phi$

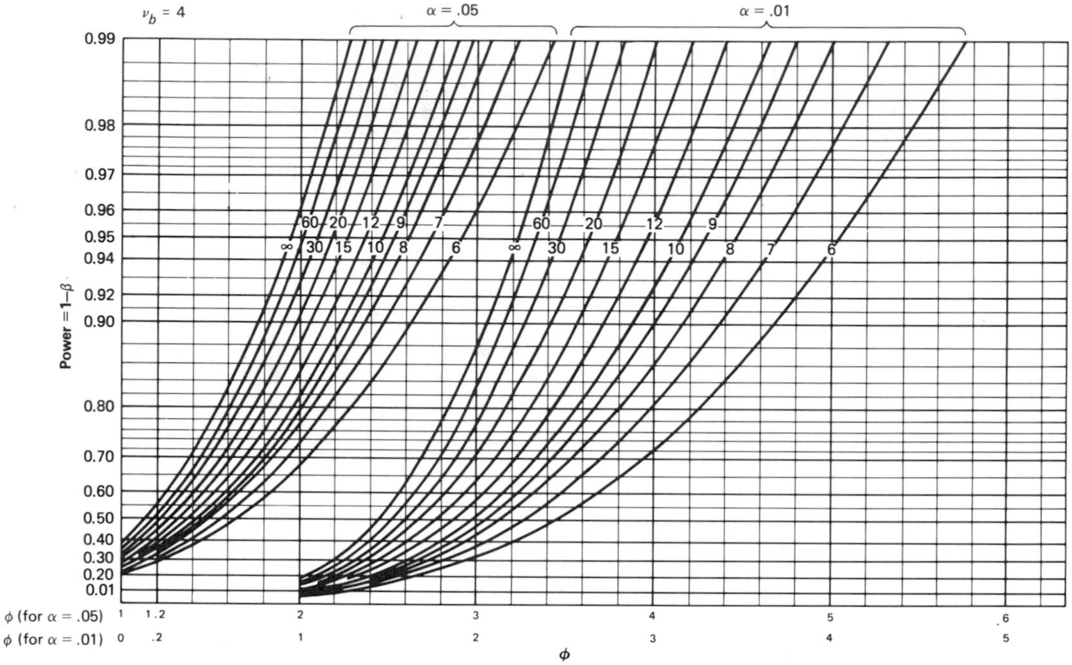

$\nu_b$ = 4
α = .05
α = .01
Power = 1−β
0.99
0.98
0.97
0.96
0.95
0.94
0.92
0.90
0.80
0.70
0.60
0.50
0.40
0.30
0.20
0.01
∞
60
30
20
15
12
10
9
8
7
6
φ (for α = .05) 1 1.2 2 3 4 5 6
φ (for α = .01) 0 .2 1 2 3 4 5
φ

TABLE H Distribution of $F_{max} = s^2_{largest}/s^2_{smallest}$ Statistic[a, b]

| $\nu$ for each $s_j^2$ | $1 - \alpha$ | *J* = Number of Variances 2 | 3 | 4 | 5 | 6 | 7 | 8 | 9 | 10 | 11 | 12 |
|---|---|---|---|---|---|---|---|---|---|---|---|---|
| 2 | .95 | 39.0 | 87.5 | 142 | 202 | 266 | 333 | 403 | 475 | 550 | 626 | 704 |
| | .99 | 199 | 448 | 729 | 1036 | 1362 | 1705 | 2063 | 2432 | 2813 | 3204 | 3605 |
| 3 | .95 | 15.4 | 27.8 | 39.2 | 50.7 | 62.0 | 72.9 | 83.5 | 93.9 | 104 | 114 | 124 |
| | .99 | 47.5 | 85 | 120 | 151 | 184 | 216 | 249 | 281 | 310 | 337 | 361 |
| 4 | .95 | 9.60 | 15.5 | 20.6 | 25.2 | 29.5 | 33.6 | 37.5 | 41.4 | 44.6 | 48.0 | 51.4 |
| | .99 | 23.2 | 37. | 49. | 59. | 69. | 79. | 89. | 97. | 106. | 113. | 120 |
| 5 | .95 | 7.15 | 10.8 | 13.7 | 16.3 | 18.7 | 20.8 | 22.9 | 24.7 | 26.5 | 28.2 | 29.9 |
| | .99 | 14.9 | 22. | 28. | 33. | 38. | 42. | 46. | 50. | 54. | 57 | 60 |
| 6 | .95 | 5.82 | 8.38 | 10.4 | 12.1 | 13.7 | 15.0 | 16.3 | 17.5 | 18.6 | 19.7 | 20.7 |
| | .99 | 11.1 | 15.5 | 19.1 | 22. | 25. | 27. | 30. | 32. | 34. | 36 | 37 |
| 7 | .95 | 4.99 | 6.94 | 8.44 | 9.70 | 10.8 | 11.8 | 12.7 | 13.5 | 14.3 | 151 | 15.8 |
| | .99 | 8.89 | 12.1 | 14.5 | 16.5 | 18.4 | 20. | 22. | 23. | 24. | 26 | 27 |
| 8 | .95 | 4.43 | 6.00 | 7.18 | 8.12 | 9.03 | 9.78 | 10.5 | 11.1 | 11.7 | 12.2 | 12.7 |
| | .99 | 7.50 | 9.9 | 11.7 | 13.2 | 14.5 | 15.8 | 16.9 | 17.9 | 18.9 | 19.8 | 21 |
| 9 | .95 | 4.03 | 5.34 | 6.31 | 7.11 | 7.80 | 8.41 | 8.95 | 9.45 | 9.91 | 10.3 | 10.7 |
| | .99 | 6.54 | 8.5 | 9.9 | 11.1 | 12.1 | 13.1 | 13.9 | 14.7 | 15.3 | 16.0 | 16.6 |
| 10 | .95 | 3.72 | 4.85 | 5.67 | 6.34 | 6.92 | 7.42 | 7.87 | 8.28 | 8.66 | 9.01 | 9.34 |
| | .99 | 5.85 | 7.4 | 8.6 | 9.6 | 10.4 | 11.1 | 11.8 | 12.4 | 12.9 | 13.4 | 13.9 |
| 12 | .95 | 3.28 | 4.16 | 4.79 | 5.30 | 5.72 | 6.09 | 6.42 | 6.72 | 7.00 | 7.25 | 7.48 |
| | .99 | 4.91 | 6.1 | 6.9 | 7.6 | 8.2 | 8.7 | 9.1 | 9.5 | 9.9 | 10.2 | 10.6 |
| 15 | .95 | 2.86 | 3.54 | 4.01 | 4.37 | 4.68 | 4.95 | 5.19 | 5.40 | 5.59 | 5.77 | 5.93 |
| | .99 | 4.07 | 4.9 | 5.5 | 6.0 | 6.4 | 6.7 | 7.1 | 7.3 | 7.5 | 7.8 | 8.0 |
| 20 | .95 | 2.46 | 2.95 | 3.29 | 3.54 | 3.76 | 3.94 | 4.10 | 4.24 | 4.37 | 4.49 | 4.59 |
| | .99 | 3.32 | 3.8 | 4.3 | 4.6 | 4.9 | 5.1 | 5.3 | 5.5 | 5.6 | 5.8 | 5.9 |
| 30 | .95 | 2.07 | 2.40 | 2.61 | 2.78 | 2.91 | 3.02 | 3.12 | 3.21 | 3.29 | 3.36 | 3.39 |
| | .99 | 2.63 | 3.0 | 3.3 | 3.4 | 3.6 | 3.7 | 3.8 | 3.9 | 4.0 | 4.1 | 4.2 |
| 60 | .95 | 1.67 | 1.85 | 1.96 | 2.04 | 2.11 | 2.17 | 2.22 | 2.26 | 2.30 | 2.33 | 2.36 |
| | .99 | 1.96 | 2.2 | 2.3 | 2.4 | 2.4 | 2.5 | 2.5 | 2.6 | 2.6 | 2.7 | 2.7 |

[a] Reproduced with permission of the trustees of *Biometrika*.

[b] For example, ${}_{1-\alpha}F_{\max_{J,\nu_j}} = {}_{.95}F_{\max_{4,6}} = 10.4$.

## TABLE I Critical Values of the Studentized Range Statistic, $q = (\overline{X}_L - \overline{X}_S)/s_{\overline{X}}$[a]

| $\nu_e$[b] | α | r (Number of Means in Set)[c] 2 | 3 | 4 | 5 | 6 | 7 | 8 | 9 | 10 | 11 | 12 | 13 | 14 | 15 | 16 | 17 | 18 | 19 | 20 |
|---|---|---|---|---|---|---|---|---|---|---|---|---|---|---|---|---|---|---|---|---|
| 1 | .10 | 8.93 | 13.4 | 16.4 | 18.5 | 20.2 | 21.5 | 22.6 | 23.6 | 24.5 | 25.2 | 25.9 | 26.5 | 27.1 | 27.6 | 28.1 | 28.5 | 29.0 | 29.3 | 29.7 |
| | .05 | 18.0 | 27.0 | 32.8 | 37.1 | 40.4 | 43.1 | 45.4 | 47.4 | 49.1 | 50.6 | 52.0 | 53.2 | 54.3 | 55.4 | 56.3 | 57.2 | 58.0 | 58.8 | 59.6 |
| | .01 | 90.0 | 13.5 | 164 | 186 | 202 | 216 | 227 | 237 | 246 | 253 | 260 | 266 | 272 | 277 | 282 | 286 | 290 | 294 | 298 |
| 2 | .10 | 4.13 | 5.78 | 6.78 | 7.54 | 8.14 | 8.63 | 9.05 | 9.41 | 9.73 | 10.0 | 10.3 | 10.5 | 10.7 | 10.9 | 11.1 | 11.2 | 11.4 | 11.5 | 11.7 |
| | .05 | 6.09 | 8.3 | 9.8 | 10.9 | 11.7 | 12.4 | 13.0 | 13.5 | 14.0 | 14.4 | 14.7 | 15.1 | 15.4 | 15.7 | 15.9 | 16.1 | 16.4 | 16.6 | 16.8 |
| | .01 | 14.0 | 19.0 | 22.3 | 24.7 | 26.6 | 28.2 | 29.5 | 30.7 | 31.7 | 32.6 | 33.4 | 34.1 | 34.8 | 35.4 | 36.0 | 36.5 | 37.0 | 37.5 | 38.0 |
| | .001 | 44.7 | 00.4 | 70.8 | 78.4 | 84.5 | 89.5 | 93.7 | 97.3 | 101. | 103 | 106 | 108 | 110 | 112 | 114. | 116 | 117 | 119 | 120 |
| 3 | .10 | 3.33 | 4.47 | 5.20 | 5.74 | 6.16 | 6.51 | 6.81 | 7.06 | 7.29 | 7.49 | 7.67 | 7.83 | 7.98 | 8.12 | 8.25 | 8.37 | 8.78 | 8.58 | 8.68 |
| | .05 | 4.50 | 5.91 | 6.82 | 7.50 | 8.04 | 8.48 | 8.85 | 9.18 | 9.46 | 9.72 | 9.95 | 10.2 | 10.4 | 10.5 | 10.7 | 10.8 | 11.0 | 11.1 | 11.2 |
| | .01 | 8.26 | 10.6 | 12.2 | 13.3 | 14.2 | 15.0 | 15.6 | 16.2 | 16.7 | 17.1 | 17.5 | 17.9 | 18.2 | 18.5 | 18.8 | 19.1 | 19.3 | 19.6 | 20.0 |
| | .001 | 18.3 | 23.3 | 20.7 | 29.1 | 31.1 | 32.7 | 34.1 | 35.3 | 36.4 | 37.3 | 38.2 | 39.0 | 39.7 | 40.4 | 41.0 | 41.5 | 42.1 | 42.6 | 43.1 |
| 4 | .10 | 3.01 | 3.98 | 4.59 | 5.04 | 5.39 | 5.69 | 5.93 | 6.14 | 6.33 | 6.50 | 6.65 | 6.78 | 6.91 | 7.03 | 7.13 | 7.23 | 7.33 | 7.41 | 7.50 |
| | .05 | 3.93 | 5.04 | 5.76 | 6.29 | 6.71 | 7.05 | 7.35 | 7.60 | 7.83 | 8.03 | 8.21 | 8.37 | 8.52 | 8.66 | 8.79 | 8.91 | 9.03 | 9.13 | 9.23 |
| | .01 | 6.51 | 8.12 | 9.17 | 9.96 | 10.6 | 11.1 | 11.5 | 11.9 | 12.3 | 12.6 | 12.8 | 13.1 | 13.3 | 13.5 | 13.7 | 13.9 | 14.1 | 14.2 | 14.4 |
| | .001 | 12.2 | 15.0 | 16.8 | 18.2 | 19.3 | 20.3 | 21.0 | 21.7 | 22.3 | 22.9 | 23.4 | 23.8 | 24.2 | 24.6 | 24.9 | 25.3 | 25.6 | 25.9 | 26.1 |
| 5 | .10 | 2.85 | 3.72 | 4.26 | 4.66 | 4.98 | 5.24 | 5.44 | 5.65 | 5.82 | 5.97 | 6.10 | 6.22 | 6.34 | 6.44 | 6.54 | 6.63 | 6.71 | 6.79 | 6.86 |
| | .05 | 3.64 | 4.60 | 5.22 | 5.67 | 6.03 | 6.33 | 6.58 | 6.80 | 6.99 | 7.17 | 7.32 | 7.47 | 7.60 | 7.72 | 7.83 | 7.93 | 8.03 | 8.12 | 8.21 |
| | .01 | 5.70 | 6.97 | 7.80 | 8.42 | 8.91 | 9.32 | 9.67 | 9.97 | 10.2 | 10.5 | 10.7 | 10.9 | 11.1 | 11.2 | 11.4 | 11.6 | 11.7 | 11.8 | 11.9 |
| | .001 | 9.71 | 11.7 | 13.0 | 13.9 | 14.7 | 15.4 | 15.9 | 16.4 | 16.8 | 17.2 | 17.5 | 17.9 | 18.1 | 18.4 | 18.7 | 18.9 | 19.1 | 19.3 | 19.5 |
| 6 | .10 | 2.75 | 3.56 | 4.07 | 4.44 | 4.73 | 4.97 | 5.17 | 5.34 | 5.50 | 5.64 | 5.76 | 5.88 | 5.98 | 6.08 | 6.16 | 6.25 | 6.33 | 6.40 | 6.47 |
| | .05 | 3.46 | 4.34 | 4.90 | 5.31 | 5.63 | 5.89 | 6.12 | 6.32 | 6.49 | 6.65 | 6.79 | 6.92 | 7.03 | 7.14 | 7.24 | 7.34 | 7.43 | 7.51 | 7.59 |
| | .01 | 5.24 | 6.33 | 7.03 | 7.56 | 7.97 | 8.32 | 8.61 | 8.87 | 9.10 | 9.30 | 9.49 | 9.65 | 9.81 | 9.95 | 10.1 | 10.2 | 10.3 | 10.4 | 10.5 |
| | .001 | 8.43 | 9.96 | 11.0 | 11.7 | 12.3 | 12.8 | 13.3 | 13.6 | 14.0 | 14.3 | 14.5 | 14.8 | 15.0 | 15.2 | 15.4 | 15.6 | 15.8 | 15.9 | 16.1 |
| 7 | .10 | 2.68 | 3.45 | 3.93 | 4.28 | 4.56 | 4.78 | 4.97 | 5.14 | 5.28 | 5.41 | 5.53 | 5.64 | 5.74 | 5.83 | 5.91 | 5.99 | 6.06 | 6.13 | 6.20 |
| | .05 | 3.34 | 4.16 | 4.69 | 5.06 | 5.36 | 5.61 | 5.82 | 6.00 | 6.16 | 6.30 | 6.43 | 6.55 | 6.66 | 6.76 | 6.85 | 6.94 | 7.02 | 7.10 | 7.17 |
| | .01 | 4.95 | 5.92 | 6.54 | 7.01 | 7.37 | 7.68 | 7.94 | 8.17 | 8.37 | 8.55 | 8.71 | 8.86 | 9.00 | 9.12 | 9.24 | 9.35 | 9.46 | 9.55 | 9.65 |
| | .001 | 7.65 | 8.93 | 9.77 | 10.4 | 10.9 | 11.3 | 11.7 | 12.0 | 12.3 | 12.5 | 12.7 | 13.0 | 13.1 | 13.3 | 13.5 | 13.6 | 13.8 | 13.9 | 14.0 |
| 8 | .10 | 2.63 | 3.37 | 3.83 | 4.17 | 4.43 | 4.65 | 4.83 | 4.99 | 5.13 | 5.25 | 5.36 | 5.46 | 5.56 | 5.64 | 5.74 | 5.83 | 5.87 | 5.94 | 6.00 |
| | .05 | 3.26 | 4.04 | 4.53 | 4.89 | 5.17 | 5.40 | 5.60 | 5.77 | 5.92 | 6.05 | 6.18 | 6.29 | 6.39 | 6.48 | 6.57 | 6.65 | 6.73 | 6.80 | 6.87 |
| | .01 | 4.74 | 5.63 | 6.20 | 6.63 | 6.96 | 7.24 | 7.47 | 7.68 | 7.78 | 8.03 | 8.18 | 8.31 | 8.44 | 8.55 | 8.66 | 8.76 | 8.85 | 8.94 | 9.03 |
| | .001 | 7.13 | 8.25 | 8.98 | 9.52 | 9.96 | 10.3 | 10.6 | 10.9 | 11.2 | 11.4 | 11.6 | 11.7 | 11.9 | 12.1 | 12.2 | 12.3 | 12.5 | 12.6 | 12.7 |

[a] Reproduced from H. Leon Harter, "Tables of range and studentized range," *Annals of Mathematical Statistics*, 31 (1960), 1122–47, by permission of the author and editor.

[b] In the one-factor ANOVA with $n$ observations in each of $J$ groups, $\nu_e = n_{\bullet} - J$. $\nu_e$ is the number of degrees of freedom for the error mean square in the ANOVA.

[c] For the Tukey method $r = J$; for the Newman-Keuls method $r$ is the number of means in the set being evaluated.

## TABLE I (cont.)

| $\nu_e$ | $\alpha$ | r (*Number of Means in Set*) 2 | 3 | 4 | 5 | 6 | 7 | 8 | 9 | 10 | 11 | 12 | 13 | 14 | 15 | 16 | 17 | 18 | 19 | 20 |
|---|---|---|---|---|---|---|---|---|---|---|---|---|---|---|---|---|---|---|---|---|
| 9 | .10 | 2.59 | 3.32 | 3.76 | 4.08 | 4.34 | 4.55 | 4.72 | 4.87 | 5.01 | 5.13 | 5.23 | 5.33 | 5.42 | 5.51 | 5.58 | 5.66 | 5.72 | 5.79 | 5.84 |
| | .05 | 3.20 | 3.95 | 4.42 | 4.76 | 5.02 | 5.24 | 5.43 | 5.60 | 5.74 | 5.87 | 5.98 | 6.09 | 6.19 | 6.28 | 6.36 | 6.44 | 6.51 | 6.53 | 6.64 |
| | .01 | 4.60 | 5.43 | 5.96 | 6.35 | 6.66 | 6.91 | 7.13 | 7.32 | 7.49 | 7.65 | 7.78 | 7.91 | 8.03 | 8.13 | 8.23 | 8.33 | 8.41 | 8.50 | 8.57 |
| | .001 | 6.76 | 7.77 | 8.42 | 8.91 | 9.30 | 9.62 | 9.90 | 10.1 | 10.4 | 10.6 | 10.7 | 10.9 | 11.0 | 11.2 | 11.3 | 11.4 | 11.5 | 11.6 | 11.8 |
| 10 | .10 | 2.56 | 3.28 | 3.70 | 4.02 | 4.26 | 4.47 | 4.64 | 4.78 | 4.91 | 5.03 | 5.13 | 5.23 | 5.32 | 5.40 | 5.47 | 5.54 | 5.61 | 5.67 | 5.73 |
| | .05 | 3.15 | 3.88 | 4.33 | 4.65 | 4.91 | 5.12 | 5.30 | 5.46 | 5.60 | 5.72 | 5.83 | 5.93 | 6.03 | 6.11 | 6.19 | 6.27 | 6.34 | 6.41 | 6.49 |
| | .01 | 4.48 | 5.27 | 5.77 | 6.14 | 6.43 | 6.67 | 6.87 | 7.05 | 7.21 | 7.36 | 7.48 | 7.60 | 7.71 | 7.81 | 7.91 | 8.00 | 8.08 | 8.15 | 8.23 |
| | .001 | 6.49 | 7.41 | 8.01 | 8.45 | 8.80 | 9.10 | 9.35 | 9. | 9.77 | 9.95 | 10.1 | 10.3 | 10.4 | 10.5 | 10.6 | 10.8 | 10.9 | 11.0 | 11.0 |
| 11 | .10 | 2.54 | 3.23 | 3.66 | 3.97 | 4.21 | 4.40 | 4.57 | 4.71 | 4.84 | 4.95 | 5.05 | 5.15 | 5.23 | 5.31 | 5.38 | 5.45 | 5.51 | 5.57 | 5.63 |
| | .05 | 3.11 | 3.82 | 4.26 | 4.57 | 4.82 | 5.03 | 5.20 | 5.35 | 5.49 | 5.61 | 5.71 | 5.81 | 5.90 | 5.99 | 6.06 | 6.18 | 6.20 | 6.27 | 6.33 |
| | .01 | 4.39 | 5.14 | 5.62 | 5.97 | 6.25 | 6.48 | 6.67 | 6.84 | 6.99 | 7.13 | 7.26 | 7.36 | 7.46 | 7.56 | 7.65 | 7.73 | 7.81 | 7.88 | 7.95 |
| | .001 | 6.28 | 7. | 7.69 | 8.10 | 8.43 | 8.70 | 8.93 | 9.14 | 9.32 | 9.48 | 9.63 | 9.77 | 9.89 | 10.0 | 10.1 | 10.2 | 10.3 | 10.4 | 10.5 |
| 12 | .10 | 2.52 | 3.20 | 3.62 | 3.92 | 4.16 | 4.35 | 4.51 | 4.65 | 4.78 | 4.89 | 4.99 | 5.08 | 5.16 | 5.24 | 5.31 | 5.37 | 5.44 | 5.50 | 5.55 |
| | .05 | 3.08 | 3.77 | 4.20 | 4.51 | 4.75 | 4.95 | 5.12 | 5.27 | 5.40 | 5.51 | 5.62 | 5.71 | 5.80 | 5.88 | 5.95 | 6.02 | 6.09 | 6.15 | 6.21 |
| | .01 | 4.32 | 5.04 | 5.50 | 5.84 | 6.10 | 6.32 | 6.51 | 6.67 | 6.81 | 6.94 | 7.06 | 7.17 | 7.26 | 7.36 | 7.44 | 7.52 | 7.50 | 7.67 | 7.73 |
| | .001 | 6.11 | 6.92 | 7.44 | 7.82 | 8.13 | 8.38 | 8.60 | 8.79 | 8.96 | 9.12 | 9.25 | 9.38 | 9.50 | 9.61 | 9.71 | 9.80 | 9.89 | 9.98 | 10.1 |
| 13 | .10 | 2.51 | 3.18 | 3.59 | 3.89 | 4.12 | 4.31 | 4.46 | 4.60 | 4.72 | 4.83 | 4.93 | 5.02 | 5.10 | 5.18 | 5.25 | 5.31 | 5.37 | 5.43 | 5.48 |
| | .05 | 3.06 | 3.73 | 4.15 | 4.45 | 4.69 | 4.88 | 5.05 | 5.19 | 5.32 | 5.43 | 5.53 | 5.63 | 5.71 | 5.79 | 5.86 | 5.93 | 6.00 | 6.06 | 6.11 |
| | .01 | 4.26 | 4.96 | 5.40 | 5.73 | 5.98 | 6.19 | 6.37 | 6.53 | 6.67 | 6.79 | 6.90 | 7.01 | 7.10 | 7.19 | 7.27 | 7.37 | 7.42 | 7.49 | 7.55 |
| | .001 | 5.97 | 6.74 | 7.23 | 7.60 | 7.89 | 8.13 | 8.33 | 8.51 | 8.67 | 8.82 | 8.95 | 9.07 | 9.18 | 9.28 | 9.38 | 9.47 | 9.55 | 9.63 | 9.70 |
| 14 | .10 | 2.99 | 3.16 | 3.56 | 3.83 | 4.08 | 4.27 | 4.42 | 4.56 | 4.68 | 4.79 | 4.88 | 4.97 | 5.05 | 5.12 | 5.19 | 5.26 | 5.32 | 5.37 | 5.43 |
| | .05 | 3.03 | 3.70 | 4.11 | 4.41 | 4.64 | 4.83 | 4.99 | 5.13 | 5.25 | 5.36 | 5.46 | 5.55 | 5.64 | 5.72 | 5.79 | 5.85 | 5.92 | 5.97 | 6.03 |
| | .01 | 4.21 | 4.89 | 5.32 | 5.63 | 5.88 | 6.08 | 6.26 | 6.41 | 6.54 | 6.66 | 6.77 | 6.87 | 6.96 | 7.05 | 7.13 | 7.20 | 7.27 | 7.33 | 7.40 |
| | .001 | 5.86 | 6.59 | 7.06 | 7.41 | 7.69 | 7.92 | 8.11 | 8.28 | 8.43 | 8.57 | 8.70 | 8.81 | 8.91 | 9.01 | 9.10 | 9.19 | 9.27 | 9.34 | 9.41 |
| 16 | .10 | 2.47 | 3.12 | 3.52 | 3.80 | 4.03 | 4.21 | 4.36 | 4.49 | 4.61 | 4.71 | 4.81 | 4.89 | 4.97 | 5.04 | 5.11 | 5.17 | 5.23 | 5.28 | 5.33 |
| | .05 | 3.00 | 3.65 | 4.05 | 4.33 | 4.56 | 4.74 | 4.90 | 5.03 | 5.15 | 5.26 | 5.35 | 5.44 | 5.52 | 5.59 | 5.66 | 5.73 | 5.79 | 5.84 | 5.90 |
| | .01 | 4.13 | 4.78 | 5.19 | 5.49 | 5.72 | 5.92 | 6.08 | 6.22 | 6.35 | 6.46 | 6.56 | 6.66 | 6.74 | 6.82 | 6.90 | 6.97 | 7.03 | 7.09 | 7.15 |
| | .001 | 5.68 | 6.37 | 6.80 | 7.12 | 7.37 | 7.59 | 7.77 | 7.92 | 8.06 | 8.19 | 8.30 | 8.41 | 8.50 | 8.59 | 8.68 | 8.76 | 8.83 | 8.90 | 8.96 |
| 18 | .10 | 2.45 | 3.10 | 3.49 | 3.77 | 3.98 | 4.16 | 4.31 | 4.44 | 4.55 | 4.66 | 4.75 | 4.83 | 4.91 | 4.98 | 5.04 | 5.10 | 5.16 | 5.21 | 5.26 |
| | .05 | 2.97 | 3.61 | 4.00 | 4.28 | 4.49 | 4.67 | 4.82 | 4.96 | 5.07 | 5.17 | 5.27 | 5.35 | 5.43 | 5.50 | 5.57 | 5.63 | 5.69 | 5.74 | 5.79 |
| | .01 | 4.07 | 4.70 | 5.09 | 5.38 | 5.60 | 5.79 | 5.94 | 6.08 | 6.20 | 6.31 | 6.41 | 6.50 | 6.58 | 6.65 | 6.73 | 6.79 | 6.85 | 6.91 | 6.97 |
| | .001 | 5.55 | 6.20 | 6.60 | 6.91 | 7.14 | 7.34 | 7.51 | 7.66 | 7.79 | 7.91 | 8.01 | 8.11 | 8.20 | 8.28 | 8.36 | 8.43 | 8.50 | 8.57 | 8.63 |
| 20 | .10 | 2.44 | 3.08 | 3.46 | 3.74 | 3.95 | 4.12 | 4.27 | 4.40 | 4.51 | 4.61 | 4.70 | 4.78 | 4.86 | 4.92 | 4.99 | 5.05 | 5.10 | 5.16 | 5.21 |
| | .05 | 2.95 | 3.58 | 3.96 | 4.23 | 4.45 | 4.62 | 4.77 | 4.90 | 5.01 | 5.11 | 5.20 | 5.28 | 5.36 | 5.43 | 5.49 | 5.55 | 5.61 | 5.66 | 5.71 |
| | .01 | 4.02 | 4.64 | 5.02 | 5.29 | 5.51 | 5.69 | 5.84 | 5.97 | 6.09 | 6.19 | 6.29 | 6.37 | 6.45 | 6.52 | 6.59 | 6.65 | 6.71 | 6.77 | 6.82 |
| | .001 | 5.44 | 6.07 | 6.45 | 6.74 | 6.97 | 7.15 | 7.31 | 7.45 | 7.58 | 7.69 | 7.79 | 7.88 | 7.97 | 8.04 | 8.12 | 8.19 | 8.25 | 8.31 | 8.37 |

**TABLE I (*Continued*)**

| $\nu_e$ | $\alpha$ | r (Number of Means in Set) 2 | 3 | 4 | 5 | 6 | 7 | 8 | 9 | 10 | 11 | 12 | 13 | 14 | 15 | 16 | 17 | 18 | 19 | 20 |
|---|---|---|---|---|---|---|---|---|---|---|---|---|---|---|---|---|---|---|---|---|
| 24 | .10 | 2.42 | 3.05 | 3.42 | 3.69 | 3.90 | 4.07 | 4.21 | 4.34 | 4.45 | 4.54 | 4.63 | 4.71 | 4.78 | 4.85 | 4.91 | 4.97 | 5.02 | 5.07 | 5.12 |
| | .05 | 2.92 | 3.53 | 3.90 | 4.17 | 4.37 | 4.54 | 4.68 | 4.81 | 4.92 | 5.01 | 5.10 | 5.18 | 5.25 | 5.32 | 5.38 | 5.44 | 5.49 | 5.55 | 5.59 |
| | .01 | 3.96 | 4.54 | 4.91 | 5.17 | 5.37 | 5.54 | 5.69 | 5.81 | 5.92 | 6.02 | 6.11 | 6.19 | 6.26 | 6.33 | 6.39 | 6.45 | 6.51 | 6.57 | 6.61 |
| | .001 | 5.30 | 5.88 | 6.24 | 6.50 | 6.71 | 6.88 | 7.03 | 7.16 | 7.27 | 7.37 | 7.47 | 7.55 | 7.63 | 7.70 | 7.77 | 7.83 | 7.89 | 7.95 | 8.00 |
| 30 | .10 | 2.40 | 3.02 | 3.39 | 3.65 | 3.85 | 4.02 | 4.16 | 4.28 | 4.38 | 4.47 | 4.56 | 4.64 | 4.71 | 4.77 | 4.83 | 4.89 | 4.94 | 4.99 | 5.03 |
| | .05 | 2.89 | 3.49 | 3.84 | 4.00 | 4.30 | 4.46 | 4.60 | 4.72 | 4.83 | 4.92 | 5.00 | 5.08 | 5.15 | 5.21 | 5.27 | 5.33 | 5.38 | 5.43 | 5.48 |
| | .01 | 3.89 | 4.45 | 4.80 | 5.05 | 5.24 | 5.40 | 5.54 | 5.56 | 5.76 | 5.85 | 5.93 | 6.01 | 6.08 | 6.14 | 6.20 | 6.26 | 6.31 | 6.36 | 6.41 |
| | .001 | 5.16 | 5.70 | 6.03 | 6.28 | 6.47 | 6.63 | 6.76 | 6.88 | 6.98 | 7.08 | 7.16 | 7.24 | 7.31 | 7.38 | 7.44 | 7.48 | 7.55 | 7.60 | 7.65 |
| 40 | .10 | 2.38 | 2.99 | 3.35 | 3.61 | 3.80 | 3.96 | 4.10 | 4.22 | 4.32 | 4.41 | 4.49 | 4.56 | 4.63 | 4.70 | 4.75 | 4.81 | 4.86 | 4.91 | 4.95 |
| | .05 | 2.86 | 3.44 | 3.79 | 4.04 | 4.23 | 4.39 | 4.52 | 4.63 | 4.74 | 4.82 | 4.91 | 4.98 | 5.05 | 5.11 | 5.16 | 5.22 | 5.27 | 5.31 | 5.36 |
| | .01 | 3.82 | 4.37 | 4.70 | 4.93 | 5.11 | 5.27 | 5.39 | 5.50 | 5.60 | 5.69 | 5.77 | 5.84 | 5.90 | 5.96 | 6.02 | 6.07 | 6.11 | 6.17 | 6.21 |
| | .001 | 5.02 | 5.53 | 5.84 | 6.06 | 6.24 | 6.39 | 6.51 | 6.62 | 6.71 | 6.80 | 6.87 | 6.94 | 7.01 | 7.07 | 7.12 | 7.17 | 7.22 | 7.27 | 7.31 |
| 60 | .10 | 2.36 | 2.96 | 3.31 | 3.56 | 3.76 | 3.91 | 4.04 | 4.16 | 4.26 | 4.34 | 4.42 | 4.49 | 4.56 | 4.62 | 4.68 | 4.73 | 4.78 | 4.82 | 4.86 |
| | .05 | 2.83 | 3.40 | 3.74 | 3.98 | 4.16 | 4.31 | 4.44 | 4.55 | 4.65 | 4.73 | 4.81 | 4.88 | 4.94 | 5.00 | 5.06 | 5.11 | 5.15 | 5.20 | 5.24 |
| | .01 | 3.76 | 4.28 | 4.60 | 4.82 | 4.99 | 5.13 | 5.25 | 5.36 | 5.45 | 5.53 | 5.60 | 5.67 | 5.73 | 5.79 | 5.84 | 5.89 | 5.93 | 5.97 | 6.02 |
| | .001 | 4.87 | 5.37 | 5.05 | 5.86 | 6.02 | 6.16 | 6.27 | 6.37 | 6.45 | 6.53 | 6.60 | 6.66 | 6.72 | 6.77 | 6.82 | 6.87 | 6.91 | 6.96 | 7.00 |
| 120 | .10 | 2.34 | 2.93 | 3.28 | 3.52 | 3.71 | 3.86 | 3.99 | 4.10 | 4.19 | 4.28 | 4.35 | 4.42 | 4.49 | 4.59 | 4.60 | 4.65 | 4.69 | 4.74 | 4.78 |
| | .05 | 2.80 | 3.36 | 3.69 | 3.92 | 4.10 | 4.24 | 4.36 | 4.48 | 4.56 | 4.64 | 4.72 | 4.78 | 4.84 | 4.90 | 4.95 | 5.00 | 5.04 | 5.09 | 5.13 |
| | .01 | 3.70 | 4.20 | 4.50 | 4.71 | 4.87 | 5.01 | 5.12 | 5.21 | 5.30 | 5.38 | 5.44 | 5.51 | 5.56 | 5.61 | 5.66 | 5.71 | 5.75 | 5.79 | 5.83 |
| | .001 | 4.77 | 5.21 | 5.48 | 5.67 | 5.82 | 5.94 | 6.04 | 6.13 | 6.21 | 6.28 | 6.34 | 6.40 | 6.45 | 6.50 | 6.54 | 6.58 | 6.62 | 6.66 | 6.70 |
| $\infty$ | .10 | 2.33 | 2.90 | 3.24 | 3.48 | 3.66 | 3.81 | 3.93 | 4.04 | 4.13 | 4.21 | 4.29 | 4.35 | 4.41 | 4.47 | 4.52 | 4.57 | 4.62 | 4.65 | 4.69 |
| | .05 | 2.77 | 3.31 | 3.63 | 3.86 | 4.03 | 4.17 | 4.29 | 4.39 | 4.47 | 4.55 | 4.62 | 4.68 | 4.74 | 4.80 | 4.85 | 4.89 | 4.93 | 4.97 | 5.01 |
| | .01 | 3.64 | 4.12 | 4.40 | 4.60 | 4.76 | 4.88 | 4.99 | 5.08 | 5.16 | 5.23 | 5.29 | 5.35 | 5.40 | 5.45 | 5.49 | 5.54 | 5.57 | 5.61 | 5.65 |
| | .001 | 4.05 | 5.06 | 5.31 | 5.48 | 5.62 | 5.73 | 5.82 | 5.90 | 5.97 | 6.04 | 6.09 | 6.14 | 6.19 | 6.23 | 6.27 | 6.31 | 6.35 | 6.38 | 6.41 |

## TABLE J Critical Values of $r$ for $H_0: \rho = 0$[a]

| $n$[b] | $\alpha_1 = .05$ $\alpha_2 = .10$ | $\alpha_1 = .025$ $\alpha_2 = .05$ | $\alpha_1 = .01$ $\alpha_2 = .02$ | $\alpha_1 = .005$ $\alpha_2 = .01$ | $\alpha_1 = .0005$ $\alpha_2 = .001$ | $\nu$[a] |
|---|---|---|---|---|---|---|
| 3 | .988 | .997 | .9995 | .9999 | .99994 | **1** |
| 4 | .900 | .950 | .980 | .990 | .999 | **2** |
| 5 | .805 | .878 | .934 | .959 | .991 | **3** |
| 6 | .729 | .811 | .882 | .917 | .974 | **4** |
| 7 | .669 | .754 | .833 | .874 | .951 | **5** |
| 8 | .622 | .707 | .789 | .834 | .925 | **6** |
| 9 | .582 | .666 | .750 | .798 | .898 | **7** |
| 10 | .549 | .632 | .716 | .765 | .872 | **8** |
| 11 | .521 | .602 | .685 | .735 | .847 | **9** |
| 12 | .497 | .576 | .658 | .708 | .823 | **10** |
| 13 | .476 | .553 | .634 | .684 | .801 | **11** |
| 14 | .458 | .532 | .612 | .661 | .780 | **12** |
| 15 | .441 | .514 | .592 | .641 | .760 | **13** |
| 16 | .426 | .497 | .574 | .623 | .742 | **14** |
| 17 | .412 | .482 | .558 | .606 | .725 | **15** |
| 18 | .400 | .468 | .542 | .590 | .708 | **16** |
| 19 | .389 | .456 | .528 | .575 | .693 | **17** |
| 20 | .378 | .444 | .516 | .561 | .679 | **18** |
| 21 | .369 | .433 | .503 | .549 | .665 | **19** |
| 22 | .360 | .423 | .492 | .537 | .652 | **20** |
| 23 | .352 | .413 | .482 | .526 | .640 | **21** |
| 24 | .344 | .404 | .472 | .515 | .629 | **22** |
| 25 | .337 | .396 | .462 | .505 | .618 | **23** |
| 26 | .330 | .388 | .453 | .496 | .607 | **24** |
| 27 | .323 | .381 | .445 | .487 | .597 | **25** |
| 28 | .317 | .374 | .437 | .479 | .588 | **26** |
| 29 | .311 | .367 | .430 | .471 | .579 | **27** |
| 30 | .306 | .361 | .423 | .463 | .570 | **28** |
| 35 | .282 | .333 | .391 | .428 | .531 | **33** |
| 40 | .264 | .312 | .366 | .402 | .501 | **38** |
| 45 | .248 | .296 | .349 | .381 | .471 | **43** |
| 50 | .235 | .276 | .328 | .361 | .451 | **48** |
| 60 | .214 | .254 | .300 | .330 | .414 | **58** |
| 70 | .198 | .235 | .277 | .305 | .385 | **68** |
| 80 | .185 | .220 | .260 | .286 | .361 | **78** |
| 90 | .174 | .208 | .245 | .270 | .342 | **88** |
| 100 | .165 | .196 | .232 | .256 | .324 | **98** |
| 150 | .135 | .161 | .190 | .210 | .267 | **148** |
| 200 | .117 | .139 | .164 | .182 | .232 | **198** |
| 250 | .104 | .124 | .147 | .163 | .207 | **248** |
| 300 | .095 | .113 | .134 | .148 | .189 | **298** |
| 400 | .082 | .098 | .115 | .128 | .169 | **398** |
| 500 | .074 | .088 | .104 | .115 | .147 | **498** |
| 1,000 | .052 | .062 | .074 | .081 | .104 | **998** |
| 5,000 | .0233 | .0278 | .0329 | .0364 | .0465 | **4,998** |
| 10,000 | .0164 | .0196 | .0233 | .0258 | .0393 | **9,998** |

[a] Column entries for $\alpha_2 = .10, .05, .02,$ and $.01$ for $n = 3$ to $n = 100$ are taken from Table 13 in E. S. Pearson and H. O. Hartley (Eds.), *Biometrika Tables for Statisticians*, 2nd ed. (1962), by permission of the *Biometrika* Trustees. Other entries were obtained using Equation 15.2.

[b] If the *value* of an $r$ from a sample of size $n$ exceeds the tabled value for $\alpha$ and $n$, the null hypothesis that $\rho = 0$ may be rejected at the $\alpha$-level of significance. For example, a sample of $r$ of .561 or more with $n = 20$ leads to rejection of the hypothesis $\rho = 0$ at $\alpha_2 = .01$. Use $n$ only for testing Pearson $r$'s.

[c] The degrees of freedom $\nu$ for a Pearson $r$ are $n - 2$; for partial correlation coefficients, $\nu = n - 2 - p$, where $p$ is the number of variables partialed out.

**TABLE K Critical Values of Spearman's Rank Correlation Coefficient, $r_{ranks}$ for Testing the Null Hypothesis of No Correlation**[a]

| $n$ | $\alpha_1 = .05$<br>$\alpha_2 = .10$ | $\alpha_1 = .025$<br>$\alpha_2 = .05$ | $\alpha_1 = .01$<br>$\alpha_2 = .02$ | $\alpha_1 = .005$<br>$\alpha_2 = .01$ | $n$ |
|---|---|---|---|---|---|
| 5 | 0.900 | — | — | — | 5 |
| 6 | 0.829 | 0.886 | 0.943 | — | 6 |
| 7 | 0.714 | 0.786 | 0.893 | — | 7 |
| 8 | 0.643 | 0.738 | 0.833 | 0.881 | 8 |
| 9 | 0.600 | 0.683 | 0.783 | 0.833 | 9 |
| 10 | 0.564 | 0.648 | 0.745 | 0.818 | 10 |
| 11 | 0.523 | 0.623 | 0.736 | 0.794 | 11 |
| 12 | 0.497 | 0.591 | 0.703 | 0.780 | 12 |
| 13 | 0.475 | 0.566 | 0.673 | 0.745 | 13 |
| 14 | 0.457 | 0.545 | 0.646 | 0.716 | 14 |
| 15 | 0.441 | 0.525 | 0.623 | 0.689 | 15 |
| 16 | 0.425 | 0.507 | 0.601 | 0.666 | 16 |
| 17 | 0.412 | 0.490 | 0.582 | 0.645 | 17 |
| 18 | 0.399 | 0.476 | 0.564 | 0.625 | 18 |
| 19 | 0.388 | 0.462 | 0.549 | 0.608 | 19 |
| 20 | 0.377 | 0.450 | 0.534 | 0.591 | 20 |
| 21 | 0.368 | 0.438 | 0.521 | 0.576 | 21 |
| 22 | 0.359 | 0.428 | 0.508 | 0.562 | 22 |
| 23 | 0.351 | 0.418 | 0.496 | 0.549 | 23 |
| 24 | 0.343 | 0.409 | 0.485 | 0.537 | 24 |
| 25 | 0.336 | 0.400 | 0.475 | 0.526 | 25 |
| 26 | 0.329 | 0.392 | 0.465 | 0.515 | 26 |
| 27 | 0.323 | 0.385 | 0.456 | 0.505 | 27 |
| 28 | 0.317 | 0.377 | 0.448 | 0.496 | 28 |
| 29 | 0.311 | 0.370 | 0.440 | 0.487 | 29 |
| 30[b] | 0.305 | 0.364 | 0.432 | 0.478 | 30[b] |

[a]Adapted from E. G. Olds, "Distributions of sums of squares of rank differences for small numbers of individuals," *Annals of Mathematical Statistics*, 9 (1938), 133–48, and "The 5% significance levels for sums of squares of rank differences and a correction," *Annals of Mathematical Statistics*, 20 (1949), 117–18, by permission of The Institute of Mathematical Statistics.

[b]Table J may be used for $n > 30$.

**TABLE L Percentile Points of the Dunn (Bonferroni) Multiple Comparison *t*-Statistic**[a]

| | | *Number of Comparisons (C)* | | | | | | | | | | | | |
|---|---|---|---|---|---|---|---|---|---|---|---|---|---|---|
| $\nu_e$ | $\alpha^*_{\Sigma 2}$ | 2 | 3 | 4 | 5 | 6 | 7 | 8 | 9 | 10 | 15 | 20 | 25 | 30 |
| 2 | .10 | 4.243 | 5.243 | 6.081 | 6.816 | 7.480 | 8.090 | 8.656 | 9.188 | 9.691 | 11.890 | 13.741 | 15.371 | 16.845 |
| | .05 | 6.164 | 7.582 | 8.774 | 9.823 | 10.769 | 11.639 | 12.449 | 13.208 | 13.927 | 17.072 | 19.721 | 22.054 | 24.163 |
| | .01 | 14.071 | 17.248 | 19.925 | 22.282 | 24.413 | 26.372 | 28.196 | 29.908 | 31.528 | 38.620 | 44.598 | 49.865 | 54.626 |
| 3 | .10 | 3.149 | 3.690 | 4.115 | 4.471 | 4.780 | 5.055 | 5.304 | 5.532 | 5.744 | 6.627 | 7.326 | 7.914 | 8.427 |
| | .05 | 4.156 | 4.826 | 5.355 | 5.799 | 6.185 | 6.529 | 6.842 | 7.128 | 7.394 | 8.505 | 9.387 | 10.129 | 10.778 |
| | .01 | 7.447 | 8.565 | 9.453 | 10.201 | 10.853 | 11.436 | 11.966 | 12.453 | 12.904 | 14.796 | 16.300 | 17.569 | 18.678 |
| 4 | .10 | 2.751 | 3.150 | 3.452 | 3.669 | 3.909 | 4.093 | 4.257 | 4.406 | 4.542 | 5.097 | 5.521 | 5.870 | 6.169 |
| | .05 | 3.481 | 3.941 | 4.290 | 4.577 | 4.822 | 5.036 | 5.228 | 5.402 | 5.562 | 6.214 | 6.714 | 7.127 | 7.480 |
| | .01 | 5.594 | 6.248 | 6.751 | 7.166 | 7.520 | 7.832 | 8.112 | 8.367 | 8.600 | 9.556 | 10.294 | 10.902 | 11.424 |
| 5 | .10 | 2.549 | 2.882 | 3.129 | 3.327 | 3.493 | 3.638 | 3.765 | 3.880 | 3.985 | 4.403 | 4.718 | 4.972 | 5.187 |
| | .05 | 3.152 | 3.518 | 3.791 | 4.012 | 4.197 | 4.358 | 4.501 | 4.630 | 4.747 | 5.219 | 5.573 | 5.861 | 6.105 |
| | .01 | 4.771 | 5.243 | 5.599 | 5.888 | 6.133 | 6.346 | 6.535 | 6.706 | 6.862 | 7.491 | 7.968 | 8.355 | 8.684 |
| 6 | .10 | 2.428 | 2.723 | 2.939 | 3.110 | 3.253 | 3.376 | 3.484 | 3.580 | 3.668 | 4.015 | 4.272 | 4.477 | 4.649 |
| | .05 | 2.959 | 3.274 | 3.505 | 3.690 | 3.845 | 3.978 | 4.095 | 4.200 | 4.296 | 4.675 | 4.956 | 5.182 | 5.372 |
| | .01 | 4.315 | 4.695 | 4.977 | 5.203 | 5.394 | 5.559 | 5.704 | 5.835 | 5.954 | 6.428 | 6.782 | 7.068 | 7.308 |
| 7 | .10 | 2.347 | 2.618 | 2.814 | 2.969 | 3.097 | 3.205 | 3.302 | 3.388 | 3.465 | 3.768 | 3.990 | 4.167 | 4.314 |
| | .05 | 2.832 | 3.115 | 3.321 | 3.484 | 3.620 | 3.736 | 3.838 | 3.929 | 4.011 | 4.336 | 4.574 | 4.764 | 4.923 |
| | .01 | 4.027 | 4.353 | 4.591 | 4.782 | 4.941 | 5.078 | 5.198 | 5.306 | 5.404 | 5.791 | 6.077 | 6.306 | 6.497 |
| 8 | .10 | 2.289 | 2.544 | 2.726 | 2.869 | 2.987 | 3.088 | 3.176 | 3.254 | 3.324 | 3.598 | 3.798 | 3.955 | 4.086 |
| | .05 | 2.743 | 3.005 | 3.193 | 3.342 | 3.464 | 3.569 | 3.661 | 3.743 | 3.816 | 4.105 | 4.316 | 4.482 | 4.621 |
| | .01 | 3.831 | 4.120 | 4.331 | 4.498 | 4.637 | 4.756 | 4.860 | 4.953 | 5.038 | 5.370 | 5.613 | 5.807 | 5.969 |
| 9 | .10 | 2.246 | 2.488 | 2.661 | 2.796 | 2.907 | 3.001 | 3.083 | 3.155 | 3.221 | 3.474 | 3.658 | 3.802 | 3.921 |
| | .05 | 2.677 | 2.923 | 3.099 | 3.237 | 3.351 | 3.448 | 3.532 | 3.607 | 3.675 | 3.938 | 4.129 | 4.280 | 4.405 |
| | .01 | 3.688 | 3.952 | 4.143 | 4.294 | 4.419 | 4.526 | 4.619 | 4.703 | 4.778 | 5.072 | 5.287 | 5.457 | 5.598 |
| 10 | .10 | 2.213 | 2.446 | 2.611 | 2.739 | 2.845 | 2.934 | 3.012 | 3.080 | 3.142 | 3.380 | 3.552 | 3.686 | 3.796 |
| | .05 | 2.626 | 2.860 | 3.027 | 3.157 | 3.264 | 3.355 | 3.434 | 3.505 | 3.568 | 3.813 | 3.989 | 4.128 | 4.243 |
| | .01 | 3.580 | 3.825 | 4.002 | 4.141 | 2.256 | 4.354 | 4.439 | 4.515 | 4.584 | 4.852 | 5.046 | 5.199 | 5.326 |
| 11 | .10 | 2.186 | 2.412 | 2.571 | 2.695 | 2.796 | 2.881 | 2.955 | 3.021 | 3.079 | 3.306 | 3.468 | 3.595 | 3.699 |
| | .05 | 2.586 | 2.811 | 2.970 | 3.094 | 3.196 | 3.283 | 3.358 | 3.424 | 3.484 | 3.715 | 3.880 | 4.010 | 4.117 |
| | .01 | 3.495 | 3.726 | 3.892 | 4.022 | 4.129 | 4.221 | 4.300 | 4.371 | 4.434 | 4.682 | 4.860 | 5.001 | 5.117 |

**TABLE L (cont.)**

| $\nu_e$ | $\alpha^*_{\Sigma_2}$ | Number of Comparisons ($C$) 2 | 3 | 4 | 5 | 6 | 7 | 8 | 9 | 10 | 15 | 20 | 25 | 30 |
|---|---|---|---|---|---|---|---|---|---|---|---|---|---|---|
| 12 | .10 | 2.164 | 2.384 | 2.539 | 2.658 | 2.756 | 2.838 | 2.910 | 2.973 | 3.029 | 3.247 | 3.402 | 3.522 | 3.621 |
| | .05 | 2.553 | 2.770 | 2.924 | 3.044 | 3.141 | 3.224 | 3.296 | 3.359 | 3.416 | 3.636 | 3.793 | 3.916 | 4.017 |
| | .01 | 3.427 | 3.647 | 3.804 | 3.927 | 4.029 | 4.114 | 4.189 | 4.256 | 4.315 | 4.547 | 4.714 | 4.845 | 4.953 |
| 13 | .10 | 2.146 | 2.361 | 2.512 | 2.628 | 2.723 | 2.803 | 2.872 | 2.933 | 2.988 | 3.196 | 3.347 | 3.463 | 3.557 |
| | .05 | 2.526 | 2.737 | 2.886 | 3.002 | 3.096 | 3.176 | 3.245 | 3.306 | 3.361 | 3.571 | 3.722 | 3.839 | 3.935 |
| | .01 | 3.371 | 3.582 | 3.733 | 3.850 | 3.946 | 4.028 | 4.099 | 4.162 | 4.218 | 4.438 | 4.595 | 4.718 | 4.819 |
| 14 | .10 | 2.131 | 2.342 | 2.489 | 2.603 | 2.696 | 2.774 | 2.841 | 2.900 | 2.953 | 3.157 | 3.301 | 3.413 | 3.504 |
| | .05 | 2.503 | 2.709 | 2.854 | 2.967 | 3.058 | 3.135 | 3.202 | 3.261 | 3.314 | 3.518 | 3.662 | 3.775 | 3.867 |
| | .01 | 3.324 | 3.528 | 3.673 | 3.785 | 3.878 | 3.956 | 4.024 | 4.084 | 4.138 | 4.347 | 4.497 | 4.614 | 4.710 |
| 15 | .10 | 2.118 | 2.325 | 2.470 | 2.582 | 2.672 | 2.748 | 2.814 | 2.872 | 2.924 | 3.122 | 3.262 | 3.370 | 3.459 |
| | .05 | 2.483 | 2.685 | 2.827 | 2.937 | 3.026 | 3.101 | 3.166 | 3.224 | 3.275 | 3.472 | 3.612 | 3.721 | 3.810 |
| | .01 | 3.285 | 3.482 | 3.622 | 3.731 | 3.820 | 3.895 | 3.961 | 4.019 | 4.071 | 4.271 | 4.414 | 4.526 | 4.618 |
| 16 | .10 | 2.106 | 2.311 | 2.453 | 2.563 | 2.652 | 2.726 | 2.791 | 2.848 | 2.898 | 3.092 | 3.228 | 3.334 | 3.420 |
| | .05 | 2.467 | 2.665 | 2.804 | 2.911 | 2.998 | 3.072 | 3.135 | 3.191 | 3.241 | 3.433 | 3.569 | 3.675 | 3.761 |
| | .01 | 3.251 | 3.443 | 3.579 | 3.684 | 3.771 | 3.844 | 3.907 | 3.963 | 4.013 | 4.206 | 4.344 | 4.451 | 4.540 |
| 18 | .10 | 2.088 | 2.287 | 2.426 | 2.532 | 2.619 | 2.691 | 2.753 | 2.808 | 2.857 | 3.043 | 3.174 | 3.275 | 3.358 |
| | .05 | 2.439 | 2.631 | 2.766 | 2.869 | 2.953 | 3.024 | 3.085 | 3.138 | 3.186 | 3.370 | 3.499 | 3.599 | 3.681 |
| | .01 | 3.195 | 3.379 | 3.508 | 3.609 | 3.691 | 3.760 | 3.820 | 3.872 | 3.920 | 4.102 | 4.231 | 4.332 | 4.414 |
| 20 | .10 | 2.073 | 2.269 | 2.405 | 2.508 | 2.593 | 2.663 | 2.724 | 2.777 | 2.824 | 3.005 | 3.132 | 3.229 | 3.309 |
| | .05 | 2.417 | 2.605 | 2.736 | 2.836 | 2.918 | 2.986 | 3.045 | 3.097 | 3.143 | 3.320 | 3.445 | 3.541 | 3.620 |
| | .01 | 3.152 | 3.329 | 3.454 | 3.550 | 3.629 | 3.695 | 3.752 | 3.802 | 3.848 | 4.021 | 4.144 | 4.239 | 4.317 |
| 25 | .10 | 2.047 | 2.236 | 2.367 | 2.466 | 2.547 | 2.614 | 2.672 | 2.722 | 2.767 | 2.938 | 3.058 | 3.149 | 3.224 |
| | .05 | 2.379 | 2.558 | 2.683 | 2.779 | 2.856 | 2.921 | 2.976 | 3.025 | 3.069 | 3.235 | 3.351 | 3.440 | 3.513 |
| | .01 | 3.077 | 3.243 | 3.359 | 3.449 | 3.521 | 3.583 | 3.635 | 3.682 | 3.723 | 3.882 | 3.995 | 4.081 | 4.152 |
| 30 | .10 | 2.030 | 2.215 | 2.342 | 2.439 | 2.517 | 2.582 | 2.638 | 2.687 | 2.731 | 2.895 | 3.010 | 3.098 | 3.169 |
| | .05 | 2.354 | 2.528 | 2.649 | 2.742 | 2.816 | 2.878 | 2.932 | 2.979 | 3.021 | 3.180 | 3.291 | 3.376 | 3.445 |
| | .01 | 3.029 | 3.188 | 3.298 | 3.384 | 3.453 | 3.511 | 2.561 | 3.605 | 3.644 | 3.794 | 3.900 | 3.981 | 4.048 |

**TABLE L (cont.)**

| $\nu_e$ | $\alpha^*_{\Sigma_2}$ | *Number of Comparisons (C)* 2 | 3 | 4 | 5 | 6 | 7 | 8 | 9 | 10 | 15 | 20 | 25 | 30 |
|---|---|---|---|---|---|---|---|---|---|---|---|---|---|---|
| 40 | .10 | 2.009 | 2.189 | 2.312 | 2.406 | 2.481 | 2.544 | 2.597 | 2.644 | 2.686 | 2.843 | 2.952 | 3.036 | 3.103 |
| | .05 | 2.323 | 2.492 | 2.608 | 2.696 | 2.768 | 2.827 | 2.878 | 2.923 | 2.963 | 3.113 | 3.218 | 3.298 | 3.363 |
| | .01 | 2.970 | 3.121 | 3.225 | 3.305 | 3.370 | 3.425 | 3.472 | 3.513 | 3.549 | 3.689 | 3.787 | 3.862 | 3.923 |
| 60 | .10 | 1.989 | 2.163 | 2.283 | 2.373 | 2.446 | 2.506 | 2.558 | 2.603 | 2.643 | 2.793 | 2.897 | 2.976 | 3.040 |
| | .05 | 2.294 | 2.456 | 2.568 | 2.653 | 2.721 | 2.777 | 2.826 | 2.869 | 2.906 | 3.049 | 3.148 | 3.223 | 3.284 |
| | .01 | 2.914 | 3.056 | 3.155 | 3.230 | 3.291 | 3.342 | 3.386 | 3.425 | 3.459 | 3.589 | 3.679 | 3.749 | 3.805 |
| 120 | .10 | 1.968 | 2.138 | 2.254 | 2.342 | 2.411 | 2.469 | 2.519 | 2.562 | 2.600 | 2.744 | 2.843 | 2.918 | 2.978 |
| | .05 | 2.265 | 2.422 | 2.529 | 2.610 | 2.675 | 2.729 | 2.776 | 2.816 | 2.852 | 2.987 | 3.081 | 3.152 | 3.209 |
| | .01 | 2.859 | 2.994 | 3.087 | 3.158 | 3.215 | 3.263 | 3.304 | 3.340 | 3.372 | 3.493 | 3.577 | 3.641 | 3.693 |
| ∞ | .10 | 1.949 | 2.114 | 2.226 | 2.311 | 2.378 | 2.434 | 2.482 | 2.523 | 2.560 | 2.697 | 2.791 | 2.862 | 2.920 |
| | .05 | 2.237 | 2.388 | 2.491 | 2.569 | 2.631 | 2.683 | 2.727 | 2.766 | 2.300 | 2.928 | 3.016 | 3.083 | 3.137 |
| | .01 | 2.806 | 2.934 | 3.022 | 3.089 | 3.143 | 3.186 | 3.226 | 3.260 | 3.289 | 3.402 | 3.480 | 3.539 | 3.587 |

[a]This table is taken from Games (1977), reproduced with permission of the editor of the *Journal of the American Statistical Association.* It is based on the work of Sidak (1967). The critical values in this table are slightly less than those in the original Dunn tables based upon the Bonferroni inequality (Eq. 17.10). Other critical values can be obtained by using the Bonferroni inequality; for example

$$_{1-(\alpha_\Sigma/2)}t_{\nu_e,C} = {}_{1-(\alpha/2C)}t_{\nu_e} = \sqrt{_{1-(\alpha/C)}F_{1,\nu_e}}.$$

*These are nondirectional alphas. For directional ("one-tailed") tests, the correct alpha value is one-half of the tabled value. For example if $C = 5$, $\nu_e = 10$, and $\alpha_{\Sigma_1} = .05$, the critical $t$ is 2.739.

## TABLE M Critical *t*-Values for the Dunnett Statistic for Comparing Treatment Means with a Control[a]

| $\nu_e$ | Alpha $\alpha_{\Sigma 2}$ | Alpha $\alpha_{\Sigma 1}$ | *J* = *Number of Means (Including Control)* 2 | 3 | 4 | 5 | 6 | 7 | 8 | 9 | 10 |
|---|---|---|---|---|---|---|---|---|---|---|---|
| 5 | .10 | .05 | 2.02 | 2.44 | 2.68 | 2.85 | 2.98 | 3.08 | 3.16 | 3.24 | 3.03 |
| | .05 | | 2.57 | 3.03 | 3.29 | 3.48 | 3.62 | 3.73 | 3.82 | 3.90 | 3.97 |
| | .02 | .01 | 3.36 | 3.90 | 4.21 | 4.43 | 4.60 | 4.73 | 4.85 | 4.94 | 5.03 |
| | .01 | | 4.03 | 4.63 | 4.98 | 5.22 | 5.41 | 5.56 | 5.69 | 5.80 | 5.89 |
| 6 | .10 | .05 | 1.94 | 2.34 | 2.56 | 2.71 | 2.83 | 2.92 | 3.00 | 3.07 | 3.12 |
| | .05 | | 2.45 | 2.86 | 3.10 | 3.26 | 3.39 | 3.49 | 3.57 | 3.64 | 3.71 |
| | .02 | .01 | 3.14 | 3.61 | 3.88 | 4.07 | 4.21 | 4.33 | 4.43 | 4.51 | 4.59 |
| | .01 | | 3.71 | 4.21 | 4.51 | 4.71 | 3.87 | 5.00 | 5.10 | 5.20 | 5.28 |
| 7 | .10 | .05 | 1.89 | 2.27 | 2.48 | 2.62 | 2.73 | 2.82 | 2.89 | 2.95 | 3.01 |
| | .05 | | 2.36 | 2.75 | 2.97 | 3.12 | 3.24 | 3.33 | 3.41 | 3.47 | 3.53 |
| | .02 | .01 | 3.00 | 3.42 | 3.66 | 3.83 | 3.96 | 4.07 | 4.15 | 4.23 | 4.30 |
| | .01 | | 3.50 | 3.95 | 4.21 | 4.39 | 4.53 | 4.64 | 4.74 | 4.82 | 4.89 |
| 8 | .10 | .05 | 1.86 | 2.22 | 2.42 | 2.55 | 2.66 | 2.74 | 2.81 | 2.87 | 2.92 |
| | .05 | | 2.31 | 2.67 | 2.88 | 3.02 | 3.13 | 3.22 | 3.29 | 3.35 | 3.41 |
| | .02 | .01 | 2.90 | 3.29 | 3.51 | 3.67 | 3.79 | 3.88 | 3.96 | 4.03 | 4.09 |
| | .01 | | 3.36 | 3.77 | 4.00 | 4.17 | 4.29 | 4.40 | 4.48 | 4.56 | 4.62 |
| 9 | .10 | .05 | 1.83 | 2.18 | 2.37 | 2.50 | 2.60 | 2.68 | 2.75 | 2.81 | 2.86 |
| | .05 | | 2.26 | 2.61 | 2.81 | 2.95 | 3.05 | 3.14 | 3.20 | 3.26 | 3.32 |
| | .02 | .01 | 2.28 | 3.19 | 3.40 | 3.55 | 3.66 | 3.75 | 3.82 | 3.89 | 3.94 |
| | .01 | | 3.25 | 3.63 | 3.85 | 4.01 | 4.12 | 4.22 | 4.30 | 4.37 | 4.43 |
| 10 | .10 | .05 | 1.81 | 2.15 | 2.34 | 2.47 | 2.56 | 2.64 | 2.70 | 2.76 | 2.81 |
| | .05 | | 2.23 | 2.57 | 2.76 | 2.89 | 2.99 | 3.07 | 3.14 | 3.19 | 3.24 |
| | .02 | .01 | 2.76 | 3.11 | 3.31 | 3.45 | 3.56 | 3.64 | 3.71 | 3.78 | 3.83 |
| | .01 | | 3.17 | 3.53 | 3.74 | 3.88 | 3.99 | 4.08 | 4.16 | 4.22 | 4.28 |
| 11 | .10 | .05 | 1.80 | 2.13 | 2.31 | 2.44 | 2.53 | 2.60 | 2.67 | 2.72 | 2.77 |
| | .05 | | 2.20 | 2.53 | 2.72 | 2.84 | 2.94 | 3.02 | 3.08 | 3.14 | 3.19 |
| | .02 | .01 | 2.72 | 3.06 | 3.25 | 3.38 | 3.48 | 3.56 | 3.63 | 3.69 | 3.74 |
| | .01 | | 3.11 | 3.45 | 3.65 | 3.79 | 3.89 | 3.98 | 4.05 | 4.11 | 4.16 |
| 12 | .10 | .05 | 1.78 | 2.11 | 2.29 | 2.41 | 2.50 | 2.58 | 2.64 | 2.69 | 2.74 |
| | .05 | | 2.18 | 2.50 | 2.68 | 2.81 | 2.90 | 2.98 | 3.04 | 3.09 | 3.14 |
| | .02 | .01 | 2.68 | 3.01 | 3.19 | 3.32 | 3.42 | 3.50 | 3.56 | 3.62 | 3.67 |
| | .01 | | 3.05 | 3.39 | 3.58 | 3.71 | 3.81 | 3.89 | 3.96 | 4.02 | 4.07 |
| 13 | .10 | .05 | 1.77 | 2.09 | 2.27 | 2.39 | 2.48 | 2.55 | 2.61 | 2.66 | 2.71 |
| | .05 | | 2.16 | 2.48 | 2.65 | 2.78 | 2.87 | 2.94 | 3.00 | 3.06 | 3.10 |
| | .02 | .01 | 2.65 | 2.97 | 3.15 | 3.27 | 3.37 | 3.44 | 3.51 | 3.56 | 3.61 |
| | .01 | | 3.01 | 3.33 | 3.52 | 3.65 | 3.74 | 3.82 | 3.89 | 3.94 | 3.99 |
| 14 | .10 | .05 | 1.76 | 2.08 | 2.25 | 2.37 | 2.46 | 2.53 | 2.59 | 2.64 | 2.69 |
| | .05 | | 2.14 | 2.46 | 2.63 | 2.75 | 2.84 | 2.91 | 2.97 | 3.02 | 3.07 |
| | .02 | .01 | 2.62 | 2.94 | 3.11 | 3.23 | 3.32 | 3.40 | 3.46 | 3.51 | 3.56 |
| | .01 | | 2.98 | 3.29 | 3.47 | 3.59 | 3.69 | 3.76 | 3.83 | 3.88 | 3.93 |

**TABLE M (cont.)**

| | *Alpha* | | *J = Number of Means (Including Control)* | | | | | | | | |
|---|---|---|---|---|---|---|---|---|---|---|---|
| $\nu_e$ | $\alpha_{\Sigma 2}$ | $\alpha_{\Sigma 1}$ | 2 | 3 | 4 | 5 | 6 | 7 | 8 | 9 | 10 |
| 16 | .10 | .05 | 1.75 | 2.06 | 2.23 | 2.34 | 2.43 | 2.50 | 2.56 | 2.61 | 2.65 |
| | .05 | | 2.12 | 2.42 | 2.59 | 2.71 | 2.80 | 2.87 | 2.92 | 2.97 | 3.02 |
| | .02 | .01 | 2.58 | 2.88 | 3.05 | 3.17 | 3.26 | 3.33 | 3.39 | 3.44 | 3.48 |
| | .01 | | 2.92 | 3.22 | 3.39 | 3.51 | 3.60 | 3.67 | 3.73 | 3.78 | 3.83 |
| 18 | .10 | .05 | 1.73 | 2.04 | 2.21 | 2.32 | 2.41 | 2.48 | 2.53 | 2.58 | 2.62 |
| | .05 | | 2.10 | 2.40 | 2.56 | 2.68 | 2.76 | 2.83 | 2.89 | 2.94 | 2.98 |
| | .02 | .01 | 2.55 | 2.84 | 3.01 | 3.12 | 3.21 | 3.27 | 3.33 | 3.38 | 3.42 |
| | .01 | | 2.88 | 3.17 | 3.33 | 3.44 | 3.53 | 3.60 | 3.66 | 3.71 | 3.75 |
| 20 | .10 | .05 | 1.72 | 2.03 | 2.19 | 2.30 | 2.39 | 2.46 | 2.51 | 2.56 | 2.60 |
| | .05 | | 2.09 | 2.38 | 2.54 | 2.65 | 2.73 | 2.80 | 2.86 | 2.90 | 2.95 |
| | .02 | .01 | 2.53 | 2.81 | 2.97 | 3.08 | 3.17 | 3.23 | 3.29 | 3.34 | 3.38 |
| | .01 | | 2.85 | 3.13 | 3.29 | 3.40 | 3.48 | 3.55 | 3.60 | 3.65 | 3.69 |
| 24 | .10 | .05 | 1.71 | 2.01 | 2.17 | 2.28 | 2.36 | 2.43 | 2.48 | 2.53 | 2.57 |
| | .05 | | 2.06 | 2.35 | 2.51 | 2.61 | 2.70 | 2.76 | 2.81 | 2.86 | 2.90 |
| | .02 | .01 | 2.49 | 2.77 | 2.92 | 3.03 | 3.11 | 3.17 | 3.22 | 3.27 | 3.31 |
| | .01 | | 2.80 | 3.07 | 3.22 | 3.32 | 3.40 | 3.47 | 3.52 | 3.57 | 3.61 |
| 30 | .10 | .05 | 1.70 | 1.99 | 2.15 | 2.25 | 2.33 | 2.40 | 2.45 | 2.50 | 2.54 |
| | .05 | | 2.04 | 2.32 | 2.47 | 2.58 | 2.66 | 2.72 | 2.77 | 2.82 | 2.86 |
| | .02 | .01 | 2.46 | 2.72 | 2.87 | 2.97 | 3.05 | 3.11 | 3.16 | 3.21 | 3.24 |
| | .01 | | 2.75 | 3.01 | 3.15 | 3.25 | 3.33 | 3.39 | 3.44 | 3.49 | 3.52 |
| 40 | .10 | .05 | 1.68 | 1.97 | 2.13 | 2.23 | 2.31 | 2.37 | 2.42 | 2.47 | 2.51 |
| | .05 | | 2.02 | 2.29 | 2.44 | 2.54 | 2.62 | 2.68 | 2.73 | 2.77 | 2.81 |
| | .02 | .01 | 2.42 | 2.68 | 2.82 | 2.92 | 2.99 | 3.05 | 3.10 | 3.14 | 3.18 |
| | .01 | | 2.80 | 2.95 | 3.09 | 3.19 | 3.26 | 3.32 | 3.37 | 3.41 | 3.44 |
| 60 | .10 | .05 | 1.67 | 1.95 | 2.10 | 2.21 | 2.28 | 2.35 | 2.39 | 2.44 | 2.48 |
| | .05 | | 2.00 | 2.27 | 2.41 | 2.51 | 2.58 | 2.64 | 2.69 | 2.73 | 2.77 |
| | .02 | .01 | 2.39 | 2.64 | 2.78 | 2.87 | 2.94 | 3.00 | 3.04 | 3.08 | 3.12 |
| | .01 | | 2.66 | 2.90 | 3.03 | 3.12 | 3.19 | 3.25 | 3.29 | 3.33 | 3.37 |
| 120 | .10 | .05 | 1.66 | 1.93 | 2.08 | 2.18 | 2.26 | 2.32 | 2.37 | 2.41 | 2.45 |
| | .05 | | 1.98 | 2.24 | 2.38 | 2.47 | 2.55 | 2.60 | 2.65 | 2.69 | 2.73 |
| | .02 | .01 | 2.36 | 2.60 | 2.73 | 2.82 | 2.89 | 2.94 | 2.99 | 3.03 | 3.06 |
| | .01 | | 2.62 | 2.85 | 2.97 | 3.06 | 3.12 | 3.18 | 3.22 | 3.26 | 3.29 |
| ∞ | .10 | .05 | 1.64 | 1.92 | 2.06 | 2.16 | 2.23 | 2.29 | 2.34 | 2.38 | 2.42 |
| | .05 | | 1.96 | 2.21 | 2.35 | 2.44 | 2.51 | 2.57 | 2.61 | 2.65 | 2.69 |
| | .02 | .01 | 2.33 | 2.56 | 2.68 | 2.77 | 2.84 | 2.89 | 2.93 | 2.97 | 3.00 |
| | .01 | | 2.58 | 2.79 | 2.92 | 3.00 | 3.06 | 3.11 | 3.15 | 3.19 | 3.22 |

[a] This table is reproduced from: A multiple comparison procedure for comparing several treatments with a control. *Journal of the American Statistical Association*, 1955, **50**, 1096–1121, and New tables for multiple comparisons with a control. *Biometrics*, 1964, **20**, 482–491, with the permission of the author, C. W. Dunnett, and the editors.

**TABLE N Coefficients of Orthogonal Polynomials for Trend Analysis**[a]

| *J* | *Trend* | *j* = 1 | 2 | 3 | 4 | 5 | 6 | 7 | 8 | 9 | 10 | 11 | 12 | $\Sigma c_j^2$ |
|---|---|---|---|---|---|---|---|---|---|---|---|---|---|---|
| 3 | Linear | −1 | 0 | 1 | | | | | | | | | | 2 |
| | Quadratic | 1 | −2 | 1 | | | | | | | | | | 6 |
| 4 | Linear | −3 | −1 | 1 | 3 | | | | | | | | | 20 |
| | Quadratic | 1 | −1 | −1 | 1 | | | | | | | | | 4 |
| | Cubic | −1 | 3 | −3 | 1 | | | | | | | | | 20 |
| 5 | Linear | −2 | −1 | 0 | 1 | 2 | | | | | | | | 10 |
| | Quadratic | 2 | −1 | −2 | −1 | 2 | | | | | | | | 14 |
| | Cubic | −1 | 2 | 0 | −2 | 1 | | | | | | | | 10 |
| | Quartic | 1 | −4 | 6 | −4 | 1 | | | | | | | | 70 |
| 6 | Linear | −5 | −3 | −1 | 1 | 3 | 5 | | | | | | | 70 |
| | Quadratic | 5 | −1 | −4 | −4 | −1 | 5 | | | | | | | 84 |
| | Cubic | −5 | 7 | 4 | −4 | −7 | 5 | | | | | | | 180 |
| | Quartic | 1 | −3 | 2 | 2 | −3 | 1 | | | | | | | 28 |
| | Quintic | −1 | 5 | −10 | 10 | −5 | 1 | | | | | | | 252 |
| 7 | Linear | −3 | −2 | −1 | 0 | 1 | 2 | 3 | | | | | | 28 |
| | Quadratic | 5 | 0 | −3 | −4 | −3 | 0 | 5 | | | | | | 84 |
| | Cubic | −1 | 1 | 1 | 0 | −1 | −1 | 1 | | | | | | 6 |
| | Quartic | 3 | −7 | 1 | 6 | 1 | −7 | 3 | | | | | | 154 |
| | Quintic | −1 | 4 | −5 | 0 | 5 | −4 | 1 | | | | | | 84 |
| 8 | Linear | −7 | −5 | −3 | −1 | 1 | 3 | 5 | 7 | | | | | 168 |
| | Quadratic | 7 | 1 | −3 | −5 | −5 | −3 | 1 | 7 | | | | | 168 |
| | Cubic | −7 | 5 | 7 | 3 | −3 | −7 | −5 | 7 | | | | | 264 |
| | Quartic | 7 | −13 | −3 | 9 | 9 | −3 | −13 | 7 | | | | | 616 |
| | Quintic | −7 | 23 | −17 | −15 | 15 | 17 | −23 | 7 | | | | | 2,184 |
| 9 | Linear | −4 | −3 | −2 | −1 | 0 | 1 | 2 | 3 | 4 | | | | 60 |
| | Quadratic | 28 | 7 | −8 | −17 | −20 | −17 | −8 | 7 | 28 | | | | 2,772 |
| | Cubic | −14 | 7 | 13 | 9 | 0 | −9 | −13 | −7 | 14 | | | | 990 |
| | Quartic | 14 | −21 | −11 | 9 | 18 | 9 | −11 | −21 | 14 | | | | 2,002 |
| | Quintic | −4 | 11 | −4 | −9 | 0 | 9 | 4 | −11 | 4 | | | | 468 |
| 10 | Linear | −9 | −7 | −5 | −3 | −1 | 1 | 3 | 5 | 7 | 9 | | | 330 |
| | Quadratic | 6 | 2 | −1 | −3 | −4 | −4 | −3 | −1 | 2 | 6 | | | 132 |
| | Cubic | −42 | 14 | 35 | 31 | 12 | −12 | −31 | −35 | −14 | 42 | | | 8,580 |
| | Quartic | 18 | −22 | −17 | 3 | 18 | 18 | 3 | −17 | −22 | 18 | | | 2,860 |
| | Quintic | −6 | 14 | −1 | −11 | −6 | 6 | 11 | 1 | −14 | 6 | | | 780 |
| 11 | Linear | −5 | −4 | −3 | −2 | −1 | 0 | 1 | 2 | 3 | 4 | 5 | | 110 |
| | Quadratic | 15 | 6 | −1 | −6 | −9 | −10 | −9 | −6 | −1 | 6 | 15 | | 858 |
| | Cubic | −30 | 6 | 22 | 23 | 14 | 0 | −14 | −23 | −22 | −6 | 30 | | 4,290 |
| | Quartic | 6 | −6 | −6 | −1 | 4 | 6 | 4 | −1 | −6 | −6 | 6 | | 286 |
| | Quintic | −3 | 6 | 1 | −4 | −4 | 0 | 4 | 4 | −1 | −6 | 3 | | 156 |
| 12 | Linear | −11 | −9 | −7 | −5 | −3 | −1 | 1 | 3 | 5 | 7 | 9 | 11 | 572 |
| | Quadratic | 55 | 25 | 1 | −17 | −29 | −35 | −35 | −29 | −17 | 1 | 25 | 55 | 12,012 |
| | Cubic | −33 | 3 | 21 | 25 | 19 | 7 | −7 | −19 | −25 | −21 | −3 | 33 | 5,148 |
| | Quartic | 33 | −27 | −33 | −13 | 12 | 28 | 28 | 12 | −13 | −33 | −27 | 33 | 8,008 |
| | Quintic | −33 | 57 | 21 | −29 | −44 | −20 | 20 | 44 | 29 | −21 | −57 | 33 | 15,912 |

*J* *Trend* *j* = 1 2 3 4 5 6 7 8 9 10 11 12 $\Sigma c_j^2$

[a] Reproduced with permission of the trustees of *Biometrika*.

# BIBLIOGRAPHY


Addelman, S., "Variability of Treatment and Experiment Units in the Design and Analysis of Experiments," *Journal of the American Statistical Association*, 65(1970), 1095-1108.

Appelbaum, M. I., and E. M. Cramer, "Some Problems in the Nonorthogonal Analysis of Variance," *Psychological Bulletin*. 81(1974), 335-43.

Allison, D. E., "Test Anxiety, Stress, and Intelligence-Test Performance," *Canadian Journal of Behavioral Science*, 2(1970), 26-37.

Augustine, N. R., "Augustine's Laws and Major System Development Programs," *Defense Systems Management Review*, 1(1978), 50-76.

Baker, F. B., "An Investigation of the Sampling Distributions of Item Discrimination Indices," *Psychometrika*, 30(1965), 165-78.

Bancroft, T. A., *Topics in Intermediate Statistical Methods.* Ames: Iowa State University Press, 1968.

Bennet, R. W., "The Magnitude of the Teacher Effect." Ph.D. thesis, University of Colorado, 1972.

Bennett, G. K., H. G. Seashore, and A. G. Wesman, *Differential Aptitude Tests: Fifth Edition Manual.* New York: Psychological Corporation, 1974.

Binder, A., "Consideration of the Place of Assumptions in Correlational Analysis," *American Psychologist*, 14(1959), 504-510.

Bolch, B. W., "More on Unbiased Estimation of the Standard Deviation," *American Statistician*, 20(June, 1968), 27.

Boneau, C. A., "The Effects of Violations of Assumptions Underlying the *t*-test," *Psychological Bulletin*, 57(1960), 49-64.

Box, G. E. P., "Non-normality and Tests on Variances," *Biometrika*, 40(1953), 318-35.

——, "Some Theorems on Quadratic Forms Applied in the Study of Analysis of Variance Problems. II, Effects of Inequality of Variance and of Correlation Between Errors in the Two-Way Classification," *Annals of Mathematical Statistics*, 25(1954), 484-98.

Box, G. E. P., and S. L. Anderson, "Permutation Theory in the Derivation of Robust Criteria and the Study of Departures from Assumptions," *Journal of the Royal Statistical Society, Series B*, 17(1955), 1-26.

Box, G. E. P., W. G. Hunter, and J. S. Hunter, *Statistics for Experimenters*. New York: John Wiley, 1978.

Brinzer, R. J., and R. L. Sinatra, Survey of statistics textbooks used by the top 100 American Educational Research Association contributors. Paper presented to the American Educational Research Association, New York, 1982.

Brown, George I., "The Relationship Between Barometric Pressure and Relative Humidity and Classroom Behavior," *Journal of Educational Research*, 57(1964), 368-70.

Camilli, G., and K. D. Hopkins, "Applicability of Chi-Square to 2 × 2 Contingency Tables with Small Expected Frequencies," *Psychological Bulletin*, 85(1978), 163-67.

——, "Testing for Association in 2 × 2 Contingency Tables with Very Small Sample Sizes," *Psychological Bulletin*, 86(1979), 1011-14.

Carlson, J. E., and N. H. Timm, "Analysis of Nonorthogonal Fixed-Effects Designs," *Psychological Bulletin*, 81(1974), 563-70.

Carrier, C. C., and A. Titus, "Effects of Notetaking Pretraining and Test Mode Expectations on Learning from Lectures," *American Educational Research Journal*, 18(1981), 385-98.

Carroll, J. B., "The Nature of the Data, or How to Choose a Correlation Coefficient," *Psychometrika*, 26(1961), 347-72.

Carter, E. S., "Comparison of Different Shrinkage Formulas in Estimating Population Multiple Correlation Coefficients," *Educational and Psychological Measurement*, 39(1979), 261-66.

Chambers, A. C., K. D. Hopkins, and B. R. Hopkins, "Anxiety, Physiologically and Psychologically Measured: Its Effects on Mental Test Performance," *Psychology in the Schools*, 9(1972), 198-206.

Cochran, W. G., "Analysis of Covariance: Its Nature and Uses," *Biometrics*, 13(1957), 261-81.

——, *Sampling Techniques*. New York: John Wiley, 1963.

Cohen, J., *Statistical Power Analysis for the Behavioral Sciences*. New York: Academic Press, 1969.

Cohen, J., and P. Cohen, *Applied Multiple Regression/Correlation Analysis for the Behavioral Sciences*. Hillsdale, NJ, 1975.

Collier, R. O., Jr., and others, "Estimates of Test Size for Several Test Procedures Based on Conventional Variance Ratios in the Repeated Measures Design," *Psychometrika*, 32(1967), 339-54.

Collins, J. R., "Jackknifing Generalizability." Ph.D. thesis, University of Colorado, 1970.

Conover, W. J., and others, "Some Reasons for not Using the Yates' Continuity Correction on 2 X 2 Contingency Tables," *Journal of the American Statistical Association*, 69(1974), 374-82.

Cook, T. D., and D. T. Campbell, *Quasi-Experimentation*. New York: Rand McNally, 1979.

Cornfield, J. and J. W. Tukey, "Average Values of Mean Squares in Factorials," *Annals of Mathematical Statistics*, 27(1956), 907-49.

Cronbach, L. J., and others, Analysis of Covariance in Nonrandomized Experiments: Parameters Affecting Bias. Occasional Paper of the Stanford Evaluation Consortium. Stanford, Calif.: Stanford University, 1977.

Cureton, E. E., "Rank-Biserial Correlation," *Psychometrika*, 21(1956), 287-90.

Darlington, R. B., "Multiple Regression in Psychological Research and Practice," *Psychological Bulletin*, 69(1968), 161-82.

DeRosia, P., "A Comparative Study of Pupil Achievement and Attitudes and Involvement of Parents of Children Enrolled in Extended-Day and Half-Day Kindergarten Programs." Ed.D. thesis, University of Colorado, 1980.

Dixon, W. J., ed., *BMD: Biomedical Computer Programs*. Berkeley: University of California Press, 1970.

Dixon, W. J., and F. J. Massey, *Introduction to Statistical Analysis* (3rd ed.). New York: McGraw-Hill, 1969.

Dunn, O. J., "Multiple Comparisons among Means," *Journal of the American Statistical Association*, 56(1961), 52-64.

Dunnett, C. W., "Pairwise Multiple Comparisons in the Homogeneous Variance, Unequal Sample Size Case," *Journal of the American Statistical Association*, 75(1980a), 789-95.

——, "Pairwise Multiple Comparisons in the Unequal Variance Case," *Journal of the American Statistical Association*, 75(1980b), 796-800.

Durrand, A. L., "Comparative Power of Various Tests of Homogeneity of Variance," M. A. thesis, University of Colorado, 1969.

Dyson, E., A Study of Ability Grouping and the Self-concept, *Journal of Educational Research*, 60(1967), 403-5.

Edgington, E. S., "A New Tabulation of Statistical Procedures Used in APA Journals," *American Psychologist*, (1974), 25-28.

Edwards, A. L., *Expected Values of Discrete Random Variables and Elementary Statistics*. New York: John Wiley, 1964.

Erlenmeyer-Kimling, L., and L. F. Jarvik, "Genetics and Intelligence: A Review," *Science*, 142(1963), 1477-79.

Federighi, E. T., "Extended Tables of the Percentage Points of Student's *t*-Distribution," *Journal of the American Statistical Association*, 54(1959), 683-88.

Feller, W., *An Introduction to Probability Theory and Its Application, Volume I*, 2nd ed. New York: John Wiley, 1957.

Fisher, R. A., *Statistical Methods for Research Workers* (eds. 1-13). Edinburgh: Oliver and Boyd, 1925-1958.

——, *The Design of Experiments* (eds. 1-8). Edinburgh: Oliver and Boyd, 1935-1966.

——, *Statistical Methods and Scientific Inference* (2nd ed.). New York: Hafner, 1959.

Flexer, R. J., and A. S. Flexer, Six booklets: 1. *Fractions*; 2. *Linear and Literal Equations*; 3. *Quadratic Equations*; 4. *Exponents and Square Roots*; 5. *Logarithms*; 6. *Introduction to Statistics.* New York: Harper & Row, 1967.

French, J. W., "Effect of Anxiety on Verbal and Mathematical Examination Scores," *Educational and Psychological Measurement*, 22(1962), 553-64.

Gabriel, R. M., and K. D. Hopkins, "Relative Merits of MANOVA Repeated Measures ANOVA, and Univariate ANOVAs for Research Utilizing Multiple Criterion Measures," *Journal of Special Education*, 8(1974), 377-89.

Games, P. A., "An Improved $t$ table for Simultaneous Control on $g$ Contrasts. *Journal of the American Statistical Association* 72(1977), 531-34.

Games, P. A., H. B. Winkler, and D. A. Probert, "Robust Tests for Homogeneity of Variance," *Educational and Psychological Measurement*, 32(1972), 887-909.

Gay, L. R., P. Campbell, and P. D. Gallagher, "SIG: Professors of Educational Research Text Analysis Survey." Paper Presented to the American Educational Research Association, Toronto, 1978.

Gehler, T. M. G., "An Analysis of Kindergarten Achievement Including the Effects of Time-of-Day and Sex," Ph.D. thesis, University of Colorado, 1979.

Glass, G. V., "Note on Rank-Biserial Correlation," *Educational and Psychological Measurement*, 26(1966), 623-31.

Glass, G. V., and J. R. Collins, "Geometric Proof of the Restriction on the Possible Values of $r_{xy}$ when $r_{xz}$ and $r_{yz}$ are Fixed," *Educational and Psychological Measurement*, 30(1970), 37-39.

Glass, G. V., and A. R. Hakstian, "Measures of Association in Comparative Experiments: Their Development and Interpretation," *American Educational Research Journal*, 6(1969), 403-14.

Glass, G. V., and J. C. Stanley, *Statistical Methods in Education and Psychology*. Englewood Cliffs, N. J.: Prentice-Hall, 1970.

Glass, G. V., B. McGaw, and M. L. Smith, *Meta-analysis in Social Research*. Beverly Hills: SAGE, 1981.

Glass, G. V., P. D. Peckham, and J. R. Sanders, "Consequences of Failure to Meet Assumptions Underlying the Fixed Effects Analysis of Variance and Covariance," *Review of Educational Research*, 42(1972), 237-88.

Glass, G. V., V. L. Willson, and J. M. Gottman, *Design and Analysis of Time-Series Experiments*. Boulder: Colorado Associated University Press, 1975.

Golladay, M. A., *The Condition of Education*. U. S. Department of Health, Education, and Welfare, National Center for Educational Statistics. Washington, D. C.: U. S. Government Printing Office, 1976.

Goodman, L. A., *Analyzing Qualitative/Categorical Data*. Cambridge, Mass.: Abt Books, 1978.

Grant, D. A., "Testing the Null Hypothesis and the Strategy and Tactics of Investigating Theoretical Models," *Psychological Review*, 69(1962), 54-61.

Graybill, F. A., *An Introduction to Linear Statistical Models, Volume 1*. New York: McGraw-Hill, 1961.

Green, B. F., and J. W. Tukey, "Complex Analysis of Variance: General Problems," *Psychometrika*, 25(1960), 127-52.

Greenhouse, S. W., and S. Geisser, "On Methods in the Analysis of Profile Data," *Psychometrika*, 24(1959), 95-112.

Guenther, W. C., *Analysis of Variance*. Englewood Cliffs, N. J.: Prentice-Hall, 1964.

Gullickson, A., and K. D. Hopkins, "Interval Estimation of Correlation Coefficients Corrected for Restriction of Range," *Educational and Psychological Measurement*, 36(1976), 9-25.

Gustav, A., "Response Set in Objective Achievement Tests," *Journal of Psychology*, 56(1963), 421-27.

Hakstian, A. R., "The Effect on Study Methods and Test Performance of Objective and Essay Examinations," *Journal of Educational Research*, 64(1971), 319-24.

Hammond, E. C., "Smoking in Relation to Mortality and Morbidity," *Journal of the National Cancer Institute*, 32(1964), 1161-87.

Hansford, B. C., and J. A. Hattie, The Relationship between Self and Achievement Measures. *Review of Educational Research*, 52(1982), 123-42.

Harrington, S. A., "Sequencing Organizers in Meaningful Verbal Learning." Research Paper No. 10. Boulder: University of Colorado, Laboratory of Educational Research, 1968.

Hartshorne, H., and M. A. May, *Studies in the Nature of Character, I: Studies in Deceit*. New York: Macmillan, 1928.

Hedges, L. V., "Distribution Theory for Glass's Estimator of Effect Size and Related Estimators," *Journal of Educational Statistics*, 6(1981), 21-32.

Heermann, E. F., and L. A. Braskamp, *Readings in Statistics for the Behavioral Sciences*. Englewood Cliffs, N. J.: Prentice-Hall, 1970.

Hendrickson, G. F., and J. R. Collins, "Note Correcting the Results in Olkin's New Formula for the Significance of $r_{13}$ vs. $r_{23}$ Compared with Hotelling's Methods," *American Educational Research Journal*, (1970), 639-64.

Herr, D. G., and J. Gaebelein, "Nonorthogonal Two-Way Analysis of Variance," *Psychological Bulletin*, 85(1978), 207-16.

Hochberg, Y., "A Modification of the *T*-Method of Multiple Comparisons for a One-Way Layout with Unequal Variances," *Journal of the American Statistical Association*, 71(1970), 200-3.

——, "An Extension of the *T*-Method to General Unbalanced Models of Fixed Effects," *Journal of the Royal Statistical Society*, Ser. B, 37(1975), 426-33.

Hollander, M., and D. A. Wolfe, *Nonparametric Statistical Inference*. New York: McGraw-Hill, 1971.

Hopkins, K. D., "Regression and the Matching Fallacy in Quasi-Experimental Research," *Journal of Special Education*, 3(1969), 329-36.

——, "Preventing the Number One Misinterpretation of Behavioral Research, or How to Increase Statistical Power," *Journal of Special Education*, 7(1973), 103-7.

——, "A Simplified Method for Determining Expected Mean Squares and Error Terms in the Analysis of Variance," *Journal of Experimental Education*, 45(1976), 13-18.

——, "The Unit of Analysis: Group Means vs. Individual Observations," *American Educational Research Journal*, 19(1982), 5-18.

——, "A Strategy for Analyzing ANOVA Designs Having One or More Random Factors," *Educational and Psychological Measurement*, 43(1983), 107-13.

Hopkins, K. D., and G. Bracht, "Ten-year Stability of Verbal and Nonverbal IQ scores," *American Educational Research Journal*, 12(1975), 469-77.

Hopkins, K. D., and L. McGuire, "Mental Measurement of the Blind: The Validity of the Wechsler Intelligence Scale for Children," *International Journal for Education of the Blind*, 15(1966), 65-73.

Hopkins, K. D., and E. G. Sitkie, "Predicting Grade One Reading Performance: Intelligence vs. Reading Readiness Tests," *Journal of Experimental Education*, 37(1969), 31-33.

Hopkins, K. D., and M. Bibelheimer, "Five-year Stability IQ's from Language and Non-Language Group Tests," *Child Development*, 42(1971), 645-49.

Hopkins, K. D., and B. L. Anderson, "Multiple Comparisons Guide," *Journal of Special Education*, 7(1973), 319-28.

Hopkins, K. D., and G. L. Kretke, "N/cell Considerations: Asking the Wrong Question for the Right Reason," *Journal of Special Education*, 10(1976), 321-24.

Hopkins, K. D., and G. V. Glass, *Basic Statistics for the Behavioral Sciences*. Englewood Cliffs, N. J.: Prentice-Hall, 1978.

Hopkins, K. D., and J. C. Stanley, *Educational and Psychological Measurement and Evaluation* (6th ed.). Englewood Cliffs, N. J.: Prentice-Hall, 1981.

Hopkins, K. D., D. K. Coulter, and B. R. Hopkins, "Tables for Quick Power Estimates when Comparing Means," *Journal of Special Education*, 15(1981), 389-94.

Hopkins, K. D., and others, "*A Technical Report on the Colorado Needs-Assessment Program, Spring 1973*." Boulder: University of Colorado, Laboratory of Educational Research, 1974.

Horst, P., "A Proof that the Point from Which the Sum of the Absolute Deviations is a Minimum is the Median," *Journal of Educational Psychology*, 22(1931), 463-64.

Hosking, J. D., and R. M. Hamer, "Nonorthogonal Analysis of Variance Programs: An Evaluation," *Journal of Educational Statistics*, 4(1979), 161-85.

Hotelling, H., "The Selection of Variates for Use in Prediction with Some Comments on the General Problem of Nuisance Parameters," *Annals of Mathematical Statistics*, 11(1940), 271-83.

Houston, S. R., C. E. Crosswhite, and R. S. King, "The Use of Judgmental Analysis in Capturing Student Policies of Rated Teacher Effectiveness," *Journal of Experimental Education*, 43(1974), 28-34.

Hsu, T. C., and L. S. Feldt, "The Effect of Limitations on the Number of Criterion Score Values on the Significance of the F-test," *American Educational Research Journal*, 6(1969), 515-27.

Huberty, C. J., and S. A. Mourad, "Estimation in Multiple Correlation/Prediction," *Educational and Psychological Measurement*, 40(1980), 101-12.

Huitema, B. E., *The Analysis of Covariance and Alternatives*. New York: John Wiley, 1980.

Jones, L. V., "Tests of Hypotheses: One-sided vs. Two-sided Alternatives," *Psychological Bulletin*, 49(1952), 43-46.

——, "A Rejoinder on One-Tailed Tests," *Psychological Bulletin*, 51(1954), 585-86.

Kaiser, H. F., "Directional Statistical Decisions," *Psychological Review*, 67(1960), 160-67.

Kaplan, A., *The Conduct of Inquiry*. San Francisco: Chandler, 1964.

Kelley, T. L., "The Selection of Upper and Lower Groups for the Validation of Test Items," *Journal of Educational Psychology*, 30(1939), 17-24.

Kendall, M. G., *Rank Correlation Methods* (3rd ed.). London: Griffin, 1962.

Kepple, G., *Design and Analysis: A Researcher's Handbook* (2nd ed.). Englewood Cliffs, N. J.: Prentice-Hall, 1982.

Kerlinger, F. N., and E. J. Pedhazer, *Multiple Regression in Behavioral Research in Behavioral Research*. New York: Holt, Rinehart, and Winston, 1973.

Kirk, R. E., *Experimental Design for the Behavioral Sciences*. Belmont, Calif.: Brooks/Cole, 1968.

Kish, L., *Survey Sampling*. New York: John Wiley, 1965.

Knoke, D., and P. J. Burke, *Log-Linear Models*. Beverly Hills, Calif.: SAGE, 1980.

Kramer, C. Y., "Extension of Multiple Range Test to Group Means with Unequal Numbers of Replications," *Biometrics*, 57(1956), 649-55.

Kruskal, W. H., "Ordinal Measures of Association," *Journal of the American Statistical Association*, 53(1958), 814-61.

——, "The Significance of Fisher: A review of *R. A. Fisher: The life of a scientist*," *Journal of the American Statistical Association*, 75(1980), 1019-29.

Lee, W., *Experimental Design and Analysis*. San Francisco: Freeman and Co, 1975.

Leinhardt, S., and S. S. Wasserman, "Teaching Regression: an Exploratory Approach," *The American Statistician*, 33(1979), 196-203.

Leinhardt, G., and S. Leinhardt, "Exploratory Data Analysis: New Tools for the Analysis of Empirical Data," in *Review of Research in Education*, ed. D. C. Berliner. American Educational Research Association, 1980.

Lewis, D., and C. J. Burke, "The Use and Misuse of the Chi-Square Test," *Psychological Bulletin*, 46(1949), 433-89.

Li, J. C. R., *Statistical Inference II*. Ann Arbor, Michigan: Edwards Brothers, 1964.

Lindquist, E. F., *Statistical Analysis in Educational Research*. New York: Houghton Mifflin, 1940.

Lord, F. M., "Elementary Models for Measuring Change," in *Problems in Measuring Change*, ed. C. W. Harris. Madison, Wisc.: University of Wisconsin Press, 1963, 21-38.

——, "A Paradox in the Interpretation of Group Comparisons," *Psychological Bulletin*, 68(1967), 304-5.

Lord, F. M., and M. R. Novick, *Statistical Theories of Mental Test Scores*. Reading, Mass.: Addison-Wesley, 1968.

Lubin, A., "The Interpretation of Significant Interaction," *Educational and Psychological Measurement*, 21(1962), 807-17.

Lunney, G. H., "Using Analysis of Variance with a Dichotomous Dependent Variable: An Empirical Study," *Journal of Educational Measurement*, 7(1970), 263-69.

Mainland, M. B., "The Use and Misuse of Statistics in Medical Publications," *Clinical Pharmacology and Therapeutics*, 1(1960), 411-22.

Mandell, A. J., and M. P. Mandell, "Suicide and the Menstrual Cycle," *Journal of the American Medical Association*, 200(1967), 132-33.

Marascuilo, L. A., "Large-Sample Multiple Comparisons," *Psychological Bulletin*, 65(1966), 280-90.

Marascuilo, L. A., and J. R. Levin, "Appropriate Post Hoc Comparisons for Interaction and Nested Hypotheses in Analysis of Variance Designs: The Elimination of Type IV Errors," *American Educational Research Journal*, 7(1970), 397-421.

Marascuilo, L. A., and M. McSweeney, *Nonparametric and Distribution-free Methods for the Social Sciences*. Monterey, Calif.: Brooks/Cole, 1978.

Martin, C. G., and P. A. Games, "ANOVA Tests for Homogeneity of Variance: Nonnormality and Unequal Samples," *Journal of Educational Statistics*, 2, no. 3 (Autumn 1977), 187-206.

McGaw, B., and G. V. Glass, "Choice of the Metric for Effect Size in Meta-analysis," *American Educational Research Journal*, 17(1980), 325-37.

McNamara, W. J., and J. W. Dunlap, "A Graphical Method for Computing the Standard Error of Biserial *r*." *Journal of Experimental Education*, 2(1934), 274-77.

McNemar, Q., *Psychological Statistics* (3rd ed.). New York: John Wiley, 1962.

Metfessel, N. S., and G. Sax, "Response Set Patterns in Published Instructors' Manuals in Education and Psychology," *California Journal of Educational Research*, 8(1957), 195-97.

Michael, W. B., "Review of Statistical Methods in Education and Psychology by G. V. Glass and J. C. Stanley," *Educational and Psychological Measurement*, 30(1970), 1015-18.

Miller, R. G., *Simultaneous Statistical Inference*. New York: McGraw-Hill, 1966.

——, "Developments in Multiple Comparisons, 1966-1976," *Journal of the American Statistical Association*, 72(1977), 779-88.

Millman, J., and G. V. Glass, "Rules of Thumb for Writing the ANOVA Table," *Journal of Educational Measurement*, 4(1967), 41-51.

Morrow, J. R., A. S. Jackson, and J. A. Bell, "The Function of Age, Sex, and Body Mass on Distance Running," *Research Quarterly*, 49(1978), 491-97.

Munsinger, H., "Children's Resemblance to Their Biological and to Their Adopting Parents in Two Ethnic Groups," *Behavior Genetics*, 5(1975), 239-54.

Myers, J. L., *Fundamentals of Experimental Design* (3rd ed.). Boston: Allyn and Bacon, 1977.

Myette, B. M., and K. R. White, "Selecting an Appropriate Multiple Comparison Technique: An Integration of Monte Carlo Studies." Paper presented to the American Educational Research Association, New York, 1982.

Nair, K. R., "Table of Confidence Interval for the Median in Sample from any Continuous Population," *Sankhya*, 4(1940), 551-58.

Newman, H. H., F. N. Freeman, and K. J. Holzinger, *Twins: A Study of Heredity and Environment*. Chicago: University of Chicago Press, 1937.

Nie, H. N., and others, *SPSS: Statistical Package for the Social Sciences* (2nd ed.). New York: McGraw-Hill, 1975.

Nunnally, J. C., "The Place of Statistics in Psychology," *Educational and Psychological Measurement*, 20(1960), 641-50.

——, *Psychometric Theory* (2nd ed.). New York: McGraw-Hill, 1979.

Olkin, I., "Correlations Revisited," in *Improving Experimental Design and Statistical Analysis*, ed. J. C. Stanley. Chicago: Rand McNally, 1967.

Olkin, I., and J. W. Pratt, "Unbiased Estimation of Certain Correlation Coefficients," *Annals of Mathematical Statistics*, 29(1958), 201-11.

O'Neill, R., and G. B. Wetherill, "The Present State of Multiple Comparison Methods," *Journal of the Royal Statistical Society*, 33(1971), 218-50.

Ostle, B., and R. W. Mensing, *Statistics for Research*. Ames, Iowa: Iowa State University Press, 1975.

Pearson, E. S., and C. J. Clopper, "The Use of Confidence Intervals or Fiducial Limits Illustrated in the Case of the Binomial," *Biometrika*, 26(1934), 404-13.

Pedhazur, E. J., *Multiple Regression in Behavioral Research* (2nd ed.). New York: Holt, Rinehart and Winston, 1982.

Peters, C. C., "The Misuse of Chi-Square–a Reply to Lewis and Burke," *Psychological Bulletin*, 47(1950), 331-37.

Petrinovich, L. F., and C. D. Hardyck, "Error Rates for Multiple Comparison Methods: Some Evidence Concerning the Frequency of Erroneous Conclusions," *Psychological Bulletin*, 71(1969), 43-54.

Poor, D. S., "Analysis of Variance for Repeated Measures Designs: Two Approaches," *Psychological Bulletin*, 80(1973), 204-09.

Ragosa, D., "Comparing Nonparallel Regression Lines," *Psychological Bulletin*, 88(1980), 307-21.

Reichardt, C. S., "The Statistical Analysis of Data from Nonequivalent Group Designs," Chapter 4 in Cook and Campbell, *Quasi-Experimentation*. New York: Rand McNally, 1979.

Reynolds, H. T., *The Analysis of Cross-classifications*. New York: Free Press, 1977.

Rogan, J. D., and H. J. Keselman, "Is the ANOVA F-test Robust to Variance Heterogeneity when Sample Sizes are Equal?: An Investigation via a Coefficient of Variation," *American Educational Research Journal*, 14(1977), 493-98.

Roscoe, J. T., and J. A. Byars, "An Investigation of the Restraints with Respect to Sample Size Commonly Imposed on the Use of the Chi-Square Statistic," *Journal of the American Statistical Association*, 66(1971), 755-59.

Rothkopf, E. Z., "Learning from Written Instructive Materials: An Exploration of the Control of Inspection Behavior by Test-Like Events," *American Educational Research Journal*, 3(1966), 241-49,

Sidak, Z., "Rectangular Confidence Regions for the Means of Multivariate Normal Distributions," *Journal of the American Statistical Association*, 62(1967), 626-33.

Scheffé, H., *The Analysis of Variance*. New York: John Wiley, 1959.

Schmidt, W., "Review of *Statistical Methods in Education and Psychology* by G. V. Glass and J. C. Stanley," *American Educational Research Journal*, 9(1972), 169-73.

Schon, I., K. D. Hopkins, and C. Vojir, "The Effects of Special Curricular Study of Mexican Culture on Anglo and Mexican-American Students' Perceptions of Mexican-Americans," *Journal of Experimental Education*, 61(1983) 215-18.

Shepard, L. A., and K. D. Hopkins, "Regression and the Matching Fallacy in Quasi-Experimental Research," *National Association for Business Teachers Education Review*, 4(1977), 11-15.

Sidák, Z., "Rectangular Confidence Regions for the Means of Multivariate Normal Distribution," *Journal of the American Statistical Association*, 62(1967), 626-33.

Smith, R. A., "The Effect of Unequal Group Size on Tukey's HSD Procedure," *Psychometrika*, 36(1971), 31-34.

Snedecor, G. W., and W. G. Cochran, *Statistical Methods* (7th ed.). Ames, Ia.: Iowa State University Press, 1980.

Solso, R. L., "Twenty-Five Years of Recommended Readings in Psychology," *American Psychologist*, 34(1979), 703-5.

Sparks, J. N., "Expository Notes on the Problem of Making Multiple Comparisons on a Completely Randomized Design," *Journal of Experimental Education*, 31(1963), 343-49.

Spinner, B., and R. M. Gabriel, "Factorial Analysis of Variance with Unequal Cell Frequencies," *Canadian Psychology*, 22(1981), 975-78.

Spjotvoll, E., and M. R. Stoline, "An Extension of the *T*-Method of Multiple Comparisons to Include the Cases with Unequal Sample Sizes," *Journal of the American Statistical Association*, 68(1973), 975-78.

Stanley, J. C., "Analysis of a Double Nested Design," *Educational and Psychological Measurement*, 21(1961), 831-37. Errata, 22(1962), ii.

——, "The Influence of Fisher's *The Design of Experiments* on Educational Research Thirty Years Later," *American Educational Research Journal*, 3(1966), 233-29.

Stein, S. L., and J. B. Kuenne, "Readability and Textbook Evaluation for Textbooks in

Educational Research and Statistics." Paper presented to the American Educational Research Association, San Francisco, 1979.

Stevens, S. S., ed., *Handbook of Experimental Psychology.* New York: John Wiley, 1951.

Stone. C. L., *Church Participation and Social Adjustment of High School and College Youth.* Rural Sociology Series on Youth, No. 12, Bulletin 550. Pullman, Wash.: Washington State University, 1954.

Terman, L. M., and M. A. Merrill, *Measuring Intelligence.* Boston: Houghton Mifflin, 1937.

——, *Stanford-Binet Intelligence Scale: Manual for the Third Revision.* Boston: Houghton Mifflin, 1973.

Thorndike, R. L., *Personnel Selection.* New York: John Wiley, 1949.

Tukey, J. W., "Conclusions vs. Decisions," *Technometrics*, 2(1960), 423-33.

——, *Exploratory Data Analysis.* Reading, Mass.: Addison-Wesley, 1977.

Vecchio, R., and F. Costin, "Predicting Teacher Effectiveness from Graduate Admissions Predictors," *American Educational Research Journal*, 14(1977), 169-76.

Vellman, P. F., and D. C. Hoaglin, *Applications, Basics, and Computers of Exploratory Data Analysis.* Boston: Duxburg Press, 1981.

Wainer, H., and D. Thissen, "Graphical Data Analysis," *Annual Review of Psychology*, 32(1981), 191-241.

Walker, H. M., "Degrees of Freedom," *Journal of Educational Psychology*, 31(1940), 253-69.

Wechsler, D., *Manual for the Wechsler Preschool and Primary Scale of Intelligence.* New York: Psychological Corporation, 1967.

——, *Manual for the Wechsler Intelligence Scale for Children–Revised.* New York: Psychological Corporation, 1974.

White, K. R., and K. D. Hopkins, "The Reliability of a Self-report Measure of Socioeconomic Status, and the Relationship of SES and Pupil Achievement in Grades 2-6," Paper presented to the National Council on Measurement in Education, Washington, D.C., 1975.

Wick, J. W., and C. Dirkes, "Characteristics of Current Doctoral Dissertations in Education," *Educational Researcher*, 2(1973), 20-22.

Wilks, S. S., *Mathematical Statistics.* New York: John Wiley, 1962.

Williams, P. A., and others, "The Impact of Leisure-Time Television on School Learning: a Research Synthesis," *American Educational Research Journal*, 19(1982), 19-50.

Willson, V. L., "Research Techniques in *AERJ* Articles: 1969 to 1978," *Educational Researcher*, 9(1980), 5-10.

Winer, B. J., *Statistical Principles in Experimental Design* (2nd ed.). New York: McGraw-Hill, 1971.

# AUTHOR INDEX

# SUBJECT INDEX